Comprehensive Structured COBOL

PWS Series in Computer Science

Abernethy/Allen
Experiments in Computing: Laboratories for Introductory Computer Science in Think Pascal

Abernethy/Allen
Experiments in Computing: Laboratories for Introductory Computer Science in Turbo Pascal

Ageloff/Mojena
Essentials of Structured BASIC

Bailey/Lundgaard
Program Design with Pseudocode, Third Edition

Beidler/Jackowitz
MODULA 2

Belcher
The COBOL Handbook

Bent/Sethares
BASIC: An Introduction to Computer Programming, Fourth Edition

Bent/Sethares
BASIC: An Introduction to Computer Programming with the Apple, Third Edition

Bent/Sethares
FORTRAN with Problem Solving: A Structured Approach

Bent/Sethares
Microsoft BASIC: Programming the IBM PC, Third Edition

Bent/Sethares
QuickBASIC: An Introduction to Computer Programming with the IBM PC

Borse
FORTRAN 77 and Numerical Methods for Engineers, Second Edition

Boyle
FORTRAN 77 PDQ, Second Edition

Brainerd
WATFIV Fundamentals and Style

Brainerd/Goldberg/Gross
FORTRAN 77 Fundamentals and Style

Burkhard
C for Programmers

Cashing
A Programmer's Guide to File Processing

Caverly/Goldstein
Introduction to Ada

Decker/Hirshfield
Pascal's Triangle: Reading, Writing, and Reasoning About Programs

Decker/Hirshfield
The Analytical Engine: An Introduction to Computer Science Using HyperCard

Decker/Hirshfield
The Analytical Engine: An Introduction to Computer Science Using ToolBook

Dershem/Jipping
Programming Languages

Firebaugh
Artificial Intelligence: A Knowledge-Based Approach

Flynn/McHoes
Understanding Operating Systems

Giarratano/Riley
Expert Systems: Principles and Programming

Goldberg/Gross/Brainerd
Pascal

Hennefeld
Using BASIC: An Introduction to Computer Programming, Third Edition

Hennefeld
Using Microsoft and IBM BASIC: An Introduction to Computer Programming

Hennefeld
Using Turbo Pascal 4.0–6.0, Second Edition

Holoien/Behforooz
FORTRAN 77 for Engineers and Scientists, Second Edition

Kapps/Stafford
Assembly Language for the PDP-II, RT-RSX-UNIX, Second Edition

Kapps/Stafford
VAX Assembly Language

Korsh
Data Structures, Algorithms, and Program Style

Korsh/Garrett
Data Structures, Algorithms, and Program Style Using C

Lane
Data Communications Software Design

Lane/Mooney
A Practical Approach to Operating Systems

Li Santi/Mann/Zlotnick
Algorithms, Programming, Pascal

Martins
Introduction to Computer Science Using Pascal

McKelvey, Jr.
The Debugger's Handbook: Turbo Pascal

Mears
Absolutely BASIC Computing

Mears
BASIC Programming with the IBM PC, Second Edition

Merchant
WATFIV S: Language and Style

Mojena
Turbo Pascal

Mojena/Ageloff
FORTRAN 77

Payne
Advanced Structured BASIC: File Processing with the IBM PC

Payne
Structured BASIC for the IBM PC with Business Applications

Payne
Structured Programming with QuickBASIC

Pollack
Effective Programming in Turbo Pascal

Popkin
Comprehensive Structured COBOL, Fourth Edition

Radford/Haigh
Turbo Pascal for the IBM PC

Reynolds
Program Design and Data Structures in Pascal

Riley
Advanced Programming and Data Structures Using Pascal

Riley
Data Abstraction and Structure, an Introduction to Computer Science II

Riley
Programming Using Turbo Pascal

Riley
Using MODULA-2

Riley
Using Pascal: An Introduction to Computer Science I

Rojiani
Programming in BASIC for Engineers

Rood
Logic and Structured Design for Computer Programmers, Second Edition

Runnion
Structured Programming in Assembly Language for the IBM PC

Shelly/Cashman
Introduction to Basic Programming

Shelly/Cashman
Introduction to Computer Programming: ANSI COBOL

Shelly/Cashman
Turbo Pascal Programming

Skvarcius
Problem Solving Using PASCAL: Algorithm Development and Programming Concepts

Smith
Design and Analysis of Algorithms

Smith
Introduction to Computers and Programming: Pascal

Steward
Software Engineering with Systems Analysis and Design

Stubbs/Webre
Data Structures with Abstract Data Types and Ada

Stubbs/Webre
Data Structures with Abstract Data Types and MODULA-2

Stubbs/Webre
Data Structures with Abstract Data Types and Pascal, Second Edition

Suhy
CICS using COBOL: A Structured Approach

Wang
An Introduction to ANSI C on UNIX

Wang
An Introduction to Berkeley UNIX

Weinman
FORTRAN for Scientists and Engineers

Weinman
VAX FORTRAN, Second Edition

Worthington
C Programming

FOURTH EDITION

Comprehensive Structured COBOL

Gary S. Popkin
New York City Technical College
of the City University of New York

PWS Publishing Company
Boston

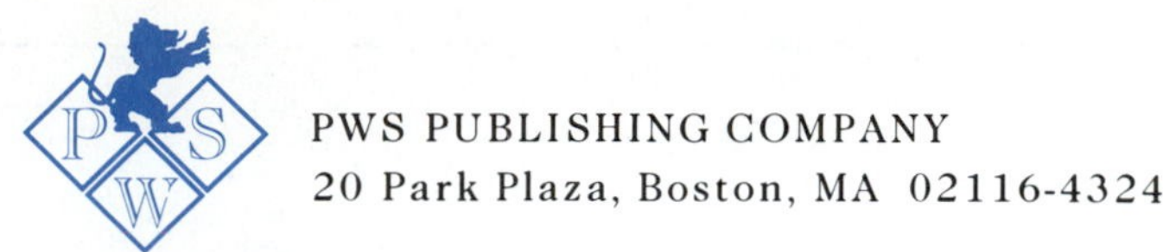
PWS PUBLISHING COMPANY
20 Park Plaza, Boston, MA 02116-4324

I(T)P™

International Thomson Publishing
The trademark ITP is used under license.

PWS Publishing Company is a division of Wadsworth, Inc.

Library of Congress Cataloging-in-Publication Data

Popkin, Gary S.
Comprehensive structured COBOL / Gary S. Popkin.—4th ed.
p. cm.
Includes index.
ISBN 0-534-93270-3
1. COBOL (Computer program language) 2. Structured programming.
I. Title.
QA76.73.C25P668 1992
005.13′3—dc20 92-32568
CIP

Printed in the United States of America.

94 95 96 97 — 10 9 8 7 6 5 4 3

Sponsoring Editor: Jonathan Plant
Assistant Editor: Mary Thomas
Production Editor: Susan M. C. Caffey
Manufacturing Coordinator: Lisa M. Flanagan
Cover Designer: DFL Publications
Text Designer: Susan M. C. Caffey
Typesetter: Pine Tree Composition, Inc.
Cover Printer: Henry N. Sawyer Co., Inc.
Text Printer: Courier/Westford

Preface

Comprehensive Structured COBOL, Fourth Edition is a complete multipurpose book. It is suitable for readers with little or no knowledge of computer programming, as well as for those readers who know one or more programming languages and wish to learn COBOL.

The book starts with the most elementary material and covers all COBOL topics except the Communication Module (the CD entry and the RECEIVE and SEND verbs). Its modular design permits the reader to cover only desired topics. The treatment of very advanced topics is useful to advanced COBOL programmers and programming professionals wishing to study selected areas of the language or to use this volume for reference.

Comprehensive Structured COBOL, Fourth Edition provides well-organized COBOL reference material for use now and later. Appendixes contain the complete reference summary of all elements of the 1985 ANSI standard COBOL language and a complete list of COBOL reserved words.

Chapter 1 provides an elementary program and successive chapters introduce additional COBOL features of increasing logical complexity. Fifty-nine complete, working COBOL programs are shown in facsimile, along with their inputs and outputs. Additional figures show the commands needed to create and use several different VSAM files, and how to use the Ryan/McFarland project-management system RM/CO* and the interactive debugger. All together, the figures in *Comprehensive Structured COBOL, Fourth Edition* constitute a valuable research tool, for they show what COBOL actually does in a variety of situations—not what the manual says it does, not what some author thinks it does, but what it does in actual performance.

Only those features needed for a particular program are discussed at each step so that complications and details are postponed until needed. All the programs in this book comply with the highest level of the 1985 ANSI COBOL standard. Those in Chapters 1–19 and 22 were compiled using IBM COBOL II, and those in Chapters 20 and 21 using Ryan/McFarland RM/COBOL-85. They should therefore run on most main-frame and PC COBOL compilers in use today. For readers wishing to obtain more information from Liant Software Corporation on the Educational Version of RM/COBOL-85 and the RM/COBOL Development System and Tools, coupons are bound in the back of the book.

Comprehensive Structured COBOL, Fourth Edition is a true 1985-standard COBOL book. The following are new in the fourth edition:

1. All programs have been rewritten using 1985 programming style and conventions and to exploit the capabilities of the language added in the 1985 standard.
2. All text material has been rewritten to refer to the totality of the COBOL language as given in the 1985 standard. Since 1985 COBOL essentially includes 1974 COBOL as a subset, a student learning 1985 COBOL learns all of 1974 COBOL and then some. There is no discussion in the book of what is new in the 1985 standard or of how COBOL programs were written in the past. All PC COBOL systems now adhere to the 1985 standard, and main-frame installations largely use the 1985 standard as well, so students of COBOL need to learn how COBOL programs are written now. They have no interest in or use for the history of COBOL.
3. A chapter on the EVALUATE verb has been added.
4. A chapter on the use of Ryan/McFarland's project-management system, RM/CO*, has been included.
5. A chapter on programming in RM/COBOL-85 and the use of the RM/CO* interactive debugger has also been added.

Program design techniques are used when suitable to particular programs. Flowcharts and hierarchy diagrams are used in appropriate circumstances, and pseudocode is discussed. The largest and most complicated programs use hierarchy diagrams to show the "big picture" in the most concise and practical way.

The book is organized into a Core part and a Modular part. In the Core, Chapters 1 through 7, all chapters must be covered in the order given in the book. In the Modular part—consisting of Chapters 8 through 22—any chapter may be covered at any time after its prerequisite chapters are covered. The chapters and their prerequisites follow.

Chapter		Prerequisite
8	Validity Checking	Chapters 1–6
9	Report Writer	Chapters 1 and 2
10	One-Dimensional Tables	Chapters 1–6
11	Tables of Higher Dimension	Chapter 10
12	Sorting and Merging	Chapters 1–6
13	Magnetic File Media	Chapter 12
14	Processing Sequential Master Files	Chapter 13
15	Indexed Files	Chapter 13
16	Relative Files	Chapter 13
17	Introduction to VSAM Processing	Chapter 13
18	String Processing	Chapters 1–6
19	Subprograms	Chapters 1–6
20	RM/COBOL-85	Chapters 1–6
21	Interactive COBOL	Chapter 20
22	The ANSI Debugging Feature	Chapter 10

If possible, I recommend that you cover Report Writer in sequence (after Chapter 8) and then use it in all subsequent chapters. The sample programs in Chapters 10–22 do not use Report Writer in deference to those to whom it is not available.

The approach used to teach programming skills is practical and intuitive. Examples are used abundantly to illustrate every concept. Exercises are placed within the body of nearly all chapters to reinforce each topic where it is discussed. Each chapter contains a summary and fill-in exercises, and nearly all of the chapters have review exercises that cover all the topics of the chapter.

Each chapter begins with a list of key points that the reader should expect to learn from the chapter, followed by a list of key words contained in the chapter. At the first appearance of each key word in the body of the chapter, the word appears in boldface, where it is explained and used in context.

Appendix D of the book contains input data for selected programming exercises.

For instructors using this book to teach a COBOL course, an *Instructor's Manual* is available from the publisher. It contains:

1. Learning objectives for each chapter
2. Chapter highlights
3. Additional exercises for each chapter
4. Answers to all nonprogramming exercises and fill-in exercises
5. Solutions to the selected programming exercises
6. The output that is produced by the solutions when run with the data in Appendix D
7. Transparency masters for all the statement formats used in the book
8. Transparency masters for item 5 above
9. Sample examinations

For the reader, a separate *Reference Guide* containing complete 1985 ANSI COBOL formats and reserved words accompanies the Fourth Edition. The Reference Guide also includes the 1985 ANSI COBOL glossary.

I wish to thank the following people for providing many helpful suggestions: Robert J. Sandler of The Grand Union Company, Michael L. Trombetta of Queensborough Community College, and Louise Popkin. I also wish to thank the following reviewers for their useful suggestions in the preparation of the manuscript:

Linda S. Barasch, *Texas Wesleyan University;* Ellen W. Gray, *Delta State University;* Lola Haskins, *University of Florida;* Joan E. Hoopes, *Marist College;* Joe Kasprzyk, *Salem State College;* Stephen J. Krebsbach, *South Dakota State University;* Gretchen Mooningham, *Saginaw Valley State University;* and Larry Nyhoff, *Calvin College.*

ing of the programming system and language. Moreover, no responsibility is assumed by any contributor, or by the committee, in connection therewith.

The authors and copyright holders of the copyrighted material used herein

> FLOW-MATIC (trademark of Sperry Rand Corporation), Programming for the UNIVAC® I and II, Data Automation Systems copyrighted 1958, 1959, by Sperry Rand Corporation; IBM Commercial Translator Form No. F 28-8013, copyrighted 1959 by IBM; FACT, DSI 27A5260–2760, copyrighted 1960 by Minneapolis-Honeywell

have specifically authorized the use of this material in whole or in part, in the COBOL specifications. Such authorization extends to the reproduction and use of COBOL specifications in programming manuals or similar publications.

Gary S. Popkin

Contents

CHAPTER 5

CHAPTER 6

CHAPTER 7

CHAPTER 8

CHAPTER 9

CHAPTER 10

CHAPTER 11

CHAPTER 12

Comprehensive Structured COBOL

CHAPTER 1

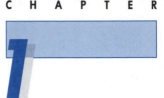

Computer Programming with COBOL

HERE ARE THE KEY POINTS YOU SHOULD LEARN FROM THIS CHAPTER

1. The steps a person must follow to obtain useful results from a computer

2. What a computer program is, and what a programmer is

3. How to write an elementary program using COBOL

4. The complete format of the Identification Division

KEY WORDS TO RECOGNIZE AND LEARN

analysis
design
coding
COBOL
program
programmer
memory
storage
output
input
division
division header
IDENTIFICATION DIVISION
ENVIRONMENT DIVISION
DATA DIVISION
PROCEDURE DIVISION
PROGRAM-ID
program name
section
Configuration Section
INPUT-OUTPUT SECTION
file
section header
FILE-CONTROL paragraph
record
FILE SECTION
FD
file description
level indicator
level number
record name
PICTURE
reserved word
user-defined word
area A
area B
paragraph header
paragraph name
OPEN
statement
MOVE
WRITE
CLOSE
STOP RUN
microcomputer
personal computer
PC
format
AUTHOR
comment-entry
DATE-COMPILED

A computer, by itself, cannot solve a problem or do anything useful. People can solve problems, using computers as tools. A person must do the following to obtain useful results from a computer:

1. Understand the problem to be solved. Only certain kinds of problems lend themselves to solution by computer. As we go through this book you will see what some of those problems are. A person must understand a problem thoroughly if a computer is to be used in its solution. This step is called **analysis** of the problem.
2. Plan how the computer can help to solve the problem. Since computers can do only certain things and not others, it is up to the human problem-solver to figure out exactly what the computer must do to contribute to the solution of the problem. This is called **designing** a solution. In this book you will study three design techniques now being used by computer professionals in industry.
3. Write instructions on a piece of paper, in a language the computer understands, that tell the computer what to do. This step is called **coding.**

   There are many languages in existence today that can be used to tell computers what to do. The language that you will study in this book is called **COBOL** (rhymes with snowball). COBOL stands for COmmon Business-Oriented Language. It is called common because the original designers of the COBOL language in 1959 envisioned a COBOL that all computers could understand. Since the 1960s, the growth of COBOL has been overseen by representatives of commerce, industry, education, and government acting through the American National Standards Institute, Inc. (ANSI) and publishing ANSI standards for the COBOL language. Three COBOL standards have been published, in 1968, 1974, and 1985. We will use 1985 standard COBOL in this book to the extent possible. You should write all of your programs in standard COBOL when possible also, using the latest system available to you.

   Any complete set of instructions that a computer uses in solving a particular problem is called a **program.** The person who prepares the program is called a **programmer.** In this book there will be many opportunities for you to create programs. When you have completed all the exercises, you will be a COBOL programmer.
4. Get the program into the computer and have the computer carry out your instructions. The program must be placed into the computer's **memory,** or **storage,** to be executed. Then you wait while the computer does exactly what you told it to do.

In real life, errors can get into this process in any of the four steps. Errors in any of the steps will cause the programmer to have to redo some of the work. Depending on the severity of the error and the step where it occurs, more or less reworking may be required.

Some errors are so easy to find that even the computer can do it. In step 4, if you make some purely mechanical error in physically getting the program into the computer, the computer usually will object in one way or another and the error can be fixed in minutes. Or in step 3, if you write an instruction that does not follow COBOL's rules of grammar, the computer will point out the error to be corrected.

In most of the programs in this book, the computer presents the results of its processing by printing its **output** onto paper. You have almost certainly seen computer-printed output. Most computers can print their output results onto continuous-form, fan-fold paper—the kind with sprocket holes along both sides.

However, computers can present their output in ways other than by printing. You have almost certainly also seen results come out of computers onto screens. And computers can present their output in still other ways; in Chapters 13 through 17 we will study several COBOL programs that deal with some of the ways.

We also must have some way of getting programs and data into computer storage. We already know that a program, once written, must be put into the computer to be executed. One common way to get a program into a computer is to enter the program on a keyboard. An example of a COBOL instruction as it might appear on a screen is as follows:

```
SUBTRACT 40 FROM HOURS-WORKED GIVING OVERTIME-HOURS
```

You will study other **input** methods in Chapters 13 through 17.

A First COBOL Program

To lend concreteness to the ideas discussed so far, we will now do a complete working COBOL program. The techniques required will be presented without unnecessary details. In this program, and with all programs in this book, only as much detail will be presented as is needed at that stage to write the particular program being discussed. If some of the material seems incomplete at any time, just wait and it will be filled out later.

Let us now set to work on Program P01-01, which is a program that does nothing but print out the author's name and (fictitious) address. Figure 1.1 shows the output as it was produced by the program.

FIGURE *1.1* Output from Program P01-01

```
G. S. POPKIN
1921 PRESIDENT ST.
BROOKLYN, NY  11221
```

The design for this program was done by the author and will not be shown here. We will save discussion of program design for more complicated programs.

Here is what the first few lines of Program P01-01 look like as they might appear on a screen:

```
00010   IDENTIFICATION DIVISION.
00020   PROGRAM-ID.  P01-01.
00030
00040 *  THIS PROGRAM PRINTS THE AUTHOR'S NAME AND
00050 *    (FICTITIOUS) ADDRESS, ON THREE LINES.  ZIP CODE IS
```

Each line contains a sequence number in character positions 1 through 5 on the screen. The sequence numbers are in intervals of 10 to allow for later insertions if necessary. Character position 6 can be used for sequence numbers also. Program P01-01 complete is shown in Figure 1.2.

FIGURE *1.2* **Program P01-01**

```
S COBOL II RELEASE 3.1 09/19/89                  P01001    DATE OCT 03,1990 T
----+-*A-1-B--+----2----+----3----+----4----+----5----+----6----+----7-%--+

00010  IDENTIFICATION DIVISION.
00020  PROGRAM-ID.  P01-01.
00030
00040 *  THIS PROGRAM PRINTS THE AUTHOR'S NAME AND
00050 *    (FICTITIOUS) ADDRESS, ON THREE LINES.  ZIP CODE IS
00060 *    INCLUDED IN THE ADDRESS.
00070 *
00080 ******************************************************************
00090
00100  ENVIRONMENT DIVISION.
00110  INPUT-OUTPUT SECTION.
00120  FILE-CONTROL.
00130      SELECT COMPLETE-ADDRESS ASSIGN TO PRINTER.
00140
00150 ******************************************************************
00160
00170  DATA DIVISION.
00180  FILE SECTION.
00190  FD  COMPLETE-ADDRESS.
00200
00210  01  ADDRESS-LINE          PICTURE X(120).
00220
00230 ******************************************************************
00240
00250  PROCEDURE DIVISION.
00260  EXECUTABLE-PROGRAM-STEPS.
00270      OPEN OUTPUT COMPLETE-ADDRESS
00280      MOVE "G. S. POPKIN"         TO ADDRESS-LINE
00290      WRITE ADDRESS-LINE
00300      MOVE "1921 PRESIDENT ST."   TO ADDRESS-LINE
00310      WRITE ADDRESS-LINE
00320      MOVE "BROOKLYN, NY  11221"  TO ADDRESS-LINE
00330      WRITE ADDRESS-LINE
00340      CLOSE COMPLETE-ADDRESS
00350      STOP RUN
00360      .
```

Program P01-01 consists of four **divisions.** Each division is identified by a **division header.** In the program shown, each division header starts in position 8 but could have begun anywhere between positions 8 and 11. The four division headers are **IDENTIFICATION DIVISION** at line 00010, **ENVIRONMENT DIVISION** at line 00100, **DATA DIVISION** at line 00170, and **PROCEDURE DIVISION** at line 00250. You must use the exact spelling and punctuation shown for the four division headers.

In COBOL a dot (.) followed by a space is taken to be a period. A dot followed by anything else is taken to be a decimal point.

The Identification Division

The Identification Division is used to give the program a name and provide other descriptive information about the program. The **PROGRAM-ID** entry, at line 00020, is required and must include a **program name** made up by the programmer. In this program the made-up program name is P01-01. The rules for making up program names are given later in this chapter.

Following the PROGRAM-ID is a brief description of the program, in lines 00040 through 00060. Each line of description has an asterisk in position 7, identifying the line as descriptive comment.

PROGRAM-ID is the only required entry in the Identification Division. There are other, optional entries. The complete form of the Identification Division is given later in this chapter.

The Environment Division

The Environment Division serves a number of purposes in COBOL. In this program the entries shown are used to indicate that the output produced by the program is to be printed on the high-speed printer.

The Environment Division has two optional **sections.** The first is the **Configuration Section.** None of the programs in this book before Chapter 21 needs a Configuration Section. If any of your programs needs one, your instructor will give you the exact entries for it.

The other section in the Environment Division is the **INPUT-OUTPUT SECTION.** It is needed whenever a program uses one or more **files,** as Program P01-01 does. It is identified by the **section header** at line 00110, and contains the required **FILE-CONTROL paragraph,** at line 00120.

It is in the Environment Division that the programmer must make up a name for every file used by the program. In Program P01-01 the output is to be three lines of name and address. Each line of printed output is considered to be one **record.** The complete printed output is a file, and its made-up name is COMPLETE-ADDRESS. The rules for making up file names are given later in this chapter.

Your instructor will give you the exact form of the Input-Output Section entries necessary for your particular computer. Later chapters contain further discussion of the Environment Division.

The Data Division

The Data Division also can be used for a number of purposes. In this program it is used to describe some details about the output to be printed. In the **FILE SECTION** of the Data Division we describe the output record and the output file. The section header for the File Section must appear exactly as shown at line 00180.

The letters **FD** stand for **file description.** There must be one FD entry for every file being used by a program. In this program there is only one file, so we need only one FD, at line 00190. The required letters FD must begin between positions 8 and 11 and be followed by the file name made up in the Environment Division. The file name and all other portions of the FD entry must begin in position 12 or to the right of position 12. In this program they begin in position 12. Each COBOL system has some rightmost position beyond which no statement may be written. In the system used to run the programs in this book, the rightmost position is position 72. There must be a period at the end of the FD entry.

FD is one of several **level indicators** in COBOL. Later in this book we will use two other level indicators.

The 01 at line 00210 indicates that we are now describing some characteristics of a single record of the output file. The 01 **level number** in position 8 must be followed by a record name made up by the programmer. Here the **record name** is ADDRESS-LINE. Rules for making up record names are given later in this chapter. The **PICTURE** clause shown tells the computer that the line of print may contain up to 120 characters. There must be at least one space between the record name and the word PICTURE, and there may be as many as you like. If your computer has a larger printer, such as a 132-character printer, you may use a larger number in the parentheses. Your instructor will give you the information you need for this.

Before going on to the next division, we can make some generalizations on the basis of what we have seen so far. First, in COBOL there are certain words that must be used exactly as given, and some that must be made up by the programmer. Those that must be used as given are called **reserved words,** and those made up by the programmer are called **user-defined words.** A reserved word must never be used where a user-defined word is required. A list of COBOL reserved words is given in Appendix A.

Also, some entries must begin in positions 8 through 11, and some must begin in position 12 or beyond. The area in positions 8 through 11 is called **area A,** and that starting in position 12 is called **area B.** Figure 1.3 shows the four areas of a line in which a COBOL statement can be written.

Area A is the place to begin division headers, section headers, **paragraph headers,** level indicators, 01 level numbers, and, as you will soon see, **paragraph names.** Later in this book you will see two other elements of COBOL that start in area A, and one that can begin in area A or area B. Everything else begins in area B. Lines that are entirely blank (except for their sequence numbers) and lines that contain an asterisk in position 7 may be included freely anywhere in the program to improve its appearance and readability.

FIGURE *1.3* **Reference format for a line of COBOL coding**

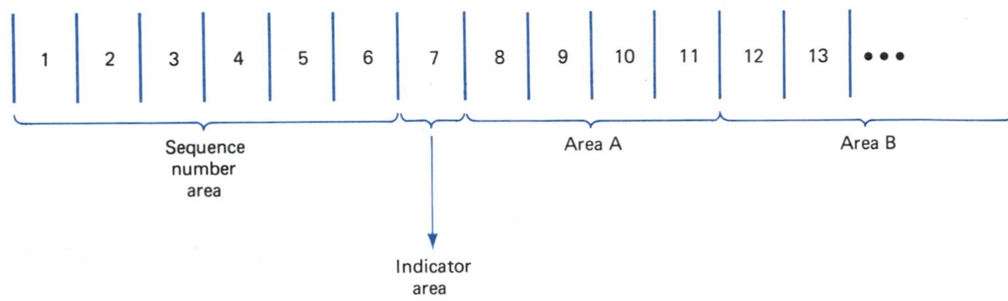

The Procedure Division

We come finally to the Procedure Division, which consists of the step-by-step procedure that the computer must follow to produce the desired output. The division header for the Procedure Division must begin in area A. There then must follow a paragraph name made up by the programmer. Whereas paragraph headers, in the Identification and Environment Divisions, must be written exactly as given, paragraph names, in the Procedure Division, must be made up. Here we have the made-up paragraph name EXECUTABLE-PROGRAM-STEPS, at line 00260. Of course it begins in area A. Rules for making up paragraph names are given later in the chapter.

We then have an instruction to **OPEN** the output file, at line 00270. All files must be OPENed before being used for an input or output operation, and the OPEN **statement** must say whether the file is going to be used for input or output or both. In our case the file will be used only for output to be printed upon. There then follow pairs of **MOVE** and **WRITE** statements, at lines 00280 through 00330. Each pair of statements causes a single line of output to be printed. There may be as many spaces as you like between words in COBOL statements. In COBOL multiple spaces are treated as one space, except when they appear inside quotation marks.

Following the instructions to print all three lines of output, we **CLOSE** the file, at line 00340. In standard COBOL all files must be CLOSEd when you are finished using them. The **STOP RUN** statement, line 00350, is the last executable statement in a program. Execution of the STOP RUN statement signals the computer to go on to its next job. Line 00360 contains a period in area B to end the paragraph.

There are two important things to notice about this Procedure Division. First, in the OPEN and CLOSE statements we use the name of the file as we made it up in the Environment Division. The name of the file in the OPEN and CLOSE statements must be spelled exactly as it was made up. The computer does not understand English, and if even one letter is wrong in spelling the file name, the computer will not understand what we mean. So when you make up user-defined words, make them whatever you like (within the rules) and then use them exactly as you made them up.

Second, our MOVE and WRITE statements used the record name that was made up in the Data Division. These usages are required by the rules of COBOL; that is, OPEN and CLOSE statements use file names, and our MOVE and WRITE statements used record names. All these rules may be a bit confusing now, but as you begin to write programs they will become automatic and even reasonable.

Statements in the Procedure Division must be completely contained in area B.

If you are going to be writing your COBOL programs on a **microcomputer,** also called a **Personal Computer** or **PC,** you may read about Program P01-01 in Chapter 20 now.

Rules for Making Up Names

User-defined words in COBOL

1. Must contain between 1 and 30 characters
2. May contain any of the letters A through Z
3. May contain any of the digits 0 through 9
4. May contain one or more hyphens
5. Must not begin or end with a hyphen
6. Must not be a reserved word

File names and record names must contain at least one letter. Paragraph names need not contain a letter, and so may consist entirely of digits, or of digits and hyphens.

The ANSI standard directs that program names be made up according to the rules that apply to file names and record names. But each COBOL system has its own requirements for program names, which may or may not comply with the standard. Check with your instructor for the rules that apply to your system.

EXERCISE 1

Which of the following are valid as paragraph names, which are valid as file names and record names as well, and which are just invalid?

a. PROG-01
b. PROGRAM-ONE
c. PROG ONE
d. 001-050
e. 001-A50
f. -001A50
g. SECTION
h. SEC-TION

EXERCISE 2

Write and execute a COBOL program to print your own name and address. Your output file may be three or more lines as needed. Make up new user-defined words for the program name, the file name, the record name, and the paragraph name.

The Complete Identification Division

The **format** of the Identification Division is shown below. In any COBOL format, words in capital letters are reserved words; items in lowercase are to be supplied by the programmer. Square brackets ([ ]) around an item indicate that it is optional. An ellipsis (. . .) following an item indicates that the item may be repeated as many times as desired. A period shown in a format is a required period.

```
IDENTIFICATION DIVISION.
PROGRAM-ID. program-identification-entry
[AUTHOR. [comment-entry] . . . ]
[INSTALLATION. [comment-entry] . . . ]
[DATE-WRITTEN. [comment-entry] . . . ]
[DATE-COMPILED. [comment-entry] . . . ]
[SECURITY. [comment-entry] . . . ]
```

The format shows that the division header and the PROGRAM-ID entry are required. The square brackets around the other entries show them to be optional. For example, the **AUTHOR** entry is optional. If you choose to include it in your program, you must write just the paragraph header AUTHOR starting in area A exactly as shown. Do not include the square brackets in the program. You then optionally follow the word AUTHOR with as many repetitions of

comment-entry as you like, all in area B. A comment-entry consists of anything you would like to write, and is ignored by the COBOL system.

If you include the **DATE-COMPILED** entry in your program, when you submit your program for a run COBOL replaces any comment-entry you may have written with the current date.

All formats shown in the body of this textbook are from the 1985 standard. Appendix B contains formats of all elements of the COBOL language from the 1985 standard.

Summary

Before a programmer can write a computer program, the problem to be solved must be completely understood. Then the programmer must plan how the computer can be used in the solution. The instructions that make up the program can be written first on a piece of paper. Then the instructions may be transferred to computer storage by being keyed on a terminal.

COBOL stands for COmmon Business-Oriented Language. Standard COBOL contains four divisions. The Identification Division can be used to give the program a name and to provide other identifying and/or descriptive information. The Input-Output Section of the Environment Division relates input and output file names to the computer's input and output devices. The Data Division describes all the details of the files and records used by the program. The Procedure Division contains the steps the computer must execute to solve the given problem.

Files must be OPENed before being used for input or output, and CLOSEd after the last input or output operation on them. A WRITE statement may be used to place a record on an output file.

Area A is the region from position 8 through position 11. Area B starts in position 12. Division headers, section headers, paragraph headers, paragraph names, level indicators, and 01 level numbers must begin in area A.

Fill-In Exercises

1. The word COBOL stands for ______ ______ ______ ______.

2. The set of instructions that a computer follows is called a(n) ______.

3. The person who makes up the computer's instructions is called a(n) ______.

4. The printed results of executing a program are called the program's ______.

5. The four divisions in standard COBOL are the ______ Division, the ______ Division, the ______ Division, and the ______ Division.

6. The PROGRAM-ID entry is part of the ______ Division.

7. The FD entry is part of the ______ Division.

8. An OPEN statement would be found in the ______ Division.

9. The ______ and ______ statements have file names as their objects.

10. The level number used for defining a record name in the File Section is ______.

11. The only required entry in the Identification Division is the ______ entry.

12. The two optional sections in the Environment Division are the ______ Section and the ______ Section.

13. In a COBOL format words in capital letters are ______ words.

14. In a COBOL format square brackets indicate that the item is ______.

15. In a COBOL format an ellipsis indicates that the preceding item may be ______.

Project

Obtain a copy of the COBOL manual for the compiler you will be using in this course. Find your compiler's reserved words. Make a list of all reserved words in your compiler that are not reserved words in the ANSI standard. Title your list ''Additional reserved words in my COBOL compiler'' and tape it onto the end of Appendix A.

CHAPTER 2

Programs Using Input, Output, and Reformatting

HERE ARE THE KEY POINTS YOU SHOULD LEARN FROM THIS CHAPTER

1. How to use the COBOL Coding Form
2. How to use a print chart
3. The rules of COBOL for reading input files
4. The general program structure for reading a variable number of input records
5. How to program column headings in COBOL
6. The format of the Environment Division

KEY WORDS TO RECOGNIZE AND LEARN

COBOL Coding Form
RECORD CONTAINS
field
data name
READ
AT END
end-of-file
END-READ
sending field
source field
literal
nonnumeric
numeric
assign
WORKING-STORAGE SECTION
initialize
VALUE
PIC
PERFORM
UNTIL
EQUAL TO
priming READ
condition
AFTER ADVANCING
FILLER
SPACES
print chart
body line
detail line
FROM
procedure name
imperative statement
BEFORE
WITH TEST AFTER
SOURCE-COMPUTER
OBJECT-COMPUTER
SPECIAL-NAMES
I-O-CONTROL
key word
implementor name
LABEL RECORDS

In this chapter we will write four programs which show more of the basic techniques of data handling. But first we will look at the **COBOL Coding Form.**

COBOL Coding Form

The COBOL Coding Form is helpful to a programmer writing COBOL programs. The forms are available in pads of about 50 at most college bookstores and wherever computer programming supplies are sold. Figure 2.1 shows a COBOL Coding Form.

FIGURE *2.1* **A COBOL Coding Form**

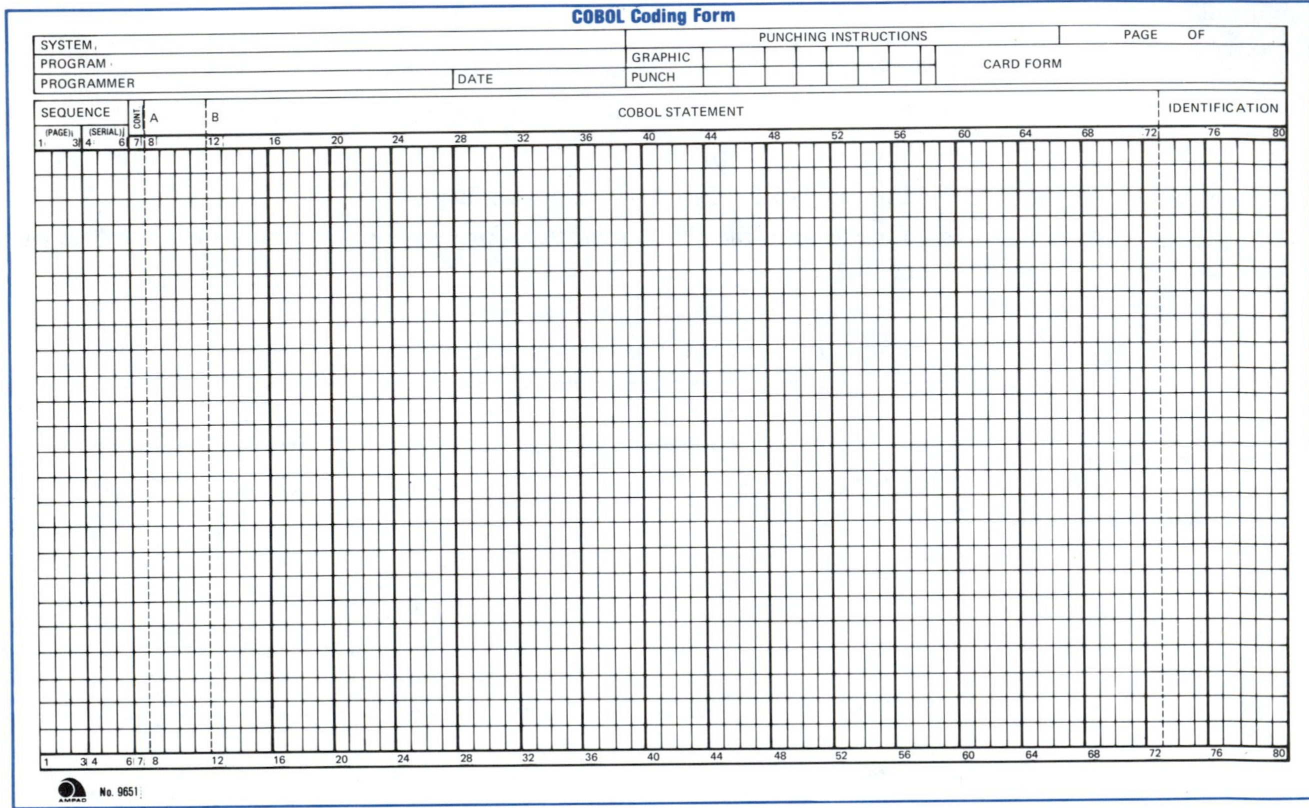

COBOL Coding Form

SYSTEM | PUNCHING INSTRUCTIONS | PAGE OF
PROGRAM | GRAPHIC | CARD FORM
PROGRAMMER | DATE | PUNCH

SEQUENCE (PAGE) (SERIAL) | CONT. | A | B | COBOL STATEMENT | IDENTIFICATION

1 3 4 6 7 8 12 16 20 24 28 32 36 40 44 48 52 56 60 64 68 72 76 80

No. 9651

The form permits a programmer to write coding line for line exactly as it will be keyed. It has room at the top for identifying information, and space below for 24 lines of COBOL code. You can see that separate areas are marked off for the sequence number for each line, column 7 for the asterisk, and areas A and B. Columns 73–80, marked "Identification," can be used by the programmer for anything and are often used for the program name. Figure 2.2 shows a COBOL Coding Form partially filled in with some of the coding from Program P01-01.

FIGURE 2.2 A COBOL Coding Form partially filled in with some of the coding from Program P01-01

COBOL Coding Form

SYSTEM	PUNCHING INSTRUCTIONS	PAGE OF
PROGRAM	GRAPHIC	CARD FORM
PROGRAMMER — DATE	PUNCH	

SEQUENCE (PAGE) (SERIAL) · CONT · A · B · COBOL STATEMENT · IDENTIFICATION

```
00010  IDENTIFICATION DIVISION.
00020  PROGRAM-ID.    P01-01.
00030
00040 *    THIS PROGRAM PRINTS THE AUTHOR'S NAME AND
00050 *        (FICTITIOUS) ADDRESS, ON THREE LINES.  ZIP CODE IS
00060 *        INCLUDED IN THE ADDRESS.
00070 *
00080 *************************************************************************
00090
00100  ENVIRONMENT DIVISION.
00110  INPUT-OUTPUT SECTION.
00120  FILE-CONTROL.
00130          SELECT COMPLETE-ADDRESS ASSIGN  TO PRINTER.
```

No. 9651

A Program to Process One Input Data Record

We now try a program slightly more complicated than Program P01-01. This program, Program P02-01, prints a three-line name and address, but this time the program obtains the name and address to be printed by reading an input record containing them. Program P01-01 was able to print only the name and address that were written into the program in the MOVE statements, but Program P02-01 is now able to print any name and address merely by being provided with a data record containing the information to be printed. Depending on the equipment available at your school, the input record may be keyed in on a terminal or it may be in some other form provided by your instructor. Let's assume that the input record to be read by Program P02-01 has the following format:

Positions	Field
1–20	Name
21–45	Street Address
46–70	City, State, ZIP
71–80	spaces

A typical input record in that format is shown in Figure 2.3.

FIGURE 2.3 Input to Program P02-01

```
--------------------------------------------------------------------------------
         1         2         3         4         5         6         7         8
12345678901234567890123456789012345678901234567890123456789012345678901234567890
--------------------------------------------------------------------------------
G. S. POPKIN         1921 PRESIDENT ST.         BROOKLYN, N. Y.  11220
```

Program P02-01 is shown in Figure 2.4. It differs from Program P01-01 in several ways. The input file,which consists of just one record, has been named ADDRESS-IN. Since we now have two files, we must have two SELECT clauses, lines 00120 and 00130, and two FD entries. The FD entry for the output file, at line 00190, is the same as in Program P01-01, but the FD entry for the input file contains the clause **RECORD CONTAINS** 80 CHARACTERS. The RECORD CONTAINS clause is optional in COBOL, but I use it here because the computer system that I used to run the programs in this book is arranged so that the most convenient size for an input record is 80 characters. Standard COBOL accepts input records of any size, but for convenience all input records in this book are 80 characters long. If my computer allowed me to use records other than 80 characters in length conveniently, I would use a 70-character record in this program, and would change line 00250 to read RECORD CONTAINS 70 CHARACTERS.

The 01 entry for the output record, at line 00210, is the same as in Program P01-01, but the 01 entry for the input record, at line 00270, introduces some new ideas. Since the input record is formatted in **fields,** we must describe those fields to the computer. The fields are described in this program by the level-05 entries, in lines 00280 through 00300. Each level-05 entry allows the programmer to make up a name for the field and indicate its length. Here the names of the three fields of input are NAME, STREET-ADDRESS, and CITY-STATE-ZIP. The names of the fields could have been any legal **data names,** of course, just as the names of files can be any legal made-up names, but it is always best to use meaningful names that describe the field contents well. The rules for data names are the same as for record names and file names. Notice that we describe only the first 70 characters of the input record, the ones we use, and ignore the remaining 10.

In the File Section of the Data Division, the 01 level always describes a record. Fields within the record may use any level number from 02 through 49. Level numbers 02 through 49 may begin anywhere in area A or B.

Although the Procedure Division in this program differs but slightly from the Procedure Division in Program P01–01, it differs in significant ways. In this program we have both an input file and an output file. Both must be OPENed before they can be used and CLOSEd after we are through using them. The OPEN statement, line 00370, OPENs both files and indicates that ADDRESS-IN is to be OPENed as an INPUT file and COMPLETE-ADDRESS is to be OPENed as an OUTPUT file. The **READ** statement at line 00390 causes the computer to READ one record from the file named in the READ statement and make that record available to the program under the record description entries associated with the file name. In this program the file being read by the READ statement is ADDRESS-

FIGURE 2.4 **Program P02-01**

```
S COBOL II RELEASE 3.1 09/19/89                  P02001    DATE MAR 23,1991 T
----+-*A-1-B--+----2----+----3----+----4----+----5----+----6----+----7-%--+

       IDENTIFICATION DIVISION.
       PROGRAM-ID.  P02-01.
      *   THIS PROGRAM READS ONE INPUT RECORD AND PRINTS
      *     ITS CONTENTS ON THREE LINES.
      *
      ******************************************************************
       ENVIRONMENT DIVISION.
       INPUT-OUTPUT SECTION.
       FILE-CONTROL.
           SELECT COMPLETE-ADDRESS   ASSIGN TO PRINTER.
           SELECT ADDRESS-IN         ASSIGN TO INFILE.
      ******************************************************************
       DATA DIVISION.
       FILE SECTION.
       FD  COMPLETE-ADDRESS.
       01  ADDRESS-LINE            PICTURE X(120).
       FD  ADDRESS-IN
           RECORD CONTAINS 80 CHARACTERS.
       01  INPUT-RECORD.
           05 NAME                 PICTURE X(20).
           05 STREET-ADDRESS       PICTURE X(25).
           05 CITY-STATE-ZIP       PICTURE X(25).
      ******************************************************************
       PROCEDURE DIVISION.
       EXECUTABLE-PROGRAM-STEPS.
           OPEN INPUT  ADDRESS-IN
                OUTPUT COMPLETE-ADDRESS
           READ ADDRESS-IN
               AT END
                   CLOSE ADDRESS-IN
                         COMPLETE-ADDRESS
                   STOP RUN
           END-READ
           MOVE NAME           TO ADDRESS-LINE
           WRITE ADDRESS-LINE
           MOVE STREET-ADDRESS TO ADDRESS-LINE
           WRITE ADDRESS-LINE
           MOVE CITY-STATE-ZIP TO ADDRESS-LINE
           WRITE ADDRESS-LINE
           CLOSE ADDRESS-IN
                 COMPLETE-ADDRESS
           STOP RUN
           .
```

IN, and the record read from the file is made available to the program under the names INPUT-RECORD, NAME, STREET-ADDRESS, and CITY-STATE-ZIP.

An **AT END** phrase in a READ statement tells COBOL what to do if and when **end-of-file** is reached on a file being read. The computer executes the AT END phrase when a READ is attempted and no more input records are found. It does not execute it when the last input record is read.

In this case, since we expect this file to contain only one record and this is the one and only READ statement to be executed on the file, the AT END phrase at line 00400 tells the computer what to do if the file accidentally contains no input record. If our input file contains no data, the AT END phrase in this program just CLOSEs both files and executes a STOP RUN. The reserved word **END-READ** at line 00440 ends the READ statement.

Of course, if all is well, our file will contain the expected input record and the computer can go on to the MOVE and WRITE statements in lines 00450 through 00500. We give the MOVE statements in the order that we want the fields to print. Notice how the MOVE statements in this program differ from those in Program P01-01. In Program P01-01 the **sending field** of the MOVE was some actual piece of data enclosed in quotation marks. Here the sending field, or **source field,** of the MOVE is a data name, so what will be MOVEd are the NAME, STREET-ADDRESS, and CITY-STATE-ZIP fields that were read from the input record, and not the words "NAME", "STREET-ADDRESS", or "CITY-STATE-ZIP". This very important difference between having a data name in a statement as distinguished from writing the actual data literally into the statement will be discussed further shortly.

After the three lines of output are MOVEd and written,we CLOSE the input and output files with a CLOSE statement, line 00510, and execute a STOP RUN in the usual way.

Program P02-01 was run with the input data shown in Figure 2.3 and produced the output shown in Figure 2.5.

FIGURE 2.5 **Output from Program P02-01**

```
G. S. POPKIN
1921 PRESIDENT ST.
BROOKLYN, N. Y.  11220
```

Literals and Assignment

In Program P01-01, where the sending fields of the MOVE statements were pieces of data enclosed in quotation marks, the pieces of data are called **literals.** There are two categories of literals in COBOL. The ones we used in Program P01-01 are called **nonnumeric** literals. A nonnumeric literal is any string of characters, except the quotation mark, enclosed in quotation marks. Thus "G.S. POPKIN" is a valid nonnumeric literal, but " "MURDER," SHE SAID." is not. If you must have quotation marks inside a literal, they can be represented by two successive quotation marks, so " " "MURDER," " SHE SAID." is valid. When such a literal is printed as output, only one of the quotation marks from each pair prints, as "MURDER," SHE SAID. Nonnumeric literals may be up to 120 characters long. The enclosing quotation marks are not part of the literal.

The other category of literals is the **numeric** literal. We have not yet used any numeric literals in our programs. A numeric literal must contain at least one of the digits 0 through 9, and may contain up to 18 digits. It may have a plus or minus sign at its left end. It may contain a decimal point anywhere except at its right end, and it must not contain a comma. An unsigned numeric literal is assumed to be positive. A numeric literal is not enclosed in quotation marks. If a numeric quantity is enclosed in quotation marks, it is treated as a nonnumeric literal. The following are legal numeric literals:

145

+14500

−1541

13.06

13.0

.68

The following are not legal numeric literals:

100,000 (Numeric literal must not contain a comma.)

13. (Decimal point, if present, must not be at right end.)

"145" (Numeric literal must not be enclosed.)

In Program P02-01, Figure 2.4, the sending fields of the MOVE statements were not literals but data names. In such a case the data that are MOVEd are whatever data happen to be **assigned** to the data name at the time. In our program, data were assigned to the data names by the READ statement; that is, the READ statement brought in an input data record and assigned the first field in the record to the name NAME, the second field to the name STREET-ADDRESS, and the third field to the name CITY-STATE-ZIP. There are many ways in which data can be assigned to data names and they will be mentioned as needed. For now, the very important difference between

```
MOVE "DOG" TO OUTPUT-LINE
```

and

```
MOVE DOG TO OUTPUT-LINE
```

is that in the first case the word DOG will be MOVEd to the output line, but in the second what will be MOVEd to the output line is whatever data value happens to have been assigned to the data name DOG by some earlier part of the program. The MOVE does not change the value assigned to the sending field; that is, the value assigned to DOG after the MOVE is the same as the value it had before the MOVE.

EXERCISE *1*

Write a program to process a single input record according to the following specifications:

Input

One record containing a name and address in the following format:

Positions	Field
1–15	Company Name
16–30	Street Address
31–45	City and State
46–65	Employee Name
66–80	Employee Title

Output

A five-line address containing, each on its own line, the Employee Name, Employee Title, Company Name, Street Address, and City and State.

A Program to Process Multiple Input Records

The usual situation in data processing is that a program will read many input records and process each one, but the number of input records to be processed is not known at the time the program is being written. In fact, it is usual for any program to be run many times, and in each running it can be expected to have to process different numbers of input records. So we must have some way to accommodate this variability in the number of input records to be read. We will do this by using the AT END phrase of the READ statement in a new way.

Program P02-02 uses data in the same format as does Program P02-01. Program P02-02 READs any number of input records whereas Program P02-01 READs only one. The contents of each input record are printed in the usual three-line format, single spaced as before, but Program P02-02 double-spaces between addresses.

Processing a Variable Number of Input Records

Program P02-02 is shown in Figure 2.6. The new things in this program are those needed to handle the unknown variable number of input records. First we need a new section in the Data Division, the **WORKING-STORAGE SECTION,** at line 00400. The Working Storage Section can be used for holding and naming any data that are neither read in nor written out; that is, any data that are not part of the File Section. In this program we use a single field called MORE-INPUT, at line 00410, to indicate to the program when there are no more input records to be processed. MORE-INPUT is a user-defined data name made up by the author. The field has been made one character long and is **initialized,** or started out, with a value of ''Y'', by use of the **VALUE** clause. This indicates that as the program begins execution we expect to find more input, since we have so far processed none at all. You will soon see how the coding in the program turns MORE-INPUT to ''N'' when there are no more input data to process.

This program also shows our first use of the abbreviation **PIC** for PICTURE. PIC is a reserved word specifically provided as an abbreviation for PICTURE. Only a few reserved words in COBOL have authorized abbreviations, and only those words for which abbreviations are given may be abbreviated. You cannot make up your own abbreviations for reserved words.

The Procedure Division in this program shows a conventional form that we will use whenever possible to process an unknown variable number of input records. The first paragraph of the program consists of three **PERFORM** statements, at lines 00470 through 00490, and a STOP RUN statement. A PERFORM statement directs the computer to carry out the paragraph named in the statement. Thus the PERFORM statement at line 00470 causes the paragraph called INITIALIZATION to be executed. Then the PERFORM statement at line 00480 causes the paragraph called MAIN-LOOP to be executed until all the input has been processed; that is, **UNTIL** MORE-INPUT has been made **EQUAL TO** ''N''.

FIGURE 2.6 **Program P02-02**

```
S COBOL II RELEASE 3.1 09/19/89                 P02002   DATE MAR 23,1991 T
----+-*A-1-B--+----2----+----3----+----4----+----5----+----6----+----7-%--+

00010  IDENTIFICATION DIVISION.
00020  PROGRAM-ID.  P02-02.
00030
00040 *      INPUT - NAMES AND ADDRESSES IN THE FOLLOWING
00050 *      FORMAT:
00060 *
00070 *      POS. 1-20               NAME
00080 *      POS. 21-45              STREET ADDRESS
00090 *      POS. 46-70              CITY, STATE, ZIP
00100 *
00110 *      OUTPUT - THREE-LINE ADDRESSES, SINGLE SPACED, WITH A DOUBLE
00120 *      SPACE BETWEEN ADDRESSES.
00130 *
00140 ******************************************************************
00150
00160  ENVIRONMENT DIVISION.
00170  INPUT-OUTPUT SECTION.
00180  FILE-CONTROL.
00190      SELECT THREE-LINE-ADDRESSES ASSIGN TO PRINTER.
00200      SELECT ADDRESSES-IN         ASSIGN TO INFILE.
00210
00220 ******************************************************************
00230
00240  DATA DIVISION.
00250  FILE SECTION.
00260  FD  THREE-LINE-ADDRESSES.
00270
00280  01  ADDRESS-LINE             PIC X(120).
00290
00300
00310  FD  ADDRESSES-IN
00320      RECORD CONTAINS 80 CHARACTERS.
00330
00340  01  INPUT-RECORD.
00350      05 NAME                  PIC X(20).
00360      05 STREET-ADDRESS        PIC X(25).
00370      05 CITY-STATE-ZIP        PIC X(25).
00380
00390
00400  WORKING-STORAGE SECTION.
00410  01  MORE-INPUT               PIC X     VALUE "Y".
00420
00430 ******************************************************************
00440
00450  PROCEDURE DIVISION.
00460  CONTROL-PARAGRAPH.
00470      PERFORM INITIALIZATION
00480      PERFORM MAIN-LOOP UNTIL MORE-INPUT IS EQUAL TO "N"
00490      PERFORM TERMINATION
00500      STOP RUN
00510
```

continued

The last PERFORM statement, line 00490, causes the TERMINATION paragraph to execute, and then the STOP RUN statement ends the execution of the program. The names of all the paragraphs in the Procedure Division of this program (and of all COBOL programs) are user-defined words.

FIGURE 2.6 *continued*

```
S COBOL II RELEASE 3.1 09/19/89                P02002   DATE MAR 23,1991 T
----+-*A-1-B--+----2----+----3----+----4----+----5----+----6----+----7-%--+

00520
00530  INITIALIZATION.
00540      OPEN INPUT  ADDRESSES-IN
00550           OUTPUT THREE-LINE-ADDRESSES
00560      READ ADDRESSES-IN
00570          AT END
00580              MOVE "N" TO MORE-INPUT
00590      .
00600
00610  TERMINATION.
00620      CLOSE ADDRESSES-IN
00630            THREE-LINE-ADDRESSES
00640      .
00650
00660  MAIN-LOOP.
00670      MOVE NAME TO ADDRESS-LINE
00680      WRITE ADDRESS-LINE AFTER ADVANCING 2 LINES
00690      MOVE STREET-ADDRESS TO ADDRESS-LINE
00700      WRITE ADDRESS-LINE
00710      MOVE CITY-STATE-ZIP TO ADDRESS-LINE
00720      WRITE ADDRESS-LINE
00730      READ ADDRESSES-IN
00740          AT END
00750              MOVE "N" TO MORE-INPUT
00760      .
```

The INITIALIZATION Paragraph

The OPEN and READ statements in the INITIALIZATION paragraph, lines 00540 and 00560, are similar to those we saw in Program P02-01. END-READ is not needed because the period in line 00590 ends both the paragraph and the READ statement. In this program the READ statement in this paragraph is used to READ only the first record from the file. This is called the **priming READ** statement. In this program all the other input records are read from the file by another READ statement elsewhere in the Procedure Division.

The AT END phrases in the READ statements in this program differ from the AT END phrase in Program P02-01. In that program, if the first (and only) READ statement discovered that there were accidentally no input data, the AT END phrase directed the computer to CLOSE the files and STOP RUN. We use here a more general procedure in both READ statements in this program. Each AT END phrase, if or when it discovers that there are no input data or no more input data, MOVEs the letter ''N'' to the working storage field MORE-INPUT.

The TERMINATION Paragraph

The function of the TERMINATION paragraph, line 00610, should be obvious. Notice that PERFORMed paragraphs can appear in any physical sequence in the program. The order in which the PERFORMed paragraphs are executed is determined by the PERFORM statements in the control paragraph. You thus can, and should, order your paragraphs in such a way that your program is easy to read and understand.

The Main Loop

The PERFORM statement at line 00480 causes the paragraph MAIN-LOOP to be executed as many times as necessary, UNTIL the specified **condition** has been met. MAIN-LOOP is first executed after the priming READ has been executed. The loop processes the first record (already read) and READs the second record; then the loop executes again to process the second record and READ the third. MAIN-LOOP executes over and over, processing each record and READing the next, until finally there are no more data to be read, and MAIN-LOOP sets MORE-INPUT to "N".

The actions carried out by MAIN-LOOP are ones we have already seen, except for the double spacing of the first line of each address. The pairs of MOVE and WRITE statements, lines 00670 through 00720, print the input data, and the READ statement at line 00730 (to READ the second and subsequent records) is identical to the priming READ. Of course, whereas we expect the priming READ never to execute its AT END phrase, the READ statement at line 00730 eventually finds no more input data and carries out the instruction in its AT END phrase.

The WRITE statement that prints the first line of each address contains the phrase **AFTER ADVANCING** 2 LINES. This gives double spacing. When the ADVANCING option is omitted, as it is in the other two WRITE statements, COBOL gives single spacing, as if you had written AFTER ADVANCING 1 LINE.[1] There is no upper limit on the size of the integer that may appear in an ADVANCING phrase. You may use AFTER ADVANCING 0 LINES to suppress spacing.

Program P02-02 was run with the input data shown in Figure 2.7. It produced the output shown in Figure 2.8.

FIGURE 2.7 **Input to Program P02-02**

```
--------------------------------------------------------------------------------
         1         2         3         4         5         6         7         8
12345678901234567890123456789012345678901234567890123456789012345678901234567890
--------------------------------------------------------------------------------
G. S. POPKIN             1921 PRESIDENT ST.        BROOKLYN, NY  11221
L. MORGAN                11 W. 42 ST.              NEW YORK, NY  10010
P. LIPPY                 44 W. 10TH ST.            NEW YORK, NY  10036
S. O'MALLEY              121 5TH AVE.              BROOKLYN, NY  11217
```

[1]Note to instructor: There is no need to reserve space for a carriage-control character. The ANSI standard does not call for such a space. In IBM COBOL II the compile-time option PARM.COB=ADV, which is the default in most installatons, provides the space and satisfies the standard. In NCR VRX COBOL, the standard is always satisfied and no space is ever needed.

FIGURE 2.8 Output from Program P02-02

```
G. S. POPKIN
1921 PRESIDENT ST.
BROOKLYN, NY  11221

L. MORGAN
11 W. 42 ST.
NEW YORK, NY  10010

P. LIPPY
44 W. 10TH ST.
NEW YORK, NY  10036

S. O'MALLEY
121 5TH AVE.
BROOKLYN, NY  11217
```

EXERCISE 2

Write a program to read and process input records according to the following specifications:

Input

Records in the following format:

Positions	Field
1–15	Company Name
16–30	Street Address
31–45	City and State
46–65	Employee Name
66–80	Employee Title

Output

For each input record, print a five-line address containing, each on its own line, an Employee Name, Employee Title, Company Name, Street Address, and City and State. The first line of each address is to be double spaced, and the address itself single spaced.

A Program with Output Line Formatting

In the programs we have done so far, only one field appeared on each output line of print. It is more usual to have several fields printed on a single line, and those fields must be properly spaced across the page to make the output easy to read. We will now consider a program to READ input records and print the entire contents of each record on one line. The format of the input records is:

Positions	Field
1–9	Social Security Number
10–34	Employee Name
35–39	Employee Number
40–46	Annual Salary (dollars and cents)
47–80	spaces

FIGURE 2.9 Input to Program P02-03

```
--------------------------------------------------------------------------------
         1         2         3         4         5         6         7         8
12345678901234567890123456789012345678901234567890123456789012345678901234567890
--------------------------------------------------------------------------------
100040002MORALES, LUIS                 105035000000
101850005JACOBSON, MRS. NELLIE         108904651000
201110008GREENWOOD, JAMES              112774302000
209560011COSTELLO, JOSEPH S.           116643953000
301810014REITER, D.                    120513604000
304870017MARRA, DITTA E.               124383255000
401710020LIPKE, VINCENT R.             128252906000
407390023KUGLER, CHARLES               132122557000
502070026JAVIER, CARLOS                135992208000
505680029GOODMAN, ISAAC                139861859000
604910032FELDSOTT, MS. SALLY           143731510000
608250035BUXBAUM, ROBERT               147601161000
703100038DUMAY, MRS. MARY              151470812000
708020041SMITH, R.                     155340463000
803220044VINCENTE, MATTHEW J.          159210114000
901050047THOMAS, THOMAS T.             163084235000
901029857WONG, TIM                     002361850000
```

There are no blanks between fields. There may be blanks within the Employee Name field, however, as part of the name, as shown in the input data listing in Figure 2.9. We will now try to write a program that will READ an input record and print all four fields from it on one output line, then READ the next record and print the four fields from that record on a line, and so on. Since there are no blanks between fields in the input record, if we print the record just as it is, the output will be difficult to read. Fortunately, in COBOL it is easy not only to insert spaces between the fields for printing, but also to rearrange the fields on the output line in any desired way. Let us say that we would like to print each line with the fields in the following print positions:

Print Positions	Field
5–9	Employee Number
12–20	Social Security Number
25–49	Employee Name
52–58	Annual Salary

Now not only have we specified spaces between the fields when printed, but also that the fields be in a different order on the output line from their order in the input record. Formatting output lines in this way is very easy in COBOL.

You can check that each output field has been made the same size as its corresponding input field. For example, the input Employee Number, positions 35 through 39, is five characters long. The Employee Number in the output, print positions 5 through 9, is also five characters. The way to compute the size of an input or output field is: Subtract the lower position number from the higher and add 1. Compute the sizes of the other three fields in the input and output before going on.

Program P02-03 is shown in Figure 2.10. In this program we can define the exact placement of the fields in the output line through the use of level-05 entries for the output record. We can arrange the fields in any desired order across the page, and by using unnamed fields we can get any desired number of blank print positions between the named fields. If you now study the level-05 entries for EMPLOYEE-LINE-OUT, lines 00430 through 00500, you will see that the organization of the fields agrees with the requirements for the output line, as given in the statement of the problem. Whenever you have fields that are not explicitly referred to in the Procedure Division, as we have here in lines 00430, 00450, 00470, and 00490, you may omit giving them names or you may name them with the reserved word **FILLER.** Although we have used unnamed fields here in an output record description, it is legal to use them in input record descriptions as well if necessary.

FIGURE *2.10* **Program P02-03**

```
S COBOL II RELEASE 3.1 09/19/89                P02003   DATE MAR 23,1991 T
----+-*A-1-B--+----2----+----3----+----4----+----5----+----6----+----7-%--+

00010  IDENTIFICATION DIVISION.
00020  PROGRAM-ID.  P02-03.
00030
00040 *     THIS PROGRAM READS INPUT RECORDS IN THE FOLLOWING FORMAT:
00050 *
00060 *     POS. 1-9           SOCIAL SECURITY NUMBER
00070 *     POS. 10-34         EMPLOYEE NAME
00080 *     POS. 35-39         EMPLOYEE NUMBER
00090 *     POS. 40-46         ANNUAL SALARY
00100 *
00110 *     FOR EACH RECORD, ONE LINE IS PRINTED IN THE FOLLOWING FORMAT:
00120 *
00130 *     PP 5-9              EMPLOYEE NUMBER
00140 *     PP 12-20            SOCIAL SECURITY NUMBER
00150 *     PP 25-49            EMPLOYEE NAME
00160 *     PP 52-58            ANNUAL SALARY
00170 *
00180 *****************************************************************
```

FIGURE 2.10 *continued*

```
 ENVIRONMENT DIVISION.
 INPUT-OUTPUT SECTION.
 FILE-CONTROL.
     SELECT EMPLOYEE-DATA-OUT ASSIGN TO PRINTER.
     SELECT EMPLOYEE-DATA-IN  ASSIGN TO INFILE.
*****************************************************************
 DATA DIVISION.
 FILE SECTION.
 FD  EMPLOYEE-DATA-IN
     RECORD CONTAINS 80 CHARACTERS.
 01  EMPLOYEE-RECORD-IN.
     05 SOCIAL-SECURITY-NUMBER-IN      PIC X(9).
     05 EMPLOYEE-NAME-IN               PIC X(25).
     05 EMPLOYEE-NUMBER-IN             PIC X(5).
     05 ANNUAL-SALARY-IN               PIC X(7).
 FD  EMPLOYEE-DATA-OUT.
 01  EMPLOYEE-LINE-OUT.
     05                                PIC X(4).
     05 EMPLOYEE-NUMBER-OUT            PIC X(5).
     05                                PIC X(2).
     05 SOCIAL-SECURITY-NUMBER-OUT     PIC X(9).
     05                                PIC X(4).
     05 EMPLOYEE-NAME-OUT              PIC X(25).
     05                                PIC X(2).
     05 ANNUAL-SALARY-OUT              PIC X(7).
 WORKING-STORAGE SECTION.
 01  MORE-INPUT                        PIC X    VALUE "Y".
*****************************************************************
 PROCEDURE DIVISION.
 CONTROL-PARAGRAPH.
     PERFORM INITIALIZATION
     PERFORM MAIN-LOOP UNTIL MORE-INPUT IS EQUAL TO "N"
     PERFORM TERMINATION
     STOP RUN
     .
 INITIALIZATION.
     OPEN INPUT  EMPLOYEE-DATA-IN
          OUTPUT EMPLOYEE-DATA-OUT
     READ EMPLOYEE-DATA-IN
         AT END
             MOVE "N" TO MORE-INPUT
     .
 TERMINATION.
     CLOSE EMPLOYEE-DATA-IN
           EMPLOYEE-DATA-OUT
     .
```

continued

FIGURE 2.10 *continued*

```
S COBOL II RELEASE 3.1 09/19/89                  P02003    DATE MAR 23,1991 T
----+-*A-1-B--+----2----+----3----+----4----+----5----+----6----+----7-%--+

00780  MAIN-LOOP.
00790      MOVE SPACES                      TO EMPLOYEE-LINE-OUT
00800      MOVE SOCIAL-SECURITY-NUMBER-IN TO SOCIAL-SECURITY-NUMBER-OUT
00810      MOVE EMPLOYEE-NUMBER-IN          TO EMPLOYEE-NUMBER-OUT
00820      MOVE ANNUAL-SALARY-IN            TO ANNUAL-SALARY-OUT
00830      MOVE EMPLOYEE-NAME-IN            TO EMPLOYEE-NAME-OUT
00840      WRITE EMPLOYEE-LINE-OUT
00850      READ EMPLOYEE-DATA-IN
00860          AT END
00870              MOVE "N" TO MORE-INPUT
00880
```

Let us now examine the paragraph MAIN-LOOP, line 00780. It begins with a MOVE **SPACES** statement that assigns blanks to all the fields in EMPLOYEE-LINE-OUT; that is, it blanks out the entire output line area. This statement is needed mainly to blank out the unnamed areas in EMPLOYEE-LINE-OUT, as there is no other way to do it. SPACES is a reserved word, and stands for as many blank characters as are indicated by the context it is used in.

The MOVE SPACES statement is followed by four MOVE statements, lines 00800 through 00830, each moving a single field from the input area to the output area. Notice that there are no intervening WRITE statements as there were in the previous program. That is so because each WRITE statement causes a line of output to print, and in this program we don't want an output line until we have MOVEd all four fields of input to the output area. In this program the four fields can be MOVEd to the output area in any order; none of the MOVEs affects any of the others, and we don't WRITE a line until all four are MOVEd. In previous programs the fields had to be MOVEd to the output area in the order in which we wanted them to print, because we wrote a line after every MOVE.

The output from Program P02-03 is shown in Figure 2.11.

FIGURE 2.11 **Output from Program P02-03**

```
10503  100040002   MORALES, LUIS                 5000000
10890  101850005   JACOBSON, MRS. NELLIE         4651000
11277  201110008   GREENWOOD, JAMES              4302000
11664  209560011   COSTELLO, JOSEPH S.           3953000
12051  301810014   REITER, D.                    3604000
12438  304870017   MARRA, DITTA E.               3255000
12825  401710020   LIPKE, VINCENT R.             2906000
13212  407390023   KUGLER, CHARLES               2557000
13599  502070026   JAVIER, CARLOS                2208000
13986  505680029   GOODMAN, ISAAC                1859000
14373  604910032   FELDSOTT, MS. SALLY           1510000
14760  608250035   BUXBAUM, ROBERT               1161000
15147  703100038   DUMAY, MRS. MARY              0812000
15534  708020041   SMITH, R.                     0463000
15921  803220044   VINCENTE, MATTHEW J.          0114000
16308  901050047   THOMAS, THOMAS T.             4235000
00236  901029857   WONG, TIM                     1850000
```

EXERCISE 3

Write a program to read and process input records according to the following specifications:

Input

Records in the following format:

Positions	Field
1–15	Company Name
16–30	Street Address
31–45	City and State
46–65	Employee Name
66–80	Employee Title

Output

For each input record, print its contents on one line in the following format:

Print Positions	Field
6–20	Company Name
23–37	Street Address
40–54	City and State
60–74	Employee Title
76–95	Employee Name

The Print Chart

A second kind of form that is helpful when writing COBOL programs is the **print chart** as shown in Figure 2.12; it can usually be bought where you buy your coding forms. The chart can be used by the programmer to plan the format of an output report or listing before starting to code a program. You can see in Figure 2.12 the print positions numbered across the top of the chart. The print position numbers are in groups of 10 for ease of locating any particular position.

In planning an output report, the programmer determines the print positions in which the various fields of output are to appear and indicates those fields on the chart. The fields should be indicated on the chart with the same character that is used in a PICTURE for that field in a COBOL program. To give an example of the use of a print chart, we will use the output specifications of Program P02-03, page 23.

Since all the output fields in that program have PICTURE characters of X, we use Xs on the print chart. In Figure 2.13 you can see that several lines have been filled in in the print positions where the fields Employee Number, Social Security Number, Employee Name, and Annual Salary would appear. In Chapters 3 and 4 you will see all the other characters that may be used in PICTUREs in COBOL programs.

FIGURE 2.12 A print chart

FIGURE 2.13 Print chart showing the output specifications of Program P02-03

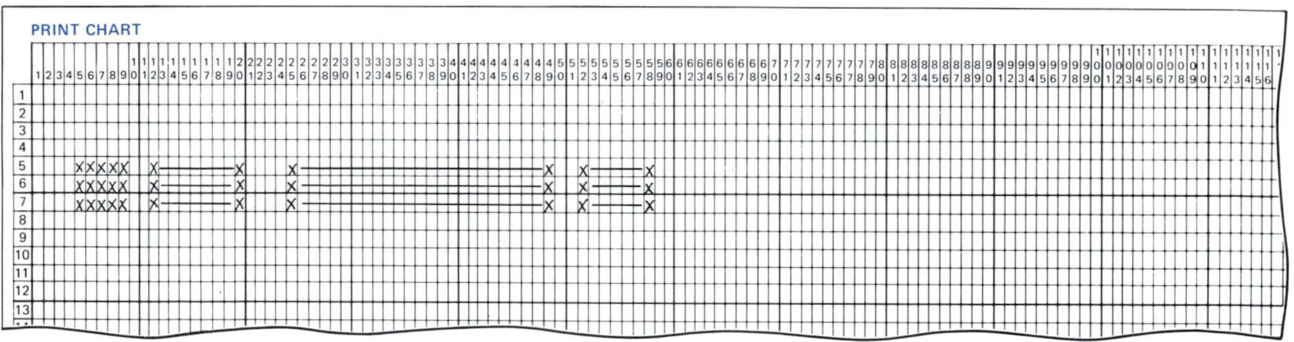

Ordinarily a print chart would not be used merely to visualize an output specification that already has been developed. Instead it is usually used to develop the output specification, that is, to plan what the output will look like. So for our next program you will be given the output requirements not in the form used previously, but in the form of a print chart. Later on you will be asked to develop your own output specifications using a print chart.

EXERCISE 4 Using a print chart, show the output specification from Exercise 3, page 27.

Column Headings

Sometimes it is useful to be able to print fixed heading information at the top of a page of output so that the reader can easily see what each column of output is supposed to contain. In the output of Program P02-03 it would have been useful to have the words EMP.NO., SOCIAL SECURITY NUMBER, EMPLOYEE NAME, and ANNUAL SALARY appear approximately over the corresponding columns of output. Figure 2.14 shows a modification of the print chart in Figure 2.13, which includes column headings.

FIGURE 2.14 **Print chart showing column headings**

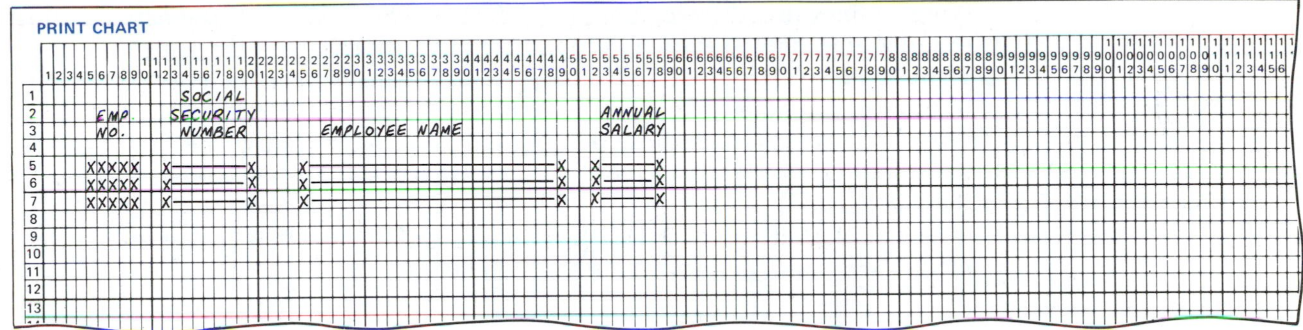

The three lines of column headings are constant information, and one place to set up such constants is in the Working Storage Section. The first heading line consists of 13 spaces and the word SOCIAL. The second heading line consists of five spaces, then the word EMP., then more spaces, then the word SECURITY, then a lot of spaces, and then the word ANNUAL. The third heading line consists of spaces and the words NO., NUMBER, EMPLOYEE NAME, and SALARY.

The first heading line can be set up in working storage as follows:

```
01 HEADING-LINE-1.
   05                    PIC X(13)   VALUE SPACES.
   05                    PIC X(6)    VALUE "SOCIAL".
```

The second heading line can be set up as follows:

```
01 HEADING-LINE-2.
   05                    PIC X(5)    VALUE SPACES.
   05                    PIC X(4)    VALUE "EMP.".
   05                    PIC X(3)    VALUE SPACES.
   05                    PIC X(8)    VALUE "SECURITY".
   05                    PIC X(32)   VALUE SPACES.
   05                    PIC X(6)    VALUE "ANNUAL".
```

You will see how to get a COBOL program to WRITE fields that have been defined in working storage when we look at Program P02-04.

EXERCISE 5 Write the working storage entries for the third heading line in Figure 2.14.

A Program with Column Headings

Program P02-04 is shown in Figure 2.15. The output records in this program have several different formats—the three heading lines and the **body line,** or **detail line,** of the report. Whenever you have more than one output-line format in a program, it is best to define all the fields of all the output lines in working storage. We have done that in this program, as you will see when we look at the Working Storage Section. You nonetheless must have some record definition in the File Section associated with the output file. Here we have OUTPUT-LINE, at line 00310. The size of OUTPUT-LINE has been made as long as the longest line that the program prints. You can see from the print chart that the longest line is 58 characters.

In the Working Storage Section you can find the definitions of the four types of lines that the program prints. EMPLOYEE-LINE-OUT, the detail line, is found at lines 00360 through 00440. The definition here is the same as in Program P02-03, except that VALUE SPACES clauses have been included in the definitions of the fields that are to be blank on the output. We did not use VALUE SPACES clauses to blank those output fields in Program P02-03 because COBOL does not permit the use of the VALUE clause to establish the value of a field in the File Section.

The definitions of HEADING-LINE-1, HEADING-LINE-2, and HEADING-LINE-3 are found in lines 00460 through 00660.

FIGURE 2.15 Program P02-04

```
S COBOL II RELEASE 3.1 09/19/89                  P02004   DATE MAR 23,1991 T
----+-*A-1-B--+----2----+----3----+----4----+----5----+----6----+----7-%--+

00010  IDENTIFICATION DIVISION.
00020  PROGRAM-ID.  P02-04.
00030
00040 *     THIS PROGRAM IS A MODIFICATION TO PROGRAM P02-03,
00050 *     WITH COLUMN HEADINGS.
00060 *
00070 *****************************************************************
00080
00090  ENVIRONMENT DIVISION.
00100  INPUT-OUTPUT SECTION.
00110  FILE-CONTROL.
00120      SELECT EMPLOYEE-DATA-OUT ASSIGN TO PRINTER.
00130      SELECT EMPLOYEE-DATA-IN  ASSIGN TO INFILE.
00140
00150 *****************************************************************
00160
00170  DATA DIVISION.
00180  FILE SECTION.
00190  FD  EMPLOYEE-DATA-IN
00200      RECORD CONTAINS 80 CHARACTERS.
00210
```

FIGURE 2.15

continued

```
 01  EMPLOYEE-RECORD-IN.
     05 SOCIAL-SECURITY-NUMBER-IN        PIC X(9).
     05 EMPLOYEE-NAME-IN                 PIC X(25).
     05 EMPLOYEE-NUMBER-IN               PIC X(5).
     05 ANNUAL-SALARY-IN                 PIC X(7).


 FD  EMPLOYEE-DATA-OUT.

 01  OUTPUT-LINE                         PIC X(58).

 WORKING-STORAGE SECTION.
 01  MORE-INPUT                          PIC X(1)    VALUE "Y".

 01  EMPLOYEE-LINE-OUT.
     05                                  PIC X(4)    VALUE SPACES.
     05 EMPLOYEE-NUMBER-OUT              PIC X(5).
     05                                  PIC X(2)    VALUE SPACES.
     05 SOCIAL-SECURITY-NUMBER-OUT       PIC X(9).
     05                                  PIC X(4)    VALUE SPACES.
     05 EMPLOYEE-NAME-OUT                PIC X(25).
     05                                  PIC X(2)    VALUE SPACES.
     05 ANNUAL-SALARY-OUT                PIC X(7).

 01  HEADING-LINE-1.
     05                    PIC X(13)  VALUE SPACES.
     05                    PIC X(6)   VALUE "SOCIAL".

 01  HEADING-LINE-2.
     05                    PIC X(5)   VALUE SPACES.
     05                    PIC X(4)   VALUE "EMP.".
     05                    PIC X(3)   VALUE SPACES.
     05                    PIC X(8)   VALUE "SECURITY".
     05                    PIC X(32)  VALUE SPACES.
     05                    PIC X(6)   VALUE "ANNUAL".

 01  HEADING-LINE-3.
     05                    PIC X(5)   VALUE SPACES.
     05                    PIC X(3)   VALUE "NO.".
     05                    PIC X(5)   VALUE SPACES.
     05                    PIC X(6)   VALUE "NUMBER".
     05                    PIC X(7)   VALUE SPACES.
     05                    PIC X(13)  VALUE "EMPLOYEE NAME".
     05                    PIC X(13)  VALUE SPACES.
     05                    PIC X(6)   VALUE "SALARY".

*****************************************************************

 PROCEDURE DIVISION.
 CONTROL-PARAGRAPH.
     PERFORM INITIALIZATION
     PERFORM MAIN-LOOP UNTIL MORE-INPUT IS EQUAL TO "N"
     PERFORM TERMINATION
     STOP RUN
     .

```

continued

In the Procedure Division we have statements to WRITE the heading lines. But where should those statements be in the program to produce heading lines once and only once before the first detail line is printed? The answer suggests itself, if we remember that everything in the MAIN-LOOP paragraph is executed once for each detail line that is printed. Since we certainly don't want heading lines to print with each detail line, the statements that print the heading lines

FIGURE 2.15

continued

```
S COBOL II RELEASE 3.1 09/19/89                P02004   DATE MAR 23,1991 T
----+-*A-1-B--+----2----+----3----+----4----+----5----+----6----+----7-%--+

00780  INITIALIZATION.
00790      OPEN INPUT  EMPLOYEE-DATA-IN
00800           OUTPUT EMPLOYEE-DATA-OUT
00810      WRITE OUTPUT-LINE FROM HEADING-LINE-1
00820      WRITE OUTPUT-LINE FROM HEADING-LINE-2
00830      WRITE OUTPUT-LINE FROM HEADING-LINE-3
00840      MOVE SPACES TO OUTPUT-LINE
00850      WRITE OUTPUT-LINE
00860      READ EMPLOYEE-DATA-IN
00870          AT END
00880              MOVE "N" TO MORE-INPUT
00890      .
00900
00910  TERMINATION.
00920      CLOSE EMPLOYEE-DATA-IN,
00930            EMPLOYEE-DATA-OUT
00940      .
00950
00960  MAIN-LOOP.
00970      MOVE SOCIAL-SECURITY-NUMBER-IN TO SOCIAL-SECURITY-NUMBER-OUT
00980      MOVE EMPLOYEE-NUMBER-IN        TO EMPLOYEE-NUMBER-OUT
00990      MOVE ANNUAL-SALARY-IN          TO ANNUAL-SALARY-OUT
01000      MOVE EMPLOYEE-NAME-IN          TO EMPLOYEE-NAME-OUT
01010      WRITE OUTPUT-LINE FROM EMPLOYEE-LINE-OUT
01020      READ EMPLOYEE-DATA-IN
01030          AT END
01040              MOVE "N" TO MORE-INPUT
01050      .
```

must be in INITIALIZATION, not in MAIN-LOOP. Statements placed in the INITIALIZATION paragraph are executed before the first detail line is printed, and statements in the TERMINATION paragraph are executed after the last detail line is printed. You can see the three WRITE . . . **FROM** statements that print the heading, at lines 00810 through 00830.

Notice the form of the WRITE . . . FROM statement. The word WRITE is followed by a record name, defined with 01 in the File Section. Following the reserved word FROM there must be a data name, which can refer to any record or field in the Working Storage Section or File Section except the output record or its component fields.

The WRITE . . . FROM statement works like a combined MOVE and WRITE. The statement

```
WRITE OUTPUT-LINE FROM HEADING-LINE-1
```

works just as if we had written:

```
MOVE HEADING-LINE-1 TO OUTPUT-LINE
WRITE OUTPUT-LINE
```

Thus there is no need to blank out OUTPUT-LINE before giving the WRITE . . . FROM statement. The implied MOVE replaces any previous contents of OUTPUT-LINE with the value assigned to HEADING-LINE-1.

The statements at lines 00840 and 00850 print one blank line after the column headings and before the first detail line. In the paragraph MAIN-LOOP, notice that we do not need to MOVE SPACES to EMPLOYEE-LINE-OUT, for the VALUE SPACES clauses in the definition of the line provide the blanks we need.

Program P02-04 was run with the same input data as Program P02-03. Program P02-04 produced the output shown in Figure 2.16.

FIGURE *2.16* **Output from Program P02-04**

EMP. NO.	SOCIAL SECURITY NUMBER	EMPLOYEE NAME	ANNUAL SALARY
10503	100040002	MORALES, LUIS	5000000
10890	101850005	JACOBSON, MRS. NELLIE	4651000
11277	201110008	GREENWOOD, JAMES	4302000
11664	209560011	COSTELLO, JOSEPH S.	3953000
12051	301810014	REITER, D.	3604000
12438	304870017	MARRA, DITTA E.	3255000
12825	401710020	LIPKE, VINCENT R.	2906000
13212	407390023	KUGLER, CHARLES	2557000
13599	502070026	JAVIER, CARLOS	2208000
13986	505680029	GOODMAN, ISAAC	1859000
14373	604910032	FELDSOTT, MS. SALLY	1510000
14760	608250035	BUXBAUM, ROBERT	1161000
15147	703100038	DUMAY, MRS. MARY	0812000
15534	708020041	SMITH, R.	0463000
15921	803220044	VINCENTE, MATTHEW J.	0114000
16308	901050047	THOMAS, THOMAS T.	4235000
00236	901029857	WONG, TIM	1850000

EXERCISE *6*

Modify your solution to Exercise 3 so that it produces output in the format shown in Figure 2.E6.

FIGURE *2.E6* **Output format for Exercise 6**

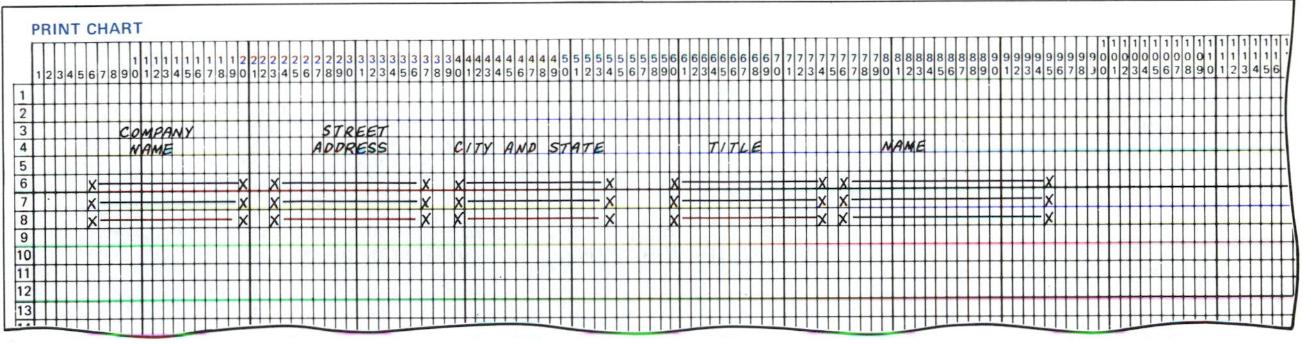

Two Formats of the PERFORM Statement

Four different formats of the PERFORM statement are given in the ANSI standard. Two of them are discussed here; the other two are discussed in Chapter 11. The simplest of the four is:

```
PERFORM [procedure-name-1 [{THROUGH} procedure-name-2]]
                           [{THRU   }                 ]

    [imperative-statement-1 END-PERFORM]
```

The format shows that the word PERFORM is required, and that it may be followed by a **procedure name** made up by the programmer or by an **imperative statement.** A procedure name is the name of a paragraph or section in the Procedure Division. We have not yet used any section names in our Procedure Divisions. We will discuss imperative statements later.

The square brackets show which portions of the statement are optional. Rules for the PERFORM statement, not shown in the format, require that the programmer use either procedure-name-1 or imperative-statement-1, but not both. We will use only procedure-name-1 at first, and will introduce the use of imperative-statement-1 later. Curly braces ({ }) in a COBOL format indicate that the programmer must choose exactly one of the items contained in the braces.

In this format, if procedure-name-1 is used, the programmer then can choose to use THROUGH or THRU and a second procedure name. THROUGH and THRU are identical in meaning. If a program is properly designed, you should never have to use the THROUGH (or THRU) option in the Procedure Division, although some programmers may want to use it to make the meaning of a program clearer. But if your program is designed so that it needs a THROUGH option to carry out its logic, then your program is more likely to be error-prone and more difficult to maintain than programs that do not use the THROUGH option. We will not use it in any Procedure Division in this book.

Two PERFORM statements using procedure names in this format that we have used so far are

```
PERFORM INITIALIZATION
```

and:

```
PERFORM TERMINATION
```

The format of the PERFORM . . . UNTIL statement is:

```
PERFORM [procedure-name-1 [{THROUGH} procedure-name-2]]
                           [{THRU   }                 ]

    [WITH TEST {BEFORE}] UNTIL condition-1
    [          {AFTER }]

    [imperatve-statement-1 END-PERFORM]
```

This format shows that the words PERFORM and UNTIL are required, and either a procedure name or an imperative statement is required, and also a condition is required. The only PERFORM . . . UNTIL statement we have used so far in this book is:

```
PERFORM MAIN-LOOP UNTIL MORE-INPUT IS EQUAL TO "N"
```

In this PERFORM statement MAIN-LOOP is procedure-name-1, and

```
MORE-INPUT IS EQUAL TO "N"
```

is condition-1. You will find the complete rules regarding conditions in Chapter 5.

In a PERFORM . . . UNTIL statement, condition-1 is ordinarily evaluated each time **BEFORE** procedure-name-1 is executed. If the condition is false, the procedure is executed; if the condition is true, control passes to the statement after the PERFORM. If the condition is already true when control first passes to the PERFORM statement, procedure-name-1 is not executed and control passes to the next statement.

If you use the **WITH TEST AFTER** phrase, condition-1 is evaluated each time AFTER procedure-name-1 is executed, instead of BEFORE. This means that when control first passes to the PERFORM statement, procedure-name-1 is first executed and then the condition is evaluated. If you leave out the WITH TEST phrase, WITH TEST BEFORE is assumed.

The Complete Environment Division

The ANSI standard format of the Environment Division is:

```
ENVIRONMENT DIVISION.
[CONFIGURATION SECTION.
[SOURCE-COMPUTER. [source-computer-entry]]
[OBJECT-COMPUTER. [object-computer-entry]]
[SPECIAL-NAMES. [special-names-entry]]]
[INPUT-OUTPUT SECTION.
 FILE-CONTROL. file-control-entry . . .
[I-O-CONTROL. input-output-control-entry] ]
```

The format shows that both the Configuration Section and the Input-Output Section are optional. If you choose to use the Configuration Section, the paragraphs **SOURCE-COMPUTER, OBJECT-COMPUTER,** and **SPECIAL-NAMES** are optional. We will use the SOURCE-COMPUTER paragraph in Chapter 21.

The Input-Output Section is considered optional because you use it only if your program has one or more input or output files. It has one required paragraph, FILE-CONTOL, and one optional paragraph, **I-O-CONTROL.** You already have seen examples of FILE-CONTROL paragraphs. There are four formats for the FILE-CONTROL entry. The one we have been using is Format 1:

```
SELECT [OPTIONAL] file-name-1

    ASSIGN TO {implementor-name-1} . . .
              {literal-1         }

    [RESERVE integer-1 [AREA ]]
                       [AREAS]

    [[ORGANIZATION IS] SEQUENTIAL]

    [PADDING CHARACTER IS {data-name-1}]
                          {literal-2  }

    [RECORD DELIMITER IS {STANDARD-1        }]
                         {implementor-name-2}

    [ACCESS MODE IS SEQUENTIAL]
    [FILE STATUS IS data-name-2].
```

All the square brackets in the format show that there are several optional clauses and entries. We will not use any of the optional portions of this format in any programs in this book.

The reserved words are, of course, in capital letters. But notice that some are not underlined. A reserved word that is not underlined is an optional word, and may be omitted without changing the meaning of the entry. That means that the ASSIGN clause

```
ASSIGN TO PRINTER
```

could just as well have been written:

```
ASSIGN PRINTER
```

An underlined reserved word is required, and is called a **key word.** The format shows that one **implementor name** or literal is required, and that the programmer may use as many as desired. We have used so far the implementor names INFILE and PRINTER. Each COBOL system has its own form of implementor names.

You will see other formats of FILE-CONTROL entries when we need them, in Chapters 15 and 16.

The I-O-CONTROL paragraph defines special control techniques to be used in the program. We will not need such techniques in any of the programs in this book.

Summary

The COBOL Coding Form permits a programmer to write coding line for line as it will be keyed or punched.

Records may be described as being composed of fields. Level numbers are used to indicate the relationship between record names and field names.

The READ verb is used to obtain data from an input file and assign the data to the record name associated with the file. The AT END phrase in a READ statement tells the computer what to do when the file contains no more data.

Reformatting of input data is accomplished easily by describing the output record in the desired format.

A nonnumeric literal consists of a string of characters, except for the quotation mark, enclosed in quotation marks.

A program to process an unknown number of input records can have a control paragraph consisting of three PERFORM statements and a STOP RUN statement. The three PERFORM statements execute the program's initialization, main loop, and termination in turn.

Fill-In Exercises

1. Area A extends from position ______ through position ______.
2. Area B extends from position ______ to the right.
3. Fields may be described in the Data Division with level numbers in the range ______ through ______.
4. The reserved word ______ may be used to end a READ statement.
5. Two kinds of literals in COBOL are ______ literals and ______ literals.
6. The ______ Section is used to describe data that are not related to any input or output file.
7. A MOVE statement always leaves the value assigned to the ______ field unchanged.
8. The statement that obtains the first input record from an input file is called a ______ READ.
9. A nonnumeric literal must be enclosed in ______ ______.
10. A ______ clause may be used to initialize data in the Working Storage Section.
11. The COBOL abbreviation for PICTURE is ______.
12. A numeric literal may have a(n) ______ anywhere except at its right end.
13. In COBOL formats ______ are used to indicate that exactly one of the items contained within them must be chosen.
14. The three paragraphs in the Configuration Section are ______, ______, and ______.
15. The required paragraph in the Input-Output Section is the ______ paragraph.

Review Exercises

1. Name the two paragraphs of the Input-Output Section in the order in which they appear.
2. In which division of a COBOL program would each of the following be found?
   a. SPECIAL-NAMES
   b. The Working Storage Section
   c. A READ statement
   d. A PERFORM statement
   e. The I-O-CONTROL paragraph

3. Which of the following statement(s) must refer to a file name, and which must refer to a record name?
   a. OPEN
   b. CLOSE
   c. READ
   d. WRITE
4. If the input file to Program P02-03 contains five records, how many times will the computer test the condition MORE-INPUT IS EQUAL TO "N", line 00600 in Figure 2.10, during execution of the program?
5. Write a COBOL program to the following specifications:

Input

Input records in the following format:

Positions	Field
1–8	Part Number
9–28	Part Description
35–37	Quantity on Hand
38–80	spaces

Output

Column headings and a listing of the contents of the records, one line per record, according to the format shown in Figure 2.RE5.

FIGURE *2.RE5* **Output format for Review Exercise 5**

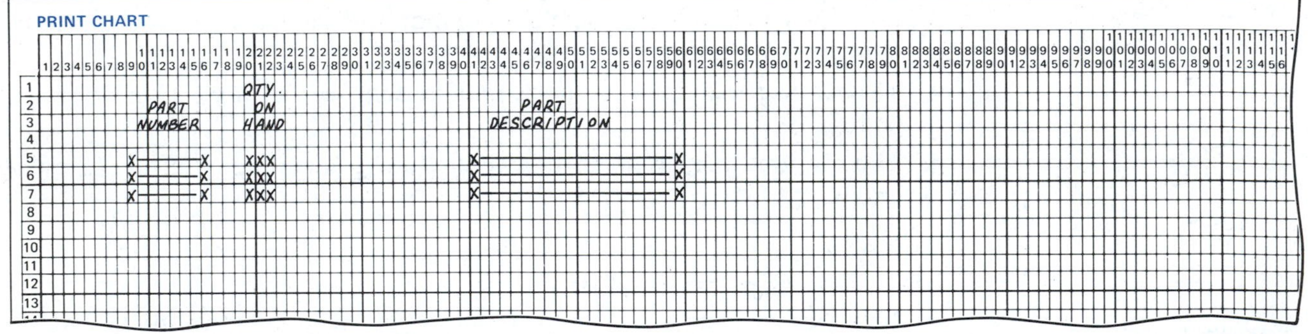

6. Here is the format of the **LABEL RECORDS** clause:

```
LABEL {RECORD IS  } {STANDARD}
      {RECORDS ARE} {OMITTED }
```

Tell whether each of the following is or is not a legal form of the clause:

a. LABEL RECORDS OMITTED
b. LABELS ARE OMITTED
c. LABEL ARE OMITTED
d. LABEL RECORD IS STANDARD
e. RECORDS ARE STANDARD
f. LABEL RECORDS IS OMITTED
g. LABEL RECORDS STANDARD
h. LABEL RECORDS ARE OMITTED

Project

Sometimes, input records contain so much data that the data cannot all fit conveniently on one output line when printed. In such a case, the data are printed on two or more lines as needed, with the columns offset horizontally for ease of reading. Column headings are correspondingly offset. The following exercise shows such an application.

Write a program to the following specifications:

Input

Records in the following format:

Positions	Field
1–8	Identification Number
9–11	Course Code 1
12	Grade 1
13–15	Course Code 2
16	Grade 2
17–19	Course Code 3
20	Grade 3
21–23	Course Code 4
24	Grade 4
25–27	Course Code 5
28	Grade 5
29–31	Course Code 6
32	Grade 6
33–35	Course Code 7
36	Grade 7
37–39	Course Code 8
40	Grade 8
41–43	Course Code 9
44	Grade 9
45–47	Course Code 10
48	Grade 10

Output

Column headings and a listing of the contents of the records, two lines per input record, according to the format shown in Figure 2.P1. Observe the single spacing within each record and the double spacing between records.

FIGURE 2.P1 Output format for Chapter 2 Project

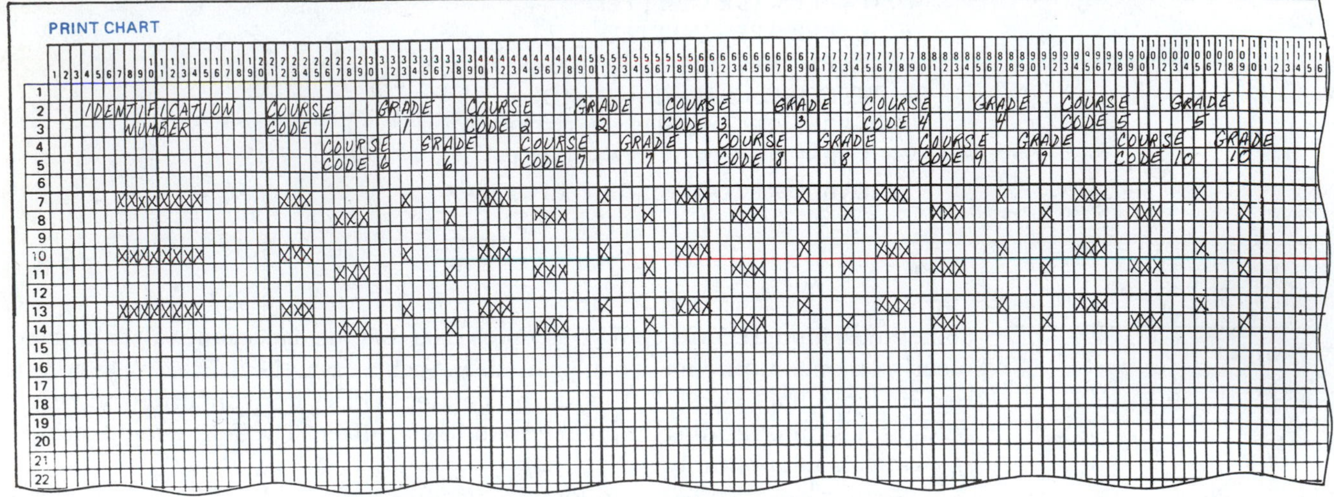

CHAPTER 3

Arithmetic: Program Design I

HERE ARE THE KEY POINTS YOU SHOULD LEARN FROM THIS CHAPTER

1. How to form PICTUREs for numeric fields
2. The formats of the verbs ADD, SUBTRACT, MULTIPLY, DIVIDE, and COMPUTE
3. The program-design technique called top-down design
4. How to develop and use hierarchy diagrams
5. How to use the arithmetic verbs in programs

KEY WORDS TO RECOGNIZE AND LEARN

ADD	END-SUBTRACT
SUBTRACT	GIVING
MULTIPLY	BY
DIVIDE	INTO
COMPUTE	REMAINDER
category of data	TO
alphanumeric	top-down design
numeric edited	subfunction
SIGN	hierarchy diagram
default	accumulate
ROUNDED	ZERO
identifier	arithmetic expression
SIZE ERROR	unary
NOT SIZE ERROR	

In this chapter we will study the arithmetic operations **ADD, SUBTRACT, MULTIPLY, DIVIDE,** and **COMPUTE,** and two sample programs using those operations. This chapter also contains the first of the three program-design techniques that we will cover in this book.

Numeric Fields

In this chapter we will be dealing, for the first time, with numeric fields in arithmetic operations. Up to now the only **category of data** we have used is **alphanumeric.** Alphanumeric data may consist of any of the computer's characters.

Numeric fields, like alphanumeric fields, may appear in input, output, or working storage. Whereas the PICTURE character X is used to describe alphanumeric fields, the PICTURE characters used to describe numeric fields are 9, S, V, and P. In this chapter we will discuss only 9, S, and V. The seldom used PICTURE character P is discussed in Chapter 11.

Numeric fields may be unsigned or signed. The only characters that legally may be assigned to an unsigned numeric field are the digits 0 through 9. The numeric value is then assumed positive. The only characters that legally may be assigned to a signed numeric field are the digits 0 through 9 and a plus or minus sign. A category of data closely related to numeric, called **numeric edited,** uses different PICTURE characters and is discussed in Chapter 4. Whereas a numeric field may not contain a decimal point, comma, or any character other than 0 through 9 and a sign, a numeric edited field may contain all those characters and more, as you will see.

Remember that a numeric literal, on the other hand, may contain digits, a plus or minus sign, and a decimal point (but not at the right end). The maximum size of a numeric field, as of a numeric literal, is 18 digits.

The PICTURE character for a single digit is 9, so to describe a three-digit integer you may use PICTURE 9(3), or PICTURE 999. To describe a number containing a decimal fractional portion, you use the PICTURE character V to show where the decimal point should be. A decimal point never appears explicitly in a numeric field, and a V is used to tell COBOL where to assume the decimal point to be. For example, a five-digit number consisting of three integer places and two decimal places could be described with PICTURE 999V99, or PICTURE 9(3)V99. Table 3.1 shows how different numeric values might be stored in working storage fields.

TABLE 3.1
How some numeric fields are stored under various PICTUREs

Value	Field Description	Digits in Computer Storage
4561	05 SAMPLE-1 PIC 9(4)	4561
4561	05 SAMPLE-2 PIC 9(5)	04561
45.61	05 SAMPLE-3 PIC 99V99	4561
45.61	05 SAMPLE-4 PIC 99V9(3)	45610
.638	05 SAMPLE-5 PIC V9(3)	638
.638	05 SAMPLE-6 PIC 99V9(4)	006380

The numeric fields shown so far lack any explicit indication of a positive or negative sign, and are assumed by COBOL to be positive. The programmer can provide for a sign in a numeric field by affixing the character S at the left end of the PICTURE for the field. COBOL then recognizes that the field has the capability of having a plus or minus sign assigned to it. Table 3.2 shows three fields and the range of values that may be assigned to each.

The programmer can designate where the sign is to appear in a numeric field in input, output, or working storage, or else can let COBOL store the sign

TABLE 3.2
Three signed numeric fields and the range of values that may be assigned to each

Field	Range of Values
05 SAMPLE-7 PIC S9(4)	−9999 through +9999
05 SAMPLE-8 PIC S9(3)V99	−999.99 through +999.99
05 SAMPLE-9 PIC SV99	−.99 through +.99

wherever it likes. The sign may appear either immediately to the left or right of the number, or it may appear in the same computer storage location with the leftmost or rightmost digit of the number. The programmer tells COBOL where to locate the sign by using the **SIGN** clause. The SIGN clause can be included anywhere after the data name in the description of a data item.

Each COBOL system has its own **default** location where the sign is stored when the SIGN clause is omitted. In the system used to run most of the programs in this book, the sign is stored in the same storage location as the rightmost digit of the number unless the programmer uses a SIGN clause to say otherwise. In input and output fields, having the sign in the same position as the rightmost digit produces a mess that is difficult to interpret. It is not recommended. The possible locations of the sign and the corresponding SIGN clauses are:

Location of Sign	SIGN Clause
With leftmost digit	SIGN IS LEADING
With rightmost digit	SIGN IS TRAILING
Immediately to left of number	SIGN IS LEADING SEPARATE CHARACTER
Immediately to right of number	SIGN IS TRAILING SEPARATE CHARACTER

So if a signed, five-digit, dollars-and-cents field with its sign to the right of the number were being read, its description might be:

```
05  MONEY-IN   PIC S9(3)V99 SIGN IS TRAILING SEPARATE CHARACTER.
```

The SIGN clause may be used only with a numeric field whose PICTURE contains the character S. The character S, if used, always appears at the left end of the PICTURE regardless of the location of the sign in the field.

Format of the SIGN Clause

The format of the SIGN clause is as follows:

```
[SIGN IS] {LEADING } [SEPARATE CHARACTER]
          {TRAILING}
```

You can see that when you use the SIGN clause, you need not use the word SIGN. The SIGN clause can be as short as

```
TRAILING
```

or

```
LEADING SEPARATE
```

The PICTURE character S counts in the size of a numeric item only if the SIGN clause and the SEPARATE phrase are present in the description of the item; otherwise, S does not count in the size of the item.

EXERCISE *1*

Write level-05 entries for the following fields:

a. An unsigned six-digit dollars-and-cents field called COMMISSION-IN

b. A signed seven-digit field with three decimal places called GAMMA-W

c. A signed eight-digit integer, called DISTANCE-IN, with the sign immediately to the left of the number

SUBTRACT

An example of a SUBTRACT statement in COBOL is:

```
SUBTRACT 37.5 FROM HOURS-WORKED
```

In this statement the difference that results from the subtraction is assigned to HOURS-WORKED and the original value of HOURS-WORKED is lost. Table 3.3 shows the results of this subtraction for different definitions and initial values of HOURS-WORKED.

Note that in the numbers in Table 3.3, no decimal points are actually stored in HOURS-WORKED. The decimal points are shown in the table only for ease of understanding. The numeric literal 37.5 legally contains an explicit decimal point, however. Notice in the last entry in the table that an unsigned field can contain only positive numbers, even if the result of arithmetic is negative. Thus it is of the greatest importance that you use signed fields whenever there is the possibility that a result could be negative.

TABLE *3.3*
Results of the statement SUBTRACT 37.5 FROM HOURS-WORKED for different definitions and initial values of HOURS-WORKED

Field		Value Before Subtraction	Value After Subtraction
05 HOURS-WORKED	PIC 99V9	40.0	02.5
05 HOURS-WORKED	PIC 99V99	50.00	12.50
05 HOURS-WORKED	PIC 99V99	37.50	00.00
05 HOURS-WORKED	PIC S99V9	+40.0	+02.5
05 HOURS-WORKED	PIC S99V9	+10.0	−27.5
05 HOURS-WORKED	PIC S99V9	−10.0	−47.5
05 HOURS-WORKED	PIC 99V9	10.0	27.5

Another legal SUBTRACT statement is:

```
SUBTRACT PAYMENT FROM BALANCE-DUE
```

In this statement the difference that results from the subtraction is assigned to BALANCE-DUE and the original value of BALANCE-DUE is lost. The value of PAYMENT is unchanged. Table 3.4 shows the results of this subtraction for different definitions and initial values of the fields PAYMENT and BALANCE-DUE.

TABLE 3.4
Results of the statement SUBTRACT PAYMENT FROM BALANCE-DUE with different definitions and initial values of the fields PAYMENT and BALANCE-DUE

Field		Value Before Subtraction	Value After Subtraction
05 BALANCE-DUE	PIC 999V99	500.00	150.00
05 PAYMENT	PIC 999V99	350.00	350.00
05 BALANCE-DUE	PIC S999V999	100.000	+049.200
05 PAYMENT	PIC S99V99	+50.80	+50.80
05 BALANCE-DUE	PIC S9(3)V99	+250.00	+239.14
05 PAYMENT	PIC S99V9(3)	+10.853	+10.853

Notice that in the last example in Table 3.4, the result assigned to BALANCE-DUE is incorrect (it should be 239.147, or 239.15 if rounded) because insufficient decimal places were provided for the answer. Such a situation may be corrected either by changing the PICTURE of BALANCE-DUE to S9(3)V9(3) to allow additional decimal places or by using the **ROUNDED** option.

The ROUNDED option is available with all the arithmetic verbs and directs COBOL to round the final result of arithmetic before assigning it to the result field. When rounding is requested, COBOL increases the least significant digit of the result by 1 whenever the most significant digit of the excess is 5 or greater. The statement

```
SUBTRACT PAYMENT FROM BALANCE-DUE ROUNDED
```

would have produced the correct result, +239.15.

Format 1 of the SUBTRACT Statement

The format of the SUBTRACT statement that we have been using is:

```
SUBTRACT {identifier-1} . . . FROM {identifier-2 [ROUNDED]} . . .
         {literal-1   }

    [ON SIZE ERROR imperative-statement-1]
    [NOT ON SIZE ERROR imperative-statement-2]
    [END-SUBTRACT]
```

The braces following the word SUBTRACT show that either an **identifier** or a literal must follow SUBTRACT. So far in this book, the only kind of identifier we know is the data name, that is, the name of a field defined in the Data Division. You will see other kinds of identifiers later. The ellipsis after the braces indicates that the contents of the braces may be repeated as many times as desired by the programmer; that is, optionally there could be a second, third, fourth, and so on, identifier and/or literal before the word FROM. We did not have a second identifier or literal in either of the sample SUBTRACT statements.

Following the required word FROM there is a required identifier. Following the identifier is the optional word ROUNDED. The format then shows that there may be as many identifiers as desired following the word FROM, and that each may be accompanied by the optional word ROUNDED or not.

The format tells us that the following statement is legal:

```
SUBTRACT
    JUNE-PAYMENT
    JULY-PAYMENT
        FROM BALANCE-DUE
```

In that statement the values of JUNE-PAYMENT and JULY-PAYMENT would first be added, and then the sum would be subtracted from BALANCE-DUE and the difference assigned to BALANCE-DUE. The following statement is also legal:

```
SUBTRACT
    BASE-HOURS
    2.5
       FROM HOURS-WORKED ROUNDED
```

Here the value of BASE-HOURS would first be added to 2.5, and then the sum would be subtracted from HOURS-WORKED. If necessary, the difference would be ROUNDED to fit into HOURS-WORKED.

The format shows that several identifiers optionally may appear after the word FROM, so the following statement is legal:

```
SUBTRACT 10.00
    FROM
        TEACHER-PAY-RATE
        JANITOR-PAY-RATE
        SWEEPER-PAY-RATE
```

In that statement 10.00 would be subtracted from the value in each of the three result fields.

The **SIZE ERROR** and **NOT SIZE ERROR** phrases, and the word **END-SUBTRACT,** are discussed in Chapter 8.

SUBTRACT with the GIVING Option

To preserve the original values of the fields in a subtraction, the **GIVING** option may be used. For example, in the statement

```
SUBTRACT 40 FROM HOURS-WORKED GIVING OVERTIME-HOURS
```

the original value assigned to HOURS-WORKED remains after the subtraction as it was before the subtraction, and the difference is assigned to OVERTIME-HOURS. Table 3.5 shows the results of the subtraction for different definitions and initial values of HOURS-WORKED and OVERTIME-HOURS.

Notice that the initial value of the result field, OVERTIME-HOURS, has no effect on the operation. The initial value of the field is replaced by the result.

In the statement

```
SUBTRACT PAYMENT FROM OLD-BALANCE GIVING NEW-BALANCE
```

the original values assigned to PAYMENT and OLD-BALANCE remain as they were before the subtraction, and the difference is assigned to NEW-BALANCE. Table 3.6 shows the result of the subtraction for different definitions and initial values of the fields.

TABLE 3.5
Results of the statement SUBTRACT 40 FROM HOURS-WORKED GIVING OVERTIME-HOURS with different definitions and initial values of the fields HOURS-WORKED and OVERTIME-HOURS

Field		Value Before Subtraction	Value After Subtraction
05 HOURS-WORKED	PIC S999V99	+010.00	+010.00
05 OVERTIME-HOURS	PIC S99V99	+99.99	−30.00
05 HOURS-WORKED	PIC 999V99	010.00	010.00
05 OVERTIME-HOURS	PIC 99V99	99.99	30.00

TABLE 3.6
Results of the statement SUBTRACT PAYMENT FROM OLD-BALANCE GIVING NEW-BALANCE with different definitions and initial values of the fields PAYMENT, OLD-BALANCE, and NEW-BALANCE

Field		Value Before Subtraction	Value After Subtraction
05 OLD-BALANCE	PIC 999V999	568.463	568.463
05 PAYMENT	PIC 99V99	25.35	25.35
05 NEW-BALANCE	PIC 999V999	999.999	543.113
05 OLD-BALANCE	PIC 999V999	568.463	568.463
05 PAYMENT	PIC 999V999	25.355	25.355
05 NEW-PAYMENT	PIC 999V99	999.99	543.10

Notice that in the last entry in Table 3.6, the result shown, 543.10, is incorrect. It should be 543.108, or 543.11 with rounding. By including the ROUNDED option, as in

```
SUBTRACT PAYMENT FROM OLD-BALANCE
    GIVING NEW-BALANCE ROUNDED
```

the correct result would be obtained.

Format 2 of the SUBTRACT Statement

The format of the SUBTRACT statement with the GIVING option is:

```
SUBTRACT {identifier-1} . . . FROM {identifier-2}
         {literal-1   }             {literal-2   }

   GIVING {identifier-3 [ROUNDED]} . . .
   [ON SIZE ERROR imperative-statement-1]
   [NOT ON SIZE ERROR imperative-statement-2]
   [END-SUBTRACT]
```

The format shows that any number of identifiers are permitted after the word GIVING. If more than one identifier appears after GIVING, the difference from the subtraction is assigned to each of the identifiers. The sample SUBTRACT statements in this format have only one such identifier each.

EXERCISE 2

Write a COBOL statement that will subtract MARKDOWN from PRICE and assign the difference to PRICE.

EXERCISE 3

Write a COBOL statement that will subtract DEDUCTIONS from GROSS-PAY and assign the difference to NET-PAY.

EXERCISE 4

Write a COBOL statement that will subtract CREDITS-EARNED from 120 and assign the difference to CREDITS-REMAINING.

MULTIPLY

Multiplication, like subtraction, can be done with or without a GIVING option. The format for MULTIPLY without the GIVING option is:

```
MULTIPLY {identifier-1} BY {identifier-2 [ROUNDED]} . . .
         {literal-1   }

    [ON SIZE ERROR imperative-statement-1]
    [NOT ON SIZE ERROR imperative-statement-2]
    [END-MULTIPLY]
```

The multiplicand is given before the word **BY,** and the multiplier is given after the word BY. There may be more than one multiplier after the word BY if desired. COBOL multiplies the multiplicand BY each multiplier in turn and replaces each multiplier with the result of the multiplication, the product. A valid MULTIPLY under this format is:

```
MULTIPLY RATE-OF-PAY BY HOURS-WORKED
```

Table 3.7 shows the results of the statement for different definitions and initial values of RATE-OF-PAY and HOURS-WORKED.

TABLE 3.7
Results of the statement MULTIPLY RATE-OF-PAY BY HOURS-WORKED with different definitions and initial values of the fields RATE-OF-PAY and HOURS-WORKED

Field		Value Before Multiplication	Value After Multiplication
05 RATE-OF-PAY	PIC 99V99	02.85	02.85
05 HOURS-WORKED	PIC 9(3)V99	010.00	028.50
05 RATE-OF-PAY	PIC S99V9	−11.3	−11.3
05 HOURS-WORKED	PIC S9(3)V99	+021.10	−238.43
05 RATE-OF-PAY	PIC S9(3)V9(3)	−011.305	−011.305
05 HOURS-WORKED	PIC S9(3)V9	−010.0	+113.0

Notice that the sign of the product is determined according to the rules of multiplication. The result in the last entry in Table 3.7 is incorrect because insufficient decimal places were allowed in the result field. The statement

```
MULTIPLY RATE-OF-PAY BY HOURS-WORKED ROUNDED
```

would have produced the correct result, +113.1.

Another valid MULTIPLY in this format is:

```
MULTIPLY 1.5 BY OVERTIME-HOURS
```

Table 3.8 shows the results of this multiplication for different definitions and initial values of the field OVERTIME-HOURS. As before, the product is assigned to the field given after the word BY.

TABLE 3.8
Results of the statement MULTIPLY 1.5 BY OVERTIME-HOURS with different definitions and initial values of the field OVERTIME-HOURS

Field		Value Before Multiplication	Value After Multiplication
05 OVERTIME-HOURS	PIC 99V99	10.50	15.75
05 OVERTIME-HOURS	PIC S99V9(3)	+10.500	+15.750
05 OVERTIME-HOURS	PIC S99V99	−10.50	−15.75
05 OVERTIME-HOURS	PIC 99V9	10.5	15.7

For the last entry in Table 3.8, the statement

```
MULTIPLY 1.5 BY OVERTIME-HOURS ROUNDED
```

would have given the correct result, 15.8.

The format of the MULTIPLY statement shows that more than one identifier is permitted after the word BY, so the following statement is valid:

```
MULTIPLY 2 BY
    WHEEL-SPINS
    PAYOFFS
```

In this case the values assigned to both WHEEL-SPINS and PAYOFFS would be doubled.

Multiplication can also be written with the GIVING option, so that the product is assigned to a field specified by the programmer. The format of MULTIPLY with the GIVING option is:

```
MULTIPLY {identifier-1} BY {identifier-2}
         {literal-1   }    {literal-2   }

    GIVING {identifier-3 [ROUNDED]} . . .
    [ON SIZE ERROR imperative-statement-1]
    [NOT ON SIZE ERROR imperative-statement-2]
    [END-MULTIPLY]
```

In this format COBOL carries out the indicated multiplication and assigns the product to each of the fields given after the word GIVING. A valid MULTIPLY in this format is:

```
MULTIPLY RATE-OF-PAY BY HOURS-WORKED GIVING GROSS-PAY
```

Table 3.9 shows the results of this statement for different definitions and initial values of RATE-OF-PAY, HOURS-WORKED, and GROSS-PAY.

TABLE 3.9 **Results of the statement MULTIPLY RATE-OF-PAY BY HOURS-WORKED GIVING GROSS-PAY with different definitions and initial values of the fields RATE-OF-PAY, HOURS-WORKED, and GROSS-PAY**

Field		Value Before Multiplication	Value After Multiplication
05 RATE-OF-PAY	PIC 99V99	02.85	02.85
05 HOURS-WORKED	PIC 9(3)V99	010.00	010.00
05 GROSS-PAY	PIC 9(3)V99	999.99	028.50
05 RATE-OF-PAY	PIC S99V9	−11.3	−11.3
05 HOURS-WORKED	PIC S9(3)V99	+021.10	+021.10
05 GROSS-PAY	PIC S9(3)V9(3)	+999.999	−238.430
05 RATE-OF-PAY	PIC S9(3)V9(3)	−011.305	−011.305
05 HOURS-WORKED	PIC S9(3)V9	−010.0	−010.0
05 GROSS-PAY	PIC S9(3)V9	+999.9	+113.0

Another legal MULTIPLY statement in this format is:

```
MULTIPLY 1.5 BY OVERTIME-HOURS
    GIVING OVERTIME-EQUIVALENT
```

Table 3.10 shows the results of this statement for different definitions and initial values of OVERTIME-HOURS and OVERTIME-EQUIVALENT.

TABLE 3.10 **Results of the statement MULTIPLY 1.5 BY OVERTIME-HOURS GIVING OVERTIME-EQUIVALENT with different definitions and initial values of the fields OVERTIME-HOURS and OVERTIME-EQUIVALENT**

Field		Value Before Multiplication	Value After Multiplication
05 OVERTIME-HOURS	PIC 99V99	10.50	10.50
05 OVERTIME-EQUIVALENT	PIC 99V99	99.99	15.75
05 OVERTIME-HOURS	PIC S99V9(3)	+10.500	+10.500
05 OVERTIME-EQUIVALENT	PIC S99V99	+99.99	+15.75
05 OVERTIME-HOURS	PIC S99V99	−10.50	−10.50
05 OVERTIME-EQUIVALENT	PIC S99V9(3)	+99.999	−15.750
05 OVERTIME-HOURS	PIC 99V99	10.50	10.50
05 OVERTIME-EQUIVALENT	PIC 99V9	99.9	15.7

EXERCISE 5

Write a COBOL statement that will triple the value assigned to the field GROSS.

EXERCISE 6

Write a COBOL statement that will multiply together the values assigned to TOTAL CREDITS and POINT-AVERAGE and assign the product to HONOR-POINTS.

DIVIDE

The DIVIDE verb is a little strange, because with the GIVING option come other options. First, DIVIDE without GIVING:

```
DIVIDE {identifier-1} INTO {identifier-2 [ROUNDED]} . . .
       {literal-1   }

    [ON SIZE ERROR imperative-statement-1]
    [NOT ON SIZE ERROR imperative-statement-2]
    [END-DIVIDE]
```

The DIVIDE statement carries out the following division:

$$\text{divisor}\,\overline{)\text{dividend}}^{\;\text{quotient}}$$

Also:

$$\text{quotient} = \frac{\text{dividend}}{\text{divisor}}$$

In a DIVIDE statement the divisor is always given before the word **INTO,** and the dividend is always given after the word INTO. More than one dividend may be given after the word INTO if desired. COBOL divides the divisor INTO each of the dividends separately and replaces each dividend with the result of the division, the quotient. A sample DIVIDE statement in this format is:

```
DIVIDE NUMBER-OF-EXAMS INTO TOTAL-GRADE
```

Table 3.11 shows the results of this division for different definitions and initial values of NUMBER-OF-EXAMS and TOTAL-GRADE.

TABLE 3.11 Results of the statement DIVIDE NUMBER-OF-EXAMS INTO TOTAL-GRADE with different definitions and initial values of the fields NUMBER-OF-EXAMS and TOTAL-GRADE

Field		Value Before Division	Value After Division
05 TOTAL-GRADE	PIC 9(3)V9	366.0	091.5
05 NUMBER-OF-EXAMS	PIC 99	04	04
05 TOTAL-GRADE	PIC S9(3)V9	−247.0	−082.3
05 NUMBER-OF-EXAMS	PIC S99V9	+03.0	+03.0
05 TOTAL-GRADE	PIC S9(3)V9	+248.0	−082.6
05 NUMBER-OF-EXAMS	PIC S99	−03	−03

COBOL determines the sign of the result according to the rules of division. In the second entry in Table 3.11, notice that although the fractional portion of the answer should be .333 . . . , only .3 is stored because only one decimal place is given in the PICTURE for the result field.

In the last entry in the table, the fractional portion of the answer should be .666 . . . , but only .6 is stored. The statement

```
DIVIDE NUMBER-OF-EXAMS INTO TOTAL-GRADE ROUNDED
```

would give the correct result, −082.7.

In Chapter 8 we discuss methods for handling cases in which the divisor may be 0.

DIVIDE with GIVING and REMAINDER

With the GIVING option, the programmer also has a choice of writing the division in either direction (that is, DIVIDE A INTO B, or DIVIDE B BY A), and also the option of having the remainder from the division assigned to a separate field. There are two formats of the DIVIDE statement with the GIVING option. First, DIVIDE with GIVING and **REMAINDER:**

```
DIVIDE {identifier-1} {INTO} {identifier-2}
       {literal-1   } {BY  } {literal-2   }

    GIVING identifier-3 [ROUNDED]
    REMAINDER identifier-4
    [ON SIZE ERROR imperative-statement-1]
    [NOT ON SIZE ERROR imperative-statement-2]
    [END-DIVIDE]
```

In this format, if INTO is used, the divisor is given before the word INTO and the dividend is given after the word INTO. If BY is used, the dividend is given before the word BY and the divisor is given after the word BY. The quotient is assigned to the field given after the word GIVING and the remainder is assigned to the field given after the word REMAINDER. The remainder is computed by COBOL by multiplying the quotient by the divisor and subtracting that product from the dividend.

A sample DIVIDE statement in this format is:

```
DIVIDE TOTAL-SCORE BY 3
    GIVING HANDICAP
    REMAINDER H-REM
```

Table 3.12 shows the results of this division for different definitions and initial values of the fields TOTAL-SCORE, HANDICAP, and H-REM. In the second entry in Table 3.12, the REMAINDER is computed by multiplying the quotient, −104, by the divisor, 3, and subtracting that product, −312, from the dividend, −314. In the last entry in the table, the REMAINDER is computed by multiplying the quotient, 104.6, by the divisor and subtracting that product, 313.8, from the dividend, 314.

TABLE 3.12
Results of the statement DIVIDE TOTAL-SCORE BY 3 GIVING HANDICAP REMAINDER H-REM with different definitions and initial values of the fields TOTAL-SCORE, HANDICAP, and H-REM

Field		Value Before Division	Value After Division
05 TOTAL-SCORE	PIC 9(4)	0313	0313
05 HANDICAP	PIC 9(3)	999	104
05 H-REM	PIC 9	9	1
05 TOTAL-SCORE	PIC S9(4)	−0314	−0314
05 HANDICAP	PIC S9(3)	+999	−104
05 H-REM	PIC S9	+9	−2
05 TOTAL-SCORE	PIC 9(4)	0314	0314
05 HANDICAP	PIC 9(3)V9	999.9	104.6
05 H-REM	PIC V9(5)	.99999	.20000

If the ROUNDED option is used in this format, the REMAINDER is computed before the quotient is ROUNDED, and then the quotient is ROUNDED. Thus for the statement

```
DIVIDE TOTAL-SCORE BY 3
    GIVING HANDICAP ROUNDED
    REMAINDER H-REM
```

the REMAINDERs would be the same as in Table 3.12. The quotient for the second entry in the table would be −105, and the quotient for the last entry would be 104.7. Only the quotient field can use the ROUNDED option. The REMAINDER field has no ROUNDED option and is truncated on the right end, if necessary, to fit.

DIVIDE with GIVING and Multiple Result Fields

The final format of the DIVIDE statement provides for multiple result fields. It is:

```
DIVIDE {identifier-1} {INTO} {identifier-2}
       {literal-1   } {BY  } {literal-2   }

    GIVING {identifier-3 [ROUNDED]} . . .
    [ON SIZE ERROR imperative-statement-1]
    [NOT ON SIZE ERROR imperative-statement-2]
    [END-DIVIDE]
```

In this format, COBOL carries out the indicated division and assigns the result to each of the fields given after the word GIVING. The two statements

```
DIVIDE NUMBER-OF-EXAMS INTO TOTAL-GRADE
    GIVING AVERAGE-GRADE
```

and

```
DIVIDE TOTAL-GRADE BY NUMBER-OF-EXAMS
    GIVING AVERAGE-GRADE
```

give the same results. Table 3.13 shows the results of the two statements for different definitions and initial values of the fields TOTAL-GRADE, NUMBER-OF-EXAMS, and AVERAGE-GRADE.

TABLE 3.13
Results of the statements DIVIDE NUMBER-OF-EXAMS INTO TOTAL-GRADE GIVING AVERAGE-GRADE and DIVIDE TOTAL-GRADE BY NUMBER-OF-EXAMS GIVING AVERAGE-GRADE with different definitions and initial values of the fields NUMBER-OF-EXAMS, TOTAL-GRADE, and AVERAGE-GRADE

Field		Value Before Division	Value After Division
05 TOTAL-GRADE	PIC 9(3)	366	366
05 NUMBER-OF-EXAMS	PIC 99	04	04
05 AVERAGE GRADE	PIC 9(3)V9	999.9	091.5
05 TOTAL-GRADE	PIC S9(3)	−247	−247
05 NUMBER-OF-EXAMS	PIC S99V9	+03.0	+03.0
05 AVERAGE GRADE	PIC S99V9(3)	+99.999	−82.333
05 TOTAL-GRADE	PIC S9(3)V9	+248.0	+248.0
05 NUMBER-OF-EXAMS	PIC S99	−03	−03
05 AVERAGE GRADE	PIC S99V99	+99.99	−82.66

For the last entry in Table 3.13, the statement

```
DIVIDE TOTAL-GRADE BY NUMBER-OF-EXAMS
    GIVING AVERAGE-GRADE ROUNDED
```

would give the correct result, −82.67.

EXERCISE 7

Write a COBOL statement that will divide the value assigned to TOTAL-SALES by the value assigned to NUMBER-OF-STORES and assign the unrounded result to TOTAL-SALES.

EXERCISE 8

Write a COBOL statement that will divide the value assigned to TOTAL-SALES by the value assigned to NUMBER-OF-STORES and assign the rounded quotient to AVERAGE-SALES.

EXERCISE 9

Write a COBOL statement that will divide the value assigned to NUMBER-TEST by 2 and assign the unrounded quotient to a field called Q and the remainder to a field called ZERO-ONE.

EXERCISE 10

Write a COBOL statement that will divide the value assigned to NUMBER-TEST by 2 and assign the unrounded quotient to a field called QU and the rounded quotient to a field called QR.

ADD

Two formats of the ADD statement will be given. One of them contains the GIVING option. The other contains the required word **TO.** The format without GIVING is:

```
ADD {identifier-1} . . . TO {identifier-2 [ROUNDED]} . . .
    {literal-1   }
    [ON SIZE ERROR imperative-statement-1]
    [NOT ON SIZE ERROR imperative-statement-2]
    [END-ADD]
```

In this format only one identifier or literal is required before the word TO, although there may be as many as the programmer desires. After the word TO, one identifier is also required, and there may be as many as desired. A sample ADD statement in this format is:

```
ADD NEW-PURCHASES TO BALANCE
```

This statement ADDs the value assigned to NEW-PURCHASES to the value assigned to BALANCE and assigns the sum to BALANCE. Table 3.14 shows the results of that statement for different definitions and initial values of the fields NEW-PURCHASES and BALANCE.

TABLE 3.14
Results of the statement ADD NEW-PURCHASES TO BALANCE with different definitions and initial values of the fields NEW-PURCHASES and BALANCE

Field		Value Before Addition	Value After Addition
05 NEW-PURCHASES	PIC 999	150	150
05 BALANCE	PIC 9999	0400	0550
05 NEW-PURCHASES	PIC S99V99	−25.15	−25.15
05 BALANCE	PIC 9(3)V9(3)	135.256	110.106
05 NEW-PURCHASES	PIC 99V99	10.43	10.43
05 BALANCE	PIC S99V9	−80.6	−70.1

For the last entry in Table 3.14, the statement

```
ADD NEW-PURCHASES TO BALANCE ROUNDED
```

would give the correct result, −70.2.

Another legal ADD statement in this format is:

```
ADD SALESPERSON-NET SALESPERSON-BONUS
         TO REGION-TOTAL
```

This statement ADDs together the values assigned to SALESPERSON-NET and SALESPERSON-BONUS, ADDs that sum to the value assigned to REGION-TOTAL, and assigns the final sum to REGION-TOTAL. Table 3.15 shows the results of that statement for different definitions and initial values of SALESPERSON-NET, SALESPERSON-BONUS, and REGION-TOTAL.

TABLE 3.15
Results of the statement ADD SALESPERSON-NET SALESPERSON-BONUS TO REGION-TOTAL with different definitions and initial values of the fields SALESPERSON-NET, SALESPERSON-BONUS, and REGION-TOTAL

Field		Value Before Addition	Value After Addition
05 SALESPERSON-NET	PIC 9(3)V99	100.75	100.75
05 SALESPERSON-BONUS	PIC 99V9(3)	50.665	50.665
05 REGION-TOTAL	PIC 9(3)V9(3)	510.675	662.090
05 SALESPERSON-NET	PIC S9(3)V99	+100.75	+100.75
05 SALESPERSON-BONUS	PIC S99V9(3)	−50.661	−50.661
05 REGION-TOTAL	PIC S9(3)V99	+510.50	+560.58

For the last entry in Table 3.15, the statement

```
ADD SALESPERSON-NET SALESPERSON-BONUS
      TO REGION-TOTAL ROUNDED
```

would give the correct result, +560.59.

Another legal ADD statement in this format is:

```
ADD OVERTIME-HOURS 40
      TO DEPARTMENT-TOTAL
         FACTORY-TOTAL
```

This statement first ADDs 40 to the value assigned to OVERTIME-HOURS, to form a temporary sum. It then ADDs the temporary sum to the value assigned to DEPARTMENT-TOTAL and assigns the final sum to DEPARTMENT-TOTAL. It then goes back and ADDs the temporary sum to the value assigned to FACTORY-TOTAL and assigns that final sum to FACTORY-TOTAL. Table 3.16 shows the results of this statement for different definitions and initial values of OVERTIME-HOURS, DEPARTMENT-TOTAL, and FACTORY-TOTAL.

TABLE 3.16
Results of the statement ADD OVERTIME-HOURS 40 TO DEPARTMENT-TOTAL FACTORY-TOTAL with different definitions and initial values of the fields OVERTIME-HOURS, DEPARTMENT-TOTAL, and FACTORY-TOTAL

Field		Value Before Addition	Value After Addition
05 OVERTIME-HOURS	PIC 99V99	12.20	12.20
05 DEPARTMENT-TOTAL	PIC 999V99	350.00	402.20
05 FACTORY-TOTAL	PIC 999V99	600.50	652.70
05 OVERTIME-HOURS	PIC S99V9(3)	−10.002	−10.002
05 DEPARTMENT-TOTAL	PIC S9(3)V99	+300.00	+329.99
05 FACTORY-TOTAL	PIC S9(3)V99	+400.00	+429.99

In the last entry in Table 3.16, the result for DEPARTMENT-TOTAL should be +329.998, but insufficient decimal places are allowed in the PICTURE for DEPARTMENTAL-TOTAL. Similarly, FACTORY-TOTAL should be +429.998. The ROUNDED option may be used on either or both of the result fields, so the statement

```
ADD OVERTIME-HOURS 40
      TO DEPARTMENT-TOTAL ROUNDED
         FACTORY-TOTAL
```

would give the same result for FACTORY-TOTAL as in Table 3.16, but would give the correct result for DEPARTMENT-TOTAL, +330.00.

The format of the ADD statement with the GIVING option is:

```
ADD {identifier-1} . . . TO {identifier-2}
    {literal-1   }          {literal-2   }

    GIVING {identifier-3 [ROUNDED]} . . .
    [ON SIZE ERROR imperative-statement-1]
    [NOT ON SIZE ERROR imperative-statement-2]
    [END-ADD]
```

In this form at least two identifiers and/or literals are required before the word GIVING, and there may be as many as desired. The format shows that any number of identifiers are allowed after the word GIVING. Notice that the word TO, since it is not underlined, is optional in this form of the ADD. ADD statements in this format ADD together the values assigned to the fields given before the word GIVING and assign the result to the fields given after the word GIVING. Two ADD statements in this format are:

```
ADD FIELD-A FIELD-B
        GIVING FIELD-C
```

and

```
ADD FIELD-A TO FIELD-B
        GIVING FIELD-C
```

These statements ADD together the values assigned to FIELD-A and FIELD-B and assign the sum to FIELD-C. Table 3.17 shows the results of these statements for different definitions and initial values of FIELD-A, FIELD-B, and FIELD-C.

TABLE 3.17
Results of the statements ADD FIELD-A FIELD-B GIVING FIELD-C and ADD FIELD-A to FIELD-B GIVING FIELD-C with different definitions and initial values of FIELD-A, FIELD-B, and FIELD-C

Field		Value Before Addition	Value After Addition
05 FIELD-A	PIC 999	150	150
05 FIELD-B	PIC 9999	0400	0400
05 FIELD-C	PIC 9(5)	99999	00550
05 FIELD-A	PIC S99V99	−25.15	−25.15
05 FIELD-B	PIC 9(3)V99	135.25	135.25
05 FIELD-C	PIC 9(3)V9(3)	999.999	110.100
05 FIELD-A	PIC 99V99	80.57	80.57
05 FIELD-B	PIC S99V9	+10.3	+10.3
05 FIELD-C	PIC S9(3)V9	+999.9	+090.8

Another ADD statement in this format is:

```
ADD OVERTIME-HOURS
    40
       GIVING TOTAL-HOURS
              SCHEDULED-HOURS
```

This statement ADDs 40 to the value assigned to OVERTIME-HOURS and assigns the sum to TOTAL-HOURS and to SCHEDULED-HOURS. Table 3.18 shows the results of this statement for different definitions and initial values of OVERTIME-HOURS, TOTAL-HOURS, and SCHEDULED-HOURS.

TABLE *3.18*
Results of the statement ADD OVERTIME-HOURS 40 GIVING TOTAL-HOURS SCHEDULED-HOURS with different definitions and initial values of the fields OVERTIME-HOURS, TOTAL-HOURS, and SCHEDULED-HOURS

Field		Value Before Addition	Value After Addition
05 OVERTIME-HOURS	PIC 99V99	12.20	12.20
05 TOTAL-HOURS	PIC 999V99	999.99	052.20
05 SCHEDULED-HOURS	PIC 999V9	999.9	052.2
		−10.002	−10.002
05 OVERTIME-HOURS	PIC S99V9(3)	+999.999	+029.998
05 TOTAL-HOURS	PIC S9(3)V9(3)	+999.99	+029.99
05 SCHEDULED-HOURS	PIC S9(3)V99		

The following ADD statement is invalid because the word TO is in the wrong place:

```
ADD FIELD-1 TO FIELD-2 FIELD-3 GIVING FIELD-4
```

EXERCISE *11*

Write a COBOL statement that will add together the values assigned to FIELD-1, FIELD-2, and FIELD-3 and assign the sum to FIELD-4.

EXERCISE *12*

Write a COBOL statement that will add the value of CASH-ADVANCES to the value of BALANCE-DUE and assign the sum to BALANCE-DUE.

A Program with Arithmetic

We will now study a program that uses addition and multiplication. Program P03-01 uses input data in the following format:

Positions	Field
1–7	Customer Number
8–15	Part Number
16–22	spaces
23–25	Quantity
26–31	Unit Price (in dollars and cents)
26–29	Unit Price dollars
30–31	Unit Price cents
32–35	Handling Charge (in dollars and cents)
32–33	Handling Charge dollars
34–35	Handling Charge cents
35–80	spaces

Each record represents a purchase of some parts by a customer. The record shows the quantity purchased, the price per unit, and a handling charge for the order. Notice that no positions have been allocated for decimal points in the numeric fields. Decimal points never appear explicitly in numeric fields in input.

The program is to read each record and compute the total cost of the merchandise (by multiplying the Quantity by the Unit Price) and a tax at 7 percent of the merchandise total. Then the program is to add together the merchandise total, the tax, and the Handling Charge to arrive at a total for the order. The information for each order is to be printed on one line as shown in Figure 3.1. Also shown in Figure 3.1 are column headings and a title for the report. At the end of the report, the program prints the total of all the merchandise amounts for all the orders and the totals of all the tax and Handling Charge amounts and a grand total of all the order totals, as shown in Figure 3.1.

FIGURE *3.1* **Output format for Program P03-01**

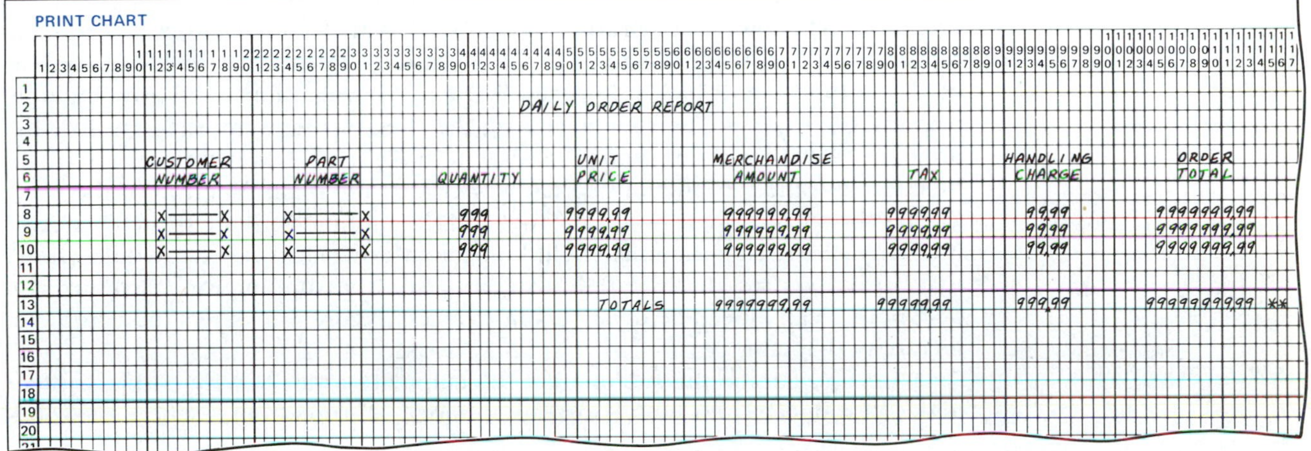

Notice that no decimal points are indicated in the money fields in Figure 3.1. Instead there are little inverted Vs to show where the decimal points are to be assumed. We show Vs instead of decimal points because COBOL does not permit explicit decimal points in fields defined as numeric. In the next chapter you will see how to get COBOL to insert decimal points into printed output easily, by using numeric edited fields.

This program is much more difficult than any we have done so far, so we will have to design the program before we begin to code it. There are a variety of program design techniques in use in industry now. For any particular program, the choice of which design technique to use often depends on the complexity and/or size of the program, personal preference, and which technique your instructor tells you to use. In this book we discuss only three of the many techniques available; among the three, all of our design needs can be served. Here we study the technique called **top-down design.** In Chapter 5 we will look at the other two.

Top-Down Design

In top-down design the programmer avoids trying to think about the whole program at once and instead first decides what the major function of the program is. In our case we can say that the major function is "Produce daily order report." The programmer then decides what **subfunctions** the program must carry out to accomplish the main function. You have already seen from the programs in Chapter 2 that coding is straightforward if you divide a program into three subfunctions:

1. What the program has to do before entering the main loop (initialization)
2. The main loop
3. What the program has to do after end-of-file (termination)

These subfunctions are recorded in the form of a **hierarchy diagram.** In Program P03-01 we can call the three subfunctions "Initialization," "Produce report body," and "Termination." "Initialization" in this program will consist of all the functions it had in Program P02-04. "Termination" will now include printing the total line as well as closing the files. A hierarchy diagram for the program "Produce order report" is shown in Figure 3.2 as it reflects the main function and the subfunctions so far. Notice that the main function of the program is shown in a single box at the top, and the subfunctions are shown beneath it. If any of the subfunctions could be broken down further, we would show that breakdown on the hierarchy diagram also. The subfunction "Produce report body" can indeed be detailed a little more. Figure 3.3 shows the complete hierarchy diagram.

Let us examine the subfunction "Accumulate totals." Why is that shown under "Produce report body" instead of under "Termination," where the total

FIGURE 3.2 **Hierarchy diagram with one level of subfunctions**

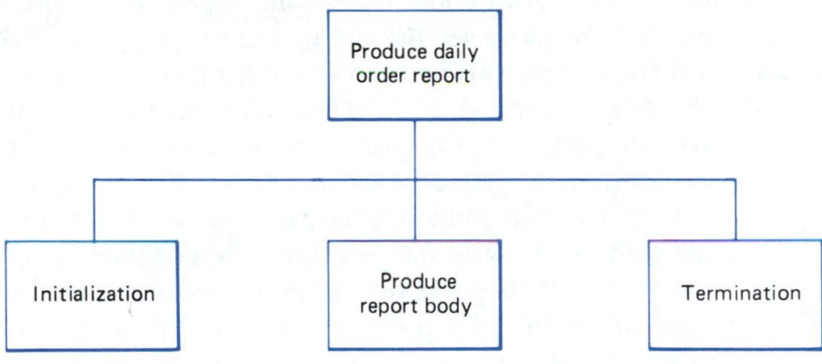

FIGURE 3.3 **Complete hierarchy diagram for Program P03-01**

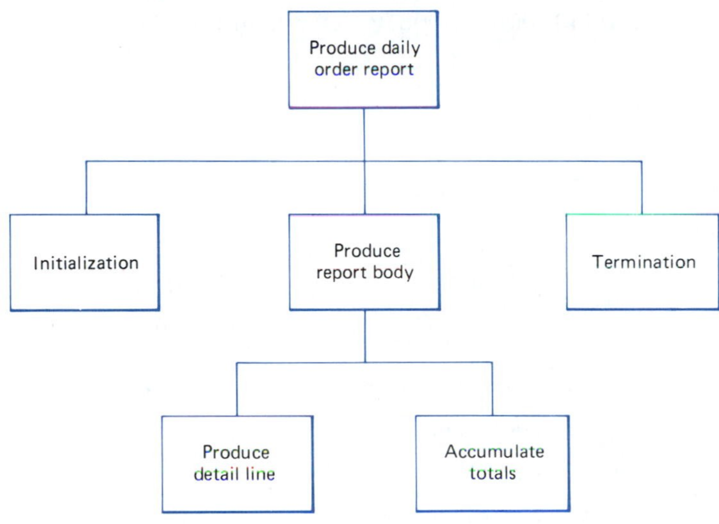

line is printed? Remember that the program can work on only one input record at a time. It must do all required processing on each input record before READ-ing in the next. So in this program, as we compute the several money amounts that we need for printing each line, we will also have to **accumulate** those amounts in some way as if we were adding them into a calculator. As each detail line is printed, therefore, we also add the money amounts into ever-growing subtotals, so that, after all the detail lines of the report have been printed, we will have the totals of the money amounts ready to be printed in the total line. COBOL provides an easy way for the programmer to do this, as you will soon see.

Using Arithmetic Statements in a Program

Program P03-01 is shown in Figure 3.4. There is nothing new in the Identification or Environment Divisions. In the Data Division the definition of ORDER-RECORD-IN, lines 00220 through 00280, shows how numeric fields in input are defined. You can see the definition of an integer, QUANTITY-IN, at line 00260, and the definitions of numbers with fractional parts at lines 00270 and 00280. The output record, REPORT-LINE, is as usual made as large as the longest line that the program is to print. You can see from the print chart in Figure 3.1 that the longest line is 116 characters.

In the Working Storage Section, we have the usual MORE-INPUT field at line 00360. We also have defined the constant .07 with the name TAX-RATE, at line 00370. It is good programming practice to define, in working storage, all constants used by a program. Notice that although the numeric literal .07 has an explicit decimal point, the PICTURE of the field contains a V and not a dot. This indicates to the system that the number is to be stored in purely numeric form, without an explicit decimal point, so that it can be used in arithmetic.

The report title line and the column heading lines are defined in lines 00390 through 00730. The detail line is defined at lines 00750 through 00910. You can see how the integer QUANTITY-OUT is defined for output, at line 00810, and how numbers with fractional parts are defined for output, at lines 00830, 00850, 00870, 00890, and 00910.

FIGURE 3.4 Program P03-01

```
S COBOL II RELEASE 3.1 09/19/89                P03001   DATE MAR 24,1991 T
----+-*A-1-B--+----2----+----3----+----4----+----5----+----6----+----7-%--+

00010  IDENTIFICATION DIVISION.
00020  PROGRAM-ID.  P03-01.
00030 *
00040 *      THIS PROGRAM READS CUSTOMER ORDER RECORDS
00050 *      AND PRODUCES A DAILY ORDER REPORT.
00060 *
00070 ******************************************************************
00080
00090  ENVIRONMENT DIVISION.
00100  INPUT-OUTPUT SECTION.
00110  FILE-CONTROL.
00120      SELECT ORDER-FILE-IN ASSIGN TO INFILE.
00130      SELECT ORDER-REPORT  ASSIGN TO PRINTER.
00140
00150 ******************************************************************
00160
00170  DATA DIVISION.
00180  FILE SECTION.
00190  FD  ORDER-FILE-IN
00200      RECORD CONTAINS 80 CHARACTERS.
00210
00220  01  ORDER-RECORD-IN.
00230      05 CUSTOMER-NUMBER-IN PIC X(7).
00240      05 PART-NUMBER-IN     PIC X(8).
00250      05                    PIC X(7).
00260      05 QUANTITY-IN        PIC 9(3).
00270      05 UNIT-PRICE-IN      PIC 9(4)V99.
00280      05 HANDLING-CHARGE-IN PIC 99V99.
00290
00300
```

FIGURE 3.4 *continued*

```
       FD  ORDER-REPORT.

       01  REPORT-LINE             PIC X(116).

       WORKING-STORAGE SECTION.
       01  MORE-INPUT              PIC X      VALUE "Y".
       01  TAX-RATE                PIC V99    VALUE .07.

       01  REPORT-TITLE.
           05                      PIC X(45) VALUE SPACES.
           05                      PIC X(18) VALUE "DAILY ORDER REPORT".

       01  COLUMN-HEADS-1.
           05                      PIC X(10) VALUE SPACES.
           05                      PIC X(8)  VALUE "CUSTOMER".
           05                      PIC X(7)  VALUE SPACES.
           05                      PIC X(4)  VALUE "PART".
           05                      PIC X(21) VALUE SPACES.
           05                      PIC X(4)  VALUE "UNIT".
           05                      PIC X(9)  VALUE SPACES.
           05                      PIC X(11) VALUE "MERCHANDISE".
           05                      PIC X(16) VALUE SPACES.
           05                      PIC X(8)  VALUE "HANDLING".
           05                      PIC X(8)  VALUE SPACES.
           05                      PIC X(5)  VALUE "ORDER".

       01  COLUMN-HEADS-2.
           05                      PIC X(11) VALUE SPACES.
           05                      PIC X(6)  VALUE "NUMBER".
           05                      PIC X(7)  VALUE SPACES.
           05                      PIC X(6)  VALUE "NUMBER".
           05                      PIC X(7)  VALUE SPACES.
           05                      PIC X(8)  VALUE "QUANTITY".
           05                      PIC X(5)  VALUE SPACES.
           05                      PIC X(5)  VALUE "PRICE".
           05                      PIC X(10) VALUE SPACES.
           05                      PIC X(6)  VALUE "AMOUNT".
           05                      PIC X(10) VALUE SPACES.
           05                      PIC X(3)  VALUE "TAX".
           05                      PIC X(7)  VALUE SPACES.
           05                      PIC X(6)  VALUE "CHARGE".
           05                      PIC X(9)  VALUE SPACES.
           05                      PIC X(5)  VALUE "TOTAL".

       01  DETAIL-LINE.
           05                             PIC X(11)    VALUE SPACES.
           05 CUSTOMER-NUMBER-OUT         PIC X(7).
           05                             PIC X(5)     VALUE SPACES.
           05 PART-NUMBER-OUT             PIC X(8).
           05                             PIC X(8)     VALUE SPACES.
           05 QUANTITY-OUT                PIC 999.
           05                             PIC X(7)     VALUE SPACES.
           05 UNIT-PRICE-OUT              PIC 9(4)V99.
           05                             PIC X(9)     VALUE SPACES.
           05 MERCHANDISE-AMOUNT-OUT      PIC 9(6)V99.
           05                             PIC X(7)     VALUE SPACES.
           05 TAX-OUT                     PIC 9(4)V99.
           05                             PIC X(7)     VALUE SPACES.
           05 HANDLING-CHARGE-OUT         PIC 99V99.
           05                             PIC X(8)     VALUE SPACES.
           05 ORDER-TOTAL-OUT             PIC 9(7)V99.
```

continued

The total line of the report is defined at lines 00930 through 01040. The numeric fields in that line serve as output fields for the four money-amount totals in the line. As you will see when we look at the Procedure Division, those numeric fields also serve as the working storage fields where the four totals are accumulated. Thus we initialize the four fields with VALUE 0, just as we would zero out a calculator before adding numbers into it. If you are inclined to mistake the letter O for the number 0, you can use VALUE **ZERO** instead. ZERO is a COBOL reserved word.

The Procedure Division begins at line 01080. Each paragraph in the Procedure Division corresponds to one box on the hierarchy diagram in Figure 3.3. For example, the main control paragraph, at line 01090, corresponds to the highest-level box on the diagram, and is given the name PRODUCE-DAILY-ORDER-REPORT. The three paragraphs at the first level of subfunctions are given the names INITIALIZATION, PRODUCE-REPORT-BODY, and TERMINATION to correspond to the hierarchy diagram. You can see in the INITIALIZATION paragraph, line 01160, how the report title and column headings are printed, and in the TERMINATION paragraph, line 01300, how the total line is printed. Remember that by the time the TERMINATION paragraph is executed, the totals have already been accumulated and there is nothing to do but print them.

The paragraph PRODUCE-REPORT-BODY, at line 01360, corresponds to the hierarchy diagram also. In the diagram the box ''Produce report body'' has two subfunctions; in the program the paragraph PRODUCE-REPORT-BODY has PERFORM statements to carry out the subfunctions. It also has a READ statement, even though such a statement is not shown on the hierarchy diagram. It is good practice for the main loop to obtain its input records either in the highest-level paragraph in the main loop, as we have done here, or directly under control of the highest-level paragraph, as we will do in later programs.

In the paragraph PRODUCE-DETAIL-LINE, you can see examples of arithmetic statements with the GIVING option, at lines 01450 through 01520. In the paragraph ACCUMULATE-TOTALS, you can see how the four money amounts are accumulated, in lines 01620 through 01650.

FIGURE *3.4* ***continued***

```
S COBOL II RELEASE 3.1 09/19/89                  P03001    DATE MAR 24,1991 T
----+-*A-1-B--+----2----+----3----+----4----+----5----+----6----+----7-%--+


00930  01   TOTAL-LINE.
00940       05                              PIC X(52)    VALUE SPACES.
00950       05                              PIC X(6)     VALUE "TOTALS".
00960       05                              PIC X(5)     VALUE SPACES.
00970       05 MERCHANDISE-AMOUNT-TOT-OUT   PIC 9(7)V99  VALUE 0.
00980       05                              PIC X(6)     VALUE SPACES.
00990       05 TAX-TOT-OUT                  PIC 9(5)V99  VALUE 0.
01000       05                              PIC X(6)     VALUE SPACES.
01010       05 HANDLING-CHARGE-TOT-OUT      PIC 999V99   VALUE 0.
01020       05                              PIC X(7)     VALUE SPACES.
01030       05 GRAND-TOT-OUT                PIC 9(8)V99  VALUE 0.
01040       05                              PIC X(3)     VALUE " **".
01050
01060 ***********************************************************************
```

FIGURE 3.4 *continued*

```
PROCEDURE DIVISION.
PRODUCE-DAILY-ORDER-REPORT.
    PERFORM INITIALIZATION
    PERFORM PRODUCE-REPORT-BODY UNTIL MORE-INPUT IS EQUAL TO "N"
    PERFORM TERMINATION
    STOP RUN
    .

INITIALIZATION.
    OPEN INPUT  ORDER-FILE-IN
         OUTPUT ORDER-REPORT
    WRITE REPORT-LINE FROM REPORT-TITLE
    WRITE REPORT-LINE FROM COLUMN-HEADS-1
        AFTER ADVANCING 3 LINES
    WRITE REPORT-LINE FROM COLUMN-HEADS-2
    MOVE SPACES TO REPORT-LINE
    WRITE REPORT-LINE
    READ ORDER-FILE-IN
        AT END
            MOVE "N" TO MORE-INPUT
    .

TERMINATION.
    WRITE REPORT-LINE FROM TOTAL-LINE AFTER ADVANCING 3 LINES
    CLOSE ORDER-FILE-IN
          ORDER-REPORT
    .

PRODUCE-REPORT-BODY.
    PERFORM PRODUCE-DETAIL-LINE
    PERFORM ACCUMULATE-TOTALS
    READ ORDER-FILE-IN
        AT END
            MOVE "N" TO MORE-INPUT
    .

PRODUCE-DETAIL-LINE.
    MULTIPLY QUANTITY-IN BY UNIT-PRICE-IN
        GIVING MERCHANDISE-AMOUNT-OUT
    MULTIPLY MERCHANDISE-AMOUNT-OUT BY TAX-RATE
        GIVING TAX-OUT ROUNDED
    ADD MERCHANDISE-AMOUNT-OUT
        TAX-OUT
        HANDLING-CHARGE-IN
            GIVING ORDER-TOTAL-OUT
    MOVE CUSTOMER-NUMBER-IN    TO CUSTOMER-NUMBER-OUT
    MOVE PART-NUMBER-IN        TO PART-NUMBER-OUT
    MOVE QUANTITY-IN           TO QUANTITY-OUT
    MOVE UNIT-PRICE-IN         TO UNIT-PRICE-OUT
    MOVE HANDLING-CHARGE-IN    TO HANDLING-CHARGE-OUT
    WRITE REPORT-LINE FROM DETAIL-LINE
    .

ACCUMULATE-TOTALS.
    ADD MERCHANDISE-AMOUNT-OUT TO MERCHANDISE-AMOUNT-TOT-OUT
    ADD TAX-OUT                TO TAX-TOT-OUT
    ADD HANDLING-CHARGE-OUT    TO HANDLING-CHARGE-TOT-OUT
    ADD ORDER-TOTAL-OUT        TO GRAND-TOT-OUT
    .
```

Program P03-01 was run with the input data shown in Figure 3.5 and produced the output shown in Figure 3.6.

FIGURE 3.5 **Input to Program P03-01**

```
--------------------------------------------------------------------------------
         1         2         3         4         5         6         7         8
12345678901234567890123456789012345678901234567890123456789012345678901234567890
--------------------------------------------------------------------------------
ABC1234F2365-09         9000000100005
09G8239836-7YT7         8000010500050
ADGH784091AN-07         0500250000500
9675473235-1287         0067000295000
```

FIGURE 3.6 **Output from Program P03-01**

```
                          DAILY ORDER REPORT

CUSTOMER     PART                   UNIT     MERCHANDISE              HANDLING     ORDER
 NUMBER     NUMBER     QUANTITY     PRICE       AMOUNT         TAX     CHARGE      TOTAL

 ABC1234    F2365-09      900      000010      00009000      000630     0005     000009635
 09G8239    836-7YT7      800      001050      00840000      058800     0050     000898850
 ADGH784    091AN-07      050      025000      01250000      087500     0500     001338000
 9675473    235-1287      006      700029      04200174      294012     5000     004499186

                                    TOTALS     006299174     0440942    05555     0006745671 **
```

EXERCISE 13 Write a program to read and process input records in the following format:

Positions	Field
1	space
2–6	Account Number
7–9	spaces
10–16	Amount (in dollars and cents)
10–14	Amount dollars
15–16	Amount cents
17–80	spaces

For each record have your program compute a 2 percent discount on the Amount and a net amount (the original Amount minus the discount). For each record have your program print the Account Number, the Amount, the computed discount, and the computed net amount. At the end of the report have your program print the total of the input Amounts, the total of the computed discounts, and the total of the computed net amounts. Have your program produce output in the format shown in Figure 3.E13.

FIGURE 3.E13 Output format for Exercise 13

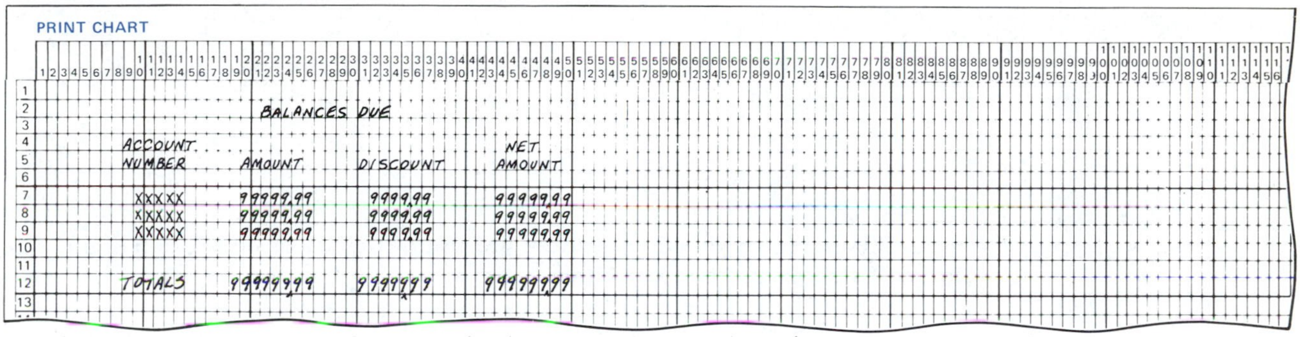

PRINT CHART

```
                    BALANCES DUE

     ACCOUNT                          NET
     NUMBER    AMOUNT    DISCOUNT     AMOUNT

      XXXXX   99999.99    9999.99    999999.99
      XXXXX   99999.99    9999.99    999999.99
      XXXXX   99999.99    9999.99    999999.99


     TOTALS  999999.99   99999.99   9999999.99
```

COMPUTE

The fifth and last arithmetic verb, COMPUTE, permits the programmer to carry out more than one arithmetic operation in a single statement. Here is an example of a COMPUTE statement:

```
COMPUTE AVERAGE-GRADE ROUNDED =
      (GRADE-1-IN +
       GRADE-2-IN +
       GRADE-3-IN +
       GRADE-4-IN) / NUMBER-OF-EXAMS.
```

In this statement COBOL would add the values of the four fields GRADE-1-IN, GRADE-2-IN, GRADE-3-IN, and GRADE-4-IN, and divide the sum by the value of NUMBER-OF-EXAMS. COBOL would then round the result and assign it to the field AVERAGE-GRADE. COBOL would set up its own field for the intermediate result, the sum.

The format of the COMPUTE statement is:

```
COMPUTE {identifier-1 [ROUNDED]} . . . = arithmetic-expression-1
    [ON SIZE ERROR imperative-statement-1]
    [NOT ON SIZE ERROR imperative-statement-2]
    [END-COMPUTE]
```

A COMPUTE statement carries out the computation indicated in the **arithmetic expression,** on the right side of the equal sign, and assigns the result of the computation to the field or fields given after the word COMPUTE, on the left side of the equal sign. The format shows that at least one identifier is required after the word COMPUTE, and that there may be as many as desired. Exactly one arithmetic expression is required to the right of the equal sign.

An arithmetic expression may consist of one numeric literal or one identifier defined as a numeric field or a combination of literals and/or identifiers connected by arithmetic operators. The arithmetic operators are:

+	addition
−	subtraction
*	multiplication
/	division
**	exponentiation

Whenever arithmetic operators are used, they must be preceded and followed by a space. The expression

```
VOLTAGE ** 2
```

would compute the square of the value assigned to VOLTAGE.

A literal or identifier in an arithmetic expression may be optionally preceded by one of the **unary** operators, + or −. A unary operator of + has no effect; a unary operator of − has the effect of multiplying the value of the literal or identifier by −1. A unary operator, if used, must be preceded and followed by a space. A unary operator may be used in addition to any + or − sign that may be part of a numeric literal. A + or − sign that is part of a numeric literal is always followed immediately by a digit.

Expressions may be enclosed in parentheses to indicate the order in which arithmetic is to be carried out. Arithmetic is carried out in the following order:

1. Contents of parentheses are evaluated first, and within nested parentheses the innermost level is evaluated first.
2. Unary plus or minus.
3. Exponentiation.
4. Multiplication and division.
5. Addition and subtraction.

If any ambiguity remains, the arithmetic is carried out from left to right.

For example, consider these three expressions:

1. A * B / C * D
2. A * (B / C) * D
3. (A * B) / (C * D)

Expression 1 is evaluated as follows: First *A* is multiplied by *B,* and then the product is divided by *C.* The quotient from the division is multiplied by *D.* Expression 2 is evaluated as follows: First *B* is divided by *C,* and *A* is multiplied by the quotient. The product of the multiplication is then multiplied by *D.* The arithmetic result is the same as in expression 1. Expression 3 in general gives a different arithmetic result from the other two. Here *A* is multiplied by *B,* and *C* is multiplied by *D.* The first product is then divided by the second. If $A = 5$, $B = 4$, $C = 2$, and $D = 10$, expressions 1 and 2 give the result 100 and expression 3 gives 1.

Do not use COMPUTE where one of the other arithmetic verbs will do. For example, if you want to ADD 1, use a statement such as

```
ADD 1 TO NUMBER-OF-STUDENTS
```

and not:

```
COMPUTE NUMBER-OF-STUDENTS = NUMBER-OF-STUDENTS + 1
```

Be careful when using COMPUTE with very large or very small intermediate results. Significant digits may sometimes be lost. In some systems a statement such as:

```
COMPUTE ONE = (10 ** 18) * (10 ** 18) / (10 ** 18) / (10 ** 18)
```

may not produce the correct result, 1.

Using the COMPUTE Verb

Our next program, Program P03-02, uses input data in the following format:

Positions	Field
1–9	Student Number
18–20	Exam Grade 1
21–23	Exam Grade 2
24–26	Exam Grade 3
27–29	Exam Grade 4
30–80	spaces

Each record contains a Student Number and the grades that the student got on each of four exams. The program is to read the data and print a list showing each Student Number, the four grades, and the average of the four grades. At the end of the list, the program is to print the average of all the grades on exam 1, the average of all the grades on exams 2, 3, and 4, and the grand class average of all the individual student averages. The output format is shown in Figure 3.7. The little inverted Vs show that the averages are computed and printed to one decimal place. In Chapter 4 you will see how to insert real decimal points into printed numbers.

FIGURE 3.7 **Output format for Program P03-02**

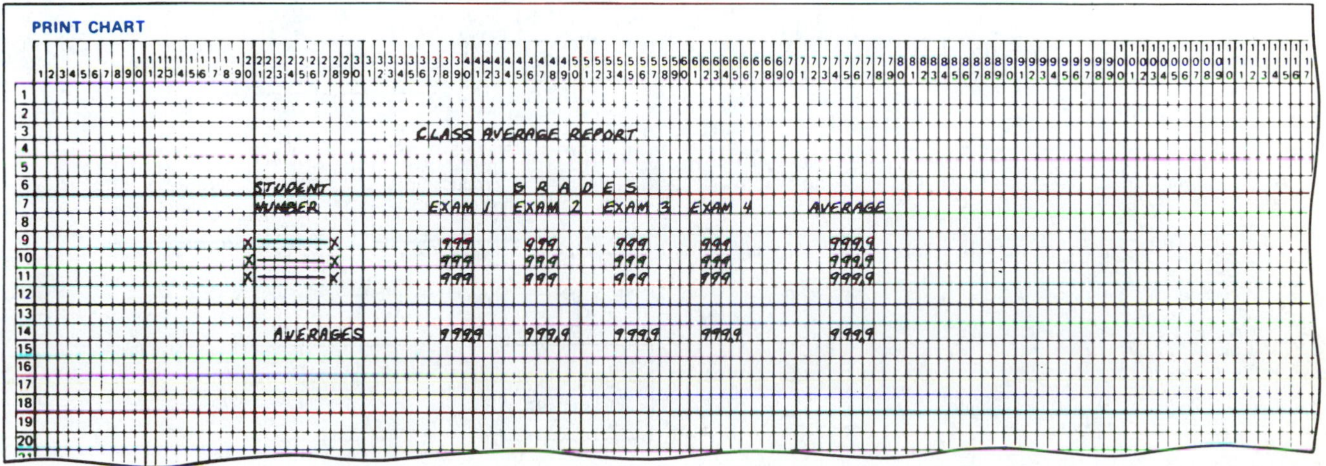

We first do the top-down design for Program P03-02. The main function of this program, "Produce class average report," and its main subfunctions are shown in Figure 3.8. Let us consider the subfunction "Termination" for a moment. What are the subfunctions of "Termination"? We know that all the subfunctions of "Termination" are things that are done after end-of-file is detected in the input, namely, producing the final print line on the list and closing the files. Producing the final print line, in turn, consists of two subfunctions. We place all of these subfunctions on the diagram as shown in Figure 3.9.

Now let us consider the subfunctions of "Produce report body." One of these subfunctions is "Produce detail line," which we already know how to do from Program P03-01. As part of "Produce report body" we will have to gener-

FIGURE 3.8 First-level hierarchy diagram for Program P03-02

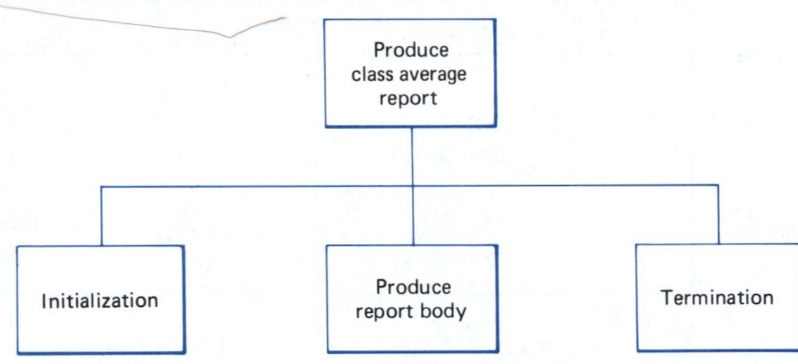

FIGURE 3.9 Hierarchy diagram for Program P03-02 showing the subfunctions of "Termination"

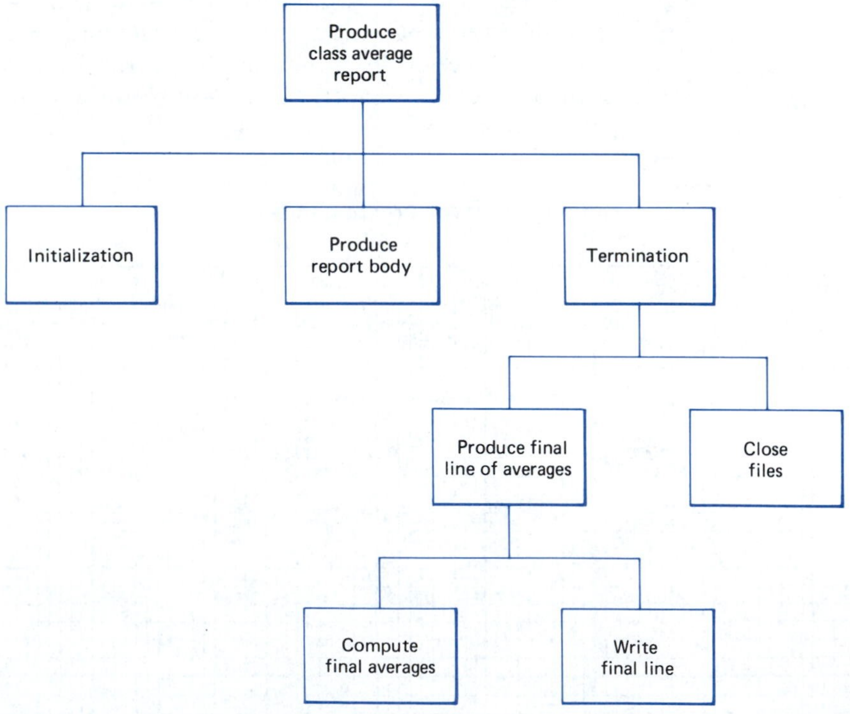

ate the data that will be needed at end-of-file for "Compute final averages" to do its work. What data will "Compute final averages" need to compute, let's say, the average grade on exam 1? It will need the sum of all the grades on exam 1 and also the number of students in the class. (For simplicity we will assume that all the students in the class took all the exams.) "Compute final averages" will need similar information about exams 2, 3, and 4. To provide this information, we show the subfunctions "Accumulate grades" and "Count number of students" as subfunctions of "Produce report body," as in Figure 3.10. These two new subfunctions are added under "Produce report body" instead of somewhere else in the diagram because this is the only place where they can be carried out. As each body line is written onto the report, the program will add the grades on the four exams into four accumulators and also the number 1 to another accumulator that will serve as a count of the number of students. When end-of-file is reached, we will have all the totals of grades that we need, as well as the number of students. The diagram in Figure 3.10 is then the complete hierarchy diagram.

FIGURE 3.10 Complete hierarchy diagram for Program P03-02

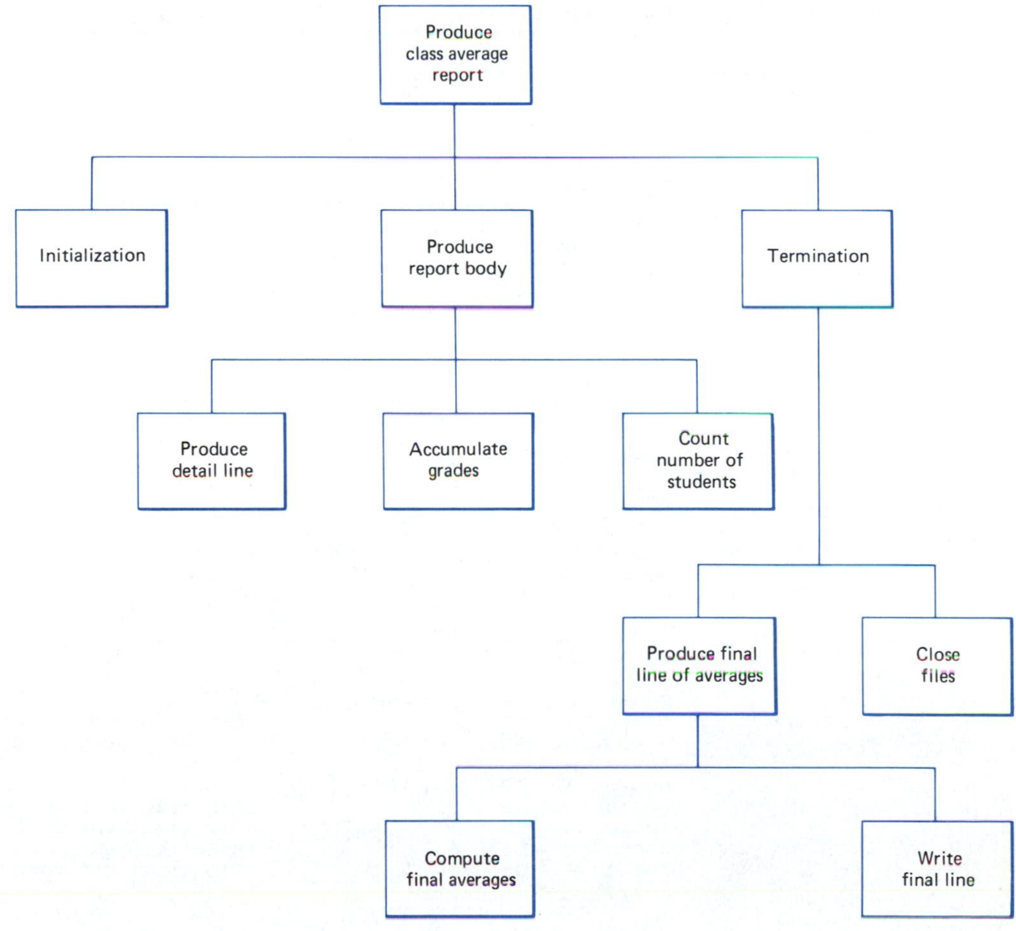

A Program Using the COMPUTE Verb

Program P03-02 is shown in Figure 3.11. Five accumulators have been set up in the Working Storage Section, at lines 00900 through 00940. EXAM-1-SUM is used for accumulating the sum of all the grades on exam 1, EXAM-2-SUM for accumulating the sum of all the grades on exam 2, and so on. NUMBER-OF-STUDENTS is used to count the number of students. Each of the accumulators is defined large enough to hold the largest possible expected sum.

FIGURE *3.11* **Program P03-02**

```
S COBOL II RELEASE 3.1 09/19/89                  P03002   DATE MAR 25,1991 T
----+-*A-1-B--+----2----+----3----+----4----+----5----+----6----+----7-%--+


00010  IDENTIFICATION DIVISION.
00020  PROGRAM-ID.  P03-02.
00030 *
00040 *      THIS PROGRAM READS A FILE OF EXAM GRADES AND
00050 *      COMPUTES EACH STUDENT'S AVERAGE AND THE CLASS AVERAGE.
00060 *
00070 ***************************************************************
00080
00090  ENVIRONMENT DIVISION.
00100  INPUT-OUTPUT SECTION.
00110  FILE-CONTROL.
00120      SELECT EXAM-GRADE-FILE-IN    ASSIGN TO INFILE.
00130      SELECT STUDENT-GRADE-REPORT  ASSIGN TO PRINTER.
00140
00150 ***************************************************************
00160
00170  DATA DIVISION.
00180  FILE SECTION.
00190  FD  EXAM-GRADE-FILE-IN
00200      RECORD CONTAINS 80 CHARACTERS.
00210
00220  01  EXAM-GRADE-RECORD.
00230      05 STUDENT-NUMBER-IN   PIC X(9).
00240      05                     PIC X(8).
00250      05 EXAM-GRADE-1-IN     PIC 9(3).
00260      05 EXAM-GRADE-2-IN     PIC 9(3).
00270      05 EXAM-GRADE-3-IN     PIC 9(3).
00280      05 EXAM-GRADE-4-IN     PIC 9(3).
00290
00300
00310  FD  STUDENT-GRADE-REPORT.
00320
00330  01  REPORT-LINE            PIC X(78).
00340
00350  WORKING-STORAGE SECTION.
00360  01  MORE-INPUT             PIC X     VALUE "Y".
00370
00380  01  REPORT-TITLE.
00390      05                     PIC X(35) VALUE SPACES.
00400      05                     PIC X(20) VALUE "CLASS AVERAGE REPORT".
00410
00420  01  COLUMN-HEADS-1.
00430      05                     PIC X(20) VALUE SPACES.
00440      05                     PIC X(7)  VALUE "STUDENT".
00450      05                     PIC X(17) VALUE SPACES.
00460      05                     PIC X(12) VALUE "G R A D E S ".
00470
```

FIGURE 3.11 *continued*

```
       01  COLUMN-HEADS-2.
           05                              PIC X(20) VALUE SPACES.
           05                              PIC X(6)  VALUE "NUMBER".
           05                              PIC X(10) VALUE SPACES.
           05                              PIC X(6)  VALUE "EXAM 1".
           05                              PIC X(2)  VALUE SPACES.
           05                              PIC X(6)  VALUE "EXAM 2".
           05                              PIC X(2)  VALUE SPACES.
           05                              PIC X(6)  VALUE "EXAM 3".
           05                              PIC X(2)  VALUE SPACES.
           05                              PIC X(6)  VALUE "EXAM 4".
           05                              PIC X(5)  VALUE SPACES.
           05                              PIC X(7)  VALUE "AVERAGE".

       01  DETAIL-LINE.
           05                                PIC X(19) VALUE SPACES.
           05 STUDENT-NUMBER-OUT             PIC X(9).
           05                                PIC X(9)  VALUE SPACES.
           05 EXAM-GRADE-1-OUT               PIC 999.
           05                                PIC X(5)  VALUE SPACES.
           05 EXAM-GRADE-2-OUT               PIC 999.
           05                                PIC X(5)  VALUE SPACES.
           05 EXAM-GRADE-3-OUT               PIC 999.
           05                                PIC X(5)  VALUE SPACES.
           05 EXAM-GRADE-4-OUT               PIC 999.
           05                                PIC X(9)  VALUE SPACES.
           05 AVERAGE-GRADE-OUT              PIC 999V9.

       01  FINAL-AVERAGE-LINE.
           05                                PIC X(22) VALUE SPACES.
           05                                PIC X(15) VALUE "AVERAGES".
           05 EXAM-1-AVERAGE-OUT             PIC 999V9.
           05                                PIC X(4)  VALUE SPACES.
           05 EXAM-2-AVERAGE-OUT             PIC 999V9.
           05                                PIC X(4)  VALUE SPACES.
           05 EXAM-3-AVERAGE-OUT             PIC 999V9.
           05                                PIC X(4)  VALUE SPACES.
           05 EXAM-4-AVERAGE-OUT             PIC 999V9.
           05                                PIC X(8)  VALUE SPACES.
           05 CLASS-AVERAGE-OUT              PIC 999V9.

       01  NUMBER-OF-EXAMS                   PIC 9     VALUE 4.
       01  EXAM-1-SUM                        PIC 9(5)  VALUE 0.
       01  EXAM-2-SUM                        PIC 9(5)  VALUE 0.
       01  EXAM-3-SUM                        PIC 9(5)  VALUE 0.
       01  EXAM-4-SUM                        PIC 9(5)  VALUE 0.
       01  NUMBER-OF-STUDENTS                PIC 9(3)  VALUE 0.
```

continued

The Procedure Division begins at line 00980. It follows the hierarchy diagram, with each box on the diagram being represented by one paragraph in the program. You can see examples of the DIVIDE statement with the GIVING option, at lines 01450 through 01520, and two COMPUTE statements, at lines 01530 and 01720.

FIGURE *3.11* ***continued***

```
S COBOL II RELEASE 3.1 09/19/89                      P03002   DATE MAR 25,1991 T
----+-*A-1-B--+----2----+----3----+----4----+----5----+----6----+----7-%--+


00960 ******************************************************************
00970
00980  PROCEDURE DIVISION.
00990  PRODUCE-CLASS-AVERAGE-REPORT.
01000      PERFORM INITIALIZATION
01010      PERFORM PRODUCE-REPORT-BODY UNTIL MORE-INPUT IS EQUAL TO "N"
01020      PERFORM TERMINATION
01030      STOP RUN
01040      .
01050
01060  INITIALIZATION.
01070      OPEN INPUT  EXAM-GRADE-FILE-IN
01080           OUTPUT STUDENT-GRADE-REPORT
01090      WRITE REPORT-LINE FROM REPORT-TITLE
01100      WRITE REPORT-LINE FROM COLUMN-HEADS-1
01110          AFTER ADVANCING 3 LINES
01120      WRITE REPORT-LINE FROM COLUMN-HEADS-2
01130      MOVE SPACES TO REPORT-LINE
01140      WRITE REPORT-LINE
01150      READ EXAM-GRADE-FILE-IN
01160          AT END
01170              MOVE "N" TO MORE-INPUT
01180      .
01190
01200  TERMINATION.
01210      PERFORM PRODUCE-FINAL-LINE-OF-AVERAGES
01220      PERFORM CLOSE-FILES
01230      .
01240
01250  CLOSE-FILES.
01260      CLOSE EXAM-GRADE-FILE-IN
01270            STUDENT-GRADE-REPORT
01280      .
01290
01300  PRODUCE-REPORT-BODY.
01310      PERFORM PRODUCE-DETAIL-LINE
01320      PERFORM ACCUMULATE-GRADES
01330      PERFORM COUNT-NUMBER-OF-STUDENTS
01340      READ EXAM-GRADE-FILE-IN
01350          AT END
01360              MOVE "N" TO MORE-INPUT
01370      .
01380
01390  PRODUCE-FINAL-LINE-OF-AVERAGES.
01400      PERFORM COMPUTE-FINAL-AVERAGES
01410      PERFORM WRITE-FINAL-LINE
01420      .
01430
01440  COMPUTE-FINAL-AVERAGES.
01450      DIVIDE EXAM-1-SUM BY NUMBER-OF-STUDENTS
01460                               GIVING EXAM-1-AVERAGE-OUT ROUNDED
01470      DIVIDE EXAM-2-SUM BY NUMBER-OF-STUDENTS
01480                               GIVING EXAM-2-AVERAGE-OUT ROUNDED
01490      DIVIDE EXAM-3-SUM BY NUMBER-OF-STUDENTS
01500                               GIVING EXAM-3-AVERAGE-OUT ROUNDED
01510      DIVIDE EXAM-4-SUM BY NUMBER-OF-STUDENTS
01520                               GIVING EXAM-4-AVERAGE-OUT ROUNDED
```

FIGURE 3.11 *continued*

```
       COMPUTE CLASS-AVERAGE-OUT ROUNDED =
           (EXAM-1-SUM +
            EXAM-2-SUM +
            EXAM-3-SUM +
            EXAM-4-SUM) /
           (NUMBER-OF-EXAMS * NUMBER-OF-STUDENTS)
       .

   WRITE-FINAL-LINE.
       WRITE REPORT-LINE FROM FINAL-AVERAGE-LINE
           AFTER ADVANCING 3 LINES
       .

   PRODUCE-DETAIL-LINE.
       MOVE STUDENT-NUMBER-IN TO STUDENT-NUMBER-OUT
       MOVE EXAM-GRADE-1-IN   TO EXAM-GRADE-1-OUT
       MOVE EXAM-GRADE-2-IN   TO EXAM-GRADE-2-OUT
       MOVE EXAM-GRADE-3-IN   TO EXAM-GRADE-3-OUT
       MOVE EXAM-GRADE-4-IN   TO EXAM-GRADE-4-OUT
       COMPUTE AVERAGE-GRADE-OUT ROUNDED =
           (EXAM-GRADE-1-IN +
            EXAM-GRADE-2-IN +
            EXAM-GRADE-3-IN +
            EXAM-GRADE-4-IN) / NUMBER-OF-EXAMS
       WRITE REPORT-LINE FROM DETAIL-LINE
       .

   ACCUMULATE-GRADES.
       ADD EXAM-GRADE-1-IN TO EXAM-1-SUM
       ADD EXAM-GRADE-2-IN TO EXAM-2-SUM
       ADD EXAM-GRADE-3-IN TO EXAM-3-SUM
       ADD EXAM-GRADE-4-IN TO EXAM-4-SUM
       .

   COUNT-NUMBER-OF-STUDENTS.
       ADD 1 TO NUMBER-OF-STUDENTS
       .
```

Program P03-02 was run with the input data shown in Figure 3.12 and produced the output shown in Figure 3.13.

FIGURE 3.12 **Input to Program P03-02**

```
--------------------------------------------------------------------------------
         1         2         3         4         5         6         7         8
12345678901234567890123456789012345678901234567890123456789012345678901234567890
--------------------------------------------------------------------------------
070543242          100078098084
091020222          090085098000
075655343          022067076057
513467845          076083082092
```

FIGURE 3.13 **Output from Program P03-02**

```
                    CLASS AVERAGE REPORT

 STUDENT                       G R A D E S
 NUMBER            EXAM 1    EXAM 2    EXAM 3    EXAM 4        AVERAGE

070543242           100       078       098       084           0900
091020222           090       085       098       000           0683
075655343           022       067       076       057           0555
513467845           076       083       082       092           0833


    AVERAGES        0720      0783      0885      0583          0743
```

EXERCISE *14*

Write a program to read and process input records in the following format:

Positions	Field
1–5	Salesperson Number
6–12	Commission 1 (in dollars and cents)
13–19	Commission 2 (in dollars and cents)
20–26	Commission 3 (in dollars and cents)
27–33	Commission 4 (in dollars and cents)
34–40	Commission 5 (in dollars and cents)
41–47	Commission 6 (in dollars and cents)
48–80	spaces

Each input record contains a Salesperson Number and six commission amounts. For each input record, have your program print the Salesperson Number, the six commission amounts, and the average commission amount, rounded to two decimal places. At the end of the report have your program print a single amount showing the average of all the commissions.

Design the output on a print chart before you begin coding. Provide for a report title, suitable column headings, and the final average line.

Summary

The arithmetic verbs in COBOL are ADD, SUBTRACT, MULTIPLY, DIVIDE, and COMPUTE. ADD, SUBTRACT, MULTIPLY, and DIVIDE can be written without the GIVING option, as ADD A TO B, SUBTRACT A FROM B, MULTIPLY A BY B, and DIVIDE A INTO B. In each such form the result is assigned to one of the terms in the operation, destroying the original value of that term. The result of arithmetic optionally can be assigned to a particular field designated by the programmer through the use of the GIVING option, as SUBTRACT A FROM B GIVING C and MULTIPLY A BY B GIVING C. When the GIVING option is used with ADD, the word TO need not be used, as in the correct statement ADD A B GIVING C. When the GIVING option is used with DIVIDE, then INTO or BY may be used, as DIVIDE A INTO B GIVING C, or DIVIDE B BY A GIVING C. The DIVIDE statement also has the optional capability of assigning a REMAINDER to a field specified by the programmer.

The COMPUTE verb can be used to carry out more than one arithmetic operation in a single statement. A COMPUTE statement always contains an equal sign, and COBOL assigns the results of the computation to the field or fields named to the left of the sign. There must be an arithmetic expression to the right of the sign.

The order of arithmetic in an expression is unary operators first, then exponentiation, then multiplication and division, then addition and subtraction. Parentheses may be used to change the order of arithmetic. The arithmetic operators are +, −, *, /; for exponentiation, **. The unary operators + and − may appear before any expression.

In all arithmetic operations, COBOL can be directed to round the result if necessary.

In top-down design, a programmer produces a hierarchy diagram showing the major function of a program broken down into lower and lower levels of subfunctions. Top-down design enables the programmer to design the whole program by concentrating on only one small portion of it at a time.

Fill-In Exercises

1. An ADD statement that does not contain the word ______ must contain the word ______.
2. In a top-down design the programmer draws a ______ diagram.
3. It is good programming practice to define and name all constants in ______.
4. In a DIVIDE statement without the GIVING option, the quotient is assigned to the field given after the word ______.
5. In a SUBTRACT statement without the GIVING option, the difference is assigned to the field given after the word ______.
6. In a MULTIPLY statement without the GIVING option, the product is assigned to the field given after the word ______.
7. In arithmetic statements with the GIVING option, the result is assigned to the field given after the word ______.
8. The ______ verb permits more than one arithmetic operation to be carried out in a single statement.
9. The order of evaluation in an arithmetic expression is parentheses first, then ______, then ______, then ______ and ______, then ______ and ______.
10. When the signs + or − appear immediately before an arithmetic expression, they are called ______.
11. The PICTURE character ______ is used to represent a digit.
12. The PICTURE character ______ is used to show the location of an assumed decimal point in a numeric field.
13. The PICTURE character ______ is used to show that COBOL may assign a plus or minus sign to a numeric field.
14. The REMAINDER in a division is found by multiplying the ______ by the ______ and subtracting the product from the ______.
15. COBOL rounds a number by increasing the least significant digit of the result by ______ when the most significant digit of the excess is ______ or greater.

Review Exercises

1. Refer to the statement formats given in the chapter and explain why each of the following statements is illegal:
   - *a.* ADD A TO B C GIVING D
   - *b.* MULTIPLY RATE BY 2
   - *c.* DIVIDE A BY B
   - *d.* DIVIDE A INTO B REMAINDER C
   - *e.* COMPUTE A + B = C
2. Write COBOL statements to accomplish the following:
   - *a.* Add the value of DEPOSITS to the value of CURRENT-BALANCE and assign the sum to CURRENT-BALANCE.

b. Subtract the value of WITHDRAWAL from the value of CURRENT-BALANCE and assign the difference to CURRENT-BALANCE.

c. Multiply the value of INTEREST-RATE by the value of CURRENT-BALANCE and assign the result to CURRENT-INTEREST.

3. Write level-05 entries for the following working-storage fields:

a. A signed nine-digit dollars-and-cents field called GROSS-REVENUES

b. A signed six-digit integer called VELOCITY

c. An unsigned seven-digit integer called BOXCARS

4. Show the digits that would appear in computer storage for each of the following fields:

Value	Field Description	Digits in Computer Storage
225	05 SAMPLE-1 PIC 9(3)	
225	05 SAMPLE-2 PIC 9(5)	
5.20	05 SAMPLE-3 PIC 9V99	
5.20	05 SAMPLE-4 PIC 99V9(3)	
.675	05 SAMPLE-5 PIC 9V9(3)	
.675	05 SAMPLE-6 PIC 99V9(4)	

5. Write a program to read and process input records in the following format:

Positions	Field
1–9	Social Security Number
10–12	Monday Hours Worked (to tenths of an hour)
13–15	Tuesday Hours Worked (to tenths of an hour)
16–18	Wednesday Hours Worked (to tenths of an hour)
19–21	Thursday Hours Worked (to tenths of an hour)
22–24	Friday Hours Worked (to tenths of an hour)
25–27	Saturday Hours Worked (to tenths of an hour)
28–80	spaces

Each input record contains the Hours Worked for one employee. For each employee have your program show the Hours Worked each day and the total hours worked during the week. Have your program show, at the end of the report, the total hours worked by all employees on Monday, the total hours worked on Tuesday, and so on, and the grand total of all hours worked during the week. Have your program produce its output in the format shown in Figure 3.RE5.

6. Write a program to read and process the input data for Program P02-03, described on page 23. Have your program print the contents of each record on one line. At the end of the report, have your program print the average salary of all employees, to the nearest cent. Plan the output format on a

FIGURE 3.RE5 Output format for Review Exercise 5

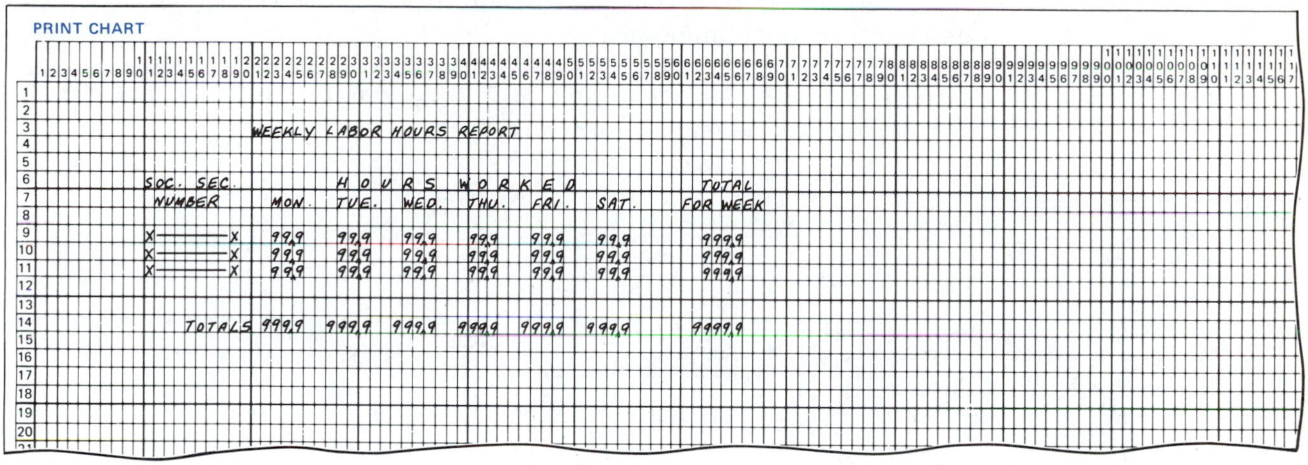

PRINT CHART

```
                                WEEKLY LABOR HOURS REPORT

                SOC. SEC.           H O U R S   W O R K E D            TOTAL
                 NUMBER     MON.   TUE.   WED.   THU.   FRI.   SAT.   FOR WEEK

                X-------X   99.9   99.9   99.9   99.9   99.9   99.9    999.9
                X-------X   99.9   99.9   99.9   99.9   99.9   99.9    999.9
                X-------X   99.9   99.9   99.9   99.9   99.9   99.9    999.9

                     TOTALS 999.9  999.9  999.9  999.9  999.9  999.9  9999.9
```

print chart before you begin coding. Provide a report title, suitable column headings, and a suitable final average line.

Project

Write a program that reads one record containing data about a single automobile loan and produces a repayment schedule in the format shown in Figure 3.P1. The input record is in the following format:

Positions	Field
1–7	Starting Loan Amount (dollars and cents)
8–9	Number of Monthly Payments
10–15	Monthly Payment (dollars and cents)
16–19	Annual Interest Rate
20–80	spaces

Define the Annual Interest Rate in the input with PICTURE V9(4). In Figure 3.P1, to print the Payment Number set up a two-digit numeric field and ADD 1 to it for each line printed. Use the following formulas for the other columns:

For Payment Number 1,

Interest = Starting Loan Amount * Annual Interest Rate / 12

Payment to Principal = Monthly Payment − Interest

Principal Remaining = Starting Loan Amount − Payment to Principal

For all payments after Payment Number 1,

Interest = Principal Remaining from previous payment * Annual Interest Rate / 12

Payment to Principal = Monthly Payment − Interest

Principal Remaining = Principal Remaining from previous payment − Payment to Principal

The minus signs in the Interest, Payment to Principal, and Principal Remaining columns in Figure 3.P1 indicate that a positive or negative sign is to print there. Define those output fields with SIGN IS TRAILING SEPARATE CHARACTER to get the printing sign.

Since only one record is read, you need not have an input data flag. Instead, you can PERFORM your main loop UNTIL PAYMENT-NUMBER IS GREATER THAN NUMBER-OF-PAYMENTS-IN.

FIGURE *3.P1* **Output format for Chapter 3 Project**

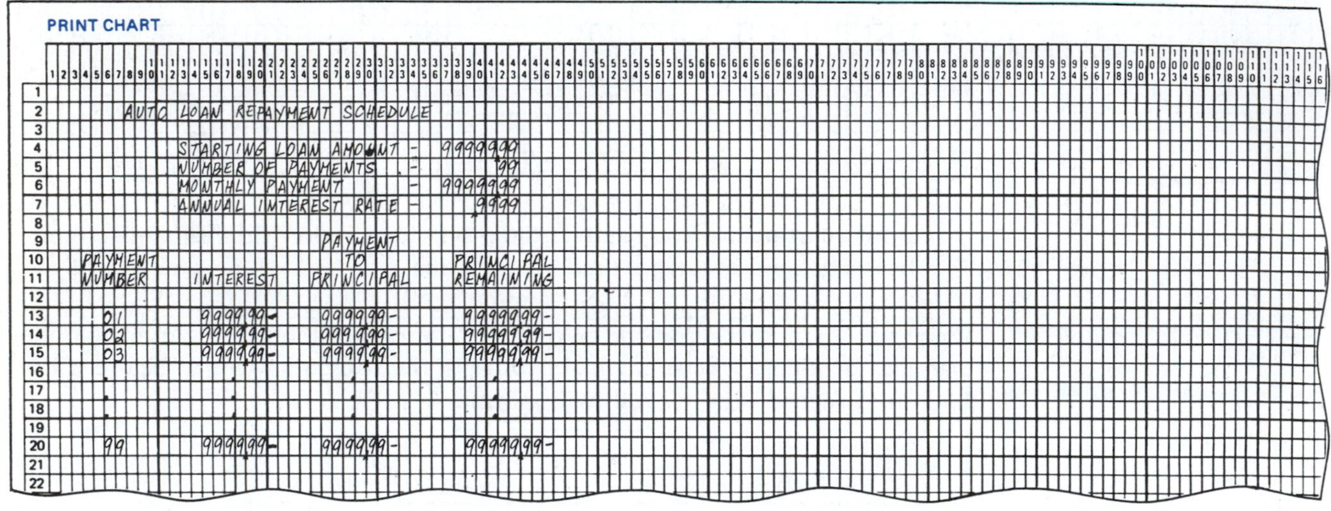

CHAPTER 4

Editing

HERE ARE THE KEY POINTS YOU SHOULD LEARN FROM THIS CHAPTER

1. How to insert today's date into an output report.
2. How to edit output data for printing.
3. The formats of the MOVE statement.

KEY WORDS TO RECOGNIZE AND LEARN

editing	TIME
validity checking	data-name qualification
alphanumeric edited	IN
zero suppression	qualified
insertion character	qualifier
check protection	OF
floating	group item
ACCEPT	elementary item
DATE	subordinate
DAY	CORRESPONDING
DAY-OF-WEEK	CORR

This chapter discusses the output **editing** features of COBOL which can be used to make output reports and listings easier to read. The word *editing* is sometimes incorrectly used to refer to automated checking and validation of input data. Validation of input is properly called **validity checking** and is discussed in Chapter 8. *Editing* refers to output.

PICTURE Characters for Editing

COBOL provides facilities for rendering numeric and alphanumeric output more readable by making it easy for the programmer to do the following:

1. Insert a decimal point into numeric output.
2. Insert commas into numeric output.
3. Insert zeros, blanks, and/or slashes (/) into numeric or alphanumeric output.
4. Suppress the printing of unwanted leading zeros in numeric output.

5. Replace leading zeros with asterisks (*) in numeric output.
6. Insert a dollar sign at the left end of numeric output.
7. Insert one of the symbols + or − to indicate the sign of numeric output.
8. Insert the characters CR or DB to indicate that numeric output is negative.

To produce numeric edited or **alphanumeric edited** output, the programmer need only specify the desired editing in the PICTURE of the output field to be edited. Then, whenever data are assigned to that output field, COBOL carries out the desired editing with no further effort on the part of the programmer. Numeric edited fields may appear in arithmetic statements, but only immediately after the words REMAINDER or COMPUTE, or anywhere after the word GIVING.

Zero Suppression

The PICTURE character Z can be used to obtain suppression of insignificant leading zeros. For example, in Program P03-01 we could have printed the QUANTITY-OUT field with **zero suppression** to eliminate unwanted zeros when the quantity amount was small by using PICTURE ZZZ instead of PICTURE 999. The use of ZZZ instead of 999 in no way would affect the printing of three-digit quantities. Table 4.1 shows how different values of QUANTITY-OUT would print using the two PICTUREs 999 and ZZZ.

TABLE *4.1*
How a three-digit integer would print using the two PICTUREs 999 and ZZZ

999	ZZZ
800	800
395	395
035	35
006	6
000	

You can see a slight difficulty with the PICTURE ZZZ (or PICTURE Z(3), which means the same). When the quantity is zero, the entire field is zero suppressed, and nothing at all prints. Usually, in a listing where we are showing the quantity of each part, if the quantity on hand is zero we probably want a zero to print. We can obtain this result by telling COBOL to zero-suppress only the first two positions of the field and print the third regardless of what it is. We would use PICTURE ZZ9 to indicate only two positions of zero suppression in a three-digit field.

Inserting Commas and Decimal Points

The **insertion characters** comma and decimal point can be used in a PICTURE to show where commas and a decimal point should appear in printed output. Commas and decimal points are, as you know, never part of numeric input data, nor are they part of numeric data as COBOL is processing them. Since COBOL cannot do arithmetic on numeric edited fields, editing can be done on numbers only just before they are printed. Thus it is the PICTURE of the output field as it is to be printed that tells COBOL how to edit the field.

To use insertion characters, the programmer simply places them in the PICTURE as they are to appear in the printed output. For example, to print a four-digit number and insert a comma after the first digit, we can use PICTURE 9,999. To obtain zero suppression of the first three digits in case the number is small, and also to allow for the insertion of a comma in case the number has four digits, we can use PICTURE Z,ZZ9. Table 4.2 shows how several numbers would print under three different PICTUREs.

TABLE 4.2
How several four-digit numbers would print under three different edit PICTUREs

Value	9,999	Z,ZZZ	Z,ZZ9
8000	8,000	8,000	8,000
3657	3,657	3,657	3,657
0657	0,657	657	657
0022	0,022	22	22
0000	0,000		0

You may have as many commas as you like in a PICTURE, and they may be anywhere you like. If a comma is the rightmost character in a PICTURE, then the PICTURE clause must be the last clause in the description of the field, and the comma in the PICTURE must be followed immediately by a period.

Decimal point insertion may be obtained in a similar way. The programmer writes the PICTURE with a decimal point, showing where it should appear in the printed output. There must be no more than one decimal point in a PICTURE. If the decimal point is the rightmost character in a PICTURE, then the PICTURE clause must be the last clause in the description of the field, and the decimal point in the PICTURE must be followed immediately by a period. To print a five-digit number as a dollars-and-cents figure, we could use PICTURE 999.99; to obtain zero suppression up to the decimal point, we would use PICTURE ZZZ.99. Zero suppression can be stopped before it reaches the decimal point with the use of PICTURE ZZ9.99 or Z99.99. Table 4.3 shows how different money amounts would print under five different PICTUREs.

TABLE 4.3
How several different money amounts would print under five different PICTUREs

Amount	999.99	ZZZ.ZZ	ZZZ.99	ZZ9.99	Z99.99
657.00	657.00	657.00	657.00	657.00	657.00
075.25	075.25	75.25	75.25	75.25	75.25
006.50	006.50	6.50	6.50	6.50	06.50
000.29	000.29	.29	.29	0.29	00.29
000.06	000.06	.06	.06	0.06	00.06
000.00	000.00		.00	0.00	00.00

If Z appears to the right of a decimal point in a PICTURE, then it must occupy every position to the right of the decimal point. In that case, if the value of the field is zero, the printed field will contain all blanks, as shown in the last line in Table 4.3. If the value of the field is not zero, then a PICTURE with Zs to the right of a decimal point acts as if the Zs stopped immediately to the left of the point, as shown in the fourth and fifth rows in Table 4.3.

EXERCISE *1*

Write an edit PICTURE for each of the following output fields:

a. A five-digit integer, comma after the second digit from the left, no zero suppression

b. A six-digit, dollars-and-cents money amount, comma after the first digit from the left, zero suppression up to the decimal point

c. A seven-digit integer, comma after the first and fourth digits from the left, entire field zero suppressed

d. A nine-digit, dollars-and-cents amount, comma after the first and fourth digits from the left, zero suppression up to one place before the decimal point

e. A six-digit number with four decimal places, zero suppression up to one place before the decimal point

Printing a Sign Designation

When a numeric field is printed, the SIGN clause can be used to say where the sign should print. But with numeric editing, the programmer has much greater flexibility in printing a sign indication. Positive numbers may have a plus sign printed at or near the right or left end of a number, and negative numbers may have either a minus sign at or near the right or left end of a number or the letters CR or DB at or near the right end of a number. Here are some ways in which a positive number can be made to print:

```
 +675.28
+ 675.28
  675.28+
  675.28 +
```

And here are some ways in which a negative number can be made to print:

```
  675.28-
 -675.28
- 675.28
  675.28CR
  675.28 DB
```

There can be as many blanks as desired between the number and its sign designation. Each digit, blank, and sign occupies one print position. The sign designations CR and DB each occupy two print positions. The programmer indicates the type of sign designation desired and the fixed location of the sign by placing the sign character in the edit PICTURE of the output field.

The following is a legal description:

```
05 FIELD-1-OUT             PIC -ZZZ.99.
```

This PICTURE tells COBOL to print a minus sign in the fixed position shown if the printed value happens to be negative. If a positive value is edited under this PICTURE, a blank will print in the position allotted to the sign. Table 4.4 shows how several values would print under two edit PICTUREs.

TABLE 4.4
How several negative, positive, and zero values print under two different PICTUREs

Value	−ZZZ.99	−ZZZ.ZZ
−675.28	−675.28	−675.28
−005.60	− 5.60	− 5.60
−000.05	− .05	− .05
+675.28	675.28	675.28
+000.07	.07	.07
000.00	.00	

Similarly, the PICTURE character − may be placed at the right end of the PICTURE, or the letters CR or DB may be placed at the right end of the PICTURE. You may not use the minus sign and the CR or DB designation in the same PICTURE. Table 4.5 shows how some values would print under four PICTUREs.

TABLE 4.5
How several negative, positive, and zero values print under four different PICTUREs

Value	ZZZ.99−	ZZZ.99CR	Z99.99DB	ZZZ.ZZDB
−675.28	675.28−	675.28CR	675.28DB	675.28DB
−005.60	5.60−	5.60CR	05.60DB	5.60DB
−000.05	.05−	.05CR	00.05DB	.05DB
+675.28	675.28	675.28	675.28	675.28
000.00	.00	.00	00.00	

To obtain a printed plus sign, the PICTURE character + may be used. But the character + works a little differently from the other three sign designators −, CR, and DB. When you use + you always get some printed sign indication, whether the printed value happens to be positive, negative, or zero, unless all the digits are zero suppressed, in which case the sign also disappears. The other three designators print only if the value happens to be negative, and they give no sign indication when the value is positive. When the PICTURE character + is used, a plus sign will print next to positive or zero values and a minus sign next to negative values. Table 4.6 shows how some values will print under four different PICTUREs.

TABLE 4.6
How several negative, positive, and zero values print under four different PICTUREs

Value	+ZZZ	ZZZ+	+ZZ9	ZZ9+
+520	+520	520+	+520	520+
−520	−520	520−	−520	520−
+006	+ 6	6+	+ 6	6+
000			+ 0	0+

Table 4.7 summarizes the result obtained for the four different kinds of sign designation and different values of edited data. Of course, in all cases if all digit positions in a field are zero suppressed and the value placed in the field is zero, the entire field will be blanked out.

TABLE 4.7
How different sign designations print for different values of data (in all cases, though, if all digit positions of a field are zero suppressed and the data value is zero, the entire field is blanked)

	PRINTED RESULT	
Sign Designation in PICTURE	***Data Item Positive or Zero***	***Data Item Negative***
—	space	—
CR	2 spaces	CR
DB	2 spaces	DB
+	+	–

If a fixed sign designation appears to the left of a number, there must be no PICTURE characters to the left of the sign. If a fixed sign designation appears to the right of a number, there must be no PICTURE characters to the right of the sign.

The Insertion Characters B, /, and 0

To obtain insertion of spaces, slashes, and zeros in numeric or alphanumeric output, the PICTURE characters B, /, and 0 are used. These PICTURE characters may be used quite freely in combination with almost all other PICTURE characters. When any of these characters appears in a PICTURE, COBOL simply inserts the appropriate character into the edited result in the position indicated in the PICTURE.

For example, the PICTURE character B may be used to obtain one or more blank spaces between a sign designation and a number. Table 4.8 shows how some values will print under several edit PICTUREs.

TABLE 4.8
How several negative, positive, and zero values prnt under four different PICTURES

Value	-BZZZ,ZZ9	+BBZZZ,ZZ9	ZZZ,ZZ9BCR	ZZZ,ZZ9BBDB
-589000	– 589,000	– 589,000	589,000 CR	589,000 DB
-006890	– 6,890	– 6,890	6,890 CR	6,890 DB
-000055	– 55	– 55	55 CR	55 DB
+589000	589,000	+ 589,000	589,000	589,000
000000	0	+ 0	0	0

As an example of the use of the PICTURE character B in alphanumeric editing, assume we have the following two fields:

```
05 SOCIAL-SECURITY-NUMBER          PIC X(9).
05 SOCIAL-SECURITY-NUMBER-EDITED   PIC X(3)BXXBX(4).
```

If the value of SOCIAL-SECURITY-NUMBER is 023456789, the statement

```
MOVE SOCIAL-SECURITY-NUMBER TO SOCIAL-SECURITY-NUMBER-EDITED
```

assigns the value 023 45 6789 to SOCIAL-SECURITY-NUMBER-EDITED. If instead SOCIAL-SECURITY-NUMBER-EDITED has the PICTURE X(3)/XX/X(4), then the statement

```
MOVE SOCIAL-SECURITY-NUMBER TO SOCIAL-SECURITY-NUMBER-EDITED
```

assigns the value 023/45/6789 to SOCIAL-SECURITY-NUMBER-EDITED.

To see the use of / with a numeric field, assume we have:

```
05  MONTH-AND-DAY-IN    PIC 9(4).
05  MONTH-AND-DAY-OUT   PIC Z9/99.
```

If the value of MONTH-AND-DAY-IN is 0915, the statement

```
MOVE MONTH-AND-DAY-IN TO MONTH-AND-DAY-OUT
```

assigns the value 9/15 to MONTH-AND-DAY-OUT.

Finally, to see how the insertion character 0 might be used, assume we have the following two fields:

```
05  MILLIONS-OF-DOLLARS    PIC 9(3).
05  DOLLARS-SPELLED-OUT    PIC ZZZ,000,000.
```

Table 4.9 shows what is assigned to DOLLARS-SPELLED-OUT for different initial values of MILLIONS-OF-DOLLARS and the statement:

```
MOVE MILLIONS-OF-DOLLARS TO DOLLARS-SPELLED-OUT
```

TABLE 4.9
Values assigned to the field DOLLARS-SPELLED-OUT with different initial values of the field MILLIONS-OF-DOLLARS

MILLIONS-OF-DOLLARS	DOLLARS-SPELLED-OUT
485	485,000,000
020	20,000,000
000	

The Dollar Sign

It is possible to have COBOL insert a dollar sign in a fixed location at the left end of a number. The PICTURE character $ is used to indicate the position of the sign. Table 4.10 shows how some money amounts print under two different PICTUREs.

TABLE 4.10
How some money amounts would print with fixed dollar sign insertion

Value	$ZZ,ZZZ.99	$ZZ,ZZZ.ZZ
58905.03	$58,905.03	$58,905.03
08905.03	$ 8,905.03	$ 8,905.03
00600.05	$ 600.05	$ 600.05
00005.29	$ 5.29	$ 5.29
00000.06	$ .06	$ .06
00000.00	$ .00	

If a single dollar sign appears to the left of a number, as in the PICTUREs in Table 4.10, the only character that may appear to the left of the dollar sign is + or −.

Asterisk Insertion

When COBOL programs are used to print checks, it is usually undesirable to leave any blank spaces in the place on the check where the money amount is printed. If the check has room for, let's say, a seven-digit number, and the particular check amount has only four or five-digits, the blanks which result from suppression of the leading zeros are an invitation to forgery. The invitation is especially appealing if the check is for an amount less than $1 and only a decimal point and some pennies are printed. For this reason COBOL provides a form of zero suppression in which leading zeros are replaced not with blanks but with asterisks (*). Replacing leading zeros with asterisks is sometimes called **check protection.** To obtain check protection, the programmer uses the PICTURE character * in the same way that the PICTURE character Z would be used. The characters * and Z may not appear in the same PICTURE. Table 4.11 shows how some money amounts print with and without check protection.

TABLE *4.11*
How some money amounts would print with and without check protection

Value	$Z,ZZZ.99CR	*,***.99-	$*,***.**DB
-8905.03	$8,905.03CR	8,905.03-	$8,905.03DB
+0600.05	$ 600.05	**600.05	$**600.05
-0005.29	$ 5.29CR	****5.29-	$****5.29DB
+0000.06	$ .06	*****.06	$*****.06
0000.00	$ .00	*****.00	******.****

When all the digit positions in a number are zero-suppressed by asterisks and the value of the field is zero, then the entire edited field is composed of asterisks except for the decimal point, as shown in the last entry in Table 4.11.

Floating Insertion

So far we have seen how a plus sign, a minus sign, or a dollar sign can be made to print in a fixed position to the left of a printed number. It is possible instead to have COBOL print those signs immediately to the left of the most significant digit in the number as printed. Such an operation is called **floating,** because the sign floats to the right until it finds the most significant digit and prints itself there. A floating sign is indicated by a string of two or more such signs in the edit PICTURE of the output field. A floating sign carries out zero suppression, so neither Z nor * may be used in any PICTURE that specifies a floating sign. Table 4.12 shows how some values would print with fixed signs and with floating signs. When all the digit positions in a number are zero-suppressed by a floating sign and the value of the field is zero, then the entire edited field is made blank, as shown in the last row in Table 4.12.

Notice that when a floating sign is used, there must be enough signs to allow for the largest possible number that might print and for the printing sign itself. So a three-digit number could have PICTURE---- to allow one sign to print even if digits occupied the other three places. Of course, a three-digit number could also have PICTURE ---9 if the programmer wanted zero suppression to stop before the rightmost digit. When a floating sign is used, there should

TABLE 4.12 How some amounts would print with fixed and with floating sign insertion

Value	-Z,ZZZ.99	--,---.--	$$,$$$.$$CR	+$$,$$$.99	$--,---.99
-5890.00	-5,890.00	-5,890.00	$5,890.00CR	-$5,890.00	$-5,890.00
+0680.09	680.09	680.09	$680.09	+ $680.09	$ 680.09
-0005.00	- 5.00	-5.00	$5.00CR	- $5.00	$ -5.00
-0000.50	- .50	-.50	$.50CR	- $.50	$ -.50
0000.00	.00			+ $.00	$ .00

always be at least two signs to the left of the leftmost comma for the PICTURE to make sense. To see why, try to figure out what size number this legal but nonsensical PICTURE is trying to represent: PICTURE −,−−−.

EXERCISE 2

Show how each of the following values would print under each of the edit PICTUREs shown:

Value	*$ZZ9−*	*$ZZZ+*	*$$$$−*	****CR*	*$***DB*	*$**9+*
+590						
−590						
+060						
−060						
+005						
−005						
000						

Precedence Rules for PICTUREs

Table 4.13 shows which characters may precede and follow which characters in a PICTURE. An X at the intersection of a row and column indicates that the PICTURE character shown at the top of the column may precede the PICTURE character shown at the left end of the row, but the two characters need not be adjacent in the PICTURE. Characters shown in curly braces are mutually exclusive and cannot be used together in the same PICTURE.

The PICTURE characters +, −, Z, *, $, and P appear in pairs in the table. The leftmost or uppermost appearance of each of those characters in a pair represents its use to the left of the decimal point position in a PICTURE; the rightmost or bottommost appearance of each character in a pair represents its use to the right of the decimal point position in a PICTURE.

For example, to determine whether the character B is legal to the left of a

TABLE 4.13 **Precedence rules for PICTURE characters. An X at the intersection of a row and a column indicates that the character at the head of the column may precede the character at the left end of the row in a PICTURE. The two characters need not be adjacent in the PICTURE.**

SECOND CHARACTER		FIRST CHARACTER																				
		Fixed Insertion Characters									Floating Insertion Characters						Other Characters					
		B	0	/	,	.	{+ −} to the left of the decimal point	{+ −} to the right of the decimal point	{CR DB}	$	{Z *} to the left of the decimal point	{Z *} to the right of the decimal point	{+ −} to the left of the decimal point	{+ −} to the right of the decimal point	$ to the left of the decimal point	$ to the right of the decimal point	9	X	S	V	P to the left of the decimal point	P to the right of the decimal point
Fixed Insertion Characters	B	x	x	x	x	x	x			x	x	x	x	x	x	x	x	x		x		x
	0	x	x	x	x	x	x			x	x	x	x	x	x	x	x	x		x		x
	/	x	x	x	x	x	x			x	x	x	x	x	x	x	x	x		x		x
	,	x	x	x	x	x	x			x	x	x	x	x	x	x	x			x		x
	.	x	x	x	x		x			x	x		x		x		x					
	{+ −} to the left of the decimal point																					
	{+ −} to the right of the decimal point	x	x	x	x	x				x	x	x			x	x	x			x	x	x
	{CR DB}	x	x	x	x	x				x	x	x			x	x	x			x	x	x
	$						x															
Floating Insertion Characters	{Z *} to the left of the decimal point	x	x	x	x		x			x	x											
	{Z *} to the right of the decimal point	x	x	x	x	x	x			x	x	x								x		x
	{+ −} to the left of the decimal point	x	x	x	x					x			x									
	{+ −} to the right of the decimal point	x	x	x	x	x				x			x	x						x		x
	$ to the left of the decimal point	x	x	x	x		x								x							
	$ to the right of the decimal point	x	x	x	x	x	x								x	x				x		x
Other Characters	9	x	x	x	x	x	x			x	x		x		x		x	x	x	x		x
	X	x	x	x													x	x				
	S																					
	V	x	x	x	x		x			x	x		x		x		x		x		x	
	P to the left of the decimal point	x	x	x	x		x			x	x		x		x		x		x		x	
	P to the right of the decimal point						x			x									x	x		x

fixed dollar sign, find B across the top of the table in the area labeled First Character. Look down the column headed B until you come to the row labeled for a fixed dollar sign in the area called Second Character. The absence of an X at the intersection of the row and column indicates that the character B may not appear to the left of a fixed dollar sign.

Now to determine whether the character B may appear to the left of a floating dollar sign, look down the column headed B until you come to the two rows labeled for floating dollar signs. The first of the two rows refers to a floating dollar sign to the left of the decimal point position, and the second refers to a floating dollar sign to the right of the decimal point position. The Xs at the intersections of the column with both rows shows that the character B may appear before a floating dollar sign whether the dollar sign is to the right or left of the decimal point position.

Obtaining Today's Date from the COBOL System

One form of the **ACCEPT** statement can be used to obtain the date, day, and time from the COBOL system at the moment the statement is executed. The ANSI standard format of that ACCEPT statement is:

```
                                  { DATE        }
ACCEPT identifier-2 FROM          { DAY         }
                                  { DAY-OF-WEEK }
                                  { TIME        }
```

This statement moves the **DATE, DAY, DAY-OF-WEEK,** or **TIME** into any desired field. The DATE is defined by COBOL as an unsigned six-digit field consisting of two digits for the year of century, two digits for the month, and two digits for the day. Thus July 1, 1994, would be expressed as 940701. DAY is defined as an unsigned five-digit field consisting of two digits for the year of century and three digits for the day of year. Thus July 1, 1994, would be expressed as 94182. DAY-OF-WEEK is an unsigned one-digit field with 1 representing Monday, 2 Tuesday, and 7 Sunday. TIME is defined as an unsigned eight-digit field consisting of two digits for hours, two digits for minutes, two digits for seconds, and two digits for hundredths of a second. TIME is expressed in so-called military time, on a 24-hour clock basis. Thus 2:41 PM would be expressed as 14410000.

As an example, if we have the following field

```
01  RUN-DATE.
    05 RUN-YEAR                     PIC 99.
    05 RUN-MONTH-AND-DAY            PIC 9(4).
```

and the statement

```
ACCEPT RUN-DATE FROM DATE
```

on July 1, 1994, COBOL will assign 94 to RUN-YEAR and 0701 to RUN-MONTH-AND-DAY.

Data-Name Qualification

Data names in COBOL need not be unique. That is, the same name may be used for more than one field in the Data Division. But COBOL still requires that every field in some way be distinguishable from every other field. Distinguishing among two or more fields may be done on the basis of some larger field and is called **data-name qualification.** For example, we might have the following fields in a program:

```
01   RUN-DATE.
     05 RUN-YEAR                       PIC 99.
     05 RUN-MONTH-AND-DAY              PIC 9(4).

01   DATE-LINE.
     05 RUN-MONTH-AND-DAY              PIC Z9/99/.
     05 RUN-YEAR                       PIC 99.
```

If it were necessary for us to distinguish one RUN-YEAR from another in the program, we could call one of the fields RUN-YEAR **IN** RUN-DATE and the other RUN-YEAR IN DATE-LINE. The name RUN-YEAR in each case would be said to be **qualified,** and the names of the larger fields, in this case RUN-DATE and DATE-LINE, would be said to be the **qualifiers.** A qualified data name is an identifier, and may be used in any statement where the format calls for an identifier. Now you know two kinds of identifiers: ordinary data names and qualified data names.

In data-name qualification the word **OF** may be used interchangeably with IN. Other legal qualified data names thus are:

```
RUN-YEAR OF RUN-DATE
RUN-MONTH-AND-DAY OF DATE-LINE
```

More than one level of qualification may be used. Consider the following definitions:

```
01   RATES-LEVEL-A.
     05 RATES-LEVEL-1.
        10 RATE-I            PIC 99V99.
        10 RATE-II           PIC 99V99.
        10 RATE-III          PIC 99V99.
        10 RATE-VII          PIC 99V99.
     05 RATES-LEVEL-2.
        10 RATE-I            PIC 99V99
        10 RATE-II           PIC 99V99
        10 RATE-VI           PIC 99V99.

01   RATES-LEVEL-B.
     05 RATES-LEVEL-1.
        10 RATE-I            PIC 99V99.
        10 RATE-II           PIC 99V99.
        10 RATE-III          PIC 99V99.
     05 RATES-LEVEL-3.
        10 RATE-I            PIC 99V99.
        10 RATE-II           PIC 99V99.
        10 RATE-VI           PIC 99V99.
        10 RATE-VII          PIC 99V99.
```

Then the following are legal names:

```
RATES-LEVEL-1  IN  RATES-LEVEL-A
RATES-LEVEL-1  IN  RATES-LEVEL-B
```

To name any of the fields called RATE-I uniquely, you would have to use a name such as:

```
RATE-I  IN  RATES-LEVEL-1  IN  RATES-LEVEL-A
```

Other legal names are:

```
RATE-VI  IN  RATES-LEVEL-2
RATE-VI  IN  RATES-LEVEL-3
RATE-VII  IN  RATES-LEVEL-A
RATE-VII  IN  RATES-LEVEL-B
```

Unnecessary qualification may be used and does no harm. The name

```
RATE-VII  IN  RATES-LEVEL-1  IN  RATES-LEVEL-A
```

means the same as either of the following:

```
RATE-VII  IN  RATES-LEVEL-1
RATE-VII  IN  RATES-LEVEL-A
```

The MOVE Verb

There are two formats for MOVE statements. Format 1 is the one we have been using all along, and is:

$$\underline{\texttt{MOVE}} \begin{Bmatrix} \texttt{identifier-1} \\ \texttt{literal-1} \end{Bmatrix} \underline{\texttt{TO}} \{\texttt{identifier-2}\} \ldots$$

The format shows that the sending field of a MOVE may be any identifier or literal, and that there may be as many receiving fields as desired. The MOVE statement assigns the contents of the sending field to each of the receiving fields, and carries out any editing indicated by the PICTURE of each receiving field. The contents of the sending field remain unchanged.

Table 4.14 shows the types of MOVEs allowed under the 1985 ANSI standard. In the table an entry of YES indicates that the MOVE is allowed. The table refers to the definitions of the sending and receiving items, and not to their contents. For example, the table shows that it is legal to MOVE an item defined as numeric noninteger to an item defined as numeric edited. When such a MOVE is executed, though, the sending field actually must contain some numeric value. Since it is possible in COBOL for a field defined as numeric accidentally to get to contain some nonnumeric value, it is the programmer's responsibility to ensure that the fields used in any operation contain valid data. There is a full discussion of valid and invalid data in Chapter 8.

TABLE 4.14
Valid and invalid MOVEs in the 1985 standard

SENDING ITEM CATEGORY	RECEIVING ITEM CATEGORY				
	Alphanumeric	Alphanumeric Edited	Numeric Integer	Numeric Noninteger	Numeric Edited
SPACES	YES	YES	NO	NO	NO
Alphanumeric	YES	YES	YES	YES	YES
Alphanumeric Edited	YES	YES	NO	NO	NO
Numeric Integer	YES	YES	YES	YES	YES
Numeric Noninteger	NO	NO	YES	YES	YES
Numeric Edited	YES	YES	YES	YES	YES

Padding and Truncation

If a receiving field in a MOVE is longer or shorter than the sending field, COBOL either will fill the extra spaces in the receiving field or truncate characters as needed. The exact treatment depends on the category of the receiving field.

If the receiving field is alphanumeric or alphanumeric edited, data from the sending field are left-aligned in the receiving field and the right end of the receiving field is filled with spaces or truncated as needed. Table 4.15 shows the value assigned to a receiving field with PICTURE X(10) for different sending fields.

TABLE 4.15
Value assigned by MOVE statement to a receiving field with PICTURE X(10) for different sending fields

PICTURE of Sending Field	Value of Sending Field	Value Assigned to Receiving Field
X(10)	TOTAL SETS	TOTAL SETS
X(12)	REGION TOTAL	REGION TOT
XXX	YES	YES
9(4)	8005	8005
9(13)	8574839574893	8574839574
ZZZ.999	5.300	5.300

If the receiving field is numeric or numeric edited, data are aligned on the decimal point, and the left and/or right end of the receiving field is filled with zeros or truncated as needed. Any filled-in zeros are subject to zero suppression if specified in the receiving field.

When an alphanumeric field is MOVEd to a numeric field, for purposes of alignment the sending field is considered to be an unsigned numeric integer. For such a MOVE to work properly and make sense, the alphanumeric source field must contain only numeric data. Table 4.16 shows the value assigned to a receiving field with PICTURE 9(4)V9(3) for different sending fields.

Table 4.17 shows one example of each of the types of MOVEs allowed to fields defined as numeric integer, numeric noninteger, and numeric edited.

TABLE 4.16
Value assigned by MOVE statement to a receiving field with PICTURE 9(4)V9(3) for different sending fields

PICTURE of Sending Field	Value of Sending Field	Value Assigned to Receiving Field
9(3)	685	0685.000
9(3)V99	685^21	0685.210
9(6)	485621	5621.000
V9(4)	^1279	0000.127
9(5)V9(5)	54634^38732	4634.387
X(10)	5463438732	8732.000

TABLE 4.17
One example of each of the types of MOVEs allowed to fields defined as numeric integer, numeric noninteger, and numeric edited

SENDING ITEM	RECEIVING ITEM Numeric Integer PIC 9(4)	Numeric Noninteger PIC 9(4)V99	Numeric Edited PIC $***,***.99
Alphanumeric PIC X(6) VALUE "001234"	1234	1234^00	$**1,234.00
Numeric integer PIC 9(4) VALUE 1234	1234	1234^00	$**1,234.00
Numeric noninteger PIC 9(4)V99 VALUE 1234.56	1234	1234^56	$**1,234.56
Numeric edited PIC $Z,ZZZ.99 VALUE "$1,234.56"	1234	1234^56	$**1,234.56

Table 4.18 shows one example of each of the types of MOVEs allowed to fields defined as alphanumeric and alphanumeric edited. When a numeric edited field is MOVEd to a field defined as numeric integer, numeric noninteger, or numeric edited, the contents of the sending field are de-edited before being placed into the receiving field. When any field is MOVEd to a field defined as alphanumeric edited, the sending field is treated as ordinary alphanumeric and is never de-edited before being placed into the receiving field.

Group-Level MOVEs

A **group item** is any field that is broken down into smaller fields, as RATES-LEVEL-A and RATES-LEVEL-B are. Any field not broken down into smaller fields is called an **elementary item.** The elementary items into which a group item is broken down are said to be **subordinate** to the group item. The fields RATE-I and RATE-II are elementary items. A group item never has a PICTURE clause; only an elementary item has a PICTURE clause.

TABLE 4.18
One example of each of the MOVEs allowed to fields defined as alphanumeric and alphanumeric edited

SENDING ITEM	RECEIVING ITEM Alphanumeric PIC X(6)	RECEIVING ITEM Alphanumeric edited PIC XX/XX/XX
SPACE or SPACES		/ /
Alphanumeric PIC X(6) VALUE "001234"	001234	00/12/34
Alphanumeric edited PIC XXBXXBXX VALUE "00 12 34"	00 12	00/ 1/2
Numeric integer PIC 9(4) VALUE 1234	1234	12/34/
Numeric edited PIC $Z,ZZZ.99 VALUE "$1,234.00"	$1,234	$1/,2/34

If the sending or receiving field of a MOVE is a group item, the sending and receiving fields both are considered to be defined with all Xs regardless of the category or categories of their elementary items. Under most conditions such treatment produces expected results. For example, consider the following definitions:

```
01    GROUP-1.
      05 FILLER                  PIC X(3)   VALUE SPACES.
      05 NUMBER-1                PIC 9(5).
      05 FILLER                  PIC X(5)   VALUE SPACES.
      05 NUMBER-2                PIC 9(4).

01    ITEM-2                     PIC X(17).
```

Then the statement

```
MOVE GROUP-1 TO ITEM-2
```

will be treated as an alphanumeric-to-alphanumeric MOVE, and all 17 characters in GROUP-1 will be MOVEd to ITEM-2 with no change. But sometimes bizarre results develop. Consider the following definitions:

```
01    NUMBER-3                   PIC 9(6).

01    GROUP-2.
      05                           PIC X(20) VALUE SPACES.
      05 NUM-ED                    PIC ZZZ,ZZ9.
```

Then the statement

```
MOVE NUMBER-3 TO GROUP-2
```

will not give the desired results. The receiving field will be treated as a 27-character field defined with Xs. The short sending field (six characters) will be left-aligned in the long receiving field and the rightmost 21 positions filled with blanks. No editing will be done on the number.

A similar problem arises if we have the following definitions:

```
01   FIELD-4                    PIC B(11)X(11).

01   GROUP-3.
     05 ELE-1                   PIC X(5).
     05 ELE-2                   PIC X(6).
```

Now the statement

```
MOVE GROUP-3 TO FIELD-4
```

will not give the desired results. The receiving field will be treated as a 22-character field defined with Xs. The short sending field will be left-aligned in the long receiving field and the rightmost 11 positions filled with blanks.

Format 2 of the MOVE Statement

Format 2 of the MOVE statement is:

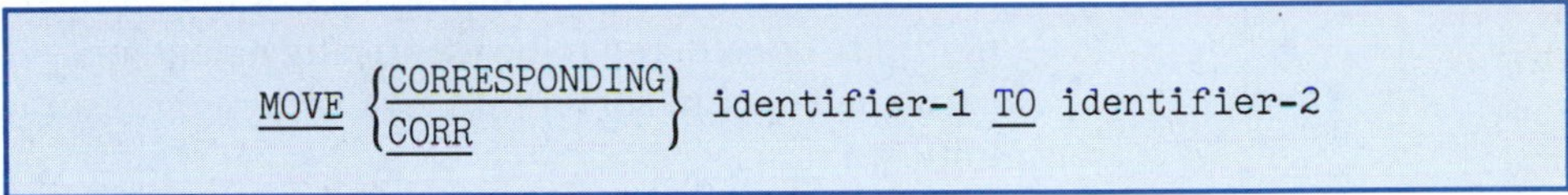

This form of the MOVE statement is sometimes called MOVE **CORRESPONDING.** The abbreviation **CORR** means exactly the same as CORRESPONDING. In this form COBOL MOVEs data from one or more sending fields to receiving fields that have names identical to the CORRESPONDING sending fields. As an example, consider the following fields:

```
01   RUN-DATE.
     05 RUN-YEAR                  PIC 99.
     05 RUN-MONTH-AND-DAY         PIC 9(4).

01   DATE-LINE.
     05 RUN-MONTH-AND-DAY         PIC Z9/99/.
     05 RUN-YEAR                  PIC 99.
```

The statement

```
MOVE CORRESPONDING RUN-DATE TO DATE-LINE
```

will carry out the same steps as the following two statements:

```
MOVE RUN-YEAR IN RUN-DATE TO RUN-YEAR IN DATE-LINE
MOVE RUN-MONTH-AND-DAY IN RUN-DATE
     TO RUN-MONTH-AND-DAY IN DATE-LINE
```

For the fields RATES-LEVEL-A and RATES-LEVEL-B, defined on page 92 the following are legal statements:

1. MOVE CORRESPONDING RATES-LEVEL-1 IN RATES-LEVEL-A TO RATES-LEVEL-1 IN RATES-LEVEL-B

2. MOVE CORRESPONDING RATES-LEVEL-1 IN RATES-LEVEL-A TO RATES-LEVEL-2
3. MOVE CORRESPONDING RATES-LEVEL-2 TO RATES-LEVEL-3
4. MOVE CORRESPONDING RATES-LEVEL-B TO RATES-LEVEL-A

For statement 1 the fields RATE-I, RATE-II, and RATE-III will be MOVEd. For statement 2 the fields RATE-I, RATE-II will be MOVEd. For statement 3, fields RATE-I, RATE-II, and RATE-VI will be MOVEd.

For statement 4 only three fields will be MOVEd. The sending fields in the MOVE are as follows:

```
RATE-I IN RATES-LEVEL-1 IN RATES-LEVEL-B
RATE-II IN RATES-LEVEL-1 IN RATES-LEVEL-B
RATE-III IN RATES-LEVEL-1 IN RATES-LEVEL-B
```

The CORRESPONDING receiving fields are:

```
RATE-I IN RATES-LEVEL-1 IN RATES-LEVEL-A
RATE-II IN RATES-LEVEL-1 IN RATES-LEVEL-A
RATE-III IN RATES-LEVEL-1 IN RATES-LEVEL-A
```

The fields that make up RATES-LEVEL-2 and RATES-LEVEL-3 do not become involved in the MOVE. For purposes of the MOVE CORRESPONDING statement, fields are considered to be identically named only if all their qualifiers are identical also. This can sometimes give surprising results. Consider the following definitions:

```
Ø1   HIGH-FIELD-1.
     Ø5 MIDDLE-FIELD-1.
        1Ø LOW-FIELD-A   PIC X.
        1Ø LOW-FIELD-B   PIC X.

Ø1   HIGH-FIELD-2.
     Ø5 MIDDLE-FIELD-2.
        1Ø LOW-FIELD-A   PIC X.
        1Ø LOW-FIELD-B   PIC X.
```

Then the statement

```
MOVE CORRESPONDING HIGH-FIELD-1 TO HIGH-FIELD-2
```

will not MOVE any fields.

Both identifiers in a MOVE CORRESPONDING statement must be group items.

A Program Using Editing

Our next program, Program P04-01, shows the use of some of the features discussed in this chapter. Program P04-01 uses input in the same format as Program P03-01 and produces output in the format shown in Figure 4.1.

The computations for merchandise amount, tax, order total, and the final totals line are the same in Program P04-01 as in Program P03-01, page 62. But there is one complication in this program that warrants construction of a new hierarchy diagram.

The complication in Program P04-01 derives from a restriction on the use of the arithmetic verbs. The restriction is this: All fields used in any ADD, SUB-

FIGURE 4.1 Output format for Program P04-01

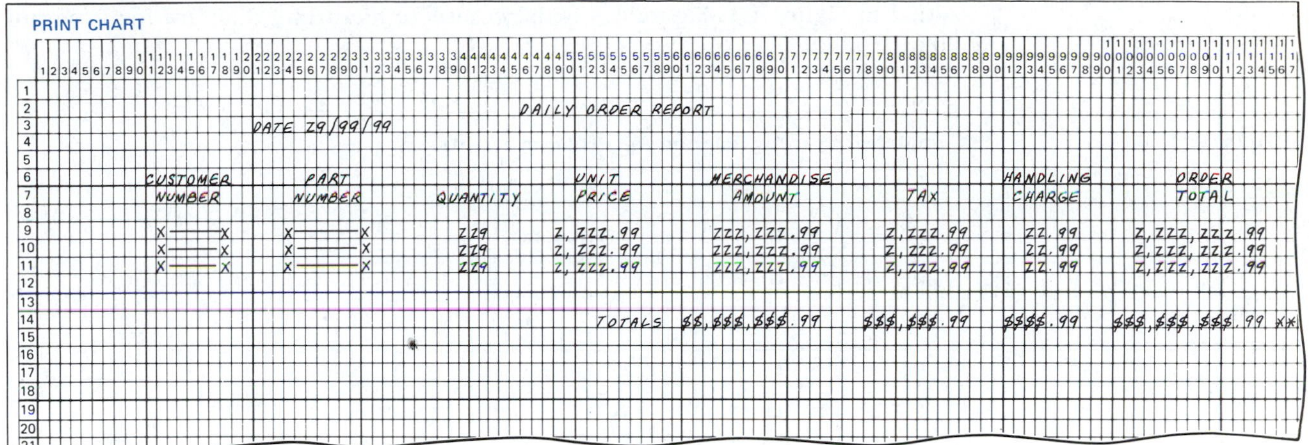

TRACT, MULTIPLY, or DIVIDE statement must be numeric except for fields appearing after the words GIVING or REMAINDER, which must be numeric or numeric edited. In a COMPUTE statement all fields must be numeric except the result field, on the left side of the equal sign, which must be numeric or numeric edited. When we look at Program P04-01, you will see the effects of this restriction.

We can create the hierarchy diagram for this program by starting with the hierarchy diagram for Program P03-01, which is repeated here as Figure 4.2. As you will see when we look at Program P04-01, the restriction on the use of the arithmetic verbs prevents us from summing the merchandise amounts, tax

FIGURE 4.2 Hierarchy diagram for Program P03-01, repeated here as the starting diagram for Program P04-01

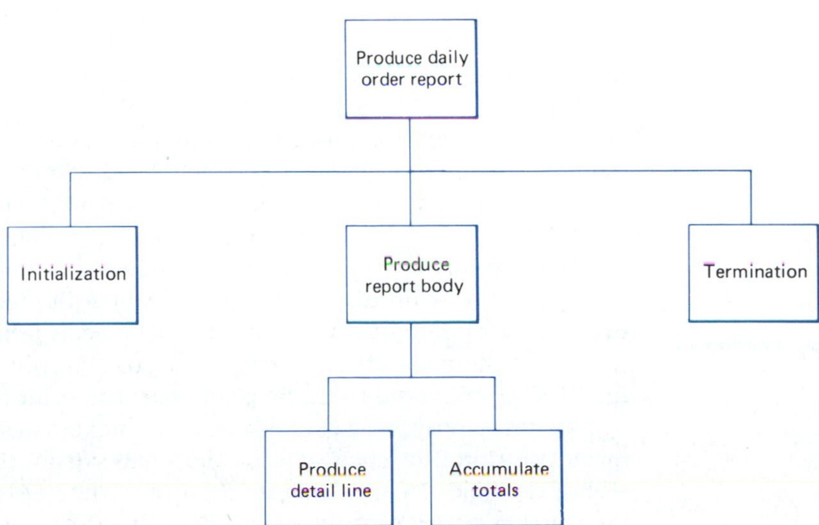

amounts, handling charge amounts, and order total amounts in the total-line output area as we did in Program P03-01. Thus, producing the total line is complicated enough to warrant its own subfunction, so "Produce total line" is added in Figure 4.3. Figure 4.3 is the complete hierarchy diagram for Program P04-01.

FIGURE 4.3 **Complete hierarchy diagram for Program P04-01**

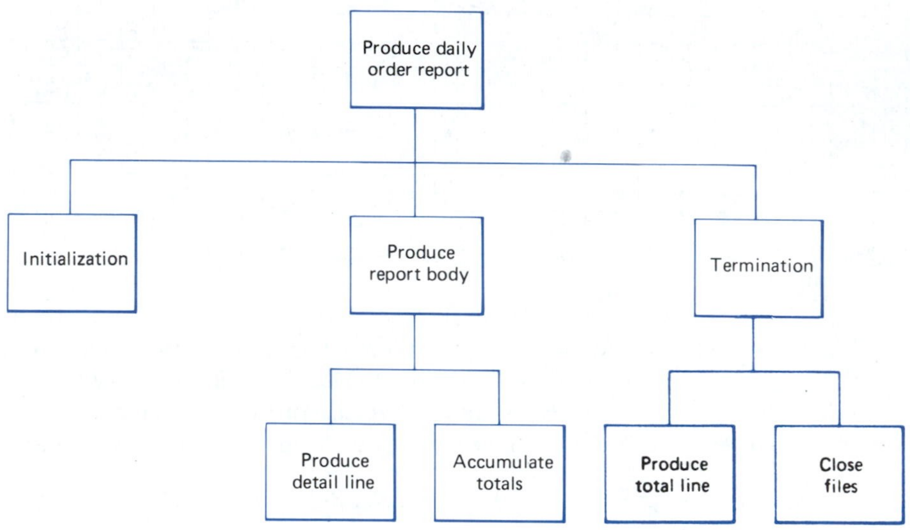

Program P04-01 is shown in Figure 4.4. The field RUN-DATE, line 00400, has been established to receive the date when it is extracted from the system by an ACCEPT statement.

This program shows a new way to enter constants such as report titles and column headings into working storage. Consider, for example, the field defined at line 00560. Although the constant, CUSTOMER, is only eight characters long, the field has a PICTURE of X(15). When the size of a constant disagrees with its PICTURE, COBOL stores the constant in the field in accordance with the rules given for the MOVE statement, as though the constant were being MOVEd to the field. In this case the word CUSTOMER is left-aligned in the field, and the remaining seven character positions are filled with spaces. This is just what we want, for you can see from the print chart in Figure 4.1 that the word CUSTOMER is followed by seven spaces. Similarly, the field at line 00570 is defined as 25 characters, producing the word PART followed by 21 blanks. There is an easy way to figure out how large to make each field without having to count spaces on the print chart. For example, to find out how big to make the field for CUSTOMER, note from the print chart the print position where CUSTOMER begins (print position 11) and where the next word on the line, PART, begins (print position 26). Then subtract the smaller from the larger, and you have the size of the field, 15. To compute the size of the field for PART, subtract 26 from the starting position of the word UNIT (print position 51).

FIGURE 4.4 **Program P04-01**

```
S COBOL II RELEASE 3.1 09/19/89                P04001   DATE MAR 25,1991 T
----+-*A-1-B--+----2----+----3----+----4----+----5----+----6----+----7-%--+

       IDENTIFICATION DIVISION.
       PROGRAM-ID.  P04-01.
      *
      *      THIS PROGRAM IS A MODIFICATION OF PROGRAM P03-01.
      *      IT DEMONSTRATES OUTPUT EDITING AND INSERTING
      *      TODAY'S DATE INTO A REPORT.
      *
      *****************************************************************
       ENVIRONMENT DIVISION.
       INPUT-OUTPUT SECTION.
       FILE-CONTROL.
           SELECT ORDER-FILE-IN ASSIGN TO INFILE.
           SELECT ORDER-REPORT  ASSIGN TO PRINTER.
      *****************************************************************
       DATA DIVISION.
       FILE SECTION.
       FD  ORDER-FILE-IN
           RECORD CONTAINS 80 CHARACTERS.
       01  ORDER-RECORD-IN.
           05 CUSTOMER-NUMBER-IN PIC X(7).
           05 PART-NUMBER-IN     PIC X(8).
           05                    PIC X(7).
           05 QUANTITY-IN        PIC 9(3).
           05 UNIT-PRICE-IN      PIC 9(4)V99.
           05 HANDLING-CHARGE-IN PIC 99V99.
       FD  ORDER-REPORT.
       01  REPORT-LINE           PIC X(117).
       WORKING-STORAGE SECTION.
       01  MORE-INPUT            PIC X      VALUE "Y".
       01  TAX-RATE              PIC V99    VALUE .07.
       01  RUN-DATE.
           05 RUN-YEAR           PIC 99.
           05 RUN-MONTH-AND-DAY  PIC 9(4).
       01  REPORT-TITLE.
           05                    PIC X(45) VALUE SPACES.
           05                    PIC X(18) VALUE "DAILY ORDER REPORT".
       01  DATE-LINE.
           05                    PIC X(20) VALUE SPACES.
           05                    PIC X(5)  VALUE "DATE".
           05 RUN-MONTH-AND-DAY  PIC Z9/99/.
           05 RUN-YEAR           PIC 99.
       01  COLUMN-HEADS-1.
           05                    PIC X(10) VALUE SPACES.
           05                    PIC X(15) VALUE "CUSTOMER".
           05                    PIC X(25) VALUE "PART".
           05                    PIC X(13) VALUE "UNIT".
           05                    PIC X(27) VALUE "MERCHANDISE".
           05                    PIC X(16) VALUE "HANDLING".
           05                    PIC X(5)  VALUE "ORDER".
```

continued

You can see some editing features in DETAIL-LINE and TOTAL-LINE, lines 00760 through 01010. The entries at lines 00770 through 00790 show the PICTURE character B used with alphanumeric and numeric edited fields. Other entries show zero suppression with replacement by blanks, insertion of commas and decimal points, and the floating dollar sign.

The INTERMEDIATE-NUMERIC-FIELDS are needed because of the restriction on the use of the arithmetic verbs. You will see exactly how the intermediate fields satisfy the restriction when we look at the Procedure Division.

The Procedure Division starts at line 01140. In the paragraph INITIALIZATION you can see how the ACCEPT and MOVE CORRESPONDING statements at lines 01230 and 01240 set up today's date in the output line DATE-LINE. Arithmetic statements in the paragraph PRODUCE-DETAIL-LINE, line 01560, show the use of multiple result fields. Why does the first MULTIPLY statement assign its result to both MERCHANDISE-AMOUNT-OUT and MERCHANDISE-AMOUNT-W? MERCHANDISE-AMOUNT-OUT is a numeric edited field, and part of an output line. MERCHANDISE-AMOUNT-W is a numeric field, and is used in the next MULTIPLY statement.

FIGURE *4.4* ***continued***

```
S COBOL II RELEASE 3.1 09/19/89                 P04001   DATE MAR 25,1991 T
----+-*A-1-B--+----2----+----3----+----4----+----5----+----6----+----7-%--+


00630  01   COLUMN-HEADS-2.
00640       05                     PIC X(11) VALUE SPACES.
00650       05                     PIC X(13) VALUE "NUMBER".
00660       05                     PIC X(13) VALUE "NUMBER".
00670       05                     PIC X(13) VALUE "QUANTITY".
00680       05                     PIC X(15) VALUE "PRICE".
00690       05                     PIC X(16) VALUE "AMOUNT".
00700       05                     PIC X(10) VALUE "TAX".
00710       05                     PIC X(15) VALUE "CHARGE".
00720       05                     PIC X(5)  VALUE "TOTAL".
00730
00740  01   BLANK-LINE             PIC X     VALUE SPACE.
00750
00760  01   DETAIL-LINE.
00770       05 CUSTOMER-NUMBER-OUT         PIC B(11)X(7).
00780       05 PART-NUMBER-OUT             PIC B(5)X(8).
00790       05 QUANTITY-OUT                PIC B(8)ZZ9.
00800       05                             PIC X(6)     VALUE SPACES.
00810       05 UNIT-PRICE-OUT              PIC Z,ZZZ.99.
00820       05                             PIC X(7)     VALUE SPACES.
00830       05 MERCHANDISE-AMOUNT-OUT      PIC ZZZ,ZZZ.99.
00840       05                             PIC X(6)     VALUE SPACES.
00850       05 TAX-OUT                     PIC Z,ZZZ.99.
00860       05                             PIC X(5)     VALUE SPACES.
00870       05 HANDLING-CHARGE-OUT         PIC ZZ.99.
00880       05                             PIC X(5)     VALUE SPACES.
00890       05 ORDER-TOTAL-OUT             PIC Z,ZZZ,ZZZ.99.
00900
00910  01   TOTAL-LINE.
00920       05                             PIC X(52)    VALUE SPACES.
00930       05                             PIC X(8)     VALUE "TOTALS".
00940       05 MERCHANDISE-AMOUNT-TOT-OUT PIC $$,$$$,$$$.99.
00950       05                             PIC X(4)     VALUE SPACES.
00960       05 TAX-TOT-OUT                 PIC $$$,$$$.99.
00970       05                             PIC X(3)     VALUE SPACES.
00980       05 HANDLING-CHARGE-TOT-OUT     PIC $$$$.99.
00990       05                             PIC X(3)     VALUE SPACES.
01000       05 GRAND-TOT-OUT               PIC $$$,$$$,$$$.99.
01010       05                             PIC X(3)     VALUE " **".
01020
```

FIGURE 4.4 *continued*

```
 01  INTERMEDIATE-NUMERIC-FIELDS.
         05 MERCHANDISE-AMOUNT-W          PIC 9(6)V99.
         05 TAX-W                         PIC 9(4)V99.
         05 ORDER-TOTAL-W                 PIC 9(7)V99.
         05 MERCHANDISE-AMOUNT-TOT-W      PIC 9(7)V99 VALUE 0.
         05 TAX-TOT-W                     PIC 9(5)V99 VALUE 0.
         05 HANDLING-CHARGE-TOT-W         PIC 9(3)V99 VALUE 0.
         05 GRAND-TOT-W                   PIC 9(8)V99 VALUE 0.

*****************************************************************

 PROCEDURE DIVISION.
 PRODUCE-DAILY-ORDER-REPORT.
     PERFORM INITIALIZATION
     PERFORM PRODUCE-REPORT-BODY UNTIL MORE-INPUT IS EQUAL TO "N"
     PERFORM TERMINATION
     STOP RUN
     .

 INITIALIZATION.
     ACCEPT RUN-DATE FROM DATE
     MOVE CORRESPONDING RUN-DATE TO DATE-LINE
     OPEN INPUT  ORDER-FILE-IN
          OUTPUT ORDER-REPORT
     READ ORDER-FILE-IN
         AT END
             MOVE "N" TO MORE-INPUT
     END-READ
     WRITE REPORT-LINE FROM REPORT-TITLE AFTER ADVANCING PAGE
     WRITE REPORT-LINE FROM DATE-LINE
     WRITE REPORT-LINE FROM COLUMN-HEADS-1 AFTER 3
     WRITE REPORT-LINE FROM COLUMN-HEADS-2
     WRITE REPORT-LINE FROM BLANK-LINE
     .

 TERMINATION.
     PERFORM PRODUCE-TOTAL-LINE
     PERFORM CLOSE-FILES
     .

 CLOSE-FILES.
     CLOSE ORDER-FILE-IN
           ORDER-REPORT
     .

 PRODUCE-REPORT-BODY.
     PERFORM PRODUCE-DETAIL-LINE
     PERFORM ACCUMULATE-TOTALS
     READ ORDER-FILE-IN
         AT END
             MOVE "N" TO MORE-INPUT
     .
```

continued

The paragraph ACCUMULATE-TOTALS, line 01760, uses more of the INTERMEDIATE-NUMERIC-FIELDS. Why do we ADD the MERCHANDISE-AMOUNT-W to MERCHANDISE-AMOUNT-TOT-W, instead of ADDing it directly to the output field, MERCHANDISE-AMOUNT-TOT-OUT? The answer is that MERCHANDISE-AMOUNT-TOT-OUT is an edited numeric field, and cannot be used in an ADD without the GIVING option.

FIGURE 4.4 *continued*

```
S COBOL II RELEASE 3.1 09/19/89                 P04001   DATE MAR 25,1991 T
----+-*A-1-B--+----2----+----3----+----4----+----5----+----6----+----7-%--+

01560  PRODUCE-DETAIL-LINE.
01570      MULTIPLY QUANTITY-IN BY UNIT-PRICE-IN
01580          GIVING MERCHANDISE-AMOUNT-OUT
01590                 MERCHANDISE-AMOUNT-W
01600      MULTIPLY MERCHANDISE-AMOUNT-W BY TAX-RATE
01610          GIVING TAX-OUT ROUNDED
01620                 TAX-W ROUNDED
01630      ADD MERCHANDISE-AMOUNT-W
01640          TAX-W
01650          HANDLING-CHARGE-IN
01660              GIVING ORDER-TOTAL-OUT
01670                     ORDER-TOTAL-W
01680      MOVE CUSTOMER-NUMBER-IN     TO CUSTOMER-NUMBER-OUT
01690      MOVE PART-NUMBER-IN         TO PART-NUMBER-OUT
01700      MOVE QUANTITY-IN            TO QUANTITY-OUT
01710      MOVE UNIT-PRICE-IN          TO UNIT-PRICE-OUT
01720      MOVE HANDLING-CHARGE-IN     TO HANDLING-CHARGE-OUT
01730      WRITE REPORT-LINE FROM DETAIL-LINE
01740      .
01750
01760  ACCUMULATE-TOTALS.
01770      ADD MERCHANDISE-AMOUNT-W    TO MERCHANDISE-AMOUNT-TOT-W
01780      ADD TAX-W                   TO TAX-TOT-W
01790      ADD HANDLING-CHARGE-IN      TO HANDLING-CHARGE-TOT-W
01800      ADD ORDER-TOTAL-W           TO GRAND-TOT-W
01810      .
01820
01830  PRODUCE-TOTAL-LINE.
01840      MOVE MERCHANDISE-AMOUNT-TOT-W TO MERCHANDISE-AMOUNT-TOT-OUT
01850      MOVE TAX-TOT-W                TO TAX-TOT-OUT
01860      MOVE HANDLING-CHARGE-TOT-W    TO HANDLING-CHARGE-TOT-OUT
01870      MOVE GRAND-TOT-W              TO GRAND-TOT-OUT
01880      WRITE REPORT-LINE FROM TOTAL-LINE AFTER 3
01890      .
```

Program P04-01 was run with the same input data as Program P03-01 and produced the output shown in Figure 4.5.

FIGURE 4.5 **Output from Program P04-01**

```
                                  DAILY ORDER REPORT
         DATE   3/25/91

CUSTOMER      PART                          UNIT          MERCHANDISE                  HANDLING          ORDER
 NUMBER      NUMBER        QUANTITY         PRICE            AMOUNT           TAX       CHARGE           TOTAL

 ABC1234     F2365-09         900             .10              90.00          6.30         .05            96.35
 09G8239     836-7YT7         800           10.50           8,400.00        588.00         .50         8,988.50
 ADGH784     091AN-07          50          250.00          12,500.00        875.00        5.00        13,380.00
 9675473     235-1287           6        7,000.29          42,001.74      2,940.12       50.00        44,991.86

                                           TOTALS         $62,991.74     $4,409.42      $55.55       $67,456.71 **
```

EXERCISE 3

Modify your solution to Exercise 13, Chapter 3, page 66, so that it produces output in the format shown in Figure 4.E3.

FIGURE 4.E3 **Output format for Exercise 3**

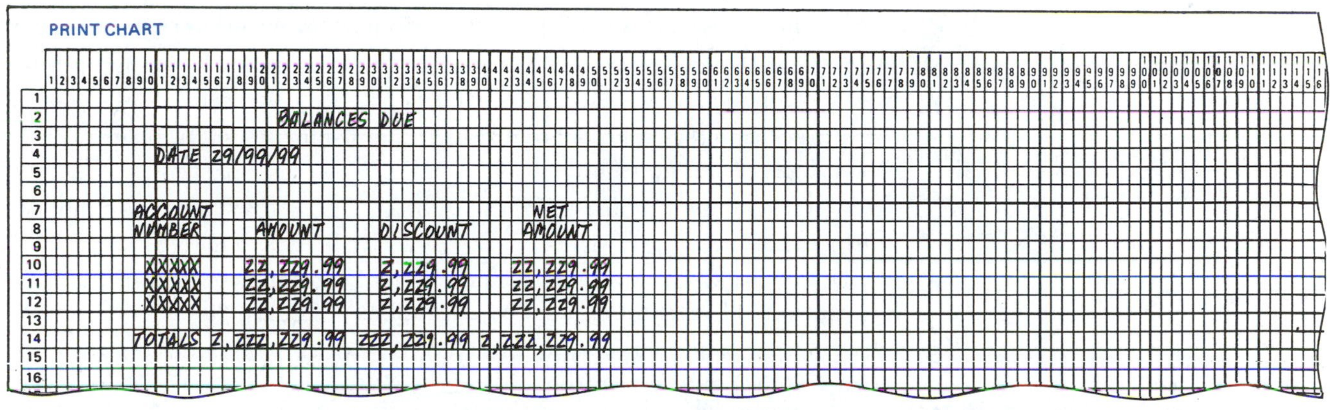

Summary

Edit PICTUREs may be used to prepare numeric and alphanumeric fields for printing. Commas and decimal points may be inserted into numeric fields, and leading zeros suppressed. Blanks, zeros, and/or slashes may be inserted into numeric or alphanumeric fields. A numeric field may have its sign designated by a fixed or floating plus or minus sign at the left end or by a fixed +, −, CR, or DB at the right end. A fixed or floating dollar sign may be printed with numeric output. Fixed positive and negative sign indications may appear to the left of a fixed or floating dollar sign.

COBOL provides a check-protection feature through the use of the PICTURE character *. In check protection, asterisks instead of blanks replace leading zeros to discourage forgery. The character * can be used in a PICTURE anywhere that a Z can be used.

The ACCEPT verb may be used to obtain the DATE, DAY, DAY-OF-WEEK, or TIME from the COBOL system when the program is run. The DATE comes into any field designated by the programmer in six-digit YYMMDD form.

Any item that is broken down into smaller fields is called a group item. Any item not broken down is called an elementary item.

The MOVE CORRESPONDING statement can be used to MOVE data from fields in one area to fields in another where the sending and receiving fields have duplicate names. Duplicate named fields can be distinguished from one another if necessary by data name qualification. They must be defined so that, through the use of IN or OF, every field is capable of being made unique. A qualified data name may be used in any COBOL statement whose format calls for an identifier.

Fill-In Exercises

1. When a fixed _____ sign is used in a PICTURE, the only PICTURE character that may appear to the left of it is a _____ or _____ sign.
2. The four fixed insertion characters that can be used as many times as you like in a PICTURE are _____, _____, _____, and _____; the special insertion character _____ can appear no more than once in a PICTURE.
3. The PICTURE character for replacing leading zeros with blanks is _____.
4. The PICTURE character for replacing leading zeros with asterisks is _____.
5. The PICTURE character _____ is used to obtain a printed decimal point.
6. When an alphanumeric constant is defined with a PICTURE having room for more characters than there are in the constant, COBOL inserts _____ to the right of the constant.
7. An ADD statement containing the word _____ may also contain the word _____.
8. In ADD, SUBTRACT, MULTIPLY, and DIVIDE statements without the GIVING option, all identifiers must be defined as _____.
9. In arithmetic statements with the GIVING option, fields given after the word GIVING must be defined as _____ or _____.
10. A floating sign is designated by _____ or more such signs in a row.
11. The _____ verb can be used to obtain the date from the COBOL system on the day a program is run.
12. The _____ option can do several independent MOVEs in one MOVE statement.
13. Distinguishing among two or more fields having identical names by using the names of some larger fields is called _____.
14. The PICTURE character _____ causes some sign to print whether the value of the output data item is positive, negative, or zero.
15. The sign designation DB prints only if the output data value is _____.

Review Exercises

1. Show how the following numbers would print if edited by each of the PICTUREs 9,999.9, Z,ZZZ.9, and Z,ZZZ.Z:

a. 4756.8
b. 0005.0
c. 0350.9
d. 0000.0
e. 0020.0

2. Modify your solution to Review Exercise 5, Chapter 3, page 78, to produce its output in the format shown in Figure 4.RE2.

3. Modify your solution to Review Exercise 6, Chapter 3, page 78, to produce its output in the format shown in Figure 4.RE3.

FIGURE *4.RE2* **Output format for Review Exercise 2**

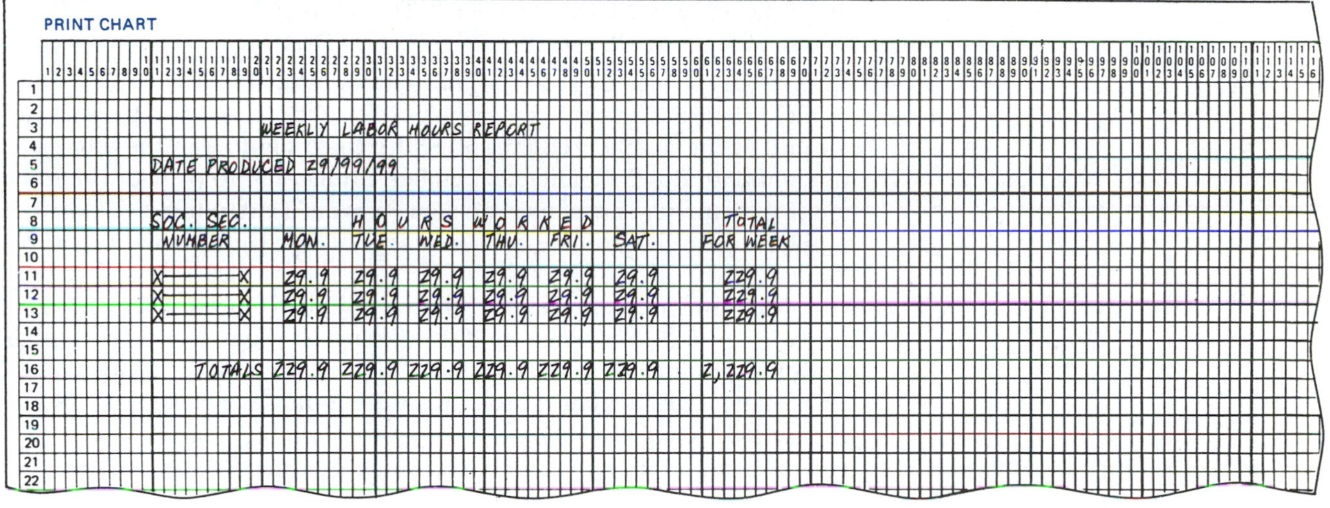

FIGURE *4.RE3* **Output format for Review Exercise 3**

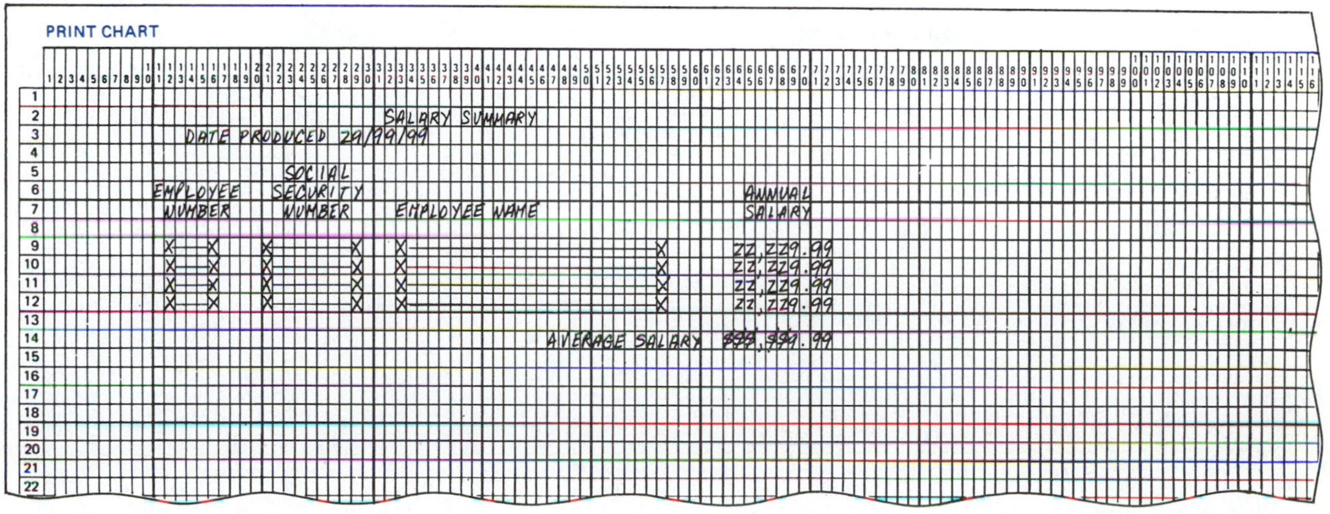

4. Given the following data definitions:

```
01   GROUP-1.
     05 FIELD-1      PIC X(5).
     05 FIELD-2      PIC X(8).
     05 FIELD-3      PIC X(6).

01 GROUP-2.
     05 FIELD-2      PIC X(8).
     05 FIELD-3      PIC X(6).
     05 FIELD-1      PIC X(5).
```

Which of the following are valid COBOL statements?

   a. MOVE FIELD-1 TO FIELD-1.
   b. MOVE FIELD-1 IN GROUP-2 TO FIELD-1 IN GROUP-1.
   c. MOVE CORRESPONDING FIELD-1- TO FIELD-1.
   d. MOVE CORRESPONDING GROUP-1 TO GROUP-2.
   e. MOVE CORRESPONDING FIELD-1 TO FIELD-2.

5. Write the PICTURE for each of the following output fields:

   a. An eight-digit dollars-and-cents number, fixed dollar sign to print at the left end of the number, comma after the third digit from the left
   b. An eight-digit dollars-and-cents number, minus sign to print at the right end if the number is negative, no sign to print if the number is positive or zero, dollar sign to float to two places before the decimal point, no comma
   c. A six-digit integer, comma after the third digit from the left, zero suppression up to but not including the rightmost digit, plus sign to float up to but not including the rightmost digit if the number is positive or zero, minus sign to float up to but not including the rightmost digit if the number is negative

Project

Modify your solution to the Project in Chapter 3, page 79. Have your program print its output in the format shown in Figure 4.P1. The minus signs in the format now indicate that you should use the PICTURE character – in that location. Multiply the Annual Interest Rate by 100 for the purpose of printing it in the page heading.

FIGURE 4.P1 Output format for Chapter 4 Project

PRINT CHART

```
 1
 2      AUTO LOAN REPAYMENT SCHEDULE
 3
 4           STARTING LOAN AMOUNT  -  ZZ,ZZ9.99
 5           NUMBER OF PAYMENTS    -         Z9
 6           PAYMENT AMOUNT        -   Z,ZZ9.99
 7           ANNUAL INTEREST RATE  -     Z9.99%
 8
 9                        PAYMENT
10   PAYMENT                 TO          PRINCIPAL
11   NUMBER    INTEREST   PRINCIPAL      REMAINING
12
13        1   -Z,ZZ9.99   -Z,ZZ9.99    -ZZ,ZZ9.99
14        2   -Z,ZZ9.99   -Z,ZZ9.99    -ZZ,ZZ9.99
15        3   -Z,ZZ9.99   -Z,ZZ9.99    -ZZ,ZZ9.99
16        4   -Z,ZZ9.99   -Z,ZZ9.99    -ZZ,ZZ9.99
17
18        .        .           .             .
19        .        .           .             .
20        .        .           .             .
21       Z9   -Z,ZZ9.99   -Z,ZZ9.99    -ZZ,ZZ9.99
22
```

CHAPTER 5

The IF Statement: Program Design II

HERE ARE THE KEY POINTS YOU SHOULD LEARN FROM THIS CHAPTER

1. How to program for page overflow and page numbering
2. How to use several forms of the IF statement
3. Flowcharts for the IF statement
4. The rules for forming nested IF statements
5. How to code IF statements with complex conditions
6. How to write abbreviated relation conditions
7. How to use condition names
8. The sign condition and the class condition
9. How to write pseudocode

KEY WORDS TO RECOGNIZE AND LEARN

conditional
PAGE
IF
END-IF
ELSE
BEFORE
program flowchart
pseudocode
CONTINUE
END-PERFORM
THEN
NEXT SENTENCE
simple condition
relation condition
class condition
condition-name condition
switch-status condition
sign condition
subject
object
relational operator
NUMERIC
ALPHABETIC
ALPHABETIC-LOWER
ALPHABETIC-UPPER
level-88
SET
TRUE
nested
outer IF statement
inner IF statement
terminate
complex condition
negated simple condition
combined condition
negated combined condition
continuation indicator

In this chapter we will study COBOL statements that permit the computer to examine the data that it is working on and decide which one out of two or more processes should be executed. For example, the computer might examine an employee's number of hours worked and decide whether or not to compute overtime pay. Or, in an inventory application, the computer might examine the quantity on hand of a certain part and decide whether to reorder.

A Program Using IF Statements

Program P05-01 reads input records in the following format:

Positions	Field
1–8	Part Number
9–28	Part Description
29–31	Quantity on Hand
32–80	spaces

Each record is for a different part, and shows the Part Number, an English description of the part, and the Quantity on Hand. Program P05-01 lists the contents of each record on one line, and in addition examines the Quantity on Hand of each part and prints the word REORDER next to any part with fewer than 400 on hand. The output format is shown in the print chart in Figure 5.1. Notice that some of the lines have the word REORDER and some do not, indicating that the printing of the word is **conditional** on something in the data. Since the print chart shows only a sample of what the output might look like, we would not expect the actual output to correspond line for line with the chart. At the time the program is being written, we may not know what data values will be used, and the program must work correctly for any combination of inputs having more or fewer than 400 on hand, or even exactly 400 on hand. (Should the word REORDER print when there are exactly 400 on hand?)

FIGURE *5.1* Output format for Program P05-01

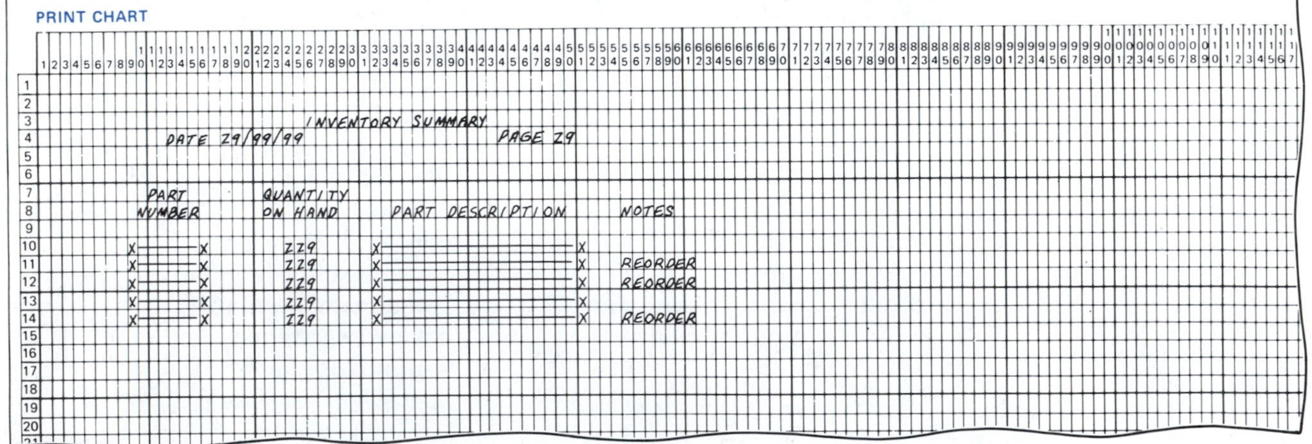

A hierarchy diagram for Program P05-01 is shown in Figure 5.2. The logic of this program is very straightforward, But, for the first time, we are going to have so much report output that it will occupy more than one page. As the program is printing detail lines, some detail line or another will find the page already full and there will be no room for it to print. The program will skip to a new page, print page headings, and then print the detail line on the new page. Thus the program will print new page headings only when it knows that it has a detail line to print on the new page. The subfunction "Produce page headings" is shown in the hierarchy diagram in Figure 5.3.

FIGURE *5.2* **Hierarchy diagram for Program P05-01 showing one level of subfunctions**

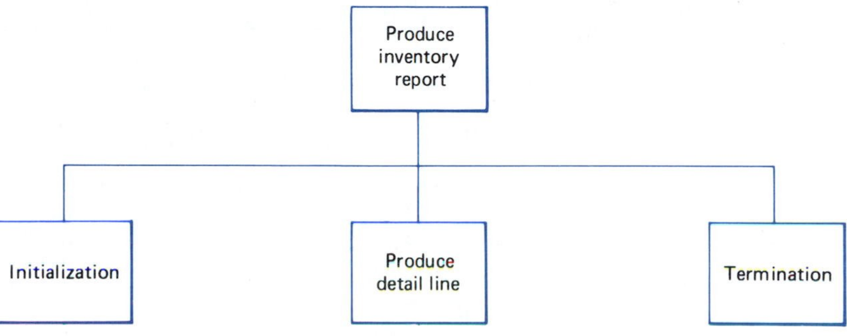

FIGURE *5.3* **Hierarchy diagram for Program P05-01 showing three levels**

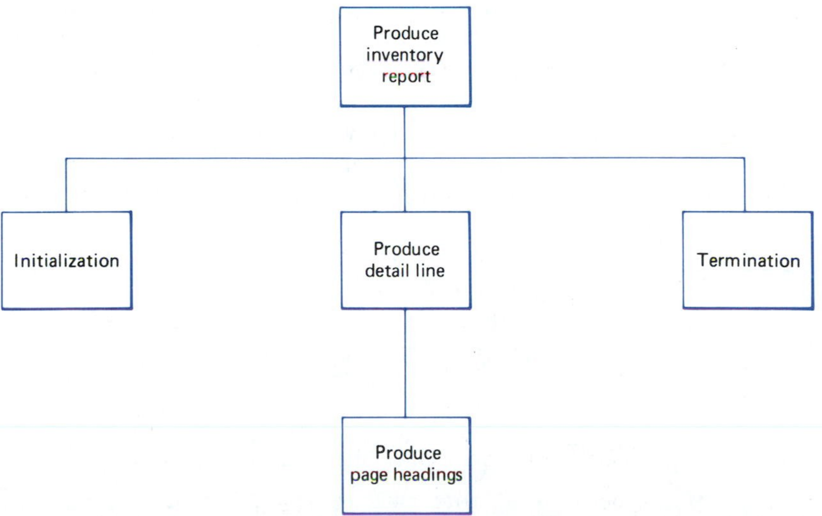

Now what does "Initialization" consist of in this program? We have the usual OPENing of the files, obtaining the DATE from the COBOL system, and the priming READ. It also turns out to be convenient to print the page headings for the first page of the report as part of "Initialization." We already have the subfunction "Produce page headings" in the diagram, so we can use that same subfunction as a subfunction of "Initialization." In Figure 5.4 we duplicate the box "Produce page headings" under the box "Initialization." The new box still represents the same coding as the original "Produce page headings." All the other functions of "Initialization" we lump together in a subfunction called "Housekeeping."

FIGURE 5.4 Complete hierarchy diagram for Program P05-01, showing the subfunctions of "Initialization"

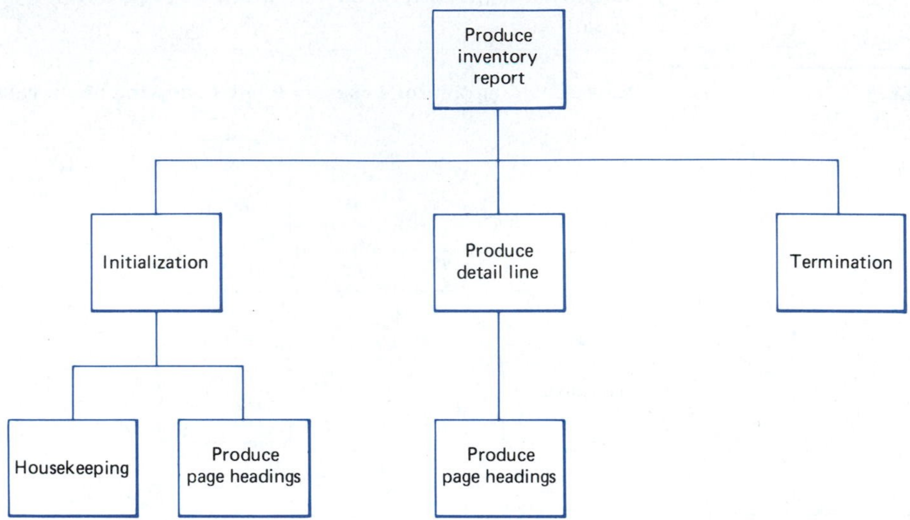

Program P05-01 is shown in Figure 5.5. In working storage the field PAGE-NUMBER-W, line 00420, is used by the program to count one page number each time it prints page headings. The field LINE-LIMIT, at line 00430, is a constant that is used to test for a full page. Its VALUE, 18, is 1 less than the last line on the page on which we want detail lines to print. The field LINE-COUNT-ER, line 00440, is used to count lines as they are printed. You will see how these fields are used to control page movement when we look at the Procedure Division.

FIGURE 5.5 Program P05-01

```
S COBOL II RELEASE 3.2 09/05/90                 P05001   DATE FEB 13,1992 T
----+-*A-1-B--+----2----+----3----+----4----+----5----+----6----+----7-%--+


00010  IDENTIFICATION DIVISION.
00020  PROGRAM-ID.  P05-01.
00030 *
00040 *    THIS PROGRAM READS RECORDS IN THE FOLLOWING FORMAT:
00050 *
00060 *    POS. 1-8         PART NUMBER
00070 *    POS. 9-28        PART DESCRIPTION
00080 *    POS. 29-31       QUANTITY ON HAND
00090 *
00100 *    THE PROGRAM PRINTS THE CONTENTS OF EACH RECORD ON ONE LINE.
00110 *    IN ADDITION, THE WORD "REORDER" IS TO BE PRINTED
00120 *    IN PRINT POSITIONS 55-61 NEXT TO ANY PART WHOSE
00130 *    QUANTITY ON HAND IS LESS THAN 400.
00140 *
00150 ******************************************************************
```

FIGURE 5.5 *continued*

```
       ENVIRONMENT DIVISION.
       INPUT-OUTPUT SECTION.
       FILE-CONTROL.
           SELECT INVENTORY-LIST      ASSIGN TO PRINTER.
           SELECT INVENTORY-FILE-IN   ASSIGN TO INFILE.
      ******************************************************************
       DATA DIVISION.
       FILE SECTION.
       FD  INVENTORY-FILE-IN
           RECORD CONTAINS 80 CHARACTERS.
       01  INVENTORY-RECORD-IN.
           05 PART-NUMBER-IN         PIC X(8).
           05 PART-DESCRIPTION-IN    PIC X(20).
           05 QUANTITY-ON-HAND-IN    PIC 9(3).
       FD  INVENTORY-LIST.
       01  OUTPUT-LINE               PIC X(61).
       WORKING-STORAGE SECTION.
       01  MORE-INPUT                PIC X(1) VALUE "Y".
       01  PAGE-NUMBER-W             PIC 99   VALUE 0.
       01  LINE-LIMIT                PIC 99   VALUE 18.
       01  LINE-COUNT-ER             PIC 99.
       01  RUN-DATE.
           05 RUN-YEAR               PIC 99.
           05 RUN-MONTH-AND-DAY      PIC 9(4).
       01  REPORT-TITLE.
           05             PIC X(25) VALUE SPACES.
           05             PIC X(17) VALUE "INVENTORY SUMMARY".
       01  DATE-LINE.
           05                        PIC X(12) VALUE SPACES.
           05                        PIC X(5)  VALUE "DATE".
           05 RUN-MONTH-AND-DAY      PIC Z9/99/.
           05 RUN-YEAR               PIC 99B(18).
           05                        PIC X(5)  VALUE "PAGE".
           05 PAGE-NUMBER-OUT        PIC Z9.
       01  COLUMN-HEADS-1.
           05                        PIC X(10) VALUE SPACES.
           05                        PIC X(11) VALUE "PART".
           05                        PIC X(8)  VALUE "QUANTITY".
       01  COLUMN-HEADS-2.
           05                        PIC X(9)  VALUE SPACES.
           05                        PIC X(12) VALUE "NUMBER".
           05                        PIC X(12) VALUE "ON HAND".
           05                        PIC X(21) VALUE "PART DESCRIPTION".
           05                        PIC X(5)  VALUE "NOTES".
       01  INVENTORY-LINE.
           05                        PIC X(8) VALUE SPACES.
           05 PART-NUMBER-OUT        PIC X(8).
           05                        PIC X(7) VALUE SPACES.
           05 QUANTITY-ON-HAND-OUT   PIC ZZ9.
           05                        PIC X(5) VALUE SPACES.
           05 PART-DESCRIPTION-OUT   PIC X(20).
           05                        PIC X(3) VALUE SPACES.
           05 MESSAGE-SPACE          PIC X(7).
      ******************************************************************
```

continued

The Procedure Division begins at line 00860. The paragraph PRODUCE-PAGE-HEADINGS, line 01090, shows a standard page heading routine that you can use in any program with more than one page of output. First, at line 01100, we ADD 1 to the page number field in working storage. Remember that we initialized PAGE-NUMBER-W with VALUE 0, so PRODUCE-PAGE-HEADINGS works for the first page as well as for all subsequent pages. Then we MOVE the page number to the output field PAGE-NUMBER-OUT, at line 01110. Why could we not just ADD 1 to PAGE-NUMBER-OUT and avoid the MOVE? The answer is that PAGE-NUMBER-OUT is a numeric edited field and must not appear in an ADD statement except after the word GIVING. Since we have no GIVING, we must use the numeric field PAGE-NUMBER-W in the ADD statement.

The WRITE statement at line 01120 uses the reserved word **PAGE** in the AFTER ADVANCING clause. This statement causes the printer to advance to the top of the next page and print the REPORT-TITLE. The program then prints the remaining lines of page headings, lines 01130 through 01180. Since the program has just printed seven lines of output, including lines of blanks, it MOVEs 7 to LINE-COUNTER-ER to keep track of how many lines have been printed on the page.

In the paragraph PRODUCE-DETAIL-LINE the three statements at lines 01280 through 01300 MOVE to the output area the three fields that are to appear unconditionally in the output line. The **IF** statement at lines 01310 through 01350 determines whether the word REORDER should be MOVEd to MESSAGE-SPACE, and if so, MOVEs it. If the value of QUANTITY-ON-HAND-IN IS LESS THAN 400, the MOVE statement at line 01320 executes. If the value of QUANTITY-ON-HAND-IN is not LESS THAN 400, the MOVE SPACES statement at line 01340 executes instead. The reserved word **END-IF** ends the IF statement, at line 01350.

The statement at lines 01360 through 01380 shows that an IF statement need not contain an **ELSE** clause. This IF statement tests whether there is any room on the page for the current detail line to print. The ADD statement at line 01400 ADDs 1 to LINE-COUNT-ER whenever a line is printed. IF the value of LINE-COUNT-ER IS GREATER THAN LINE-LIMIT, the PERFORM statement at line 01370 executes. If the value of LINE-COUNT-ER is not GREATER THAN LINE-LIMIT, the PERFORM statement is skipped. Then the WRITE statement at line 01390 executes unconditionally.

FIGURE 5.5 *continued*

```
S COBOL II RELEASE 3.2 09/05/90                P05001   DATE FEB 13,1992 T
----+-*A-1-B--+----2----+----3----+----4----+----5----+----6----+----7-%--+


00850
00860  PROCEDURE DIVISION.
00870  PRODUCE-INVENTORY-REPORT.
00880      PERFORM INITIALIZATION
00890      PERFORM PRODUCE-DETAIL-LINE UNTIL MORE-INPUT IS EQUAL TO "N"
00900      PERFORM TERMINATION
00910      STOP RUN
00920      .
```

FIGURE 5.5 *continued*

```

 INITIALIZATION.
     PERFORM HOUSEKEEPING
     PERFORM PRODUCE-PAGE-HEADINGS
     .

 HOUSEKEEPING.
     OPEN INPUT  INVENTORY-FILE-IN
          OUTPUT INVENTORY-LIST
     ACCEPT RUN-DATE FROM DATE
     MOVE CORRESPONDING RUN-DATE TO DATE-LINE
     READ INVENTORY-FILE-IN
         AT END
             MOVE "N" TO MORE-INPUT
     .

 PRODUCE-PAGE-HEADINGS.
     ADD 1 TO PAGE-NUMBER-W
     MOVE PAGE-NUMBER-W TO PAGE-NUMBER-OUT
     WRITE OUTPUT-LINE FROM REPORT-TITLE AFTER ADVANCING PAGE
     WRITE OUTPUT-LINE FROM DATE-LINE
     WRITE OUTPUT-LINE FROM COLUMN-HEADS-1
                          AFTER ADVANCING 3 LINES
     WRITE OUTPUT-LINE FROM COLUMN-HEADS-2
     MOVE SPACES TO OUTPUT-LINE
     WRITE OUTPUT-LINE
     MOVE 7 TO LINE-COUNT-ER
     .

 TERMINATION.
     CLOSE INVENTORY-FILE-IN
           INVENTORY-LIST
     .

 PRODUCE-DETAIL-LINE.
     MOVE PART-NUMBER-IN      TO PART-NUMBER-OUT
     MOVE PART-DESCRIPTION-IN TO PART-DESCRIPTION-OUT
     MOVE QUANTITY-ON-HAND-IN TO QUANTITY-ON-HAND-OUT
     IF QUANTITY-ON-HAND-IN IS LESS THAN 400
         MOVE "REORDER" TO MESSAGE-SPACE
     ELSE
         MOVE SPACES TO MESSAGE-SPACE
     END-IF
     IF LINE-COUNT-ER IS GREATER THAN LINE-LIMIT
         PERFORM PRODUCE-PAGE-HEADINGS
     END-IF
     WRITE OUTPUT-LINE FROM INVENTORY-LINE
     ADD 1 TO LINE-COUNT-ER
     READ INVENTORY-FILE-IN
         AT END
             MOVE "N" TO MORE-INPUT
     .
```

Program P05-01 was run with the input data shown in Figure 5.6 and produced the output shown in Figure 5.7. Notice that three pages of output are produced. Whenever you have a page heading routine in a program, you should test it with enough data to produce at least three pages of output.

FIGURE 5.6 Input to Program P05-01

```
--------------------------------------------------------------------------------
         1         2         3         4         5         6         7         8
12345678901234567890123456789012345678901234567890123456789012345678901234567890
--------------------------------------------------------------------------------
100103341/8" WASHER           489
200335473/16" WASHER          301
300489291/4" WASHER           400
345543115/16" WASHER          259
555994326" HAMMER             999
000123498" HAMMER             557
0012343110" HAMMER            207
012567426' FOLDING LADDER     399
321098858' FOLDING LADDER     019
5667721210' FOLDING LADDER    456
0202340012' EXTENSION LADDER367
0473927416' EXTENSION LADDER000
4783926420' EXTENSION LADDER005
7462962224' EXTENSION LADDER500
7483613430' EXTENSION LADDER658
4738161935' EXTENSION LADDER400
2659172340' EXTENSION LADDER399
4738261225-GALLON TANK        401
8372040330-GALLON TANK        999
9164831235-GALLON TANK        000
2648103340-GALLON TANK        478
8371023850-GALLON TANK        582
6572650160-GALLON TANK        124
7583659275-GALLON TANK        231
732127431" PAINT BRUSH        238
829105241 1/4" PAINT BRUSH    145
375629111 1/2" PAINT BRUSH    563
748399212" PAINT BRUSH        123
```

FIGURE 5.7 Output from Program P05-01

```
                    INVENTORY SUMMARY
     DATE   2/13/92                  PAGE   1

  PART          QUANTITY
 NUMBER         ON HAND       PART DESCRIPTION      NOTES

10010334          489      1/8" WASHER
20033547          301      3/16" WASHER             REORDER
30048929          400      1/4" WASHER
34554311          259      5/16" WASHER             REORDER
55599432          999      6" HAMMER
00012349          557      8" HAMMER
00123431          207      10" HAMMER               REORDER
01256742          399      6' FOLDING LADDER        REORDER
32109885           19      8' FOLDING LADDER        REORDER
56677212          456      10' FOLDING LADDER
02023400          367      12' EXTENSION LADDER     REORDER
04739274            0      16' EXTENSION LADDER     REORDER
```

FIGURE 5.7 *continued*

```
                 INVENTORY SUMMARY
    DATE   2/13/92                    PAGE   2

  PART        QUANTITY
 NUMBER       ON HAND      PART DESCRIPTION       NOTES

47839264          5      20'  EXTENSION LADDER    REORDER
74629622        500      24'  EXTENSION LADDER
74836134        658      30'  EXTENSION LADDER
47381619        400      35'  EXTENSION LADDER
26591723        399      40'  EXTENSION LADDER    REORDER
47382612        401      25-GALLON TANK
83720403        999      30-GALLON TANK
91648312          0      35-GALLON TANK           REORDER
26481033        478      40-GALLON TANK
83710238        582      50-GALLON TANK
65726501        124      60-GALLON TANK           REORDER
75836592        231      75-GALLON TANK           REORDER


                 INVENTORY SUMMARY
    DATE   2/13/92                    PAGE   3

  PART        QUANTITY
 NUMBER       ON HAND      PART DESCRIPTION       NOTES

73212743        238      1" PAINT BRUSH           REORDER
82910524        145      1 1/4" PAINT BRUSH       REORDER
37562911        563      1 1/2" PAINT BRUSH
74839921        123      2" PAINT BRUSH           REORDER
```

Format 1 of the WRITE Statement

The format of the WRITE statement that we have been using is:

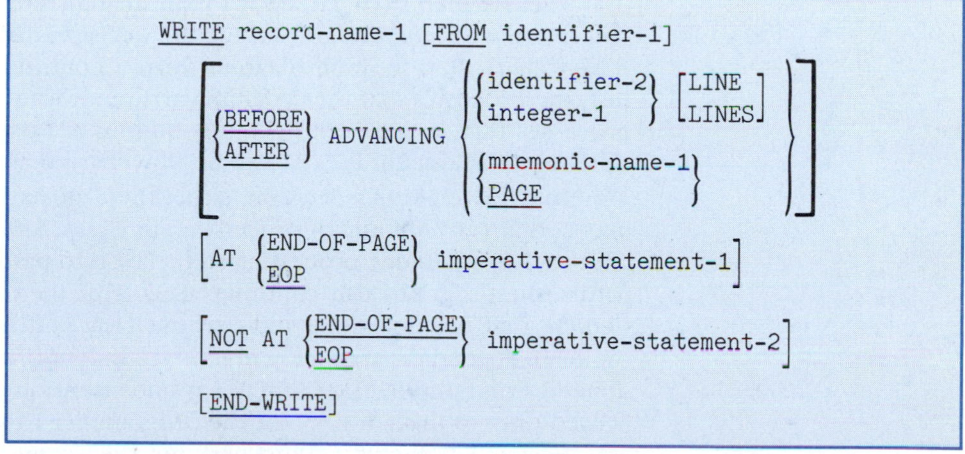

```
WRITE record-name-1 [FROM identifier-1]

  [ {BEFORE}  ADVANCING  { {identifier-2} [LINE ] } ]
  [ {AFTER }             { {integer-1   } [LINES] } ]
  [                      {                        } ]
  [                      { {mnemonic-name-1}      } ]
  [                      { {PAGE           }      } ]

  [AT {END-OF-PAGE} imperative-statement-1]
      {EOP        }

  [NOT AT {END-OF-PAGE} imperative-statement-2]
          {EOP        }

  [END-WRITE]
```

You can see that a line can be written BEFORE the paper is advanced, as well as AFTER. We will use only AFTER in this book. Also, ADVANCING, LINE, and LINES are optional words, so the statement

```
WRITE REPORT-LINE FROM COLUMN-HEADS-1 AFTER 3
```

means the same as:

```
WRITE REPORT-LINE FROM COLUMN-HEADS-1
    AFTER ADVANCING 3 LINES
```

An identifier may be used instead of an integer to indicate the line spacing desired. The identifier must be defined as an integer. For example, if the value of LINE-SPACING is 2, the following statement

```
WRITE REPORT-LINE FROM DETAIL-LINE AFTER LINE-SPACING
```

will execute just as:

```
WRITE REPORT-LINE FROM DETAIL-LINE AFTER 2
```

We will not use mnemonic name for paper control in this book.

Program Design with Conditions

We will now look at the other two design tools that we discuss in this book. They are the **program flowchart** and **pseudocode.** Program flowcharts are most useful in designing the parts of programs where IF statements would be used. Pseudocode can be used both in the way that hierarchy diagrams are used, to design the overall structure of a program, or as flowcharts would be used, to design the detailed logic in a program. We look at the program flowchart first.

The Program Flowchart

The program flowchart is one of the oldest tools for program design. It has drawbacks which have caused it to fall into disrepute in recent years, but it is still the most useful design tool for the decision-making portions of programs. A flowchart may show in diagram form a condition that the program has to test, the processes that the program carries out if the condition is True, and the processes that it carries out if the condition is False. For example, the first IF statement in Program P05-01 can be flowcharted as shown in Figure 5.8.

In a flowchart of a decision, either the True path or the False path, or both, may contain any amount of processing. In Figure 5.8 the True path and the False path each contain one processing step. The two paths of a decision must rejoin before the flowchart can continue. END-IF at the end of an IF statement tells COBOL that the IF is done and that the True and False paths are rejoined. Although it is good programming practice to indent IF statements the way we have done in Program P05-01, COBOL pays no attention to the indenting. Indenting is used only to make it easy for the programmer to see where the paths rejoin.

Figure 5.9 shows a flowchart for the second IF statement in Program P05-01. Here there is no processing in the False path.

Another form of the IF statement is one where there is no processing in the True path but one or more steps in the False path. An example of such a situation is shown in the flowchart in Figure 5.10. The IF statement for that logic

FIGURE 5.8 Flowchart of the statement

```
IF QUANTITY-ON-HAND IS LESS THAN 400
    MOVE "REORDER" TO MESSAGE-SPACE
ELSE
    MOVE SPACES TO MESSAGE-SPACE
END-IF
```

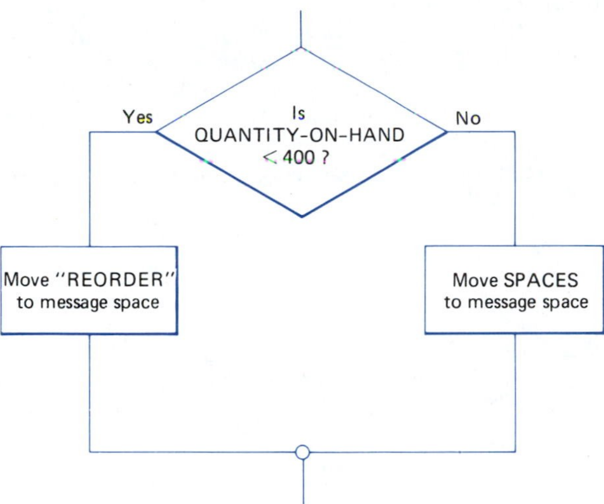

FIGURE 5.9 Flowchart of the statement

```
IF LINE-COUNT-ER IS GREATER THAN LINE-LIMIT
    PERFORM PRODUCE-PAGE-HEADINGS
END-IF
```

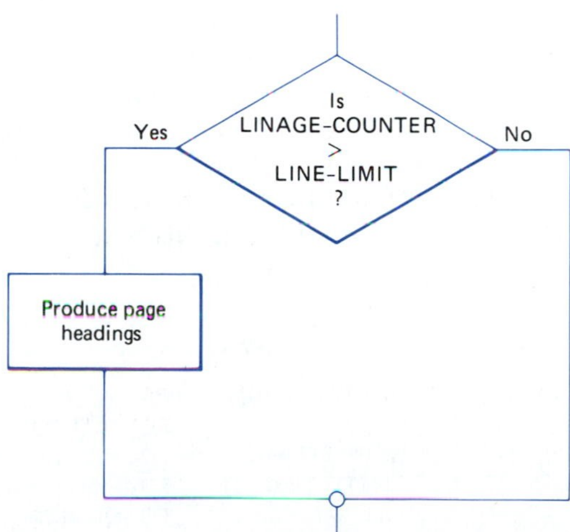

uses the **CONTINUE** statement, as follows:

```
IF RESPONSE-1 IS EQUAL TO RESPONSE-2
    CONTINUE
ELSE
    PERFORM RESPONSES-DIFFER
END-IF
```

FIGURE 5.10 **Flowchart of logic requiring processing in the False path only**

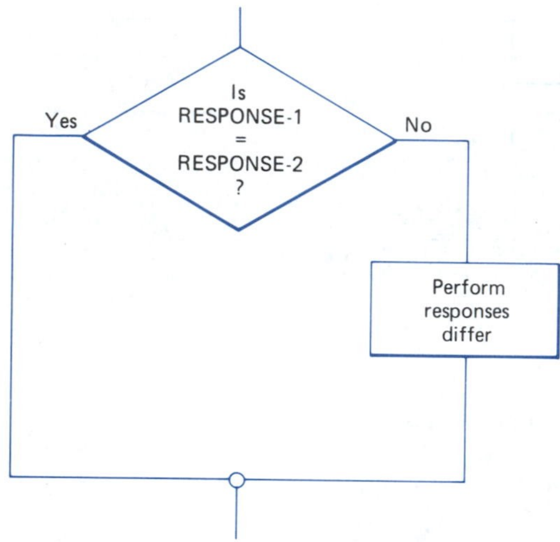

The word CONTINUE in the True path here indicates that no processing is to take place in that path, and that processing is to proceed following the END-IF. Since CONTINUE is an ordinary COBOL statement, it can be used also in the False path of an IF statement, as you will see later.

A flowchart with more than one processing step in a path is shown in Figure 5.11. That flowchart is coded in this way:

```
IF QUANTITY-IN IS LESS THAN 400
    MOVE SPACES                    TO OUTPUT-LINE
    MOVE PART-NUMBER-IN            TO PART-NUMBER-OUT
    MOVE PART-DESCRIPTION-IN       TO PART-DESCRIPTION-OUT
    MOVE QUANTITY-IN               TO QUANTITY-OUT
    WRITE REPORT-LINE FROM OUTPUT-LINE
END-IF
```

FIGURE 5.11 **Flowchart with more than one processing step in a path**

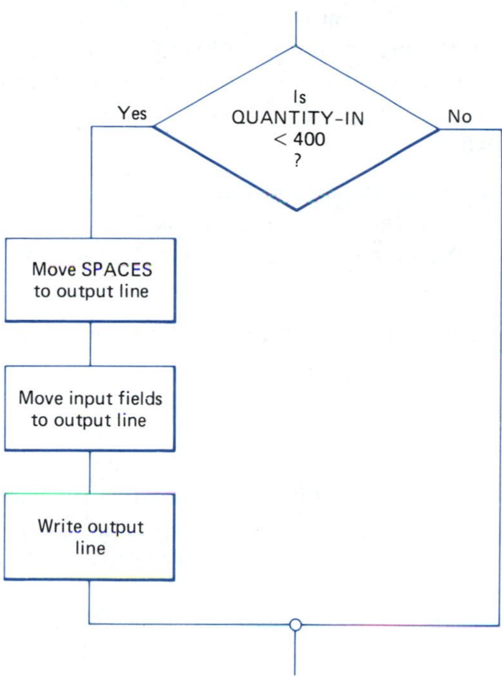

This IF statement will execute all the MOVE statements and the WRITE statement when QUANTITY-IN IS LESS THAN 400, and skip all the statements when it is not.

Pseudocode

Pseudocode has some of the advantages of hierarchy diagrams and some of the advantages of flowcharts. One of the advantages of pseudocode over all other methods of program design is that it can be written in plain English and does not require drawing any diagrams or charts. Pseudocode is written in a form that resembles COBOL code, but since pseudocode is English it has none of the language rules of COBOL (or any programming language). As an example, here is the pseudocode for the HOUSEKEEPING paragraph in Program P05-01:

Open files

Accept Run-date

Move corresponding Run-date to Date-line

Read Inventory-file-in at end move "N" to More-input

There are some important differences between pseudocode and COBOL. In pseudocode, only procedural steps are written; there is no reference in pseudocode to data descriptions or identification or environment details. Pseudocode may be written in as much or as little detail as desired. In the example given, the Move and Read operations are given in complete detail but the Open and Accept operations are not.

Pseudocode may be used to design a program in the same manner that top-down design is used. That is, we may first write pseudocode at a summary level, showing only the major subfunctions of the program, and fill in the details later. For example, if we were to use pseudocode to design Program P05-01, we could first write only as much detail as is shown in Figure 5.4. The pseudocode might look like this:

```
Perform initialization module
        Perform housekeeping module
        Perform produce page headings module
End-perform
Perform produce detail line module until More-input is equal to "N"
Perform termination module
Stop run
```

Notice that in pseudocode a performed procedure can be written directly under the Perform statement that controls it instead of in a paragraph by itself, as we have been doing in our programs. The scope of the Perform statement is shown by indenting the performed procedure and ending it with the statement End-perform.

Pseudocode for the paragraph PRODUCE-DETAIL-LINE shows how decision logic is written:

```
Move Part-number-in to Part-number-out
Move Part-description-in to Part-description-out
Move Quantity-on-hand-in to Quantity-on-hand-out
If Quantity-on-hand-in is less than 400
        Move "REORDER" to Message-space
else
        Move spaces to Message-space
End-if
If Line-count-er is greater than Line-limit
        Perform Produce-page-headings-module
End-if
Write output line
Read Inventory-file-in at end move "N" to More-input
```

Each End-if statement matches the previous If and rejoins the True and False paths.

In actual practice, a programmer would probably not use both hierarchy diagrams and pseudocode to design a program. Notice that in pseudocode, performed procedures can be written right where they are performed. So far in our COBOL programs, PERFORMed paragraphs were always written elsewhere in the program. It is possible in COBOL, by using the reserved word **END-PERFORM,** to write PERFORMed procedures right where they are PERFORMed, as in pseudocode. You will see how later in the book.

EXERCISE *1*

Write a program to read input records in the following format:

Positions	Field
1–5	Employee Number
6–14	Social Security Number
15–16	Hours Worked (whole numbers)
17–80	spaces

Have your program print one line for each record in the format shown in Figure 5.E1. Have your program print the word OVERTIME next to each employee who worked more than 37.5 hours. Have your program produce at least three pages of output.

FIGURE *5.E1* **Output format for Exercise 1**

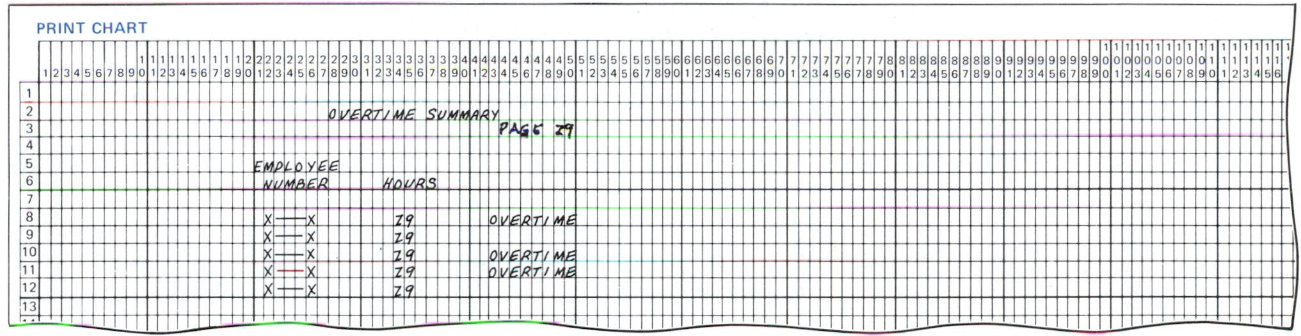

EXERCISE *2*

Using the same input and output formats as in Exercise 1, write a program that reads all the input records and prints only those employees who worked fewer than 30 hours. Do not print the word OVERTIME for any employee.

The Format of the IF Statement

```
IF condition-1 THEN { {statement-1} ... }  { ELSE {statement-2} ... [END-IF] }
                    { NEXT SENTENCE     }  { ELSE NEXT SENTENCE               }
                                           { END-IF                           }
```

The format shows that the word IF must be followed by a condition supplied by the programmer. A condition is any expression in a program that can be true or false. The condition we used in Chapter 2, in a PERFORM statement,

```
MORE-INPUT IS EQUAL TO "N"
```

is true when the value "N" is assigned to MORE-INPUT, and it is false when any other value is assigned to MORE-INPUT.

In Program P05-01 we use two conditions in IF statements:

```
QUANTITY-ON-HAND-IN IS LESS THAN 400
```

and

```
LINE-COUNT-ER IS GREATER THAN LINE-LIMIT
```

The first of those two conditions is true when any number LESS THAN 400 is assigned to QUANTITY-ON-HAND, and it is false when any other number is assigned to QUANTITY-ON-HAND. The second of the two conditions is true when the value assigned to LINE-COUNT-ER IS GREATER THAN the value assigned to LINE-LIMIT, and it is false otherwise. You will find a complete discussion of conditions in the next section.

Following the optional word **THEN** we see braces, which mean that one of the items within must be chosen. We have used only statement-1 in our IF statements, and have never chosen the reserved words **NEXT SENTENCE.** The rules of COBOL forbid the use of the words NEXT SENTENCE in an IF statement when the word END-IF is used in it, and since we always use END-IF in our IF statements, use of the words NEXT SENTENCE is forbidden to us.

The ellipsis following statement-1 shows that as many statements as desired may be included in the True path of the IF statement. The next set of braces shows that either ELSE or END-IF may be used to terminate the True path. If ELSE is used, then the False path may contain as many statements as desired.

The format says nothing about indenting in the IF statement because COBOL does not examine the indenting. Indenting is only for the programmer's convenience and should be used to improve the readability of programs.

Conditions

The **simple conditions** in COBOL are the **relation condition,** the **class condition,** the **condition-name condition,** the **switch-status condition,** and the **sign condition.** The relation condition is the only kind we have used so far in this book.

The Relation Condition

The format of the relation condition is:

```
           ⎧ IS [NOT] GREATER THAN                ⎫
           ⎪ IS [NOT] >                           ⎪
           ⎪ IS [NOT] LESS THAN                   ⎪
           ⎪ IS [NOT] <                           ⎪
           ⎪ IS [NOT] EQUAL TO                    ⎪
operand-1  ⎨ IS [NOT] =                           ⎬ operand-2
           ⎪ IS GREATER THAN OR EQUAL TO          ⎪
           ⎪ IS >=                                ⎪
           ⎪ IS LESS THAN OR EQUAL TO             ⎪
           ⎩ IS <=                                ⎭
```

Operand-1 is called the **subject** of the relation condition. Operand-2 is called the **object** of the relation condition. Operand-1 and operand-2 may each be an identifier, a literal, or an arithmetic expression. The relation condition must contain at least one reference to an identifier.

Note the optional words in this format. In

```
IF QUANTITY-ON-HAND-IN IS LESS THAN 400 ...
```

both IS and THAN are optional, and the statement could have begun with

```
IF QUANTITY-ON-HAND-IN LESS THAN 400 ...
```

or

```
IF QUANTITY-ON-HAND-IN IS LESS 400 ...
```

or

```
IF QUANTITY-ON-HAND-IN LESS 400 ...
```

but the optional words were used to improve the readability. The signs >, <, =, >=, and <= may be used instead of the corresponding words. The signs, if used, are required, and we refrain from underlining them here because underlining might make them confusing. In the condition

```
MORE-INPUT IS EQUAL TO "N"
```

we could have used the equal sign instead:

```
MORE-INPUT = "N"
```

The brackets around the appearances of the word NOT in the format show that the programmer may choose to use NOT or omit it. The underlining shows that if the programmer chooses to use the contents of the brackets, the word NOT must be used and spelled exactly as shown. Note that the **relational operator** NOT GREATER THAN means exactly the same as LESS THAN OR EQUAL TO, and NOT LESS THAN means exactly the same as GREATER THAN OR EQUAL TO.

Comparison of numeric operands. If both operands are defined as purely numeric, their true algebraic values are compared. The COBOL system carries out automatically any decimal-point alignment needed for the comparison. Zero is always equal to zero regardless of its sign.

Comparison of nonnumeric operands. If both operands are defined as other than purely numeric, comparison is made character by character, left to right in the operands until an inequality is found between corresponding characters in the two operands or the right end of the fields is reached. If the right end of the fields is reached with no inequality being found, the fields are considered equal. If the two operands are of unequal size, the comparison is done as though the shorter field were padded with blanks on the right end to the size of the larger.

Comparison of an elementary-level nonnumeric operand with a numeric operand. The comparison is made as though the numeric operand were first MOVEd to a nonnumeric field of suitable length, in accordance with the rules for MOVE given in Chapter 4. A numeric operand with decimal positions cannot be compared to a nonnumeric operand.

Comparison of a group-level operand with a numeric operand. The comparison is made as though the numeric operand were first MOVEd to a group-level item of suitable length. This kind of comparison sometimes may not work as expected because the MOVE of the numeric operand to the group item sometimes may not give the desired result (see "Group-level MOVEs." Chapter 4, page 95).

The Class Condition

The class condition allows a program to check whether a particular field contains only numbers; or whether it contains only the lowercase characters a through z, the uppercase characters A through Z, and the character space; or whether it contains only some characters specified by the programmer. The format of the class condition is:

```
                                  ⎧NUMERIC           ⎫
                                  ⎪ALPHABETIC        ⎪
identifier-1 IS [NOT]             ⎨ALPHABETIC-LOWER  ⎬
                                  ⎪ALPHABETIC-UPPER  ⎪
                                  ⎩class-name-1      ⎭
```

To see how the class test works, assume we have the following fields:

```
05 MONEY-AMOUNT-IN     PIC 9(5)V99.
05 MONEY-AMOUNT-W      PIC S9(5)V99.
05 ALPHA-FIELD         PIC X(8).
```

The test

```
IF MONEY-AMOUNT-IN IS NOT NUMERIC ...
```

will execute the True path if any of the characters in MONEY-AMOUNT-IN are other than the digits 0 through 9. The field MONEY-AMOUNT-W, however, will be considered **NUMERIC** if it contains the digits 0 through 9 and a valid plus or minus sign. MONEY-AMOUNT-IN, which contains no S in its PICTURE, would be considered NOT NUMERIC if it were found to contain a sign.

The **ALPHABETIC** class condition permits a program to test whether all the characters in a field are the alphabetic characters, which are defined in COBOL as the lower- and uppercase letters and the character space. So the test

```
IF ALPHA-FIELD IS ALPHABETIC ...
```

would execute the False path if any of the characters in ALPHA-FIELD were other than the letters or space. **ALPHABETIC-LOWER** is defined as the lowercase letters a through z and the character space, so the test

```
IF ALPHA-FIELD IS ALPHABETIC-LOWER ...
```

would execute the False path if any of the characters in ALPHA-FIELD were other than the lowercase letters or space. **ALPHABETIC-UPPER** is defined as the uppercase A through Z and the character space, so the test

```
IF ALPHA-FIELD IS ALPHABETIC-UPPER ...
```

would execute the False path if any of the characters in ALPHA-FIELD were other than the uppercase letters or space. Finally, class-name-1 can consist of any set of characters defined by the programmer in the Special Names paragraph of the Environment Division, so if class-name-1 has been defined as, let's say, SPECIAL-CLASS, the test

```
IF ALPHA-FIELD IS SPECIAL-CLASS ...
```

would execute the False path if any of the characters in ALPHA-FIELD were other than the characters defined in SPECIAL-CLASS.

It is legal and sometimes useful to be able to determine whether a field described with Xs contains all numbers. The test

```
IF ALPHA-FIELD IS NUMERIC ...
```

would execute the True path only if all the characters in ALPHA-FIELD were the digits 0 through 9. The ALPHABETIC class test may not be executed on a field defined as numeric.

The Condition-Name Condition

To use a condition-name test, the programmer must first define one or more condition names. A condition name is a name given to one or more values that might be assigned to a field. A condition name is defined by using a **level-88** entry in the Data Division. When a level-88 entry is used with a field, the field must still be described in the usual way. That is, the field must have an ordinary level number (from 01 to 49) and, if it is an elementary field, must have a PICTURE, and may have other optional clauses, such as SIGN and/or VALUE.

As an example, assume we have the following input field:

```
05 CODE-IN               PIC 9.
```

Let us say that valid values of CODE-IN are 1, 2, and 3. We can use a level-88 entry with this field to give a condition name to the valid codes. A level-88 entry, when used, must follow immediately the description of the field it applies to. If we want to give the condition name VALID-CODE to the values 1, 2, and 3, we can write

```
05 CODE-IN               PIC 9.
   88 VALID-CODE         VALUES ARE 1 THROUGH 3.
```

or

```
05 CODE-IN               PIC 9.
   88 VALID-CODE               VALUES 1, 2, 3.
```

When you use a level-88 entry with a field defined as numeric, the literals in the VALUE clause in the level-88 entry must all be numeric. When the field is defined as alphanumeric, alphanumeric edited, or numeric edited, the literals must all be nonnumeric.

The format of the level-88 entry is:

$$\text{88 condition-name-1} \left\{\begin{matrix}\underline{\text{VALUE}}\ \text{IS} \\ \underline{\text{VALUES}}\ \text{ARE}\end{matrix}\right\} \left\{\text{literal-1} \left[\left\{\begin{matrix}\underline{\text{THROUGH}} \\ \underline{\text{THRU}}\end{matrix}\right\} \text{literal-2}\right]\right\} \ldots .$$

The words VALUE and VALUES are equivalent. The words THROUGH and THRU are equivalent. Although there is never any need to use the word THROUGH in the Procedure Division, it is quite proper to use it in the Data Division. The rules for making up condition names are the same as for making up data names. You can see from the format that exactly one VALUE clause is required in a level-88 entry and that no other clauses are permitted. Note especially that the PICTURE clause is not permitted in a level-88 entry. Level-88 entries must be contained entirely in area B.

In the Procedure Division a condition name may be tested in an IF statement. For example, the statement

```
IF VALID-CODE
    CONTINUE
ELSE
    PERFORM ERROR-ROUTINE
END-IF
```

will skip to the END-IF if CODE-IN is equal to 1 or 2 or 3 and will PERFORM the paragraph ERROR-ROUTINE otherwise. It is legal to use the word NOT before a condition name, so the following statement will do the same as the previous:

```
IF NOT VALID-CODE
    PERFORM ERROR-ROUTINE
END-IF
```

Notice that there is no relational operator in these IF statements. The condition name alone constitutes the entire condition in the IF statement.

The use of a level-88 entry in connection with coded fields such as CODE-IN makes it very convenient to see at a glance what all the valid codes are. The program is also very easy to change if the set of valid codes should change, and the Procedure Division coding is clearer when condition names are properly used.

EXERCISE 3

Write a level-05 entry and a level-88 entry for the following field: a three digit, unsigned integer called WORK-STATION. Give the condition name VALID-WORK-STATION to the valid work stations, whose numbers lie in the range 100 to 999 inclusive.

We have so far examined the use of level-88 entries with input data fields. Level-88 entries can be used also with intermediate-result fields in working storage. For example, consider this definition of the input-data flag:

```
01 MORE-INPUT       PIC X       VALUE "Y".
   88 THERE-IS-MORE-INPUT                   VALUE "Y".
   88 THERE-IS-NO-MORE-INPUT                VALUE "N".
```

This is a legal definition, and it shows that the VALUE clause may be used both to establish the initial VALUE of a field and to give names to particular VALUEs that might appear in the field. Now the following is a legal statement:

```
PERFORM MAIN-LOOP UNTIL THERE-IS-NO-MORE-INPUT
```

This statement reads very nicely and is clear English. Any valid condition is legal following the word UNTIL in a PERFORM statement, whether relation condition, condition-name condition, or any of the others. Now we have to change the READ statements in our programs to use the **SET** statement and the reserved word **TRUE,** as for example:

```
READ INPUT-FILE
     AT END
          SET THERE-IS-NO-MORE-INPUT TO TRUE
END-READ
```

END-READ is of course required only if the READ statement is not the last statement of a paragraph.

When end-of-file is encountered on the input file, the SET statement here SETs the condition name THERE-IS-NO-MORE-INPUT to TRUE by moving "N" to the field MORE-INPUT.

The Sign Condition

The sign condition determines whether the algebraic value of a numeric operand is less than, greater than, or equal to zero. The format of the sign condition is:

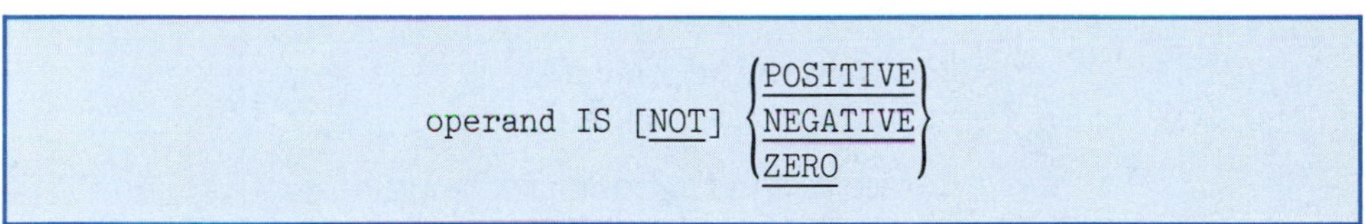

```
                    {POSITIVE}
operand IS [NOT]    {NEGATIVE}
                    {ZERO    }
```

The operand being tested must be a field defined as numeric or it must be an arithmetic expression that contains at least one reference to an identifier. An operand greater than zero is considered POSITIVE, less than zero NEGATIVE. An operand of zero value is considered ZERO regardless of whether it is signed or unsigned.

An example of the use of the sign condition is:

```
IF BALANCE-DUE IS POSITIVE
    PERFORM BALANCE-DUE-ROUTINE
END-IF
```

The Switch-Status Condition

The switch-status condition permits the programmer to give names to switches which can be set on or off by the programmer or the computer operator at the time a COBOL program is executed. Entries in the SPECIAL-NAMES paragraph of the Environment Division are used to assign the names, and the names may then be used as conditions in the Procedure Division to determine whether a particular switch is on or off. The switches are set on or off externally to the COBOL program. In IBM COBOL systems, the switches are set through the use of the UPSI parameter in an EXEC statement. In NCR VRX COBOL, the switches are set by use of the OPTS parameter in the JOB statement.

Format 4 of the SET Statement

The format of the SET statement that contains the word TRUE is as follows:

```
SET {condition-name-1} . . . TO TRUE
```

The ellipsis shows that more than one condition name can be SET to TRUE with a single statement. If more than one condition name is given in a SET statement, then each condition name is SET to TRUE separately in the order given in the statement.

If a condition name is defined with more than one literal in its VALUE clause, for example, as follows:

```
05 CODE-IN          PIC X.
   88 VALID-CODE          VALUES 1, 2, 3.
```

or

```
05 CODE-IN          PIC X.
   88 VALID-CODE          VALUES 1 THRU 3.
```

then the statement

```
SET VALID-CODE TO TRUE
```

would MOVE 1 to the field CODE-IN.

Nested IF Statements

A **nested** IF statement is one where one or more IF statements appear in the True path or the False path, or both, of an IF statement. Figure 5.12 shows logic that may be coded with a nested IF statement. The coding is:

```
IF QUANTITY-IN LESS THAN 400
    MOVE SPACES                 TO OUTPUT-LINE
    MOVE PART-NUMBER-IN         TO PART-NUMBER-OUT
    MOVE PART-DESCRIPTION-IN    TO PART-DESCRIPTION-OUT
    MOVE QUANTITY-IN            TO QUANTITY-OUT
    IF LINE-COUNT-ER GREATER THAN LINE-LIMIT
        PERFORM PRODUCE-PAGE-HEADINGS
        WRITE REPORT-LINE FROM OUTPUT-LINE
    ELSE
        WRITE REPORT-LINE FROM OUTPUT-LINE
    END-IF
END-IF
```

FIGURE 5.12 **Flowchart of logic that may be coded using a nested IF statement**

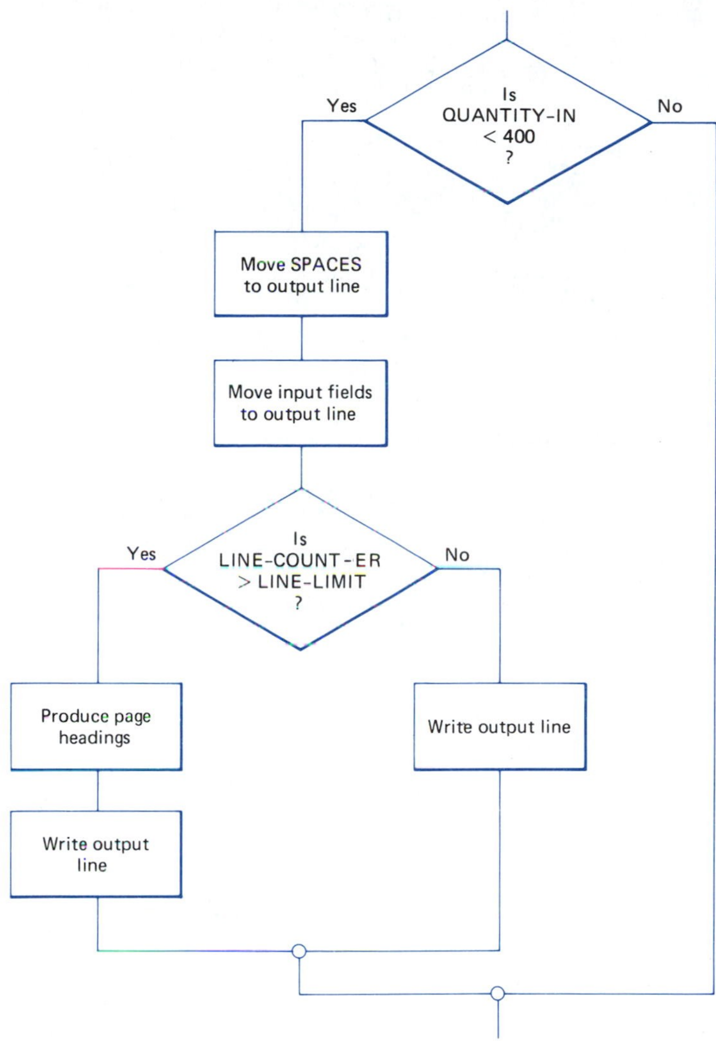

This nested IF statement consists of an **outer IF statement** containing an **inner IF statement** in its True path. Figure 5.13 shows a flowchart for a slightly more complex nested IF statement. In Figure 5.13 both the True and False paths of the outer IF contain an IF. Figure 5.13 may be coded as follows:

```
IF C1
    PERFORM P1
    IF C2
        CONTINUE
    ELSE
        PERFORM P2
        PERFORM P3
    END-IF
ELSE
    IF C3
        PERFORM P4
    ELSE
        PERFORM P5
    END-IF
END-IF
```

FIGURE 5.13 Flowchart of logic in which each path of the outer decision contains a decision

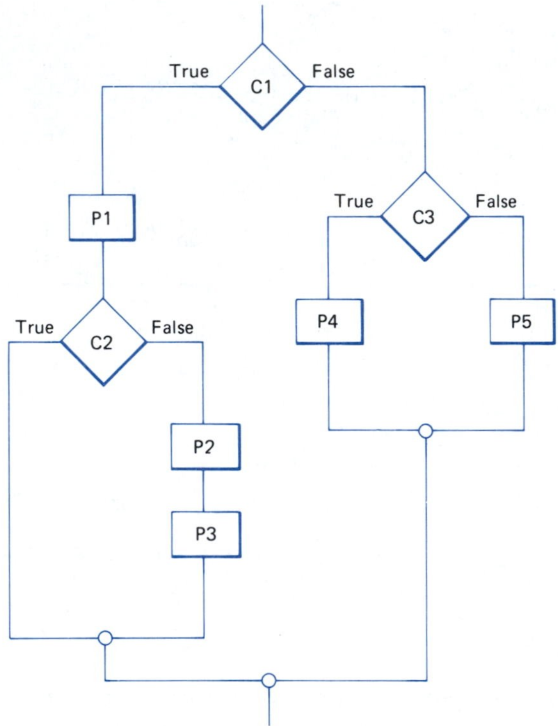

The word END-IF appearing immediately after PERFORM P3 is said to **terminate** the inner IF statement that begins with IF C2. That END-IF optionally could have been omitted, because the ELSE immediately following it terminates the inner IF statement also. For clarity, it is best to use END-IF to terminate all IF statements.

Nested IF statements should always be written with proper indentation so that the programmer can see which ELSE and which END-IF belong to which IF, and where the True and False paths of each of the IF tests are. In the IF statement above, the first IF tests the condition C1 and starts the True path for that condition. The ELSE aligned with the first IF starts the False path for that same condition, C1, and the END-IF aligned with the first IF ends the entire IF statement. Indented further are other IFs, ELSEs, and END-IFs, and ELSE and END-IF aligned with its corresponding IF. Each ELSE ends the True path for its corresponding IF and starts the False path, and each END-IF ends the False path (and the IF statement) for its corresponding IF.

In flowcharts of IF statements the rejoining of True and False paths is shown by a little circle. You can see in Figure 5.13 that there are three places where True and False paths rejoin, and in the IF statement each such joining is represented by an END-IF.

It has already been mentioned that COBOL does not examine indenting in IF statements (or in any others) and that indenting is only for the programmer's convenience. Here the programmer would use indenting to keep track of which ELSE and which END-IF belong to which IF. But since COBOL does not examine indenting, it uses the following rule to determine for itself which ELSE and END-IF belong to which IF: Any ELSE encountered in the statement is considered to apply to the immediately preceding IF that has neither been terminated nor already paired with an ELSE; any END-IF encountered in the statement is considered to apply to the immediately preceding IF that has not already been terminated.

Figure 5.14 shows a flowchart where there are two paths with no processing. The coding for the flowchart in Figure 5.14 is as follows:

```
IF C1
    IF C2
        PERFORM P1
        PERFORM P2
        PERFORM P3
    ELSE
        CONTINUE
    END-IF
ELSE
    IF C3
        CONTINUE
    ELSE
        PERFORM P4
    END-IF
END-IF
```

Notice that in this statement the CONTINUE statement is used whenever there is no processing in a path.

FIGURE 5.14 **Flowchart of logic in which two paths contain no processing**

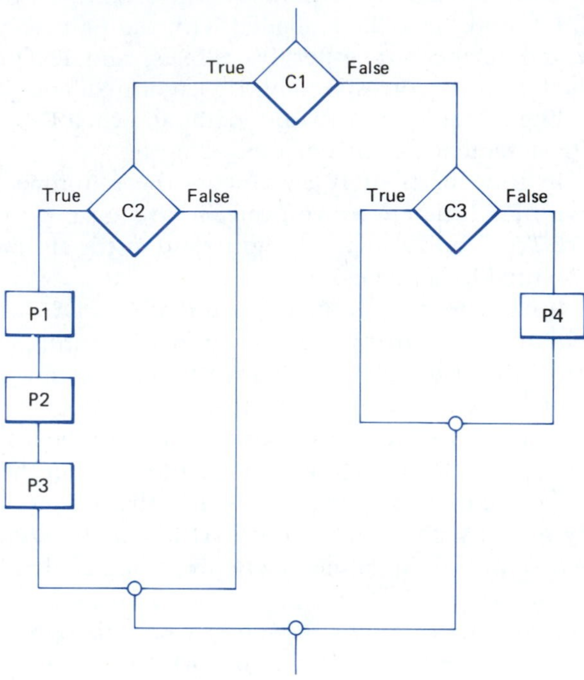

Figure 5.15 shows another flowchart with no processing in two paths. One way of coding Figure 5.15 is:

```
IF C1
     IF C2
          PERFORM P1
     ELSE
          CONTINUE
     END-IF
ELSE
     IF C3
          PERFORM P2
     ELSE
          CONTINUE
     END-IF
END-IF
```

But the words ELSE CONTINUE may be omitted wherever they appear if the word END-IF has been used consistently as recommended, so Figure 5.15 may be coded equally well as follows:

```
IF C1
     IF C2
          PERFORM P1
     END-IF
ELSE
     IF C3
          PERFORM P2
     END-IF
END-IF
```

FIGURE 5.15 **Another flowchart in which two paths contain no processing**

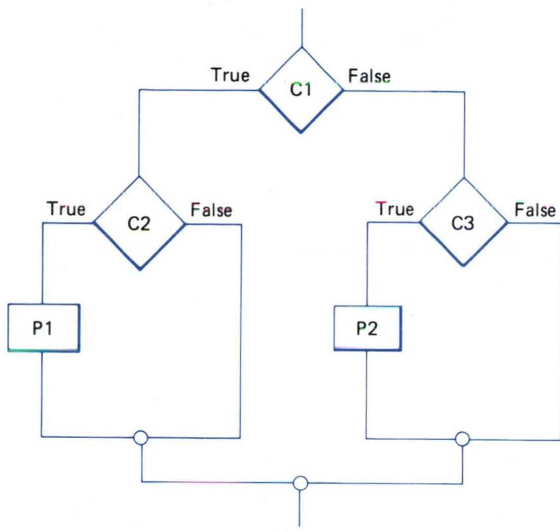

Figure 5.16 shows logic that requires a statement immediately after an END-IF. It is coded as follows:

```
IF C1
     IF C2
          PERFORM P1
     ELSE
          PERFORM P2
     END-IF
     PERFORM P3
ELSE
     IF C3
          PERFORM P4
     ELSE
          PERFORM P5
     END-IF
END-IF
```

FIGURE 5.16 **Flowchart of logic that requires a statement immediately after an END-IF**

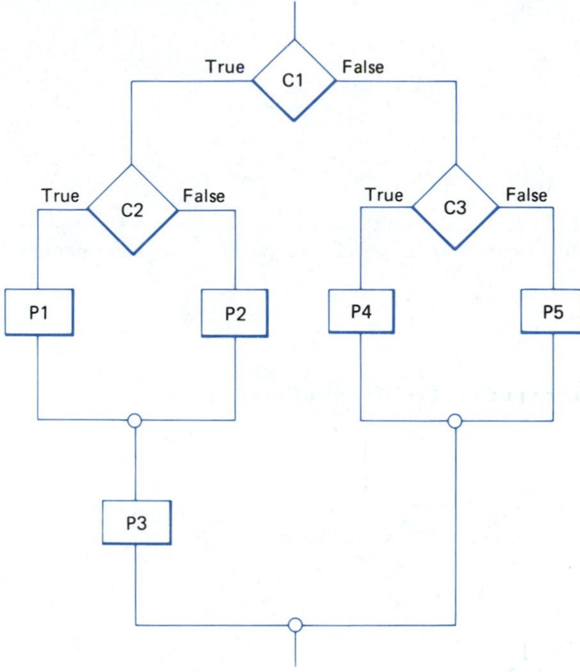

IF statements may be nested to any level within the limits of the size of the computer. That is, an IF statement in one of the paths of an outer IF statement may itself have an IF statement in one of its own paths. The logic shown in Figure 5.17 may be coded as:

```
IF C1
    PERFORM P1
    IF C2
        CONTINUE
    ELSE
        PERFORM P2
        IF C3
            PERFORM P3
            PERFORM P4
        ELSE
            CONTINUE
        END-IF
    END-IF
ELSE
    CONTINUE
END-IF
```

Or, by removing the ELSE CONTINUE phrases:

```
IF C1
    PERFORM P1
    IF C2
        CONTINUE
    ELSE
        PERFORM P2
        IF C3
            PERFORM P3
            PERFORM P4
        END-IF
    END-IF
END-IF
```

FIGURE 5.17 Logic requiring three levels of nesting in an IF statement

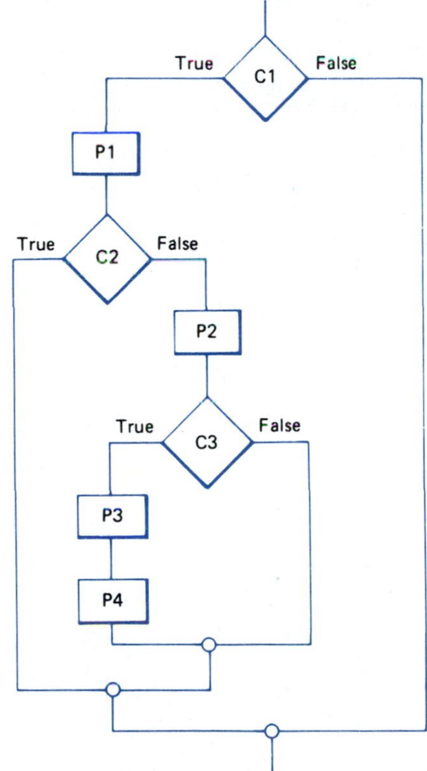

One possible realistic use of nested IF statements is shown in the following example:

```
IF JOB-CODE-1
    IF UNION-CODE-1
        IF HOURS-WORKED > 40
            PERFORM OV1
        ELSE
            PERFORM OV0
        END-IF
    ELSE
        IF UNION-CODE-2
            IF HOURS-WORKED > 37.5
                PERFORM OV2
            ELSE
                PERFORM OV0
            END-IF
        END-IF
    END-IF
    PERFORM JOB-ROUTINE-1
ELSE
    IF JOB-CODE-2
        IF MARRIED
            PERFORM TAX-1
        ELSE
            IF SINGLE
                PERFORM TAX-2
            ELSE
                PERFORM TAX-3
            END-IF
        END-IF
        PERFORM JOB-ROUTINE-2
    ELSE
        PERFORM JOB-ROUTINE-0
    END-IF
END-IF
```

EXERCISE 4 Code the logic shown in Figure 5.E4 using nested IF statements.

FIGURE 5.E4 **Flowcharts for Exercise 4**

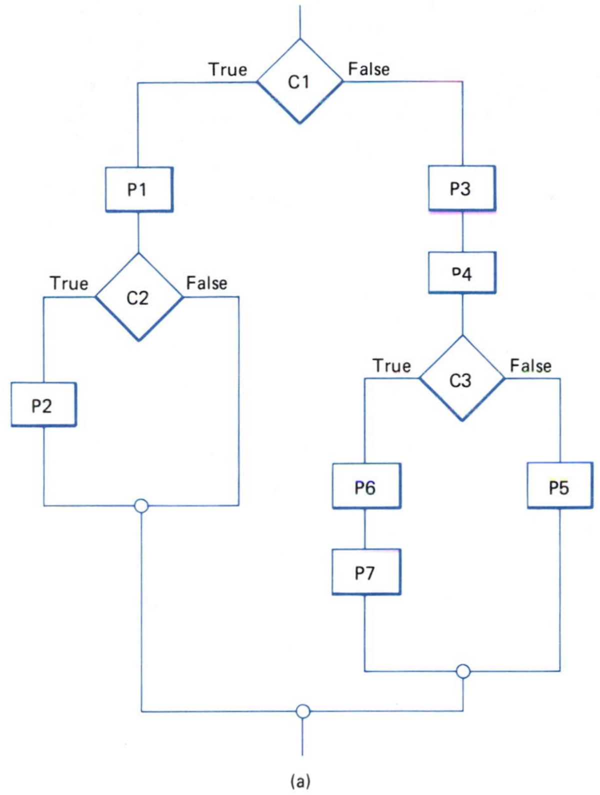

(a)

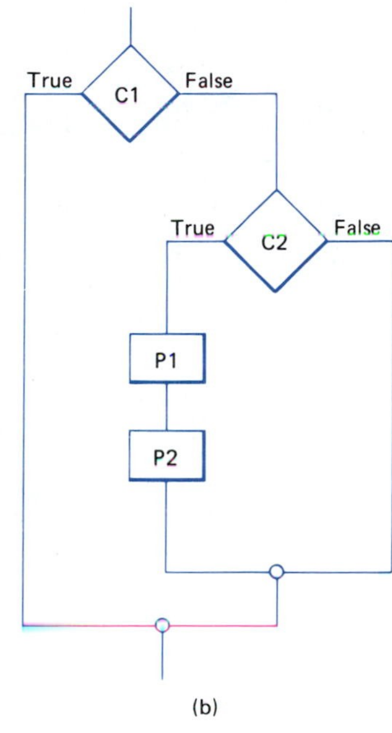

(b)

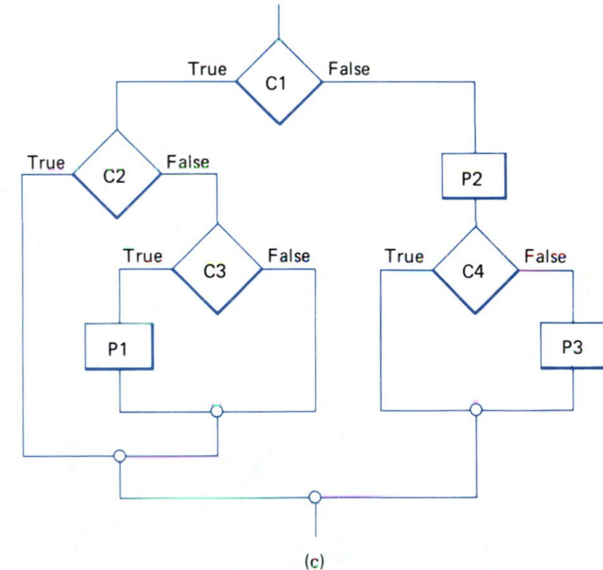

(c)

continued

FIGURE *5.E4* *continued*

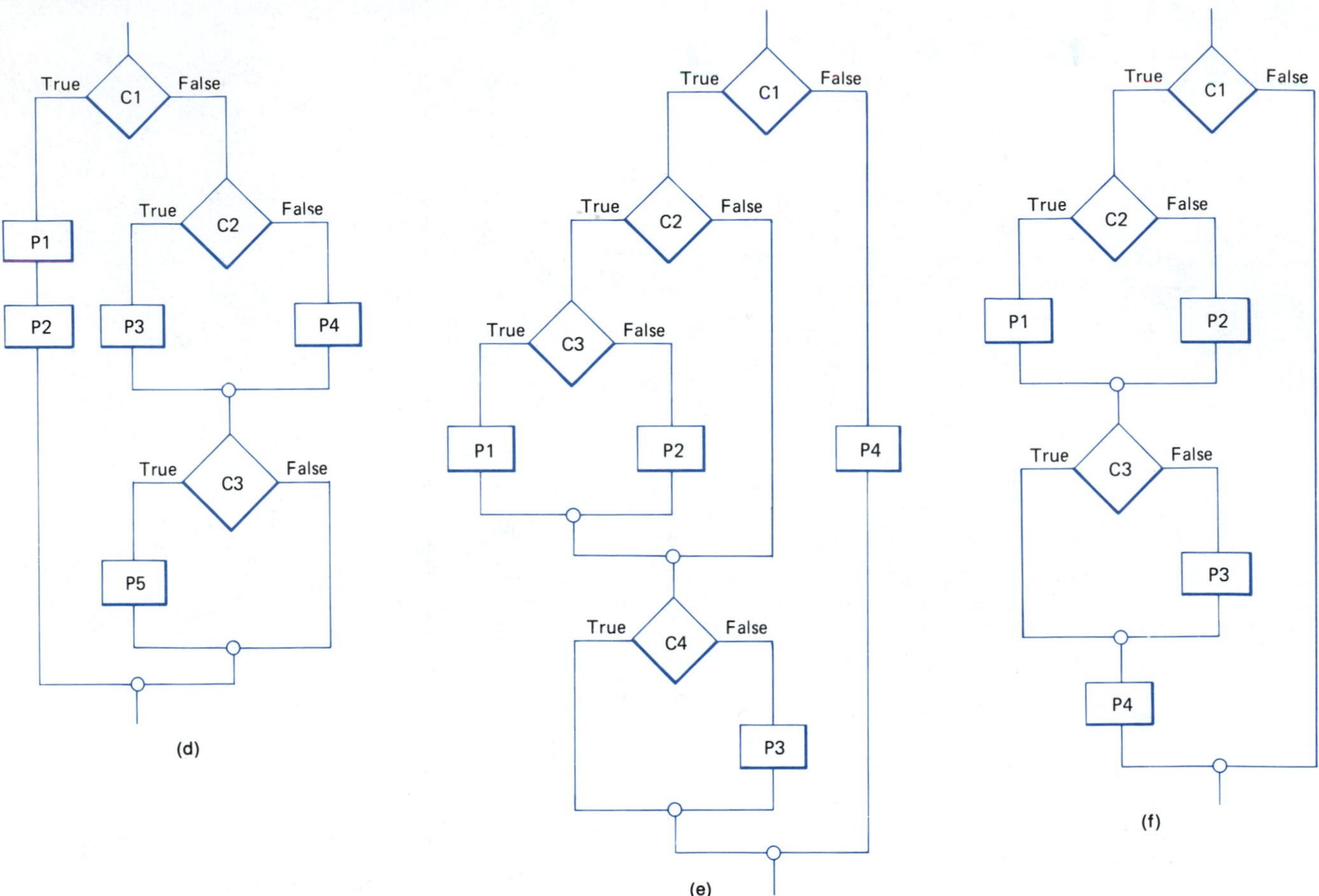

EXERCISE *5*

Draw a flowchart showing the logic of each of the following statements:

a.
```
IF C1
     PERFORM P1
     IF C2
          CONTINUE
     ELSE
          PERFORM P2
     END-IF
ELSE
     IF C3
          PERFORM P3
     END-IF
END-IF
```

b.
```
IF C1
     IF C2
          PERFORM P1
          PERFORM P2
     END-IF
ELSE
     IF C3
          CONTINUE
     ELSE
          PERFORM P3
          PERFORM P4
     END-IF
END-IF
```

c.
```
IF C1
     IF C2
          IF C3
               PERFORM P1
          END-IF
     END-IF
END-IF
```

Complex Conditions

There are three kinds of **complex conditions** in COBOL. They are the **negated simple condition,** the **combined condition,** and the **negated combined condition.** A negated simple condition is formed by placing the word NOT before any simple condition. Earlier we saw a negated simple condition, in the section on condition-name conditions:

```
IF NOT VALID-CODE
     PERFORM ERROR-ROUTINE
```

The word NOT can be placed before any simple condition, so the following is legal:

```
IF NOT A IS EQUAL TO B ...
```

The simple condition may be placed in parentheses without changing the meaning, so

```
IF NOT (A IS EQUAL TO B) ...
```

has the same effect. Both negated conditions have the same meaning as:

```
IF A IS NOT EQUAL TO B ...
```

A combined condition is one that uses the words AND and/or OR. An example of a combined condition used in an IF statement is:

```
IF QUANTITY-ON-HAND-IN IS LESS THAN 400 AND
   UNIT-PRICE IS GREATER THAN 10.00
     PERFORM REORDER-HIGH-PRICE
ELSE
     PERFORM TEST-2
END-IF
```

In the preceding IF statement both simple conditions would have to be true for the True path of the IF statement to be executed. In the statement

```
IF A = B OR
   C = D
    PERFORM FOUND-A-MATCH
ELSE
    PERFORM NO-MATCH
END-IF
```

if either A equals B or C equals D, the True path will be executed.

ANDs and ORs may be used together in a combined condition. Ordinarily, ANDs are evaluated first, followed by ORs. So the condition

```
IF A = B OR C = D AND E NOT = F ...
```

would be evaluated as if it were written:

```
IF A = B OR (C = D AND E NOT = F) . . .
```

This statement would execute the True path if either:

1. A is equal to B, OR

2. C is equal to D and E is not equal to F.

In general a different result would be obtained from the statement:

```
IF (A = B OR C = D) AND E NOT = F ...
```

This statement would execute the True path only if:

1. Either A is equal to B or C is equal to D, AND

2. E is not equal to F.

A negated combined condition consists of the word NOT followed by a combined condition in parentheses, as in:

```
IF NOT (A = B AND C = D)
    PERFORM NOT-BOTH-EQUAL
ELSE
    PERFORM BOTH-EQUAL
END-IF
```

In this statement the False path would be executed if A is equal to B and C is equal to D.

Complex conditions can become extremely complicated. You should use them only when their use makes the meaning of the program clearer than it would be without the complex condition.

EXERCISE *6*

Given the following statement:

```
IF AMOUNT IS LESS THAN 1000000
    PERFORM ERROR-ROUTINE
ELSE
    IF CHARGE-CODE NOT = "H"
        CONTINUE
    ELSE
        PERFORM ERROR-ROUTINE
    END-IF
END-IF
```

Rewrite this statement using a combined condition so that the logic is made clearer.

Abbreviated Combined Relation Conditions

In a combined condition having two or more relation conditions in a row, more than one of the relation conditions sometimes have the same subject and/or the same relational operator. For example, in the condition

```
IF A = B OR A IS GREATER THAN C ...
```

there are two relation conditions and they both have A as their subject. Such a condition can be abbreviated by leaving out the repetition of the subject, so the following would be legal:

```
IF A = B OR IS GREATER THAN C
    PERFORM IN-RANGE
END-IF
```

If the simple conditions in a complex condition have the same subject and the same relational operator, repetition of the subject and the operator may be omitted. So the condition

```
IF A NOT = B AND A NOT = C ...
```

can be abbreviated to the following:

```
IF A NOT = B AND C
    PERFORM EQUALS-NEITHER
END-IF
```

You may mix omitting just the subject with omitting the subject and the operator. In the condition

```
IF A IS NOT GREATER THAN B AND
   A IS LESS THAN C        OR
   A IS LESS THAN D ...
```

you can first omit the repetitious subject A, and then later omit the operator LESS THAN when it becomes repetitious, as:

```
IF A IS NOT GREATER THAN B AND LESS THAN C OR D
    PERFORM IN-RANGE
END-IF
```

Parentheses are not permitted within an abbreviated condition, even to improve readability.

A word of warning about a common error made by even experienced programmers. In testing whether the value of some data name is not equal to any of several values, the incorrect connective is sometimes used, and the abbreviation masks the error. For example, with the field CODE-IN, described earlier, where the legal values of CODE-IN are 1, 2, and 3, we might want to use an abbreviated relation condition to test for the legal values. Unfortunately COBOL does not permit us to say:

```
IF CODE-IN IS NEITHER 1 NOR 2 NOR 3
    PERFORM ERROR-ROUTINE
END-IF
```

Whenever you find this NEITHER . . . NOR situation, there are three correct ways to code it and one commonly used incorrect way (which, of course, eventually must be corrected by the programmer if the program is to work). You may write it as an OR and negate the whole condition, as in:

```
IF NOT (CODE-IN = 1 OR 2 OR 3)
    PERFORM ERROR-ROUTINE
END-IF
```

You may reverse the True and False paths, as:

```
IF CODE-IN = 1 OR 2 OR 3
    CONTINUE
ELSE
    PERFORM ERROR-ROUTINE
END-IF
```

Or in the form that is closest to the original wording:

```
IF CODE-IN NOT = 1 AND 2 AND 3
    PERFORM ERROR-ROUTINE
END-IF
```

This last form may look a little strange but it makes sense when you realize that in its fully expanded, unabbreviated form, the statement would be:

```
IF CODE-IN NOT = 1 AND
   CODE-IN NOT = 2 AND
   CODE-IN NOT = 3
    PERFORM ERROR-ROUTINE
END-IF
```

For the common wrong way of coding this situation, see Exercise 7. Of course, a better way to handle a situation like this is to use a condition name, as described earlier in the chapter.

EXERCISE 7

Expand the following statement into its unabbreviated form. Then answer the questions below.

```
IF CODE-IN NOT = 1 OR 2 OR 3
    PERFORM ERROR-ROUTINE
END-IF
```

How would the statement execute if CODE-IN is equal to:

a. 1

b. 2

c. 4

EXERCISE 8

Rewrite the following conditions using abbreviated subjects and/or operators, as appropriate:

a. IF FIELD-1 GREATER THAN FIELD-2 AND FIELD-1 LESS THAN FIELD 3 . . .

b. IF FIELD-1 NOT GREATER THAN FIELD-2 AND FIELD-1 NOT GREATER THAN FIELD-3 . . .

c. IF FIELD-1 LESS THAN FIELD-2 OR FIELD-1 GREATER THAN FIELD-3 AND FIELD-1 EQUAL TO FIELD-4 AND FIELD-1 EQUAL TO FIELD-5 . . .

A Program with Complicated Condition Testing

We now do a program for computing commissions on sales, using a somewhat involved schedule of commission rates. This program shows the use of a nested IF statement, a negated simple condition, a combined condition, and level-88 entries in context.

In this problem, salespeople are each assigned to some class. The salespeople classes are A through H. All salespeople assigned to classes A through F are considered junior salespeople; salespeople in class G are associate salespeople; and class H salespeople are senior. Salespeople in different titles have different annual quotas, and their commission rates on current sales depend on whether or not they met their quota last year. The quotas are as follows: for junior salespeople, none; for associates, \$150,000; for seniors, \$250,000. The commission rates for each of the salespeople titles are shown in Table 5.1.

TABLE *5.1*
Commission schedules for three salespeople titles for Program P05-02

Title	*Commission Schedule If Quota Was Not Met*	*Commission Schedule If Quota Was Met*
Junior	10% of sale amount on all sales	10% of sale amount on all sales
Associate	5% of first \$10,000 of sale amount; 20% of sale amount in excess of \$10,000	20% of first \$10,000 of sale amount; 30% of sale amount in excess of \$10,000
Senior	20% of first \$50,000 of sale amount; 30% of sale amount in excess of \$50,000	30% of first \$50,000 of sale amount; 40% of sale amount in excess of \$50,000

For example, suppose that an associate salesperson met the quota last year and has just made a sale of \$25,000. The commission on that sale would be 20% of \$10,000 plus 30% of the excess. Now suppose that a senior salesperson did not meet the quota last year and has just made a sale of \$40,000. The commission on that sale would be 20% of \$40,000.

The input format for Program P05-02 is:

Positions	*Field*
1–5	Salesperson Number
6	Class
7–12	Last Year's Sales (in whole dollars)
13–20	Current Sale (in dollars and cents)
21–80	spaces

The output format is shown in Figure 5.18. Two types of error lines are shown. This program checks the salesperson Class in each input record before processing it, and if the Class is missing or invalid, the program prints an appropriate error message.

FIGURE 5.18 Output format for Program P05-02

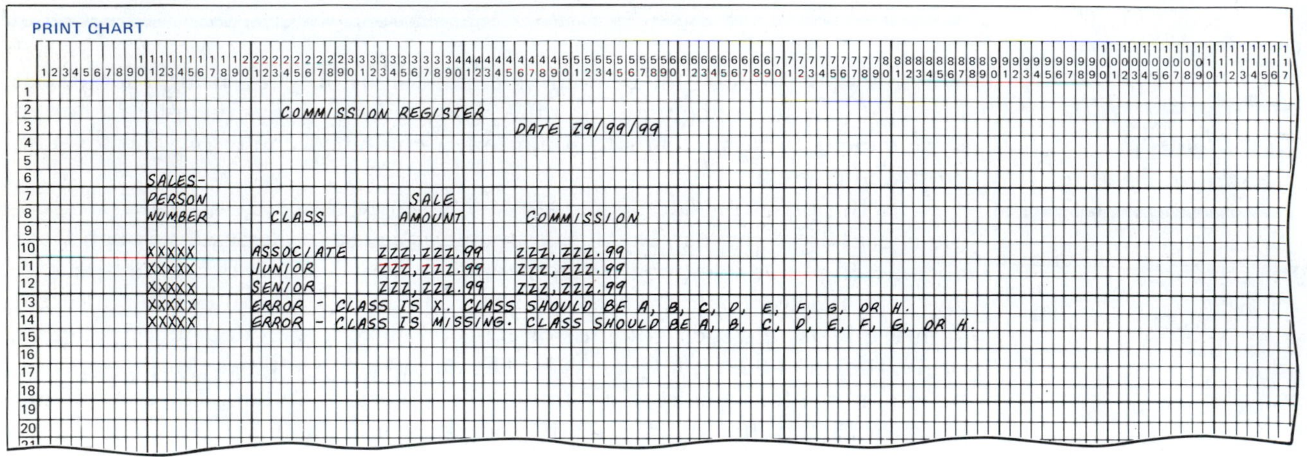

FIGURE 5.19 Hierarchy diagram for Program P05-02

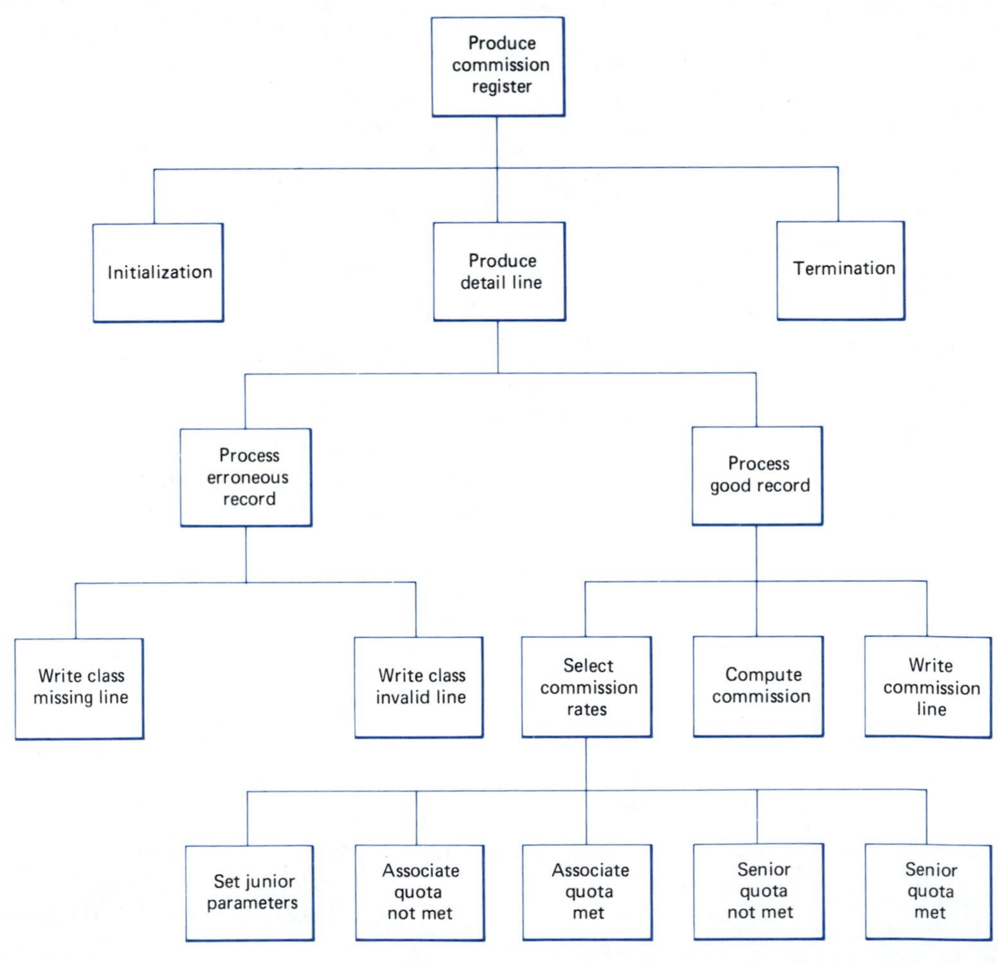

A hierarchy diagram for Program P05-02 is shown in Figure 5.19. Under "Produce detail line" there is shown one way to handle error checking in programs. We first separate the good records from the bad, and then execute either "Process erroneous record" or "Process good record," but not both. "Process erroneous record" determines whether the Class is missing or invalid and writes an appropriate error line.

"Process good record" is divided into three subfunctions. The first, "Select commission rates," determines which commission schedule to use on the basis of the salesperson's class and whether the salesperson met last year's quota. The remaining two subfunctions compute the commission on the Current Sale and write a detail line.

Program P05-02 is shown in Figure 5.20. Level-88 entries for the field CLASS-IN are shown in lines 00250 through 00290. Notice that it is legal to

FIGURE 5.20 **Program P05-02**

```
S COBOL II RELEASE 3.2 09/05/90                  P05002   DATE FEB 13,1992 T
----+-*A-1-B--+----2----+----3----+----4----+----5----+----6----+----7-%--+


00010  IDENTIFICATION DIVISION.
00020  PROGRAM-ID.  P05-02.
00030 *
00040 *     THIS PROGRAM COMPUTES SALESPERSON COMMISSIONS FOR JUNIOR
00050 *     SALESPERSONS, ASSOCIATE SALESPERSONS, AND SENIOR SALESPERSONS
00060 *
00070 *****************************************************************
00080
00090  ENVIRONMENT DIVISION.
00100  INPUT-OUTPUT SECTION.
00110  FILE-CONTROL.
00120      SELECT COMMISSION-REPORT ASSIGN TO PRINTER.
00130      SELECT SALES-FILE-IN     ASSIGN TO INFILE.
00140
00150 *****************************************************************
00160
00170  DATA DIVISION.
00180  FILE SECTION.
00190  FD  SALES-FILE-IN
00200      RECORD CONTAINS 80 CHARACTERS.
00210
00220  01  SALES-RECORD-IN.
00230      05 SALESPERSON-NUMBER-IN     PIC X(5).
00240      05 CLASS-IN                  PIC X.
00250         88 SALESPERSON-IS-JUNIOR     VALUES "A" THRU "F".
00260         88 SALESPERSON-IS-ASSOCIATE VALUE "G".
00270         88 SALESPERSON-IS-SENIOR     VALUE "H".
00280         88 VALID-CLASS-CODE          VALUES "A" THRU "H".
00290         88 CLASS-CODE-IS-MISSING     VALUE SPACE.
00300      05 LAST-YEARS-SALES-IN       PIC 9(6).
00310      05 CURRENT-SALE-IN           PIC 9(6)V99.
00320
00330
00340  FD  COMMISSION-REPORT.
00350
00360  01  REPORT-LINE                  PIC X(88).
00370
```

continued

have as many level-88 entries as desired, and they may have any VALUEs or combinations of VALUEs that you like.

A constant called NO-INPUT-DATA appears at line 00420. In this and nearly all subsequent programs, the program will check whether the input file contains no data and, if it does, will print out this constant.

At lines 00870 and 00880 we see for the first time a nonnumeric literal that is too long to fit on one line. The complete literal is supposed to be:

```
ERROR - CLASS IS MISSING. CLASS SHOULD BE A, B, C, D, E, F, G, OR H.
```

FIGURE 5.20 *continued*

```
S COBOL II RELEASE 3.2 09/05/90                    P05002   DATE FEB 13,1992 T
----+-*A-1-B--+----2----+----3----+----4----+----5----+----6----+----7-%--+

00380  WORKING-STORAGE SECTION.
00390  01  MORE-INPUT              PIC X      VALUE "Y".
00400      88 THERE-IS-NO-MORE-INPUT          VALUE "N".
00410      88 THERE-IS-NO-INPUT               VALUE "N".
00420  01  NO-INPUT-DATA           PIC X(15) VALUE "  NO INPUT DATA".
00430
00440  01  PAGE-HEAD-1.
00450      05                      PIC X(23) VALUE SPACES.
00460      05                      PIC X(19) VALUE "COMMISSION REGISTER".
00470
00480  01  PAGE-HEAD-2.
00490      05                      PIC X(45) VALUE SPACES.
00500      05                      PIC X(5)  VALUE "DATE".
00510      05 RUN-MONTH-AND-DAY    PIC Z9/99/.
00520      05 RUN-YEAR             PIC 99.
00530
00540  01  PAGE-HEAD-3.
00550      05                      PIC X(10) VALUE SPACES.
00560      05                      PIC X(6)  VALUE "SALES-".
00570
00580  01  PAGE-HEAD-4.
00590      05                      PIC X(10) VALUE SPACES.
00600      05                      PIC X(25) VALUE "PERSON".
00610      05                      PIC X(4)  VALUE "SALE".
00620
00630  01  PAGE-HEAD-5.
00640      05                      PIC X(10) VALUE SPACES.
00650      05                      PIC X(12) VALUE "NUMBER".
00660      05                      PIC X(12) VALUE "CLASS".
00670      05                      PIC X(12) VALUE "AMOUNT".
00680      05                      PIC X(10) VALUE "COMMISSION".
00690
00700  01  DETAIL-LINE.
00710      05 SALESPERSON-NUMBER-OUT     PIC B(10)X(5).
00720      05 CLASS-TITLE-OUT            PIC B(5)X(9)BBB.
00730      05 CURRENT-SALE-OUT           PIC ZZZ,ZZZ.99BBB.
00740      05 COMMISSION-OUT             PIC ZZZ,ZZZ.99.
00750
00760  01  CLASS-INVALID-LINE.
00770      05 SALESPERSON-NUMBER         PIC B(10)X(5)B(5).
00780      05                            PIC X(17)
00790                                    VALUE "ERROR - CLASS IS".
00800      05 INVALID-CLASS              PIC X.
00810      05                            PIC X(44)
00820          VALUE ". CLASS SHOULD BE A, B, C, D, E, F, G, OR H.".
00830
00840  01  CLASS-MISSING-LINE.
00850      05 SALESPERSON-NUMBER         PIC B(10)X(5)B(5).
00860      05                            PIC X(68)
00870          VALUE "ERROR - CLASS IS MISSING. CLASS SHOULD BE A, B, C,
00880 -        "D, E, F, G, OR H.".
```

Whenever a nonnumeric literal cannot fit on a line, you must write as much of it as you can all the way up through the rightmost position of area B of the line, even if it means breaking a word in the middle. All spaces and punctuation that you write up through the rightmost position of area B also count as part of the literal. Then in position 7 of the next line you must use a hyphen to indicate that this line is a continuation. Then you must write a quotation mark in area B to indicate that a nonnumeric literal is being continued, and then the rest of the literal followed by its closing quotation mark. Remember that we use the **continuation indicator** in position 7 only for continuing a literal from one line to the next and not to continue ordinary statements and entries. Also remember that we have gotten this far without previously using the continuation indicator.

The COMMISSION-RATES used by this program are written in lines 01060 through 01270. These entries show a hierarchy of fields. The field COMMISSION-RATES is defined as consisting of the three fields: ASSOCIATE-

FIGURE 5.20 *continued*

```
S COBOL II RELEASE 3.2 09/05/90                 P05002   DATE FEB 13,1992 T
----+-*A-1-B--+----2----+----3----+----4----+----5----+----6----+----7-%--+


00890
00900  01  COMMISSION-BREAK-POINTS.
00910      05 JUNIOR-BREAK-POINT          PIC 9       VALUE 0.
00920      05 ASSOCIATE-BREAK-POINT       PIC 9(5)    VALUE 10000.
00930      05 SENIOR-BREAK-POINT          PIC 9(5)    VALUE 50000.
00940
00950  01  SELECTED-COMMISSION-RATES.
00960      05 LOW-COMMISSION-RATE         PIC V99.
00970      05 HIGH-COMMISSION-RATE        PIC V99.
00980
00990  01  SELECTED-BREAK-POINT           PIC 9(5).
01000
01010  01  SALE-QUOTAS.
01020      05 JUNIOR-SALE-QUOTA           PIC 9       VALUE 0.
01030      05 ASSOCIATE-SALE-QUOTA        PIC 9(6)    VALUE 150000.
01040      05 SENIOR-SALE-QUOTA           PIC 9(6)    VALUE 250000.
01050
01060  01  COMMISSION-RATES.
01070      05 ASSOCIATE-RATES.
01080         10 QUOTA-NOT-MET.
01090            15 LOW-RATE              PIC V99     VALUE .05.
01100            15 HIGH-RATE             PIC V99     VALUE .20.
01110         10 QUOTA-MET.
01120            15 LOW-RATE              PIC V99     VALUE .20.
01130            15 HIGH-RATE             PIC V99     VALUE .30.
01140      05 SENIOR-RATES.
01150         10 QUOTA-NOT-MET.
01160            15 LOW-RATE              PIC V99     VALUE .20.
01170            15 HIGH-RATE             PIC V99     VALUE .30.
01180         10 QUOTA-MET.
01190            15 LOW-RATE              PIC V99     VALUE .30.
01200            15 HIGH-RATE             PIC V99     VALUE .40.
01210      05 JUNIOR-RATES.
01220         10 QUOTA-NOT-MET.
01230            15 LOW-RATE              PIC V99     VALUE .10.
01240            15 HIGH-RATE             PIC V99     VALUE .10.
01250         10 QUOTA-MET.
01260            15 LOW-RATE              PIC V99     VALUE .10.
01270            15 HIGH-RATE             PIC V99     VALUE .10.
```

continued

RATES, SENIOR-RATES, and JUNIOR-RATES. In turn, each of those fields consists of two fields called QUOTA-NOT-MET and QUOTA-MET. And each of those consists of the elementary items LOW-RATE and HIGH-RATE. In this way all the commission rates from the problem are written into the program. Even though junior salespeople have only one commission rate, 10%, it was entered in a form consistent with the rates for associate and senior salespeople.

At line 01700 there is a negated simple condition, formed by placing the word NOT before the condition name VALID-CLASS-CODE. Lines 01950 through 02140 show a nested IF statement which contains a combined condition at lines 01980 and 01990.

FIGURE 5.20 ***continued***

```
S COBOL II RELEASE 3.2 09/05/90                     P05002    DATE FEB 13,1992 T
----+-*A-1-B--+----2----+----3----+----4----+----5----+----6----+----7-%--+

01280
01290  01  TODAYS-DATE.
01300      05 RUN-YEAR                     PIC 99.
01310      05 RUN-MONTH-AND-DAY            PIC 9(4).
01320
01330 *******************************************************************
01340
01350  PROCEDURE DIVISION.
01360  PRODUCE-COMMISSION-REGISTER.
01370      PERFORM INITIALIZATION
01380      PERFORM PRODUCE-DETAIL-LINE UNTIL THERE-IS-NO-MORE-INPUT
01390      PERFORM TERMINATION
01400      STOP RUN
01410      .
01420
01430  INITIALIZATION.
01440      OPEN INPUT  SALES-FILE-IN
01450           OUTPUT COMMISSION-REPORT
01460      ACCEPT TODAYS-DATE FROM DATE
01470      MOVE CORR TODAYS-DATE TO PAGE-HEAD-2
01480      WRITE REPORT-LINE FROM PAGE-HEAD-1 AFTER PAGE
01490      WRITE REPORT-LINE FROM PAGE-HEAD-2
01500      WRITE REPORT-LINE FROM PAGE-HEAD-3 AFTER 3
01510      WRITE REPORT-LINE FROM PAGE-HEAD-4
01520      WRITE REPORT-LINE FROM PAGE-HEAD-5
01530      MOVE SPACES TO REPORT-LINE
01540      WRITE REPORT-LINE
01550      READ SALES-FILE-IN
01560          AT END
01570              SET THERE-IS-NO-INPUT TO TRUE
01580      END-READ
01590      IF THERE-IS-NO-INPUT
01600          WRITE REPORT-LINE FROM NO-INPUT-DATA AFTER 2
01610      END-IF
01620      .
01630
01640  TERMINATION.
01650      CLOSE SALES-FILE-IN
01660            COMMISSION-REPORT
01670      .
```

FIGURE 5.20 *continued*

```
PRODUCE-DETAIL-LINE.
    IF NOT VALID-CLASS-CODE
        PERFORM PROCESS-ERRONEOUS-RECORD
    ELSE
        PERFORM PROCESS-GOOD-RECORD
    END-IF
    READ SALES-FILE-IN
        AT END
            SET THERE-IS-NO-MORE-INPUT TO TRUE
    .

PROCESS-ERRONEOUS-RECORD.
    IF CLASS-CODE-IS-MISSING
        PERFORM WRITE-CLASS-MISSING-LINE
    ELSE
        PERFORM WRITE-CLASS-INVALID-LINE
    END-IF
    .

PROCESS-GOOD-RECORD.
    PERFORM SELECT-COMMISSION-RATES
    PERFORM COMPUTE-COMMISSION
    PERFORM WRITE-COMMISSION-LINE
    .

SELECT-COMMISSION-RATES.
    IF SALESPERSON-IS-JUNIOR
        PERFORM SET-JUNIOR-PARAMETERS
    ELSE
        IF SALESPERSON-IS-ASSOCIATE AND
           LAST-YEARS-SALES-IN LESS THAN ASSOCIATE-SALE-QUOTA
            PERFORM ASSOCIATE-QUOTA-NOT-MET
        ELSE
            IF SALESPERSON-IS-ASSOCIATE
                PERFORM ASSOCIATE-QUOTA-MET
            ELSE
                IF LAST-YEARS-SALES-IN LESS THAN
                                         SENIOR-SALE-QUOTA
                    PERFORM SENIOR-QUOTA-NOT-MET
                ELSE
                    PERFORM SENIOR-QUOTA-MET
                END-IF
            END-IF
        END-IF
    END-IF
    .

WRITE-CLASS-MISSING-LINE.
    MOVE SALESPERSON-NUMBER-IN TO
         SALESPERSON-NUMBER IN CLASS-MISSING-LINE
    WRITE REPORT-LINE FROM CLASS-MISSING-LINE
    .

WRITE-CLASS-INVALID-LINE.
    MOVE CLASS-IN TO INVALID-CLASS
    MOVE SALESPERSON-NUMBER-IN TO
         SALESPERSON-NUMBER IN CLASS-INVALID-LINE
    WRITE REPORT-LINE FROM CLASS-INVALID-LINE
    .
```

continued

There are many examples of data-name qualification. Many of them show that more than one level of qualification may sometimes be needed to identify a field uniquely. The name

```
HIGH-RATE IN QUOTA-MET IN JUNIOR-RATES
```

at line 02320 could not be made unique except with the two levels of qualification shown.

FIGURE 5.20 *continued*

```
S COBOL II RELEASE 3.2 09/05/90                    P05002   DATE FEB 13,1992 T
----+-*A-1-B--+----2----+----3----+----4----+----5----+----6----+----7-%--+

02280
02290  SET-JUNIOR-PARAMETERS.
02300      MOVE JUNIOR-BREAK-POINT TO SELECTED-BREAK-POINT
02310      MOVE "JUNIOR"           TO CLASS-TITLE-OUT
02320      MOVE HIGH-RATE IN QUOTA-MET IN JUNIOR-RATES TO
02330           HIGH-COMMISSION-RATE
02340      MOVE LOW-RATE  IN QUOTA-MET IN JUNIOR-RATES TO
02350           LOW-COMMISSION-RATE
02360      .
02370
02380  ASSOCIATE-QUOTA-NOT-MET.
02390      MOVE ASSOCIATE-BREAK-POINT TO SELECTED-BREAK-POINT
02400      MOVE "ASSOCIATE"           TO CLASS-TITLE-OUT
02410      MOVE HIGH-RATE IN QUOTA-NOT-MET IN ASSOCIATE-RATES TO
02420           HIGH-COMMISSION-RATE
02430      MOVE LOW-RATE  IN QUOTA-NOT-MET IN ASSOCIATE-RATES TO
02440           LOW-COMMISSION-RATE
02450      .
02460
02470  ASSOCIATE-QUOTA-MET.
02480      MOVE ASSOCIATE-BREAK-POINT TO SELECTED-BREAK-POINT
02490      MOVE "ASSOCIATE"           TO CLASS-TITLE-OUT
02500      MOVE HIGH-RATE IN QUOTA-MET IN ASSOCIATE-RATES TO
02510           HIGH-COMMISSION-RATE
02520      MOVE LOW-RATE  IN QUOTA-MET IN ASSOCIATE-RATES TO
02530           LOW-COMMISSION-RATE
02540      .
02550
02560  SENIOR-QUOTA-NOT-MET.
02570      MOVE SENIOR-BREAK-POINT TO SELECTED-BREAK-POINT
02580      MOVE "SENIOR"           TO CLASS-TITLE-OUT
02590      MOVE HIGH-RATE IN QUOTA-NOT-MET IN SENIOR-RATES TO
02600           HIGH-COMMISSION-RATE
02610      MOVE LOW-RATE  IN QUOTA-NOT-MET IN SENIOR-RATES TO
02620           LOW-COMMISSION-RATE
02630      .
02640
02650  SENIOR-QUOTA-MET.
02660      MOVE SENIOR-BREAK-POINT TO SELECTED-BREAK-POINT
02670      MOVE "SENIOR"           TO CLASS-TITLE-OUT
02680      MOVE HIGH-RATE IN QUOTA-MET IN SENIOR-RATES TO
02690           HIGH-COMMISSION-RATE
02700      MOVE LOW-RATE  IN QUOTA-MET IN SENIOR-RATES TO
02710           LOW-COMMISSION-RATE
02720      .
```

FIGURE 5.20 *continued*

```

COMPUTE-COMMISSION.
    IF CURRENT-SALE-IN GREATER THAN SELECTED-BREAK-POINT
        COMPUTE COMMISSION-OUT ROUNDED =
            LOW-COMMISSION-RATE * SELECTED-BREAK-POINT +
            HIGH-COMMISSION-RATE *
                (CURRENT-SALE-IN - SELECTED-BREAK-POINT)
    ELSE
        COMPUTE COMMISSION-OUT ROUNDED =
            LOW-COMMISSION-RATE * CURRENT-SALE-IN
    END-IF
    .

WRITE-COMMISSION-LINE.
    MOVE SALESPERSON-NUMBER-IN TO SALESPERSON-NUMBER-OUT
    MOVE CURRENT-SALE-IN       TO CURRENT-SALE-OUT
    WRITE REPORT-LINE FROM DETAIL-LINE
    .
```

Program P05-02 was run with the input data shown in Figure 5.21 and produced the output shown in Figure 5.22. Then it was run with an empty input file and produced the output shown in Figure 5.23.

FIGURE 5.21 **Input to Program P05-02**

```
--------------------------------------------------------------------------------
         1         2         3         4         5         6         7         8
12345678901234567890123456789012345678901234567890123456789012345678901234567890
--------------------------------------------------------------------------------
14756G08994307059243
14758G22342101000000
15008H07076399804299
19123H17036705376542
14689 16900001245968
10089G08054604307865
17665G15000008870099
15699A00000003000099
15003H06576305000000
12231B19630024367921
14769G21991219445399
15013H06920000782135
15014H42310003596299
14770G17630008235643
14771G29342100936951
15000Z24936204345621
15002H03421601934526
15004H02632105732123
12352G16030000698234
15006H07962303922431
14757G10009900198499
15010H25192304736554
13834F12989604598799
15011H25743205078654
14764I15054320909324
15015H28996507987523
14759G02980004783965
15016H48990008535942
14761G06597600643912
15012H25000009368342
```

FIGURE 5.22 Output from Program P05-02

```
                    COMMISSION REGISTER
                                          DATE   2/13/92


SALES-
PERSON                      SALE
NUMBER       CLASS         AMOUNT        COMMISSION

14756      ASSOCIATE      70,592.43     12,618.49
14758      ASSOCIATE      10,000.00      2,000.00
15008      SENIOR        998,042.99    294,412.90
19123      SENIOR         53,765.42     11,129.63
14689      ERROR - CLASS IS MISSING. CLASS SHOULD BE A, B, C, D, E, F, G, OR H.
10089      ASSOCIATE      43,078.65      7,115.73
17665      ASSOCIATE      88,700.99     25,610.30
15699      JUNIOR         30,000.99      3,000.10
15003      SENIOR         50,000.00     10,000.00
12231      JUNIOR        243,679.21     24,367.92
14769      ASSOCIATE     194,453.99     57,336.20
15013      SENIOR          7,821.35      1,564.27
15014      SENIOR         35,962.99     10,788.90
14770      ASSOCIATE      82,356.43     23,706.93
14771      ASSOCIATE       9,369.51      1,873.90
15000      ERROR - CLASS IS Z. CLASS SHOULD BE A, B, C, D, E, F, G, OR H.
15002      SENIOR         19,345.26      3,869.05
15004      SENIOR         57,321.23     12,196.37
12352      ASSOCIATE       6,982.34      1,396.47
15006      SENIOR         39,224.31      7,844.86
14757      ASSOCIATE       1,984.99         99.25
15010      SENIOR         47,365.54     14,209.66
13834      JUNIOR         45,987.99      4,598.80
15011      SENIOR         50,786.54     15,314.62
14764      ERROR - CLASS IS 1. CLASS SHOULD BE A, B, C, D, E, F, G, OR H.
15015      SENIOR         79,875.23     26,950.09
14759      ASSOCIATE      47,839.65      8,067.93
15016      SENIOR         85,359.42     29,143.77
14761      ASSOCIATE       6,439.12        321.96
15012      SENIOR         93,683.42     32,473.37
```

FIGURE 5.23 Output produced when Program P05-02 was run with an empty input file

```
                    COMMISSION REGISTER
                                          DATE   2/13/92


SALES-
PERSON                      SALE
NUMBER       CLASS         AMOUNT        COMMISSION


NO INPUT DATA
```

A Special Kind of IF Statement

The nested IF statement in Program P05-02 is of a special type, in that the words IF and ELSE alternate. In this kind of IF statement, it is very easy to see which ELSE belongs to which IF since there are no unrelated IFs and ELSEs in the way. In such a statement only one, or none, of the True paths is executed each time the statement is executed. Since it is easy to know which ELSE belongs to which IF, it is not important to indent the levels of the nest as we have done. In fact, some programmers feel that since one of the True paths at most will be executed, it is clearer to write it this way:

```
IF SALESPERSON-IS-JUNIOR
    PERFORM SET-JUNIOR-PARAMETERS
ELSE
IF SALESPERSON-IS-ASSOCIATE AND
   LAST-YEARS-SALES-IN-LESS THAN ASSOCIATE-SALE-QUOTA
    PERFORM ASSOCIATE-QUOTA-NOT-MET
ELSE
IF SALESPERSON-IS-ASSOCIATE
    PERFORM ASSOCIATE-QUOTA-MET
ELSE
IF LAST-YEARS-SALES-IN LESS THAN SENIOR-SALE-QUOTA
    PERFORM SENIOR-QUOTA-NOT-MET
ELSE
    PERFORM SENIOR-QUOTA-MET
END-IF
END-IF
END-IF
END-IF
```

EXERCISE 9

Rewrite the IF statement in lines 01950 through 02130 of Program P05-02 without using a combined condition. The resulting IF statement no longer will have alternating IFs and ELSEs. Which of the two forms of the IF statement do you think is easier to understand? What are the good and bad features of each form of the statement?

Summary

The IF statement enables a COBOL program to make decisions on the basis of data. The decision determines which of two paths will be executed. Either or both of the paths may contain as many processing steps as needed. When the True path contains no processing, the CONTINUE statement may be used. If the False path contains processing, the reserved word ELSE must be used to show where the False path begins. The reserved word END-IF terminates the IF statement and shows where the True and False paths rejoin. The coding of the True and False paths is indented to improve program readability. Indenting is not examined by the COBOL system.

A nested IF statement consists of one or more IF statements in the True and/or False paths of another IF statement. An IF statement may be nested to essentially any level. It is recommended that each IF statement in the nest be terminated with END-IF. For the programmer to keep track of which ELSE and which END-IF belong to which IF, conventional indenting should be adhered to. There may be as many processing steps as desired in any of the paths at any level of the nest, and any path containing no processing may use the CONTINUE statement. The phrase ELSE CONTINUE may be omitted wherever it may happen to appear if END-IF is used to terminate each IF statement.

The five simple conditions are the relation condition, the condition-name condition, the class condition, the sign condition, and the switch-status condition. Condition-name conditions depend on level-88 entries.

A level-88 entry may be used to give a condition name to particular values of fields. When a level-88 entry is used, the field must still be defined in the usual way. Condition names can be used in the File Section and the Working Storage Section. When a level-88 entry is used, it must immediately follow the description of the field to which it applies. A level-88 entry must contain exactly one VALUE clause and no other clauses, especially no PICTURE clause.

The complex conditions are the negated simple condition, as IF NOT VALID-CODE, the combined condition, as IF A = B AND C = D, and the negated combined condition, as IF NOT (A = B AND C = D). Care should be taken to avoid writing IF statements whose meaning is not clear to the human reader.

A special kind of nested IF statement is one in which the IFs and ELSEs alternate and there are no intervening IFs or ELSEs. Special indenting conventions different from the indenting used for regular nested IF statements are often used in writing such a statement.

Fill-In Exercises

1. The ______ statement may be used whenever an IF statement contains processing in the False path but not in the True path.
2. The phrase ______ ______ may be omitted wherever it happens to appear if every IF statement is terminated with END-IF.
3. In a nested IF statement the ______ appearance of the word IF begins the outer IF.
4. Use of proper ______ enables the programmer to see which ELSE belongs to which IF.
5. IF statements may be ______ to any level.
6. Simple conditions may be connected by the words ______ and ______ to form combined conditions.
7. Placing the word NOT before a simple condition forms a ______ ______ ______.
8. Placing the word NOT before a combined condition in parentheses forms a ______ ______ ______.
9. The order of evaluation in a combined condition is ______ first and then ______.
10. If the same ______ and/or ______ appears in more than one relation condition in a combined condition, the repetitions may be omitted.
11. A level-88 entry can be used to give a ______ to one or more values that might be assigned to a field.
12. Exactly one ______ clause is required in a level-88 entry.
13. In a flowchart of a decision the True path and the False path must ______ before the flowchart can continue.
14. The five simple conditions in COBOL are the relation condition, the ______ condition, the ______ condition, the ______ condition, and the ______ condition.
15. The continuation indicator is the character ______ in position ______ of the continuation line.

Review Exercises

1. Write a program to the following specifications:

Input

Records in the following format:

Positions	Field
1–5	Employee Number
6	Overtime Eligibility Indicator E—Exempt (not eligible for overtime pay) N—Nonexempt (eligible for overtime pay)
7–9	Hours Worked (to one decimal place)
10–80	spaces

Output

Use the output format shown in Figure 5.RE1.

FIGURE *5.RE1* Output format for Review Exercise 1

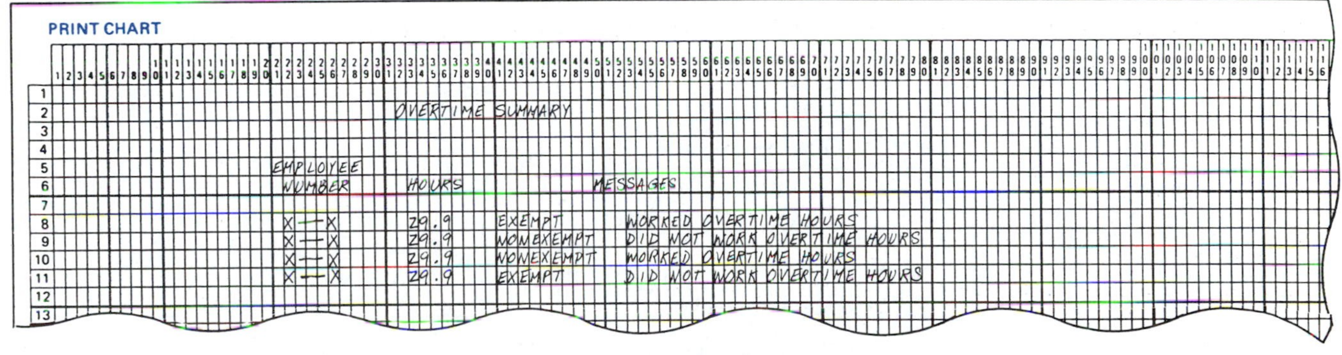

Processing

For each employee print the Employee Number and the Hours Worked. If the employee is exempt from overtime pay, print the word EXEMPT. If the employee is nonexempt, print the word NONEXEMPT. If the Hours Worked are more than 40, print WORKED OVERTIME HOURS. If the Hours Worked are not more than 40, print DID NOT WORK OVERTIME HOURS.

2. Write a program using the same input format as in Review Exercise 1, and produce output in the format shown in Figure 5.RE2. For each input record, have your program print the Employee Number and the Hours Worked. Also, if the employee is eligible for overtime pay and the Hours Worked are more than 40, have your program print the words OVERTIME PAY. Have your program produce at least three pages of output.

FIGURE 5.RE2 Output format for Review Exercise 2

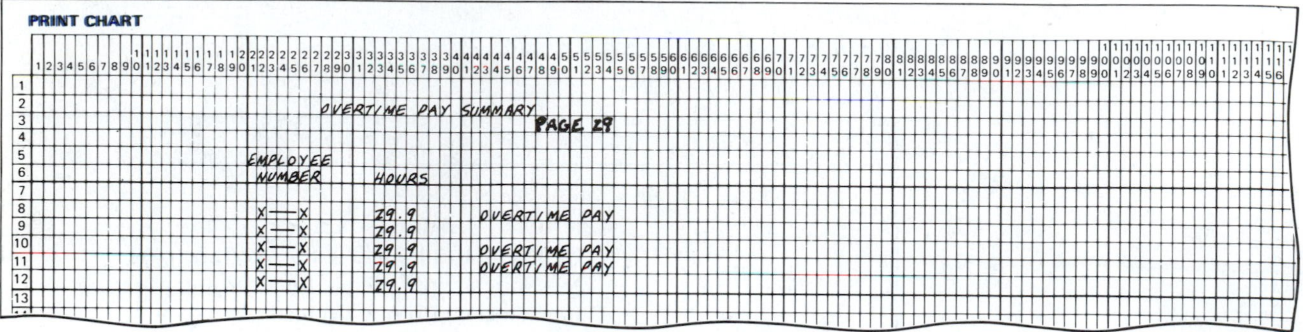

3. Write a program to process input data in the following format:

Positions	Field
1–9	Social Security Number
10	Job Grade
11–18	Annual Salary (to two decimal places)
19–80	spaces

Each input record is for one employee and shows the employee's Job Grade and current Annual Salary. The Job Grades are V through Z and 1 through 6. The titles for each grade are:

Z Smelter apprentice
Y Junior smelter
X Smelter
W Gang chief
V Foreman
6 Superintendent
5–1 Plant manager

The program is required to compute a cost-of-living raise for each employee on the basis of the employee's Job Grade and current Annual Salary and to print the results in the format shown in Figure 5.RE3. The schedule for cost-of-living increases is as follows:

Job Grade	Annual Salary	Increase
Any	Less than $15,000	15% of current salary
Z	Any	15% of curent salary
V–Y	$15,000–	7% of current salary, plus $1200
V–Y	$20,000 and over	5% of current salary, plus $1600
4–6	$15,000–19,999.99	15% of current salary
4–6	$20,000 and over	$3,000
1–3	$15,000 and over	$2,250

Have your program produce at least three pages of output.

FIGURE 5.RE3 Output format for Review Exercise 3

```
PRINT CHART

                          COST-OF-LIVING INCREASES SCHEDULE
          PAGE Z9                                DATE PRODUCED Z9/99/99

           EMPLOYEE SOCIAL                 CURRENT                      NEW
           SECURITY NUMBER      GRADE       SALARY       INCREASE      SALARY

              XXX-XX-XXXX         X      ZZZ,ZZZ.99     Z,ZZZ.99    ZZZ,ZZZ.99
              XXX-XX-XXXX         X      ZZZ,ZZZ.99     Z,ZZZ.99    ZZZ,ZZZ.99
              XXX-XX-XXXX         X      ZZZ,ZZZ.99     Z,ZZZ.99    ZZZ,ZZZ.99
          **  XXX-XX-XXXX         X ERROR - INVALID GRADE.
          **  XXX-XX-XXXX           ERROR - GRADE MISSING.
```

4. Modify your solution to Review Exercise 3 to count the number of employees in each Job Grade and also to compute the total current salaries, the total increases, and the total salaries after the increase. The program should produce output in the format shown in Figure 5.RE4.

FIGURE 5.RE4 Output format for Review Exercise 4

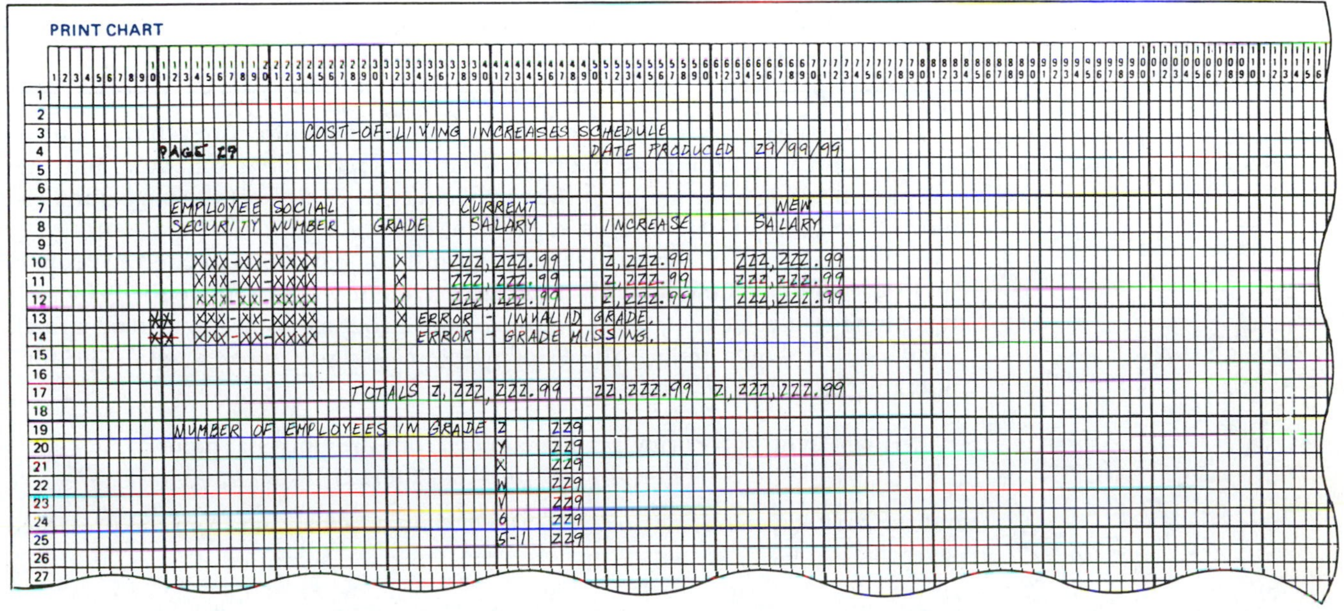

5. Draw a flowchart showing the logic of the following statement:

```
IF C1
    CONTINUE
ELSE
    IF C2
        PERFORM P2
        PERFORM P3
        IF C3
            IF C4
                PERFORM P4
            ELSE
                CONTINUE
            END-IF
        ELSE
            CONTINUE
        END-IF
    ELSE
        PERFORM P5
    END-IF
    PERFORM P1
END-IF
```

6. Rewrite the statement in Review Exercise 5 by combining C3 and C4 into a combined condition. Reduce the depth of nesting by one level.

Project

Modify your solution to the Project in Chapter 4, page 108. Have your program READ any number of input records, each relating to a different automobile loan, and produce a separate repayment schedule for each loan in the format shown in Figure 5.P1. Have your program read input records in the following format:

Positions	Field
1–7	Starting Loan Amount (dollars and cents)
8–13	Monthly Payment (dollars and cents)
14–17	Annual Interest Rate
18–80	spaces

Have your program skip to a new page at the beginning of each repayment schedule and when the page overflows within a repayment schedule. Put the complete heading information at the top of every page. Restart the page numbering at 1 at the beginning of each repayment schedule.

Have your repayment schedules print just the payments needed to reduce the Principal Remaining to zero. If the last payment would reduce the Principal Remaining to a value less than zero, have your program compute instead a final payment that would reduce the Principal Remaining to zero exactly. The formula for the final payment is:

$$\text{Final Payment} = \text{Principal Remaining from previous payment} * (1 + \text{Annual Interest Rate}/12)$$

and the final Payment to Principal is the Principal Remaining from the previous payment.

FIGURE 5.P1 Output format for Chapter 5 Project

PRINT CHART

```
          AUTO LOAN REPAYMENT SCHEDULE                  PAGE Z9

                  STARTING LOAN AMOUNT =  ZZ,ZZ9.99
                  PAYMENT AMOUNT       =   Z,ZZ9.99
                  ANNUAL INTEREST RATE =     Z9.99%


                                PAYMENT
    PAYMENT                       TO           PRINCIPAL
    NUMBER       INTEREST      PRINCIPAL       REMAINING

         1       Z,ZZ9.99       Z,ZZ9.99       ZZ,ZZ9.99
         2       Z,ZZ9.99       Z,ZZ9.99       ZZ,ZZ9.99
         3       Z,ZZ9.99       Z,ZZ9.99       ZZ,ZZ9.99
         4       Z,ZZ9.99       Z,ZZ9.99       ZZ,ZZ9.99
         .           .              .               .
         .           .              .               .
         .           .              .               .

        Z9       Z,ZZ9.99       Z,ZZ9.99       ZZ,ZZ9.99
        Z9       Z,ZZ9.99       Z,ZZ9.99            0.00   FINAL PAYMENT = Z,ZZ9.99
```

You will need two PERFORM loops in this program, one inside the other. You will need an ordinary main loop, controlled by a PERFORM statement and executed until there is no more input. Somewhere within the main loop, you will need a PERFORM statement to generate one repayment schedule (PERFORM . . . UNTIL PRINCIPAL-REMAINING = ZERO). Each PERFORM statement will need its own kind of initialization immediately preceding it, similar to the initialization each has had in previous programs.

Design this program carefully and draw a hierarchy diagram before you begin coding. When you make up your input data, be sure your monthly payments are large enough to reduce the Principal Remaining each month; else the Principal Remaining will never get to zero and your program will be in an endless loop.

CHAPTER 6 The EVALUATE Statement

HERE ARE THE KEY POINTS YOU SHOULD LEARN FROM THIS CHAPTER

1. The main forms of the EVALUATE statement
2. The purpose of the EVALUATE statement
3. How to use EVALUATE statements to implement multi-branch flowchart decision logic
4. How to construct and use decision tables
5. How to use EVALUATE statements to implement decision-table logic

KEY WORDS TO RECOGNIZE AND LEARN

EVALUATE	OTHER
case	TRUE
multi-branch	FALSE
decision table	ANY
selection subject	ALSO
selection object	set of selection subjects
WHEN	set of selection objects
END-EVALUATE	explicit scope terminator

The **EVALUATE** statement is intended to be used to code the kind of program logic called **case.** A case arises in a flowchart when a decision box has more than two branches out and when the several branches out of the decision box have no processing in common. Figure 6.1 shows such a **multi-branch** situation. Notice that all branches of the case eventually rejoin so that the program logic may continue.

In Figure 6.1 a single field is being tested, and the results of the test direct the program to one of four branches. Another and very powerful use of the EVALUATE statement occurs when the flow of program control is dependent not on the value of a single field as in Figure 6.1 but on the values of several fields in combination. Often, such logic is too complicated to be shown clearly in a flowchart, and a **decision table** can be used to show the logic instead. We will look at complicated logic and complicated uses of the EVALUATE statement

FIGURE 6.1 A case

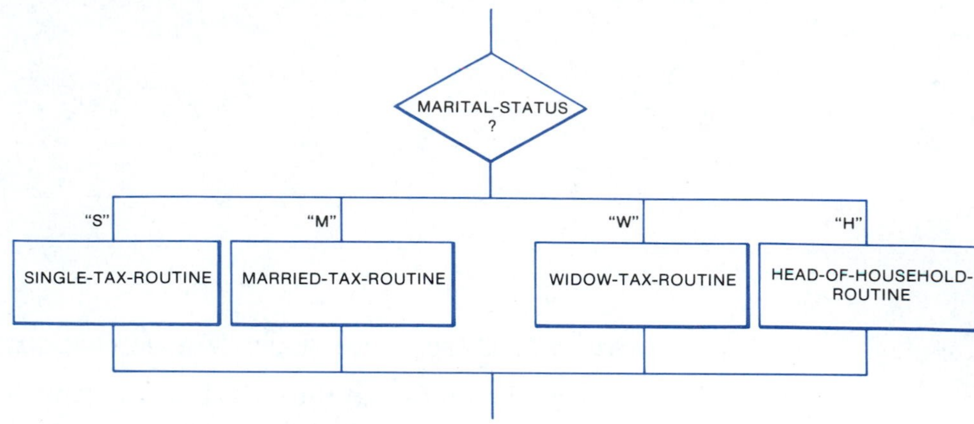

later in the chapter, but first let's look at a straightforward one and see how to code the logic shown in Figure 6.1.

An Easy EVALUATE Statement

The logic in Figure 6.1 can be coded as follows:

```
EVALUATE MARITAL-STATUS
    WHEN "S"
        PERFORM SINGLE-TAX-ROUTINE
    WHEN "M"
        PERFORM MARRIED-TAX-ROUTINE
    WHEN "W"
        PERFORM WIDOW-TAX-ROUTINE
    WHEN "H"
        PERFORM HEAD-OF-HOUSEHOLD-ROUTINE
END-EVALUATE
```

The field MARITAL-STATUS is called the **selection subject** in this EVALUATE statement. Each of the literals, S, M, W, and H, in the statement is called a **selection object.** When an EVALUATE statement executes, the **WHEN** phrases are evaluated in turn, in the order in which they appear in the statement, until one of the WHEN phrases is satisfied. In this statement, a WHEN phrase is satisfied when the literal in it equals the contents of the field MARITAL-STATUS. Once a WHEN phrase is satisfied, the next executable statement following it is executed, and then program control passes to **END-EVALUATE** and the program continues from there. If none of the WHEN phrases can be satisfied, program control passes to END-EVALUATE and the program continues.

Forms of the EVALUATE Statement

The EVALUATE statement can be written in many different forms, and so can provide for a great variety of types of condition testing. To demonstrate several ways in which an EVALUATE statement can be written, let us look for a moment at one of the IF statements from Chapter 5:

```
IF QUANTITY-ON-HAND IS LESS THAN 400
    MOVE "REORDER" TO MESSAGE-SPACE
ELSE
    MOVE SPACES TO MESSAGE-SPACE
END-IF
```

This same logic can be written in several ways using an EVALUATE statement. In actual practice, you would not use an EVALUATE statement where a straightforward IF statement such as this one would do. Here we are using it only to demonstrate the great flexibility of the EVALUATE statement. We now show six of the ways the logic of the IF statement can be written. There are many more.

1.
```
EVALUATE QUANTITY-ON-HAND
      WHEN 0 THROUGH 399
            MOVE "REORDER" TO MESSAGE-SPACE
      WHEN 400 THROUGH 999
            MOVE SPACES TO MESSAGE-SPACE
END-EVALUATE
```

or

2.
```
EVALUATE QUANTITY-ON-HAND
     WHEN 0 THROUGH 399
           MOVE "REORDER" TO MESSAGE-SPACE
     WHEN NOT 0 THROUGH 399
           MOVE SPACES TO MESSAGE-SPACE
END-EVALUATE
```

or, using the reserved word **OTHER:**

3.
```
EVALUATE QUANTITY-ON-HAND
     WHEN 0 THROUGH 399
           MOVE "REORDER" TO MESSAGE-SPACE
     WHEN OTHER
           MOVE SPACES TO MESSAGE-SPACE
END-EVALUATE
```

or, using the reserved words **TRUE** and **FALSE:**

4.
```
EVALUATE QUANTITY-ON-HAND LESS THAN 400
     WHEN TRUE
         MOVE "REORDER" TO MESSAGE-SPACE
     WHEN FALSE
         MOVE SPACES TO MESSAGE-SPACE
END-EVALUATE
```

or

5.
```
EVALUATE QUANTITY-ON-HAND LESS THAN 400
     WHEN TRUE
           MOVE "REORDER" TO MESSAGE-SPACE
     WHEN OTHER
           MOVE SPACES TO MESSAGE-SPACE
END-EVALUATE
```

or, using the reserved word **ANY:**

```
6. EVALUATE TRUE
       WHEN QUANTITY-ON-HAND IS LESS THAN 400
               MOVE "REORDER" TO MESSAGE-SPACE
       WHEN ANY
               MOVE SPACES TO MESSAGE-SPACE
   END-EVALUATE
```

Notice that the phrases THROUGH and NOT . . . THROUGH using literals can serve as selection objects, as in statements 1 and 2. Whenever literals are used in selection objects or subjects, they must agree in category with the selection subjects or objects to which they correspond. In this statement, QUANTITY-ON-HAND is defined as numeric, and so the literals must be numeric. If the selection subject had been defined as alphanumeric, as in the very first EVALUATE statement in this chapter, then the literals in the selection object would be nonnumeric.

When the reserved word OTHER is used, as in statements 3 and 5, it must appear only in the last WHEN phrase of the statement. A conditional expression may appear as a selection subject (as in statements 4 and 5) or selection object (as in statement 6). Any conditions that are legal in IF statements are legal in EVALUATE statements, and so may include relation conditions, condition-name conditions, combined conditions, negated conditions, and so on. The reserved words TRUE and FALSE may appear as selection subjects (as in statement 6) and selection objects (as in statements 4 and 5).

We will examine the format of the EVALUATE statement at the end of this chapter.

EVALUATE Statements with Multiple Conditions

EVALUATE statements can handle the same kind of flow found in nested IF statements, sometimes more conveniently and sometimes less so. Let's look at the logic of a nested IF statement from Chapter 5 and see whether an EVALUATE statement can do the job better. Figure 5.13 is reproduced here for convenience as Figure 6.2. The logic of the flowchart can be coded as follows, using the reserved word **ALSO:**

```
EVALUATE C1    ALSO C2     ALSO C3
    WHEN TRUE  ALSO TRUE   ALSO ANY
                                PERFORM P1
    WHEN TRUE  ALSO FALSE  ALSO ANY
                                PERFORM P1
                                PERFORM P2
                                PERFORM P3
    WHEN FALSE ALSO ANY    ALSO TRUE
                                PERFORM P4
    WHEN FALSE ALSO ANY    ALSO FALSE
                                PERFORM P5
END-EVALUATE
```

In this form of the EVALUATE statement all the conditions to be tested, C1, C2, and C3, are written immediately following the word EVALUATE, to form what is called a **set of selection subjects.** Then in each WHEN phrase there must be a **set of selection objects,** where each selection object in the set matches a corresponding selection subject. Each WHEN phrase lists the out-

FIGURE 6.2 **Flowchart of logic in which each path of the outer decision contains a decision**

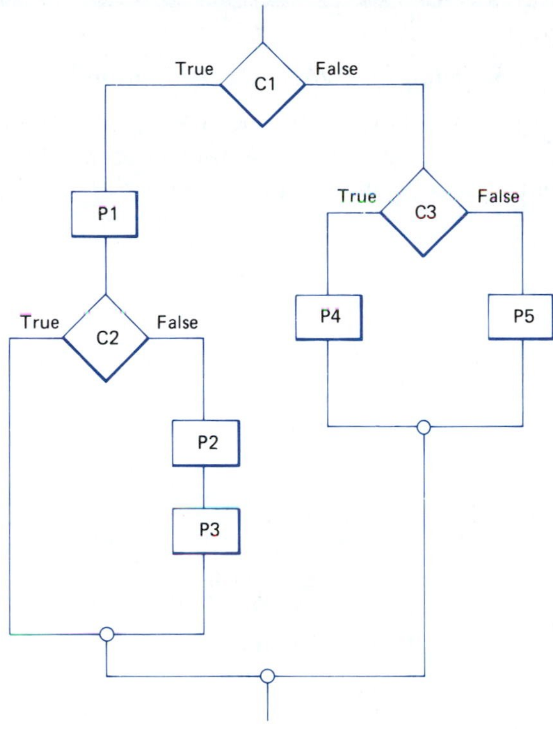

comes of all the condition tests, or the reserved word ANY is used if a particular outcome is immaterial to the processing. For example in the first WHEN phrase, where C1 and C2 are TRUE, C3 is immaterial, and so the selection object corresponding to it is shown as ANY. Notice that in this statement it was necessary to write PERFORM P1 twice. PERFORM P1 must be written twice because the flowchart of Figure 6.2 does not describe a true case. In a true case, the several paths have no processing in common, and only one True path at most can ever be executed in a single pass through the logic. In Figure 6.2, P1 is executed whether C2 is True or False, and the True paths of both C1 and C2 could be executed in a single pass through the logic.

One advantage of writing this logic as an EVALUATE statement instead of an IF is that the programmer can see at a glance which procedures are always PERFORMed together and which can never be PERFORMed together in one pass through the logic. For example, the EVALUATE statement shows clearly that under certain conditions, P1, P2, and P3 can be PERFORMed one after the other in one pass through the statement, but that P1 and P4 can never be PERFORMed together in one pass through.

EXERCISE 1 Code the logic of the flowchart shown in Figure 5.14, Chapter 5, page 136, using an EVALUATE statement. Is the logic described in the flowchart a true case? Why is it possible to write the EVALUATE statement without repeating any PERFORM statements?

A Program Using an EVALUATE Statement

Program P06-01, shown in Figure 6.3, demonstrates the use of the EVALUATE statement. It is a rewritten version of Program P05-02, with the big nested IF statement of that program replaced with an EVALUATE statement. You can see

FIGURE 6.3 **Program P06-01**

```
S COBOL II RELEASE 3.2 09/05/90                  P06001   DATE FEB 18,1992 T
----+-*A-1-B--+----2----+----3----+----4----+----5----+----6----+----7-|--+

 IDENTIFICATION DIVISION.
 PROGRAM-ID.  P06-01.
*
*    THIS PROGRAM IS A MODIFICATION TO PROGRAM P05-02 AND
*    DEMONSTRATES THE USE OF THE EVALUATE STATEMENT
*
*****************************************************************

 ENVIRONMENT DIVISION.
 INPUT-OUTPUT SECTION.
 FILE-CONTROL.
     SELECT COMMISSION-REPORT ASSIGN TO PRINTER.
     SELECT SALES-FILE-IN     ASSIGN TO INFILE.

*****************************************************************

 DATA DIVISION.
 FILE SECTION.
 FD  SALES-FILE-IN
     RECORD CONTAINS 80 CHARACTERS.

 01  SALES-RECORD-IN.
     05 SALESPERSON-NUMBER-IN     PIC X(5).
     05 CLASS-IN                  PIC X.
        88 SALESPERSON-IS-JUNIOR     VALUES "A" THRU "F".
        88 SALESPERSON-IS-ASSOCIATE VALUE "G".
        88 SALESPERSON-IS-SENIOR     VALUE "H".
        88 VALID-CLASS-CODE          VALUES "A" THRU "H".
        88 CLASS-CODE-IS-MISSING     VALUE SPACE.
     05 LAST-YEARS-SALES-IN       PIC 9(6).
     05 CURRENT-SALE-IN           PIC 9(6)V99.

 FD  COMMISSION-REPORT.

 01  REPORT-LINE                  PIC X(88).

 WORKING-STORAGE SECTION.
 01  MORE-INPUT             PIC X      VALUE "Y".
     88 THERE-IS-NO-MORE-INPUT         VALUE "N".
     88 THERE-IS-NO-INPUT              VALUE "N".
 01  NO-INPUT-DATA          PIC X(15) VALUE "  NO INPUT DATA".

 01  PAGE-HEAD-1.
     05                     PIC X(23) VALUE SPACES.
     05                     PIC X(19) VALUE "COMMISSION REGISTER".

```

FIGURE 6.3 *continued*

```
       01  PAGE-HEAD-2.
           05                        PIC X(45) VALUE SPACES.
           05                        PIC X(5)  VALUE "DATE".
           05  RUN-MONTH-AND-DAY     PIC Z9/99/.
           05  RUN-YEAR              PIC 99.

       01  PAGE-HEAD-3.
           05                        PIC X(10) VALUE SPACES.
           05                        PIC X(6)  VALUE "SALES-".

       01  PAGE-HEAD-4.
           05                        PIC X(10) VALUE SPACES.
           05                        PIC X(25) VALUE "PERSON".
           05                        PIC X(4)  VALUE "SALE".

       01  PAGE-HEAD-5.
           05                        PIC X(10) VALUE SPACES.
           05                        PIC X(12) VALUE "NUMBER".
           05                        PIC X(12) VALUE "CLASS".
           05                        PIC X(12) VALUE "AMOUNT".
           05                        PIC X(10) VALUE "COMMISSION".

       01  DETAIL-LINE.
           05  SALESPERSON-NUMBER-OUT    PIC B(10)X(5).
           05  CLASS-TITLE-OUT           PIC B(5)X(9)BBB.
           05  CURRENT-SALE-OUT          PIC ZZZ,ZZZ.99BBB.
           05  COMMISSION-OUT            PIC ZZZ,ZZZ.99.

       01  CLASS-INVALID-LINE.
           05  SALESPERSON-NUMBER        PIC B(10)X(5)B(5).
           05                            PIC X(17)
                                         VALUE "ERROR - CLASS IS".
           05  INVALID-CLASS             PIC X.
           05                            PIC X(44)
               VALUE ". CLASS SHOULD BE A, B, C, D, E, F, G, OR H.".

       01  CLASS-MISSING-LINE.
           05  SALESPERSON-NUMBER        PIC B(10)X(5)B(5).
           05                            PIC X(68)
               VALUE "ERROR - CLASS IS MISSING. CLASS SHOULD BE A, B, C,
      -        "D, E, F, G, OR H.".

       01  COMMISSION-BREAK-POINTS.
           05  JUNIOR-BREAK-POINT        PIC 9     VALUE 0.
           05  ASSOCIATE-BREAK-POINT     PIC 9(5)  VALUE 10000.
           05  SENIOR-BREAK-POINT        PIC 9(5)  VALUE 50000.

       01  SELECTED-COMMISSION-RATES.
           05  LOW-COMMISSION-RATE       PIC V99.
           05  HIGH-COMMISSION-RATE      PIC V99.

       01  SELECTED-BREAK-POINT          PIC 9(5).

       01  SALE-QUOTAS.
           05  JUNIOR-SALE-QUOTA         PIC 9     VALUE 0.
           05  ASSOCIATE-SALE-QUOTA      PIC 9(6)  VALUE 150000.
           05  SENIOR-SALE-QUOTA         PIC 9(6)  VALUE 250000.

```

continued

FIGURE 6.3 *continued*

```
S COBOL II RELEASE 3.2 09/05/90                    P06001    DATE FEB 18,1992 T
----+-*A-1-B--+----2----+----3----+----4----+----5----+----6----+----7-|--+

        01  COMMISSION-RATES.
            05 ASSOCIATE-RATES.
               10 QUOTA-NOT-MET.
                  15 LOW-RATE              PIC V99    VALUE .05.
                  15 HIGH-RATE             PIC V99    VALUE .20.
               10 QUOTA-MET.
                  15 LOW-RATE              PIC V99    VALUE .20.
                  15 HIGH-RATE             PIC V99    VALUE .30.
            05 SENIOR-RATES.
               10 QUOTA-NOT-MET.
                  15 LOW-RATE              PIC V99    VALUE .20.
                  15 HIGH-RATE             PIC V99    VALUE .30.
               10 QUOTA-MET.
                  15 LOW-RATE              PIC V99    VALUE .30.
                  15 HIGH-RATE             PIC V99    VALUE .40.
            05 JUNIOR-RATES.
               10 QUOTA-NOT-MET.
                  15 LOW-RATE              PIC V99    VALUE .10.
                  15 HIGH-RATE             PIC V99    VALUE .10.
               10 QUOTA-MET.
                  15 LOW-RATE              PIC V99    VALUE .10.
                  15 HIGH-RATE             PIC V99    VALUE .10.

        01  TODAYS-DATE.
            05 RUN-YEAR                    PIC 99.
            05 RUN-MONTH-AND-DAY           PIC 9(4).

       *****************************************************************

        PROCEDURE DIVISION.
        PRODUCE-COMMISSION-REGISTER.
            PERFORM INITIALIZATION
            PERFORM PRODUCE-DETAIL-LINE UNTIL THERE-IS-NO-MORE-INPUT
            PERFORM TERMINATION
            STOP RUN
            .

        INITIALIZATION.
            OPEN INPUT  SALES-FILE-IN
                 OUTPUT COMMISSION-REPORT
            ACCEPT TODAYS-DATE FROM DATE
            MOVE CORR TODAYS-DATE TO PAGE-HEAD-2
            WRITE REPORT-LINE FROM PAGE-HEAD-1 AFTER PAGE
            WRITE REPORT-LINE FROM PAGE-HEAD-2
            WRITE REPORT-LINE FROM PAGE-HEAD-3 AFTER 3
            WRITE REPORT-LINE FROM PAGE-HEAD-4
            WRITE REPORT-LINE FROM PAGE-HEAD-5
            MOVE SPACES TO REPORT-LINE
            WRITE REPORT-LINE
            READ SALES-FILE-IN
                AT END
                    SET THERE-IS-NO-INPUT TO TRUE
            END-READ
            IF THERE-IS-NO-INPUT
                WRITE REPORT-LINE FROM NO-INPUT-DATA AFTER 2
            END-IF
            .

        TERMINATION.
            CLOSE SALES-FILE-IN
                  COMMISSION-REPORT
            .
```

that the EVALUATE statement, lines 01940 through 02060, is clearer and neater than the nested IF statement from Program P05-02.That is because it carries out genuine case logic.

The statement shows that a variety of conditions are allowed in an EVALUATE statement. In lines 01950 and 02000 there is a condition-name condition; in lines 01970 and 01980 a combined condition using the word AND, consisting of a condition-name condition and a relation condition; and in line 02020 just a relation condition. Remember that the conditions in an EVALUATE statement are evaluated in the order in which the WHEN phrases appear in the program. As soon as one WHEN phrase is satisfied, the next executable statement is executed and no other WHEN phrases are evaluated. Instead, control passes to END-EVALUATE and the program continues from there.

Notice that the selection subject in this EVALUATE statement is TRUE. When you are coding case logic in which each branch depends on the outcome of a single different condition, as we have here, the most convenient way to do it is to have one selection subject, TRUE, and write the conditions as the selection objects. Soon, we will see a case with more than one selection subject.

FIGURE *6.3* ***continued***

```
01680 PRODUCE-DETAIL-LINE.
01690     IF NOT VALID-CLASS-CODE
01700         PERFORM PROCESS-ERRONEOUS-RECORD
01710     ELSE
01720         PERFORM PROCESS-GOOD-RECORD
01730     END-IF
01740     READ SALES-FILE-IN
01750         AT END
01760             SET THERE-IS-NO-MORE-INPUT TO TRUE
01770     .
01780
01790 PROCESS-ERRONEOUS-RECORD.
01800     IF CLASS-CODE-IS-MISSING
01810         PERFORM WRITE-CLASS-MISSING-LINE
01820     ELSE
01830         PERFORM WRITE-CLASS-INVALID-LINE
01840     END-IF
01850     .
01860
01870 PROCESS-GOOD-RECORD.
01880     PERFORM SELECT-COMMISSION-RATES
01890     PERFORM COMPUTE-COMMISSION
01900     PERFORM WRITE-COMMISSION-LINE
01910     .
01920
01930 SELECT-COMMISSION-RATES.
01940     EVALUATE TRUE
01950         WHEN SALESPERSON-IS-JUNIOR
01960                 PERFORM SET-JUNIOR-PARAMETERS
01970         WHEN SALESPERSON-IS-ASSOCIATE AND
01980              LAST-YEARS-SALES-IN LESS THAN ASSOCIATE-SALE-QUOTA
01990                 PERFORM ASSOCIATE-QUOTA-NOT-MET
02000         WHEN SALESPERSON-IS-ASSOCIATE
02010                 PERFORM ASSOCIATE-QUOTA-MET
02020         WHEN LAST-YEARS-SALES-IN LESS THAN SENIOR-SALE-QUOTA
02030                 PERFORM SENIOR-QUOTA-NOT-MET
02040         WHEN OTHER
02050                 PERFORM SENIOR-QUOTA-MET
02060     END-EVALUATE
02070     .
02080
```

continued

FIGURE 6.3 *continued*

```
S COBOL II RELEASE 3.2 09/05/90              P06001   DATE FEB 18,1992 T
----+-*A-1-B--+----2----+----3----+----4----+----5----+----6----+----7-|--+

 WRITE-CLASS-MISSING-LINE.
     MOVE SALESPERSON-NUMBER-IN TO
          SALESPERSON-NUMBER IN CLASS-MISSING-LINE
     WRITE REPORT-LINE FROM CLASS-MISSING-LINE
     .

 WRITE-CLASS-INVALID-LINE.
     MOVE CLASS-IN TO INVALID-CLASS
     MOVE SALESPERSON-NUMBER-IN TO
          SALESPERSON-NUMBER IN CLASS-INVALID-LINE
     WRITE REPORT-LINE FROM CLASS-INVALID-LINE
     .

 SET-JUNIOR-PARAMETERS.
     MOVE JUNIOR-BREAK-POINT TO SELECTED-BREAK-POINT
     MOVE "JUNIOR"           TO CLASS-TITLE-OUT
     MOVE HIGH-RATE IN QUOTA-MET IN JUNIOR-RATES TO
          HIGH-COMMISSION-RATE
     MOVE LOW-RATE  IN QUOTA-MET IN JUNIOR-RATES TO
          LOW-COMMISSION-RATE
     .

 ASSOCIATE-QUOTA-NOT-MET.
     MOVE ASSOCIATE-BREAK-POINT TO SELECTED-BREAK-POINT
     MOVE "ASSOCIATE"           TO CLASS-TITLE-OUT
     MOVE HIGH-RATE IN QUOTA-NOT-MET IN ASSOCIATE-RATES TO
          HIGH-COMMISSION-RATE
     MOVE LOW-RATE  IN QUOTA-NOT-MET IN ASSOCIATE-RATES TO
          LOW-COMMISSION-RATE
     .

 ASSOCIATE-QUOTA-MET.
     MOVE ASSOCIATE-BREAK-POINT TO SELECTED-BREAK-POINT
     MOVE "ASSOCIATE"           TO CLASS-TITLE-OUT
     MOVE HIGH-RATE IN QUOTA-MET IN ASSOCIATE-RATES TO
          HIGH-COMMISSION-RATE
     MOVE LOW-RATE  IN QUOTA-MET IN ASSOCIATE-RATES TO
          LOW-COMMISSION-RATE
     .

 SENIOR-QUOTA-NOT-MET.
     MOVE SENIOR-BREAK-POINT TO SELECTED-BREAK-POINT
     MOVE "SENIOR"           TO CLASS-TITLE-OUT
     MOVE HIGH-RATE IN QUOTA-NOT-MET IN SENIOR-RATES TO
          HIGH-COMMISSION-RATE
     MOVE LOW-RATE  IN QUOTA-NOT-MET IN SENIOR-RATES TO
          LOW-COMMISSION-RATE
     .

 SENIOR-QUOTA-MET.
     MOVE SENIOR-BREAK-POINT TO SELECTED-BREAK-POINT
     MOVE "SENIOR"           TO CLASS-TITLE-OUT
     MOVE HIGH-RATE IN QUOTA-MET IN SENIOR-RATES TO
          HIGH-COMMISSION-RATE
     MOVE LOW-RATE  IN QUOTA-MET IN SENIOR-RATES TO
          LOW-COMMISSION-RATE
     .
```

FIGURE 6.3 *continued*

```
COMPUTE-COMMISSION.
    IF CURRENT-SALE-IN GREATER THAN SELECTED-BREAK-POINT
        COMPUTE COMMISSION-OUT ROUNDED =
            LOW-COMMISSION-RATE * SELECTED-BREAK-POINT +
            HIGH-COMMISSION-RATE *
                (CURRENT-SALE-IN - SELECTED-BREAK-POINT)
    ELSE
        COMPUTE COMMISSION-OUT ROUNDED =
            LOW-COMMISSION-RATE * CURRENT-SALE-IN
    END-IF
    .

WRITE-COMMISSION-LINE.
    MOVE SALESPERSON-NUMBER-IN TO SALESPERSON-NUMBER-OUT
    MOVE CURRENT-SALE-IN       TO CURRENT-SALE-OUT
    WRITE REPORT-LINE FROM DETAIL-LINE
    .
```

Program P06-01 was run with same input data as Program P05-02 and produced the same output, shown here in Figure 6.4.

FIGURE 6.4 **Output from Program P06-01**

```
             COMMISSION REGISTER
                                     DATE  2/18/92


SALES-
PERSON                    SALE
NUMBER       CLASS       AMOUNT       COMMISSION

14756      ASSOCIATE     70,592.43     12,618.49
14758      ASSOCIATE     10,000.00      2,000.00
15008      SENIOR       998,042.99    294,412.90
19123      SENIOR        53,765.42     11,129.63
14689      ERROR - CLASS IS MISSING.  CLASS SHOULD BE A, B, C, D, E, F, G, OR H
10089      ASSOCIATE     43,078.65      7,115.73
17665      ASSOCIATE     88,700.99     25,610.30
15699      JUNIOR        30,000.99      3,000.10
15003      SENIOR        50,000.00     10,000.00
12231      JUNIOR       243,679.21     24,367.92
14769      ASSOCIATE    194,453.99     57,336.20
15013      SENIOR         7,821.35      1,564.27
15014      SENIOR        35,962.99     10,788.90
14770      ASSOCIATE     82,356.43     23,706.93
14771      ASSOCIATE      9,369.51      1,873.90
15000      ERROR - CLASS IS Z.  CLASS SHOULD BE A, B, C, D, E, F, G, OR H.
15002      SENIOR        19,345.26      3,869.05
15004      SENIOR        57,321.23     12,196.37
12352      ASSOCIATE      6,982.34      1,396.47
15006      SENIOR        39,224.31      7,844.86
14757      ASSOCIATE      1,984.99         99.25
15010      SENIOR        47,365.54     14,209.66
13834      JUNIOR        45,987.99      4,598.80
15011      SENIOR        50,786.54     15,314.62
14764      ERROR - CLASS IS 1.  CLASS SHOULD BE A, B, C, D, E, F, G, OR H.
15015      SENIOR        79,875.23     26,950.09
14759      ASSOCIATE     47,839.65      8,067.93
15016      SENIOR        85,359.42     29,143.77
14761      ASSOCIATE      6,439.12        321.96
15012      SENIOR        93,683.42     32,473.37
```

EXERCISE 2

Rewrite your solution to Review Exercise 3, Chapter 5, page 160, using an EVALUATE statement.

Executable Statements in an EVALUATE Statement

Following each WHEN phrase in an EVALUATE statement you may have executable statements of any complexity, including IF statements and nested IF statements, and even other EVALUATE statements. You may thus construct nested EVALUATE statements by placing EVALUATE statements within other EVALUATE statements. Here is an example of an EVALUATE statement that contains nested IF statements. This statement carries out the same logic as one of the nested IF statements from Chapter 5:

```
EVALUATE TRUE
     WHEN JOB-CODE-1
          IF UNION-CODE-1
               IF HOURS-WORKED > 40
                    PERFORM OV1
          ELSE
               PERFORM OV0
          END-IF
          ELSE
               IF UNION-CODE-2
                    IF HOURS-WORKED > 37.5
                         PERFORM OV2
                    ELSE
                         PERFORM OV0
                    END-IF
               END-IF
          END-IF
          PERFORM JOB-ROUTINE-1
     WHEN JOB-CODE-2
          IF MARRIED
               PERFORM TAX-1
          ELSE
               IF SINGLE
                    PERFORM TAX-2
               ELSE
                    PERFORM TAX-3
               END-IF
          END-IF
          PERFORM JOB-ROUTINE-2
     WHEN OTHER
          PERFORM JOB-ROUTINE-0
END-EVALUATE
```

Another way to write the same logic, which demonstrates the nesting of EVALUATE statements, is as follows:

```
EVALUATE TRUE
     WHEN JOB-CODE-1
          EVALUATE TRUE
               WHEN UNION-CODE-1
                    IF HOURS-WORKED > 40
                        PERFORM OV1
                    ELSE
                        PERFORM OV0
                    END-IF
               WHEN UNION-CODE-2
                    IF HOURS-WORKED > 37.5
                        PERFORM OV2
                    ELSE
                        PERFORM OV0
                    END-IF
          END-EVALUATE
          PERFORM JOB-ROUTINE-1
     WHEN JOB-CODE-2
          EVALUATE TRUE
               WHEN MARRIED
                    PERFORM TAX-1
               WHEN SINGLE
                    PERFORM TAX-2
               WHEN OTHER
                    PERFORM TAX-3
          END-EVALUATE
          PERFORM JOB-ROUTINE-2
     WHEN OTHER
          PERFORM JOB-ROUTINE-0
END-EVALUATE
```

Notice that indenting conventions are adhered to strictly, so that the writer and reader of the statements can see easily which WHEN phrases and which END-EVALUATEs belong to which EVALUATE, and which executable statements belong to which WHEN phrases.

Decision Tables

In the two EVALUATE statements just given in the previous section, the flow of control depends on the outcomes of various condition tests in various combinations. A decision table can be used to describe clearly that kind of complex logic.

A decision table for the logic of the two EVALUATE statements in the previous section is shown in Table 6.1. You can see that the table is divided into four sections. In the upper left section we list all the conditions to be tested in the logic. In the decision table the conditions may be listed in any order. They do not have to be listed in the order in which they are tested in the logic. This means that even if a condition is tested in more than one place in the logic, it needs to be listed in the decision table only once.

TABLE 6.1
Decision table showing logic that depends on the outcome of several conditions in combination

	1	2	3	4	5	6	7	8
JOB-CODE-1	T	T	T	T	F	F	F	F
JOB-CODE-2	—	—	—	—	T	T	T	F
UNION-CODE-1	T	T	F	F	—	—	—	—
UNION-CODE-2	—	—	T	T	—	—	—	—
HOURS-WORKED > 40	T	F	—	—	—	—	—	—
HOURS-WORKED > 37.5	—	—	T	F	—	—	—	—
MARRIED	—	—	—	—	T	F	F	—
SINGLE	—	—	—	—	—	T	F	—
OV0		X		X				
OV1	X							
OV2			X					
TAX-1					X			
TAX-2						X		
TAX-3							X	
JOB-ROUTINE-0								X
JOB-ROUTINE-1	X	X	X	X				
JOB-ROUTINE-2					X	X	X	

In the lower left section we list all of the procedures that are carried out anywhere in the logic. Procedures must appear in the table in the order in which they are executed in the logic. In the upper right section of the table we list and number different combinations of outcomes of the conditions (True, False, or immaterial), and in the lower right we indicate with Xs which procedures are carried out for the different combinations of outcomes. If you study the table and the two previous EVALUATE statements, you will see that they all describe the same logic. For example, the column numbered 1 in the table shows that when the conditions JOB-CODE-1, UNION-CODE-1, and HOURS-WORKED > 40 are all True, then the procedures OV1 and JOB-ROUTINE-1 are to be carried out in that order. If you now examine the two EVALUATE statements in the previous section you will see that they carry out those same procedures when the same three conditions are True.

Coding a Decision Table Using an EVALUATE Statement

A decision table can be coded easily and mechanically with an EVALUATE statement. You write all the conditions as the set of condition subjects in the EVALUATE statement, and each numbered column of the table as a WHEN phrase consisting of some combination of the reserved words TRUE, FALSE, ALSO, and ANY. The decision table in Table 6.1 can be coded as follows:

```
EVALUATE JOB-CODE-1
    ALSO JOB-CODE-2
    ALSO UNION-CODE-1
    ALSO UNION-CODE-2
    ALSO HOURS-WORKED > 40
    ALSO HOURS-WORKED > 37.5
    ALSO MARRIED
    ALSO SINGLE
    WHEN TRUE  ALSO ANY   ALSO TRUE  ALSO ANY  ALSO TRUE  ALSO ANY   ALSO ANY    ALSO ANY
                                                                              PERFORM OV1
                                                                              PERFORM JOB-ROUTINE-1
    WHEN TRUE  ALSO ANY   ALSO TRUE  ALSO ANY  ALSO FALSE ALSO ANY   ALSO ANY    ALSO ANY
    WHEN TRUE  ALSO ANY   ALSO FALSE ALSO TRUE ALSO ANY   ALSO FALSE ALSO ANY    ALSO ANY
                                                                              PERFORM OV0
                                                                              PERFORM JOB-ROUTINE-1
    WHEN TRUE  ALSO ANY   ALSO FALSE ALSO TRUE ALSO ANY   ALSO TRUE  ALSO ANY    ALSO ANY
                                                                              PERFORM OV2
                                                                              PERFORM JOB-ROUTINE-1
    WHEN FALSE ALSO TRUE  ALSO ANY   ALSO ANY  ALSO ANY   ALSO ANY   ALSO TRUE   ALSO ANY
                                                                              PERFORM TAX-ROUTINE-1
                                                                              PERFORM JOB-ROUTINE-2
    WHEN FALSE ALSO TRUE  ALSO ANY   ALSO ANY  ALSO ANY   ALSO ANY   ALSO FALSE ALSO TRUE
                                                                              PERFORM TAX-ROUTINE-2
                                                                              PERFORM JOB-ROUTINE-2
    WHEN FALSE ALSO TRUE  ALSO ANY   ALSO ANY  ALSO ANY   ALSO ANY   ALSO FALSE ALSO FALSE
                                                                              PERFORM TAX-ROUTINE-3
                                                                              PERFORM JOB-ROUTINE-2
    WHEN FALSE ALSO FALSE ALSO ANY   ALSO ANY  ALSO ANY   ALSO ANY   ALSO ANY   ALSO ANY
                                                                              PERFORM JOB-ROUTINE-0
END-EVALUATE
```

Notice that it is legal to have WHEN phrases one after the other followed by one or more executable statements. In the decision table it just happened that columns 2 and 4 called for execution of the same procedures. The two columns were coded with successive WHEN phrases and it was not necessary to write the procedures twice. Both WHEN phrases refer to the same procedures.

EXERCISE 3

Construct a decision table to describe the logic found in the flowchart in Exercise 4(a), Chapter 5, page 141.

Format of the EVALUATE Statement

The format of the EVALUATE statement follows on page 180.

In the format, expression-1 and expression-2 may be arithmetic expressions or conditions. Imperative-statement-1 and imperative-statement-2 must be one or more imperative statements. An imperative statement is a statement that begins with an imperative verb and specifies some unconditional action to be taken, or any statement that ends with an **explicit scope terminator.** Two typical statements that begin with imperative verbs are

```
MOVE HANDLING-CHARGE-IN TO HANDLING-CHARGE-OUT
```

and

```
PERFORM INITIALIZATION
```

```
        ⎧identifier-1⎫ ⎡      ⎧identifier-2⎫⎤
        ⎪literal-1   ⎪ ⎢      ⎪literal-2   ⎪⎥
EVALUATE⎨expression-1⎬ ⎢ ALSO ⎨expression-2⎬⎥ ...
        ⎪TRUE        ⎪ ⎢      ⎪TRUE        ⎪⎥
        ⎩FALSE       ⎭ ⎣      ⎩FALSE       ⎭⎦

 {{WHEN

  ⎧ANY                                                                                   ⎫
  ⎪condition-1                                                                           ⎪
  ⎪TRUE                                                                                  ⎪
  ⎨FALSE                                                                                 ⎬
  ⎪      ⎧⎧identifier-3             ⎫ ⎧THROUGH⎫ ⎧identifier-4             ⎫⎤⎫            ⎪
  ⎪[NOT]⎨⎨literal-3                 ⎬ ⎨       ⎬ ⎨literal-4                ⎬⎥⎬            ⎪
  ⎩      ⎩⎩arithmetic-expression-1  ⎭ ⎩THRU   ⎭ ⎩arithmetic-expression-2  ⎭⎦⎭            ⎭

  [ALSO

  ⎧ANY                                                                                   ⎫
  ⎪condition-2                                                                           ⎪
  ⎪TRUE                                                                                  ⎪
  ⎨FALSE                                                                                 ⎬ ]...}...
  ⎪      ⎧⎧identifier-5             ⎫⎡⎧THROUGH⎫ ⎧identifier-6             ⎫⎤⎫            ⎪
  ⎪[NOT]⎨⎨literal-5                 ⎬⎢⎨       ⎬ ⎨literal-6                ⎬⎥⎬            ⎪
  ⎩      ⎩⎩arithmetic-expression-3  ⎭⎣⎩THRU   ⎭ ⎩arithmetic-expression-4  ⎭⎦⎭            ⎭

   imperative-statement-1} ...
 [WHEN OTHER imperative-statement-2]
 [END-EVALUATE]
```

A complete list of imperative verbs is given on page 802. Some typical explicit scope terminators are END-IF, END-READ, and END-SUBTRACT. A complete list of explicit scope terminators is given on page 803.

The ellipsis after imperative-statement-1 indicates that you may have as many WHEN phrases and imperative statements as you like. The ellipsis after the brace on the preceding line indicates that you may have as many WHEN phrases as you like before imperative-statement-1, all referring to imperative-statement-1. And the ellipsis following the square bracket on that line indicates that you may have as many ALSO phrases as you like to make up a set of selection objects.

The first brace on the line with the word WHEN matches the brace after imperative-statement-1. The second brace on the line with the word WHEN matches the last brace on the line preceding imperative-statement-1. And the bracket on the line with the word ALSO matches the last bracket on the line preceding imperative-statement-1.

Summary

EVALUATE can be used to code case logic, in which a flowchart decision has more than two branches out. In an EVALUATE statement, a set of selection subjects consists of one or more selection subjects connected by the word ALSO. A selection subject may be an identifier, a literal, an arithmetic expression, a condition, the word TRUE, or the word FALSE. In each WHEN phrase, the set of selection objects must contain selection objects that correspond to the selection subjects. A selection object may be the word ANY, a condition, the word TRUE, the word FALSE, an identifier, a literal, an arithmetic expression, the word NOT followed by an identifier, literal, or arithmetic expression, a THROUGH phrase using identifiers, literals, or arithmetic expressions, or a NOT . . . THROUGH phrase using identifiers, literals, or arithmetic expressions. Whenever literals are used in selection objects or subjects, they must agree in category with the selection subjects or objects to which they correspond.

WHEN phrases in an EVALUATE statement are evaluated in turn, in the order in which they appear in the statement. Once a WHEN phrase is satisfied, the next executable statement following it is carried out, and control then passes to END-EVALUATE and the program continues. WHEN phrases may appear successively, and they all apply to the next executable statement following them.

Decision tables may be used to describe logic in which the processing depends on the outcomes of several conditions in different combinations. In a decision table, all the conditions to be tested in the logic are listed in any order. Also, all the procedures to be carried out are listed, in the order in which they are to be executed. Numbered columns show the combinations of outcomes of the conditions, and the procedures that are to be executed for each such combination. To code an EVALUATE statement from a decision table, you write all the conditions as the set of selection subjects and each numbered column as a WHEN phrase using the words TRUE, FALSE, ANY, and ALSO.

Fill-In Exercises

1. In an EVALUATE statement, the set of ______ ______ follows the word EVALUATE.
2. In an EVALUATE statement, a set of ______ ______ follows the word WHEN.
3. The EVALUATE statement is used to code the kind of program logic called ______.
4. The reserved word ______ is used to end an EVALUATE statement.
5. In a single execution of an EVALUATE statement, at most ______ WHEN phrase(s) can be satisfied.
6. The word OTHER, when used, must appear only in the ______ WHEN phrase in the statement.
7. The word ANY may be used as a selection ______.

8. The words ______ and ______ may be used as selection subjects and selection objects.
9. When a particular selection subject is immaterial to the evaluation of a particular WHEN phrase, the word ______ is used as the corresponding selection object.
10. If no WHEN phrase can be satisfied, control passes to the word ______ and the program proceeds from there.
11. A ______ EVALUATE statement is one that contains another EVALUATE statement in one or more of its WHEN phrases.
12. A decision table is divided into ______ sections.
13. All the conditions to be tested in a segment of logic can be listed in the ______ ______ section of a decision table.
14. All the procedures to be carried out in a segment of logic can be listed in the ______ ______ of a decision table.
15. Numbered columns in a decision table show combinations of outcomes of the ______ and the ______ to be carried out.

Review Exercises

1. Code the logic of the flowchart shown in Figure 5.15, Chapter 5, page 137, using an EVALUATE statement. Use the following set of selection subjects: C1 ALSO C2 ALSO C3.
2. Code the logic of the flowchart shown in Figure 5.16, Chapter 5, page 138, using an EVALUATE statement. Use the following set of selection subjects: C1 ALSO C3. Use an IF statement to test condition C2.
3. Code the logic of the flowchart shown in Figure 5.17, Chapter 5, page 139, using an EVALUATE statement. Use the following set of selection subjects: C1 ALSO C2 ALSO C3.
4. Construct decision tables to describe the logic in the flowcharts in Exercises 4(b) through 4(f), Chapter 5, pages 141–142.
5. Code the decision tables you constructed in Review Exercise 4 immediately above.
6. Construct decision tables to describe the logic in the coding in Exercises 5(a) through 5(c), Chapter 5, pages 142–143.

CHAPTER 7

Control Breaks: Program Design III

HERE ARE THE KEY POINTS YOU SHOULD LEARN FROM THIS CHAPTER

1. What control breaks are and why they are important in data processing
2. A generalized approach to developing hierarchy diagrams for programs with control breaks
3. How to program control breaks in COBOL

KEY WORDS TO RECOGNIZE AND LEARN

control break	QUOTE
control field	QUOTES
PACKED-DECIMAL	READ . . . INTO
COMPUTATIONAL	INITIALIZE
SYNCHRONIZED	REPLACING
COMP	rolling
SYNC	forward
USAGE	group indicating
DISPLAY	ADD CORRESPONDING
figurative constant	sort
ZEROS	major sort field
ZEROES	minor sort field
SPACE	intermediate sort field
HIGH-VALUE	minor control field
HIGH-VALUES	major control field
LOW-VALUE	group printing
LOW-VALUES	summary reporting

In this chapter we will study techniques for printing totals throughout a report as well as at its end. This kind of processing is carried out in almost every COBOL installation in the world and can become quite complicated. By starting at the beginning and using top-down design, we will be able to keep the difficulties under control. In the course of studying these totaling techniques we will also see some other useful COBOL features.

A Report with One Control Break

The first program in this chapter uses input in the following format:

Positions	Field
1	Indicator
2–6	Account Number
7–9	spaces
10–16	Amount (to two decimal places)
17–80	spaces

Each record contains an Indicator to say whether the Amount is a credit or a debit. If there is a dash in the Indicator field, the Amount is a debit; if the Indicator is anything else, the Amount is a credit. There may be any number of input records for a single Account Number, and there may be any number of credits and/or debits for a single Account Number. The records for each Account Number will be grouped together in the input. The program is to READ the input file, print the contents of each record, and also print the total debits and the total credits for each Account Number. The totals for each Account Number are to be printed immediately following the printing of the group of lines for that Account Number. The output from Program P07-01 is to look like Figure 7.1, from the input shown in Figure 7.2.

FIGURE 7.1 **Output from Program P07-01**

```
                         ACCOUNT ACTIVITY REPORT

 DATE  2/18/92                                                      PAGE  1


                    ACCT. NO.         DEBITS       CREDITS

                      02005            30.34
                      02005                              .00
                      02005                        98,762.01
                      02005              .06
                      02005        89,235.51
                      02005                        34,859.10

TOTALS FOR ACCOUNT NUMBER 02005   $89,265.91     $133,621.11

                      04502                        99,999.99
                      04502            83.99
                      04502        45,672.12

TOTALS FOR ACCOUNT NUMBER 04502   $45,756.11      $99,999.99

                      12121        75,499.00
                      12121              .02
                      12121              .00
                      12121                        23,411.11
                      12121                            66.67
                      12121        66,662.22

TOTALS FOR ACCOUNT NUMBER 12121  $142,161.24      $23,477.78

                      19596                        92,929.29
                      19596        12,547.20
                      19596        23,487.64
```

FIGURE 7.1 *continued*

```
                         ACCOUNT ACTIVITY REPORT

DATE   2/18/92                                                    PAGE  2

                        ACCT. NO.        DEBITS        CREDITS

                         19596              .20
                         19596                            2.39
                         19596                          213.45

TOTALS FOR ACCOUNT NUMBER 19596    $36,035.04    $93,145.13

                         20023         99,999.99
                         20023         87,654.99
                         20023         86,868.68
                         20023                        88,888.80
                         20023                        88,553.32
                         20023                        56,789.23

TOTALS FOR ACCOUNT NUMBER 20023   $274,523.66   $234,231.35

                         23456              2.11
                         23456              4.53
                         23456             12.00
                         23456                              .12
                         23456                            18.00
                         23456                              .54

TOTALS FOR ACCOUNT NUMBER 23456        $18.64        $18.66

                         30721              1.01
                         30721                            99.12
                         30721             98.44

TOTALS FOR ACCOUNT NUMBER 30721        $99.45        $99.12
```

continued

FIGURE 7.1 *continued*

```
                                ACCOUNT ACTIVITY REPORT

      DATE  2/18/92                                                            PAGE  3

                         ACCT. NO.          DEBITS        CREDITS

                          40101             342.87
                          40101                             212.45
                          40101          60,002.01
                          40101                              67.00
                          40101          32,343.23
                          40101                          90,023.41

TOTALS FOR ACCOUNT NUMBER 40101         $92,688.11     $90,302.86

                          67689              11.14
                          67689                           1,010.10
                          67689              33.35
                          67689                           2,203.30
                          67689           3,040.20
                          67689                          10,000.00

TOTALS FOR ACCOUNT NUMBER 67689          $3,084.69     $13,213.40

                          72332                .04
                          72332                              44.44
                          72332             444.44
                          72332                               4.44
                          72332                .44
                          72332                           4,040.40

TOTALS FOR ACCOUNT NUMBER 72332            $444.92      $4,089.28
```

You can see that for a single Account Number there may be several debits and/or credits. All the lines for an Account Number print consecutively, and at the end of the group of lines there is a line showing the total of the debits and the total of the credits for the Account Number. At the end of the next Account Number are its totals, and so on for all the Account Numbers. The input to this program is in Account Number order, that is, each Account Number in the input is higher than the Account Number before it, and all records for a single Account Number are together in the input. This program would have worked as well even if the Account Numbers were not in order, just as long as all records for a single account come in one after the other in the input. The Account Numbers were ordered so that it would be easy to find them on the output.

Before doing a hierarchy diagram for this program, let's try to think about how this program can be done. We already know how to accumulate totals, so there is no problem in accumulating the total of the debits and the total of the credits for the first Account Number as we print each line. But how will the program know when all the records have been read for the first Account Number and that it is time to print the totals for that account? The program will know that all of the first account is processed when it READs the first record of the second Account Number. As the program READs records, it compares the Account Number in each record to the Account Number in the previous record, until it detects a change in Account Number. The change in the Account Number is called a **control break,** and the Account Number field itself is called a **control field.**

FIGURE 7.2 **Input to Program P07-01**

```
--------------------------------------------------------------------------------
         1         2         3         4         5         6         7         8
12345678901234567890123456789012345678901234567890123456789012345678901234567890
--------------------------------------------------------------------------------
-02005    0003034
 02005    0000000
 02005    9876201
-02005    0000006
-02005    8923551
 02005    3485910
 04502    9999999
-04502    0008399
-04502    4567212
-12121    7549900
-12121    0000002
-12121    0000000
 12121    2341111
 12121    0006667
-12121    6666222
 19596    9292929
-19596    1254720
-19596    2348764
-19596    0000020
 19596    0000239
 19596    0021345
-20023    9999999
-20023    8765499
-20023    8686868
 20023    8888880
 20023    8855332
 20023    5678923
-23456    0000211
-23456    0000453
-23456    0001200
 23456    0000012
 23456    0001800
 23456    0000054
-30721    0000101
 30721    0009912
-30721    0009844
-40101    0034287
 40101    0021245
-40101    6000201
 40101    0006700
-40101    3234323
 40101    9002341
-67689    0001114
 67689    0101010
-67689    0003335
 67689    0220330
-67689    0304020
 67689    1000000
-72332    0000004
 72332    0004444
-72332    0044444
 72332    0000444
-72332    0000044
 72332    0404040
```

Once a control break is detected, the program will print the total line for the first Account Number and prepare to process the second Account Number. The preparation consists mainly of zeroing out the accumulator fields that were used to total the debits and credits for the first Account Number, so that the same fields may be used to total the debits and credits for the second. When the second control break is detected, the total line for the second Account Number can be printed, and the accumulators zeroed again in preparation for processing the third Account Number. In this way we can process an indefinite number of Account Numbers without having to provide endless numbers of accumulator fields.

Printing the very last total line sometimes presents a problem to programmers. Since a total line is printed only after the first record of the next group is detected, what will be printed when there is no next group? When end-of-file is detected on the input file, we still have not printed the totals of the debits and credits for the last Account Number, for the program has not detected a control break, a change in Account Number. So when doing the hierarchy diagram, we need only remember that, after end-of-file is detected, one more total line has to be written, and that is the total line for the last Account Number.

A Hierarchy Diagram for a Program with One Control Break

We can now begin to create the hierarchy diagram for this program. The first level of main subfunctions, as shown in Figure 7.3, is of the same form as in other first-level diagrams. We have an initialization box, a main loop, and termination. In this program, what is carried out in "Termination," after end-of-file is detected on the input, aside from closing the files, is only printing the last total line on the report—just the total line for the last group. All the other total lines on the report are printed by the main loop as we go along.

FIGURE 7.3 First-level hierarchy diagram for Program P07-01

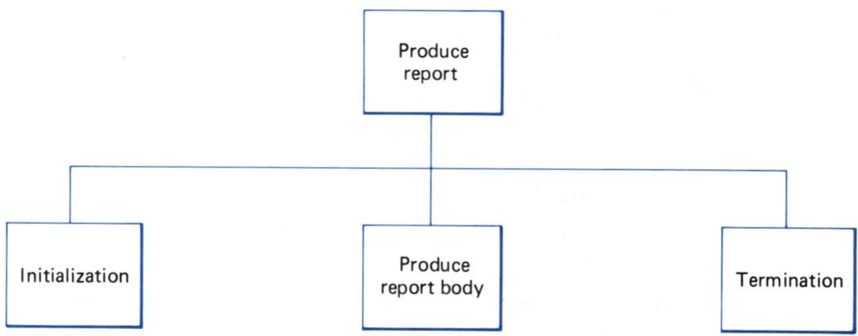

We next add to the hierarchy diagram two boxes showing that the main loop produces both detail lines and total lines. The hierarchy diagram showing "Produce a detail line" and "Account number break" is in Figure 7.4. The box "Account number break" will produce all total lines except the last one on the report, and the "Termination" box will produce the final line. We now add to the diagram the boxes "Print a detail line" and "Accumulate debits and credits," as shown in Figure 7.5. The relationship between printing a detail line and accumulating sums is similar here to what we have seen in earlier programs.

FIGURE 7.4 Partial hierarchy diagram for Program P07-01 showing "Produce a detail line" and "Account number break"

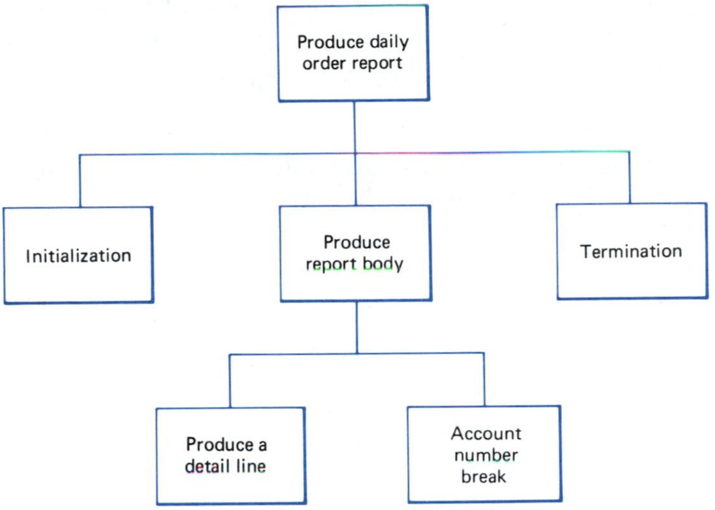

FIGURE 7.5 Partial hierarchy diagram for Program P07-01 showing subfunctions of "Produce a detail line"

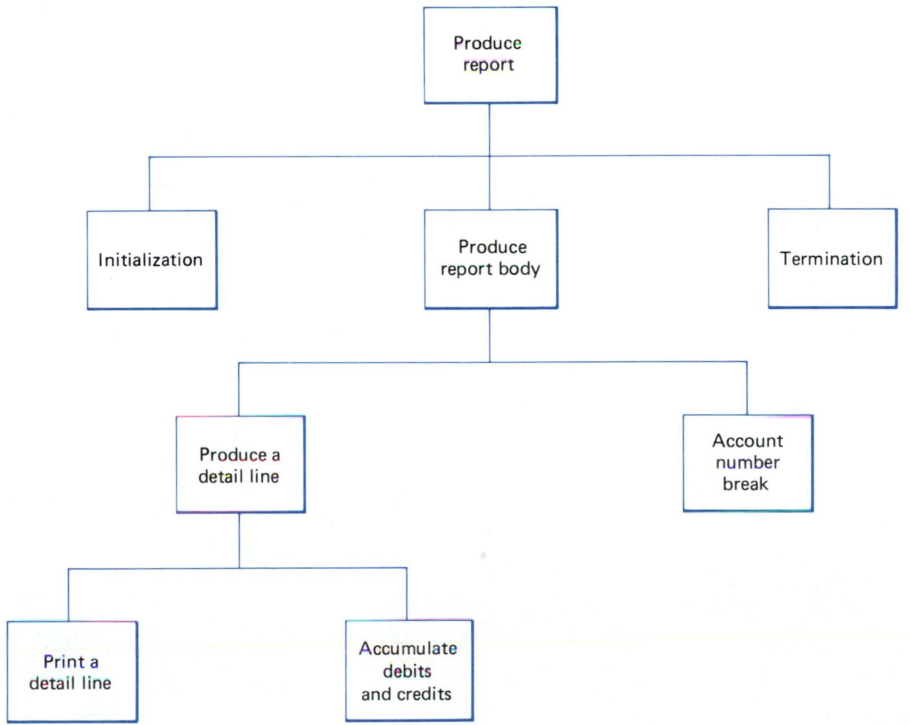

The customary subfunctions of "Initialization" are added to the diagram, and "Print page headings" has been added as a subfunction of "Print a detail line," in Figure 7.6.

Finally, what are the subfunctions of "Termination"? The box "Account number break" is all that is needed to produce the last total line, and so we add that as shown in Figure 7.7.

FIGURE 7.6 **Partial hierarchy diagram for Program P07-01 showing subfunctions of "Initialization" and "Print a detail line"**

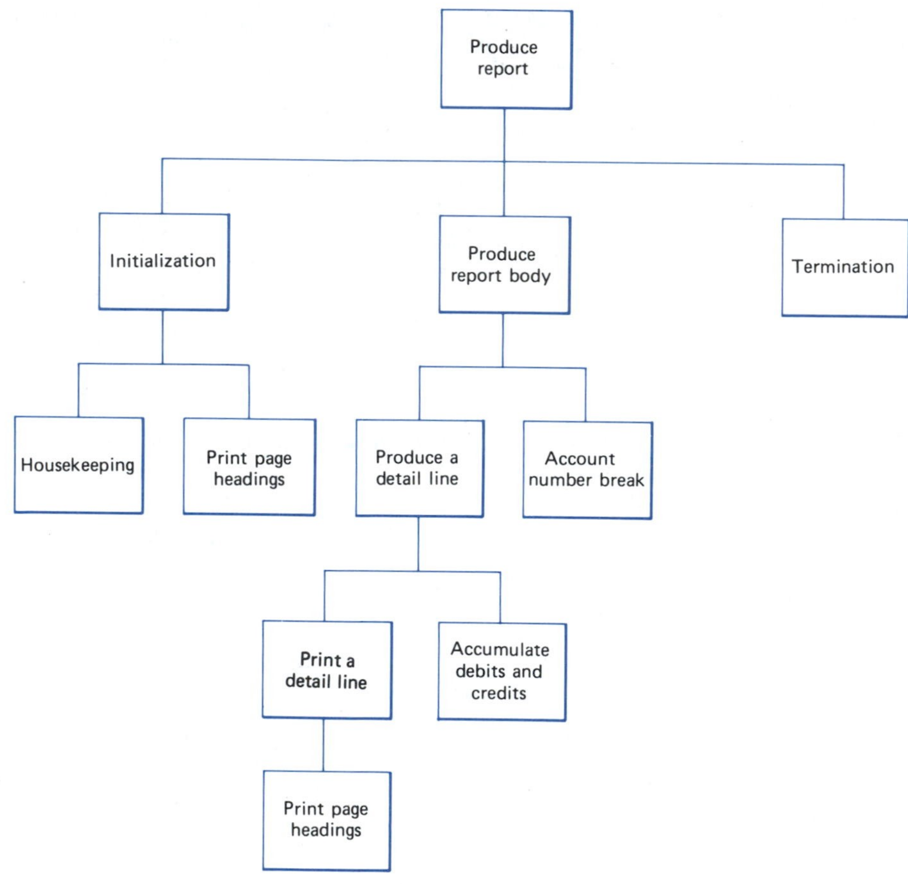

FIGURE 7.7 Complete hierarchy diagram for Program P07-01

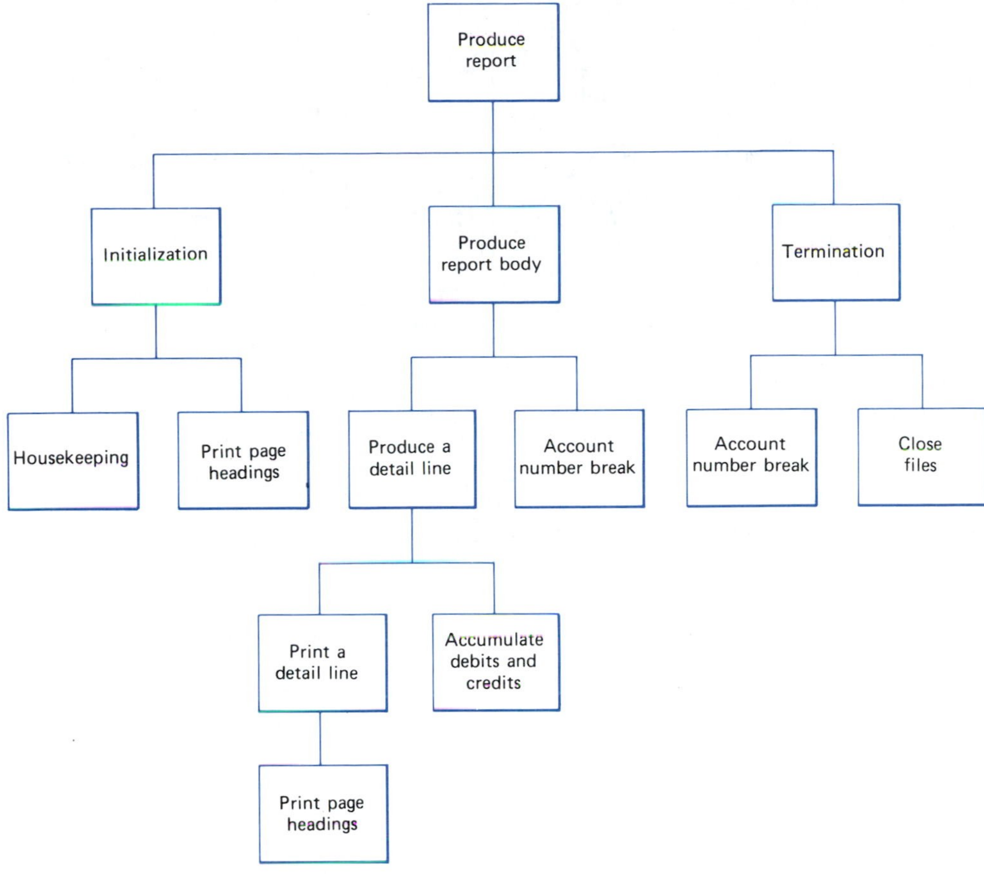

Notice that we have not shown "Print page headings" as a subfunction of "Account number break," for if a control break occurs when a page is already full, we don't want to skip to a new page, print page headings, and then print the total line at the top of the page without the detail group that it belongs to. In fact, in this kind of processing it is customary never to have total lines print at the top of a new page away from their corresponding detail lines. Sufficient space must be left at the bottom of each page of report output to accommodate any total lines that might appear. Figure 7.7 is the complete hierarchy diagram.

The First Control Break Program

The output format for Program P07-01 is shown in Figure 7.8. Program P07-01 is shown in Figure 7.9.

FIGURE 7.8 Output format for Program P07-01

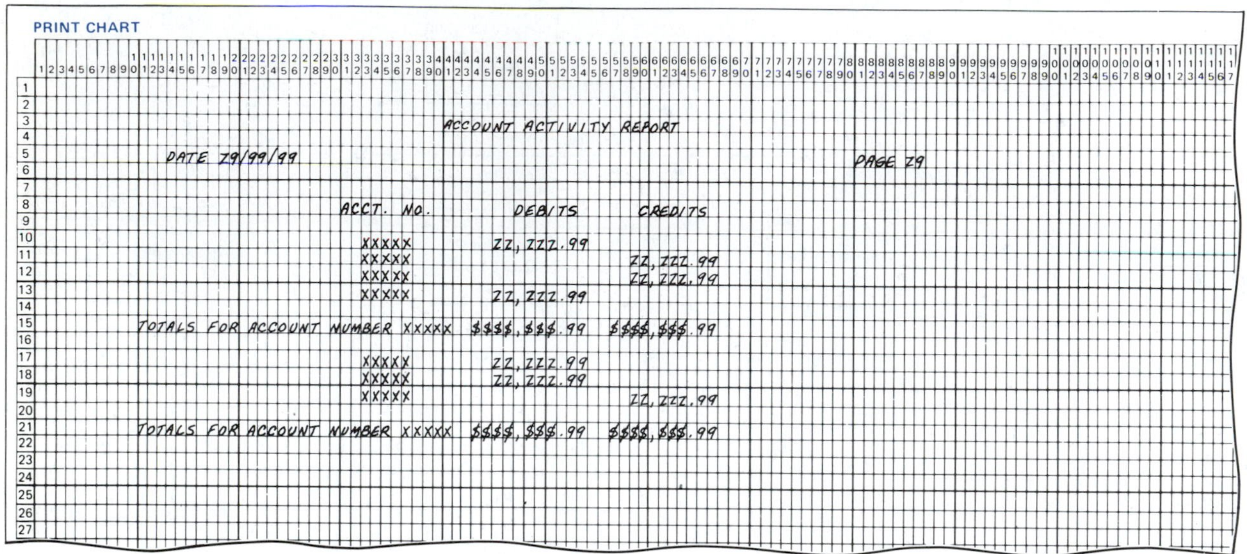

FIGURE 7.9 Program P07-01

```
S COBOL II RELEASE 3.2 09/05/90                    P07001    DATE FEB 18,1992 T
----+-*A-1-B--+----2----+----3----+----4----+----5----+----6----+----7-|--+


       IDENTIFICATION DIVISION.
       PROGRAM-ID.  P07-01.
      *
      *     THIS PROGRAM PRODUCES AN ACCOUNT ACTIVITY REPORT
      *     WITH TOTALS OF DEBITS AND CREDITS FOR EACH ACCOUNT.
      *
      *****************************************************************

       ENVIRONMENT DIVISION.
       INPUT-OUTPUT SECTION.
       FILE-CONTROL.
           SELECT ACCOUNT-ACTIVITY-REPORT  ASSIGN TO PRINTER.
           SELECT ACCOUNT-FILE-IN          ASSIGN TO INFILE.

      *****************************************************************

       DATA DIVISION.
       FILE SECTION.
       FD  ACCOUNT-FILE-IN
           RECORD CONTAINS 80 CHARACTERS.

       01  ACCOUNT-RECORD-IN         PIC X(80).

       FD  ACCOUNT-ACTIVITY-REPORT.

       01  REPORT-LINE               PIC X(87).

       WORKING-STORAGE SECTION.
       01  MORE-INPUT                PIC X      VALUE "Y".
           88 THERE-IS-NO-INPUT                 VALUE "N".
           88 THERE-IS-NO-MORE-INPUT            VALUE "N".
       01  NO-INPUT-DATA             PIC X(15) VALUE "  NO INPUT DATA".

```

FIGURE 7.9 *continued*

```
00340  01  ACCOUNT-RECORD-W.
00350      05 INDICATOR                 PIC X.
00360         88 AMOUNT-IS-DEBIT        VALUE "-".
00370      05 ACCOUNT-NUMBER-IN         PIC X(5)   VALUE SPACES.
00380      05                           PIC X(3).
00390      05 AMOUNT                    PIC 9(5)V99.
00400
00410  01  PAGE-HEAD-1.
00420      05                      PIC X(40) VALUE SPACES.
00430      05                 PIC X(23) VALUE "ACCOUNT ACTIVITY REPORT".
00440
00450  01  PAGE-HEAD-2.
00460      05                           PIC X(13) VALUE SPACES.
00470      05                           PIC X(5)   VALUE "DATE".
00480      05 RUN-MONTH-AND-DAY         PIC Z9/99/.
00490      05 RUN-YEAR                  PIC 99.
00500      05                           PIC X(54) VALUE SPACES.
00510      05                           PIC X(5)   VALUE "PAGE".
00520      05 PAGE-NUMBER-OUT           PIC Z9.
00530
00540  01  PAGE-HEAD-3.
00550      05                           PIC X(30) VALUE SPACES.
00560      05                           PIC X(17) VALUE "ACCT. NO.".
00570      05                           PIC X(12) VALUE "DEBITS".
00580      05                           PIC X(7)   VALUE "CREDITS".
00590
00600  01  DETAIL-LINE.
00610      05 ACCOUNT-NUMBER-OUT        PIC B(32)X(5).
00620      05 DEBITS                    PIC B(8)ZZ,ZZZ.99.
00630      05 CREDITS                   PIC B(4)ZZ,ZZZ.99.
00640
00650  01  CONTROL-BREAK-LINE.
00660      05                           PIC X(10) VALUE SPACES.
00670      05                 PIC X(26) VALUE "TOTALS FOR ACCOUNT NUMBER".
00680      05 ACCOUNT-NUMBER-SAVE       PIC X(5)BB.
00690      05 DEBITS-TOTAL              PIC $$$$,$$$.99BB.
00700      05 CREDITS-TOTAL             PIC $$$$,$$$.99.
00710
00720  01  ACCUMULATORS-W    PACKED-DECIMAL.
00730      05 DEBITS-TOTAL   PIC S9(6)V99 VALUE 0.
00740      05 CREDITS-TOTAL  PIC S9(6)V99 VALUE 0.
00750
```

continued

Notice the definition of the input file and input record at lines 00190 through 00220. In this and all subsequent control break programs in this book, the input record is defined in the File Section as just one 80-character field. Each input record, after being read, is transferred to an area in working storage, in this program ACCOUNT-RECORD-W, line 00340, where it is worked on. Whenever you use the kind of control break logic we have in this program, you must work on your input records in working storage and not in the File Section. The reason we set up our input area in working storage is that the logic of this program requires access to the input area after end-of-file has been read on the input file, and the rules of COBOL prohibit any reference to an input area in the File Section after end-of-file has been read on the input file associated with that area. All areas in the Working Storage Section, however, can be accessed at any time. Notice that the work area in working storage does not have to be 80 character positions long, but only as long as you need to handle all the input fields.

All fields being used for intermediate working-storage results, such as the two accumulator fields at lines 00730 and 00740, are described with the PIC-

TURE character S even though we expect all values to be positive. In most COBOL systems if you use the character S on numeric fields in working storage you will get programs that run faster and occupy less computer storage space.

In addition, in most COBOL systems, such fields should be described either as **PACKED-DECIMAL** or as **COMPUTATIONAL** and **SYNCHRONIZED,** also to obtain more efficient processing. We have described three fields as COMPUTATIONAL and SYNCHRONIZED, using the authorized abbreviations **COMP** and **SYNC,** at lines 00760, 00770, and 00790. Three fields have been described as PACKED-DECIMAL, also. The designation PACKED-DECIMAL at the group level in line 00720 causes the two elementary items within the group to be PACKED-DECIMAL.

Designating a field COMPUTATIONAL and SYNCHRONIZED directs the COBOL system to store the field in the form most efficient for computation. Those designations should always be used on numeric fields that are neither read in nor written out and that have no operations performed on them with fields that are read in or written out. An example of such a field is LINE-LIMIT. LINE-LIMIT is used to compare against LINE-COUNT-ER to determine whether a report page is full. No input or output ever interacts with this field, so it should be designated COMPUTATIONAL SYNCHRONIZED. The other COMPUTATIONAL SYNCHRONIZED field also does not interact with input or output.

All other intermediate numeric working-storage fields should be designated as PACKED-DECIMAL. This designation directs the COBOL system to store these fields in a form efficient for computation, but as decimal numbers so that they may interact efficiently with the decimal numbers in input and output.

COMPUTATIONAL and PACKED-DECIMAL each are referred to as a **USAGE** of a field. A field whose USAGE is not explicitly specified is said to have the USAGE **DISPLAY.**

The field called LINE-SPACING, at line 00770, is used to control the spacing of detail lines as they are printed. The print chart shows that a detail line should be double-spaced if it appears immediately after the column headings or after a total line and should be single-spaced if it appears after another detail line. When we look at the Procedure Division, you will see how LINE-SPACING controls the variable spacing. LINE-SPACING has been made COMPUTATIONAL and SYNCHRONIZED because it is used only internally to the program.

The word ZERO, as in line 00780, is a **figurative constant.** It can be used wherever a numeric or nonnumeric literal of zero would be legal. COBOL interprets ZERO as being numeric or nonnumeric depending on its context. The figurative constants **ZEROS** and **ZEROES** have exactly the same meaning as ZERO. They are provided only for the programmer's convenience.

Another figurative constant that we have been using all along is SPACES. It may be used interchangeably with the word **SPACE,** whose meaning in COBOL is identical to SPACES. SPACE and SPACES are always interpreted as nonnumeric literals consisting of as many blank characters as are required by the context in which they are used.

There is no great advantage in using the word ZERO instead of the numeral 0 when a numeric literal is desired, except perhaps to avoid confusion between O and 0. But when a nonnumeric literal consisting of a string of zeros is desired, then ZERO (or ZEROS or ZEROES) will be interpreted by COBOL to give the exact number of characters needed.

Other figurative constants are **HIGH-VALUE** and **HIGH-VALUES,** which both stand for the highest character that can be stored in the computer, **LOW-VALUE** and **LOW-VALUES,** which both stand for the lowest character that can be stored in the computer, and **QUOTE** and **QUOTES,** which both stand for the character ".

The Procedure Division begins at line 00870. The paragraph PRINT-PAGE-HEADINGS, at line 01030, carries out the usual page heading functions, and it also sets LINE-SPACING to 2. This will mean, as you will see, that the first detail line following the printing of page headings will be double-spaced. In fact, throughout the execution of the program, the field LINE-SPACING will always contain either 2 or 1, and you will see how the 2 and 1 are used to control the spacing of the detail lines.

FIGURE 7.9 *continued*

```
S COBOL II RELEASE 3.2 09/05/90                  P07001    DATE FEB 18,1992 T
----+-*A-1-B--+----2----+----3----+----4----+----5----+----6----+----7-|--+

00760  01  LINE-LIMIT        PIC S99 VALUE 34 COMP SYNC.
00770  01  LINE-SPACING      PIC S9           COMP SYNC.
00780  01  PAGE-NUMBER-W     PIC S99 VALUE ZERO PACKED-DECIMAL.
00790  01  LINE-COUNT-ER     PIC S99          COMP SYNC.
00800
00810  01  TODAYS-DATE.
00820      05 RUN-YEAR       PIC 99.
00830      05 RUN-MONTH-AND-DAY      PIC 9(4).
00840
00850 ************************************************************************
00860
00870  PROCEDURE DIVISION.
00880  PRODUCE-REPORT.
00890      PERFORM INITIALIZATION
00900      PERFORM PRODUCE-REPORT-BODY UNTIL THERE-IS-NO-MORE-INPUT
00910      PERFORM TERMINATION
00920      STOP RUN
00930      .
00940
00950  INITIALIZATION.
00960      PERFORM HOUSEKEEPING
00970      PERFORM PRINT-PAGE-HEADINGS
00980      IF THERE-IS-NO-INPUT
00990          WRITE REPORT-LINE FROM NO-INPUT-DATA AFTER 2
01000      END-IF
01010      .
01020
01030  PRINT-PAGE-HEADINGS.
01040      ADD 1              TO PAGE-NUMBER-W
01050      MOVE PAGE-NUMBER-W TO PAGE-NUMBER-OUT
01060      WRITE REPORT-LINE FROM PAGE-HEAD-1 AFTER PAGE
01070      WRITE REPORT-LINE FROM PAGE-HEAD-2 AFTER 2
01080      WRITE REPORT-LINE FROM PAGE-HEAD-3 AFTER 3
01090      MOVE 6 TO LINE-COUNT-ER
01100      MOVE 2 TO LINE-SPACING
01110      .
```

continued

The **READ ... INTO** statement at line 01180 shows how a record can be read from an input file and transferred to working storage with a single statement. The READ . . . INTO works like a combined READ and MOVE, so

```
READ ACCOUNT-FILE-IN INTO ACCOUNT-RECORD-W ...
```

does exactly the same thing as:

```
READ ACCOUNT-FILE-IN
MOVE ACCOUNT-RECORD-IN TO ACCOUNT-RECORD-W
```

The receiving field of the MOVE need not be the same size as the record defined in the File Section. The receiving field may be any field in working storage or in an output area in the File Section. If a READ . . . INTO statement finds an end-of-file condition, no MOVE is carried out and the contents of the receiving field remain unchanged.

The statement at line 01220 MOVEs the Account Number from the first input record to a field called ACCOUNT-NUMBER-SAVE, which happens to be part of CONTROL-BREAK-LINE but could have been described anywhere in working storage. ACCOUNT-NUMBER-SAVE is the field to which we assign the Account Number currently being worked on by the program. As the program READs each input record, it compares the Account Number in the record to the value of ACCOUNT-NUMBER-SAVE to see whether a control break has occurred. If the Account Number in the just-read record is the same as ACCOUNT-NUMBER-SAVE, that means that the program is still working on the same Account Number. If the two are different, it means that all the records for the previous account have been read and that a control break has occurred.

Let us now look at PRODUCE-REPORT-BODY, line 01250. The program always enters PRODUCE-REPORT-BODY with a newly read record waiting to be processed. The IF statement at line 01260 checks to see whether this new record is the first record of a group. If it is, a control break has occurred, so the program PERFORMs the paragraph ACCOUNT-NUMBER-BREAK and then goes to PRODUCE-A-DETAIL-LINE for the first record of the new group. If not, it goes directly to PRODUCE-A-DETAIL-LINE for the record.

In the paragraph ACCOUNT-NUMBER-BREAK, line 01350, the program formats and prints a total line. The totals it needs are already accumulated in the two ACCUMULATORS-W fields, and those merely have to be MOVEd to the total line, which in this program is called CONTROL-BREAK-LINE. The only other variable field in CONTROL-BREAK-LINE, ACCOUNT-NUMBER-SAVE, had the Account Number MOVEd to it when the program first started processing the group; so there is no further formatting needed in this line, and it is written with double spacing.

In line 01390, 2 is MOVEd to LINE-SPACING. This indicates, as you will see, that a detail line following an Account Number break is to be double-spaced. The fields in ACCUMULATORS-W are then zeroed by the **INITIALIZE** statement at line 01400.

An INITIALIZE statement such as this can be used to set to zero or space elementary fields defined within a group item. When a group name is the object of the INITIALIZE verb, as it is here, any fields within the group defined as

FIGURE 7.9 *continued*

```
S COBOL II RELEASE 3.2 09/05/90                P07001    DATE FEB 18,1992 T
----+-*A-1-B--+----2----+----3----+----4----+----5----+----6----+----7-|--+

01120
01130  HOUSEKEEPING.
01140      OPEN INPUT  ACCOUNT-FILE-IN
01150            OUTPUT ACCOUNT-ACTIVITY-REPORT
01160      ACCEPT TODAYS-DATE FROM DATE
01170      MOVE CORRESPONDING TODAYS-DATE TO PAGE-HEAD-2
01180      READ ACCOUNT-FILE-IN INTO ACCOUNT-RECORD-W
01190          AT END
01200              SET THERE-IS-NO-INPUT TO TRUE
01210      END-READ
01220      MOVE ACCOUNT-NUMBER-IN TO ACCOUNT-NUMBER-SAVE
01230      .
01240
01250  PRODUCE-REPORT-BODY.
01260      IF ACCOUNT-NUMBER-IN NOT = ACCOUNT-NUMBER-SAVE
01270          PERFORM ACCOUNT-NUMBER-BREAK
01280      END-IF
01290      PERFORM PRODUCE-A-DETAIL-LINE
01300      READ ACCOUNT-FILE-IN INTO ACCOUNT-RECORD-W
01310          AT END
01320              SET THERE-IS-NO-MORE-INPUT TO TRUE
01330      .
01340
01350  ACCOUNT-NUMBER-BREAK.
01360      MOVE CORRESPONDING ACCUMULATORS-W TO CONTROL-BREAK-LINE
01370      WRITE REPORT-LINE FROM CONTROL-BREAK-LINE AFTER ADVANCING 2
01380      ADD 2                      TO LINE-COUNT-ER
01390      MOVE 2                     TO LINE-SPACING
01400      INITIALIZE ACCUMULATORS-W
01410      MOVE ACCOUNT-NUMBER-IN TO ACCOUNT-NUMBER-SAVE
01420      .
01430
01440  PRODUCE-A-DETAIL-LINE.
01450      PERFORM PRINT-A-DETAIL-LINE
01460      PERFORM ACCUMULATE-DEBITS-AND-CREDITS
01470      .
```

continued

numeric or numeric edited are set to zero, and all other fields are set to spaces, except fields without names or fields named FILLER, which are ignored by the INITIALIZE statement. Each elementary item being INITIALIZEd is treated as though it were the receiving field of an elementary MOVE operation. This makes the INITIALIZE statement especially useful when you want to zero out COMPUTATIONAL or PACKED-DECIMAL fields, for each field has zeros MOVEd to it in the appropriate form. The INITIALIZE statement can be used also to MOVE values other than zero and space. You will see how when we look at the format of the INITIALIZE statement later in this chapter.

Finally, the new ACCOUNT-NUMBER-IN is MOVEd to ACCOUNT-NUMBER-SAVE in preparation for processing the new Account Number, in line 01410.

Let us look at PRINT-A-DETAIL-LINE, line 01490, to see how it handles page overflow and how it uses LINE-SPACING to get most detail lines single-spaced, but double-spaced after page headings and total lines.

Line 01600 shows how to use an identifier in an AFTER phrase to get variable line spacing. If the field LINE-SPACING has a value of 2 at the time the WRITE statement is executed, COBOL gives double spacing. If LINE-SPACING has a 1 at that time, the paper will be single-spaced. Both paragraphs PRINT-PAGE-HEADINGS and ACCOUNT-NUMBER-BREAK set LINE-SPACING to 2, so the first detail line printed after the page headings or at the beginning of a new group will have double spacing. PRINT-A-DETAIL-LINE itself turns LINE-SPACING to 1, at line 01620, so that subsequent detail lines will be single-spaced.

The IF statement at line 01570 shows how page overflow can be detected when variable line spacing is in use. The IF statement determines whether the next detail line to be printed will fall beyond the LINE-LIMIT and, if so, PERFORMs PRINT-PAGE-HEADINGS.

FIGURE 7.9 *continued*

```
S COBOL II RELEASE 3.2 09/05/90                  P07001   DATE FEB 18,1992 T
----+-*A-1-B--+----2----+----3----+----4----+----5----+----6----+----7-|--+

01480
01490  PRINT-A-DETAIL-LINE.
01500      MOVE SPACES TO DETAIL-LINE
01510      MOVE ACCOUNT-NUMBER-IN TO ACCOUNT-NUMBER-OUT
01520      IF AMOUNT-IS-DEBIT
01530          MOVE AMOUNT TO DEBITS
01540      ELSE
01550          MOVE AMOUNT TO CREDITS
01560      END-IF
01570      IF LINE-COUNT-ER + LINE-SPACING > LINE-LIMIT
01580          PERFORM PRINT-PAGE-HEADINGS
01590      END-IF
01600      WRITE REPORT-LINE FROM DETAIL-LINE AFTER LINE-SPACING
01610      ADD LINE-SPACING TO LINE-COUNT-ER
01620      MOVE 1 TO LINE-SPACING
01630      .
01640
01650  ACCUMULATE-DEBITS-AND-CREDITS.
01660      IF AMOUNT-IS-DEBIT
01670          ADD AMOUNT TO DEBITS-TOTAL IN ACCUMULATORS-W
01680      ELSE
01690          ADD AMOUNT TO CREDITS-TOTAL IN ACCUMULATORS-W
01700      END-IF
01710      .
01720
01730  TERMINATION.
01740      PERFORM ACCOUNT-NUMBER-BREAK
01750      PERFORM CLOSE-FILES
01760      .
01770
01780  CLOSE-FILES.
01790      CLOSE ACCOUNT-FILE-IN
01800            ACCOUNT-ACTIVITY-REPORT
01810      .
```

EXERCISE 1

Explain why some working storage fields in Program P07-01 need a VALUE clause and some do not. These are fields with a VALUE clause:

```
PAGE-NUMBER-W
LINE-LIMIT
```

These fields do not have a VALUE clause:

```
PAGE-NUMBER-OUT
LINE-SPACING
LINE-COUNT-ER
```

EXERCISE 2

Write a program to read and process data in the following format:

Positions	Field
1–7	Customer Number
8–15	Part Number
16–22	spaces
23–25	Quantity
26–31	Unit Price (in dollars and cents)
26–29	Unit Price dollars
30–31	Unit Price cents
32–35	Handling Charge (in dollars and cents)
32–33	Handling Charge dollars
34–35	Handling Charge cents
36–80	spaces

Assume that there are several input records for each customer, each record containing a different Part Number. For each record have your program print a line showing the Customer Number, Part Number, Quantity, Unit Price, Handling Charge, and merchandise amount (compute the merchandise amount by multiplying the Unit Price by the Quantity). For each customer have your program print a total line showing the total Handling Charge and the total merchandise amount. Design your output on a print chart before you begin coding.

The INITIALIZE Statement

The format of the INITIALIZE statement is as follows:

```
INITIALIZE {identifier-1} ...

[          {ALPHABETIC          }                            ]
[          {ALPHANUMERIC        }                            ]
[ REPLACING{NUMERIC             } DATA BY {identifier-2} } ...]
[          {ALPHANUMERIC-EDITED }         {literal-1   } }    ]
[          {NUMERIC-EDITED      }                            ]
```

The ellipsis after identifier-1 shows that you may have as many receiving fields as you like in an INITIALIZE statement. The receiving fields are INITIALIZEd in the order in which they appear in the statement.

The entire **REPLACING** phrase is optional. The INITIALIZE statements used in the programs in this chapter lack the REPLACING phrase. When the REPLACING phrase is omitted, the INITIALIZE statement MOVEs zeros to fields that are defined as numeric or numeric edited, and spaces to all other fields.

When the REPLACING phrase is used, the programmer can specify how fields of different categories are to be filled. Several categories of fields may be given in a single INITIALIZE statement, although the word REPLACING appears only once. For example, the statement

```
INITIALIZE GROUP-1 REPLACING ALPHANUMERIC    BY HIGH-VALUES
                             NUMERIC         BY 999999
                             NUMERIC-EDITED  BY ZERO
```

would MOVE HIGH-VALUES to all the fields in GROUP-1 that are defined as alphanumeric, 999999 to all the fields in GROUP-1 that are defined as numeric, and zeros to all fields in GROUP-1 that are defined as numeric edited. All MOVEs would be done as individual elementary MOVEs in accordance with the rules for MOVE. Unnamed elementary fields and fields named FILLER are always ignored by the INITIALIZE statement.

One Control Break and a Final Total

Our next program uses the same input as Program P07-01 and produces all of the same output. But in addition, Program P07-02 prints, at the end of the report, a final total of the debits for all the Account Numbers and of the credits for all the Account Numbers. To do this, we will use a technique called **rolling** the accumulators **forward.** Program P07-02 will contain a final total accumulator for the debits and a final total accumulator for the credits in addition to the accumulators we had in Program P07-01. Then, whenever a total line for an Account Number prints, the debits total for the Account Number will be added into the final debits accumulator and the credits total for the Account Number will be added into the final credits accumulator before the Account Number accumulators are zeroed.

Program P07-02 also introduces **group indicating.** Group indicating means that control fields are printed only the first time they appear on a page or the first time they appear after a control break. You will see in the output from Program P07-02 that the Account Number field prints only in the first detail line on each page and the first detail line after every control break, instead of printing in every detail line. In Program P07-01 we did not have group indicating; we printed the control field, Account Number, in every detail line.

The output format for Program P07-02 is shown in Figure 7.10. You can see there the format of the final total line. Also you can see the Account Numbers shown with group indicating.

To produce a hierarchy diagram for this program, we can modify the final hierarchy diagram for Program P07-01, shown in Figure 7.7. To produce the hierarchy diagram for Program P07-02, we need to change only the "Termination" procedure. When Program P07-02 comes to end-of-file on the input file, we have to print the total line for the last Account Number, and then produce the final total line. Thus the box "Final break" is added as a subfunction of "Termination," as shown in Figure 7.11.

FIGURE 7.10 Output format for Program P07-02

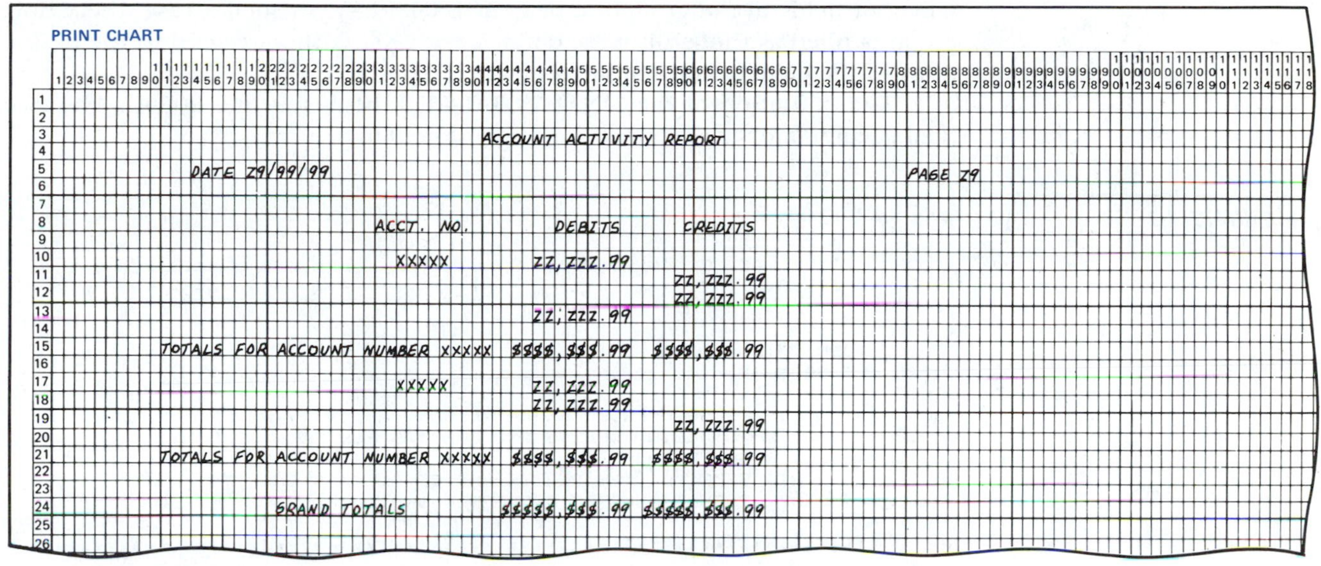

FIGURE 7.11 Hierarchy diagram for Program P07-02

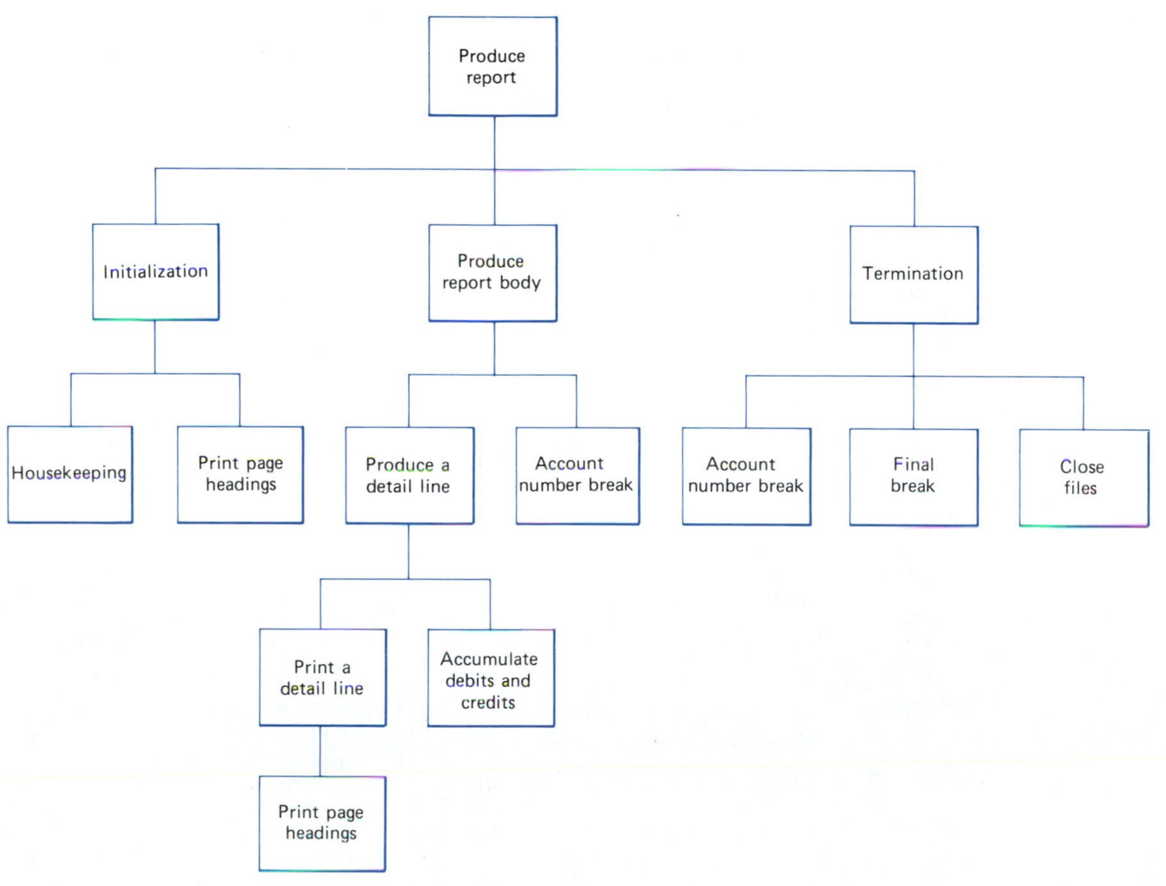

Program P07-02 is shown in Figure 7.12. Notice the VALUE clause at the group level in line 00620. A VALUE clause is permitted at the group level only when all fields in the group are of USAGE DISPLAY. In such a case, the whole group is filled as though it were defined with Xs, without regard to the definitions of the elementary items.

The definition of the FINAL-TOTAL-LINE begins at line 00740. The two final accumulators are defined starting at line 00840.

FIGURE 7.12 **Program P07-02**

```
S COBOL II RELEASE 3.2 09/05/90                          P07002    DATE FEB 22,1992 T
----+-*A-1-B--+----2----+----3----+----4----+----5----+----6----+----7-!--+

00010  IDENTIFICATION DIVISION.
00020  PROGRAM-ID.  P07-02.
00030 *
00040 *      THIS PROGRAM PRODUCES AN ACCOUNT ACTIVITY REPORT
00050 *      WITH TOTALS OF DEBITS AND CREDITS FOR EACH ACCOUNT.
00060 *      IT ALSO PRODUCES A FINAL TOTAL LINE SHOWING THE
00070 *      TOTALS OF ALL THE DEBITS AND OF ALL THE CREDITS.
00080 *      THE ACCOUNT NUMBERS ARE GROUP INDICATED.
00090 *
00100 *****************************************************************
00110
00120  ENVIRONMENT DIVISION.
00130  INPUT-OUTPUT SECTION.
00140  FILE-CONTROL.
00150      SELECT ACCOUNT-ACTIVITY-REPORT  ASSIGN TO PRINTER.
00160      SELECT ACCOUNT-FILE-IN          ASSIGN TO INFILE.
00170
00180 *****************************************************************
00190
00200  DATA DIVISION.
00210  FILE SECTION.
00220  FD  ACCOUNT-FILE-IN
00230      RECORD CONTAINS 80 CHARACTERS.
00240
00250  01  ACCOUNT-RECORD-IN         PIC X(80).
00260
00270  FD  ACCOUNT-ACTIVITY-REPORT.
00280
00290  01  REPORT-LINE               PIC X(87).
00300
00310  WORKING-STORAGE SECTION.
00320  01  MORE-INPUT                PIC X      VALUE "Y".
00330      88 THERE-IS-NO-INPUT                 VALUE "N".
00340      88 THERE-IS-NO-MORE-INPUT            VALUE "N".
00350  01  NO-INPUT-DATA             PIC X(15) VALUE "   NO INPUT DATA".
00360
00370  01  ACCOUNT-RECORD-W.
00380      05 INDICATOR              PIC X.
00390      05 ACCOUNT-NUMBER-IN      PIC X(5)   VALUE SPACES.
00400      05                        PIC X(3).
00410      05 AMOUNT                 PIC 9(5)V99.
00420
00430  01  PAGE-HEAD-1.
00440      05                        PIC X(40) VALUE SPACES.
00450      05                PIC X(23) VALUE "ACCOUNT ACTIVITY REPORT".
00460
00470  01  PAGE-HEAD-2.
00480      05                        PIC X(13) VALUE SPACES.
00490      05                        PIC X(5)   VALUE "DATE".
00500      05 RUN-MONTH-AND-DAY      PIC Z9/99/.
00510      05 RUN-YEAR               PIC 99.
00520      05                        PIC X(54) VALUE SPACES.
00530      05                        PIC X(5)   VALUE "PAGE".
00540      05 PAGE-NUMBER-OUT        PIC Z9.
00550
```

FIGURE 7.12 *continued*

```
 01  PAGE-HEAD-3.
     05                             PIC X(30) VALUE SPACES.
     05                             PIC X(17) VALUE "ACCT. NO.".
     05                             PIC X(12) VALUE "DEBITS".
     05                             PIC X(7)  VALUE "CREDITS".

 01  DETAIL-LINE                    VALUE SPACES.
     05 ACCOUNT-NUMBER-OUT          PIC B(32)X(5).
     05 DEBITS                      PIC B(8)ZZ,ZZZ.99.
     05 CREDITS                     PIC B(4)ZZ,ZZZ.99.

 01  CONTROL-BREAK-LINE.
     05                             PIC X(10) VALUE SPACES.
     05               PIC X(26)     VALUE "TOTALS FOR ACCOUNT NUMBER".
     05 ACCOUNT-NUMBER-SAVE         PIC X(5)BB.
     05 DEBITS-TOTAL                PIC $$$$,$$$.99BB.
     05 CREDITS-TOTAL               PIC $$$$,$$$.99.

 01  FINAL-TOTAL-LINE.
     05                             PIC X(21) VALUE SPACES.
     05                             PIC X(21) VALUE "GRAND TOTALS".
     05 DEBITS-TOTAL                PIC $$$$$,$$$.99B.
     05 CREDITS-TOTAL               PIC $$$$$,$$$.99.

 01  ACCUMULATORS-W         PACKED-DECIMAL.
     05 DEBITS-TOTAL                PIC S9(6)V99 VALUE 0.
     05 CREDITS-TOTAL               PIC S9(6)V99 VALUE 0.

 01  FINAL-ACCUMULATORS-W PACKED-DECIMAL.
     05 DEBITS-TOTAL                PIC S9(7)V99 VALUE 0.
     05 CREDITS-TOTAL               PIC S9(7)V99 VALUE 0.

 01  LINE-LIMIT         PIC S99 VALUE 34 COMP SYNC.
 01  LINE-SPACING       PIC S9           COMP SYNC.
 01  PAGE-NUMBER-W      PIC S99 VALUE ZERO PACKED-DECIMAL.
 01  LINE-COUNT-ER      PIC S99          COMP SYNC.

 01  TODAYS-DATE.
     05 RUN-YEAR                    PIC 99.
     05 RUN-MONTH-AND-DAY           PIC 9(4).

******************************************************************

PROCEDURE DIVISION.
PRODUCE-REPORT.
    PERFORM INITIALIZATION
    PERFORM PRODUCE-REPORT-BODY UNTIL THERE-IS-NO-MORE-INPUT
    PERFORM TERMINATION
    STOP RUN
    .

INITIALIZATION.
    PERFORM HOUSEKEEPING
    PERFORM PRINT-PAGE-HEADINGS
    IF THERE-IS-NO-INPUT
        WRITE REPORT-LINE FROM NO-INPUT-DATA AFTER 2
    END-IF
    .

```

continued

Three statements are needed in this program to accomplish group indication of the Account Number. Remember that group indication means that the Account Number will print in the first detail line after page headings and the first detail line after a control break. Thus, the statement at line 01230 MOVEs the Account Number to the detail line output area after page headings are printed, and the statement at line 01550 MOVEs the Account Number to the detail line output area after a control break. At line 01760, SPACES are MOVEd to the detail line to blank out the Account Number so that it does not print on subsequent detail lines.

The **ADD CORRESPONDING** statement, at line 01530, shows how the two ACCUMULATORS-W are rolled forward into the FINAL-ACCUMULATORS-W, just before the ACCUMULATORS-W are zeroed during an ACCOUNT-NUMBER-BREAK. The CORRESPONDING option is available with the SUBTRACT verb, also.

FIGURE 7.12 *continued*

```
S COBOL II RELEASE 3.2 09/05/90                 P07002   DATE FEB 22,1992 T
----+-*A-1-B--+----2----+----3----+----4----+----5----+----6----+----7-|--+

01150  PRINT-PAGE-HEADINGS.
01160      ADD 1                  TO PAGE-NUMBER-W
01170      MOVE PAGE-NUMBER-W TO PAGE-NUMBER-OUT
01180      WRITE REPORT-LINE FROM PAGE-HEAD-1 AFTER PAGE
01190      WRITE REPORT-LINE FROM PAGE-HEAD-2 AFTER 2
01200      WRITE REPORT-LINE FROM PAGE-HEAD-3 AFTER 3
01210      MOVE 6 TO LINE-COUNT-ER
01220      MOVE 2 TO LINE-SPACING
01230      MOVE ACCOUNT-NUMBER-SAVE TO ACCOUNT-NUMBER-OUT
01240      .
01250
01260  HOUSEKEEPING.
01270      OPEN INPUT  ACCOUNT-FILE-IN
01280           OUTPUT ACCOUNT-ACTIVITY-REPORT
01290      ACCEPT TODAYS-DATE FROM DATE
01300      MOVE CORRESPONDING TODAYS-DATE TO PAGE-HEAD-2
01310      READ ACCOUNT-FILE-IN INTO ACCOUNT-RECORD-W
01320          AT END
01330              SET THERE-IS-NO-INPUT TO TRUE
01340      END-READ
01350      MOVE ACCOUNT-NUMBER-IN TO ACCOUNT-NUMBER-SAVE
01360      .
01370
01380  PRODUCE-REPORT-BODY.
01390      IF ACCOUNT-NUMBER-IN NOT = ACCOUNT-NUMBER-SAVE
01400          PERFORM ACCOUNT-NUMBER-BREAK
01410      END-IF
01420      PERFORM PRODUCE-A-DETAIL-LINE
01430      READ ACCOUNT-FILE-IN INTO ACCOUNT-RECORD-W
01440          AT END
01450              SET THERE-IS-NO-MORE-INPUT TO TRUE
01460       .
01470
01480  ACCOUNT-NUMBER-BREAK.
01490      MOVE CORRESPONDING ACCUMULATORS-W TO CONTROL-BREAK-LINE
01500      WRITE REPORT-LINE FROM CONTROL-BREAK-LINE AFTER ADVANCING 2
01510      ADD 2                     TO LINE-COUNT-ER
01520      MOVE 2                    TO LINE-SPACING
01530      ADD CORRESPONDING ACCUMULATORS-W TO FINAL-ACCUMULATORS-W
01540      INITIALIZE ACCUMULATORS-W
01550      MOVE ACCOUNT-NUMBER-IN TO ACCOUNT-NUMBER-SAVE
01560                                ACCOUNT-NUMBER-OUT
01570      .
```

FIGURE *7.12* ***continued***

```
PRODUCE-A-DETAIL-LINE.
    PERFORM PRINT-A-DETAIL-LINE
    PERFORM ACCUMULATE-DEBITS-AND-CREDITS
    .

PRINT-A-DETAIL-LINE.
    IF INDICATOR IS EQUAL TO "-"
        MOVE AMOUNT TO DEBITS
    ELSE
        MOVE AMOUNT TO CREDITS
    END-IF
    IF LINE-COUNT-ER + LINE-SPACING > LINE-LIMIT
        PERFORM PRINT-PAGE-HEADINGS
    END-IF
    WRITE REPORT-LINE FROM DETAIL-LINE AFTER LINE-SPACING
    ADD LINE-SPACING TO LINE-COUNT-ER
    MOVE 1 TO LINE-SPACING
    MOVE SPACES TO DETAIL-LINE
    .

ACCUMULATE-DEBITS-AND-CREDITS.
    IF INDICATOR IS EQUAL TO "-"
        ADD AMOUNT TO DEBITS-TOTAL IN ACCUMULATORS-W
    ELSE
        ADD AMOUNT TO CREDITS-TOTAL IN ACCUMULATORS-W
    END-IF
    .

TERMINATION.
    PERFORM ACCOUNT-NUMBER-BREAK
    PERFORM FINAL-BREAK
    PERFORM CLOSE-FILES
    .

FINAL-BREAK.
    MOVE CORRESPONDING FINAL-ACCUMULATORS-W TO FINAL-TOTAL-LINE
    WRITE REPORT-LINE FROM FINAL-TOTAL-LINE AFTER 3
    .

CLOSE-FILES.
    CLOSE ACCOUNT-FILE-IN
          ACCOUNT-ACTIVITY-REPORT
    .
```

Program P07-02 was run with the same input as Program P07-01. Program P07–02 produced the output shown in Figure 7.13 on page 206.

FIGURE 7.13 **Output from Program P07-02**

```
                                   ACCOUNT ACTIVITY REPORT

  DATE  2/22/92                                                          PAGE  1

                         ACCT. NO.          DEBITS       CREDITS

                           02005             30.34
                                                             .00
                                                       98,762.01
                                               .06
                                         89,235.51
                                                       34,859.10

TOTALS FOR ACCOUNT NUMBER 02005       $89,265.91    $133,621.11

                           04502                       99,999.99
                                             83.99
                                         45,672.12

TOTALS FOR ACCOUNT NUMBER 04502       $45,756.11     $99,999.99

                           12121         75,499.00
                                               .02
                                               .00
                                                       23,411.11
                                                           66.67
                                         66,662.22

TOTALS FOR ACCOUNT NUMBER 12121      $142,161.24     $23,477.78

                           19596                       92,929.29
                                         12,547.20
                                         23,487.64



                                   ACCOUNT ACTIVITY REPORT

  DATE  2/22/92                                                          PAGE  2

                         ACCT. NO.          DEBITS       CREDITS

                           19596               .20
                                                            2.39
                                                          213.45

TOTALS FOR ACCOUNT NUMBER 19596       $36,035.04     $93,145.13

                           20023         99,999.99
                                         87,654.99
                                         86,868.68
                                                       88,888.80
                                                       88,553.32
                                                       56,789.23

TOTALS FOR ACCOUNT NUMBER 20023      $274,523.66    $234,231.35

                           23456              2.11
                                              4.53
                                             12.00
                                                             .12
                                                           18.00
                                                             .54

TOTALS FOR ACCOUNT NUMBER 23456           $18.64         $18.66

                           30721              1.01
                                                           99.12
                                             98.44

TOTALS FOR ACCOUNT NUMBER 30721           $99.45         $99.12
```

FIGURE 7.13 *continued*

```
                              ACCOUNT ACTIVITY REPORT

DATE  2/22/92                                                      PAGE  3

                         ACCT. NO.         DEBITS       CREDITS

                           40101           342.87
                                                         212.45
                                        60,002.01
                                                          67.00
                                        32,343.23
                                                      90,023.41

TOTALS FOR ACCOUNT NUMBER 40101       $92,688.11    $90,302.86

                           67689            11.14
                                                       1,010.10
                                            33.35
                                                       2,203.30
                                         3,040.20
                                                      10,000.00

TOTALS FOR ACCOUNT NUMBER 67689        $3,084.69    $13,213.40

                           72332              .04
                                                          44.44
                                           444.44
                                                           4.44
                                              .44
                                                       4,040.40

TOTALS FOR ACCOUNT NUMBER 72332          $444.92     $4,089.28

                GRAND TOTALS         $684,077.77   $692,198.68
```

Multiple Control Breaks

It is not uncommon for input data to have more than one control field and for reports to have several different kinds of total lines, each kind showing totals for a different control field. For example, consider input records in the following format:

Positions	Field
1–3	Store Number
4–6	Salesperson Number
7–12	Customer Number
13–19	Sale Amount (to two decimal places)
20–80	spaces

Each input record shows the dollars-and-cents amount of a purchase made by a customer. The record also shows the number of the salesperson who serviced the customer and the store number where the sale took place. Program P07-03 will produce a list of all these sales and show the total amount of sales made by each salesperson, the total amount of sales in each store, and the total amount of all sales. The output should look like Figure 7.14, from the input in Figure 7.15. The output format is shown in Figure 7.16.

Obviously, many of the ideas from Program P07-02 can be used in Program P07-03. The new ideas that we will need in order to create a report with three levels of totals are general enough that you will be able to apply them to reports of four or more levels.

FIGURE 7.14 **Output from P07-03**

```
                SALES REPORT
DATE   2/22/92                                    PAGE   1


     STORE      SALES-      CUSTOMER       SALE
      NO.       PERSON       NUMBER       AMOUNT

      010        101         003001      1,234.56
                             007002          2.24
                             011003      6,665.70
                             039004      8,439.20
                             046005      8,448.48
                             053006         12.34
                             060006      9,494.93
                             067007      4,000.03

                                        38,297.48 *

      010        102         074212      5,454.99
                             081012           .33
                             088013      5,849.58
                             095015        393.90

                                        11,698.80 *

      010        103         003234        303.03

                                           303.03 *

       TOTAL FOR STORE NO. 010      $ 50,299.31 **


      020        011         007567      9,999.99
                             011454        456.00
                             015231      8,484.39
                             019345      8,459.44
                             023345      8,333.33

                                        35,733.15 *
```

FIGURE 7.14

continued

```
                  SALES REPORT
DATE   2/22/92                                  PAGE   2

         STORE     SALES-     CUSTOMER     SALE
          NO.      PERSON      NUMBER      AMOUNT

          020       222        027345     4,343.43
                               031567     9,903.30
                               035001        34.21

                                         14,280.94 *

          020       266        039903     4,539.87
                               043854     5,858.30

                                         10,398.17 *

           TOTAL  FOR STORE NO. 020   $ 60,412.26 **


          030       193        047231     9,391.93
                               051342     5,937.43
                               055034     9,383.22
                               059932     5,858.54
                               063419     3,949.49

                                         34,520.61 *

           TOTAL  FOR STORE NO. 030   $ 34,520.61 **


          040       045        067333          .00
                               071323     5,959.50

                                          5,959.50 *

          040       403        048399     3,921.47


                  SALES REPORT
DATE   2/22/92                                  PAGE   3

         STORE     SALES-     CUSTOMER     SALE
          NO.      PERSON      NUMBER      AMOUNT

          040       403        054392          .00

                                          3,921.47 *

          040       412        060111     9,999.99

                                          9,999.99 *

           TOTAL  FOR STORE NO. 040   $ 19,880.96 **

          046       012        013538          .00
                               017521       690.78
                               021504     1,381.56
                               025487     2,072.34
                               029470     2,763.12

                                          6,907.80 *

          046       028        033453     3,453.90
                               037436     4,144.68
                               041419     4,835.46

                                         12,434.04 *

           TOTAL  FOR STORE NO. 046   $ 19,341.84 **

                    GRAND TOTAL     $  184,454.98 ***
```

FIGURE 7.15 **Input to Program P07-03**

```
--------------------------------------------------------------------------------
         1         2         3         4         5         6         7         8
12345678901234567890123456789012345678901234567890123456789012345678901234567890
--------------------------------------------------------------------------------
010101003001123456
010101007002000224
010101011003666570
010101039004843920
010101046005844848
010101053006001234
010101060006949493
010101067007400003
010102074212545499
010102081012000033
010102088013584958
010102095015039390
010103003234030303
020011007567999999
020011011454045600
020011015231848439
020011019345845944
020011023345833333
020222027345434343
020222031567990330
020222035001003421
020266039903453987
020266043854585830
030193047231939193
030193051342593743
030193055034938322
030193059932585854
030193063419394949
040045067333000000
040045071323595950
040403048399392147
040403054392000000
040412060111999999
046012013538000000
046012017521069078
046012021504138156
046012025487207234
046012029470276312
046028033453345390
046028037436414468
046028041419483546
```

The input data for Program P07-03 are grouped so that the printed output will be in the correct order for the totals to print. All sales for each store are grouped together in the input. Within each group of sales for a store, all sales made by one salesperson are grouped together; within each group of sales made by one salesperson, the customer numbers are in order. The input is thus **sorted** on the three fields: Store Number, Salesperson Number, and Customer Number. The Store Number is the most significant field and is called the **major sort field.** The Customer Number is the least significant field and is called the **minor sort field.** The Salesperson Number, whose significance falls between that of the Store Number and the Customer Number, is called the **intermediate sort field.** If there had been more than three fields used for ordering the data, the most significant would be the major, the least significant the minor, and all those between major and minor would be called intermediate. This input is said to be sorted by Store Number by Salesperson Number by Customer Number. Alternatively, the input can be described as being sorted by Customer Number within Salesperson Number within Store Number.

FIGURE 7.16 **Output format for Program P07–03**

PRINT CHART

```
                            SALES REPORT
                  DATE Z9/99/99                            PAGE Z9

                     STORE    SALES-    CUSTOMER     SALE
                      NO.     PERSON     NUMBER     AMOUNT

                      XXX      XXX       XXXXXX     Z,ZZZ.99
                                         XXXXXX     Z,ZZZ.99
                                         XXXXXX     Z,ZZZ.99

                                                   ZZ,ZZZ.99 *

                      XXX      XXX       XXXXXX     Z,ZZZ.99
                                         XXXXXX     Z,ZZZ.99

                                                   ZZ,ZZZ.99 *
                       TOTAL FOR STORE NO. XXX   $ZZZ,ZZZ.99 **

                      XXX      XXX       XXXXXX     Z,ZZZ.99
                                         XXXXXX     Z,ZZZ.99

                                                   ZZ,ZZZ.99 *

                      XXX      XXX       XXXXXX     Z,ZZZ.99
                                         XXXXXX     Z,ZZZ.99
                                         XXXXXX     Z,ZZZ.99

                                                   ZZ,ZZZ.99 *

                       TOTAL FOR STORE NO. XXX   $ZZZ,ZZZ.99 **

                               GRAND TOTAL     $Z,ZZZ,ZZZ.99 ***
```

In this program control breaks will be taken only on Salesperson Number and Store Number and totals printed for those breaks. Salesperson Number will be the **minor control field,** and Store Number will be the **major control field.** There will also be a final total line.

In this program there are three accumulators: one to accumulate the total of all sales for a salesperson, one for the total of all the sales in a store, and one for the total of all the sales. As each input record is read, the program prints it and adds the Sale Amount to the salesperson accumulator. When a salesperson break occurs, the total in the salesperson accumulator is printed, added into the store accumulator, and zeroed. When a break occurs on Store Number, the total in the store accumulator is printed, added into the final accumulator and zeroed. Thus the accumulators are rolled forward from the most minor level to the most major.

The program will have to check each input record to see whether there is a control break on Salesperson Number and/or on Store Number. If there is a break on Salesperson Number, the program will print a total for the previous salesperson, roll the salesperson accumulator into the store accumulator, zero the salesperson accumulator, and prepare to process the next salesperson group. But if there is a break on Store Number, that means that all the data have been read not only for the previous store but also for the last salesperson of the previous store. So a break on Store Number first requires carrying out all the steps of a salesperson break for the last salesperson of the previous store and then carrying out the Store Number break for the previous store: printing the store total line, rolling the store accumulator into the final accumulator, and preparing to process the next Store Number. When end-of-file is reached on the input, there still remain to be printed the total line for the last salesperson in the last store, the total line for the last store, and the grand total line.

Hierarchy Diagram for Program P07-03

Using the ideas and rationale from the hierarchy diagram for Program P07-02, we can start with the diagram for Program P07-03 shown in Figure 7.17. Here the box ''Produce report body'' has three subfunctions instead of two. Now its subfunctions are ''Produce a detail line,'' ''Salesperson Number break,'' and ''Store Number break.'' The diagram is not complete, though, for we have not filled in the subfunctions of ''Initialization'' and ''Termination.'' For ''Initialization'' we need the same subfunctions that we had in Program P07-02. For ''Termination'' we must print the total line for the last salesperson in the last store, the total line for the last store, and the grand total line. The hierarchy diagram can be completed by duplicating the boxes ''Salesperson Number break'' and ''Store Number break,'' and adding the box ''Final break.'' This is done in Figure 7.18.

FIGURE 7.17 **Partial hierarchy diagram for Program P07-03**

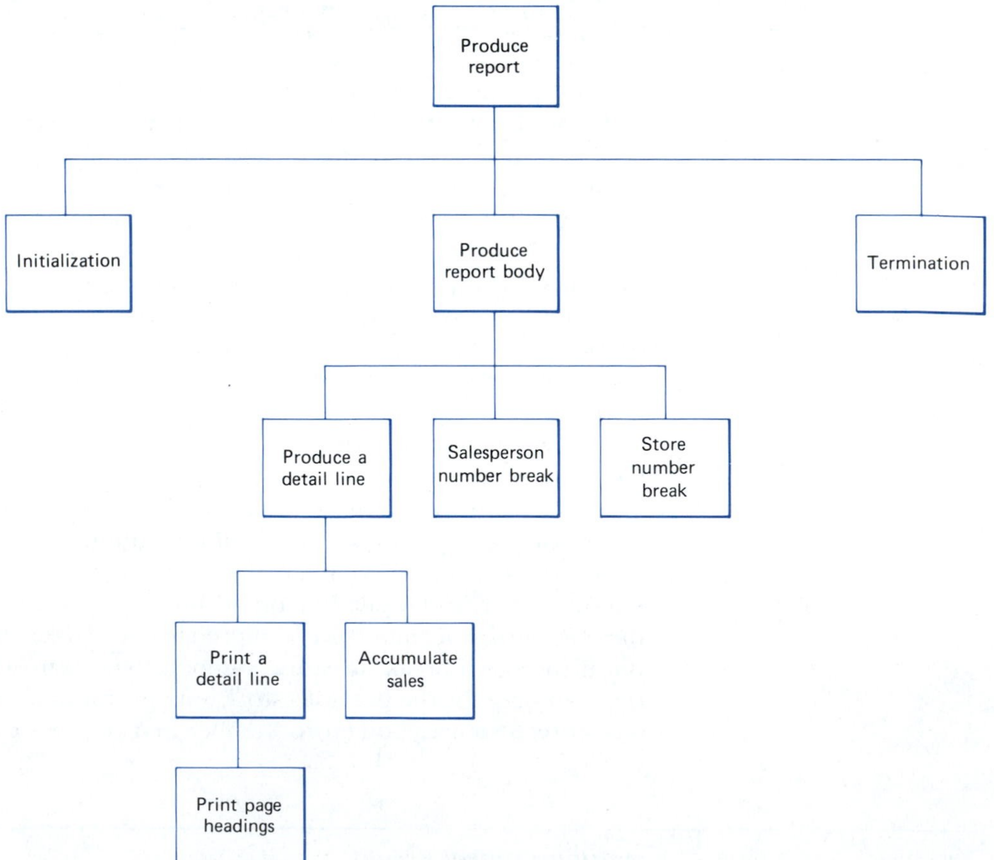

FIGURE 7.18 Complete hierarchy diagram for Program P07-03

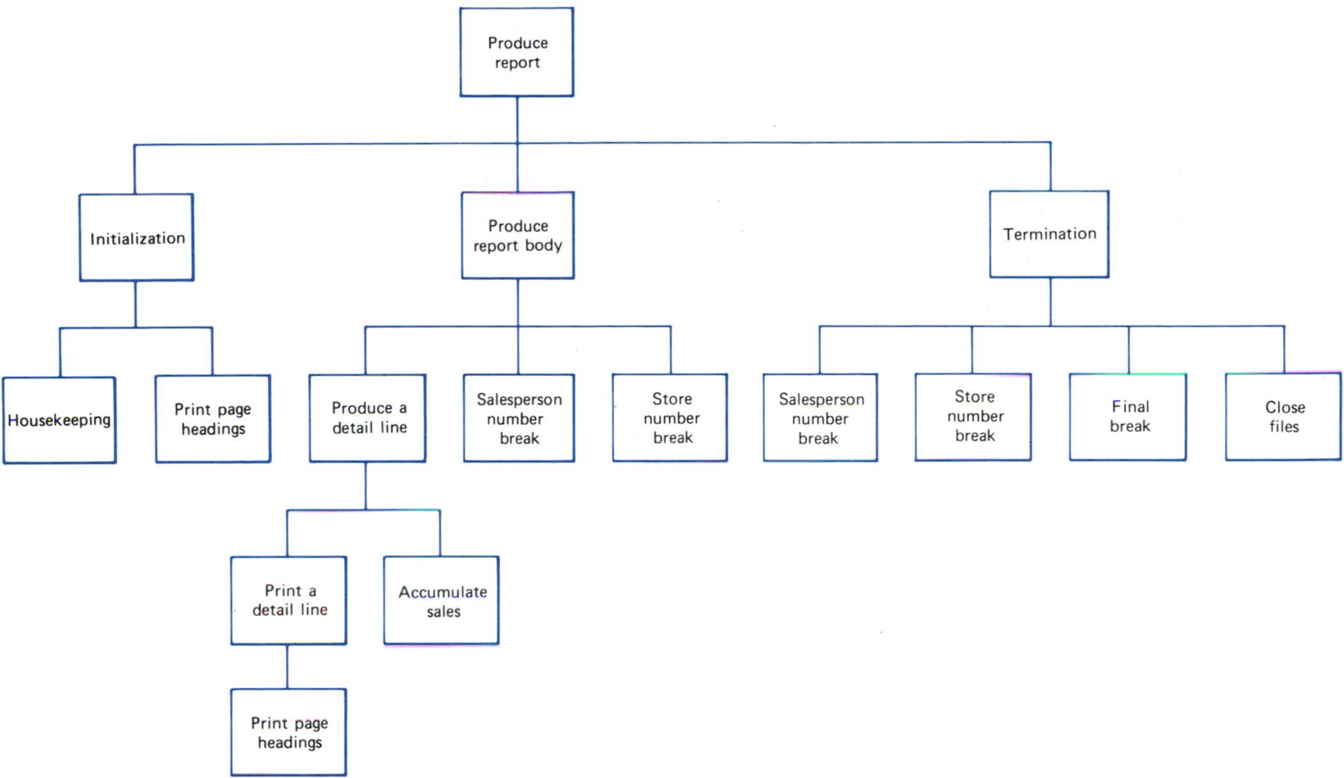

A Program with Three Levels of Totals

Program P07-03 is shown in Figure 7.19. You can follow the Procedure Division easily if you refer to the hierarchy diagram in Figure 7.18.

FIGURE 7.19 Program P07-03

```
S COBOL II RELEASE 3.2 09/05/90                P07003   DATE FEB 22,1992 T
----+-*A-1-B--+----2----+----3----+----4----+----5----+----6----+----7-|--+

  IDENTIFICATION DIVISION.
  PROGRAM-ID.  P07-03.
 *
 *     THIS PROGRAM PRODUCES A SALES REPORT
 *     WITH THREE LEVELS OF TOTALS.
 *
 *****************************************************************
```

FIGURE 7.19 *continued*

```
S COBOL II RELEASE 3.2 09/05/90                  P07003   DATE FEB 22,1992 T
----+-*A-1-B--+----2----+----3----+----4----+----5----+----6----+----7-|--+

ENVIRONMENT DIVISION.
INPUT-OUTPUT SECTION.
FILE-CONTROL.
    SELECT SALES-REPORT  ASSIGN TO PRINTER.
    SELECT SALES-FILE-IN ASSIGN TO INFILE.

******************************************************************

DATA DIVISION.
FILE SECTION.
FD  SALES-FILE-IN
    RECORD CONTAINS 80 CHARACTERS.

01  SALES-RECORD-IN          PIC X(80).

FD  SALES-REPORT.

01  REPORT-LINE              PIC X(69).

WORKING-STORAGE SECTION.
01  MORE-INPUT               PIC X     VALUE "Y".
    88 THERE-IS-NO-INPUT               VALUE "N".
    88 THERE-IS-NO-MORE-INPUT          VALUE "N".
01  NO-INPUT-DATA            PIC X(15) VALUE "  NO INPUT DATA".

01  SALES-RECORD-W.
    05 STORE-NUMBER-IN       PIC 9(3)  VALUE 0.
    05 SALESPERSON-NUMBER-IN PIC 9(3)  VALUE 0.
    05 CUSTOMER-NUMBER       PIC 9(6).
    05 SALE-AMOUNT           PIC 9(4)V99.

01  PAGE-HEAD-1.
    05                       PIC X(35) VALUE SPACES.
    05                       PIC X(12) VALUE "SALES REPORT".

01  PAGE-HEAD-2.
    05                       PIC X(19) VALUE SPACES.
    05                       PIC X(5)  VALUE "DATE".
    05 RUN-MONTH-AND-DAY     PIC Z9/99/.
    05 RUN-YEAR              PIC 99.
    05                       PIC X(29) VALUE SPACES.
    05                       PIC X(5)  VALUE "PAGE".
    05 PAGE-NUMBER-OUT       PIC Z9.

01  PAGE-HEAD-3.
    05                       PIC X(24) VALUE SPACES.
    05                       PIC X(9)  VALUE "STORE".
    05                       PIC X(10) VALUE "SALES-".
    05                       PIC X(13) VALUE "CUSTOMER".
    05                       PIC X(4)  VALUE "SALE".

01  PAGE-HEAD-4.
    05                       PIC X(25) VALUE SPACES.
    05                       PIC X(8)  VALUE "NO.".
    05                       PIC X(11) VALUE "PERSON".
    05                       PIC X(11) VALUE "NUMBER".
    05                       PIC X(6)  VALUE "AMOUNT".

01  DETAIL-LINE.
    05 STORE-NUMBER-OUT      PIC B(25)9(3).
    05 SALESPERSON-NUMBER-OUT   PIC B(6)9(3).
    05 CUSTOMER-NUMBER       PIC B(7)9(6).
    05 SALE-AMOUNT           PIC B(4)Z,ZZZ.99.
```

FIGURE 7.19 *continued*

```
 01  SALESPERSON-TOTAL-LINE.
     05 SALESPERSON-TOTAL-OUT PIC B(53)ZZ,ZZZ.99B.
     05                       PIC X     VALUE "*".

 01  STORE-TOTAL-LINE.
     05                       PIC X(26) VALUE SPACES.
     05             PIC X(20) VALUE "TOTAL FOR STORE NO.".
     05 STORE-NUMBER-SAVE     PIC 9(3).
     05                       PIC X(2)  VALUE SPACES.
     05 STORE-TOTAL-OUT       PIC $ZZZ,ZZZ.99B.
     05                       PIC X(2)  VALUE "**".

 01  GRAND-TOTAL-LINE.
     05                       PIC X(34) VALUE SPACES.
     05                       PIC X(15) VALUE "GRAND TOTAL".
     05 GRAND-TOTAL-OUT       PIC $Z,ZZZ,ZZZ.99B.
     05                       PIC X(3)  VALUE "***".

 01  PAGE-NUMBER-W            PIC S99 VALUE 0      PACKED-DECIMAL.
 01  PAGE-LIMIT               PIC S99 VALUE 38 COMP SYNC.
 01  LINE-SPACING             PIC S9           COMP SYNC.
 01  LINE-COUNT-ER            PIC S99          COMP SYNC.
 01  SALESPERSON-TOTAL-W      PIC S9(5)V99 VALUE 0 PACKED-DECIMAL.
 01  STORE-TOTAL-W            PIC S9(6)V99 VALUE 0 PACKED-DECIMAL.
 01  GRAND-TOTAL-W            PIC S9(7)V99 VALUE 0 PACKED-DECIMAL.
 01  SALESPERSON-NUMBER-SAVE  PIC 9(3).

 01  TODAYS-DATE.
     05 RUN-YEAR              PIC 99.
     05 RUN-MONTH-AND-DAY     PIC 9(4).

******************************************************************

 PROCEDURE DIVISION.
 PRODUCE-REPORT.
     PERFORM INITIALIZATION
     PERFORM PRODUCE-REPORT-BODY UNTIL THERE-IS-NO-MORE-INPUT
     PERFORM TERMINATION
     STOP RUN
     .

 INITIALIZATION.
     PERFORM HOUSEKEEPING
     PERFORM PRINT-PAGE-HEADING
     IF THERE-IS-NO-INPUT
         WRITE REPORT-LINE FROM NO-INPUT-DATA AFTER 2
     END-IF
     .

 HOUSEKEEPING.
     OPEN INPUT  SALES-FILE-IN
          OUTPUT SALES-REPORT
     ACCEPT TODAYS-DATE FROM DATE
     MOVE CORRESPONDING TODAYS-DATE TO PAGE-HEAD-2
     READ SALES-FILE-IN INTO SALES-RECORD-W
         AT END
             SET THERE-IS-NO-INPUT TO TRUE
     END-READ
     MOVE SALESPERSON-NUMBER-IN TO SALESPERSON-NUMBER-SAVE
     MOVE STORE-NUMBER-IN       TO STORE-NUMBER-SAVE
     .

```

continued

The EVALUATE statement at line 01360 determines whether any control break has occurred. As each input record is read, it is tested first by the WHEN phrase in line 01370 to see whether a major control break has occurred. If so, the minor and major control break routines are PERFORMed; if not, it is then necessary to see whether the lower-level break has occurred. The WHEN phrase at line 01400 does so.

Group indication of the Salesperson Number and Store Number is carried out by five statements in the program. The two statements at lines 01640 and 01660 MOVE the Salesperson Number and Store Number to the output line after every control break. The two statements at lines 02000 and 02010 MOVE the Salesperson Number and Store Number to the output line at the beginning of each new page. And the MOVE statement at line 01840 blanks the output line so that the control fields do not print on subsequent detail lines.

FIGURE 7.19 *continued*

```
S COBOL II RELEASE 3.2 09/05/90                 P07003    DATE FEB 22,1992 T
----+-*A-1-B--+----2----+----3----+----4----+----5----+----6----+----7-|--+

01350  PRODUCE-REPORT-BODY.
01360      EVALUATE TRUE
01370         WHEN STORE-NUMBER-IN NOT = STORE-NUMBER-SAVE
01380                                   PERFORM SALESPERSON-NUMBER-BREAK
01390                                   PERFORM STORE-NUMBER-BREAK
01400         WHEN SALESPERSON-NUMBER-IN NOT = SALESPERSON-NUMBER-SAVE
01410                                   PERFORM SALESPERSON-NUMBER-BREAK
01420      END-EVALUATE
01430      PERFORM PRODUCE-A-DETAIL-LINE
01440      READ SALES-FILE-IN INTO SALES-RECORD-W
01450          AT END
01460              SET THERE-IS-NO-MORE-INPUT TO TRUE
01470      .
01480
01490  STORE-NUMBER-BREAK.
01500      MOVE STORE-TOTAL-W TO STORE-TOTAL-OUT
01510      WRITE REPORT-LINE FROM STORE-TOTAL-LINE AFTER 2
01520      ADD 2 TO LINE-COUNT-ER
01530      ADD STORE-TOTAL-W TO GRAND-TOTAL-W
01540      MOVE STORE-NUMBER-IN TO STORE-NUMBER-SAVE
01550      MOVE 0 TO STORE-TOTAL-W
01560      MOVE 3 TO LINE-SPACING
01570      .
01580
01590  SALESPERSON-NUMBER-BREAK.
01600      MOVE SALESPERSON-TOTAL-W TO SALESPERSON-TOTAL-OUT
01610      WRITE REPORT-LINE FROM SALESPERSON-TOTAL-LINE AFTER 2
01620      ADD 2                      TO LINE-COUNT-ER
01630      ADD SALESPERSON-TOTAL-W    TO STORE-TOTAL-W
01640      MOVE SALESPERSON-NUMBER-IN TO SALESPERSON-NUMBER-OUT
01650                                    SALESPERSON-NUMBER-SAVE
01660      MOVE STORE-NUMBER-IN       TO STORE-NUMBER-OUT
01670      MOVE 0                     TO SALESPERSON-TOTAL-W
01680      MOVE 2                     TO LINE-SPACING
01690      .
01700
01710  PRODUCE-A-DETAIL-LINE.
01720      PERFORM PRINT-A-DETAIL-LINE
01730      PERFORM ACCUMULATE-SALES
01740      .
01750
```

```
PRINT-A-DETAIL-LINE.
    MOVE CORRESPONDING SALES-RECORD-W TO DETAIL-LINE
    IF LINE-COUNT-ER + LINE-SPACING > PAGE-LIMIT
        PERFORM PRINT-PAGE-HEADING
    END-IF
    WRITE REPORT-LINE FROM DETAIL-LINE AFTER LINE-SPACING
    ADD LINE-SPACING TO LINE-COUNT-ER
    MOVE 1            TO LINE-SPACING
    MOVE SPACES       TO DETAIL-LINE
    .

ACCUMULATE-SALES.
    ADD SALE-AMOUNT IN SALES-RECORD-W TO SALESPERSON-TOTAL-W
    .

PRINT-PAGE-HEADING.
    ADD 1 TO PAGE-NUMBER-W
    MOVE PAGE-NUMBER-W TO PAGE-NUMBER-OUT
    WRITE REPORT-LINE FROM PAGE-HEAD-1 AFTER PAGE
    WRITE REPORT-LINE FROM PAGE-HEAD-2
    WRITE REPORT-LINE FROM PAGE-HEAD-3 AFTER 3
    WRITE REPORT-LINE FROM PAGE-HEAD-4
    MOVE 6                        TO LINE-COUNT-ER
    MOVE 2                        TO LINE-SPACING
    MOVE STORE-NUMBER-SAVE        TO STORE-NUMBER-OUT
    MOVE SALESPERSON-NUMBER-SAVE TO SALESPERSON-NUMBER-OUT
    .

FINAL-BREAK.
    MOVE GRAND-TOTAL-W TO GRAND-TOTAL-OUT
    WRITE REPORT-LINE FROM GRAND-TOTAL-LINE AFTER 2
    .

TERMINATION.
    PERFORM SALESPERSON-NUMBER-BREAK
    PERFORM STORE-NUMBER-BREAK
    PERFORM FINAL-BREAK
    PERFORM CLOSE-FILES
    .

CLOSE-FILES.
    CLOSE SALES-FILE-IN
          SALES-REPORT
    .
```

EXERCISE *3*

Rewrite the program in Exercise 2 with group indication of the Customer Number. That is, have each Customer Number print on only the first detail line after a control break and on the first detail line of a page.

EXERCISE *4*

Using the input of Program P07-03, write a program that will print a line for each input record showing the Customer Number, the Sale Amount, a tax amount on the sale (at 8%), and the total of the Sale amount and the tax. On each total line for salesperson, store, and grand total, show the total of all the appropriate Sale Amounts, tax amounts, and the totals of the Sale Amounts and the tax amounts. Group indicate the Store Numbers and Salesperson Numbers.

EXERCISE *5*

Modify your solution to Exercise 4 so that no detail lines print; have your program print only the various levels of total lines. This is called **group printing** or **summary reporting.** On salesperson total lines, show the Store Number and the Salesperson Number. On store total lines, show the Store Number. Arrange the page overflow logic so that a salesperson total line may be the first line on a page (after the page headings) but so that a store total line will never print at the top of a page right after the headings.

EXERCISE 6

Modify your solution to Exercise 5 so that on each total line there also prints the number of sale amounts that make up the total.

Any Number of Control Breaks

You can see now how to plan and write a program having any number of control breaks. Let's say we have an application with five levels of breaks, called Level-A through Level-E, with Level-A being the lowest-level break and Level-E being the highest. You would of course need a save field for each control field A through E. One possible way to code the control break logic is as follows:

```
EVALUATE TRUE
     WHEN LEVEL-E-FIELD-IN NOT = LEVEL-E-FIELD-SAVE
                                          PERFORM LEVEL-A-BREAK
                                          PERFORM LEVEL-B-BREAK
                                          PERFORM LEVEL-C-BREAK
                                          PERFORM LEVEL-D-BREAK
                                          PERFORM LEVEL-E-BREAK
     WHEN LEVEL-D-FIELD-IN NOT = LEVEL-D-FIELD-SAVE
                                          PERFORM LEVEL-A-BREAK
                                          PERFORM LEVEL-B-BREAK
                                          PERFORM LEVEL-C-BREAK
                                          PERFORM LEVEL-D-BREAK
     WHEN LEVEL-C-FIELD-IN NOT = LEVEL-C-FIELD-SAVE
                                          PERFORM LEVEL-A-BREAK
                                          PERFORM LEVEL-B-BREAK
                                          PERFORM LEVEL-C-BREAK
     WHEN LEVEL-B-FIELD-IN NOT = LEVEL-B-FIELD-SAVE
                                          PERFORM LEVEL-A-BREAK
                                          PERFORM LEVEL-B-BREAK
     WHEN LEVEL-A-FIELD-IN NOT = LEVEL-A-FIELD-SAVE
                                          PERFORM LEVEL-A-BREAK

END-EVALUATE
```

The TERMINATION paragraph could include the following statements:

```
PERFORM LEVEL-A-BREAK
PERFORM LEVEL-B-BREAK
PERFORM LEVEL-C-BREAK
PERFORM LEVEL-D-BREAK
PERFORM LEVEL-E-BREAK
PERFORM FINAL-BREAK
```

There are methods for handling multiple levels of control breaks other than the ones shown in this chapter. These methods were chosen for ease of learning, understanding, and application.

Summary

COBOL programs must often produce reports that have total lines throughout, as well as at the end. There may also be one or more levels of totals. There must be at least one accumulator for each level of total, including one accumulator for a final total if desired. Programs with any number of levels of control breaks can be organized in this same way. The input data are added into the minor accumulator. When a minor total line is printed, the contents of the minor accumulator are added into the next higher-level accumulator. When a total line for that accumulator is printed, its contents are added into the next higher-level accumulator, and so on.

COMPUTATIONAL or PACKED-DECIMAL may be designated as the USAGE of a field. Numeric fields that are used entirely for operations internal to the program should be designated as COMPUTATIONAL. Other independent numeric fields in working storage should be designated as PACKED-DECIMAL. Any field designated as COMPUTATIONAL should also be SYNCHRONIZED. The abbreviations for COMPUTATIONAL and SYNCHRONIZED are COMP and SYNC. A field whose USAGE is not given explicitly is a DISPLAY field.

The figurative constants ZERO, ZEROS, and ZEROES may be used whenever a numeric or nonnumeric constant of zero would otherwise be legal. COBOL interprets the figurative constant as numeric or nonnumeric, depending on the context. If a nonnumeric literal of zeros is called for, COBOL provides as many zeros as are needed, depending on the context.

SPACE and SPACES are equivalent, and both are treated as nonnumeric constants. When SPACE or SPACES is used, COBOL provides a string of blanks, the exact number of blank characters being determined by the context.

Other figurative constants are HIGH-VALUE, HIGH-VALUES, LOW-VALUE, LOW-VALUES, QUOTE, and QUOTES.

A VALUE clause may be used at the group level only if all the items within the group are of USAGE DISPLAY. In such a case, the group is filled as if it were defined with all Xs and without regard to the definitions of the fields within it.

Group indicating is printing each control field only the first time it appears on a page or the first time it appears after a control break. Group printing, also called summary reporting, is printing total lines only but not any detail lines.

Fill-In Exercises

1. A change in the value of a control ______ is called a control ______.
2. When end-of-file is detected on the input file, the last ______ line(s) still remain to be printed.
3. Designating fields which do not interact with input or output fields as ______ can improve program efficiency.
4. Using the PICTURE character ______ on numeric fields in working storage can improve program efficiency.
5. The three field USAGEs we have studies so far are ______, ______, and ______.
6. SPACE and ZERO are ______ constants.
7. ______ and ______ stand for the highest character that can be stored in the computer.
8. A field that is broken down into smaller fields is called a(n) ______ ______.
9. A field that is not broken down into smaller fields is called a(n) ______ ______.

10. Printing only total lines and not printing any detail lines is called ______.
11. ______ and ______ stand for the lowest character that can be stored in the computer.
12. ______ and ______ stand for the character ".
13. The most significant field used for sequencing data is called the ______ sort field.
14. Two COBOL words with the same meaning as ZERO are ______ and ______.
15. A VALUE clause may be used at the group level only if all items within the group are of USAGE ______.

Review Exercises

1. Modify your solution to Exercise 3, page 217, to provide a grand total line in addition to the customer total lines.
2. Using the input for Program P07-01, write a program that will print and accumulate only the debits. Have your program print one line for each input record containing a debit. Have your program print a total line for each account, showing the total of only the debits for that account. Also show a final total line. Group indicate the Account Number.
3. Modify your solution to Exercise 4, page 217, so that on each salesperson total line there also prints the average Sale Amount (before tax) and, if the average Sale Amount is equal to or greater than $200, the words ABOVE QUOTA.
4. Modify your solution to Exercise 4, page 217, so that only Sale Amounts of $200 or less are printed and added into the totals. Sale Amounts greater than $200 should be ignored by the program.
5. Modify your solution to Exercise 4, page 217, so that on each total line there prints the number of sales less than $200 included in the total and the number of sales of $200 included in the total.

Project

Modify your solution to the Project in Chapter 5, page 162. Use input records in the following format:

Positions	Field
1–7	Starting Loan Amount (dollars and cents)
8–13	Monthly Payment (dollars and cents)
14–15	Month of First Payment
16–19	Year of First Payment
20–23	Annual Interest Rate
24–80	spaces

Have your program produce output in the format shown in Figure 7.P1. Use control break logic to print the field Total Interest For Year, in the following way:

1. Set up an accumulator for the total interest for the year.

2. Every time you print an interest amount, add it to the accumulator.
3. At the end of each calendar year, print the accumulator and zero it out. Add 1 to the Year of Payment.

Group indicate the Year of Payment as shown in Figure 7.P1. Don't forget to print the Total Interest For Year in the last year of the loan.

FIGURE 7.P1 **Output format for Chapter 7 Project**

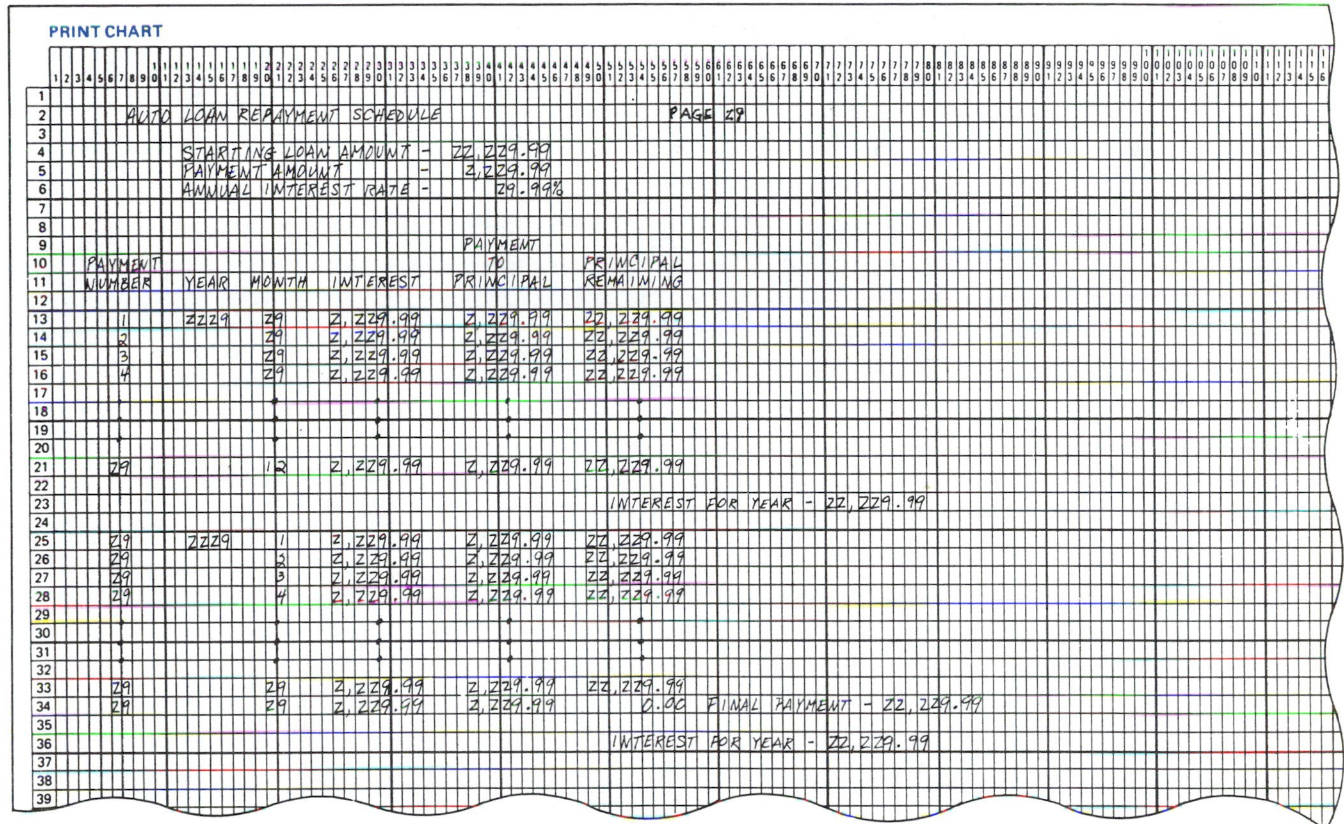

CHAPTER 8 Validity Checking

HERE ARE THE KEY POINTS YOU SHOULD LEARN FROM THIS CHAPTER

1. The importance of checking the validity of input data
2. How to check for presence of data, class of data, valid codes, and reasonableness
3. How to program for arithmetic overflow

KEY WORDS TO RECOGNIZE AND LEARN

REDEFINES	END-ADD
overflow	END-COMPUTE

COBOL has several features that permit a program to check the validity of the data it is working on. Invalid data can arise in essentially two ways, the more common of which is invalid data in program input. Most input data are prepared by people, usually on key machines such as a terminal. Even though such data are proofread and verified in other ways before being processed by the program, it is usual to expect that the input data still will contain errors, and the variety of errors will be literally impossible to imagine. After you think you have seen all the possible kinds of input errors, ''you ain't seen nothing yet.''

Obviously, programs should not execute on incorrect or invalid data. The worst thing that can happen if a program processes incorrect data is that the output will be incorrect and no one will notice the error until it is too late. Another is that incorrect data will cause the program to behave in such an obviously nonsensical way that the error becomes apparent to all. The best thing, though, is for the program itself to be able to detect errors and to handle them in a rational, planned way.

Aside from program input, the other source of invalid data is the program itself. It sometimes happens that in the course of execution the program generates unexpected intermediate results that cannot be further processed properly. COBOL provides ways for a program to protect itself against certain kinds of invalid input data and certain kinds of internally generated invalid data.

Validity Check of Input Data

Since the variety of possible invalid inputs is infinite, it is customary for COBOL programs to make just a few kinds of checks on the data before proceeding. The program can check that fields that are required in the input are in fact present; that fields that are supposed to contain only numbers are in fact purely numeric (and that fields that are supposed to contain only letters are in fact alphabetic); and that the contents of fields are reasonable values. We now look at these in order.

Checking for Presence of Data

In all the programs we have done so far, every field of input data was required to be present. For example, in Program P05-02 each input record had to contain some Salesperson Number, some Class, a figure for Last Year's Sales, and a figure for Current Sale. If any of those fields accidentally had been left blank in any record, the program would not have been able to process the record. Program P05-02 did check that the Class field was present, but the absence of any of the other fields also would have been a fatal error.

In real data processing in industry, not all input records always need to have all their fields present, but when the presence of a field is required, there are ways that COBOL can check that the field is filled in. One technique may be used for fields defined as alphanumeric and other techniques used for numeric fields.

Checking for the presence of data in alphanumeric fields. As in Program P05-02, the programmer may attach a level-88 entry to the field. A suitable condition name may be given and the VALUE SPACE or VALUE SPACES clause used, as in:

```
05  CLASS-IN              PIC X.
    88  CLASS-CODE-IS-MISSING     VALUE SPACE.
```

Then in the Procedure Division, the test

```
IF CLASS-CODE-IS-MISSING ...
```

may be used. The following relation test would work as well:

```
IF CLASS-IN = SPACE ...
```

The choice of which form to use is a matter of programmer preference.

Checking for the presence of unsigned integers. It is illegal in COBOL to use a VALUE SPACES clause with an item described as numeric. Thus a level-88 entry cannot be used to test for a missing integer. (Level-88 entries may be used with numeric fields in other contexts, however; see, for example, Exercise 3, Chapter 5, page 130.) The easiest way to check for the absence of an unsigned integer is with a relation condition in an IF statement, as, for example:

```
IF STORE-NUMBER-IN = SPACES ...
```

Notice that it is legal to use SPACES in an IF statement with an unsigned integer field.

Checking for the presence of signed fields and numeric noninteger fields. It is illegal to use SPACES in an IF statement with a numeric noninteger field. And if you use SPACES in an IF statement with a signed field, the IF test may not work properly. So the best way to test for the presence of a signed or noninteger field is to take advantage of the COBOL feature that permits a single field to have more than one PICTURE and more than one name if necessary.

The **REDEFINES** clause permits the programmer to give as many different PICTUREs as desired to a single field, and so for purposes of testing the field, the programmer can assign an alphanumeric PICTURE to the field and use the techniques given earlier for testing for the presence of data in an alphanumeric field. For example, the entries

```
05 MONEY-AMOUNT-IN               PIC 9(6)V99.
05 MONEY-AMOUNT-IN-X
   REDEFINES MONEY-AMOUNT-IN     PIC X(8).
```

will let the programmer refer to the same field by either of two names—MONEY-AMOUNT-IN or MONEY-AMOUNT-IN-X. The choice of which name the programmer will use in any particular place in the Procedure Division depends on how the field is used: If the program were to do arithmetic with the field, the name MONEY-AMOUNT-IN would be used. But if the program were to use the field in some context where only alphanumeric fields are allowed, the name MONEY-AMOUNT-IN-X would be used. So to test MONEY-AMOUNT-IN for absence of data, the following would be legal:

```
IF MONEY-AMOUNT-IN-X = SPACES ...
```

But it is permissible to attach a level-88 entry to a field defined with a REDEFINES clause, so the following would be legal:

```
05 MONEY-AMOUNT-IN             PIC 9(6)V99.
05 MONEY-AMOUNT-IN-X
REDEFINES MONEY-AMOUNT-IN      PIC X(8).
88 MONEY-AMOUNT-IS-MISSING     VALUE SPACES.
```

Then in the Procedure Division, the programmer may write:

```
IF MONEY-AMOUNT-IS-MISSING ...
```

The presence of the REDEFINES clause does not interfere with other uses of the field MONEY-AMOUNT-IN. For example, MONEY-AMOUNT-IN still could have its own numeric level-88 entries if desired, as follows:

```
05 MONEY-AMOUNT-IN                  PIC 9(6)V99.
   88 MONEY-AMOUNT-IS-LOW      VALUES 0 THRU 4999.99.
   88 MONEY-AMOUNT-IS-HIGH     VALUES 700000 THRU 999999.99.
05 MONEY-AMOUNT-IN-X
   REDEFINES MONEY-AMOUNT-IN        PIC X(8).
   88 MONEY-AMOUNT-IS-MISSING       VALUE SPACES.
```

This REDEFINES technique also can be used, of course, with unsigned integer fields as well. Names used to redefine fields are ignored by the CORRESPONDING option. In Chapter 10 we will see an entirely different use of the REDEFINES clause.

EXERCISE 1

Given the following COBOL statement:

```
05 PART-DESCRIPTION-IN               PIC X(20).
```

a. Without using a level-88 entry, write an IF statement to check for the absence of data in the field.

b. Write a level-88 entry using a VALUE SPACES clause and write an IF statement to check for the absence of data in the field.

EXERCISE 2

Given the following COBOL statement:

```
05 NUMBER-OF-SHEEP-IN                    PIC 9(5).
```

a. Without using a REDEFINES entry or a level-88 entry, write an IF statement to check for the absence of data in the field.

b. Using a REDEFINES entry and a level-88 entry with a VALUE SPACES clause, write an IF statement to check for the absence of data in the field.

Checking the Class of Data

The class condition should be used to check whether input fields do or do not contain only numbers, or do or do not contain only alphabetic characters. The format of the class condition is given in Chapter 5, page 128.

These types of test are needed because the READ statement does not check that data being read agree with the PICTUREs of the fields the data are being read into. That is, if nonnumeric data are read into a field defined as numeric, the READ statement will not detect the error.

The results of not testing a numeric field for absence or invalidity of data can range from insignificant to disastrous. If the field is merely printed on a report, then its absence or invalidity will appear in the report and cause just that one item to be unreadable. If, instead, the missing or invalid field is a control field, then the control breaks for that group will not operate properly and a whole section of the output may be useless. The remainder of the output may be usable, however.

If a field used for numeric comparisons, numeric editing, or arithmetic is missing or invalid, any of several very unpleasant things can happen. Depending on the nature of the error in the numeric field and on the COBOL system being used, the program just might make up its own number and go merrily along using that number in processing. Of course, the output will be totally wrong and the error might not be noticed until too late. Another thing that might happen is that the program will terminate execution. At least that way everyone will know that an error has occurred, but none of the input records following the bad one will be processed. It is best to have the program check all numeric input fields and take care of the erroneous ones before they take care of you.

Checking Data for Reasonableness

Incorrect input data can often slip past tests for presence and tests of class. For example, a field described as

```
05 HOURS-WORKED       PIC 99V9.
```

with room for three digits accidentally might contain 93.0 instead of the correct value of 39.0. This kind of error, which would not be detected by a class test or a presence test, can be detected by the program because it is so much larger than one would expect. The test could be coded as

```
05 HOURS-WORKED                      PIC 99V9.
   88 HOURS-WORKED-IS-VERY-HIGH VALUES 60.1 THRU 99.9.
```

and

```
IF HOURS-WORKED-IS-VERY-HIGH ...
```

Fields that are supposed to contain only certain valid codes can be checked to see that one of the valid codes is present:

```
05 MARITAL-STATUS                   PIC X.
   88 SINGLE                        VALUE "S".
   88 MARRIED                       VALUE "M".
   88 LEGALLY-SEPARATED             VALUE "L".
   88 LIVING-APART                  VALUE "V".
   88 LIVING-TOGETHER               VALUE "T".
   88 MENAGE-A-TROIS                VALUE "3".
   88 DONT-KNOW-MARITAL-STATUS VALUE "U".
   88 WIDOW-OR-WIDOWER              VALUE "W".
   88 DIVORCED                      VALUE "D".
   88 MARITAL-CODE-IS-MISSING       VALUE SPACE.
   88 VALID-MARITAL-STATUS          VALUE "3"
                                          "S" "M" "L"
                                          "T" THRU "W"
                                          "D".
```

Then for processing the field the program may refer to any of the level-88 names, and for checking the field we can have

```
IF MARITAL-CODE-IS-MISSING ...
```

and

```
IF NOT VALID-MARITAL-STATUS ...
```

Sometimes individual fields cannot be tested for reasonableness in cases where data can be detected as invalid only because of an unlikely combination of fields in the input. For example, in a certain payroll application it may be reasonable to have annual salaries in the range \$5,000 to \$200,000, because everyone from janitor to vice-president is processed by the one program. Combined conditions sometimes can be used to detect unlikely combinations of data, as in:

```
IF WORK-CODE-IS-JANITOR AND
   SALARY GREATER THAN JANITOR-SALARY-LIMIT ...
```

It usually is not wise to go to great lengths to include complicated and extensive reasonableness testing in a program. No matter how thorough the validity checking might be, some creative input clerk will make a keying error that gets through it. The easiest tests to make, like those for presence, class, and valid codes, and some straightforward reasonableness tests, are the ones that catch the greatest number of errors.

EXERCISE 3

Given the following field:

```
05 HOURS-WORKED                          PIC 99V9.
```

Write a level-88 entry and an IF statement to determine whether the contents of the field are outside the reasonable range. Fewer than 8 hours worked, or more than 65, is outside the reasonable range. Write the IF statement so that the True path will be executed if the field contents are found unreasonable.

EXERCISE 4

Given the following field:

```
05 TYPE-OF-SALE                          PIC X.
```

Write level-88 entries giving suitable names to the following codes for the different types of sales: wholesale, W; retail, R; return, N; preferred customer, P. Also write a level-88 entry giving a name to a missing code and a level-88 entry giving a name to the valid codes. Write IF statements to check for the absence of data in the field and for an invalid code.

A Program with Validity Checking of Input Data

In Program P08-01 you will see how to program validity checking of input data. In Program P08-01 each input record is supposed to contain a numeric Salesperson Number, a valid salesperson Class, a numeric value for Last Year's Sales, and a numeric value for Current Sale. The valid salesperson Classes are the letters A through H as before. The program is to check each input record for validity. If a record contains no validity errors, the program is to compute the ratio of the Current Sale to Last Year's Sales and print a line of output as shown in Figure 8.1. The format of the input record is given on page 235.

Figure 8.1 also shows the different kinds of error messages that the program might produce and thus implies the kinds of errors the program is supposed to check for. The error message about the Current Sale amount being

FIGURE 8.1 Output format for Program P08-01

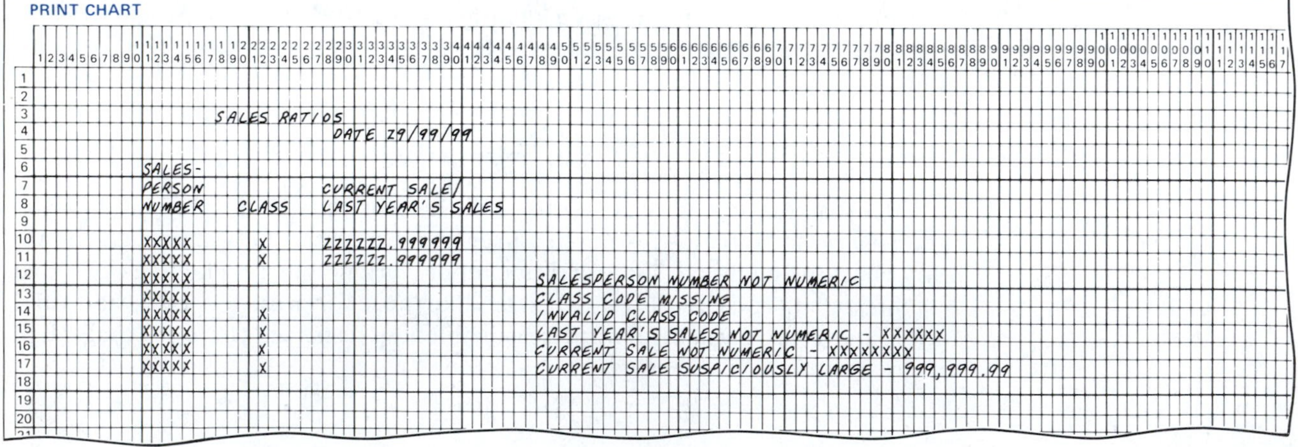

suspiciously large refers to Current Sales of more than $500,000. In this sales application it is assumed that so large a Current Sale amount is probably an error.

The program is to check for all possible errors in each input record. If there is more than one error in a single record, the program is to print an error line for each error found. A line is to be printed showing the ratio of the Current Sale to Last Year's Sales only if the input record contains no errors. If any errors are found in an input record, only the error lines are to print for that record.

A hierarchy diagram for Program P08-01 is shown in Figure 8.2. The subfunctions of "Check for errors" are the different validity checks that the program makes on each input record. For each type of error that may be found, the

FIGURE 8.2 **Hierarchy diagram for Program P08-01**

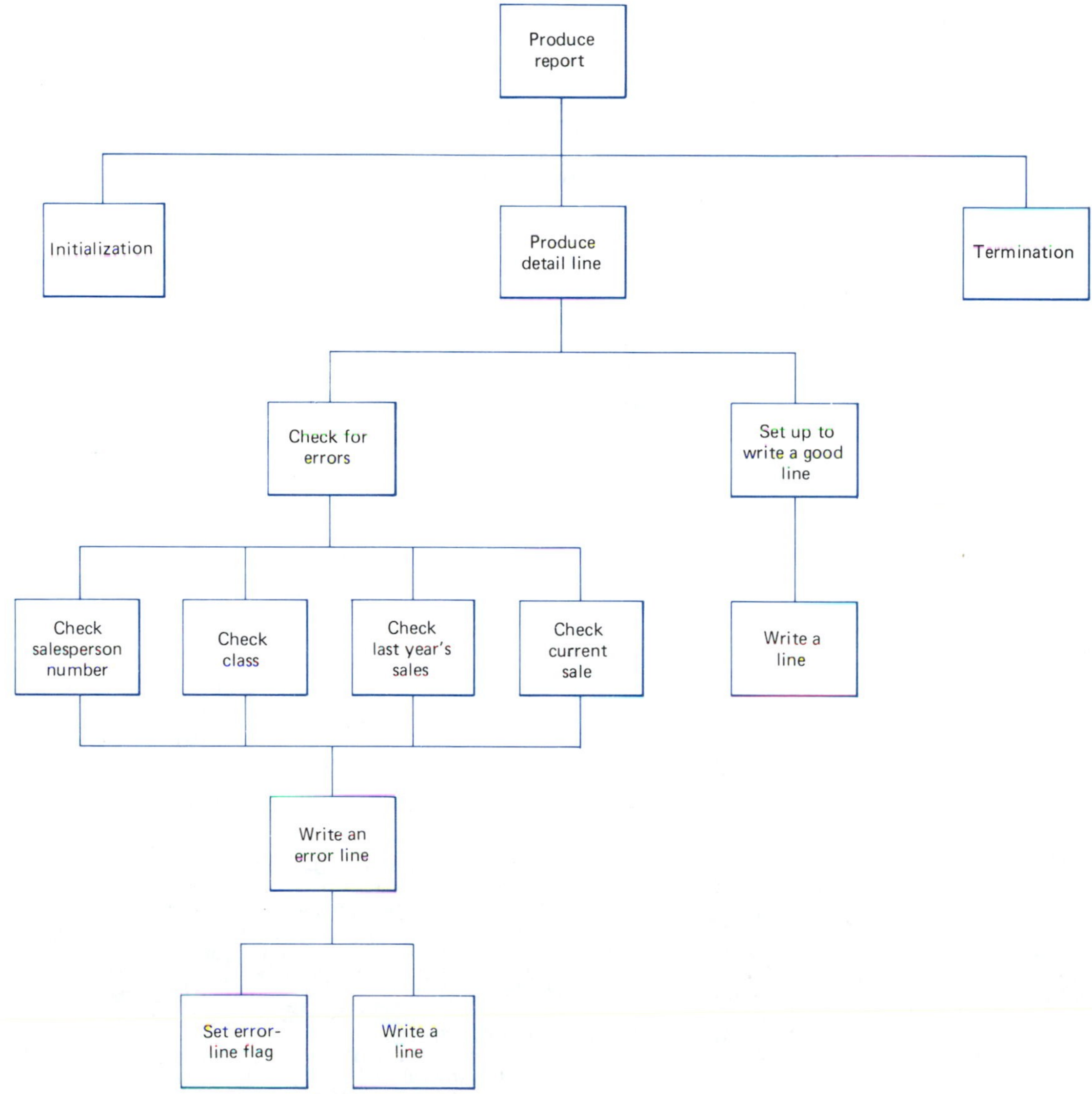

program will set up an appropriate error line and PERFORM a common routine called "Write an error line." If no errors are found in an input record, the program will carry out the step "Set up to write a good line." The error-line flag referred to in the hierarchy diagram is used to indicate to the program whether any errors have been found in the input record being processed. Its use will become clear when we look at the coding for Program P08-01, shown in Figure 8.3.

We see here for the first time the use of the AUTHOR paragraph, in the Identification Division at line 00040. An asterisk has been placed in position 7 of the line to make it a comment, because the AUTHOR paragraph is going to be dropped from COBOL in the next standard. Making the AUTHOR paragraph a comment here ensures that this program will operate under future versions of COBOL.

In the description of SALES-RECORD-IN, a level-88 entry has been assigned

FIGURE ***8.3***

Program P08-01

```
S COBOL II RELEASE 3.2 09/05/90                   P08001   DATE FEB 22,1992 T
----+-*A-1-B--+----2----+----3----+----4----+----5----+----6----+----7-|--+

00010  IDENTIFICATION DIVISION.
00020  PROGRAM-ID.  P08-01.
00030
00040 *  AUTHOR. WENDEL KELLER.
00050 *  THIS PROGRAM CHECKS THE VALIDITY OF EACH FIELD
00060 *  IN EACH INPUT RECORD AND WRITES A LINE FOR EACH
00070 *  ERROR FOUND.
00080 *
00090 *****************************************************************
00100
00110  ENVIRONMENT DIVISION.
00120  INPUT-OUTPUT SECTION.
00130  FILE-CONTROL.
00140      SELECT SALES-RATIO-REPORT ASSIGN TO PRINTER.
00150      SELECT SALES-FILE-IN      ASSIGN TO INFILE.
00160
00170 *****************************************************************
00180
00190  DATA DIVISION.
00200  FILE SECTION.
00210  FD  SALES-FILE-IN
00220      RECORD CONTAINS 80 CHARACTERS.
00230
00240  01  SALES-RECORD-IN.
00250      05 SALESPERSON-NUMBER-IN          PIC X(5).
00260      05 CLASS-IN                       PIC X.
00270         88 CLASS-CODE-IS-MISSING       VALUE SPACE.
00280         88 VALID-CLASS-CODE            VALUES "A" THRU "H".
00290      05 LAST-YEARS-SALES-IN            PIC 9(6).
00300      05 CURRENT-SALE-IN                PIC 9(6)V99.
00310        88 CURRENT-SALE-VERY-LARGE VALUES 500000.01 THRU 999999.99.
00320      05 CURRENT-SALE-IN-X
00330         REDEFINES CURRENT-SALE-IN      PIC X(8).
00340
00350  FD  SALES-RATIO-REPORT.
00360
00370  01  REPORT-LINE                       PIC X(91).
00380
00390  WORKING-STORAGE SECTION.
00400  01  MORE-INPUT          VALUE "Y"     PIC X.
00410      88 THERE-IS-NO-INPUT              VALUE "N".
00420      88 THERE-IS-NO-MORE-INPUT         VALUE "N".
00430  01  ERROR-LINE-FLAG                   PIC X.
```

FIGURE 8.3 *continued*

```
00440
00450  01  PAGE-HEAD-1.
00460      05                      PIC X(17) VALUE SPACES.
00470      05                      PIC X(12) VALUE "SALES RATIOS".
00480
00490  01  PAGE-HEAD-2.
00500      05                      PIC X(28) VALUE SPACES.
00510      05                      PIC X(5)  VALUE "DATE".
00520      05 RUN-MONTH-AND-DAY    PIC Z9/99/.
00530      05 RUN-YEAR             PIC 99.
00540
00550  01  PAGE-HEAD-3.
00560      05                      PIC X(10) VALUE SPACES.
00570      05                      PIC X(6)  VALUE "SALES-".
00580
00590  01  PAGE-HEAD-4.
00600      05                      PIC X(10) VALUE SPACES.
00610      05                      PIC X(17) VALUE "PERSON".
00620      05                      PIC X(13) VALUE "CURRENT SALE/".
00630
00640  01  PAGE-HEAD-5.
00650      05                      PIC X(10) VALUE SPACES.
00660      05                      PIC X(9)  VALUE "NUMBER".
00670      05                      PIC X(8)  VALUE "CLASS".
00680      05                      PIC X(17) VALUE "LAST YEAR'S SALES".
00690
00700  01  BODY-LINE.
00710      05 SALESPERSON-NUMBER-OUT           PIC B(10)X(5).
00720      05 CLASS-OUT                        PIC B(6)X.
00730      05 SALE-RATIO-OUT                   PIC B(5)Z(6).9(6)B(7).
00740      05 ERROR-MESSAGE-OUT                PIC X(44).
00750
00760  01  ERROR-MESSAGES.
00770      05 LAST-YEARS-SALES-NOT-NUMERIC.
00780         10 PIC X(32) VALUE "LAST YEAR'S SALES NOT NUMERIC -".
00790         10 NONNUMERIC-LAST-YEARS-SALES PIC X(6).
00800      05 CURRENT-SALE-NOT-NUMERIC.
00810         10 PIC X(27) VALUE "CURRENT SALE NOT NUMERIC - ".
00820         10 NONNUMERIC-CURRENT-SALE       PIC X(8).
00830      05 LARGE-SALE-MESSAGE.
00840         10 PIC X(34) VALUE "CURRENT SALE SUSPICIOUSLY LARGE - ".
00850         10 LARGE-CURRENT-SALE            PIC 999,999.99.
```

continued

to suspiciously large sale amounts, at line 00310. The ERROR-LINE-FLAG is shown at line 00430. You will see how it is used when we look at the Procedure Division.

The formatting of the error lines in this program is handled a little differently from Program P05-02. Here all lines on the report, whether they contain an error message or the sale ratio, are written from the same area in working storage, BODY-LINE, at line 00700. BODY-LINE has space for both the sale ratio and the longest possible error message, in fields called SALE-RATIO-OUT, line 00730, and ERROR-MESSAGE-OUT, line 00740. For any single printed line, of course, either the sale ratio or an error message will print, but never both. Some of the different kinds of error messages that may be MOVEd to ERROR-MESSAGE-OUT in the course of processing are defined in the level-01 entry ERROR-MESSAGES, line 00760. Within ERROR-MESSAGES we have, for example, the message called LAST-YEARS-SALES-NOT-NUMERIC, at line 00770. This message will be printed if the field LAST-YEARS-SALES-IN is found to be not numeric. Part of this message is the field NONNUMERIC-LAST-YEARS-SALES, at line 00790. To this field will be assigned the actual nonnumeric value found in

LAST-YEARS-SALES-IN. As a general rule, whenever you are printing an erroneous field, the output PICTURE should be all Xs. In this way you will be able to see on the output exactly what the field looked like in the input, with no editing or other modifications.

CURRENT-SALE-IN, at line 00300, was redefined with Xs for error processing because it is illegal to MOVE a noninteger field to an alphanumeric field. If there had been any signed integer fields in the input, they too would have been redefined with Xs for it is unwise, though legal, to MOVE a signed integer to an alphanumeric field.

The Procedure Division begins at line 00950. The Paragraph PRODUCE-DETAIL-LINE, line 01290, starts by setting the ERROR-LINE-FLAG to "N" to indicate that no error lines have been printed for the input record being processed. SALESPERSON-NUMBER-IN is MOVEd to SALESPERSON-NUMBER-OUT because the Salesperson Number is to print regardless of whether or not the line is an error line and regardless of whether or not the Salesperson Number is valid.

FIGURE 8.3 ***continued***

```
S COBOL II RELEASE 3.2 09/05/90                  P08001   DATE FEB 22,1992 T
----+-*A-1-B--+----2----+----3----+----4----+----5----+----6----+----7-|--+

00860
00870  01  RUN-DATE.
00880      05 RUN-YEAR              PIC 99.
00890      05 RUN-MONTH-AND-DAY     PIC 9(4).
00900
00910  01  NO-INPUT-DATA            PIC X(15) VALUE "  NO INPUT DATA".
00920
00930 ************************************************************************
00940
00950  PROCEDURE DIVISION.
00960  PRODUCE-REPORT.
00970      PERFORM INITIALIZATION
00980      PERFORM PRODUCE-DETAIL-LINE UNTIL THERE-IS-NO-MORE-INPUT
00990      PERFORM TERMINATION
01000      STOP RUN
01010      .
01020
01030  INITIALIZATION.
01040      OPEN INPUT  SALES-FILE-IN
01050           OUTPUT SALES-RATIO-REPORT
01060      ACCEPT RUN-DATE FROM DATE
01070      MOVE CORRESPONDING RUN-DATE TO PAGE-HEAD-2
01080      WRITE REPORT-LINE FROM PAGE-HEAD-1 AFTER PAGE
01090      WRITE REPORT-LINE FROM PAGE-HEAD-2
01100      WRITE REPORT-LINE FROM PAGE-HEAD-3 AFTER 2
01110      WRITE REPORT-LINE FROM PAGE-HEAD-4
01120      WRITE REPORT-LINE FROM PAGE-HEAD-5
01130      MOVE SPACES TO REPORT-LINE
01140      WRITE REPORT-LINE
01150      READ SALES-FILE-IN
01160          AT END
01170              SET THERE-IS-NO-INPUT TO TRUE
01180      END-READ
01190      IF THERE-IS-NO-INPUT
01200          WRITE REPORT-LINE FROM NO-INPUT-DATA AFTER 2
01210      END-IF
01220      .
01230
01240  TERMINATION.
01250      CLOSE SALES-FILE-IN
01260            SALES-RATIO-REPORT
01270      .
```

FIGURE 8.3 *continued*

```
01280
01290  PRODUCE-DETAIL-LINE.
01300      MOVE "N" TO ERROR-LINE-FLAG
01310      MOVE SPACES TO BODY-LINE
01320      MOVE SALESPERSON-NUMBER-IN TO SALESPERSON-NUMBER-OUT
01330      PERFORM CHECK-FOR-ERRORS
01340      IF ERROR-LINE-FLAG = "N"
01350          PERFORM SET-UP-TO-WRITE-A-GOOD-LINE
01360      END-IF
01370      READ SALES-FILE-IN
01380          AT END
01390              SET THERE-IS-NO-MORE-INPUT TO TRUE
01400      .
01410
01420  WRITE-AN-ERROR-LINE.
01430      PERFORM SET-ERROR-LINE-FLAG
01440      PERFORM WRITE-A-LINE
01450      .
01460
01470  CHECK-FOR-ERRORS.
01480      PERFORM CHECK-SALESPERSON-NUMBER
01490      PERFORM CHECK-CLASS
01500      PERFORM CHECK-LAST-YEARS-SALES
01510      PERFORM CHECK-CURRENT-SALE
01520      .
01530
01540  CHECK-SALESPERSON-NUMBER.
01550      IF SALESPERSON-NUMBER-IN NOT NUMERIC
01560          MOVE "SALESPERSON NUMBER NOT NUMERIC"
01570                TO ERROR-MESSAGE-OUT
01580          PERFORM WRITE-AN-ERROR-LINE
01590      END-IF
01600      .
01610
01620  CHECK-CLASS.
01630      MOVE CLASS-IN TO CLASS-OUT
01640      EVALUATE TRUE
01650        WHEN CLASS-CODE-IS-MISSING
01660          MOVE "CLASS CODE MISSING" TO ERROR-MESSAGE-OUT
01670          PERFORM WRITE-AN-ERROR-LINE
01680        WHEN NOT VALID-CLASS-CODE
01690          MOVE "INVALID CLASS CODE" TO ERROR-MESSAGE-OUT
01700          PERFORM WRITE-AN-ERROR-LINE
01710      END-EVALUATE
01720      .
01730
01740  CHECK-LAST-YEARS-SALES.
01750      IF LAST-YEARS-SALES-IN NOT NUMERIC
01760          MOVE LAST-YEARS-SALES-IN TO NONNUMERIC-LAST-YEARS-SALES
01770          MOVE LAST-YEARS-SALES-NOT-NUMERIC TO ERROR-MESSAGE-OUT
01780          PERFORM WRITE-AN-ERROR-LINE
01790      END-IF
01800      .
```

continued

The PERFORM statement at line 01330 checks for all errors. Whenever an error is found, an appropriate error message is set up and the paragraph WRITE-AN-ERROR-LINE, line 01420, is PERFORMed. When WRITE-AN-ERROR-LINE executes, it sets the ERROR-LINE-FLAG to "Y" to indicate that at least one error has been found in the input record. The IF statement at line 01340 tests to see whether any errors were found in the input record. If no errors are found even after all the error checks have been made, normal processing may be done and the sales ratio computed and printed.

The paragraph CHECK-CURRENT-SALE, line 01820, shows a field being checked for numeric before being used in a numeric comparison. Whenever a field must be checked for numeric and also used in a numeric comparison, the NUMERIC test must be done first.

FIGURE 8.3 ***continued***

```
S COBOL II RELEASE 3.2 09/05/90                  P08001    DATE FEB 22,1992 T
----+-*A-1-B--+----2----+----3----+----4----+----5----+----6----+----7-|--+

01810
01820  CHECK-CURRENT-SALE.
01830      EVALUATE TRUE
01840        WHEN CURRENT-SALE-IN NOT NUMERIC
01850          MOVE CURRENT-SALE-IN-X TO NONNUMERIC-CURRENT-SALE
01860          MOVE CURRENT-SALE-NOT-NUMERIC TO ERROR-MESSAGE-OUT
01870          PERFORM WRITE-AN-ERROR-LINE
01880        WHEN CURRENT-SALE-VERY-LARGE
01890          MOVE CURRENT-SALE-IN TO LARGE-CURRENT-SALE
01900          MOVE LARGE-SALE-MESSAGE TO ERROR-MESSAGE-OUT
01910          PERFORM WRITE-AN-ERROR-LINE
01920      END-EVALUATE
01930      .
01940
01950  SET-ERROR-LINE-FLAG.
01960      MOVE "Y" TO ERROR-LINE-FLAG
01970      .
01980
01990  SET-UP-TO-WRITE-A-GOOD-LINE.
02000      DIVIDE CURRENT-SALE-IN BY LAST-YEARS-SALES-IN
02010         GIVING SALE-RATIO-OUT
02020      PERFORM WRITE-A-LINE
02030      .
02040
02050  WRITE-A-LINE.
02060      WRITE REPORT-LINE FROM BODY-LINE
02070      .
```

Program P08-01 was run with the input data shown in Figure 8.4 and produced the output shown in Figure 8.5.

FIGURE 8.4 **Input for Program P08-01**

```
--------------------------------------------------------------------------------
         1         2         3         4         5         6         7         8
12345678901234567890123456789012345678901234567890123456789012345678901234567890
--------------------------------------------------------------------------------
34ABA 06543X843961V9
78121H10000038745231
00000ACDEFGHIJKLMNOP
14758H22342101000000
45 4150 79218 542165
9#121H19087055089733
91A00A08749002384009
99121H19087045089733
82423 17142109865022
73315I04396001925035
64876D099 4201000042
6745HA0953Z1043942)9
55252E054320043#0066
46701F21005054365281
374  317329907279823
00322A00000149999999
28421B06923Z50000000
14756A08994307059243
89  6 9"942117642972
78932ZA9324167632075
569$2 00943259239651
15008B07076306804299
05))6LO*923570092151
03442A03500004808989
19123G17036705376542
```

FIGURE 8.5 **Output from Program P08-01**

```
              SALES RATIOS
                           DATE   2/22/92

SALES-
PERSON                CURRENT SALE/
NUMBER    CLASS       LAST YEAR'S SALES

34ABA                                        SALESPERSON NUMBER NOT NUMERIC
34ABA                                        CLASS CODE MISSING
34ABA                                        LAST YEAR'S SALES NOT NUMERIC - 06543X
34ABA                                        CURRENT SALE NOT NUMERIC - 843961V9
78121      H                 3.874523
00000      A                                 LAST YEAR'S SALES NOT NUMERIC - CDEFGH
00000      A                                 CURRENT SALE NOT NUMERIC - IJKLMNOP
14758      H                  .044758
45 41                                        SALESPERSON NUMBER NOT NUMERIC
45 41      5                                 INVALID CLASS CODE
45 41      5                                 LAST YEAR'S SALES NOT NUMERIC - 0 7921
45 41      5                                 CURRENT SALE NOT NUMERIC - 8 542165
9#121                                        SALESPERSON NUMBER NOT NUMERIC
9#121      H                                 CURRENT SALE SUSPICIOUSLY LARGE - 550,897.33
91A00                                        SALESPERSON NUMBER NOT NUMERIC
99121      H                 2.362326
82423                                        CLASS CODE MISSING
73315      I                                 INVALID CLASS CODE
64876      D                                 LAST YEAR'S SALES NOT NUMERIC - 099 42
6745H                                        SALESPERSON NUMBER NOT NUMERIC
6745H      A                                 LAST YEAR'S SALES NOT NUMERIC - 0953Z1
6745H      A                                 CURRENT SALE NOT NUMERIC - 043942)9
55252      E                                 CURRENT SALE NOT NUMERIC - 043#0066
46701      F                                 CURRENT SALE SUSPICIOUSLY LARGE - 543,652.81
374                                          SALESPERSON NUMBER NOT NUMERIC
374        3                                 INVALID CLASS CODE
00322      A            499999.990000
28421      B                                 LAST YEAR'S SALES NOT NUMERIC - 06923Z
14756      A                  .784857
89   6                                       SALESPERSON NUMBER NOT NUMERIC
89   6                                       CLASS CODE MISSING
89   6                                       LAST YEAR'S SALES NOT NUMERIC - 9"9421
78932      Z                                 INVALID CLASS CODE
78932      Z                                 LAST YEAR'S SALES NOT NUMERIC - A93241
78932      Z                                 CURRENT SALE SUSPICIOUSLY LARGE - 676,320.75
569$2                                        SALESPERSON NUMBER NOT NUMERIC
569$2                                        CLASS CODE MISSING
569$2                                        LAST YEAR'S SALES NOT NUMERIC - 009432
569$2                                        CURRENT SALE SUSPICIOUSLY LARGE - 592,396.51
15008      B                  .961561
05))6                                        SALESPERSON NUMBER NOT NUMERIC
05))6      L                                 INVALID CLASS CODE
05))6      L                                 LAST YEAR'S SALES NOT NUMERIC - 0*9235
05))6      L                                 CURRENT SALE SUSPICIOUSLY LARGE - 700,921.51
03442      A                 1.373996
19123      G                  .315585
```

EXERCISE 5

Write a program to process input records in the following format:

Positions	*Field*
1–9	Social Security Number
10	Job Grade
11–18	Annual Salary (to two decimal places)
10–80	spaces

Have your program make the following validity checks on each input record:

a. Social Security Number numeric
b. Grade present
c. Grade valid (V through Z or 1 through 6)
d. Annual Salary numeric
e. Annual Salary not greater than $400,000

Have your program check each input record for all five possible types of errors. Print an error line for each error found. If a record is completely free of errors, print its contents on one line (formatted so that it can be read easily). At the end of the report, have your program print a total of all the salaries printed, that is, the total of all the salaries in the error-free records.

Design a report format with a suitable title and suitable column headings. Include the date in the heading.

Arithmetic Overflow

Sometimes invalid data in the form of arithmetic **overflow** can be generated during execution of a program. An arithmetic result is considered to overflow if there are more places to the left of the decimal point in the answer than to the left of the point in the field provided by the programmer. Excess places to the right of the decimal point are never considered an overflow condition. Excess places to the right of the point are either truncated or rounded, depending on whether the ROUNDED option is present in the arithmetic statement.

The programmer can test for arithmetic overflow by using the SIZE ERROR or NOT SIZE ERROR phrase. The two phrases are optional with all five arithmetic verbs—ADD, SUBTRACT, MULTIPLY, DIVIDE, and COMPUTE. The formats of the SIZE ERROR and NOT SIZE ERROR phrases were given in Chapter 3:

```
[ON SIZE ERROR imperative-statement-1]
[NOT ON SIZE ERROR imperative-statement-2]
```

A single arithmetic statement may contain either an optional SIZE ERROR phrase or an optional NOT SIZE ERROR phrase, or both. Following the words SIZE ERROR and NOT SIZE ERROR there must be one or more imperative statements. Remember that whenever an imperative statement is called for in a format, you may have as many imperative statements as you like.

Here are two examples of the SIZE ERROR and NOT SIZE ERROR phrases in ADD statements:

```
ADD A TO B
      SIZE ERROR
            MOVE "Y" TO SIZE-ERROR-FLAG
END-ADD

ADD A TO B ROUNDED
      SIZE ERROR
            MOVE SIZE-ERROR-MESSAGE TO ERRØR-MESSAGE-OUT
            WRITE ERROR-LINE
            MOVE Ø TO B
      NOT SIZE ERROR
            MOVE Ø TO A
END-ADD
```

In the first ADD statement the SIZE ERROR phrase is terminated by the explicit scope terminator **END-ADD.** In the second ADD statement the SIZE ERROR phrase is terminated by the NOT SIZE ERROR phrase, which is in turn terminated by END-ADD. One rule about the termination of any conditional phrase (such as SIZE ERROR, NOT SIZE ERROR, or AT END) in any statement is: A conditional phrase can be terminated by an explicit scope terminator or by the beginning of some other phrase in the same statement.

You should always terminate any arithmetic statement containing a SIZE ERROR or NOT SIZE ERROR phrase with an appropriate explicit scope terminator. In an arithmetic statement that uses neither a SIZE ERROR nor NOT SIZE ERROR phrase, an explicit scope terminator is never needed.

If the ROUNDED option is specified in an arithmetic operation, rounding is carried out before the field is tested for SIZE ERROR. Division by zero always causes a SIZE ERROR condition. If more than one result field is given in an arithmetic statement, a SIZE ERROR on one of the fields will not interfere with normal execution of arithmetic on the others. If a size error occurs during execution of a statement that contains a SIZE ERROR phrase, the result field is left unchanged from before the operation. If a size error occurs in a statement where the SIZE ERROR phrase is not specified, the results may be unpredictable.

Nesting of Conditions and Conditional Phrases

Figure 8.6 shows a flowchart of logic in which SIZE ERROR and NOT SIZE ERROR conditions are nested in an IF condition, and an IF condition is nested in the NOT SIZE ERROR condition. The only limit to the depth and complexity of such nesting is the size of your computer. The flowchart can be coded as follows:

```
IF CURRENT-SALE-IN GREATER THAN SELECTED-BREAK-POINT
     COMPUTE COMMISSION-W    ROUNDED
               COMMISSION-OUT ROUNDED =
           LOW-COMMISSION-RATE * SELECTED-BREAK-POINT +
           HIGH-COMMISSION-RATE *
                (CURRENT-SALE-IN - SELECTED-BREAK-POINT)
     SIZE ERROR
           PERFORM SIZE-ERROR-ROUTINE
     NOT SIZE ERROR
           IF COMMISSION-IS-HIGH
                MOVE "!" TO COMMISSION-CODE
           ELSE
                MOVE "B" TO COMMISSION-CODE
           END-IF
     END-COMPUTE
ELSE
     COMPUTE COMMISSION-W    ROUNDED
               COMMISSION-OUT ROUNDED =
           LOW-COMMISSION-RATE * CURRENT-SALE-IN
     IF COMMISSION-IS-LOW
           MOVE "L" TO COMMISSION-CODE
     ELSE
           MOVE "*" TO COMMISSION-CODE
     END-IF
END-IF
```

The terminator **END-COMPUTE** before the ELSE is not strictly needed, since an ELSE terminates all conditions that are nested more deeply than itself and not already terminated. For safety, clarity, and consistency of programming style, though, you should always use an explicit scope terminator where appropriate. Notice that the COMPUTE statement after the ELSE needs no explicit scope terminator, for it lacks both the SIZE ERROR and NOT SIZE ERROR phrases.

A Program with SIZE ERROR and NOT SIZE ERROR Phrases

We now do a program that shows the SIZE ERROR and NOT SIZE ERROR phrases in context. Program P08-02 is a modification to Program P05-02, which computes commissions for junior, associate, and senior salespeople. In Program P08-02, a commission is limited to a maximum of $99,999.99. If any commission computation comes out larger than that, Program P08-02 prints a message so indicating. Also, the program prints either !, B, L, or * next to each commission amount depending on whether the commission amount is over $70,000 or under $10,000 and on whether the sale amount is high or low. Program P08-02 is shown in Figure 8.7.

FIGURE 8.6 **Logic in which SIZE ERROR and NOT SIZE ERROR conditions are nested in an IF condition, and an IF condition is nested in the NOT SIZE ERROR condition**

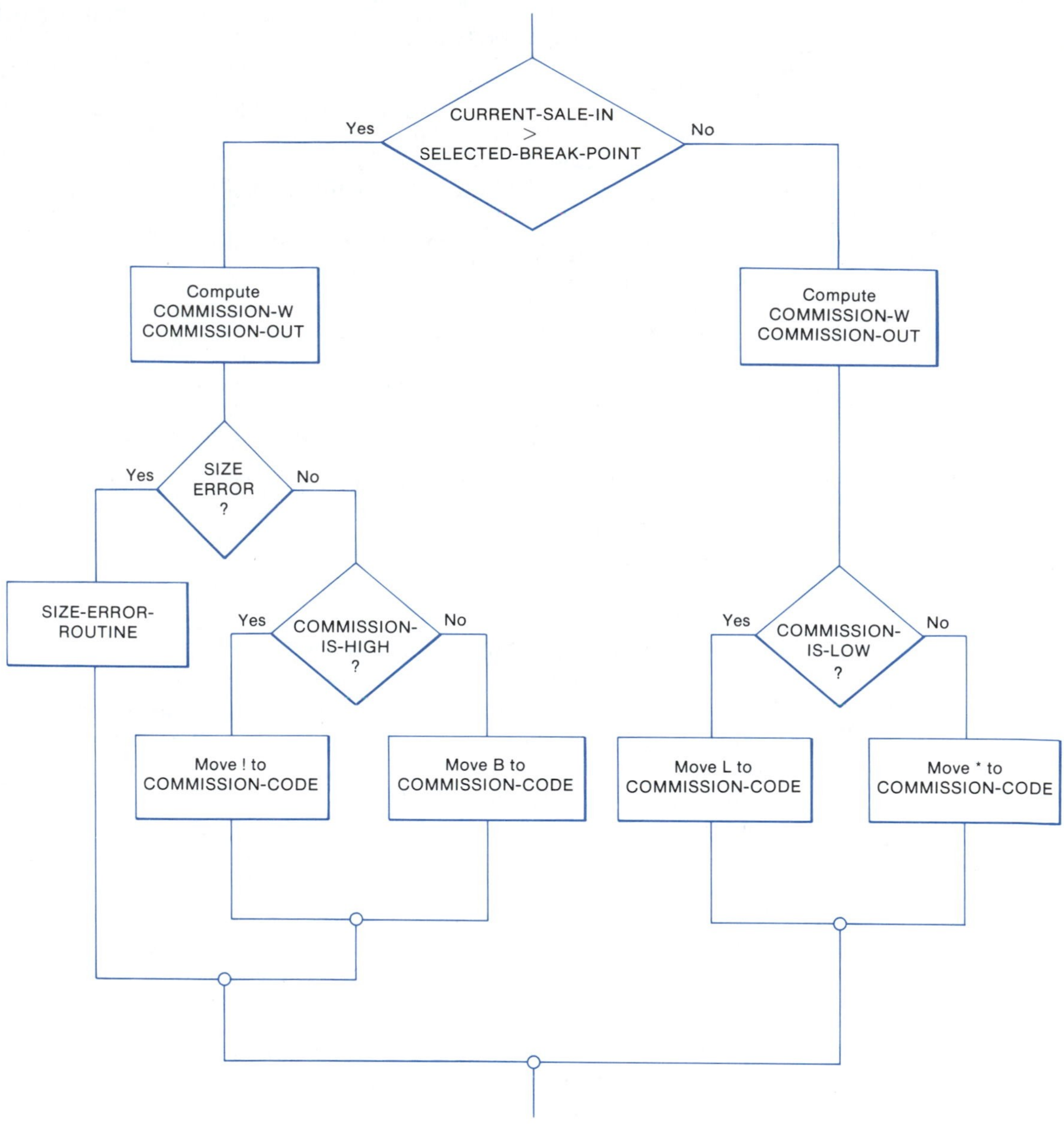

FIGURE 8.7 **Program P08-02**

```
S COBOL II RELEASE 3.2 09/05/90              P08002   DATE FEB 22,1992 T
----+-*A-1-B--+----2----+----3----+----4----+----5----+----6----+----7-|--+


       IDENTIFICATION DIVISION.
       PROGRAM-ID.  P08-02.
      *
```

FIGURE *8.7* ***continued***

```
*     AUTHOR. WENDEL KELLER.
*     THIS PROGRAM COMPUTES SALESPERSON COMMISSIONS FOR JUNIOR
*     SALESPERSONS, ASSOCIATE SALESPERSONS, AND SENIOR SALESPERSONS
*     ANY COMMISSION AMOUNT OVER $99,999.99 IS CONSIDERED A
*     SIZE ERROR.
*
*****************************************************************

 ENVIRONMENT DIVISION.
 INPUT-OUTPUT SECTION.
 FILE-CONTROL.
     SELECT COMMISSION-REPORT ASSIGN TO PRINTER.
     SELECT SALES-FILE-IN     ASSIGN TO INFILE.

*****************************************************************

 DATA DIVISION.
 FILE SECTION.
 FD  SALES-FILE-IN
     RECORD CONTAINS 80 CHARACTERS.

 01  SALES-RECORD-IN.
     05 SALESPERSON-NUMBER-IN     PIC X(5).
     05 CLASS-IN                  PIC X.
        88 SALESPERSON-IS-JUNIOR     VALUES "A" THRU "F".
        88 SALESPERSON-IS-ASSOCIATE VALUE "G".
        88 SALESPERSON-IS-SENIOR     VALUE "H".
        88 CLASS-CODE-IS-VALID       VALUES "A" THRU "H".
        88 CLASS-CODE-IS-MISSING     VALUE SPACE.
     05 LAST-YEARS-SALES-IN       PIC 9(6).
     05 CURRENT-SALE-IN           PIC 9(6)V99.

 FD  COMMISSION-REPORT.

 01  REPORT-LINE                  PIC X(88).

 WORKING-STORAGE SECTION.
 01  MORE-INPUT             PIC X      VALUE "Y".
     88 THERE-IS-NO-INPUT              VALUE "N".
     88 THERE-IS-NO-MORE-INPUT         VALUE "N".
 01  NO-INPUT-DATA          PIC X(15) VALUE "  NO INPUT DATA".
 01  COMMISSION-W           PIC S9(5)V99 PACKED-DECIMAL.
     88 COMMISSION-IS-LOW   VALUES 0 THRU 9999.99.
     88 COMMISSION-IS-HIGH VALUES 70000.01 THRU 99999.99.

 01  PAGE-HEAD-1.
     05                     PIC X(23) VALUE SPACES.
     05                     PIC X(19) VALUE "COMMISSION REGISTER".

 01  PAGE-HEAD-2.
     05                     PIC X(45) VALUE SPACES.
     05                     PIC X(5)  VALUE "DATE".
     05 RUN-MONTH-AND-DAY   PIC Z9/99/.
     05 RUN-YEAR            PIC 99.

 01  PAGE-HEAD-3.
     05                     PIC X(10) VALUE SPACES.
     05                     PIC X(6)  VALUE "SALES-".

 01  PAGE-HEAD-4.
     05                     PIC X(10) VALUE SPACES.
     05                     PIC X(25) VALUE "PERSON".
     05                     PIC X(4)  VALUE "SALE".

 01  PAGE-HEAD-5.
     05                     PIC X(10) VALUE SPACES.
     05                     PIC X(12) VALUE "NUMBER".
     05                     PIC X(12) VALUE "CLASS".
     05                     PIC X(12) VALUE "AMOUNT".
     05                     PIC X(10) VALUE "COMMISSION".
```

continued

FIGURE 8.7 *continued*

```
S COBOL II RELEASE 3.2 09/05/90                     P08002   DATE FEB 22,1992 T
----+-*A-1-B--+----2----+----3----+----4----+----5----+----6----+----7-|--+

       01  DETAIL-LINE.
           05 SALESPERSON-NUMBER-OUT    PIC B(10)X(5).
           05 CLASS-TITLE-OUT           PIC B(5)X(9)BBB.
           05 CURRENT-SALE-OUT          PIC ZZZ,ZZZ.99BBB.
           05 COMMISSION-AND-CODE.
              06 COMMISSION-OUT         PIC ZZ,ZZZ.99.
              06 COMMISSION-CODE        PIC BXB(16).
           05 DETAIL-ERROR REDEFINES COMMISSION-AND-CODE
                                        PIC X(27).

       01  CLASS-INVALID-LINE.
           05 SALESPERSON-NUMBER        PIC B(10)X(5)B(5).
           05                           PIC X(17)
                                        VALUE "ERROR - CLASS IS".
           05 INVALID-CLASS             PIC X.
           05                           PIC X(44)
              VALUE ". CLASS SHOULD BE A, B, C, D, E, F, G, OR H.".

       01  CLASS-MISSING-LINE.
           05 SALESPERSON-NUMBER        PIC B(10)X(5)B(5).
           05                           PIC X(68)
              VALUE "ERROR - CLASS IS MISSING. CLASS SHOULD BE A, B, C,
      -       "D, E, F, G, OR H.".

       01  COMMISSION-BREAK-POINTS      PACKED-DECIMAL.
           05 JUNIOR-BREAK-POINT        PIC S9    VALUE 0.
           05 ASSOCIATE-BREAK-POINT     PIC S9(5) VALUE 10000.
           05 SENIOR-BREAK-POINT        PIC S9(5) VALUE 50000.

       01  SELECTED-COMMISSION-RATES    PACKED-DECIMAL.
           05 LOW-COMMISSION-RATE       PIC SV99.
           05 HIGH-COMMISSION-RATE      PIC SV99.

       01  SELECTED-BREAK-POINT         PIC S9(5) PACKED-DECIMAL.

       01  SALE-QUOTAS                  PACKED-DECIMAL.
           05 JUNIOR-SALE-QUOTA         PIC S9    VALUE 0.
           05 ASSOCIATE-SALE-QUOTA      PIC S9(6) VALUE 150000.
           05 SENIOR-SALE-QUOTA         PIC S9(6) VALUE 250000.

       01  COMMISSION-RATES             PACKED-DECIMAL.
           05 ASSOCIATE-RATES.
              10 QUOTA-NOT-MET.
                 15 LOW-RATE            PIC SV99  VALUE .05.
                 15 HIGH-RATE           PIC SV99  VALUE .20.
              10 QUOTA-MET.
                 15 LOW-RATE            PIC SV99  VALUE .20.
                 15 HIGH-RATE           PIC SV99  VALUE .30.
           05 SENIOR-RATES.
              10 QUOTA-NOT-MET.
                 15 LOW-RATE            PIC SV99  VALUE .20.
                 15 HIGH-RATE           PIC SV99  VALUE .30.
              10 QUOTA-MET.
                 15 LOW-RATE            PIC SV99  VALUE .30.
                 15 HIGH-RATE           PIC SV99  VALUE .40.
           05 JUNIOR-RATES.
              10 QUOTA-NOT-MET.
                 15 LOW-RATE            PIC SV99  VALUE .10.
                 15 HIGH-RATE           PIC SV99  VALUE .10.
              10 QUOTA-MET.
                 15 LOW-RATE            PIC SV99  VALUE .10.
                 15 HIGH-RATE           PIC SV99  VALUE .10.
```

FIGURE 8.7 *continued*

```
01   TODAYS-DATE.
     05 RUN-YEAR                       PIC 99.
     05 RUN-MONTH-AND-DAY              PIC 9(4).

*****************************************************************

PROCEDURE DIVISION.
PRODUCE-COMMISSION-REPORT.
     PERFORM INITIALIZATION
     PERFORM PRODUCE-DETAIL-LINE UNTIL THERE-IS-NO-MORE-INPUT
     PERFORM TERMINATION
     STOP RUN
     .

INITIALIZATION.
     OPEN INPUT  SALES-FILE-IN
          OUTPUT COMMISSION-REPORT
     ACCEPT TODAYS-DATE FROM DATE
     MOVE CORR TODAYS-DATE TO PAGE-HEAD-2
     WRITE REPORT-LINE FROM PAGE-HEAD-1 AFTER PAGE
     WRITE REPORT-LINE FROM PAGE-HEAD-2
     WRITE REPORT-LINE FROM PAGE-HEAD-3 AFTER 3
     WRITE REPORT-LINE FROM PAGE-HEAD-4
     WRITE REPORT-LINE FROM PAGE-HEAD-5
     MOVE SPACES TO REPORT-LINE
     WRITE REPORT-LINE
     READ SALES-FILE-IN
         AT END
             SET THERE-IS-NO-INPUT TO TRUE
     END-READ
     IF THERE-IS-NO-INPUT
         WRITE REPORT-LINE FROM NO-INPUT-DATA AFTER 2
     END-IF
     .

TERMINATION.
     CLOSE SALES-FILE-IN
           COMMISSION-REPORT
     .

PRODUCE-DETAIL-LINE.
     IF NOT CLASS-CODE-IS-VALID
         PERFORM PROCESS-ERRONEOUS-RECORD
     ELSE
         PERFORM PROCESS-GOOD-RECORD
     END-IF
     READ SALES-FILE-IN
         AT END
             SET THERE-IS-NO-MORE-INPUT TO TRUE
     .

PROCESS-ERRONEOUS-RECORD.
     IF CLASS-CODE-IS-MISSING
         PERFORM WRITE-CLASS-MISSING-LINE
     ELSE
         PERFORM WRITE-CLASS-INVALID-LINE
     END-IF
     .

PROCESS-GOOD-RECORD.
     PERFORM SELECT-COMMISSION-RATES
     PERFORM COMPUTE-COMMISSION
     PERFORM WRITE-COMMISSION-LINE
     .
```

continued

FIGURE 8.7 *continued*

```
S COBOL II RELEASE 3.2 09/05/90                P08002   DATE FEB 22,1992 T
----+-*A-1-B--+----2----+----3----+----4----+----5----+----6----+----7-|--+

       SELECT-COMMISSION-RATES.
           EVALUATE TRUE
               WHEN SALESPERSON-IS-JUNIOR
                       PERFORM SET-JUNIOR-PARAMETERS
               WHEN SALESPERSON-IS-ASSOCIATE AND
                    LAST-YEARS-SALES-IN LESS THAN ASSOCIATE-SALE-QUOTA
                       PERFORM ASSOCIATE-QUOTA-NOT-MET
               WHEN SALESPERSON-IS-ASSOCIATE
                       PERFORM ASSOCIATE-QUOTA-MET
               WHEN LAST-YEARS-SALES-IN LESS THAN SENIOR-SALE-QUOTA
                       PERFORM SENIOR-QUOTA-NOT-MET
               WHEN OTHER
                       PERFORM SENIOR-QUOTA-MET
           END-EVALUATE
           .

       WRITE-CLASS-MISSING-LINE.
           MOVE SALESPERSON-NUMBER-IN TO
                SALESPERSON-NUMBER IN CLASS-MISSING-LINE
           WRITE REPORT-LINE FROM CLASS-MISSING-LINE
           .

       WRITE-CLASS-INVALID-LINE.
           MOVE CLASS-IN TO INVALID-CLASS
           MOVE SALESPERSON-NUMBER-IN TO
                SALESPERSON-NUMBER IN CLASS-INVALID-LINE
           WRITE REPORT-LINE FROM CLASS-INVALID-LINE
           .

       SET-JUNIOR-PARAMETERS.
           MOVE JUNIOR-BREAK-POINT TO SELECTED-BREAK-POINT
           MOVE "JUNIOR"           TO CLASS-TITLE-OUT
           MOVE HIGH-RATE IN QUOTA-MET IN JUNIOR-RATES TO
                HIGH-COMMISSION-RATE
           MOVE LOW-RATE  IN QUOTA-MET IN JUNIOR-RATES TO
                LOW-COMMISSION-RATE
           .

       ASSOCIATE-QUOTA-NOT-MET.
           MOVE ASSOCIATE-BREAK-POINT TO SELECTED-BREAK-POINT
           MOVE "ASSOCIATE"           TO CLASS-TITLE-OUT
           MOVE HIGH-RATE IN QUOTA-NOT-MET IN ASSOCIATE-RATES TO
                HIGH-COMMISSION-RATE
           MOVE LOW-RATE  IN QUOTA-NOT-MET IN ASSOCIATE-RATES TO
                LOW-COMMISSION-RATE
           .

       ASSOCIATE-QUOTA-MET.
           MOVE ASSOCIATE-BREAK-POINT TO SELECTED-BREAK-POINT
           MOVE "ASSOCIATE"           TO CLASS-TITLE-OUT
           MOVE HIGH-RATE IN QUOTA-MET IN ASSOCIATE-RATES TO
                HIGH-COMMISSION-RATE
           MOVE LOW-RATE  IN QUOTA-MET IN ASSOCIATE-RATES TO
                LOW-COMMISSION-RATE
           .

       SENIOR-QUOTA-NOT-MET.
           MOVE SENIOR-BREAK-POINT TO SELECTED-BREAK-POINT
           MOVE "SENIOR"           TO CLASS-TITLE-OUT
           MOVE HIGH-RATE IN QUOTA-NOT-MET IN SENIOR-RATES TO
                HIGH-COMMISSION-RATE
           MOVE LOW-RATE  IN QUOTA-NOT-MET IN SENIOR-RATES TO
                LOW-COMMISSION-RATE
           .
```

FIGURE 8.7 ***continued***

```
02680 SENIOR-QUOTA-MET.
02690     MOVE SENIOR-BREAK-POINT TO SELECTED-BREAK-POINT
02700     MOVE "SENIOR"           TO CLASS-TITLE-OUT
02710     MOVE HIGH-RATE IN QUOTA-MET IN SENIOR-RATES TO
02720          HIGH-COMMISSION-RATE
02730     MOVE LOW-RATE  IN QUOTA-MET IN SENIOR-RATES TO
02740          LOW-COMMISSION-RATE
02750     .
02760
02770 COMPUTE-COMMISSION.
02780     IF CURRENT-SALE-IN GREATER THAN SELECTED-BREAK-POINT
02790         COMPUTE COMMISSION-W   ROUNDED
02800                 COMMISSION-OUT ROUNDED =
02810             LOW-COMMISSION-RATE * SELECTED-BREAK-POINT +
02820             HIGH-COMMISSION-RATE *
02830                 (CURRENT-SALE-IN - SELECTED-BREAK-POINT)
02840         SIZE ERROR
02850             PERFORM SIZE-ERROR-ROUTINE
02860         NOT SIZE ERROR
02870             IF COMMISSION-IS-HIGH
02880                 MOVE "!" TO COMMISSION-CODE
02890             ELSE
02900                 MOVE "B" TO COMMISSION-CODE
02910             END-IF
02920         END-COMPUTE
02930     ELSE
02940         COMPUTE COMMISSION-W   ROUNDED
02950                 COMMISSION-OUT ROUNDED =
02960             LOW-COMMISSION-RATE * CURRENT-SALE-IN
02970         IF COMMISSION-IS-LOW
02980             MOVE "L" TO COMMISSION-CODE
02990         ELSE
03000             MOVE "*" TO COMMISSION-CODE
03010         END-IF
03020     END-IF
03030     .
03040
03050 SIZE-ERROR-ROUTINE.
03060     MOVE "COMMISSION AMOUNT TOO LARGE" TO DETAIL-ERROR
03070     .
03080
03090 WRITE-COMMISSION-LINE.
03100     MOVE SALESPERSON-NUMBER-IN TO SALESPERSON-NUMBER-OUT
03110     MOVE CURRENT-SALE-IN       TO CURRENT-SALE-OUT
03120     WRITE REPORT-LINE FROM DETAIL-LINE
03130     .
```

You can see the coding for the logic of Figure 8.6 starting at line 02780. Program P08-02 was run with the input shown in Figure 8.8 and produced the output shown in Figure 8.9.

FIGURE 8.8 Input to Program P08-02

```
--------------------------------------------------------------------------------
         1         2         3         4         5         6         7         8
12345678901234567890123456789012345678901234567890123456789012345678901234567890
--------------------------------------------------------------------------------
14756G08994307059243
14758G22342101000000
15008H07076399804299
19123H17036705376542
14689 16900001245968
10089G08054604307865
17665G15000008870099
15699A00000003000099
15003H06576305000000
12231B19630024367921
14769G21991226445399
15013H06920000782135
15014H42310003596299
14770G17630008235643
14771G29342100936951
15000Z24936204345621
15002H03421601934526
15004H02632105732123
12352G16030000698234
15006H07962303922431
14757G10009900198499
15010H25192304736554
13834F12989604598799
15011H25743205078654
14764115054320909324
15015H28996507987523
14759G02980004783965
15016H48990008535942
14761G06597600643912
15012H25000009368342
```

FIGURE 8.9 **Output from Program P08-02**

```
                     COMMISSION REGISTER
                                       DATE  2/22/92

SALES-
PERSON                      SALE
NUMBER       CLASS         AMOUNT        COMMISSION

14756     ASSOCIATE     70,592.43    12,618.49 B
14758     ASSOCIATE     10,000.00     2,000.00 L
15008     SENIOR       998,042.99    COMMISSION AMOUNT TOO LARGE
19123     SENIOR        53,765.42    11,129.63 B
14689     ERROR - CLASS IS MISSING. CLASS SHOULD BE A, B, C, D, E, F, G, OR H.
10089     ASSOCIATE     43,078.65     7,115.73 B
17665     ASSOCIATE     88,700.99    25,610.30 B
15699     JUNIOR        30,000.99     3,000.10 B
15003     SENIOR        50,000.00    10,000.00 *
12231     JUNIOR       243,679.21    24,367.92 B
14769     ASSOCIATE    264,453.99    78,336.20 !
15013     SENIOR         7,821.35     1,564.27 L
15014     SENIOR        35,962.99    10,788.90 *
14770     ASSOCIATE     82,356.43    23,706.93 B
14771     ASSOCIATE      9,369.51     1,873.90 L
15000     ERROR - CLASS IS Z. CLASS SHOULD BE A, B, C, D, E, F, G, OR H.
15002     SENIOR        19,345.26     3,869.05 L
15004     SENIOR        57,321.23    12,196.37 B
12352     ASSOCIATE      6,982.34     1,396.47 L
15006     SENIOR        39,224.31     7,844.86 L
14757     ASSOCIATE      1,984.99        99.25 L
15010     SENIOR        47,365.54    14,209.66 *
13834     JUNIOR        45,987.99     4,598.80 B
15011     SENIOR        50,786.54    15,314.62 B
14764     ERROR - CLASS IS 1. CLASS SHOULD BE A, B, C, D, E, F, G, OR H.
15015     SENIOR        79,875.23    26,950.09 B
14759     ASSOCIATE     47,839.65     8,067.93 B
15016     SENIOR        85,359.42    29,143.77 B
14761     ASSOCIATE      6,439.12       321.96 L
15012     SENIOR        93,683.42    32,473.37 B
```

EXERCISE 6

Write a program to read the same input data used in Exercise 5. The program is to compute a 20% Christmas bonus based on the employee's Annual Salary. For each record read, have your program print the employee's Social Security Number, Annual Salary, and computed bonus amount, except if the bonus amount exceeds $99,999.99. If the bonus amount exceeds $99,999.99, print no bonus amount, but instead print the message BONUS AMOUNT SUSPICIOUSLY LARGE. Accumulate the total of the bonus amounts printed and print the total at the end of the report.

Summary

Whenever a program reads input data that have been prepared by people, the program should check the validity of the data before proceeding to process them. The program should check that required data fields are in fact filled in. Different techniques may be used to check for the presence of alphanumeric data and for signed and unsigned integers and fractions. Among the COBOL features that can be used to check one or another kind of field are a level-88 entry with a VALUE SPACES clause, a relation condition where the field is compared with SPACES, and a REDEFINES clause.

The REDEFINES clause permits the programmer to assign more than one name and one PICTURE to a single field. Then the programmer may use any of the names of the field in the Procedure Division, depending on the requirements of each context.

If a program reads a coded field as input data, the program should check that the field contains one of the valid codes. If numeric fields are being read, the program should use the class test to check that the numeric fields contain only numbers. Sometimes there can be disastrous results if a program tries to do numeric comparisons, numeric editing, or arithmetic with fields containing characters other than numbers. Alphabetic fields can be checked for all letters and spaces.

Input data should be checked for reasonableness. That is, the program should check to the extent possible that the values present in input data fields are values that reasonably could be expected to be there. Sometimes it is possible to test individual fields for reasonable values, and sometimes fields must be tested in combinations to see whether their contents are reasonable.

The SIZE ERROR and NOT SIZE ERROR phrases may be used with arithmetic verbs to check for arithmetic overflow. Overflow is considered to occur when a result of arithmetic has more places to the left of the decimal point than the programmer has allowed for in the result field. The COBOL statements following the words SIZE ERROR and NOT SIZE ERROR must be imperative statements. The SIZE ERROR and NOT SIZE ERROR phrases are terminated by the beginning of another phrase in the same statement, an explicit scope terminator, or ELSE. If a size error occurs during execution of an arithmetic statement where the SIZE ERROR phrase is specified, the result field remains unchanged from what it was before the operation. If a size error occurs in a statement where the SIZE ERROR phrase is not specified, the results may be unpredictable.

Fill-In Exercises

1. A VALUE SPACES clause may appear in a level-88 entry only if the field is defined as ______.
2. To use a VALUE SPACES clause with a numeric field, the field must be ______.
3. The four classes of data that may be tested for with a class condition test are ______, ______, ______, and ______.
4. Testing the contents of fields to determine whether the fields contain valid codes or values within an expected range of values is called checking data for ______.
5. Arithmetic overflow can be tested for with the ______ phrase.
6. Arithmetic overflow occurs if there are too many places in the answer to the ______ of the decimal point.
7. A SIZE ERROR phrase may be terminated by ______, ______, or ______.
8. Overflow never occurs when there are more places to the ______ of the decimal point in the answer than have been provided for in the result field.
9. If the ROUNDED option is specified in an arithmetic operation, rounding takes place ______ the field is tested for size error.
10. A(n) ______ terminates all conditions that are nested more deeply than itself and are not already terminated.

11. Under certain conditions nonnumeric data in numeric fields will cause a program to ______ execution.

12. Excess places to the right of the decimal point in arithmetic results are ______ if the ROUNDED option is not used.

13. The SIZE ERROR phrase may be used with the verbs ______, ______, ______, ______, and ______.

14. Only ______ statements may appear in a SIZE ERROR phrase.

15. Division by ______ always causes a size error.

Review Exercises

1. For each of the three fields defined below, write IF statements to test for the absence of data:
   a. Without using any level-88 entries or REDEFINES clauses, if possible
   b. Using level-88 entries but no REDEFINES clause, if possible
   c. Using level-88 entries and/or REDEFINES clauses

```
  I.  05 OFFICE-NAME-IN                PIC X(25).
 II.  05 NUMBER-OF-DAYS-IN             PIC 999.
III.  05 PURCHASE-IN                   PIC 9(4)V99.
```

2. Write an IF statement that will determine whether the field PURCHASE-IN, described in Review Exercise 1, contains all numbers, and execute the True path if it does not.

3. Given the following field:

```
05 SAME-AMOUNT-IN                      PIC 999V99.
```

   Write a level-88 entry and an IF statement that will execute the True path if the contents of the field SALE-AMOUNT-IN are outside the reasonable range of $5 through $750.

4. Given the following field:

```
05 SKILL-CODE                          PIC X.
```

   Write level-88 entries giving suitable names to the following codes for the different skills: machinist, M; carpenter, C; press operator, P; riveter, R. Also write a level-88 entry giving a name to a missing code. Write IF statements to check for the absence of data in the field and for an invalid code.

5. Write a program to read data in the following format:

Positions	Field
1–3	Customer Number
4–6	Store Number
7–12	Salesperson Number
13–19	Sale Amount (to two decimal places)
20–80	spaces

   Have the program check the validity of the input as follows:
   a. Store Number numeric
   b. Salesperson Number numeric

c. Customer Number present
d. Customer Number numeric
e. Sale Amount numeric
f. Sale Amount not less than $10 or greater than $50,000

Have your program list the contents of each error-free record. Have your program accumulate the Sale Amounts from the error-free records and print the total at the end of the report. Have your program check for all five types of errors in each record. If more than one error is found in a record, have your program print an error line for each error.

6. Write a program to read input data in the following format:

Positions	Fields
1–7	Customer Number
8–15	Part Number
16–22	spaces
23–25	Quantity
26–31	Unit Price (in dollars and cents)
26–29	Unit Price dollars
30–31	Unit Price cents
32–35	Handling Charge (in dollars and cents)
32–33	Handling Charge dollars
34–35	Handling Charge cents
35–80	spaces

Have your program check that all Quantity and all Unit Price fields contain only numbers. If a field is found not to contain only numbers, a suitable error line is to be printed. For each valid record have your program print the Customer Number, Part Number, Quantity, Unit Price, and a merchandise amount (the Quantity times the Unit Price), except if the merchandise amount is greater than 999,999.99. If the merchandise amount is greater than 999,999.99, have your program print only the Customer Number, Part Number, Quantity, Unit Price, and a message MERCHANDISE AMOUNT SUSPICIOUSLY LARGE. At the end of the report, have your program print the total of the valid merchandise amounts.

Project

Modify your solution to the project in Chapter 7, page 220, to include checking the input data for validity before processing. Make the following checks on each input record:

a. Starting Loan Amount numeric
b. Monthly Payment numeric
c. Month of First Payment numeric
d. Month of First Payment within the range 1 through 12
e. Year of First Payment numeric

f. Year of First Payment within the range 1960 through 2011

g. Annual Interest Rate numeric

h. Annual Interest Rate within the range .04 through .23

Have your program check each input record for all eight possible errors. If one error is found in an input record, have your program print an error message and the entire input record on a page by themselves. If more than one error is found in the record, print an additional error message for each error on the same page as the first. Design your error messages before you begin coding.

CHAPTER 9

Report Writer

HERE ARE THE KEY POINTS YOU SHOULD LEARN FROM THIS CHAPTER

1. The concept of automatic generation of coding for report output
2. The features of the COBOL Report Writer
3. How to use Report Writer to produce a variety of reports
4. How to use declaratives in connection with Report Writer

KEY WORDS TO RECOGNIZE AND LEARN

Report Writer	PAGE
declarative	FIRST DETAIL
Report Section	absolute LINE NUMBER clause
REPORT	relative LINE NUMBER clause
report name	SUM
RD	sum counter
report description entry	LAST DETAIL
report group	FOOTING
TYPE	PAGE-COUNTER
DETAIL	LINE-COUNTER
REPORT HEADING	GROUP INDICATE
PAGE HEADING	NEXT GROUP
CONTROL FOOTING	ALL
PAGE FOOTING	declarative section
REPORT FOOTING	NEXT PAGE
LINE	DECLARATIVES
PLUS	USE
COLUMN	BEFORE REPORTING
SOURCE	SUPPRESS
INITIATE	END
GENERATE	CONTROL HEADING
TERMINATE	UPON
CONTROL	RESET ON
FINAL	

The Report Writer feature of COBOL makes programming for report output easier. The Report Writer provides, automatically, coding that otherwise would have to be written step by step by the programmer. With Report Writer, the programmer can describe certain characteristics that the output report is to have, and Report Writer generates the coding needed to make the report look that way. For example, Report Writer can provide all the page overflow coding needed in a program. The programmer need only tell Report Writer how big the page is, and Report Writer provides coding that will count lines as they print, test for page overflow, and skip to a new page and print headings when necessary. Report Writer can also provide coding that will take totals. If a total line is to print at the end of a report, the programmer need not code any of the totaling logic but just tell Report Writer which fields are to be totaled, and all the necessary coding will be provided automatically.

Report Writer also contains control break logic. If control breaks are needed on a report, the programmer need only say what the control fields are, and Report Writer provides coding to test for control breaks and print the appropriate total lines.

Another feature of Report Writer that makes programming easier is the way that output line formats are specified in Report Writer. Just tell Report Writer in which print positions each field is to print, and it provides all the necessary coding. There is no need to count blank spaces.

There have been many schemes to produce automatically programs that print reports. But Report Writer is more than a means of producing reports. Report Writer is the printing component of the whole powerful COBOL language. In using Report Writer, the programmer does not give up any of the capabilities of COBOL; the programmer still has command over all the output editing features, the nested IF, and complex conditions. Thus Report Writer should be used in any COBOL program that produces printed output. No matter what else the program might be doing, no matter how large the program is or how involved the logic, and no matter what volume of printed output is produced by the program, Report Writer should handle the formatting and printing of all lines. We refrain from using Report Writer in subsequent chapters of this book because it is not always available in the COBOL systems in use at some schools.

Even though Report Writer is extremely flexible and powerful, it sometimes happens that the programmer needs one or more features that Report Writer does not contain. Such features can be hand-coded using a **declarative** section, as will be shown later in the chapter.

The Report Section and Report Groups

The first program we will write using Report Writer reads input records and prints the contents of each one, reformatted, on one line. There are no page or column headings. Program P09-01 uses input records in the following format:

Positions	Field
1–9	Social Security Number
10–14	Employee Number
15–21	Annual Salary (in dollars and cents)
22–46	Employee Name
47–80	spaces

Program P09-01 produces output in the format shown in Figure 9.1. The program is shown in Figure 9.2.

FIGURE 9.1 **Output format for Program P09-01**

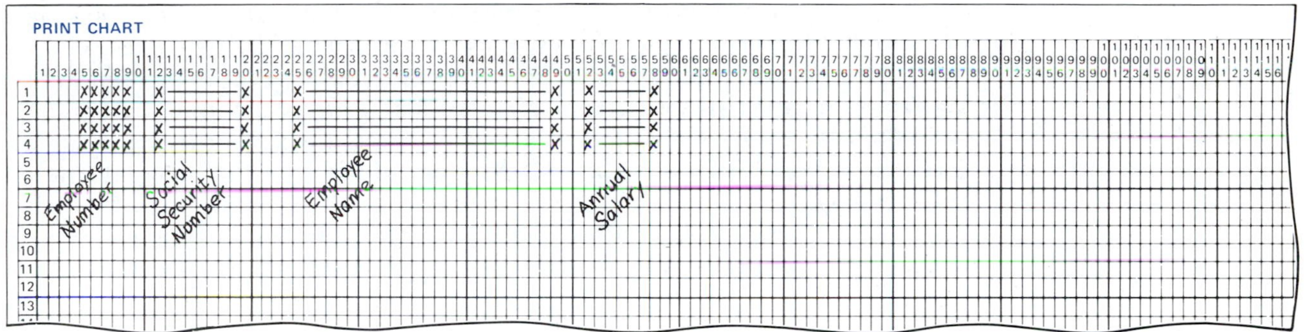

FIGURE 9.2 **Program P09-01**

```
S COBOL II RELEASE 3.2 09/05/90                    P09001    DATE FEB 22,1992 T
----+-*A-1-B--+----2----+----3----+----4----+----5----+----6----+----7-|--+

       IDENTIFICATION DIVISION.
       PROGRAM-ID.  P09-01.
      *AUTHOR.  WENDEL KELLER.
      *
      *     THIS PROGRAM READS INPUT RECORDS
      *     PRINTS THE CONTENTS OF EACH RECORD ON ONE LINE.
      *
      *****************************************************************

       ENVIRONMENT DIVISION.
       INPUT-OUTPUT SECTION.
       FILE-CONTROL.
           SELECT EMPLOYEE-DATA-FILE-IN     ASSIGN TO INFILE.
           SELECT EMPLOYEE-DATA-FILE-OUT    ASSIGN TO PRINTER.

      *****************************************************************

       DATA DIVISION.
       FILE SECTION.
       FD  EMPLOYEE-DATA-FILE-IN
           RECORD CONTAINS 80 CHARACTERS.

       01  EMPLOYEE-DATA-RECORD-IN.
           05  SOCIAL-SECURITY-NUMBER-IN     PIC X(9).
           05  EMPLOYEE-NUMBER-IN            PIC X(5).
           05  ANNUAL-SALARY-IN              PIC X(7).
           05  EMPLOYEE-NAME-IN              PIC X(25).

       FD  EMPLOYEE-DATA-FILE-OUT
           REPORT IS EMPLOYEE-REPORT.
```

continued

In the Data Division we see the **Report Section,** beginning at line 00360. The Report Section must appear whenever Report Writer is used, and it must be the last section in the Data Division. In the File Section the output file FD entry, line 00290, has no level-01 entry associated with it. Instead, the **REPORT** clause in the FD entry tells COBOL that Report Writer will be writing out a report on this file. The REPORT clause gives a name to the report that is being produced. In this program the **report name** is EMPLOYEE-REPORT. The rules for making up report names are the same as for making up file names.

Every report name given in the File Section must appear in the Report Section as part of an **RD** entry (**report description entry**). Within the RD entry and the level numbers that follow it, many characteristics of the report are described. Report Writer uses these descriptions of the report to create the necessary coding.

Each level-01 entry following the RD entry describes a different type of line, or group of related lines, that may appear on the report. The line or lines appearing under a level-01 entry is called a **report group.** In Program P09-01 the level-01 entry, shown in line 00390, describes a report group called REPORT-LINE. In this case the report group consists of only one line. The rules for making up report group names are the same as for making up data names.

The report group REPORT-LINE is shown as **TYPE DETAIL,** meaning that this is a detail line on the report. Some other TYPEs of report groups that may be described are

1. **REPORT HEADING,** one or more lines to print only once on the report at the beginning
2. **PAGE HEADING,** one or more lines to print at the top of every page
3. **CONTROL FOOTING,** one or more lines to print after a control break has been detected
4. **PAGE FOOTING,** one or more lines to print at the bottom of each page before skipping to a new page
5. **REPORT FOOTING,** one or more lines to print at the end of the report

The clause **LINE PLUS** 1, at line 00410, tells Report Writer that the detail lines on this report are to be single-spaced. The clause LINE PLUS 1 means that each detail line is to be printed on whatever LINE the previous one was printed, PLUS 1. By one means or another, you always must tell Report Writer explicitly where to put every line it prints.

We come now to the level-05 entries, beginning with line 00420, where we describe the individual fields that make up REPORT-LINE. Using the **COLUMN** clause, we tell Report Writer the print position where each field on the line begins. The column numbers shown in these COLUMN clauses were taken directly from the print chart in Figure 9.1. There is no need for counting the number of blanks between fields.

The **SOURCE** clause tells Report Writer where the data come from in the Data Division to fill each field. The SOURCE of a print field may be any identifier anywhere in the File Section or Working Storage Section or certain fields in the Report Section.

The Procedure Division introduces three new verbs. The **INITIATE** statement, line 00600, must be issued to initialize the report file. It must be issued after the output file has been OPENed in the usual way and before a **GENERATE**

FIGURE *9.2* *continued*

```
S COBOL II RELEASE 3.2 09/05/90                P09001    DATE FEB 22,1992 T
----+-*A-1-B--+----2----+----3----+----4----+----5----+----6----+----7-|--+

00310
00320  WORKING-STORAGE SECTION.
00330  01  MORE-INPUT                        PIC X        VALUE "Y".
00340      88 THERE-IS-NO-MORE-INPUT         VALUE "N".
00350
00360  REPORT SECTION.
00370  RD  EMPLOYEE-REPORT.
00380
00390  01  REPORT-LINE
00400      TYPE DETAIL
00410      LINE PLUS 1.
00420      05  COLUMN 5     PIC X(5)     SOURCE EMPLOYEE-NUMBER-IN.
00430      05  COLUMN 12    PIC X(9)     SOURCE SOCIAL-SECURITY-NUMBER-IN.
00440      05  COLUMN 25    PIC X(25)    SOURCE EMPLOYEE-NAME-IN.
00450      05  COLUMN 52    PIC X(7)     SOURCE ANNUAL-SALARY-IN.
00460
00470 ******************************************************************
00480
00490  PROCEDURE DIVISION.
00500  CONTROL-PARAGRAPH.
00510      PERFORM INITIALIZATION
00520      PERFORM MAIN-PROCESS UNTIL THERE-IS-NO-MORE-INPUT
00530      PERFORM TERMINATION
00540      STOP RUN
00550      .
00560
00570  INITIALIZATION.
00580      OPEN INPUT  EMPLOYEE-DATA-FILE-IN
00590           OUTPUT EMPLOYEE-DATA-FILE-OUT
00600      INITIATE EMPLOYEE-REPORT
00610      PERFORM READ-A-RECORD
00620      .
00630
00640  MAIN-PROCESS.
00650      GENERATE REPORT-LINE
00660      PERFORM READ-A-RECORD
00670      .
00680
00690  TERMINATION.
00700      TERMINATE EMPLOYEE-REPORT
00710      CLOSE EMPLOYEE-DATA-FILE-IN
00720            EMPLOYEE-DATA-FILE-OUT
00730      .
00740
00750  READ-A-RECORD.
00760      READ EMPLOYEE-DATA-FILE-IN
00770          AT END
00780              SET THERE-IS-NO-MORE-INPUT TO TRUE
00790      .
```

verb is issued for that report. The INITIATE statement must include the report name as it appears in the RD entry. The GENERATE verb may be used to print a report group. In this case we have only the one report group, REPORT-LINE. The statement GENERATE REPORT-LINE, at line 00650, does everything: It blanks the output areas that should be blank, moves data from the input area to the print line, single-spaces the paper, and writes a line.

After the complete report is written, a **TERMINATE** statement must be issued for the report name, as shown in line 00700. This must be done before the file is CLOSEd. Program P09-01 was run with the input data shown in Figure 9.3 and produced the output shown in Figure 9.4.

FIGURE 9.3 Input to Program P09-01

```
---------------------------------------------------------------------------------
         1         2         3         4         5         6         7         8
12345678901234567890123456789012345678901234567890123456789012345678901234567890
---------------------------------------------------------------------------------
100040002105035000000MORALES, LUIS
101850005108904651000JACOBSON, MRS. NELLIE
201110008112774302000GREENWOOD, JAMES
209560011116643953000COSTELLO, JOSEPH S.
301810014120513604000REITER, D.
304870017124383255000MARRA, DITTA E.
401710020128252906000LIPKE, VINCENT R.
407390023132122557000KUGLER, CHARLES
502070026135992208000JAVIER, CARLOS
505680029139861859000GOODMAN, ISAAC
604910032143731510000FELDSOTT, MS. SALLY
608250035147601161000BUXBAUM, ROBERT
703100038151470812000DUMAY, MRS. MARY
708020041155340463000SMITH, R.
803220044159210114000VINCENTE, MATTHEW J.
901050047163084235000THOMAS, THOMAS T.
```

FIGURE 9.4 Output from Program P09-01

```
10503   100040002      MORALES, LUIS              5000000
10890   101850005      JACOBSON, MRS. NELLIE      4651000
11277   201110008      GREENWOOD, JAMES           4302000
11664   209560011      COSTELLO, JOSEPH S.        3953000
12051   301810014      REITER, D.                 3604000
12438   304870017      MARRA, DITTA E.            3255000
12825   401710020      LIPKE, VINCENT R.          2906000
13212   407390023      KUGLER, CHARLES            2557000
13599   502070026      JAVIER, CARLOS             2208000
13986   505680029      GOODMAN, ISAAC             1859000
14373   604910032      FELDSOTT, MS. SALLY        1510000
14760   608250035      BUXBAUM, ROBERT            1161000
15147   703100038      DUMAY, MRS. MARY           0812000
15534   708020041      SMITH, R.                  0463000
15921   803220044      VINCENTE, MATTHEW J.       0114000
16308   901050047      THOMAS, THOMAS T.          4235000
```

EXERCISE 1 Using Report Writer, write a program to read and process input records in the following format:

Positions	*Field*
1–20	Company Name
21–35	Street Address
36–50	City and State
51–65	Employee Name
66–80	Employee Title

Have your program print the contents of each record on one line in the format shown in Figure 9.E1.

FIGURE 9.E1 Output format for Exercise 1

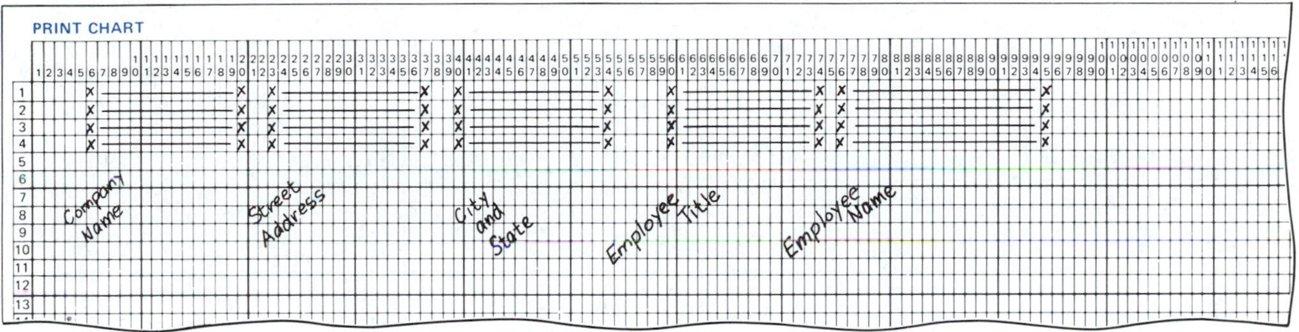

A Final Total Using Report Writer

We will now do a program that shows how Report Writer handles page and column headings, arithmetic manipulation of data before they are printed on a detail line, and totaling. Program P09-02 reads input records in the following format:

Positions	Field
1–7	Customer Number
8–15	Part Number
16–22	spaces
23–25	Quantity
26–31	Unit Price (in dollars and cents)
26–29	Unit Price dollars
30–31	Unit Price cents
32–35	Handling Charge (in dollars and cents)
32–33	Handling Charge dollars
34–35	Handling Charge cents
35–80	spaces

Each input record represents the purchase of some parts by a customer. The record shows the quantity purchased, the price per unit, and a handling charge for the order. The program is to read each record and compute the cost of the merchandise (by multiplying the Quantity by the Unit Price) and a tax at 7% of the merchandise amount. Then the program is to add together the merchandise amount, the tax, and the handling charge to arrive at a total for the order. The information for each order is to be printed on one line as shown in Figure 9.5. At the end of the report, the program is to print the total of all the merchandise amounts for all the orders, the totals of all the tax and handling charge amounts, and a grand total of all the order totals, as shown in Figure 9.5. The program is also to print a report title and column headings as shown in Figure 9.5.

FIGURE 9.5 Output format for Program P09-02

PRINT CHART

```
2                               DAILY ORDER REPORT

5       CUSTOMER      PART       QUANTITY   UNIT      MERCHANDISE    TAX        HANDLING   TOTAL
6       NUMBER        NUMBER                PRICE       AMOUNT

8       X-----X       X-----X    ZZ9        Z,ZZZ.99  ZZZ,ZZZ.99     Z,ZZZ.99   ZZ.99      Z,ZZZ,ZZZ.99
9       X-----X       X-----X    ZZ9        Z,ZZZ.99  ZZZ,ZZZ.99     Z,ZZZ.99   ZZ.99      Z,ZZZ,ZZZ.99
10      X-----X       X-----X    ZZ9        Z,ZZZ.99  ZZZ,ZZZ.99     Z,ZZZ.99   ZZ.99      Z,ZZZ,ZZZ.99

13                                          TOTALS  Z,ZZZ,ZZZ.99   ZZ,ZZZ.99  ZZZ.99    ZZ,ZZZ,ZZZ.99 **
```

Program P09-02 will handle an empty input file by printing the report title, the column headings, the words "No input data," and a total line with all zero totals. Later you will see how to suppress the printing of column headings and total lines by using declarative sections. Program P09-02 is shown in Figure 9.6.

The Working Storage Section, beginning on line 00340, contains fields that we will need for the results of arithmetic. The RD entry, line 00430, has a few clauses that we are seeing for the first time. The **CONTROL** clause tells Report Writer that **FINAL** totals are to be printed. In a later program we will see how totals for minor, intermediate, and major control breaks are indicated in the CONTROL clause. The **PAGE** clause is required if you want to control the vertical spacing of lines on the page. From the print chart in Figure 9.5, you can see that the first detail line of the report is to print on line 8 of the page, and we indicate this to Report Writer by saying **FIRST DETAIL** 8. We are also required to tell Report Writer how many lines can fit on a page, and here we arbitrarily said 50.

For this report we have five report groups: a REPORT HEADING group that consists of one line (the report title); a PAGE HEADING group that consists of two lines (the column headings); a DETAIL group of one line to handle the normal detail printing shown on the print chart; a DETAIL group consisting of one line containing the words "No input data"; and a FINAL total line. So we need five level-01 entries, one for each report group. The first level-01 entry is for the REPORT HEADING group and is indicated by the clause TYPE REPORT HEADING, line 00480. The print chart shows that the REPORT HEADING is to print on line 2 of the page, so that line number is indicated in the clause LINE 2. You can see that a VALUE clause is used in the level-05 entry when constant information is to print. Whenever you have the word LINE followed by an integer, you are using what is called an **absolute LINE NUMBER clause.** When you use the words LINE PLUS followed by an integer, you are using a **relative LINE NUMBER clause.**

The next level-01 entry is for the column headings, and is indicated by the clause TYPE PAGE HEADING, line 00520. The print chart shows that the two lines that make up the PAGE HEADING are to print on lines 5 and 6 of the page, and so those line numbers are indicated in the level-05 entries, lines 00530 and 00620. The level-10 entries describe the individual fields that make up the two column heading lines.

FIGURE 9.6 **Program P09-02**

```
S COBOL II RELEASE 3.1 09/19/89                    P09002   DATE AUG 13,1991 T
----+-*A-1-B--+----2----+----3----+----4----+----5----+----6----+----7-|--+

        IDENTIFICATION DIVISION.
        PROGRAM-ID.  P09-02.
       *AUTHOR.  WENDEL KELLER.
       *
       *    THIS PROGRAM PRINTS A REPORT TITLE, COLUMN HEADINGS,
       *    DETAIL LINES, AND A FINAL TOTAL LINE.
       *
       *****************************************************************

        ENVIRONMENT DIVISION.
        INPUT-OUTPUT SECTION.
        FILE-CONTROL.
            SELECT ORDER-FILE-IN             ASSIGN TO INFILE.
            SELECT ORDER-REPORT-FILE-OUT     ASSIGN TO PRINTER.

       *****************************************************************

        DATA DIVISION.
        FILE SECTION.
        FD  ORDER-FILE-IN
            RECORD CONTAINS 80 CHARACTERS.

        01  ORDER-RECORD-IN.
            05  CUSTOMER-NUMBER-IN       PIC X(7).
            05  PART-NUMBER-IN           PIC X(8).
            05                           PIC X(7).
            05  QUANTITY-IN              PIC 999.
            05  UNIT-PRICE-IN            PIC 9(4)V99.
            05  HANDLING-IN              PIC 99V99.

        FD  ORDER-REPORT-FILE-OUT
            REPORT IS DAILY-ORDER-REPORT.

        WORKING-STORAGE SECTION.
        01  MORE-INPUT                   PIC X             VALUE "Y".
            88 THERE-IS-NO-MORE-INPUT    VALUE "N".
        01  TAX-RATE                     PIC V99           VALUE .07.
        01  MERCHANDISE-AMOUNT-W         PIC 9(6)V99.
        01  TAX-W                        PIC 9(4)V99.
        01  ORDER-TOTAL-W                PIC 9(7)V99.

        REPORT SECTION.
        RD  DAILY-ORDER-REPORT
            CONTROL FINAL
            PAGE 50 LINES
            FIRST DETAIL 8.

        01  TYPE REPORT HEADING
            LINE 2.
            05  COLUMN 46        PIC X(18)    VALUE "DAILY ORDER REPORT".

        01  TYPE PAGE HEADING.
            05  LINE 5.
                10  COLUMN 11    PIC X(8)          VALUE "CUSTOMER".
                10  COLUMN 26    PIC X(4)          VALUE "PART".
                10  COLUMN 38    PIC X(8)          VALUE "QUANTITY".
                10  COLUMN 51    PIC X(4)          VALUE "UNIT".
                10  COLUMN 64    PIC X(11)         VALUE "MERCHANDISE".
                10  COLUMN 82    PIC XXX           VALUE "TAX".
                10  COLUMN 91    PIC X(8)          VALUE "HANDLING".
                10  COLUMN 107   PIC X(5)          VALUE "TOTAL".
            05  LINE 6.
                10  COLUMN 12    PIC X(6)          VALUE "NUMBER".
                10  COLUMN 25    PIC X(6)          VALUE "NUMBER".
                10  COLUMN 51    PIC X(5)          VALUE "PRICE".
                10  COLUMN 66    PIC X(6)          VALUE "AMOUNT".
```

continued

Whenever there is only one line in a report group, the entries that describe the fields on the line may have any level number in the range 02–49. When there is more than one line in a group and some line has only one field, that line and its field may be described in a single entry that has a level number in the range 02–49. Otherwise the level number of an entry immediately following a level-01 entry can be any number in the range 02–48; in our program it is 05. Then the entries that describe the fields in each line can have level numbers in the range 03–49; in our program they have level number 10.

The normal detail line in the program, called DETAIL-LINE and described in line 00680, is similar to the one in Program P09-01. But here we have some output editing. Note that the PICTUREs included in these descriptions are PICTUREs of the output fields as they are to print. Any PICTURE features may be used in the Report Section, including floating signs, check protection, and insertion, to obtain any kind of output editing.

The next level-01 entry, at line 00820, describes the DETAIL line that is to print when there are no input data. The clause LINE 8 says that this line is to print on LINE 8 of the page. You will see how this DETAIL line is used when we look at the Procedure Division.

The last level-01 entry, at line 00870, describes the final total line. Since Report Writer considers final total a control break, the final total line must be described as CONTROL FOOTING FINAL. The clause LINE PLUS 3 will cause the final total line to be triple-spaced down from the last detail line on the report.

In the FINAL total line we see the use of the **SUM** clause, as in line 00910, which tells Report Writer that a particular field is to be printed as the SUM of the values of the field named. For example, the clause SUM MERCHANDISE-AMOUNT-W will cause Report Writer to set up a field called a **sum counter** to accumulate the total of the MERCHANDISE-AMOUNT-W amounts. Whenever a GENERATE statement is executed, Report Writer adds the value of MERCHANDISE-AMOUNT-W into the sum counter. The sum counter is defined by Report Writer as purely numeric. The PICTURE given in the level-05 entry with the clause SUM MERCHANDISE-AMOUNT-W is the PICTURE that Report Writer uses to edit the sum when it is finally printed. The SUM clause may appear only in a CONTROL FOOTING report group.

The Procedure Division of this program has very little that is new. The INITIALIZATION paragraph, starting at line 01070, contains the usual initialization, and also the processing needed to handle an empty input file. The IF statement at line 01120 does it. The MAIN-PROCESS routine, starting at line 01170, shows that any regular COBOL processing may be done on an input record. In this case some arithmetic is done, and the results are assigned to working storage fields, which are then used as SOURCE fields in the Report Section.

Notice that nowhere in the Procedure Division do we tell Report Writer when to print the REPORT HEADING group, the PAGE HEADING group, or the FINAL total line, nor do we code any of the logic for accumulating the sums or printing them. Report Writer automatically prints the REPORT HEADING and the PAGE HEADING when we give the first GENERATE statement. It accumulates SUMs with the execution of each GENERATE statement. And it automatically prints the FINAL total line when we give the TERMINATE statement.

Since we never had to refer to the REPORT HEADING, PAGE HEADING, or FINAL total line groups by name, their level-01 entries were written without

FIGURE 9.6 *continued*

```
S COBOL II RELEASE 3.1 09/19/89                P09002   DATE AUG 13,1991 T
----+-*A-1-B--+----2----+----3----+----4----+----5----+----6----+----7-|--+

 01  DETAIL-LINE
     TYPE DETAIL
     LINE PLUS 1.
     05  COLUMN 12         PIC X(7)          SOURCE CUSTOMER-NUMBER-IN.
     05  COLUMN 24         PIC X(8)          SOURCE PART-NUMBER-IN.
     05  COLUMN 40         PIC ZZ9           SOURCE QUANTITY-IN.
     05  COLUMN 49         PIC Z,ZZZ.99      SOURCE UNIT-PRICE-IN.
     05  COLUMN 64         PIC ZZZ,ZZZ.99
                           SOURCE MERCHANDISE-AMOUNT-W.
     05  COLUMN 80         PIC Z,ZZZ.99      SOURCE TAX-W.
     05  COLUMN 93         PIC ZZ.99         SOURCE HANDLING-IN.
     05  COLUMN 103        PIC Z,ZZZ,ZZZ.99
                           SOURCE ORDER-TOTAL-W.

 01  NO-INPUT-DATA
     TYPE DETAIL
     LINE 8.
     05  COLUMN 49         PIC X(13)            VALUE "NO INPUT DATA".

 01  TYPE CONTROL FOOTING FINAL
     LINE PLUS 3.
     05  COLUMN 53         PIC X(6)             VALUE "TOTALS".
     05  COLUMN 62         PIC Z,ZZZ,ZZZ.99
                           SUM MERCHANDISE-AMOUNT-W.
     05  COLUMN 79         PIC ZZ,ZZZ.99        SUM TAX-W.
     05  COLUMN 92         PIC ZZZ.99           SUM HANDLING-IN.
     05  COLUMN 102        PIC ZZ,ZZZ,ZZZ.99    SUM ORDER-TOTAL-W.
     05  COLUMN 116        PIC XX               VALUE "**".

*****************************************************************

 PROCEDURE DIVISION.
 CONTROL-PARAGRAPH.
     PERFORM INITIALIZATION
     PERFORM MAIN-PROCESS UNTIL THERE-IS-NO-MORE-INPUT
     PERFORM TERMINATION
     STOP RUN
     .

 INITIALIZATION.
     OPEN INPUT  ORDER-FILE-IN
          OUTPUT ORDER-REPORT-FILE-OUT
     INITIATE DAILY-ORDER-REPORT
     PERFORM READ-A-RECORD
     IF THERE-IS-NO-MORE-INPUT
         GENERATE NO-INPUT-DATA
     END-IF
     .

 MAIN-PROCESS.
     MULTIPLY QUANTITY-IN BY UNIT-PRICE-IN
             GIVING MERCHANDISE-AMOUNT-W
     MULTIPLY MERCHANDISE-AMOUNT-W BY TAX-RATE
             GIVING TAX-W ROUNDED
     ADD MERCHANDISE-AMOUNT-W
         TAX-W
         HANDLING-IN
             GIVING ORDER-TOTAL-W
     GENERATE DETAIL-LINE
     PERFORM READ-A-RECORD
     .
```

continued

FIGURE 9.6 *continued*

```
S COBOL II RELEASE 3.1 09/19/89                         P09002   DATE AUG 13,1991 T
----+-*A-1-B--+----2----+----3----+----4----+----5----+----6----+----7-|--+

       TERMINATION.
           TERMINATE DAILY-ORDER-REPORT
           CLOSE ORDER-FILE-IN
                 ORDER-REPORT-FILE-OUT
           .

       READ-A-RECORD.
           READ ORDER-FILE-IN
               AT END
                   SET THERE-IS-NO-MORE-INPUT TO TRUE
           .
```

names. The only groups that needed names were the DETAIL groups, so that they could be referred to in GENERATE statements. A level-01 entry needs a name only if the name is referred to in a GENERATE statement, in a declarative section, or in an entry elsewhere in the Report Section.

Program P09-02 was run first on the input data shown in Figure 9.7 and produced the output shown in Figure 9.8. Then it was run with an empty input file and produced the output shown in Figure 9.9.

FIGURE 9.7 **Input to Program P09-02**

```
--------------------------------------------------------------------------------
         1         2         3         4         5         6         7         8
12345678901234567890123456789012345678901234567890123456789012345678901234567890
--------------------------------------------------------------------------------
ABC1234F2365-09      9000000100005
09G8239836-7YT7      8000010500050
ADGH784091AN-07      0500250000500
9675473235-1287      0067000295000
```

FIGURE 9.8 **Output from Program P09-02**

DAILY ORDER REPORT

CUSTOMER NUMBER	PART NUMBER	QUANTITY	UNIT PRICE	MERCHANDISE AMOUNT	TAX	HANDLING	TOTAL
ABC1234	F2365-09	900	.10	90.00	6.30	.05	96.35
09G8239	836-7YT7	800	10.50	8,400.00	588.00	.50	8,988.50
ADGH784	091AN-07	50	250.00	12,500.00	875.00	5.00	13,380.00
9675473	23S-1287	6	7,000.29	42,001.74	2,940.12	50.00	44,991.86
			TOTALS	62,991.74	4,409.42	55.55	67,456.71 **

FIGURE 9.9 Output produced when Program P09-02 was run with an empty input file

```
                              DAILY ORDER REPORT

CUSTOMER       PART          QUANTITY     UNIT          MERCHANDISE         TAX        HANDLING          TOTAL
 NUMBER       NUMBER                      PRICE            AMOUNT

                                     NO INPUT DATA

                                          TOTALS                .00               .00          .00                .00 **
```

EXERCISE 2

Write a program to read input records in the following format:

Positions	Field
1–5	Account Number
6–10	spaces
11–17	Amount (to two decimal places)
11–15	Amount dollars
16–17	Amount cents
18–80	spaces

Have your program compute a 4% discount on the amount shown in each record and a net amount (the original amount minus the discount). For each record read, have your program print the Account Number, the Amount, the computed discount, and the computed net amount. At the end of the report, have your program print a total line showing the sum of all the input Amounts, the sum of all the discount amounts, and the sum of the net amounts.

Have your program print a report title "Discount Report" and column headings "Account Number," "Amount," "Discount," and "Net Amount." Use a print chart to plan the spacing of the output; the placement of decimal points and commas; zero suppression; the alignment of the report title, the column headings, and the columns of data; and the format of the total line.

Multiple Control Breaks Using Report Writer

Program P09-03 has a report title, column headings, three levels of control breaks, the date, page overflow, page numbering, and group indication of the control fields. Program P09-03 uses input data in the following format:

Positions	Field
1–3	Store Number
4–6	Salesperson Number
7–12	Customer Number
13–19	Sale Amount (to two decimal places)
20–80	spaces

The program produces output in the format shown in Figure 9.10. The program was run using the input data shown in Figure 9.11, and produced the output shown in Figure 9.12.

Program P09-03 is shown in Figure 9.13 beginning on page 269. In the Working Storage Section the field TODAYS-DATE, at line 00350, is set up to be used with the Procedure Division statement ACCEPT TODAYS-DATE FROM DATE. The fields TODAYS-YEAR and TODAYS-MONTH-AND-DAY will be used as SOURCE fields in the Report Section for printing the date on the report.

FIGURE *9.10* **Output format for Program P09-03**

PRINT CHART

```
                                  SALES REPORT
                  DATE Z9/99/99                          PAGE Z9

                         STORE     SALES-     CUSTOMER      SALE
                          NO.      PERSON      NUMBER      AMOUNT

                          XXX       XXX        XXXXXX     ZZ,ZZZ.99
                                               XXXXXX     ZZ,ZZZ.99
                                               XXXXXX     ZZ,ZZZ.99

                                                         ZZZ,ZZZ.99 *

                          XXX       XXX        XXXXXX     ZZ,ZZZ.99
                                               XXXXXX     ZZ,ZZZ.99

                                                         ZZZ,ZZZ.99 *

                         TOTAL FOR STORE NO. XXX    $Z,ZZZ,ZZZ.99 **
                         ****************************************

                          XXX       XXX        XXXXXX     ZZ,ZZZ.99
                                               XXXXXX     ZZ,ZZZ.99

                                                         ZZZ,ZZZ.99 *

                          XXX       XXX        XXXXXX     ZZ,ZZZ.99
                                               XXXXXX     ZZ,ZZZ.99

                                                         ZZZ,ZZZ.99 *

                         TOTAL FOR STORE NO. XXX    $Z,ZZZ,ZZZ.99 **
                         ****************************************

                                GRAND TOTAL        $ZZ,ZZZ,ZZZ.99 ***

                         ****************************************
```

FIGURE 9.11 **Input to Program P09-03**

```
--------------------------------------------------------------------------------
         1         2         3         4         5         6         7         8
12345678901234567890123456789012345678901234567890123456789012345678901234567890
--------------------------------------------------------------------------------
010101003001123456
010101007002000224
010101039004843920
010101046005844848
010101053006001234
010101060006949493
010101067007400003
010102074212545499
010102081012000033
010102088013584958
010102095015039390
010103003234030303
020011007567999999
020011011454045600
020011023345833333
020222027345434343
020222031567990330
020222035001003421
020266039903453987
020266043854585830
030193059932585854
030193063419394949
040045067333000000
040045071323595950
040403048399392147
040403054392000000
040412060111999999
046012013538000000
046012017521069078
046012021504138156
046012025487207234
046012029470276312
046028033453345390
046028037436414468
046028041419483546
```

FIGURE 9.12 Output from Program P09-03

```
                    SALES REPORT
DATE  6/18/91                                         PAGE   1

          STORE     SALES-     CUSTOMER      SALE
           NO.      PERSON      NUMBER      AMOUNT

           010       101        003001     1,234.56
                                007002         2.24
                                039004     8,439.20
                                046005     8,448.48
                                053006        12.34
                                060006     9,494.93
                                067007     4,000.03

                                          31,631.78 *

           010       102        074212     5,454.99
                                081012          .33
                                088013     5,849.58
                                095015       393.90

                                          11,698.80 *

           010       103        003234       303.03

                                             303.03 *

          TOTAL FOR STORE NO. 010  $      43,633.61 **
          ************************************

           020       011        007567     9,999.99
                                011454       456.00
                                023345     8,333.33

                                          18,789.32 *

           020       222        027345     4,343.43
```

FIGURE 9.12 *continued*

```
DATE  6/18/91                                  PAGE  2

     STORE      SALES-      CUSTOMER       SALE
      NO.       PERSON       NUMBER       AMOUNT

      020        222         031567     9,903.30
                             035001        34.21

                                       14,280.94 *

      020        266         039903     4,539.87
                             043854     5,858.30

                                       10,398.17 *

     TOTAL FOR STORE NO. 020  $        43,468.43 **
     *************************************

      030        193         059932     5,858.54
                             063419     3,949.49

                                        9,808.03 *

     TOTAL FOR STORE NO. 030  $         9,808.03 **
     *************************************

      040        045         067333          .00
                             071323     5,959.50

                                        5,959.50 *

      040        403         048399     3,921.47
                             054392          .00

                                        3,921.47 *
```

```
DATE  6/18/91                                  PAGE  3

     STORE      SALES-      CUSTOMER       SALE
      NO.       PERSON       NUMBER       AMOUNT

      040        412         060111     9,999.99

                                        9,999.99 *

     TOTAL FOR STORE NO. 040  $        19,880.96 **
     *************************************

      046        012         013538          .00
                             017521       690.78
                             021504     1,381.56
                             025487     2,072.34
                             029470     2,763.12

                                        6,907.80 *

      046        028         033453     3,453.90
                             037436     4,144.68
                             041419     4,835.46

                                       12,434.04 *

     TOTAL FOR STORE NO. 046  $        19,341.84 **
     *************************************

             GRAND TOTAL      $       136,132.87 ***

     *************************************
```

FIGURE 9.13 **Program P09-03**

```
S COBOL II RELEASE 3.1 09/19/89                  P09003    DATE JUN 18,1991 T
----+-*A-1-B--+----2----+----3----+----4----+----5----+----6----+----7-|--+

 IDENTIFICATION DIVISION.
 PROGRAM-ID.  P09-03.
*AUTHOR.  WENDEL KELLER.
*
*    THIS PROGRAM PRINTS A REPORT TITLE, COLUMN HEADINGS,
*    DETAIL LINES, AND THREE LEVELS OF TOTALS.
*
*****************************************************************

 ENVIRONMENT DIVISION.
 INPUT-OUTPUT SECTION.
 FILE-CONTROL.
     SELECT SALES-FILE-IN             ASSIGN TO INFILE.
     SELECT SALES-REPORT-FILE-OUT     ASSIGN TO PRINTER.

*****************************************************************

 DATA DIVISION.
 FILE SECTION.
 FD  SALES-FILE-IN
     RECORD CONTAINS 80 CHARACTERS.

```

continued

In the RD entry, line 00400, we now must provide Report Writer with more information than in earlier programs. The CONTROL clause now must name all the levels of control breaks from the highest level to the most minor, in that order. Since a FINAL total is considered a control break, it must be named along with the two control fields STORE-NUMBER-IN and SALESPERSON-NUMBER-IN.

Since we have page overflow in this program, the PAGE clause must be more elaborate than before. The size of the overall page is still arbitrarily given as 50. From the print chart you can see that the FIRST DETAIL line is on line 9, so the PAGE clause includes FIRST DETAIL 9. We now include the **LAST DETAIL** phrase to tell Report Writer on which line of the page it may print the last detail line. Here LAST DETAIL 39 will permit Report Writer to print DETAIL lines up through line 39 of the page. Any DETAIL line that would print past line 39 will instead cause Report Writer to skip to a new page automatically and print the PAGE HEADING report group.

Report Writer recognizes that programmers usually will want to leave extra space at the bottom of each page for the printing of totals. That is, even though DETAIL lines may print up through line 39 of the page, we want to allow total lines to print beyond line 39 so that they will not appear on the next page separated from the control group being totaled. The **FOOTING** clause allows for this. With the FOOTING clause we can specify the last line of the page on which total lines (CONTROL FOOTING lines) may print. From the print chart you can see that we can have a maximum of nine lines of totals on this report (the last set of totals: three total lines, two lines of asterisks, and four blank lines). Since DETAIL lines can print up through line 39 of the page, we must permit the total lines to print up through line 48 to ensure that there will be room for them all. Thus we make the FOOTING limit 48. The depth of the full page, which we here made 50, could have been used to allow space beyond the limit of the

FIGURE 9.13 ***continued***

```
S COBOL II RELEASE 3.1 09/19/89                    P09003   DATE JUN 18,1991 T
----+-*A-1-B--+----2----+----3----+----4----+----5----+----6----+----7-|--+

00230  01  SALES-RECORD-IN.
00240      05  STORE-NUMBER-IN          PIC XXX.
00250      05  SALESPERSON-NUMBER-IN    PIC XXX.
00260      05  CUSTOMER-NUMBER-IN       PIC X(6).
00270      05  SALE-AMOUNT-IN           PIC 9(4)V99.
00280
00290  FD  SALES-REPORT-FILE-OUT
00300      REPORT IS SALES-REPORT-OUT.
00310
00320  WORKING-STORAGE SECTION.
00330  01  MORE-INPUT                   PIC X             VALUE "Y".
00340      88 THERE-IS-NO-MORE-INPUT    VALUE "N".
00350  01  TODAYS-DATE.
00360      05  TODAYS-YEAR              PIC 99.
00370      05  TODAYS-MONTH-AND-DAY     PIC 9(4).
00380
00390  REPORT SECTION.
00400  RD  SALES-REPORT-OUT
00410      CONTROLS FINAL, STORE-NUMBER-IN, SALESPERSON-NUMBER-IN
00420      PAGE 50 LINES, FIRST DETAIL 9, LAST DETAIL 39, FOOTING 48.
00430
```

total lines for PAGE FOOTINGs and a REPORT FOOTING. We have neither PAGE FOOTING nor REPORT FOOTING, so the depth of page could have been any number 48 or larger and the program would work the same way.

In the PAGE HEADING report group, which begins on line 00480, LINE 3 is the most interesting. You can see how the fields TODAYS-MONTH-AND-DAY and TODAYS-YEAR are used to print the date. The SOURCE field used for printing the page number is a special register called **PAGE-COUNTER.** Report Writer sets up a PAGE-COUNTER, with PICTURE 9(6), for every RD entry. The INITIATE statement for a report sets the PAGE-COUNTER to 1, and then Report Writer adds 1 to PAGE-COUNTER each time just before printing the PAGE HEADING report group (except the first PAGE HEADING). PAGE-COUNTER may be referred to and changed by ordinary Procedure Division statements. In this way the programmer may begin page-numbering a report with any desired page number. If a program contains more than one PAGE-COUNTER (because there is more than one RD entry in the program), then PAGE-COUNTER must be qualified by the RD name whenever it is referred to in the Procedure Division or in a report description other than the one it was set up for. Our program has only one PAGE-COUNTER, so it need not be qualified.

Report Writer also sets up a special register called **LINE-COUNTER** for every RD entry. The LINE-COUNTER is used by Report Writer to position print lines on the page and to detect page overflow. LINE-COUNTER may be referred to in the Procedure Division. An INITIATE statement for a report sets LINE-COUNTER to 0. If there is more than one LINE-COUNTER in a program, the name LINE-COUNTER must be qualified by the RD name whenever it is referred to in the Procedure Division or outside its own report description.

FIGURE 9.13 *continued*

```
00440  01  TYPE REPORT HEADING
00450      LINE 2.
00460      05  COLUMN 36        PIC X(12)      VALUE "SALES REPORT".
00470
00480  01  TYPE PAGE HEADING.
00490      05  LINE 3.
00500          10  COLUMN 20    PIC X(4)       VALUE "DATE".
00510          10  COLUMN 25    PIC Z9/99/
00520                           SOURCE TODAYS-MONTH-AND-DAY.
00530          10  COLUMN 31    PIC 99         SOURCE TODAYS-YEAR.
00540          10  COLUMN 62    PIC X(4)       VALUE "PAGE".
00550          10  COLUMN 67    PIC Z9         SOURCE PAGE-COUNTER.
00560      05  LINE 6.
00570          10  COLUMN 25    PIC X(5)       VALUE "STORE".
00580          10  COLUMN 34    PIC X(6)       VALUE "SALES-".
00590          10  COLUMN 44    PIC X(8)       VALUE "CUSTOMER".
00600          10  COLUMN 57    PIC X(4)       VALUE "SALE".
00610      05  LINE 7.
00620          10  COLUMN 26    PIC XXX        VALUE "NO.".
00630          10  COLUMN 34    PIC X(6)       VALUE "PERSON".
00640          10  COLUMN 45    PIC X(6)       VALUE "NUMBER".
00650          10  COLUMN 56    PIC X(6)       VALUE "AMOUNT".
00660
```

continued

In the description of the DETAIL line we see for the first time the **GROUP INDICATE** clause, at lines 00700 and 00720. These will cause the STORE-NUMBER-IN and SALESPERSON-NUMBER-IN fields to be group indicated; that is, to be printed only the first time this DETAIL line is printed after a control break or the first time it is printed on a page. The GROUP INDICATE clause may be used only in a TYPE DETAIL report group.

In this report description we have three different CONTROL FOOTING report groups, one each for a control break on SALESPERSON-NUMBER-IN and STORE-NUMBER-IN and for a FINAL total. Each report group is defined with its own level-01 entry.

The Salesperson Total Line

This is the minor total line, the lowest level of totals, at line 00820. The clause LINE PLUS 2 that appears in the description of the salesperson total line causes the total line to be double-spaced from the last detail line before it. In the description of the salesperson total line, we see for the first time the use of the **NEXT GROUP** clause. The NEXT GROUP clause is used for spacing or skipping the report output after printing a report group. Here we use NEXT GROUP PLUS 1 to give one blank line after a salesperson total line. When a NEXT GROUP clause appears in a CONTROL FOOTING group, as this one does, it is effective only for a control break at the same level as the CONTROL FOOTING line; that is, the NEXT GROUP PLUS 1 is effective only when a salesperson total line is being printed because of a salesperson break. The clause is ignored when a salesperson total line is printed as a result of a break on store number or on the FINAL break. This is an extremely useful feature and allows the programmer great flexibility in spacing output lines of the report.

The total field itself is described as being the SUM of all the SALE-AMOUNT-IN fields. The total field is given the name SALESPERSON-TOTAL. A SUMmed field has to be given a name only if it is referred to somewhere in the Procedure Division or elsewhere in the Report Section. In earlier programs our SUMmed fields were not referred to, and so they were not given names.

The Store Total Line

The CONTROL FOOTING group for the store total consists of two lines, one containing the total of all the SALESPERSON-TOTALs for that store, and the other a line of asterisks, as shown on the print chart in Figure 9.10. The clause NEXT GROUP PLUS 1 on line 00910 will give one blank line following the printing of the line of asterisks, but only if the line is printed as a result of a break on store number. When the store total report group is printed as part of the FINAL break, the NEXT GROUP clause is ignored. The NEXT GROUP clause, when used, must appear only in a level-01 entry, and it must not be used in a TYPE PAGE HEADING description or in TYPE REPORT FOOTING.

The clause LINE PLUS 2 in line 00920 will give double spacing for the total line. When a break on store number occurs, both a salesperson total line and a store total line print. First the salesperson total line prints, and the clause LINE PLUS 2 in the description of the salesperson total line causes it to be double-spaced from the last detail line. The clause NEXT GROUP PLUS 1 is ignored. The store total line is printed, and the clause LINE PLUS 2 in the description of the store total line causes it to be double-spaced from the salesperson total report group.

FIGURE 9.13 *continued*

```
S COBOL II RELEASE 3.1 09/19/89                    P09003    DATE JUN 18,1991 T
----+-*A-1-B--+----2----+----3----+----4----+----5----+----6----+----7-|--+

00670  01  DETAIL-LINE
00680      TYPE DETAIL
00690      LINE PLUS 1.
00700      05  COLUMN 26        PIC XXX        GROUP INDICATE
00710                           SOURCE STORE-NUMBER-IN.
00720      05  COLUMN 35        PIC XXX        GROUP INDICATE
00730                           SOURCE SALESPERSON-NUMBER-IN.
00740      05  COLUMN 45        PIC X(6)       SOURCE CUSTOMER-NUMBER-IN.
00750      05  COLUMN 54        PIC ZZ,ZZZ.99 SOURCE SALE-AMOUNT-IN.
00760
00770  01  NO-INPUT-DATA
00780      TYPE DETAIL
00790      LINE 9.
00800      05  COLUMN 36        PIC X(13)      VALUE "NO INPUT DATA".
00810
00820  01  TYPE CONTROL FOOTING SALESPERSON-NUMBER-IN
00830      LINE PLUS 2
00840      NEXT GROUP PLUS 1.
00850      05  SALESPERSON-TOTAL
00860          COLUMN 53        PIC ZZZ,ZZZ.99
00870                           SUM SALE-AMOUNT-IN.
00880      05  COLUMN 64        PIC X          VALUE "*".
00890
00900  01  TYPE CONTROL FOOTING STORE-NUMBER-IN
00910      NEXT GROUP PLUS 1.
00920      05  LINE PLUS 2.
00930          10  COLUMN 25    PIC X(19)
00940                           VALUE "TOTAL FOR STORE NO.".
00950          10  COLUMN 45    PIC XXX        SOURCE STORE-NUMBER-IN.
00960          10  STORE-TOTAL
00970              COLUMN 50    PIC $Z,ZZZ,ZZZ.99
00980                           SUM SALESPERSON-TOTAL.
00990          10  COLUMN 64    PIC XX         VALUE "**".
01000      05  LINE PLUS 1
01010          COLUMN 25        PIC X(38)      VALUE ALL "*".
01020
```

continued

In the store total line, the total field is described as being the SUM of all the SALESPERSON-TOTAL values. It could have been defined as the SUM of all the SALE-AMOUNT-IN values but the processing would have been slower. SALESPERSON-TOTAL is a SUMmed field and is defined in the Report Section. Whenever a SUMmed field such as SALESPERSON-TOTAL is itself used as the operand in some other SUM clause, it must be defined either at a level lower than where it is used in the control break hierarchy or at the same level. Our SUM fields meet that condition: SALESPERSON-TOTAL is defined in the salesperson line, which is at a lower level than the store total line, where it is used. The field that is the SUM of all the SALESPERSON-TOTAL amounts is given the name STORE-TOTAL. This name is used elsewhere in the Report Section.

The field whose SOURCE is STORE-NUMBER-IN shows that when a control break occurs, the previous value of the control field is used in producing total lines. That is, even though some new value of STORE-NUMBER-IN caused the break and is already assigned to the input area, Report Writer has saved and uses the correct, previous value.

The description of the line of asterisks, line 01010, shows the use of the figurative constant **ALL.** Whenever the word ALL is used, it must be followed by a nonnumeric literal or a figurative constant other than ALL. When a figurative constant follows the word ALL, the word ALL is redundant and is used for readability only.

The Final Total Line

The FINAL total report group is described in the CONTROL FOOTING FINAL entry beginning on line 01030. It consists of one line showing the SUM of all the STORE-TOTAL values and one line of asterisks. The grand total field itself needs no name, for it is not referred to anywhere.

The Procedure Division

The single GENERATE statement in MAIN-PROCESS, line 01340, creates nearly the entire report. When the first GENERATE is issued, Report Writer prints the

FIGURE 9.13 *continued*

```
S COBOL II RELEASE 3.1 09/19/89                    P09003   DATE JUN 18,1991 T
----+-*A-1-B--+----2----+----3----+----4----+----5----+----6----+----7-|--+

01030  01  TYPE CONTROL FOOTING FINAL.
01040      05  LINE PLUS 2.
01050          10  COLUMN 33    PIC X(11)      VALUE "GRAND TOTAL".
01060          10  COLUMN 49    PIC $ZZ,ZZZ,ZZZ.99
01070                           SUM STORE-TOTAL.
01080          10  COLUMN 64    PIC XXX        VALUE "***".
01090      05  LINE PLUS 2
01100          COLUMN 25        PIC X(38)      VALUE ALL "*".
01110
01120 *****************************************************************
01130
01140  PROCEDURE DIVISION.
01150  CONTROL-PARAGRAPH.
01160      PERFORM INITIALIZATION
01170      PERFORM MAIN-PROCESS UNTIL THERE-IS-NO-MORE-INPUT
01180      PERFORM TERMINATION
01190      STOP RUN
01200      .
01210
01220  INITIALIZATION.
01230      OPEN INPUT  SALES-FILE-IN
01240           OUTPUT SALES-REPORT-FILE-OUT
01250      ACCEPT TODAYS-DATE FROM DATE
01260      INITIATE SALES-REPORT-OUT
01270      PERFORM READ-A-RECORD
01280      IF THERE-IS-NO-MORE-INPUT
01290          GENERATE NO-INPUT-DATA
01300      END-IF
01310      .
01320
01330  MAIN-PROCESS.
01340      GENERATE DETAIL-LINE
01350      PERFORM READ-A-RECORD
01360      .
01370
01380  TERMINATION.
01390      TERMINATE SALES-REPORT-OUT
01400      CLOSE SALES-FILE-IN
01410            SALES-REPORT-FILE-OUT
01420      .
01430
01440  READ-A-RECORD.
01450      READ SALES-FILE-IN
01460          AT END
01470              SET THERE-IS-NO-MORE-INPUT TO TRUE
01480      .
```

page and column headings and then the first DETAIL line. After that, for every GENERATE statement that is issued, Report Writer checks for control breaks and page overflow, and takes the action indicated in the Report Section. Execution of the TERMINATE statement produces the last set of total lines on the report.

It is illegal to try to issue a GENERATE statement for a PAGE HEADING group or a CONTROL FOOTING group, or for any group other than TYPE DETAIL. There is no need to tell Report Writer when to print page headings or total lines, for all the necessary logic is built in and tested.

EXERCISE 3

Write a program to read and process data in the following format:

Positions	Field
1–7	Customer Number
8–9	spaces
10–15	Part Number
16–22	spaces
23–25	Quantity
26–31	Unit Price (in dollars and cents)
26–29	Unit Price dollars
30–31	Unit Price cents
32–35	Handling Charge (in dollars and cents)
32–33	Handling Charge dollars
34–35	Handling Charge cents
35–80	spaces

Assume that there are several input records for each customer, each record containing a different part number. For each record, print a line showing the Customer Number, Part Number, Quantity, Unit Price, Handling Charge, and merchandise amount (compute the merchandise amount by multiplying the Unit Price by the Quantity). For each customer, print a total line showing the total Handling Charge and the total merchandise amount. Design the output on a print chart before you begin coding.

EXERCISE 4

Using the input of Program P09-03, write a program that will print a line for each record showing the Customer Number, the Sale Amount, a tax amount on the sale (at $8\frac{1}{4}$%), and the total of the sale amount and the tax. On each total line for salesperson, store, and grand total, show the total of all the appropriate sale amounts, tax amounts, and the totals of the sale amounts and the tax amounts. Group indicate the store numbers and salesperson numbers.

Declaratives

Sometimes it happens that Report Writer does not contain some feature needed to produce exactly the report that is wanted. In that case the programmer may use a **declarative section** to insert the needed coding into the program. Declaratives may be used for other purposes as well, and we will discuss them in Chapter 22.

Using a Declarative Section to Suppress Printing

Sometimes a programmer may want to prevent Report Writer from printing certain lines that otherwise would be printed in the course of Report Writer's normal processing. For example, we might want the final total line in Program P09-03 to print on a separate page of the report, with no detail lines present. In that case we would not want the PAGE HEADING group, which contains column headings, to appear on the page with the final total, for the column headings refer to fields that do not appear in the final total line. In the normal course of processing, Report Writer prints the PAGE HEADING group at the top of every page, whether it is wanted or not. Declarative sections can be used to prevent the printing of unwanted lines. Program P09-04, in Figure 9.14, shows how.

In the Report Section we have now given a name to the PAGE HEADING group, at line 00480. Any group that is referred to in a declarative section must be given a name. We have also specified LINE 9 **NEXT PAGE** for the final total,

FIGURE *9.14* **Program P09-04**

```
S COBOL II RELEASE 3.1 09/19/89                  P09004   DATE JUN 18,1991 T
----+-*A-1-B--+----2----+----3----+----4----+----5----+----6----+----7-|--+

00010  IDENTIFICATION DIVISION.
00020  PROGRAM-ID.  P09-04.
00030 *AUTHOR.  WENDEL KELLER.
00040 *
00050 *      THIS PROGRAM PRINTS A REPORT TITLE, COLUMN HEADINGS,
00060 *      DETAIL LINES, AND THREE LEVELS OF TOTALS.
00070
00080 *****************************************************************
00090
00100  ENVIRONMENT DIVISION.
00110  INPUT-OUTPUT SECTION.
00120  FILE-CONTROL.
00130      SELECT SALES-FILE-IN              ASSIGN TO INFILE.
00140      SELECT SALES-REPORT-FILE-OUT      ASSIGN TO PRINTER.
00150
00160 *****************************************************************
00170
00180  DATA DIVISION.
00190  FILE SECTION.
00200  FD  SALES-FILE-IN
00210      RECORD CONTAINS 80 CHARACTERS.
00220
00230  01  SALES-RECORD-IN.
00240      05  STORE-NUMBER-IN          PIC XXX.
00250      05  SALESPERSON-NUMBER-IN    PIC XXX.
00260      05  CUSTOMER-NUMBER-IN       PIC X(6).
00270      05  SALE-AMOUNT-IN           PIC 9(4)V99.
00280
00290  FD  SALES-REPORT-FILE-OUT
00300      REPORT IS SALES-REPORT-OUT.
00310
00320  WORKING-STORAGE SECTION.
00330  01  MORE-INPUT                   PIC X            VALUE "Y".
00340      88 THERE-IS-NO-MORE-INPUT    VALUE "N".
00350  01  TODAYS-DATE.
00360      05  TODAYS-YEAR              PIC 99.
00370      05  TODAYS-MONTH-AND-DAY     PIC 9(4).
00380
```

FIGURE 9.14 *continued*

```
REPORT SECTION.
RD  SALES-REPORT-OUT
    CONTROLS FINAL, STORE-NUMBER-IN, SALESPERSON-NUMBER-IN
    PAGE 50 LINES, FIRST DETAIL 9, LAST DETAIL 39, FOOTING 48.

01  TYPE REPORT HEADING
    LINE 2.
    05  COLUMN 36        PIC X(12)      VALUE "SALES REPORT".

01  COLUMN-HEADINGS
    TYPE PAGE HEADING.
    05  LINE 3.
        10  COLUMN 20    PIC X(4)       VALUE "DATE".
        10  COLUMN 25    PIC Z9/99/
                         SOURCE TODAYS-MONTH-AND-DAY.
        10  COLUMN 31    PIC 99         SOURCE TODAYS-YEAR.
        10  COLUMN 62    PIC X(4)       VALUE "PAGE".
        10  COLUMN 67    PIC Z9         SOURCE PAGE-COUNTER.
    05  LINE 6.
        10  COLUMN 25    PIC X(5)       VALUE "STORE".
        10  COLUMN 34    PIC X(6)       VALUE "SALES-".
        10  COLUMN 44    PIC X(8)       VALUE "CUSTOMER".
        10  COLUMN 57    PIC X(4)       VALUE "SALE".
    05  LINE 7.
        10  COLUMN 26    PIC XXX        VALUE "NO.".
        10  COLUMN 34    PIC X(6)       VALUE "PERSON".
        10  COLUMN 45    PIC X(6)       VALUE "NUMBER".
        10  COLUMN 56    PIC X(6)       VALUE "AMOUNT".

01  DETAIL-LINE
    TYPE DETAIL
    LINE PLUS 1.
    05  COLUMN 26        PIC XXX        GROUP INDICATE
                         SOURCE STORE-NUMBER-IN.
    05  COLUMN 35        PIC XXX        GROUP INDICATE
                         SOURCE SALESPERSON-NUMBER-IN.
    05  COLUMN 45        PIC X(6)       SOURCE CUSTOMER-NUMBER-IN.
    05  COLUMN 54        PIC ZZ,ZZZ.99 SOURCE SALE-AMOUNT-IN.

01  NO-INPUT-DATA
    TYPE DETAIL
    LINE 9.
    05  COLUMN 36        PIC X(13)      VALUE "NO INPUT DATA".

01  TYPE CONTROL FOOTING SALESPERSON-NUMBER-IN
    LINE PLUS 2
    NEXT GROUP PLUS 1.
    05  SALESPERSON-TOTAL
        COLUMN 53        PIC ZZZ,ZZZ.99
                         SUM SALE-AMOUNT-IN.
    05  COLUMN 64        PIC X          VALUE "*".

01  TYPE CONTROL FOOTING STORE-NUMBER-IN
    NEXT GROUP PLUS 1.
    05  LINE PLUS 2.
        10  COLUMN 25    PIC X(19)
                         VALUE "TOTAL FOR STORE NO.".
        10  COLUMN 45    PIC XXX        SOURCE STORE-NUMBER-IN.
        10  STORE-TOTAL
            COLUMN 50    PIC $Z,ZZZ,ZZZ.99
                         SUM SALESPERSON-TOTAL.
        10  COLUMN 64    PIC XX         VALUE "**".
    05  LINE PLUS 1
        COLUMN 25        PIC X(38)      VALUE ALL "*".

```

continued

at line 01050. This clause causes Report Writer to skip to line 9 on a new page before printing this report group. It also would be legal to use the clause NEXT GROUP NEXT PAGE if the context of a problem were to require it.

In the Procedure Division, line 01220, we see that to use a declarative section you must have the reserved word **DECLARATIVES,** followed by a period, right after the division header and starting in area A. That must be followed by a section header. This is the first time we have seen a section in the Procedure Division. We have been using sections in the Environment Division and Data Division all along. In those two divisions the names of sections are always reserved words, such as INPUT-OUTPUT SECTION or REPORT SECTION. But when you use a section in the Procedure Division, its name must be made up by the programmer. Here the made-up section name is SUPPRESS-COLUMN-HEADINGS. The section header is shown in line 01250. The rules for making up section names are the same as for making up paragraph names.

The section header must be followed by a **USE** sentence. When a declarative section is being used in connection with Report Writer, the USE sentence must consist of the reserved words USE **BEFORE REPORTING,** followed by the name of the report group related to this declarative section, followed by a period. In this case we wish to suppress the printing of the report group called COLUMN-HEADINGS, so we have the USE sentence shown in line 01260.

Following the USE sentence you may have one or more paragraphs containing the processing you want for the report group. Each paragraph must have its own made-up paragraph name. In this case the processing is very simple and can fit into one paragraph. When more than one paragraph is needed in a declarative section, the following rule must be followed: A PERFORM statement in a declarative section may refer only to a paragraph that is among the DECLARATIVES. The PERFORMed paragraph need not be in the same section as the PERFORM statement, however.

Here we want only to determine whether we should suppress the printing of the COLUMN-HEADINGS group or let Report Writer print it. If THERE-IS-NO-MORE-INPUT we want to suppress the printing of COLUMN-HEADINGS, for we know we are at end-of-file and doing the final total. Otherwise, we should do nothing and Report Writer will print the column headings as part of its normal processing. The **SUPPRESS** verb is used to suppress printing. Each time a SUPPRESS command is given, it prevents the printing of a report group for that one time only. You can see how the IF statement at line 01280 controls the printing of COLUMN-HEADINGS.

If more than one declarative section is to appear in a program, the additional sections follow immediately after the first. Each declarative section must have a section header, a USE sentence, and zero, one, or more paragraphs. The last declarative section in a program must be followed by the reserved words **END** DECLARATIVES followed by a period, as shown in line 01320. The end of a USE BEFORE REPORTING section is indicated by the beginning of another section or the words END DECLARATIVES.

The regular Procedure Division statements then follow the declarative sections, in a section of their own. Whenever declarative sections are used, the remainder of the Procedure Division must be organized into sections. Here the section header for the remainder of the Procedure Division is shown in line 01340. The name of the section at line 01340 could have been any made-up name. The SECTION did not have to be called NONDECLARATIVE.

FIGURE 9.14 *continued*

```
S COBOL II RELEASE 3.1 09/19/89                 P09004   DATE JUN 18,1991 T
----+-*A-1-B--+----2----+----3----+----4----+----5----+----6----+----7-|--+

 01  TYPE CONTROL FOOTING FINAL.
     05  LINE 9 NEXT PAGE.
         10  COLUMN 20   PIC X(4)       VALUE "DATE".
         10  COLUMN 25   PIC Z9/99/
                         SOURCE TODAYS-MONTH-AND-DAY.
         10  COLUMN 31   PIC 99         SOURCE TODAYS-YEAR.
         10  COLUMN 62   PIC X(4)       VALUE "PAGE".
         10  COLUMN 67   PIC Z9         SOURCE PAGE-COUNTER.
     05  LINE PLUS 3.
         10  COLUMN 33   PIC X(11)      VALUE "GRAND TOTAL".
         10  COLUMN 49   PIC $ZZ,ZZZ,ZZZ.99
                         SUM STORE-TOTAL.
         10  COLUMN 64   PIC XXX        VALUE "***".
     05  LINE PLUS 2
         COLUMN 25       PIC X(38)      VALUE ALL "*".

*****************************************************************

 PROCEDURE DIVISION.

 DECLARATIVES.
 SUPPRESS-COLUMN-HEADINGS SECTION.
      USE BEFORE REPORTING COLUMN-HEADINGS.
 COLUMN-HEADINGS-PARAGRAPH.
      IF THERE-IS-NO-MORE-INPUT
          SUPPRESS PRINTING
      END-IF
      .
 END DECLARATIVES.

 NONDECLARATIVE SECTION.
 CONTROL-PARAGRAPH.
     PERFORM INITIALIZATION
     PERFORM MAIN-PROCESS UNTIL THERE-IS-NO-MORE-INPUT
     PERFORM TERMINATION
     STOP RUN
     .

 INITIALIZATION.
     OPEN INPUT  SALES-FILE-IN
          OUTPUT SALES-REPORT-FILE-OUT
     ACCEPT TODAYS-DATE FROM DATE
     INITIATE SALES-REPORT-OUT
     PERFORM READ-A-RECORD
     IF THERE-IS-NO-MORE-INPUT
         GENERATE NO-INPUT-DATA
     END-IF
     .

 MAIN-PROCESS.
     GENERATE DETAIL-LINE
     PERFORM READ-A-RECORD
     .

 TERMINATION.
     TERMINATE SALES-REPORT-OUT
     CLOSE SALES-FILE-IN
           SALES-REPORT-FILE-OUT
     .

 READ-A-RECORD.
     READ SALES-FILE-IN
         AT END
             SET THERE-IS-NO-MORE-INPUT TO TRUE
     .
```

When a program containing DECLARATIVES is executed, the computer begins execution at the beginning of the first paragraph after the END DECLARATIVES statement. In this program execution begins at the beginning of CONTROL-PARAGRAPH. The procedures written in the declarative sections are executed only at the specified times, in this case just BEFORE REPORTING the report group COLUMN-HEADINGS.

Program P09-04 was run with the same input data as Program P09-03 and produced the results shown in Figure 9.15.

FIGURE *9.15* **Output from Program P09-04**

```
                 SALES REPORT
DATE   6/18/91                                        PAGE   1

        STORE     SALES-      CUSTOMER      SALE
         NO.      PERSON       NUMBER      AMOUNT

         010       101         003001     1,234.56
                               007002         2.24
                               039004     8,439.20
                               046005     8,448.48
                               053006        12.34
                               060006     9,494.93
                               067007     4,000.03

                                         31,631.78 *

         010       102         074212     5,454.99
                               081012          .33
                               088013     5,849.58
                               095015       393.90

                                         11,698.80 *

         010       103         003234       303.03

                                            303.03 *

        TOTAL FOR STORE NO. 010  $   43,633.61 **
        *************************************

         020       011         007567     9,999.99
                               011454       456.00
                               023345     8,333.33

                                         18,789.32 *

         020       222         027345     4,343.43
```

FIGURE 9.15 *continued*

```
DATE   6/18/91                                    PAGE   2

     STORE     SALES-     CUSTOMER     SALE
      NO.      PERSON      NUMBER      AMOUNT

      020       222        031567     9,903.30
                           035001        34.21

                                     14,280.94 *

      020       266        039903     4,539.87
                           043854     5,858.30

                                     10,398.17 *

     TOTAL FOR STORE NO. 020  $      43,468.43 **
     ***************************************

      030       193        059932     5,858.54
                           063419     3,949.49

                                      9,808.03 *

     TOTAL FOR STORE NO. 030  $       9,808.03 **
     ***************************************

      040       045        067333          .00
                           071323     5,959.50

                                      5,959.50 *

      040       403        048399     3,921.47
                           054392          .00

                                      3,921.47 *

DATE   6/18/91                                    PAGE   3

     STORE     SALES-     CUSTOMER     SALE
      NO.      PERSON      NUMBER      AMOUNT

      040       412        060111     9,999.99

                                      9,999.99 *

     TOTAL FOR STORE NO. 040  $      19,880.96 **
     ***************************************

      046       012        013538          .00
                           017521       690.78
                           021504     1,381.56
                           025487     2,072.34
                           029470     2,763.12

                                      6,907.80 *

      046       028        033453     3,453.90
                           037436     4,144.68
                           041419     4,835.46

                                     12,434.04 *

     TOTAL FOR STORE NO. 046  $      19,341.84 **
     ***************************************
```

continued

FIGURE 9.15 *continued*

```
DATE  6/18/91                                    PAGE  4

              GRAND TOTAL      $    136,132.87 ***

     ***************************************
```

The SUPPRESS Statement

The format of the SUPPRESS statement is

```
SUPPRESS PRINTING
```

The SUPPRESS statement may appear only in a USE BEFORE REPORTING section. Its execution causes the associated report group not to be printed, and any LINE or NEXT GROUP clauses that appear in the description of the report group to be ignored.

Report Writer Entries in the Data Division

The format of the RD entry is

```
RD report-name-1
    [CODE literal-1]
    [{CONTROL IS  } {{data-name-1} . . .        }]
    [{CONTROLS ARE} {FINAL [data-name-1] . . .  }]
    [PAGE [LIMIT IS  ] integer-1 [LINE ] [HEADING integer-2]
          [LIMITS ARE]           [LINES]
       [FIRST DETAIL integer-3 [LAST DETAIL integer-4]
       [FOOTING integer-5] ] .
```

The clauses that follow the report name are optional, and may appear in any order. The CODE clause is used to distinguish reports when more than one report is written on a file. We do not use the CODE clause in this book.

Integer-2 is the first line on the page in which anything may print. If the HEADING option is omitted, integer-2 is assumed to be 1. If all report groups in the report use absolute line spacing, all the options in the PAGE clause may be omitted.

If any relative line spacing is used in a report, then it is illegal to provide conflicting or nonsensical information in the PAGE clause. For example, you cannot have a HEADING option here that conflicts with any LINE clauses that may appear in the definitions of any TYPE REPORT HEADING or TYPE PAGE HEADING report group. You cannot specify a line number for the FIRST DETAIL line that conflicts with the actual number of lines occupied by the REPORT HEADING or the PAGE HEADING. That is, if a REPORT HEADING and/or PAGE

HEADING is to appear on the same page with DETAIL lines, then the headings must not run over into the line reserved for the FIRST DETAIL. If a REPORT HEADING or a REPORT FOOTING is to appear on a page by itself, then it may appear anywhere on the page.

The overall depth of the page, given by integer-1, must not be less than any of the other integers in the clause. Integer-5 must not be less than integer-4. Integer-4 must not be less than integer-3. And integer-3 must not be less than integer-2. All integers in the clause must be positive.

As mentioned earlier in this chapter, the line number given in the FOOTING option specifies the last line on which CONTROL FOOTING lines may print. Any additional space provided by the overall depth of the page can be used for PAGE FOOTING and REPORT FOOTING groups.

The TYPE Clause

The TYPE clause is the only required clause in a level-01 entry in the Report Section. The format of the TYPE clause is

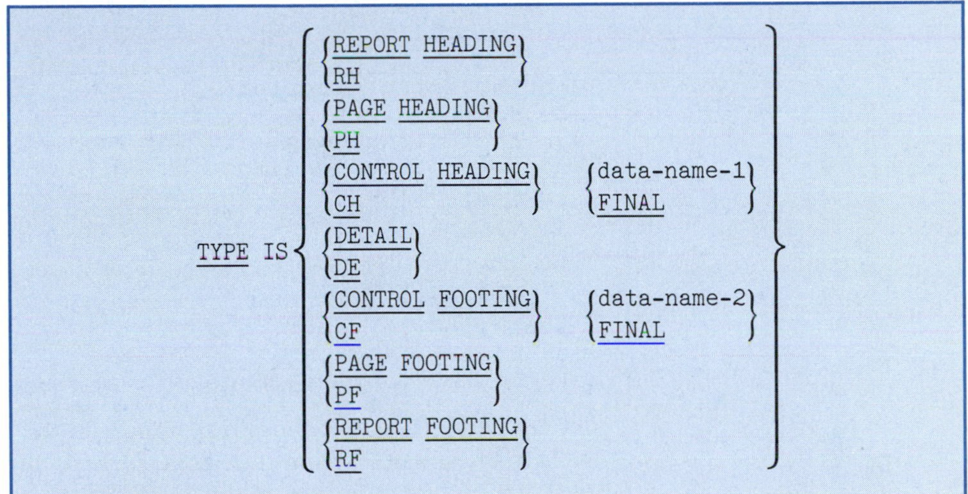

RH is the abbreviation for REPORT HEADING; PH is the abbreviation for PAGE HEADING; DE is the abbreviation for DETAIL; CF is the abbreviation for CONTROL FOOTING; PF is the abbreviation for PAGE FOOTING; and RF is the abbreviation for REPORT FOOTING. Data-name-1 and data-name-2 must be names that are given in the CONTROL clause of the RD entry; that is, they must be fields that control breaks are taken on. We refrained from using abbreviations in the sample programs because their meanings are not at all obvious, as are PIC, COMP, and SYNC.

A **CONTROL HEADING** report group is one or more lines to be printed before the detail lines of a control group. It usually serves as a title for the control group. For example, consider the following entry:

```
RD SAMPLE-REPORT
    CONTROLS FINAL, YEAR, MONTH
    PAGE 50 LINES.
```

Then if there were entries of

```
01   TYPE CONTROL HEADING FINAL
01   TYPE CONTROL HEADING  YEAR
01   TYPE CONTROL HEADING   MONTH
01   TYPE CONTROL FOOTING   MONTH
01   TYPE CONTROL FOOTING  YEAR
01   TYPE CONTROL FOOTING FINAL
```

the report groups would print as follows:

```
final control heading (once on the report)
  year control heading
    month control heading
      first detail line on the report
      detail lines
           .
           .
           .
    month control footing
    month control heading (for the next month)
      detail lines
           .
           .
           .
    month control footing
  year control footing
  year control heading (for the next year)
    month control heading
      detail lines
           .
           .
           .
      last detail line on the report
    month control footing
  year control footing
final control footing (once on the report)
```

CONTROL HEADING lines may appear in the same areas of a report page as DETAIL lines, that is, from the FIRST DETAIL line number through the LAST DETAIL line number as given in the PAGE clause.

The SUM Clause

The format of the SUM clause is

```
{SUM {identifier-1} . . . [UPON {data-name-1} . . . ]} . . .

     [RESET ON {data-name-2}]
               {FINAL      }
```

The last ellipsis in the format shows that there may be as many SUM clauses as desired in a single entry. If there is more than one SUM clause in an entry, all the identifiers named in all the SUM clauses are added into the sum counter.

The **UPON** phrase, when used, causes the SUM clause to be executed only when a GENERATE statement is issued for one of the DETAIL report groups given as data-name-1 and data-name-2. The data name(s) given in the UPON phrase must be the names of DETAIL report groups in the same report as the SUM clause.

The **RESET ON** phrase gives the programmer the ability to delay resetting sum counters until after their normal time. Normally a sum counter is reset to zero automatically by Report Writer when a control break occurs and after the contents of the counter are printed. With the RESET phrase, the programmer can direct Report Writer not to reset the counter until some specified higher-level break occurs. This provides for printing ever-growing lower-level subtotals. The RESET ON phrase really should be called the DON'T RESET UNTIL phrase. Using RESET ON FINAL delays resetting the counter for the entire report, and so the report output shows only ever-growing subtotals for that SUM field.

Summary

Report Writer is a COBOL feature that permits the programmer to describe characteristics of a report rather than write the step-by-step coding needed to produce the report. Report Writer automatically provides the coding needed to format output lines, sum into accumulators, print report headings, test for page overflow, skip to a new page, print page headings, test for control breaks, print total lines, reset accumulators, and print page footings and report footings. At the same time, the programmer has complete command over all the logical capabilities of COBOL.

Before giving a GENERATE statement to print a DETAIL line, the program may carry out any desired processing on the input data. Before any other TYPEs of report groups are printed, any processing may be carried out in a declarative section with a USE BEFORE REPORTING sentence.

The characteristics of all the reports produced by a program may be described in the Report Section. There, each report has an RD entry with a report name. Within the RD entry, report groups are described. Report groups may be of TYPE REPORT HEADING, PAGE HEADING, CONTROL HEADING, DETAIL, CONTROL FOOTING, PAGE FOOTING, and REPORT FOOTING.

The LINE clause directs Report Writer to space or skip before printing a single line or a report group. The NEXT GROUP clause directs Report Writer to space or skip after printing a report group. The LINE clause can be written as an absolute LINE NUMBER clause or a relative LINE NUMBER clause. The NEXT GROUP clause can be written as an absolute NEXT GROUP clause or a relative NEXT GROUP clause. The NEXT PAGE option may be used in a LINE clause or a NEXT GROUP clause. When a NEXT GROUP clause appears in a CONTROL FOOTING report group, the clause is executed only when a control break occurs at the exact level of the CONTROL FOOTING. The NEXT GROUP clause is always effective when it appears in report groups other than TYPE CONTROL FOOTING.

Within each report group definition, fields to be printed may be defined. A printable item is recognized by the appearance of a COLUMN clause, a PICTURE clause, and one of the clauses SOURCE, SUM, or VALUE. It also must have a LINE clause properly related to it in order to tell Report Writer where it is to be printed.

The CONTROL clause in the RD entry indicates the fields on which control breaks are to be taken. The PAGE clause in the RD entry indicates the areas of the report output page where different TYPEs of report groups may print.

The INITIATE, GENERATE, and TERMINATE statements are used in the Procedure Division to control the printing of the report. The INITIATE statement must be given for each report after the report output file is OPENed and before any GENERATE statements are given. The GENERATE statement directs Report Writer to produce a DETAIL report group and at the same time to test whether any other report groups should be printed. For each DETAIL group printed, Report Writer tests for page overflow and control breaks. If any conditions are found that require printing lines in addition to the DETAIL line, Report Writer automatically prints them with no further effort on the part of the programmer. The programmer may suppress the printing of any report group by using a SUPPRESS statement.

The TERMINATE statement is given after the last GENERATE statement and before the report output file is CLOSEd. The TERMINATE statement signals the production of the last CONTROL FOOTING groups, the last PAGE FOOTING group, and any REPORT FOOTING group.

Fill-In Exercises

1. In the FD entry for a report file, the ______ clause must be used to name the report.
2. In the Report Section each report name must have a(n) ______ entry.
3. The TYPEs of report groups that Report Writer can process are ______, ______, ______, ______, ______, ______, and ______.
4. The beginning print position of each printable item is given by a(n) ______ clause.
5. Vertical spacing of the paper is controlled by the ______ and ______ clauses.
6. The words USE ______ ______ indicate that a declarative section is to be used with Report Writer.
7. The statement that is used to begin processing a report is the ______ statement.
8. The statement that causes a DETAIL report group to print is the ________ statement.
9. The areas on the page where different TYPEs of report groups may print are described by the ______ clause.
10. The control fields of a report are listed in the ______ clause in the RD entry.
11. The control fields of a report are listed in order from ______ to ______.
12. The clause LINE ______ ______ may be used to obtain single spacing.
13. The ______ clause indicates to Report Writer where data are to be obtained to fill an output field.
14. The ______ statement is used to end the processing of a report.
15. The ______ clause is used to delay zeroing a sum counter until a specified control break has been executed.

Review Exercises

1. Write a program to read input records in the following format:

Positions	Field
1–8	Part Number
9–28	Part Description
29–31	Quantity on hand
32–80	spaces

Have your program print the contents of each record on one line in the format shown in Figure 9.RE1.

FIGURE *9.RE1* Output format for Review Exercise 1

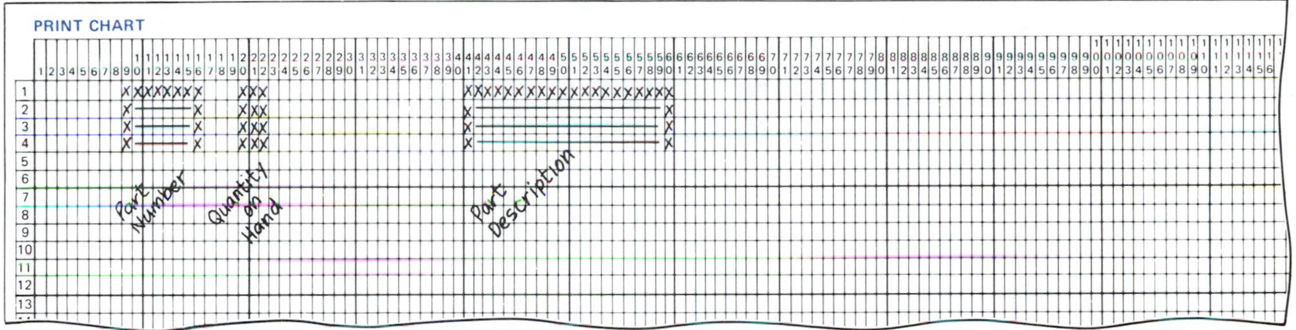

2. Write a program to read input records in the following format:

Positions	Field
1–5	Employee Number
6	Code
7–9	Hours Worked (to one decimal place)
10–80	spaces

Each record contains an Employee Number, a Code indicating whether the employee is eligible for overtime pay or is exempt from overtime pay, and the Hours Worked. The Code field contains an E if the employee is exempt from overtime pay and an N if the employee is eligible for overtime pay (nonexempt).

Have your program print one line for each employee in the format shown in Figure 9.RE2. If an employee worked more than 40 hours and is eligible for overtime pay, print the words OVERTIME PAY as shown in the print chart. Otherwise print only the Employee Number and the Hours Worked.

FIGURE 9.RE2 Output format for Review Exercise 2

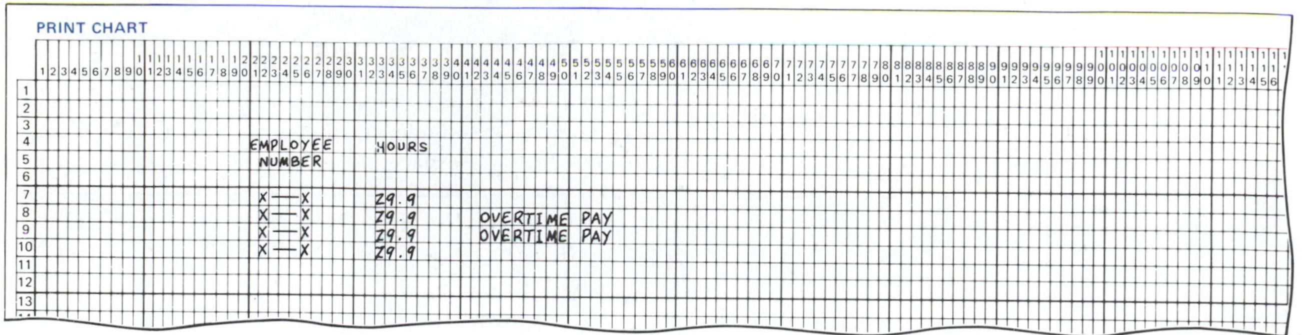

3. Write a program to read input records in the following format:

Positions	Field
1–9	Social Security Number
10–12	Monday Hours (to one decimal place)
13–15	Tuesday Hours (to one decimal place)
16–18	Wednesday Hours (to one decimal place)
19–21	Thursday Hours (to one decimal place)
22–24	Friday Hours (to one decimal place)
25–80	spaces

Have your program produce a report in the format shown in Figure 9.RE3. On the report list only those employees who worked more than 37.5 hours during the week. Compute each employee's number of overtime hours (hours worked during the week minus 37.5).

FIGURE 9.RE3 Output format for Review Exercise 3

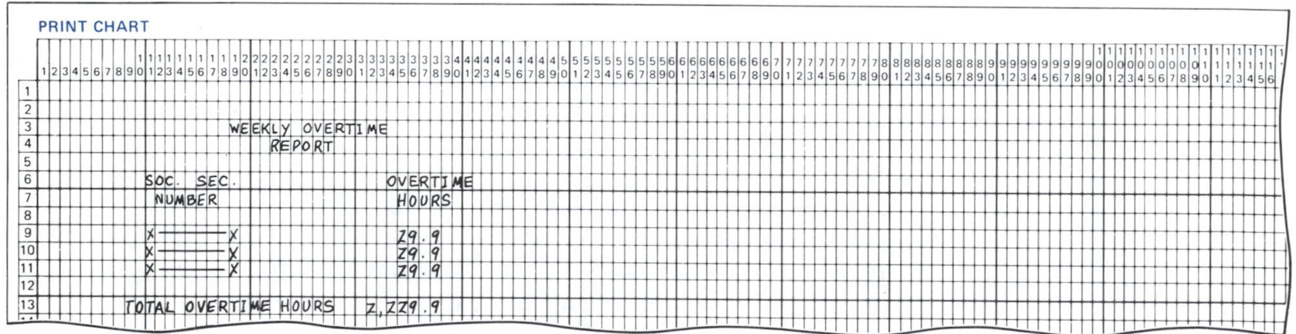

4. Write a program to read input records in the following format:

Positions	Field
1–5	Department Number
6–11	Employee Number
12–19	Annual Salary (to two decimal places)
20–44	Employee Name
45–80	spaces

Have your program produce a report in the format shown in Figure 9.RE4. Use a DECLARATIVES section to compute the averages in the CONTROL FOOTING lines.

FIGURE 9.RE4 Output format for Review Exercise 4

PRINT CHART

```
                                        SALARY SUMMARY REPORT
          DATE Z9/99/99                                                        PAGE Z9

          DEPARTMENT   EMPLOYEE           EMPLOYEE NAME                  ANNUAL
            NUMBER      NUMBER                                           SALARY

            XXXXX       XXXXXX      X-------------------------X      ZZZ,ZZZ.99
                        XXXXXX      X-------------------------X      ZZZ,ZZZ.99
                        XXXXXX      X-------------------------X      ZZZ,ZZZ.99


                      NUMBER OF EMPLOYEES IN DEPARTMENT NUMBER XXXXX  -  ZZ9
                           AVERAGE SALARY IN DEPARTMENT NUMBER XXXXX  -  ZZZ,ZZZ.99


            XXXXX       XXXXXX      X-------------------------X      ZZZ,ZZZ.99
                        XXXXXX      X-------------------------X      ZZZ,ZZZ.99
                        XXXXXX      X-------------------------X      ZZZ,ZZZ.99
                        XXXXXX      X-------------------------X      ZZZ,ZZZ.99


                      NUMBER OF EMPLOYEES IN DEPARTMENT NUMBER XXXXX  -  ZZ9
                           AVERAGE SALARY IN DEPARTMENT NUMBER XXXXX  -  ZZZ,ZZZ.99
```

5. Modify your solution to Review Exercise 4 so that at the end of the report your program prints a final total of the number of employees and the average salary of all the employees. Design suitable final lines.

6. Write a program to read input records in the following format:

Positions	Field
1–7	Customer Number
8–9	spaces
10–15	Part Number
16–22	spaces
23–25	Quantity
26–31	Unit Price (to two decimal places)
32–80	spaces

The program is to check that all Quantity and all Unit Price fields contain only numbers. If a field is found not to contain only numbers, a suitable error line is to be printed. For each valid record have your program print the Customer Number, Part Number, Quantity, Unit Price, and a merchandise amount (the Quantity times the Unit Price), except if the merchandise amount is greater than 999,999.99. If the merchandise amount is greater than 999,999.99, print only the Customer Number, Part Number, Quantity, Unit Price, and a message MERCHANDISE AMOUNT SUSPICIOUSLY LARGE.

Project

Rewrite your solution to the Project in Chapter 8, page 250, using Report Writer.

CHAPTER

One-Dimensional Tables

HERE ARE THE KEY POINTS YOU SHOULD LEARN FROM THIS CHAPTER

1. The need for tables in computer programs
2. How to set up one-dimensional tables in COBOL
3. How to program for one-dimensional tables
4. How to load a table from an external file

KEY WORDS TO RECOGNIZE AND LEARN

table
OCCURS
subscript
index
SEARCH
VARYING
one-dimensional
array
direct-reference table
search table
element
argument
function
INDEXED BY
index name
direct indexing
relative indexing
SEARCH ALL
ASCENDING KEY
DESCENDING KEY
binary search

It often happens that computer programs must operate on related fields of data that all have the same description. In many such cases the data can be arranged in a COBOL program in the form of a **table** and processed conveniently using the table-handling features of COBOL. The first program in this chapter shows how some of the table-handling features operate, and later programs show additional features. Also, later in the chapter you will see the exact definition of a table.

A Program Using Subscripting

Program P10-01 reads and processes input data in the following format:

Positions	Field
1–7	Salesperson Number
8–13	Sale Amount 1 (in dollars and cents)
14–19	Sale Amount 2 (in dollars and cents)
20–25	Sale Amount 3 (in dollars and cents)
26–31	Sale Amount 4 (in dollars and cents)
32–37	Sale Amount 5 (in dollars and cents)
38–43	Sale Amount 6 (in dollars and cents)
44–49	Sale Amount 7 (in dollars and cents)
50–55	Sale Amount 8 (in dollars and cents)
56–61	Sale Amount 9 (in dollars and cents)
62–67	Sale Amount 10 (in dollars and cents)
68–80	spaces

Each input record contains a salesperson number and 10 sale amounts. The program is to compute a commission on each sale according to the following schedule:

Sale Amount	Commission
0–100.00	5% of the sale amount
Over 100.00	5% of the first $100 of the sale amount plus 10% of the sale amount in excess of $100

The paragraph needed to test each sale amount and compute the commission obviously will be at least a little complicated. It would be a nuisance to have to write the paragraph 10 times in the program in order to compute each of the 10 commission amounts. Worse, even if we did get it correct in one place in the program, we might make a keying error and get it wrong somewhere else. So the program might compute the commission for sale 1 correctly but not for sale 2. Fortunately, we can use the table-handling features of COBOL to avoid having to write anything in the program 10 times.

The output format for Program P10-01 is shown in Figure 10.1. Program P10-01 is shown in Figure 10.2. The input record description, which begins at line 00250, does not name 10 different sale amount fields but instead uses an **OCCURS** clause. An OCCURS clause may be used whenever several fields have identical descriptions, as our 10 sale amount fields do. The OCCURS clause permits the programmer to describe the field once and tell COBOL how many such fields there are. Our OCCURS clause at line 00270 tells COBOL that there are 10 sale amount fields, one right after the other in the input record, and that each has PICTURE 9(4)V99. The OCCURS clause may appear before or after the PICTURE clause, so either of the following is legal:

```
05 SALE-AMOUNT-IN   PIC 9(4)V99   OCCURS 10 TIMES.
05 SALE-AMOUNT-IN   OCCURS 10 TIMES   PIC 9(4)V99.
```

FIGURE 10.1 Output format for Program P10-01

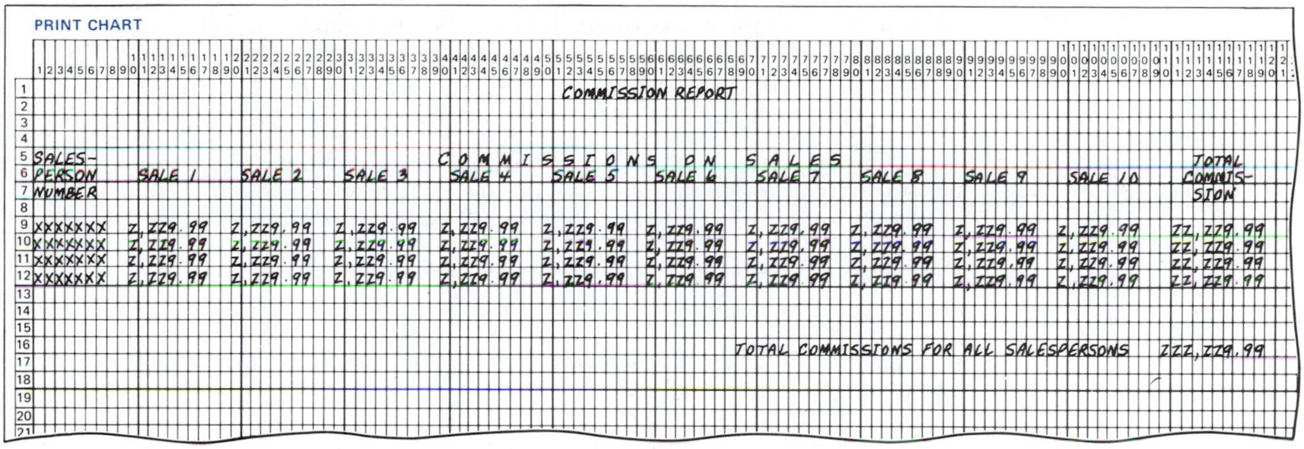

PRINT CHART

```
                                  COMMISSION REPORT



SALES-                           C O M M I S S I O N S   O N   S A L E S                       TOTAL
PERSON   SALE 1    SALE 2    SALE 3    SALE 4    SALE 5    SALE 6    SALE 7    SALE 8    SALE 9    SALE 10     COMMIS-
NUMBER                                                                                                        SION

XXXXXXX  Z,ZZ9.99  Z,ZZ9.99  Z,ZZ9.99  Z,ZZ9.99  Z,ZZ9.99  Z,ZZ9.99  Z,ZZ9.99  Z,ZZ9.99  Z,ZZ9.99  Z,ZZ9.99    ZZ,ZZ9.99
XXXXXXX  Z,ZZ9.99  Z,ZZ9.99  Z,ZZ9.99  Z,ZZ9.99  Z,ZZ9.99  Z,ZZ9.99  Z,ZZ9.99  Z,ZZ9.99  Z,ZZ9.99  Z,ZZ9.99    ZZ,ZZ9.99
XXXXXXX  Z,ZZ9.99  Z,ZZ9.99  Z,ZZ9.99  Z,ZZ9.99  Z,ZZ9.99  Z,ZZ9.99  Z,ZZ9.99  Z,ZZ9.99  Z,ZZ9.99  Z,ZZ9.99    ZZ,ZZ9.99
XXXXXXX  Z,ZZ9.99  Z,ZZ9.99  Z,ZZ9.99  Z,ZZ9.99  Z,ZZ9.99  Z,ZZ9.99  Z,ZZ9.99  Z,ZZ9.99  Z,ZZ9.99  Z,ZZ9.99    ZZ,ZZ9.99



                                              TOTAL COMMISSIONS FOR ALL SALESPERSONS   ZZZ,ZZ9.99
```

FIGURE 10.2 Program P10-01

```
S COBOL II RELEASE 3.1 09/19/89                  P10001   DATE JUN 21,1991 T
----+-*A-1-B--+----2----+----3----+----4----+----5----+----6----+----7-%--+

 IDENTIFICATION DIVISION.
 PROGRAM-ID.  P10-01.
*AUTHOR. DEBORAH ANN SENIOR.
*
*     THIS PROGRAM PRODUCES A SALESPERSON COMMISSION
*     REPORT SHOWING TEN COMMISSION AMOUNTS
*     AND THE TOTAL FOR EACH SALESPERSON.
*
*
*****************************************************************

 ENVIRONMENT DIVISION.
 INPUT-OUTPUT SECTION.
 FILE-CONTROL.
     SELECT SALES-FILE-IN                  ASSIGN TO INFILE.
     SELECT COMMISSION-REPORT-FILE-OUT     ASSIGN TO PRINTER.

*****************************************************************

 DATA DIVISION.
 FILE SECTION.
 FD  SALES-FILE-IN
     RECORD CONTAINS 80 CHARACTERS.

 01  SALES-RECORD-IN.
     05  SALESPERSON-NUMBER-IN    PIC X(7).
     05  SALE-AMOUNT-IN           PIC 9(4)V99     OCCURS 10 TIMES.

 FD  COMMISSION-REPORT-FILE-OUT.

 01  REPORT-LINE                  PIC X(119).

```

continued

All 10 SALE-AMOUNT-IN fields have, in a sense, the same name now. They are all called SALE-AMOUNT-IN, and COBOL must have some way of distinguishing one from the other. This is accomplished by means of a **subscript.** In COBOL a subscript is a positive or unsigned integer (or a field defined as an integer) that is written in parentheses following the data name being subscripted. The 10 SALE-AMOUNT-IN fields can be referred to in the Procedure Division as

```
SALE-AMOUNT-IN (1)   (pronounced "SALE-AMOUNT-IN sub one")
SALE-AMOUNT-IN (2)   (pronounced "SALE-AMOUNT-IN sub two")
SALE-AMOUNT-IN (3)   (pronounced "SALE-AMOUNT-IN sub three")
```

and so on. So the following would be a legal statement:

```
MOVE SALE-AMOUNT-IN (1) TO SALE-OUT
```

It would be read as "MOVE SALE-AMOUNT-IN sub one TO SALE-OUT." Here are other legal statements:

```
IF SALE-AMOUNT-IN (2) GREATER THAN 50.00
    PERFORM 50-DOLLAR-ROUTINE
END-IF
ADD SALE-AMOUNT-IN (3) TO SALE-ACCUMULATOR ROUNDED
```

Try reading the IF and ADD statements aloud before going on.

The subscript following the data name SALE-AMOUNT-IN in each statement tells COBOL which of the 10 SALE-AMOUNT-IN fields is being referred to in the statement.

Whenever a field is defined with an OCCURS clause, you must use a subscript (or an **index,** discussed later in this chapter) whenever you refer to that field (except with the **SEARCH** verb, also to be discussed later in this chapter). Also, whenever you want to use a subscript on a field, the field must be defined with an OCCURS clause. An OCCURS clause may not be used at the 01 level.

A subscript doesn't have to be just an integer; a subscript can be given in the form of a data name or a qualified data name. Any data name or qualified data name can be used as a subscript provided it is defined as an integer. So we could make up the following field to serve as a subscript:

```
05 SALE-SUBSCRIPT  PIC S99.
```

The field SALE-SUBSCRIPT looks like an ordinary field and it is. It could be used wherever a numeric variable would be legal. But, because it is defined as an integer, it could also be used as a subscript. So it would be legal to refer to the 10 fields called SALE-AMOUNT-IN this way:

```
SALE-AMOUNT-IN (SALE-SUBSCRIPT)
```

(pronounced "SALE-AMOUNT-IN subscripted by SALE-SUBSCRIPT").

The field SALE-SUBSCRIPT could be assigned any value 1 through 10, so that a statement such as

```
MOVE SALE-AMOUNT-IN (SALE-SUBSCRIPT) TO SALE-OUT
```

would execute in a way that depends on the value assigned to SALE-SUBSCRIPT at the time the statement executes. If SALE-SUBSCRIPT happened to have the integer 4 assigned to it, the MOVE statement would execute as though it were written:

```
MOVE SALE-AMOUNT-IN (4) TO SALE-OUT
```

If SALE-SUBSCRIPT has a 5 assigned when the MOVE executes, it will execute as:

```
MOVE SALE-AMOUNT-IN (5) TO SALE-OUT
```

It would be illegal for SALE-SUBSCRIPT to have a value larger than 10 when the MOVE statement executes, since the OCCURS clause in the definition of SALE-AMOUNT-IN says that there are only 10 such fields. You can see that, by using a data name as a subscript, it is possible to get a statement such as:

```
MOVE SALE-AMOUNT-IN (SALE-SUBSCRIPT) TO SALE-OUT
```

to refer to all 10 of the fields SALE-AMOUNT-IN merely by changing the value assigned to SALE-SUBSCRIPT.

You will see in Program P10-01 that the field we use to subscript SALE-AMOUNT-IN is not called SALE-SUBSCRIPT. The name of a subscript need not have any special form; for a field to be used as a subscript, it need only be defined as an integer. A subscript in a COBOL program may be used on any field in the program that is defined with an OCCURS clause.

EXERCISE 1

Which of the following would be valid as a subscript?

a. `05 DOG              PIC S999.`

b. `05 SUBSCRIPT-1      PIC 299V99.`

c. `05 SUBSCRIPT-2      PIC X(3).`

d. `05 I                PIC 99.`

EXERCISE 2

Given the following fields:

```
05 PURCHASES      PIC 9(4)V99    OCCURS 5 TIMES.
05 RETURNS        PIC 9(3)V99    OCCURS 4 TIMES.
05 SUBSC-1        PIC S9.
05 SUBSC-2        PIC S99.
```

a. Which of the following statements could be legal in a COBOL program?

1. `ADD PURCHASES (SUBSC-1)    TO ACCUMULATOR`

2. `ADD PURCHASES (SUBSC-2)    TO ACCUMULATOR`

3. `ADD SUBSC-1 (PURCHASES)    TO ACCUMULATOR`

4. `ADD RETURNS (SUBSC-1)      TO ACCUMULATOR`

5. `ADD 1 TO SUBSC-1`

b. What is the highest value that may legally be assigned to SUBSC-1 at the time statement 1 above executes?

c. What is the highest value that may legally be assigned to SUBSC-2 at the time statement 2 above executes?

FIGURE 10.2 *continued*

```
S COBOL II RELEASE 3.1 09/19/89                    P10001    DATE JUN 21,1991 T
----+-*A-1-B--+----2----+----3----+----4----+----5----+----6----+----7-%--+

WORKING-STORAGE SECTION.
01  MORE-INPUT                    PIC X            VALUE "Y".
    88 THERE-IS-NO-MORE-INPUT     VALUE "N".
01  PACKED-DECIMAL-CONSTANTS      PACKED-DECIMAL.
    05  COMMISSION-RATE-1         PIC V99          VALUE .05.
    05  COMMISSION-RATE-2         PIC V99          VALUE .10.
    05  BRACKET-MAXIMUM           PIC 999V99       VALUE 100.00.
01  NUMBER-OF-SALES               PIC S99          VALUE 10
                                  COMP             SYNC.
01  GRAND-TOTAL-COMMISSIONS-W     PIC S9(6)V99     PACKED-DECIMAL
                                                   VALUE 0.
01  COMMISSION-AMOUNT-W           PIC S9(4)V99     PACKED-DECIMAL.
01  COMMISSION-FOR-SALESPERSON    PIC S9(5)V99     PACKED-DECIMAL.
01  I.                            PIC S99          COMP SYNC.
01  LINE-SPACING  VALUE 1         PIC S9           COMP SYNC.
01  PAGE-HEADING-1.
    05            PIC X(51)       VALUE SPACES.
    05            PIC X(17)       VALUE "COMMISSION REPORT".
01  PAGE-HEADING-2.
    05            PIC X(39)       VALUE "SALES-".
    05            PIC X(73)
        VALUE "C O M M I S S I O N S   O N   S A L E S".
    05            PIC X(5)        VALUE "TOTAL".
01  PAGE-HEADING-3.
    05            PIC X(10)       VALUE "PERSON".
    05            PIC X(10)       VALUE "SALE 1".
    05            PIC X(10)       VALUE "SALE 2".
    05            PIC X(10)       VALUE "SALE 3".
    05            PIC X(10)       VALUE "SALE 4".
    05            PIC X(10)       VALUE "SALE 5".
    05            PIC X(10)       VALUE "SALE 6".
    05            PIC X(10)       VALUE "SALE 7".
    05            PIC X(10)       VALUE "SALE 8".
    05            PIC X(10)       VALUE "SALE 9".
    05            PIC X(11)       VALUE "SALE 10".
    05            PIC X(7)        VALUE "COMMIS-".
01  PAGE-HEADING-4.
    05            PIC X(112)      VALUE "NUMBER".
    05            PIC X(4)        VALUE "SION".
01  DETAIL-LINE.
    05  SALESPERSON-NUMBER-OUT    PIC X(9).
    05  COMMISSION-AMOUNT-OUT     PIC Z,ZZ9.99BB
                                  OCCURS 10 TIMES.
    05  COMMISSION-FOR-SALESPERSON-OUT
                                  PIC BZZ,ZZ9.99.
01  NO-INPUT-DATA.
    05                            PIC X(53) VALUE SPACES.
    05                            PIC X(13) VALUE "NO INPUT DATA".
01  TOTAL-LINE.
    05                            PIC X(68) VALUE SPACES.
    05                            PIC X(41)
    VALUE "TOTAL COMMISSION FOR ALL SALESPERSONS".
    05  GRAND-TOTAL-COMMISSIONS PIC ZZZ,ZZ9.99.
******************************************************************
```

continued

The Working Storage Section begins at line 00330. The commission rates for this problem have been written into working storage as constants, lines 00370 and 00380. This is better programming practice than writing the commission rates into the Procedure Division. First, all the commission rates for the problem can easily be seen since they are all written in one place. If the commission rates should change while this program is still being used, the program can be changed more easily than if the rates were written into the Procedure Division. Also, the use of the names COMMISSION-RATE-1 and COMMISSION-RATE-2 will make the Procedure Division clearer than if we just had the numbers .05 and .10 in it. Similar reasoning applies to the sale amount at which the commission rate changes. It too is written into working storage, instead of the number 100 being written into the Procedure Division.

Similarly, the NUMBER-OF-SALES is defined as a constant in working storage. Furthermore, it has been designated COMPUTATIONAL and SYNCHRONIZED. Since the field is used only internally to the program and does not interact with input or output, it should be COMPUTATIONAL.

The field COMMISSION-FOR-SALESPERSON is used to accumulate the sum of the 10 commission amounts for each salesperson, for printing on the report. You will see how it is used when we look at the Procedure Division.

Also in working storage, a subscript has been defined, at line 00460. It is called I, but of course it could have had any legal data name. It will be used to permit the program to refer to all 10 of the SALE-AMOUNT-IN fields and all 10 of the COMMISSION-AMOUNT-OUT fields, defined at line 00790. It was made large enough to accommodate the highest value that the subscript can take on. Since it often happens in COBOL that a subscript gets to take on a value that is one larger than the number of fields being subscripted, I should be big enough to hold the value 11. A two-digit field does it, and I was given the PICTURE S99. You will see exactly how I is used when we look at the Procedure Division.

I has been designated COMPUTATIONAL and SYNCHRONIZED. Fields used as subscripts don't have to be COMPUTATIONAL, and the decision whether to make them COMPUTATIONAL is the same as with any other field: If a subscript is used only internally to the program, it should certainly be made COMPUTATIONAL; if, on the other hand, a field is used as a subscript and also interacts with input and/or output, then a COMPUTATIONAL designation may improve or worsen program efficiency.

Controlling the Value of a Subscript with a PERFORM Statement

In the MAIN-PROCESS paragraph of the Procedure Division, we see a new form of the PERFORM statement, at line 01200. This is the PERFORM statement with the **VARYING** option. When you use the VARYING option, you must also use the required words FROM, BY, and UNTIL. The format of this PERFORM statement is given in the next chapter.

The VARYING option is often used when one or more subscripted fields are involved in the processing, but it can also be used in certain circumstances where there are no subscripted fields. The meaning of the PERFORM . . . VARYING statement in Program P10-01 is almost self-evident. The paragraph COMMISSION-CALCULATION is to be PERFORMed over and over. The first time the COMMISSION-CALCULATION is PERFORMed, I will be set to 1 by the PERFORM statement. Then the value of I will be increased by 1 and the UNTIL condition tested. As long as the UNTIL condition is false, COMMISSION-CALCULATION will be PERFORMed again. This will go on until the value of I IS GREATER THAN the NUMBER-OF-SALES. So the PERFORM statement causes COMMISSION-CALCULATION to be executed with I set to 1, 2, 3, and so on to 10. When I finally gets to assume the value of 11, the PERFORM statement notices that I IS GREATER THAN the NUMBER-OF-SALES and does not execute the paragraph COMMISSION-CALCULATION.

In the paragraph COMMISSION-CALCULATION, which begins at line 01390, all references to SALE-AMOUNT-IN and COMMISSION-AMOUNT-OUT are subscripted. All such references must be subscripted, since SALE-AMOUNT-IN and COMMISSION-AMOUNT-OUT are both defined with OCCURS clauses. But the subscripting permits the entire paragraph to refer to all 10 SALE-AMOUNT-IN fields and all 10 COMMISSION-AMOUNT-OUT fields, even though the coding is written only once. You can see how each of the 10 COMMISSION-AMOUNT-W values is computed and how the 10 amounts are accumulated to obtain the COMMISSION-FOR-SALESPERSON.

FIGURE *10.2* ***continued***

```
S COBOL II RELEASE 3.1 09/19/89                    P10001    DATE JUN 21,1991 T
----+-*A-1-B--+----2----+----3----+----4----+----5----+----6----+----7-%--+

00950
00960  PROCEDURE DIVISION.
00970  CONTROL-PARAGRAPH.
00980      PERFORM INITIALIZATION
00990      PERFORM MAIN-PROCESS UNTIL THERE-IS-NO-MORE-INPUT
01000      PERFORM TERMINATION
01010      STOP RUN
01020      .
01030
01040  INITIALIZATION.
01050      OPEN INPUT  SALES-FILE-IN
01060           OUTPUT COMMISSION-REPORT-FILE-OUT
01070      WRITE REPORT-LINE FROM PAGE-HEADING-1 AFTER PAGE
01080      WRITE REPORT-LINE FROM PAGE-HEADING-2 AFTER 4
01090      WRITE REPORT-LINE FROM PAGE-HEADING-3
01100      WRITE REPORT-LINE FROM PAGE-HEADING-4
01110      MOVE 2 TO LINE-SPACING
01120      PERFORM READ-A-RECORD
01130      IF THERE-IS-NO-MORE-INPUT
01140          WRITE REPORT-LINE FROM NO-INPUT-DATA AFTER 2
01150      END-IF
01160      .
01170
01180  MAIN-PROCESS.
01190      MOVE ZERO TO COMMISSION-FOR-SALESPERSON
01200      PERFORM COMMISSION-CALCULATION
01210          VARYING I FROM 1 BY 1 UNTIL
01220          I IS GREATER THAN NUMBER-OF-SALES
01230      PERFORM PRODUCE-THE-REPORT
01240      PERFORM READ-A-RECORD
01250      .
01260
01270  TERMINATION.
01280      PERFORM PRODUCE-FINAL-TOTAL-LINE
01290      CLOSE SALES-FILE-IN
01300            COMMISSION-REPORT-FILE-OUT
01310      .
01320
```

FIGURE 10.2 *continued*

```
READ-A-RECORD.
    READ SALES-FILE-IN
        AT END
            SET THERE-IS-NO-MORE-INPUT TO TRUE
    .

COMMISSION-CALCULATION.
    IF SALE-AMOUNT-IN (I) IS NOT GREATER THAN BRACKET-MAXIMUM
        COMPUTE
          COMMISSION-AMOUNT-W ROUNDED
          COMMISSION-AMOUNT-OUT (I) ROUNDED
             = SALE-AMOUNT-IN (I) * COMMISSION-RATE-1
    ELSE
        COMPUTE
          COMMISSION-AMOUNT-W ROUNDED
          COMMISSION-AMOUNT-OUT (I) ROUNDED
             = BRACKET-MAXIMUM * COMMISSION-RATE-1 +
               (SALE-AMOUNT-IN (I) - BRACKET-MAXIMUM) *
               COMMISSION-RATE-2
    END-IF
    ADD COMMISSION-AMOUNT-W TO COMMISSION-FOR-SALESPERSON
    .

PRODUCE-THE-REPORT.
    MOVE SALESPERSON-NUMBER-IN TO SALESPERSON-NUMBER-OUT
    MOVE COMMISSION-FOR-SALESPERSON TO
         COMMISSION-FOR-SALESPERSON-OUT
    ADD COMMISSION-FOR-SALESPERSON TO GRAND-TOTAL-COMMISSIONS-W
    WRITE REPORT-LINE FROM DETAIL-LINE AFTER LINE-SPACING
    MOVE 1 TO LINE-SPACING
    .

PRODUCE-FINAL-TOTAL-LINE.
    MOVE GRAND-TOTAL-COMMISSIONS-W TO GRAND-TOTAL-COMMISSIONS
    WRITE REPORT-LINE FROM TOTAL-LINE AFTER 4
    .
```

Program P10-01 was run using the input data shown in Figure 10.3 and produced the output shown in Figure 10.4.

FIGURE 10.3 **Input to Program P10-01**

```
--------------------------------------------------------------------------------
         1         2         3         4         5         6         7         8
12345678901234567890123456789012345678901234567890123456789012345678901234567890
--------------------------------------------------------------------------------
000128950075000125680010004871218149200060001100000480001050008 7593
```

```
0001289500750001256800100048712181492000600011000004800010500087593
0942386010000200000051927009550002795020000012500041225006000036150
3684420020000012165007495010000000000000000000000000000000000000000
5236714008412004519072368006850029518000000000000000000000000000000
6612364001000022358001873099500006515024512010368008995017360060287
7747119005200016500119500007350044895012500006875001425009999000000
```

FIGURE 10.4 **Output from Program P10-01**

COMMISSION REPORT

SALES-PERSON NUMBER	C O M M I S S I O N S O N S A L E S SALE 1	SALE 2	SALE 3	SALE 4	SALE 5	SALE 6	SALE 7	SALE 8	SALE 9	SALE 10	TOTAL COMMIS-SION
0001289	495.75	0.63	795.10	43.71	176.49	0.30	6.00	2.40	5.50	82.59	1,608.47
0942386	5.00	195.00	46.93	4.78	1.40	15.00	7.50	36.23	3.00	31.15	345.99
3684420	15.00	7.17	3.75	5.00	0.00	0.00	0.00	0.00	0.00	0.00	30.92
5236714	4.21	2.26	67.37	3.43	24.52	0.00	0.00	0.00	0.00	0.00	101.79
6612364	0.50	17.36	0.94	94.50	3.26	19.51	5.37	4.50	12.36	55.29	213.59
7747119	2.60	11.50	114.50	3.68	39.90	7.50	3.44	0.71	5.00	0.00	188.83

TOTAL COMMISSION FOR ALL SALESPERSONS 2,489.59

EXERCISE 3

Draw a hierarchy diagram of Program P10-01, using the program for reference. Tell how many times each box on the diagram will be executed if the program is run with 55 input records. Tell how many times each box on the diagram will be executed if the program is run with no input records.

EXERCISE 4

Write a program to read input records in the following format:

Positions	Field
1–9	Social Security Number
10–12	Monday Hours (to one decimal place)
13–15	Tuesday Hours (to one decimal place)
16–18	Wednesday Hours (to one decimal place)
19–21	Thursday Hours (to one decimal place)
22–24	Friday Hours (to one decimal place)
25–80	spaces

For each record have your program print the number of hours worked each day, unless the number of hours worked in any day is greater than 7.5. If the number of hours worked in a day is greater than 7.5, have your program compute and print the number of effective hours worked that day according to the following formula:

$$\text{Effective hours} = \text{hours worked} + \frac{\text{hours worked} - 7.5}{2}$$

Have your program print its output in the format shown in Figure 10.E4.

FIGURE 10.E4 Output format for Exercise 4

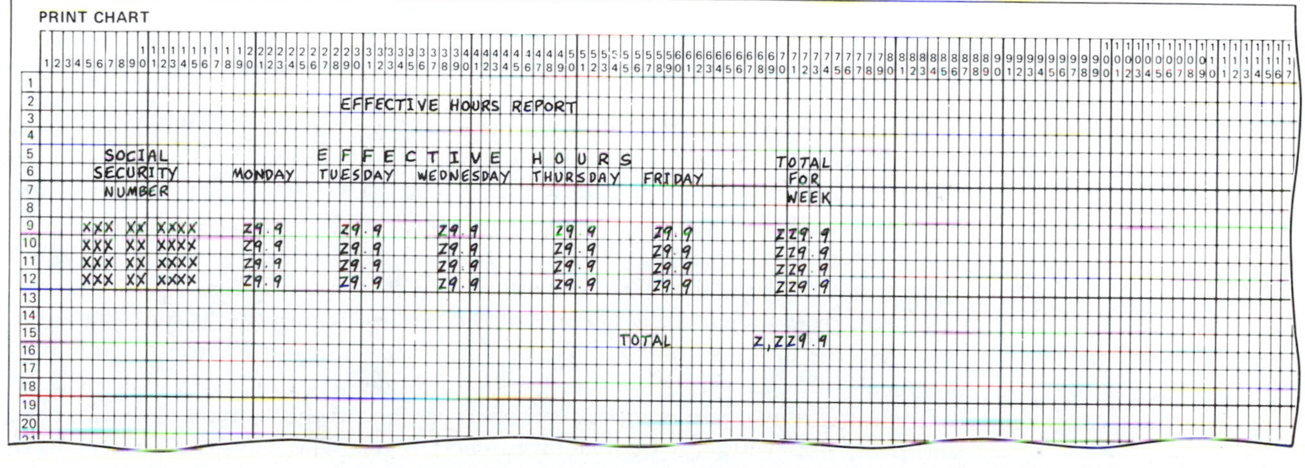

Tables

In COBOL, a table is a group of fields defined with an OCCURS clause. COBOL is capable of handling **one-dimensional** tables, as well as tables of up to seven dimensions. In this chapter, we will discuss only one-dimensional tables. Tables of higher dimension will be discussed in Chapter 11.

In computer terminology, tables are often referred to as **arrays.** Whereas in mathematics the words "table" and "array" may mean different things (as in an array of coefficients, but a table of trigonometric functions), in computer terminology they mean exactly the same thing. We will use only the word "table."

For our purposes, there are only two kinds of tables: **direct-reference tables** and **search tables.** Program P10-01 used direct-reference tables. The next section shows another way that a program can use a direct-reference table.

Direct-Reference Tables

A direct-reference table is one whose fields are referred to by their numerical position in the table; for example, a list of the names of the 12 months January, February, March, and so on. If we had such a list, and wanted to know the name of month 8, we would only have to look at the eighth entry in the table to find our answer, August. Actually it is easier for a COBOL program to find any particular item in such a list than it would be for you or me. We would have to count, either from the beginning or the end of the list, to find the item wanted. A COBOL program can go directly to the desired item without having to count. That is why such a table is called a direct-reference table.

Program P10-02 shows how such a table can be written into a COBOL program and how it might be used. Program P10-02 reads input records in the following format:

Positions	Field
1–2	Month Number (01 through 12)
3–4	Day Number (01 through 31)
5–6	Year of Century (01 through 99)
7–80	spaces

Each record contains a date in the usual American format MMDDYY. For each record read, Program P10-02 expands the date and prints the input and the expanded date on one line, as shown in Figure 10.5. Notice that the dates are formatted rather crudely; the short names such as May and June have a lot of space after them. COBOL provides a method of eliminating those unwanted spaces, which we will cover in Chapter 18.

For Program P10-02 to print out the names of months, it must have the names of the months in it somewhere. Tables that are written into COBOL programs are always written in the Working Storage Section. Most tables can be written into a program in more than one way, but in this book you will not see all the possible ways in which tables can be written. The ways shown here were selected for ease of use and clarity of meaning.

Program P10-02 is shown in Figure 10.6, and the table of month names

FIGURE ***10.5*** **Output format for Program P10-02**

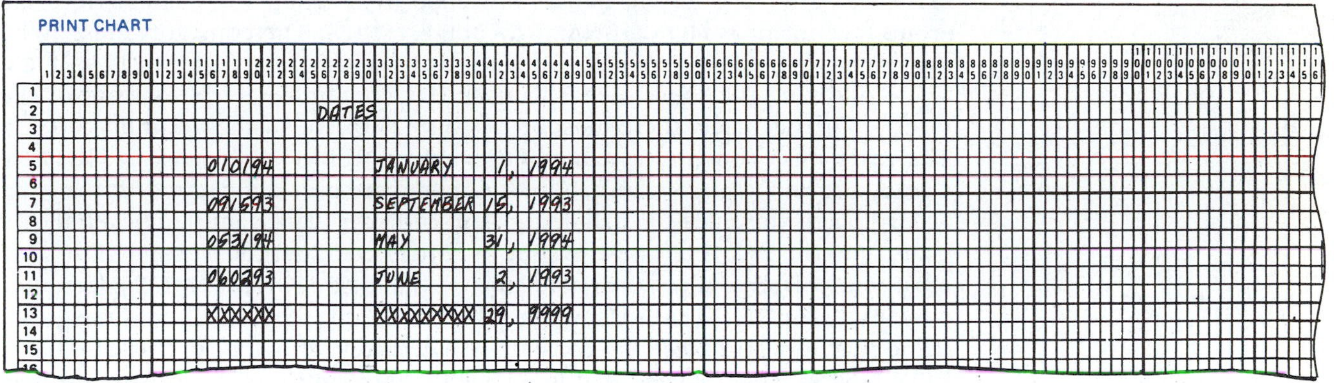

FIGURE ***10.6*** **Program P10-02**

```
S COBOL II RELEASE 3.1 09/19/89                    P10002   DATE AUG 18,1991 T
----+-*A-1-B--+----2----+----3----+----4----+----5----+----6----+----7-|--+

 IDENTIFICATION DIVISION.
 PROGRAM-ID.  P10-02.
*AUTHOR.  DEBORAH ANN SENIOR.
*
*    THIS PROGRAM READS DATES IN MMDDYY FORM AND PRINTS THEM
*    WITH THE MONTH NAME SPELLED OUT
*
******************************************************************

 ENVIRONMENT DIVISION.
 INPUT-OUTPUT SECTION.
 FILE-CONTROL.
     SELECT DATE-FILE-IN              ASSIGN TO INFILE.
     SELECT DATE-REPORT-FILE-OUT      ASSIGN TO PRINTER.

******************************************************************

 DATA DIVISION.
 FILE SECTION.
 FD  DATE-FILE-IN
     RECORD CONTAINS 80 CHARACTERS.

 01  DATE-RECORD-IN.
     05  DATE-IN.
         10  MONTH-IN     PIC 99.
         10  DAY-IN       PIC 99.
         10  YEAR-IN      PIC 99.

 FD  DATE-REPORT-FILE-OUT.

 01  REPORT-LINE          PIC X(48).

```

continued

begins at line 00380. A direct-reference table can be written into a program in several ways. The method used here is convenient for most applications. It consists of a series of constant entries preceded by a group-level name. Here the group-level name is MONTH-NAME-TABLE-ENTRIES. The constants must all be the same size, and so they were all made as large as the largest, SEPTEMBER.

Following the series of constant entries containing the **elements** of the direct-reference table, there must be an entry in the form shown in line 00510. The entry must contain the name of the table, a REDEFINES clause, a PICTURE clause, and an OCCURS clause. Names of tables are user-defined words made up according to the rules for making up any ordinary data names. The PICTURE clause and the OCCURS clause may be in either order, but the REDEFINES clause must immediately follow the data name, in this case MONTH-NAME. The entry containing the REDEFINES clause must have the same level number as the group name that appears before the constants immediately above it, in this case 05. A REDEFINES clause may be used in a level-01 entry in the Working Storage Section; an OCCURS clause must not be used in a level-01 entry anywhere.

The dummy entry, line 00370, is needed to prevent the OCCURS clause in line 00520 from ending up at the 01 level. Remember that the entry in line 00510 must be at the same level as the group name in line 00380. Line 00370 was included in the program so that 00380 could be written at some level other than 01. If you have more than one table in a program, they may all be written under the same dummy level-01 entry.

We have already used a REDEFINES clause to give a single field more than one PICTURE in connection with validity checking, but here REDEFINES is used for an entirely different purpose. In this entry the PICTURE is the same as the PICTURE in the constant entries that were used for writing the table values, X(9). The OCCURS clause, of course, tells how many entries there are in the table. This whole set of entries—the 12 constant entries, their group-level name, and the REDEFINES entry—now permits us to refer to the 12 different names of the months by the names

```
MONTH-NAME (1)
MONTH-NAME (2)
MONTH-NAME (3)
```

and so on up to:

```
MONTH-NAME (12)
```

Better yet, we can have a data name be the subscript, let's say MONTH-SUBSCRIPT, and then we can refer to any of the month names as

```
MONTH-NAME (MONTH-SUBSCRIPT)
```

with MONTH-SUBSCRIPT assigned some value from 1 through 12. Of course, the field used for subscripting MONTH-NAME doesn't have to be called MONTH-SUBSCRIPT; it can be any field defined as an integer.

The MOVE statement at line 00930 shows how we can use subscripting to get the desired month name directly. Line 00930 has as its sending field MONTH-NAME (MONTH-IN). MONTH-IN is defined as an integer and so can be used as a subscript. Furthermore, it is defined in the File Section as part of the input area, and so the month number as it appears in the input record can be used as the subscript in the MOVE statement.

FIGURE 10.6 *continued*

```
S COBOL II RELEASE 3.1 09/19/89               P10002   DATE AUG 18,1991 T
----+-*A-1-B--+----2----+----3----+----4----+----5----+----6----+----7-|--+

WORKING-STORAGE SECTION.
01  MORE-INPUT              PIC X           VALUE "Y".
    88 THERE-IS-NO-MORE-INPUT               VALUE "N".
01  LINE-SPACING            PIC S9          COMP SYNC.
01  .
    05  MONTH-NAME-TABLE-ENTRIES.
        10                  PIC X(9)        VALUE "JANUARY".
        10                  PIC X(9)        VALUE "FEBRUARY".
        10                  PIC X(9)        VALUE "MARCH".
        10                  PIC X(9)        VALUE "APRIL".
        10                  PIC X(9)        VALUE "MAY".
        10                  PIC X(9)        VALUE "JUNE".
        10                  PIC X(9)        VALUE "JULY".
        10                  PIC X(9)        VALUE "AUGUST".
        10                  PIC X(9)        VALUE "SEPTEMBER".
        10                  PIC X(9)        VALUE "OCTOBER".
        10                  PIC X(9)        VALUE "NOVEMBER".
        10                  PIC X(9)        VALUE "DECEMBER".
    05  MONTH-NAME          REDEFINES MONTH-NAME-TABLE-ENTRIES
                            PIC X(9)        OCCURS 12 TIMES.

01  PAGE-HEADING.
    05                      PIC X(25)       VALUE SPACES.
    05                      PIC X(5)        VALUE "DATES".

01  DETAIL-LINE.
    05                      PIC X(16)       VALUE SPACES.
    05 DATE-OUT             PIC X(6).
    05 MONTH-OUT            PIC B(8)X(9).
    05 DAY-OUT              PIC BZ9.
    05                      PIC X(4)        VALUE ", 19".
    05 YEAR-OUT             PIC 99.

01  NO-INPUT-DATA.
    05                      PIC X(21)       VALUE SPACES.
    05                      PIC X(13)       VALUE "NO INPUT DATA".

******************************************************************

PROCEDURE DIVISION.
CONTROL-PARAGRAPH.
    PERFORM INITIALIZATION
    PERFORM MAIN-PROCESS UNTIL THERE-IS-NO-MORE-INPUT
    PERFORM TERMINATION
    STOP RUN
    .

INITIALIZATION.
    OPEN INPUT  DATE-FILE-IN
         OUTPUT DATE-REPORT-FILE-OUT
    WRITE REPORT-LINE FROM PAGE-HEADING AFTER PAGE
    MOVE 3 TO LINE-SPACING
    PERFORM READ-A-RECORD
    IF THERE-IS-NO-MORE-INPUT
        WRITE REPORT-LINE FROM NO-INPUT-DATA AFTER 3
    END-IF
    .

MAIN-PROCESS.
    MOVE DATE-IN                    TO DATE-OUT
    MOVE MONTH-NAME (MONTH-IN)      TO MONTH-OUT
    MOVE DAY-IN                     TO DAY-OUT
    MOVE YEAR-IN                    TO YEAR-OUT
    WRITE REPORT-LINE FROM DETAIL-LINE AFTER LINE-SPACING
    MOVE 2 TO LINE-SPACING
    PERFORM READ-A-RECORD
    .
```

continued

FIGURE 10.6 *continued*

```
S COBOL II RELEASE 3.1 09/19/89                  P10002   DATE AUG 18,1991 T
----+-*A-1-B--+----2----+----3----+----4----+----5----+----6----+----7-|--+

     TERMINATION.
         CLOSE DATE-FILE-IN
               DATE-REPORT-FILE-OUT
         .

     READ-A-RECORD.
         READ DATE-FILE-IN
             AT END
                 SET THERE-IS-NO-MORE-INPUT TO TRUE
         .
```

Program P10-02 was run with the input data shown in Figure 10.7 and produced the output shown in Figure 10.8.

FIGURE 10.7 **Input to Program P10-02**

```
--------------------------------------------------------------------------------
         1         2         3         4         5         6         7         8
12345678901234567890123456789012345678901234567890123456789012345678901234567890
--------------------------------------------------------------------------------
010194
091593
053194
060294
071494
112793
050794
090393
063094
021494
```

FIGURE 10.8 **Output from Program P10-02**

```
         DATES

010194        JANUARY    1, 1994

091593        SEPTEMBER 15, 1993

053194        MAY       31, 1994

060294        JUNE       2, 1994

071494        JULY      14, 1994

112793        NOVEMBER  27, 1993

050794        MAY        7, 1994

090393        SEPTEMBER  3, 1993

063094        JUNE      30, 1994

021494        FEBRUARY  14, 1994
```

A Direct-Reference Table in Storage

Figure 10.9 shows how the month-name table in Program P10-02 is arranged in computer storage. The 12 entries in lines 00390 through 00500 establish 12 fields, containing the words JANUARY, FEBRUARY, and so on, in adjacent areas of storage. The REDEFINES entry with its OCCURS clause, line 00510, then establishes the 12 occurrences of MONTH-NAME, with each being assigned to one of the 12 fields.

FIGURE *10.9* **How the MONTH-NAME-TABLE-ENTRIES of Program P10-02 are arranged in computer storage**

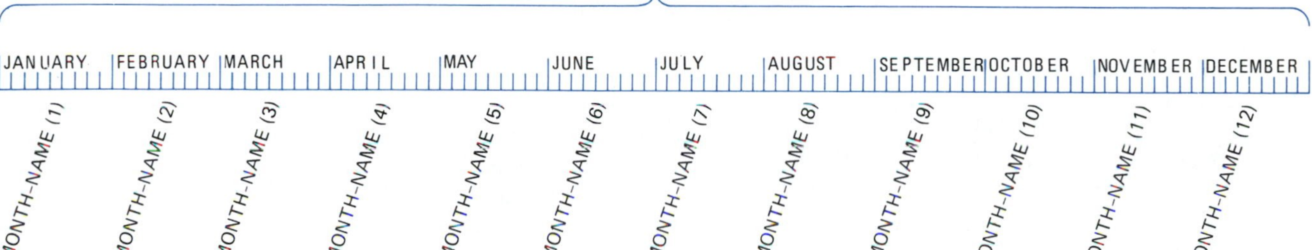

EXERCISE *5*

Write a program to read and process input records in the following format:

Positions	Field
1–2	State Code
3–22	City Name
23–80	spaces

Each record contains a two-digit state code and the name of a city spelled out. For each record read, print the input data in their original form, and also print the city name and state name in the format shown in Figure 10.E5. Use the 16 state names listed in Table 10.E5. Include in your test data for this program at least one record with a state code of 01, at least one record with a state code of 16, and some with state codes in between.

FIGURE 10.E5 Output format for Exercise 5

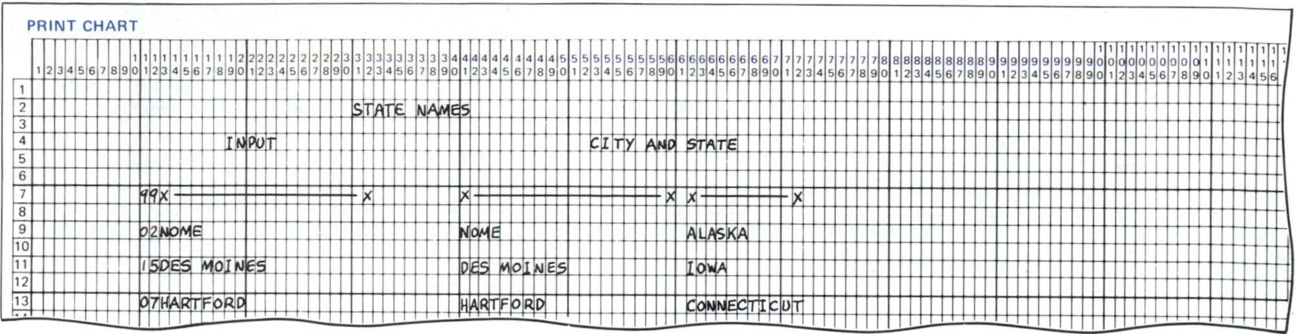

TABLE 10.E5 Sixteen state names in alphabetic order

Alabama
Alaska
Arizona
Arkansas
California
Colorado
Connecticut
Delaware
Florida
Georgia
Hawaii
Idaho
Illinois
Indiana
Iowa
Kansas

A Search Table with Indexing

A search table is one whose contents must be examined in some way before any data can be extracted from the table. An example of such a table is Table 10.1, which might be used by the U.S. Postal Service.

This table can be used two ways. If you know a state code, you can get the corresponding state name out of the table. Or you can enter the table knowing a state name and find the code. The entry keys to a table are called the **arguments,** and the pieces of data we want to extract are called **functions.** If we have the state code GA, for example, and want to find the state name, GA is the argument. The name we are looking for, Georgia, is the function. If we want to find the state code for California, then California is the argument. The code CA is the function.

With a table such as this, neither you nor I nor COBOL can find what we want without searching through the table arguments. Whenever you have to

TABLE *10.1*
Sixteen state codes and their corresponding state names

State Code	State Name
AL	Alabama
AK	Alaska
AZ	Arizona
AR	Arkansas
CA	California
CO	Colorado
CT	Connecticut
DE	Delaware
FL	Florida
GA	Georgia
HI	Hawaii
ID	Idaho
IL	Illinois
IN	Indiana
IA	Iowa
KS	Kansas

search a table in a COBOL program, it is best to use indexing with it, because the SEARCH verb can be used only with an indexed table and not with a subscripted one. Although using the SEARCH verb is not the only way to search a table, it is the best because it makes the program coding most easily understandable.

Indexes work essentially differently from subscripts. Subscripts are stored in the computer as the numbers 1, 2, 3, and so on, referring to the first, second, third, and so forth, entry in the table. Every time a subscript is used, COBOL must compute, using the subscript, the storage location of the corresponding table entry. Indexes, on the other hand, are stored in a form that reflects the actual storage locations of table entries, and so such computations are unnecessary when they are used. The programmer need never be concerned with storage locations, however, and can always think of an index simply as referring to the first, second, third, and so on, entry in a table.

To set up a table for indexing, you merely include an **INDEXED BY** phrase in the OCCURS clause that defines the table. For example, if we were to use indexing on the table in Program P10-02, then instead of the entry

```
05 MONTH-NAME REDEFINES MONTH-NAME-TABLE-ENTRIES
              PIC X(9)  OCCURS 12 TIMES.
```

we would have

```
05 MONTH-NAME REDEFINES MONTH-NAME-TABLE-ENTRIES
              PIC X(9)
              OCCURS 12 TIMES INDEXED BY MONTH-INDEX.
```

The made-up name referred to in the INDEXED BY phrase is called an **index name.** The rules for making up index names are the same as for making up ordinary data names. Once a name is given as an index name in an INDEXED BY phrase, it must not be defined further. COBOL will set up the index name field in its most efficient form. Unlike a subscript, which can be used to subscript any field in a program that is defined with an OCCURS clause, an index name can be used to index only the one table that it is defined with.

Once an index name is established, we can refer to fields by using **direct indexing.** Direct indexing looks just like subscripting. Here's how we could refer to some of the MONTH-NAME fields with direct indexing:

```
MONTH-NAME (1)
MONTH-NAME (2)
MONTH-NAME (12)
```

and

```
MONTH-NAME (MONTH-INDEX)
```

(pronounced "MONTH-NAME indexed by MONTH-INDEX"). It is also possible to refer to indexed fields by using **relative indexing,** which will be discussed in the next chapter, and by subscripting, in which we use an ordinary identifier defined as an integer.

We now will do a program using the Postal Service table of state names and two-letter state codes. The input to Program P10-03 is similar to the input for Exercise 5 (page 307) except that the State Code, in positions 1 and 2 of the input, is two letters instead of two digits. The City Name field remains the same as in Exercise 5, and the output is to be the same (Figure 10.E5).

In this program we have to write both the state names and the two-letter state codes into the program. We already know how to write a table of state names from Exercise 5. In Program P10-03 we will also have to write a table of two-letter state codes. The state codes will have to be in the same order as their corresponding state names. The state names are in alphabetic order, but the program would work regardless of the order of the state names as long as the codes were in the same order as the names. Then, for each input record the program reads, it will take the two-letter state code from the input and search the table of state codes looking for a match. Once a match is found between the input state code and a state code in the table, the program will be able to find the corresponding state name to print on the output report.

Program P10-03 is shown in Figure 10.10. In the Working Storage Section you can see the table of state names, set up for indexing, beginning at line 00370. The entries for this table should resemble very strongly the entries you wrote for the state-names table in Exercise 5, except that now we have an INDEXED BY phrase in the OCCURS clause at line 00550. Of course, once we establish the index name STATE-NAME-INDEX, we must not define it elsewhere. You can see that the table of state codes is set up just below, starting at line 00570. It gets its own index, STATE-CODE-INDEX, in line 00750.

FIGURE 10.10 **Program 10-03**

```
S COBOL II RELEASE 3.1 09/19/89                P10003   DATE AUG 19,1991 T
----+-*A-1-B--+----2----+----3----+----4----+----5----+----6----+----7-%--+

00010  IDENTIFICATION DIVISION.
00020  PROGRAM-ID.  P10-03.
00030 *AUTHOR.  DEBORAH ANN SENIOR.
00040 *
00050 *     THIS PROGRAM PERFORMS A SEARCH OF STATE CODES AND PRINTS
00060 *     STATE NAMES.
00070 *
00080 *****************************************************************
```

FIGURE ***10.10*** ***continued***

```
       ENVIRONMENT DIVISION.
       INPUT-OUTPUT SECTION.
       FILE-CONTROL.
           SELECT ADDRESS-FILE-IN          ASSIGN TO INFILE.
           SELECT ADDRESS-REPORT-FILE-OUT  ASSIGN TO PRINTER.

      *****************************************************************

       DATA DIVISION.
       FILE SECTION.
       FD  ADDRESS-FILE-IN
           RECORD CONTAINS 80 CHARACTERS.

       01  ADDRESS-RECORD-IN.
           05  STATE-AND-CITY-IN.
               10  STATE-CODE-IN                PIC XX.
               10  CITY-NAME-IN                 PIC X(20).

       FD  ADDRESS-REPORT-FILE-OUT.

       01  REPORT-LINE          PIC X(72).

       WORKING-STORAGE SECTION.
       01  LINE-SPACING         PIC S9          COMP SYNC.
       01  MORE-INPUT           PIC X           VALUE "Y".
           88 THERE-IS-NO-MORE-INPUT            VALUE "N".
       01  .
           05  STATE-NAME-TABLE-ENTRIES.
               10               PIC X(11)       VALUE "ALABAMA".
               10               PIC X(11)       VALUE "ALASKA".
               10               PIC X(11)       VALUE "ARIZONA".
               10               PIC X(11)       VALUE "ARKANSAS".
               10               PIC X(11)       VALUE "CALIFORNIA".
               10               PIC X(11)       VALUE "COLORADO".
               10               PIC X(11)       VALUE "CONNECTICUT".
               10               PIC X(11)       VALUE "DELAWARE".
               10               PIC X(11)       VALUE "FLORIDA".
               10               PIC X(11)       VALUE "GEORGIA".
               10               PIC X(11)       VALUE "HAWAII".
               10               PIC X(11)       VALUE "IDAHO".
               10               PIC X(11)       VALUE "ILLINOIS".
               10               PIC X(11)       VALUE "INDIANA".
               10               PIC X(11)       VALUE "IOWA".
               10               PIC X(11)       VALUE "KANSAS".
           05  STATE-NAME       REDEFINES STATE-NAME-TABLE-ENTRIES
               OCCURS 16 TIMES  INDEXED BY STATE-NAME-INDEX
                                PIC X(11).
           05  STATE-CODE-TABLE-ENTRIES.
               10               PIC XX          VALUE "AL".
               10               PIC XX          VALUE "AK".
               10               PIC XX          VALUE "AZ".
               10               PIC XX          VALUE "AR".
               10               PIC XX          VALUE "CA".
               10               PIC XX          VALUE "CO".
               10               PIC XX          VALUE "CT".
               10               PIC XX          VALUE "DE".
               10               PIC XX          VALUE "FL".
               10               PIC XX          VALUE "GA".
               10               PIC XX          VALUE "HI".
               10               PIC XX          VALUE "ID".
               10               PIC XX          VALUE "IL".
               10               PIC XX          VALUE "IN".
               10               PIC XX          VALUE "IA".
               10               PIC XX          VALUE "KS".
           05  STATE-CODE       REDEFINES STATE-CODE-TABLE-ENTRIES
               OCCURS 16 TIMES  INDEXED BY STATE-CODE-INDEX
                                PIC XX.
```

continued

The statement at line 01280 will MOVE a STATE-NAME to the report output area. In that statement, STATE-NAME is indexed by its table index, STATE-NAME-INDEX. How will STATE-NAME-INDEX get the correct value assigned to it so that the correct STATE-NAME will print? In Program P10-02 and Exercise 5 we were able to subscript our output fields directly by using input data as the subscript because in those programs we were dealing with direct-reference tables. Here we have a search table, and for the program to get the value it needs for STATE-NAME-INDEX, it will have to search the STATE-CODE-TABLE-ENTRIES. You will soon see how.

In the MAIN-PROCESS paragraph in the Procedure Division are the two statements needed to search the STATE-CODE-TABLE-ENTRIES and assign the correct value to STATE-NAME-INDEX so that the MOVE statement in line 01280 will work correctly. The first is the SET statement in line 01210. Whenever you SEARCH a table sequentially as we are doing here, that is, whenever you examine the table entries one after another in order, you must tell COBOL where the SEARCH should begin. Here we want to begin the SEARCH at the beginning of the table, so we SET both table indexes to point to the first element in their respective tables. Then we give a SEARCH statement.

In a SEARCH statement the word SEARCH must be followed by the name of the field to be SEARCHed. The field to be SEARCHed must be defined with an OCCURS clause having an INDEXED BY phrase. In this case the field to be SEARCHed is STATE-CODE. This directs COBOL to step through the STATE-CODEs, stepping up the STATE-CODE-INDEX to point to successive elements of the state code table until the SEARCH finds what it is looking for.

Following the name of the field to be SEARCHed, you may have a VARYING phrase. The VARYING phrase is used when you are SEARCHing through a table and you want one index name to keep pace with another, as when there are two tables in a program. In our case, we want the STATE-NAME-INDEX to

FIGURE *10.10* ***continued***

```
S COBOL II RELEASE 3.1 09/19/89                    P10003    DATE AUG 19,1991 T
----+-*A-1-B--+----2----+----3----+----4----+----5----+----6----+----7-%--+


00770
00780  01   PAGE-HEADING-1.
00790       05                      PIC X(30)        VALUE SPACE.
00800       05                      PIC X(11)        VALUE "STATE NAMES".
00810
00820  01   PAGE-HEADING-2.
00830       05                      PIC X(18)        VALUE SPACES.
00840       05                      PIC X(5)         VALUE "INPUT".
00850       05                      PIC X(29)        VALUE SPACES.
00860       05                      PIC X(14)        VALUE "CITY AND STATE".
00870
00880  01   DETAIL-LINE.
00890       05                            PIC X(10) VALUE SPACES.
00900       05 STATE-AND-CITY-OUT         PIC X(22).
00910       05 CITY-NAME-OUT              PIC B(8)X(20).
00920       05 STATE-NAME-OUT             PIC BX(11).
00930
00940  01   NO-INPUT-DATA.
00950       05                      PIC X(29)        VALUE SPACES.
00960       05                      PIC X(13)        VALUE "NO INPUT DATA".
00970
00980 ************************************************************************
```

FIGURE 10.10 *continued*

```
PROCEDURE DIVISION.
CONTROL-PARAGRAPH.
    PERFORM INITIALIZATION
    PERFORM MAIN-PROCESS UNTIL THERE-IS-NO-MORE-INPUT
    PERFORM TERMINATION
    STOP RUN
    .

INITIALIZATION.
    OPEN INPUT  ADDRESS-FILE-IN
         OUTPUT ADDRESS-REPORT-FILE-OUT
    WRITE REPORT-LINE FROM PAGE-HEADING-1 AFTER PAGE
    WRITE REPORT-LINE FROM PAGE-HEADING-2 AFTER 2
    MOVE 3 TO LINE-SPACING
    PERFORM READ-A-RECORD
    IF THERE-IS-NO-MORE-INPUT
        WRITE REPORT-LINE FROM NO-INPUT-DATA AFTER 3
    END-IF
    .

MAIN-PROCESS.
    SET STATE-CODE-INDEX
        STATE-NAME-INDEX TO 1
    SEARCH STATE-CODE
        VARYING STATE-NAME-INDEX
        WHEN STATE-CODE-IN = STATE-CODE (STATE-CODE-INDEX)
            MOVE STATE-AND-CITY-IN     TO STATE-AND-CITY-OUT
            MOVE CITY-NAME-IN          TO CITY-NAME-OUT
            MOVE STATE-NAME (STATE-NAME-INDEX) TO STATE-NAME-OUT
            WRITE REPORT-LINE FROM DETAIL-LINE
                   AFTER LINE-SPACING
            MOVE 2 TO LINE-SPACING
    END-SEARCH
    PERFORM READ-A-RECORD
    .

TERMINATION.
    CLOSE ADDRESS-FILE-IN
          ADDRESS-REPORT-FILE-OUT
    .

READ-A-RECORD.
    READ ADDRESS-FILE-IN
        AT END
            SET THERE-IS-NO-MORE-INPUT TO TRUE
    .
```

keep pace with the STATE-CODE-INDEX as the STATE-CODEs are SEARCHed. That is, when STATE-CODE-INDEX is pointing to the second STATE-CODE in the state code table, we want STATE-NAME-INDEX to be pointing to the second STATE-NAME in the state name table. If STATE-CODE-INDEX should get to point to the third STATE-CODE, we would want STATE-NAME-INDEX to point to the third STATE-NAME at the same time. Then when a match is found between STATE-CODE-IN and a STATE-CODE in the table, STATE-NAME-INDEX will be pointing to the corresponding STATE-NAME in the state name table.

The WHEN clause in a SEARCH statement tells COBOL under what conditions the SEARCH is to stop, and what to do then. Here we want the SEARCH to end WHEN STATE-CODE-IN is equal to one of the table STATE-CODEs. At that time, the STATE-NAME-INDEX has been set to its proper value by the VARYING phrase. We then give statements to format and print the output line. You may have as many imperative statements as you like in a WHEN phrase. Alternatively, you may use just a CONTINUE statement if you want the flow of control to proceed to the next statement after the SEARCH when the SEARCH is completed.

Program P10-03 was run with the input data shown in Figure 10.11 and produced the output shown in Figure 10.12.

FIGURE *10.11* **Input to Program P10-03**

```
--------------------------------------------------------------------------------
         1         2         3         4         5         6         7         8
12345678901234567890123456789012345678901234567890123456789012345678901234567890
--------------------------------------------------------------------------------
AKNOME
IADES MOINES
CTHARTFORD
KSWICHITA
CASAN FRANCISCO
FLMIAMI
HIHONOLULU
```

FIGURE *10.12* **Output from Program P10-03**

```
                          STATE NAMES

          INPUT                               CITY AND STATE

AKNOME                        NOME                    ALASKA

IADES MOINES                  DES MOINES              IOWA

CTHARTFORD                    HARTFORD                CONNECTICUT

KSWICHITA                     WICHITA                 KANSAS

CASAN FRANCISCO               SAN FRANCISCO           CALIFORNIA

FLMIAMI                       MIAMI                   FLORIDA

HIHONOLULU                    HONOLULU                HAWAII
```

Format 1 of the SET Statement

The SET statement in Program P10-03 has the following format:

$$\underline{\text{SET}} \begin{Bmatrix} \text{index-name-1} \\ \text{identifier-1} \end{Bmatrix} \ldots \ \underline{\text{TO}} \begin{Bmatrix} \text{index-name-2} \\ \text{identifier-2} \\ \text{integer-1} \end{Bmatrix}$$

The first set of braces, before the word TO, shows that index names and identifiers may have values assigned to them by the SET statement. An identifier is a data name followed by any legal combination of qualifiers, subscripts, and/or indexes. The ellipsis after the braces show that more than one index name or more than one identifier may have a value assigned to them with a single SET statement. The second set of braces, after the word TO, shows that the sending field of the SET statement may be either an index name, an identifier, or a literal. If a literal is used, it must be an integer numeric literal.

In Program P10-03, the receiving fields of the SET statement were the index names STATE-CODE-INDEX and STATE-NAME-INDEX. The sending field was the numeric literal 1. Execution of the SET statement caused the literal 1 to be converted to a number that reflected the storage location of the first STATE-CODE, and to store that number in STATE-CODE-INDEX. It also caused the literal 1 to be converted to a number that reflected the storage location of the first STATE-NAME, and to store that number in STATE-NAME-INDEX.

If a SET statement of the form

```
SET index-name-1 TO identifier-3
```

is used, identifier-3 must be defined as an integer. The SET statement takes the number in identifier-3 (a 1, 2, or 3, and so on) and converts it to point to the first, second, or third (and so on) entry in the table related to index-name-1.

If a SET statement of the form

```
SET identifier-1 TO index-name-3
```

is used, the SET statement determines which entry in its table index-name-3 is pointing to (the first, second, or third, and so on) and converts it to the number 1, 2, or 3, and so on, and stores the number in identifier-1.

If a SET statement of the form

```
SET index-name-1 TO index-name-3
```

is used, the SET statement determines which entry in its table index-name-3 is pointing to and stores in index-name-1 a number that points to the corresponding entry in its table. Remember that in a SET statement, the sending field appears after the word TO, and the receiving field before, opposite to the order of sending and receiving fields in a MOVE statement.

Any other combination of sending and receiving fields is illegal. You cannot use

```
SET identifier-1 TO identifier-3
```

Use instead:

```
MOVE identifier-3 TO identifier-1
```

You cannot use

```
SET identifier-1 TO literal-1
```

Use instead:

```
MOVE literal-1 TO identifier-1
```

The only statements that can change the value of an index name are SET, SEARCH, and PERFORM . . . VARYING. An index name can be used in a relation condition anywhere that such a condition is legal. Its value in the relation condition is taken to be 1, 2, or 3, and so on, depending on whether the index name is pointing to the first, second, or third, and so on, entry in its table. An index name by itself cannot be used as the sending or receiving field in any statement other than SET.

The SEARCH Statement

The format of the SEARCH statement is as follows:

```
SEARCH identifier-1 [VARYING {identifier-1  }]
                             {index-name-1  }

    [AT END imperative-statement-1]

    {WHEN condition-1 {imperative-statement-2}} ...
                      {NEXT SENTENCE         }

    [END-SEARCH]
```

The first set of square brackets shows that the VARYING phrase is optional. The braces accompanying the VARYING phrase show that the SEARCH statement can vary either an index name or an identifier. In Program P10-03 we used it to vary the index name STATE-NAME-INDEX. When the VARYING phrase is used to vary an identifier, the identifier is assigned the value 1, 2, 3, and so on, as the SEARCH points to the first, second, third, and so on, entry of the table being SEARCHed. The AT END phrase is optional and is used when there is the possibility that the SEARCH may run off the end of the table. We will use an AT END phrase in our next program.

Any legal COBOL condition may be used in a WHEN phrase to terminate a SEARCH (such as GREATER THAN, LESS THAN, and so on, and complex conditions). The ellipsis accompanying the WHEN phrase shows that any number of WHEN phrases may be written into a SEARCH statement, and that each may have its own imperative statement or statements. If a SEARCH statement contains more than one WHEN phrase, then for each setting of the search index the WHEN conditions are tested in the order in which they are written in the SEARCH statement. The first WHEN condition that is satisfied terminates the SEARCH, and the appropriate imperative statement or statements are carried out.

EXERCISE 6

Write a program to read input records in the following format:

Positions	Field
1–2	Branch Office Number
3–32	Agent Name
33–80	spaces

Each record contains an Agent Name and a Branch Office Number. For each record read, have your program print on one line the Agent Name, the Branch Office Number, and the branch office name. Use the following table for the branch office names:

Branch Office Number	Branch Office Name
02	Allentown
05	Bethlehem
07	Blue Ball
11	Delaware Water Gap
13	Dingmans Ferry
15	Harrisburg
20	King of Prussia
21	Philadelphia
37	Pittsburgh
39	Scranton
44	Wilkes-Barre

Design the output for this program before you begin coding. Provide a suitable report title and column headings. Include in your input data at least one record with Branch Office Number 44, at least one record with Branch Office Number 02, and at least two records with Branch Office Number 11.

A Program Using an Argument-Function Table

In Program P10-03 we wrote the table arguments into the program separately from the table functions. That is, the state names and the state codes were written into working storage as two separate tables. It is possible instead to arrange each argument and its corresponding function in a single working-storage entry. This approach is most convenient when all the arguments and functions are alphanumeric or can be treated as alphanumeric. If the arguments or functions, or both, are numeric, it is still possible to arrange each argument with its function in one entry, but less conveniently than if they are all alphanumeric. In Program P11-02, Chapter 11, you will see the inconvenience connected with having each argument in the same entry with its functions when the arguments and functions are not all alphanumeric.

In Program P10-03, we had tables in which all the arguments and functions were alphanumeric. In Exercise 6, although the arguments are branch office numbers, they can easily be treated as alphanumeric without affecting the working of the program (Did you define the branch office numbers with 9s or did you define them with Xs?).

There are several advantages to having each argument and its function in one entry. It takes less coding—often much less—to enter the table into the program. It usually makes the meaning of the table clearer. And it permits the whole table and all its entries to be referred to by a single index, without the need for two indexes as in Program P10-03 and Exercise 6.

In Program P10-04 we will rewrite Program P10-03 to show how each argument of a table and its function can be arranged in a single working-storage entry. We will also show how table entries can be read in from a file instead of being written into the program, and we will introduce the **SEARCH ALL** statement.

Program P10-04 uses two input files. One is a file of state codes and city names similar to the input to Program P10-03. The other is read by Program P10-04 and placed into working storage to serve as the table of state codes and state names. The table file is shown in Figure 10.13. Each input record contains one entire row of the table. The first record shows both AK and ALASKA, one right after the other. The second record similarly shows the argument and function for ALABAMA. In this way all the arguments and functions are written into the file. When we look at Program P10-04, you will see how this file is read and stored in working storage as a table. One of the advantages of having each argument with its function is that you can see at a glance which argument belongs to which function. In the tables of Program P10-03 it was necessary to count down the entries of both tables to find that AR belongs to ARKANSAS.

FIGURE *10.13* **Table-file input for Program P10-04**

```
--------------------------------------------------------------------------------
         1         2         3         4         5         6         7         8
12345678901234567890123456789012345678901234567890123456789012345678901234567890
--------------------------------------------------------------------------------
AKALASKA
ALALABAMA
ARARKANSAS
AZARIZONA
CACALIFORNIA
COCOLORADO
CTCONNECTICUT
DEDELAWARE
FLFLORIDA
GAGEORGIA
HIHAWAII
IAIOWA
IDIDAHO
ILILLINOIS
ININDIANA
KSKANSAS
```

You may notice that the states are not in the same order in this table as they were in Program P10-03. The order has been changed so that we can use a SEARCH ALL statement in this program. SEARCH ALL provides a faster search than an ordinary SEARCH statement (except with very small tables), but SEARCH ALL can be used only when the SEARCH arguments are in alphabetic or numeric order. In Program P10-04 we want to use a SEARCH ALL on the state codes, and so the table was arranged so that the state codes are in alphabetic order.

Program P10-04 is shown in Figure 10.14. There are now three FILE-CONTROL entries, lines 00130 through 00150, for the two input files and the print file. The table of state codes and names, lines 00470 through 00520, is now defined without VALUE clauses or a REDEFINES clause. In Program P10-04 the table is initialized instead by READ and MOVE statements, as you will see. Each input record will be assigned to one of the 16 STATE-ENTRY fields, with the first two characters of each input record being assigned to a STATE-CODE field and characters 3 through 13 of the input record assigned to a STATE-NAME field.

The OCCURS clause, line 00490, now contains an **ASCENDING KEY** phrase. The ASCENDING KEY phrase tells COBOL the field that the table is ordered on. In this case our table is in order on STATE-CODE. A table may also be stored in descending order, and then the programmer would specify a **DE-**

FIGURE 10.14 **Program P10-04**

```
S COBOL II RELEASE 3.1 09/19/89                   P10004   DATE AUG 19,1991 T
----+-*A-1-B--+----2----+----3----+----4----+----5----+----6----+----7-%--+

       IDENTIFICATION DIVISION.
       PROGRAM-ID.  P10-04.
      *AUTHOR.  DEBORAH ANN SENIOR.
      *
      *     THIS PROGRAM SHOWS HOW AN ARGUMENT AND A FUNCTION MAY
      *     APPEAR AS A SINGLE TABLE ENTRY
      *
      *****************************************************************

       ENVIRONMENT DIVISION.
       INPUT-OUTPUT SECTION.
       FILE-CONTROL.
           SELECT TABLE-FILE-IN              ASSIGN TO TABLEIN.
           SELECT ADDRESS-FILE-IN            ASSIGN TO INFILE.
           SELECT ADDRESS-REPORT-FILE-OUT    ASSIGN TO PRINTER.

      *****************************************************************

       DATA DIVISION.
       FILE SECTION.
       FD  ADDRESS-FILE-IN
           RECORD CONTAINS 80 CHARACTERS.

       01  ADDRESS-RECORD-IN.
           05  STATE-AND-CITY-IN.
               10  STATE-CODE-IN                    PIC XX.
               10  CITY-NAME-IN                     PIC X(20).

       FD  ADDRESS-REPORT-FILE-OUT.

       01  REPORT-LINE                              PIC X(79).

       FD  TABLE-FILE-IN
           RECORD CONTAINS 80 CHARACTERS.

       01  TABLE-RECORD-IN                          PIC X(80).

       WORKING-STORAGE SECTION.
       01  MORE-INPUT              PIC X           VALUE "Y".
           88 THERE-IS-NO-MORE-INPUT               VALUE "N".
       01  MORE-TABLE-INPUT        PIC X           VALUE "Y".
           88 THERE-IS-NO-MORE-TABLE-INPUT         VALUE "N".
       01  NUMBER-OF-TABLE-ENTRIES
               COMP SYNC           PIC S99         VALUE 16.
       01  LINE-SPACING            PIC S9          COMP SYNC.

       01  .
           05  STATE-ENTRY
               OCCURS 16 TIMES ASCENDING KEY STATE-CODE
               INDEXED BY STATE-INDEX.
               10  STATE-CODE   PIC XX.
               10  STATE-NAME   PIC X(11).

       01  PAGE-HEADING-1.
           05                      PIC X(30)       VALUE SPACES.
           05                      PIC X(11)       VALUE "STATE NAMES".

       01  PAGE-HEADING-2.
           05                      PIC X(18)       VALUE SPACES.
           05                      PIC X(5)        VALUE "INPUT".
           05                      PIC X(29)       VALUE SPACES.
           05                      PIC X(14)       VALUE "CITY AND STATE".
```

continued

SCENDING KEY.** Whenever a SEARCH ALL is to be used on a table, the table must be defined with an ASCENDING KEY or DESCENDING KEY phrase. It is the programmer's responsibility to ensure that each and every entry in the table is in the order indicated by the ASCENDING KEY or DESCENDING KEY phrase. If an ASCENDING KEY or DESCENDING KEY phrase is used, it must appear before the INDEXED BY phrase in the OCCURS clause.

The INDEXED BY phrase names a single index name for the whole table. The single index name STATE-INDEX can now be used to refer to all the state codes and all the state names. One index does the job instead of two.

Since each input record in the table file contains two fields, both a state code and a state name, two PICTUREs are needed to describe them. The two PICTUREs are shown in the level-10 entries in lines 00510 and 00520. These level-10 entries also permit us to give the names STATE-CODE and STATE-NAME to the appropriate parts of each input record.

This table could have been written into working storage using VALUE clauses and a REDEFINES clause. In that case the table would have been written this way:

```
01 .
    05 STATE-TABLE ENTRIES.
        10          PIC X(13) VALUE "AKALASKA".
        10          PIC X(13) VALUE "ALALABAMA".
        10          PIC X(13) VALUE "AZARIZONA".
        10          PIC X(13) VALUE "ARARKANSAS".
        10          PIC X(13) VALUE "CACALIFORNIA".
        10          PIC X(13) VALUE "COCOLORADO".
        10          PIC X(13) VALUE "CTCONNECTICUT".
        10          PIC X(13) VALUE "DEDELAWARE".
        10          PIC X(13) VALUE "FLFLORIDA".
        10          PIC X(13) VALUE "GAGEORGIA".
        10          PIC X(13) VALUE "HIHAWAII".
        10          PIC X(13) VALUE "IAIOWA".
        10          PIC X(13) VALUE "IDIDAHO".
        10          PIC X(13) VALUE "ILILLINOIS".
        10          PIC X(13) VALUE "ININDIANA".
        10          PIC X(13) VALUE "KSKANSAS".
    05 STATE-ENTRY REDEFINES STATE-TABLE-ENTRIES
        OCCURS 16 TIMES ASCENDING KEY STATE-CODE
        INDEXED BY STATE-INDEX.
        10 STATE-CODE PIC XX.
        10 STATE-NAME PIC X(11).
```

The level-10 entries for STATE-CODE and STATE-NAME are subordinate to the level-05 entry called STATE-ENTRY. Items subordinate to an entry that contains an OCCURS clause must be subscripted or indexed whenever they appear in the program. In this case both STATE-CODE and STATE-NAME would be indexed by STATE-INDEX. You will see how when we look at the Procedure Division.

At line 00720 there is a level-01 entry for an output line called NOT-IN-TABLE-DETAIL-LINE. This will be used if an invalid state code should appear in the input and no match can be found in the table. In earlier programs in this chapter we made no provision for invalid input data, but in Program P10-04 we will print the words "State code invalid" if no match can be found between the STATE-CODE-IN and the STATE-CODEs in the table. Notice that the error message "State code invalid" is superior to an error message such as "State code not in table." The latter message is clear to the programmer but would not be clear to users of the report. Users are unaware of any table; on seeing a message such as "State code not in table" they would not know what to do—whether to fix the state code, fix the table, or do nothing. The message "State code invalid," on the other hand, alerts users to an error and implies action on their part.

The CONTROL-PARAGRAPH of the Procedure Division begins at line 00860. Before any of the usual processing is done, we first PERFORM the steps needed to load the table of state codes and names from the external table file. Those steps are shown in lines 00940 through 01080. Here we are assuming that the table file contains exactly the number of records needed to fill the table, 16.

FIGURE ***10.14*** ***continued***

```
S COBOL II RELEASE 3.1 09/19/89                    P10004    DATE AUG 19,1991 T
----+-*A-1-B--+----2----+----3----+----4----+----5----+----6----+----7-%--+

00650  01  IN-TABLE-DETAIL-LINE.
00660      05                            PIC X(10) VALUE SPACES.
00670      05 STATE-AND-CITY-OUT         PIC X(22).
00680      05                            PIC X(8)  VALUE SPACES.
00690      05 CITY-NAME-OUT              PIC X(20)B.
00700      05 STATE-NAME-OUT             PIC X(11).
00710
00720  01  NOT-IN-TABLE-DETAIL-LINE.
00730      05                            PIC X(10) VALUE SPACES.
00740      05 STATE-AND-CITY-ERR         PIC X(22).
00750      05 CITY-NAME-ERR              PIC B(8)X(20)B.
00760      05                            PIC X(18)
00770         VALUE "STATE CODE INVALID".
00780
00790  01  NO-INPUT-DATA.
00800      05                  PIC X(29)       VALUE SPACES.
00810      05                  PIC X(13)       VALUE "NO INPUT DATA".
00820
00830 ******************************************************************
00840
00850  PROCEDURE DIVISION.
00860  CONTROL-PARAGRAPH.
00870      PERFORM LOAD-STATE-TABLE
00880      PERFORM INITIALIZATION
00890      PERFORM MAIN-PROCESS UNTIL THERE-IS-NO-MORE-INPUT
00900      PERFORM TERMINATION
00910      STOP RUN
00920      .
00930
00940  LOAD-STATE-TABLE.
00950      OPEN INPUT TABLE-FILE-IN
00960      PERFORM LOAD-ONE-TABLE-ENTRY VARYING STATE-INDEX
00970          FROM 1 BY 1 UNTIL
00980          STATE-INDEX GREATER THAN NUMBER-OF-TABLE-ENTRIES
00990      CLOSE TABLE-FILE-IN
01000      .
01010
01020  LOAD-ONE-TABLE-ENTRY.
01030      READ TABLE-FILE-IN
01040          AT END
01050              SET THERE-IS-NO-MORE-TABLE-INPUT TO TRUE
01060      END-READ
01070      MOVE TABLE-RECORD-IN TO STATE-ENTRY (STATE-INDEX)
01080      .
```

continued

In that case end-of-file would never be read because the statement at line 00960 would execute the paragraph LOAD-ONE-TABLE-ENTRY only 16 times. If the table file should accidentally contain more than 16 records, only the first 16 would be read. If it should accidentally contain fewer than 16 records, the program would terminate abnormally when the READ statement at line 01030 tried to READ past end-of-file. In either case, the table file would have to be fixed by hand and the program run again.

In MAIN-PROCESS, beginning at line 01220, there is a SEARCH ALL statement, but no SET statement. The SEARCH ALL statement searches the entire table, unlike the ordinary SEARCH statement, which starts its sequential search from wherever we SET the index initially. Different COBOL systems may carry out a SEARCH ALL in different ways. Usually SEARCH ALL will not search sequentially but will hop around the table in some way.[1] Remember that SEARCH ALL will usually search a table faster than an ordinary SEARCH statement will. The improvement in speed becomes more noticeable with very large tables. Of course, to use SEARCH ALL the tables arguments must be in ASCENDING or DESCENDING order. To use an ordinary SEARCH, the table arguments may be in any order.

Following the words SEARCH ALL is the data name STATE-ENTRY. Even though it's the STATE-CODE fields that we want to examine during the search, the data name following the words SEARCH or SEARCH ALL must always be the name that has attached to it an OCCURS clause with an INDEXED BY phrase.

This SEARCH ALL statement shows the use of the optional AT END phrase. The AT END phrase may be used to tell COBOL what to do if the SEARCH examines the whole table without satisfying the WHEN conditions. In our case we will print a line containing the words ''State code invalid'' if the SEARCH ALL finds no match. The AT END phrase may be used in a SEARCH statement as well as in a SEARCH ALL statement.

The WHEN condition, line 01260, is written slightly differently in this program than in Program P10-03. In standard COBOL the index name being used for the SEARCH ALL must appear as an index on the left side of the equal sign. This requirement applies only to the SEARCH ALL statement and not to an ordinary SEARCH. Another requirement of the SEARCH ALL is that the only condition allowed in a WHEN clause is an equal condition. In SEARCH any condition may appear in a WHEN clause.

You can see how the STATE-NAME is printed on the output report, in the MOVE statement at line 01460. The SEARCH statement, line 01230, assigns the correct value to STATE-INDEX, so the correct STATE-NAME is MOVEd to the output area.

Program P10-04 was run with the state code and city name input data shown in Figure 10.15 and produced the output shown in Figure 10.16.

[1]In the system used to run the programs in this book, SEARCH ALL is implemented with a **binary search.** Binary search is not specified in the ANSI standard.

FIGURE ***10.14*** ***continued***

```
S COBOL II RELEASE 3.1 09/19/89                P10004   DATE AUG 19,1991 T
----+-*A-1-B--+----2----+----3----+----4----+----5----+----6----+----7-%--+

 INITIALIZATION.
     OPEN INPUT  ADDRESS-FILE-IN
          OUTPUT ADDRESS-REPORT-FILE-OUT
     WRITE REPORT-LINE FROM PAGE-HEADING-1 AFTER PAGE
     WRITE REPORT-LINE FROM PAGE-HEADING-2 AFTER 2
     MOVE 3 TO LINE-SPACING
     PERFORM READ-A-CARD
     IF MORE-INPUT IS EQUAL TO "N"
         WRITE REPORT-LINE FROM NO-INPUT-DATA AFTER 3
     END-IF
     .

 MAIN-PROCESS.
     SEARCH ALL STATE-ENTRY
         AT END
             PERFORM PRODUCE-NOT-IN-TABLE-DETAIL
         WHEN STATE-CODE (STATE-INDEX) = STATE-CODE-IN
             PERFORM PRODUCE-IN-TABLE-DETAIL
     END-SEARCH
     PERFORM READ-A-CARD
     .

 TERMINATION.
     CLOSE ADDRESS-FILE-IN
           ADDRESS-REPORT-FILE-OUT
     .

 READ-A-CARD.
     READ ADDRESS-FILE-IN
         AT END
             SET THERE-IS-NO-MORE-INPUT TO TRUE
     .

 PRODUCE-IN-TABLE-DETAIL.
     MOVE STATE-AND-CITY-IN              TO STATE-AND-CITY-OUT
     MOVE CITY-NAME-IN                   TO CITY-NAME-OUT
     MOVE STATE-NAME (STATE-INDEX)       TO STATE-NAME-OUT
     WRITE REPORT-LINE FROM IN-TABLE-DETAIL-LINE
                       AFTER LINE-SPACING
     MOVE 2                              TO LINE-SPACING
     .

 PRODUCE-NOT-IN-TABLE-DETAIL.
     MOVE STATE-AND-CITY-IN              TO STATE-AND-CITY-ERR
     MOVE CITY-NAME-IN                   TO CITY-NAME-ERR
     WRITE REPORT-LINE FROM NOT-IN-TABLE-DETAIL-LINE
                       AFTER LINE-SPACING
     MOVE 2                              TO LINE-SPACING
     .
```

FIGURE 10.15 State code and city input to Program P10-04

```
--------------------------------------------------------------------------------
         1         2         3         4         5         6         7         8
12345678901234567890123456789012345678901234567890123456789012345678901234567890
--------------------------------------------------------------------------------
AKNOME
IADES MOINES
PQMONTREAL
KSWICHITA
CTHARTFORD
CASAN FRANCISCO
NYBROOKLYN
FLMIAMI
HIHONOLULU
```

FIGURE 10.16 Output from Program P10-04

```
                          STATE NAMES

             INPUT                              CITY AND STATE

AKNOME                          NOME                   ALASKA

IADES MOINES                    DES MOINES             IOWA

PQMONTREAL                      MONTREAL               STATE CODE INVALID

KSWICHITA                       WICHITA                KANSAS

CTHARTFORD                      HARTFORD               CONNECTICUT

CASAN FRANCISCO                 SAN FRANCISCO          CALIFORNIA

NYBROOKLYN                      BROOKLYN               STATE CODE INVALID

FLMIAMI                         MIAMI                  FLORIDA

HIHONOLULU                      HONOLULU               HAWAII
```

The SEARCH ALL Statement

The format of the SEARCH ALL statement is as follows:

```
SEARCH ALL identifier-1 [AT END imperative-statement-1]

        { data-name-1 {IS EQUAL TO} {identifier-3              } }
   WHEN {             {IS =       } {literal-1                 } }
        {                           {arithmetic-expression-1   } }
        { condition-name-1                                        }

   [     { data-name-2 {IS EQUAL TO} {identifier-4            } } ]
   [ AND {             {IS =       } {literal-2               } } ] ...
   [     {                           {arithmetic-expression-2 } } ]
   [     { condition-name-2                                      } ]

   {imperative-statement-2}
   {NEXT SENTENCE         }

   [END-SEARCH]
```

If one or more condition names are used, each condition name specified must have only a single value.

The format shows that a SEARCH ALL statement must contain exactly one WHEN clause, but the clause may contain as many conditions as desired, connected by AND. A SEARCH ALL terminates WHEN all conditions are satisfied. An ordinary SEARCH, on the other hand, may contain as many WHEN conditions as desired, and the SEARCH terminates when any of them is satisfied.

The index name associated with the table being searched must appear on the left side of the condition and must not appear on the right side.

EXERCISE 7

Write a program to read input and produce output in the same formats as in Exercise 6. Have your program read in the branch office table from an external file containing records in the following format:

Positions	Field
1–2	Branch Office Number
3–25	Branch Office Name
26–80	spaces

Arrange the table in working storage so that you need only one index.

Include in your test data several records with invalid Branch Office Numbers. For each such input record, have your program print on one line the Agent Name, the Branch Office Number, and the words ''Branch office number invalid.''

The OCCURS Clause

There are two formats of the OCCURS clause. The one we have been using is as follows:

```
OCCURS integer-1 TIMES

    [{ASCENDING }
     {DESCENDING} KEY IS {data-name-2} ... ] ...

    [INDEXED BY {index-name-1} ... ]
```

The format shows that an OCCURS clause may have more than one index associated with it. Having more than one index associated with a single OCCURS clause provides a convenient way to point to more than one element in an indexed table at a time. Any given index, though, can be associated with only one OCCURS clause.

The format also shows that the table elements may be ordered on more than one ASCENDING KEY or DESCENDING KEY. If so, the keys must be listed in the OCCURS clause from major to minor.

The other format of the OCCURS clause, used for variable-length tables, is as follows:

```
OCCURS integer-1 TO integer-2 TIMES DEPENDING ON data-name-1

 [{ASCENDING }
  {DESCENDING} KEY IS {data-name-2 ... ] ...
 [INDEXED BY {index-name-1} ... ]
```

In this format, the table always contains a number of elements equal to the value assigned to data-name-1. Data-name-1 must be a positive integer within the range of integer-1 through integer-2.

Format 2 of the SET Statement

Format 2 of the SET statement may be used to increase or decrease the setting of one or more indexes. The format is given in the ANSI standard exactly as follows:

```
SET {index-name-3} ... {UP BY  } {identifier-3}
                       {DOWN BY} {integer-2   }
```

The receiving fields in this format are index-name-3, index-name-4, etc. After the SET statement is executed, the receiving field indexes must be within the range of their tables.

The sending fields are identifier-3, which must be an integer, or integer-2. They refer to the number of table elements (1, 2, 3, and so on) that the indexes are to be increased or decreased by.

Identifier-3, if used, may be a subscripted or indexed data name and may be indexed by one of the receiving fields. Receiving fields are acted upon in the order in which they appear in the SET statement. The value of the sending field at the beginning of execution of the SET statement is used for all receiving fields.

Summary

If a program has to process several related fields all having the same description, the fields may be defined with an OCCURS clause and then subscripted or indexed. A subscript may be an integer literal or an identifier defined as an integer. An index may be an integer literal or an index name.

If a field is to be indexed, its OCCURS clause must contain an INDEXED BY phrase. An index name, given in an INDEXED BY phrase, must not be otherwise defined in the program.

Any table can be written into working storage with VALUE clauses or be read in from an external file.

A direct-reference table can be written in working storage as a series of constant entries preceded by a group-level name. Any field defined as an integer may be used as a subscript to refer to any item in the table directly.

A search table may be entered into a COBOL program with each argument and each function a separate entry. Alternatively, each argument and its corresponding function may appear together as a single entry.

The SET statement may be used to assign a value to an index. The SEARCH statement may be used to step through a table until one or more specified conditions are met. The SEARCH ALL statement will usually search a table faster than an ordinary SEARCH statement. If SEARCH ALL is used, the OCCURS clause that defines the table must contain either the ASCENDING KEY or DESCENDING KEY phrase, or both, and the table items must be ordered on the key or keys named in the phrase.

Fill-In Exercises

1. In order for a field to be subscripted or indexed, it must be defined with a(n) ______ clause.
2. For a field to be indexed, its OCCURS clause must include a(n) ______ phrase.
3. If a SEARCH ALL statement is used on a table, its OCCURS clause must include a(n) ______ phrase or a(n) ______ phrase.
4. The field "TAX-AMOUNT subscripted by TAX-SUBSCRIPT" would be written in COBOL as ______.
5. A subscript may be a positive or unsigned integer numeric literal or a field defined as a(n) ______.
6. The value of a subscript may be controlled by a PERFORM statement with the ______ option.
7. A table that can be used without being searched is called a(n) ______ table.
8. COBOL can process tables of up to ______ dimensions.
9. A name given in an INDEXED BY phrase is called a(n) ______ ______.
10. The ______ clause can be used to specify the conditions under which a SEARCH or SEARCH ALL should terminate.
11. A table in COBOL is any group of fields defined with a(n) ______ clause.
12. A REDEFINES clause may be used in a level-01 entry in the ______ Section.
13. If an ASCENDING KEY phrase in an OCCURS clause contains the names of more than one field, the fields must be listed in order from ______ to ______.
14. The only relational operator allowed in a relation condition in a SEARCH ALL statement is ______.
15. The ______ phrase may be used in a SEARCH statement when one index name is to keep pace with another.

Review Exercises

1. Given the following fields:

```
05 AGE-RANGE            PIC 9(3)      OCCURS 15 TIMES.
05 OCCUPATION-CLASS PIC X            OCCURS 10 TIMES.
05 A-SUBSCRIPT          PIC S99.
05 B-SUBSCRIPT          PIC S99.
```

a. Which of the following statements could be legal in a COBOL program?

1. MOVE A-SUBSCRIPT (OCCUPATION-CLASS) TO LINE-OUT.

2. MOVE OCCUPATION-CLASS (B-SUBSCRIPT) TO LINE-OUT.

3. SUBTRACT 1 FROM A-SUBSCRIPT.

b. What is the highest value that may legally be assigned to B-SUBSCRIPT at the time statement 2 executes?

2. Given the following table:

```
01 CITY-TABLE.
   05 CITY-TABLE-ENTRIES.
      10          PIC X(12) VALUE "PEEKSKILL".
      10          PIC X(12) VALUE "PLATTSBURGH".
      10          PIC X(12) VALUE "PORT JERVIS".
      10          PIC X(12) VALUE "POUGHKEEPSIE".
   05 CITY REDEFINES CITY-TABLE-ENTRIES
                  PIC X(12) OCCURS 4 TIMES.
```

What will be MOVEd to LINE-OUT by the following pair of statements?

```
MOVE 2 TO CITY-SUBSCRIPT
MOVE CITY (CITY-SUBSCRIPT) TO LINE-OUT
```

3. Write a program to read input records in the following format:

Positions	Field
1–6	Store Number
7–12	January Sales (in whole dollars)
13–18	February Sales (in whole dollars)
19–24	March Sales (in whole dollars)
25–30	April Sales (in whole dollars)
31–36	May Sales (in whole dollars)
37–42	June Sales (in whole dollars)
43–48	July Sales (in whole dollars)
49–54	August Sales (in whole dollars)
55–60	September Sales (in whole dollars)
61–66	October Sales (in whole dollars)
67–72	November Sales (in whole dollars)
73–78	December Sales (in whole dollars)
79–80	spaces

Each record contains a Store Number and a sales amount for each month of the year. For each record, have your program compute the sales tax for each month (at 4 percent of the sales amount) and print on one line the Store Number, the sales tax for each month, and the total sales tax for the year. At the end of the report print the total sales tax for the year for all stores.

4. A program can determine the day of the week that a particular date falls on if it is given the date (as a number from 1 to 365 or 366) and the day of the week that the year begins on. Assign each day of the week a number 1 through 7 in order from Sunday through Saturday. 1993 began on day 6 (a Friday). 1994 begins on day 7 (a Saturday).

   Write a program to read input data in the following format:

Positions	Field
1–3	Day Number of Year
4	Day Number of the Day on which the year begins (1 through 7)
5–80	spaces

   Each input record contains a date as a number from 1 to 366 and the day number that the year begins on.

   For each input record, have your program print on one line the original input and the name of the day of the week that the date falls on.

5. Write a program to read input records in the following format:

Positions	Field
1–5	Employee Number
6	Job Classification Code
7–14	Annual Salary (to two decimal places)
15–80	spaces

   There is one record for each employee. Each record contains a Job Classification Code and an Annual Salary. For each input record, print on one line the Employee Number, the employee's Job Classification Code, the employee's job title and the employee's Annual Salary. At the end of the report print a total of all the salaries.

   Use the table below for Job Classification Codes and job titles. In your program, enter each argument and each function as a separate entry. Use two indexes. Use an ordinary SEARCH statement.

   Include in your test data several records with invalid Job Classification Codes. For each such input record print on one line the employee number, the words "Job classification code invalid," and the employee's Annual Salary. Use the following Job Classification Codes and job titles in your program:

Job Classification Code	Job Title
Z	Smelter apprentice
Y	Junior smelter
X	Smelter
W	Gang chief
V	Foreman
6	Superintendent
5	Section manager
4	Division manager
3	Plant manager
2	Assistant vice-president
1	Vice-president
0	President

6. Write a program to read input and produce output in the same formats as in Review Exercise 5. Write each row of the job table as a single entry in your program. Arrange the entries so that the Job Classification Codes are in ascending order on your computer. Use a SEARCH ALL statement.
7. Modify your solution to Review Exercise 6 so that the job table entries are read in from an external file.

Project

Write a program to read records in the following format:

Positions	Field
1–9	Employee Number
10–15	Gross Pay
16–80	spaces

Each record contains an Employee Number and a Gross Pay amount for the employee. Have your program compute a tax on the gross Pay according to the following table:

If Gross Pay is:	Tax is
less than \$100	3% of Gross Pay
at least \$100 but less than \$200	\$3 plus 4% of the excess over \$100
at least \$200 but less than \$500	\$7 plus 5% of the excess over \$200
at least \$500 but less than \$1000	\$22 plus 6% of the excess over \$500
at least \$1000 but less than \$2000	\$52 plus 7% of the excess over \$1000
at least \$2000 but less than \$5000	\$122 plus 8% of the excess over \$2000
at least \$5000	\$362 plus 9% of the excess over \$5000

Write the tax rates and the ranges of Gross Pay into one or more tables in your program as constants. Use a SEARCH statement to find the tax rates for each input record. For each record read, have your program print the Employee Number, the Gross Pay, and the tax amount computed by the program. Design a report with suitable headings before you begin coding.

CHAPTER 11

Tables of Higher Dimension

HERE ARE THE KEY POINTS YOU SHOULD LEARN FROM THIS CHAPTER

1. The need for tables of higher dimension
2. How to set up two- and three-dimensional tables in COBOL programs
3. How to program for two- and three-dimensional tables
4. How to load a table of more than three dimensions

KEY WORDS TO RECOGNIZE AND LEARN

row
column
caption
in-line PERFORM
out-of-line PERFORM
END-PERFORM
AFTER
END-SEARCH

A two-dimensional table is one in which two arguments are needed to find a function. One example of a two-dimensional table is a table showing the monthly payment per $1 of loan amount for loans of various interest rates and numbers of payments. If we wanted to find the monthly payment per $1 of principal for a 20-year home-mortgage loan (240 payments) at 12.5%, we could do so in such a table. A three-dimensional table needs three arguments to find a function. An example of a three-dimensional table is a table of insurance premiums for 5-year renewable term insurance where a person's age and sex and the face amount of the policy are needed to find a particular premium amount.

The first program in this chapter deals with a sales application. The program uses accumulators arranged as a two-dimensional table to compute the total sales in each of five stores in each of 6 months. Each accumulator is one element of the table and is identified by two arguments—a store number and a month number.

A Program with a Two-Dimensional Table

Program P11-01 processes input data in the following format:

Positions	Field
1	Store Number
2–6	Customer Number
7–12	January Sales (to two decimal places)
13–18	February Sales (to two decimal places)
19–24	March Sales (to two decimal places)
25–30	April Sales (to two decimal places)
31–36	May Sales (to two decimal places)
37–42	June Sales (to two decimal places)
43–80	spaces

Each record contains a Store Number, a Customer Number, and Sales for 6 months, January through June. Naturally, each store services many customers, and so the input will contain many records for each store. The stores are numbered 1 through 5. The input data might be in any random order; that is, we cannot assume that all records for a store are grouped together in the input.

Program P11-01 is to accumulate the total sales for each store for each month and produce a report in the format shown in Figure 11.1. The body of the report has the appearance of a typical two-dimensional table. It has **rows,** going across the page from left to right, and **columns,** going from top to bottom. The rows and columns have **captions,** saying what the rows and columns stand for. In our case each row represents a different store number and each column a different month. At the intersection of each row and column is a sales amount for that store and month.

FIGURE *11.1* **Output format for Program P11-01**

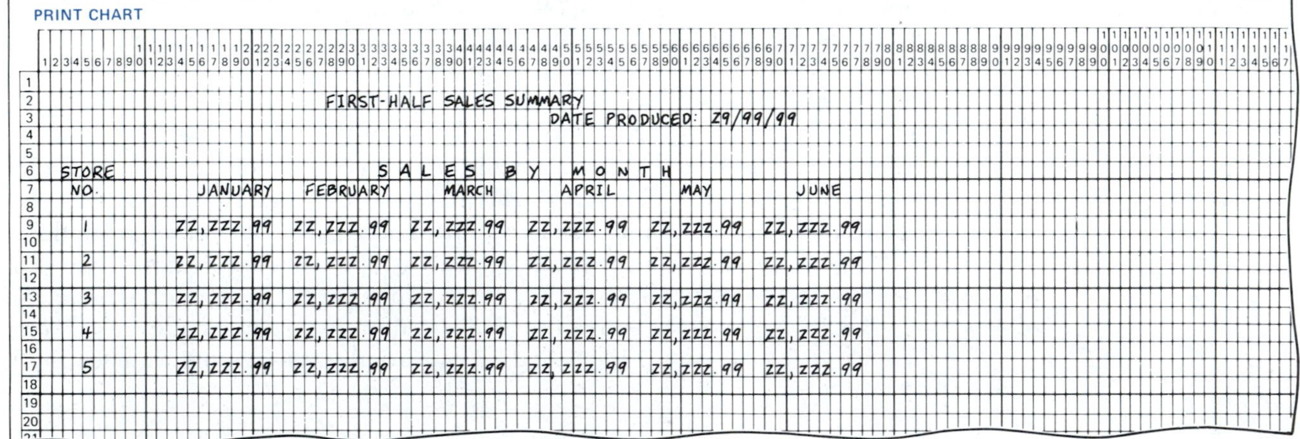

Since the input data are in no particular order, this report cannot be produced in the same way that our earlier reports were produced. That is, we cannot accumulate all the data for store 1, print them, and then go on to process store 2, because we cannot be sure that all the records for store 1 precede the records for store 2. Thus we must set up 30 accumulators in storage, one for each store for each month. Then, as the program reads each input record, it can determine which accumulators to add the various sales amounts into. After all the data have been read and accumulated, the report can be printed.

Top-Down Design for Program P11-01

This program is sufficiently difficult that we should do a top-down design before we begin coding. As we do the design, we must remember that for each input record we can do no more than add the sales amounts to the appropriate accumulators. We cannot print anything until after all the input records have been read and processed.

The first stage of the design is shown in the hierarchy diagram in Figure 11.2. There we have broken the main function of the program into the usual three subfunctions:

a. What we have to do before entering the main loop of the program

b. The main loop

c. What we do after end-of-file

FIGURE *11.2* **The first stage of a hierarchy diagram for Program P11-01**

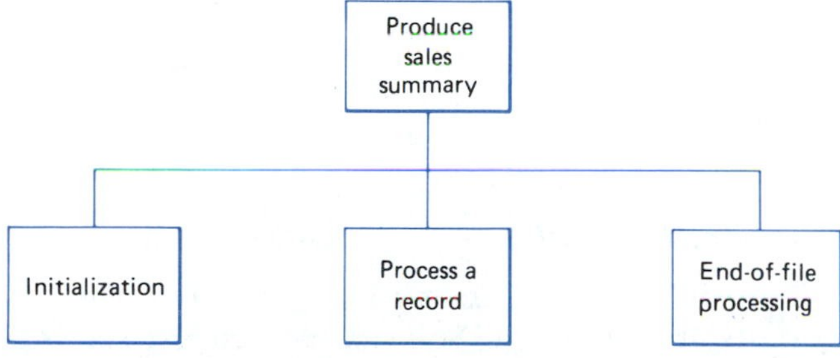

Now we can elaborate on the three subfunctions as necessary. The "Initialization" procedure contains nothing except the usual initializing steps that we have in earlier programs. The box "Process a record" needs a lower-level subfunction to show that each input record has its sales fields added to the appropriate six accumulators in storage. No printing is done.

The box "End-of-file processing" needs subfunctions to show exactly what processes are executed after end-of-file is reached on the input. Figure 11.3 shows that after end-of-file we can "Print the report" and then "Close files." The subfunction of "Print the report" shows that the report can be printed line after line with no further processing of input data. The subfunction of "Print a line" shows that we will need a separate paragraph to format each line of the report. You will see why when we look at the program. The hierarchy diagram in Figure 11.3 thus shows the complete design.

FIGURE *11.3* Complete hierarchy diagram for Program P11-01

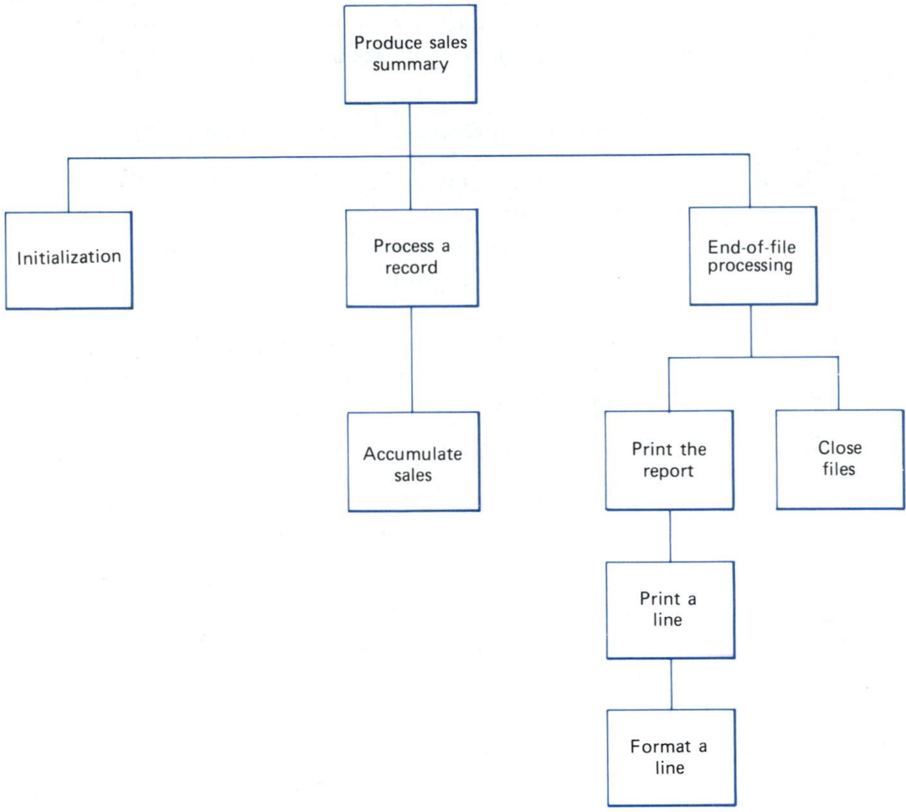

Program P11-01

Program P11-01 is shown in Figure 11.4. The definition of the input record starts at line 00230. You can see that the six SALE-AMOUNT-IN fields in the input record have been defined with an OCCURS clause, at line 00260. The value of STORE-NUMBER-IN, line 00240, used together with the month numbers 1 through 6, enables the program to refer to the six accumulators that the SALE-AMOUNT-IN amounts are to be added into.

The Working Storage Section begins at line 00320. The fields NUMBER-OF-STORES and NUMBER-OF-MONTHS have been established. The reasons for having these fields are the usual: If the number of stores changes or the number of months covered by the report changes, the program will be easier to modify than if we had the numbers 5 or 6 appear in the Procedure Division. Also, the Procedure Division is made more readable by the use of the names NUMBER-OF-STORES and NUMBER-OF-MONTHS rather than the numbers 5 and 6.

You can see how the 30 sales accumulators have been set up, at SALES-ACCUMULATOR-TABLE in line 00400. The level-05 entry names the row caption and says how many rows there are. The level-10 entry names the column caption and says how many columns there are. Finally the level-15 entry names the table item itself, SALES-ACCUMULATOR, and gives its PICTURE. The VALUE clause in line 00430 initializes all 30 accumulators to 0. The OCCURS clauses at lines 00410 and 00420 contain no INDEXED BY phrases because it turns out to be more convenient to use subscripting in this program than indexing.

FIGURE *11.4*

Program P11-01

```
S COBOL II RELEASE 3.1 09/19/89                  P11001   DATE JUL 09,1991 T
----+-*A-1-B--+----2----+----3----+----4----+----5----+----6----+----7-|--+

00010  IDENTIFICATION DIVISION.
00020  PROGRAM-ID.  P11-01.
00030 *AUTHOR.  DEBORAH ANN SENIOR.
00040 *
00050 *     THIS PROGRAM ACCUMULATES AND PRINTS SALES TOTALS
00060 *     FOR 5 STORES FOR 6 MONTHS
00070 *
00080 ******************************************************************
00090
00100  ENVIRONMENT DIVISION.
00110  INPUT-OUTPUT SECTION.
00120  FILE-CONTROL.
00130      SELECT SALES-FILE-IN          ASSIGN TO INFILE.
00140      SELECT SALES-REPORT-FILE-OUT  ASSIGN TO PRINTER.
00150
00160 ******************************************************************
00170
00180  DATA DIVISION.
00190  FILE SECTION.
00200  FD  SALES-FILE-IN
00210      RECORD CONTAINS 80 CHARACTERS.
00220
00230  01  SALES-RECORD-IN.
00240      05  STORE-NUMBER-IN          PIC 9.
00250      05  CUSTOMER-NUMBER-IN       PIC X(5).
00260      05  SALE-AMOUNT-IN           PIC 9(4)V99      OCCURS 6 TIMES.
00270
00280  FD  SALES-REPORT-FILE-OUT.
00290
00300  01  REPORT-LINE          PIC X(77).
00310
00320  WORKING-STORAGE SECTION.
00330  01  MORE-INPUT           PIC X           VALUE "Y".
00340      88 THERE-IS-NO-MORE-INPUT            VALUE "N".
00350  01  NUMBER-OF-STORES     PIC S99         VALUE 5
00360                           COMP            SYNC.
00370  01  NUMBER-OF-MONTHS     PIC S99         VALUE 6
00380                           COMP            SYNC.
00390  01  LINE-SPACING         PIC S9          COMP SYNC.
00400  01  SALES-ACCUMULATOR-TABLE              PACKED-DECIMAL.
00410      05  STORE            OCCURS 5 TIMES.
00420          10  MONTH        OCCURS 6 TIMES.
00430              15  SALES-ACCUMULATOR        PIC S9(5)V99 VALUE 0.
00440  01  MONTH-SUBSCRIPT      PIC S99         COMP SYNC.
00450  01  STORE-SUBSCRIPT      PIC S99         COMP SYNC.
00460
00470  01  PAGE-HEAD-1.
00480      05                   PIC X(27)       VALUE SPACES.
00490      05                   PIC X(24)
00500                           VALUE "FIRST-HALF SALES SUMMARY".
00510
```

continued

You should consider using subscripting instead of indexing on a table whenever an input field is used directly as a subscript to refer to elements of the table and/or whenever the subscript value itself is to be used as an output field. Both situations are present in this program. The input field STORE-NUMBER-IN is used to refer to elements in the SALES-ACCUMULATOR-TABLE, and the subscript STORE-SUBSCRIPT is printed as part of the output.

Whenever we refer to one of the 30 SALES-ACCUMULATORS, we must use two subscripts to say which row and which column we are referring to. The subscripts must appear in parentheses in the order in which the OCCURS clauses are written. In Program P11-01 a reference to SALES-ACCUMULATOR could be

```
SALES-ACCUMULATOR (STORE-SUBSCRIPT, MONTH-SUBSCRIPT)
```

Either or both of these subscripts could be given as integer literals, if desired. For example, SALES-ACCUMULATOR (3, 2) refers to the sales in store 3 for February. Also

```
SALES-ACCUMULATOR (STORE-SUBSCRIPT, 4)
```

could refer to any of the April accumulators, depending on the value of STORE-SUBSCRIPT.

There is another way in which this table could have been set up. The MONTHs could have been named at the 05 level and the STORE-NUMBERs at the 10 level. That is, we could have had

```
05 MONTH      OCCURS 6 TIMES
   10 STORE   OCCURS 5 TIMES
```

In either case, the individual table entry would be given at the 15 level.

If the table had been set up as shown above, with the MONTHs named at the 05 level, then references to SALES-ACCUMULATOR would have to be of the form

```
SALES-ACCUMULATOR (MONTH-SUBSCRIPT, STORE-SUBSCRIPT)
```

and SALES-ACCUMULATOR (3, 2) would refer to the March sales in store 2.

Two detail lines have been defined, at lines 00740 and 00780. One of them is used only when there are no input data, and the other is used to print all five lines of accumulators. When the detail line at line 00740 is to be printed the first time, STORE-SUBSCRIPT will be assigned the value 1 and all the accumulators for store 1 will print. Then STORE-SUBSCRIPT will be assigned the value 2, and the accumulators for store 2 will print, and so on. You will see exactly how it all happens when we look at the Procedure Division.

The Procedure Division begins at line 00880. In the paragraph PROCESS-A-RECORD there is a PERFORM . . . VARYING statement, at line 01130. Each time the program enters PROCESS-A-RECORD, it has in its input area a record containing sales for 6 months and a store number. We want to add, from the input record, January's sales into the January accumulator for that store, and then add, from the input record, February's sales into the February accumulator for that store, and so on. That is, we want to vary the MONTH-SUBSCRIPT through all the months. The PERFORM statement at line 01130 does it. The

FIGURE 11.4 *continued*

```
S COBOL II RELEASE 3.1 09/19/89                    P11001    DATE JUL 09,1991 T
----+-*A-1-B--+----2----+----3----+----4----+----5----+----6----+----7-|--+

       01  PAGE-HEAD-2.
           05                     PIC X(48)        VALUE SPACES.
           05                     PIC X(15)        VALUE "DATE PRODUCED:".
           05 RUN-MONTH-DAY       PIC Z9/99/.
           05 RUN-YEAR            PIC 99.

       01  PAGE-HEAD-3.
           05                     PIC XX           VALUE SPACES.
           05                     PIC X(30)        VALUE "STORE".
           05                     PIC X(27)
                                  VALUE "S A L E S   B Y   M O N T H".

       01  PAGE-HEAD-4.
           05                     PIC X(3)         VALUE SPACES.
           05                     PIC X(12)        VALUE "NO.".
           05                     PIC X(10)        VALUE "JANUARY".
           05                     PIC X(13)        VALUE "FEBRUARY".
           05                     PIC X(11)        VALUE "MARCH".
           05                     PIC X(11)        VALUE "APRIL".
           05                     PIC X(11)        VALUE "MAY".
           05                     PIC X(4)         VALUE "JUNE".

       01  STORE-LINE.
           05 STORE-NUMBER-OUT   PIC B(4)9B(6).
           05 SALES-TOTAL-OUT    PIC BBZZ,ZZZ.99 OCCURS 6 TIMES.

       01  NO-INPUT-DATA.
           05                     PIC X(33)        VALUE SPACES.
           05                     PIC X(13)        VALUE "NO INPUT DATA".

       01  TODAYS-DATE.
           05 RUN-YEAR            PIC 99.
           05 RUN-MONTH-DAY       PIC 9(4).

      ******************************************************************

       PROCEDURE DIVISION.
       PRODUCE-SALES-SUMMARY.
           PERFORM INITIALIZATION
           PERFORM PROCESS-A-RECORD UNTIL THERE-IS-NO-MORE-INPUT
           PERFORM END-OF-FILE-PROCESSING
           STOP RUN
           .

       INITIALIZATION.
           ACCEPT TODAYS-DATE FROM DATE
           MOVE CORR TODAYS-DATE TO PAGE-HEAD-2
           OPEN INPUT  SALES-FILE-IN
                OUTPUT SALES-REPORT-FILE-OUT
           WRITE REPORT-LINE FROM PAGE-HEAD-1 AFTER PAGE
           WRITE REPORT-LINE FROM PAGE-HEAD-2
           WRITE REPORT-LINE FROM PAGE-HEAD-3 AFTER 3
           WRITE REPORT-LINE FROM PAGE-HEAD-4
           MOVE 2 TO LINE-SPACING
           PERFORM READ-A-RECORD
           IF THERE-IS-NO-MORE-INPUT
               WRITE REPORT-LINE FROM NO-INPUT-DATA AFTER 2
           END-IF
           .

       PROCESS-A-RECORD.
           PERFORM ACCUMULATE-SALES
               VARYING MONTH-SUBSCRIPT FROM 1 BY 1 UNTIL
                   MONTH-SUBSCRIPT IS GREATER THAN NUMBER-OF-MONTHS
           PERFORM READ-A-RECORD
           .
```

continued

paragraph ACCUMULATE–SALES begins at line 01300. You can see how, each time it executes, it fetches the correct SALE-AMOUNT-IN from the input area and adds it to the correct SALES-ACCUMULATOR. Notice that SALES-ACCUMULATOR is subscripted by the input field STORE-NUMBER-IN in the ADD statement at line 01310.

We enter the paragraph PRINT-THE-REPORT, line 01350, ready to print the entire report with no further reading of input data. We have five lines of data to print, one for each store. The PERFORM statement at line 01360 steps through all five stores. To build a print line for one store, we must step through the 6 months. The PERFORM statement at line 01470 does it.

Program P11-01 was run using the input shown in Figure 11.5 and produced the output shown in Figure 11.6.

FIGURE *11.4* ***continued***

```
S COBOL II RELEASE 3.1 09/19/89                  P11001    DATE JUL 09,1991 T
----+-*A-1-B--+----2----+----3----+----4----+----5----+----6----+----7-|--+

01180
01190  END-OF-FILE-PROCESSING.
01200      PERFORM PRINT-THE-REPORT
01210      PERFORM CLOSE-FILES
01220      .
01230
01240  READ-A-RECORD.
01250      READ SALES-FILE-IN
01260          AT END
01270              SET THERE-IS-NO-MORE-INPUT TO TRUE
01280      .
01290
01300  ACCUMULATE-SALES.
01310      ADD SALE-AMOUNT-IN (MONTH-SUBSCRIPT) TO
01320          SALES-ACCUMULATOR (STORE-NUMBER-IN, MONTH-SUBSCRIPT)
01330      .
01340
01350  PRINT-THE-REPORT.
01360      PERFORM PRINT-A-LINE
01370          VARYING STORE-SUBSCRIPT FROM 1 BY 1 UNTIL
01380              STORE-SUBSCRIPT IS GREATER THAN NUMBER-OF-STORES
01390      .
01400
01410  CLOSE-FILES.
01420      CLOSE SALES-FILE-IN
01430            SALES-REPORT-FILE-OUT
01440      .
01450
01460  PRINT-A-LINE.
01470      PERFORM FORMAT-A-LINE
01480          VARYING MONTH-SUBSCRIPT FROM 1 BY 1 UNTIL
01490              MONTH-SUBSCRIPT IS GREATER THAN NUMBER-OF-MONTHS
01500      MOVE STORE-SUBSCRIPT TO STORE-NUMBER-OUT
01510      WRITE REPORT-LINE FROM STORE-LINE AFTER 2
01520      .
01530
01540  FORMAT-A-LINE.
01550      MOVE SALES-ACCUMULATOR (STORE-SUBSCRIPT, MONTH-SUBSCRIPT)
01560           TO SALES-TOTAL-OUT (MONTH-SUBSCRIPT)
01570      .
```

FIGURE 11.5 **Input to Program P11-01**

```
--------------------------------------------------------------------------------
         1         2         3         4         5         6         7         8
12345678901234567890123456789012345678901234567890123456789012345678901234567890
--------------------------------------------------------------------------------
162947029438105368000000010647374398001618
527394000000000000000000027530240694729301 4
340268701268050275006453168927687941502000
345192942000627413000000080100000000712423
280628000000000000000000029450800000000000
514771231056289473962710643859711372969821
525168612943712900001124500295314000000000
171439091973050743063039081809013106090370
262437295368000000666804293000002937428536
327142000000680187000000000000000000000000
198104000000000000000000000000000006400000
472168302946095381673893847290399388274308
478527000295300042693937427290000138793814
172965039384293984893388392649030000188827
440463844392849683837939211682773904400055
```

FIGURE 11.6 **Output from Program P11-01**

```
                         FIRST-HALF SALES SUMMARY
                                           DATE PRODUCED:   7/09/91

STORE                          S A L E S   B Y   M O N T H
 NO.         JANUARY   FEBRUARY    MARCH       APRIL       MAY         JUNE

  1         1,607.95   4,500.95   9,564.27   4,851.05   4,175.10   6,808.15

  2         2,953.68        .00   6,668.04   5,875.08      29.37   4,285.36

  3        16,432.68  13,578.75      64.53   9,699.27   6,879.41  12,144.23

  4        11,476.33  12,451.06  22,057.69  14,862.62  11,734.30  14,681.77

  5         8,439.99  10,023.73   9,638.34  14,194.56  14,323.19  12,628.35
```

In-Line PERFORM

The PERFORM statement at line 01130 in Program P11-01 PERFORMs a very small paragraph, ACCUMULATE-SALES, line 01300, which contains only one statement, an ADD. Whenever you have a PERFORM statement carrying out a very small paragraph, you can consider using an **in-line PERFORM** statement instead of the kinds of PERFORM statements we have been using, which are called **out-of-line PERFORM** statements. When you use an in-line PERFORM statement, the statement or statements being PERFORMed do not appear in a separate paragraph, but appear instead right inside the PERFORM statement. So, for example, the PERFORM statement at line 01130 could have been written with the ADD statement right inside it, and then we could leave out the paragraph ACCUMULATE-SALES. The in-line PERFORM statement is as follows:

```
PERFORM VARYING MONTH-SUBSCRIPT FROM 1 BY 1 UNTIL
  MONTH-SUBSCRIPT IS GREATER THAN NUMBER-OF-MONTHS
    ADD SALE-AMOUNT-IN (MONTH-SUBSCRIPT) TO
      SALES-ACCUMULATOR (STORE-NUMBER-IN, MONTH-SUBSCRIPT)
END-PERFORM
```

Notice that the word VARYING follows immediately the word PERFORM; no paragraph name is given after the word PERFORM because there is no out-of-line paragraph to be PERFORMed. Also notice that an in-line PERFORM statement must include the explicit scope terminator **END-PERFORM.** The entire paragraph PROCESS-A-RECORD, line 01120, would then contain one in-line PERFORM statement and one out-of-line PERFORM statement, as follows:

```
PROCESS-A-RECORD.
    PERFORM VARYING MONTH-SUBSCRIPT FROM 1 BY 1 UNTIL
      MONTH-SUBSCRIPT IS GREATER THAN NUMBER-OF-MONTHS
        ADD SALE-AMOUNT-IN (MONTH-SUBSCRIPT) TO
          SALES-ACCUMULATOR (STORE-NUMBER-IN, MONTH-SUBSCRIPT)
    END-PERFORM
    PERFORM READ-A-RECORD
```

An out-of-line PERFORM statement must never contain the word END-PERFORM.

Another opportunity to use an in-line PERFORM statement is found at line 01470 of Program P11-01. The PERFORM statement there carries out a paragraph, FORMAT-A-LINE, that contains only one statement, a MOVE. We could rewrite the paragraph PRINT-A-LINE and leave out the paragraph FORMAT-A-LINE, as follows:

```
PRINT-A-LINE.
    PERFORM VARYING MONTH-SUBSCRIPT FROM 1 BY 1 UNTIL
      MONTH-SUBSCRIPT IS GREATER THAN NUMBER-OF-MONTHS
        MOVE SALES-ACCUMULATOR (STORE-SUBSCRIPT, MONTH-SUBSCRIPT)
          TO SALES-TOTAL-OUT (MONTH-SUBSCRIPT)
    END-PERFORM
    MOVE STORE-SUBSCRIPT TO STORE-NUMBER-OUT
    WRITE REPORT-LINE FROM STORE-LINE AFTER 2
```

You may have as many statements as you like in an in-line PERFORM statement. All four formats of the PERFORM statement can be written as in-line or out-of-line statements. See the formats in Appendix B.

Two More Formats of the PERFORM Statement

There are four formats of the PERFORM statement. Two of them were given in Chapter 2. A PERFORM statement in the third format, which can vary the values of fields, was used first in Chapter 10. And a PERFORM statement in the fourth format will be used in Chapter 19.

The format of the PERFORM statement that can vary the values of fields is as follows:

```
PERFORM [procedure-name-1 [{THROUGH} procedure-name-2]]
                           {THRU   }

   [WITH TEST {BEFORE}]
              {AFTER }

                                   {identifier-3}
   VARYING {identifier-2}   FROM  {index-name-2}
           {index-name-1}          {literal-1   }

         BY {identifier-4} UNTIL condition-1
            {literal-2   }

                                     {identifier-6}
         [ AFTER {identifier-5}  FROM {index-name-4}
                 {index-name-3}       {literal-3   }

         BY {identifier-7} UNTIL condition-2 ] ...
            {literal-4   }

   [imperative-statement-1 END-PERFORM]
```

This is the form of the PERFORM statement that we used to vary the subscripts in Program P11-01. Whenever an identifier is used in a PERFORM . . . VARYING statement, the identifier must be described as a numeric elementary item. (Remember that an identifier can be a data name itself or a data name followed by any legal combination of qualifiers, subscripts, and indexes.) A PERFORM . . . VARYING statement can vary the value of any numeric field; it is not limited to VARYING only subscripts and indexes. When it is used to vary a field other than a subscript or index, the field being varied need not be described as an integer. Subscripts and indexes, of course, must always be integers.

In Program P11-01 the phrases FROM 1 and BY 1 use literal-1 and literal-2 in the format. Any literal used in a PERFORM . . . VARYING statement must be a numeric literal. If the literal is used in connection with a subscript or an index, it must be an integer as well.

Condition-1 in the PERFORM statement at line 01380 in Program P11-01 is

```
STORE-SUBSCRIPT IS GREATER THAN NUMBER-OF-STORES
```

You can see from the format that any number of fields can be varied by a single PERFORM . . . VARYING statement, through use of the reserved word **AFTER.** But no matter how many fields are being varied, the word VARYING appears only once in the statement.

A PERFORM . . . VARYING statement having one condition executes as shown in the flowcharts in Figures 11.7 and 11.8.

Figure 11.7 shows the usual operation of a PERFORM . . . VARYING statement, where the condition is tested before the procedure is carried out for the first time. This is its operation when you use the WITH TEST BEFORE phrase or omit the WITH TEST phrase, for then WITH TEST BEFORE is assumed. Figure 11.8 shows the operation of the PERFORM . . . VARYING statement when

FIGURE 11.7 The VARYING option of a PERFORM statement with the TEST BEFORE phrase having one condition

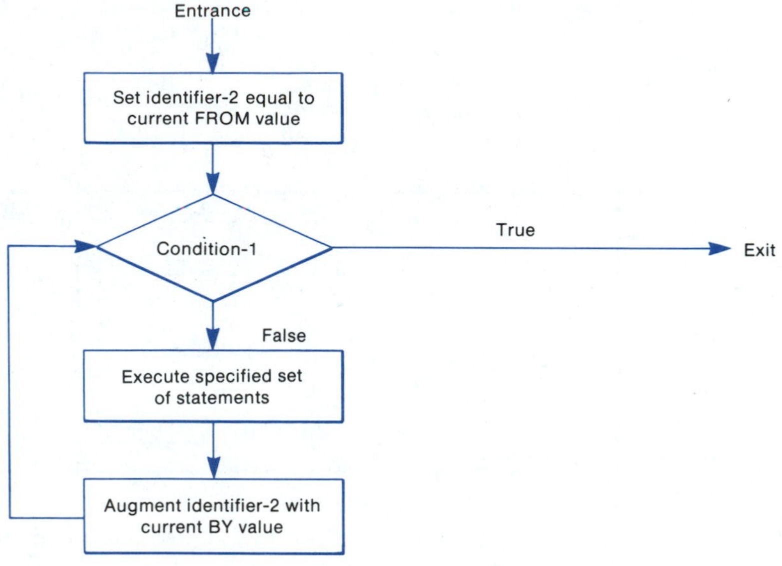

FIGURE 11.8 The VARYING option of a PERFORM statement with the TEST AFTER phrase having one condition

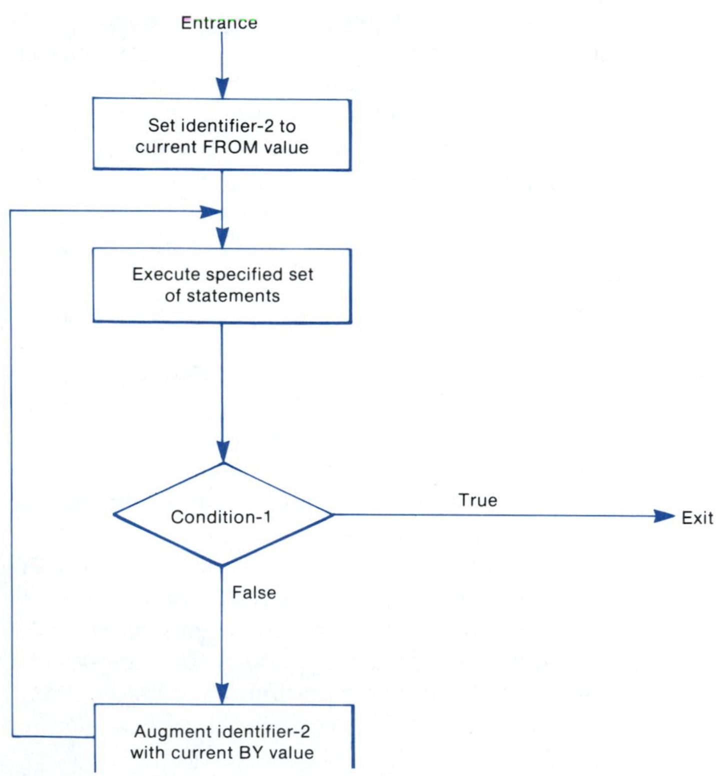

WITH TEST AFTER is used. With WITH TEST AFTER, the procedure is carried out once before the condition is tested the first time. Everything else is the same whether you use WITH TEST BEFORE or WITH TEST AFTER—the initial setting, the incrementing, and the testing of the field being varied are all done in the same order and with the same effects.

Figure 11.9 shows the operation of a PERFORM . . . VARYING statement having two conditions and WITH TEST BEFORE; Figure 11.10 shows its operation with two conditions and WITH TEST AFTER.

FIGURE *11.9* **The VARYING option of a PERFORM statement with the TEST BEFORE phrase having two conditions**

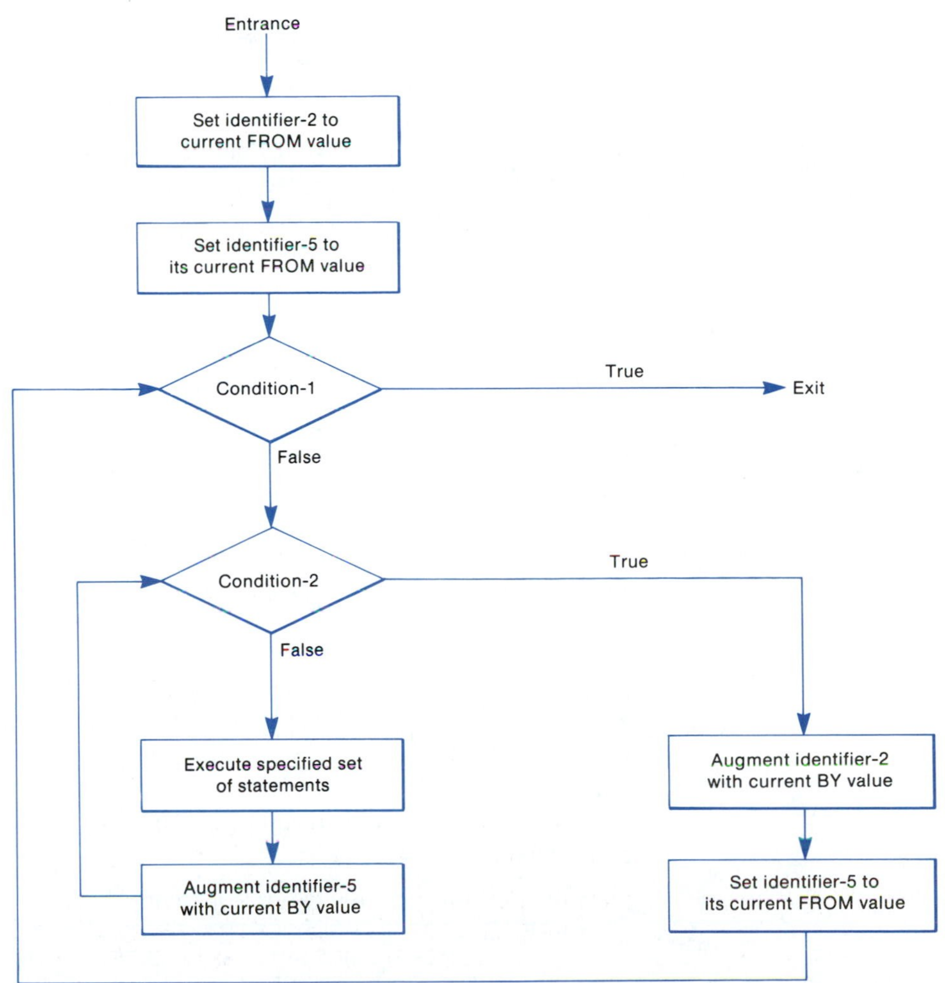

Notice that in each case the value of the field being varied is changed after the procedure is executed.

An example of a PERFORM . . . VARYING statement with an AFTER phrase could arise if we wanted to carry out some operation on every accumulator in

FIGURE 11.10 **The VARYING option of a PERFORM statement with the TEST AFTER phrase having two conditions**

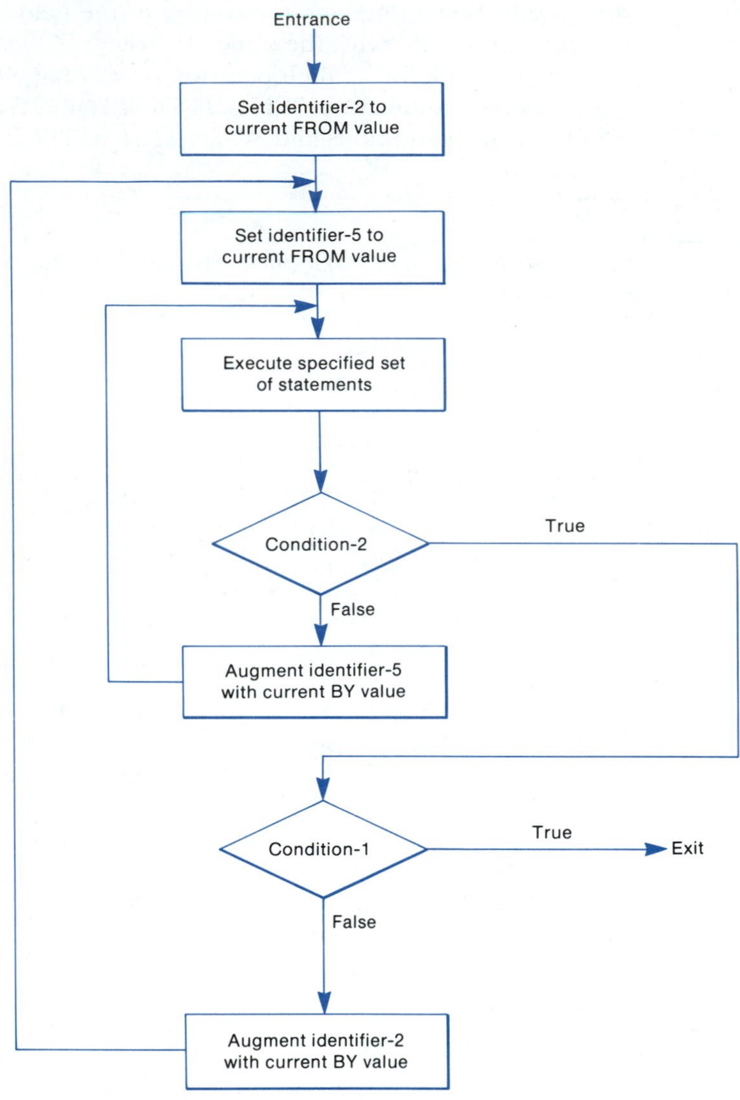

Program P11-01, such as zeroing each one individually. We might have a statement such as:

```
PERFORM PROCESS-ONE-ACCUMULATOR
    VARYING STORE-SUBSCRIPT FROM 1 BY 1 UNTIL
        STORE-SUBSCRIPT IS GREATER THAN
        NUMBER-OF-STORES
    AFTER MONTH-SUBSCRIPT FROM 1 BY 1 UNTIL
        MONTH-SUBSCRIPT IS GREATER THAN
        NUMBER-OF-MONTHS
```

The paragraph PROCESS-ONE-ACCUMULATOR would contain some processing on just one of the 30 accumulators, and the PERFORM statement would control the subscripts so that each time PROCESS-ONE-ACCUMULATOR executes, the subscripts would be pointing to a different one of the 30 accumulators. When more than one field is being varied in a PERFORM . . . VARYING statement, the last named varies most rapidly and the first named varies least rapidly. In the PERFORM . . . VARYING statement given, the subscripts would be set in the order shown in Table 11.1. Thus the paragraph PROCESS-ONE-ACCUMULATOR is PERFORMed 30 times, with the subscripts pointing to a different one of the accumulators each time.

TABLE *11.1*
The settings of the subscripts STORE-SUBSCRIPT and MONTH-SUBSCRIPT for the 30 executions of the paragraph PROCESS-ONE-ACCUMULATOR

STORE-SUBSCRIPT	*MONTH-SUBSCRIPT*
1	1
1	2
1	3
1	4
1	5
1	6
2	1
2	2
2	3
2	4
2	5
2	6
3	1
.	.
.	.
.	.
4	5
4	6
5	1
5	2
5	3
5	4
5	5
5	6

The fourth format of the PERFORM statement is as follows:

```
PERFORM [procedure-name-1 [{THROUGH} procedure-name-2]]
                           {THRU   }
    {identifier-1} TIMES [imperative-statement-1 END-PERFORM]
    {integer-1   }
```

This format permits the program to execute a paragraph a specific number of times. The number of times may be given as identifier-1 or integer-1. If identifier-1 is used, it must be defined as an integer. We use this kind of PERFORM statement in Chapter 19.

EXERCISE 1

Rewrite Program P11-01, defining the table with its MONTHs at the 05 level and the STORE-NUMBERs at the 10 level. Rearrange whatever subscripting needs rearranging. Change any of the PERFORM statements that need changing.

A Two-Dimensional Table with VALUE Clauses

In Program P11-01 you saw how to write a two-dimensional table in working storage and how to initialize all the elements of the table to zero with one VALUE clause. In Program P11-02 we see how to initialize the elements of a table to different values.

Program P11-02 reads input records in the following format:

Positions	Field
1–6	Loan Number
7–14	Principal (to two decimal places)
15–17	Number of Payments
18–20	Annual Interest Rate (to tenths of 1%)
21–80	spaces

Each record contains information about a home-mortgage loan—the Loan Number, the original Principal amount, the Number of monthly Payments, and the Annual Interest Rate. The program is to determine the monthly payment on the loan and print one line for each loan in the format shown in Figure 11.11.

FIGURE 11.11 Output format for Program P11-02

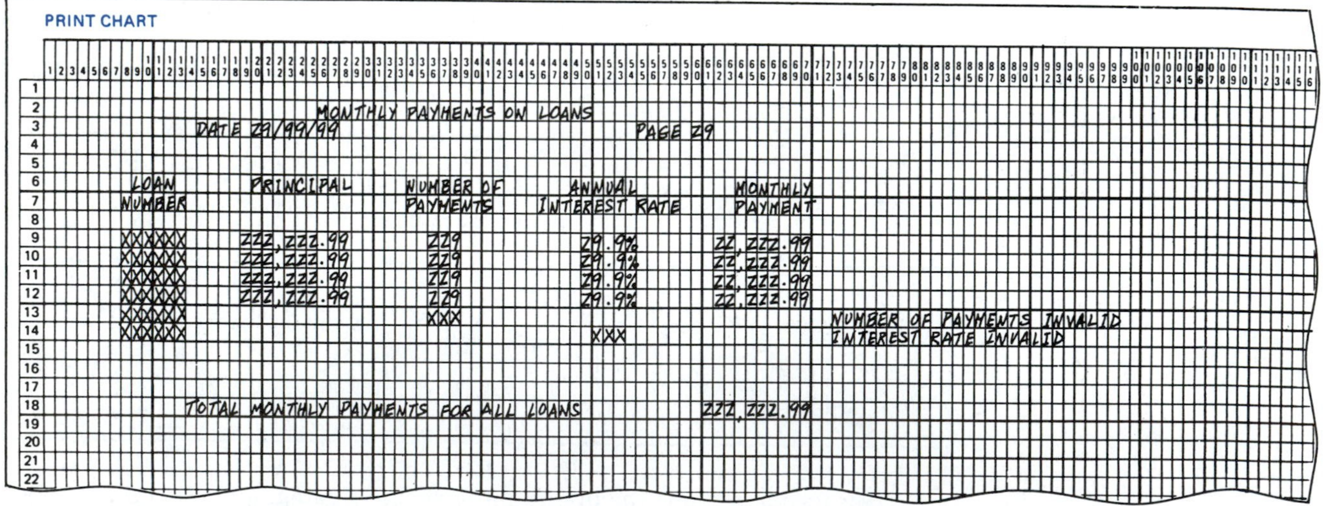

The program uses Table 11.2. For each input record, the program looks up in the table the interest rate and number of payments for that particular loan to find the payment per $1 of loan. Then the program multiplies the table function by the full loan amount to arrive at the monthly payment for the loan.

TABLE *11.2*

Monthly payments required per $1 of loan amount on loans of different interest rates and numbers of payments

ANNUAL INTEREST RATE, %	NUMBER OF MONTHLY PAYMENTS					
	60	120	180	240	300	360
10	.0212471	.0132151	.0107461	.0096503	.0090871	.0087758
10.5	.0214940	.0134935	.0110540	.0099838	.0094419	.0091474
11	.0217425	.0137751	.0113660	.0103219	.0098012	.0095233
11.5	.0219927	.0140596	.0116819	.0106643	.0101647	.0099030
12	.0222445	.0143471	.0120017	.0110109	.0105323	.0102862
12.5	.0224980	.0146377	.0123253	.0113615	.0109036	.0106726
13	.0227531	.0149311	.0126525	.0117158	.0112784	.0110620
13.5	.0230099	.0152275	.0129832	.0120738	.0116565	.0114542
14	.0232683	.0155267	.0133175	.0124353	.0120377	.0118488
14.5	.0235283	.0158287	.0136551	.0128000	.0124217	.0122456
15	.0237900	.0161335	.0139959	.0131679	.0128084	.0126445
15.5	.0240532	.0164411	.0143400	.0135389	.0131975	.0130452
16	.0243181	.0167514	.0146871	.0139126	.0135889	.0134476
16.5	.0245846	.0170643	.0150371	.0142891	.0139825	.0138515
17	.0248526	.0173798	.0153901	.0146681	.0143780	.0142568

If an input record contains an Annual Interest Rate or a Number of Payments that has no match in the table, an error line is to be printed as shown in Figure 11.11. The program is to check for valid Annual Interest Rate and valid Number of Payments and print two error lines if both fields are invalid. At the end of the report, the program is to print a total of the monthly payments for all the loans.

Program P11-02 is shown in Figure 11.12. In the File Section, the fields NUMBER-OF-PAYMENTS-IN and ANNUAL-INTEREST-RATE-IN have been REDEFINED with Xs. The reason for this is that either or both of these fields might be invalid and might contain nonnumeric values. We will use the alphanumeric redefinitions of the fields in the program up to the point where the program knows that the fields are numeric and valid.

FIGURE *11.12*

Program P11-02

```
S COBOL II RELEASE 3.1 09/19/89                 P11002   DATE JUL 18,1991 T
----+-*A-1-B--+----2----+----3----+----4----+----5----+----6----+----7-%--+

 IDENTIFICATION DIVISION.
 PROGRAM-ID.  P11-02.
*AUTHOR.  DEBORAH ANN SENIOR.
*
*     THIS PROGRAM COMPUTES THE MONTHLY PAYMENT NEEDED
*     TO REPAY A LOAN
*
*****************************************************************
```

continued

The Working Storage Section begins at line 00370. In it there is a field called ANY-INPUT-ERRORS, at line 00400. This field is used to signal the program if either the ANNUAL-INTEREST-RATE-IN or the NUMBER-OF-PAYMENTS-IN, or both, is invalid.

The tables that we need for this program start at line 00570. First the ROW-ENTRIES are written, each complete row as a single level-10 entry. Whenever you write more than one numeric field into a single entry, as we are doing here, you may use a PICTURE of 9s and write all the numbers one after another (only the digits, no decimal points) as one big numeric literal. If you do that, you must write all the leading and trailing zeros of all the numbers, except the leftmost zeros of the leftmost number, to make the fields come out the right size. But numeric literals are limited to 18 digits. Our rows are longer than 18 digits, so we must make them alphanumeric. We must define them with Xs, put quotation marks around the numbers, and write all the leading and trailing zeros (including the leftmost zeros).

Following the entries for all the rows, we have a REDEFINES entry. Whenever you write a two-dimensional table into a program row by row, as we have done here, you must write the OCCURS clause for the rows as part of the REDEFINES entry and take care of the OCCURS clause for the columns later. Our REDEFINES entry in line 00890 says that there are 15 rows, and also sets up the rows with an ASCENDING KEY phrase and an INDEXED BY phrase so that we can use SEARCH ALL to find the row of the table that we want. You will see how we find the correct row for any particular loan when we look at the Procedure Division.

FIGURE *11.12* ***continued***

```
S COBOL II RELEASE 3.1 09/19/89                       P11002    DATE JUL 18,1991 T
----+-*A-1-B--+----2----+----3----+----4----+----5----+----6----+----7-%--+

00090
00100  ENVIRONMENT DIVISION.
00110  INPUT-OUTPUT SECTION.
00120  FILE-CONTROL.
00130      SELECT LOAN-FILE-IN                ASSIGN TO INFILE.
00140      SELECT PAYMENT-REPORT-FILE-OUT     ASSIGN TO PRINTER.
00150
00160 *****************************************************************
00170
00180  DATA DIVISION.
00190  FILE SECTION.
00200  FD  LOAN-FILE-IN
00210      RECORD CONTAINS 80 CHARACTERS.
00220
00230  01  LOAN-RECORD-IN.
00240      05  LOAN-NUMBER-IN           PIC X(6).
00250      05  PRINCIPAL-IN             PIC 9(6)V99.
00260      05  NUMBER-OF-PAYMENTS-IN    PIC 999.
00270      05  NUMBER-OF-PAYMENTS-XXX-IN
00280          REDEFINES NUMBER-OF-PAYMENTS-IN      PIC XXX.
00290      05  ANNUAL-INTEREST-RATE-IN PIC 99V9.
00300      05  ANNUAL-INTEREST-RATE-XXX-IN
00310          REDEFINES ANNUAL-INTEREST-RATE-IN    PIC XXX.
00320
00330  FD  PAYMENT-REPORT-FILE-OUT.
00340
00350  01  REPORT-LINE          PIC X(98).
00360
```

FIGURE 11.12 *continued*

```
00370  WORKING-STORAGE SECTION.
00380  01  MORE-INPUT          PIC X          VALUE "Y".
00390      88 THERE-IS-NO-MORE-INPUT          VALUE "N".
00400  01  ANY-INPUT-ERRORS    PIC X.
00410  01  TODAYS-DATE.
00420      05  TODAYS-YEAR     PIC 99.
00430      05  TODAYS-MONTH-AND-DAY           PIC 9(4).
00440  01  MONTHLY-PAYMENT-W   PIC S9(5)V99   PACKED-DECIMAL.
00450  01  TOTAL-MONTHLY-PAYMENTS-W           PACKED-DECIMAL
00460                          PIC S9(6)V99   VALUE ZERO.
00470  01  LINE-LIMIT          PIC S99        VALUE 40 COMP SYNC.
00480  01  LINE-COUNT-ER       PIC S99                 COMP SYNC.
00490  01  LINE-SPACING        PIC S9                  COMP SYNC.
00500  01  PAGE-NUMBER-W       PIC S99        VALUE 0
00510                                         PACKED-DECIMAL.
00520  01  ERROR-MESSAGE-RATE                 PIC X(21)
00530                  VALUE "INTEREST RATE INVALID".
00540  01  ERROR-MESSAGE-PAYMENT              PIC X(26)
00550                  VALUE "NUMBER OF PAYMENTS INVALID".
00560
00570  01  PAYMENT-TABLES.
00580      05  ROW-ENTRIES.
00590          10              PIC X(45)
00600             VALUE "100021247101321510107461009650300908710087758".
00610          10              PIC X(45)
00620             VALUE "105021494001349350110540009983800944190091474".
00630          10              PIC X(45)
00640             VALUE "110021742501377510113660010321900980120095233".
00650          10              PIC X(45)
00660             VALUE "115021992701405960116819010664301016470099030".
00670          10              PIC X(45)
00680             VALUE "120022244501434710120017011010901053230102862".
00690          10              PIC X(45)
00700             VALUE "125022498001463770123253011361501090360106726".
00710          10              PIC X(45)
00720             VALUE "130022753101493110126525011715801127840110620".
00730          10              PIC X(45)
00740             VALUE "135023009901522750129832012073801165650114542".
00750          10              PIC X(45)
00760             VALUE "140023268301552670133175012435301203770118488".
00770          10              PIC X(45)
00780             VALUE "145023528301582870136551012800001242170122456".
00790          10              PIC X(45)
00800             VALUE "150023790001613350139959013167901280840126445".
00810          10              PIC X(45)
00820             VALUE "155024053201644110143400013538901319750130452".
00830          10              PIC X(45)
00840             VALUE "160024318101675140146871013912601358890134476".
00850          10              PIC X(45)
00860             VALUE "165024584601706430150371014289101398250138515".
00870          10              PIC X(45)
00880             VALUE "170024852601737980153901014668101437800142568".
00890      05  ROW             REDEFINES ROW-ENTRIES
00900          OCCURS 15 TIMES ASCENDING KEY TABLE-INTEREST-RATE
00910          INDEXED BY ROW-INDEX.
00920          10  TABLE-INTEREST-RATE        PIC XXX.
00930          10  MONTHLY-PAYMENT-PER-DOLLAR  PIC V9(7)
00940              OCCURS 6 TIMES INDEXED BY COLUMN-INDEX.
```

continued

Since each row consists of two different types of data, two entries are needed to describe them. The level-10 entries at lines 00920 and 00930 do it. The first level-10 entry defines the first field in the row, TABLE-INTEREST-RATE. The second level-10 entry, line 00930, defines the remaining six fields in the row, using the name MONTHLY-PAYMENT-PER-DOLLAR and an OCCURS clause. MONTHLY-PAYMENT-PER-DOLLAR has an OCCURS clause in its description and is subordinate to an entry that has an OCCURS clause. Thus, whenever the name MONTHLY-PAYMENT-PER-DOLLAR is referred to, it must be followed by two subscripts or two indexes in parentheses, or one subscript and one index in parentheses, in the order in which the OCCURS clauses are written.

This is all jolly good as far as it goes, but we still have not entered into the program anywhere the different numbers of months of payments, the constants 60, 120, 180, and so on. We have entered the rows and their captions, but not the column captions. These must be entered as a separate one-dimensional table, as shown starting at line 00960. This table has been set up for SEARCH ALL, as you can see by the ASCENDING KEY and INDEXED BY phrases in lines 01050 and 01060.

For each input record the program can SEARCH ALL of the rows looking for a TABLE-INTEREST-RATE that matches the ANNUAL-INTEREST-RATE-IN, and SEARCH ALL of the column captions looking for a TABLE-NUMBER-OF-PAYMENTS equal to the NUMBER-OF-PAYMENTS-IN. The program will then have two index values it needs to do its further processing. The SEARCH ALL statements have suitable AT END clauses to take care of situations in which no match(es) is (are) found.

Four detail lines are defined. GOOD-DETAIL-LINE, line 01370, is the ordinary line that prints when the input record is error-free. Two other definitions, lines 01510 through 01610, describe the two types of error lines.

FIGURE *11.12* ***continued***

```
S COBOL II RELEASE 3.1 09/19/89                    P11002   DATE JUL 18,1991 T
----+-*A-1-B--+----2----+----3----+----4----+----5----+----6----+----7-%--+

00950
00960          05  NUMBER-OF-PAYMENTS-ENTRIES.
00970              10              PIC 999           VALUE 60.
00980              10              PIC 999           VALUE 120.
00990              10              PIC 999           VALUE 180.
01000              10              PIC 999           VALUE 240.
01010              10              PIC 999           VALUE 300.
01020              10              PIC 999           VALUE 360.
01030          05. TABLE-NUMBER-OF-PAYMENTS
01040              REDEFINES NUMBER-OF-PAYMENTS-ENTRIES
01050              OCCURS 6 TIMES ASCENDING KEY TABLE-NUMBER-OF-PAYMENTS
01060              INDEXED BY NUMBER-OF-PAYMENTS-INDEX
01070                              PIC XXX.
01080
01090      01  PAGE-HEAD-1.
01100          05                  PIC X(25)         VALUE SPACES.
01110          05                  PIC X(25)
01120                              VALUE "MONTHLY PAYMENTS ON LOANS".
01130
01140      01  PAGE-HEAD-2.
01150          05                  PIC X(14)         VALUE SPACES.
01160          05                  PIC X(5)          VALUE "DATE".
01170          05 TODAYS-MONTH-AND-DAY               PIC Z9/99/.
01180          05 TODAYS-YEAR      PIC 99B(27).
01190          05                  PIC X(5)          VALUE "PAGE".
01200          05 PAGE-NUMBER-OUT  PIC Z9.
01210
```

FIGURE 11.12 *continued*

```
       01  PAGE-HEAD-3.
           05                         PIC X(8)        VALUE SPACES.
           05                         PIC X(11)       VALUE "LOAN".
           05                         PIC X(14)       VALUE "PRINCIPAL".
           05                         PIC X(15)       VALUE "NUMBER OF".
           05                         PIC X(15)       VALUE "ANNUAL".
           05                         PIC X(7)        VALUE "MONTHLY".

       01  PAGE-HEAD-4.
           05                         PIC X(7)        VALUE SPACES.
           05                         PIC X(26)       VALUE "NUMBER".
           05                         PIC X(12)       VALUE "PAYMENTS".
           05                         PIC X(18)       VALUE "INTEREST RATE".
           05                         PIC X(7)        VALUE "PAYMENT".

       01  GOOD-DETAIL-LINE.
           05 LOAN-NUMBER-OUT             PIC B(7)X(6).
           05 PRINCIPAL-OUT               PIC B(5)ZZZ,ZZZ.99.
           05 NUMBER-OF-PAYMENTS-OUT      PIC B(7)ZZ9.
           05 ANNUAL-INTEREST-RATE-OUT    PIC B(11)Z9.9.
           05                             PIC X           VALUE "%".
           05 MONTHLY-PAYMENT-OUT         PIC B(7)ZZ,ZZZ.99.

       01  TOTAL-LINE.
           05                             PIC X(13)       VALUE SPACES.
           05                             PIC X(47)
               VALUE "TOTAL MONTHLY PAYMENTS FOR ALL LOANS".
           05 TOTAL-PAYMENT-OUT           PIC ZZZ,ZZZ.99.

       01  RATE-ERROR-DETAIL-LINE.
           05 LOAN-NUMBER-R-ERROR         PIC B(7)X(6).
           05 ANNUAL-INTEREST-RATE-XXX-OUT
                                          PIC B(37)X(3)B(19).
           05 RATE-ERROR-MESSAGE          PIC X(21).

       01  PAYMENTS-ERROR-DETAIL-LINE.
           05 LOAN-NUMBER-P-ERROR         PIC B(7)X(6).
           05 NUMBER-OF-PAYMENTS-XXX-OUT
                                          PIC B(22)X(3)B(34).
           05 PAYMENT-ERROR-MESSAGE       PIC X(26).

       01  NO-INPUT-DATA.
           05                         PIC X(31)       VALUE SPACES.
           05                         PIC X(13)       VALUE "NO INPUT DATA".

      *****************************************************************

       PROCEDURE DIVISION.
       CONTROL-PARAGRAPH.
           PERFORM INITIALIZATION
           PERFORM MAIN-PROCESS UNTIL THERE-IS-NO-MORE-INPUT
           PERFORM TERMINATION
           STOP RUN
           .

       INITIALIZATION.
           ACCEPT TODAYS-DATE FROM DATE
           MOVE CORR TODAYS-DATE TO PAGE-HEAD-2
           OPEN INPUT  LOAN-FILE-IN
                OUTPUT PAYMENT-REPORT-FILE-OUT
           PERFORM PRINT-PAGE-HEADING-LINES
           PERFORM READ-A-RECORD
           IF THERE-IS-NO-MORE-INPUT
               WRITE REPORT-LINE FROM NO-INPUT-DATA AFTER 2
           END-IF
           .

```

continued

In the Procedure Division MAIN-PROCESS begins at line 01890. As we enter MAIN-PROCESS each time with an input record, the flag ANY-INPUT-ERRORS is first set to indicate that no errors have yet been found in this record. The program then SEARCHes ALL the ROWs looking for the condition given in the WHEN clause at line 01940:

```
TABLE-INTEREST-RATE (ROW-INDEX) IS EQUAL TO
    ANNUAL-INTEREST-RATE-XXX-IN
```

Notice that TABLE-INTEREST-RATE is indexed by ROW-INDEX even though TABLE-INTEREST-RATE has no OCCURS clause. That is because TABLE-INTEREST-RATE is subordinate to an entry that has an OCCURS clause with the phrase INDEXED BY ROW-INDEX.

If this SEARCH ALL fails to satisfy the WHEN condition, the AT END clause, line 01920, is executed. The paragraph INTEREST-RATE-INVALID, line 02150, prints an error line and sets ANY-INPUT-ERRORS to "Y" to indicate that at least one error was found in this input record.

Regardless of whether or not the row search was successful, the SEARCH ALL statement at line 01980 executes next. This SEARCH ALL examines the one-dimensional table TABLE-NUMBER-OF-PAYMENTS looking for the condition:

```
TABLE-NUMBER-OF-PAYMENTS (NUMBER-OF-PAYMENTS-INDEX)
    IS EQUAL TO NUMBER-OF-PAYMENTS-XXX-IN
```

If this SEARCH ALL fails to satisfy the condition, the AT END clause at line 01990 is executed. The paragraph NUMBER-OF-PAYMENTS-INVALID writes an error line and sets ANY-INPUT-ERRORS to "Y" to indicate that the input record contains at least one error.

If no errors are found in the input record, the two SEARCH ALLs leave ROW-INDEX pointing to the row containing the desired interest rate, and NUMBER-OF-PAYMENTS-INDEX pointing to the entry in the NUMBER-OF-PAYMENTS-ENTRIES that represents the desired number of payments. Now we are ready to try to fetch the correct MONTHLY-PAYMENT-PER-DOLLAR and multiply it by the loan amount, PRINCIPAL-IN.

MONTHLY-PAYMENT-PER-DOLLAR is defined with the phrase INDEXED BY COLUMN-INDEX and is subordinate to an entry that is defined with the phrase INDEXED BY ROW-INDEX. That means that whenever MONTHLY-PAYMENT-PER-DOLLAR is referred to, it must be referred to either this way:

```
MONTHLY-PAYMENT-PER-DOLLAR (ROW-INDEX, COLUMN-INDEX)
```

or with integer literals or integer identifiers in place of the words ROW-INDEX and/or COLUMN-INDEX. It is not possible to use any other index names to refer to MONTHLY-PAYMENT-PER-DOLLAR. Unlike subscripting, where any field defined as an integer may be used to subscript any field defined with an OCCURS clause, indexing requires that if a field is referred to by index names, they must be the index names given in the INDEXED BY phrases that the field is defined with or is subordinate to.

When the IF statement at line 02050 executes, COLUMN-INDEX has not yet been assigned any value. The column we want to refer to corresponds to the setting of the NUMBER-OF-PAYMENTS-INDEX resulting from the SEARCH ALL at line 01980. We can use the SET statement at line 02060 to SET COLUMN-INDEX to point to the column we want. Remember that the sending field of a

SET statement comes after the word TO, and the receiving field before. Notice that the SET, MULTIPLY, and PERFORM statements at lines 02060 through 02100 are executed only if ANY-INPUT-ERRORS indicates that the record is free of errors.

Program P11-02 was run with the input data shown in Figure 11.13 and produced the output shown in Figure 11.14.

FIGURE *11.12*

continued

```
S COBOL II RELEASE 3.1 09/19/89                 P11002   DATE JUL 18,1991 T
----+-*A-1-B--+----2----+----3----+----4----+----5----+----6----+----7-%--+

01890  MAIN-PROCESS.
01900      MOVE "N" TO ANY-INPUT-ERRORS
01910      SEARCH ALL ROW
01920          AT END
01930              PERFORM INTEREST-RATE-INVALID
01940          WHEN TABLE-INTEREST-RATE (ROW-INDEX) IS EQUAL TO
01950              ANNUAL-INTEREST-RATE-XXX-IN
01960              CONTINUE
01970      END-SEARCH
01980      SEARCH ALL TABLE-NUMBER-OF-PAYMENTS
01990          AT END
02000              PERFORM NUMBER-OF-PAYMENTS-INVALID
02010          WHEN TABLE-NUMBER-OF-PAYMENTS (NUMBER-OF-PAYMENTS-INDEX)
02020              IS EQUAL TO NUMBER-OF-PAYMENTS-XXX-IN
02030              CONTINUE
02040      END-SEARCH
02050      IF ANY-INPUT-ERRORS IS EQUAL TO "N"
02060          SET COLUMN-INDEX TO NUMBER-OF-PAYMENTS-INDEX
02070          MULTIPLY PRINCIPAL-IN BY
02080              MONTHLY-PAYMENT-PER-DOLLAR (ROW-INDEX, COLUMN-INDEX)
02090              GIVING MONTHLY-PAYMENT-W ROUNDED
02100          PERFORM PRINT-A-GOOD-LINE
02110      END-IF
02120      PERFORM READ-A-RECORD
02130      .
02140
02150  INTEREST-RATE-INVALID.
02160      MOVE LOAN-NUMBER-IN                TO LOAN-NUMBER-R-ERROR
02170      MOVE ANNUAL-INTEREST-RATE-XXX-IN
02180                            TO ANNUAL-INTEREST-RATE-XXX-OUT
02190      MOVE ERROR-MESSAGE-RATE            TO RATE-ERROR-MESSAGE
02200      IF LINE-COUNT-ER + LINE-SPACING > LINE-LIMIT
02210         PERFORM PRINT-PAGE-HEADING-LINES
02220      END-IF
02230      WRITE REPORT-LINE FROM RATE-ERROR-DETAIL-LINE
02240            AFTER LINE-SPACING
02250      ADD LINE-SPACING TO LINE-COUNT-ER
02260      MOVE 1                             TO LINE-SPACING
02270      MOVE "Y" TO ANY-INPUT-ERRORS
02280      .
02290
02300  TERMINATION.
02310      PERFORM PRODUCE-TOTAL-LINE
02320      CLOSE LOAN-FILE-IN
02330            PAYMENT-REPORT-FILE-OUT
02340      .
02350
02360  READ-A-RECORD.
02370      READ LOAN-FILE-IN
02380          AT END
02390              SET THERE-IS-NO-MORE-INPUT TO TRUE
02400      .
02410
```

continued

FIGURE 11.12 *continued*

```
S COBOL II RELEASE 3.1 09/19/89                   P11002   DATE JUL 18,1991 T
----+-*A-1-B--+----2----+----3----+----4----+----5----+----6----+----7-%--+

       PRINT-PAGE-HEADING-LINES.
           ADD 1                            TO PAGE-NUMBER-W
           MOVE PAGE-NUMBER-W               TO PAGE-NUMBER-OUT
           WRITE REPORT-LINE FROM PAGE-HEAD-1 AFTER PAGE
           WRITE REPORT-LINE FROM PAGE-HEAD-2
           WRITE REPORT-LINE FROM PAGE-HEAD-3 AFTER 3
           WRITE REPORT-LINE FROM PAGE-HEAD-4
           MOVE 6                           TO LINE-COUNT-ER
           MOVE 2                           TO LINE-SPACING
           .

       PRODUCE-TOTAL-LINE.
           MOVE TOTAL-MONTHLY-PAYMENTS-W  TO TOTAL-PAYMENT-OUT
           WRITE REPORT-LINE FROM TOTAL-LINE AFTER 4
           .

       NUMBER-OF-PAYMENTS-INVALID.
           MOVE LOAN-NUMBER-IN              TO LOAN-NUMBER-P-ERROR
           MOVE NUMBER-OF-PAYMENTS-XXX-IN TO NUMBER-OF-PAYMENTS-XXX-OUT
           MOVE ERROR-MESSAGE-PAYMENT       TO PAYMENT-ERROR-MESSAGE
           IF LINE-COUNT-ER + LINE-SPACING > LINE-LIMIT
              PERFORM PRINT-PAGE-HEADING-LINES
           END-IF
           WRITE REPORT-LINE FROM PAYMENTS-ERROR-DETAIL-LINE
                 AFTER LINE-SPACING
           ADD LINE-SPACING                 TO LINE-COUNT-ER
           MOVE 1                           TO LINE-SPACING
           MOVE "Y" TO ANY-INPUT-ERRORS
           .

       PRINT-A-GOOD-LINE.
           MOVE LOAN-NUMBER-IN              TO LOAN-NUMBER-OUT
           MOVE PRINCIPAL-IN                TO PRINCIPAL-OUT
           MOVE NUMBER-OF-PAYMENTS-IN       TO NUMBER-OF-PAYMENTS-OUT
           MOVE ANNUAL-INTEREST-RATE-IN     TO ANNUAL-INTEREST-RATE-OUT
           MOVE MONTHLY-PAYMENT-W           TO MONTHLY-PAYMENT-OUT
           IF LINE-COUNT-ER + LINE-SPACING > LINE-LIMIT
              PERFORM PRINT-PAGE-HEADING-LINES
           END-IF
           WRITE REPORT-LINE FROM GOOD-DETAIL-LINE
                 AFTER LINE-SPACING
           ADD LINE-SPACING                 TO LINE-COUNT-ER
           MOVE 1                           TO LINE-SPACING
           ADD MONTHLY-PAYMENT-W            TO TOTAL-MONTHLY-PAYMENTS-W
           .
```

FIGURE 11.13 **Input to Program P11-02**

```
--------------------------------------------------------------------------------
         1         2         3         4         5         6         7         8
12345678901234567890123456789012345678901234567890123456789012345678901234567890
--------------------------------------------------------------------------------
002683100000000060100
071439010000000360100
178294000500000060170
248371005000000360170
572829016827883360125
662714684611212230115
728605200000000240115
744618001005001201350
822277004000001201800
900026000800004001750
953641001000000601400
```

FIGURE 11.14 Output from Program P11-02

```
                    MONTHLY PAYMENTS ON LOANS
          DATE  7/18/91                                PAGE  1

    LOAN          PRINCIPAL        NUMBER OF       ANNUAL            MONTHLY
    NUMBER                         PAYMENTS     INTEREST RATE        PAYMENT

    002683       100,000.00           60            10.0%            2,124.71
    071439        10,000.00          360            10.0%               87.76
    178294           500.00           60            17.0%               12.43
    248371         5,000.00          360            17.0%               71.28
    572829        16,827.88          360            12.5%              179.60
    662714                           230                                        NUMBER OF PAYMENTS INVALID
    728605       200,000.00          240            11.5%            2,132.86
    744618         1,005.00          120            13.5%               15.30
    822277                                           180                        INTEREST RATE INVALID
    900026                                           175                        INTEREST RATE INVALID
    900026                           400                                        NUMBER OF PAYMENTS INVALID
    953641         1,000.00           60            14.0%               23.27


         TOTAL MONTHLY PAYMENTS FOR ALL LOANS                        4,647.21
```

The PICTURE Character P

The character P is useful in PICTUREs that describe very large or very small numeric quantities. In this context "very large" numbers are those that have one or more zeros at the right end of the number; "very small" numbers have one or more zeros immediately to the right of the decimal point. In Table 11.2 all the entries in the body of the table have one zero just to the right of the decimal point. By using the PICTURE character P in one place in the program, we can indicate to COBOL the presence of all those zeros and not have to write them. Here's how we would change Program P11-02 to take advantage of P.

First we would write the ROW-ENTRIES without those leading zeros. For example, the first entry, line 00590, instead of having the VALUE

```
100021247101321510107461009650300908710087758
```

would have the VALUE:

```
100212471132151107461096503090871087758
```

Of course, the PICTURE for that entry and all the other ROW-ENTRIES would be X(39) now instead of X(45).

Then the PICTURE for MONTHLY-PAYMENT-PER-DOLLAR, line 00930, would be changed to indicate that the zeros are missing. Instead of PIC V9(7), we would use:

```
10 MONTHLY-PAYMENT-PER-DOLLAR PIC P9(6)
   OCCURS 6 TIMES INDEXED BY COLUMN-INDEX.
```

The 9(6) in the PICTURE indicates that six digits were actually written into the ROW-ENTRIES. The P in the PICTURE tells COBOL to assume a zero at the left end of the number whenever the field is used for arithmetic or printing or anything. You may have one or more Ps at the left or right end of a PICTURE, but not both in the same PICTURE. P may be followed by an integer inside parentheses to indicate repetitions of P. For example, PIC PPPPPP9(5) is the same as PIC P(6)9(5). One or more Ps at the left end of a PICTURE tell the system that a decimal point is assumed to the left of the Ps. You may use a V to the left of one or more Ps, but it would be redundant. P is not counted in the size of a field. You may use an S to the left of one or more Ps.

One or more Ps at the right end of a PICTURE tell the system that a decimal point is assumed to the right of the Ps. You wouldn't be using V at the right end of an integer anyway.

We have been using P here in a purely numeric field in a table in working storage. P may be used equally well to describe fields not in tables, and may also be used in PICTUREs for numeric fields in input records, and in PICTUREs for numeric and edited numeric fields in output records. As an example of its use in an input record, let's say that an input record contains fields in the form .000000nnn, where the ns stand for digits in the number. The field may be defined with PICTURE P(6)9(3) and only the three digits indicated by n need to be keyed in the input.

P may be used in an edited numeric field in a print line when you don't want the digits at the right or left end of a number to print. For example, you might have a field in working storage that contains hundreds of millions of dollars and is defined with PICTURE 9(9). When you print this field, you may want only the three high-order digits to print, in millions of dollars. Then you could define the output field with PICTURE $ZZ9P(6).

EXERCISE *2*

Write a program to read input records in the following format:

Positions	Field
1–5	Employee Number
6	Job Classification Code
7	Education Code
8–80	spaces

There is one input record for each employee. Each record contains an Employee Number, the employee's Job Classification Code, and the employee's Education Code.

Table 11.E2 shows the minimum annual salary for employees as a function of their Job Classification Code and their Education Code. For each employee, have your program compute the minimum weekly salary (annual salary divided by 52) and the minimum monthly salary (annual salary divided by 12) and print on one line the Employee Number, Job Classification Code, Education Code, minimum weekly salary, and minimum monthly salary. If any input record contains an invalid Job Classification Code or Education Code, or both, have your program print an error line showing the Employee Number and a suitable error message. At the end of the report have your program print totals of the minimum weekly salaries and the minimum monthly salaries.

Set up the salary figures in the table in your program without their two low-order zeros. Use two Ps in the description of the salary amount to tell the system that the zeros are missing.

TABLE 11.E2
Minimum annual salary for employees as a function of Job Classification Code and Education Code

JOB CLASSIFICATION CODE	EDUCATION CODE			
	A	B	C	D
Z	7,200	8,000	9,100	10,500
Y	7,800	8,500	9,800	11,100
X	8,800	9,600	10,800	12,600
W	10,400	11,300	12,700	14,900
V	13,800	16,000	19,200	21,100
6	15,600	18,900	23,000	25,400
5	20,200	24,100	27,600	31,000

Searching a Table for a Range of Values

In all our search tables so far we have always been SEARCHing for a specific value of a table argument. We have SEARCHed for state codes and interest rates and numbers of months of payment, always looking for an equal match between a table argument and a search argument. Our WHEN conditions have always been tests for equal. We will now write a program in which a condition other than EQUAL TO is used.

Program P11-03 reads input data in the following format:

Positions	Field
1–5	Salesperson Number
6	Grade
7–13	Sale Amount (to two decimal places)
14–80	spaces

Each record represents a sale made by a salesperson. The record contains a Salesperson Number, a Salesperson Grade, and a Sale Amount. The commission rate on the sale depends on the Sale Amount and the Salesperson Grade as shown in Table 11.3. Assume that there are several sales for each salesperson, grouped together in the input. For each record, the program is to look up the commission rate in the table, compute the commission by multiplying the commission rate by the Sale Amount, and print a line of output as shown in Figure 11.15. For each salesperson, the total sales and the total commission are to be shown.

TABLE 11.3
Commission rates on sales as a function of Sale Amount and Salesperson Grade

SALE AMOUNT	SALESPERSON GRADE				
	1	2	3	4	5
0–1,000.00	5%	5%	10%	10%	15%
1,000.01–10,000.00	10%	15%	15%	20%	25%
10,000.01–50,000.00	15%	20%	25%	30%	35%
over 50,000	25%	30%	35%	45%	50%

FIGURE 11.15 Output format for Program P11-03

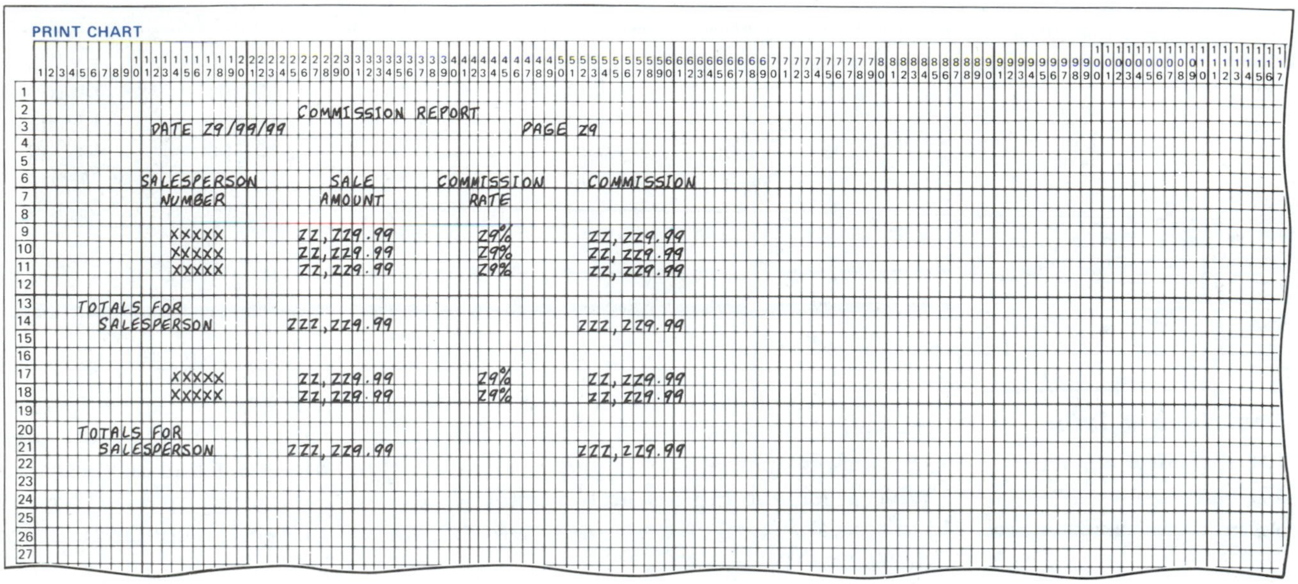

PRINT CHART

```
                    COMMISSION REPORT
       DATE Z9/99/99                       PAGE Z9

       SALESPERSON      SALE      COMMISSION     COMMISSION
         NUMBER        AMOUNT        RATE

          XXXXX       ZZ,ZZ9.99      Z9%         ZZ,ZZ9.99
          XXXXX       ZZ,ZZ9.99      Z9%         ZZ,ZZ9.99
          XXXXX       ZZ,ZZ9.99      Z9%         ZZ,ZZ9.99

  TOTALS FOR
    SALESPERSON      ZZZ,ZZ9.99                 ZZZ,ZZ9.99


          XXXXX       ZZ,ZZ9.99      Z9%         ZZ,ZZ9.99
          XXXXX       ZZ,ZZ9.99      Z9%         ZZ,ZZ9.99

  TOTALS FOR
    SALESPERSON      ZZZ,ZZ9.99                 ZZZ,ZZ9.99
```

In Program P11-03 we have to write the rows of Table 11.3 into working storage. Whenever table captions involve contiguous ranges of values, or brackets, as our row captions do, it is best to write into the program only the high end of each bracket. In Program P11-03 we can determine into which bracket each input Sale Amount falls by comparing the Sale Amount to the table bracket amounts and using some sort of GREATER THAN or LESS THAN test to determine when the correct bracket is found. You will see how when we look at the Procedure Division.

There is no need to write both the high and low ends of the brackets, since each bracket begins where another leaves off. Experience has shown that writing the high end of each bracket into a program leads to far simpler coding than writing the low end. If the brackets were not contiguous, both the high and low ends of each would have to be written into the program. The fourth row of Table 11.3 doesn't seem at first glance to have a high end, but it really does. The largest possible Sale Amount allowed by the size of the input field is $99,999.99, so we use that as the high end of row 4.

Program P11-03 is shown in Figure 11.16. In the Working Storage Section there is a field called COMMISSION-W, at line 00390. This is used to hold the product of the Sale Amount by the commission rate found in the table.

FIGURE 11.16 **Program P11-03**

```
S COBOL II RELEASE 3.1 09/19/89                    P11003   DATE JUL 20,1991 T
----+-*A-1-B--+----2----+----3----+----4----+----5----+----6----+----7-|--+

 IDENTIFICATION DIVISION.
 PROGRAM-ID.  P11-03.
*
*      THIS PROGRAM DEMONSTRATES SEARCHING A TABLE FOR A RANGE
*      OF VALUES TO CALCULATE COMMISSIONS
*
*****************************************************************

 ENVIRONMENT DIVISION.
 INPUT-OUTPUT SECTION.
 FILE-CONTROL.
     SELECT SALES-FILE-IN                  ASSIGN TO INFILE.
     SELECT COMMISSION-REPORT-FILE-OUT     ASSIGN TO PRINTER.

*****************************************************************

 DATA DIVISION.
 FILE SECTION.
 FD  SALES-FILE-IN.

 01  SALES-RECORD-IN                PIC X(80).

 FD  COMMISSION-REPORT-FILE-OUT.

 01  COMMISSION-REPORT-RECORD-OUT           PIC X(62).

 WORKING-STORAGE SECTION.
 01  MORE-INPUT              PIC X            VALUE "Y".
     88 THERE-IS-NO-MORE-INPUT                VALUE "N".

 01  SALES-RECORD-W.
     05  SALESPERSON-NUMBER-IN    PIC X(5).
     05  SALESPERSON-GRADE-IN     PIC 9.
     05  SALE-AMOUNT-IN           PIC 9(5)V99.

 01  TODAYS-DATE.
     05  TODAYS-YEAR        PIC 99.
     05  TODAYS-MONTH-AND-DAY                 PIC 9(4).
 01  COMMISSION-W            PIC S9(5)V99             PACKED-DECIMAL.
 01  PAGE-NUMBER-W           PIC S99          VALUE 0 PACKED-DECIMAL.
 01  LINE-LIMIT              PIC S99 COMP SYNC VALUE 40.
 01  LINE-COUNT-ER           PIC S99 COMP SYNC.
 01  LINE-SPACING            PIC S9  COMP SYNC.
 01  SALESPERSON-NUMBER-SAVE                  PIC X(5).

```

continued

Table 11.3 starts at line 00500. Here the rows are less than 18 digits long, so they are defined with 9s. There is no big advantage in defining them with 9s instead of Xs, except that the leftmost zeros of the leftmost number can be omitted when the field is defined with 9s. It was done here mainly to show the idea.

In the redefinition of the ROW-ENTRIES there is no ASCENDING KEY clause, just an INDEXED BY clause. This table is set up for use of the SEARCH statement but not for the SEARCH ALL. Remember that the only condition permitted in a SEARCH ALL statement is the EQUAL TO condition, and in Program P11-03 we are going to have to use some form of a GREATER THAN or LESS THAN condition.

The COMMISSION-RATE, line 00590, is defined both as a fraction (line 00610) and as an integer (line 00620). Each definition has a different name. We use the name COMMISSION-RATE-F when we want to treat the percentage COMMISSION-RATE as a fraction, and we use COMMISSION-RATE-I when we want to treat it as an integer. This coding shows that an entry containing a REDEFINES clause may be subordinate to one containing an OCCURS clause.

We won't need a separate one-dimensional table for the column captions in this program, for the columns in Table 11.3 are numbered 1 through 5. The program will be able to use the value of SALESPERSON-GRADE-IN, a number from 1 through 5, to refer to the columns directly, without having to SEARCH.

Lines 00470 and 00480 show that level numbers other than 01 can begin anywhere in area A or B.

FIGURE *11.16* ***continued***

```
S COBOL II RELEASE 3.1 09/19/89                P11003   DATE JUL 20,1991 T
----+-*A-1-B--+----2----+----3----+----4----+----5----+----6----+----7-¦--+

00460  01  ACCUMULATORS                                     PACKED-DECIMAL.
00470    05 SALES-TOTAL-W       PIC S9(6)V99    VALUE 0.
00480    05 COMMISSION-TOTAL-W PIC S9(6)V99    VALUE 0.
00490
00500  01  COMMISSION-TABLE.
00510      05  ROW-ENTRIES.
00520          10               PIC 9(17)       VALUE  1000000505101015.
00530          10               PIC 9(17)       VALUE 10000001015152025.
00540          10               PIC 9(17)       VALUE 50000001520253035.
00550          10               PIC 9(17)       VALUE 99999992530354550.
00560      05  ROW              REDEFINES ROW-ENTRIES
00570          OCCURS 4 TIMES   INDEXED BY SALES-BRACKET-INDEX.
00580          10  TOP-OF-SALES-BRACKET         PIC 9(5)V99.
00590          10  COMMISSION-RATE
00600                           OCCURS 5 TIMES  INDEXED BY GRADE-INDEX.
00610              15  COMMISSION-RATE-F        PIC V99.
00620              15  COMMISSION-RATE-I
00630                           REDEFINES COMMISSION-RATE-F
00640                           PIC 99.
00650
00660  01  HEADING-LINE-2.
00670      05                   PIC X(25)       VALUE SPACES.
00680      05                   PIC X(17) VALUE "COMMISSION REPORT".
00690
00700  01  HEADING-LINE-3.
00710      05                   PIC X(11)       VALUE SPACES.
00720      05                   PIC X(5)        VALUE "DATE".
00730      05  TODAYS-MONTH-AND-DAY             PIC Z9/99/.
00740      05  TODAYS-YEAR                      PIC 99B(22).
00750      05                   PIC X(5)        VALUE "PAGE".
00760      05  PAGE-NUMBER-OUT PIC Z9.
00770
```

FIGURE 11.16 ***continued***

```
 01  HEADING-LINE-6.
     05                         PIC X(10)        VALUE SPACES.
     05                         PIC X(18)        VALUE "SALESPERSON".
     05                         PIC X(10)        VALUE "SALE".
     05                         PIC X(14)        VALUE "COMMISSION".
     05                         PIC X(10)        VALUE "COMMISSION".
 01  HEADING-LINE-7.
     05                         PIC X(12)        VALUE SPACES.
     05                         PIC X(15)        VALUE "NUMBER".
     05                         PIC X(14)        VALUE "AMOUNT".
     05                         PIC X(4)         VALUE "RATE".
 01  DETAIL-LINE.
     05  SALESPERSON-NUMBER-OUT                  PIC B(13)X(5).
     05  SALE-AMOUNT-OUT                         PIC B(7)ZZ,ZZ9.99.
     05  COMMISSION-RATE-OUT                     PIC B(8)Z9.
     05                         PIC X            VALUE "%".
     05  COMMISSION-OUT                          PIC B(7)ZZ,ZZ9.99.
 01  TOTAL-LINE-1.
     05                         PIC X(4)         VALUE SPACES.
     05                         PIC X(10)        VALUE "TOTALS FOR".
 01  TOTAL-LINE-2.
     05                         PIC X(6)         VALUE SPACES.
     05                         PIC X(18)        VALUE "SALESPERSON".
     05  SALES-TOTAL-OUT                         PIC ZZZ,ZZ9.99B(17).
     05  COMMISSION-TOTAL-OUT                    PIC ZZZ,ZZ9.99.
 01  NO-INPUT-DATA.
     05                         PIC X(27)        VALUE SPACES.
     05                         PIC X(13)        VALUE "NO INPUT DATA".
************************************************************************
 PROCEDURE DIVISION.
 CONTROL-PARAGRAPH.
     PERFORM INITIALIZATION
     PERFORM MAIN-PROCESS UNTIL THERE-IS-NO-MORE-INPUT
     PERFORM TERMINATION
     STOP RUN
     .
 INITIALIZATION.
     ACCEPT TODAYS-DATE FROM DATE
     MOVE CORR TODAYS-DATE TO HEADING-LINE-3
     OPEN INPUT  SALES-FILE-IN
          OUTPUT COMMISSION-REPORT-FILE-OUT
     PERFORM PRINT-PAGE-HEADINGS
     PERFORM READ-A-RECORD
     MOVE SALESPERSON-NUMBER-IN TO SALESPERSON-NUMBER-SAVE
     IF THERE-IS-NO-MORE-INPUT
         WRITE COMMISSION-REPORT-RECORD-OUT FROM NO-INPUT-DATA
             AFTER 2
     END-IF
     .
 PRINT-PAGE-HEADINGS.
     ADD 1 TO PAGE-NUMBER-W
     MOVE PAGE-NUMBER-W TO PAGE-NUMBER-OUT
     WRITE COMMISSION-REPORT-RECORD-OUT FROM HEADING-LINE-2
         AFTER PAGE
     WRITE COMMISSION-REPORT-RECORD-OUT FROM HEADING-LINE-3
     WRITE COMMISSION-REPORT-RECORD-OUT FROM HEADING-LINE-6
         AFTER 3
     WRITE COMMISSION-REPORT-RECORD-OUT FROM HEADING-LINE-7
     MOVE 6 TO LINE-COUNT-ER
     MOVE 2 TO LINE-SPACING
     .
```

continued

PRODUCE-DETAIL-LINE begins at line 01570. In it, the program does a serial SEARCH of the ROWs looking for the correct sales bracket. First, SALES-BRACKET-INDEX must be SET to 1 to start the SEARCH at the first ROW of the table. Then, as the SEARCH statement steps through the ROWs, it tests the condition given in the WHEN clause in line 01600. SALE-AMOUNT-IN is compared with each of the different TOP-OF-SALES-BRACKET figures until the condition is met. You can see that IS NOT GREATER THAN is the relational operator we need to terminate the SEARCH, for as long as SALE-AMOUNT-IN is greater than the top of some sales bracket, we want the SEARCH to continue and try

FIGURE *11.16* ***continued***

```
S COBOL II RELEASE 3.1 09/19/89                  P11003   DATE JUL 20,1991 T
----+-*A-1-B--+----2----+----3----+----4----+----5----+----6----+----7-|--+

01480
01490  MAIN-PROCESS.
01500      IF SALESPERSON-NUMBER-IN NOT = SALESPERSON-NUMBER-SAVE
01510          PERFORM CONTROL-BREAK
01520      END-IF
01530      PERFORM PRODUCE-DETAIL-LINE
01540      PERFORM READ-A-RECORD
01550      .
01560
01570  PRODUCE-DETAIL-LINE.
01580      SET SALES-BRACKET-INDEX TO 1
01590      SEARCH ROW
01600          WHEN SALE-AMOUNT-IN IS NOT GREATER THAN
01610              TOP-OF-SALES-BRACKET (SALES-BRACKET-INDEX)
01620              CONTINUE
01630      END-SEARCH
01640      SET GRADE-INDEX TO SALESPERSON-GRADE-IN
01650      MULTIPLY SALE-AMOUNT-IN BY
01660          COMMISSION-RATE-F (SALES-BRACKET-INDEX, GRADE-INDEX)
01670          GIVING COMMISSION-W   ROUNDED,
01680                 COMMISSION-OUT ROUNDED
01690      ADD SALE-AMOUNT-IN TO SALES-TOTAL-W
01700      ADD COMMISSION-W   TO COMMISSION-TOTAL-W
01710      IF LINE-COUNT-ER + LINE-SPACING > LINE-LIMIT
01720          PERFORM PRINT-PAGE-HEADINGS
01730      END-IF
01740      MOVE SALESPERSON-NUMBER-IN TO SALESPERSON-NUMBER-OUT
01750      MOVE SALE-AMOUNT-IN        TO SALE-AMOUNT-OUT
01760      MOVE COMMISSION-RATE-I (SALES-BRACKET-INDEX, GRADE-INDEX)
01770          TO COMMISSION-RATE-OUT
01780      WRITE COMMISSION-REPORT-RECORD-OUT FROM DETAIL-LINE
01790          AFTER LINE-SPACING
01800      ADD LINE-SPACING TO LINE-COUNT-ER
01810      MOVE 1           TO LINE-SPACING
01820      .
01830
01840  CONTROL-BREAK.
01850      MOVE COMMISSION-TOTAL-W    TO COMMISSION-TOTAL-OUT
01860      MOVE SALES-TOTAL-W         TO SALES-TOTAL-OUT
01870      WRITE COMMISSION-REPORT-RECORD-OUT FROM TOTAL-LINE-1
01880          AFTER 2
01890      WRITE COMMISSION-REPORT-RECORD-OUT FROM TOTAL-LINE-2
01900      ADD 3                      TO LINE-COUNT-ER
01910      MOVE 0                     TO SALES-TOTAL-W
01920      MOVE 0                     TO COMMISSION-TOTAL-W
01930      MOVE SALESPERSON-NUMBER-IN TO SALESPERSON-NUMBER-SAVE
01940      MOVE 3                     TO LINE-SPACING
01950      .
01960
```

FIGURE *11.16* *continued*

```
01970 TERMINATION.
01980     PERFORM CONTROL-BREAK
01990     CLOSE SALES-FILE-IN
02000           COMMISSION-REPORT-FILE-OUT
02010     .
02020
02030 READ-A-RECORD.
02040     READ SALES-FILE-IN INTO SALES-RECORD-W
02050         AT END
02060             SET THERE-IS-NO-MORE-INPUT TO TRUE
02070     .
```

another, higher bracket. Table 11.4 shows how three different values of SALE-AMOUNT-IN would cause the SEARCH to end.

TABLE *11.4*
The value of TOP-OF-SALES-BRACKET (SALES-BRACKET-INDEX) that causes the SEARCH statement in line 01590 of Program P11-03 to terminate, for three different values of SALE-AMOUNT-IN

SALE-AMOUNT-IN	*TOP-OF-SALES-BRACKET (SALES-BRACKET-INDEX)*
$15,000.00	$50,000.00
950.00	1,000.00
10,000.00	10,000.00

EXERCISE *3*

What value of TOP-OF-SALES-BRACKET (SALES-BRACKET-INDEX) would cause the SEARCH statement in line 01590 of Program P11-03 to terminate, for each of the following values of SALE-AMOUNT-IN?

a. $500.00

b. $75,000.00

c. $50,000.00

In Program P11-03 we make no checks on the validity of the input data. We are assuming that it will all be correct. If we were to check for validity, we would check that SALE-AMOUNT-IN is numeric and that SALESPERSON-GRADE-IN is a number within the range 1 through 5. There would be no need to check that SALE-AMOUNT-IN is within a correct range, for any of its possible values 0 through 99,999.99 is valid. No AT END clause would be needed in the SEARCH statement, for the SEARCH cannot run off the end of the table if SALE-AMOUNT-IN is numeric.

WHEN the SEARCH in line 01590 terminates, the program proceeds past END-SEARCH. The SET statement at line 01640 SETs the GRADE-INDEX to point to the correct COMMISSION-RATE-F. We use the input value of SALESPERSON-GRADE-IN to SET the value of GRADE-INDEX.

Program P11-03 was run with the input data shown in Figure 11.17 and produced the output shown in Figure 11.18.

FIGURE 11.17 Input to Program P11-03

```
-------------------------------------------------------------------------------
         1         2         3         4         5         6         7         8
12345678901234567890123456789012345678901234567890123456789012345678901234567890
-------------------------------------------------------------------------------
1072820012500
6530742500000
6530740012500
6530745000000
6530741000000
6530746000000
7143950012500
7143951200000
7143955432198
7143950200000
9037010010000
9037010020000
9037011100000
```

FIGURE 11.18 Output from Program P11-03

```
                    COMMISSION REPORT
          DATE  7/20/91                      PAGE  1


         SALESPERSON       SALE       COMMISSION     COMMISSION
           NUMBER         AMOUNT         RATE

             10728          125.00          5%              6.25

      TOTALS FOR
        SALESPERSON         125.00                          6.25

             65307       25,000.00         30%          7,500.00
             65307          125.00         10%             12.50
             65307       50,000.00         30%         15,000.00
             65307       10,000.00         20%          2,000.00
             65307       60,000.00         45%         27,000.00

      TOTALS FOR
        SALESPERSON     145,125.00                     51,512.50

             71439          125.00         15%             18.75
             71439       12,000.00         35%          4,200.00
             71439       54,321.98         50%         27,160.99
             71439        2,000.00         25%            500.00

      TOTALS FOR
        SALESPERSON      68,446.98                     31,879.74

             90370          100.00          5%              5.00
             90370          200.00          5%             10.00
             90370       11,000.00         15%          1,650.00

      TOTALS FOR
        SALESPERSON      11,300.00                      1,665.00
```

EXERCISE 4 Write a program to process input records in the following format:

Positions	Field
1–5	Employee Number
6–7	Years Employed
8	Job Code
9–15	Annual Salary (to two decimal places)
16–80	spaces

Each record is for one employee and contains an Employee Number, the number of Years Employed, a Job Code, and the employee's current Annual Salary. Each employee is to receive a percentage salary increase based on the Job Code and the number of Years Employed. Table 11.E4 shows the percentage increase for the different Job Codes and Years Employed.

TABLE *11.E4*
Percentage salary increases as a function of Job Code and Years Employed

YEARS EMPLOYED	JOB CODE			
	1	2	3	4
0–2	5%	5%	10%	10%
2–5	15%	20%	22%	25%
6–10	20%	22%	28%	30%
11–20	20%	25%	30%	35%
21–99	25%	28%	32%	36%

The program is to determine for each employee the dollar amount of the increase and print on one line the Employee Number, the increase, and the new salary after the increase. At the end of the report, have your program print the total of all the increases and the total of all the new salaries. Assume that all input data are valid.

Relative Subscripting and Indexing

It is sometimes convenient to be able to refer to a certain item in a table even when its subscript or index is not pointing to it. It is especially useful during table SEARCHes to be able to examine neighboring items in a table. For example, if a table index is pointing to the sixth item in a table, it might be useful to be able to refer to the fifth item or the seventh. With relative indexing, it is possible to do so easily.

Even though we have no use for relative subscripting or relative indexing in Program P11-03, we can use some fields from that program to give an example of relative indexing. Let's say that sometime during the SEARCH in Program P11-03 SALES-BRACKET-INDEX was pointing to the third ROW of Table 11.3. Then it would have been legal to refer to

```
TOP-OF-SALES-BRACKET (SALES-BRACKET-INDEX)
```

and that, of course, would have been the third TOP-OF-SALES-BRACKET figure,

$50,000.00. Using relative indexing, it also would have been legal to refer to

```
TOP-OF-SALES-BRACKET (SALES-BRACKET-INDEX + 1)
```

and that would have been the fourth TOP-OF-SALES-BRACKET figure, $99,999.99. Subtraction as well as addition may be used in relative indexing, and so this would be legal:

```
TOP-OF-SALES-BRACKET (SALES-BRACKET-INDEX - 1)
```

and that would refer to the second TOP-OF-SALES-BRACKET figure.

The general form of a relative subscript or relative index is the data name or index name followed by a space, followed by a plus or minus sign, followed by another space, followed by an integer literal. Note that after the plus or minus sign you may have only an unsigned numeric literal, never an identifier. Relative subscripting and relative indexing may be used wherever direct subscripting or indexing is allowed. It is the programmer's responsibility to ensure that a relative subscript or relative index always comes out within the range of the table being subscripted or indexed.

Programming for a Three-Dimensional Table

A three-dimensional table can be visualized most easily as a book full of two-dimensional tables. In the example given at the beginning of the chapter, for 5-year renewable term insurance, a person's age and sex and the face amount of the policy were needed to find a particular premium amount. We will arrange our three-dimensional table of age versus face amount, with each sex being on a different page of the book. Table 11.5 shows the first page of the book, the annual premium for different ages and face amounts for males, and Table 11.6 shows the second page of the book, the annual premium for different ages and face amounts for females.

TABLE *11.5*
Annual premium for 5-year renewable term life insurance for males

Age	$10,000 Policy	$25,000 Policy	$30,000 Policy
18	$30.30	$55.75	$66.90
19	30.70	56.75	68.10
20	31.00	57.50	69.00
21	31.30	58.25	69.90
22	31.50	58.75	70.50
23	31.90	59.75	71.70
24	32.20	60.50	72.60
25	32.50	61.25	73.50
26	32.90	62.25	74.70
27	33.30	63.25	75.90
28	33.80	64.50	77.40
29	34.50	66.25	79.50

TABLE 11.6
Annual premium for 5-year renewable term life insurance for females

Age	$10,000 Policy	$25,000 Policy	$30,000 Policy
18	$28.40	$51.00	$61.20
19	29.10	52.75	63.30
20	29.80	54.50	65.40
21	30.30	55.75	66.90
22	30.70	56.75	68.10
23	31.00	57.50	69.00
24	31.30	58.25	69.90
25	31.50	58.75	70.50
26	31.90	59.75	71.70
27	32.20	60.50	72.60
28	32.50	61.25	73.50
29	32.90	62.25	74.70

Program P11-04 reads input records in the following format:

Positions	Field
1–25	Customer Name
26–27	Age
28	Sex
29–33	Face Amount (in whole dollars)
34–80	spaces

Each record represents a potential customer for life insurance, and contains the Customer Name, Age, Sex (M or F), and the Face Amount of the policy that the customer is interested in. For each error-free input record, Program P11-04 produces a page of output in the format shown in Figure 11.19.

FIGURE 11.19 Output format for error-free records in Program P11-04

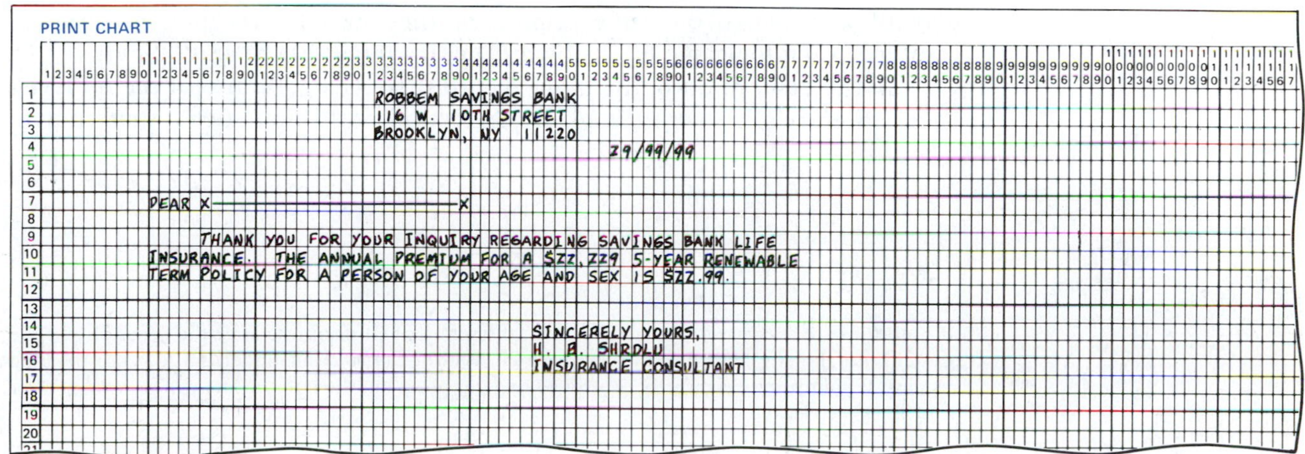

Program P11-04 checks all input for valid Age, Sex, and Face Amount. Each input record is checked for all possible errors. For each error found, a line is printed on a separate error report in the format shown in Figure 11.20.

FIGURE *11.20* **Output format for error report in Program P11-04**

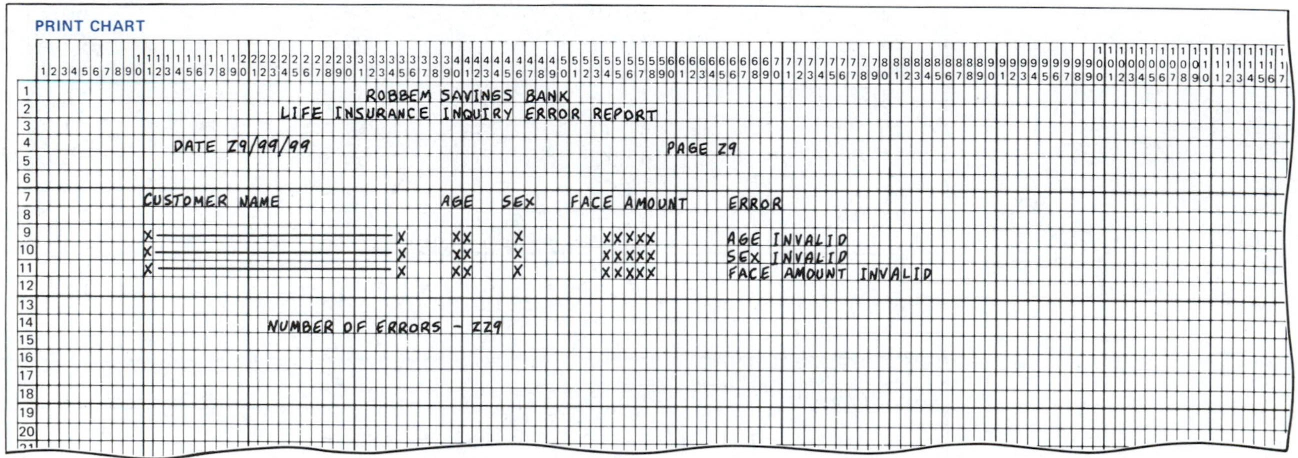

A hierarchy diagram for Program P11-04 is shown in Figure 11.21. The box "Process a record" consists of two subfunctions. The first, "Assign index values," does all the SEARCHing and validity checking needed to determine the values of all the indexes that are needed for the box "Print an inquiry letter." Any or all of three types of errors might be found by "Assign index values"—an invalid Sex code, an invalid Age, and/or an invalid Face Amount. The separate routines that handle each type of error are shown in the hierarchy diagram. The diagram also shows that all three error routines can use a common print routine to create the error report. For each input record, the box "Print an inquiry letter" executes only if the record is error-free.

Program P11-04 is shown in Figure 11.22. This program has one input file and two output files. Each of the two reports prints as a separate file. Both files may be assigned to the same printer, or they may be assigned to different printers.[1] Each file name has its own FD entry (lines 00350 and 00390).

In the description of the input record there is a good use of the 88 level. Level-88 entries are very useful in connection with input fields that contain

[1]If both files are assigned to the same printer, the reports will print one after the other only if the printer is not directly controlled by your program, as is the case with all modern large-scale operating systems. If your printer is directly controlled by your program, the two reports will print with their print lines interleaved.

FIGURE 11.21 **Hierarchy diagram for Program P11-04**

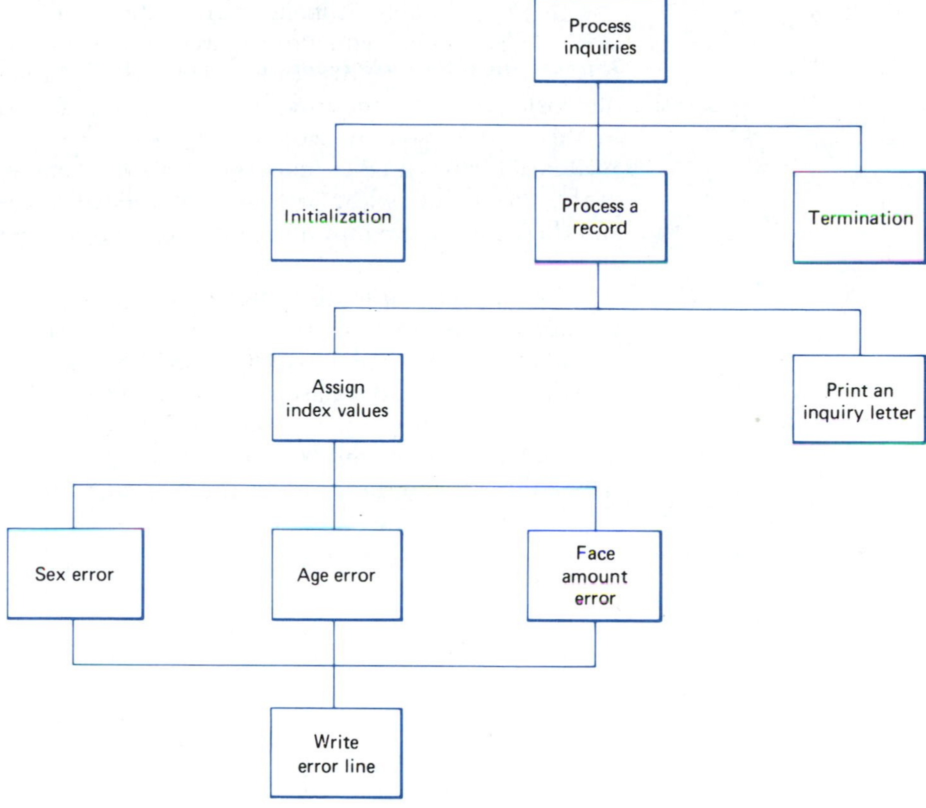

FIGURE 11.22 **Program P11-04**

```
S COBOL II RELEASE 3.2 09/05/90                P11004   DATE FEB 26,1992 T
----+-*A-1-B--+----2----+----3----+----4----+----5----+----6----+----7-|--+

 IDENTIFICATION DIVISION.
 PROGRAM-ID.  P11-04.
*
*     THIS PROGRAM USES A THREE-DIMENSIONAL TABLE TO FIND
*     INSURANCE PREMIUMS AS A FUNCTION OF AGE, SEX, AND
*     FACE AMOUNT OF POLICY, AND PRODUCES INQUIRY-RESPONSE
*     LETTERS AND AN ERROR REPORT
*
*****************************************************************

 ENVIRONMENT DIVISION.
 INPUT-OUTPUT SECTION.
 FILE-CONTROL.
     SELECT INQUIRY-FILE-IN              ASSIGN TO INFILE.
     SELECT INQUIRY-LETTERS-FILE-OUT     ASSIGN TO PRINTER1.
     SELECT ERROR-REPORT-FILE-OUT        ASSIGN TO PRINTER2.

*****************************************************************

```

continued

coded values, as our SEX-IN field at line 00280 does. The use of level-88 entries here to give the names MALE and FEMALE to the coded input values M and F makes the Procedure Division coding clearer.

In the Working Storage Section, the table of insurance premiums begins at line 00580. When you write a three-dimensional table into a COBOL program, it is best to write the row captions and the column captions into separate one-dimensional tables, and to write just the table functions in entries of their own. By this method you can avoid having to write the row captions more than once. Write each row of table functions as a single entry, starting with the first page of the "book" of tables. First, write all the rows from the first page of the book, and then continue right on with the rows from the second page and so on until all the rows are written.

Whenever you write a three-dimensional table into a program in this way, you must write the OCCURS clause for the pages of the book as part of the REDEFINES entry. The next OCCURS clause after that must refer to the rows, and the last OCCURS clause must refer to the columns. You can see the REDEFINES entry in Program P11-04 at line 00830 and the three OCCURS clauses in lines 00840, 00850, and 00870. The one-dimensional table for the ages begins at line 00880, and the table for the face amounts begins at line 01050.

FIGURE 11.22 ***continued***

```
S COBOL II RELEASE 3.2 09/05/90                    P11004   DATE FEB 26,1992 T
----+-*A-1-B--+----2----+----3----+----4----+----5----+----6----+----7-|--+

00200  DATA DIVISION.
00210  FILE SECTION.
00220  FD   INQUIRY-FILE-IN
00230       RECORD CONTAINS 80 CHARACTERS.
00240
00250  01   INQUIRY-RECORD-IN.
00260       05   CUSTOMER-NAME-IN         PIC X(25).
00270       05   AGE-IN                   PIC XX.
00280       05   SEX-IN                   PIC X.
00290            88   MALE                VALUE "M".
00300            88   FEMALE              VALUE "F".
00310       05   FACE-AMOUNT-IN           PIC 9(5).
00320       05   FACE-AMOUNT-X5-IN        REDEFINES FACE-AMOUNT-IN
00330                                     PIC X(5).
00340
00350  FD   INQUIRY-LETTERS-FILE-OUT.
00360
00370  01   INQUIRY-LETTER-RECORD-OUT    PIC X(71).
00380
00390  FD   ERROR-REPORT-FILE-OUT.
00400
00410  01   ERROR-REPORT-RECORD-OUT      PIC X(84).
00420
00430  WORKING-STORAGE SECTION.
00440  01   MORE-INPUT              PIC X              VALUE "Y".
00450       88 THERE-IS-NO-MORE-INPUT                  VALUE "N".
00460  01   ANY-INPUT-ERRORS        PIC X.
00470  01   ERROR-REPORT-LINE-SPACING                  PIC S9  COMP SYNC.
00480  01   ERROR-REPORT-LINE-COUNT                    PIC S99 COMP SYNC.
00490  01   ERROR-REPORT-LINE-LIMIT                    PIC S99 COMP SYNC
00500                                                  VALUE 40.
00510  01   PAGE-NUMBER-W          PIC S99 VALUE 0 PACKED-DECIMAL.
00520  01   NUMBER-OF-ERRORS-W     PIC S99 VALUE 0 PACKED-DECIMAL.
00530  01   TODAYS-DATE.
00540       05   TODAYS-YEAR                           PIC 99.
00550       05   TODAYS-MONTH-AND-DAY                  PIC 9(4).
00560
```

FIGURE 11.22 *continued*

```
       01  .
           05  PREMIUM-ROW-ENTRIES.
               10              PIC 9(12)        VALUE 303055756690.
               10              PIC 9(12)        VALUE 307056756810.
               10              PIC 9(12)        VALUE 310057506900.
               10              PIC 9(12)        VALUE 313058256990.
               10              PIC 9(12)        VALUE 315058757050.
               10              PIC 9(12)        VALUE 319059757170.
               10              PIC 9(12)        VALUE 322060507260.
               10              PIC 9(12)        VALUE 325061257350.
               10              PIC 9(12)        VALUE 329062257470.
               10              PIC 9(12)        VALUE 333063257590.
               10              PIC 9(12)        VALUE 338064507740.
               10              PIC 9(12)        VALUE 345066257950.
               10              PIC 9(12)        VALUE 284051006120.
               10              PIC 9(12)        VALUE 291052756330.
               10              PIC 9(12)        VALUE 298054506540.
               10              PIC 9(12)        VALUE 303055756690.
               10              PIC 9(12)        VALUE 307056756810.
               10              PIC 9(12)        VALUE 310057506900.
               10              PIC 9(12)        VALUE 313058256990.
               10              PIC 9(12)        VALUE 315058757050.
               10              PIC 9(12)        VALUE 319059757170.
               10              PIC 9(12)        VALUE 322060507260.
               10              PIC 9(12)        VALUE 325061257350.
               10              PIC 9(12)        VALUE 329062257470.
           05  SEX             REDEFINES PREMIUM-ROW-ENTRIES
                               OCCURS 2 TIMES   INDEXED BY SEX-INDEX.
               10  ROW         OCCURS 12 TIMES  INDEXED BY ROW-INDEX.
                   15  ANNUAL-PREMIUM           PIC 99V99
                               OCCURS 3 TIMES   INDEXED BY COLUMN-INDEX.
           05  AGE-TABLE-ENTRIES.
               10              PIC XX           VALUE "18".
               10              PIC XX           VALUE "19".
               10              PIC XX           VALUE "20".
               10              PIC XX           VALUE "21".
               10              PIC XX           VALUE "22".
               10              PIC XX           VALUE "23".
               10              PIC XX           VALUE "24".
               10              PIC XX           VALUE "25".
               10              PIC XX           VALUE "26".
               10              PIC XX           VALUE "27".
               10              PIC XX           VALUE "28".
               10              PIC XX           VALUE "29".
           05  TABLE-AGE       REDEFINES AGE-TABLE-ENTRIES
                               PIC XX           OCCURS 12 TIMES
               ASCENDING KEY TABLE-AGE INDEXED BY AGE-INDEX.

           05  FACE-AMOUNT-TABLE-ENTRIES.
               10              PIC X(5)         VALUE "10000".
               10              PIC X(5)         VALUE "25000".
               10              PIC X(5)         VALUE "30000".
           05  TABLE-FACE-AMOUNT
                               REDEFINES FACE-AMOUNT-TABLE-ENTRIES
               OCCURS 3 TIMES  ASCENDING KEY TABLE-FACE-AMOUNT
               INDEXED BY FACE-AMOUNT-INDEX     PIC X(5).

           05  ERROR-TABLE.
               10              PIC X(19)        VALUE "SEX INVALID".
               10              PIC X(19)        VALUE "AGE INVALID".
               10              PIC X(19)
                               VALUE "FACE AMOUNT INVALID".
           05  ERROR-MESSAGE   REDEFINES ERROR-TABLE
                               OCCURS 3 TIMES   INDEXED BY ERROR-INDEX
                               PIC X(19).

       01  PAGE-HEAD-1.
           05                  PIC X(31) VALUE SPACES.
           05                  PIC X(19) VALUE "ROBBEM SAVINGS BANK".
```

continued

The three different error messages that this program can produce are shown starting at line 01140. When the program discovers an error in an input field, it SETs ERROR-INDEX to point to the appropriate ERROR-MESSAGE. ERROR-MESSAGE (ERROR-INDEX) is used as the sending field of a MOVE statement to MOVE the correct error message to the output area.

The Procedure Division, which begins at line 02200, follows the hierarchy diagram. Program P11-04 was run with the input data shown in Figure 11.23 and produced the output shown in Figure 11.24.

FIGURE *11.22* ***continued***

```
S COBOL II RELEASE 3.2 09/05/90                  P11004    DATE FEB 26,1992 T
----+-*A-1-B--+----2----+----3----+----4----+----5----+----6----+----7-|--+

01260
01270  01  ERROR-REPORT-PAGE-HEAD-2.
01280      05                      PIC X(23) VALUE SPACES.
01290      05                      PIC X(35)
01300          VALUE "LIFE INSURANCE INQUIRY ERROR REPORT".
01310
01320  01  ERROR-REPORT-PAGE-HEAD-3.
01330      05                      PIC X(13) VALUE SPACES.
01340      05                      PIC X(5)  VALUE "DATE".
01350      05  TODAYS-MONTH-AND-DAY          PIC Z9/99/.
01360      05  TODAYS-YEAR                   PIC 99B(33).
01370      05                      PIC X(5)  VALUE "PAGE".
01380      05  PAGE-NUMBER-OUT               PIC Z9.
01390
01400  01  ERROR-REPORT-PAGE-HEAD-4.
01410      05                                PIC X(10) VALUE SPACES.
01420      05                      PIC X(28) VALUE "CUSTOMER NAME".
01430      05                      PIC X(6)  VALUE "AGE".
01440      05                      PIC X(6)  VALUE "SEX".
01450      05                      PIC X(15) VALUE "FACE AMOUNT".
01460      05                      PIC X(5)  VALUE "ERROR".
01470
01480  01  NO-INPUT-DATA.
01490      05                      PIC X(34) VALUE SPACES.
01500      05                      PIC X(13) VALUE "NO INPUT DATA".
01510
01520  01  ERROR-LINE.
01530      05                      PIC X(10) VALUE SPACES.
01540      05  CUSTOMER-NAME-E               PIC X(25)B(4).
01550      05  AGE-E                         PIC XXB(4).
01560      05  SEX-E                         PIC XB(7).
01570      05  FACE-AMOUNT-X5-OUT            PIC X(5)B(7).
01580      05  ERROR-MESSAGE-OUT             PIC X(19).
01590
01600  01  ERROR-REPORT-TOTAL-LINE.
01610      05                      PIC X(22) VALUE SPACES.
01620      05                      PIC X(19) VALUE "NUMBER OF ERRORS -".
01630      05  NUMBER-OF-ERRORS-OUT          PIC ZZ9.
01640
01650  01  LETTER-LINE-2.
01660      05                      PIC X(31) VALUE SPACES.
01670      05                      PIC X(18) VALUE "116 W. 10TH STREET".
01680
01690  01  LETTER-LINE-3.
01700      05                      PIC X(31) VALUE SPACES.
01710      05                      PIC X(19) VALUE "BROOKLYN, NY  11220".
01720
01730  01  LETTER-LINE-4.
01740      05                      PIC X(53) VALUE SPACES.
01750      05  TODAYS-MONTH-AND-DAY          PIC ZZ/99/.
01760      05  TODAYS-YEAR                   PIC 99.
```

FIGURE 11.22 *continued*

```
 01  LETTER-LINE-7.
     05                     PIC X(10) VALUE SPACES.
     05                     PIC X(5)  VALUE "DEAR".
     05  CUSTOMER-NAME-OUT            PIC X(25).

 01  LETTER-LINE-9.
     05                     PIC X(15) VALUE SPACES.
     05                     PIC X(27)
         VALUE "THANK YOU FOR YOUR INQUIRY".
     05                     PIC X(27)
         VALUE "REGARDING SAVINGS BANK LIFE".

 01  LETTER-LINE-10.
     05                     PIC X(10) VALUE SPACES.
     05                     PIC X(37)
         VALUE "INSURANCE.  THE ANNUAL PREMIUM FOR A".
     05  FACE-AMOUNT-OUT PIC $ZZ,ZZ9B.
     05                     PIC X(16) VALUE "5-YEAR RENEWABLE".

 01  LETTER-LINE-11.
     05                     PIC X(10) VALUE SPACES.
     05                     PIC X(28)
         VALUE "TERM POLICY FOR A PERSON OF".
     05                     PIC X(20)
         VALUE "YOUR AGE AND SEX IS".
     05  ANNUAL-PREMIUM-OUT           PIC $ZZ.99.
     05                     PIC X     VALUE ".".

 01  LETTER-LINE-14.
     05                     PIC X(46) VALUE SPACES.
     05                     PIC X(16) VALUE "SINCERELY YOURS,".

 01  LETTER-LINE-15.
     05                     PIC X(46) VALUE SPACES.
     05                     PIC X(12) VALUE "H. B. SHRDLU".

 01  LETTER-LINE-16.
     05                     PIC X(46) VALUE SPACES.
     05                     PIC X(20) VALUE "INSURANCE CONSULTANT".

*****************************************************************

 PROCEDURE DIVISION.
 PROCESS-INQUIRIES.
     PERFORM INITIALIZATION
     PERFORM PROCESS-A-RECORD UNTIL THERE-IS-NO-MORE-INPUT
     PERFORM TERMINATION
     STOP RUN
     .

 INITIALIZATION.
     ACCEPT TODAYS-DATE FROM DATE
     MOVE CORR TODAYS-DATE TO LETTER-LINE-4
     MOVE CORR TODAYS-DATE TO ERROR-REPORT-PAGE-HEAD-3
     OPEN INPUT  INQUIRY-FILE-IN
          OUTPUT INQUIRY-LETTERS-FILE-OUT
                 ERROR-REPORT-FILE-OUT
     PERFORM PRINT-PAGE-HEADINGS
     PERFORM READ-A-RECORD
     IF THERE-IS-NO-MORE-INPUT
         WRITE ERROR-REPORT-RECORD-OUT FROM NO-INPUT-DATA AFTER 2
     END-IF
     .

```

continued

FIGURE 11.22 *continued*

```
S COBOL II RELEASE 3.2 09/05/90                P11004   DATE FEB 26,1992 T
----+-*A-1-B--+----2----+----3----+----4----+----5----+----6----+----7-|--+

PRINT-PAGE-HEADINGS.
    ADD 1 TO PAGE-NUMBER-W
    MOVE PAGE-NUMBER-W TO PAGE-NUMBER-OUT
    WRITE ERROR-REPORT-RECORD-OUT FROM PAGE-HEAD-1
               AFTER ADVANCING PAGE
    WRITE ERROR-REPORT-RECORD-OUT FROM ERROR-REPORT-PAGE-HEAD-2
    WRITE ERROR-REPORT-RECORD-OUT FROM ERROR-REPORT-PAGE-HEAD-3
              AFTER ADVANCING 2
    WRITE ERROR-REPORT-RECORD-OUT FROM ERROR-REPORT-PAGE-HEAD-4
              AFTER ADVANCING 3
    MOVE 2 TO ERROR-REPORT-LINE-SPACING
    MOVE 7 TO ERROR-REPORT-LINE-COUNT
    .

PROCESS-A-RECORD.
    MOVE "N" TO ANY-INPUT-ERRORS
    PERFORM ASSIGN-INDEX-VALUES
    IF ANY-INPUT-ERRORS IS EQUAL TO "N"
        PERFORM PRINT-AN-INQUIRY-LETTER
    END-IF
    PERFORM READ-A-RECORD
    .

TERMINATION.
    MOVE NUMBER-OF-ERRORS-W TO NUMBER-OF-ERRORS-OUT
    WRITE ERROR-REPORT-RECORD-OUT FROM ERROR-REPORT-TOTAL-LINE
              AFTER ADVANCING 3
    CLOSE INQUIRY-FILE-IN
          INQUIRY-LETTERS-FILE-OUT
          ERROR-REPORT-FILE-OUT
    .

READ-A-RECORD.
    READ INQUIRY-FILE-IN
        AT END
            SET THERE-IS-NO-MORE-INPUT TO TRUE
    .

ASSIGN-INDEX-VALUES.
    IF MALE
        SET SEX-INDEX TO 1
    ELSE
        IF FEMALE
            SET SEX-INDEX TO 2
        ELSE
            PERFORM SEX-ERROR
        END-IF
    END-IF
    SEARCH ALL TABLE-AGE
        AT END
            PERFORM AGE-ERROR
        WHEN TABLE-AGE (AGE-INDEX) IS EQUAL TO AGE-IN
            SET ROW-INDEX TO AGE-INDEX
    END-SEARCH
    SEARCH ALL TABLE-FACE-AMOUNT
        AT END
            PERFORM FACE-AMOUNT-ERROR
        WHEN TABLE-FACE-AMOUNT (FACE-AMOUNT-INDEX) IS EQUAL TO
            FACE-AMOUNT-X5-IN
            SET COLUMN-INDEX TO FACE-AMOUNT-INDEX
     END-SEARCH
     .
```

FIGURE 11.22 ***continued***

```
PRINT-AN-INQUIRY-LETTER.
    WRITE INQUIRY-LETTER-RECORD-OUT FROM PAGE-HEAD-1
                      AFTER ADVANCING PAGE
    WRITE INQUIRY-LETTER-RECORD-OUT FROM LETTER-LINE-2
    WRITE INQUIRY-LETTER-RECORD-OUT FROM LETTER-LINE-3
    WRITE INQUIRY-LETTER-RECORD-OUT FROM LETTER-LINE-4
    MOVE CUSTOMER-NAME-IN TO CUSTOMER-NAME-OUT
    WRITE INQUIRY-LETTER-RECORD-OUT FROM LETTER-LINE-7 AFTER 3
    WRITE INQUIRY-LETTER-RECORD-OUT FROM LETTER-LINE-9 AFTER 2
    MOVE FACE-AMOUNT-IN TO FACE-AMOUNT-OUT
    WRITE INQUIRY-LETTER-RECORD-OUT FROM LETTER-LINE-10
    MOVE ANNUAL-PREMIUM (SEX-INDEX, ROW-INDEX, COLUMN-INDEX)
        TO ANNUAL-PREMIUM-OUT
    WRITE INQUIRY-LETTER-RECORD-OUT FROM LETTER-LINE-11
    WRITE INQUIRY-LETTER-RECORD-OUT FROM LETTER-LINE-14 AFTER 3
    WRITE INQUIRY-LETTER-RECORD-OUT FROM LETTER-LINE-15
    WRITE INQUIRY-LETTER-RECORD-OUT FROM LETTER-LINE-16
    .

SEX-ERROR.
    SET ERROR-INDEX TO 1
    PERFORM WRITE-ERROR-LINE
    .

AGE-ERROR.
    SET ERROR-INDEX TO 2
    PERFORM WRITE-ERROR-LINE
    .

FACE-AMOUNT-ERROR.
    SET ERROR-INDEX TO 3
    PERFORM WRITE-ERROR-LINE
    .

WRITE-ERROR-LINE.
    MOVE "Y" TO ANY-INPUT-ERRORS
    ADD 1 TO NUMBER-OF-ERRORS-W
    MOVE CUSTOMER-NAME-IN  TO CUSTOMER-NAME-E
    MOVE AGE-IN            TO AGE-E
    MOVE SEX-IN            TO SEX-E
    MOVE FACE-AMOUNT-X5-IN TO FACE-AMOUNT-X5-OUT
    MOVE ERROR-MESSAGE (ERROR-INDEX) TO ERROR-MESSAGE-OUT
    IF ERROR-REPORT-LINE-COUNT + ERROR-REPORT-LINE-SPACING >
       ERROR-REPORT-LINE-LIMIT
        PERFORM PRINT-PAGE-HEADINGS
    END-IF
    WRITE ERROR-REPORT-RECORD-OUT FROM ERROR-LINE
                      AFTER ERROR-REPORT-LINE-SPACING
    ADD ERROR-REPORT-LINE-SPACING TO ERROR-REPORT-LINE-COUNT
    MOVE 1 TO ERROR-REPORT-LINE-SPACING
    .
```

FIGURE 11.23 **Input to Program P11-04**

```
--------------------------------------------------------------------------------
         1         2         3         4         5         6         7         8
12345678901234567890123456789012345678901234567890123456789012345678901234567890
--------------------------------------------------------------------------------
MARY WILLIAMS            18F10000
DEBORAH THOMPSON         25F25000
MARTIN JONES             16Z18000
GEORGE JOHN O'SHAUGHNESSY29M30000
AMY SUSAN RICHARDS       20F15000
LAURA JANE BROWN         30F30000
ELLEN JOY SMITH          29Q10000
HENRY ANDREWS            19M25000
THOMAS CARTER            18Z11000
MARY BETH LINCOLN        33F40000
CARL JACKSON             16R25000
```

FIGURE 11.24 **Output from Program P11-04**

```
                           ROBBEM SAVINGS BANK
                           116 W. 10TH STREET
                           BROOKLYN, NY  11220
                                                 2/26/92


DEAR MARY WILLIAMS

     THANK YOU FOR YOUR INQUIRY REGARDING SAVINGS BANK LIFE
INSURANCE.  THE ANNUAL PREMIUM FOR A $10,000 5-YEAR RENEWABLE
TERM POLICY FOR A PERSON OF YOUR AGE AND SEX IS $28.40.

                                          SINCERELY YOURS,
                                          H. B. SHRDLU
                                          INSURANCE CONSULTANT




                           ROBBEM SAVINGS BANK
                           116 W. 10TH STREET
                           BROOKLYN, NY  11220
                                                 2/26/92


DEAR DEBORAH THOMPSON

     THANK YOU FOR YOUR INQUIRY REGARDING SAVINGS BANK LIFE
INSURANCE.  THE ANNUAL PREMIUM FOR A $25,000 5-YEAR RENEWABLE
TERM POLICY FOR A PERSON OF YOUR AGE AND SEX IS $58.75.

                                          SINCERELY YOURS,
                                          H. B. SHRDLU
                                          INSURANCE CONSULTANT
```

FIGURE 11.24 *continued*

```
                    ROBBEM SAVINGS BANK
                    116 W. 10TH STREET
                    BROOKLYN, NY  11220
                                        2/26/92

DEAR GEORGE JOHN O'SHAUGHNESSY

     THANK YOU FOR YOUR INQUIRY REGARDING SAVINGS BANK LIFE
INSURANCE.  THE ANNUAL PREMIUM FOR A $30,000 5-YEAR RENEWABLE
TERM POLICY FOR A PERSON OF YOUR AGE AND SEX IS $79.50.

                              SINCERELY YOURS,
                              H. B. SHRDLU
                              INSURANCE CONSULTANT
```

```
                    ROBBEM SAVINGS BANK
                    116 W. 10TH STREET
                    BROOKLYN, NY  11220
                                        2/26/92

DEAR HENRY ANDREWS

     THANK YOU FOR YOUR INQUIRY REGARDING SAVINGS BANK LIFE
INSURANCE.  THE ANNUAL PREMIUM FOR A $25,000 5-YEAR RENEWABLE
TERM POLICY FOR A PERSON OF YOUR AGE AND SEX IS $56.75.

                              SINCERELY YOURS,
                              H. B. SHRDLU
                              INSURANCE CONSULTANT
```

```
                    ROBBEM SAVINGS BANK
           LIFE INSURANCE INQUIRY ERROR REPORT

   DATE  2/26/92                              PAGE  1

CUSTOMER NAME                AGE   SEX   FACE AMOUNT    ERROR

MARTIN JONES                  16    Z       18000       SEX INVALID
MARTIN JONES                  16    Z       18000       AGE INVALID
MARTIN JONES                  16    Z       18000       FACE AMOUNT INVALID
AMY SUSAN RICHARDS            20    F       15000       FACE AMOUNT INVALID
LAURA JANE BROWN              30    F       30000       AGE INVALID
ELLEN JOY SMITH               29    Q       10000       SEX INVALID
THOMAS CARTER                 18    Z       11000       SEX INVALID
THOMAS CARTER                 18    Z       11000       FACE AMOUNT INVALID
MARY BETH LINCOLN             33    F       40000       AGE INVALID
MARY BETH LINCOLN             33    F       40000       FACE AMOUNT INVALID
CARL JACKSON                  16    R       25000       SEX INVALID
CARL JACKSON                  16    R       25000       AGE INVALID

             NUMBER OF ERRORS -  12
```

EXERCISE 5

Write a program to read input records in the following format:

Positions	Field
1–3	Country Code
4	Time-of-Day Code
5	Type of Call
6–80	spaces

Each record relates to an overseas telephone call and contains a code indicating the Country Called, a Time-of-Day Code indicating whether the call was made during peak hours (P) or during off-peak hours (O), and a code indicating the Type of Call—whether the call was direct-dialed (D), operator-assisted station-to-station (S), or person-to-person (P). For each record, the program is to print on one line the name of the country called and the cost of the first 3 minutes of the call.

Check each input record for all possible invalid codes. For each error print on one line the field in error and a suitable message.

Tables 11.E5.1 and 11.E5.2 show the cost of the first 3 minutes of certain overseas calls.

TABLE 11.E5.1 Cost of the first 3 minutes for calls to certain countries made during peak hours

	COUNTRY CALLED	TYPE OF CALL		
		D	S	P
55	Brazil	$4.75	$9.45	$12.60
49	West Germany	4.05	7.05	12.60
353	Ireland	3.00	5.70	10.10
972	Israel	4.95	9.45	12.60
39	Italy	4.05	7.05	12.60
886	Taiwan	4.95	9.45	12.60
44	United Kingdom	3.00	5.70	10.10

TABLE 11.E5.2 Cost of the first 3 minutes for calls to certain countries made during off-peak hours

	COUNTRY CALLED	TYPE OF CALL		
		D	S	P
55	Brazil	$3.75	$7.05	$9.45
49	West Germany	3.15	5.40	9.45
353	Ireland	2.40	4.25	7.50
972	Israel	3.75	7.05	9.45
39	Italy	3.15	5.40	9.45
886	Taiwan	3.75	7.05	9.45
44	United Kingdom	2.40	4.25	7.50

Tables of Four and More Dimensions

COBOL systems adhering to the 1985 standard can process tables of up to at least seven dimensions. We give here an example of a four-dimensional table.

Let us say that we want to construct a table showing the cost of the initial period of certain telephone calls, and the cost of each additional minute of those calls. To find a function in this table, one would have to know the location of the calling number, the location of the called number, the time of day (day, evening, or night), and the type of call (direct-dialed, operator-assisted, or pay phone). We could define a table for the three types of calls, three different times of day, two calling locations, and 15 called locations as follows:

```
01 TABLES.
   02 TYPE-OF-CALL OCCURS 3 TIMES.
      03 TIME-0F-DAY OCCURS 3 TIMES.
         04 CALLING-LOCATION OCCURS 2 TIMES.
            05 CALLED-LOCATION OCCURS 15 TIMES.
               06 COST-OF-INITIAL-PERIOD       PIC V999.
               06 COST-PER-ADDITIONAL-MINUTE   PIC V999.
```

The number of computer storage locations occupied by a single element of this table is six—the sum of the sizes of COST-OF-INITIAL PERIOD and COST-PER-ADDITIONAL-MINUTE. The number of elements in the table is found by multiplying together the integers in all the OCCURS clauses, 3 by 3 by 2 by 15, to give 270 elements. The number of computer storage locations occupied by the entire table is found by multiplying the number of elements by the size of one element, in this case 270 by 6, or 1,620. If you wanted to write this table into a program, you would have to write 1,620 digits in many lines of entries.

This table could be loaded easily from an external file. Let us assume that the external file contains 270 records, with each record containing one value for COST-OF-INITIAL-PERIOD and one for COST-PER-ADDITIONAL-MINUTE. Then the following routine will load the table:

```
PERFORM LOAD-TABLE
     VARYING TYPE-OF-CALL-SUBSCRIPT FROM 1 BY 1 UNTIL
             TYPE-OF-CALL-SUBSCRIPT GREATER THAN 3
        AFTER TIME-OF-DAY-SUBSCRIPT FROM 1 BY 1 UNTIL
             TIME-OF-DAY-SUBSCRIPT GREATER THAN 3
        AFTER CALLING-LOCATION-SUBSCRIPT FROM 1 BY 1 UNTIL
             CALLING-LOCATION-SUBSCRIPT GREATER THAN 2
        AFTER CALLED-LOCATION-SUBSCRIPT FROM 1 BY 1 UNTIL
             CALLED-LOCATION-SUBSCRIPT GREATER THAN 15
```

Remember that the CALLED-LOCATION-SUBSCRIPT varies most rapidly and the TYPE-OF-CALL SUBSCRIPT least rapidly. The paragraph LOAD-TABLE, which could be anywhere in the Procedure Division, could be:

```
LOAD-TABLE.
    READ TABLE-FILE AT END MOVE "N" TO END-TABLE-FILE
    END-READ
    MOVE COST-OF-INITIAL-PERIOD-IN TO
          COST-OF-INITIAL-PERIOD (TYPE-OF-CALL-SUBSCRIPT
                                  TIME-OF-DAY-SUBSCRIPT
                                  CALLING-LOCATION-SUBSCRIPT
                                  CALLED-LOCATION-SUBSCRIPT)
    MOVE COST-PER-ADDITIONAL-MINUTE-IN TO
          COST-PER-ADDITIONAL-MINUTE (TYPE-OF-CALL-SUBSCRIPT
                                      TIME-OF-DAY-SUBSCRIPT
                                      CALLING-LOCATION-SUBSCRIPT
                                      CALLED-LOCATION-SUBSCRIPT)
```

Summary

Two-dimensional tables may be written in the Working Storage Section row by row. The OCCURS clause appearing in the REDEFINES entry must refer to the rows, and the OCCURS clause subordinate to it must refer to the columns.

A three-dimensional table may be thought of as a book full of two-dimensional tables. A three-dimensional table may be written into working storage row by row starting with the first row of the first page of the book. The OCCURS clause in the REDEFINES entry for such a table must refer to the pages of the book, the next subordinate OCCURS clause to the rows, and the last OCCURS clause to the columns.

A PERFORM . . . VARYING statement may be used to vary fields. Any identifiers used in a PERFORM . . . VARYING must be defined as numeric items. Any literals used in a PERFORM . . . VARYING must be numeric. Tables may have up to at least seven dimensions and a PERFORM . . . VARYING statement can vary up to at least seven fields.

The PICTURE character P may be used in definitions of fields in input, working storage, or output. In input and working storage the use of the character P can eliminate writing or keying low-order zeros, or zeros immediately to the right of a decimal point. In output P can eliminate the printing of unwanted high- or low-order digits.

Relative subscripting and relative indexing permit a program to refer to an entry in a table even if the subscript or index is not pointing to it. A relative subscript or relative index consists of a data name or index name followed by a space, followed by a plus or minus sign, followed by another space, followed by an integer.

Fill-In Exercises

1. The columns in a table run from ______ to ______, and the rows run from ______ to ______.
2. The labels that say what the rows and columns of a table stand for are called ______.
3. If a field is referred to with two indexes, either or both of the indexes may be given as a(n) ______, a(n) ______, or a(n) ______.
4. When a PERFORM . . . VARYING statement is used to vary more than one field, the reserved word ______ must be used.
5. In a three-dimensional table, ______ arguments are needed to locate a function.
6. You should consider using subscripting instead of indexing whenever a(n) ______ ______ is to be used to subscript a table.
7. The maximum size of a numeric literal is ______ digits.
8. When a two-dimensional table is written in the Working Storage Section row by row, only the ______ captions can be written into the table; the ______ captions must be written into a separate one-dimensional table.
9. When a three-dimensional table is written in the Working Storage Section row by row, it is best to write the ______ ______ and the ______ ______ in separate one-dimensional tables.
10. The PICTURE character ______ may be used to eliminate the printing of unwanted low-order zeros.

11. An in-line PERFORM statement never uses a(n) ______ ______ and always uses the word ______.

12. A PERFORM statement that contains the name of a paragraph to be executed is called a(n) ______ PERFORM.

13. When the WITH TEST phrase is omitted from a PERFORM statement, WITH TEST ______ is assumed.

14. Fields subordinate to an OCCURS clause may have more than one PICTURE because the ______ clause is permitted in an entry that is subordinate to an entry containing an OCCURS clause.

15. In a PERFORM statement that is varying more than one field, the first-named field varies ______ rapidly; the last-named field varies ______ rapidly.

Review Exercises

1. Given the following statement:

```
PERFORM PARAGRAPH-1
    VARYING SUBSCRIPT-1 FROM 1 BY 1 UNTIL
            SUBSCRIPT-1 IS GREATER THAN 5
    AFTER   SUBSCRIPT-2 FROM 1 BY 1 UNTIL
            SUBSCRIPT-2 IS GREATER THAN 6
```

   a. How many times will PARAGRAPH-1 execute?
   b. What will be the values of SUBSCRIPT-1 and SUBSCRIPT-2 the second time that PARAGRAPH-1 executes?
   c. Make a list showing the values of SUBSCRIPT-1 and SUBSCRIPT-2 for each execution of PARAGRAPH-1.

2. Write a program to read input records in the following format:

Positions	Field
1–2	County Code
3–7	Ranch Number
8–13	1987 Slaughter
14–19	1988 Slaughter
20–25	1989 Slaughter
26–31	1990 Slaughter
32–37	1991 Slaughter
38–43	1992 Slaughter
44–80	spaces

Each record contains data relating to the slaughter of cattle in seven counties in Wyoming in the years 1987 through 1992. There is one record for each cattle ranch in the seven counties, showing the Ranch Number, a County Code telling the location of the ranch, and six fields showing the number of head of cattle sent to slaughter in each of the six years 1987 through 1992.

Have your program sum the figures for each county for each year and produce a report in the format shown in Figure 11.RE2. Assume that the input data may be in any random order.

FIGURE *11.RE2* **Output format for Review Exercise 2**

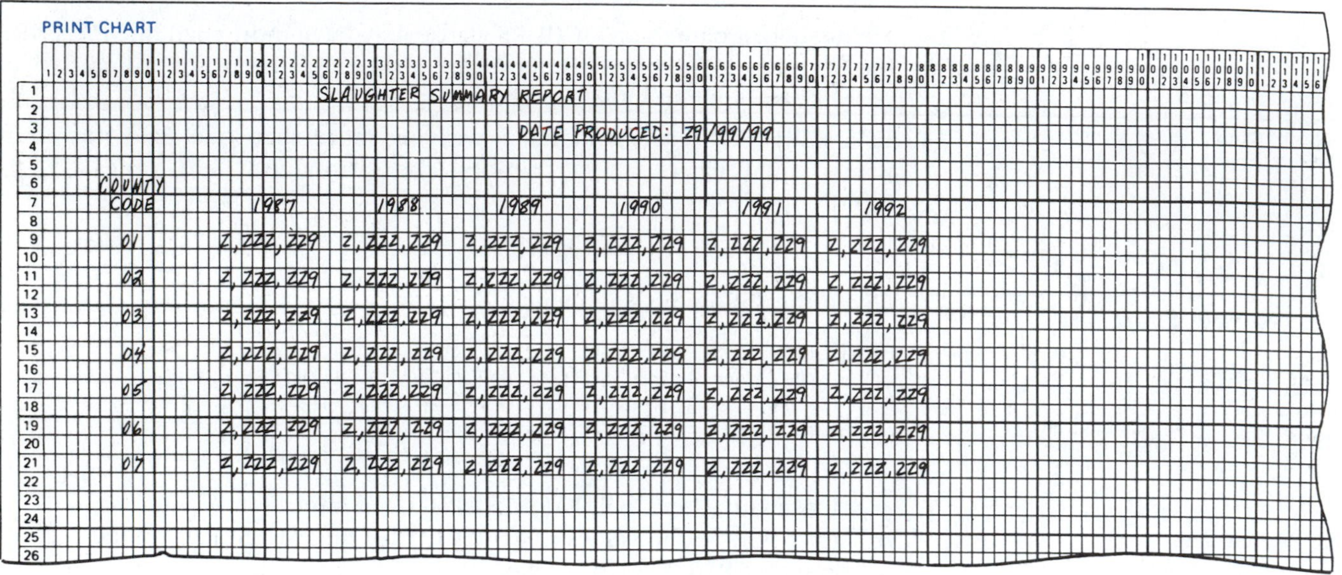

3. Write a program to read data in the following format:

Positions	Field
1–6	Policy Number
7–8	Age
9–10	Years to Run
11–18	Amount (to two decimal places)
19–80	spaces

Each record relates to a mortgage-protection life insurance policy and shows the Policy Number, the Age of the policy holder, the number of Years to Run on the mortgage, and the Amount of the mortgage. The program is to look up the monthly premium per $1 of mortgage amount in Table 11.RE3 and compute the monthly premium on the policy by multiplying the table function by the Amount of the mortgage. For each input record have your program print on one line the Policy Number, the Amount of the mortgage, and the computed premium. Check each input record for valid Age and valid Years to Run and print suitable error lines if any errors are found.

TABLE 11.RE3
Monthly premium per $1 of mortgage protection life insurance as a function of Age of policyholder and number of Years to Run on Mortgage

AGE OF POLICYHOLDER	YEARS TO RUN ON MORTGAGE		
	Over 15 but not over 20	Over 20 but not over 25	Over 25 but not over 30
26	.17	.19	.22
27	.17	.20	.22
28	.18	.21	.23
29	.19	.22	.24
30	.20	.23	.25
31	.21	.24	.26
32	.22	.25	.27
33	.23	.26	.29
34	.25	.28	.31
35	.26	.29	.32

Project

Rewrite your solution to the Project in Chapter 10. Use the following format for your input records instead of the one you used in Chapter 10:

Positions	Field
1–9	Employee Number
10–15	Gross Pay
16–17	Number of Exemptions
18–80	spaces

Write the following tax tables into your program as a two-dimensional table, and use it instead of the table you used in the Project in Chapter 10:

For 1 exemption:

If Gross Pay is:	Tax is:
less than $100	3% of Gross Pay
at least $100 but less than $200	$3 plus 4% of the excess over $100
at least $200 but less than $500	$7 plus 5% of the excess over $200
at least $500 but less than $1000	$22 plus 6% of the excess over $500
at least $1000 but less than $2000	$52 plus 7% of the excess over $1000
at least $2000 but less than $5000	$122 plus 8% of the excess over $2000
at least $5000	$362 plus 9% of the excess over $5000

For 2 exemptions:

If Gross Pay is:	Tax is:
less than $100	2% of Gross Pay
at least $100 but less than $200	$2 plus 3% of the excess over $100
at least $200 but less than $500	$5 plus 4% of the excess over $200
at least $500 but less than $1000	$17 plus 5% of the excess over $500
at least $1000 but less than $2000	$32 plus 6% of the excess over $1000
at least $2000 but less than $5000	$92 plus 7% of the excess over $2000
at least $5000	$302 plus 8% of the excess over $5000

For 3 exemptions:

If Gross Pay is:	Tax is:
less than $100	1% of Gross Pay
at least $100 but less than $200	$1 plus 2% of the excess over $100
at least $200 but less than $500	$3 plus 3% of the excess over $200
at least $500 but less than $1000	$12 plus 4% of the excess over $500
at least $1000 but less than $2000	$32 plus 5% of the excess over $1000
at least $2000 but less than $5000	$82 plus 6% of the excess over $2000
at least $5000	$262 plus 7% of the excess over $5000

For 4 or more exemptions:

If Gross Pay is:	Tax is:
less than $100	0
at least $100 but less than $200	1% of the excess over $100
at least $200 but less than $500	$1 plus 2% of the excess over $200
at least $500 but less than $1000	$4 plus 3% of the excess over $500
at least $1000 but less than $2000	$19 plus 4% of the excess over $1000
at least $2000 but less than $5000	$59 plus 5% of the excess over $2000
at least $5000	$209 plus 6% of the excess over $5000

CHAPTER 12

Sorting and Merging

HERE ARE THE KEY POINTS YOU SHOULD LEARN FROM THIS CHAPTER

1. What sorting and merging are

2. How to use the SORT verb

3. How to use the MERGE verb

4. How to write procedures that process data before or after they are sorted

5. How to write procedures that process data after they are merged

KEY WORDS TO RECOGNIZE AND LEARN

SORT	alphabet-name
MERGE	RELEASE
SD	master file
sort-merge file description entry	transaction file
key field	NATIVE
USING	alphabet-name clause
OUTPUT PROCEDURE	STANDARD-1
RETURN	STANDARD-2
INPUT PROCEDURE	ALPHABET
DUPLICATES	BCD
COLLATING SEQUENCE	binary-coded decimal

Arranging records in a particular order or sequence is a common requirement in data processing. Such record ordering can be accomplished using sorting or merging operations. A **SORT** produces an ordered file from one or more files that may be completely unordered. A **MERGE** produces an ordered file from two or more input files, each of which is already in sequence.

Sorting and merging have always constituted a large percentage of the work load in business data processing. COBOL has special language features that assist in sort and merge operations so that the user need not program these operations in detail. The COBOL sort and merge feature makes these operations easy to specify and to modify.

Using the SORT Verb

Our first program using the SORT verb, Program P12-01, reads input records in the following format:

Positions	Field
1–9	Social Security Number
10–14	Employee Number
15–21	Annual Salary (to two decimal places)
22–46	Employee Name
47–80	spaces

The program uses a SORT statement to SORT the input records into alphabetic order on Employee Name. The program then prints the SORTed records, and shows that the SORT process does not change the format of the records but only reorders them.

Program P12-01 is shown in Figure 12.1. The Environment Division shows a new FILE-CONTROL entry, one for a SORT-WORK-FILE, line 00140. SORTing and merging operations require a work file, which must be provided by the programmer. Here we provide SORT-WORK-FILE. SORT-WORK-FILE is a user-defined name. The name of the work file for a SORT or MERGE operation can be any legal name made up in accordance with the rules for making up file names.

In the Data Division there is a description of the input file and input record, lines 00200 through 00220. It turns out that we don't have to refer to any fields in the input record area, so we use just PIC X(80) to define it.

Then, at line 00240, there is an **SD** entry (**sort-merge file description entry**) for the SORT-WORK-FILE. An SD entry must contain the file name made up in the SELECT clause and must not contain a LABEL RECORDS clause. The SD entry must have associated with it at least one level-01 entry. The level-01 entry for a SORT or MERGE file must be the same size as the records being SORTed or MERGEd. In this program we are SORTing 80-character records, but you will see in later programs that the size of the records being SORTed need not be the same as the size of the input records. Ordinarily, the level-01 entry is broken down into fields, at least one of which must be a **key field,** which the records are to be SORTed or MERGEd on. Other fields in the level-01 entry may serve other uses in the program, and in later programs you will see what those uses are.

In lines 00270 through 00310 you can see how the format of SORT-RECORD corresponds to the format of the input records being SORTed. It turns out that some of the fields defined here are not referred to in the program. Only EMPLOYEE-NAME-S is referred to, so SORT-RECORD could just as well have been defined as

```
01 SORT-RECORD.
    05                      PIC X(21).
    05  EMPLOYEE-NAME-S     PIC X(25).
```

with EMPLOYEE-NAME-S positioned properly in the 80-character record.

The Procedure Division begins at line 00390. The ONLY-PARAGRAPH in this program consists of just a SORT statement and a STOP RUN statement. Ordinarily you would not write a COBOL program just to do a SORT in this manner if you have a sort utility program available on your computer to do the job. Here you see just how to use a SORT statement. Later you will see how to incorporate a SORT statement into a useful COBOL program.

Following the word SORT must be the name of the file as given in the SD entry. Then we must say whether the records are to be SORTed in ASCENDING or DESCENDING order on their KEY field, and we must say what that field is. In this case we want to SORT the records into alphabetic order on Employee Name, so we say ASCENDING KEY EMPLOYEE-NAME-S. The field named in the ASCENDING KEY or DESCENDING KEY phrase must be defined within a level-01 entry associated with the file named after the word SORT, or as the level-01

FIGURE *12.1* **Program P12-01**

```
S COBOL II RELEASE 3.1 09/19/89                  P12001    DATE JUL 26,1991 T
----+-*A-1-B--+----2----+----3----+----4----+----5----+----6----+----7-|--+

       IDENTIFICATION DIVISION.
       PROGRAM-ID.  P12-01.
      *
      *     THIS PROGRAM SORTS A FILE OF EMPLOYEE RECORDS AND
      *     PRINTS EACH RECORD ON ONE LINE.
      *
      ******************************************************************

       ENVIRONMENT DIVISION.
       INPUT-OUTPUT SECTION.
       FILE-CONTROL.
           SELECT EMPLOYEE-DATA-FILE-IN     ASSIGN TO INFILE.
           SELECT EMPLOYEE-DATA-FILE-OUT    ASSIGN TO PRINTER.
           SELECT SORT-WORK-FILE            ASSIGN TO SORTWK.

      ******************************************************************

       DATA DIVISION.
       FILE SECTION.
       FD  EMPLOYEE-DATA-FILE-IN.

       01                                   PIC X(80).

       SD  SORT-WORK-FILE
           RECORD CONTAINS 80 CHARACTERS.

       01  SORT-RECORD.
           05  SOCIAL-SECURITY-NUMBER-S     PIC X(9).
           05  EMPLOYEE-NUMBER-S            PIC X(5).
           05  ANNUAL-SALARY-S              PIC 9(5)V99.
           05  EMPLOYEE-NAME-S              PIC X(25).

       FD  EMPLOYEE-DATA-FILE-OUT.

       01                                  PIC X(80).
      ******************************************************************

       PROCEDURE DIVISION.
       ONLY-PARAGRAPH.
           SORT SORT-WORK-FILE
               ASCENDING KEY EMPLOYEE-NAME-S
               USING  EMPLOYEE-DATA-FILE-IN
               GIVING EMPLOYEE-DATA-FILE-OUT
           STOP RUN
           .
```

entry itself. More than one key field may be given in this phrase. We will use more than one key field later, in Program P12-02.

The third entry in our SORT statement names the input file to be SORTed, after the reserved word **USING.** And the last entry in the statement uses the reserved word GIVING to tell the SORT where to put the SORTed records when done. In this program we put the SORTed records directly onto the printer file, EMPLOYEE-DATA-FILE-OUT.

You can now follow how the program works. First, the contents of EMPLOYEE-DATA-FILE-IN are read in, SORTed, and written onto EMPLOYEE-DATA-FILE-OUT. Then the STOP RUN statement executes. The original input records, in EMPLOYEE-DATA-FILE-IN, remain in that file in their original order.

Program P12-01 was run with the input data shown in Figure 12.2 and produced the output shown in Figure 12.3.

FIGURE *12.2* **Input to Program P12-01**

```
--------------------------------------------------------------------------------
         1         2         3         4         5         6         7         8
12345678901234567890123456789012345678901234567890123456789012345678901234567890
--------------------------------------------------------------------------------
100040002105035000000MORALES, LUIS
209560011116643953000COSTELLO, JOSEPH S.
502070026135992208000JAVIER, CARLOS
703100038151470812000DUMAY, MRS. MARY
401710020128252906000LIPKE, VINCENT R.
608250035147601161000BUXBAUM, ROBERT
708020041155340463000SMITH, R.
604910032143731510000FELDSOTT, MS. SALLY
101850005108904651000JACOBSON, MRS. NELLIE
201110008112774302000GREENWOOD, JAMES
301810014120513604000REITER, D.
304870017124383255000MARRA, DITTA E.
407390023132122557000KUGLER, CHARLES
046302813714393604000MILLER, D.
505680029139861859000GOODMAN, ISAAC
987654321917735000000JANES, LAURA M.
803220044159210114000VINCENTE, MATTHEW J.
901050047163084235000THOMAS, THOMAS T.
007360661626394651000LAMBERT, GEORGE
```

FIGURE *12.3* **Output from Program P12-01**

```
608250035147601161000BUXBAUM, ROBERT
209560011116643953000COSTELLO, JOSEPH S.
703100038151470812000DUMAY, MRS. MARY
604910032143731510000FELDSOTT, MS. SALLY
505680029139861859000GOODMAN, ISAAC
201110008112774302000GREENWOOD, JAMES
101850005108904651000JACOBSON, MRS. NELLIE
987654321917735000000JANES, LAURA M.
502070026135992208000JAVIER, CARLOS
407390023132122557000KUGLER, CHARLES
007360661626394651000LAMBERT, GEORGE
401710020128252906000LIPKE, VINCENT R.
304870017124383255000MARRA, DITTA E.
046302813714393604000MILLER, D.
100040002105035000000MORALES, LUIS
301810014120513604000REITER, D.
708020041155340463000SMITH, R.
901050047163084235000THOMAS, THOMAS T.
803220044159210114000VINCENTE, MATTHEW J.
```

EXERCISE 1

Write a program to read input records in the following format:

Positions	Field
1–15	Company Name
16–30	Street Address
31–45	City and State
46–65	Employee Name
66–80	Employee Title

SORT them, and list them. Use a SORT statement to SORT the input data into alphabetic order on Company Name.

The SORT Verb with USING and GIVING

In Program P12-01 we had a SORT statement with a USING phrase and a GIVING phrase. The USING phrase told the SORT from which file to get the records to be SORTed, and the GIVING phrase told the SORT on which file to put the SORTed records when done. Not all SORT statements have USING or GIVING phrases. Later we will see some that don't.

A SORT statement with a USING and a GIVING phrase goes through the following steps to complete the SORT:

1. It OPENs the USING file as INPUT.
2. It READs each record in the file and releases it to the sorting process.
3. It CLOSEs the USING file.
4. It SORTs the records.
5. It OPENs the GIVING file as OUTPUT.
6. It returns each record from the sorting process and WRITEs it onto the GIVING file.
7. It CLOSEs the GIVING file.

Figure 12.4 shows the flow of records in a program having a SORT statement with USING and GIVING. Remember that the sorting takes place only after all the input records have been released to the sort system.

FIGURE 12.4 **Flow of records in a program having a SORT statement with USING and GIVING**

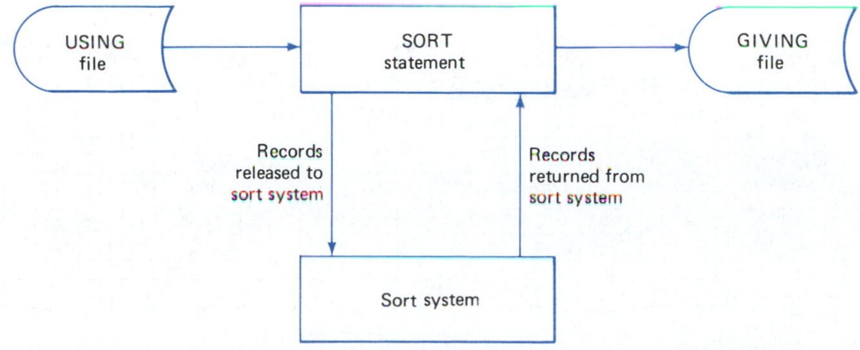

Since the SORT statement OPENs and CLOSEs both the USING file and the GIVING file, the files must not already be OPENed when the SORT statement is executed, and you must not try to CLOSE them when the SORT is done. You may OPEN the USING and GIVING files yourself outside of the SORT in order to use them for your own purposes, and then you must CLOSE them when you are through with them.

You must not issue an OPEN, CLOSE, READ, or WRITE statement to a SORT or MERGE work file itself.

Using an OUTPUT PROCEDURE

Now let us say that we would like to be able to process the input records after they are SORTed, rather than having the SORT just dump the records out onto some GIVING file. As it happens, we can easily get the SORT to hold onto the records after SORTing them and return them one at a time, in SORTed order, to the processing portion of a program as they are needed. We do this by using an **OUTPUT PROCEDURE** phrase instead of a GIVING phrase in the SORT statement. This tells the SORT that there is no GIVING file, no place for it to put its SORTed results.

Program P12-02 shows how an OUTPUT PROCEDURE is used and also some other features of SORTing. Program P12-02 uses the same input data as Program P12-01 and produces output in the format shown in Figure 12.5. This time the data are SORTed in a different order. This time the output prints so that all the employees who have the highest salary are first, followed by all the employees with the second-highest salary, and so on down to the employees with the lowest salary. If there is more than one employee with the same salary, such employees are printed one right after the other in order on Employee Number.

The output from Program P12-02 may be said to be sorted on Annual Salary as a descending key and Employee Number as an ascending key. Alternatively it can be said to be sorted on Employee Number as an ascending key within Annual Salary as a descending key. Annual Salary is the major sort field and Employee Number the minor sort field.

FIGURE *12.5* **Output format for Program P12-02**

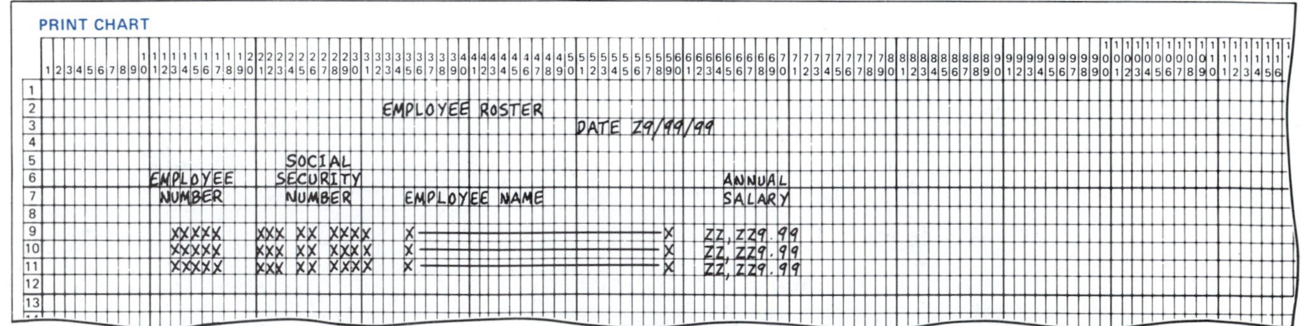

A Program with an OUTPUT PROCEDURE

Program P12-02 is shown in Figure 12.6. In the File Section, the input file is defined in the usual way, at line 00200, and the input record, at line 00220, once again is not broken down into fields. As a general rule, if you don't OPEN an input file in a program, you need not break down the input record into fields. You will soon see how we avoid OPENing the input file in this program.

The SD and level-01 entries for SORT-WORK-FILE and SORT-RECORD follow, at lines 00240 through 00310. This time we need all the level-05 entries in SORT-RECORD.

FIGURE 12.6

Program P12-02

```
S COBOL II RELEASE 3.1 09/19/89                      P12002   DATE JUL 26,1991 T
----+-*A-1-B--+----2----+----3----+----4----+----5----+----6----+----7-|--+

00010  IDENTIFICATION DIVISION.
00020  PROGRAM-ID.  P12-02.
00030 *
00040 *     THIS PROGRAM SORTS A FILE OF EMPLOYEE RECORDS AND
00050 *     PRINTS THE CONTENTS OF EACH RECORD ON ONE LINE.
00060 *
00070 *****************************************************************
00080
00090  ENVIRONMENT DIVISION.
00100  INPUT-OUTPUT SECTION.
00110  FILE-CONTROL.
00120      SELECT EMPLOYEE-DATA-FILE-IN     ASSIGN TO INFILE.
00130      SELECT EMPLOYEE-DATA-FILE-OUT    ASSIGN TO PRINTER.
00140      SELECT SORT-WORK-FILE            ASSIGN TO SORTWK.
00150
00160 *****************************************************************
00170
00180  DATA DIVISION.
00190  FILE SECTION.
00200  FD  EMPLOYEE-DATA-FILE-IN.
00210
00220  01                                   PIC X(80).
00230
00240  SD  SORT-WORK-FILE
00250      RECORD CONTAINS 80 CHARACTERS.
00260
00270  01  SORT-RECORD.
00280      05  SOCIAL-SECURITY-NUMBER-S     PIC X(9).
00290      05  EMPLOYEE-NUMBER-S            PIC X(5).
00300      05  ANNUAL-SALARY-S              PIC 9(5)V99.
00310      05  EMPLOYEE-NAME-S              PIC X(25).
00320
00330  FD  EMPLOYEE-DATA-FILE-OUT.
00340
00350  01  REPORT-LINE                      PIC X(71).
00360
00370  WORKING-STORAGE SECTION.
00380  01  MORE-INPUT                       PIC X        VALUE "Y".
00390      88 THERE-IS-NO-MORE-INPUT        VALUE "N".
00400  01  TODAYS-DATE.
00410      05  TODAYS-YEAR                  PIC 99.
00420      05  TODAYS-MONTH-AND-DAY         PIC 9(4).
00430
00440  01  HEADING-LINE-1.
00450      05                     PIC X(32) VALUE SPACES.
00460      05                     PIC X(15) VALUE "EMPLOYEE ROSTER".
00470
00480  01  HEADING-LINE-2.
00490      05                     PIC X(50) VALUE SPACES.
00500      05                     PIC X(5)  VALUE "DATE".
00510      05  TODAYS-MONTH-AND-DAY         PIC Z9/99/.
00520      05  TODAYS-YEAR                  PIC 99.
```

continued

The Procedure Division begins at line 00850. The SORT statement at line 00870 contains a DESCENDING KEY phrase and an ASCENDING KEY phrase, to describe the desired SORT sequence fully. Whenever there is more than one KEY field in a SORT, they must be listed in order from major to minor. Although each KEY field must be indicated as ASCENDING or DESCENDING, you will see when we look at the format of the SORT statement that it is sometimes not necessary to repeat the words ASCENDING KEY or DESCENDING KEY for each KEY field.

At line 00910 there is an OUTPUT PROCEDURE phrase instead of a GIVING phrase. An OUTPUT PROCEDURE contains processing steps to be carried out after the SORT is complete, and the OUTPUT PROCEDURE phrase gives the name of the procedure. In this program the OUTPUT PROCEDURE has been given the name PRODUCE-REPORT. PRODUCE-REPORT is shown as the name of a paragraph at line 00950.

The paragraph PRODUCE-REPORT contains three familiar-looking PERFORM statements. When these three PERFORM statements are through executing, the program executes the STOP RUN statement at line 00920.

Our read routine, at line 01320, now contains a **RETURN** statement where we would ordinarily expect a READ. A RETURN statement, like a READ statement, brings records into a program one at a time for processing. But whereas a READ statement brings a record into the program from an external file, a RETURN statement brings in a SORTed or MERGEd record from the SORT or MERGE process. Notice that the file name given in the SD entry is the one that must be used in the RETURN statement. A RETURN statement makes the next SORTed or MERGEd record available to the program in the level-01 entry associated with the work file.

The MOVE statements at lines 01190 through 01230 show that fields that are part of a level-01 entry associated with a work file can be operated on just like any other fields. You can now see why we don't have to OPEN the input file in this program. The SORT statement OPENs the input file originally to READ the records for SORTing and then RETURNs the SORTed records to the level-01 area associated with the SD entry.

FIGURE 12.6 *continued*

```
S COBOL II RELEASE 3.1 09/19/89                    P12002   DATE JUL 26,1991 T
----+-*A-1-B--+----2----+----3----+----4----+----5----+----6----+----7-|--+


00530
00540  01  COLUMN-HEADS-1.
00550      05                    PIC X(23) VALUE SPACES.
00560      05                    PIC X(6)  VALUE "SOCIAL".
00570
00580  01  COLUMN-HEADS-2.
00590      05                    PIC X(10) VALUE SPACES.
00600      05                    PIC X(12) VALUE "EMPLOYEE".
00610      05                    PIC X(42) VALUE "SECURITY".
00620      05                    PIC X(6)  VALUE "ANNUAL".
00630
00640  01  COLUMN-HEADS-3.
00650      05                    PIC X(11) VALUE SPACES.
00660      05                    PIC X(12) VALUE "NUMBER".
00670      05                    PIC X(11) VALUE "NUMBER".
00680      05                    PIC X(30) VALUE "EMPLOYEE NAME".
00690      05                    PIC X(6)  VALUE "SALARY".
```

FIGURE 12.6 *continued*

```
 01  DETAIL-LINE.
     05                                PIC X(12) VALUE SPACES.
     05  EMPLOYEE-NUMBER-OUT           PIC X(5)B(3).
     05  SOCIAL-SECURITY-NUMBER-OUT
                                       PIC X(3)BXXBX(4)B(3).
     05  EMPLOYEE-NAME-OUT             PIC X(25)B(3).
     05  ANNUAL-SALARY-OUT             PIC ZZ,ZZ9.99.

 01  NO-INPUT-DATA.
     05                      PIC X(33) VALUE SPACES.
     05                      PIC X(13) VALUE "NO INPUT DATA".

******************************************************************

 PROCEDURE DIVISION.
 CONTROL-PARAGRAPH.
     SORT SORT-WORK-FILE
         DESCENDING KEY ANNUAL-SALARY-S
         ASCENDING  KEY EMPLOYEE-NUMBER-S
         USING EMPLOYEE-DATA-FILE-IN
         OUTPUT PROCEDURE IS PRODUCE-REPORT
     STOP RUN
     .

 PRODUCE-REPORT.
     PERFORM INITIALIZATION
     PERFORM MAIN-PROCESS UNTIL THERE-IS-NO-MORE-INPUT
     PERFORM TERMINATION
     .

 INITIALIZATION.
     OPEN OUTPUT EMPLOYEE-DATA-FILE-OUT
     ACCEPT TODAYS-DATE FROM DATE
     MOVE CORRESPONDING TODAYS-DATE TO HEADING-LINE-2
     WRITE REPORT-LINE FROM HEADING-LINE-1 AFTER PAGE
     WRITE REPORT-LINE FROM HEADING-LINE-2
     WRITE REPORT-LINE FROM COLUMN-HEADS-1 AFTER 2
     WRITE REPORT-LINE FROM COLUMN-HEADS-2
     WRITE REPORT-LINE FROM COLUMN-HEADS-3
     MOVE SPACES TO REPORT-LINE
     WRITE REPORT-LINE
     PERFORM READ-A-RECORD
     IF THERE-IS-NO-MORE-INPUT
         WRITE REPORT-LINE FROM NO-INPUT-DATA
     END-IF
     .

 MAIN-PROCESS.
     MOVE EMPLOYEE-NUMBER-S TO EMPLOYEE-NUMBER-OUT
     MOVE SOCIAL-SECURITY-NUMBER-S
                           TO SOCIAL-SECURITY-NUMBER-OUT
     MOVE EMPLOYEE-NAME-S   TO EMPLOYEE-NAME-OUT
     MOVE ANNUAL-SALARY-S   TO ANNUAL-SALARY-OUT
     WRITE REPORT-LINE FROM DETAIL-LINE
     PERFORM READ-A-RECORD
     .

 TERMINATION.
     CLOSE EMPLOYEE-DATA-FILE-OUT
     .

 READ-A-RECORD.
     RETURN SORT-WORK-FILE
         AT END
             SET THERE-IS-NO-MORE-INPUT TO TRUE
     .
```

When this program executes, the SORT statement first brings in and SORTs all the records in the file EMPLOYEE-DATA-FILE-IN. The program then executes the OUTPUT PROCEDURE. When a RETURN statement is encountered in the OUTPUT PROCEDURE, the SORT provides the next SORTed record for processing. When execution of the OUTPUT PROCEDURE is complete, the program executes the STOP RUN statement. Figure 12.7 shows the flow of records in a program having a SORT statement with USING and an OUTPUT PROCEDURE.

Program P12-02 was run with the same input data as Program P12–01 and produced the output shown in Figure 12.8.

FIGURE 12.7 **Flow of records in a program having a SORT statement with USING and an OUTPUT PROCEDURE**

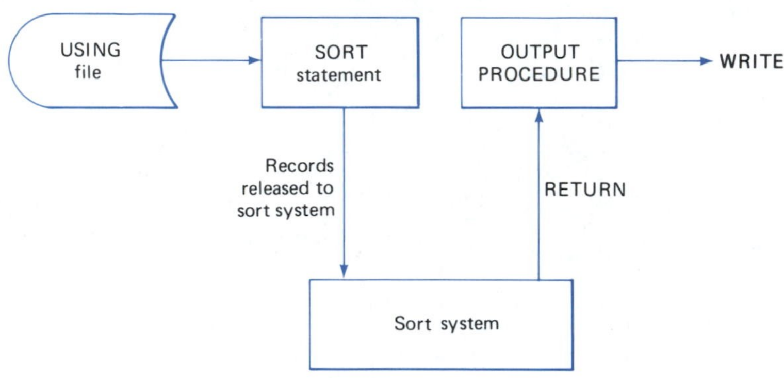

FIGURE 12.8 **Output from Program P12-02**

```
                          EMPLOYEE ROSTER
                                             DATE   7/26/91

                SOCIAL
EMPLOYEE       SECURITY                                          ANNUAL
 NUMBER         NUMBER        EMPLOYEE NAME                      SALARY

  10503      100 04 0002     MORALES, LUIS                    50,000.00
  91773      987 65 4321     JANES, LAURA M.                  50,000.00
  10890      101 85 0005     JACOBSON, MRS. NELLIE            46,510.00
  62639      007 36 0661     LAMBERT, GEORGE                  46,510.00
  11277      201 11 0008     GREENWOOD, JAMES                 43,020.00
  16308      901 05 0047     THOMAS, THOMAS T.                42,350.00
  11664      209 56 0011     COSTELLO, JOSEPH S.              39,530.00
  12051      301 81 0014     REITER, D.                       36,040.00
  71439      046 30 2813     MILLER, D.                       36,040.00
  12438      304 87 0017     MARRA, DITTA E.                  32,550.00
  12825      401 71 0020     LIPKE, VINCENT R.                29,060.00
  13212      407 39 0023     KUGLER, CHARLES                  25,570.00
  13599      502 07 0026     JAVIER, CARLOS                   22,080.00
  13986      505 68 0029     GOODMAN, ISAAC                   18,590.00
  14373      604 91 0032     FELDSOTT, MS. SALLY              15,100.00
  14760      608 25 0035     BUXBAUM, ROBERT                  11,610.00
  15147      703 10 0038     DUMAY, MRS. MARY                  8,120.00
  15534      708 02 0041     SMITH, R.                         4,630.00
  15921      803 22 0044     VINCENTE, MATTHEW J.              1,140.00
```

The SORT Statement

The format of the SORT statement is as follows:

```
SORT file-name-1 {ON {ASCENDING } KEY {data-name-1} ... } ...
                     {DESCENDING}

    [WITH DUPLICATES IN ORDER]
    [COLLATING SEQUENCE IS alphabet-name-1]

    {INPUT PROCEDURE IS procedure-name-1 [{THROUGH} procedure-name-2]}
    {                                     [{THRU   }                 ]}
    {USING {file-name-2} ...                                          }

    {OUTPUT PROCEDURE IS procedure-name-3 [{THROUGH} procedure-name-4]}
    {                                      [{THRU   }                 ]}
    {GIVING {file-name-3} ...                                          }
```

The format shows that the programmer may specify as many KEY fields as desired to control the SORT. The fields must be specified in order from major to minor. There may be as many ASCENDING KEY and DESCENDING KEY phrases as desired, and each phrase may contain as many data names as desired.

For input to the SORT the programmer must choose either the **INPUT PROCEDURE** phrase or the USING phrase. If more than one file name is contained in a USING phrase, the contents of all USING files are SORTed together.

Then, regardless of the choice made for input, the programmer must choose either OUTPUT PROCEDURE or GIVING for the output from the SORT. If more than one file name is contained in a GIVING phrase, the same SORTed output is placed onto each of the GIVING files.

If the **DUPLICATES** phrase is used, any records having the contents of their SORT fields identical will appear in the output from the SORT in the same order as they appeared in the input. If the DUPLICATES phrase is omitted, the order of such records in the output is unpredictable.

COLLATING SEQUENCE and **alphabet-name** will be discussed later in this chapter.

The RETURN Statement

The format of the RETURN statement is as follows:

```
RETURN file-name-1 RECORD [INTO identifier-1]
    AT END imperative-statement-1
    [NOT AT END imperative-statement-2]
    [END-RETURN]
```

The RETURN statement may be used only within an OUTPUT PROCEDURE, and every OUTPUT PROCEDURE must contain at least one RETURN statement. After all SORTed records have been RETURNed, the AT END phrase is executed, and no more RETURN statements may be executed.

The INTO option in a RETURN statement works the same way that it does in a READ statement. You will see it used in a RETURN statement later in this chapter.

EXERCISE *2*

Explain why the paragraph PRODUCE-REPORT in Program P12-02 lacks a STOP RUN statement.

EXERCISE *3*

Write a program that uses the same input format as Exercise 1, page 391, and produces output in the format shown in Figure 12.E3. Use a SORT statement to SORT the input data into alphabetic order on Employee Name within Company Name. Use an OUTPUT PROCEDURE to print the output.

FIGURE *12.E3* Output format for Exercise 3

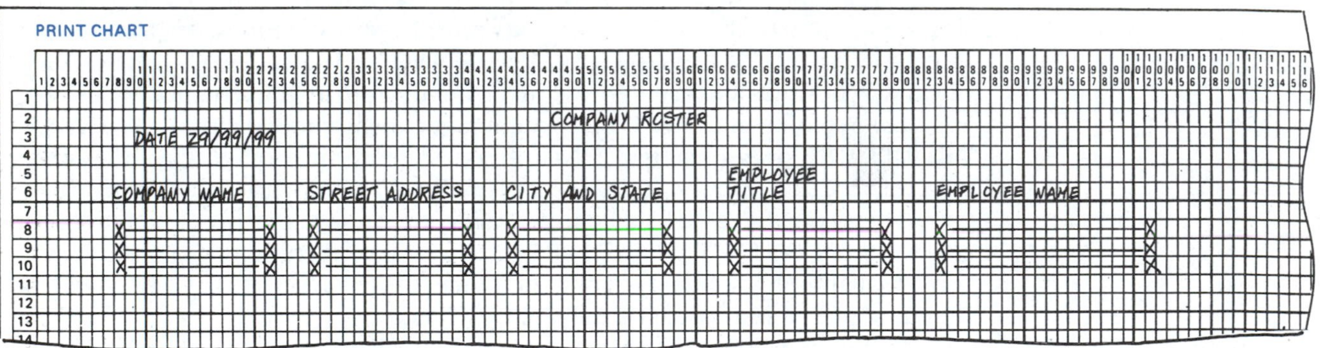

Using an INPUT PROCEDURE

An INPUT PROCEDURE contains processing steps to be carried out before SORTing begins. In Program P12-03 we will use an INPUT PROCEDURE to select certain input records for SORTing. An INPUT PROCEDURE may also be used to modify input records before they are SORTed.

Program P12-03 reads input records in the following format:

Positions	*Field*
1–6	Part Number
7–26	Description
27–31	Reorder Quantity
32–36	Reorder Point
37–41	Quantity on Hand
42–80	spaces

Each record contains a Part Number, a Description of the part, a Reorder Quantity, a Reorder Point, and a Quantity on Hand. The program is to print a reorder report showing the parts that have a Quantity on Hand less than their Reorder Point. The output is to be in Part Number order and is to have the format shown in Figure 12.9.

In Program P12-03 we want to SORT only the records that are going to be printed; namely, the ones whose Quantity on Hand is less than their Reorder Point. We will use an INPUT PROCEDURE to select out only those records and release them to the SORT process.

FIGURE *12.9* **Output format for Program P12-03**

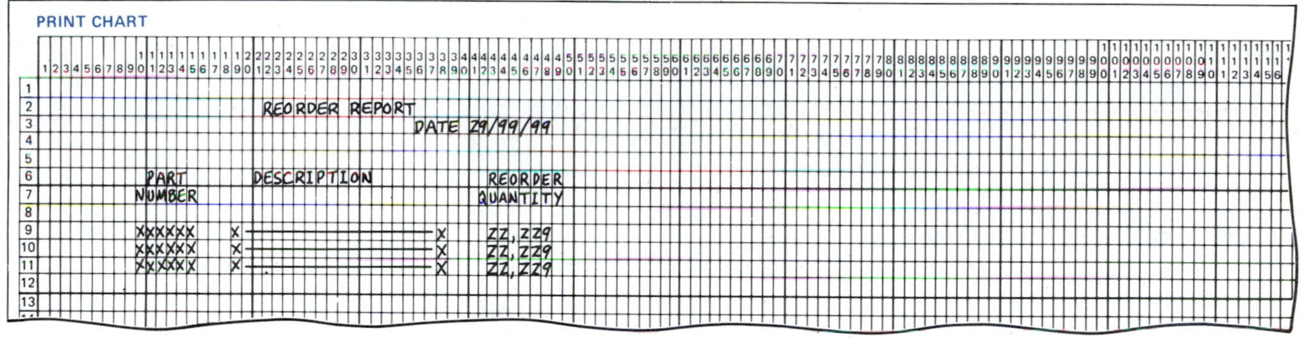

A Program with an INPUT PROCEDURE

Program P12-03 is shown in Figure 12.10. The input file is defined starting at line 00210. The input record is broken down into fields in this program because the field names are needed for processing in the INPUT PROCEDURE. The description of SORT-RECORD, starting at line 00340, includes only the fields that are needed for the SORT and for processing after the SORT is complete. As a general rule you should arrange a SORT so that you SORT as few and as small records as possible.

SORTing is one of the most time-consuming operations in data processing, and if you can make your records small and few, you can save a lot of computer time. Also, the capacity of the COBOL SORT is limited. For any given record size and work-file size, only a certain maximum number of records can be SORTed. The smaller the records, the more that can be SORTed. If you have more records to SORT than the SORT can handle, you must SORT the records in groups of manageable size and then MERGE the results (more about MERGE later in this chapter).

The Working Storage Section begins at line 00430. In this program we use two flags to signal end-of-file, MORE-INPUT at line 00440 and MORE-SORTED-RECORDS at line 00460. The first is used during the original input and selection process to signal that there are no more input records. The other is used during the printing of the report to signal that the SORT has no more records to RETURN to the program. You will see how both are used when we look at the Procedure Division.

The Procedure Division of Program P12-03 starts at line 00860. The SORT and STOP RUN statements are of course in their own paragraph. The SORT statement names SELECT-RECORDS as its INPUT PROCEDURE and PRODUCE-REPORT as its OUTPUT PROCEDURE. The paragraph SELECT-RECORDS can be

FIGURE 12.10 **Program P12-03**

```
S COBOL II RELEASE 3.1 09/19/89                    P12003   DATE AUG 06,1991 T
----+-*A-1-B--+----2----+----3----+----4----+----5----+----6----+----7-|--+

00010  IDENTIFICATION DIVISION.
00020  PROGRAM-ID.  P12-03.
00030 *
00040 *     THIS PROGRAM SORTS SOME FIELDS OF SELECTED INVENTORY RECORDS
00050 *     AND THEN PRINTS THE SELECTED FIELDS OF EACH SELECTED RECORD
00060 *     ON ONE LINE.
00070 *
00080 ******************************************************************
00090
00100  ENVIRONMENT DIVISION.
00110  INPUT-OUTPUT SECTION.
00120  FILE-CONTROL.
00130      SELECT INVENTORY-FILE-IN          ASSIGN TO INFILE.
00140      SELECT REORDER-REPORT-FILE-OUT    ASSIGN TO PRINTER.
00150      SELECT SORT-WORK-FILE             ASSIGN TO SORTWK.
00160
00170 ******************************************************************
00180
00190  DATA DIVISION.
00200  FILE SECTION.
00210  FD  INVENTORY-FILE-IN
00220      RECORD CONTAINS 80 CHARACTERS.
00230
00240  01  INVENTORY-RECORD-IN.
00250      05  PART-NUMBER-IN                PIC X(6).
00260      05  DESCRIPTION-IN                PIC X(20).
00270      05  REORDER-QUANTITY-IN           PIC 9(5).
00280      05  REORDER-POINT-IN              PIC 9(5).
00290      05  QUANTITY-ON-HAND-IN           PIC 9(5).
00300
```

FIGURE 12.10 *continued*

```
SD  SORT-WORK-FILE
    RECORD CONTAINS 31 CHARACTERS.

01  SORT-RECORD.
    05  PART-NUMBER-S                PIC X(6).
    05  DESCRIPTION-S                PIC X(20).
    05  REORDER-QUANTITY-S           PIC 9(5).

FD  REORDER-REPORT-FILE-OUT.

01  REPORT-LINE                      PIC X(49).

WORKING-STORAGE SECTION.
01  MORE-INPUT                       PIC X         VALUE "Y".
    88 THERE-IS-NO-MORE-INPUT                      VALUE "N".
01  MORE-SORTED-RECORDS              PIC X         VALUE "Y".
    88 THERE-IS-NO-MORE-SORTED-INPUT               VALUE "N".
01  TODAYS-DATE.
    05  TODAYS-YEAR                  PIC 99.
    05  TODAYS-MONTH-AND-DAY         PIC 9(4).

01  HEADING-LINE-1.
    05                     PIC X(21) VALUE SPACES.
    05                     PIC X(14) VALUE "REORDER REPORT".

01  HEADING-LINE-2.
    05                     PIC X(35) VALUE SPACES.
    05                     PIC X(5)  VALUE "DATE".
    05  TODAYS-MONTH-AND-DAY
                           PIC Z9/99/.
    05  TODAYS-YEAR        PIC 99.

01  COLUMN-HEADS-1.
    05                     PIC X(10) VALUE SPACES.
    05                     PIC X(10) VALUE "PART".
    05                     PIC X(22) VALUE "DESCRIPTION".
    05                     PIC X(7)  VALUE "REORDER".

01  COLUMN-HEADS-2.
    05                     PIC X(9)  VALUE SPACES.
    05                     PIC X(32) VALUE "NUMBER".
    05                     PIC X(8)  VALUE "QUANTITY".

01  DETAIL-LINE.
    05                         PIC X(9)  VALUE SPACES.
    05  PART-NUMBER-OUT        PIC X(6)B(3).
    05  DESCRIPTION-OUT        PIC X(20)B(4).
    05  REORDER-QUANTITY-OUT   PIC ZZ,ZZ9.

01  NO-INPUT-DATA.
    05                         PIC X(21) VALUE SPACES.
    05                         PIC X(13) VALUE "NO INPUT DATA".

*****************************************************************

PROCEDURE DIVISION.
CONTROL-PARAGRAPH.
    SORT SORT-WORK-FILE
        ASCENDING KEY PART-NUMBER-S
        INPUT  PROCEDURE IS SELECT-RECORDS
        OUTPUT PROCEDURE IS PRODUCE-REPORT
    STOP RUN
    .
```

continued

found at line 00950, and PRODUCE-REPORT at line 01260. When this program executes, it first carries out the INPUT PROCEDURE, then SORTs the records that have been released to it by the INPUT PROCEDURE, then carries out the OUTPUT PROCEDURE, and then executes the STOP RUN.

The INPUT PROCEDURE

The paragraph SELECT-RECORDS is organized like the OUTPUT PROCEDURE in Program P12-03, with three PERFORM statements.

The INITIALIZATION-I paragraph, at line 01010, OPENs only the INPUT file. This INPUT PROCEDURE deals only with the INPUT file and the SORT-WORK-FILE. Later, the OUTPUT PROCEDURE will operate on the SORT-WORK-FILE and the OUTPUT file. So we need to OPEN only the INPUT file now. The OUTPUT PROCEDURE will later OPEN only the OUTPUT file. After the priming READ, we do not test for an empty INPUT file. Later, in the OUTPUT PROCEDURE, we will test to see whether any input records were selected.

In the SELECTION paragraph, line 01060, each input record is tested to see whether it meets the condition for being printed on the output report. If it does, the three MOVE statements set up the record that is to be SORTed, and the **RELEASE** statement RELEASEs the record to the sorting process. Whereas a WRITE statement transfers a record from the program to an external file, a RELEASE statement transfers a record from the program to the SORT process. Notice that the object of the RELEASE verb is the record name in the level-01 entry associated with the sort work file. The format of the RELEASE statement will be given shortly.

Any source fields may be used to build the record that is RELEASEd to the SORT system. In this program the three source fields used were PART-NUMBER-IN, DESCRIPTION-IN, and REORDER-QUANTITY-IN. But fields used to build a SORT record need not all come from input areas. They can come from fields in working storage as well, or they can be the result of computation. There is no limit to the amount or complexity of coding that may be contained in an INPUT PROCEDURE and executed before any records are SORTed.

The OUTPUT PROCEDURE

The paragraph PRODUCE-REPORT begins at line 01260 and contains the usual three PERFORM statements.

FIGURE *12.10* ***continued***

```
S COBOL II RELEASE 3.1 09/19/89                 P12003   DATE AUG 06,1991 T
----+-*A-1-B--+----2----+----3----+----4----+----5----+----6----+----7-|--+


00940
00950  SELECT-RECORDS.
00960      PERFORM INITIALIZATION-I
00970      PERFORM SELECTION UNTIL THERE-IS-NO-MORE-INPUT
00980      PERFORM TERMINATION-I
00990      .
01000
```

FIGURE 12.10 *continued*

```
INITIALIZATION-I.
    OPEN INPUT INVENTORY-FILE-IN
    PERFORM READ-A-RECORD
    .
SELECTION.
    IF QUANTITY-ON-HAND-IN IS LESS THAN REORDER-POINT-IN
        MOVE PART-NUMBER-IN      TO PART-NUMBER-S
        MOVE DESCRIPTION-IN      TO DESCRIPTION-S
        MOVE REORDER-QUANTITY-IN TO REORDER-QUANTITY-S
        RELEASE SORT-RECORD
    END-IF
    PERFORM READ-A-RECORD
    .
TERMINATION-I.
    CLOSE INVENTORY-FILE-IN
    .
READ-A-RECORD.
    READ INVENTORY-FILE-IN
        AT END
            SET THERE-IS-NO-MORE-INPUT TO TRUE
    .
PRODUCE-REPORT.
    PERFORM INITIALIZATION-O
    PERFORM PRINT-REPORT UNTIL THERE-IS-NO-MORE-SORTED-INPUT
    PERFORM TERMINATION-O
    .
INITIALIZATION-O.
    OPEN OUTPUT REORDER-REPORT-FILE-OUT
    ACCEPT TODAYS-DATE FROM DATE
    MOVE CORRESPONDING TODAYS-DATE TO HEADING-LINE-2
    WRITE REPORT-LINE FROM HEADING-LINE-1 AFTER PAGE
    WRITE REPORT-LINE FROM HEADING-LINE-2
    WRITE REPORT-LINE FROM COLUMN-HEADS-1 AFTER 3
    WRITE REPORT-LINE FROM COLUMN-HEADS-2
    MOVE SPACES TO REPORT-LINE
    WRITE REPORT-LINE
    PERFORM READ-A-SORTED-RECORD
    IF THERE-IS-NO-MORE-SORTED-INPUT
        WRITE REPORT-LINE FROM NO-INPUT-DATA
    END-IF
    .
PRINT-REPORT.
    MOVE PART-NUMBER-S TO PART-NUMBER-OUT
    MOVE DESCRIPTION-S TO DESCRIPTION-OUT
    MOVE REORDER-QUANTITY-S TO REORDER-QUANTITY-OUT
    WRITE REPORT-LINE FROM DETAIL-LINE
    PERFORM READ-A-SORTED-RECORD
    .
TERMINATION-O.
    CLOSE REORDER-REPORT-FILE-OUT
    .
READ-A-SORTED-RECORD.
    RETURN SORT-WORK-FILE
        AT END
            SET THERE-IS-NO-MORE-SORTED-INPUT TO TRUE
    .
```

In INITIALIZATION-O, the OPEN statement OPENs only the OUTPUT file. After the priming RETURN, the usual test is made to see if there are any data. The RETURN statement at line 01610 signals the program when there are no more records to be RETURNed by SETting THERE-IS-NO-MORE-SORTED-INPUT TO TRUE.

Figure 12.11 shows the flow of records in a program having a SORT statement with an INPUT PROCEDURE and OUTPUT PROCEDURE. Remember that sorting takes place only after execution of the INPUT PROCEDURE is completed.

Program P12-03 was run with the input data shown in Figure 12.12 and produced the output shown in Figure 12.13.

FIGURE *12.11* **Flow of records in a program having a SORT statement with an INPUT PROCEDURE and an OUTPUT PROCEDURE**

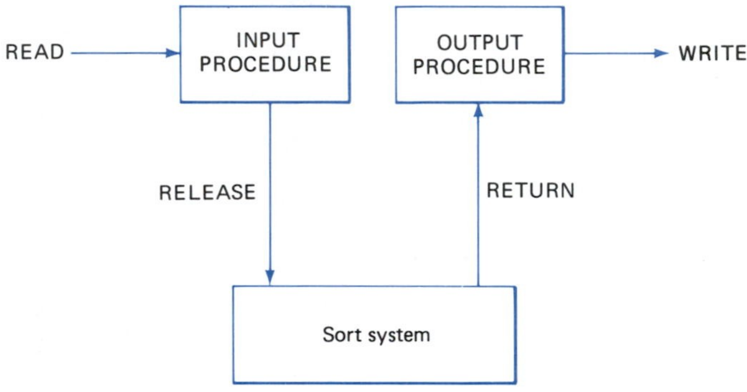

FIGURE *12.12* **Input to Program P12-03**

```
--------------------------------------------------------------------------------
         1         2         3         4         5         6         7         8
12345678901234567890123456789012345678901234567890123456789012345678901234567890
--------------------------------------------------------------------------------
071439BALL-PEEN HAMMER    002500001000009
8028371/2 IN. FLAT WASHER 020000050000400
2836419/16 IN. STOVE BOLT 001000005000110
002363CROSS-CUT SAW       000100000800006
001042RIP SAW             001000000800007
8028389/16 IN. FLAT WASHER025000120001100
283741DRAWER HANDLE       000300001000009
58374350 FT. GARDEN HOSE  001800012000110
583744100 FT. GARDEN HOSE 001250008000100
```

FIGURE 12.13 Output from Program P12-03

```
              REORDER REPORT
                             DATE  8/06/91

  PART      DESCRIPTION            REORDER
 NUMBER                            QUANTITY

001042   RIP SAW                       100
002363   CROSS-CUT SAW                  10
071439   BALL-PEEN HAMMER              250
283741   DRAWER HANDLE                  30
583743   50 FT. GARDEN HOSE            180
802837   1/2 IN. FLAT WASHER         2,000
802838   9/16 IN. FLAT WASHER        2,500
```

The RELEASE Statement

The format of the RELEASE statement is as follows:

```
RELEASE record-name-1 [FROM identifier-1]
```

A RELEASE statement may be given only within an INPUT PROCEDURE, and every INPUT PROCEDURE must contain at least one RELEASE statement. The FROM option serves the same purpose in a RELEASE statement as it does in a WRITE statement.

EXERCISE 4 Write a program to read input records in the following format:

Positions	Field
1–3	Department Number
4–8	Employee Number
9–11	Monday Hours (to one decimal place)
12–14	Tuesday Hours (to one decimal place)
15–17	Wednesday Hours (to one decimal place)
18–20	Thursday Hours (to one decimal place)
21–23	Friday Hours (to one decimal place)
24–26	Saturday Hours (to one decimal place)
27–80	spaces

Have your program select for printing only those employees who worked more than 30 hours in the week. For each such employee, have your program print on one line the Employee Number, the number of hours worked in the week, and the difference between 30 and the number of hours worked.

Have your program produce its output in ascending order by Employee Number within Department Number.

The MERGE Statement

The MERGE statement may be used to combine two or more files into one such that the resulting file is in ASCENDING or DESCENDING order on one or more KEY fields. The files used as input to a MERGE must already be in the same order that the resulting file is to be.

The format of the MERGE statement is as follows:

```
MERGE file-name-1 {ON {ASCENDING } KEY {data-name-1} ... } ...
                      {DESCENDING}

    [COLLATING SEQUENCE IS alphabet-name-1]
    USING file-name-2 {file-name-3} ...

    {OUTPUT PROCEDURE IS procedure-name-1 [{THROUGH} procedure-name-2]}
    {                                      [{THRU   }                 ]}
    {GIVING {file-name-4} ...                                          }
```

The file name given after the word MERGE must be a name defined in an SD entry. The MERGE statement has an optional OUTPUT PROCEDURE, as the SORT statement does, but no INPUT PROCEDURE capability.

The USING clause names the files to be used as input, and, of course, there must be at least two of them. It makes no sense to try to MERGE only one file.

Using the MERGE Statement

Program P12-04 shows a typical use of a MERGE capability. The program produces customer invoices in the format shown in Figure 12.14. The customer's name and address may occupy as many as five lines and are printed on lines 6 through 10 of the invoice. If the name and address of any particular customer occupy fewer than five lines, the unneeded lines are left blank. The column headings are printed on lines 13 and 14 regardless of the number of lines in the name and address. The detail lines, showing the items being billed on this invoice, print on lines 16 through 25. The invoice total always prints on line 26 regardless of the number of detail lines. If there are more than 10 detail lines, the excess lines print on successive pages, and the invoice total prints on line 26 of the last page for that customer.

These invoices are prepared from two input files. One file is a more or less permanent one containing the names and addresses of all of Northwestern Hard-Pressed Hardware Company's customers. This file is changed only when a customer's name or address changes, when a new customer opens an account, or when an inactive customer is removed from the file. This is a typical **master file.** In this application the master file might be called the "customer name and address master." Its records are in the following format:

Positions	Field
1	Code
2–6	Customer Number
7–26	Name and Address Line
27–80	spaces

FIGURE *12.14* **Output format for Program P12-04**

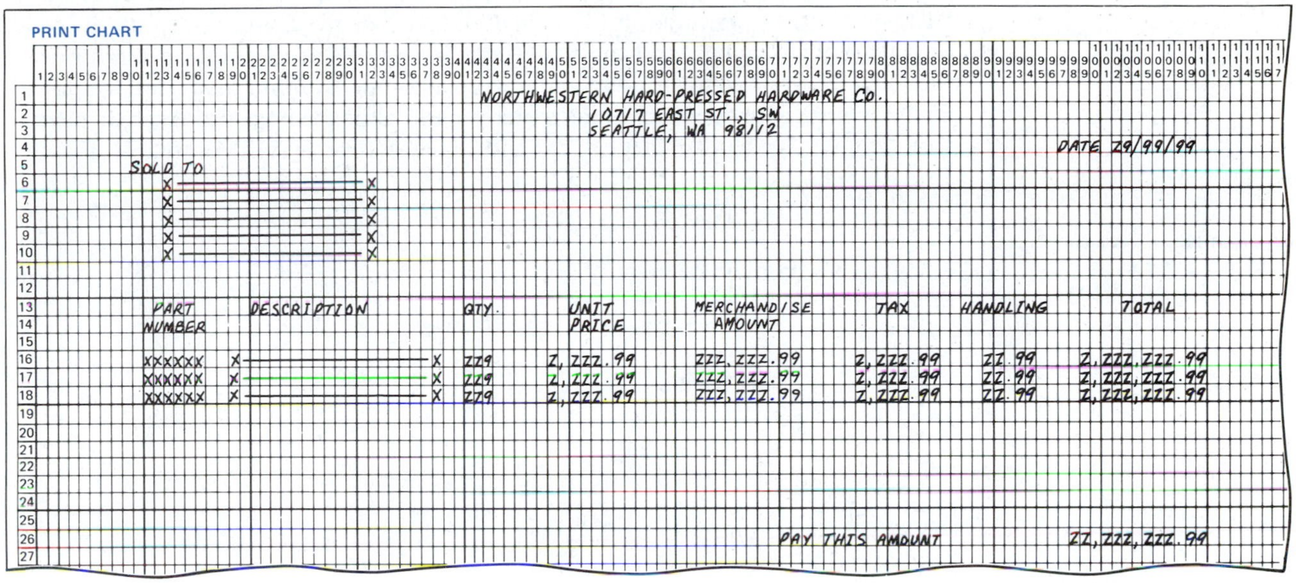

PRINT CHART

```
1                                    NORTHWESTERN HARD-PRESSED HARDWARE CO.
2                                                 10717 EAST ST., SW
3                                                 SEATTLE, WA 98112
4                                                                                       DATE Z9/99/99
5          SOLD TO
6             X-------------------X
7             X-------------------X
8             X-------------------X
9             X-------------------X
10            X-------------------X
11
12
13            PART       DESCRIPTION            QTY     UNIT       MERCHANDISE      TAX        HANDLING       TOTAL
14            NUMBER                                    PRICE        AMOUNT
15
16            XXXXXX  X-------------------X    ZZ9     Z,ZZZ.99    ZZZ,ZZZ.99     Z,ZZZ.99    ZZ.99      Z,ZZZ,ZZZ.99
17            XXXXXX  X-------------------X    ZZ9     Z,ZZZ.99    ZZZ,ZZZ.99     Z,ZZZ.99    ZZ.99      Z,ZZZ,ZZZ.99
18            XXXXXX  X-------------------X    ZZ9     Z,ZZZ.99    ZZZ,ZZZ.99     Z,ZZZ.99    ZZ.99      Z,ZZZ,ZZZ.99
19
20
21
22
23
24
25
26                                                                PAY THIS AMOUNT              ZZ,ZZZ,ZZZ.99
27
```

The Code in position 1, which can be a number from 1 through 5, tells which line of the name and address this record represents.

The second input file contains records relating to purchases by customers, for which they will now be billed. The records in this file contain the data the program needs to make up the line items which are to appear on the invoices. The record format is as follows:

Positions	Field
1	Code
2–6	Customer Number
7–12	Part Number
13–32	Description
33–35	Quantity
36–41	Unit Price (to two decimal places)
42–45	Handling (to two decimal places)
46–80	spaces

This is a typical **transaction file.** Position 1 of each transaction contains the number 6.

The program also produces a separate error report, whose format is not shown. The error report lists erroneous transactions or indicates that there are no input data. A transaction is in error if it does not contain a 6 in position 1 or if the Customer Number in the transaction does not match any Customer Number on the master file.

A Hierarchy Diagram for a MERGE Program

The hierarchy diagram in Figure 12.15 shows the approach taken in Program P12-04. First the transaction file is SORTed so that the transactions are in order on Customer Number, and the SORTed transactions are stored on a temporary file. The master file must be in order on Customer Number also, but we do not SORT it in this program. Since the master file is used over and over, it pays to sort it once, by hand if necessary, and leave it that way. Presumably that has already been done.

FIGURE *12.15* **Hierarchy diagram for Program P12-04**

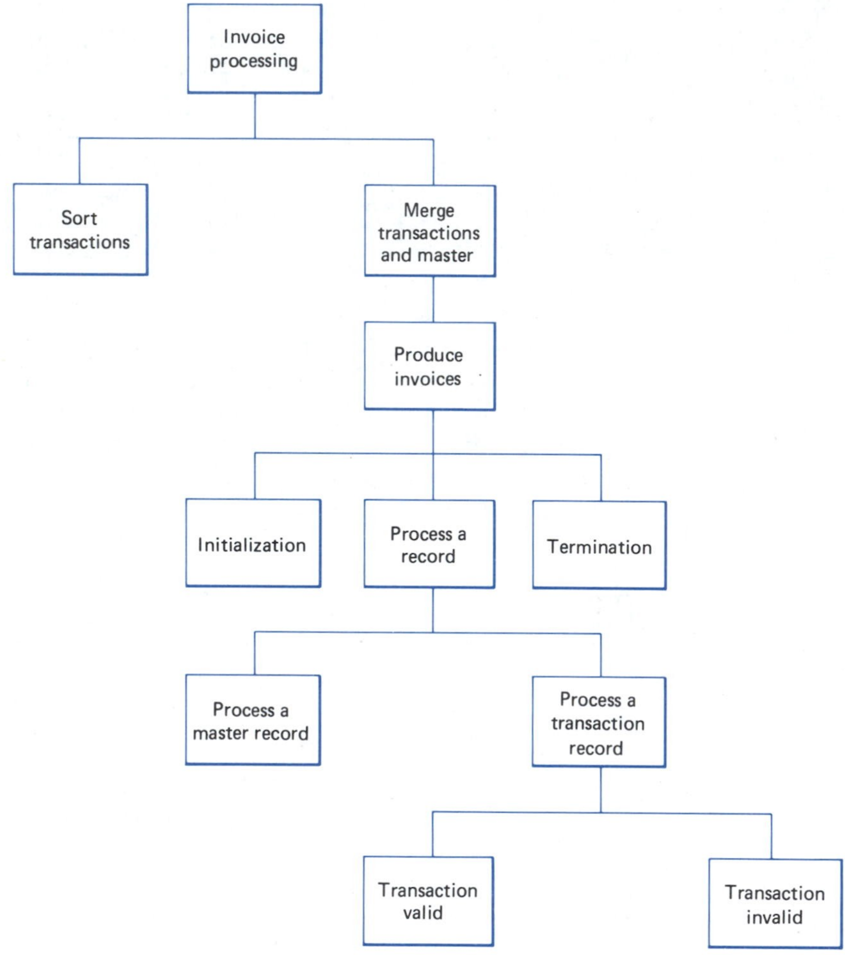

Then the master file and the SORTed transaction file are MERGEd on Customer Number. The MERGE statement has an OUTPUT PROCEDURE phrase, and the OUTPUT PROCEDURE is the entire remainder of the hierarchy diagram, "Produce invoices" and its subfunctions. The MERGE feeds records one at a time to "Produce invoices" from the master file and the transaction file such that for any customer the master name and address records are RETURNed from the MERGE first, followed by the transactions for that customer. If there are no transactions for a particular customer, only the master name and address records are RETURNed from the MERGE. If there are no name and address records to match a particular transaction, the transaction is in error.

"Produce invoices" is organized like any ordinary program. You will see what the "Initialization" and "Termination" consist of when we look at the program. The box "Process a record" is entered with each record RETURNed from the MERGE. "Process a record" first determines whether a master record or a transaction record has been RETURNed, and handles it accordingly. If it is a transaction record, the box "Process a transaction record" determines whether the transaction is valid or invalid, and processes it accordingly.

A Program with a MERGE Statement

Program P12-04 is shown in Figure 12.16. The SD entry has now been given the name SORT-MERGE-WORK-FILE, for in this program it is used for both SORTing and merging. Although two different types of records are being MERGEd in this program, only the transaction record is described under the SD entry for the SORT-MERGE-WORK-FILE, at line 00240. The format of the master record is described in the Working Storage Section, as you will see. The program uses control break logic to determine when the first master record for each customer is RETURNed from the MERGE, and so master records are worked on in working storage in the manner discussed in Chapter 7. Transaction records are worked on in the File Section.

FIGURE 12.16 **Program P12-04**

```
S COBOL II RELEASE 3.1 09/19/89                    P12004    DATE AUG 13,1991 T
----+-*A-1-B--+----2----+----3----+----4----+----5----+----6----+----7-%--+

00010  IDENTIFICATION DIVISION.
00020  PROGRAM-ID.  P12-04.
00030 *
00040 *    THIS PROGRAM SORTS TRANSACTION RECORDS AND THEN MERGES THEM
00050 *    WITH THE MASTER FILE WHICH IS ALREADY IN SEQUENCE.  IT THEN
00060 *    PRODUCES INVOICES AND AN ERROR REPORT.
00070 *
00080 *****************************************************************
00090
00100  ENVIRONMENT DIVISION.
00110  INPUT-OUTPUT SECTION.
00120  FILE-CONTROL.
00130      SELECT SORT-MERGE-WORK-FILE      ASSIGN TO SORTWK.
00140      SELECT CUSTOMER-MASTER-FILE-IN   ASSIGN TO INFILE1.
00150      SELECT TRANSACTION-FILE-IN       ASSIGN TO INFILE2.
00160      SELECT TRANSACTION-FILE-SRT      ASSIGN TO TEMPFILE.
00170      SELECT INVOICE-FILE-OUT          ASSIGN TO PRINTER1.
00180      SELECT ERROR-FILE-OUT            ASSIGN TO PRINTER2.
00190
00200 *****************************************************************
00210
00220  DATA DIVISION.
00230  FILE SECTION.
00240  SD  SORT-MERGE-WORK-FILE
00250      RECORD CONTAINS 80 CHARACTERS.
00260
```

continued

When a record is RETURNed or read from a file that contains records in more than one format, your program must have some way of determining which type of record it is. In Program P12-04 we can tell the master records from the transactions, for each master record has some number 1 through 5 in position 1, whereas the transactions have the number 6.

CUSTOMER-MASTER-FILE-IN is defined starting at line 00380, and TRANSACTION-FILE-IN is defined starting at line 00420. The level-01 entries in those files have not been broken down into fields because neither of the files is OPENed by us. In this program, they are OPENed and CLOSEd only by the SORT and MERGE statements. The file TRANSACTION-FILE-SRT, at line 00460, is used by the SORT statement as a place to put the SORTed transactions temporarily before they are MERGEd. It too is not OPENed by us.

The Working Storage Section begins at line 00580. There we have defined five fields to hold the customer names and addresses in preparation for printing on the invoices, at line 00890. We also have defined CUSTOMER-NUMBER-W, at line 00900, and CUSTOMER-NUMBER-SAVE, at line 00680. CUSTOMER-NUMBER-W is used to hold the Customer Number of the master records being worked on, and CUSTOMER-NUMBER-SAVE is used to hold the Customer Number of the transaction records being worked on. You will see how both fields are used when we look at the Procedure Division. Also in working storage are fields that we need to hold the results of arithmetic.

FIGURE *12.16* ***continued***

```
S COBOL II RELEASE 3.1 09/19/89                    P12004    DATE AUG 13,1991 T
----+-*A-1-B--+----2----+----3----+----4----+----5----+----6----+----7-%--+

00270  01   TRANSACTION-WORK-RECORD.
00280       05  CODE-T                          PIC 9.
00290       05  CODE-T-X REDEFINES CODE-T       PIC X.
00300           88  CODE-T-VALID                VALUE "6".
00310       05  CUSTOMER-NUMBER-T               PIC X(5).
00320       05  PART-NUMBER-T                   PIC X(6).
00330       05  DESCRIPTION-T                   PIC X(20).
00340       05  QUANTITY-T                      PIC 999.
00350       05  UNIT-PRICE-T                    PIC 9(4)V99.
00360       05  HANDLING-T                      PIC 99V99.
00370
00380  FD   CUSTOMER-MASTER-FILE-IN.
00390
00400  01   CUSTOMER-MASTER-RECORD-IN          PIC X(80).
00410
00420  FD   TRANSACTION-FILE-IN.
00430
00440  01   TRANSACTION-RECORD-IN              PIC X(80).
00450
00460  FD   TRANSACTION-FILE-SRT.
00470
00480  01   TRANSACTION-RECORD-SRT             PIC X(80).
00490
00500  FD   INVOICE-FILE-OUT.
00510
00520  01   INVOICE-RECORD-OUT                 PIC X(110).
00530
00540  FD   ERROR-FILE-OUT.
00550
00560  01   ERROR-RECORD-OUT                   PIC X(120).
00570
```

FIGURE ***12.16*** ***continued***

```
WORKING-STORAGE SECTION.
01  CUSTOMER-MASTER-WORK-RECORD.
    05  CODE-M                          PIC 9.
    05  CODE-M-X REDEFINES CODE-M       PIC X.
        88  CODE-M-VALID                VALUES "1" THRU "5".
    05  CUSTOMER-NUMBER-M               PIC X(5).
    05  NAME-AND-ADDRESS-LINE-M         PIC X(20).
    05                                  PIC X(54).
01  LINE-SPACING                        PIC S9  COMP SYNC.
01  CUSTOMER-NUMBER-SAVE                PIC X(5).
01  LINE-LIMIT                          PIC S99 COMP SYNC VALUE 24.
01  INVOICE-LINE-COUNTER                PIC S99 COMP SYNC VALUE 0.
01  INVOICE-TOTAL-W PACKED-DECIMAL      PIC S9(7)V99      VALUE 0.
01  MORE-INPUT                          PIC X        VALUE "Y".
    88 THERE-IS-NO-MORE-INPUT                        VALUE "N".
01  MASTER-RECORD-FLAG                  PIC X        VALUE "N".
    88 MASTER-RECORDS-EXIST                          VALUE "Y".
    88 MASTER-RECORDS-DONT-EXIST                     VALUE "N".
01  TRANSACTION-RECORD-FLAG             PIC X        VALUE "N".
    88 TRANSACTION-RECORDS-EXIST                     VALUE "Y".
    88 TRANSACTION-RECORDS-DONT-EXIST                VALUE "N".
01  TODAYS-DATE.
    05  TODAYS-YEAR                     PIC 99.
    05  TODAYS-MONTH-AND-DAY            PIC 9(4).
01  PACKED-DECIMAL-WORK-FIELDS PACKED-DECIMAL.
     02 TAX-RATE                        PIC V999     VALUE .085.
     02 MERCHANDISE-AMOUNT-W            PIC S9(6)V99.
     02 TAX-AMOUNT-W                    PIC S9(4)V99.
     02 LINE-ITEM-TOTAL-W               PIC S9(7)V99.
01  NAME-AND-ADDRESS-TABLE.
    05  NAME-AND-ADDRESS                PIC X(20)    OCCURS 5 TIMES.
01  CUSTOMER-NUMBER-W                   PIC X(5)     VALUE SPACES.
01  INVOICE-REPORT-HEAD-1.
    05                    PIC X(42) VALUE SPACES.
    05                    PIC X(48)
        VALUE "NORTHWESTERN HARD-PRESSED HARDWARE CO.".
01  INVOICE-REPORT-HEAD-2.
    05                    PIC X(52)    VALUE SPACES.
    05                    PIC X(18)    VALUE "10717 EAST ST., SW".
01  INVOICE-REPORT-HEAD-3.
    05                    PIC X(52)    VALUE SPACES.
    05                    PIC X(18)    VALUE "SEATTLE, WA  98112".
01  INVOICE-REPORT-HEAD-4.
    05                    PIC X(96)    VALUE SPACES.
    05                    PIC X(5)     VALUE "DATE".
    05  TODAYS-MONTH-AND-DAY            PIC Z9/99/.
    05  TODAYS-YEAR                     PIC 99.
01  INVOICE-REPORT-HEAD-5.
    05                    PIC X(9)     VALUE SPACES.
    05                    PIC X(7)     VALUE "SOLD TO".
01  NAME-AND-ADDRESS-LINE.
    05                    PIC X(12)    VALUE SPACES.
    05  NAME-AND-ADDRESS-OUT            PIC X(20).
```

continued

FIGURE 12.16 *continued*

```
S COBOL II RELEASE 3.1 09/19/89                    P12004    DATE AUG 13,1991 T
----+-*A-1-B--+----2----+----3----+----4----+----5----+----6----+----7-%--+

 01   INVOICE-COLUMN-HEAD-1.
      05                     PIC X(11)    VALUE SPACES.
      05                     PIC X(9)     VALUE "PART".
      05                     PIC X(20)    VALUE "DESCRIPTION".
      05                     PIC X(10)    VALUE "QTY.".
      05                     PIC X(12)    VALUE "UNIT".
      05                     PIC X(17)    VALUE "MERCHANDISE".
      05                     PIC X(8)     VALUE "TAX".
      05                     PIC X(15)    VALUE "HANDLING".
      05                     PIC X(5)     VALUE "TOTAL".

 01   INVOICE-COLUMN-HEAD-2.
      05                     PIC X(10)    VALUE SPACES.
      05                     PIC X(40)    VALUE "NUMBER".
      05                     PIC X(14)    VALUE "PRICE".
      05                     PIC X(6)     VALUE "AMOUNT".

 01   LINE-ITEM.
      05                                  PIC X(10) VALUE SPACES.
      05  PART-NUMBER-OUT                 PIC X(6)BB.
      05  DESCRIPTION-OUT                 PIC X(20)BB.
      05  QUANTITY-OUT                    PIC ZZ9B(5).
      05  UNIT-PRICE-OUT                  PIC Z,ZZZ.99B(6).
      05  MERCHANDISE-AMOUNT-OUT          PIC ZZZ,ZZZ.99B(5).
      05  TAX-OUT                         PIC Z,ZZZ.99B(4).
      05  HANDLING-OUT                    PIC ZZ.99B(4).
      05  LINE-ITEM-TOTAL-OUT             PIC Z,ZZZ,ZZZ.99.

 01   INVOICE-TOTAL-LINE.
      05                     PIC X(70)    VALUE SPACES.
      05                     PIC X(27)    VALUE "PAY THIS AMOUNT".
      05  INVOICE-TOTAL-OUT               PIC ZZ,ZZZ,ZZZ.99.

 01   ERROR-REPORT-HEADING-1.
      05                     PIC X(96)
          VALUE "INVOICE PROGRAM ERROR REPORT".
      05                     PIC X(5)     VALUE "DATE".
      05  TODAYS-MONTH-AND-DAY            PIC Z9/99/.
      05  TODAYS-YEAR                     PIC 99.

 01   ERROR-REPORT-HEADING-2.
      05                     PIC X(6)     VALUE "TRANS".
      05                     PIC X(9)     VALUE "CUSTOMER".
      05                     PIC X(81)    VALUE "INPUT RECORD".
      05                     PIC X(5)     VALUE "ERROR".

 01   ERROR-REPORT-HEADING-3.
      05                     PIC X(7)     VALUE " CODE".
      05                     PIC X(8)     VALUE "NUMBER".
      05                     PIC X(40)
              VALUE "....+....1....+....2....+....3....+....4".
      05                     PIC X(41)
              VALUE "....+....5....+....6....+....7....+....8".
      05                     PIC X(7)     VALUE "MESSAGE".

 01   NO-MASTER-DATA.
      05                     PIC X(96)    VALUE SPACES.
      05                     PIC X(14)    VALUE "NO MASTER DATA".

 01   NO-TRANSACTION-DATA.
      05                     PIC X(96)    VALUE SPACES.
      05                     PIC X(19)    VALUE "NO TRANSACTION DATA".
```

ERROR-LINE, line 01820, defines an output area that is used for printing error messages. This program detects invalid transaction codes in transaction input records and also transaction records that have no matching master records. Error messages are printed in ERROR-FILE-OUT, separate from the invoices, which are printed in INVOICE-FILE-OUT. When you have more than one printer output file in a COBOL program, the outputs may be assigned to different printers if your installation has more than one, or the outputs can be made to print one after the other on a single printer if the operating system provides such capability. Otherwise, the print lines of the several output files will be interleaved in an unpredictable manner.

The Procedure Division starts at line 01910. In the SORT statement, at line 01990, you can see that the transactions are SORTed on Customer Number and Part Number (or, alternatively, on Part Number within Customer Number). This causes each customer's invoice to print in Part Number order. The MERGE statement, at line 02070, MERGEs on CUSTOMER-NUMBER-T and CODE-T-X. This assures that each customer's name and address records, with Codes 1 through 5, will MERGE in before its transactions, with Code 6.

FIGURE *12.16* ***continued***

```
01810
01820  01  ERROR-LINE.
01830      05                                  PIC XX VALUE SPACES.
01840      05  CODE-T-E                        PIC XB(5).
01850      05  CUSTOMER-NUMBER-E               PIC X(5)BB.
01860      05  TRANSACTION-WORK-RECORD-E       PIC X(80)B.
01870      05  ERROR-MESSAGE-E                 PIC X(24).
01880
01890 *****************************************************************
01900
01910  PROCEDURE DIVISION.
01920  INVOICE-PROCESSING.
01930      PERFORM SORT-TRANSACTIONS
01940      PERFORM MERGE-TRANSACTIONS-AND-MASTER
01950      STOP RUN
01960      .
01970
01980  SORT-TRANSACTIONS.
01990      SORT SORT-MERGE-WORK-FILE
02000           ASCENDING KEY CUSTOMER-NUMBER-T
02010                         PART-NUMBER-T
02020           USING  TRANSACTION-FILE-IN
02030           GIVING TRANSACTION-FILE-SRT
02040      .
02050
02060  MERGE-TRANSACTIONS-AND-MASTER.
02070      MERGE SORT-MERGE-WORK-FILE
02080            ASCENDING KEY CUSTOMER-NUMBER-T
02090                          CODE-T-X
02100            USING CUSTOMER-MASTER-FILE-IN
02110                  TRANSACTION-FILE-SRT
02120            OUTPUT PROCEDURE IS PRODUCE-INVOICES
02130      .
02140
02150  PRODUCE-INVOICES.
02160      PERFORM INITIALIZATION
02170      PERFORM PROCESS-A-RECORD UNTIL THERE-IS-NO-MORE-INPUT
02180      PERFORM TERMINATION
02190      .
02200
```

continued

The Procedure Division follows the hierarchy diagram. The paragraph PROCESS-A-MASTER-RECORD, line 02740, saves each customer's number, name, and address in working storage. The name and address are used for printing on the invoice, and the customer number is used to determine whether there are any valid transactions for this customer.

The statement at line 02690 shows the use of the INTO option in a RETURN statement. You saw the INTO option used with a READ statement in Chapter 7. RETURN . . . INTO acts like a combined RETURN and MOVE. The RETURN . . . INTO statement at line 02690 works just like the following two statements:

```
RETURN SORT-MERGE-WORK-FILE
MOVE TRANSACTION-WORK-RECORD TO CUSTOMER-MASTER-WORK-RECORD
```

After the RETURN . . . INTO executes, the RETURNed record is available both in the level-01 area associated with the file—in this case TRANSACTION-WORK-RECORD, and the working-storage area that the record was MOVEd INTO—in this case CUSTOMER-MASTER-WORK-RECORD.

In PROCESS-A-TRANSACTION-RECORD, line 02840, the program determines whether each transaction is valid or invalid. For a transaction to be valid it must have a 6 in position 1 and its Customer Number must match a Customer Number from the name and address file.

FIGURE *12.16* *continued*

```
S COBOL II RELEASE 3.1 09/19/89                 P12004   DATE AUG 13,1991 T
----+-*A-1-B--+----2----+----3----+----4----+----5----+----6----+----7-%--+


02210   INITIALIZATION.
02220       OPEN OUTPUT INVOICE-FILE-OUT
02230                   ERROR-FILE-OUT
02240       ACCEPT TODAYS-DATE FROM DATE
02250       MOVE CORRESPONDING TODAYS-DATE TO INVOICE-REPORT-HEAD-4
02260       MOVE CORRESPONDING TODAYS-DATE TO ERROR-REPORT-HEADING-1
02270       WRITE ERROR-RECORD-OUT FROM ERROR-REPORT-HEADING-1
02280                              AFTER PAGE
02290       WRITE ERROR-RECORD-OUT FROM ERROR-REPORT-HEADING-2 AFTER 3
02300       WRITE ERROR-RECORD-OUT FROM ERROR-REPORT-HEADING-3
02310       MOVE SPACES TO ERROR-RECORD-OUT
02320       WRITE ERROR-RECORD-OUT
02330       PERFORM READ-A-RECORD
02340       MOVE CUSTOMER-NUMBER-M TO CUSTOMER-NUMBER-SAVE
02350       .
02360
02370   PROCESS-A-RECORD.
02380       IF CODE-M-VALID
02390           PERFORM PROCESS-A-MASTER-RECORD
02400       ELSE
02410           PERFORM PROCESS-A-TRANSACTION-RECORD
02420       END-IF
02430       PERFORM READ-A-RECORD
02440       .
02450
```

FIGURE 12.16 *continued*

```
INVOICE-TOTAL-BREAK.
    MOVE INVOICE-TOTAL-W TO INVOICE-TOTAL-OUT
    MOVE 0 TO INVOICE-TOTAL-W
    MOVE CUSTOMER-NUMBER-M TO CUSTOMER-NUMBER-SAVE
    COMPUTE LINE-SPACING = LINE-LIMIT + 2 - INVOICE-LINE-COUNTER
    WRITE INVOICE-RECORD-OUT FROM INVOICE-TOTAL-LINE
                             AFTER LINE-SPACING
    ADD LINE-SPACING TO INVOICE-LINE-COUNTER
    .

TERMINATION.
    PERFORM INVOICE-TOTAL-BREAK
    IF MASTER-RECORDS-DONT-EXIST
        WRITE ERROR-RECORD-OUT FROM NO-MASTER-DATA
    END-IF
    IF TRANSACTION-RECORDS-DONT-EXIST
        WRITE ERROR-RECORD-OUT FROM NO-TRANSACTION-DATA
    END-IF
    CLOSE INVOICE-FILE-OUT
          ERROR-FILE-OUT
    .

READ-A-RECORD.
    RETURN SORT-MERGE-WORK-FILE INTO CUSTOMER-MASTER-WORK-RECORD
        AT END
            SET THERE-IS-NO-MORE-INPUT TO TRUE
    .

PROCESS-A-MASTER-RECORD.
    SET MASTER-RECORDS-EXIST TO TRUE
    IF CUSTOMER-NUMBER-M IS NOT EQUAL TO CUSTOMER-NUMBER-W
        MOVE CUSTOMER-NUMBER-M TO CUSTOMER-NUMBER-W
        MOVE SPACES            TO NAME-AND-ADDRESS-TABLE
    END-IF
    MOVE NAME-AND-ADDRESS-LINE-M
         TO NAME-AND-ADDRESS (CODE-M)
    .

PROCESS-A-TRANSACTION-RECORD.
    SET TRANSACTION-RECORDS-EXIST TO TRUE
    IF CODE-T-VALID
        AND CUSTOMER-NUMBER-T IS EQUAL TO CUSTOMER-NUMBER-W
            PERFORM TRANSACTION-VALID
    ELSE
        PERFORM TRANSACTION-INVALID
    END-IF
    .

TRANSACTION-VALID.
    IF CUSTOMER-NUMBER-M NOT = CUSTOMER-NUMBER-SAVE
        PERFORM INVOICE-TOTAL-BREAK
    END-IF
    MULTIPLY QUANTITY-T BY UNIT-PRICE-T
        GIVING MERCHANDISE-AMOUNT-W
    MULTIPLY MERCHANDISE-AMOUNT-W BY TAX-RATE
        GIVING TAX-AMOUNT-W ROUNDED
    ADD MERCHANDISE-AMOUNT-W,
        TAX-AMOUNT-W,
        HANDLING-T GIVING LINE-ITEM-TOTAL-W
    PERFORM PRODUCE-INVOICE-LINE
    .

TRANSACTION-INVALID.
    IF NOT CODE-T-VALID
        PERFORM PRODUCE-INVALID-TRANS-CODE
    END-IF
    IF CUSTOMER-NUMBER-T IS NOT EQUAL TO CUSTOMER-NUMBER-W
        PERFORM PRODUCE-INVALID-CUST-NUMB
    END-IF
    .
```

continued

FIGURE 12.16 *continued*

```
S COBOL II RELEASE 3.1 09/19/89                    P12004   DATE AUG 13,1991 T
----+-*A-1-B--+----2----+----3----+----4----+----5----+----6----+----7-%--+

 PRODUCE-INVOICE-LINE.
     IF INVOICE-LINE-COUNTER IS LESS THAN 2 OR
        GREATER THAN LINE-LIMIT
         WRITE INVOICE-RECORD-OUT FROM INVOICE-REPORT-HEAD-1
                                  AFTER PAGE
         WRITE INVOICE-RECORD-OUT FROM INVOICE-REPORT-HEAD-2
         WRITE INVOICE-RECORD-OUT FROM INVOICE-REPORT-HEAD-3
         WRITE INVOICE-RECORD-OUT FROM INVOICE-REPORT-HEAD-4
         WRITE INVOICE-RECORD-OUT FROM INVOICE-REPORT-HEAD-5
         PERFORM WRITE-CUSTMER-NAME-AND-ADDRESS
                 VARYING CODE-M FROM 1 BY 1 UNTIL CODE-M > 5
         WRITE INVOICE-RECORD-OUT FROM INVOICE-COLUMN-HEAD-1
                                  AFTER 3
         WRITE INVOICE-RECORD-OUT FROM INVOICE-COLUMN-HEAD-2
         MOVE 14 TO INVOICE-LINE-COUNTER
         MOVE 2 TO LINE-SPACING
     END-IF
     MOVE PART-NUMBER-T         TO PART-NUMBER-OUT
     MOVE DESCRIPTION-T         TO DESCRIPTION-OUT
     MOVE QUANTITY-T            TO QUANTITY-OUT
     MOVE UNIT-PRICE-T          TO UNIT-PRICE-OUT
     MOVE MERCHANDISE-AMOUNT-W  TO MERCHANDISE-AMOUNT-OUT
     MOVE TAX-AMOUNT-W          TO TAX-OUT
     MOVE HANDLING-T            TO HANDLING-OUT
     MOVE LINE-ITEM-TOTAL-W     TO LINE-ITEM-TOTAL-OUT
     ADD LINE-ITEM-TOTAL-W TO INVOICE-TOTAL-W
     WRITE INVOICE-RECORD-OUT FROM LINE-ITEM AFTER LINE-SPACING
     ADD LINE-SPACING           TO INVOICE-LINE-COUNTER
     MOVE 1                     TO LINE-SPACING
     .

 PRODUCE-INVALID-TRANS-CODE.
     MOVE "INVALID TRANSACTION CODE" TO ERROR-MESSAGE-E
     PERFORM PRODUCE-ERROR-LINE
     .

 WRITE-CUSTMER-NAME-AND-ADDRESS.
     MOVE NAME-AND-ADDRESS (CODE-M) TO NAME-AND-ADDRESS-OUT
     WRITE INVOICE-RECORD-OUT FROM NAME-AND-ADDRESS-LINE
     .

 PRODUCE-ERROR-LINE.
     MOVE CODE-T-X             TO CODE-T-E
     MOVE CUSTOMER-NUMBER-T TO CUSTOMER-NUMBER-E
     MOVE TRANSACTION-WORK-RECORD
                               TO TRANSACTION-WORK-RECORD-E
     WRITE ERROR-RECORD-OUT FROM ERROR-LINE
     .

 PRODUCE-INVALID-CUST-NUMB.
     MOVE "INVALID CUSTOMER NUMBER" TO ERROR-MESSAGE-E
     PERFORM PRODUCE-ERROR-LINE
     .
```

Program P12-04 was run with the customer name-and-address master file shown in Figure 12.17 and the transactions shown in Figure 12.18. It produced the invoices shown in Figure 12.19 and the error report shown in Figure 12.20.

FIGURE *12.17* **Customer name-and-address master-file input to Program P12-04**

```
--------------------------------------------------------------------------------
         1         2         3         4         5         6         7         8
12345678901234567890123456789012345678901234567890123456789012345678901234567890
--------------------------------------------------------------------------------
100112JERRY PARKS
200112106 WEST 10TH ST.
300112BROOKLYN NY 11221
100189ROBERT S. BAUXBAUM
200189BOND EXTERMINATORS
300189458 LITTLE NECK PKWY
400189NORTHERN BLVD.
500189LITTLE NECK NY 11261
100217W & W HOUSEWARES INC
200217127-91 ELLIOT AV.
300217FLUSHING NY 11423
100513FILONE NICHOLAS
20051364-21 SMITH ST.
300513FOREST DRIVE NY
100561PARKER BROS. INC.
20056146 BEACH PKWY BLVD.
30056 SPRINGFIELD GARDENS
400561NEWPORT NJ 11468
100579JUAN ALVAREZ
200579SUNNYSIDE SUPPLIES
3005791375 EARLE COPIAG ST
400579FRESH MEADOW PARK
500579QUEENS VILLAGE NY
```

FIGURE *12.18* **Transaction input to Program P12-04**

```
--------------------------------------------------------------------------------
         1         2         3         4         5         6         7         8
12345678901234567890123456789012345678901234567890123456789012345678901234567890
--------------------------------------------------------------------------------
600579234110HAND SAWS           0640034590131
900513096310LIGHT BULB          0090001490014
600561100241CIRCULAR SAW        0010129160967
600579712346LEVEL               0290015790102
600561146312LAWNMOWER           0050106310512
600579641139RUBBER WASHERS      2160000120089
600112241321HAMMER              0020029190106
600579413821MEASURING TAPE      1090003990084
600561846329WORK BENCH          0090094670413
601421246317SANDER              0010094890431
600561004267LATHE               0010219631315
600579817390TEN FOOT LADDER     0080064990812
600561091426BAND SAW            0010640901519
600579041210PAINT               0710021160143
600195631789CLAMPS              0030016990431
600579114316PAINT BRUSH         1350011990091
600579121613SCREWDRIVER         0870009470110
```

FIGURE *12.19* **Invoices produced by Program P12-04**

```
                         NORTHWESTERN HARD-PRESSED HARDWARE CO.
                                10717 EAST ST., SW
                                SEATTLE, WA  98112
                                                                  DATE  8/13/91
SOLD TO
   JERRY PARKS
   106 WEST 10TH ST.
   BROOKLYN NY 11221


 PART     DESCRIPTION          QTY.      UNIT      MERCHANDISE      TAX     HANDLING      TOTAL
NUMBER                                   PRICE       AMOUNT

241321   HAMMER                  2       29.19        58.38         4.96      1.06         64.40




                                                   PAY THIS AMOUNT                         64.40




                         NORTHWESTERN HARD-PRESSED HARDWARE CO.
                                10717 EAST ST., SW
                                SEATTLE, WA  98112
                                                                  DATE  8/13/91
SOLD TO
   PARKER BROS. INC.
   46 BEACH PKWY BLVD.
   SPRINGFIELD GARDENS
   NEWPORT NJ 11468


 PART     DESCRIPTION          QTY.      UNIT      MERCHANDISE      TAX     HANDLING      TOTAL
NUMBER                                   PRICE       AMOUNT

004267   LATHE                   1      219.63       219.63        18.67     13.15        251.45
091426   BAND SAW                1      640.90       640.90        54.48     15.19        710.57
100241   CIRCULAR SAW            1      129.16       129.16        10.98      9.67        149.81
146312   LAWNMOWER               5      106.31       531.55        45.18      5.12        581.85
846329   WORK BENCH              9       94.67       852.03        72.42      4.13        928.58



                                                   PAY THIS AMOUNT                      2,622.26
```

FIGURE 12.19 *continued*

```
                                       NORTHWESTERN HARD-PRESSED HARDWARE CO.
                                                10717 EAST ST., SW
                                                SEATTLE, WA  98112
                                                                                      DATE  8/13/91
SOLD TO
   JUAN ALVAREZ
   SUNNYSIDE SUPPLIES
   1375 EARLE COPIAG ST
   FRESH MEADOW PARK
   QUEENS VILLAGE NY

 PART      DESCRIPTION                 QTY.       UNIT        MERCHANDISE       TAX     HANDLING        TOTAL
NUMBER                                            PRICE          AMOUNT

041210   PAINT                          71        21.16        1,502.36       127.70      1.43        1,631.49
114316   PAINT BRUSH                   135        11.99        1,618.65       137.59       .91        1,757.15
121613   SCREWDRIVER                    87         9.47          823.89        70.03      1.10          895.02
234110   HAND SAWS                      64        34.59        2,213.76       188.17      1.31        2,403.24
413821   MEASURING TAPE                109         3.99          434.91        36.97       .84          472.72
641139   RUBBER WASHERS                216          .12           25.92         2.20       .89           29.01
712346   LEVEL                          29        15.79          457.91        38.92      1.02          497.85
817390   TEN FOOT LADDER                 8        64.99          519.92        44.19      8.12          572.23

                                                                  PAY THIS AMOUNT                     8,258.71
```

FIGURE 12.20 **Error report produced by Program P12-04**

```
INVOICE PROGRAM ERROR REPORT                                                                  DATE  8/13/91

TRANS CUSTOMER INPUT RECORD                                                                   ERROR
 CODE  NUMBER  ....+....1....+....2....+....3....+....4....+....5....+....6....+....7....+....8 MESSAGE

  6     00195  600195631789CLAMPS              0030016990431                                  INVALID CUSTOMER NUMBE
  9     00513  900513096310LIGHT BULB          0090001490014                                  INVALID TRANSACTION CO
  6     01421  601421246317SANDER              0010094890431                                  INVALID CUSTOMER NUMBE
```

EXERCISE 5

Write a program to produce the gross pay computation report shown in Figure 12.E5. Have your program use two input files. One file is an employee master file, with records in the following format:

Positions	Field
1	Code
2–4	Department Number
5–9	Employee Number
10–12	Monday Hours (to one decimal place)
13–15	Tuesday Hours (to one decimal place)
16–18	Wednesday Hours (to one decimal place)
19–21	Thursday Hours (to one decimal place)
22–24	Friday Hours (to one decimal place)
25–27	Saturday Hours (to one decimal place)
28–80	spaces

The other file is a transaction file showing the hours worked for each day of the week, with records in the following format:

Positions	Field
1	Code
2–4	Department Number
5–9	Employee Number
10–12	Monday Hours (to one decimal place)
13–15	Tuesday Hours (to one decimal place)
16–18	Wednesday Hours (to one decimal place)
19–21	Thursday Hours (to one decimal place)
22–24	Friday Hours (to one decimal place)
25–80	spaces

Have your program SORT the transactions in order by Employee Number within Department Number. Make sure your master file is in that order. Then have your program MERGE the two files and compute the gross pay for each employee who worked that week by multiplying the total hours worked during the week by the employee's Hourly Rate of Pay.

Produce a separate error report showing each transaction that has no matching master record.

FIGURE *12.E5* Output format for Exercise 5

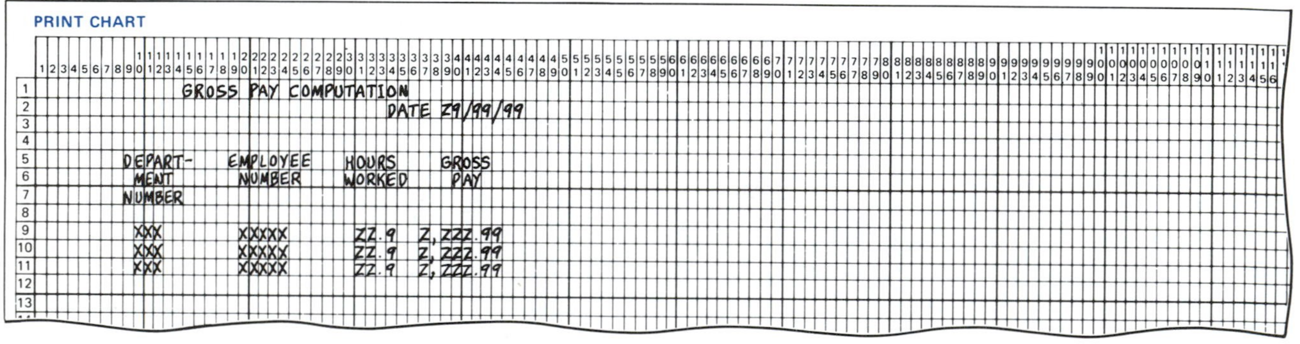

COLLATING SEQUENCE and Alphabet Name

Every computer has its own sequence for ordering characters, from the lowest character to the highest. That is, whenever a computer compares two unequal characters, one of the characters must be the lower and one must be the higher. This holds true whether the two characters being compared are both numbers, both letters, or one a number and one a letter, or even if special characters like $, %, the comma, and the decimal point are being compared. The order of the characters from lowest to highest is called the COLLATING SEQUENCE.

The COLLATING SEQUENCE on the computer used to run most of the programs in this book is called the Extended Binary-Coded Decimal Interchange Code (EBCDIC). It is as follows:

Blank

Special characters

Lowercase letters a through z

Uppercase letters A through Z

Digits 0 through 9

The COLLATING SEQUENCE on the computer used to run the programs in Chapter 20 is called the American National Standard Code for Information Interchange (ASCII). It is as follows:

Blank

Some special characters

Digits 0 through 9

A few more special characters

Uppercase letters A through Z

A few more special characters

Lowercase letters a through z

A few more special characters

Sometimes a programmer would like to use a COLLATING SEQUENCE different from the one that is **NATIVE** to the computer that the program is being run on. For example, if I wanted to use the SORT verb to help prepare the index for this book I would want lowercase "a" and uppercase "A" both to fall before lowercase "b" and uppercase "B." Furthermore, I would want "a" and "A" both to have the same position in the COLLATING SEQUENCE. That is, I would not want "a" to be considered lower or higher than "A."

A COLLATING SEQUENCE other than the NATIVE one may be defined by including an **alphabet-name clause** in the SPECIAL-NAMES paragraph of the Environment Division. The format of the alphabet-name clause is:

```
[ALPHABET alphabet-name-1 IS

  { STANDARD-1                                                    }
  { STANDARD-2                                                    }
  { NATIVE                                                        }
  { implementor-name-2                                            } ...]
  {                                                               }
  { { literal-1 [ {THROUGH} literal-2          ] } ...            }
  { {           [ {THRU   }                    ] }                }
  { {           [ {ALSO literal-3} ...         ] }                }
```

If **STANDARD-1** is used, the ASCII COLLATING SEQUENCE is used. **STANDARD-2** is the same as STANDARD-1 except for the currency symbol, which is $ in STANDARD-1. In some COBOL systems, one or more implementor names define COLLATING SEQUENCEs used in those systems other than the NATIVE sequence. For example, in the system used in Chapter 20 of this book the implementor name EBCDIC specifies that the Extended Binary-Coded Decimal Interchange Code should be used.

Literals used in the alphabet-name clause may be nonnumeric or numeric. If nonnumeric, the literals specify the desired COLLATING SEQUENCE of the characters. If numeric, the literals specify the desired COLLATING SEQUENCE of the characters that occupy the ordinal positions of the literals in the computer's NATIVE character set. For example, in the COLLATING SEQUENCE that is NATIVE to this computer the character blank is in ordinal position 65 and the character zero is in ordinal position 241. A numeric literal in an alphabet-name clause cannot be larger than the number of characters in the computer's character set, in this computer 256.

To use the SORT verb to help prepare the index for this book we could use an alphabet-name clause such as the following, with the made-up alphabet name INDEX-SEQUENCE and the reserved words **ALPHABET** and ALSO:

```
ALPHABET INDEX-SEQUENCE IS
              "a" ALSO "A"
              "b" ALSO "B"
              "c" ALSO 196
              "d" ALSO 197
              "e" ALSO "E"
              "f" ALSO "F"
              "g" ALSO "G"
              "h" ALSO "H"
              "i" ALSO 202
              "j" ALSO 210
              "k" ALSO 211
              "l" ALSO "L"
              "m" ALSO "M"
              "n" ALSO "N"
              "o" ALSO "O"
              "p" ALSO "P"
              "q" ALSO "Q"
              "r" ALSO "R"
              "s" ALSO "S"
              "t" ALSO "T"
              "u" ALSO "U"
              "v" ALSO "V"
              "w" ALSO "W"
              "x" ALSO "X"
              "y" ALSO "Y"
              "z" ALSO "Z"
```

Characters not explicitly specified in the definition of an alphabet name are placed at the end in their NATIVE order.

You may define as many alphabet names as you like in a COBOL program, each with a different alphabet name. Then in any SORT or MERGE statement in the program, you may indicate which is to be used for the collating sequence by including a COLLATING SEQUENCE phrase in the SORT or MERGE statement.

For example, the statement

```
SORT SORT-WORK-FILE
     ASCENDING KEY INDEX-WORD
     COLLATING SEQUENCE IS INDEX-SEQUENCE
     USING INDEX-WORD-FILE
     OUTPUT PROCEDURE PRODUCE-INDEX
```

uses the INDEX-SEQUENCE alphabet described above. The index words to be SORTed are contained in a file called INDEX-WORD-FILE, and the field INDEX-WORD is defined in the 01 area associated with the SORT-WORK-FILE.

Summary

The SORT/MERGE feature of COBOL permits programs to rearrange the order of records and to combine two or more files in order.

Records may be SORTed directly from an input file, or else an INPUT PROCEDURE may be carried out before the records are SORTed. After the records are SORTed they may be placed directly onto an output file, or else an OUTPUT PROCEDURE may be carried out on the records in their new sequence.

Records may be MERGEd from two or more files in order on one or more specified KEY fields. The input files must be in the same order as the final MERGEd result. An OUTPUT PROCEDURE may be used, but no INPUT PROCEDURE.

An SD entry must be used to describe the file that the SORT and/or MERGE is to use for a work area.

The RELEASE verb can be used only in an INPUT PROCEDURE. It is executed after all the necessary input processing has been carried out on an input record and the record is ready for SORTing. The RETURN verb is used in an OUTPUT PROCEDURE to fetch SORTed and MERGEd records for processing.

An alphabet-name may be defined in the SPECIAL-NAMES paragraph to establish a COLLATING SEQUENCE different from the NATIVE one. The COLLATING SEQUENCE phrase may be used in a SORT or MERGE statement to indicate that the sequence defined in the alphabet-name clause is to be used for ordering the records.

Fill-In Exercises

1. The work file for a SORT or MERGE statement must be defined in a(n) ______ entry.
2. One or more ______ ______ or ______ ______ phrases must be used in each SORT or MERGE statement to indicate which field(s) is (are) to be used for ordering the records.
3. The ______ phrase may be used to name the file or files that contain the records to be used as input to a SORT or MERGE.
4. The ______ phrase may be used to name the file where the output records from a SORT or MERGE are to be placed.
5. If records are to be SORTed or MERGEd before being processed, the programmer must specify a(n) ______ PROCEDURE.
6. If records are to be processed before being SORTed, the programmer must specify a(n) ______ PROCEDURE.

7. In a SORT or MERGE statement, the KEY fields must be listed in order from ______ to ______.
8. To keep in their original order records whose SORT-field contents are identical you must use the ______ phrase.
9. You may define as many alphabet ______ as you like in a COBOL program.
10. The ______ phrase causes a SORT statement to open a file for input.
11. Alphabet names are defined in the ______ paragraph of the ______ Division.
12. The RETURN verb may be used only in a(n) ______ PROCEDURE.
13. The RELEASE verb may be used only in a(n) ______ PROCEDURE.
14. The use of STANDARD-1 in an alphabet-name clause causes the ______ COLLATING SEQUENCE to be used.
15. You need not define the fields of a record if you do not ______ the file that the record is associated with.

Review Exercises

1. Write a program to SORT the input data you used in Review Exercise 1, Chapter 9, page 287, into alphabetic order on Part Description. Use GIVING in the SORT statement, and ASSIGN a printer as the GIVING file.
2. Write a program to read the same input data you used in Review Exercise 1 above. Have your program SORT the input data into alphabetical order on Part Description and produce a report in the format shown in Figure 12.RE2. Use an OUTPUT PROCEDURE to produce the report.

FIGURE *12.RE2* Output format for Review Exercise 2

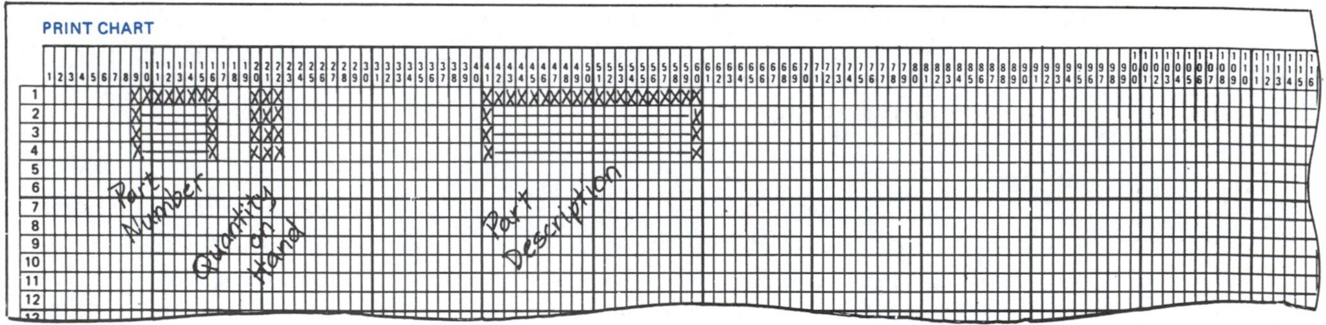

3. Write a program to read input records in the following format:

Positions	Field
1–5	Employee Number
6	Code
7–9	Hours Worked (to one decimal place)
10–80	spaces

Each record contains an Employee Number, a Code indicating whether the employee is eligible for overtime pay or is exempt from overtime pay, and the Hours Worked. The Code field contains an E if the employee is exempt from overtime pay and an N if the employee is eligible for overtime pay (nonexempt).

Use an INPUT PROCEDURE to select for SORTing only those employees who are eligible for overtime pay and who worked more than 40 hours. Have your program SORT the selected records into order on Employee Number and produce a list of the SORTed records showing each Employee Number and the Hours Worked.

4. Write the ASCENDING KEY and DESCENDING KEY phrases that would be needed to SORT the records in the employee master file in Exercise 5, page 419, into ascending order on Department Number. Within each Department Number, employees with the highest Hourly Rate of Pay should fall together first, followed by employees with the second-highest hourly rate, down to employees with the lowest hourly rate. If, within a department, there is more than one employee with the same hourly rate, they should fall together SORTed on Employee Number.

5. Write an alphabet-name definition to establish the following COLLATING SEQUENCE: the digits 0 through 9, the uppercase letters A through R, the character /, and the uppercase letters S through Z. This is part of the COLLATING SEQUENCE of the Hollerith card code and the **BCD** code (**binary-coded decimal** code). There are no lowercase letters in the Hollerith or BCD codes.

Project

Write a program to read records in the following format:

Positions	Field
1–6	Course Code
7–15	Student Number
16–18	Exam Grade 1
19–21	Exam Grade 2
22–24	Exam Grade 3
25–27	Exam Grade 4
28–80	spaces

Each record contains a Course Code, a Student Number, and the grades that the student got on each of four exams. The program is to READ the data and select for SORTing those records where the average grade on the four exams is less than 75. The selected records are to be SORTed in ascending order on Student Number within descending order on average grade within ascending order on Course Code.

Have your program print a report from the SORTed records in the format shown in Figure 12.P1 on the following page. Group indicate the Course Code. Double-space between courses, single-space within courses.

FIGURE *12.P1* **Output format for Chapter 12 Project**

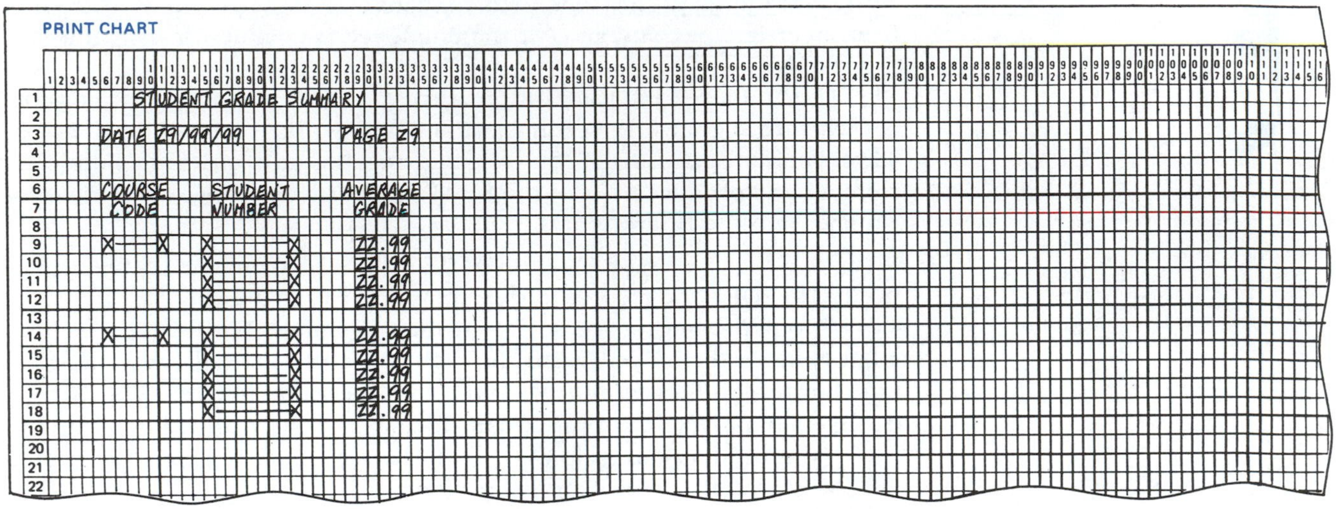

CHAPTER 13

Magnetic File Media

HERE ARE THE KEY POINTS YOU SHOULD LEARN FROM THIS CHAPTER

1. The nature of files stored on magnetic media
2. Types of master files and their uses
3. How to create a sequential file
4. How to delete records from a sequential file

KEY WORDS TO RECOGNIZE AND LEARN

magnetic file media	DASD
magnetic tape	mass storage device
magnetic disk	block
magnetic drum	physical record
data cell	logical record
mass storage system	update
tape deck	record key
tape transport	file activity
tape drive	file volatility
read-write head	LABEL RECORDS ARE STANDARD
sequential	BLOCK CONTAINS
access	balance-line algorithm
direct-access	NOT AT END
random access	END-RETURN
direct-access storage device	

Up to this point all of our programs have written their output files onto paper, producing what is usually called a list, a listing, or a report. Your input files may have been entered on a keyboard or punched in cards. There are other kinds of materials, though, that computers can read input data from and write output onto. In this chapter we will discuss one such material, **magnetic file media.** There are a number of forms of magnetic media commonly processed by COBOL programs, such as **magnetic tape, magnetic disk, magnetic drum, data cell,** and **mass storage system.**

Magnetic computer tape is very much like audio recording tape, except that computer tape is wider, thicker, and stronger. It is available on reels or cassettes just as audio recording tape is, and just as music can be stored on tape as magnetic patterns, computer tape can store characters as a series of magnetic impulses. The characters are stored one after another along the length of the tape, forming fields and records. Fields and records on tape can be thousands of characters long.

A computer installation that uses magnetic tape files will usually have one or more **tape decks** attached to the computer. The tape deck, or **tape transport** or **tape drive** as it is sometimes called, works just like a tape deck for audio tape. It moves the tape from one reel to the other and back, so that the computer can read data from the tape and write data onto it. Computer tapes can be removed from the transport when not in use and stored in a cabinet or on a rack.

A magnetic disk looks like a large phonograph record coated on both sides with a thin layer of magnetizable material. Characters, fields, and records can be stored one after another in circular tracks on both sides of the disk. Data can be written onto and read from the disk by a device called a **read-write head.** The read-write head can be directed by the computer to any location on the disk surface to read any particular desired record or to write a record into any particular location.

You can now see the fundamental difference between files on tape and files on disk. Tape is a **sequential** medium; records on tape can be **accessed** only sequentially, which means that they can be read and written on tape only one after another, in order. Disk is a **direct-access** medium, which means that the computer can go to any location on the disk directly for reading or writing. So a file on disk can enjoy **random access.** A file on disk can also be accessed sequentially, just as a phonograph record can be played through from beginning to end.

All other magnetic media, aside from magnetic tape, can be thought of as operating the same way that disk does. Even though the actual principles of operation may be quite different, for our purposes we need differentiate only between magnetic tape and magnetic disk. Disk and all the other media that work the same way are called **direct-access storage devices (DASD).**[1]

On both sequential and direct-access media, records are often grouped into larger units called **blocks.** Blocks have no logical meaning for a program; our tape and disk programs will still READ and WRITE one record at a time. The programmer has no responsibility regarding blocks except to decide how many records should be grouped into each one. Grouping a large number of records into a block saves storage space on tape or disk and increases the amount of primary storage space needed to run the program. Having large blocks in a sequential file usually reduces execution time of the program; having large blocks in a random-access file usually increases it. A block is sometimes called a **physical record.** What we have been calling a record is sometimes called a **logical record.** At this point in your study of COBOL it is best to have your instructor decide how many records you should have in your blocks.

[1]COBOL literature refers to direct-access storage devices as **mass storage devices.** We prefer the term "direct-access storage device" to avoid confusion with IBM's Model 3850 Mass Storage System.

Advantages of Magnetic Media

Keyed input files and printed output are good for computers to use to receive data from the outside world and to communicate results back. They are easy for people to handle, and their contents can be ready fairly easily. They have their role in data processing.

The big advantage of magnetic media is that the computer can write data onto them and then, at a later time, read the same data in again; the later time may be seconds later, weeks later, or, due to the extremely stable nature of magnetic media, years later. Other advantages of magnetic media over paper ones are as follows:

1. Magnetic media are reusable; obsolete data can be erased and new data written in their place.
2. Computers can read and write magnetic media much faster than paper media.
3. Huge volumes of data can be stored more compactly on magnetic media than on paper.

Uses of Magnetic Media

The characteristics of magnetic media just given make them ideally suited for storing master files of data. In Chapter 12 we had a customer name-and-address master file. In the file we had up to five records for each customer, each record containing one line of the customer's name and address. If the file were to be stored on tape or disk, the records could be made as big as we like, and all five lines of name and address data for a single customer could fit into one record. When a master file is stored on magnetic media, changes to the file cannot be made by hand, but instead by a computer program. Such a program is called an **update** program.

A master file quite different from our name-and-address master might be found in a sales application. The file could be a catalog master file with one record for every part number. Each record would contain a part number, a description of the part, a price, a shipping weight, and perhaps other data. In this application the entire file would be used for reference and would be changed only when a new catalog was issued, perhaps every 6 months. Then the old master file could be thrown out (erased would be better) and a complete new catalog master created.

A catalog master could be used daily by a program that prints invoices. The program would read the day's orders and look in the master file to see that the part numbers in the orders were valid. Then it would get the description of the part for printing on the invoice and the price for computing the merchandise amount.

EXERCISE *1*

Think of another application of a master file. Tell the following about the file:

a. What does each record on the file represent? That is, is there one record for each customer or one record for each part number or one record for each what?

b. What are some of the fields that would be in the record?

c. Under what circumstances would each of the fields in the master file have to be changed?

d. In what ways would the file be used?

A Master File

In this and the next three chapters we will be discussing master files and how to handle them. Many of the programming examples deal with the same master file, a bank savings-account master. There is one record on the file for each savings account in the bank. Each record contains a unique account number. The account number is used to order and locate records in the file, and is the **record key.** Each record also contains the depositor's name, the date of the last transaction to the account (either the date the account was opened or the date of the last deposit or withdrawal), and the current balance. When a new account is opened it must be accompanied by an initial deposit; when an account is closed, the former balance is assumed to be the final withdrawal.

You will see how to create and maintain the savings-account master file first as a sequential file on tape or disk and then as a random-access file on disk. In industry practice, several criteria may be used to decide whether a file should be sequential or random-access.

1. The use to which the file will be put. A master file is maintained in an up-to-date condition so that the information on it can be used for some data processing purpose. The uses made of a file, aside from updating it, are often the most important considerations in determining whether the file will be sequential or random-access.
2. **File activity.** Activity refers to the average number of master records changed in an update run. For example, if on the average 15% of the records in a master file are changed in an update run, the file activity would be said to be 15%. Files with high activity tend to be stored as sequential files; those with low activity, as random-access files.
3. **File volatility.** Volatility refers to the number of additions and deletions from a file. Files with high volatility tend to be stored as sequential files, those with low volatility as random-access files.
4. File size. File size can sometimes be a determining factor. Sequential files can often be of any size. If necessary, sequential files may extend over several reels of tape or over several disks. When the file is used, only one reel or disk need be mounted at any one time. Since the file is processed sequentially, when a reel or disk is read completely it can be removed and the next one mounted. With random-access files, the entire file must be mounted during a processing run since any portion of the file may be needed at any time during the run. Random-access files are thus limited in size by the available equipment.

Validity of Data on a Master File

It is very important to ensure that data on a master file are valid. Erroneous data on a master file can cause much more trouble than erroneous input to a program that merely produces a report. There are three general kinds of difficulty that can be caused by invalid data on a master file, each one worse than the previous.

Master Records Out of Sequence

As you will see, much of the program logic dealing with master file updating requires that the records be in sequence on the record key and that there be no duplicate keys. In our master file it means that the records must be in order on account number and that there not be two records with the same account number. A duplicate or out-of-sequence condition in a master file will ruin the execution of any update program that uses the file as input. The master file would have to be recreated correctly and the update program tried again.

Invalid Numeric Field

If a numeric field on a master file somehow gets to contain something other than numbers, the field may cause abnormal termination of any program that tries to use it in arithmetic, numeric editing, or numeric comparison. Since the field might not be used until months or years after it is put on the master file, it sits there like a time bomb waiting to cause an abnormal termination when one is least expected.

Erroneous Data

Worst of all is a field whose contents are simply wrong. It doesn't do anything dramatic, such as cause a program to terminate suddenly. It just comes out wrong week after week, month after month, and maybe no one notices the error until it is too late.

Creating a Sequential Master File

Program P13-01 shows one way to create a savings-account master file on magnetic tape or disk. The input to Program P13-01 is a batch of new accounts to create the file. The new account data are in the following format:

Positions	Field
1	Code 1
2–6	Account Number
7–26	Depositor Name
27–32	Date of Transaction
33–40	Amount (to two decimal places)
41–80	spaces

The 1 in position 1 of the input record is a Code that identifies this as a new account. The Amount field is the initial deposit, which becomes the account's current balance on the master file. To create this master file, the input records must be in order on the key field, which in this application is the Account Number. Program P13-01 SORTs the input into order on Account Number and then, in the OUTPUT PROCEDURE of the SORT, checks the input for validity, creates a master file out of the good input records, and produces two reports. One report lists the good records, which were placed on the master file, and the other shows the erroneous transactions. The two report formats are shown in Figures 13.1 and 13.2.

FIGURE *13.1* **Output format for good records for Program P13-01**

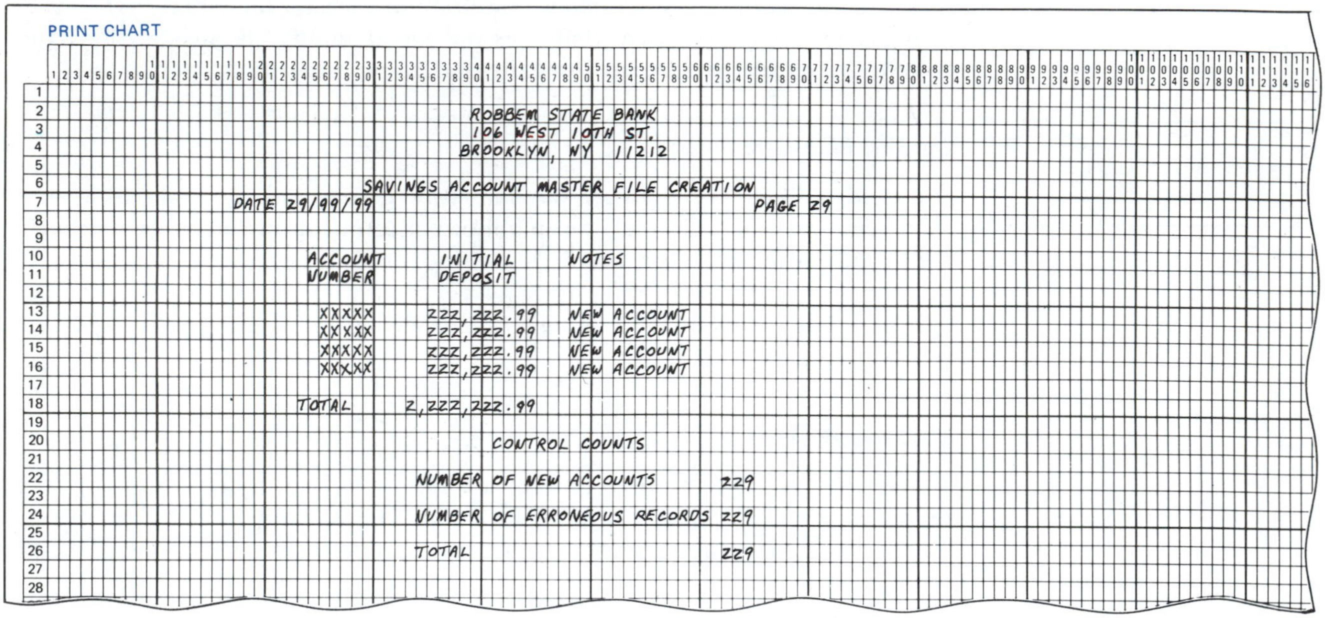

PRINT CHART

```
                                ROBBEM STATE BANK
                                 106 WEST 10TH ST.
                                BROOKLYN, NY  11212

                      SAVINGS ACCOUNT MASTER FILE CREATION
            DATE Z9/99/99                                          PAGE Z9

                  ACCOUNT        INITIAL        NOTES
                  NUMBER         DEPOSIT

                   XXXXX       ZZZ,ZZZ.99      NEW ACCOUNT
                   XXXXX       ZZZ,ZZZ.99      NEW ACCOUNT
                   XXXXX       ZZZ,ZZZ.99      NEW ACCOUNT
                   XXXXX       ZZZ,ZZZ.99      NEW ACCOUNT

                 TOTAL       Z,ZZZ,ZZZ.99

                                 CONTROL COUNTS

                         NUMBER OF NEW ACCOUNTS              ZZ9

                         NUMBER OF ERRONEOUS RECORDS         ZZ9

                         TOTAL                               ZZ9
```

FIGURE *13.2* **Output format for error report for Program P13-01**

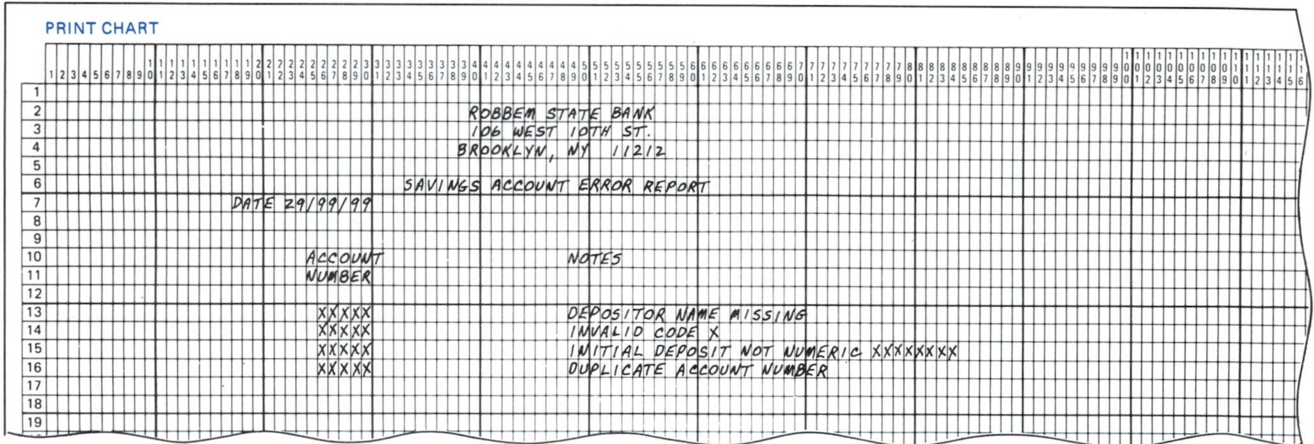

A Hierarchy Diagram for Creating a Master File

The hierarchy diagram for Program P13-01 is shown in Figure 13.3. The OUTPUT PROCEDURE consists of the box "Produce master file" and its subfunctions. The box "Process a record" is entered with each input record. Each record is checked to see that all its fields are valid. For each field found invalid, the program prints an error message onto the error report. If an input record is found to be error-free, the program writes it onto the output master file and prints a NEW ACCOUNT line, as shown in Figure 13.1.

FIGURE *13.3* Hierarchy diagram for Program P13-01

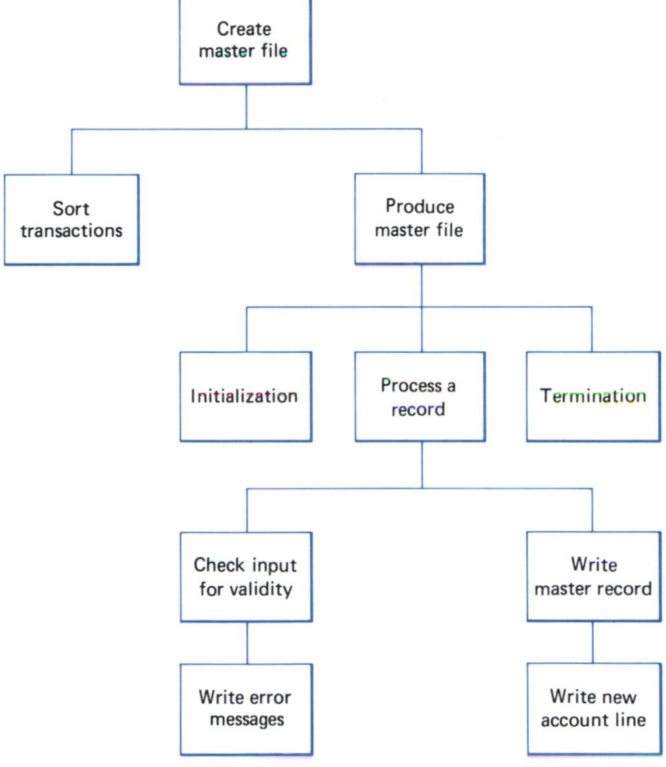

A Program to Create a Sequential Master File

Program P13-01 is shown in Figure 13.4. In the File Section you can find the FD entry for the master file that is to be created on tape or disk, at line 00410. We have the clause **LABEL RECORDS ARE STANDARD.** Label records are special records written onto tape and disk files by the COBOL system and used by the system to identify the file. You should always use STANDARD labels on all your tape and disk files unless there is some compelling reason to do otherwise.

In the **BLOCK CONTAINS** clause we have indicated that the system should process 100 records as a single block. We need do nothing else regarding BLOCKs.

In working storage we have three fields that are used for counting records: NUMBER-OF-INPUT-RECORDS-W, NUMBER-OF-ERRONEOUS-RECORDS-W, and NUMBER-OF-NEW-ACCOUNTS-W. We use the field NUMBER-OF-NEW-ACCOUNTS-W to count the number of good records as they are written onto the master file. We use NUMBER-OF-ERRONEOUS-RECORDS-W to count the number of input records that contain one or more errors and were not written onto the master. The sum of NUMBER-OF-NEW-ACCOUNTS-W and NUMBER-OF-ERRONEOUS-RECORDS-W should equal NUMBER-OF-INPUT-RECORDS-W.

Also we have a field called ACCOUNT-NUMBER-SAVE, at line 00670. This field is used to check that every input record contains a different Account Number. As mentioned earlier, it is of the greatest importance that records on a master file be in sequence on their key and that there be no duplicate keys. The SORT in Program P13-01 will assure that the input records are in nondescending order on Account Number, but the SORT does not check for duplicates. We will have to do that with coding in the Data Division and the Procedure Division.

The Data Division coding connected with checking for duplicate Account Numbers is in line 00670. There ACCOUNT-NUMBER-SAVE was given a VALUE that could not be a legal Account Number in the COBOL system used to run this program, the figurative constant HIGH-VALUES. In your own COBOL system you would use an initial VALUE for ACCOUNT-NUMBER-SAVE that could not be a legal Account Number in that system. If there is no VALUE in your COBOL system that could not be a legal Account Number, the cleanest way to handle the matter is to define ACCOUNT-NUMBER-SAVE to be one character longer than the Account Number and initialize ACCOUNT-NUMBER-SAVE to any VALUE that is neither blanks nor zeros.

FIGURE 13.4 **Program P13-01**

```
S COBOL II RELEASE 3.1 09/19/89                P13001   DATE AUG 16,1991 T
----+-*A-1-B--+----2----+----3----+----4----+----5----+----6----+----7-|--+

00010  IDENTIFICATION DIVISION.
00020  PROGRAM-ID. P13-01.
00030 * AUTHOR. SHAMEZE SULTAN
00040 *         REVISED BY GAETANO MURATORE
00050 *
00060 *    THIS PROGRAM CREATES A SEQUENTIAL MASTER FILE.
00070 *
00080 *******************************************************************
```

FIGURE 13.4 ***continued***

```

       ENVIRONMENT DIVISION.
       INPUT-OUTPUT SECTION.
       FILE-CONTROL.
           SELECT SAVINGS-ACCOUNT-DATA-FILE-IN      ASSIGN TO INFILE.
           SELECT SORT-WORK-FILE                    ASSIGN TO SORTWK.
           SELECT SAVINGS-ACCOUNT-MASTER-FLE-OUT    ASSIGN TO MASTER.
           SELECT TRANSACTION-REGISTER-FILE-OUT     ASSIGN TO PRINTER1.
           SELECT ERROR-FILE-OUT                    ASSIGN TO PRINTER2.

      ******************************************************************

       DATA DIVISION.
       FILE SECTION.
       FD  SAVINGS-ACCOUNT-DATA-FILE-IN
           RECORD CONTAINS 80 CHARACTERS.

       01  SAVINGS-ACCOUNT-DATA-RECORD-IN       PIC X(80).

       SD  SORT-WORK-FILE
           RECORD CONTAINS 80 CHARACTERS.

       01  SORT-WORK-RECORD.
           05 CODE-IN                           PIC X.
              88  VALID-CODE                  VALUE "1".
           05 ACCOUNT-NUMBER-IN                 PIC X(5).
           05 DEPOSITOR-NAME-IN                 PIC X(20).
              88  DEPOSITOR-NAME-MISSING      VALUE SPACES.
           05 DATE-OF-LAST-TRANSACTION-IN       PIC 9(6).
           05 AMOUNT-IN                         PIC 9(6)V99.
           05 AMOUNT-IN-X REDEFINES AMOUNT-IN   PIC X(8).

       FD  SAVINGS-ACCOUNT-MASTER-FLE-OUT
           LABEL RECORDS ARE STANDARD
           RECORD CONTAINS 80 CHARACTERS
           BLOCK CONTAINS 100 RECORDS.

       01  SAVINGS-ACCOUNT-MASTER-REC-OUT       PIC X(80).

       FD  TRANSACTION-REGISTER-FILE-OUT.

       01  TRANSACTION-REGISTER-RECORD          PIC X(72).

       FD  ERROR-FILE-OUT.

       01  ERROR-RECORD-OUT                     PIC X(84).

       WORKING-STORAGE SECTION.
       01  MORE-INPUT                           PIC X VALUE "Y".
           88 THERE-IS-NO-MORE-INPUT            VALUE "N".
       01  ANY-ERRORS                           PIC X.
       01  PACKED-DECIMAL-COUNTERS PACKED-DECIMAL.
        02 NUMBER-OF-INPUT-RECORDS-W            PIC S9(3)    VALUE ZERO.
        02 NUMBER-OF-ERRONEOUS-RECORDS-W        PIC S9(3)    VALUE ZERO.
        02 NUMBER-OF-NEW-ACCOUNTS-W             PIC S9(3)    VALUE ZERO.
        02 AMOUNT-IN-COUNTER                    PIC 9(7)V99  VALUE 0.
        02 PAGE-NUMBER-W                        PIC S9       VALUE 0.
        02 ERROR-PAGE-NUMBER-W                  PIC S9       VALUE 0.
       01  ACCOUNT-NUMBER-SAVE          PIC X(5) VALUE HIGH-VALUES.
       01  TODAYS-DATE.
           05 TODAYS-YEAR                       PIC 99.
           05 TODAYS-MONTH-AND-DAY              PIC 9(4).
       01  BLANK-LINE                           PIC X  VALUE SPACE.
       01  LINE-LIMIT                       PIC S99 COMP SYNC VALUE 34.
       01  LINE-COUNT-ER                    PIC S99 COMP SYNC.
       01  ERROR-LINE-LIMIT                 PIC S99 COMP SYNC VALUE 54.
       01  ERROR-LINE-COUNTER               PIC S99 COMP SYNC.
```

continued

The Procedure Division, which starts at line 01780, follows the hierarchy diagram. Upon entering PROCESS-A-RECORD each time, we ADD 1 to the count of the number of input records. Later, as we find each record to be either free of errors or erroneous, we will ADD 1 to either the number of good records written onto the master or the count of the number of erroneous records.

FIGURE *13.4* ***continued***

```
S COBOL II RELEASE 3.1 09/19/89                  P13001   DATE AUG 16,1991 T
----+-*A-1-B--+----2----+----3----+----4----+----5----+----6----+----7-|--+

00760
00770  01  REPORT-HEADING-1.
00780      05                                    PIC X(39) VALUE SPACES.
00790      05                  PIC X(17) VALUE "ROBBEM STATE BANK".
00800
00810  01  REPORT-HEADING-2.
00820      05                                    PIC X(39) VALUE SPACES.
00830      05                  PIC X(17) VALUE "106 WEST 10TH ST.".
00840
00850  01  REPORT-HEADING-3.
00860      05                                    PIC X(38) VALUE SPACES.
00870      05                  PIC X(19) VALUE "BROOKLYN, NY  11212".
00880
00890  01  PAGE-HEADING-1.
00900      05                                    PIC X(29) VALUE SPACES.
00910      05                                    PIC X(36)
00920                VALUE "SAVINGS ACCOUNT MASTER FILE CREATION".
00930
00940  01  ERROR-HEADING-1.
00950      05                                    PIC X(33) VALUE SPACES.
00960      05                                    PIC X(29)
00970                         VALUE "SAVINGS ACCOUNT ERROR REPORT".
00980
00990  01  PAGE-HEADING-2.
01000      05                                    PIC X(17) VALUE SPACES.
01010      05                                    PIC X(5) VALUE "DATE".
01020      05 TODAYS-MONTH-AND-DAY               PIC Z9/99/.
01030      05 TODAYS-YEAR                        PIC 99.
01040      05                                    PIC X(35) VALUE SPACES.
01050      05                                    PIC X(4)  VALUE "PAGE".
01060      05 PAGE-NUMBER-OUT                    PIC Z9.
01070
01080  01  PAGE-HEADING-3.
01090      05                                  PIC X(24) VALUE SPACES.
01100      05                                  PIC X(7)  VALUE "ACCOUNT".
01110      05                                  PIC X(5)  VALUE SPACES.
01120      05                                  PIC X(7)  VALUE "INITIAL".
01130      05                                  PIC X(5)  VALUE SPACES.
01140      05                                  PIC X(5)  VALUE "NOTES".
01150
01160  01  ERROR-PAGE-HEADING-3.
01170      05                                  PIC X(24) VALUE SPACES.
01180      05                                  PIC X(7)  VALUE "ACCOUNT".
01190      05                                  PIC X(17) VALUE SPACES.
01200      05                                  PIC X(5)  VALUE "NOTES".
01210
01220  01  PAGE-HEADING-4.
01230      05                                  PIC X(24) VALUE SPACES.
01240      05                                  PIC X(6)  VALUE "NUMBER".
01250      05                                  PIC X(6)  VALUE SPACES.
01260      05                                  PIC X(7) VALUE  "DEPOSIT".
01270
01280  01  ERROR-PAGE-HEADING-4.
01290      05                                  PIC X(24) VALUE SPACES.
01300      05                                  PIC X(6)  VALUE "NUMBER".
01310
```

FIGURE 13.4 *continued*

```
       01  REPORT-LINE.
           05 ACCOUNT-NUMBER-OUT                      PIC B(25)X(5).
           05 AMOUNT-OUT                              PIC B(5)ZZZ,ZZZ.99B(3).
           05                                   PIC X(11) VALUE "NEW ACCOUNT".

       01  ERROR-LINE.
           05 ACCOUNT-NUMBER-E                        PIC B(25)X(5).
           05 LONG-MESSAGES.
               10 MSG                                 PIC B(18)X(27).
               10 AMOUNT-E                            PIC BX(9).
           05 SHORT-MESSAGES REDEFINES LONG-MESSAGES.
               10 SHORT-MESSAGE                       PIC B(18)X(12).
               10 CODE-E                              PIC BXB(23).

       01  TOTAL-LINE-1.
           05                                         PIC X(23) VALUE SPACES.
           05                                      PIC X(5)B(5) VALUE "TOTAL".
           05 AMOUNT-OUT-TOTAL                        PIC Z,ZZZ,ZZZ.99.

       01  TOTAL-LINE-2.
           05                                         PIC X(41) VALUE SPACES.
           05                               PIC X(14) VALUE "CONTROL COUNTS".

       01  TOTAL-LINE-3.
           05                                         PIC X(34) VALUE SPACES.
           05                                         PIC X(22)
                                    VALUE "NUMBER OF NEW ACCOUNTS".
           05 NUMBER-OF-NEW-ACCOUNTS                  PIC B(6)ZZ9.

       01  TOTAL-LINE-4.
           05                                         PIC X(34) VALUE SPACES.
           05                                         PIC X(27)
                                      VALUE "NUMBER OF ERRONEOUS RECORDS".
           05 NUMBER-OF-ERRONEOUS-RECORDS             PIC BZZ9.

       01  TOTAL-LINE-5.
           05                                         PIC X(34) VALUE SPACES.
           05                                         PIC X(5)  VALUE "TOTAL".
           05 NUMBER-OF-INPUT-RECORDS                 PIC B(23)ZZ9.

       01  NO-INPUT-DATA.
           05                                         PIC X(21) VALUE SPACES.
           05              VALUE "NO INPUT DATA"      PIC X(13).

      *****************************************************************

       PROCEDURE DIVISION.
       CREATE-MASTER-FILE.
           SORT SORT-WORK-FILE
                ASCENDING KEY ACCOUNT-NUMBER-IN
                USING SAVINGS-ACCOUNT-DATA-FILE-IN
                OUTPUT PROCEDURE IS PRODUCE-MASTER-FILE
           STOP RUN
           .
```

continued

In WRITE-MASTER-RECORD we MOVE the KEY field to ACCOUNT-NUMBER-SAVE, at line 02180. This is part of the processing to check for duplicate Account Numbers. The rest of that processing is in the paragraph CHECK-INPUT-FOR-VALIDITY, at line 02310. You can now see why we gave ACCOUNT-NUMBER-SAVE an initial VALUE of HIGH-VALUES—to cause the first input record to have an Account Number different from ACCOUNT-NUMBER-SAVE.

FIGURE *13.4* ***continued***

```
S COBOL II RELEASE 3.1 09/19/89                   P13001    DATE AUG 16,1991 T
----+-*A-1-B--+----2----+----3----+----4----+----5----+----6----+----7-|--+

01860
01870  PRODUCE-MASTER-FILE.
01880      PERFORM INITIALIZATION
01890      PERFORM PROCESS-A-RECORD UNTIL THERE-IS-NO-MORE-INPUT
01900      PERFORM TERMINATION
01910      .
01920
01930  INITIALIZATION.
01940      OPEN OUTPUT SAVINGS-ACCOUNT-MASTER-FLE-OUT
01950                  ERROR-FILE-OUT
01960                  TRANSACTION-REGISTER-FILE-OUT
01970      ACCEPT TODAYS-DATE FROM DATE
01980      MOVE CORR TODAYS-DATE TO PAGE-HEADING-2
01990      PERFORM PRINT-REPORT-HEADINGS
02000      PERFORM READ-A-RECORD
02010      IF THERE-IS-NO-MORE-INPUT
02020          WRITE TRANSACTION-REGISTER-RECORD FROM NO-INPUT-DATA
02030      END-IF
02040      .
02050
02060  PROCESS-A-RECORD.
02070      ADD 1 TO NUMBER-OF-INPUT-RECORDS-W
02080      MOVE "N" TO ANY-ERRORS
02090      PERFORM CHECK-INPUT-FOR-VALIDITY
02100      IF ANY-ERRORS = "N"
02110          PERFORM WRITE-MASTER-RECORD
02120      END-IF
02130      PERFORM READ-A-RECORD
02140      .
02150
02160  WRITE-MASTER-RECORD.
02170      WRITE SAVINGS-ACCOUNT-MASTER-REC-OUT FROM SORT-WORK-RECORD
02180      MOVE ACCOUNT-NUMBER-IN TO ACCOUNT-NUMBER-SAVE
02190      ADD 1 TO NUMBER-OF-NEW-ACCOUNTS-W
02200      PERFORM WRITE-NEW-ACCOUNT-LINE
02210      .
02220
```

FIGURE 13.4 *continued*

```
CHECK-INPUT-FOR-VALIDITY.
    MOVE SPACES TO ERROR-LINE
    IF NOT VALID-CODE
        MOVE "Y" TO ANY-ERRORS
        MOVE CODE-IN TO CODE-E
        MOVE "INVALID CODE" TO SHORT-MESSAGE
        PERFORM WRITE-ERROR-MESSAGE
    END-IF
    IF ACCOUNT-NUMBER-IN = ACCOUNT-NUMBER-SAVE
        MOVE "Y" TO ANY-ERRORS
        MOVE "DUPLICATE ACCOUNT NUMBER" TO MSG
        PERFORM WRITE-ERROR-MESSAGE
    END-IF
    IF DEPOSITOR-NAME-MISSING
        MOVE "Y" TO ANY-ERRORS
        MOVE "DEPOSITOR NAME MISSING" TO MSG
        PERFORM WRITE-ERROR-MESSAGE
    END-IF
    IF AMOUNT-IN NOT NUMERIC
        MOVE "Y" TO ANY-ERRORS
        MOVE AMOUNT-IN-X TO AMOUNT-E
        MOVE "INITIAL DEPOSIT NOT NUMERIC" TO MSG
        PERFORM WRITE-ERROR-MESSAGE
    END-IF
    IF ANY-ERRORS = "Y"
        ADD 1 TO NUMBER-OF-ERRONEOUS-RECORDS-W
    END-IF
    .

WRITE-ERROR-MESSAGE.
    MOVE ACCOUNT-NUMBER-IN TO ACCOUNT-NUMBER-E
    PERFORM ERROR-LINE-COUNT-CHECK
    WRITE ERROR-RECORD-OUT FROM ERROR-LINE
    ADD 1 TO ERROR-LINE-COUNTER
    .

ERROR-LINE-COUNT-CHECK.
    IF 1 + ERROR-LINE-COUNTER > ERROR-LINE-LIMIT
        PERFORM PRINT-ERROR-REPORT-HEAD
    END-IF
    .

TERMINATION.
    PERFORM WRITE-TOTALS
    CLOSE SAVINGS-ACCOUNT-MASTER-FLE-OUT
          ERROR-FILE-OUT
          TRANSACTION-REGISTER-FILE-OUT
    .

READ-A-RECORD.
    RETURN SORT-WORK-FILE
        AT END
            SET THERE-IS-NO-MORE-INPUT TO TRUE
    .

LINE-COUNT-CHECK.
    IF 1 + LINE-COUNT-ER
       GREATER THAN LINE-LIMIT
        PERFORM PRINT-REGISTER-HEAD
    END-IF
    .
```

continued

FIGURE 13.4 *continued*

```
S COBOL II RELEASE 3.1 09/19/89                    P13001    DATE AUG 16,1991 T
----+-*A-1-B--+----2----+----3----+----4----+----5----+----6----+----7-|--+


       WRITE-TOTALS.
           MOVE AMOUNT-IN-COUNTER TO AMOUNT-OUT-TOTAL
           WRITE TRANSACTION-REGISTER-RECORD FROM TOTAL-LINE-1 AFTER 2
           WRITE TRANSACTION-REGISTER-RECORD FROM TOTAL-LINE-2 AFTER 2
           MOVE NUMBER-OF-NEW-ACCOUNTS-W TO NUMBER-OF-NEW-ACCOUNTS
           WRITE TRANSACTION-REGISTER-RECORD FROM TOTAL-LINE-3 AFTER 2
           MOVE NUMBER-OF-ERRONEOUS-RECORDS-W TO
                                      NUMBER-OF-ERRONEOUS-RECORDS
           WRITE TRANSACTION-REGISTER-RECORD FROM TOTAL-LINE-4 AFTER 2
           MOVE NUMBER-OF-INPUT-RECORDS-W TO
                                       NUMBER-OF-INPUT-RECORDS
           WRITE TRANSACTION-REGISTER-RECORD FROM TOTAL-LINE-5 AFTER 2
           .

       PRINT-REPORT-HEADINGS.
           PERFORM PRINT-REGISTER-HEAD
           PERFORM PRINT-ERROR-REPORT-HEAD
           .

       PRINT-ERROR-REPORT-HEAD.
           ADD 1 TO ERROR-PAGE-NUMBER-W
           MOVE ERROR-PAGE-NUMBER-W TO PAGE-NUMBER-OUT
           WRITE ERROR-RECORD-OUT FROM REPORT-HEADING-1
                                       AFTER ADVANCING PAGE
           WRITE ERROR-RECORD-OUT FROM REPORT-HEADING-2 .
           WRITE ERROR-RECORD-OUT FROM REPORT-HEADING-3
           WRITE ERROR-RECORD-OUT FROM ERROR-HEADING-1 AFTER 2
           WRITE ERROR-RECORD-OUT FROM PAGE-HEADING-2
           WRITE ERROR-RECORD-OUT FROM ERROR-PAGE-HEADING-3
                                       AFTER ADVANCING 3
           WRITE ERROR-RECORD-OUT FROM ERROR-PAGE-HEADING-4
           WRITE ERROR-RECORD-OUT FROM BLANK-LINE
           MOVE 11 TO ERROR-LINE-COUNTER
           .

       PRINT-REGISTER-HEAD.
           ADD 1 TO PAGE-NUMBER-W
           MOVE PAGE-NUMBER-W TO PAGE-NUMBER-OUT
           WRITE TRANSACTION-REGISTER-RECORD FROM REPORT-HEADING-1
                                       AFTER ADVANCING PAGE
           WRITE TRANSACTION-REGISTER-RECORD FROM REPORT-HEADING-2
           WRITE TRANSACTION-REGISTER-RECORD FROM REPORT-HEADING-3
           WRITE TRANSACTION-REGISTER-RECORD FROM PAGE-HEADING-1
                                       AFTER ADVANCING 2
           WRITE TRANSACTION-REGISTER-RECORD FROM PAGE-HEADING-2
           WRITE TRANSACTION-REGISTER-RECORD FROM PAGE-HEADING-3
                                       AFTER ADVANCING 3
           WRITE TRANSACTION-REGISTER-RECORD FROM PAGE-HEADING-4
           WRITE TRANSACTION-REGISTER-RECORD FROM BLANK-LINE
           MOVE 11 TO LINE-COUNT-ER
           .

       WRITE-NEW-ACCOUNT-LINE.
           MOVE ACCOUNT-NUMBER-IN TO ACCOUNT-NUMBER-OUT
           MOVE AMOUNT-IN TO AMOUNT-OUT
           PERFORM LINE-COUNT-CHECK
           WRITE TRANSACTION-REGISTER-RECORD FROM REPORT-LINE
           ADD 1 TO LINE-COUNT-ER
           ADD AMOUNT-IN TO AMOUNT-IN-COUNTER
           .
```

Program P13-01 was run with the input data shown in Figure 13.5 and produced the report output shown in Figure 13.6. The output that was written onto the master file is shown in Figure 13.7. In the installation where this program was run, both the error report and the transaction register were printed on the same printer, one report after the other.

FIGURE *13.5* **Input to Program P13-01**

```
--------------------------------------------------------------------------------
         1         2         3         4         5         6         7         8
12345678901234567890123456789012345678901234567890123456789012345678901234567890
--------------------------------------------------------------------------------
100063                    10269000007500
100070PATRICK J. LEE      11249000050000
100077LESLIE MINSKY       10269000001037
100084JOHN DAPRINO        10149000150000
100091JOE'S DELI          10159000010000
100098GEORGE CULHANE      10169000050000
100105LENORE MILLER       10039000005000
100112ROSEMARY LANE       10019000025000
300007MICHELE CAPUANO     1020900CA00000
100126JAMES BUDD          11049000075000
100133PAUL LERNER, D.D.S. 11019000100000
100035JOHN J. LEHMAN      11299000015000
100032JOSEPH CAMILLO      11139000002500
100049JAY GREENE          10169000015000
100056EVELYN SLATER       10179000000100
200182BOB LANIGAN         11069000007500
100189J. & L. CAIN        11069000003500
100196IMPERIAL FLORIST    10309000015000
100203JOYCE MITCHELL      10279000000500
100210JERRY PARKS         10289000025000
100217CARL CALDERON       11079000005000
100224JOHN WILLIAMS       11189000017550
100231BILL WILLIAMS       11279000055500
100238KEVIN PARKER        11199000001000
100245FRANK CAPUTO        11149000003500
100252GENE GALLI          12089000001500
100259                    11209000002937
100266MARTIN LANG         11289000009957
100140BETH FALLON         11039000002575
100098JANE HALEY          11059000002000
100105ONE DAY CLEANERS    11059000005000
100161ROBERT RYAN         11059000002450
100168KELLY HEDERMAN      11059000012550
100175MARY KEATING        11069000001000
100007ROSEBUCCI           10259000100784
100014ROBERT DAVIS M.D.   10269000001000
100021LORICE MONTI        10279000012500
100028MICHAEL SMITH       11049000700159
100273VITO CACACI         12049000027500
100280COMMUNITY DRUGS     11169000002000
100287SOLOMON CHAPELS     11239000001500
100294JOHN BURKE          12199000150000
100301PAT P. POWERS       1212900FG15750
100308JOE GARCIA          11279000200000
100315GRACE MICELI        11299000025000
100322                    11249000002000
100329GUY VOLPONE         12289000001000
100336SALVATORE CALI      121890))))!%))
100343JOE & MARY SESSA    12139000100000
100350ROGER SHAW          12319000250000
```

FIGURE 13.6 Report output from Program P13-01

```
                              ROBBEM STATE BANK
                              106 WEST 10TH ST.
                             BROOKLYN, NY  11212

                        SAVINGS ACCOUNT ERROR REPORT
DATE  8/16/91                                                PAGE 1

        ACCOUNT                    NOTES
        NUMBER

         00007                     INVALID CODE 3
         00007                     INITIAL DEPOSIT NOT NUMERIC 0CA00000
         00063                     DEPOSITOR NAME MISSING
         00098                     DUPLICATE ACCOUNT NUMBER
         00105                     DUPLICATE ACCOUNT NUMBER
         00182                     INVALID CODE 2
         00259                     DEPOSITOR NAME MISSING
         00301                     INITIAL DEPOSIT NOT NUMERIC 0FG15750
         00322                     DEPOSITOR NAME MISSING
         00336                     INITIAL DEPOSIT NOT NUMERIC ))))!%))
```

```
                              ROBBEM STATE BANK
                              106 WEST 10TH ST.
                             BROOKLYN, NY  11212

                    SAVINGS ACCOUNT MASTER FILE CREATION
DATE  8/16/91                                                PAGE 1

        ACCOUNT      INITIAL       NOTES
        NUMBER       DEPOSIT

         00007       1,007.84      NEW ACCOUNT
         00014          10.00      NEW ACCOUNT
         00021         125.00      NEW ACCOUNT
         00028       7,001.59      NEW ACCOUNT
         00032          25.00      NEW ACCOUNT
         00035         150.00      NEW ACCOUNT
         00049         150.00      NEW ACCOUNT
         00056           1.00      NEW ACCOUNT
         00070         500.00      NEW ACCOUNT
         00077          10.37      NEW ACCOUNT
         00084       1,500.00      NEW ACCOUNT
         00091         100.00      NEW ACCOUNT
         00098         500.00      NEW ACCOUNT
         00105          50.00      NEW ACCOUNT
         00112         250.00      NEW ACCOUNT
         00126         750.00      NEW ACCOUNT
         00133       1,000.00      NEW ACCOUNT
         00140          25.75      NEW ACCOUNT
         00161          24.50      NEW ACCOUNT
         00168         125.50      NEW ACCOUNT
         00175          10.00      NEW ACCOUNT
         00189          35.00      NEW ACCOUNT
         00196         150.00      NEW ACCOUNT
```

FIGURE 13.6 *continued*

```
                    ROBBEM STATE BANK
                    106 WEST 10TH ST.
                   BROOKLYN, NY  11212

           SAVINGS ACCOUNT MASTER FILE CREATION
DATE  8/16/91                                      PAGE 2

       ACCOUNT        INITIAL       NOTES
       NUMBER         DEPOSIT

        00203            5.00       NEW ACCOUNT
        00210          250.00       NEW ACCOUNT
        00217           50.00       NEW ACCOUNT
        00224          175.50       NEW ACCOUNT
        00231          555.00       NEW ACCOUNT
        00238           10.00       NEW ACCOUNT
        00245           35.00       NEW ACCOUNT
        00252           15.00       NEW ACCOUNT
        00266           99.57       NEW ACCOUNT
        00273          275.00       NEW ACCOUNT
        00280           20.00       NEW ACCOUNT
        00287           15.00       NEW ACCOUNT
        00294        1,500.00       NEW ACCOUNT
        00308        2,000.00       NEW ACCOUNT
        00315          250.00       NEW ACCOUNT
        00329           10.00       NEW ACCOUNT
        00343        1,000.00       NEW ACCOUNT
        00350        2,500.00       NEW ACCOUNT

      TOTAL          22,266.62

                          CONTROL COUNTS

                 NUMBER OF NEW ACCOUNTS          41

                 NUMBER OF ERRONEOUS RECORDS      9

                 TOTAL                           50
```

FIGURE 13.7 **Master file produced by Program P13-01**

```
--------------------------------------------------------------------------------
         1         2         3         4         5         6         7         8
12345678901234567890123456789012345678901234567890123456789012345678901234567890
--------------------------------------------------------------------------------
100007ROSEBUCCI                10259000100784
100014ROBERT DAVIS M.D.        10269000001000
100021LORICE MONTI             10279000012500
100028MICHAEL SMITH            11049000700159
100032JOSEPH CAMILLO           11139000002500
100035JOHN J. LEHMAN           11299000015000
100049JAY GREENE               10169000015000
100056EVELYN SLATER            10179000000100
100070PATRICK J. LEE           11249000050000
100077LESLIE MINSKY            10269000001037
100084JOHN DAPRINO             10149000150000
100091JOE'S DELI               10159000010000
100098GEORGE CULHANE           10169000050000
100105ONE DAY CLEANERS         11059000005000
100112ROSEMARY LANE            10019000025000
100126JAMES BUDD               11049000075000
100133PAUL LERNER, D.D.S.      11019000100000
100140BETH FALLON              11039000002575
100161ROBERT RYAN              11059000002450
100168KELLY HEDERMAN           11059000012550
100175MARY KEATING             11069000001000
100189J. & L. CAIN             11069000003500
100196IMPERIAL FLORIST         10309000015000
100203JOYCE MITCHELL           10279000000500
100210JERRY PARKS              10289000025000
100217CARL CALDERON            11079000005000
100224JOHN WILLIAMS            11189000017550
100231BILL WILLIAMS            11279000055500
100238KEVIN PARKER             11199000001000
100245FRANK CAPUTO             11149000003500
100252GENE GALLI               12089000001500
100266MARTIN LANG              11289000009957
100273VITO CACACI              12049000027500
100280COMMUNITY DRUGS          11169000002000
100287SOLOMON CHAPELS          11239000001500
100294JOHN BURKE               12199000150000
100308JOE GARCIA               11279000200000
100315GRACE MICELI             11299000025000
100329GUY VOLPONE              12289000001000
100343JOE & MARY SESSA         12139000100000
100350ROGER SHAW               12319000250000
```

EXERCISE 2

Write a program to create a sequential inventory master file. Use the following input format:

Positions	Field
1–5	Part Number
6–25	Part Description
26	Units E–each L–pound G–gross D–dozen
27–29	Quantity on Hand
30–35	Unit Cost (dollars and cents)
36–41	Date of Last Withdrawal from Inventory (yymmdd)
42–47	Date of Last Receipt into Inventory (yymmdd)
48–80	spaces

Make the following validity checks on the input records:

Part Number	—numeric
Part Description	—present
Units	—valid code
Quantity on Hand	—numeric
Unit Cost	—numeric
Date of Last Withdrawal	—numeric
Date of Last Receipt	—numeric

Design appropriate reports for your program to show the error messages and the good records that were placed on the file. Create your master file on tape if your computer has facilities for doing so. Otherwise, create the sequential file on disk.

Building a Master Record in Storage

In Program P13-01 we wrote a master file containing no small amount of garbage. For example, positions 41 through 80 of the input records contained blanks or perhaps random useless characters. We wrote those characters as part of the master records. Also, the 1 in position 1 of the input records was written onto the master file even though it was not needed there. It was needed only in the input record for validity checking.

Program P13-02 shows how to build master records from input records so that only the fields worth saving get onto the master file. Program P13-02 and the programs following also introduce some general techniques relating to file creation and updating. Some of these techniques may not seem extremely useful at the time they are presented, but their usefulness will become evident as we get into more complex file-handling situations.

Program P13-02 uses input data in the following format:

Positions	Field
1	Code 1
2–6	Account Number
7–14	Amount (to two decimal places)
15–34	Depositor Name
35–80	spaces

You will soon see why there is no need to key the Date of Transaction into the input records. Program P13-02 produces report output in the same formats as Program P13-01.

The master records produced by Program P13-02 will contain only the following fields:

Account Number—5 characters

Depositor Name—20 characters

Date of Last Transaction—6 characters

Current Balance—8 characters

The master records will contain no Code field nor any useless character positions. Each master record will be only 39 characters long.

Program P13-02 is shown in Figure 13.8. It is very similar to Program P13-01. In the File Section, the output record is now defined as containing 39 characters, at line 00450. The master record is broken down into fields in the Working Storage Section, at line 00760. Although this program would have worked if the master record had been broken down into fields in the File Section instead, it is better programming practice to have the breakdown in working storage. Having the fields defined in working storage allows for greater complexity of master-file organization and results in a more general program.

FIGURE *13.8* **Program P13-02**

```
S COBOL II RELEASE 3.1 09/19/89                P13002   DATE AUG 19,1991 T
----+-*A-1-B--+----2----+----3----+----4----+----5----+----6----+----7-|--+

00010  IDENTIFICATION DIVISION.
00020  PROGRAM-ID. P13-02.
00030 * AUTHOR. SHAMEZE SULTAN
00040 *         REVISED BY GAETANO MURATORE
00050 *
00060 *     THIS PROGRAM CREATES A SEQUENTIAL MASTER FILE.
00070 *
00080 ************************************************************************
00090
```

FIGURE 13.8 *continued*

```
 ENVIRONMENT DIVISION.
 CONFIGURATION SECTION.
 INPUT-OUTPUT SECTION.
 FILE-CONTROL.
     SELECT SAVINGS-ACCOUNT-DATA-FILE-IN      ASSIGN TO INFILE.
     SELECT SORT-WORK-FILE                    ASSIGN TO SORTWK.
     SELECT SAVINGS-ACCOUNT-MASTER-FLE-OUT    ASSIGN TO MASTER.
     SELECT TRANSACTION-REGISTER-FILE-OUT     ASSIGN TO PRINTER1.
     SELECT ERROR-FILE-OUT                    ASSIGN TO PRINTER2.

*****************************************************************

 DATA DIVISION.
 FILE SECTION.
 FD  SAVINGS-ACCOUNT-DATA-FILE-IN.

 01  SAVINGS-ACCOUNT-DATA-RECORD-IN       PIC X(80).

 SD  SORT-WORK-FILE
     RECORD CONTAINS 34 CHARACTERS.

 01  SORT-WORK-RECORD.
     05 CODE-IN                           PIC X.
        88  VALID-CODE                   VALUE "1".
     05 ACCOUNT-NUMBER-IN                 PIC X(5).
     05 AMOUNT-IN                         PIC 9(6)V99.
     05 AMOUNT-IN-X REDEFINES AMOUNT-IN   PIC X(8).
     05 DEPOSITOR-NAME-IN                 PIC X(20).
        88  DEPOSITOR-NAME-MISSING       VALUE SPACES.

 FD  SAVINGS-ACCOUNT-MASTER-FLE-OUT
     LABEL RECORDS ARE STANDARD
     RECORD CONTAINS 39 CHARACTERS
     BLOCK CONTAINS 100 RECORDS.

 01  SAVINGS-ACCOUNT-MASTER-REC-OUT       PIC X(39).

 FD  TRANSACTION-REGISTER-FILE-OUT.

 01  TRANSACTION-REGISTER-RECORD          PIC X(72).

 FD  ERROR-FILE-OUT.

 01  ERROR-RECORD-OUT                     PIC X(84).

 WORKING-STORAGE SECTION.
 01  MORE-INPUT                           PIC X VALUE "Y".
     88 THERE-IS-NO-MORE-INPUT            VALUE "N".
 01  ANY-ERRORS                           PIC X.
 01                                       PACKED-DECIMAL.
  02 NUMBER-OF-INPUT-RECORDS-W            PIC S9(3)   VALUE ZERO.
  02 NUMBER-OF-ERRONEOUS-RECORDS-W        PIC S9(3)   VALUE ZERO.
  02 NUMBER-OF-NEW-ACCOUNTS-W             PIC S9(3)   VALUE ZERO.
  02 AMOUNT-IN-COUNTER                    PIC 9(7)V99 VALUE 0.
  02 PAGE-NUMBER-W                        PIC S9 VALUE 0.
  02 ERROR-PAGE-NUMBER-W                  PIC S9 VALUE 0.
 01  ACCOUNT-NUMBER-SAVE         PIC X(5) VALUE HIGH-VALUES.
 01  TODAYS-DATE.
     05 TODAYS-YEAR                       PIC 99.
     05 TODAYS-MONTH-AND-DAY              PIC 9(4).
 01  BLANK-LINE                           PIC X  VALUE SPACE.
 01  LINE-LIMIT                        PIC S99 COMP SYNC VALUE 34.
 01  LINE-COUNT-ER                     PIC S99 COMP SYNC.
 01  ERROR-LINE-LIMIT                  PIC S99 COMP SYNC VALUE 54.
 01  ERROR-LINE-COUNTER                PIC S99 COMP SYNC.

 01  MASTER-RECORD-W.
     05 ACCOUNT-NUMBER                    PIC X(5).
     05 DEPOSITOR-NAME                    PIC X(20).
     05 DATE-OF-LAST-TRANSACTION          PIC 9(6).
     05 CURRENT-BALANCE                   PIC 9(6)V99.
```

continued

FIGURE 13.8 *continued*

```
S COBOL II RELEASE 3.1 09/19/89                    P13002   DATE AUG 19,1991 T
----+-*A-1-B--+----2----+----3----+----4----+----5----+----6----+----7-|--+

       01  REPORT-HEADING-1.
           05                                      PIC X(39) VALUE SPACES.
           05                     PIC X(17) VALUE "ROBBEM STATE BANK".

       01  REPORT-HEADING-2.
           05                                      PIC X(39) VALUE SPACES.
           05                     PIC X(17) VALUE "106 WEST 10TH ST.".

       01  REPORT-HEADING-3.
           05                                      PIC X(38) VALUE SPACES.
           05                     PIC X(19) VALUE "BROOKLYN, NY  11212".

       01  PAGE-HEADING-1.
           05                                      PIC X(29) VALUE SPACES.
           05                                      PIC X(36)
                      VALUE "SAVINGS ACCOUNT MASTER FILE CREATION".

       01  ERROR-HEADING-1.
           05                                      PIC X(33) VALUE SPACES.
           05                                      PIC X(29)
                            VALUE "SAVINGS ACCOUNT ERROR REPORT".

       01  PAGE-HEADING-2.
           05                                      PIC X(17) VALUE SPACES.
           05                                      PIC X(5) VALUE "DATE".
           05  TODAYS-MONTH-AND-DAY                PIC Z9/99/.
           05  TODAYS-YEAR                         PIC 99.
           05                                      PIC X(35) VALUE SPACES.
           05                                      PIC X(4)  VALUE "PAGE".
           05  PAGE-NUMBER-OUT                     PIC Z9.

       01  PAGE-HEADING-3.
           05                                  PIC X(24) VALUE SPACES.
           05                                  PIC X(7)  VALUE "ACCOUNT".
           05                                  PIC X(5)  VALUE SPACES.
           05                                  PIC X(7)  VALUE "INITIAL".
           05                                  PIC X(5)  VALUE SPACES.
           05                                  PIC X(5)  VALUE "NOTES".

       01  ERROR-PAGE-HEADING-3.
           05                                  PIC X(24) VALUE SPACES.
           05                                  PIC X(7)  VALUE "ACCOUNT".
           05                                  PIC X(17) VALUE SPACES.
           05                                  PIC X(5)  VALUE "NOTES".

       01  PAGE-HEADING-4.
           05                                  PIC X(24) VALUE SPACES.
           05                                  PIC X(6)  VALUE "NUMBER".
           05                                  PIC X(6)  VALUE SPACES.
           05                                  PIC X(7) VALUE  "DEPOSIT".

       01  ERROR-PAGE-HEADING-4.
           05                                  PIC X(24) VALUE SPACES.
           05                                  PIC X(6)  VALUE "NUMBER".

       01  REPORT-LINE.
           05  ACCOUNT-NUMBER-OUT                PIC B(25)X(5).
           05  AMOUNT-OUT                        PIC B(5)ZZZ,ZZZ.99B(3).
           05                              PIC X(11) VALUE "NEW ACCOUNT".
```

FIGURE ***13.8*** ***continued***

```
 01   ERROR-LINE.
      05 ACCOUNT-NUMBER-E                      PIC B(25)X(5).
      05 LONG-MESSAGES.
         10 MSG                                PIC B(18)X(27).
         10 AMOUNT-E                           PIC BX(9).
      05 SHORT-MESSAGES REDEFINES LONG-MESSAGES.
         10 SHORT-MESSAGE                      PIC B(18)X(12).
         10 CODE-E                             PIC BXB(23).

 01   TOTAL-LINE-1.
      05                                       PIC X(23) VALUE SPACES.
      05                                    PIC X(5)B(5) VALUE "TOTAL".
      05 AMOUNT-OUT-TOTAL                      PIC Z,ZZZ,ZZZ.99.

 01   TOTAL-LINE-2.
      05                                       PIC X(41) VALUE SPACES.
      05                              PIC X(14) VALUE "CONTROL COUNTS".

 01   TOTAL-LINE-3.
      05                                       PIC X(34) VALUE SPACES.
      05                                       PIC X(22)
                                  VALUE "NUMBER OF NEW ACCOUNTS".
      05 NUMBER-OF-NEW-ACCOUNTS                PIC B(6)ZZ9.

 01   TOTAL-LINE-4.
      05                                       PIC X(34) VALUE SPACES.
      05                                       PIC X(27)
                                    VALUE "NUMBER OF ERRONEOUS RECORDS".
      05 NUMBER-OF-ERRONEOUS-RECORDS           PIC BZZ9.

 01   TOTAL-LINE-5.
      05                                       PIC X(34) VALUE SPACES.
      05                                       PIC X(5)  VALUE "TOTAL".
      05 NUMBER-OF-INPUT-RECORDS               PIC B(23)ZZ9.

 01   NO-INPUT-DATA.
      05                                       PIC X(21) VALUE SPACES.
      05                VALUE "NO INPUT DATA"  PIC X(13).

*****************************************************************

 PROCEDURE DIVISION.
 CREATE-MASTER-FILE.
     SORT SORT-WORK-FILE
          ASCENDING KEY ACCOUNT-NUMBER-IN
          USING SAVINGS-ACCOUNT-DATA-FILE-IN
          OUTPUT PROCEDURE IS PRODUCE-MASTER-FILE
     STOP RUN
     .

 PRODUCE-MASTER-FILE.
     PERFORM INITIALIZATION
     PERFORM PROCESS-A-RECORD UNTIL THERE-IS-NO-MORE-INPUT
     PERFORM TERMINATION
     .

 INITIALIZATION.
     OPEN OUTPUT SAVINGS-ACCOUNT-MASTER-FLE-OUT
                 ERROR-FILE-OUT
                 TRANSACTION-REGISTER-FILE-OUT
     ACCEPT TODAYS-DATE FROM DATE
     MOVE CORR TODAYS-DATE TO PAGE-HEADING-2
     PERFORM PRINT-REPORT-HEADINGS
     PERFORM READ-A-RECORD
     IF THERE-IS-NO-MORE-INPUT
         WRITE TRANSACTION-REGISTER-RECORD FROM NO-INPUT-DATA
     END-IF
     .
```

continued

In the paragraph PROCESS-A-RECORD we now have a new PERFORM statement, at line 02160. The paragraph BUILD-MASTER-RECORD, at line 02220, constructs the master record in working storage in preparation for writing it onto the master file. It is good practice to have separate paragraphs for building the master record and for writing it, even though in this program the functions of the two paragraphs could easily have been combined in one. Program P13-02 was run with the input data shown in Figure 13.9 and produced the report output shown in Figure 13.10. The master file produced by the program is shown in Figure 13.11.

FIGURE *13.8* ***continued***

```
S COBOL II RELEASE 3.1 09/19/89                    P13002   DATE AUG 19,1991 T
----+-*A-1-B--+----2----+----3----+----4----+----5----+----6----+----7-|--+

02110  PROCESS-A-RECORD.
02120      ADD 1 TO NUMBER-OF-INPUT-RECORDS-W
02130      MOVE "N" TO ANY-ERRORS
02140      PERFORM CHECK-INPUT-FOR-VALIDITY
02150      IF ANY-ERRORS = "N"
02160          PERFORM BUILD-MASTER-RECORD
02170          PERFORM WRITE-MASTER-RECORD
02180      END-IF
02190      PERFORM READ-A-RECORD
02200      .
02210
02220  BUILD-MASTER-RECORD.
02230      MOVE ACCOUNT-NUMBER-IN TO ACCOUNT-NUMBER
02240      MOVE DEPOSITOR-NAME-IN TO DEPOSITOR-NAME
02250      MOVE AMOUNT-IN         TO CURRENT-BALANCE
02260      MOVE TODAYS-DATE       TO DATE-OF-LAST-TRANSACTION
02270      .
02280
02290  WRITE-MASTER-RECORD.
02300      WRITE SAVINGS-ACCOUNT-MASTER-REC-OUT FROM MASTER-RECORD-W
02310      MOVE ACCOUNT-NUMBER-IN TO ACCOUNT-NUMBER-SAVE
02320      ADD 1 TO NUMBER-OF-NEW-ACCOUNTS-W
02330      PERFORM WRITE-NEW-ACCOUNT-LINE
02340      .
02350
02360  CHECK-INPUT-FOR-VALIDITY.
02370      MOVE SPACES TO ERROR-LINE
02380      IF NOT VALID-CODE
02390          MOVE "Y" TO ANY-ERRORS
02400          MOVE CODE-IN TO CODE-E
02410          MOVE "INVALID CODE" TO SHORT-MESSAGE
02420          PERFORM WRITE-ERROR-MESSAGE
02430      END-IF
02440      IF ACCOUNT-NUMBER-IN = ACCOUNT-NUMBER-SAVE
02450          MOVE "Y" TO ANY-ERRORS
02460          MOVE "DUPLICATE ACCOUNT NUMBER" TO MSG
02470          PERFORM WRITE-ERROR-MESSAGE
02480      END-IF
02490      IF DEPOSITOR-NAME-MISSING
02500          MOVE "Y" TO ANY-ERRORS
02510          MOVE "DEPOSITOR NAME MISSING" TO MSG
02520          PERFORM WRITE-ERROR-MESSAGE
02530      END-IF
02540      IF AMOUNT-IN NOT NUMERIC
02550          MOVE "Y" TO ANY-ERRORS
02560          MOVE AMOUNT-IN-X TO AMOUNT-E
02570          MOVE "INITIAL DEPOSIT NOT NUMERIC" TO MSG
02580          PERFORM WRITE-ERROR-MESSAGE
02590      END-IF
02600      IF ANY-ERRORS = "Y"
02610          ADD 1 TO NUMBER-OF-ERRONEOUS-RECORDS-W
02620      END-IF
02630      .
```

FIGURE ***13.8*** ***continued***

```
WRITE-ERROR-MESSAGE.
    MOVE ACCOUNT-NUMBER-IN TO ACCOUNT-NUMBER-E
    PERFORM ERROR-LINE-COUNT-CHECK
    WRITE ERROR-RECORD-OUT FROM ERROR-LINE
    ADD 1 TO ERROR-LINE-COUNTER
    .

ERROR-LINE-COUNT-CHECK.
    IF 1 + ERROR-LINE-COUNTER > ERROR-LINE-LIMIT
        PERFORM PRINT-ERROR-REPORT-HEAD
    END-IF
    .

TERMINATION.
    PERFORM WRITE-TOTALS
    CLOSE SAVINGS-ACCOUNT-MASTER-FLE-OUT
          ERROR-FILE-OUT
          TRANSACTION-REGISTER-FILE-OUT
    .

READ-A-RECORD.
    RETURN SORT-WORK-FILE
        AT END
            SET THERE-IS-NO-MORE-INPUT TO TRUE
    .

LINE-COUNT-CHECK.
    IF 1 + LINE-COUNT-ER GREATER THAN LINE-LIMIT
        PERFORM PRINT-REGISTER-HEAD
    END-IF
    .

WRITE-TOTALS.
    MOVE AMOUNT-IN-COUNTER TO AMOUNT-OUT-TOTAL
    WRITE TRANSACTION-REGISTER-RECORD FROM TOTAL-LINE-1 AFTER 2
    WRITE TRANSACTION-REGISTER-RECORD FROM TOTAL-LINE-2 AFTER 2
    MOVE NUMBER-OF-NEW-ACCOUNTS-W TO NUMBER-OF-NEW-ACCOUNTS
    WRITE TRANSACTION-REGISTER-RECORD FROM TOTAL-LINE-3 AFTER 2
    MOVE NUMBER-OF-ERRONEOUS-RECORDS-W TO
                                NUMBER-OF-ERRONEOUS-RECORDS
    WRITE TRANSACTION-REGISTER-RECORD FROM TOTAL-LINE-4 AFTER 2
    MOVE NUMBER-OF-INPUT-RECORDS-W TO
                                 NUMBER-OF-INPUT-RECORDS
    WRITE TRANSACTION-REGISTER-RECORD FROM TOTAL-LINE-5 AFTER 2
    .

PRINT-REPORT-HEADINGS.
    PERFORM PRINT-REGISTER-HEAD
    PERFORM PRINT-ERROR-REPORT-HEAD
    .

PRINT-ERROR-REPORT-HEAD.
    ADD 1 TO ERROR-PAGE-NUMBER-W
    MOVE ERROR-PAGE-NUMBER-W TO PAGE-NUMBER-OUT
    WRITE ERROR-RECORD-OUT FROM REPORT-HEADING-1
                                 AFTER ADVANCING PAGE
    WRITE ERROR-RECORD-OUT FROM REPORT-HEADING-2
    WRITE ERROR-RECORD-OUT FROM REPORT-HEADING-3
    WRITE ERROR-RECORD-OUT FROM ERROR-HEADING-1 AFTER 2
    WRITE ERROR-RECORD-OUT FROM PAGE-HEADING-2
    WRITE ERROR-RECORD-OUT FROM ERROR-PAGE-HEADING-3
                                 AFTER ADVANCING 3
    WRITE ERROR-RECORD-OUT FROM ERROR-PAGE-HEADING-4
    WRITE ERROR-RECORD-OUT FROM BLANK-LINE
    MOVE 11 TO ERROR-LINE-COUNTER
    .
```

continued

FIGURE 13.8 *continued*

```
S COBOL II RELEASE 3.1 09/19/89                    P13002   DATE AUG 19,1991 T
----+-*A-1-B--+----2----+----3----+----4----+----5----+----6----+----7-|--+

       PRINT-REGISTER-HEAD.
           ADD 1 TO PAGE-NUMBER-W
           MOVE PAGE-NUMBER-W TO PAGE-NUMBER-OUT
           WRITE TRANSACTION-REGISTER-RECORD FROM REPORT-HEADING-1
                                        AFTER ADVANCING PAGE
           WRITE TRANSACTION-REGISTER-RECORD FROM REPORT-HEADING-2
           WRITE TRANSACTION-REGISTER-RECORD FROM REPORT-HEADING-3
           WRITE TRANSACTION-REGISTER-RECORD FROM PAGE-HEADING-1
                                        AFTER ADVANCING 2
           WRITE TRANSACTION-REGISTER-RECORD FROM PAGE-HEADING-2
           WRITE TRANSACTION-REGISTER-RECORD FROM PAGE-HEADING-3
                                        AFTER ADVANCING 3
           WRITE TRANSACTION-REGISTER-RECORD FROM PAGE-HEADING-4
           WRITE TRANSACTION-REGISTER-RECORD FROM BLANK-LINE
           MOVE 11 TO LINE-COUNT-ER
           .

       WRITE-NEW-ACCOUNT-LINE.
           MOVE ACCOUNT-NUMBER-IN TO ACCOUNT-NUMBER-OUT
           MOVE AMOUNT-IN TO AMOUNT-OUT
           PERFORM LINE-COUNT-CHECK
           WRITE TRANSACTION-REGISTER-RECORD FROM REPORT-LINE
           ADD 1 TO LINE-COUNT-ER
           ADD AMOUNT-IN TO AMOUNT-IN-COUNTER
           .
```

FIGURE 13.9 Input to Program P13-02

```
--------------------------------------------------------------------------------
         1         2         3         4         5         6         7         8
12345678901234567890123456789012345678901234567890123456789012345678901234567890
--------------------------------------------------------------------------------
10010500005000LENORE MILLER
10011200025000ROSEMARY LANE
3000070CA00000MICHELE CAPUANO
10012600075000JAMES BUDD
10013300100000PAUL LERNER, D.D.S.
10014000002575BETH FALLON
10009800002000JANE HALEY
10010500005000ONE DAY CLEANERS
10016100002450ROBERT RYAN
10016800012550KELLY HEDERMAN
10017500001000MARY KEATING
20018200007500BOB LANIGAN
10018900003500J. & L. CAIN
10019600015000IMPERIAL FLORIST
10020300000500JOYCE MITCHELL
10021000025000JERRY PARKS
10021700005000CARL CALDERON
10022400017550JOHN WILLIAMS
10003500015000JOHN J. LEHMAN
10003200002500JOSEPH CAMILLO
10004900015000JAY GREENE
10005600000100EVELYN SLATER
10006300007500
10007000050000PATRICK J. LEE
10007700001037LESLIE MINSKY
10008400150000JOHN DAPRINO
10009100010000JOE'S DELI
10009800050000GEORGE CULHANE
10026600009957MARTIN LANG
10027300027500VITO CACACI
10028000002000COMMUNITY DRUGS
10028700001500SOLOMON CHAPELS
10029400150000JOHN BURKE
1003010FG15750PAT P. POWERS
10030800200000JOE GARCIA
10031500025000GRACE MICELI
10032200002000
10032900001000GUY VOLPONE
100336))))!%))SALVATORE CALI
10023100055500BILL WILLIAMS
10023800001000KEVIN PARKER
10024500003500FRANK CAPUTO
10025200001500GENE GALLI
10025900002937
10000700100784ROSEBUCCI
10001400001000ROBERT DAVIS M.D.
10002100012500LORICE MONTI
10002800700159MICHAEL SMITH
10034300100000JOE & MARY SESSA
10035000250000ROGER SHAW
```

FIGURE 13.10 **Report output produced by Program P13-02**

```
                         ROBBEM STATE BANK
                         106 WEST 10TH ST.
                        BROOKLYN, NY  11212

                   SAVINGS ACCOUNT ERROR REPORT
DATE  8/19/91                                           PAGE 1


       ACCOUNT                 NOTES
       NUMBER

        00007                  INVALID CODE 3
        00007                  DUPLICATE ACCOUNT NUMBER
        00007                  INITIAL DEPOSIT NOT NUMERIC OCA00000
        00063                  DEPOSITOR NAME MISSING
        00098                  DUPLICATE ACCOUNT NUMBER
        00105                  DUPLICATE ACCOUNT NUMBER
        00182                  INVALID CODE 2
        00259                  DEPOSITOR NAME MISSING
        00301                  INITIAL DEPOSIT NOT NUMERIC OFG15750
        00322                  DEPOSITOR NAME MISSING
        00336                  INITIAL DEPOSIT NOT NUMERIC ))))!%))
```

```
                         ROBBEM STATE BANK
                         106 WEST 10TH ST.
                        BROOKLYN, NY  11212

                SAVINGS ACCOUNT MASTER FILE CREATION
DATE  8/19/91                                           PAGE 1


       ACCOUNT     INITIAL     NOTES
       NUMBER      DEPOSIT

        00007      1,007.84    NEW ACCOUNT
        00014         10.00    NEW ACCOUNT
        00021        125.00    NEW ACCOUNT
        00028      7,001.59    NEW ACCOUNT
        00032         25.00    NEW ACCOUNT
        00035        150.00    NEW ACCOUNT
        00049        150.00    NEW ACCOUNT
        00056          1.00    NEW ACCOUNT
        00070        500.00    NEW ACCOUNT
        00077         10.37    NEW ACCOUNT
        00084      1,500.00    NEW ACCOUNT
        00091        100.00    NEW ACCOUNT
        00098        500.00    NEW ACCOUNT
        00105         50.00    NEW ACCOUNT
        00112        250.00    NEW ACCOUNT
        00126        750.00    NEW ACCOUNT
        00133      1,000.00    NEW ACCOUNT
        00140         25.75    NEW ACCOUNT
        00161         24.50    NEW ACCOUNT
        00168        125.50    NEW ACCOUNT
        00175         10.00    NEW ACCOUNT
        00189         35.00    NEW ACCOUNT
        00196        150.00    NEW ACCOUNT
```

FIGURE 13.10 *continued*

```
                       ROBBEM STATE BANK
                       106 WEST 10TH ST.
                      BROOKLYN, NY  11212

              SAVINGS ACCOUNT MASTER FILE CREATION
DATE  8/19/91                                          PAGE 2


       ACCOUNT      INITIAL     NOTES
       NUMBER       DEPOSIT

        00203          5.00     NEW ACCOUNT
        00210        250.00     NEW ACCOUNT
        00217         50.00     NEW ACCOUNT
        00224        175.50     NEW ACCOUNT
        00231        555.00     NEW ACCOUNT
        00238         10.00     NEW ACCOUNT
        00245         35.00     NEW ACCOUNT
        00252         15.00     NEW ACCOUNT
        00266         99.57     NEW ACCOUNT
        00273        275.00     NEW ACCOUNT
        00280         20.00     NEW ACCOUNT
        00287         15.00     NEW ACCOUNT
        00294      1,500.00     NEW ACCOUNT
        00308      2,000.00     NEW ACCOUNT
        00315        250.00     NEW ACCOUNT
        00329         10.00     NEW ACCOUNT
        00343      1,000.00     NEW ACCOUNT
        00350      2,500.00     NEW ACCOUNT

      TOTAL        22,266.62

                          CONTROL COUNTS

                 NUMBER OF NEW ACCOUNTS        41

                 NUMBER OF ERRONEOUS RECORDS    9

                 TOTAL                         50
```

FIGURE 13.11 **Master file produced by Program P13-02**

```
--------------------------------------------------------------------------------
         1         2         3         4         5         6         7         8
12345678901234567890123456789012345678901234568790123456789012345678901234567890
--------------------------------------------------------------------------------
00007ROSEBUCCI           91081900100784
00014ROBERT DAVIS M.D.   91081900001000
00021LORICE MONTI        91081900012500
00028MICHAEL SMITH       91081900700159
00032JOSEPH CAMILLO      91081900002500
00035JOHN J. LEHMAN      91081900015000
00049JAY GREENE          91081900015000
00056EVELYN SLATER       91081900000100
00070PATRICK J. LEE      91081900050000
00077LESLIE MINSKY       91081900001037
00084JOHN DAPRINO        91081900150000
00091JOE'S DELI          91081900010000
00098GEORGE CULHANE      91081900050000
00105ONE DAY CLEANERS    91081900005000
00112ROSEMARY LANE       91081900025000
00126JAMES BUDD          91081900075000
00133PAUL LERNER, D.D.S. 91081900100000
00140BETH FALLON         91081900002575
00161ROBERT RYAN         91081900002450
00168KELLY HEDERMAN      91081900012550
00175MARY KEATING        91081900001000
00189J. & L. CAIN        91081900003500
00196IMPERIAL FLORIST    91081900015000
00203JOYCE MITCHELL      91081900000500
00210JERRY PARKS         91081900025000
00217CARL CALDERON       91081900005000
00224JOHN WILLIAMS       91081900017550
00231BILL WILLIAMS       91081900055500
00238KEVIN PARKER        91081900001000
00245FRANK CAPUTO        91081900003500
00252GENE GALLI          91081900001500
00266MARTIN LANG         91081900009957
00273VITO CACAÇI         91081900027500
00280COMMUNITY DRUGS     91081900002000
00287SOLOMON CHAPELS     91081900001500
00294JOHN BURKE          91081900150000
00308JOE GARCIA          91081900200000
00315GRACE MICELI        91081900025000
00329GUY VOLPONE         91081900001000
00343JOE & MARY SESSA    91081900100000
00350ROGER SHAW          91081900250000
```

EXERCISE 3

Write a program to create a sequential inventory master file using input in the following format:

Positions	*Field*
1–5	Part Number
6–25	Part Description
26	Units
	E–each
	L–pound
	G–gross
	D–dozen
27–32	Unit Cost (dollars and cents)
33–36	Supplier Code
37–41	Storage Location
42–44	Reorder Point
45–47	Reorder Quantity
48–80	spaces

Have your program build the master records in working storage. Have each master record contain the following fields:

Part Number—5 characters

Part Description—20 characters

Units—1 character

Quantity on Hand—3 characters

Unit Cost (dollars and cents)—6 characters

Supplier Code—4 characters

Storage Location—5 characters

Reorder Point—3 characters

Reorder Quantity—3 characters

Date of Last Withdrawal from Inventory (yymmdd)—6 characters

Date of Last Receipt into Inventory (yymmdd)—6 characters

Date Created (yymmdd)—6 characters

Date of Last Access (yymmdd)—6 characters

Create the Quantity on Hand field and the Dates of Last Withdrawal and Last Receipt with values of zero. Have your program insert today's date into the Date Created and Date of Last Access fields in each master record. Use 15 records per block. Have your program make the following validity checks on the input records:

Part Number	—numeric
Part Description	—present
Units	—valid code

Unit Cost	—numeric
Supplier Code	—first character alphabetic, second through fourth characters numeric
Storage Location	—first two characters alphabetic, third through fifth characters numeric
Reorder Point	—numeric
Reorder Quantity	—numeric

Have your program produce a report showing the good records and a report showing the errors.

Save the file that you create in this exercise for use in later exercises in this chapter and the next.

Deleting Records from a Sequential File

We will now study the first of the several file-update programs in this book, one that deletes records from a master file. You will see other update programs, which change existing records and add new ones, in the following chapters.

A master file needs to have records deleted from it when they become obsolete. In our savings-account master file a record would be deleted when a depositor closes an account. Any balance remaining in the account would be paid to the depositor as a final withdrawal. The format of the transaction input to Program P13-03 is:

Positions	Field
1	Code 5
2–6	Account Number
7–80	spaces

There is one transaction for each record that is to be removed from the master file. The transaction contains only the Code 5, identifying the transaction as a deletion, and the Account Number of the master record to be deleted.

If a deletion transaction contains an Account Number that is not on the master file, the transaction is in error. If there is more than one transaction with the same Account Number, only one of them could be valid. If one were valid and successfully deleted a master record, the other transaction records with the same Account Number would be invalid because there would no longer be a master record with that Account Number. Program P13-03 produces a report in the format shown in Figure 13.12 showing the records deleted. The erroneous transactions are shown in the format given in Figure 13.13. Notice that neither report shows the complete contents of the master file.

When records are to be deleted from a tape file, we cannot remove them with scissors. Nor can we erase the obsolete records and somehow move the remaining ones up along the tape to fill the gaps. Even if COBOL permitted that kind of processing, which it does not, it would involve too much time-consuming movement of tape back and forth. The way that records are deleted

FIGURE ***13.12*** **Output format for deletion report for Program P13-03**

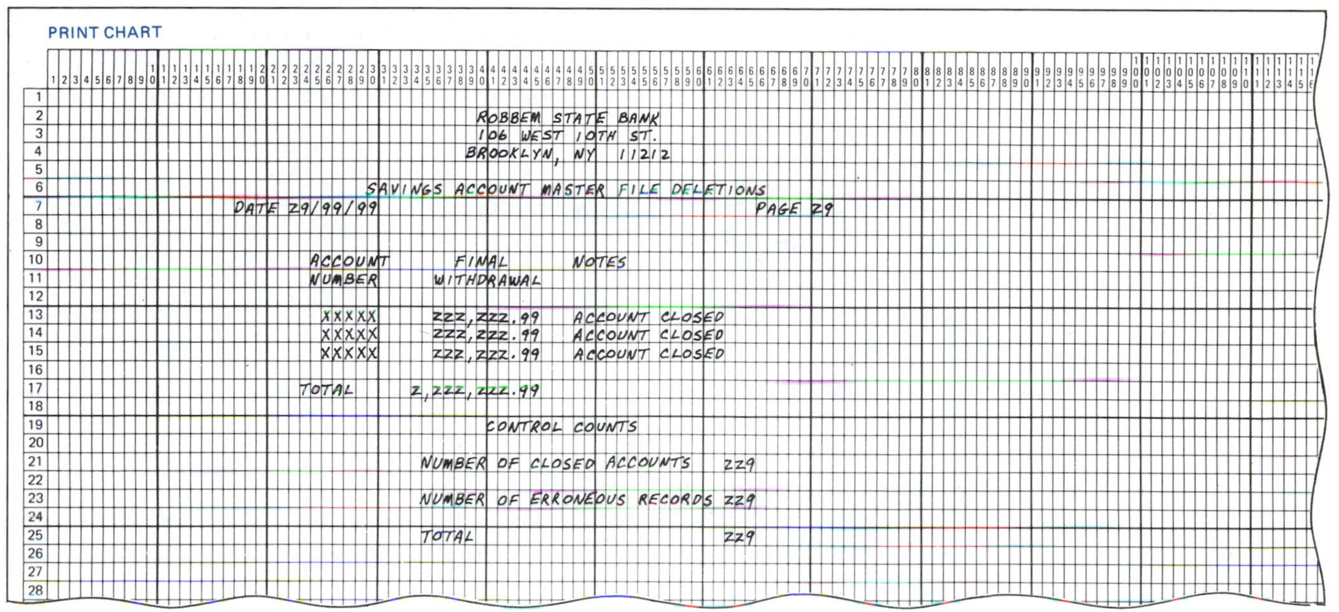

FIGURE ***13.13*** **Output format for error report for Program P13-03**

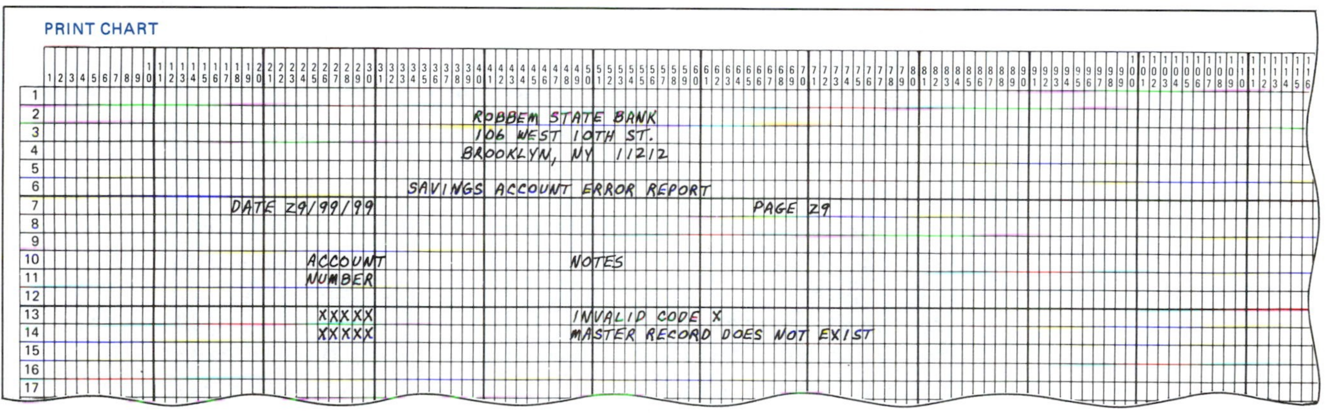

from a tape file is this: The update program reads the existing master file and, by referring to the deletion transactions, copies the master onto a new tape, omitting the deleted records. The transactions must be in sequence on the same key field as the master file—in this case, Account Number. The same procedure is followed for deleting records from a sequential file on disk.

All the update programs in this book use the well-known **balance-line algorithm.** This is a widely published and widely accepted algorithm, and is known to be correct.[2] Its use is certain to become more widespread as programmers recognize that it can easily accommodate update logic of any imaginable complexity. The algorithm uses a transaction input area in working storage with space for one transaction record, a master input area with space for one incoming master record, and a master work area for working on each master record. There is a field in working storage called CURRENT-KEY, to which is assigned the key of the record being worked on.

A Hierarchy Diagram for Deleting Records from a Sequential File

The hierarchy diagram for Program P13-03 is shown in Figure 13.14. The diagram is more complex than is absolutely necessary for doing deletions. The logic contained in the diagram is very general, though, and will be able easily to accommodate all the additional features of all the update programs to come. You will see that if you learn the logic of this hierarchy diagram, there will be very little more to learn. The diagram is not easy to follow, but the effort expended in learning it is extremely worthwhile.

The boxes of the hierarchy diagram are described briefly in this section. In the next section, we will step through the diagram with sample data to see how it would handle some deletions and some error conditions.

In the diagram, the program SORTs the transactions into order on their key, in this case Account Number, and the OUTPUT PROCEDURE of the SORT is the rest of the hierarchy diagram. As part of the "Initialization" the program reads the first master record and the first transaction record, in the boxes "Read a master record" and "Read a transaction record." These two records are assigned to their respective input areas in working storage. Later in the program, whenever we get done with either a master record or a transaction record in its input area, we immediately replace it with the next incoming master or transaction record. In that way we always have in the input areas in working storage the next master record and the next transaction record.

The box "Choose current key" determines the key of the next record to be worked on and assigns it to the field CURRENT-KEY. In a sequential update, you must always work on the record in storage with the lowest key. If the record in the master input area has a lower key than the record in the transaction input area, the program assigns the key of the master record to CURRENT-KEY; if the transaction has a lower key than the master record, the program assigns the key of the transaction to CURRENT-KEY. If the two keys are equal, the program assigns their common key to CURRENT-KEY. Master records are worked on in the master work area, and transaction records are worked on in the transaction input area. In the course of execution of the hierarchy diagram, every key on the master and transaction files is assigned to CURRENT-KEY, in ascending order.

"Process one key" is the main loop of the program. It executes once for each different value of CURRENT-KEY. Each time CURRENT-KEY is assigned a new value, the four subfunctions of "Process one key" execute left to right. In

[2]See, for example, Dwyer, Barry. January 1981. One more time—How to update a master file, *Communications of the ACM* 24:1, pp. 3–8; Grauer, Robert T. 1983. *Structured Methods Through COBOL.* Englewood Cliffs, NJ: Prentice Hall, pp. 140–167.

FIGURE 13.14 Hierarchy diagram for Program P13-03

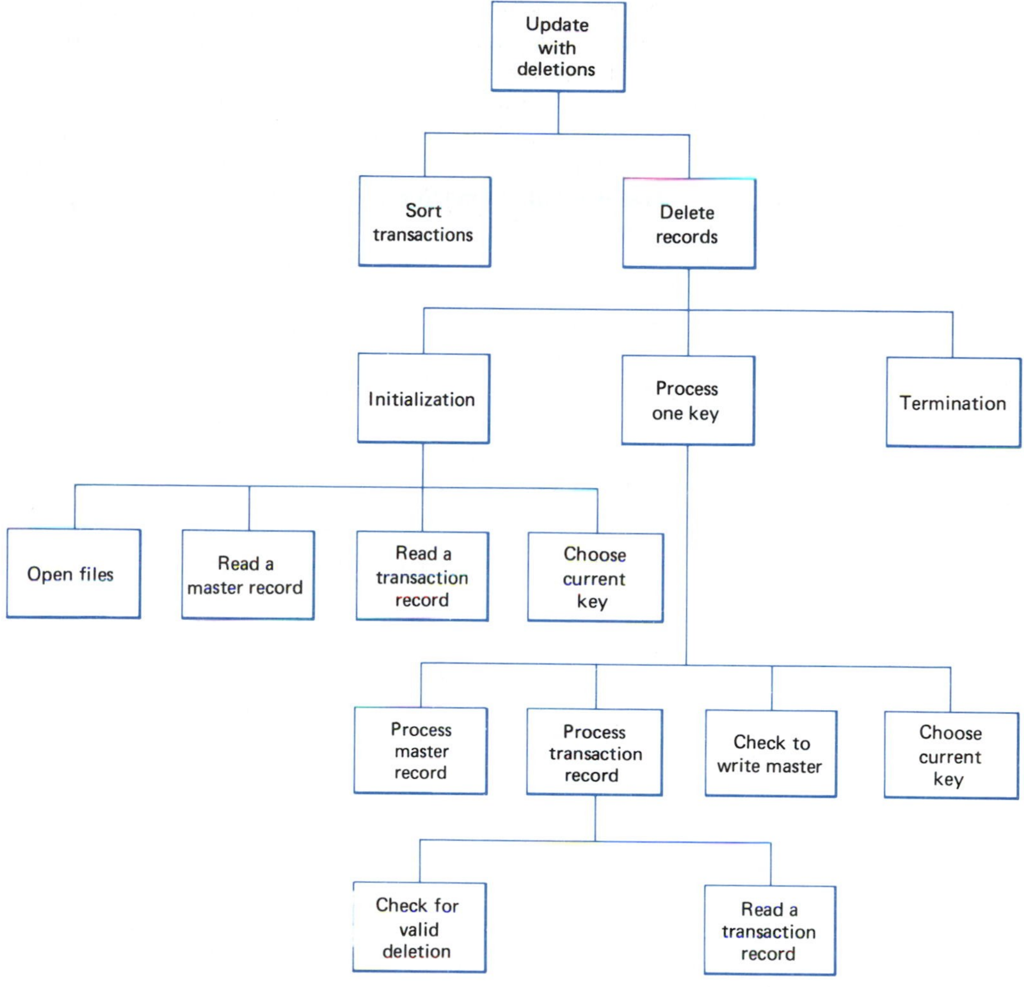

so doing, they process any master record whose key is equal to CURRENT-KEY (if there is one), and all the transactions whose keys are equal to CURRENT-KEY (if there are any). The subfunctions "Process master record," "Process transaction record," "Check to write master," and "Choose current key" thus keep executing over and over until all the keys on the master and transaction files have been processed.

The box "Process master record" determines whether the record in the master input area should be moved to the master work area. It does this by comparing the key of the record in the master input area to CURRENT-KEY. If they are equal then "Process master record"

a. moves the contents of the master input area to the master work area

b. reads the next incoming master record and assigns it to the master input area *c.* moves "Y" to a flag to indicate that a record was moved to the master work area

If the key of the record in the master input area is not equal to CURRENT-KEY, "Process master record" moves "N" to the flag to indicate that no record was moved to the master work area.

"Process transaction record" executes only if the key of the record in the transaction input area is equal to CURRENT-KEY. If there is more than one transaction whose key is equal to CURRENT-KEY, "Process transaction record" processes all of them. In our deletion program there can be no more than one valid transaction for any key.

"Check to write master" looks to see if there is a master record in the work area, by checking whether the flag is "Y" or "N." If the flag is "Y," "Check to write master" writes the contents of the master work area onto the new master output tape. If the flag is "N," "Check to write master" does nothing.

This hierarchy diagram allows for erroneous transactions of both types mentioned earlier; that is, a deletion transaction whose key does not match the key of any master record, and more than one deletion transaction against a single master record.

How the Hierarchy Diagram Works

Let us look at a few master records and a few deletion transactions to see how the hierarchy diagram would execute. For this example we will assume that we have the master file that was created by Program P13-02. The Account Numbers of the first eight records in that file are listed here:

00007

00014

00021

00028

00032

00035

00049

00056

Now let us assume that we have the following four deletion transactions, two of which are in error:

5 00021

5 00021

5 00029

5 00035

One of the transactions is in error because it has no match on the master file; one of the others is in error because it is a duplicate and will be trying to delete a record that will have already been deleted. Now let us follow the hierarchy diagram as it processes the master records and deletion transactions shown.

First, ''Initialization'' reads the first master record, 00007, into the master input area in working storage. It then reads the first transaction, 00021, into the transaction input area in working storage. ''Choose current key'' assigns the lower of the two keys, 00007, to CURRENT-KEY.

Now we enter the main loop. First, ''Process master record'' compares the key of the master record in the master input area to CURRENT-KEY. Since they are equal, ''Process master record'' moves the master record to the work area and reads the next master record, 00014, into the master input area. It also sets a flag to ''Y'' to indicate that a master record was moved. Then the program goes on to ''Process transaction record.'' Since there are no transactions whose key is equal to the CURRENT-KEY, 00007, the program goes to ''Check to write master.'' ''Check to write master'' looks to see whether there is a master record in the work area, and since there is one, writes it onto the new output master file. ''Choose current key'' now executes, and chooses between the master key in the master input area, 00014, and the transaction key, which is still 00021. The master key is again lower, so 00014 is assigned to CURRENT-KEY.

We now go around the main loop again. ''Process master record'' determines that the key of the master record in the master input area is equal to CURRENT-KEY, and so moves master record 00014 to the work area, reads master record 00021 into the master input area, and sets the flag to ''Y'' to indicate that the move was made. Once again there are no transactions for the CURRENT-KEY, so we go directly to ''Check to write master.'' ''Check to write master'' finds that the work area contains a master record, and so writes it onto the new output master file. Now ''Choose current key'' finds the keys of the master record and the transaction the same, 00021. It assigns 00021 to CURRENT-KEY.

As we go around the main loop again, ''Process master record'' moves master record 00021 to the work area, reads master record 00028 into the master input area, and sets the flag to ''Y'' to reflect the move. Now we have a transaction in the transaction input area whose key is equal to CURRENT-KEY, so ''Process transaction record'' executes. Since there is more than one transaction with this same key, ''Process transaction record'' will execute over and over until they are all processed. ''Check for valid deletion'' checks that the transaction contains a Code of 5 and that the flag is ''Y,'' indicating that there is a master record in the work area that can be deleted. It then processes the deletion as follows: It takes the Current Balance in master record 00021 to be the final withdrawal and prints a line on the transaction report showing the amount. Then it sets the flag to ''N'' to indicate that master record 00021 is no longer present. Of course, the record is still sitting in the work area, but as far as the program cares, the record has disappeared. The transaction is thus processed, and ''Read a transaction record'' reads in the next transaction, the second of the 00021s.

Since this transaction has the same key as the previous one, ''Process transaction record'' executes again. This time the transaction is found invalid because there is no longer a master record with a key of 00021. The program writes an error message saying that there is no such master record. The next transaction, 00029, is then read into the transaction input area.

Since all transactions with a key of 00021 have been processed, ''Check to write master'' executes. Now ''Check to write master'' finds no master record in the work area, because the processing of the valid deletion transaction made it disappear. So the program goes on to "Choose current key." The lower of the two keys, 00028, is assigned to CURRENT-KEY.

You can now trace the execution of the main loop and see that master record 00028 gets written onto the output master tape. "Choose current key" then chooses between the master key, 00032, and the transaction key, 00029. It assigns the lower, 00029, to CURRENT-KEY.

As we go around the loop again, "Process master record" notes that the key of the master record in the input area is not equal to CURRENT-KEY, so it does not move anything to the work area. It sets the flag to "N" to indicate that no master record was moved. In "Process transaction record" the program checks that the transaction contains a Code of 5 and whether there is a master record in the work area. Since the flag is "N," indicating that there is no master record in the work area, the program knows that this transaction is in error. Indeed, the transaction is trying to delete master record 00029, and no such master record exists. The program writes an error message, and "Read a transaction record" reads transaction 00035. "Check to write master" of course finds the flag "N," indicating that there is no master record in the work area, and so the program goes on to "Choose current key."

EXERCISE *4*

Step through the hierarchy diagram in Figure 13.14 and show how the master records 00032, 00035, 00049, and 00056 are processed. Answer the following questions:

a. Which of the three master records 00032, 00035, and 00049 gets written onto the new output master tape?

b. What is the value assigned to CURRENT-KEY at the time the last transaction is processed?

c. What is the value assigned to CURRENT-KEY at the time master record 00056 is written onto the new master tape?

How the Hierarchy Diagram Handles End-of-File

We now discuss how the hierarchy diagram handles end-of-file on the transaction file and the master file. In an update program such as this, there is no field such as MORE-INPUT, for there are two input files, and both must reach end-of-file before the program can proceed to the termination routine. In the sample data that we were using to step through the hierarchy diagram, an end-of-file would be detected on the transaction file after transaction 00035 was processed. At that time, master records 00049 and 00056 still need to be copied from the incoming master file to the new output master file.

The simplest way to handle transaction end-of-file is this: When end-of-file is detected on the transaction file, move HIGH-VALUES to the transaction input area. That way, "Choose current key" will keep choosing master keys as lower, and the remaining master records will be copied.

When end-of-file is detected on the incoming master file, HIGH-VALUES is moved to the master input area. When CURRENT-KEY finally gets HIGH-

VALUES assigned to it, that means that both the master and transaction files have been completely processed, and then the "Termination" box is executed.

A Program to Delete Records from a Sequential File

Program P13-03 is shown in Figure 13.15. The definition of the SORT-WORK-FILE, line 00420, shows that only the first six characters of each record from the transaction file will be processed by the SORT. Those are the only characters needed for later processing.

FIGURE *13.15*

Program P13-03

```
S COBOL II RELEASE 3.1 09/19/89                     P13003   DATE SEP 02,1991 T
----+-*A-1-B--+----2----+----3----+----4----+----5----+----6----+----7-|--+

00010  IDENTIFICATION DIVISION.
00020  PROGRAM-ID. P13-03.
00030 * AUTHOR. SHAMEZE SULTAN
00040 *         REVISED BY GAETANO MURATORE
00050 *
00060 *    THIS PROGRAM DELETES RECORDS FROM A SEQUENTIAL MASTER
00070 *    FILE.
00080 *
00090 *****************************************************************
00100
00110  ENVIRONMENT DIVISION.
00120  INPUT-OUTPUT SECTION.
00130  FILE-CONTROL.
00140      SELECT ACCOUNT-MASTER-FILE-IN            ASSIGN TO MASTIN.
00150      SELECT ACCOUNT-MASTER-FILE-OUT           ASSIGN TO MASTOUT.
00160      SELECT TRANSACTION-FILE-IN               ASSIGN TO INFILE.
00170      SELECT TRANSACTION-REGISTER-FILE-OUT     ASSIGN TO PRINTER1.
00180      SELECT ERROR-FILE-OUT                    ASSIGN TO PRINTER2.
00190      SELECT SORT-WORK-FILE                    ASSIGN TO SORTWK.
00200
00210 *****************************************************************
00220
00230  DATA DIVISION.
00240  FILE SECTION.
00250  FD  ACCOUNT-MASTER-FILE-IN
00260      LABEL RECORDS ARE STANDARD
00270      RECORD CONTAINS 39 CHARACTERS
00280      BLOCK CONTAINS 100 RECORDS.
00290
00300  01  ACCOUNT-MASTER-RECORD-IN         PIC X(39).
00310
00320  FD  ACCOUNT-MASTER-FILE-OUT
00330      LABEL RECORDS ARE STANDARD
00340      RECORD CONTAINS 39 CHARACTERS
00350      BLOCK CONTAINS 100 RECORDS.
00360
00370  01  ACCOUNT-MASTER-RECORD-OUT        PIC X(39).
00380
00390  SD  SORT-WORK-FILE
00400      RECORD CONTAINS 6 CHARACTERS.
00410
00420  01  SORT-WORK-RECORD.
00430      05  TRANSACTION-CODE-S           PIC X.
00440      05  ACCOUNT-NUMBER-S             PIC X(5).
00450
```

continued

In the Working Storage Section you can find CURRENT-KEY, at line 00600. The field IS-MASTER-RECORD-IN-WORK-AREA is the flag that it used to record whether or not there is a master record in the work area. You will see how the flag is set to "Y" and "N" as needed when we look at the Procedure Division. Level-88 entries are used here, in CURRENT-KEY to facilitate testing for when THERE-IS-NO-MORE-INPUT and for when THERE-IS-NO-INPUT whatsoever, and in IS-MASTER-RECORD-IN-WORK-AREA to facilitate both SETting and testing the flag.

The three areas in working storage that are used to store master and transaction records are shown in lines 00780 through 00940. Remember that a master record is worked on only when it is in the WORK-AREA. The level-88 entries at lines 00790 and 00840 apply to their entire respective level-01 entries. They will be used in the Procedure Division to facilitate filling the input areas with HIGH-VALUES and testing their contents. The level-88 entry at line 00860 applies only to the TRANSACTION-CODE.

FIGURE 13.15 ***continued***

```
S COBOL II RELEASE 3.1 09/19/89                  P13003   DATE SEP 02,1991 T
----+-*A-1-B--+----2----+----3----+----4----+----5----+----6----+----7-|--+

00460  FD   TRANSACTION-FILE-IN
00470       RECORD CONTAINS 80 CHARACTERS.
00480
00490  01   TRANSACTION-RECORD-IN             PIC X(80).
00500
00510  FD   TRANSACTION-REGISTER-FILE-OUT.
00520
00530  01   TRANSACTION-REGISTER-RECORD       PIC X(72).
00540
00550  FD   ERROR-FILE-OUT.
00560
00570  01   ERROR-RECORD-OUT                  PIC X(76).
00580
00590  WORKING-STORAGE SECTION.
00600  01   CURRENT-KEY                       PIC X(5).
00610       88 THERE-IS-NO-MORE-INPUT         VALUE HIGH-VALUES.
00620       88 THERE-IS-NO-INPUT              VALUE HIGH-VALUES.
00630  01   IS-MASTER-RECORD-IN-WORK-AREA     PIC X.
00640       88 MASTER-RECORD-IS-IN-WORKAREA             VALUE "Y".
00650       88 MASTER-RECORD-ISNT-IN-WORKAREA           VALUE "N".
00660  01   PACKED-DECIMAL.
00670   02 NUMBER-OF-INPUT-RECORDS-W          PIC S9(3) VALUE ZERO.
00680   02 NUMBER-OF-DELETIONS-W              PIC S9(3) VALUE ZERO.
00690   02 PAGE-NUMBER-W                      PIC S9(3) VALUE ZERO.
00700   02 ERROR-PAGE-NUMBER-W                PIC S9(3) VALUE ZERO.
00710   02 NUMBER-OF-ERRONEOUS-RECORDS-W      PIC S9(3) VALUE ZERO.
00720   02 CURRENT-BALANCE-TOTAL              PIC 9(7)V99 VALUE ZERO.
00730  01   BLANK-LINE                        PIC X     VALUE SPACE.
00740  01   TODAYS-DATE.
00750       05  TODAYS-YEAR                   PIC 99.
00760       05  TODAYS-MONTH-AND-DAY          PIC 9(4).
00770
00780  01   MASTER-INPUT-AREA.
00790       88 NO-MORE-MASTER-RECORDS         VALUE HIGH-VALUES.
00800       05  ACCOUNT-NUMBER                PIC X(5).
00810       05                                PIC X(34).
00820
```

FIGURE 13.15 *continued*

```
 01  TRANSACTION-INPUT-AREA.
     88 NO-MORE-TRANSACTION-RECORDS   VALUE HIGH-VALUES.
     05  TRANSACTION-CODE             PIC X.
         88 DELETION                  VALUE "5".
     05  ACCOUNT-NUMBER               PIC X(5).
     05                               PIC X(74).

 01  WORK-AREA.
     05  ACCOUNT-NUMBER-W             PIC X(5).
     05  DEPOSITOR-NAME-W             PIC X(20).
     05  DATE-OF-LAST-TRANSACTION-W   PIC 9(6).
     05  CURRENT-BALANCE-W            PIC 9(6)V99.

 01  REPORT-HEADING-1.
     05                                   PIC X(39) VALUE SPACES.
     05                  PIC X(17) VALUE "ROBBEM STATE BANK".

 01  REPORT-HEADING-2.
     05                                   PIC X(39) VALUE SPACES.
     05                  PIC X(17) VALUE "106 WEST 10TH ST.".

 01  REPORT-HEADING-3.
     05                                   PIC X(38) VALUE SPACES.
     05                  PIC X(19) VALUE "BROOKLYN, NY  11212".

 01  PAGE-HEADING-1.
     05                                   PIC X(29) VALUE SPACES.
     05                                   PIC X(37)
                 VALUE "SAVINGS ACCOUNT MASTER FILE DELETIONS".

 01  ERROR-PAGE-HEADING-1.
     05                                   PIC X(33) VALUE SPACES.
     05                                   PIC X(28)
                 VALUE     "SAVINGS ACCOUNT ERROR REPORT".

 01  PAGE-HEADING-2.
     05                                   PIC X(17) VALUE SPACES.
     05                                   PIC X(5) VALUE "DATE".
     05 TODAYS-MONTH-AND-DAY              PIC Z9/99/.
     05 TODAYS-YEAR                       PIC 99.
     05                                   PIC X(35) VALUE SPACES.
     05                                   PIC X(4)  VALUE "PAGE".
     05 PAGE-NUMBER-OUT                   PIC Z9.

 01  PAGE-HEADING-3.
     05                                   PIC X(24) VALUE SPACES.
     05                                 PIC X(7)  VALUE "ACCOUNT".
     05                                   PIC X(6) VALUE SPACES.
     05                                 PIC X(5)  VALUE "FINAL".
     05                                   PIC X(6) VALUE SPACES.
     05                                   PIC X(5)  VALUE "NOTES".

 01  ERROR-PAGE-HEADING-3.
     05                                   PIC X(24) VALUE SPACES.
     05                                 PIC X(7)  VALUE "ACCOUNT".
     05                                   PIC X(17) VALUE SPACES.
     05                                   PIC X(5)  VALUE "NOTES".

 01  PAGE-HEADING-4.
     05                                   PIC X(24) VALUE SPACES.
     05                                  PIC X(6)  VALUE "NUMBER".
     05                                   PIC X(5) VALUE SPACES.
     05                                   PIC X(10)
                                          VALUE "WITHDRAWAL".

 01  ERROR-PAGE-HEADING-4.
     05                                   PIC X(24) VALUE SPACES.
     05                                  PIC X(6)  VALUE "NUMBER".
```

continued

The Procedure Division begins at line 02010. The main control paragraph of the OUTPUT PROCEDURE begins at line 02100. The PERFORM statement that controls the main loop is at line 02120. Remember that in this program the conditions THERE-IS-NO-MORE-INPUT and THERE-IS-NO-INPUT signal the end of both the master and transaction files. If there are no input data on either the master or transaction files, the IF statement at line 02270 prints the words "No input data."

The paragraph PROCESS-ONE-KEY, line 02320, executes exactly once for each different value of CURRENT-KEY. The PERFORM statement at line 02330 causes a master record to be moved to the master work area if the Account Number in the master record is equal to CURRENT-KEY, and the PERFORM statement at line 02340 executes PROCESS-TRANSACTION-RECORD over and over as long as the transaction Account Number is equal to CURRENT-KEY.

FIGURE *13.15* ***continued***

```
S COBOL II RELEASE 3.1 09/19/89                  P13003   DATE SEP 02,1991 T
----+-*A-1-B--+----2----+----3----+----4----+----5----+----6----+----7-|--+

01520  01  REPORT-LINE.
01530      05 ACCOUNT-NUMBER-OUT                  PIC B(25)X(5).
01540      05 CURRENT-BALANCE-OUT                 PIC B(5)ZZZ,ZZZ.99B(3).
01550      05                                     PIC X(14)
01560                                             VALUE "ACCOUNT CLOSED".
01570
01580  01  INVALID-CODE-LINE.
01590      05 ACCOUNT-NUMBER-E                    PIC B(25)X(5)B(18).
01600      05 MSG                                 PIC X(12)
01610                                             VALUE "INVALID CODE".
01620      05 TRANSACTION-CODE-OUT                PIC BX.
01630
01640  01  MASTER-MISSING-LINE.
01650      05 ACCOUNT-NUMBER-MISSING              PIC B(25)X(5)B(18).
01660      05                                     PIC X(28)
01670          VALUE "MASTER RECORD DOES NOT EXIST".
01680
01690  01  TOTAL-LINE-1.
01700      05                                     PIC X(23) VALUE SPACES.
01710      05                                  PIC X(5)B(5) VALUE "TOTAL".
01720      05 CURRENT-BALANCE-TOTAL-OUT           PIC Z,ZZZ,ZZZ.99.
01730
01740  01  TOTAL-LINE-2.
01750      05                                     PIC X(41) VALUE SPACES.
01760      05                              PIC X(14) VALUE "CONTROL COUNTS".
01770
01780  01  TOTAL-LINE-3.
01790      05                                     PIC X(34) VALUE SPACES.
01800      05                                     PIC X(25)
01810                             VALUE "NUMBER OF CLOSED ACCOUNTS".
01820      05 NUMBER-OF-DELETIONS                 PIC B(3)ZZ9.
01830
01840  01  TOTAL-LINE-4.
01850      05                                     PIC X(34) VALUE SPACES.
01860      05                                     PIC X(27)
01870                               VALUE "NUMBER OF ERRONEOUS RECORDS".
01880      05 NUMBER-OF-ERRONEOUS-RECORDS         PIC BZZ9.
01890
01900  01  TOTAL-LINE-5.
01910      05                                     PIC X(34) VALUE SPACES.
01920      05                                     PIC X(5)  VALUE "TOTAL".
01930      05 NUMBER-OF-INPUT-RECORDS             PIC B(23)ZZ9.
01940
```

FIGURE 13.15 *continued*

```
 01  NO-INPUT-DATA.
     05                                  PIC X(21) VALUE SPACES.
     05                        PIC X(13) VALUE "NO INPUT DATA".

*****************************************************************

 PROCEDURE DIVISION.
 UPDATE-WITH-DELETIONS.
     SORT SORT-WORK-FILE
          ASCENDING KEY ACCOUNT-NUMBER-S
          USING TRANSACTION-FILE-IN
          OUTPUT PROCEDURE IS DELETE-RECORDS
     STOP RUN
     .

 DELETE-RECORDS.
     PERFORM INITIALIZATION
     PERFORM PROCESS-ONE-KEY UNTIL THERE-IS-NO-MORE-INPUT
     PERFORM TERMINATION
     .

 INITIALIZATION.
     OPEN INPUT  ACCOUNT-MASTER-FILE-IN
          OUTPUT ACCOUNT-MASTER-FILE-OUT
                 ERROR-FILE-OUT
                 TRANSACTION-REGISTER-FILE-OUT
     ACCEPT TODAYS-DATE FROM DATE
     MOVE CORR TODAYS-DATE TO PAGE-HEADING-2
     PERFORM PRINT-REPORT-HEADINGS
     PERFORM READ-A-MASTER-RECORD
     PERFORM READ-A-TRANSACTION-RECORD
     PERFORM CHOOSE-CURRENT-KEY
     IF THERE-IS-NO-INPUT
         WRITE TRANSACTION-REGISTER-RECORD FROM NO-INPUT-DATA
     END-IF
     .

 PROCESS-ONE-KEY.
     PERFORM PROCESS-MASTER-RECORD
     PERFORM PROCESS-TRANSACTION-RECORD UNTIL
         ACCOUNT-NUMBER IN TRANSACTION-INPUT-AREA
         IS NOT EQUAL TO CURRENT-KEY
     PERFORM CHECK-TO-WRITE-MASTER
     PERFORM CHOOSE-CURRENT-KEY
     .

 PROCESS-TRANSACTION-RECORD.
     PERFORM CHECK-FOR-VALID-DELETION
     PERFORM READ-A-TRANSACTION-RECORD
     .

 CHECK-TO-WRITE-MASTER.
     IF MASTER-RECORD-IS-IN-WORKAREA
         WRITE ACCOUNT-MASTER-RECORD-OUT FROM WORK-AREA
     END-IF
     .
```

continued

In CHOOSE-CURRENT-KEY, line 02520, the program chooses the lower of two keys. CHECK-FOR-VALID-DELETION, line 02890, checks each transaction for validity. The successful deletion of a master record is shown in lines 02980 through 03000.

The paragraphs at lines 02740 and 02830 show the use of the INTO option in RETURN and READ statements. The INTO option permits a record to be read from a file and placed in working storage, just as the FROM option permits a record to be written FROM working storage. When the INTO option is used with a READ statement, a record is first transferred from the external file to the File Section and then moved to working storage as we have seen earlier, in Chapter 7. When the INTO option is used with a RETURN statement, a record is first RETURNed from the SORT into the File Section and then moved to working storage.

At line 02780 you see the use of the **NOT AT END** condition. NOT AT END may be used in a RETURN or READ statement, and executes whenever the RETURN or READ does not detect end-of-file. Here we add 1 to a count of the number of transaction records each time the RETURN statement brings in a record from the sort system. The explicit scope delimiter **END-RETURN** is not strictly needed here, because the dot that ends the paragraph would also end the RETURN statement.

FIGURE *13.15* ***continued***

```
S COBOL II RELEASE 3.1 09/19/89                P13003    DATE SEP 02,1991 T
----+-*A-1-B--+----2----+----3----+----4----+----5----+----6----+----7-|--+

02520  CHOOSE-CURRENT-KEY.
02530      IF ACCOUNT-NUMBER IN TRANSACTION-INPUT-AREA IS LESS THAN
02540         ACCOUNT-NUMBER IN MASTER-INPUT-AREA
02550          MOVE ACCOUNT-NUMBER IN TRANSACTION-INPUT-AREA TO
02560              CURRENT-KEY
02570      ELSE
02580          MOVE ACCOUNT-NUMBER IN MASTER-INPUT-AREA TO
02590              CURRENT-KEY
02600      END-IF
02610      .
02620
02630  PROCESS-MASTER-RECORD.
02640      IF ACCOUNT-NUMBER IN MASTER-INPUT-AREA IS EQUAL TO
02650         CURRENT-KEY
02660          MOVE MASTER-INPUT-AREA TO WORK-AREA
02670          PERFORM READ-A-MASTER-RECORD
02680          SET MASTER-RECORD-IS-IN-WORKAREA TO TRUE
02690      ELSE
02700          SET MASTER-RECORD-ISNT-IN-WORKAREA TO TRUE
02710      END-IF
02720      .
02730
02740  READ-A-TRANSACTION-RECORD.
02750      RETURN SORT-WORK-FILE INTO TRANSACTION-INPUT-AREA
02760          AT END
02770              SET NO-MORE-TRANSACTION-RECORDS TO TRUE
02780          NOT AT END
02790              ADD 1 TO NUMBER-OF-INPUT-RECORDS-W
02800      END-RETURN
02810      .
02820
02830  READ-A-MASTER-RECORD.
02840      READ ACCOUNT-MASTER-FILE-IN INTO MASTER-INPUT-AREA
02850          AT END
02860              SET NO-MORE-MASTER-RECORDS TO TRUE
02870      .
```

FIGURE 13.15 *continued*

```
CHECK-FOR-VALID-DELETION.
    IF NOT DELETION
        PERFORM WRITE-INVALID-CODE-LINE
        ADD 1 TO NUMBER-OF-ERRONEOUS-RECORDS-W
    ELSE
    IF MASTER-RECORD-ISNT-IN-WORKAREA
        PERFORM WRITE-MASTER-MISSING-LINE
        ADD 1 TO NUMBER-OF-ERRONEOUS-RECORDS-W
    ELSE
        PERFORM WRITE-REPORT-LINE
        SET MASTER-RECORD-ISNT-IN-WORKAREA TO TRUE
        ADD 1 TO NUMBER-OF-DELETIONS-W
    END-IF
    END-IF
    .

WRITE-REPORT-LINE.
    MOVE ACCOUNT-NUMBER-W TO ACCOUNT-NUMBER-OUT
    MOVE CURRENT-BALANCE-W TO CURRENT-BALANCE-OUT
    WRITE TRANSACTION-REGISTER-RECORD FROM REPORT-LINE
    ADD CURRENT-BALANCE-W TO CURRENT-BALANCE-TOTAL
    .

WRITE-INVALID-CODE-LINE.
    MOVE ACCOUNT-NUMBER IN TRANSACTION-INPUT-AREA TO
                                   ACCOUNT-NUMBER-E
    MOVE TRANSACTION-CODE TO TRANSACTION-CODE-OUT
    WRITE ERROR-RECORD-OUT FROM INVALID-CODE-LINE
    .

WRITE-MASTER-MISSING-LINE.
    MOVE ACCOUNT-NUMBER IN TRANSACTION-INPUT-AREA TO
                                   ACCOUNT-NUMBER-MISSING
    WRITE ERROR-RECORD-OUT FROM MASTER-MISSING-LINE
    .

TERMINATION.
    PERFORM WRITE-TOTALS
    CLOSE ACCOUNT-MASTER-FILE-IN
          ACCOUNT-MASTER-FILE-OUT
          ERROR-FILE-OUT
          TRANSACTION-REGISTER-FILE-OUT
    .

WRITE-TOTALS.
    MOVE CURRENT-BALANCE-TOTAL TO CURRENT-BALANCE-TOTAL-OUT
    WRITE TRANSACTION-REGISTER-RECORD FROM TOTAL-LINE-1 AFTER 2
    WRITE TRANSACTION-REGISTER-RECORD FROM TOTAL-LINE-2 AFTER 2
    MOVE NUMBER-OF-DELETIONS-W TO NUMBER-OF-DELETIONS
    WRITE TRANSACTION-REGISTER-RECORD FROM TOTAL-LINE-3 AFTER 2
    MOVE NUMBER-OF-ERRONEOUS-RECORDS-W TO
                                 NUMBER-OF-ERRONEOUS-RECORDS
    WRITE TRANSACTION-REGISTER-RECORD FROM TOTAL-LINE-4 AFTER 2
    MOVE NUMBER-OF-INPUT-RECORDS-W TO
                                 NUMBER-OF-INPUT-RECORDS
    WRITE TRANSACTION-REGISTER-RECORD FROM TOTAL-LINE-5 AFTER 2
    .

PRINT-REPORT-HEADINGS.
    PERFORM PRINT-REGISTER-HEADINGS
    PERFORM PRINT-ERROR-HEADINGS
    .
```

continued

FIGURE *13.15* ***continued***

```
S COBOL II RELEASE 3.1 09/19/89                   P13003   DATE SEP 02,1991 T
----+-*A-1-B--+----2----+----3----+----4----+----5----+----6----+----7-|--+

PRINT-REGISTER-HEADINGS.
    ADD 1 TO PAGE-NUMBER-W
    MOVE PAGE-NUMBER-W TO PAGE-NUMBER-OUT
    WRITE TRANSACTION-REGISTER-RECORD FROM REPORT-HEADING-1
                                AFTER ADVANCING PAGE
    WRITE TRANSACTION-REGISTER-RECORD FROM REPORT-HEADING-2
    WRITE TRANSACTION-REGISTER-RECORD FROM REPORT-HEADING-3
    WRITE TRANSACTION-REGISTER-RECORD FROM PAGE-HEADING-1
                                AFTER 2
    WRITE TRANSACTION-REGISTER-RECORD FROM PAGE-HEADING-2
    WRITE TRANSACTION-REGISTER-RECORD FROM PAGE-HEADING-3
                                AFTER 3
    WRITE TRANSACTION-REGISTER-RECORD FROM PAGE-HEADING-4
    WRITE TRANSACTION-REGISTER-RECORD FROM BLANK-LINE
    .

PRINT-ERROR-HEADINGS.
    ADD 1 TO ERROR-PAGE-NUMBER-W
    MOVE ERROR-PAGE-NUMBER-W TO PAGE-NUMBER-OUT
    WRITE ERROR-RECORD-OUT FROM REPORT-HEADING-1 AFTER PAGE
    WRITE ERROR-RECORD-OUT FROM REPORT-HEADING-2
    WRITE ERROR-RECORD-OUT FROM REPORT-HEADING-3
    WRITE ERROR-RECORD-OUT FROM ERROR-PAGE-HEADING-1 AFTER 2
    WRITE ERROR-RECORD-OUT FROM PAGE-HEADING-2
    WRITE ERROR-RECORD-OUT FROM ERROR-PAGE-HEADING-3 AFTER 3
    WRITE ERROR-RECORD-OUT FROM ERROR-PAGE-HEADING-4
    WRITE ERROR-RECORD-OUT FROM BLANK-LINE
    .
```

Program P13-03 was run with the transaction input shown in Figure 13.16 and the master file that was created in Program P13-02. The report output produced by Program P13-03 is shown in Figure 13.17. The contents of the new output master file are shown in Figure 13.18.

FIGURE *13.16* **Input to Program P13-03**

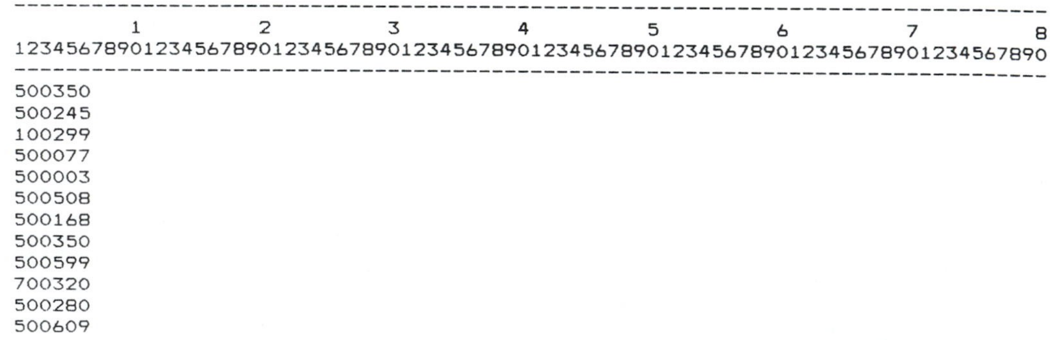

```
--------------------------------------------------------------------------------
         1         2         3         4         5         6         7         8
12345678901234567890123456789012345678901234567890123456789012345678901234567890
--------------------------------------------------------------------------------
500350
500245
100299
500077
500003
500508
500168
500350
500599
700320
500280
500609
```

FIGURE 13.17 Report output from Program P13-03

```
                     ROBBEM STATE BANK
                     106 WEST 10TH ST.
                    BROOKLYN, NY  11212

              SAVINGS ACCOUNT ERROR REPORT
DATE  9/02/91                                  PAGE 1

       ACCOUNT               NOTES
       NUMBER

        00003                MASTER RECORD DOES NOT EXIST
        00299                INVALID CODE 1
        00320                INVALID CODE 7
        00350                MASTER RECORD DOES NOT EXIST
        00508                MASTER RECORD DOES NOT EXIST
        00599                MASTER RECORD DOES NOT EXIST
        00609                MASTER RECORD DOES NOT EXIST
```

```
                     ROBBEM STATE BANK
                     106 WEST 10TH ST.
                    BROOKLYN, NY  11212

          SAVINGS ACCOUNT MASTER FILE DELETIONS
DATE  9/02/91                                  PAGE 1

       ACCOUNT     FINAL     NOTES
       NUMBER    WITHDRAWAL

        00077        10.37   ACCOUNT CLOSED
        00168       125.50   ACCOUNT CLOSED
        00245        35.00   ACCOUNT CLOSED
        00280        20.00   ACCOUNT CLOSED
        00350     2,500.00   ACCOUNT CLOSED

      TOTAL       2,690.87

                       CONTROL COUNTS

             NUMBER OF CLOSED ACCOUNTS        5

             NUMBER OF ERRONEOUS RECORDS      7

             TOTAL                           12
```

FIGURE 13.18 **Master file produced by Program P13-03**

```
--------------------------------------------------------------------------------
         1         2         3         4         5         6         7         8
12345678901234567890123456789012345678901234567890123456789012345678901234567890
--------------------------------------------------------------------------------
00007ROSEBUCCI               91081900100784
00014ROBERT DAVIS M.D.       91081900001000
00021LORICE MONTI            91081900012500
00028MICHAEL SMITH           91081900700159
00032JOSEPH CAMILLO          91081900002500
00035JOHN J. LEHMAN          91081900015000
00049JAY GREENE              91081900015000
00056EVELYN SLATER           91081900000100
00070PATRICK J. LEE          91081900050000
00084JOHN DAPRINO            91081900150000
00091JOE'S DELI              91081900010000
00098GEORGE CULHANE          91081900050000
00105ONE DAY CLEANERS        91081900005000
00112ROSEMARY LANE           91081900025000
00126JAMES BUDD              91081900075000
00133PAUL LERNER, D.D.S.     91081900100000
00140BETH FALLON             91081900002575
00161ROBERT RYAN             91081900002450
00175MARY KEATING            91081900001000
00189J. & L. CAIN            91081900003500
00196IMPERIAL FLORIST        91081900015000
00203JOYCE MITCHELL          91081900000500
00210JERRY PARKS             91081900025000
00217CARL CALDERON           91081900005000
00224JOHN WILLIAMS           91081900017550
00231BILL WILLIAMS           91081900055500
00238KEVIN PARKER            91081900001000
00252GENE GALLI              91081900001500
00266MARTIN LANG             91081900009957
00273VITO CACACI             91081900027500
00287SOLOMON CHAPELS         91081900001500
00294JOHN BURKE              91081900150000
00308JOE GARCIA              91081900200000
00315GRACE MICELI            91081900025000
00329GUY VOLPONE             91081900001000
00343JOE & MARY SESSA        91081900100000
```

EXERCISE 5 Write a program to update the master file you created in Exercise 3 with deletion transactions in the following format:

Positions	Field
1	Code 8
2–6	Part Number
7–80	spaces

Design reports to show the records deleted and the erroneous transactions. Have your program check all transactions for validity. Save the updated file for use in Chapter 14.

Summary

Magnetic storage media include magnetic tape, magnetic disk, magnetic drum, data cell, and mass storage system. Magnetic tape is a sequential medium, and disk is a direct-access medium. Records on tape may be accessed only sequentially, whereas records on disk may be accessed sequentially or randomly.

Master files of data may be stored on magnetic media. A computer can write data onto the files, and then later read or change the data. Huge volumes of data can be stored on modern magnetic media.

It is especially important that data on a master file be correct. Much of the program logic dealing with master files relies on the sequence of the records in the file.

A sequential master file may be created from data entered on a keyboard or punched in cards. A program may read the data, check them for validity, and write a master file. The file so created may later be used as input to an update program.

Records may be deleted from a master file. A program to delete records reads the master file and, by referring to a file of deletion transactions, copies the old file onto a new one, omitting the deleted records.

Fill-In Exercises

1. Five kinds of magnetic storage media that computers can read input data from and write output onto are ______, ______, ______, ______, and ______.
2. The only access method available for tape files is ______ access.
3. Three advantages of magnetic media over paper media are:
   a. ______________________________
   b. ______________________________
   c. ______________________________
4. The ______ clause tells the system how many records are in a block.
5. Special records written onto magnetic files for identification are called ______ records.
6. Magnetic media that can enjoy sequential or random access are called ______ - ______ storage devices.
7. A block of records is sometimes called a(n) ______ record.
8. In a program that deletes records from a master file, there can be no more than ______ valid transaction(s) for a single master record.
9. In a sequential update, the program must always work on the record in storage with the ______ key.
10. The best way to handle end-of-file in a sequential update is to move ______ to the file input areas in working storage.
11. The average number of records on a master file changed during an update run is referred to as file ______.
12. The average number of records added to or deleted from a master file during an update run is referred to as file ______.
13. A numeric field containing nonnumeric data may cause abnormal termination of a run if the field is used for ______, ______ ______, or ______ ______.
14. In a program to delete records from a sequential file, the field ______ gets assigned in turn every key on the master and transaction files.

15. In the hierarchy diagram for a program to delete records from a master file, the box "Process one key" executes once for every different ______ on the master file and the transaction file.

Review Exercises

1. A school wishes to maintain a file of alumni names and addresses. Write a program to create a sequential master file on tape or disk using transaction input in the following format:

Positions	Field
1	Code 1
2–10	Social Security Number
11–30	Student Name
31–50	Street Address
51–70	City State Zip
71–72	Major Department
73–74	Year of Graduation
75–80	spaces

Have your program check for the presence of all fields in each input record.

For each error-free input record, have your program write the entire 80-character record onto the master file. Have your program print a report showing the good records written onto the master file and a report showing the erroneous transactions. Create your master file with 50 records per block.

2. Using the same input data as in Review Exercise 1, write a program to create a sequential master file on tape or disk. Have your program build the master records in working storage. Each master record should contain the following fields:

Social Security Number

Student Name

Street Address

City, State, Zip

Major Department

Year of Graduation

Create your master file with 25 records per block. Have your program check for the presence of all fields in each input record. Have your program print a report showing the records written onto the master file and a report showing the erroneous transactions. Save the master file for use in Chapter 14.

3. Write a program to update the master file you created in Review Exercise 2. Use deletion transactions in the following format:

Positions	Field
1	Code 7
2–10	Social Security Number
11–80	spaces

Have your program print a report showing the complete contents of the records deleted from the file, and a report showing the erroneous transactions. Save the updated file for use in Review Exercises in Chapter 14.

4. Step through the hierarchy diagram in Figure 13.14 and show what would happen if the very first transaction had an Account Number lower than the Account Number of the first incoming master record. Would the hierarchy diagram work in such a situation?

Project

Write a program to create a sequential customer-name-and-address master file using input in the format described on page 406. Each master record should have room for up to five lines of name and address data, and should be in the following format:

Positions	Field
1–5	Customer Number
6–25	First line of name and address
26–45	Second line of name and address
46–65	Third line of name and address
66–85	Fourth line of name and address, if any
86–105	Fifth line of name and address, if any

Master records should contain blanks in any unused fields not needed for names-and-address lines. Have your program SORT the input transactions on the Code in position 1 within Customer Number, and check each input record to see that the Code it contains is valid. Have your program produce reports showing any errors found in the input and showing, for each good record written onto the master file, the Customer Number and the first line of the name and address. Save the master file for use in Chapter 14.

CHAPTER 14

Processing Sequential Master Files

HERE ARE THE KEY POINTS YOU SHOULD LEARN FROM THIS CHAPTER

1. How to develop a hierarchy diagram for any program that reads a master file and a transaction file

2. How to list selected records from a master file

3. How to update a master file with additions, changes, and deletions

4. How to list the complete contents of a master file

There are no new key words in this chapter.

In this chapter we develop four programs. Three of them read a master file and a transaction file, and one reads only a master file. You will see that the hierarchy diagrams for the three programs that read a master and a transaction file differ from one another only at the lowest level. The upper portions of the three hierarchy diagrams will be identical, and also identical to the upper portion of the hierarchy diagram we used for the update program in Chapter 13. Thus you will see that the balance-line algorithm can be used for reading the master and transaction files in any program that reads such files. About the only things that change from one program to the next are the details of the box "Process transaction record."

Listing Selected Records from a Master File

To return to our savings-account master file, let us assume that the bank would like to list the complete contents of certain master records each evening. That is, the bank would like to see printed, for certain accounts, the Account Number, the Current Balance, the Depositor Name, and the Date of Last Transaction.

Program P14-01 lists selected records from a master file. The program uses two input files. One is the master file itself, and the other is a transaction file indicating which master records are to be listed. The format of the transactions is:

Positions	*Field*
1	Code 6
2–6	Account Number
7–80	spaces

Each record contains the Account Number of the master record to be listed, and a transaction Code of 6 designating this transaction as a request to list a master record. Nothing else is needed in the transaction, since all of the information to be listed comes from the master record. The listing of the selected master records has the format shown in Figure 14.1. The program also lists erroneous transactions, in the format shown in Figure 14.2.

FIGURE *14.1* Output format for selected records in Program P14-01

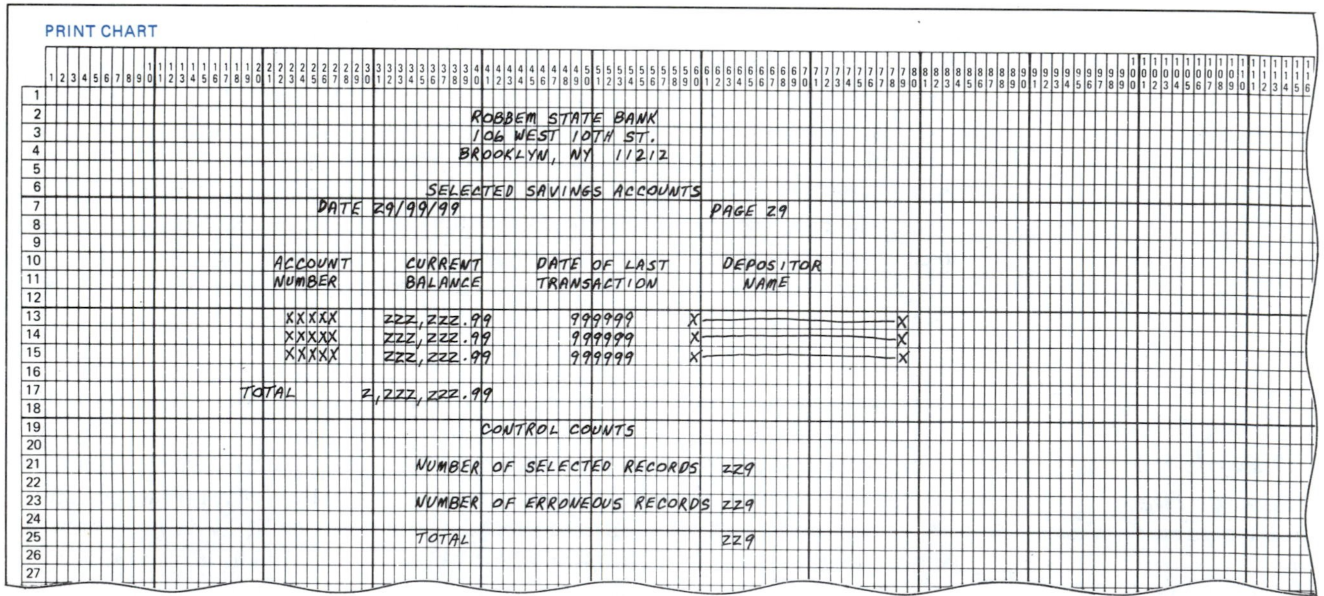

FIGURE 14.2 Output format for error report for Program P14-01

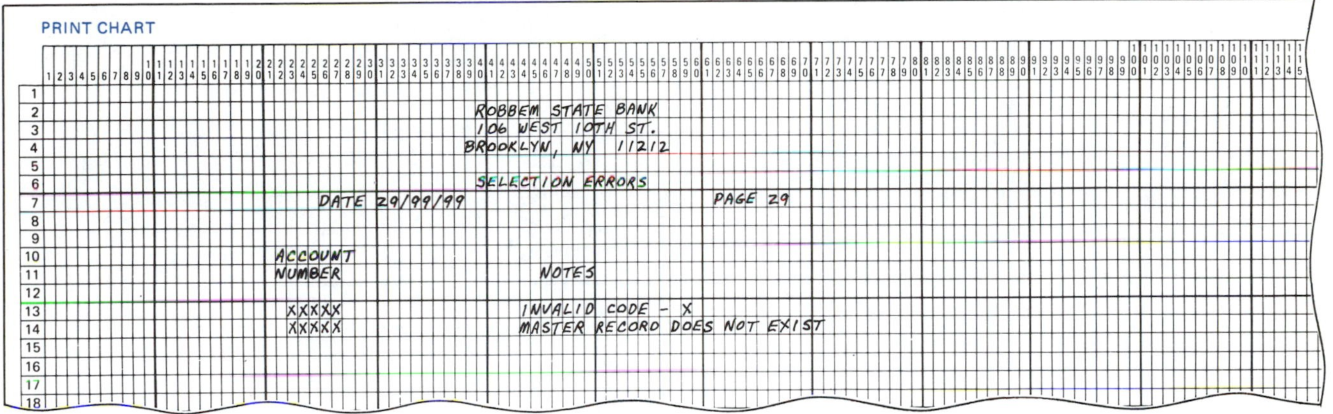

PRINT CHART
ROBBEM STATE BANK
106 WEST 10TH ST.
BROOKLYN, NY 11212
SELECTION ERRORS
DATE Z9/99/99
PAGE Z9
ACCOUNT
NUMBER
NOTES
XXXXX
INVALID CODE - X
XXXXX
MASTER RECORD DOES NOT EXIST

A Hierarchy Diagram for Listing Selected Records from a Master File

The hierarchy diagram for Program P14-01 is shown in Figure 14.3. Almost all of the boxes are the same as in the hierarchy diagram for Program P13-03, in Figure 13.14, page 461. One difference is in the box ''Process transaction record.'' In Program P13-03 processing a transaction involved deleting a master record from the file. In Program 14-01 processing a transaction means listing a master record on a report.

Also, in Program P14-01 we will not be writing a new output master file. Program P14-01 is not an update program and does not create a new file. It merely reads the old master file and lists some of its records. So in the hierarchy diagram of Figure 14.3, we have simply omitted the box ''Check to write master'' and left a gap to remind you where it once was.

Listing selected records from a master file is really not a very complicated operation, and this hierarchy diagram is much more elaborate than is needed to do the job. We have included it here to show how the hierarchy diagram introduced in Chapter 13 can easily be modified to handle any kind of program that reads a master file and a transaction file.

This hierarchy diagram will handle erroneous transactions. In this program errors could include an invalid transaction Code, or a transaction to list a master record that does not exist. We will also consider duplicate transactions an error. That is, we will not list a master record more than once, even if there is more than one transaction with an Account Number that matches the Account Number of a master record. We will treat duplicate transactions as errors and print a message saying that no master record exists for them.

FIGURE 14.3 **Hierarchy diagram for Program P14-01**

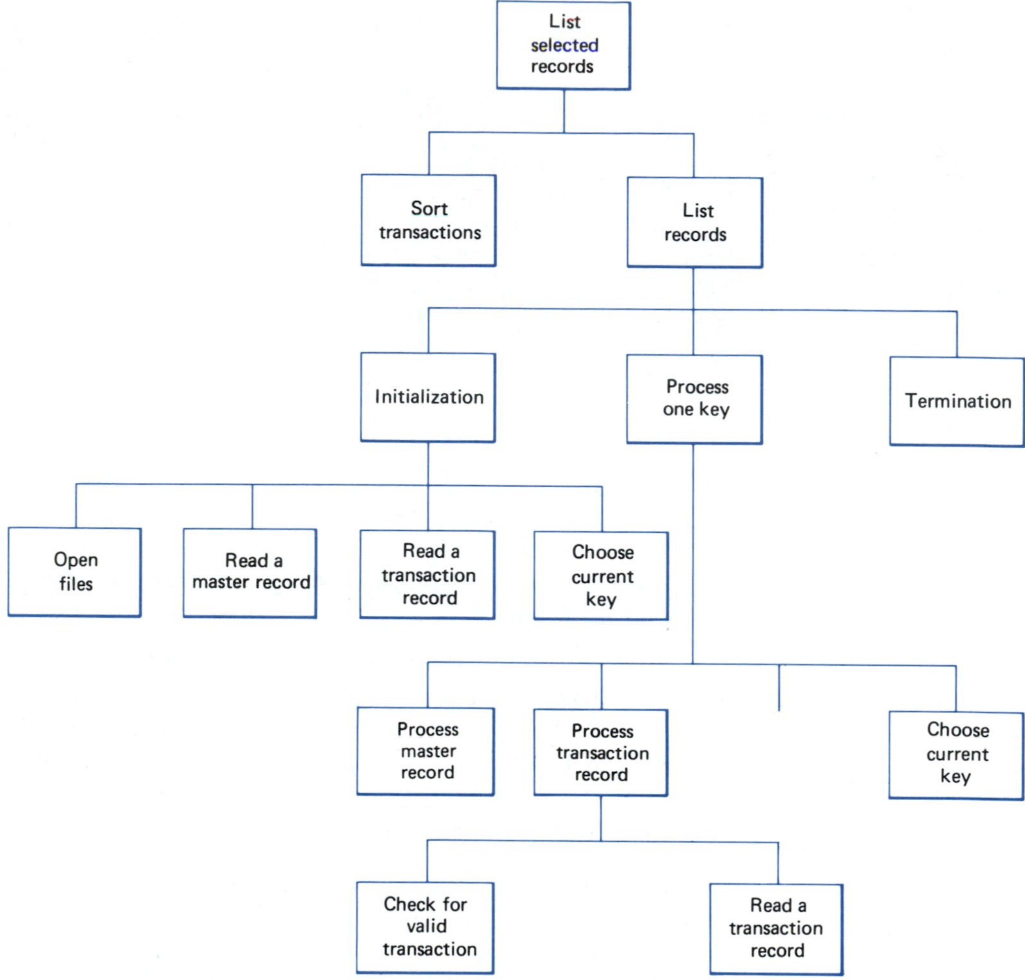

Stepping Through the Hierarchy Diagram

As before, we will use a few master records and transactions to step through the execution of the hierarchy diagram and see that it does its job of listing only those master records having matching transactions. We will also see that it handles erroneous transactions properly.

We can use the same savings-account master file as before. The Account Numbers of the first seven records of that file are:

00007
00014
00021
00028
00032

00035

00049

Assume we have the following transactions:

6 00006

6 00021

6 00021

6 00035

6 00064

Of these transactions, three are in error. Two are asking us to list master records that don't exist, and one is a duplicate. As we step through the hierarchy diagram you will see what happens when the first input transaction has a key lower than the key of the first incoming master record, and the last transaction a key higher than the key of the last master record.

"Initialization" brings master record 00007 and transaction 00006 into their respective areas in working storage. "Choose current key" assigns 00006 to CURRENT-KEY, and we enter the main loop of the program with CURRENT-KEY equal to 00006.

Now "Process master record" executes. Since the key of the master record in the master input area is not equal to CURRENT-KEY, "Process master record" sets the flag to "N" to indicate that no master record was moved to the work area. "Process transaction record" executes, since the key of the transaction in the transaction input area is equal to CURRENT-KEY. For transaction 00006 to be valid it must have a Code of 6 and there must be a master record in the work area waiting to be listed. Since the flag is "N," the program knows that there is no master record to match this transaction. The program writes an error message and "Read a transaction record" reads transaction 00021 into the transaction input area.

"Choose current key" assigns 00007 to CURRENT-KEY. "Process master record" moves master record 00007 to the work area, reads master record 00014 into the master input area, and sets the flag to "Y." Since there are no transactions whose key is equal to CURRENT-KEY, "Process transaction record" does not execute. "Choose current key" next assigns 00014 to CURRENT-KEY.

"Process master record" moves master record 00014 to the work area, reads master record 00021 into the master input area, and sets the flag to "Y." "Process transaction record" is skipped, and "Choose current key" assigns 00021 to CURRENT-KEY. "Process master record" moves master record 00021 to the work area, reads master record 00028 into the master input area, and sets the flag to "Y." Since there now is a transaction whose key is equal to CURRENT-KEY, "Process transaction record" executes. Of course, "Process transaction record" will execute over and over until all transactions whose key is equal to CURRENT-KEY are processed. For the present transaction to be valid, its Code must be 6 and the flag must indicate that there is a master record in the work area. The flag is "Y," so the contents of master record 00021 are listed out from the work area. The program now sets the flag to "N" to indicate that the record in the work area is not available for any further processing. It is as if the record were not there. Note that if we wanted to allow duplicate transactions to list the contents of a record more than once, we would simply omit the step that turns the flag to "N."

"Read a transaction record" reads the second of the transactions with a key of 00021. Since this is still equal to CURRENT-KEY, "Process transaction record" executes again. This time it finds no master record in the work area waiting to be listed. An error message is printed for this transaction, and "Read a transaction record" reads transaction 00035 into the transaction input area. "Choose current key" assigns 00028 to CURRENT-KEY.

"Process master record" moves master record 00028 to the work area, reads master record 00032 into the master input area, and sets the flag to "Y." "Choose current key" now executes, and assigns 00032 to CURRENT-KEY. "Process master record" moves master record 00032 to the work area, reads master record 00035 into the master input area, and sets the flag to "Y." "Choose current key" then assigns 00035 to CURRENT-KEY. "Process master record" moves master record 00035 to the work area, reads master record 00049 into the master input area, and sets the flag to "Y." "Process transaction record" processes transaction 00035 by printing out the contents of master record 00035 from the work area and reading transaction 00064 into the transaction input area. "Choose current key" assigns 00049 to CURRENT-KEY.

"Process master record" moves master record 00049 to the work area. In attempting to read the next master record, the program encounters end-of-file on the master file and so moves HIGH-VALUES to the master input area. It sets the flag to "Y" to indicate that master record 00049 was moved to the work area.

Since there is no transaction whose key is equal to CURRENT-KEY, "Process transaction record" does not execute. "Choose current key" assigns 00064 to CURRENT-KEY, since 00064 is lower than HIGH-VALUES. "Process master record" finds that the key of the master record in the master input area is not equal to CURRENT-KEY, and so sets the flag to "N."

Since there is a transaction whose key is equal to CURRENT-KEY, "Process transaction record" executes. Since the flag is set to "N," the program knows that there is no matching master record for this transaction. An error line is printed, and "Read a transaction record" reads end-of-file on the transaction file. The program moves HIGH-VALUES to the transaction input area. "Choose current key" assigns HIGH-VALUES to CURRENT-KEY, and the program goes to "Termination."

You can now review how the five transactions were processed. The three erroneous transactions caused error messages to be printed, and the two valid transactions caused the contents of master records 00021 and 00035 to be printed.

A Program to List Selected Records from a Master File

Program P14-01 is shown in Figure 14.4. It is very similar to Program P13-03. There is no output master file in this program, nor a FILE-CONTROL entry or an FD for such a file. There is no paragraph CHECK-TO-WRITE-MASTER, since none is written. And of course the paragraph PROCESS-ONE-KEY, line 02210, does not have PERFORM CHECK-TO-WRITE-MASTER.

FIGURE 14.4 **Program P14-01**

```
S COBOL II RELEASE 3.1 09/19/89                    P14001   DATE SEP 01,1991 T
----+-*A-1-B--+----2----+----3----+----4----+----5----+----6----+----7-|--+

 IDENTIFICATION DIVISION.
 PROGRAM-ID. P14-01.
* AUTHOR. SHAMEZE SULTAN
*          REVISED BY GAETANO MURATORE
*
*     THIS PROGRAM LISTS SELECTED RECORDS FROM A SEQUENTIAL
*     MASTER FILE.
*
******************************************************************

 ENVIRONMENT DIVISION.
 INPUT-OUTPUT SECTION.
 FILE-CONTROL.
     SELECT ACCOUNT-MASTER-FILE-IN       ASSIGN TO MASTER.
     SELECT TRANSACTION-FILE-IN          ASSIGN TO INFILE.
     SELECT LISTING-FILE-OUT             ASSIGN TO PRINTER1.
     SELECT ERROR-FILE-OUT               ASSIGN TO PRINTER2.
     SELECT SORT-WORK-FILE               ASSIGN TO SORTWK.

******************************************************************

 DATA DIVISION.
 FILE SECTION.
 FD  ACCOUNT-MASTER-FILE-IN
     LABEL RECORDS ARE STANDARD
     RECORD CONTAINS 39 CHARACTERS
     BLOCK CONTAINS 100 RECORDS.

 01  ACCOUNT-MASTER-RECORD-IN            PIC X(39).

 SD  SORT-WORK-FILE
     RECORD CONTAINS 6 CHARACTERS.

 01  SORT-WORK-RECORD.
     05  TRANSACTION-CODE-S              PIC X.
     05  ACCOUNT-NUMBER-S                PIC X(5).

 FD  TRANSACTION-FILE-IN.

 01  TRANSACTION-RECORD-IN               PIC X(80).

 FD  LISTING-FILE-OUT.

 01  LISTING-RECORD                      PIC X(79).

 FD  ERROR-FILE-OUT.

 01  ERROR-RECORD-OUT                    PIC X(71).

 WORKING-STORAGE SECTION.
 01  CURRENT-KEY                         PIC X(5).
     88 THERE-IS-NO-INPUT                VALUE "N".
 01  IS-MASTER-RECORD-IN-WORK-AREA       PIC X.
     88 MASTER-RECORD-IS-IN-WORKAREA       VALUE "Y".
     88 MASTER-RECORD-ISNT-IN-WORKAREA   VALUE "N".
 01  PACKED-DECIMAL.
  02 NUMBER-OF-INPUT-RECORDS-W           PIC S9(3) VALUE ZERO.
  02 NUMBER-OF-SELECTED-RECORDS-W        PIC S9(3) VALUE ZERO.
  02 PAGE-NUMBER-W                       PIC S9(2) VALUE ZERO.
  02 ERROR-PAGE-NUMBER-W                 PIC S9(2) VALUE ZERO.
  02 NUMBER-OF-ERRONEOUS-RECORDS-W       PIC S9(3) VALUE ZERO.
  02 CURRENT-BALANCE-TOTAL               PIC 9(7)V99 VALUE ZERO.
 01  BLANK-LINE                          PIC X      VALUE SPACE.
 01  TODAYS-DATE.
     05  TODAYS-YEAR                     PIC 99.
     05  TODAYS-MONTH-AND-DAY            PIC 9(4).
```

continued

FIGURE 14.4 *continued*

```
S COBOL II RELEASE 3.1 09/19/89                    P14001    DATE SEP 01,1991 T
----+-*A-1-B--+----2----+----3----+----4----+----5----+----6----+----7-|--+
       01  MASTER-INPUT-AREA.
           88  NO-MORE-MASTER-RECORDS        VALUE HIGH-VALUES.
           05  ACCOUNT-NUMBER                PIC X(5).
           05                                PIC X(34).
       01  TRANSACTION-INPUT-AREA.
           88  NO-MORE-TRANSACTION-RECORDS   VALUE HIGH-VALUES.
           05  TRANSACTION-CODE              PIC X.
               88  LISTING-REQUEST           VALUE "6".
           05  ACCOUNT-NUMBER                PIC X(5).
       01  WORK-AREA.
           05  ACCOUNT-NUMBER-W              PIC X(5).
           05  DEPOSITOR-NAME-W              PIC X(20).
           05  DATE-OF-LAST-TRANSACTION-W    PIC 9(6).
           05  CURRENT-BALANCE-W             PIC 9(6)V99.
       01  REPORT-HEADING-1.
           05                                        PIC X(39) VALUE SPACES.
           05                  PIC X(17) VALUE "ROBBEM STATE BANK".
       01  REPORT-HEADING-2.
           05                                        PIC X(39) VALUE SPACES.
           05                  PIC X(17) VALUE "106 WEST 10TH ST.".
       01  REPORT-HEADING-3.
           05                                        PIC X(38) VALUE SPACES.
           05                  PIC X(19) VALUE "BROOKLYN, NY  11212".
       01  PAGE-HEADING-1.
           05                                        PIC X(35) VALUE SPACES.
           05                                        PIC X(25)
                       VALUE "SELECTED SAVINGS ACCOUNTS".
       01  ERROR-PAGE-HEADING-1.
           05                                        PIC X(39) VALUE SPACES.
           05                                        PIC X(16)
                       VALUE     "SELECTION ERRORS".
       01  PAGE-HEADING-2.
           05                                        PIC X(25) VALUE SPACES.
           05                                        PIC X(5) VALUE "DATE".
           05 TODAYS-MONTH-AND-DAY                   PIC Z9/99/.
           05 TODAYS-YEAR                            PIC 99.
           05                                        PIC X(23) VALUE SPACES.
           05                                        PIC X(5)  VALUE "PAGE".
           05 PAGE-NUMBER-OUT                        PIC Z9.
       01  PAGE-HEADING-3.
           05                                      PIC X(21) VALUE SPACES.
           05                                      PIC X(7) VALUE "ACCOUNT".
           05                                      PIC X(5) VALUE SPACES.
           05                                      PIC X(7) VALUE "CURRENT".
           05                                      PIC X(5) VALUE SPACES.
           05          VALUE "DATE OF LAST"  PIC X(17).
           05          VALUE "DEPOSITOR"     PIC X(9).
       01  ERROR-PAGE-HEADING-3.
           05                                      PIC X(21) VALUE SPACES.
           05                                      PIC X(7) VALUE "ACCOUNT".
```

FIGURE 14.4 *continued*

```
 01  PAGE-HEADING-4.
     05                                        PIC X(21) VALUE SPACES.
     05                                        PIC X(12) VALUE "NUMBER".
     05                                        PIC X(12) VALUE "BALANCE".
     05                                        PIC X(19)
                                                    VALUE "TRANSACTION".
     05                                        PIC X(4)  VALUE "NAME".

 01  ERROR-PAGE-HEADING-4.
     05                                        PIC X(21) VALUE SPACES.
     05                                        PIC X(24) VALUE "NUMBER".
     05                                        PIC X(5)  VALUE "NOTES".

 01  REPORT-LINE.
     05 ACCOUNT-NUMBER-OUT                       PIC B(22)X(5)B(4).
     05 CURRENT-BALANCE-OUT                      PIC ZZZ,ZZZ.99B(7).
     05 DATE-OF-LAST-TRANSACTION                 PIC 9(6)B(5).
     05 DEPOSITOR-NAME                           PIC X(20).

 01  INVALID-CODE-LINE.
     05 ACCOUNT-NUMBER-E                         PIC B(22)X(5)B(16).
     05                                          PIC X(15)
                                                 VALUE "INVALID CODE - ".
     05 TRANSACTION-CODE-OUT                     PIC BX.

 01  MASTER-MISSING-LINE.
     05 ACCOUNT-NUMBER-MISSING                   PIC B(22)X(5)B(16).
     05                                          PIC X(28)
         VALUE "MASTER RECORD DOES NOT EXIST".

 01  TOTAL-LINE-1.
     05                                          PIC X(18) VALUE SPACES.
     05                                          PIC X(11) VALUE "TOTAL".
     05 CURRENT-BALANCE-TOTAL-OUT                PIC Z,ZZZ,ZZZ.99.

 01  TOTAL-LINE-2.
     05                                          PIC X(40) VALUE SPACES.
     05                                PIC X(14) VALUE "CONTROL COUNTS".

 01  TOTAL-LINE-3.
     05                                          PIC X(34) VALUE SPACES.
     05                                          PIC X(27)
                                 VALUE "NUMBER OF SELECTED ACCOUNTS".
     05 NUMBER-OF-SELECTED-RECORDS               PIC BZZ9.

 01  TOTAL-LINE-4.
     05                                          PIC X(34) VALUE SPACES.
     05                                          PIC X(27)
                                 VALUE "NUMBER OF ERRONEOUS RECORDS".
     05 NUMBER-OF-ERRONEOUS-RECORDS              PIC BZZ9.

 01  TOTAL-LINE-5.
     05                                          PIC X(34) VALUE SPACES.
     05                                          PIC X(5)  VALUE "TOTAL".
     05 NUMBER-OF-INPUT-RECORDS                  PIC B(23)ZZ9.

 01  NO-INPUT-DATA.
     05                                          PIC X(21) VALUE SPACES.
     05                               PIC X(13) VALUE "NO INPUT DATA".

******************************************************************

 PROCEDURE DIVISION.
 LIST-SELECTED-RECORDS.
     SORT SORT-WORK-FILE
          ASCENDING KEY ACCOUNT-NUMBER-S
          USING TRANSACTION-FILE-IN
          OUTPUT PROCEDURE IS LIST-RECORDS
     STOP RUN
     .
```

continued

The main loop of this program terminates a little differently from the main loop in Program P13-03. In Program P14-01 the PERFORM statement at line 02020 ceases executing when there are no more transactions; that is, when the TRANSACTION-INPUT-AREA is equal to HIGH-VALUES. In Program P13-03 the main loop ceased executing only when CURRENT-KEY got to be equal to HIGH-VALUES, that is, after both the master and transaction files had reached end-of-file. The reason for the difference lies in the fact that Program P13-03 is an update program and creates a new output master file. Thus the entire input master file must be processed to ensure that all records from the incoming master file are copied onto the output master if they are not deleted. Program P14-01 is not an update program and does not create an output master file. The input master file is read and used, but remains unchanged. In Program P14-01, as soon as the transaction file reaches end-of-file, there is no reason to read the remainder of the input master file.

FIGURE *14.4* ***continued***

```
S COBOL II RELEASE 3.1 09/19/89                  P14001    DATE SEP 01,1991 T
----+-*A-1-B--+----2----+----3----+----4----+----5----+----6----+----7-|--+

01990
02000  LIST-RECORDS.
02010      PERFORM INITIALIZATION
02020      PERFORM PROCESS-ONE-KEY UNTIL NO-MORE-TRANSACTION-RECORDS
02030      PERFORM TERMINATION
02040      .
02050
02060  INITIALIZATION.
02070      OPEN INPUT  ACCOUNT-MASTER-FILE-IN
02080           OUTPUT LISTING-FILE-OUT
02090                  ERROR-FILE-OUT
02100      ACCEPT TODAYS-DATE FROM DATE
02110      MOVE CORR TODAYS-DATE TO PAGE-HEADING-2
02120      PERFORM PRINT-REPORT-HEADINGS
02130      PERFORM READ-A-MASTER-RECORD
02140      PERFORM READ-A-TRANSACTION-RECORD
02150      PERFORM CHOOSE-CURRENT-KEY
02160      IF THERE-IS-NO-INPUT
02170          WRITE LISTING-RECORD FROM NO-INPUT-DATA
02180      END-IF
02190      .
02200
02210  PROCESS-ONE-KEY.
02220      PERFORM PROCESS-MASTER-RECORD
02230      PERFORM PROCESS-TRANSACTION-RECORD UNTIL
02240          ACCOUNT-NUMBER IN TRANSACTION-INPUT-AREA
02250          IS NOT EQUAL TO CURRENT-KEY
02260      PERFORM CHOOSE-CURRENT-KEY
02270      .
02280
02290  PROCESS-TRANSACTION-RECORD.
02300      PERFORM CHECK-FOR-VALID-LIST-REQUEST
02310      PERFORM READ-A-TRANSACTION-RECORD
02320      .
02330
02340  CHOOSE-CURRENT-KEY.
02350      IF ACCOUNT-NUMBER IN TRANSACTION-INPUT-AREA IS LESS THAN
02360         ACCOUNT-NUMBER IN MASTER-INPUT-AREA
02370          MOVE ACCOUNT-NUMBER IN TRANSACTION-INPUT-AREA TO
02380               CURRENT-KEY
02390      ELSE
02400          MOVE ACCOUNT-NUMBER IN MASTER-INPUT-AREA TO
02410               CURRENT-KEY
02420      END-IF
02430      .
```

FIGURE 14.4 *continued*

```
PROCESS-MASTER-RECORD.
    IF ACCOUNT-NUMBER IN MASTER-INPUT-AREA IS EQUAL TO
       CURRENT-KEY
        MOVE MASTER-INPUT-AREA TO WORK-AREA
        PERFORM READ-A-MASTER-RECORD
        SET MASTER-RECORD-IS-IN-WORKAREA TO TRUE
    ELSE
        SET MASTER-RECORD-ISNT-IN-WORKAREA TO TRUE
    END-IF
    .

READ-A-TRANSACTION-RECORD.
    RETURN SORT-WORK-FILE INTO TRANSACTION-INPUT-AREA
        AT END
            SET NO-MORE-TRANSACTION-RECORDS TO TRUE
        NOT AT END
            ADD 1 TO NUMBER-OF-INPUT-RECORDS-W
    .

READ-A-MASTER-RECORD.
    READ ACCOUNT-MASTER-FILE-IN INTO MASTER-INPUT-AREA
        AT END
            SET NO-MORE-MASTER-RECORDS TO TRUE
    .

CHECK-FOR-VALID-LIST-REQUEST.
    IF NOT LISTING-REQUEST
        PERFORM WRITE-INVALID-CODE-LINE
        ADD 1 TO NUMBER-OF-ERRONEOUS-RECORDS-W
    ELSE
    IF MASTER-RECORD-ISNT-IN-WORKAREA
        PERFORM WRITE-MASTER-MISSING-LINE
        ADD 1 TO NUMBER-OF-ERRONEOUS-RECORDS-W
    ELSE
        PERFORM WRITE-REPORT-LINE
        SET MASTER-RECORD-ISNT-IN-WORKAREA TO TRUE
        ADD 1 TO NUMBER-OF-SELECTED-RECORDS-W
    END-IF
    END-IF
    .

WRITE-REPORT-LINE.
    MOVE ACCOUNT-NUMBER-W TO ACCOUNT-NUMBER-OUT
    MOVE CURRENT-BALANCE-W TO CURRENT-BALANCE-OUT
    MOVE DATE-OF-LAST-TRANSACTION-W TO DATE-OF-LAST-TRANSACTION
    MOVE DEPOSITOR-NAME-W TO DEPOSITOR-NAME
    WRITE LISTING-RECORD FROM REPORT-LINE
    ADD CURRENT-BALANCE-W TO CURRENT-BALANCE-TOTAL
    .

WRITE-INVALID-CODE-LINE.
    MOVE ACCOUNT-NUMBER IN TRANSACTION-INPUT-AREA TO
                                   ACCOUNT-NUMBER-E
    MOVE TRANSACTION-CODE TO TRANSACTION-CODE-OUT
    WRITE ERROR-RECORD-OUT FROM INVALID-CODE-LINE
    .

WRITE-MASTER-MISSING-LINE.
    MOVE ACCOUNT-NUMBER IN TRANSACTION-INPUT-AREA TO
                                   ACCOUNT-NUMBER-MISSING
    WRITE ERROR-RECORD-OUT FROM MASTER-MISSING-LINE
    .
```

continued

FIGURE ***14.4*** ***continued***

```
S COBOL II RELEASE 3.1 09/19/89                   P14001   DATE SEP 01,1991 T
----+-*A-1-B--+----2----+----3----+----4----+----5----+----6----+----7-|--+

 TERMINATION.
     PERFORM WRITE-TOTALS
     CLOSE ACCOUNT-MASTER-FILE-IN
            LISTING-FILE-OUT
            ERROR-FILE-OUT
     .

 WRITE-TOTALS.
     MOVE CURRENT-BALANCE-TOTAL TO CURRENT-BALANCE-TOTAL-OUT
     WRITE LISTING-RECORD FROM TOTAL-LINE-1 AFTER 2
     WRITE LISTING-RECORD FROM TOTAL-LINE-2 AFTER 2
     MOVE NUMBER-OF-SELECTED-RECORDS-W
                       TO NUMBER-OF-SELECTED-RECORDS
     WRITE LISTING-RECORD FROM TOTAL-LINE-3 AFTER 2
     MOVE NUMBER-OF-ERRONEOUS-RECORDS-W TO
                                NUMBER-OF-ERRONEOUS-RECORDS
     WRITE LISTING-RECORD FROM TOTAL-LINE-4 AFTER 2
     MOVE NUMBER-OF-INPUT-RECORDS-W TO
                                NUMBER-OF-INPUT-RECORDS
     WRITE LISTING-RECORD FROM TOTAL-LINE-5 AFTER 2
     .

 PRINT-REPORT-HEADINGS.
     PERFORM PRINT-LISTING-HEADINGS
     PERFORM PRINT-ERROR-REPORT-HEADINGS
     .

 PRINT-LISTING-HEADINGS.
     ADD 1 TO PAGE-NUMBER-W
     MOVE PAGE-NUMBER-W TO PAGE-NUMBER-OUT
     WRITE LISTING-RECORD FROM REPORT-HEADING-1
                                 AFTER ADVANCING PAGE
     WRITE LISTING-RECORD FROM REPORT-HEADING-2
     WRITE LISTING-RECORD FROM REPORT-HEADING-3
     WRITE LISTING-RECORD FROM PAGE-HEADING-1
                                 AFTER 2
     WRITE LISTING-RECORD FROM PAGE-HEADING-2
     WRITE LISTING-RECORD FROM PAGE-HEADING-3
                                 AFTER 3
     WRITE LISTING-RECORD FROM PAGE-HEADING-4
     WRITE LISTING-RECORD FROM BLANK-LINE
     .

 PRINT-ERROR-REPORT-HEADINGS.
     ADD 1 TO ERROR-PAGE-NUMBER-W
     MOVE ERROR-PAGE-NUMBER-W TO PAGE-NUMBER-OUT
     WRITE ERROR-RECORD-OUT FROM REPORT-HEADING-1
                                 AFTER ADVANCING PAGE
     WRITE ERROR-RECORD-OUT FROM REPORT-HEADING-2
     WRITE ERROR-RECORD-OUT FROM REPORT-HEADING-3
     WRITE ERROR-RECORD-OUT FROM ERROR-PAGE-HEADING-1
                                 AFTER 2
     WRITE ERROR-RECORD-OUT FROM PAGE-HEADING-2
     WRITE ERROR-RECORD-OUT FROM ERROR-PAGE-HEADING-3
                                 AFTER 3
     WRITE ERROR-RECORD-OUT FROM ERROR-PAGE-HEADING-4
     WRITE ERROR-RECORD-OUT FROM BLANK-LINE
     .
```

Program P14-01 was run with the transaction input shown in Figure 14.5 and the input master file created by Program P13-02, and produced the output shown in Figure 14.6.

FIGURE 14.5 Transaction input to Program P14-01

```
--------------------------------------------------------------------------------
         1         2         3         4         5         6         7         8
12345678901234567890123456789012345678901234567890123456789012345678901234567890
--------------------------------------------------------------------------------
600350
600245
100299
600077
600003
600508
600168
600350
600599
700320
600280
600609
500390
```

FIGURE 14.6 Output from Program P14-01

```
                    ROBBEM STATE BANK
                    106 WEST 10TH ST.
                   BROOKLYN, NY  11212

                SELECTED SAVINGS ACCOUNTS
      DATE  9/01/91                              PAGE  1


    ACCOUNT      CURRENT      DATE OF LAST      DEPOSITOR
    NUMBER       BALANCE      TRANSACTION         NAME

     00077          10.37        910819       LESLIE MINSKY
     00168         125.50        910819       KELLY HEDERMAN
     00245          35.00        910819       FRANK CAPUTO
     00280          20.00        910819       COMMUNITY DRUGS
     00350       2,500.00        910819       ROGER SHAW

 TOTAL           2,690.87

                      CONTROL COUNTS

             NUMBER OF SELECTED ACCOUNTS     5

             NUMBER OF ERRONEOUS RECORDS     8

             TOTAL                          13


                   ROBBEM STATE BANK
                   106 WEST 10TH ST.
                  BROOKLYN, NY  11212

                   SELECTION ERRORS
     DATE  9/01/91                              PAGE  1


ACCOUNT
NUMBER                   NOTES

 00003                 MASTER RECORD DOES NOT EXIST
 00299                 INVALID CODE -  1
 00320                 INVALID CODE -  7
 00350                 MASTER RECORD DOES NOT EXIST
 00390                 INVALID CODE -  5
 00508                 MASTER RECORD DOES NOT EXIST
 00599                 MASTER RECORD DOES NOT EXIST
 00609                 MASTER RECORD DOES NOT EXIST
```

EXERCISE *1*

Write a program to list selected records from the inventory master file you created in Exercise 3, Chapter 13, page 457. List the following fields from each record selected:

Part Number

Part Description

Quantity on Hand

Reorder Point

The Quantity on Hand should show as zero in each record. Use input transactions in the following format:

Positions	Field
1	Code 9
2–6	Part Number
7–80	spaces

Design suitable reports for your program. Have your program check the input transactions for validity, and print error messages and the selected master records.

An Update Program with Changes and Deletions

We will now develop a program to handle four different kinds of transactions in a single run. Program P14-02 will be able to update a sequential master file using an input transaction file that may contain any combination of changes to existing master records and deletions of existing master records.

Records on our savings-account master file can be changed in the following ways: A depositor may make a deposit or withdrawal, or a depositor may change his or her name. If a deposit were made, we would want to add the deposit amount to the Current balance field in the master record for the account; if a withdrawal were made, we would want to subtract the withdrawal amount from the Current Balance field. If a depositor name change occurs, we would want to change the Depositor Name field in the master record. There may be any combination of these kinds of changes to a single master record in one run. A depositor may make one or more deposits and/or one or more withdrawals in a single day, and may change his or her name during the day. Each of these different events would be reflected in a single transaction record, and Program P14-02 would be able to process all transactions against any master record.

There may even be one or more changes and a deletion against a single master record in one run. A depositor may make a deposit and then close the account all in the same day. The transaction input would then contain one record for the deposit and one for the deletion. Of course, any change transactions to a master record must precede the deletion in the transaction input.

The formats of the four types of transactions that can be processed by Program P14-02 are:

Positions	Field
1	Code 2 (Deposit)
2–6	Account Number
7–14	Deposit Amount (to two decimal places)
15–80	spaces
1	Code 3 (Withdrawal)
2–6	Account Number
7–14	Withdrawal Amount (to two decimal places)
15–80	spaces
1	Code 4 (Depositor name change)
2–6	Account Number
7–26	Depositor Name
27–80	spaces
1	Code 5 (Close account)
2–6	Account number
7–80	spaces

Even though the different types of transactions have different formats, they can all be processed in one transaction input area in working storage. When we look at Program P14-02, you will see how the transaction input area can be defined to accommodate the different formats.

The format of the transaction register produced by Program P14-02 is shown in Figure 14.7. The format shows the output that is printed for a valid deposit, a valid withdrawal, a valid name change, and a valid closing of an account. The format of the error report for this program, Figure 14.8, shows the types of errors that can be detected by the program.

In this update program it is legal for there to be more than one transaction against a master record in a single run. The several transactions may all have the same transaction Code (as when several deposits are being made to one account) or they may have different transaction Codes (as when a deposit and a withdrawal are being made). Thus the program must examine the transaction Code of each input transaction to determine how the transaction is to be processed.

FIGURE *14.7* **Output format for transaction register for Program P14-02**

```
PRINT CHART

                                      ROBBEM STATE BANK
                                      106 WEST 10TH ST.
                                     BROOKLYN, NY 11212

                          SAVINGS ACCOUNT TRANSACTION REGISTER
            DATE Z9/99/99                                          PAGE Z9

                ACCOUNT     DEPOSITS          WITHDRAWALS          NOTES
                NUMBER

                 XXXXX     ZZZ,ZZZ.99
                 XXXXX                        ZZZ,ZZZ.99
                 XXXXX     X-------------------X                NAME CHANGE
                 XXXXX     ZZZ,ZZZ.99
                 XXXXX                        ZZZ,ZZZ.99        ACCOUNT CLOSED

            TOTALS       Z,ZZZ,ZZZ.99  Z,ZZZ,ZZZ.99

                                     CONTROL COUNTS

                              NUMBER OF DEPOSITS               ZZ9

                              NUMBER OF WITHDRAWALS            ZZ9

                              NUMBER OF NAME CHANGES           ZZ9

                              NUMBER OF CLOSED ACCOUNTS        ZZ9

                              NUMBER OF ERRORS                 ZZ9

                              TOTAL                          Z,ZZ9
```

FIGURE *14.8* **Output format for error report for Program P14-02**

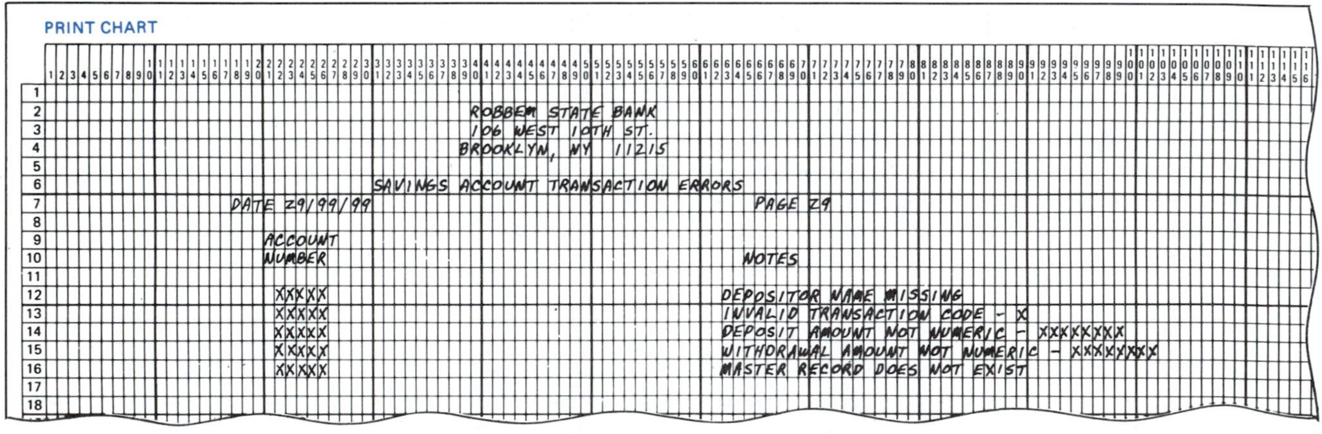

A Hierarchy Diagram for Making Changes and Deletions to a Master File

In a hierarchy diagram for Program P14-02, the box "Process transaction record" would be much more elaborate than in any program we have done so far. However, all of the boxes above "Process transaction record" would be identical to those in the hierarchy diagram for deleting records from a master file, Figure 13.14.

Figure 14.9 shows just the box "Process transaction record" and its subfunctions for Program P14-02. Here there is one subfunction, "Apply transaction," just to determine which of the several types of transactions is being processed. Then, at lower levels, the program coding carries out the validity checking and processing suitable to each type of transaction.

FIGURE *14.9* **Hierarchy diagram for "Process transaction record" for Program P14-02**

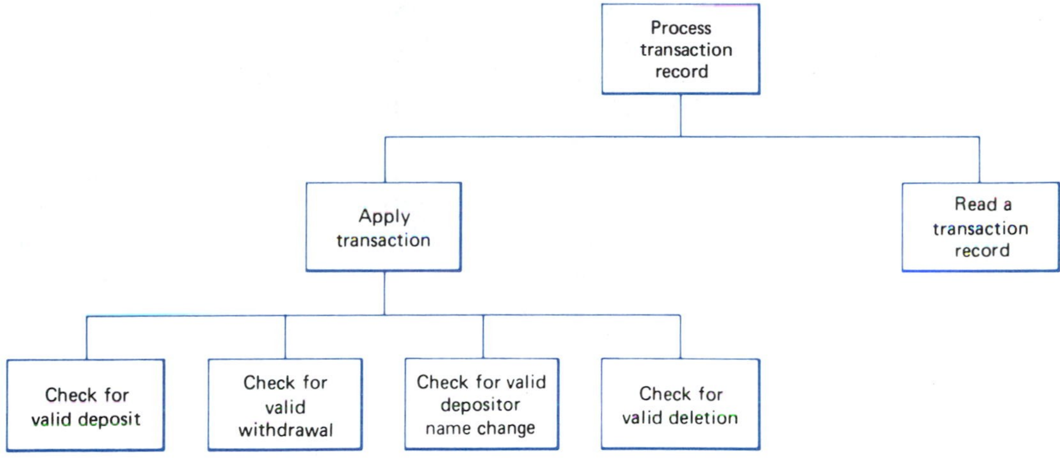

A Program to Make Changes and Deletions to a Master File

Program P14-02 is shown in Figure 14.10. The TRANSACTION-INPUT-AREA, at line 00910, is defined so that it can accommodate the several transaction types with their different formats. The transaction Code and Account Number occupy positions 1 through 6 in all the transaction input, so those fields are defined at lines 00930 through 00980. The TRANSACTION-CODE has level-88 entries for the valid Codes.

The next fields in the transaction input record are the deposit and withdrawal amount fields, and the name-change field. We first define the Amount fields, under the heading DEPOSIT-AND-WITHDRAWAL-AMTS at line 00990,

FIGURE *14.10* **Program P14-02**

```
S COBOL II RELEASE 3.2 09/05/90                    P14002   DATE MAR 13,1992 T
----+-*A-1-B--+----2----+----3----+----4----+----5----+----6----+----7-|--+

00010  IDENTIFICATION DIVISION.
00020  PROGRAM-ID. P14-02.
00030 *
00040 *     THIS PROGRAM UPDATES A SEQUENTIAL MASTER FILE
00050 *     WITH CHANGES AND DELETIONS.
00060 *
00070 *****************************************************************
00080
```

continued

and later we will define the Depositor Name field. Since the Deposit Amount and the Withdrawal Amount both occupy the same eight positions of the transaction input, the field WITHDRAWAL-AMOUNT is used to redefine the field DEPOSIT-AMOUNT. The two fields have also been redefined as alphanumeric in case it turns out that they contain one or more nonnumeric characters and must be printed without editing. Notice that when a field is redefined more than once, as DEPOSIT-AMOUNT is, all the redefinitions must refer to the original name of the field, DEPOSIT-AMOUNT. That is, you cannot redefine a field whose definition contains a REDEFINES clause.

Line 01070 is needed so that we can process transactions of Code 4 properly. The Depositor Name field in those transactions presents a slight difficulty because part of it overlaps the Deposit and Withdrawal Amount fields in transactions of Codes 2 and 3. We accommodate type-4 transactions as shown in lines 01080 through 01110. We first redefine the entire TRANSACTION-INPUT-AREA. Then, by using line 01090, we can position the DEPOSITOR-NAME field to correspond to the position of the Depositor Name in the transaction record. Since a redefining entry must occupy the same number of character positions as the entry being redefined, line 01070 is included in the definition of TRANSACTION-INPUT-AREA to make it the same size as TRANSACTION-4-INPUT-AREA.

FIGURE *14.10* ***continued***

```
S COBOL II RELEASE 3.2 09/05/90                  P14002   DATE MAR 13,1992 T
----+-*A-1-B--+----2----+----3----+----4----+----5----+----6----+----7-|--+

00090  ENVIRONMENT DIVISION.
00100  INPUT-OUTPUT SECTION.
00110  FILE-CONTROL.
00120      SELECT ACCOUNT-MASTER-FILE-IN           ASSIGN TO MASTIN.
00130      SELECT ACCOUNT-MASTER-FILE-OUT          ASSIGN TO MASTOUT.
00140      SELECT TRANSACTION-FILE-IN              ASSIGN TO INFILE.
00150      SELECT TRANSACTION-REGISTER-FILE-OUT    ASSIGN TO PRINTER1.
00160      SELECT ERROR-FILE-OUT                   ASSIGN TO PRINTER2.
00170      SELECT SORT-WORK-FILE                   ASSIGN TO SORTWK.
00180
00190 *****************************************************************
00200
00210  DATA DIVISION.
00220  FILE SECTION.
00230  FD  ACCOUNT-MASTER-FILE-IN
00240      LABEL RECORDS ARE STANDARD
00250      RECORD CONTAINS 39 CHARACTERS
00260      BLOCK CONTAINS 100 RECORDS.
00270
00280  01  ACCOUNT-MASTER-RECORD-IN         PIC X(39).
00290
00300  FD  ACCOUNT-MASTER-FILE-OUT
00310      LABEL RECORDS ARE STANDARD
00320      RECORD CONTAINS 39 CHARACTERS
00330      BLOCK CONTAINS 100 RECORDS.
00340
00350  01  ACCOUNT-MASTER-RECORD-OUT        PIC X(39).
00360
00370  SD  SORT-WORK-FILE
00380      RECORD CONTAINS 26 CHARACTERS.
00390
00400  01  SORT-WORK-RECORD.
00410      05  TRANSACTION-CODE-S           PIC X.
00420      05  ACCOUNT-NUMBER-S             PIC X(5).
00430      05                               PIC X(20).
00440
```

FIGURE ***14.10*** ***continued***

```
FD   TRANSACTION-FILE-IN
     RECORD CONTAINS 80 CHARACTERS.
01   TRANSACTION-RECORD-IN              PIC X(80).
FD   TRANSACTION-REGISTER-FILE-OUT.
01   TRANSACTION-REGISTER-RECRD-OUT     PIC X(76).
FD   ERROR-FILE-OUT.
01   ERROR-RECORD-OUT                   PIC X(102).
WORKING-STORAGE SECTION.
01   CURRENT-KEY                        PIC X(5).
     88 THERE-IS-NO-MORE-INPUT            VALUE HIGH-VALUES.
     88 THERE-IS-NO-INPUT                 VALUE HIGH-VALUES.
01   IS-MASTER-RECORD-IN-WORK-AREA      PIC X.
     88 MASTER-RECORD-IS-IN-WORKAREA      VALUE "Y".
     88 MASTER-RECORD-ISNT-IN-WORKAREA VALUE "N".
01   PACKED-DECIMAL.
 02 NUMBER-OF-INPUT-RECORDS-W           PIC S9(3) VALUE ZERO.
 02 NUMBER-OF-ERRONEOUS-RECORDS-W       PIC S9(3) VALUE ZERO.
 02 DEPOSIT-TOTAL-W                     PIC S9(7)V99 VALUE ZERO.
 02 WITHDRAWAL-TOTAL-W                  PIC S9(7)V99 VALUE ZERO.
 02 NUMBER-OF-DEPOSITS-W                PIC S9(3) VALUE ZERO.
 02 NUMBER-OF-WITHDRAWALS-W             PIC S9(3) VALUE ZERO.
 02 NUMBER-OF-NAME-CHANGES-W            PIC S9(3) VALUE ZERO.
 02 NUMBER-OF-CLOSED-ACCOUNTS-W         PIC S9(3) VALUE ZERO.
 02 PAGE-NUMBER-W                       PIC S99   VALUE 0.
 02 ERROR-PAGE-NUMBER-W                 PIC S99   VALUE 0.
01   BLANK-LINE                         PIC X     VALUE SPACE.
01   PAGE-LIMIT            COMP SYNC    PIC S99   VALUE 28.
01   LINE-COUNT-ER         COMP SYNC    PIC S99.
01   ERROR-PAGE-LIMIT      COMP SYNC    PIC S99   VALUE 45.
01   ERROR-LINE-COUNTER    COMP SYNC    PIC S99.
01   TODAYS-DATE.
     05   TODAYS-YEAR                   PIC 99.
     05   TODAYS-MONTH-AND-DAY          PIC 9(4).
01   MASTER-INPUT-AREA.
     88 NO-MORE-MASTER-RECORDS          VALUE HIGH-VALUES.
     05   ACCOUNT-NUMBER                PIC X(5).
     05                                 PIC X(34).
01   TRANSACTION-INPUT-AREA.
     88 NO-MORE-TRANSACTION-RECORDS     VALUE HIGH-VALUES.
     05   TRANSACTION-CODE              PIC X.
          88   DEPOSIT                  VALUE "2".
          88   WITHDRAWAL               VALUE "3".
          88   NAME-CHANGE              VALUE "4".
          88   DELETION                 VALUE "5".
     05   ACCOUNT-NUMBER                PIC X(5).
     05   DEPOSIT-AND-WITHDRAWAL-AMTS.
          10   DEPOSIT-AMOUNT           PIC 9(6)V99.
          10   DEPOSIT-AMOUNT-X      REDEFINES DEPOSIT-AMOUNT
                                        PIC X(8).
          10   WITHDRAWAL-AMOUNT     REDEFINES DEPOSIT-AMOUNT
                                        PIC 9(6)V99.
          10   WITHDRAWAL-AMOUNT-X REDEFINES DEPOSIT-AMOUNT
                                        PIC X(8).
     05                                 PIC X(12).
01   TRANSACTION-4-INPUT-AREA REDEFINES TRANSACTION-INPUT-AREA.
     05                                 PIC X(6).
     05   DEPOSITOR-NAME                PIC X(20).
          88   DEPOSITOR-NAME-MISSING   VALUE SPACES.
```

continued

FIGURE 14.10 *continued*

```
S COBOL II RELEASE 3.2 09/05/90                        P14002    DATE MAR 13,1992 T
----+-*A-1-B--+----2----+----3----+----4----+----5----+----6----+----7-|--+

       01  WORK-AREA.
           05  ACCOUNT-NUMBER-W                PIC X(5).
           05  DEPOSITOR-NAME-W                PIC X(20).
           05  DATE-OF-LAST-TRANSACTION-W      PIC 9(6).
           05  CURRENT-BALANCE-W               PIC S9(6)V99.
       01  REPORT-HEADING-1.
           05              PIC X(39) VALUE SPACES.
           05              PIC X(17) VALUE "ROBBEM STATE BANK".
       01  REPORT-HEADING-2.
           05              PIC X(39) VALUE SPACES.
           05              PIC X(17) VALUE "106 WEST 10TH ST.".
       01  REPORT-HEADING-3.
           05              PIC X(38) VALUE SPACES.
           05              PIC X(19) VALUE "BROOKLYN, NY  11212".
       01  PAGE-HEADING-1.
           05              PIC X(29) VALUE SPACES.
           05              PIC X(36)
                           VALUE "SAVINGS ACCOUNT TRANSACTION REGISTER".
       01  ERROR-PAGE-HEADING-1.
           05              PIC X(30) VALUE SPACES.
           05              PIC X(34)
                           VALUE  "SAVINGS ACCOUNT TRANSACTION ERRORS".
       01  PAGE-HEADING-2.
           05                  PIC X(17) VALUE SPACES.
           05                  PIC X(5)  VALUE "DATE".
           05  TODAYS-MONTH-AND-DAY                        PIC Z9/99/.
           05  TODAYS-YEAR                                 PIC 99B(35).
           05                  PIC X(5)  VALUE "PAGE".
           05  PAGE-NUMBER-OUT                             PIC Z9.
       01  PAGE-HEADING-3.
           05                  PIC X(20) VALUE SPACES.
           05                  PIC X(12) VALUE "ACCOUNT".
           05                  PIC X(14) VALUE "DEPOSITS".
           05                  PIC X(18) VALUE "WITHDRAWALS".
           05                  PIC X(5)  VALUE "NOTES".
       01  ERROR-PAGE-HEADING-3.
           05                  PIC X(20) VALUE SPACES.
           05                  PIC X(44) VALUE "ACCOUNT".
           05                  PIC X(5)  VALUE "NOTES".
       01  PAGE-HEADING-4.
           05                  PIC X(20) VALUE SPACES.
           05                  PIC X(6)  VALUE "NUMBER".
       01  DEPOSIT-LINE.
           05                  PIC X(21) VALUE SPACES.
           05  ACCOUNT-NUMBER-OUT        PIC X(5)B(5).
           05  DEPOSIT-AMOUNT-OUT        PIC ZZZ,ZZZ.99.
       01  WITHDRAWAL-LINE.
           05                  PIC X(21) VALUE SPACES.
           05  ACCOUNT-NUMBER-OUT        PIC X(5)B(19).
           05  WITHDRAWAL-AMOUNT-OUT     PIC ZZZ,ZZZ.99.
       01  NAME-CHANGE-LINE.
           05                  PIC X(21) VALUE SPACES.
           05  ACCOUNT-NUMBER-OUT        PIC X(5)B(5).
           05  DEPOSITOR-NAME-OUT        PIC X(20)B(11).
           05                  PIC X(11) VALUE "NAME CHANGE".
```

FIGURE 14.10 *continued*

```
       01  DELETION-LINE.
           05                    PIC X(21) VALUE SPACES.
           05  ACCOUNT-NUMBER-OUT          PIC X(5)B(19).
           05  CURRENT-BALANCE-OUT         PIC ZZZ,ZZZ.99B(7).
           05                    PIC X(14) VALUE "ACCOUNT CLOSED".

       01  DEPOSIT-AMOUNT-INVALID-MSG.
           05                    PIC X(29)
                          VALUE "DEPOSIT AMOUNT NOT NUMERIC -".
           05  DEPOSIT-AMOUNT-OUT          PIC X(8).

       01  WITHDRAWAL-AMOUNT-INVALID-MSG.
           05                              PIC X(32)
                          VALUE "WITHDRAWAL AMOUNT NOT NUMERIC -".
           05  WITHDRAWAL-AMOUNT-OUT       PIC X(8).

       01  INVALID-CODE-MSG.
           05                 PIC X(27) VALUE "INVALID TRANSACTION CODE -".
           05  TRANSACTION-CODE-OUT        PIC X.

       01  ERROR-LINE.
           05  ACCOUNT-NUMBER-E            PIC B(21)X(5)B(36).
           05  ERROR-MESSAGE               PIC X(40).

       01  FINAL-LINE-1.
           05                    PIC X(17) VALUE SPACES.
           05                    PIC X(12) VALUE "TOTALS".
           05  DEPOSIT-TOTAL-OUT                 PIC Z,ZZZ,ZZZ.99BB.
           05  WITHDRAWAL-TOTAL-OUT              PIC Z,ZZZ,ZZZ.99.

       01  FINAL-LINE-2.
           05                    PIC X(40) VALUE SPACES.
           05                    PIC X(14) VALUE "CONTROL COUNTS".

       01  FINAL-LINE-3.
           05                    PIC X(34) VALUE SPACES.
           05                    PIC X(26)
                                 VALUE "NUMBER OF DEPOSITS".
           05  NUMBER-OF-DEPOSITS-OUT            PIC ZZ9.

       01  FINAL-LINE-4.
           05                    PIC X(34) VALUE SPACES.
           05                    PIC X(26)
                                 VALUE "NUMBER OF WITHDRAWALS".
           05  NUMBER-OF-WITHDRAWALS-OUT         PIC ZZ9.

       01  FINAL-LINE-5.
           05                    PIC X(34) VALUE SPACES.
           05                    PIC X(26)
                                 VALUE "NUMBER OF NAME CHANGES".
           05  NUMBER-OF-NAME-CHANGES-OUT        PIC ZZ9.

       01  FINAL-LINE-6.
           05                    PIC X(34) VALUE SPACES.
           05                    PIC X(26)
                                 VALUE "NUMBER OF CLOSED ACCOUNTS".
           05  NUMBER-OF-CLOSED-ACCOUNTS-OUT     PIC ZZ9.

       01  FINAL-LINE-7.
           05                    PIC X(34) VALUE SPACES.
           05                    PIC X(26)
                                 VALUE "NUMBER OF ERRORS".
           05  NUMBER-OF-ERRONEOUS-RECRDS-OUT    PIC ZZ9.

       01  FINAL-LINE-8.
           05                    PIC X(34) VALUE SPACES.
           05                    PIC X(26) VALUE "TOTAL".
           05  NUMBER-OF-INPUT-RECORDS-OUT       PIC ZZ9.
```

continued

The Procedure Division, which follows the hierarchy diagram, begins at line 02560. It is nearly identical to the Procedure Division of Program P14-02 except at the lowest level. The SORT statement, at line 02580, SORTs the input transactions on their transaction Code as well as their Account Number. This assures that if there is more than one transaction against a single master record, a deletion transaction, if present, will fall after all other transactions.

FIGURE *14.10* ***continued***

```
S COBOL II RELEASE 3.2 09/05/90                  P14002   DATE MAR 13,1992 T
----+-*A-1-B--+----2----+----3----+----4----+----5----+----6----+----7-|--+

02500  01  NO-INPUT-DATA.
02510      05                   PIC X(21) VALUE SPACES.
02520      05                   PIC X(13) VALUE "NO INPUT DATA".
02530
02540 ************************************************************************
02550
02560  PROCEDURE DIVISION.
02570  UPDATE-PARAGRAPH.
02580      SORT SORT-WORK-FILE
02590           ASCENDING KEY ACCOUNT-NUMBER-S
02600                         TRANSACTION-CODE-S
02610           USING TRANSACTION-FILE-IN
02620           OUTPUT PROCEDURE IS UPDATE-RECORDS
02630      STOP RUN
02640      .
02650
02660  UPDATE-RECORDS.
02670      PERFORM INITIALIZATION
02680      PERFORM PROCESS-ONE-KEY UNTIL THERE-IS-NO-MORE-INPUT
02690      PERFORM TERMINATION
02700      .
02710
02720  INITIALIZATION.
02730      OPEN INPUT  ACCOUNT-MASTER-FILE-IN
02740           OUTPUT ACCOUNT-MASTER-FILE-OUT
02750                  ERROR-FILE-OUT
02760                  TRANSACTION-REGISTER-FILE-OUT
02770      ACCEPT TODAYS-DATE FROM DATE
02780      MOVE CORR TODAYS-DATE TO PAGE-HEADING-2
02790      PERFORM PRODUCE-REPORT-HEADINGS
02800      PERFORM READ-A-MASTER-RECORD
02810      PERFORM READ-A-TRANSACTION-RECORD
02820      PERFORM CHOOSE-CURRENT-KEY
02830      IF THERE-IS-NO-INPUT
02840          WRITE TRANSACTION-REGISTER-RECRD-OUT FROM NO-INPUT-DATA
02850      END-IF
02860      .
02870
02880  PRODUCE-REPORT-HEADINGS.
02890      PERFORM WRITE-REGISTER-HEADINGS
02900      PERFORM WRITE-ERROR-REPORT-HEADINGS
02910      .
02920
```

FIGURE 14.10 *continued*

```
WRITE-REGISTER-HEADINGS.
    ADD 1 TO PAGE-NUMBER-W
    MOVE PAGE-NUMBER-W TO PAGE-NUMBER-OUT
    WRITE TRANSACTION-REGISTER-RECRD-OUT FROM
        REPORT-HEADING-1 AFTER ADVANCING PAGE
    WRITE TRANSACTION-REGISTER-RECRD-OUT FROM REPORT-HEADING-2
    WRITE TRANSACTION-REGISTER-RECRD-OUT FROM REPORT-HEADING-3
    WRITE TRANSACTION-REGISTER-RECRD-OUT FROM PAGE-HEADING-1
                                                         AFTER 2
    WRITE TRANSACTION-REGISTER-RECRD-OUT FROM PAGE-HEADING-2
    WRITE TRANSACTION-REGISTER-RECRD-OUT FROM PAGE-HEADING-3
                                                         AFTER 3
    WRITE TRANSACTION-REGISTER-RECRD-OUT FROM PAGE-HEADING-4
    WRITE TRANSACTION-REGISTER-RECRD-OUT FROM BLANK-LINE
    MOVE 11 TO LINE-COUNT-ER
    .

WRITE-ERROR-REPORT-HEADINGS.
    ADD 1 TO ERROR-PAGE-NUMBER-W
    MOVE ERROR-PAGE-NUMBER-W TO PAGE-NUMBER-OUT
    WRITE ERROR-RECORD-OUT FROM REPORT-HEADING-1 AFTER PAGE
    WRITE ERROR-RECORD-OUT FROM REPORT-HEADING-2
    WRITE ERROR-RECORD-OUT FROM REPORT-HEADING-3
    WRITE ERROR-RECORD-OUT FROM ERROR-PAGE-HEADING-1 AFTER 2
    WRITE ERROR-RECORD-OUT FROM PAGE-HEADING-2
    WRITE ERROR-RECORD-OUT FROM ERROR-PAGE-HEADING-3 AFTER 3
    WRITE ERROR-RECORD-OUT FROM PAGE-HEADING-4
    WRITE ERROR-RECORD-OUT FROM BLANK-LINE
    MOVE 11 TO ERROR-LINE-COUNTER
    .

PROCESS-ONE-KEY.
    PERFORM PROCESS-MASTER-RECORD
    PERFORM PROCESS-TRANSACTION-RECORD UNTIL
        ACCOUNT-NUMBER IN TRANSACTION-INPUT-AREA IS NOT EQUAL TO
        CURRENT-KEY
    PERFORM CHECK-TO-WRITE-MASTER
    PERFORM CHOOSE-CURRENT-KEY
    .

PROCESS-TRANSACTION-RECORD.
    PERFORM APPLY-TRANSACTION
    PERFORM READ-A-TRANSACTION-RECORD
    .

CHECK-TO-WRITE-MASTER.
    IF MASTER-RECORD-IS-IN-WORKAREA
        WRITE ACCOUNT-MASTER-RECORD-OUT FROM WORK-AREA
    END-IF
    .

CHOOSE-CURRENT-KEY.
    IF ACCOUNT-NUMBER IN TRANSACTION-INPUT-AREA IS LESS THAN
       ACCOUNT-NUMBER IN MASTER-INPUT-AREA
        MOVE ACCOUNT-NUMBER IN TRANSACTION-INPUT-AREA TO
            CURRENT-KEY
    ELSE
        MOVE ACCOUNT-NUMBER IN MASTER-INPUT-AREA TO
            CURRENT-KEY
    END-IF
    .
```

continued

The paragraph APPLY-TRANSACTION, at line 03800, determines the TRANSACTION-CODE of the transaction, in the transaction input area, and PERFORMs the appropriate paragraph to apply the transaction to the master record in the work area. Each of the paragraphs CHECK-FOR-VALID-DEPOSIT, CHECK-FOR-VALID-WITHDRAWAL, CHECK-FOR-VALID-NAME-CHANGE, and CHECK-FOR-VALID-DELETION makes suitable validity checks before applying the transaction. Each of the four paragraphs checks that there is a master record in the work area whose key is equal to the transaction key. They do so by checking the flag IS-MASTER-RECORD-IN-WORK-AREA.

FIGURE *14.10* ***continued***

```
S COBOL II RELEASE 3.2 09/05/90                  P14002   DATE MAR 13,1992 T
----+-*A-1-B--+----2----+----3----+----4----+----5----+----6----+----7-|--+


03550  PROCESS-MASTER-RECORD.
03560      IF ACCOUNT-NUMBER IN MASTER-INPUT-AREA
03570         IS EQUAL TO CURRENT-KEY
03580          MOVE MASTER-INPUT-AREA TO WORK-AREA
03590          PERFORM READ-A-MASTER-RECORD
03600          SET MASTER-RECORD-IS-IN-WORKAREA TO TRUE
03610      ELSE
03620          SET MASTER-RECORD-ISNT-IN-WORKAREA TO TRUE
03630      END-IF
03640      .
03650
03660  READ-A-TRANSACTION-RECORD.
03670      RETURN SORT-WORK-FILE INTO TRANSACTION-INPUT-AREA
03680          AT END
03690              SET NO-MORE-TRANSACTION-RECORDS TO TRUE
03700          NOT AT END
03710              ADD 1 TO NUMBER-OF-INPUT-RECORDS-W
03720      .
03730
03740  READ-A-MASTER-RECORD.
03750      READ ACCOUNT-MASTER-FILE-IN INTO MASTER-INPUT-AREA
03760          AT END
03770              SET NO-MORE-MASTER-RECORDS TO TRUE
03780      .
03790
03800  APPLY-TRANSACTION.
03810      EVALUATE TRUE
03820      WHEN DEPOSIT
03830          PERFORM CHECK-FOR-VALID-DEPOSIT
03840      WHEN WITHDRAWAL
03850          PERFORM CHECK-FOR-VALID-WITHDRAWAL
03860      WHEN NAME-CHANGE
03870          PERFORM CHECK-FOR-VALID-NAME-CHANGE
03880      WHEN DELETION
03890          PERFORM CHECK-FOR-VALID-DELETION
03900      WHEN OTHER
03910          ADD 1 TO NUMBER-OF-ERRONEOUS-RECORDS-W
03920          PERFORM WRITE-INVALID-CODE-LINE
03930      END-EVALUATE
03940      .
03950
```

Lines 04490 and 04500 show the application of a valid deletion transaction to a master record. The flag is set to "N" to indicate that the master record is no longer considered present in the work area. The other paragraphs that apply transactions to master records do not change the flag, because a deposit or withdrawal or name change does not make the master record disappear. The flag must remain set to "Y" to indicate that the master record is still present, in case there are more transactions against this master still to come, and so that CHECK-TO-WRITE-MASTER will write the updated master record out onto the new master file.

FIGURE *14.10* *continued*

```
CHECK-FOR-VALID-DEPOSIT.
    IF DEPOSIT-AMOUNT NOT NUMERIC
        ADD 1 TO NUMBER-OF-ERRONEOUS-RECORDS-W
        PERFORM WRITE-DEPOSIT-INVALID-LINE
    ELSE
    IF MASTER-RECORD-ISNT-IN-WORKAREA
        ADD 1 TO NUMBER-OF-ERRONEOUS-RECORDS-W
        PERFORM WRITE-MASTER-MISSING-LINE
    ELSE
        ADD DEPOSIT-AMOUNT TO CURRENT-BALANCE-W
        MOVE TODAYS-DATE TO DATE-OF-LAST-TRANSACTION-W
        PERFORM WRITE-DEPOSIT-LINE
    END-IF
    END-IF
    .

CHECK-FOR-VALID-WITHDRAWAL.
    IF WITHDRAWAL-AMOUNT NOT NUMERIC
        ADD 1 TO NUMBER-OF-ERRONEOUS-RECORDS-W
        PERFORM WRITE-WITHDRAWAL-INVALID-LINE
    ELSE
    IF MASTER-RECORD-ISNT-IN-WORKAREA
        ADD 1 TO NUMBER-OF-ERRONEOUS-RECORDS-W
        PERFORM WRITE-MASTER-MISSING-LINE
    ELSE
        SUBTRACT WITHDRAWAL-AMOUNT FROM CURRENT-BALANCE-W
        MOVE TODAYS-DATE TO DATE-OF-LAST-TRANSACTION-W
        PERFORM WRITE-WITHDRAWAL-LINE
    END-IF
    END-IF
    .

CHECK-FOR-VALID-NAME-CHANGE.
    IF DEPOSITOR-NAME-MISSING
        ADD 1 TO NUMBER-OF-ERRONEOUS-RECORDS-W
        PERFORM WRITE-NAME-MISSING-LINE
    ELSE
    IF MASTER-RECORD-ISNT-IN-WORKAREA
        ADD 1 TO NUMBER-OF-ERRONEOUS-RECORDS-W
        PERFORM WRITE-MASTER-MISSING-LINE
    ELSE
        MOVE DEPOSITOR-NAME TO DEPOSITOR-NAME-W
        MOVE TODAYS-DATE TO DATE-OF-LAST-TRANSACTION-W
        PERFORM WRITE-NAME-CHANGE-LINE
    END-IF
    END-IF
    .

CHECK-FOR-VALID-DELETION.
    IF MASTER-RECORD-ISNT-IN-WORKAREA
        ADD 1 TO NUMBER-OF-ERRONEOUS-RECORDS-W
        PERFORM WRITE-MASTER-MISSING-LINE
    ELSE
        PERFORM WRITE-DELETION-LINE
        SET MASTER-RECORD-ISNT-IN-WORKAREA TO TRUE
    END-IF
    .
```

continued

FIGURE 14.10 *continued*

```
S COBOL II RELEASE 3.2 09/05/90                P14002   DATE MAR 13,1992 T
----+-*A-1-B--+----2----+----3----+----4----+----5----+----6----+----7-|--+

WRITE-DEPOSIT-LINE.
    MOVE CURRENT-KEY TO ACCOUNT-NUMBER-OUT     IN DEPOSIT-LINE
    MOVE DEPOSIT-AMOUNT TO DEPOSIT-AMOUNT-OUT IN DEPOSIT-LINE
    IF 1 + LINE-COUNT-ER GREATER THAN PAGE-LIMIT
        PERFORM WRITE-REGISTER-HEADINGS
    END-IF
    WRITE TRANSACTION-REGISTER-RECRD-OUT FROM DEPOSIT-LINE
    ADD 1 TO LINE-COUNT-ER
    ADD DEPOSIT-AMOUNT TO DEPOSIT-TOTAL-W
    ADD 1 TO NUMBER-OF-DEPOSITS-W
    .

WRITE-WITHDRAWAL-LINE.
    MOVE CURRENT-KEY TO ACCOUNT-NUMBER-OUT IN WITHDRAWAL-LINE
    MOVE WITHDRAWAL-AMOUNT TO
         WITHDRAWAL-AMOUNT-OUT IN WITHDRAWAL-LINE
    IF 1 + LINE-COUNT-ER GREATER THAN PAGE-LIMIT
        PERFORM WRITE-REGISTER-HEADINGS
    END-IF
    WRITE TRANSACTION-REGISTER-RECRD-OUT FROM WITHDRAWAL-LINE
    ADD 1 TO LINE-COUNT-ER
    ADD WITHDRAWAL-AMOUNT TO WITHDRAWAL-TOTAL-W
    ADD 1 TO NUMBER-OF-WITHDRAWALS-W
    .

WRITE-DEPOSIT-INVALID-LINE.
    MOVE DEPOSIT-AMOUNT-X TO
         DEPOSIT-AMOUNT-OUT IN DEPOSIT-AMOUNT-INVALID-MSG
    MOVE DEPOSIT-AMOUNT-INVALID-MSG TO ERROR-MESSAGE
    PERFORM WRITE-ERROR-LINE
    .

 WRITE-WITHDRAWAL-INVALID-LINE.
    MOVE WITHDRAWAL-AMOUNT-X TO
         WITHDRAWAL-AMOUNT-OUT IN WITHDRAWAL-AMOUNT-INVALID-MSG
    MOVE WITHDRAWAL-AMOUNT-INVALID-MSG TO ERROR-MESSAGE
    PERFORM WRITE-ERROR-LINE
    .

WRITE-NAME-MISSING-LINE.
    MOVE "DEPOSITOR NAME MISSING" TO ERROR-MESSAGE
    PERFORM WRITE-ERROR-LINE
    .

WRITE-NAME-CHANGE-LINE.
    MOVE CURRENT-KEY TO ACCOUNT-NUMBER-OUT IN NAME-CHANGE-LINE
    MOVE DEPOSITOR-NAME TO DEPOSITOR-NAME-OUT
    IF 1 + LINE-COUNT-ER GREATER THAN PAGE-LIMIT
        PERFORM WRITE-REGISTER-HEADINGS
    END-IF
    WRITE TRANSACTION-REGISTER-RECRD-OUT FROM NAME-CHANGE-LINE
    ADD 1 TO LINE-COUNT-ER
    ADD 1 TO NUMBER-OF-NAME-CHANGES-W
    .

WRITE-DELETION-LINE.
    MOVE CURRENT-KEY TO ACCOUNT-NUMBER-OUT IN DELETION-LINE
    MOVE CURRENT-BALANCE-W TO CURRENT-BALANCE-OUT
    IF 1 + LINE-COUNT-ER GREATER THAN PAGE-LIMIT
        PERFORM WRITE-REGISTER-HEADINGS
    END-IF
    WRITE TRANSACTION-REGISTER-RECRD-OUT FROM DELETION-LINE
    ADD 1 TO LINE-COUNT-ER
    ADD CURRENT-BALANCE-W TO WITHDRAWAL-TOTAL-W
    ADD 1 TO NUMBER-OF-CLOSED-ACCOUNTS-W
    .
```

FIGURE 14.10 *continued*

```

WRITE-INVALID-CODE-LINE.
     MOVE TRANSACTION-CODE TO TRANSACTION-CODE-OUT
     MOVE INVALID-CODE-MSG TO ERROR-MESSAGE
     PERFORM WRITE-ERROR-LINE
     .

WRITE-MASTER-MISSING-LINE.
     MOVE "MASTER RECORD DOES NOT EXIST" TO ERROR-MESSAGE
     PERFORM WRITE-ERROR-LINE
     .

WRITE-ERROR-LINE.
     IF 1 + ERROR-LINE-COUNTER GREATER THAN
        ERROR-PAGE-LIMIT
         PERFORM WRITE-ERROR-REPORT-HEADINGS
     END-IF
     MOVE CURRENT-KEY TO ACCOUNT-NUMBER-E
     WRITE ERROR-RECORD-OUT FROM ERROR-LINE
     ADD 1 TO ERROR-LINE-COUNTER
     .

TERMINATION.
     PERFORM PRODUCE-TOTAL-LINES
     CLOSE ACCOUNT-MASTER-FILE-IN
           ACCOUNT-MASTER-FILE-OUT
           ERROR-FILE-OUT
           TRANSACTION-REGISTER-FILE-OUT
     .

PRODUCE-TOTAL-LINES.
     MOVE DEPOSIT-TOTAL-W    TO DEPOSIT-TOTAL-OUT
     MOVE WITHDRAWAL-TOTAL-W TO WITHDRAWAL-TOTAL-OUT
     WRITE TRANSACTION-REGISTER-RECRD-OUT FROM FINAL-LINE-1
                                          AFTER 3
     WRITE TRANSACTION-REGISTER-RECRD-OUT FROM FINAL-LINE-2
                                          AFTER 2
     MOVE NUMBER-OF-DEPOSITS-W TO NUMBER-OF-DEPOSITS-OUT
     WRITE TRANSACTION-REGISTER-RECRD-OUT FROM FINAL-LINE-3
                                          AFTER 2
     MOVE NUMBER-OF-WITHDRAWALS-W TO NUMBER-OF-WITHDRAWALS-OUT
     WRITE TRANSACTION-REGISTER-RECRD-OUT FROM FINAL-LINE-4
                                          AFTER 2
     MOVE NUMBER-OF-NAME-CHANGES-W TO NUMBER-OF-NAME-CHANGES-OUT
     WRITE TRANSACTION-REGISTER-RECRD-OUT FROM FINAL-LINE-5
                                          AFTER 2
     MOVE NUMBER-OF-CLOSED-ACCOUNTS-W
          TO NUMBER-OF-CLOSED-ACCOUNTS-OUT
     WRITE TRANSACTION-REGISTER-RECRD-OUT FROM FINAL-LINE-6
                                          AFTER 2
     MOVE NUMBER-OF-ERRONEOUS-RECORDS-W
          TO NUMBER-OF-ERRONEOUS-RECRDS-OUT
     WRITE TRANSACTION-REGISTER-RECRD-OUT FROM FINAL-LINE-7
                                          AFTER 2
     MOVE NUMBER-OF-INPUT-RECORDS-W
          TO NUMBER-OF-INPUT-RECORDS-OUT
     WRITE TRANSACTION-REGISTER-RECRD-OUT FROM FINAL-LINE-8
                                          AFTER 2
     .
```

Program P14-02 was run with the transaction input shown in Figure 14.11 and the input master file created in Program P13-02. It produced the report output shown in Figure 14.12. The output master file produced is shown in Figure 14.13.

The rightmost position of the Current Balance field prints strangely because the sign of the field is in the same storage location as the rightmost digit.

FIGURE *14.11* **Transaction input to Program P14-01**

```
--------------------------------------------------------------------------------
         1         2         3         4         5         6         7         8
12345678901234567890123456789012345678901234567890123456789012345678901234567890
--------------------------------------------------------------------------------
20007700015000
20037100015000
70038500007500JAMES WASHINGTON
10039200007500INEZ WASHINGTON
400084JOHN & SALLY DUPRINO
20016100125634
30002800150050
10042000150000JOHN RICE
20008400357429
20009100150000
400140BETH DENNY
10039900014Z00GARY NASTI
200007)))$%)))
30001400100000
20002100012750
30011900002735
70042700002500GREG PRUITT
20006300007500
20013300256300
20012600035000
30016800011000
400266
20002800015327
20009100120000
20021000025000
20021000025000
500232
30009100050000
30025929390000
20027300172500
400098GEORGE & ANN CULHANE
500168
20017500019202
500182
20021000025000
20028000231700
80031500013798
200182
20030100005763
5
10030800017000AL MARRELLA
20030800005000
10037100001000THOMAS HERR
20032200006875
10035700001000ROBIN RATANSKI
10036400150000JOSE TORRES
10037100015000ALISE MARKOVITZ
10040600120000
10041300010000BILL HAYES
10039800001000JUAN ALVAREZ
30010500015025
```

FIGURE 14.12 Report output from Program P14-02

```
                         ROBBEM STATE BANK
                         106 WEST 10TH ST.
                        BROOKLYN, NY  11212

                 SAVINGS ACCOUNT TRANSACTION ERRORS
DATE   3/13/92                                  PAGE  1


   ACCOUNT                                    NOTES
   NUMBER


                                   MASTER RECORD DOES NOT EXIST
    00007                          DEPOSIT AMOUNT NOT NUMERIC - )))$%)))
    00063                          MASTER RECORD DOES NOT EXIST
    00105                          WITHDRAWAL AMOUNT NOT NUMERIC - 00015025
    00119                          MASTER RECORD DOES NOT EXIST
    00182                          DEPOSIT AMOUNT NOT NUMERIC -
    00182                          MASTER RECORD DOES NOT EXIST
    00232                          MASTER RECORD DOES NOT EXIST
    00259                          MASTER RECORD DOES NOT EXIST
    00266                          DEPOSITOR NAME MISSING
    00301                          MASTER RECORD DOES NOT EXIST
    00308                          INVALID TRANSACTION CODE - 1
    00315                          INVALID TRANSACTION CODE - 8
    00322                          MASTER RECORD DOES NOT EXIST
    00357                          INVALID TRANSACTION CODE - 1
    00364                          INVALID TRANSACTION CODE - 1
    00371                          INVALID TRANSACTION CODE - 1
    00371                          INVALID TRANSACTION CODE - 1
    00371                          MASTER RECORD DOES NOT EXIST
    00385                          INVALID TRANSACTION CODE - 7
    00392                          INVALID TRANSACTION CODE - 1
    00398                          INVALID TRANSACTION CODE - 1
    00399                          INVALID TRANSACTION CODE - 1
    00406                          INVALID TRANSACTION CODE - 1
    00413                          INVALID TRANSACTION CODE - 1
    00420                          INVALID TRANSACTION CODE - 1
    00427                          INVALID TRANSACTION CODE - 7
```

```
                         ROBBEM STATE BANK
                         106 WEST 10TH ST.
                        BROOKLYN, NY  11212

                SAVINGS ACCOUNT TRANSACTION REGISTER
DATE   3/13/92                                  PAGE  1


   ACCOUNT     DEPOSITS      WITHDRAWALS       NOTES
   NUMBER

    00014                      1,000.00
    00021        127.50
    00028        153.27
    00028                      1,500.50
    00077        150.00
    00084      3,574.29
    00084     JOHN & SALLY DUPRINO            NAME CHANGE
    00091      1,500.00
    00091      1,200.00
    00091                        500.00
    00098     GEORGE & ANN CULHANE            NAME CHANGE
    00126        350.00
    00133      2,563.00
    00140     BETH DENNY                      NAME CHANGE
    00161      1,256.34
    00168                        110.00
    00168                         15.50       ACCOUNT CLOSED
```

continued

FIGURE 14.12 *continued*

```
                    ROBBEM STATE BANK
                    106 WEST 10TH ST.
                   BROOKLYN, NY  11212

            SAVINGS ACCOUNT TRANSACTION REGISTER
DATE   3/13/92                                        PAGE  2

   ACCOUNT      DEPOSITS       WITHDRAWALS        NOTES
   NUMBER

    00175          192.02
    00210          250.00
    00210          250.00
    00210          250.00
    00273        1,725.00
    00280        2,317.00
    00308           50.00


TOTALS          15,908.42       3,126.00

                      CONTROL COUNTS

                NUMBER OF DEPOSITS            16

                NUMBER OF WITHDRAWALS          4

                NUMBER OF NAME CHANGES         3

                NUMBER OF CLOSED ACCOUNTS      1

                NUMBER OF ERRORS              27

                TOTAL                         51
```

FIGURE *14.13* **Output master file from Program P14-02**

```
------------------------------------------------------------------------------------
          1         2         3         4         5         6         7         8
12345678901234567890123456789012345678901234567890123456789012345678901234567890
------------------------------------------------------------------------------------
00007ROSEBUCCI           91081900100784
00014ROBERT DAVIS M.D.   9203130009900}
00021LORICE MONTI        9203130002525{
00028MICHAEL SMITH       9203130056543F
00032JOSEPH CAMILLO      91081900002500
00035JOHN J. LEHMAN      91081900015000
00049JAY GREENE          91081900015000
00056EVELYN SLATER       91081900000100
00070PATRICK J. LEE      91081900050000
00077LESLIE MINSKY       9203130001603G
00084JOHN & SALLY DUPRINO9203130050742I
00091JOE'S DELI          9203130023000{
00098GEORGE & ANN CULHANE92031300050000
00105ONE DAY CLEANERS    91081900005000
00112ROSEMARY LANE       91081900025000
00126JAMES BUDD          9203130011000{
00133PAUL LERNER, D.D.S. 9203130035630{
00140BETH DENNY          92031300002575
00161ROBERT RYAN         9203130012808D
00175MARY KEATING        9203130002020B
00189J. & L. CAIN        91081900003500
00196IMPERIAL FLORIST    91081900015000
00203JOYCE MITCHELL      91081900000500
00210JERRY PARKS         9203130010000{
00217CARL CALDERON       91081900005000
00224JOHN WILLIAMS       91081900017550
00231BILL WILLIAMS       91081900055500
00238KEVIN PARKER        91081900001000
00245FRANK CAPUTO        91081900003500
00252GENE GALLI          91081900001500
00266MARTIN LANG         91081900009957
00273VITO CACACI         9203130020000{
00280COMMUNITY DRUGS     9203130023370{
00287SOLOMON CHAPELS     91081900001500
00294JOHN BURKE          91081900150000
00308JOE GARCIA          9203130020500{
00315GRACE MICELI        91081900025000
00329GUY VOLPONE         91081900001000
00343JOE & MARY SESSA    91081900100000
00350ROGER SHAW          91081900250000
```

EXERCISE *2*

Write a program to update the master file you created in Exercise 3, Chapter 13, page 457. Use transactions in the formats shown on the next page.

Design suitable reports for your program. Have your program check the input transactions for validity. Have your program print a line for each transaction processed. For each master record that is updated, have your program insert today's date in the Date of Last Access field. Also for each master record that is updated, have your program check whether the Quantity on Hand is equal to or less than the Reorder Point, and print a message showing the Reorder Quantity and the word REORDER if it is. If an attempt is made to delete a Part Number having a nonzero Quantity on Hand, do not delete it. Instead, count the transaction as erroneous and have your program print the Quantity on Hand and a message NONZERO QUANTITY ON HAND on the error report.

Positions	Field
1	Code B (Receipt of goods into inventory)
2–6	Part Number
7–9	Quantity Received
10–80	spaces
1	Code C (Withdrawal of goods from inventory)
2–6	Part Number
7–9	Quantity Withdrawn
10–80	spaces
1	Code D (Part Description change)
2–6	Part Number
7–26	Part Description
27–80	spaces
1	Code 1 (Units change)
2–6	Part Number
7	Units
8–80	spaces
1	Code 2 (Quantity on Hand correction)
2–6	Part Number
7	Sign of correction (+ or −)
8–10	Quantity on Hand correction
11–80	spaces
1	Code 3 (Unit cost change)
2–6	Part Number
7–12	Unit Cost (dollars and cents)
13–80	spaces
1	Code 4 (Supplier Code change)
2–6	Part Number
7–10	Supplier Code
11–80	spaces
1	Code 5 (Storage Location change)
2–6	Part Number
7–11	Storage Location
12–80	spaces
1	Code 6 (Reorder Point change)
2–6	Part Number
7–9	Reorder Point
10–80	spaces
1	Code 7 (Reorder Quantity change)
2–6	Part Number
7–9	Reorder Quantity
10–80	spaces

A Complete Update Program

We will now develop a program to process additions of new savings-account records to the master file in the same run as changes and deletions to existing records. We have only to make a few small changes to Program P14-02 and we will have our complete update program, Program P14-03. Program P14-03 will be able to create a new master record and process changes to it in the same run, just as Program P14-02 could change a record and delete it in one run. Program P14-03 will check for all kinds of errors. For example, if a transaction attempts to add to the master file a record whose key is already present on the file, the transaction will be detected as an error. If a valid transaction to add a record to the file is followed by another transaction to add a record with the same key, the second add will be detected as an error. And of course all of the error checking that is present in Program P14-02 will be used in Program P14-03.

For Program P14-03 the formats of input transactions having transaction Codes 2 through 5 are the same as for Program P14-02. In addition, Program P14-03 will accept transactions in the following format, to add new records to the master file:

Positions	Field
1	Code 1
2–6	Account Number
7–14	Amount (to two decimal places)
15–34	Depositor Name
35–80	spaces

Notice that the Depositor Name field in this transaction partially overlaps the Depositor Name field in the depositor name-change transaction described on page 493. Such overlapping presents no problem. All five transaction types can be defined in a single transaction input area by using redefinition, as you will see when we look at Program P14-03.

The format of the transaction register produced by Program P14-03 is shown in Figure 14.14. It is very similar to the transaction register produced by Program P14-02, except that provision is made for handling new accounts. The format of the error report, Figure 14.15, has provision for all the usual errors and for those dealing with new accounts.

A Hierarchy Diagram for a Complete Update Program

The hierarchy diagram for ''Process transaction record'' for Program P14-03 is shown in Figure 14.16. It is the same as the hierarchy diagram for ''Process transaction record'' for Program P14-02 except that this diagram includes the ability to add new savings-account master records to the output master file. The box ''Check for valid new account'' is now included as one of the subfunctions of ''Apply transaction.''

FIGURE 14.14 Output format for transaction register for Program P14-03

PRINT CHART

```
                                        ROBBEM STATE BANK
                                        106 WEST 10TH ST.
                                        BROOKLYN, NY  11212

                          SAVINGS ACCOUNT TRANSACTION REGISTER
              DATE Z9/99/99                                        PAGE Z9

                    ACCOUNT     DEPOSITS        WITHDRAWALS        NOTES
                    NUMBER

                     XXXXX    ZZZ,ZZZ.99
                     XXXXX                   ZZZ,ZZZ.99
                     XXXXX    ZZZ,ZZZ.99                         NEW ACCOUNT
                     XXXXX                   ZZZ,ZZZ.99          ACCOUNT CLOSED
                     XXXXX    X-------------------------X        NAME CHANGED
                     XXXXX    ZZZ,ZZZ.99


              TOTALS        Z,ZZZ,ZZZ.99  Z,ZZZ,ZZZ.99

                                   CONTROL COUNTS

                         NUMBER OF NEW ACCOUNTS          ZZ9

                         NUMBER OF DEPOSITS              ZZ9

                         NUMBER OF WITHDRAWALS           ZZ9

                         NUMBER OF NAME CHANGES          ZZ9

                         NUMBER OF CLOSED ACCOUNTS       ZZ9

                         NUMBER OF ERRORS                ZZ9

                         TOTAL                         Z,ZZ9
```

FIGURE 14.15 Output format for error report for Program P14-03

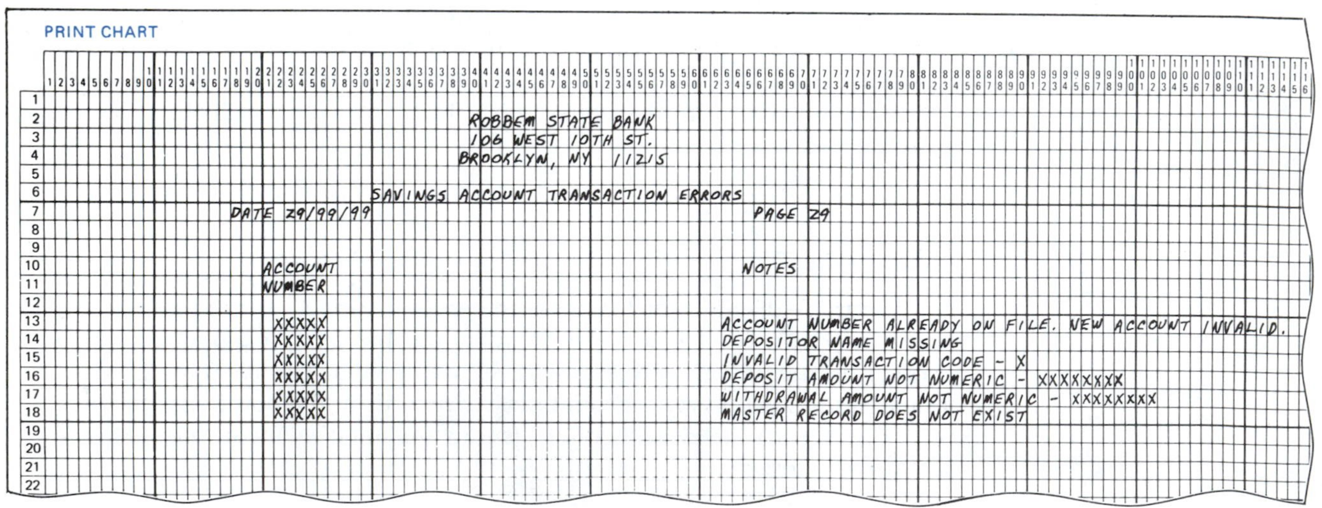

PRINT CHART

```
                                        ROBBEM STATE BANK
                                        106 WEST 10TH ST.
                                        BROOKLYN, NY  11215

                          SAVINGS ACCOUNT TRANSACTION ERRORS
              DATE Z9/99/99                                        PAGE Z9

                    ACCOUNT                                        NOTES
                    NUMBER

                     XXXXX                          ACCOUNT NUMBER ALREADY ON FILE. NEW ACCOUNT INVALID.
                     XXXXX                          DEPOSITOR NAME MISSING
                     XXXXX                          INVALID TRANSACTION CODE - X
                     XXXXX                          DEPOSIT AMOUNT NOT NUMERIC - XXXXXXXX
                     XXXXX                          WITHDRAWAL AMOUNT NOT NUMERIC - XXXXXXXX
                     XXXXX                          MASTER RECORD DOES NOT EXIST
```

FIGURE 14.16 Hierarchy diagram for "Process transaction record" for Program P14-03

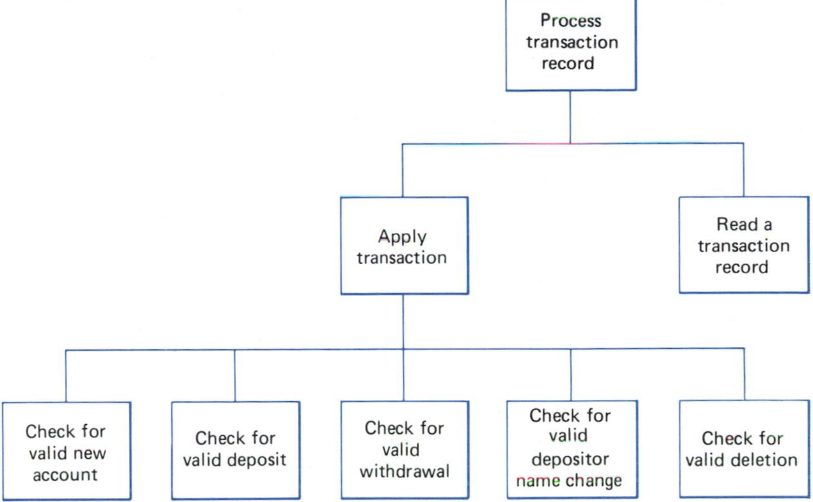

Stepping Through the Hierarchy Diagram

To see how this hierarchy diagram would add a record to the output master file, assume we have a master file containing records with the following Account Numbers:

00007

00014

00021

00028

Now assume that we have transactions with the following Codes and Account Numbers:

2 00007

1 00018

2 00018

3 00028

These transactions are all valid. The first transaction is a deposit to Account Number 00007. The second transaction is to create a new master record for Account Number 00018. The third transaction makes a deposit to the newly created master record, and the last transaction is a withdrawal from Account Number 00028. Of course the program must write the new master record into its proper place on the output master file, that is, between master records 00014 and 00021.

When the program executes, 00007 is first assigned to CURRENT-KEY. Master record 00007 is updated with the deposit and the updated record written onto the output master file. Then 00014 is assigned to CURRENT-KEY, and master record 00014 is written onto the output master file unchanged. CHOOSE-

CURRENT-KEY then chooses between 00018 and 00021. 00018 is assigned to CURRENT-KEY. Since the key of the master record in the master input area is not equal to CURRENT-KEY, PROCESS-MASTER-RECORD moves nothing to the work area and sets the flag to "N."

This is exactly the situation we need in order to create a new master record and insert it in the correct place in the output master file. There must be no master record in the work area, so that we can build the new master record there. The flag must be set to "N." Whereas in all of our other types of transactions there had to be a matching master record in the work area for the transaction to be applied to, when we are creating a new master record we want no matching master record in the work area. If there were one, it would mean that a transaction is trying to create a new master record having an Account Number that is already on the file. So in all our previous update programs a transaction could be immediately recognized as erroneous if the flag were set to "N"; when we are trying to create a new master record the transaction is erroneous if the flag is set to "Y."

The box "Check for valid new account" now makes the usual validity checks on the input transaction. If the transaction passes all the checks, a new master record with Account Number 00018 is created in the work area the same way that we created master records in Program P13-02 when we were first creating the master file.

Then, after the master record is created in the work area, the program must set the flag to "Y" to indicate that now there is in the work area a master record whose key matches CURRENT-KEY. The flag must be set to "Y" so that the deposit transaction to Account Number 00018, which is coming in next, finds a matching master record in the work area, and so that CHECK-TO-WRITE-MASTER, when its time comes to execute, recognizes that there is a master record, 00018, waiting in the work area to be written out.

A Program to Update a Sequential Master File with Additions, Changes, and Deletions

Program P14-03 is shown in Figure 14.17. It is of course very similar to Program P14-02. The TRANSACTION-INPUT-AREA now has a level-88 entry for the TRANSACTION-CODE for a NEW-ACCOUNT, at line 00940.

FIGURE *14.17* **Program P14-03**

```
S COBOL II RELEASE 3.1 09/19/89                P14003   DATE SEP 06,1991 T
----+-*A-1-B--+----2----+----3----+----4----+----5----+----6----+----7-%--+

00010  IDENTIFICATION DIVISION.
00020  PROGRAM-ID. P14-03.
00030 *
00040 *    THIS PROGRAM UPDATES A SEQUENTIAL MASTER FILE
00050 *    WITH ADDITIONS, CHANGES, AND DELETIONS.
00060 *
00070 ***********************************************************************
00080
```

FIGURE 14.17 *continued*

```
ENVIRONMENT DIVISION.
INPUT-OUTPUT SECTION.
FILE-CONTROL.
    SELECT ACCOUNT-MASTER-FILE-IN             ASSIGN TO MFILEIN.
    SELECT ACCOUNT-MASTER-FILE-OUT            ASSIGN TO MFILEOUT.
    SELECT TRANSACTION-FILE-IN                ASSIGN TO INFILE.
    SELECT TRANSACTION-REGISTER-FILE-OUT      ASSIGN TO PRINTER1.
    SELECT ERROR-FILE-OUT                     ASSIGN TO PRINTER2.
    SELECT SORT-WORK-FILE                     ASSIGN TO SORTWK.

*****************************************************************

DATA DIVISION.
FILE SECTION.
FD  ACCOUNT-MASTER-FILE-IN
    LABEL RECORDS ARE STANDARD
    RECORD CONTAINS 39 CHARACTERS
    BLOCK CONTAINS 100 RECORDS.

01  ACCOUNT-MASTER-RECORD-IN          PIC X(39).

FD  ACCOUNT-MASTER-FILE-OUT
    LABEL RECORDS ARE STANDARD
    RECORD CONTAINS 39 CHARACTERS
    BLOCK CONTAINS 100 RECORDS.

01  ACCOUNT-MASTER-RECORD-OUT         PIC X(39).

SD  SORT-WORK-FILE
    RECORD CONTAINS 34 CHARACTERS.

01  SORT-WORK-RECORD.
    05  TRANSACTION-CODE-S            PIC X.
    05  ACCOUNT-NUMBER-S              PIC X(5).
    05                                PIC X(28).

FD  TRANSACTION-FILE-IN.

01  TRANSACTION-RECORD-IN             PIC X(80).

FD  TRANSACTION-REGISTER-FILE-OUT.

01  REGISTER-RECORD-OUT               PIC X(76).

FD  ERROR-FILE-OUT.

01  ERROR-RECORD-OUT                  PIC X(114).
```

continued

FIGURE 14.17 *continued*

```
S COBOL II RELEASE 3.1 09/19/89                P14003   DATE SEP 06,1991 T
----+-*A-1-B--+----2----+----3----+----4----+----5----+----6----+----7-%--+

00570  WORKING-STORAGE SECTION.
00580  01  CURRENT-KEY                               PIC X(5).
00590      88 THERE-IS-NO-MORE-INPUT                 VALUE HIGH-VALUES.
00600      88 THERE-IS-NO-INPUT                      VALUE HIGH-VALUES.
00610  01  IS-MASTER-RECORD-IN-WORK-AREA             PIC X.
00620      88 MASTER-RECORD-IS-IN-WORKAREA            VALUE "Y".
00630      88 MASTER-RECORD-ISNT-IN-WORKAREA         VALUE "N".
00640  01  PACKED-DECIMAL.
00650   02 NUMBER-OF-INPUT-RECORDS-W                 PIC S9(3) VALUE ZERO.
00660   02 NUMBER-OF-ERRONEOUS-RECORDS-W             PIC S9(3) VALUE ZERO.
00670   02 DEPOSIT-TOTAL-W                           PIC S9(7)V99 VALUE ZERO.
00680   02 WITHDRAWAL-TOTAL-W                        PIC S9(7)V99 VALUE ZERO.
00690   02 NUMBER-OF-NEW-ACCOUNTS-W                  PIC S9(3) VALUE ZERO.
00700   02 NUMBER-OF-DEPOSITS-W                      PIC S9(3) VALUE ZERO.
00710   02 NUMBER-OF-WITHDRAWALS-W                   PIC S9(3) VALUE ZERO.
00720   02 NUMBER-OF-NAME-CHANGES-W                  PIC S9(3) VALUE ZERO.
00730   02 NUMBER-OF-CLOSED-ACCOUNTS-W               PIC S9(3) VALUE ZERO.
00740   02 PAGE-NUMBER-W                             PIC S99   VALUE 0.
00750   02 ERROR-PAGE-NUMBER-W                       PIC S99   VALUE 0.
00760  01  BLANK-LINE                                PIC X     VALUE SPACE.
00770  01  PAGE-LIMIT                 COMP SYNC      PIC S99   VALUE 28.
00780  01  LINE-COUNT-ER              COMP SYNC      PIC S99.
00790  01  ERROR-PAGE-LIMIT           COMP SYNC      PIC S99   VALUE 45.
00800  01  ERROR-LINE-COUNTER         COMP SYNC      PIC S99.
00810
00820  01  TODAYS-DATE.
00830      05  TODAYS-YEAR                           PIC 99.
00840      05  TODAYS-MONTH-AND-DAY                  PIC 9(4).
00850
00860  01  MASTER-INPUT-AREA.
00870      88  NO-MORE-MASTER-RECORDS                VALUE HIGH-VALUES.
00880      05  ACCOUNT-NUMBER                        PIC X(5).
00890      05                                        PIC X(34).
00900
00910  01  TRANSACTION-INPUT-AREA.
00920      88  NO-MORE-TRANSACTION-RECORDS           VALUE HIGH-VALUES.
00930      05  TRANSACTION-CODE                      PIC X.
00940          88  NEW-ACCOUNT                       VALUE "1".
00950          88  DEPOSIT                           VALUE "2".
00960          88  WITHDRAWAL                        VALUE "3".
00970          88  NAME-CHANGE                       VALUE "4".
00980          88  DELETION                          VALUE "5".
00990      05  ACCOUNT-NUMBER                        PIC X(5).
01000      05  DEPOSIT-AND-WITHDRAWAL-AMTS.
01010          10  DEPOSIT-AMOUNT                    PIC 9(6)V99.
01020          10  DEPOSIT-AMOUNT-X          REDEFINES DEPOSIT-AMOUNT
01030                                                PIC X(8).
01040          10  WITHDRAWAL-AMOUNT         REDEFINES DEPOSIT-AMOUNT
01050                                                PIC 9(6)V99.
01060          10  WITHDRAWAL-AMOUNT-X       REDEFINES DEPOSIT-AMOUNT
01070                                                PIC X(8).
01080      05  DEPOSITOR-NAME-NEW-ACCOUNT            PIC X(20).
01090          88  DEPOSITOR-NAME-MISSING            VALUE SPACES.
01100  01  TRANSACTION-4-INPUT-AREA REDEFINES TRANSACTION-INPUT-AREA.
01110      05                                        PIC X(6).
01120      05  DEPOSITOR-NAME                        PIC X(20).
01130          88  REPLACEMENT-NAME-MISSING          VALUE SPACES.
01140      05                                        PIC X(8).
01150
```

You can see how the transaction input area has been defined to accommodate the formats of all the transaction types. The level-05 entries at lines 00930 through 01080 provide for all the fields in transactions with Codes 1, 2, 3, and 5. The redefined transaction input area at lines 01100 through 01140 provides for the DEPOSITOR-NAME as it appears in transactions with Code 4.

FIGURE 14.17 ***continued***

```
       01  WORK-AREA.
           05  ACCOUNT-NUMBER-W                 PIC X(5).
           05  DEPOSITOR-NAME-W                 PIC X(20).
           05  DATE-OF-LAST-TRANSACTION-W       PIC 9(6).
           05  CURRENT-BALANCE-W                PIC S9(6)V99.

       01  REPORT-HEADING-1.
           05               PIC X(39) VALUE SPACES.
           05               PIC X(17) VALUE "ROBBEM STATE BANK".

       01  REPORT-HEADING-2.
           05               PIC X(39) VALUE SPACES.
           05               PIC X(17) VALUE "106 WEST 10TH ST.".

       01  REPORT-HEADING-3.
           05               PIC X(38) VALUE SPACES.
           05               PIC X(19) VALUE "BROOKLYN, NY  11212".

       01  PAGE-HEADING-1.
           05               PIC X(29) VALUE SPACES.
           05               PIC X(36)
                            VALUE "SAVINGS ACCOUNT TRANSACTION REGISTER".

       01  ERROR-PAGE-HEADING-1.
           05               PIC X(30) VALUE SPACES.
           05               PIC X(34)
                            VALUE  "SAVINGS ACCOUNT TRANSACTION ERRORS".

       01  PAGE-HEADING-2.
           05                   PIC X(17) VALUE SPACES.
           05                   PIC X(5)  VALUE "DATE".
           05  TODAYS-MONTH-AND-DAY                      PIC Z9/99/.
           05  TODAYS-YEAR                               PIC 99B(35).
           05                   PIC X(5)  VALUE "PAGE".
           05  PAGE-NUMBER-OUT                           PIC Z9.

       01  PAGE-HEADING-3.
           05                   PIC X(20) VALUE SPACES.
           05                   PIC X(12) VALUE "ACCOUNT".
           05                   PIC X(14) VALUE "DEPOSITS".
           05                   PIC X(18) VALUE "WITHDRAWALS".
           05                   PIC X(5)  VALUE "NOTES".

       01  ERROR-PAGE-HEADING-3.
           05                   PIC X(20) VALUE SPACES.
           05                   PIC X(44) VALUE "ACCOUNT".
           05                   PIC X(5)  VALUE "NOTES".

       01  PAGE-HEADING-4.
           05                   PIC X(20) VALUE SPACES.
           05                   PIC X(6)  VALUE "NUMBER".

       01  NEW-ACCOUNT-LINE.
           05                   PIC X(21) VALUE SPACES.
           05  ACCOUNT-NUMBER-OUT       PIC X(5)B(5).
           05  DEPOSIT-AMOUNT-OUT       PIC ZZZ,ZZZ.99B(21).
           05                   PIC X(11) VALUE "NEW ACCOUNT".

       01  DEPOSIT-LINE.
           05                   PIC X(21) VALUE SPACES.
           05  ACCOUNT-NUMBER-OUT       PIC X(5)B(5).
           05  DEPOSIT-AMOUNT-OUT       PIC ZZZ,ZZZ.99.

       01  WITHDRAWAL-LINE.
           05                   PIC X(21) VALUE SPACES.
           05  ACCOUNT-NUMBER-OUT       PIC X(5)B(19).
           05  WITHDRAWAL-AMOUNT-OUT    PIC ZZZ,ZZZ.99.
```

continued

FIGURE 14.17 *continued*

```
S COBOL II RELEASE 3.1 09/19/89                    P14003   DATE SEP 06,1991 T
----+-*A-1-B--+----2----+----3----+----4----+----5----+----6----+----7-%--+

       01  NAME-CHANGE-LINE.
           05                    PIC X(21) VALUE SPACES.
           05  ACCOUNT-NUMBER-OUT        PIC X(5)B(5).
           05  DEPOSITOR-NAME-OUT        PIC X(20)B(11).
           05                    PIC X(11) VALUE "NAME CHANGE".

       01  DELETION-LINE.
           05                    PIC X(21) VALUE SPACES.
           05  ACCOUNT-NUMBER-OUT        PIC X(5)B(19).
           05  CURRENT-BALANCE-OUT       PIC ZZZ,ZZZ.99B(7).
           05                    PIC X(14) VALUE "ACCOUNT CLOSED".

       01  DEPOSIT-AMOUNT-INVALID-MSG.
           05                    PIC X(29)
                             VALUE "DEPOSIT AMOUNT NOT NUMERIC -".
           05  DEPOSIT-AMOUNT-OUT        PIC X(8).

       01  WITHDRAWAL-AMOUNT-INVALID-MSG.
           05                            PIC X(32)
                             VALUE "WITHDRAWAL AMOUNT NOT NUMERIC -".
           05  WITHDRAWAL-AMOUNT-OUT     PIC X(8).

       01  INVALID-CODE-MSG.
           05                PIC X(27) VALUE "INVALID TRANSACTION CODE -".
           05  TRANSACTION-CODE-OUT      PIC X.

       01  ERROR-LINE.
           05  ACCOUNT-NUMBER-E          PIC B(21)X(5)B(36).
           05  ERROR-MESSAGE             PIC X(52).

       01  FINAL-LINE-1.
           05                    PIC X(17) VALUE SPACES.
           05                    PIC X(12) VALUE "TOTALS".
           05  DEPOSIT-TOTAL-OUT               PIC Z,ZZZ,ZZZ.99BB.
           05  WITHDRAWAL-TOTAL-OUT            PIC Z,ZZZ,ZZZ.99.

       01  FINAL-LINE-2.
           05                    PIC X(40) VALUE SPACES.
           05                    PIC X(14) VALUE "CONTROL COUNTS".

       01  FINAL-LINE-3.
           05                    PIC X(34) VALUE SPACES.
           05                    PIC X(26)
                                 VALUE "NUMBER OF NEW ACCOUNTS".
           05  NUMBER-OF-NEW-ACCOUNTS-OUT      PIC ZZ9.

       01  FINAL-LINE-4.
           05                    PIC X(34) VALUE SPACES.
           05                    PIC X(26)
                                 VALUE "NUMBER OF DEPOSITS".
           05  NUMBER-OF-DEPOSITS-OUT          PIC ZZ9.

       01  FINAL-LINE-5.
           05                    PIC X(34) VALUE SPACES.
           05                    PIC X(26)
                                 VALUE "NUMBER OF WITHDRAWALS".
           05  NUMBER-OF-WITHDRAWALS-OUT       PIC ZZ9.

       01  FINAL-LINE-6.
           05                    PIC X(34) VALUE SPACES.
           05                    PIC X(26)
                                 VALUE "NUMBER OF NAME CHANGES".
           05  NUMBER-OF-NAME-CHANGES-OUT      PIC ZZ9.
```

FIGURE 14.17 *continued*

```
 01  FINAL-LINE-7.
     05                      PIC X(34) VALUE SPACES.
     05                      PIC X(26)
                             VALUE "NUMBER OF CLOSED ACCOUNTS".
     05  NUMBER-OF-CLOSED-ACCOUNTS-OUT  PIC ZZ9.
 01  FINAL-LINE-8.
     05                      PIC X(34) VALUE SPACES.
     05                      PIC X(26)
                             VALUE "NUMBER OF ERRORS".
     05  NUMBER-OF-ERRONEOUS-RECRDS-OUT PIC ZZ9.
 01  FINAL-LINE-9.
     05                      PIC X(34) VALUE SPACES.
     05                      PIC X(24) VALUE "TOTAL".
     05  NUMBER-OF-INPUT-RECORDS-OUT    PIC Z,ZZ9.
 01  NO-INPUT-DATA.
     05                      PIC X(21) VALUE SPACES.
     05                      PIC X(13) VALUE "NO INPUT DATA".
*****************************************************************
 PROCEDURE DIVISION.
 UPDATE-PARAGRAPH.
     SORT SORT-WORK-FILE
          ASCENDING KEY ACCOUNT-NUMBER-S
                        TRANSACTION-CODE-S
          USING TRANSACTION-FILE-IN
          OUTPUT PROCEDURE IS UPDATE-RECORDS
     STOP RUN
     .
 UPDATE-RECORDS.
     PERFORM INITIALIZATION
     PERFORM PROCESS-ONE-KEY UNTIL THERE-IS-NO-MORE-INPUT
     PERFORM TERMINATION
     .
 INITIALIZATION.
     OPEN INPUT  ACCOUNT-MASTER-FILE-IN
          OUTPUT ACCOUNT-MASTER-FILE-OUT
                 ERROR-FILE-OUT
                 TRANSACTION-REGISTER-FILE-OUT
     ACCEPT TODAYS-DATE FROM DATE
     MOVE CORR TODAYS-DATE TO PAGE-HEADING-2
     PERFORM PRODUCE-REPORT-HEADINGS
     PERFORM READ-A-MASTER-RECORD
     PERFORM READ-A-TRANSACTION-RECORD
     PERFORM CHOOSE-CURRENT-KEY
     IF THERE-IS-NO-INPUT
         WRITE REGISTER-RECORD-OUT FROM NO-INPUT-DATA
     END-IF
     .
 PRODUCE-REPORT-HEADINGS.
     PERFORM WRITE-REGISTER-HEADINGS
     PERFORM WRITE-ERROR-REPORT-HEADINGS
     .
```

continued

FIGURE *14.17* *continued*

```
S COBOL II RELEASE 3.1 09/19/89                 P14003   DATE SEP 06,1991 T
----+-*A-1-B--+----2----+----3----+----4----+----5----+----6----+----7-%--+

       WRITE-REGISTER-HEADINGS.
           ADD 1 TO PAGE-NUMBER-W
           MOVE PAGE-NUMBER-W TO PAGE-NUMBER-OUT
           WRITE REGISTER-RECORD-OUT FROM
               REPORT-HEADING-1 AFTER ADVANCING PAGE
           WRITE REGISTER-RECORD-OUT FROM REPORT-HEADING-2
           WRITE REGISTER-RECORD-OUT FROM REPORT-HEADING-3
           WRITE REGISTER-RECORD-OUT FROM PAGE-HEADING-1 AFTER 2
           WRITE REGISTER-RECORD-OUT FROM PAGE-HEADING-2
           WRITE REGISTER-RECORD-OUT FROM PAGE-HEADING-3 AFTER 3
           WRITE REGISTER-RECORD-OUT FROM PAGE-HEADING-4
           WRITE REGISTER-RECORD-OUT FROM BLANK-LINE
           MOVE 11 TO LINE-COUNT-ER
           .

       WRITE-ERROR-REPORT-HEADINGS.
           ADD 1 TO ERROR-PAGE-NUMBER-W
           MOVE ERROR-PAGE-NUMBER-W TO PAGE-NUMBER-OUT
           WRITE ERROR-RECORD-OUT FROM REPORT-HEADING-1 AFTER PAGE
           WRITE ERROR-RECORD-OUT FROM REPORT-HEADING-2
           WRITE ERROR-RECORD-OUT FROM REPORT-HEADING-3
           WRITE ERROR-RECORD-OUT FROM ERROR-PAGE-HEADING-1 AFTER 2
           WRITE ERROR-RECORD-OUT FROM PAGE-HEADING-2
           WRITE ERROR-RECORD-OUT FROM ERROR-PAGE-HEADING-3 AFTER 3
           WRITE ERROR-RECORD-OUT FROM PAGE-HEADING-4
           WRITE ERROR-RECORD-OUT FROM BLANK-LINE
           MOVE 11 TO ERROR-LINE-COUNTER
           .

       PROCESS-ONE-KEY.
           PERFORM PROCESS-MASTER-RECORD
           PERFORM PROCESS-TRANSACTION-RECORD UNTIL
               ACCOUNT-NUMBER IN TRANSACTION-INPUT-AREA
               IS NOT EQUAL TO CURRENT-KEY
           PERFORM CHECK-TO-WRITE-MASTER
           PERFORM CHOOSE-CURRENT-KEY
           .

       PROCESS-TRANSACTION-RECORD.
           PERFORM APPLY-TRANSACTION
           PERFORM READ-A-TRANSACTION-RECORD
           .

       CHECK-TO-WRITE-MASTER.
           IF MASTER-RECORD-IS-IN-WORKAREA
               WRITE ACCOUNT-MASTER-RECORD-OUT FROM WORK-AREA
           END-IF
           .

       CHOOSE-CURRENT-KEY.
           IF ACCOUNT-NUMBER IN TRANSACTION-INPUT-AREA IS LESS THAN
              ACCOUNT-NUMBER IN MASTER-INPUT-AREA
               MOVE ACCOUNT-NUMBER IN TRANSACTION-INPUT-AREA TO
                   CURRENT-KEY
           ELSE
               MOVE ACCOUNT-NUMBER IN MASTER-INPUT-AREA TO
                   CURRENT-KEY
           END-IF
           .
```

FIGURE 14.17 ***continued***

```
03680 PROCESS-MASTER-RECORD.
03690     IF ACCOUNT-NUMBER IN MASTER-INPUT-AREA
03700        IS EQUAL TO CURRENT-KEY
03710         MOVE MASTER-INPUT-AREA TO WORK-AREA
03720         PERFORM READ-A-MASTER-RECORD
03730         SET MASTER-RECORD-IS-IN-WORKAREA TO TRUE
03740     ELSE
03750         SET MASTER-RECORD-ISNT-IN-WORKAREA TO TRUE
03760     END-IF
03770     .
03780
03790 READ-A-TRANSACTION-RECORD.
03800     RETURN SORT-WORK-FILE INTO TRANSACTION-INPUT-AREA
03810         AT END
03820             SET NO-MORE-TRANSACTION-RECORDS TO TRUE
03830         NOT AT END
03840             ADD 1 TO NUMBER-OF-INPUT-RECORDS-W
03850     .
03860
03870 READ-A-MASTER-RECORD.
03880     READ ACCOUNT-MASTER-FILE-IN INTO MASTER-INPUT-AREA
03890         AT END
03900             SET NO-MORE-MASTER-RECORDS TO TRUE
03910     .
03920
03930 APPLY-TRANSACTION.
03940     EVALUATE TRUE
03950     WHEN NEW-ACCOUNT
03960         PERFORM CHECK-FOR-VALID-NEW-ACCOUNT
03970     WHEN DEPOSIT
03980         PERFORM CHECK-FOR-VALID-DEPOSIT
03990     WHEN WITHDRAWAL
04000         PERFORM CHECK-FOR-VALID-WITHDRAWAL
04010     WHEN NAME-CHANGE
04020         PERFORM CHECK-FOR-VALID-NAME-CHANGE
04030     WHEN DELETION
04040         PERFORM CHECK-FOR-VALID-DELETION
04050     WHEN OTHER
04060         ADD 1 TO NUMBER-OF-ERRONEOUS-RECORDS-W
04070         PERFORM WRITE-INVALID-CODE-LINE
04080     END-EVALUATE
04090     .
04100
04110 CHECK-FOR-VALID-NEW-ACCOUNT.
04120     EVALUATE TRUE
04130     WHEN MASTER-RECORD-IS-IN-WORKAREA
04140         ADD 1 TO NUMBER-OF-ERRONEOUS-RECORDS-W
04150         PERFORM WRITE-NEW-ACCT-INVALID-LINE
04160     WHEN DEPOSIT-AMOUNT NOT NUMERIC
04170         ADD 1 TO NUMBER-OF-ERRONEOUS-RECORDS-W
04180         PERFORM WRITE-DEPOSIT-INVALID-LINE
04190     WHEN DEPOSITOR-NAME-MISSING
04200         ADD 1 TO NUMBER-OF-ERRONEOUS-RECORDS-W
04210         PERFORM WRITE-NAME-MISSING-LINE
04220     WHEN OTHER
04230         MOVE ACCOUNT-NUMBER IN TRANSACTION-INPUT-AREA
04240              TO ACCOUNT-NUMBER-W
04250         MOVE DEPOSITOR-NAME-NEW-ACCOUNT
04260              TO DEPOSITOR-NAME-W
04270         MOVE TODAYS-DATE TO DATE-OF-LAST-TRANSACTION-W
04280         MOVE DEPOSIT-AMOUNT TO CURRENT-BALANCE-W
04290         PERFORM WRITE-NEW-ACCOUNT-LINE
04300         SET MASTER-RECORD-IS-IN-WORKAREA TO TRUE
04310     END-EVALUATE
04320     .
```

In the Procedure Division, the paragraph APPLY-TRANSACTION now has an additional WHEN condition, at line 03950. We also have the paragraph CHECK-FOR-VALID-NEW-ACCOUNT, at line 04110, and the paragraphs that are

PERFORMed by CHECK-FOR-VALID-NEW-ACCOUNT. Program P14-03 was run using the same master file input and transaction input as Program P14-02 and produced the report output shown in Figure 14.18. The output master file produced is shown in Figure 14.19.

FIGURE *14.17* ***continued***

```
S COBOL II RELEASE 3.1 09/19/89                 P14003   DATE SEP 06,1991 T
----+-*A-1-B--+----2----+----3----+----4----+----5----+----6----+----7-%--+


 CHECK-FOR-VALID-DEPOSIT.
     IF DEPOSIT-AMOUNT NOT NUMERIC
         ADD 1 TO NUMBER-OF-ERRONEOUS-RECORDS-W
         PERFORM WRITE-DEPOSIT-INVALID-LINE
     ELSE
     IF MASTER-RECORD-ISNT-IN-WORKAREA
         ADD 1 TO NUMBER-OF-ERRONEOUS-RECORDS-W
         PERFORM WRITE-MASTER-MISSING-LINE
     ELSE
         ADD DEPOSIT-AMOUNT TO CURRENT-BALANCE-W
         MOVE TODAYS-DATE TO DATE-OF-LAST-TRANSACTION-W
         PERFORM WRITE-DEPOSIT-LINE
     END-IF
     END-IF
     .

  CHECK-FOR-VALID-WITHDRAWAL.
     IF WITHDRAWAL-AMOUNT NOT NUMERIC
         ADD 1 TO NUMBER-OF-ERRONEOUS-RECORDS-W
         PERFORM WRITE-WITHDRAWAL-INVALID-LINE
     ELSE
     IF MASTER-RECORD-ISNT-IN-WORKAREA
         ADD 1 TO NUMBER-OF-ERRONEOUS-RECORDS-W
         PERFORM WRITE-MASTER-MISSING-LINE
     ELSE
         SUBTRACT WITHDRAWAL-AMOUNT FROM CURRENT-BALANCE-W
         MOVE TODAYS-DATE TO DATE-OF-LAST-TRANSACTION-W
         PERFORM WRITE-WITHDRAWAL-LINE
     END-IF
     END-IF
     .

 CHECK-FOR-VALID-NAME-CHANGE.
     IF REPLACEMENT-NAME-MISSING
         ADD 1 TO NUMBER-OF-ERRONEOUS-RECORDS-W
         PERFORM WRITE-NAME-MISSING-LINE
     ELSE
     IF MASTER-RECORD-ISNT-IN-WORKAREA
         ADD 1 TO NUMBER-OF-ERRONEOUS-RECORDS-W
         PERFORM WRITE-MASTER-MISSING-LINE
     ELSE
         MOVE DEPOSITOR-NAME TO DEPOSITOR-NAME-W
         MOVE TODAYS-DATE TO DATE-OF-LAST-TRANSACTION-W
         PERFORM WRITE-NAME-CHANGE-LINE
     END-IF
     END-IF
     .

 CHECK-FOR-VALID-DELETION.
     IF MASTER-RECORD-ISNT-IN-WORKAREA
         ADD 1 TO NUMBER-OF-ERRONEOUS-RECORDS-W
         PERFORM WRITE-MASTER-MISSING-LINE
     ELSE
         PERFORM WRITE-DELETION-LINE
         SET MASTER-RECORD-ISNT-IN-WORKAREA TO TRUE
     END-IF
     .
```

FIGURE 14.17 *continued*

```
WRITE-NEW-ACCOUNT-LINE.
    MOVE CURRENT-KEY TO ACCOUNT-NUMBER-OUT IN NEW-ACCOUNT-LINE
    MOVE DEPOSIT-AMOUNT
         TO DEPOSIT-AMOUNT-OUT IN NEW-ACCOUNT-LINE
    IF 1 + LINE-COUNT-ER GREATER THAN PAGE-LIMIT
        PERFORM WRITE-REGISTER-HEADINGS
    END-IF
    WRITE REGISTER-RECORD-OUT FROM NEW-ACCOUNT-LINE
    ADD 1 TO LINE-COUNT-ER
    ADD DEPOSIT-AMOUNT TO DEPOSIT-TOTAL-W
    ADD 1 TO NUMBER-OF-NEW-ACCOUNTS-W
    .

WRITE-DEPOSIT-LINE.
    MOVE CURRENT-KEY TO ACCOUNT-NUMBER-OUT     IN DEPOSIT-LINE
    MOVE DEPOSIT-AMOUNT TO DEPOSIT-AMOUNT-OUT IN DEPOSIT-LINE
    IF 1 + LINE-COUNT-ER GREATER THAN PAGE-LIMIT
        PERFORM WRITE-REGISTER-HEADINGS
    END-IF
    WRITE REGISTER-RECORD-OUT FROM DEPOSIT-LINE
    ADD 1 TO LINE-COUNT-ER
    ADD DEPOSIT-AMOUNT TO DEPOSIT-TOTAL-W
    ADD 1 TO NUMBER-OF-DEPOSITS-W
    .

WRITE-WITHDRAWAL-LINE.
    MOVE CURRENT-KEY TO ACCOUNT-NUMBER-OUT IN WITHDRAWAL-LINE
    MOVE WITHDRAWAL-AMOUNT TO
         WITHDRAWAL-AMOUNT-OUT IN WITHDRAWAL-LINE
    IF 1 + LINE-COUNT-ER GREATER THAN PAGE-LIMIT
        PERFORM WRITE-REGISTER-HEADINGS
    END-IF
    WRITE REGISTER-RECORD-OUT FROM WITHDRAWAL-LINE
    ADD 1 TO LINE-COUNT-ER
    ADD WITHDRAWAL-AMOUNT TO WITHDRAWAL-TOTAL-W
    ADD 1 TO NUMBER-OF-WITHDRAWALS-W
    .

WRITE-DEPOSIT-INVALID-LINE.
    MOVE DEPOSIT-AMOUNT-X TO
         DEPOSIT-AMOUNT-OUT IN DEPOSIT-AMOUNT-INVALID-MSG
    MOVE DEPOSIT-AMOUNT-INVALID-MSG TO ERROR-MESSAGE
    PERFORM WRITE-ERROR-LINE
    .

WRITE-WITHDRAWAL-INVALID-LINE.
    MOVE WITHDRAWAL-AMOUNT-X TO
         WITHDRAWAL-AMOUNT-OUT IN WITHDRAWAL-AMOUNT-INVALID-MSG
    MOVE WITHDRAWAL-AMOUNT-INVALID-MSG TO ERROR-MESSAGE
    PERFORM WRITE-ERROR-LINE
    .

WRITE-NAME-MISSING-LINE.
    MOVE "DEPOSITOR NAME MISSING" TO ERROR-MESSAGE
    PERFORM WRITE-ERROR-LINE
    .

WRITE-NAME-CHANGE-LINE.
    MOVE CURRENT-KEY TO ACCOUNT-NUMBER-OUT IN NAME-CHANGE-LINE
    MOVE DEPOSITOR-NAME TO DEPOSITOR-NAME-OUT
    IF 1 + LINE-COUNT-ER GREATER THAN PAGE-LIMIT
        PERFORM WRITE-REGISTER-HEADINGS
    END-IF
    WRITE REGISTER-RECORD-OUT FROM NAME-CHANGE-LINE
    ADD 1 TO LINE-COUNT-ER
    ADD 1 TO NUMBER-OF-NAME-CHANGES-W
    .
```

continued

FIGURE 14.17 *continued*

```
S COBOL II RELEASE 3.1 09/19/89                P14003   DATE SEP 06,1991 T
----+-*A-1-B--+----2----+----3----+----4----+----5----+----6----+----7-%--+

WRITE-DELETION-LINE.
    MOVE CURRENT-KEY TO ACCOUNT-NUMBER-OUT IN DELETION-LINE
    MOVE CURRENT-BALANCE-W TO CURRENT-BALANCE-OUT
    IF 1 + LINE-COUNT-ER GREATER THAN PAGE-LIMIT
        PERFORM WRITE-REGISTER-HEADINGS
    END-IF
    WRITE REGISTER-RECORD-OUT FROM DELETION-LINE
    ADD 1 TO LINE-COUNT-ER
    ADD CURRENT-BALANCE-W TO WITHDRAWAL-TOTAL-W
    ADD 1 TO NUMBER-OF-CLOSED-ACCOUNTS-W
    .

WRITE-INVALID-CODE-LINE.
    MOVE TRANSACTION-CODE TO TRANSACTION-CODE-OUT
    MOVE INVALID-CODE-MSG TO ERROR-MESSAGE
    PERFORM WRITE-ERROR-LINE
    .

WRITE-MASTER-MISSING-LINE.
    MOVE "MASTER RECORD DOES NOT EXIST" TO ERROR-MESSAGE
    PERFORM WRITE-ERROR-LINE
    .

WRITE-NEW-ACCT-INVALID-LINE.
    MOVE "ACCOUNT NUMBER ALREADY ON FILE NEW ACCOUNT INVALID"
         TO ERROR-MESSAGE
    PERFORM WRITE-ERROR-LINE
    .

WRITE-ERROR-LINE.
    IF 1 + ERROR-LINE-COUNTER GREATER THAN ERROR-PAGE-LIMIT
        PERFORM WRITE-ERROR-REPORT-HEADINGS
    END-IF
    MOVE CURRENT-KEY TO ACCOUNT-NUMBER-E
    WRITE ERROR-RECORD-OUT FROM ERROR-LINE
    ADD 1 TO ERROR-LINE-COUNTER
    .

TERMINATION.
    PERFORM PRODUCE-TOTAL-LINES
    CLOSE ACCOUNT-MASTER-FILE-IN
          ACCOUNT-MASTER-FILE-OUT
          ERROR-FILE-OUT
          TRANSACTION-REGISTER-FILE-OUT
    .
```

FIGURE *14.17* ***continued***

```
PRODUCE-TOTAL-LINES.
      MOVE DEPOSIT-TOTAL-W    TO DEPOSIT-TOTAL-OUT
      MOVE WITHDRAWAL-TOTAL-W TO WITHDRAWAL-TOTAL-OUT
      WRITE REGISTER-RECORD-OUT FROM FINAL-LINE-1 AFTER 3
      WRITE REGISTER-RECORD-OUT FROM FINAL-LINE-2 AFTER 2
      MOVE NUMBER-OF-NEW-ACCOUNTS-W TO NUMBER-OF-NEW-ACCOUNTS-OUT
      WRITE REGISTER-RECORD-OUT FROM FINAL-LINE-3 AFTER 2
      MOVE NUMBER-OF-DEPOSITS-W TO NUMBER-OF-DEPOSITS-OUT
      WRITE REGISTER-RECORD-OUT FROM FINAL-LINE-4 AFTER 2
      MOVE NUMBER-OF-WITHDRAWALS-W TO NUMBER-OF-WITHDRAWALS-OUT
      WRITE REGISTER-RECORD-OUT FROM FINAL-LINE-5 AFTER 2
      MOVE NUMBER-OF-NAME-CHANGES-W TO NUMBER-OF-NAME-CHANGES-OUT
      WRITE REGISTER-RECORD-OUT FROM FINAL-LINE-6 AFTER 2
      MOVE NUMBER-OF-CLOSED-ACCOUNTS-W
           TO NUMBER-OF-CLOSED-ACCOUNTS-OUT
      WRITE REGISTER-RECORD-OUT FROM FINAL-LINE-7 AFTER 2
      MOVE NUMBER-OF-ERRONEOUS-RECORDS-W
           TO NUMBER-OF-ERRONEOUS-RECRDS-OUT
      WRITE REGISTER-RECORD-OUT FROM FINAL-LINE-8 AFTER 2
      MOVE NUMBER-OF-INPUT-RECORDS-W
           TO NUMBER-OF-INPUT-RECORDS-OUT
      WRITE REGISTER-RECORD-OUT FROM FINAL-LINE-9 AFTER 2
      .
```

FIGURE *14.18* **Report output from Program P14-03**

```
                         ROBBEM STATE BANK
                         106 WEST 10TH ST.
                        BROOKLYN, NY  11212

              SAVINGS ACCOUNT TRANSACTION ERRORS
    DATE  9/06/91                                  PAGE  1


       ACCOUNT                                     NOTES
       NUMBER


                                                MASTER RECORD DOES NOT EXIST
        00007                                   DEPOSIT AMOUNT NOT NUMERIC - )))$%)))
        00063                                   MASTER RECORD DOES NOT EXIST
        00105                                   WITHDRAWAL AMOUNT NOT NUMERIC - 00015025
        00119                                   MASTER RECORD DOES NOT EXIST
        00182                                   DEPOSIT AMOUNT NOT NUMERIC -
        00182                                   MASTER RECORD DOES NOT EXIST
        00232                                   MASTER RECORD DOES NOT EXIST
        00259                                   MASTER RECORD DOES NOT EXIST
        00266                                   DEPOSITOR NAME MISSING
        00301                                   MASTER RECORD DOES NOT EXIST
        00308                                   ACCOUNT NUMBER ALREADY ON FILE NEW ACCOUNT INVALID
        00315                                   INVALID TRANSACTION CODE - 8
        00322                                   MASTER RECORD DOES NOT EXIST
        00371                                   ACCOUNT NUMBER ALREADY ON FILE NEW ACCOUNT INVALID
        00385                                   INVALID TRANSACTION CODE - 7
        00399                                   DEPOSIT AMOUNT NOT NUMERIC - 00014Z00
        00406                                   DEPOSITOR NAME MISSING
        00427                                   INVALID TRANSACTION CODE - 7
```

FIGURE 14.19 Master file produced by Program P14-03

```
--------------------------------------------------------------------------------
         1         2         3         4         5         6         7         8
12345678901234567890123456789012345678901234567890123456789012345678901234567890
--------------------------------------------------------------------------------
00007ROSEBUCCI           91081900100784
00014ROBERT DAVIS M.D.   9109060009900%
00021LORICE MONTI        9109060002525%
00028MICHAEL SMITH       9109060056543F
00032JOSEPH CAMILLO      91081900002500
00035JOHN J. LEHMAN      91081900015000
00049JAY GREENE          91081900015000
00056EVELYN SLATER       91081900000100
00070PATRICK J. LEE      91081900050000
00077LESLIE MINSKY       9109060001603G
00084JOHN & SALLY DUPRINO9109060050742I
00091JOE'S DELI          9109060023000%
00098GEORGE & ANN CULHANE91090600050000
00105ONE DAY CLEANERS    91081900005000
00112ROSEMARY LANE       91081900025000
00126JAMES BUDD          9109060011000%
00133PAUL LERNER, D.D.S. 9109060035630%
00140BETH DENNY          91090600002575
00161ROBERT RYAN         9109060012808D
00175MARY KEATING        9109060002020B
00189J. & L. CAIN        91081900003500
00196IMPERIAL FLORIST    91081900015000
00203JOYCE MITCHELL      91081900000500
00210JERRY PARKS         9109060010000%
00217CARL CALDERON       91081900005000
00224JOHN WILLIAMS       91081900017550
00231BILL WILLIAMS       91081900055500
00238KEVIN PARKER        91081900001000
00245FRANK CAPUTO        91081900003500
00252GENE GALLI          91081900001500
00266MARTIN LANG         91081900009957
00273VITO CACACI         9109060020000%
00280COMMUNITY DRUGS     9109060023370%
00287SOLOMON CHAPELS     91081900001500
00294JOHN BURKE          91081900150000
00308JOE GARCIA          9109060020500%
00315GRACE MICELI        91081900025000
00329GUY VOLPONE         91081900001000
00343JOE & MARY SESSA    91081900100000
00350ROGER SHAW          91081900250000
00357ROBIN RATANSKI      9109060000100%
00364JOSE TORRES         9109060015000%
00371ALISE MARKOVITZ     9109060003000%
00392INEZ WASHINGTON     9109060000750%
00398JUAN ALVAREZ        9109060000100%
00413BILL HAYES          9109060001000%
00420JOHN RICE           9109060015000%
```

ROBBEM STATE BANK
106 WEST 10TH ST.
BROOKLYN, NY 11212

SAVINGS ACCOUNT TRANSACTION REGISTER

DATE 9/06/91 PAGE 1

ACCOUNT NUMBER	DEPOSITS	WITHDRAWALS	NOTES
00014		1,000.00	
00021	127.50		
00028	153.27		
00028		1,500.50	
00077	150.00		
00084	3,574.29		
00084	JOHN & SALLY DUPRIND		NAME CHANGE
00091	1,500.00		
00091	1,200.00		
00091		500.00	
00098	GEORGE & ANN CULHANE		NAME CHANGE
00126	350.00		
00133	2,563.00		
00140	BETH DENNY		NAME CHANGE
00161	1,256.34		
00168		110.00	
00168		15.50	ACCOUNT CLOSED

ROBBEM STATE BANK
106 WEST 10TH ST.
BROOKLYN, NY 11212

SAVINGS ACCOUNT TRANSACTION REGISTER

DATE 9/06/91 PAGE 2

ACCOUNT NUMBER	DEPOSITS	WITHDRAWALS	NOTES
00175	192.02		
00210	250.00		
00210	250.00		
00210	250.00		
00273	1,725.00		
00280	2,317.00		
00308	50.00		
00357	10.00		NEW ACCOUNT
00364	1,500.00		NEW ACCOUNT
00371	150.00		NEW ACCOUNT
00371	150.00		
00392	75.00		NEW ACCOUNT
00398	10.00		NEW ACCOUNT
00413	100.00		NEW ACCOUNT
00420	1,500.00		NEW ACCOUNT
TOTALS	19,403.42	3,126.00	

CONTROL COUNTS

NUMBER OF NEW ACCOUNTS	7
NUMBER OF DEPOSITS	17
NUMBER OF WITHDRAWALS	4
NUMBER OF NAME CHANGES	3
NUMBER OF CLOSED ACCOUNTS	1
NUMBER OF ERRORS	19
TOTAL	51

EXERCISE 3

Write a program to update the accounts-receivable master file you created in Exercise 3, Chapter 13, page 457. Have your program accept transactions in the formats described in Exercise 2, page 509, and also transactions to create new inventory records, in the following format:

Positions	Field
1	Code A
2–6	Part Number
7–26	Part Description
27	Units
	E–each
	L–pound
	G–gross
	D–dozen
28–33	Unit Cost (dollars and cents)
34–37	Supplier Code
38–42	Storage Location
43–45	Reorder Point
46–48	Reorder Quantity
49–80	spaces

Have your program carry out all the processing required in Exercise 2, page 509. In addition, for a new inventory record created on the master file, set the Quantity on Hand field and the Dates of Last Withdrawal and Last Receipt to zero, and insert today's date into the Date Created and Date of Last Access fields.

Listing the Contents of a Sequential File

Listing the complete contents of a sequential file is no different in concept from listing the contents of a file entered on a keyboard. Program P14-04, to list the contents of the output master file created in Program P14-03, just reads in one record after another and lists its contents reformatted. Program P14-04 is shown in Figure 14.20. The output produced by the program is shown in Figure 14.21. In the output you can see that all the deposits, withdrawals, and name changes were made correctly, new records added, and the records for the closed accounts removed. Provision was made to show any negative Current Balance amount.

FIGURE *14.20* **Program P14-04**

```
S COBOL II RELEASE 3.1 09/19/89                    P14004   DATE SEP 06,1991 T
----+-*A-1-B--+----2----+----3----+----4----+----5----+----6----+----7-|--+


       IDENTIFICATION DIVISION.
       PROGRAM-ID. P14-04.
      *
      *     THIS PROGRAM LISTS A SEQUENTIAL FILE.
      *
      *****************************************************************

       ENVIRONMENT DIVISION.
       INPUT-OUTPUT SECTION.
       FILE-CONTROL.
           SELECT LIST-FILE-OUT     ASSIGN TO PRINTER.
           SELECT MASTER-FILE-IN    ASSIGN TO MFILEIN.

      *****************************************************************

       DATA DIVISION.
       FILE SECTION.
       FD  MASTER-FILE-IN
           LABEL RECORDS ARE STANDARD
           RECORD CONTAINS 39 CHARACTERS
           BLOCK CONTAINS 100 RECORDS.

       01  MASTER-RECORD-IN.
           05  ACCOUNT-NUMBER                              PIC X(5).
           05  DEPOSITOR-NAME                              PIC X(20).
           05  TRANSACTION-YEAR                            PIC 99.
           05  TRANSACTION-MONTH                           PIC 99.
           05  TRANSACTION-DAY                             PIC 99.
           05  CURRENT-BALANCE                             PIC S9(6)V99.

       FD  LIST-FILE-OUT.

       01  LIST-RECORD-OUT                               PIC X(81).

       WORKING-STORAGE SECTION.
       01  MORE-INPUT          VALUE   "Y"                 PIC X.
           88 THERE-IS-NO-MORE-INPUT                       VALUE "N".
           88 THERE-IS-NO-INPUT                            VALUE "N".
       01  PAGE-NUMBER-W       VALUE 0  PACKED-DECIMAL     PIC S99.
       01  PAGE-LIMIT          VALUE 38 COMP SYNC          PIC S99.
       01  LINE-COUNT-ER                COMP SYNC          PIC S99.
       01  BLANK-LINE          VALUE SPACE                 PIC X.

       01  RUN-DATE.
           05  RUN-YEAR                                    PIC 99.
           05  RUN-MONTH-AND-DAY                           PIC 9(4).

       01  PAGE-HEADING-1.
           05                    VALUE SPACES              PIC X(40).
           05                    VALUE  "SAVINGS ACCOUNT MASTER"
                                                           PIC X(22).
```

continued

FIGURE 14.20 *continued*

```
S COBOL II RELEASE 3.1 09/19/89                 P14004   DATE SEP 06,1991 T
----+-*A-1-B--+----2----+----3----+----4----+----5----+----6----+----7-|--+


 01  PAGE-HEADING-2.
     05                    VALUE SPACES             PIC X(28).
     05                    VALUE  "DATE"            PIC X(5).
     05  RUN-MONTH-AND-DAY                          PIC Z9/99/.
     05  RUN-YEAR                                   PIC 99B(21).
     05                    VALUE  "PAGE"            PIC X(5).
     05  PAGE-NUMBER-OUT                            PIC Z9.

 01  PAGE-HEADING-3.
     05                    VALUE SPACES             PIC X(46).
     05                    VALUE  "DATE OF LAST"    PIC X(12).

 01  PAGE-HEADING-4.
     05                    VALUE SPACES             PIC X(20).
     05                    VALUE  "ACCOUNT"         PIC X(13).
     05                    VALUE  "CURRENT"         PIC X(13).
     05                    VALUE  "TRANSACTION"     PIC X(15).
     05                    VALUE  "DEPOSITOR NAME"  PIC X(14).

 01  PAGE-HEADING-5.
     05                    VALUE SPACES             PIC X(20).
     05                    VALUE  "NUMBER"          PIC X(13).
     05                    VALUE  "BALANCE"         PIC X(14).
     05                    VALUE  "YR  MO  DA"      PIC X(10).

 01  DETAIL-LINE.
     05                    VALUE SPACES           PIC X(21).
     05  ACCOUNT-NUMBER                           PIC X(5)B(4).
     05  CURRENT-BALANCE                          PIC Z,ZZZ,ZZZ.99-.
     05  TRANSACTION-YEAR                         PIC B(4)99BB.
     05  TRANSACTION-MONTH                        PIC 99BB.
     05  TRANSACTION-DAY                          PIC 99B(4).
     05  DEPOSITOR-NAME                           PIC X(20).

 01  NO-INPUT-DATA.
     05                 VALUE SPACES              PIC X(21).
     05                 VALUE "NO INPUT DATA"     PIC X(13).

*****************************************************************

 PROCEDURE DIVISION.
 CONTROL-PARAGRAPH.
     PERFORM INITIALIZATION
     PERFORM MAIN-PROCESS UNTIL THERE-IS-NO-MORE-INPUT
     PERFORM TERMINATION
     STOP RUN
     .

 INITIALIZATION.
     OPEN INPUT  MASTER-FILE-IN
          OUTPUT LIST-FILE-OUT
     ACCEPT RUN-DATE FROM DATE
     MOVE CORR RUN-DATE TO PAGE-HEADING-2
     PERFORM PRODUCE-PAGE-HEADINGS
     READ MASTER-FILE-IN
         AT END
             SET THERE-IS-NO-INPUT TO TRUE
     END-READ
     IF THERE-IS-NO-INPUT
         WRITE LIST-RECORD-OUT FROM NO-INPUT-DATA
     END-IF
     .
```

FIGURE 14.20 *continued*

```
PRODUCE-PAGE-HEADINGS.
    ADD 1 TO PAGE-NUMBER-W
    MOVE PAGE-NUMBER-W TO PAGE-NUMBER-OUT
    WRITE LIST-RECORD-OUT FROM PAGE-HEADING-1 AFTER PAGE
    WRITE LIST-RECORD-OUT FROM PAGE-HEADING-2
    WRITE LIST-RECORD-OUT FROM PAGE-HEADING-3 AFTER 3
    WRITE LIST-RECORD-OUT FROM PAGE-HEADING-4
    WRITE LIST-RECORD-OUT FROM PAGE-HEADING-5
    WRITE LIST-RECORD-OUT FROM BLANK-LINE
    MOVE 8 TO LINE-COUNT-ER
    .

TERMINATION.
    CLOSE MASTER-FILE-IN,
          LIST-FILE-OUT
    .

MAIN-PROCESS.
    MOVE CORR MASTER-RECORD-IN TO DETAIL-LINE
    IF 1 + LINE-COUNT-ER > PAGE-LIMIT
        PERFORM PRODUCE-PAGE-HEADINGS
    END-IF
    WRITE LIST-RECORD-OUT FROM DETAIL-LINE
    ADD 1 TO LINE-COUNT-ER
    READ MASTER-FILE-IN
        AT END
            SET THERE-IS-NO-MORE-INPUT TO TRUE
```

FIGURE 14.21 Output from Program P14-04

```
                    SAVINGS ACCOUNT MASTER
          DATE   9/06/91                         PAGE   1


                                     DATE OF LAST
ACCOUNT         CURRENT             TRANSACTION        DEPOSITOR NAME
NUMBER          BALANCE              YR   MO   DA

 00007          1,007.84             91   08   19      ROSEBUCCI
 00014            990.00-            91   09   06      ROBERT DAVIS M.D.
 00021            252.50             91   09   06      LORICE MONTI
 00028          5,654.36             91   09   06      MICHAEL SMITH
 00032             25.00             91   08   19      JOSEPH CAMILLO
 00035            150.00             91   08   19      JOHN J. LEHMAN
 00049            150.00             91   08   19      JAY GREENE
 00056              1.00             91   08   19      EVELYN SLATER
 00070            500.00             91   08   19      PATRICK J. LEE
 00077            160.37             91   09   06      LESLIE MINSKY
 00084          5,074.29             91   09   06      JOHN & SALLY DUPRINO
 00091          2,300.00             91   09   06      JOE'S DELI
 00098            500.00             91   09   06      GEORGE & ANN CULHANE
 00105             50.00             91   08   19      ONE DAY CLEANERS
 00112            250.00             91   08   19      ROSEMARY LANE
 00126          1,100.00             91   09   06      JAMES BUDD
 00133          3,563.00             91   09   06      PAUL LERNER, D.D.S.
 00140             25.75             91   09   06      BETH DENNY
 00161          1,280.84             91   09   06      ROBERT RYAN
 00175            202.02             91   09   06      MARY KEATING
 00189             35.00             91   08   19      J. & L. CAIN
 00196            150.00             91   08   19      IMPERIAL FLORIST
 00203              5.00             91   08   19      JOYCE MITCHELL
 00210          1,000.00             91   09   06      JERRY PARKS
 00217             50.00             91   08   19      CARL CALDERON
 00224            175.50             91   08   19      JOHN WILLIAMS
 00231            555.00             91   08   19      BILL WILLIAMS
 00238             10.00             91   08   19      KEVIN PARKER
 00245             35.00             91   08   19      FRANK CAPUTO
 00252             15.00             91   08   19      GENE GALLI



                    SAVINGS ACCOUNT MASTER
          DATE   9/06/91                         PAGE   2


                                     DATE OF LAST
ACCOUNT         CURRENT             TRANSACTION        DEPOSITOR NAME
NUMBER          BALANCE              YR   MO   DA

 00266             99.57             91   08   19      MARTIN LANG
 00273          2,000.00             91   09   06      VITO CACACI
 00280          2,337.00             91   09   06      COMMUNITY DRUGS
 00287             15.00             91   08   19      SOLOMON CHAPELS
 00294          1,500.00             91   08   19      JOHN BURKE
 00308          2,050.00             91   09   06      JOE GARCIA
 00315            250.00             91   08   19      GRACE MICELI
 00329             10.00             91   08   19      GUY VOLPONE
 00343          1,000.00             91   08   19      JOE & MARY SESSA
 00350          2,500.00             91   08   19      ROGER SHAW
 00357             10.00             91   09   06      ROBIN RATANSKI
 00364          1,500.00             91   09   06      JOSE TORRES
 00371            300.00             91   09   06      ALISE MARKOVITZ
 00392             75.00             91   09   06      INEZ WASHINGTON
 00398             10.00             91   09   06      JUAN ALVAREZ
 00413            100.00             91   09   06      BILL HAYES
 00420          1,500.00             91   09   06      JOHN RICE
```

EXERCISE 4

Write a program to list the contents of the master files produced by the programs in Chapter 13, Exercise 3, page 457 and Exercise 5, page 474; and Exercises 2 and 3 in this chapter. Show whether any of the Quantity on Hand fields on the master file are negative. For any record whose Quantity on Hand is equal to or less than the Reorder Point, print a message showing the Reorder Quantity and the word REORDER.

Summary

The balance-line algorithm can be used to design all programs that read a sequential master file and a transaction file. The algorithm was first used in Chapter 13 to design a program to delete records from a master file. The same algorithm also can be used to design a program to list selected records from a master file and to design programs to add new master records, delete obsolete ones, and make all kinds of changes to master records in a single run.

For the algorithm to work, the input master file and the transaction file must both be in sequence on the record key. The master file must contain no duplicate values of any key. If the program is designed to process more than one kind of transaction, every transaction record must contain a code to say what kind of transaction it is. The algorithm contains in its main loop a comparison between the record key in the master input area and the record key in the transaction input area. The lower of the two keys is always processed first. Master records are processed in the master work area; transaction records are processed in the transaction input area.

The main difference among the different program designs lies in the box on the hierarchy diagram called "Process transaction record." By properly designing and coding the function "Process transaction record" it is possible to create a file-update program of any imaginable complexity.

An input area can be defined to process records with different formats by redefining the input area for as many formats as necessary. A redefining entry must specify exactly as many computer storage locations as the entry being redefined.

Listing the complete contents of a sequential tape or disk file is conceptually identical to listing any ordinary sequential file. The input records are read one after another and their contents are printed.

Fill-In Exercises

1. In a program to list selected records from a master file, the keys of the master records to be listed are provided by way of a ______ file.
2. Five files needed in a sequential file update program are the ______ input file, the ______ input file, the transaction register file, the error report file, and the ______ output file.
3. Of the five files named in Fill-in Exercise 2, the one that is not used in a program to list selected records from a master file is the ______.
4. Master records are always worked on in the master ______ area.
5. "Process transaction record" executes when there are one or more transactions whose key is equal to ______.

6. "Choose current key" assigns to CURRENT-KEY the ______ of the two keys in the master ______ area and the transaction ______ area.

7. "Process master record" moves a master record from the master ______ area to the master ______ area when the key of the master record in the master ______ is equal to ______.

8. "Check to write master" writes a master record onto the output master tape when the flag is set to ______.

9. A deposit transaction is considered to have a matching master record in the master work area when the flag is set to ______.

10. A master record for a new account may be built in the master work area when the flag is set to ______.

11. In a program to list the contents of selected master records, only the Account Number is needed in the transaction record because all the other information listed comes from the ______ record.

12. The contents of a selected master record can be listed only when the flag is set to ______.

13. In a program to list selected records from a master file, processing can cease when end-of-file is reached on the ______ file.

14. If a new master record is created, and changes are made to it in the same run, the transaction that creates the record must fall ______ any of the transactions that change it.

15. A redefining entry must specify the same number of ______ ______ ______ as the entry being redefined.

Review Exercises

1. Write a program to list the complete contents of records selected from the master file you created in Review Exercise 2, Chapter 13, page 476. Use transactions in the following format:

Positions	Field
1–9	Social Security Number
10–80	spaces

2. Write a program to list selected fields from records selected from the master file you created in Review Exercise 2, Chapter 13, page 476. Use transactions in the following format:

Positions	Field
1	Code (8 or 9)
2–10	Social Security Number
11–80	spaces

Do not treat duplicate transactions as erroneous.

For transactions with Code 8, have your program print the following fields from the records selected:

Social Security Number

Student Name

Major Department

For transactions with a Code of 9, have your program print the following fields from the records selected:

Social Security Number

Student Name

Year of Graduation

Design suitable reports for your program before you begin coding.

3. Write a program to update the master file you created in Review Exercise 2, Chapter 13, page 476, with changes and deletions. Use transactions in the following formats:

Positions	Field
1	Code 2 (Student Name change)
2–10	Social Security Number
11–30	Student Name
31–80	spaces
1	Code 3 (Street Address change)
2–10	Social Security Number
11–30	Street Address
31–80	spaces
1	Code 4 (City, State, Zip change)
2–10	Social Security Number
11–30	City, State, Zip
31–80	spaces
1	Code 5 (Major Department change)
2–10	Social Security Number
11–12	Major Department
13–80	spaces
1	Code 6 (Year of Graduation change)
2–10	Social Security Number
11–12	Year of Graduation
13–80	spaces
1	Code 7 (Delete record)
2–10	Social Security Number

Have your program make all suitable validity checks on each transaction, and print a line on one of the output reports for each transaction. For any change to an existing master record, have your program print the Social Security Number and the contents of the changed field from the master record. For a record deleted from the master file, have your program print the Social Security Number, the Student Name, and the Year of Graduation from the master file.

4. Write a program to update the master file you created in Review Exercise 2, Chapter 13, page 476, with transactions in the formats given in Review Exercise 3 above. Have your program accept also transactions in the following format, to add new records to the master file:

Positions	Field
1	Code 1
2–10	Social Security Number
11–30	Student Name
31–50	Street Address
51–70	City, State, Zip
71–72	Major Department
73–74	Year of Graduation
75–80	spaces

For a record added to the master file, print the Social Security Number and the Student Name.

5. Explain why each of the REDEFINES entries below is illegal:

a.
```
01  RECORD-NAME.
    05  FIELD-1.
        10  FIELD-2   PIC X(4).
        10  FIELD-3   PIC X(5).
01  NEW-FIELD REDEFINES RECORD-NAME    PIC X(80).
```

b.
```
01  RECORD-NAME.
    05  FIELD-1.
        10  FIELD-2   PIC X(4).
        10  FIELD-3   PIC X(5).
    05  FIELD-4 REDEFINES FIELD-1.
```

6. Write a program to produce customer invoices in the format shown in Figure 12.14, page 407. Use as inputs the customer-name-and-address master file you created in the Project in Chapter 13, page 477, and transactions in the format used for Program 12-04 and described on page 407. Have your program SORT the transactions into order on Customer Number. Have your program make all suitable validity checks on the transactions and produce an error report separate from the invoices.

Project

Write a program to update the sequential master file you created in the Project in Chapter 13, page 477. Use input transactions in the following formats:

Positions	Field
1	Transaction Code: 1–Add customer to file 2–Change a Name and Address Line
2	Line Number of Address—1 through 5
3–7	Customer Number
8–27	Name and Address Line
28–80	spaces
1	Transaction Code: 3—Delete customer from file
3–7	Customer Number
8–80	spaces

Have your program SORT the input transactions on Line Number of Address within Transaction Code within Customer Number. Have your program make all suitable validity checks on each transaction, and print a line on one of the output reports for each transaction. For any change to an existing master record, have your program print the Customer Number and the contents of the changed field from the master record. For a record deleted from the master file, have your program print the Customer Number and the first line of the Customer Name and Address from the master file. For a record added to the master file, have your program print the Customer Number and the first line of the Customer Name and Address.

CHAPTER 15

Indexed Files

HERE ARE THE KEY POINTS YOU SHOULD LEARN FROM THIS CHAPTER

1. What an indexed file is
2. Why indexed files are useful
3. How to get COBOL to create an indexed file
4. How to access an indexed file randomly
5. How to update an indexed file
6. How to access an indexed file sequentially and randomly in a single run
7. How to list the contents of an indexed file

KEY WORDS TO RECOGNIZE AND LEARN

organization
indexed file
indexed organization
DELETE
relative organization
standard sequential organization
indexed-sequential organization
dynamic access
prime record key
alternate record key
ORGANIZATION
INDEXED
RECORD KEY IS
ALTERNATE RECORD KEY IS
WITH DUPLICATES
STATUS IS
DISPLAY
INVALID KEY
standard exception procedure
NO ADVANCING
ACCESS
RANDOM
I-O
OPEN mode
EXTEND
REWRITE
DYNAMIC
START
key of reference
NEXT

In Chapters 13 and 14 we worked with sequential master files on tape or disk. Our transaction files were sequential files also. Even our printed reports were sequential files. A sequential file is said to have sequential **organization.** A characteristic of sequential organization is that all the records in a file sit there in the order in which they were written. All files having sequential organization must be accessed sequentially. A characteristic of sequential access is that a program must read or write the first record of a file before it can read or write the second. When a program is reading a tape file, a card file, or a file entered on a keyboard, it must read the first record in the file before it can read the second; when a program is writing a tape file or a printer file, it must write the first record before it writes the second.

On the other hand, **indexed files,** or files having **indexed organization,** may be accessed randomly. An indexed file cannot be stored on magnetic tape. It must be stored on disk or some other direct-access storage device. An indexed file has its records stored more or less in sequence on some key field; also it has indexes, which tell COBOL where each record on the file is located. COBOL constructs and maintains the indexes automatically, with almost no effort on the part of the programmer.

The indexes permit COBOL to do some very remarkable things with an indexed file. Imagine that our savings-account master file was an indexed file instead of a sequential one. Then if we wanted to make a deposit to an account, COBOL could find on the disk just the master record we need, and READ it into the File Section. There we could update it by adding the deposit to the current balance. Then we could ask COBOL to put the updated record back onto the disk in the same place it came from, erasing the old record in that location on the disk and replacing it with the new. Thus there would be no need to READ the entire master file in order to change some of the records on it.

Random access of an indexed file also permits COBOL to add new records to the file without having to create a whole new file. If we have a record to add, we just WRITE it. COBOL automatically finds the place in the file where the new record should go, moves a few existing records around if necessary to make space for the new one, and slips it in.

Similarly, random access of an indexed file permits COBOL to delete a record without having to create a whole new file. The **DELETE** verb enables a program to remove a record from a file.

A Summary of File Terminology

Before discussing indexed files further, it is worthwhile to review all the terminology we have studied so far relating to file storage media, file organization, and file access methods. In doing so, we will also see some new related terminology.

File Storage Media

As mentioned in Chapter 13, for our purposes there are only two types of storage media—sequential media and direct-access media. Examples of sequential media are punched cards, magnetic tape, and printed output. Examples of direct-access media are magnetic disk and magnetic drum. Direct-access media are also sometimes called mass storage media.

File Organization

Three types of file organization are supported by modern COBOL systems—sequential organization, indexed organization, and **relative organization.** All of the files we have used up through Chapter 14 have had sequential organization. In this chapter we will study a file having indexed organization. In Chapter 16 we will study files with relative organization.

Sequential organization is also sometimes called **standard sequential organization.** Sequentially organized files can be stored on punched cards and on magnetic tape. Of course a printed file is sequential also, since the records appear in the file in the order in which they are written there. Sequential files can also be stored on direct-access storage devices.

An indexed file contains indexes as well as data records. Since most of the records in an indexed file are in sequence on the record key, indexed organization is also sometimes called **indexed-sequential organization.** An indexed file can be stored only on a direct-access storage device.

File Access

There are really only two ways to READ records from a file or WRITE records onto a file—sequentially and randomly. When a program READs a file sequentially, the first READ statement brings in the first record on the file; the second READ issued by the program brings in the second record on the file. When a program WRITEs a file sequentially, the first WRITE statement issued by the program puts the first record onto the file; the second WRITE statement puts the second record.

When a program READs a file randomly, however, any READ statement issued by the program can bring in any record from anywhere on the file. When a program WRITEs a file randomly, the program can insert a new record into any location in the file.

A sequential file may be accessed only sequentially. Indexed files and relative files may be accessed sequentially or randomly.

A third form of access, called **dynamic access,** is merely a combination of sequential access and random access. COBOL programs have the ability to switch back and forth between sequential access and random access in a single run. In this chapter we will use all three access methods on our indexed file.

Creating an Indexed File on Disk

We are now ready to write a program to create an indexed file. The program will create a savings-account master file on disk, using the same formats for transaction and master records that we had for Program P13-02, when we created a sequential master file. The input format for Program P13-02 (and Program P15-01) is repeated here:

Positions	Field
1	Code 1
2–6	Account Number
7–14	Amount (to two decimal places)
15–34	Depositor Name
35–80	spaces

Our indexed master file will have its records in order on Account Number, just as our sequential master file did. But now our master file will be indexed so that COBOL can find the record for any Account Number in the file. In addition, we will have COBOL index the file on Depositor Name also, so that a program can find the record or records for any Depositor Name in the file. Since the master records are in order on Account Number, the Account Number field is called the **prime record key** of the file. The Depositor Name field is called an **alternate record key.** An indexed file may have more than one alternate key. The maximum number of alternate keys that an indexed file may have is different in different COBOL systems.

The input to Program P15-01 will be a batch of new accounts to create the master file, in the format just given. The input will be in order on the prime record key field, Account Number, so that the system can create the file and the indexes sequentially. It is possible for COBOL to create an indexed file randomly if the input records are not in order on the prime key field, but doing so usually uses much more computer time than if the input records are in order. After the file is created, we will be able to access the master records randomly with transactions in any order.

Program P15-01 is shown in Figure 15.1. It is, of course, very similar to Program P13-02. Some differences are found in the FILE-CONTROL entry for the output master file, at line 00160. Here we use the **ORGANIZATION** clause to tell COBOL that we would like it to create the output master file as an indexed file. Whenever you use ORGANIZATION **INDEXED,** you must use the **RECORD KEY IS** clause to tell COBOL the prime key on which the file is ordered. The prime key must be a field defined within a level-01 entry in the File Section associated with this file.

The **ALTERNATE RECORD KEY IS** clause, lines 00190 and 00200, tells COBOL that we would like to be able to access records in this file on the basis of the alternate record key. The ALTERNATE RECORD KEY field, like the prime key, must be defined within a level-01 entry in the File Section associated with this file. The **WITH DUPLICATES** phrase tells COBOL that any given value of the alternate key may appear more than once in the file. In this case it means that a depositor may have more than one account. Duplicate appearances of the prime record key in an indexed file are never allowed.

If an indexed file has more than one ALTERNATE RECORD KEY, the FILE-CONTROL entry for the file must contain a separate ALTERNATE RECORD KEY clause for each such KEY. The ALTERNATE RECORD KEY clauses must follow one immediately after the other in the FILE-CONTROL entry, and each clause may have a WITH DUPLICATES phrase or not as appropriate.

A **STATUS IS** clause, such as the one shown in line 00210, should always be used with any indexed or relative file and can be used with sequential files also. The STATUS IS clause is used to name a two-character alphanumeric field in working storage. The field is used by COBOL to record the STATUS of input and output operations on the file. Statements in the Procedure Division can use the contents of the STATUS field at any time.

After each input or output operation on a file, COBOL places two characters into the STATUS field for the file if such a field is specified. The ANSI standard meanings of the STATUS codes related to writing an indexed file sequentially are shown in Table 15.1.

FIGURE *15.1*

Program P15-01

```
S COBOL II RELEASE 3.1 09/19/89                P15001    DATE SEP 15,1991 T
----+-*A-1-B--+----2----+----3----+----4----+----5----+----6----+----7-|--+

       IDENTIFICATION DIVISION.
       PROGRAM-ID. P15-01.
      *
      *     THIS PROGRAM CREATES AN INDEXED
      *     MASTER FILE OF SAVINGS ACCOUNT RECORDS.
      *
      ******************************************************************

       ENVIRONMENT DIVISION.
       INPUT-OUTPUT SECTION.
       FILE-CONTROL.
           SELECT TRANSACTION-REGISTER-FILE-OUT ASSIGN TO PRINTER1.
           SELECT ERROR-FILE-OUT                ASSIGN TO PRINTER2.
           SELECT SAVINGS-ACCOUNT-DATA-FILE-IN  ASSIGN TO INFILE.
           SELECT SORT-WORK-FILE                ASSIGN TO SORTWK.
           SELECT ACCOUNT-MASTER-FILE-OUT       ASSIGN TO DISKOUT
               ORGANIZATION INDEXED
               RECORD KEY IS ACCOUNT-NUMBER-M
               ALTERNATE RECORD KEY IS DEPOSITOR-NAME-M
                   WITH DUPLICATES
               STATUS IS FILE-CHECK.

      ******************************************************************
```

continued

TABLE *15.1*
ANSI standard STATUS codes related to writing an indexed file sequentially

Status Code	Meaning
00	Successful completion
02	Successful completion, and the record just written created a duplicate key value for an ALTERNATE RECORD KEY for which DUPLICATES are allowed[a]
21	Invalid key—prime RECORD KEY out of order
22	Invalid key—an attempt has been made to WRITE a record that would create an invalid duplicate key value[a]
24	Invalid key—boundary violation (attempt to WRITE past the physical end of the file)
30	Permanent error (hardware malfunction)
48	Output file not properly OPENed

[a]Under certain conditions some COBOL systems do not check for the presence of duplicate values of alternate keys during file creation. In such situations, the condition described for STATUS code 02 would return a STATUS code of 00, and an attempt to WRITE a record that would create an invalid duplicate value of an ALTERNATE RECORD KEY would also return a STATUS code of 00. An attempt to WRITE a record that would create a duplicate value of the prime RECORD KEY always returns a STATUS code of 22. Any error condition resulting from invalid duplicate values of alternate keys would be discovered in later processing. See Chapter 17 for a full discussion of this matter.

Your own COBOL system may have additional codes in the range 90 through 99. The sequence error, STATUS code 21, arises if an attempt is made to WRITE on the file a record whose prime key is less than a prime key already on the file. Our input records are SORTed on the prime key, Account Number, so Program P15-01 could not be writing a record with a key lower than one already on the file. It could be erroneously attempting to WRITE a record with a duplicate key, however, and such a situation would cause the STATUS field to be set to 22.

The STATUS code reflecting the successful execution of an OPEN statement is 00.

The description of SORT-WORK-RECORD, line 00340, is only 34 characters long. Only 34 characters from each input record are SORTed in this program. SORT time is reduced by not SORTing all 80 characters of each input record, since only 34 are needed for processing after the SORT is complete.

The level-88 entries associated with FILE-CHECK, defined at line 00750, will be used to check the success or failure of the OPEN and WRITE statements to the indexed master file being created. A successful OPEN will assign 00 to FILE-CHECK and make the condition name MASTER-FILE-OPENED true. A successful WRITE will assign 00 or 02 to FILE-CHECK and make the condition name WRITE-WAS-SUCCESSFUL true. And finally, an attempt to WRITE a master record with an Account Number that is a duplicate of an Account Number that is already on the file will assign 22 to FILE-CHECK and make the condition name DUPLICATE-PRIME-RECORD-KEY true. You will see how the condition names are used when we look at the Procedure Division.

FIGURE *15.1* ***continued***

```
S COBOL II RELEASE 3.1 09/19/89                 P15001   DATE SEP 15,1991 T
----+-*A-1-B--+----2----+----3----+----4----+----5----+----6----+----7-|--+

00240
00250    DATA DIVISION.
00260    FILE SECTION.
00270    FD   SAVINGS-ACCOUNT-DATA-FILE-IN.
00280
00290    01   SAVINGS-ACCOUNT-DATA-RECORD-IN               PIC X(80).
00300
00310    SD   SORT-WORK-FILE
00320         RECORD CONTAINS 34 CHARACTERS.
00330
00340    01   SORT-WORK-RECORD.
00350         05 CODE-IN                                    PIC X.
00360            88 VALID-CODE                                  VALUE "1".
00370         05 ACCOUNT-NUMBER-IN                          PIC X(5).
00380         05 AMOUNT-IN                                  PIC 9(6)V99.
00390         05 AMOUNT-IN-X
00400            REDEFINES AMOUNT-IN                        PIC X(8).
00410         05 DEPOSITOR-NAME-IN                          PIC X(20).
00420            88 DEPOSITOR-NAME-IS-MISSING                   VALUE SPACES.
00430
00440    FD   ACCOUNT-MASTER-FILE-OUT
00450         LABEL RECORDS ARE STANDARD
00460         RECORD CONTAINS 39 CHARACTERS.
00470
00480    01   ACCOUNT-MASTER-RECORD-OUT.
00490         05 ACCOUNT-NUMBER-M                           PIC X(5).
00500         05 DEPOSITOR-NAME-M                           PIC X(20).
00510         05 DATE-OF-LAST-TRANSACTION-M                 PIC 9(6).
00520         05 CURRENT-BALANCE-M                          PIC S9(6)V99.
00530
00540    FD   TRANSACTION-REGISTER-FILE-OUT.
00550
00560    01   REGISTER-RECORD-OUT                           PIC X(72).
00570
00580    FD   ERROR-FILE-OUT.
00590
```

FIGURE 15.1 *continued*

```
01  ERROR-RECORD-OUT                           PIC X(84).

WORKING-STORAGE SECTION.
01  BLANKS                                     PIC X        VALUE SPACE.
01  PACKED-DECIMAL.
 02 REGISTER-PAGE-NUMBER-W                     PIC S99      VALUE 0.
 02 ERROR-PAGE-NUMBER-W                        PIC S99      VALUE 0.
 02 DEPOSIT-TOTAL-W                            PIC S9(7)V99 VALUE 0.
 02 NUMBER-OF-INPUT-RECORDS-W                  PIC S9(3)    VALUE ZERO.
 02 NUMBER-OF-ERRONEOUS-RECORDS-W              PIC S9(3)    VALUE ZERO.
 02 NUMBER-OF-NEW-ACCOUNTS-W                   PIC S9(3)    VALUE ZERO.
01  REGISTER-PAGE-LIMIT   COMP SYNC            PIC S99      VALUE 35.
01  LINE-COUNT-ER         COMP SYNC            PIC S99.
01  ERROR-PAGE-LIMIT      COMP SYNC            PIC S99      VALUE 50.
01  ERROR-LINE-COUNTER    COMP SYNC            PIC S99.
01  FILE-CHECK.
    88 MASTER-FILE-OPENED                      VALUE "00".
    88 DUPLICATE-PRIME-RECORD-KEY              VALUE "22".
    05  STATUS-KEY-1                           PIC X.
        88 WRITE-WAS-SUCCESSFUL                VALUE "0".
    05  STATUS-KEY-2                           PIC X.
01  MORE-INPUT                                 PIC X        VALUE "Y".
    88 THERE-IS-NO-MORE-INPUT                  VALUE "N".
01  ANY-ERRORS                                 PIC X.
01  TODAYS-DATE.
    05  TODAYS-YEAR                            PIC 99.
    05  TODAYS-MONTH-AND-DAY                   PIC 9(4).

01  REPORT-HEADING-1.
    05               PIC X(39) VALUE SPACES.
    05               PIC X(17) VALUE "ROBBEM STATE BANK".

01  REPORT-HEADING-2.
    05               PIC X(39) VALUE SPACES.
    05               PIC X(17) VALUE "106 WEST 10TH ST.".

01  REPORT-HEADING-3.
    05               PIC X(38) VALUE SPACES.
    05               PIC X(19) VALUE "BROOKLYN, NY  11212".

01  REGISTER-PAGE-HEADING-1.
    05               PIC X(29) VALUE SPACES.
    05               PIC X(36)
                     VALUE "SAVINGS ACCOUNT MASTER FILE CREATION".

01  ERROR-PAGE-HEADING-1.
    05               PIC X(30) VALUE SPACES.
    05               PIC X(34)
                     VALUE "SAVINGS ACCOUNT MASTER FILE ERRORS".

01  PAGE-HEADING-2.
    05                      PIC X(17) VALUE SPACES.
    05                      PIC X(5)  VALUE "DATE".
    05  TODAYS-MONTH-AND-DAY      PIC Z9/99/.
    05  TODAYS-YEAR         PIC 99B(35).
    05                      PIC X(5)  VALUE "PAGE".
    05  PAGE-NUMBER-OUT           PIC Z9.

01  REGISTER-PAGE-HEADING-3.
    05                      PIC X(24) VALUE SPACES.
    05                      PIC X(12) VALUE "ACCOUNT".
    05                      PIC X(12) VALUE "INITIAL".
    05                      PIC X(5)  VALUE "NOTES".

01  ERROR-PAGE-HEADING-3.
    05                      PIC X(24) VALUE SPACES.
    05                      PIC X(24) VALUE "ACCOUNT".
    05                      PIC X(5)  VALUE "NOTES".
```

continued

The Procedure Division of this program, which starts at line 01880, is very much like the Procedure Division of Program 13-02. One difference can be found at line 02070, where the program determines whether the indexed file was OPENed successfully by the statement at line 02040. If the OPEN was successful, FILE-CHECK will be equal to zeroes and the condition name MASTER-FILE-OPENED will be true. If FILE-CHECK is anything other than zeros, the OPEN was not successful. We used a **DISPLAY** statement to print an error message, and then we terminate the run.

FIGURE *15.1* ***continued***

```
S COBOL II RELEASE 3.1 09/19/89                P15001   DATE SEP 15,1991 T
----+-*A-1-B--+----2----+----3----+----4----+----5----+----6----+----7-|--+

01280
01290  01  REGISTER-PAGE-HEADING-4.
01300      05                  PIC X(24) VALUE SPACES.
01310      05                  PIC X(12) VALUE "NUMBER".
01320      05                  PIC X(7)  VALUE "DEPOSIT".
01330
01340  01  ERROR-PAGE-HEADING-4.
01350      05                  PIC X(24) VALUE SPACES.
01360      05                  PIC X(6)  VALUE "NUMBER".
01370
01380  01  NEW-ACCOUNT-LINE.
01390      05              PIC X(25)       VALUE SPACES.
01400      05  ACCOUNT-NUMBER-OUT-G        PIC X(5)B(5).
01410      05  AMOUNT-OUT-G                PIC ZZZ,ZZZ.99B(3).
01420      05              PIC X(11)       VALUE "NEW ACCOUNT".
01430
01440  01  ERROR-LINE.
01450      05              PIC X(25) VALUE SPACES.
01460      05  ACCOUNT-NUMBER-OUT-E PIC X(5)B(18).
01470      05  MESSAGE-E            PIC X(36).
01480
01490  01  INVALID-CODE-MSG.
01500      05              PIC X(13) VALUE "INVALID CODE".
01510      05  CODE-OUT    PIC X.
01520
01530  01  AMOUNT-NOT-NUMERIC-MSG.
01540      05              PIC X(28) VALUE "INITIAL DEPOSIT NOT NUMERIC".
01550      05  AMOUNT-OUT-X         PIC X(9).
01560
01570  01  FINAL-LINE-1.
01580      05                  PIC X(23) VALUE SPACES.
01590      05                  PIC X(10) VALUE "TOTAL".
01600      05  AMOUNT-TOTAL-OUT           PIC Z,ZZZ,ZZZ.99.
01610
01620  01  FINAL-LINE-2.
01630      05                  PIC X(40) VALUE SPACES.
01640      05                  PIC X(14) VALUE "CONTROL COUNTS".
01650
01660  01  FINAL-LINE-3.
01670      05                  PIC X(34) VALUE SPACES.
01680      05                  PIC X(28) VALUE "NUMBER OF NEW ACCOUNTS".
01690      05  NUMBER-OF-NEW-ACCOUNTS-OUT PIC ZZ9.
01700
01710  01  FINAL-LINE-4.
01720      05                  PIC X(34) VALUE SPACES.
01730      05                  PIC X(28)
01740                          VALUE "NUMBER OF ERRONEOUS RECORDS".
01750      05  NUMBER-OF-ERRONEOUS-RCDS-OUT PIC ZZ9.
01760
01770  01  FINAL-LINE-5.
01780      05                  PIC X(34) VALUE SPACES.
01790      05                  PIC X(28) VALUE "TOTAL".
01800      05  NUMBER-OF-INPUT-RECORDS-OUT PIC ZZ9.
```

FIGURE 15.1 *continued*

```
 01  NO-INPUT-DATA.
     05                  PIC X(21) VALUE SPACES.
     05                  PIC X(13) VALUE "NO INPUT DATA".
*****************************************************************
 PROCEDURE DIVISION.
 CREATE-MASTER-FILE.
     SORT SORT-WORK-FILE
          ASCENDING KEY ACCOUNT-NUMBER-IN
          USING SAVINGS-ACCOUNT-DATA-FILE-IN
          OUTPUT PROCEDURE IS PRODUCE-MASTER-FILE
     STOP RUN
     .
 PRODUCE-MASTER-FILE.
     PERFORM INITIALIZATION.
     PERFORM PROCESS-A-RECORD UNTIL THERE-IS-NO-MORE-INPUT
     PERFORM TERMINATION
     .
 INITIALIZATION.
     OPEN OUTPUT ACCOUNT-MASTER-FILE-OUT
                 ERROR-FILE-OUT
                 TRANSACTION-REGISTER-FILE-OUT
     IF NOT MASTER-FILE-OPENED
         DISPLAY " MASTER FILE OPEN STATUS = ", FILE-CHECK
         CLOSE TRANSACTION-REGISTER-FILE-OUT,
               ERROR-FILE-OUT,
               ACCOUNT-MASTER-FILE-OUT
         STOP RUN
     END-IF
     ACCEPT TODAYS-DATE FROM DATE
     MOVE CORRESPONDING TODAYS-DATE TO PAGE-HEADING-2
     PERFORM PRODUCE-REGISTER-HEAD
     PERFORM PRODUCE-ERROR-HEAD
     PERFORM READ-A-RECORD
     IF THERE-IS-NO-MORE-INPUT
         WRITE ERROR-RECORD-OUT FROM NO-INPUT-DATA
     END-IF
     .
```

continued

A DISPLAY statement can place its output onto a printer, a screen, or other output devices. It is not limited to handling error messages. The DISPLAY verb, when used for printing, has severe limitations, and should not be used for printing normal report output. It is convenient to use when precise formatting of printed output is not needed. Output printed by a DISPLAY statement normally appears on a separate report from output printed by WRITE or GENERATE statements. The two reports can be printed on separate printers, or they can be printed one after the other on a single printer if the printer is not directly under the control of your program, as is the case with most modern operating systems. If only one printer directly under the control of your program is available, the report lines will be interleaved in an unpredictable manner.

When used for printing, a DISPLAY statement prints the values of the literals and/or data names listed in the statement, one right after the other from left to right on the print line. You must not have any entries in the File Section in connection with DISPLAY print output, and, of course, you cannot OPEN or CLOSE a DISPLAY file, since there is no such file defined. This is one of the advantages of using DISPLAY for printing error messages. You can print the message even if you are unable to OPEN any output print files.

The WRITE statement at line 02730 attempts to place each master record onto the output master file. When COBOL is writing an indexed file, it will not WRITE duplicate prime keys. That is, if we tell COBOL to WRITE a record sequentially on the file, and COBOL finds that there is already on the file a record with the same Account Number as the one we are trying to WRITE, COBOL will not WRITE the record but will instead set the STATUS code to 22. For this reason, we do not have to check for duplicate Account Numbers the way we did in Program P13-02. In Program P15-01 COBOL does it for us. COBOL checks for duplicate keys when it is working with indexed files, but not when it is working with sequential files.

And so, in the paragraph CHECK-INPUT-FOR-VALIDITY, line 02920, we don't have to check the ACCOUNT-NUMBER-IN against any ACCOUNT-NUMBER-SAVE field. Instead, in the paragraph WRITE-MASTER-RECORD, line 02720, we can detect a duplicate Account Number by testing the STATUS code for 22 after trying to WRITE each output record.

Notice that the WRITE statement at line 02730 contains an **INVALID KEY** phrase. In this program an INVALID KEY condition can arise if we try to WRITE onto the master file a record with a duplicate prime record key, or if we try to WRITE beyond the physical end of the file. If either condition occurs, the imperative statement in the INVALID KEY clause will be executed, in this case CONTINUE. You might wonder why we test for INVALID KEY if we then do nothing upon finding it. The answer is that the ANSI standard requires that every operation on an indexed or relative file that could cause a invalid key condition have either an INVALID KEY phrase or something called a **standard exception procedure.** In order to avoid the complications of using a standard exception procedure, we will just include an INVALID KEY phrase wherever it is needed to avoid having to use one.

Program P15-01 was run with the input data shown in Figure 15.2 and produced the report output shown in Figure 15.3.

FIGURE *15.1* ***continued***

```
S COBOL II RELEASE 3.1 09/19/89                    P15001   DATE SEP 15,1991 T
----+-*A-1-B--+----2----+----3----+----4----+----5----+----6----+----7-|--+

02240  PRODUCE-REGISTER-HEAD.
02250      WRITE REGISTER-RECORD-OUT FROM REPORT-HEADING-1 AFTER PAGE
02260      WRITE REGISTER-RECORD-OUT FROM REPORT-HEADING-2
02270      WRITE REGISTER-RECORD-OUT FROM REPORT-HEADING-3
02280      ADD 1 TO REGISTER-PAGE-NUMBER-W
02290      MOVE REGISTER-PAGE-NUMBER-W TO PAGE-NUMBER-OUT
02300      WRITE REGISTER-RECORD-OUT FROM REGISTER-PAGE-HEADING-1
02310                                     AFTER 2
02320      WRITE REGISTER-RECORD-OUT FROM PAGE-HEADING-2
02330      WRITE REGISTER-RECORD-OUT FROM REGISTER-PAGE-HEADING-3
02340                                     AFTER 3
02350      WRITE REGISTER-RECORD-OUT FROM REGISTER-PAGE-HEADING-4
02360      WRITE REGISTER-RECORD-OUT FROM BLANKS
02370      MOVE 11 TO LINE-COUNT-ER
02380      .
```

FIGURE *15.1* ***continued***

```

PRODUCE-ERROR-HEAD.
    WRITE ERROR-RECORD-OUT FROM REPORT-HEADING-1 AFTER PAGE
    WRITE ERROR-RECORD-OUT FROM REPORT-HEADING-2
    WRITE ERROR-RECORD-OUT FROM REPORT-HEADING-3
    ADD 1 TO ERROR-PAGE-NUMBER-W
    MOVE ERROR-PAGE-NUMBER-W TO PAGE-NUMBER-OUT
    WRITE ERROR-RECORD-OUT FROM ERROR-PAGE-HEADING-1 AFTER 2
    WRITE ERROR-RECORD-OUT FROM PAGE-HEADING-2
    WRITE ERROR-RECORD-OUT FROM ERROR-PAGE-HEADING-3 AFTER 3
    WRITE ERROR-RECORD-OUT FROM ERROR-PAGE-HEADING-4
    WRITE ERROR-RECORD-OUT FROM BLANKS
    MOVE 11 TO ERROR-LINE-COUNTER
    .

PROCESS-A-RECORD.
    ADD 1 TO NUMBER-OF-INPUT-RECORDS-W
    MOVE "N" TO ANY-ERRORS
    PERFORM CHECK-INPUT-FOR-VALIDITY
    IF ANY-ERRORS = "N"
        PERFORM BUILD-MASTER-RECORD
        PERFORM WRITE-MASTER-RECORD
    END-IF
    PERFORM READ-A-RECORD
    .

BUILD-MASTER-RECORD.
    MOVE ACCOUNT-NUMBER-IN TO ACCOUNT-NUMBER-M
    MOVE DEPOSITOR-NAME-IN TO DEPOSITOR-NAME-M
    MOVE AMOUNT-IN         TO CURRENT-BALANCE-M
    MOVE TODAYS-DATE       TO DATE-OF-LAST-TRANSACTION-M
    .

WRITE-MASTER-RECORD.
    WRITE ACCOUNT-MASTER-RECORD-OUT
        INVALID KEY CONTINUE
    END-WRITE
    IF WRITE-WAS-SUCCESSFUL
        ADD 1 TO NUMBER-OF-NEW-ACCOUNTS-W
        ADD AMOUNT-IN TO DEPOSIT-TOTAL-W
        PERFORM WRITE-NEW-ACCOUNT-LINE
    ELSE
    IF DUPLICATE-PRIME-RECORD-KEY
        ADD 1 TO NUMBER-OF-ERRONEOUS-RECORDS-W
        PERFORM WRITE-DUPLICATE-ERROR-MESSAGE
    ELSE
        DISPLAY " MASTER FILE WRITE STATUS = ", FILE-CHECK
        PERFORM TERMINATION
        STOP RUN
    END-IF
    END-IF
    .

CHECK-INPUT-FOR-VALIDITY.
    IF NOT VALID-CODE
        MOVE "Y" TO ANY-ERRORS
        PERFORM WRITE-INVALID-CODE-LINE
    END-IF
    IF DEPOSITOR-NAME-IS-MISSING
        MOVE "Y" TO ANY-ERRORS
        PERFORM WRITE-NAME-ERROR-MESSAGE
    END-IF
    IF AMOUNT-IN NOT NUMERIC
        MOVE "Y" TO ANY-ERRORS
        PERFORM WRITE-AMOUNT-MESSAGE
    END-IF
    IF ANY-ERRORS = "Y"
        ADD 1 TO NUMBER-OF-ERRONEOUS-RECORDS-W
    END-IF
    .
```

continued

FIGURE 15.1 *continued*

```
S COBOL II RELEASE 3.1 09/19/89                     P15001   DATE SEP 15,1991 T
----+-*A-1-B--+----2----+----3----+----4----+----5----+----6----+----7-|--+


 WRITE-NEW-ACCOUNT-LINE.
     MOVE ACCOUNT-NUMBER-IN TO ACCOUNT-NUMBER-OUT-G
     MOVE AMOUNT-IN         TO AMOUNT-OUT-G
     IF LINE-COUNT-ER + 1 > REGISTER-PAGE-LIMIT
         PERFORM PRODUCE-REGISTER-HEAD
     END-IF
     WRITE REGISTER-RECORD-OUT FROM NEW-ACCOUNT-LINE
     ADD 1 TO LINE-COUNT-ER
     .

 WRITE-INVALID-CODE-LINE.
     MOVE ACCOUNT-NUMBER-IN TO ACCOUNT-NUMBER-OUT-E
     MOVE CODE-IN           TO CODE-OUT
     MOVE INVALID-CODE-MSG  TO MESSAGE-E
     PERFORM WRITE-ERROR-LINE
     .

 WRITE-ERROR-LINE.
     IF ERROR-LINE-COUNTER + 1 > ERROR-PAGE-LIMIT
         PERFORM PRODUCE-ERROR-HEAD
     END-IF
     WRITE ERROR-RECORD-OUT FROM ERROR-LINE
     ADD 1 TO ERROR-LINE-COUNTER
     .

 WRITE-DUPLICATE-ERROR-MESSAGE.
     MOVE "DUPLICATE ACCOUNT NUMBER" TO MESSAGE-E
     MOVE ACCOUNT-NUMBER-IN          TO ACCOUNT-NUMBER-OUT-E
     PERFORM WRITE-ERROR-LINE
     .

 WRITE-NAME-ERROR-MESSAGE.
     MOVE "DEPOSITOR NAME MISSING" TO MESSAGE-E
     MOVE ACCOUNT-NUMBER-IN        TO ACCOUNT-NUMBER-OUT-E
     PERFORM WRITE-ERROR-LINE
     .

 WRITE-AMOUNT-MESSAGE.
     MOVE AMOUNT-IN-X             TO AMOUNT-OUT-X
     MOVE AMOUNT-NOT-NUMERIC-MSG TO MESSAGE-E
     MOVE ACCOUNT-NUMBER-IN       TO ACCOUNT-NUMBER-OUT-E
     PERFORM WRITE-ERROR-LINE
     .

 TERMINATION.
     PERFORM PRODUCE-TOTAL-LINES
     CLOSE ACCOUNT-MASTER-FILE-OUT
           ERROR-FILE-OUT
           TRANSACTION-REGISTER-FILE-OUT
     .

 PRODUCE-TOTAL-LINES.
     MOVE DEPOSIT-TOTAL-W TO AMOUNT-TOTAL-OUT
     MOVE NUMBER-OF-NEW-ACCOUNTS-W TO NUMBER-OF-NEW-ACCOUNTS-OUT
     MOVE NUMBER-OF-ERRONEOUS-RECORDS-W
         TO NUMBER-OF-ERRONEOUS-RCDS-OUT
     MOVE NUMBER-OF-INPUT-RECORDS-W
         TO NUMBER-OF-INPUT-RECORDS-OUT
     WRITE REGISTER-RECORD-OUT FROM FINAL-LINE-1 AFTER 2
     WRITE REGISTER-RECORD-OUT FROM FINAL-LINE-2 AFTER 2
     WRITE REGISTER-RECORD-OUT FROM FINAL-LINE-3 AFTER 2
     WRITE REGISTER-RECORD-OUT FROM FINAL-LINE-4 AFTER 2
     WRITE REGISTER-RECORD-OUT FROM FINAL-LINE-5 AFTER 2
     .
```

FIGURE 15.1 *continued*

```
 READ-A-RECORD.
     RETURN SORT-WORK-FILE
         AT END
             SET THERE-IS-NO-MORE-INPUT TO TRUE
     .
```

FIGURE 15.2 **Input to Program P15-01**

```
--------------------------------------------------------------------------------
         1         2         3         4         5         6         7         8
12345678901234567890123456789012345678901234567890123456789012345678901234567890
--------------------------------------------------------------------------------
10002300110000ROSEMARY LANE
10010500005000LENORE MILLER
10022000002460GENE GALLI
10017500001000MARY KEATING
20018200007500BOB LANIGAN
10018900003500J. & L. CAIN
10011200025000ROSEMARY LANE
3000070CA00000MICHELE CAPUANO
10012600075000JAMES BUDD
10041000031800GENE GALLI
10013300100000PAUL LERNER, D.D.S.
10014000002575BETH FALLON
10009800002000JANE HALEY
10010500005000ONE DAY CLEANERS
10016100002450ROBERT RYAN
10039100064200GENE GALLI
10016800012550KELLY HEDERMAN
10021000025000JERRY PARKS
10003500015000JOHN J. LEHMAN
10003200002500JOSEPH CAMILLO
10030600049300COMMUNITY DRUGS
10005600000100EVELYN SLATER
10006300007500
10007000050000PATRICK J. LEE
10027300027500VITO CACACI
10028000002000COMMUNITY DRUGS
10009600087100GENE GALLI
1003010FG15750PAT P. POWERS
10030800200000JOE GARCIA
10007700001037LESLIE MINSKY
10008400150000JOHN DAPRINO
10009100010000JOE'S DELI
10009800050000GEORGE CULHANE
10026600009957MARTIN LANG
10031500025000GRACE MICELI
10032200002000
10019900002100COMMUNITY DRUGS
10032900001000GUY VOLPONE
100336))))!%))SALVATORE CALI
10023100055500BILL WILLIAMS
10024500003500FRANK CAPUTO
10034900123400COMMUNITY DRUGS
10025200001500GENE GALLI
10025900002937
10000700100784ROSEBUCCI
10001400001000ROBERT DAVIS M.D.
10002100012500LORICE MONTI
10001500070000LENORE MILLER
10002000080000LENORE MILLER
10002100090000ROSEMARY LANE
10002200100000ROSEMARY LANE
10002800700159MICHAEL SMITH
10034300100000JOE & MARY SESSA
1000880021A000COMMUNITY DRUGS
10035000250000ROGER SHAW
```

FIGURE. 15.3 Report output from Program P15-01

```
                         ROBBEM STATE BANK
                         106 WEST 10TH ST.
                        BROOKLYN, NY  11212

                SAVINGS ACCOUNT MASTER FILE ERRORS
DATE   9/15/91                                          PAGE   1

       ACCOUNT                  NOTES
       NUMBER

        00007                   INVALID CODE 3
        00007                   INITIAL DEPOSIT NOT NUMERIC 0CA00000
        00021                   DUPLICATE ACCOUNT NUMBER
        00063                   DEPOSITOR NAME MISSING
        00088                   INITIAL DEPOSIT NOT NUMERIC 0021A000
        00098                   DUPLICATE ACCOUNT NUMBER
        00105                   DUPLICATE ACCOUNT NUMBER
        00182                   INVALID CODE 2
        00259                   DEPOSITOR NAME MISSING
        00301                   INITIAL DEPOSIT NOT NUMERIC 0FG15750
        00322                   DEPOSITOR NAME MISSING
        00336                   INITIAL DEPOSIT NOT NUMERIC ))))!%))


                         ROBBEM STATE BANK
                         106 WEST 10TH ST.
                        BROOKLYN, NY  11212

               SAVINGS ACCOUNT MASTER FILE CREATION
DATE   9/15/91                                          PAGE   1

       ACCOUNT     INITIAL      NOTES
       NUMBER      DEPOSIT

        00007      1,007.84     NEW ACCOUNT
        00014         10.00     NEW ACCOUNT
        00015        700.00     NEW ACCOUNT
        00020        800.00     NEW ACCOUNT
        00021        900.00     NEW ACCOUNT
        00022      1,000.00     NEW ACCOUNT
        00023      1,100.00     NEW ACCOUNT
        00028      7,001.59     NEW ACCOUNT
        00032         25.00     NEW ACCOUNT
        00035        150.00     NEW ACCOUNT
        00056          1.00     NEW ACCOUNT
        00070        500.00     NEW ACCOUNT
        00077         10.37     NEW ACCOUNT
        00084      1,500.00     NEW ACCOUNT
        00091        100.00     NEW ACCOUNT
        00096        871.00     NEW ACCOUNT
        00098        500.00     NEW ACCOUNT
        00105         50.00     NEW ACCOUNT
        00112        250.00     NEW ACCOUNT
        00126        750.00     NEW ACCOUNT
        00133      1,000.00     NEW ACCOUNT
        00140         25.75     NEW ACCOUNT
        00161         24.50     NEW ACCOUNT
        00168        125.50     NEW ACCOUNT
```

FIGURE 15.3 *continued*

```
                    ROBBEM STATE BANK
                    106 WEST 10TH ST.
                   BROOKLYN, NY  11212

             SAVINGS ACCOUNT MASTER FILE CREATION
DATE   9/15/91                                      PAGE  2

        ACCOUNT      INITIAL      NOTES
        NUMBER       DEPOSIT

         00175          10.00     NEW ACCOUNT
         00189          35.00     NEW ACCOUNT
         00199          21.00     NEW ACCOUNT
         00210         250.00     NEW ACCOUNT
         00220          24.60     NEW ACCOUNT
         00231         555.00     NEW ACCOUNT
         00245          35.00     NEW ACCOUNT
         00252          15.00     NEW ACCOUNT
         00266          99.57     NEW ACCOUNT
         00273         275.00     NEW ACCOUNT
         00280          20.00     NEW ACCOUNT
         00306         493.00     NEW ACCOUNT
         00308       2,000.00     NEW ACCOUNT
         00315         250.00     NEW ACCOUNT
         00329          10.00     NEW ACCOUNT
         00343       1,000.00     NEW ACCOUNT
         00349       1,234.00     NEW ACCOUNT
         00350       2,500.00     NEW ACCOUNT
         00391         642.00     NEW ACCOUNT
         00410         318.00     NEW ACCOUNT

       TOTAL         28,189.72

                       CONTROL COUNTS

                NUMBER OF NEW ACCOUNTS          44

                NUMBER OF ERRONEOUS RECORDS     11

                TOTAL                           55
```

The DISPLAY Statement

The ANSI standard format of the DISPLAY statement is as follows:

```
DISPLAY {identifier-1} ... [UPON mnemonic-name-1] [WITH NO ADVANCING]
        {literal-1   }
```

The standard DISPLAY statement can be used to print output on a high-speed printer or console typewriter, or to show output on the screen of a computer or terminal. The DISPLAY statement prints or shows the literals and identifiers in order from left to right in the order in which they appear in the DISPLAY statement, using as many output records or lines as are needed for all the data items listed. A mnemonic name can be used in the optional UPON phrase to direct the output to a specific output device. Each COBOL system has its own default output device in case the UPON clause is omitted.

In the usual case, when the **NO ADVANCING** phrase is omitted, a printer or a cursor will advance to the next line when a DISPLAY statement is through executing. If the NO ADVANCING phrase is included, a printer will remain positioned at the line just printed and a cursor will remain in its final position after a DISPLAY statement executes.

The standard DISPLAY statement has very limited capabilities for line formatting, line skipping and spacing, and output editing. It is best used for transmitting messages to the computer operator. We will discuss much more powerful nonstandard DISPLAY statements in Chapter 21.

EXERCISE *1*

Write a program to create an indexed inventory master file. Use the same formats for transaction and master records that you used when you created your sequential master file in Exercise 3, Chapter 13, page 457. Specify the Supplier Code and Storage Location as alternate keys. Decide for yourself whether either or both of the alternate keys should be specified WITH DUPLICATES. Save the master file for use later in this chapter.

Updating an Indexed File

The big difference between updating a sequential master file and updating an indexed master file is that when you are updating an indexed file there is no need to copy the old file in order to make the desired changes. COBOL can take advantage of its random-access capability to update existing master records in place on the file, add new records in their proper places, and delete existing master records from the file.

The hierarchy diagram for Program P15-02 is shown in Figure 15.4. The "Initialization" includes a priming read of the transaction file. The program READs each transaction and determines from the Account Number of the transaction which master record it should try to READ from the master file.

"Process master record" tries to READ into the master input area the master record whose key is equal to the transaction key, regardless of the type of transaction that is being processed. Even if the current transaction is to add a new record to the master file, "Process master record" nevertheless READs the master file in search of a record having the same key as the transaction. If there is such a record, "Process master record" sets a flag to "Y"; if not, it sets the flag to "N."

"Process transaction record" applies the transaction record to the master record in the master input area. For each of the five different types of transactions, suitable validity checks are carried out. If the transaction is valid, it is applied to the master record in the master input area. For a valid transaction of Code 1, to add a new record to the file, there will be no record in the master input area, and the new master record is built there.

FIGURE 15.4 Hierarchy diagram for Program P15-02

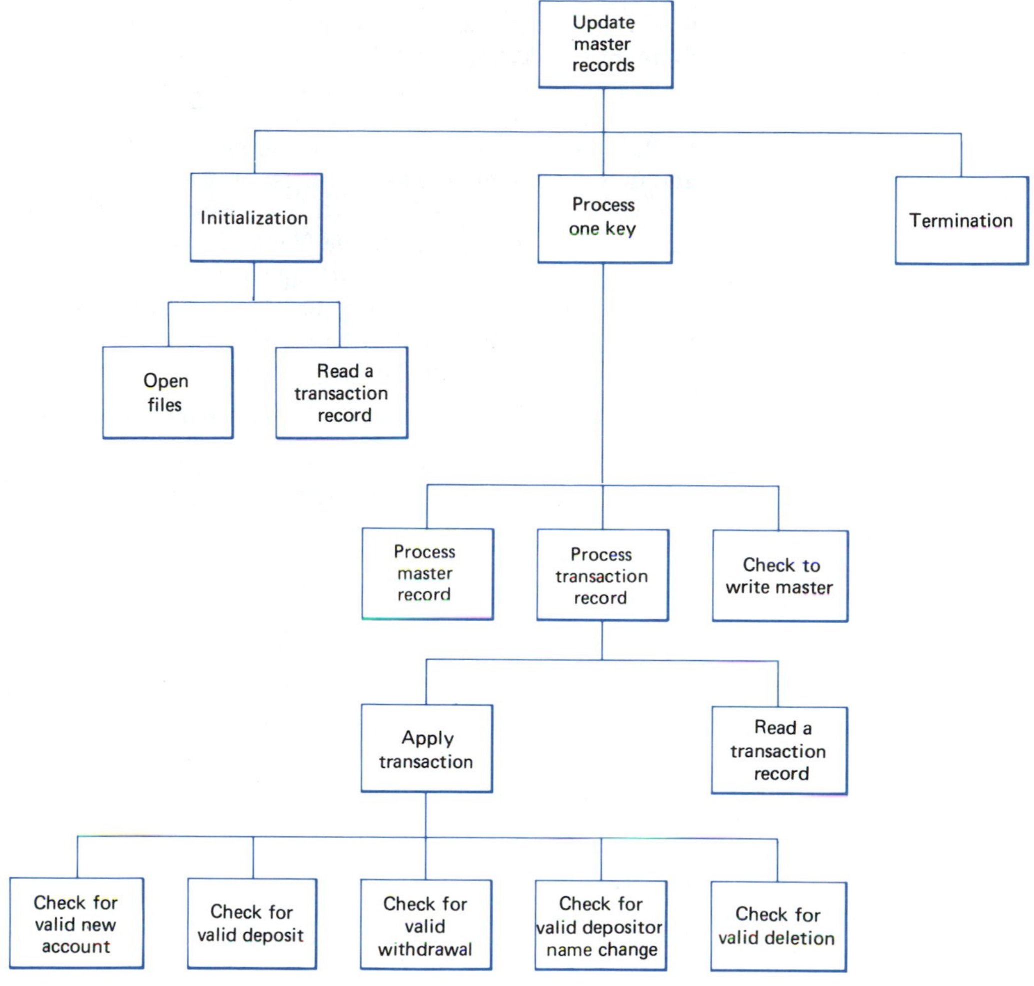

"Check to write master" determines whether a master record should be written from the master input area to replace an existing master record on the file, whether a new master record should be written from the input area to the file, whether a master record should be deleted from the file, or whether none of those actions should be taken. "Check to write master" then carries out any action it finds necessary.

A Program to Update an Indexed File

The transaction input formats for Program P15-02 are the same as the ones we used when we updated a sequential master file, in Program P14-03. The formats are described on pages 493 and 511.

Program P15-02 is shown in Figure 15.5. There is only one FILE-CONTROL entry for the master file, at line 00120, because there is only one master file. The one master file serves as both the input and output file. It has its records read in, updated, and put back in the same place. The FILE-CONTROL entry includes the **ACCESS RANDOM** clause, line 00180, to tell COBOL that in this program the ACCOUNT-MASTER-FILE-I-O will be accessed randomly.

In the Data Division the TRANSACTION-FILE-IN and the TRANSACTION-INPUT-AREA are defined as in Program P14-03, at lines 00370 through 00390 and 00850 through 01040, respectively. The TRANSACTION-INPUT-AREA is redefined as in Program P14-03 to accommodate all the different transaction formats. Notice that the TRANSACTION-INPUT-AREA is only 34 characters long. This shows that an area in working storage INTO which an input record will be read need not be 80 characters long. In this case the first 34 of the 80 characters in each input record will be read INTO the TRANSACTION-INPUT-AREA.

The master area is defined a little differently from the way it was defined in Chapter 14. It turns out that we don't need a master input area separate from a master work area in this program, as we did in Program P14-03. So the master input area is defined in the File Section as ACCOUNT-MASTER-RECORD-I-O, at line 00310, and serves as both the master input area and the place where we work on master records.

And of course we don't need any sort file. In this program the transactions can be processed in random order and do not need to be SORTed. Some programmers might want to SORT the transaction file so that the transaction register and the error report will print in Account Number sequence, but such SORTing is not needed for the update to take place correctly. The random-access capability of indexed files is used to advantage even if the transaction file is SORTed, for the program can still READ just the master records it needs and no others.

FIGURE *15.5* **Program P15-02**

```
S COBOL II RELEASE 3.1 09/19/89                 P15002   DATE SEP 16,1991 T
----+-*A-1-B--+----2----+----3----+----4----+----5----+----6----+----7-%--+

00010  IDENTIFICATION DIVISION.
00020  PROGRAM-ID. P15-02.
00030 *
00040 *     THIS PROGRAM UPDATES AN INDEXED MASTER FILE ON DISK
00050 *     WITH ADDITIONS, CHANGES, AND DELETIONS.
00060 *
00070 *****************************************************************
00080
00090  ENVIRONMENT DIVISION.
00100  INPUT-OUTPUT SECTION.
00110  FILE-CONTROL.
00120      SELECT ACCOUNT-MASTER-FILE-I-O         ASSIGN TO MSTRDISK
00130          ORGANIZATION INDEXED
00140          RECORD KEY IS ACCOUNT-NUMBER-M
00150          ALTERNATE RECORD KEY IS DEPOSITOR-NAME-M
00160              WITH DUPLICATES
00170          STATUS IS FILE-CHECK
00180          ACCESS RANDOM.
00190      SELECT TRANSACTION-FILE-IN             ASSIGN TO INFILE.
00200      SELECT TRANSACTION-REGISTER-FILE-OUT   ASSIGN TO PRINTER1.
00210      SELECT ERROR-FILE-OUT                  ASSIGN TO PRINTER2.
00220
00230 *****************************************************************
```

FIGURE *15.5* *continued*

```
00240
00250  DATA DIVISION.
00260  FILE SECTION.
00270  FD  ACCOUNT-MASTER-FILE-I-O
00280      LABEL RECORDS ARE STANDARD
00290      RECORD CONTAINS 39 CHARACTERS.
00300
00310  01  ACCOUNT-MASTER-RECORD-I-O.
00320      05  ACCOUNT-NUMBER-M                 PIC X(5).
00330      05  DEPOSITOR-NAME-M                 PIC X(20).
00340      05  DATE-OF-LAST-TRANSACTION-M       PIC 9(6).
00350      05  CURRENT-BALANCE-M                PIC S9(6)V99.
00360
00370  FD  TRANSACTION-FILE-IN.
00380
00390  01  TRANSACTION-RECORD-IN                PIC X(80).
00400
00410  FD  TRANSACTION-REGISTER-FILE-OUT.
00420
00430  01  REGISTER-RECORD-OUT                  PIC X(76).
00440
00450  FD  ERROR-FILE-OUT.
00460
00470  01  ERROR-RECORD-OUT                     PIC X(114).
00480
00490  WORKING-STORAGE SECTION.
00500  01  FILE-CHECK.
00510      88 MASTER-FILE-OPENED                VALUE "00".
00520      88 MASTER-RECORD-FOUND               VALUE "00".
00530      88 NO-FILE-OPERATION                 VALUE "00".
00540      88 MASTER-RECORD-NOT-FOUND           VALUE "23".
00550      05  STATUS-KEY-1                     PIC X.
00560          88 FILE-OPERATION-FAILED         VALUES "1" THRU "9".
00570      05  STATUS-KEY-2                     PIC X.
00580  01  IS-MASTER-RECORD-IN-WORK-AREA        PIC X.
00590      88 MASTER-RECORD-IS-IN-WORKAREA        VALUE "Y".
00600      88 MASTER-RECORD-ISNT-IN-WORKAREA    VALUE "N".
00610  01  IS-MASTER-RECORD-IN-THE-FILE         PIC X.
00620      88 MASTER-RECORD-IS-IN-THE-FILE        VALUE "Y".
00630      88 MASTER-RECORD-ISNT-IN-THE-FILE    VALUE "N".
00640  01  PACKED-DECIMAL.
00650   02 NUMBER-OF-INPUT-RECORDS-W            PIC S9(3) VALUE ZERO.
00660   02 NUMBER-OF-ERRONEOUS-RECORDS-W        PIC S9(3) VALUE ZERO.
00670   02 DEPOSIT-TOTAL-W                      PIC S9(7)V99 VALUE ZERO.
00680   02 WITHDRAWAL-TOTAL-W                   PIC S9(7)V99 VALUE ZERO.
00690   02 NUMBER-OF-DEPOSITS-W                 PIC S9(3) VALUE 0.
00700   02 NUMBER-OF-WITHDRAWALS-W              PIC S9(3) VALUE 0.
00710   02 NUMBER-OF-NAME-CHANGES-W             PIC S9(3) VALUE 0.
00720   02 NUMBER-OF-CLOSED-ACCOUNTS-W          PIC S9(3) VALUE 0.
00730   02 NUMBER-OF-NEW-ACCOUNTS-W             PIC S9(3) VALUE 0.
00740   02 PAGE-NUMBER-W                        PIC S99    VALUE 0.
00750   02 ERROR-PAGE-NUMBER-W                  PIC S99    VALUE 0.
00760  01  BLANK-LINE                           PIC X      VALUE SPACE.
00770  01  PAGE-LIMIT              COMP SYNC    PIC S99    VALUE 28.
00780  01  LINE-COUNT-ER           COMP SYNC    PIC S99.
00790  01  ERROR-PAGE-LIMIT        COMP SYNC    PIC S99    VALUE 45.
00800  01  ERROR-LINE-COUNTER      COMP SYNC    PIC S99.
00810  01  TODAYS-DATE.
00820      05  TODAYS-YEAR                      PIC 99.
00830      05  TODAYS-MONTH-AND-DAY             PIC 9(4).
```

continued

A flag IS-MASTER-RECORD-IN-THE-FILE has been defined, at line 00610. This flag is needed in addition to the usual flag IS-MASTER-RECORD-IN-WORK-AREA, line 00580. You will see how the two flags are used when we look at the Procedure Division.

FIGURE *15.5* *continued*

```
S COBOL II RELEASE 3.1 09/19/89              P15002    DATE SEP 16,1991 T
----+-*A-1-B--+----2----+----3----+----4----+----5----+----6----+----7-%--+

       01  TRANSACTION-INPUT-AREA.
           88  NO-MORE-TRANSACTION-RECORDS  VALUE HIGH-VALUES.
           88  NO-TRANSACTION-RECORDS       VALUE HIGH-VALUES.
           05  TRANSACTION-CODE             PIC X.
               88  NEW-ACCOUNT              VALUE "1".
               88  DEPOSIT                  VALUE "2".
               88  WITHDRAWAL               VALUE "3".
               88  NAME-CHANGE              VALUE "4".
               88  DELETION                 VALUE "5".
           05  ACCOUNT-NUMBER-T             PIC X(5).
           05  DEPOSIT-AND-WITHDRAWAL-AMTS.
               10  DEPOSIT-AMOUNT           PIC 9(6)V99.
               10  DEPOSIT-AMOUNT-X     REDEFINES DEPOSIT-AMOUNT
                                            PIC X(8).
               10  WITHDRAWAL-AMOUNT    REDEFINES DEPOSIT-AMOUNT
                                            PIC 9(6)V99.
               10  WITHDRAWAL-AMOUNT-X REDEFINES DEPOSIT-AMOUNT
                                            PIC X(8).
           05  DEPOSITOR-NAME-NEW-ACCOUNT   PIC X(20).
               88 DEPOSITOR-NAME-MISSING    VALUE SPACES.
       01  TRANSACTION-4-INPUT-AREA REDEFINES TRANSACTION-INPUT-AREA.
           05                               PIC X(6).
           05  DEPOSITOR-NAME               PIC X(20).
               88  REPLACEMENT-NAME-MISSING VALUE SPACES.
           05                               PIC X(8).

       01  REPORT-HEADING-1.
           05               PIC X(39) VALUE SPACES.
           05               PIC X(17) VALUE "ROBBEM STATE BANK".

       01  REPORT-HEADING-2.
           05               PIC X(39) VALUE SPACES.
           05               PIC X(17) VALUE "106 WEST 10TH ST.".

       01  REPORT-HEADING-3.
           05               PIC X(38) VALUE SPACES.
           05               PIC X(19) VALUE "BROOKLYN, NY  11212".

       01  PAGE-HEADING-1.
           05               PIC X(29) VALUE SPACES.
           05               PIC X(36)
                            VALUE "SAVINGS ACCOUNT TRANSACTION REGISTER".

       01  PAGE-HEADING-2.
           05               PIC X(17)      VALUE SPACES.
           05               PIC X(5)       VALUE "DATE".
           05  TODAYS-MONTH-AND-DAY        PIC Z9/99/.
           05  TODAYS-YEAR                 PIC 99B(35).
           05               PIC X(5)       VALUE "PAGE".
           05  PAGE-NUMBER-OUT             PIC Z9.

       01  PAGE-HEADING-3.
           05                    PIC X(20) VALUE SPACES.
           05                    PIC X(12) VALUE "ACCOUNT".
           05                    PIC X(14) VALUE "DEPOSITS".
           05                    PIC X(18) VALUE "WITHDRAWALS".
           05                    PIC X(5)  VALUE "NOTES".

       01  PAGE-HEADING-4.
           05                    PIC X(20) VALUE SPACES.
           05                    PIC X(6)  VALUE "NUMBER".

       01  ERROR-PAGE-HEADING-1.
           05                    PIC X(33) VALUE SPACES.
           05                    PIC X(28) VALUE
                                 "SAVINGS ACCOUNT ERROR REPORT".
```

FIGURE 15.5 *continued*

```
 01  ERROR-PAGE-HEADING-3.
     05                       PIC X(20) VALUE SPACES.
     05                       PIC X(44) VALUE "ACCOUNT".
     05                       PIC X(5)  VALUE "NOTES".
 01  NEW-ACCOUNT-LINE.
     05                       PIC X(21) VALUE SPACES.
     05  ACCOUNT-NUMBER-OUT             PIC 9(5)B(5).
     05  DEPOSIT-AMOUNT-OUT             PIC ZZZ,ZZZ.99B(21).
     05                       PIC X(11) VALUE "NEW ACCOUNT".
 01  DEPOSIT-LINE.
     05                       PIC X(21) VALUE SPACES.
     05  ACCOUNT-NUMBER-OUT             PIC 9(5)B(5).
     05  DEPOSIT-AMOUNT-OUT             PIC ZZZ,ZZZ.99.
 01  WITHDRAWAL-LINE.
     05                       PIC X(21) VALUE SPACES.
     05  ACCOUNT-NUMBER-OUT             PIC 9(5)B(19).
     05  WITHDRAWAL-AMOUNT-OUT          PIC ZZZ,ZZZ.99.
 01  NAME-CHANGE-LINE.
     05                       PIC X(21) VALUE SPACES.
     05  ACCOUNT-NUMBER-OUT             PIC 9(5)B(5).
     05  DEPOSITOR-NAME-OUT             PIC X(20)B(11).
     05                       PIC X(11) VALUE "NAME CHANGE".
 01  DELETION-LINE.
     05                       PIC X(21) VALUE SPACES.
     05  ACCOUNT-NUMBER-OUT             PIC 9(5)B(19).
     05  CURRENT-BALANCE-M-OUT          PIC ZZZ,ZZZ.99B(7).
     05                       PIC X(14) VALUE "ACCOUNT CLOSED".
 01  ERROR-LINE.
     05                 PIC X(21) VALUE SPACES.
     05  ACCOUNT-NUMBER-E     PIC X(5)B(36).
     05  ERROR-MESSAGE        PIC X(52).
 01  DEPOSIT-AMOUNT-INVALID-MSG.
     05                 PIC X(29) VALUE
                        "DEPOSIT AMOUNT NOT NUMERIC -".
     05  DEPOSIT-AMOUNT-OUT   PIC X(8).
 01  WITHDRAWAL-AMOUNT-INVALID-MSG.
     05                 PIC X(32) VALUE
                        "WITHDRAWAL AMOUNT NOT NUMERIC -".
     05  WITHDRAWAL-AMOUNT-E    PIC X(8).
 01  INVALID-CODE-MSG.
     05                 PIC X(27) VALUE "INVALID TRANSACTION CODE -".
     05  TRANSACTION-CODE-OUT PIC X.
 01  FINAL-LINE-1.
     05                       PIC X(17) VALUE SPACES.
     05                       PIC X(12) VALUE "TOTALS".
     05  DEPOSIT-TOTAL-OUT              PIC Z,ZZZ,ZZZ.99BB.
     05  WITHDRAWAL-TOTAL-OUT           PIC Z,ZZZ,ZZZ.99.
 01  FINAL-LINE-2.
     05                       PIC X(40) VALUE SPACES.
     05                       PIC X(14) VALUE "CONTROL COUNTS".
 01  FINAL-LINE-3.
     05                       PIC X(34) VALUE SPACES.
     05                       PIC X(26)
                              VALUE "NUMBER OF NEW ACCOUNTS".
     05  NUMBER-OF-NEW-ACCOUNTS-OUT PIC ZZ9.
```

continued

FIGURE 15.5 *continued*

```
S COBOL II RELEASE 3.1 09/19/89                P15002   DATE SEP 16,1991 T
----+-*A-1-B--+----2----+----3----+----4----+----5----+----6----+----7-%--+

02190
02200  01  FINAL-LINE-4.
02210      05                    PIC X(34) VALUE SPACES.
02220      05                    PIC X(26)
02230                            VALUE "NUMBER OF DEPOSITS".
02240      05  NUMBER-OF-DEPOSITS-OUT   PIC ZZ9.
02250
02260  01  FINAL-LINE-5.
02270      05                    PIC X(34) VALUE SPACES.
02280      05                    PIC X(26)
02290                            VALUE "NUMBER OF WITHDRAWALS".
02300      05  NUMBER-OF-WITHDRAWALS-OUT PIC ZZ9.
02310
02320  01  FINAL-LINE-6.
02330      05                    PIC X(34) VALUE SPACES.
02340      05                    PIC X(26)
02350                            VALUE "NUMBER OF NAME CHANGES".
02360      05  NUMBER-OF-NAME-CHANGES-OUT PIC ZZ9.
02370
02380  01  FINAL-LINE-7.
02390      05                    PIC X(34) VALUE SPACES.
02400      05                    PIC X(26)
02410                            VALUE "NUMBER OF CLOSED ACCOUNTS".
02420      05  NUMBER-OF-CLOSED-ACCOUNTS-OUT  PIC ZZ9.
02430
02440  01  FINAL-LINE-8.
02450      05                    PIC X(34) VALUE SPACES.
02460      05                    PIC X(26)
02470                            VALUE "NUMBER OF ERRORS".
02480      05  NUMBER-OF-ERRONEOUS-RECRDS-OUT
02490                            PIC ZZ9.
02500
02510  01  FINAL-LINE-9.
02520      05                    PIC X(34) VALUE SPACES.
02530      05                    PIC X(24) VALUE "TOTAL".
02540      05  NUMBER-OF-INPUT-RECORDS-OUT PIC Z,ZZ9.
02550
02560  01  NO-TRANSACTIONS.
02570      05                    PIC X(21) VALUE SPACES.
02580      05                    PIC X(15) VALUE "NO TRANSACTIONS".
02590
02600 *****************************************************************
```

The Procedure Division begins at line 02620. We have no SORTing to do in this program, so the structure of the Procedure Division is simplified by the omission of the SORT statement.

Notice that ACCOUNT-MASTER-FILE-I-O is OPENed as both an input and output file, at line 02740. **I-O** is a third **OPEN mode,** in addition to the OPEN modes that you already know, INPUT and OUTPUT. Be careful how you spell I-O when you use it in an OPEN statement. You must not spell it INPUT-OUTPUT. INPUT-OUTPUT is the name of a section in the Environment Division, the INPUT-OUTPUT SECTION. And the section header INPUT-OUTPUT SECTION cannot be written I-O SECTION.

There is a fourth OPEN mode, **EXTEND,** that is used only to add records to the end of a file. We will not discuss the EXTEND mode in this book.

The paragraph PROCESS-MASTER-RECORD shows how to READ an indexed file randomly on its prime key. First, the key of the desired record must be MOVEd to whatever field was named in the RECORD KEY clause in the FILE-

FIGURE 15.5 *continued*

```
PROCEDURE DIVISION.
UPDATE-MASTER-RECORDS.
    PERFORM INITIALIZATION
    PERFORM PROCESS-ONE-KEY UNTIL NO-MORE-TRANSACTION-RECORDS
    PERFORM TERMINATION
    STOP RUN
    .

INITIALIZATION.
    OPEN INPUT  TRANSACTION-FILE-IN
         OUTPUT TRANSACTION-REGISTER-FILE-OUT
                ERROR-FILE-OUT
         I-O    ACCOUNT-MASTER-FILE-I-O
    IF NOT MASTER-FILE-OPENED
        DISPLAY " MASTER FILE OPEN STATUS = ", FILE-CHECK
        CLOSE TRANSACTION-FILE-IN
              TRANSACTION-REGISTER-FILE-OUT
              ERROR-FILE-OUT
              ACCOUNT-MASTER-FILE-I-O
        STOP RUN
    END-IF
    ACCEPT TODAYS-DATE FROM DATE
    MOVE CORR TODAYS-DATE TO PAGE-HEADING-2
    PERFORM PRODUCE-REPORT-HEADINGS
    PERFORM READ-A-TRANSACTION-RECORD
    IF NO-TRANSACTION-RECORDS
        WRITE REGISTER-RECORD-OUT FROM NO-TRANSACTIONS
    END-IF
    .

PRODUCE-REPORT-HEADINGS.
    PERFORM WRITE-REGISTER-HEADINGS
    PERFORM WRITE-ERROR-REPORT-HEADINGS
    .

WRITE-REGISTER-HEADINGS.
    ADD 1 TO PAGE-NUMBER-W
    MOVE PAGE-NUMBER-W TO PAGE-NUMBER-OUT
    WRITE REGISTER-RECORD-OUT FROM
        REPORT-HEADING-1 AFTER ADVANCING PAGE
    WRITE REGISTER-RECORD-OUT FROM REPORT-HEADING-2
    WRITE REGISTER-RECORD-OUT FROM REPORT-HEADING-3
    WRITE REGISTER-RECORD-OUT FROM PAGE-HEADING-1 AFTER 2
    WRITE REGISTER-RECORD-OUT FROM PAGE-HEADING-2
    WRITE REGISTER-RECORD-OUT FROM PAGE-HEADING-3 AFTER 3
    WRITE REGISTER-RECORD-OUT FROM PAGE-HEADING-4
    WRITE REGISTER-RECORD-OUT FROM BLANK-LINE
    MOVE 11 TO LINE-COUNT-ER
    .

WRITE-ERROR-REPORT-HEADINGS.
    ADD 1 TO ERROR-PAGE-NUMBER-W
    MOVE ERROR-PAGE-NUMBER-W TO PAGE-NUMBER-OUT
    WRITE ERROR-RECORD-OUT FROM REPORT-HEADING-1 AFTER PAGE
    WRITE ERROR-RECORD-OUT FROM REPORT-HEADING-2
    WRITE ERROR-RECORD-OUT FROM REPORT-HEADING-3
    WRITE ERROR-RECORD-OUT FROM ERROR-PAGE-HEADING-1 AFTER 2
    WRITE ERROR-RECORD-OUT FROM PAGE-HEADING-2
    WRITE ERROR-RECORD-OUT FROM ERROR-PAGE-HEADING-3 AFTER 3
    WRITE ERROR-RECORD-OUT FROM PAGE-HEADING-4
    WRITE ERROR-RECORD-OUT FROM BLANK-LINE
    MOVE 11 TO ERROR-LINE-COUNTER
    .

PROCESS-ONE-KEY.
    PERFORM PROCESS-MASTER-RECORD
    PERFORM PROCESS-TRANSACTION-RECORD
    PERFORM CHECK-TO-WRITE-MASTER
    .
```

continued

CONTROL entry for the file. That is done by the MOVE statement at line 03380. Then a READ statement is given, naming the file to be read. A random READ statement of an indexed file sets the STATUS field if one is given for the file. The ANSI standard meanings of the STATUS codes related to READing an indexed file randomly on its prime key are given in Table 15.2.

TABLE *15.2*
ANSI standard STATUS codes related to READing an indexed file randomly on its prime RECORD KEY

Status Code	Meaning
00	Successful completion
23	Invalid key—no record found
30	Permanent error (hardware malfunction)
47	File not OPENed as INPUT or I-O

Your own COBOL system may have additional codes in the range 90 through 99. STATUS code 23 arises from an attempt to READ a master record not on the file. That is, if we give COBOL an Account Number and ask it to READ a master record from the file having that Account Number, and the record is not found on the file, COBOL sets the STATUS field to 23. As with the WRITE statement, an IF statement and the STATUS code are all we need to determine the outcome of the READ.

If PROCESS-MASTER-RECORD finds a master record whose key is equal to the key of the current transaction, it READs the master record into the master area and sets both flags, IS-MASTER-RECORD-IN-WORK-AREA and IS-MASTER-RECORD-IN-THE-FILE, to "Y." If no master record is found with a key equal to the key of the current transaction, nothing is placed in the master area and both flags are set to "N."

After PROCESS-MASTER-RECORD executes, the paragraph PROCESS-TRANSACTION-RECORD executes APPLY-TRANSACTION. APPLY-TRANSACTION performs validity checks and carries out the actions implied by each particular transaction. Among the validity checks is one to see that a master record is in the master area if one is supposed to be there and that nothing is in the master area if nothing is supposed to be there. Remember that for most transactions, namely a deposit, a withdrawal, a name change, and a deletion, there must be in the master area a master record whose key is equal to the key of the transaction. But for adding a new account, there most definitely must not be a master record with the key of the transaction, for that would mean that the transaction was trying to create a record for an Account Number that is already in the file.

So in the course of its execution, APPLY-TRANSACTION might leave both flags alone (if it does a deposit, a withdrawal, or a name change), or it might set IS-MASTER-RECORD-IN-WORK-AREA to "N" (if it does a deletion), or it might set IS-MASTER-RECORD-IN-WORK-AREA to "Y" (if it builds a new master record in the master area). Notice that APPLY-TRANSACTION can never change the flag IS-MASTER-RECORD-IN-THE-FILE, for APPLY-TRANSACTION never acts directly on the file on disk.

After APPLY-TRANSACTION has applied the transaction to the master record in the master area, CHECK-TO-WRITE-MASTER executes. CHECK-TO-WRITE-MASTER determines whether or not there is a master record in the master area and what to do about it. If there is a master record in the master area,

FIGURE 15.5 *continued*

```
S COBOL II RELEASE 3.1 09/19/89                P15002   DATE SEP 16,1991 T
----+-*A-1-B--+----2----+----3----+----4----+----5----+----6----+----7-%--+

03310
03320  PROCESS-TRANSACTION-RECORD.
03330      PERFORM APPLY-TRANSACTION
03340      PERFORM READ-A-TRANSACTION-RECORD
03350      .
03360
03370  PROCESS-MASTER-RECORD.
03380      MOVE ACCOUNT-NUMBER-T TO ACCOUNT-NUMBER-M
03390      READ ACCOUNT-MASTER-FILE-I-O
03400          INVALID KEY CONTINUE
03410      END-READ
03420      IF MASTER-RECORD-FOUND
03430          SET MASTER-RECORD-IS-IN-THE-FILE
03440              MASTER-RECORD-IS-IN-WORKAREA   TO TRUE
03450      ELSE
03460      IF MASTER-RECORD-NOT-FOUND
03470          SET MASTER-RECORD-ISNT-IN-THE-FILE
03480              MASTER-RECORD-ISNT-IN-WORKAREA TO TRUE
03490      ELSE
03500          DISPLAY " MASTER FILE READ STATUS = ", FILE-CHECK
03510          PERFORM TERMINATION
03520          STOP RUN
03530      END-IF
03540      END-IF
03550      .
03560
03570  CHECK-TO-WRITE-MASTER.
03580      EVALUATE MASTER-RECORD-IS-IN-WORKAREA
03590          ALSO MASTER-RECORD-IS-IN-THE-FILE
03600      WHEN TRUE ALSO FALSE
03610          WRITE ACCOUNT-MASTER-RECORD-I-O
03620              INVALID KEY CONTINUE
03630          END-WRITE
03640      WHEN TRUE ALSO TRUE
03650          REWRITE ACCOUNT-MASTER-RECORD-I-O
03660              INVALID KEY CONTINUE
03670          END-REWRITE
03680      WHEN FALSE ALSO TRUE
03690          DELETE ACCOUNT-MASTER-FILE-I-O
03700              INVALID KEY CONTINUE
03710          END-DELETE
03720      WHEN OTHER
03730          SET NO-FILE-OPERATION TO TRUE
03740      END-EVALUATE
03750      IF FILE-OPERATION-FAILED
03760          DISPLAY " MASTER FILE WRITE STATUS = ", FILE-CHECK
03770          PERFORM TERMINATION
03780          STOP RUN
03790      END-IF
03800      .
```

continued

CHECK-TO-WRITE-MASTER will want to put the record onto the master file. But what about this master record to be put onto the file—is it a new record being added to the file or is it replacing a record already on the file? CHECK-TO-WRITE-MASTER examines the flag IS-MASTER-RECORD-IN-THE-FILE to determine whether it should WRITE a new record onto the master file, as at line 03610, or **REWRITE** an existing master record, as at line 03650. Any successful WRITE statement to a file with any kind of organization always adds a record to the file. A random WRITE to an indexed file tells COBOL to find the place on the file where this new record should be slipped in and to move some existing records around if necessary to make space for it. A REWRITE statement tells

COBOL to find the place on the file where this key is already located, and replace the existing record with a new one.

On the other hand, if there is no master record in the work area but there is one in the file, the DELETE statement at line 03690 removes the record from the file.

FIGURE *15.5* *continued*

```
S COBOL II RELEASE 3.1 09/19/89                P15002   DATE SEP 16,1991 T
----+-*A-1-B--+----2----+----3----+----4----+----5----+----6----+----7-%--+

03810
03820  READ-A-TRANSACTION-RECORD.
03830      READ TRANSACTION-FILE-IN INTO TRANSACTION-INPUT-AREA
03840          AT END
03850              SET NO-MORE-TRANSACTION-RECORDS TO TRUE
03860          NOT AT END
03870              ADD 1 TO NUMBER-OF-INPUT-RECORDS-W
03880      .
03890
03900  APPLY-TRANSACTION.
03910      EVALUATE TRUE
03920      WHEN NEW-ACCOUNT
03930          PERFORM CHECK-FOR-VALID-NEW-ACCOUNT
03940      WHEN DEPOSIT
03950          PERFORM CHECK-FOR-VALID-DEPOSIT
03960      WHEN WITHDRAWAL
03970          PERFORM CHECK-FOR-VALID-WITHDRAWAL
03980      WHEN NAME-CHANGE
03990          PERFORM CHECK-FOR-VALID-NAME-CHANGE
04000      WHEN DELETION
04010          PERFORM CHECK-FOR-VALID-DELETION
04020      WHEN OTHER
04030          ADD 1 TO NUMBER-OF-ERRONEOUS-RECORDS-W
04040          PERFORM WRITE-INVALID-CODE-LINE
04050      END-EVALUATE
04060      .
04070
04080  CHECK-FOR-VALID-NEW-ACCOUNT.
04090      EVALUATE TRUE
04100      WHEN MASTER-RECORD-IS-IN-WORKAREA
04110          ADD 1 TO NUMBER-OF-ERRONEOUS-RECORDS-W
04120          PERFORM WRITE-NEW-ACCT-INVALID-LINE
04130      WHEN DEPOSIT-AMOUNT NOT NUMERIC
04140          ADD 1 TO NUMBER-OF-ERRONEOUS-RECORDS-W
04150          PERFORM WRITE-DEPOSIT-INVALID-LINE
04160      WHEN DEPOSITOR-NAME-MISSING
04170          ADD 1 TO NUMBER-OF-ERRONEOUS-RECORDS-W
04180          PERFORM WRITE-NAME-MISSING-LINE
04190      WHEN OTHER
04200          MOVE DEPOSITOR-NAME-NEW-ACCOUNT TO DEPOSITOR-NAME-M
04210          MOVE TODAYS-DATE TO DATE-OF-LAST-TRANSACTION-M
04220          MOVE DEPOSIT-AMOUNT TO CURRENT-BALANCE-M
04230          PERFORM WRITE-NEW-ACCOUNT-LINE
04240          SET MASTER-RECORD-IS-IN-WORKAREA TO TRUE
04250      END-EVALUATE
04260      .
04270
```

FIGURE 15.5 *continued*

```
CHECK-FOR-VALID-DEPOSIT.
    IF DEPOSIT-AMOUNT NOT NUMERIC
        ADD 1 TO NUMBER-OF-ERRONEOUS-RECORDS-W
        PERFORM WRITE-DEPOSIT-INVALID-LINE
    ELSE
    IF MASTER-RECORD-ISNT-IN-WORKAREA
        ADD 1 TO NUMBER-OF-ERRONEOUS-RECORDS-W
        PERFORM WRITE-MASTER-MISSING-LINE
    ELSE
        ADD DEPOSIT-AMOUNT TO CURRENT-BALANCE-M
        MOVE TODAYS-DATE TO DATE-OF-LAST-TRANSACTION-M
        PERFORM WRITE-DEPOSIT-LINE
    END-IF
    END-IF
    .

CHECK-FOR-VALID-WITHDRAWAL.
    IF WITHDRAWAL-AMOUNT NOT NUMERIC
        ADD 1 TO NUMBER-OF-ERRONEOUS-RECORDS-W
        PERFORM WRITE-WITHDRAWAL-INVALID-LINE
    ELSE
    IF MASTER-RECORD-ISNT-IN-WORKAREA
        ADD 1 TO NUMBER-OF-ERRONEOUS-RECORDS-W
        PERFORM WRITE-MASTER-MISSING-LINE
    ELSE
        SUBTRACT WITHDRAWAL-AMOUNT FROM CURRENT-BALANCE-M
        MOVE TODAYS-DATE TO DATE-OF-LAST-TRANSACTION-M
        PERFORM WRITE-WITHDRAWAL-LINE
    END-IF
    END-IF
    .

CHECK-FOR-VALID-NAME-CHANGE.
    IF REPLACEMENT-NAME-MISSING
        ADD 1 TO NUMBER-OF-ERRONEOUS-RECORDS-W
        PERFORM WRITE-NAME-MISSING-LINE
    ELSE
    IF MASTER-RECORD-ISNT-IN-WORKAREA
        ADD 1 TO NUMBER-OF-ERRONEOUS-RECORDS-W
        PERFORM WRITE-MASTER-MISSING-LINE
    ELSE
        MOVE DEPOSITOR-NAME TO DEPOSITOR-NAME-M
        MOVE TODAYS-DATE TO DATE-OF-LAST-TRANSACTION-M
        PERFORM WRITE-NAME-CHANGE-LINE
    END-IF
    END-IF
    .

CHECK-FOR-VALID-DELETION.
    IF MASTER-RECORD-ISNT-IN-WORKAREA
        ADD 1 TO NUMBER-OF-ERRONEOUS-RECORDS-W
        PERFORM WRITE-MASTER-MISSING-LINE
    ELSE
        PERFORM WRITE-DELETION-LINE
        SET MASTER-RECORD-ISNT-IN-WORKAREA TO TRUE
    END-IF
    .

WRITE-NEW-ACCOUNT-LINE.
    MOVE ACCOUNT-NUMBER-T
         TO ACCOUNT-NUMBER-OUT IN NEW-ACCOUNT-LINE
    MOVE DEPOSIT-AMOUNT
         TO DEPOSIT-AMOUNT-OUT IN NEW-ACCOUNT-LINE
    IF 1 + LINE-COUNT-ER GREATER THAN PAGE-LIMIT
       PERFORM WRITE-REGISTER-HEADINGS
    END-IF
    WRITE REGISTER-RECORD-OUT FROM NEW-ACCOUNT-LINE
    ADD 1 TO LINE-COUNT-ER
    ADD DEPOSIT-AMOUNT TO DEPOSIT-TOTAL-W
    ADD 1 TO NUMBER-OF-NEW-ACCOUNTS-W
    .
```

continued

FIGURE 15.5 *continued*

```
S COBOL II RELEASE 3.1 09/19/89              P15002   DATE SEP 16,1991 T
----+-*A-1-B--+----2----+----3----+----4----+----5----+----6----+----7-%--+

       WRITE-DEPOSIT-LINE.
           MOVE ACCOUNT-NUMBER-T TO ACCOUNT-NUMBER-OUT IN DEPOSIT-LINE
           MOVE DEPOSIT-AMOUNT TO DEPOSIT-AMOUNT-OUT IN DEPOSIT-LINE
           IF 1 + LINE-COUNT-ER GREATER THAN PAGE-LIMIT
               PERFORM WRITE-REGISTER-HEADINGS
           END-IF
           WRITE REGISTER-RECORD-OUT FROM DEPOSIT-LINE
           ADD 1 TO LINE-COUNT-ER
           ADD DEPOSIT-AMOUNT TO DEPOSIT-TOTAL-W
           ADD 1 TO NUMBER-OF-DEPOSITS-W
           .

       WRITE-WITHDRAWAL-LINE.
           MOVE ACCOUNT-NUMBER-T
                TO ACCOUNT-NUMBER-OUT IN WITHDRAWAL-LINE
           MOVE WITHDRAWAL-AMOUNT TO
                WITHDRAWAL-AMOUNT-OUT IN WITHDRAWAL-LINE
           IF 1 + LINE-COUNT-ER GREATER THAN PAGE-LIMIT
               PERFORM WRITE-REGISTER-HEADINGS
           END-IF
           WRITE REGISTER-RECORD-OUT FROM WITHDRAWAL-LINE
           ADD 1 TO LINE-COUNT-ER
           ADD WITHDRAWAL-AMOUNT TO WITHDRAWAL-TOTAL-W
           ADD 1 TO NUMBER-OF-WITHDRAWALS-W
           .

       WRITE-DEPOSIT-INVALID-LINE.
           MOVE DEPOSIT-AMOUNT-X TO
                DEPOSIT-AMOUNT-OUT IN DEPOSIT-AMOUNT-INVALID-MSG
           MOVE DEPOSIT-AMOUNT-INVALID-MSG TO ERROR-MESSAGE
           PERFORM WRITE-ERROR-LINE
           .

       WRITE-WITHDRAWAL-INVALID-LINE.
           MOVE WITHDRAWAL-AMOUNT-X TO WITHDRAWAL-AMOUNT-E
           MOVE WITHDRAWAL-AMOUNT-INVALID-MSG TO ERROR-MESSAGE
           PERFORM WRITE-ERROR-LINE
           .

       WRITE-NAME-MISSING-LINE.
           MOVE "DEPOSITOR NAME MISSING" TO ERROR-MESSAGE
           PERFORM WRITE-ERROR-LINE
           .

       WRITE-NAME-CHANGE-LINE.
           MOVE ACCOUNT-NUMBER-T
                TO ACCOUNT-NUMBER-OUT IN NAME-CHANGE-LINE
           MOVE DEPOSITOR-NAME TO DEPOSITOR-NAME-OUT
           IF 1 + LINE-COUNT-ER GREATER THAN PAGE-LIMIT
               PERFORM WRITE-REGISTER-HEADINGS
           END-IF
           WRITE REGISTER-RECORD-OUT FROM NAME-CHANGE-LINE
           ADD 1 TO LINE-COUNT-ER
           ADD 1 TO NUMBER-OF-NAME-CHANGES-W
           .

       WRITE-DELETION-LINE.
           MOVE ACCOUNT-NUMBER-T TO ACCOUNT-NUMBER-OUT IN DELETION-LINE
           MOVE CURRENT-BALANCE-M TO CURRENT-BALANCE-M-OUT
           IF 1 + LINE-COUNT-ER GREATER THAN PAGE-LIMIT
               PERFORM WRITE-REGISTER-HEADINGS
           END-IF
           WRITE REGISTER-RECORD-OUT FROM DELETION-LINE
           ADD 1 TO LINE-COUNT-ER
           ADD CURRENT-BALANCE-M TO WITHDRAWAL-TOTAL-W
           ADD 1 TO NUMBER-OF-CLOSED-ACCOUNTS-W
           .
```

FIGURE 15.5 *continued*

```
WRITE-INVALID-CODE-LINE.
    MOVE TRANSACTION-CODE TO TRANSACTION-CODE-OUT
    MOVE INVALID-CODE-MSG TO ERROR-MESSAGE
    PERFORM WRITE-ERROR-LINE
    .

WRITE-MASTER-MISSING-LINE.
    MOVE "MASTER RECORD DOES NOT EXIST" TO ERROR-MESSAGE
    PERFORM WRITE-ERROR-LINE
    .

WRITE-NEW-ACCT-INVALID-LINE.
    MOVE "ACCOUNT NUMBER ALREADY ON FILE NEW ACCOUNT INVALID"
         TO ERROR-MESSAGE
    PERFORM WRITE-ERROR-LINE
    .

WRITE-ERROR-LINE.
    IF 1 + ERROR-LINE-COUNTER GREATER THAN ERROR-PAGE-LIMIT
        PERFORM WRITE-ERROR-REPORT-HEADINGS
    END-IF
    MOVE ACCOUNT-NUMBER-T TO ACCOUNT-NUMBER-E
    WRITE ERROR-RECORD-OUT FROM ERROR-LINE
    ADD 1 TO ERROR-LINE-COUNTER
    .

TERMINATION.
    PERFORM PRODUCE-TOTAL-LINES
    CLOSE TRANSACTION-FILE-IN
          ACCOUNT-MASTER-FILE-I-O
          ERROR-FILE-OUT
          TRANSACTION-REGISTER-FILE-OUT
    .

PRODUCE-TOTAL-LINES.
    MOVE DEPOSIT-TOTAL-W    TO DEPOSIT-TOTAL-OUT
    MOVE WITHDRAWAL-TOTAL-W TO WITHDRAWAL-TOTAL-OUT
    WRITE REGISTER-RECORD-OUT FROM FINAL-LINE-1 AFTER 3
    WRITE REGISTER-RECORD-OUT FROM FINAL-LINE-2 AFTER 2
    MOVE NUMBER-OF-NEW-ACCOUNTS-W TO NUMBER-OF-NEW-ACCOUNTS-OUT
    WRITE REGISTER-RECORD-OUT FROM FINAL-LINE-3 AFTER 2
    MOVE NUMBER-OF-DEPOSITS-W TO NUMBER-OF-DEPOSITS-OUT
    WRITE REGISTER-RECORD-OUT FROM FINAL-LINE-4 AFTER 2
    MOVE NUMBER-OF-WITHDRAWALS-W TO NUMBER-OF-WITHDRAWALS-OUT
    WRITE REGISTER-RECORD-OUT FROM FINAL-LINE-5 AFTER 2
    MOVE NUMBER-OF-NAME-CHANGES-W TO NUMBER-OF-NAME-CHANGES-OUT
    WRITE REGISTER-RECORD-OUT FROM FINAL-LINE-6 AFTER 2
    MOVE NUMBER-OF-CLOSED-ACCOUNTS-W
         TO NUMBER-OF-CLOSED-ACCOUNTS-OUT
    WRITE REGISTER-RECORD-OUT FROM FINAL-LINE-7 AFTER 2
    MOVE NUMBER-OF-ERRONEOUS-RECORDS-W
         TO NUMBER-OF-ERRONEOUS-RECRDS-OUT
    WRITE REGISTER-RECORD-OUT FROM FINAL-LINE-8 AFTER 2
    MOVE NUMBER-OF-INPUT-RECORDS-W
         TO NUMBER-OF-INPUT-RECORDS-OUT
    WRITE REGISTER-RECORD-OUT FROM FINAL-LINE-9 AFTER 2
    .
```

A random WRITE, REWRITE, or DELETE to an indexed file sets the STATUS code if one is specified for the file. The ANSI standard meanings of the STATUS codes for a random WRITE to an indexed file are given in Table 15.3. The meanings of the STATUS codes for a random REWRITE to an indexed file are given in Table 15.4.

TABLE 15.3
ANSI standard STATUS codes related to writing an indexed file randomly

Status Code	Meaning
00	Successful completion
02	Successful completion, and the record just written created a duplicate key value for an ALTERNATE RECORD KEY for which DUPLICATES are allowed
22	Invalid key—an attempt has been made to WRITE a record that would create an invalid duplicate key
24	Invalid key—boundary violation (attempt to WRITE past the physical end of the file)
30	Permanent error (hardware malfunction)
48	File not OPENed as OUTPUT, I-O, or EXTEND

TABLE 15.4
ANSI standard STATUS codes related to rewriting an indexed file randomly

Status Code	Meaning
00	Successful completion
02	Successful completion, and the record just written created a duplicate key value for an ALTERNATE RECORD KEY for which DUPLICATES are allowed
22	Invalid key—an attempt has been made to REWRITE a record that would create an invalid duplicate key
23	Invalid key—the record to be rewritten over is not on the file
30	Permanent error (hardware malfunction)
49	File not OPENed as I-O

The meanings of the STATUS codes for a random DELETE to an indexed file are given in Table 15.5.

TABLE 15.5
ANSI standard STATUS codes related to deleting records from an indexed file randomly

Status Code	Meaning
00	Successful completion
23	Invalid key—the record to be DELETEd is not on the file
30	Permanent error (hardware malfunction)
49	File not OPENed as I-O

In all cases, your own COBOL system may have additional codes in the range 90 through 99.

Program P15-02 was run with the transaction input data shown in Figure 15.6 and the master file created by Program P15-01. Program P15-02 produced the report output shown in Figure 15.7.

FIGURE 15.6 Transaction input to Program P15-02

```
--------------------------------------------------------------------------------
         1         2         3         4         5         6         7         8
12345678901234567890123456789012345678901234567890123456789012345678901234567890
--------------------------------------------------------------------------------
20007700015000
20037100015000
70038500007500JAMES WASHINGTON
10039200007500INEZ WASHINGTON
400084JOHN & SALLY DUPRINO
20016100125634
30002800150050
10042000150000JOHN RICE
30022000002460
20008400357429
20009100150000
400140BETH DENNY
10039900014Z00GARY NASTI
200007)))$%)))
20039100064200
30001400100000
20002100012750
30011900002735
70042700002500GREG PRUITT
20013300256300
400220GENE & THERESA GALLI
20012600035000
30016800011000
400266
20002800015327
20009100120000
20021000025000
20021000025000
10009200043200GENE GALLI
30009100050000
20027300172500
400098GEORGE & ANN CULHANE
500168
20017500019202
500182
20021000025000
20028000231700
80031500013798
200182
5
10030800017000AL MARRELLA
20030800005000
10037100001000THOMAS HERR
400032GENE GALLI
10037100015000ALISE MARKOVITZ
10040600120000
10041300010000BILL HAYES
10039800001000JUAN ALVAREZ
30010500015025
```

FIGURE 15.7 **Report output from Program P15-02**

```
                         ROBBEM STATE BANK
                         106 WEST 10TH ST.
                        BROOKLYN, NY  11212

             SAVINGS ACCOUNT TRANSACTION REGISTER
DATE  9/16/91                                          PAGE  1


   ACCOUNT     DEPOSITS      WITHDRAWALS       NOTES
   NUMBER

    00077         150.00
    00392          75.00                     NEW ACCOUNT
    00084      JOHN & SALLY DUPRINO          NAME CHANGE
    00161       1,256.34
    00028                       1,500.50
    00420       1,500.00                     NEW ACCOUNT
    00220                          24.60
    00084       3,574.29
    00091       1,500.00
    00140      BETH DENNY                    NAME CHANGE
    00391         642.00
    00014                       1,000.00
    00021         127.50
    00133       2,563.00
    00220      GENE & THERESA GALLI          NAME CHANGE
    00126         350.00
    00168                         110.00
```

FIGURE 15.7 *continued*

```
                         ROBBEM STATE BANK
                         106 WEST 10TH ST.
                        BROOKLYN, NY   11212

               SAVINGS ACCOUNT TRANSACTION REGISTER
DATE   9/16/91                                          PAGE   2

   ACCOUNT      DEPOSITS       WITHDRAWALS        NOTES
   NUMBER

    00028         153.27
    00091       1,200.00
    00210         250.00
    00210         250.00
    00092         432.00                        NEW ACCOUNT
    00091                          500.00
    00273       1,725.00
    00098      GEORGE & ANN CULHANE             NAME CHANGE
    00168                           15.50       ACCOUNT CLOSED
    00175         192.02
    00210         250.00
    00280       2,317.00
    00308          50.00
    00371          10.00                        NEW ACCOUNT
    00032      GENE GALLI                       NAME CHANGE
    00413         100.00                        NEW ACCOUNT
    00398          10.00                        NEW ACCOUNT


TOTALS         18,677.42       3,150.60

                          CONTROL COUNTS

                NUMBER OF NEW ACCOUNTS       6

                NUMBER OF DEPOSITS          17

                NUMBER OF WITHDRAWALS        5

                NUMBER OF NAME CHANGES       5

                NUMBER OF CLOSED ACCOUNTS    1

                NUMBER OF ERRORS            15

                TOTAL                       49
```

continued

FIGURE 15.7 *continued*

```
                    ROBBEM STATE BANK
                    106 WEST 10TH ST.
                   BROOKLYN, NY  11212

             SAVINGS ACCOUNT ERROR REPORT
DATE  9/16/91                                   PAGE  1

   ACCOUNT                                     NOTES
   NUMBER

    00371                               MASTER RECORD DOES NOT EXIST
    00385                               INVALID TRANSACTION CODE - 7
    00399                               DEPOSIT AMOUNT NOT NUMERIC - 00014Z00
    00007                               DEPOSIT AMOUNT NOT NUMERIC - )))$%)))
    00119                               MASTER RECORD DOES NOT EXIST
    00427                               INVALID TRANSACTION CODE - 7
    00266                               DEPOSITOR NAME MISSING
    00182                               MASTER RECORD DOES NOT EXIST
    00315                               INVALID TRANSACTION CODE - 8
    00182                               DEPOSIT AMOUNT NOT NUMERIC -
                                        MASTER RECORD DOES NOT EXIST
    00308                               ACCOUNT NUMBER ALREADY ON FILE NEW ACCOUNT INVALID
    00371                               ACCOUNT NUMBER ALREADY ON FILE NEW ACCOUNT INVALID
    00406                               DEPOSITOR NAME MISSING
    00105                               WITHDRAWAL AMOUNT NOT NUMERIC - 00015025
```

EXERCISE 2

Write a program to randomly update the indexed inventory master file you created in Exercise 1, page 554. Use the same transaction formats that you used when you updated your sequential inventory master file in Exercise 3, Chapter 14, Page 528.

Use the same report formats you used in Exercise 3, Chapter 14. Have your program print a line for each transaction processed. For a new inventory record created on the master file, set the Quantity on Hand field and the Dates of Last Withdrawal and Last Receipt to zero, and insert today's date into the Date Created and Date of Last Access fields.

For each existing master record that is updated, have your program insert today's date into the Date of Last Access field. Also for each existing master record that is updated, have your program check whether the Quantity on Hand is equal to or less than the Reorder Point, and print a message showing the Reorder Quantity and the word REORDER if it is. If an attempt is made to delete a Part Number having a nonzero Quantity on Hand, do not delete it. Instead, count the transaction as erroneous and have your program print the Quantity on Hand and a message NONZERO QUANTITY ON HAND on the error report. Save the updated file for use later in this chapter.

Using Dynamic Access

Our next program demonstrates how an indexed file can be accessed sequentially and randomly in a single run. Program P15-03 lists selected records, and the records to be listed may be selected in either of two ways. We can ask Program P15-03 to list the contents of the master record for a particular Account Number, or we can ask it to list the contents of all the master records for all the Depositor Names that start with a particular letter of the alphabet. The requests may be in any order and the two types of requests may be mixed in any desired way.

To find a record on the master file for a particular Account Number, Program P15-03 does a random READ the way Program P15-02 did. But to find all the master records for all Depositor Names beginning with a given letter, Program P15-03 has to combine random access with sequential access. First it uses its random-access capability to find the first record for the given letter of the alphabet and then READs the file sequentially on Depositor Name, listing out the contents of all master records for that same letter. The formats of the two types of transactions accepted by Program P15-03 are:

Positions	Field
1	Code 6
2–6	Account Number
1	Code 7
2	First letter of Depositor Name

The meanings of the transaction codes are:

6—List the contents of the master record for this Account Number

7—List the contents of all the master records for all Depositor Names that start with this letter

The hierarchy diagram for Program P15-03 is similar to the one for Program P14-01, which listed selected records from our sequential savings-account master file. Program P14-01 listed records only on their Account Number and so had only one type of input transaction. In Program P15-03 we have two types of transactions, so the procedure for processing a transaction is more involved. The portion of the hierarchy diagram for "Process transaction record" and its subfunctions is shown in Figure 15.8. The box "Process one transaction" determines whether the transaction is asking for a listing of one master record by Account Number or for a listing of all the Depositor Names beginning with a certain letter and processes it accordingly.

FIGURE 15.8 Hierarchy diagram for "Process transaction record" and its subfunctions for Program P15-03

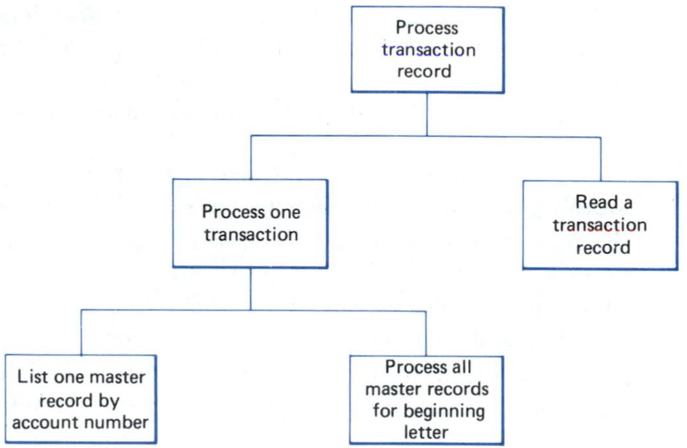

A Program Using Dynamic Access

Program P15-03 is shown in Figure 15.9. The FILE-CONTROL entry at line 00120 shows the use of the ACCESS **DYNAMIC** clause. In ACCOUNT-MASTER-RECORD-IN, line 00310, the DEPOSITOR-NAME-M field is broken down into two elementary items. As you already know, COBOL can access an indexed file

FIGURE 15.9 Program P15-03

```
S COBOL II RELEASE 3.1 09/19/89                P15003   DATE SEP 17,1991 T
----+-*A-1-B--+----2----+----3----+----4----+----5----+----6----+----7-|--+

00010  IDENTIFICATION DIVISION.
00020  PROGRAM-ID. P15-03.
00030 *
00040 *    THIS PROGRAM LISTS SELECTED RECORDS FROM AN INDEXED
00050 *    MASTER FILE.
00060 *
00070 *****************************************************************
00080
00090  ENVIRONMENT DIVISION.
00100  INPUT-OUTPUT SECTION.
00110  FILE-CONTROL.
00120      SELECT ACCOUNT-MASTER-FILE-IN      ASSIGN TO DISKUNIT
00130          ORGANIZATION INDEXED
00140          ACCESS DYNAMIC
00150          RECORD KEY IS ACCOUNT-NUMBER-M
00160          ALTERNATE RECORD KEY IS DEPOSITOR-NAME-M
00170              WITH DUPLICATES
00180          STATUS IS MASTER-FILE-CHECK.
00190      SELECT TRANSACTION-FILE-IN         ASSIGN TO INFILE.
00200      SELECT LISTING-FILE-OUT            ASSIGN TO PRINTER1.
00210      SELECT ERROR-FILE-OUT              ASSIGN TO PRINTER2.
00220
00230 *****************************************************************
00240
00250  DATA DIVISION.
00260  FILE SECTION.
00270  FD  ACCOUNT-MASTER-FILE-IN
00280      LABEL RECORDS ARE STANDARD
00290      RECORD CONTAINS 39 CHARACTERS.
00300
```

on its prime key and its alternate key(s). COBOL can also access an indexed file on any field that is a subordinate part of an alternate key field, provided that the subordinate field is at the left end of the alternate key field. Our field FIRST-LETTER-OF-DEPOSITOR-NAME is subordinate to and at the left end of the alternate key field DEPOSITOR-NAME-M, so Program P15-03 can access the master file on the basis of FIRST-LETTER-OF-DEPOSITOR-NAME. You will see how this feature is used when we look at the Procedure Division.

The TRANSACTION-INPUT-AREA, at line 00790, is defined a little differently from before. Since the two different kinds of transactions contain two different kinds of fields that will be used to access the master file, the TRANSACTION-KEY field has been broken into two level-10 fields. You will see how Program P15-03 uses these definitions to access the master file on the basis of either the Account Number or the Depositor Name, when we look at the Procedure Division.

Program P15-03 has some complications that we have not seen in earlier programs. All of the complications stem from the fact that the two different types of transactions provide two different kinds of access keys to the master file. In all our earlier programs dealing with master files, only the Account Number was used to access the master file regardless of what kind of transaction the program was processing. In Program P15-03, on the other hand, we use a single field, TRANSACTION-KEY, to hold the key of the current transaction whether that key is a letter of the alphabet followed by four blanks or a five-character Account Number.

Nearly all the complications relating to the TRANSACTION-KEY can be confined to the portion of the program that READs transaction records. This shows a general principle of the logic we are using to process our master files: Any complications regarding the formats of the transaction or master records can usually be confined to the lowest levels of the hierarchy diagram, namely to the READing of the files. The logic expressed in the upper levels of the diagram remains unchanged, or nearly so.

FIGURE *15.9* *continued*

```
00310  01  ACCOUNT-MASTER-RECORD-IN.
00320      05  ACCOUNT-NUMBER-M             PIC X(5).
00330      05  DEPOSITOR-NAME-M.
00340          10  FIRST-LETTER-OF-DEPOSITOR-NAME
00350                                       PIC X.
00360          10                           PIC X(19).
00370      05  DATE-OF-LAST-TRANSACTION-M   PIC 9(6).
00380      05  CURRENT-BALANCE-M            PIC S9(6)V99.
00390
00400  FD  TRANSACTION-FILE-IN.
00410
00420  01  TRANSACTION-RECORD-IN           PIC X(80).
00430
00440  FD  LISTING-FILE-OUT.
00450
00460  01  LISTING-RECORD-OUT              PIC X(79).
00470
```

continued

FIGURE 15.9 *continued*

```
S COBOL II RELEASE 3.1 09/19/89                  P15003   DATE SEP 17,1991 T
----+-*A-1-B--+----2----+----3----+----4----+----5----+----6----+----7-|--+

       FD  ERROR-FILE-OUT.

       01  ERROR-RECORD-OUT                    PIC X(71).

       WORKING-STORAGE SECTION.
       01  MASTER-FILE-CHECK.
           88  MASTER-FILE-OPENED              VALUE "00".
           88  RECORD-NOT-FOUND                VALUE "23".
           88  END-OF-MASTER-FILE-REACHED      VALUE "10".
           05  MASTER-STATUS-KEY-1             PIC X.
               88 FILE-OPERATION-WAS-SUCCESSFUL VALUE "0".
           05                                  PIC X.
       01  IS-THERE-A-MASTER-RECORD            PIC X.
           88 THERE-IS-A-MASTER-RECORD         VALUE "Y".
           88 THERE-ISNT-A-MASTER-RECORD       VALUE "N".
       01  PACKED-DECIMAL.
        02 NUMBER-OF-INPUT-RECORDS-W           PIC S9(3) VALUE ZERO.
        02 NUMBER-OF-ERRONEOUS-RECORDS-W       PIC S9(3) VALUE ZERO.
        02 NUMBER-OF-SELECTED-RECORDS-W        PIC S9(3) VALUE ZERO.
        02 CURRENT-BALANCE-TOTAL-W             PIC S9(7)V99    VALUE 0.
        02 PAGE-NUMBER-W                       PIC S99   VALUE 0.
        02 ERROR-PAGE-NUMBER-W                 PIC S99   VALUE 0.
       01  PAGE-LIMIT        COMP SYNC         PIC S99   VALUE 35.
       01  LINE-COUNT-ER     COMP SYNC         PIC S99.
       01  ERROR-PAGE-LIMIT COMP SYNC          PIC S99   VALUE 45.
       01  ERROR-LINE-COUNTER COMP SYNC        PIC S99.
       01  BLANK-LINE                          PIC X     VALUE SPACE.
       01  TODAYS-DATE.
           05  TODAYS-YEAR                     PIC 99.
           05  TODAYS-MONTH-AND-DAY            PIC 9(4).

       01  TRANSACTION-INPUT-AREA.
           88  NO-MORE-TRANSACTION-RECORDS     VALUE HIGH-VALUES.
           88  NO-TRANSACTION-RECORDS          VALUE HIGH-VALUES.
           05  TRANSACTION-CODE-T              PIC X.
               88  ACCOUNT-NUMBER-REQUEST      VALUE "6".
               88  DEPOSITOR-NAMES-REQUEST     VALUE "7".
               88  TRANSACTION-CODE-IS-VALID
                                               VALUES "6" "7".
           05  TRANSACTION-KEY.
               10  STARTING-LETTER-T           PIC X.
               10  UNUSED-PORTION-OF-KEY       PIC X(4).

       01  REPORT-HEADING-1.
           05                  PIC X(39) VALUE SPACES.
           05                  PIC X(17) VALUE "ROBBEM STATE BANK".

       01  REPORT-HEADING-2.
           05                  PIC X(39) VALUE SPACES.
           05                  PIC X(17) VALUE "106 WEST 10TH ST.".

       01  REPORT-HEADING-3.
           05                  PIC X(38) VALUE SPACES.
           05                  PIC X(19) VALUE "BROOKLYN, NY  11212".

       01  PAGE-HEADING-1.
           05                  PIC X(35) VALUE SPACES.
           05                  PIC X(25) VALUE "SELECTED SAVINGS ACCOUNTS".

       01  ERROR-HEADING-1.
           05                  PIC X(39) VALUE SPACES.
           05                  PIC X(16) VALUE "SELECTION ERRORS".
```

FIGURE 15.9 *continued*

```
 01  PAGE-HEADING-2.
     05                        PIC X(25) VALUE SPACES.
     05                        PIC X(5)  VALUE "DATE".
     05  TODAYS-MONTH-AND-DAY      PIC  Z9/99/.
     05  TODAYS-YEAR       PIC 99B(23).
     05                        PIC X(5)  VALUE "PAGE".
     05  PAGE-NUMBER-OUT             PIC Z9.

 01  PAGE-HEADING-3.
     05                        PIC X(21) VALUE SPACES.
     05                        PIC X(12) VALUE "ACCOUNT".
     05                        PIC X(12) VALUE "CURRENT".
     05                        PIC X(19) VALUE "DATE OF LAST".
     05                        PIC X(9)  VALUE "DEPOSITOR".

 01  ERROR-HEADING-3.
     05                        PIC X(21) VALUE SPACES.
     05                        PIC X(12) VALUE "ACCOUNT".

 01  PAGE-HEADING-4.
     05                        PIC X(21) VALUE SPACES.
     05                        PIC X(12) VALUE "NUMBER".
     05                        PIC X(12) VALUE "BALANCE".
     05                        PIC X(19) VALUE "TRANSACTION".
     05                        PIC X(4)  VALUE "NAME".

 01  ERROR-HEADING-4.
     05                        PIC X(21) VALUE SPACES.
     05                        PIC X(12) VALUE "NUMBER".

 01  REPORT-LINE.
     05                        PIC X(22)  VALUE SPACES.
     05  ACCOUNT-NUMBER-OUT          PIC X(5)B(4).
     05  CURRENT-BALANCE-OUT         PIC ZZZ,ZZZ.99B(7).
     05  DATE-OF-LAST-TRANSACTION-OUT PIC 9(6)B(5).
     05  DEPOSITOR-NAME-OUT          PIC X(20).

 01  INVALID-CODE-LINE.
     05                    PIC X(22)   VALUE SPACES.
     05  TRANSACTION-KEY-OUT   PIC X(5)B(16).
     05                    PIC X(15)   VALUE "INVALID CODE - ".
     05  TRANSACTION-CODE-OUT    PIC X.

 01  MASTER-MISSING-LINE.
     05                    PIC X(22)   VALUE SPACES.
     05  TRANSACTION-KEY-OUT   PIC X(5)B(16).
     05                    PIC X(28)
         VALUE "MASTER RECORD DOES NOT EXIST".

 01  FINAL-LINE-1.
     05                        PIC X(23) VALUE SPACES.
     05                        PIC X(6)  VALUE "TOTAL".
     05  CURRENT-BALANCE-TOTAL-OUT PIC Z,ZZZ,ZZZ.99.

 01  FINAL-LINE-2.
     05                        PIC X(40) VALUE SPACES.
     05                        PIC X(14) VALUE "CONTROL COUNTS".

 01  FINAL-LINE-3.
     05                        PIC X(34) VALUE SPACES.
     05                        PIC X(28)
                               VALUE "NUMBER OF SELECTED RECORDS".
     05  NUMBER-OF-SELECTED-RECORDS-OUT  PIC ZZ9.

 01  FINAL-LINE-4.
     05                        PIC X(34) VALUE SPACES.
     05                        PIC X(28)
                               VALUE "NUMBER OF ERRONEOUS RECORDS".
     05  NUMBER-OF-ERRONEOUS-RECRDS-OUT PIC ZZ9.
```

continued

FIGURE 15.9 *continued*

```
S COBOL II RELEASE 3.1 09/19/89                    P15003   DATE SEP 17,1991 T
----+-*A-1-B--+----2----+----3----+----4----+----5----+----6----+----7-|--+

01800
01810  01  FINAL-LINE-5.
01820      05                        PIC X(34) VALUE SPACES.
01830      05                        PIC X(28)
01840                                VALUE "NUMBER OF INPUT RECORDS".
01850      05  NUMBER-OF-INPUT-RECORDS-OUT      PIC ZZ9.
01860
01870  01  NO-TRANSACTIONS.
01880      05                        PIC X(21) VALUE SPACES.
01890      05                        PIC X(20) VALUE "NO TRANSACTION INPUT".
01900
01910 *****************************************************************
01920
01930  PROCEDURE DIVISION.
01940  LIST-RECORDS.
01950      PERFORM INITIALIZATION
01960      PERFORM PROCESS-ONE-KEY UNTIL NO-MORE-TRANSACTION-RECORDS
01970      PERFORM TERMINATION
01980      STOP RUN
01990      .
02000
02010  INITIALIZATION.
02020      OPEN INPUT  ACCOUNT-MASTER-FILE-IN
02030                  TRANSACTION-FILE-IN
02040           OUTPUT LISTING-FILE-OUT
02050                  ERROR-FILE-OUT
02060      IF NOT MASTER-FILE-OPENED
02070          DISPLAY " MASTER FILE OPEN STATUS = " MASTER-FILE-CHECK
02080          CLOSE ACCOUNT-MASTER-FILE-IN
02090                TRANSACTION-FILE-IN
02100                LISTING-FILE-OUT
02110                ERROR-FILE-OUT
02120          STOP RUN
02130      END-IF
02140      ACCEPT TODAYS-DATE FROM DATE
02150      MOVE CORR TODAYS-DATE TO PAGE-HEADING-2
02160      PERFORM PRODUCE-REPORT-HEADINGS
02170      PERFORM READ-A-TRANSACTION-RECORD
02180      IF NO-TRANSACTION-RECORDS
02190          WRITE LISTING-RECORD-OUT FROM NO-TRANSACTIONS
02200      END-IF
02210      .
02220
02230  PROCESS-ONE-KEY.
02240      PERFORM PROCESS-MASTER-RECORD
02250      PERFORM PROCESS-TRANSACTION-RECORD
02260      .
02270
```

Consider the section of the program that READs transaction records. It consists of the two paragraphs READ-A-TRANSACTION-RECORD and READ-TRANSACTION-FILE, at lines 02280 through 02380. READ-A-TRANSACTION-RECORD returns to the upper portions of the hierarchy diagram only records having a valid transaction code, 6 or 7. Furthermore, READ-A-TRANSACTION-RECORD makes sure that TRANSACTION-KEY is set properly regardless of what type of transaction is being processed. The upper portions of the diagram can then operate on TRANSACTION-KEY.

Notice the WITH TEST AFTER phrase in the PERFORM . . . UNTIL statement at line 02290. Ordinarily a PERFORM . . . UNTIL evaluates its condition before executing the PERFORMed paragraph, so you must be sure before you enter the PERFORM that the condition is not true if you want the PERFORMed paragraph to be executed at least once. Here the condition TRANSACTION-CODE-IS-VALID might be true from some previously read transaction. So to ensure that the paragraph READ-TRANSACTION-FILE will be executed we include the WITH TEST AFTER phrase. Without the WITH TEST AFTER phrase, once the condition TRANSACTION-CODE-IS-VALID became true the paragraph READ-TRANSACTION-FILE would never again be carried out.

Now examine the paragraph PROCESS-MASTER-RECORD, line 02500. If a transaction is asking for a master record to be retrieved on its Account Number, the program tries to do a random READ in the usual way, at lines 02520 through 02550. But if a transaction is asking for a listing of master records on the basis of the first letter of the Depositor Name, the program uses a **START** statement to locate the first record in the file (if any) whose Depositor Name begins with the desired letter of the alphabet, in lines 02580 through 02610. The START

FIGURE *15.9* ***continued***

```
02280 READ-A-TRANSACTION-RECORD.
02290     PERFORM READ-TRANSACTION-FILE
02300        WITH TEST AFTER UNTIL
02310         TRANSACTION-CODE-IS-VALID OR
02320         NO-MORE-TRANSACTION-RECORDS
02330     IF DEPOSITOR-NAMES-REQUEST
02340         MOVE SPACES TO UNUSED-PORTION-OF-KEY
02350     END-IF
02360     .
02370
02380 READ-TRANSACTION-FILE.
02390     READ TRANSACTION-FILE-IN INTO TRANSACTION-INPUT-AREA
02400         AT END
02410             SET NO-MORE-TRANSACTION-RECORDS TO TRUE
02420         NOT AT END
02430             ADD 1 TO NUMBER-OF-INPUT-RECORDS-W
02440             IF NOT TRANSACTION-CODE-IS-VALID
02450                 ADD 1 TO NUMBER-OF-ERRONEOUS-RECORDS-W
02460                 PERFORM WRITE-INVALID-CODE-LINE
02470             END-IF
02480     .
02490
02500 PROCESS-MASTER-RECORD.
02510     IF ACCOUNT-NUMBER-REQUEST
02520         MOVE TRANSACTION-KEY TO ACCOUNT-NUMBER-M
02530         READ ACCOUNT-MASTER-FILE-IN
02540             INVALID KEY CONTINUE
02550         END-READ
02560     ELSE
02570         MOVE TRANSACTION-KEY TO DEPOSITOR-NAME-M
02580         START ACCOUNT-MASTER-FILE-IN
02590             KEY = FIRST-LETTER-OF-DEPOSITOR-NAME
02600             INVALID KEY CONTINUE
02610         END-START
02620     END-IF
02630     IF FILE-OPERATION-WAS-SUCCESSFUL
02640         SET THERE-IS-A-MASTER-RECORD TO TRUE
02650     ELSE
02660     IF RECORD-NOT-FOUND
02670         SET THERE-ISNT-A-MASTER-RECORD TO TRUE
02680     ELSE
02690         DISPLAY " MASTER FILE RANDOM READ/START STATUS = "
02700                   MASTER-FILE-CHECK,
02710         PERFORM TERMINATION
02720         STOP RUN
02730     END-IF
02740     END-IF
02750     .
```

continued

statement does not bring a record in from the file; it merely locates a particular record, if it exists, so that sequential READ statements issued later can bring in the records wanted. Successful execution of a START statement establishes a **key of reference** for later sequential READs. In our case, the START statement used a field subordinate to DEPOSITOR-NAME-M, so DEPOSITOR-NAME-M becomes the key of reference. Only the prime RECORD KEY or any ALTERNATE RECORD KEY may be the key of reference. The complete format of the START statement will be given shortly.

The START statement may be used on an indexed file in any program using ACCESS DYNAMIC, as we are doing here, or ACCESS SEQUENTIAL. It is not permitted in a program using ACCESS RANDOM. We will not use the START statement in any other programs in this book.

Execution of the START statement sets the STATUS field if one is specified for the file. The ANSI standard meanings of the STATUS codes related to executing a START statement on an indexed file are given in Table 15.6.

TABLE *15.6*
ANSI standard STATUS codes related to executing a START statement on an indexed file

Status Code	Meaning
00	Successful completion
23	Invalid key—no record found
30	Permanent error (hardware malfunction)
47	File not OPENed as INPUT or I-O

As usual, your own system may have additional codes in the range 90 through 99. Since the STATUS codes for START are the same as for a random READ, the IF statement at line 02630 does its job regardless of whether the preceding IF statement executes the READ at line 02530 or the START at line 02580.

We now come to the portion of the program corresponding to the hierarchy diagram in Figure 15.8. The paragraphs PROCESS-TRANSACTION-RECORD, PROCESS-ONE-TRANSACTION, and LIST-1-MASTER-REC-BY-ACCT-NUM, at lines 02770, 02820, and 02900, respectively, are all straightforward. The paragraph PROCESS-ALL-MSTR-RECS-FOR-LTR shows how the program finds all the master records having a Depositor Name beginning with the letter given in the transaction. First, at line 03010, it tests whether the START statement found any such records at all. If so, it brings in the first such record by PERFORMing the paragraph READ-MASTER-FILE-SEQUENTIALLY.

The paragraph READ-MASTER-FILE-SEQUENTIALLY, at line 03190, shows how to READ an indexed file sequentially when ACCESS DYNAMIC is given. The reserved word **NEXT** must follow the file name, indicating to COBOL that records are to be read sequentially. A READ . . . NEXT statement may be given after a successful START, READ, or OPEN statement. If given after a START statement, the READ . . . NEXT brings in from the file the record that the START statement found. If given after an OPEN statement, a READ . . . NEXT brings in the first record in the file. If given after a READ or READ . . . NEXT, it brings in from the file the next record in sequence. In our case, the READ . . . NEXT brings into the master work area the record that the START statement found.

FIGURE 15.9 *continued*

```
S COBOL II RELEASE 3.1 09/19/89                    P15003   DATE SEP 17,1991 T
----+-*A-1-B--+----2----+----3----+----4----+----5----+----6----+----7-|--+

       PROCESS-TRANSACTION-RECORD.
           PERFORM PROCESS-ONE-TRANSACTION
           PERFORM READ-A-TRANSACTION-RECORD
           .

       PROCESS-ONE-TRANSACTION.
           IF ACCOUNT-NUMBER-REQUEST
               PERFORM LIST-1-MASTR-REC-BY-ACCT-NUM
           ELSE
               PERFORM PROCESS-ALL-MSTR-RECS-FOR-LTR
           END-IF
           .

       LIST-1-MASTR-REC-BY-ACCT-NUM.
           IF THERE-ISNT-A-MASTER-RECORD
               ADD 1 TO NUMBER-OF-ERRONEOUS-RECORDS-W
               PERFORM WRITE-MASTER-MISSING-LINE
           ELSE
               ADD 1 TO NUMBER-OF-SELECTED-RECORDS-W
               PERFORM WRITE-REPORT-LINE
           END-IF
           .

       PROCESS-ALL-MSTR-RECS-FOR-LTR.
           IF THERE-ISNT-A-MASTER-RECORD
               ADD 1 TO NUMBER-OF-ERRONEOUS-RECORDS-W
               PERFORM WRITE-MASTER-MISSING-LINE
           ELSE
               PERFORM READ-MASTER-FILE-SEQUENTIALLY
               PERFORM LIST-ALL-MSTR-RECS-FOR-LTR UNTIL
                   FIRST-LETTER-OF-DEPOSITOR-NAME
                   NOT = STARTING-LETTER-T OR
                   END-OF-MASTER-FILE-REACHED
           END-IF
           .

       LIST-ALL-MSTR-RECS-FOR-LTR.
           ADD 1 TO NUMBER-OF-SELECTED-RECORDS-W
           PERFORM WRITE-REPORT-LINE
           PERFORM READ-MASTER-FILE-SEQUENTIALLY
           .

       READ-MASTER-FILE-SEQUENTIALLY.
           READ ACCOUNT-MASTER-FILE-IN NEXT
               AT END
                   CONTINUE
               NOT AT END
                   IF FILE-OPERATION-WAS-SUCCESSFUL
                       CONTINUE
                   ELSE
                       DISPLAY " SEQUENTIAL MASTER READ STATUS = "
                               MASTER-FILE-CHECK
                       PERFORM TERMINATION
                       STOP RUN
                   END-IF
           .

```

continued

FIGURE *15.9* *continued*

```
S COBOL II RELEASE 3.1 09/19/89                    P15003   DATE SEP 17,1991 T
----+-*A-1-B--+----2----+----3----+----4----+----5----+----6----+----7-|--+

       WRITE-REPORT-LINE.
           MOVE ACCOUNT-NUMBER-M TO ACCOUNT-NUMBER-OUT
           MOVE CURRENT-BALANCE-M TO CURRENT-BALANCE-OUT
           MOVE DATE-OF-LAST-TRANSACTION-M
                TO DATE-OF-LAST-TRANSACTION-OUT
           MOVE DEPOSITOR-NAME-M TO DEPOSITOR-NAME-OUT
           IF 1 + LINE-COUNT-ER > PAGE-LIMIT
               PERFORM PRINT-LISTING-HEADINGS
           END-IF
           WRITE LISTING-RECORD-OUT FROM REPORT-LINE
           ADD 1 TO LINE-COUNT-ER
           ADD CURRENT-BALANCE-M TO CURRENT-BALANCE-TOTAL-W
           .

       WRITE-INVALID-CODE-LINE.
           MOVE TRANSACTION-KEY TO TRANSACTION-KEY-OUT IN
                                        INVALID-CODE-LINE
           MOVE TRANSACTION-CODE-T TO TRANSACTION-CODE-OUT
           IF 1 + ERROR-LINE-COUNTER > ERROR-PAGE-LIMIT
               PERFORM PRINT-ERROR-REPORT-HEADINGS
           END-IF
           WRITE ERROR-RECORD-OUT FROM INVALID-CODE-LINE
           ADD 1 TO ERROR-LINE-COUNTER
           .

       WRITE-MASTER-MISSING-LINE.
           MOVE TRANSACTION-KEY TO TRANSACTION-KEY-OUT IN
                                        MASTER-MISSING-LINE
           IF 1 + ERROR-LINE-COUNTER > ERROR-PAGE-LIMIT
               PERFORM PRINT-ERROR-REPORT-HEADINGS
           END-IF
           WRITE ERROR-RECORD-OUT FROM MASTER-MISSING-LINE
           ADD 1 TO ERROR-LINE-COUNTER
           .

       TERMINATION.
           PERFORM PRODUCE-FINAL-LINES
           CLOSE ACCOUNT-MASTER-FILE-IN
                 TRANSACTION-FILE-IN
                 LISTING-FILE-OUT
                 ERROR-FILE-OUT
           .

       PRODUCE-FINAL-LINES.
           MOVE CURRENT-BALANCE-TOTAL-W TO CURRENT-BALANCE-TOTAL-OUT
           WRITE LISTING-RECORD-OUT FROM FINAL-LINE-1 AFTER 2
           WRITE LISTING-RECORD-OUT FROM FINAL-LINE-2 AFTER 2
           MOVE NUMBER-OF-SELECTED-RECORDS-W
                              TO NUMBER-OF-SELECTED-RECORDS-OUT
           WRITE LISTING-RECORD-OUT FROM FINAL-LINE-3 AFTER 2
           MOVE NUMBER-OF-ERRONEOUS-RECORDS-W TO
                                        NUMBER-OF-ERRONEOUS-RECRDS-OUT
           WRITE LISTING-RECORD-OUT FROM FINAL-LINE-4 AFTER 2
           MOVE NUMBER-OF-INPUT-RECORDS-W TO
                                         NUMBER-OF-INPUT-RECORDS-OUT
           WRITE LISTING-RECORD-OUT FROM FINAL-LINE-5 AFTER 2
           .

       PRODUCE-REPORT-HEADINGS.
           PERFORM PRINT-LISTING-HEADINGS
           PERFORM PRINT-ERROR-REPORT-HEADINGS
           .
```

FIGURE 15.9 *continued*

```
PRINT-LISTING-HEADINGS.
    ADD 1 TO PAGE-NUMBER-W
    MOVE PAGE-NUMBER-W TO PAGE-NUMBER-OUT
    WRITE LISTING-RECORD-OUT FROM REPORT-HEADING-1
                             AFTER ADVANCING PAGE
    WRITE LISTING-RECORD-OUT FROM REPORT-HEADING-2
    WRITE LISTING-RECORD-OUT FROM REPORT-HEADING-3
    WRITE LISTING-RECORD-OUT FROM PAGE-HEADING-1
                             AFTER 2
    WRITE LISTING-RECORD-OUT FROM PAGE-HEADING-2
    WRITE LISTING-RECORD-OUT FROM PAGE-HEADING-3
                             AFTER 3
    WRITE LISTING-RECORD-OUT FROM PAGE-HEADING-4
    WRITE LISTING-RECORD-OUT FROM BLANK-LINE
    MOVE 11 TO LINE-COUNT-ER
    .

PRINT-ERROR-REPORT-HEADINGS.
    ADD 1 TO ERROR-PAGE-NUMBER-W
    MOVE ERROR-PAGE-NUMBER-W TO PAGE-NUMBER-OUT
    WRITE ERROR-RECORD-OUT FROM REPORT-HEADING-1
                             AFTER ADVANCING PAGE
    WRITE ERROR-RECORD-OUT FROM REPORT-HEADING-2
    WRITE ERROR-RECORD-OUT FROM REPORT-HEADING-3
    WRITE ERROR-RECORD-OUT FROM ERROR-HEADING-1
                             AFTER 2
    WRITE ERROR-RECORD-OUT FROM PAGE-HEADING-2
    WRITE ERROR-RECORD-OUT FROM ERROR-HEADING-3
                             AFTER 3
    WRITE ERROR-RECORD-OUT FROM ERROR-HEADING-4
    WRITE ERROR-RECORD-OUT FROM BLANK-LINE
    MOVE 11 TO ERROR-LINE-COUNTER
    .
```

Subsequent READ . . . NEXT statements bring records in from the file in sequence on the key of reference. In our case, the key of reference is DEPOSITOR-NAME-M, so READ . . . NEXT statements will bring in records sequentially on Depositor Name. READ . . . NEXT statements given after an OPEN statement bring in records sequentially on the prime key of the file.

When an indexed file is read sequentially on an alternate key for which duplicate key values exist, the records are brought in from the file in the order in which they were placed on the file. If during an update operation the value of an alternate key in a record is changed to a value that already exists on the file, the updated record is considered to be the last of the records with that value of the alternate key placed on the file. If the file were to be accessed sequentially on that value of the alternate key, the newly updated record would be the last retrieved.

A READ . . . NEXT statement sets the STATUS field if one is specified for the file. The ANSI standard meanings of the STATUS codes related to READing an indexed file sequentially are given in Table 15.7.

TABLE 15.7

ANSI standard STATUS codes related to READing an indexed file sequentially

Status Code	Meaning
00	Successful completion
02	Successful completion, and the NEXT record on the file has the same key value as the record just read (this can happen only when an indexed file is being read on a key other than its prime key)
10	At end—end-of-file encountered
30	Permanent error (hardware malfunction)
47	File not OPENed as INPUT or I-O

In this application, a code of 02 will be returned if the next record in the file after the record just read has the same Depositor Name as the record just read. Your system may have additional codes in the range 90–99.

After a master record has been read sequentially, the PERFORM statement at line 03060 brings in records UNTIL the first letter of the depositor name changes or end-of-file is encountered in READing the master file sequentially.

Program P15-03 was run with the transaction input shown in Figure 15.10 and the updated master file created by Program P15-02. Program P15-03 produced the output shown in Figure 15.11.

FIGURE 15.10 **Transaction input to Program P15-03**

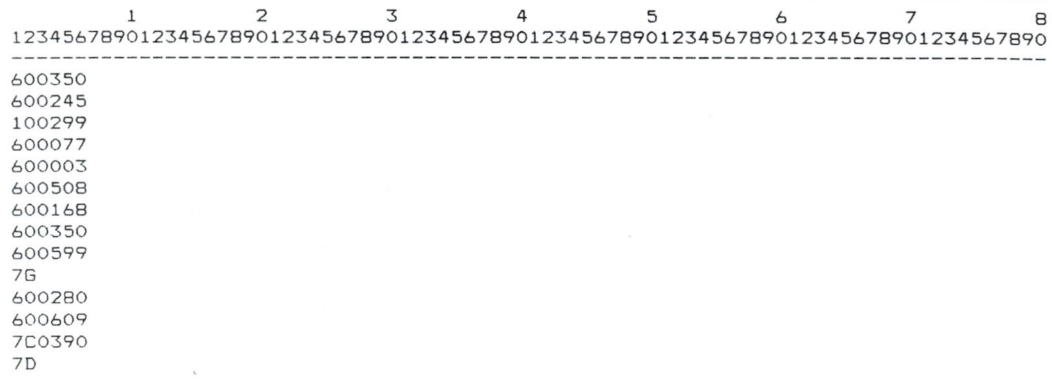

```
--------------------------------------------------------------------------------
         1         2         3         4         5         6         7         8
12345678901234567890123456789012345678901234567890123456789012345678901234567890
--------------------------------------------------------------------------------
600350
600245
100299
600077
600003
600508
600168
600350
600599
7G
600280
600609
7C0390
7D
```

FIGURE 15.11 Output from Program P15-03

```
                    ROBBEM STATE BANK
                   106 WEST 10TH ST.
                  BROOKLYN, NY  11212

                SELECTED SAVINGS ACCOUNTS
    DATE  9/17/91                          PAGE  1

ACCOUNT      CURRENT      DATE OF LAST      DEPOSITOR
NUMBER       BALANCE      TRANSACTION       NAME

 00350      2,500.00         910915      ROGER SHAW
 00245         35.00         910915      FRANK CAPUTO
 00077        160.37         910916      LESLIE MINSKY
 00350      2,500.00         910915      ROGER SHAW
 00220           .00         910916      GENE & THERESA GALLI
 00096        871.00         910915      GENE GALLI
 00252         15.00         910915      GENE GALLI
 00391      1,284.00         910916      GENE GALLI
 00410        318.00         910915      GENE GALLI
 00092        432.00         910916      GENE GALLI
 00032         25.00         910916      GENE GALLI
 00098        500.00         910916      GEORGE & ANN CULHANE
 00315        250.00         910915      GRACE MICELI
 00329         10.00         910915      GUY VOLPONE
 00280      2,337.00         910916      COMMUNITY DRUGS
 00199         21.00         910915      COMMUNITY DRUGS
 00280      2,337.00         910916      COMMUNITY DRUGS
 00306        493.00         910915      COMMUNITY DRUGS
 00349      1,234.00         910915      COMMUNITY DRUGS

  TOTAL    15,322.37

                     CONTROL COUNTS

             NUMBER OF SELECTED RECORDS     19

             NUMBER OF ERRONEOUS RECORDS     7

             NUMBER OF INPUT RECORDS        14



                    ROBBEM STATE BANK
                   106 WEST 10TH ST.
                  BROOKLYN, NY  11212

                    SELECTION ERRORS
    DATE  9/17/91                          PAGE  1

ACCOUNT
NUMBER

 00299                 INVALID CODE - 1
 00003                 MASTER RECORD DOES NOT EXIST
 00508                 MASTER RECORD DOES NOT EXIST
 00168                 MASTER RECORD DOES NOT EXIST
 00599                 MASTER RECORD DOES NOT EXIST
 00609                 MASTER RECORD DOES NOT EXIST
 D                     MASTER RECORD DOES NOT EXIST
```

The START Statement

The format of the START statement is as follows:

```
                    ┌     ⎧ IS EQUAL TO                   ⎫              ┐
                    │     ⎪ IS =                          ⎪              │
                    │     ⎪ IS GREATER THAN               ⎪              │
                    │     ⎪ IS >                          ⎪              │
START file-name-1   │ KEY ⎨ IS NOT LESS THAN              ⎬ data-name-1  │
                    │     ⎪ IS NOT <                      ⎪              │
                    │     ⎪ IS GREATER THAN OR EQUAL TO   ⎪              │
                    └     ⎩ IS >=                         ⎭              ┘
    [INVALID KEY imperative-statement-1]
    [NOT INVALID KEY imperative-statement-2]
    [END-START]
```

The START statement locates the first record in an indexed file that satisfies the condition given in the KEY clause. If the KEY clause is omitted, the EQUAL condition is assumed and the comparison is made on the prime RECORD KEY of the file. If the KEY clause is given, data-name-1 may be either the prime key, an alternate key, or an alphanumeric data item subordinate to an alternate key and at the left end of the alternate key.

If the condition in the KEY clause is satisfied, the START is considered successful, and the key field used for the START becomes the key of reference for subsequent READ . . . NEXT statements. If no record is found that satisfies the condition given in the KEY clause, the STATUS field is set to 23 and the imperative-statement in the INVALID KEY clause is executed.

If the symbols for equal, greater than, less than, or greater than or equal are used, they are required. We refrain from underlining them here to avoid possible confusion with other mathematical symbols.

For example, the statement

```
START ACCOUNT-MASTER-FILE-IN
      KEY > ACCOUNT-NUMBER-M
END-START
```

would locate (but not READ) the first record in the file having an Account Number greater than the value in the field ACCOUNT-NUMBER-M.

The Sequential READ Statement

A READ statement, when used for any kind of sequential retrieval of records from a file with any kind of organization, has the following format:

```
READ file-name-1 [NEXT] RECORD [INTO identifier-1]
    [AT END imperative-statement-1]
    [NOT AT END imperative-statement-2]
    [END-READ]
```

When this READ statement is used with a file in dynamic access mode, the word NEXT is required to obtain sequential retrieval of records. When used with a file in sequential access mode, the word NEXT may appear and has no effect.

If end-of-file is encountered, the STATUS code is set to 10 and the imperative statement in the AT END clause is executed.

EXERCISE 3

Write a program to list selected records from the files you created in Exercises 1 and 2 in this chapter. Have your program accept transactions in the following formats:

Positions	Field
1	Code A
2–6	Account Number
7–80	spaces
1	Code B
2	First character of Supplier Code
3–80	spaces
1	Code C
2	First character of Storage Location
3–80	spaces

The meanings of the transaction codes are as follows:

A—list the contents of the master record having this Account Number

B—list the contents of all master records whose Supplier Code begins with this character

C—list the contents of all master records whose Storage Location begins with this character

For each record listed, have your program determine whether the Quantity on Hand is equal to or less than the Reorder Point, and print the message REORDER if it is.

Listing the Complete Contents of an Indexed File

Listing an indexed file sequentially on its prime key is very much like doing any sequential listing. Program P15-04, shown in Figure 15.12, lists the contents of our savings-account master file.

In the FILE-CONTROL entry for the master file, line 00120, we can omit the ALTERNATE RECORD KEY clause because this program makes no reference to the Depositor Name field as a key. In the Working Storage Section, we can use FILE-CHECK, line 00390, instead of MORE-INPUT to signal the end-of-file. Program P15-04 was run using the updated master file created in Program P15-02. Program P15-04 produced the output shown in Figure 15.13.

FIGURE *15.12* **Program P15-04**

```
S COBOL II RELEASE 3.2 09/05/90                 P15004   DATE MAR 04,1992 T
----+-*A-1-B--+----2----+----3----+----4----+----5----+----6----+----7-|--+

 IDENTIFICATION DIVISION.
 PROGRAM-ID. P15-04.
*
*     THIS PROGRAM LISTS AN INDEXED FILE.
*
************************************************************************

 ENVIRONMENT DIVISION.
 INPUT-OUTPUT SECTION.
 FILE-CONTROL.
     SELECT LIST-FILE-OUT     ASSIGN TO PRINTER.
     SELECT MASTER-FILE-IN    ASSIGN TO DISKUNIT
         ORGANIZATION INDEXED
         RECORD KEY IS ACCOUNT-NUMBER IN MASTER-RECORD-IN
         STATUS IS FILE-CHECK.

************************************************************************

 DATA DIVISION.
 FILE SECTION.
 FD  MASTER-FILE-IN
     LABEL RECORDS ARE STANDARD
     RECORD CONTAINS 39 CHARACTERS
     BLOCK CONTAINS 100 RECORDS.

 01  MASTER-RECORD-IN.
     05  ACCOUNT-NUMBER                                  PIC X(5).
     05  DEPOSITOR-NAME                                  PIC X(20).
     05  TRANSACTION-YEAR                                PIC 99.
     05  TRANSACTION-MONTH                               PIC 99.
     05  TRANSACTION-DAY                                 PIC 99.
     05  CURRENT-BALANCE                                 PIC S9(6)V99.

 FD  LIST-FILE-OUT.

 01  LIST-RECORD-OUT                                   PIC X(81).

 WORKING-STORAGE SECTION.
 01  FILE-CHECK                                          PIC XX.
     88 THERE-IS-NO-MORE-INPUT                           VALUE "10".
     88 THERE-IS-NO-INPUT                                VALUE "10".
     88 MASTER-FILE-IS-OPENED                            VALUE "00".
     88 READ-WAS-SUCCESSFUL                              VALUE "00".
 01  PAGE-NUMBER-W      VALUE 0  PACKED-DECIMAL          PIC S99.
 01  PAGE-LIMIT         VALUE 38 COMP SYNC               PIC S99.
 01  LINE-COUNT-ER               COMP SYNC               PIC S99.
 01  BLANK-LINE         VALUE SPACE                      PIC X.

 01  RUN-DATE.
     05  RUN-YEAR                                        PIC 99.
     05  RUN-MONTH-AND-DAY                               PIC 9(4).

 01  PAGE-HEADING-1.
     05                   VALUE SPACES                   PIC X(40).
     05                   VALUE  "SAVINGS ACCOUNT MASTER"
                                                         PIC X(22).

 01  PAGE-HEADING-2.
     05                   VALUE SPACES                   PIC X(28).
     05                   VALUE  "DATE"                  PIC X(5).
     05  RUN-MONTH-AND-DAY                               PIC Z9/99/.
     05  RUN-YEAR                                        PIC 99B(21).
     05                   VALUE  "PAGE"                  PIC X(5).
     05  PAGE-NUMBER-OUT                                 PIC Z9.
```

FIGURE *15.12* *continued*

```
 01  PAGE-HEADING-3.
     05                    VALUE SPACES            PIC X(46).
     05                    VALUE  "DATE OF LAST"   PIC X(12).
 01  PAGE-HEADING-4.
     05                    VALUE SPACES            PIC X(20).
     05                    VALUE  "ACCOUNT"        PIC X(13).
     05                    VALUE  "CURRENT"        PIC X(13).
     05                    VALUE  "TRANSACTION"    PIC X(15).
     05                    VALUE  "DEPOSITOR NAME" PIC X(14).
 01  PAGE-HEADING-5.
     05                    VALUE SPACES            PIC X(20).
     05                    VALUE  "NUMBER"         PIC X(13).
     05                    VALUE  "BALANCE"        PIC X(14).
     05                    VALUE  "YR  MO  DA"     PIC X(10).
 01  DETAIL-LINE.
     05                    VALUE SPACES         PIC X(21).
     05  ACCOUNT-NUMBER                         PIC X(5)B(4).
     05  CURRENT-BALANCE                        PIC Z,ZZZ,ZZZ.99-.
     05  TRANSACTION-YEAR                       PIC B(4)99BB.
     05  TRANSACTION-MONTH                      PIC 99BB.
     05  TRANSACTION-DAY                        PIC 99B(4).
     05  DEPOSITOR-NAME                         PIC X(20).
 01  NO-INPUT-DATA.
     05              VALUE SPACES               PIC X(21).
     05              VALUE "NO INPUT DATA"      PIC X(13).
******************************************************************

PROCEDURE DIVISION.
CONTROL-PARAGRAPH.
    PERFORM INITIALIZATION
    PERFORM MAIN-PROCESS UNTIL THERE-IS-NO-MORE-INPUT
    PERFORM TERMINATION
    STOP RUN
    .
INITIALIZATION.
    OPEN INPUT  MASTER-FILE-IN
         OUTPUT LIST-FILE-OUT
    IF NOT MASTER-FILE-IS-OPENED
        DISPLAY " MASTER FILE OPEN STATUS = " FILE-CHECK
        CLOSE MASTER-FILE-IN
              LIST-FILE-OUT
        STOP RUN
    END-IF
    ACCEPT RUN-DATE FROM DATE
    MOVE CORR RUN-DATE TO PAGE-HEADING-2
    PERFORM PRODUCE-PAGE-HEADINGS
    READ MASTER-FILE-IN
        AT END
            WRITE LIST-RECORD-OUT FROM NO-INPUT-DATA
        NOT AT END
            IF READ-WAS-SUCCESSFUL
                CONTINUE
            ELSE
                DISPLAY " MASTER FILE READ STATUS = " FILE-CHECK
                CLOSE MASTER-FILE-IN
                      LIST-FILE-OUT
                 STOP RUN
            END-IF
    END-READ
    .
```

continued

FIGURE ***15.12*** ***continued***

```
S COBOL II RELEASE 3.2 09/05/90                    P15004    DATE MAR 04,1992 T
----+-*A-1-B--+----2----+----3----+----4----+----5----+----6----+----7-|--+

       PRODUCE-PAGE-HEADINGS.
           ADD 1 TO PAGE-NUMBER-W
           MOVE PAGE-NUMBER-W TO PAGE-NUMBER-OUT
           WRITE LIST-RECORD-OUT FROM PAGE-HEADING-1 AFTER PAGE
           WRITE LIST-RECORD-OUT FROM PAGE-HEADING-2
           WRITE LIST-RECORD-OUT FROM PAGE-HEADING-3 AFTER 3
           WRITE LIST-RECORD-OUT FROM PAGE-HEADING-4
           WRITE LIST-RECORD-OUT FROM PAGE-HEADING-5
           WRITE LIST-RECORD-OUT FROM BLANK-LINE
           MOVE 8 TO LINE-COUNT-ER
           .

       TERMINATION.
           CLOSE MASTER-FILE-IN,
                 LIST-FILE-OUT
           .

       MAIN-PROCESS.
           MOVE CORR MASTER-RECORD-IN TO DETAIL-LINE
           IF 1 + LINE-COUNT-ER > PAGE-LIMIT
               PERFORM PRODUCE-PAGE-HEADINGS
           END-IF
           WRITE LIST-RECORD-OUT FROM DETAIL-LINE
           ADD 1 TO LINE-COUNT-ER
           READ MASTER-FILE-IN
               AT END
                   CONTINUE
               NOT AT END
                   IF READ-WAS-SUCCESSFUL
                       CONTINUE
                   ELSE
                       DISPLAY " MASTER FILE READ STATUS = " FILE-CHECK
                       CLOSE MASTER-FILE-IN
                             LIST-FILE-OUT
                       STOP RUN
                   END-IF
           .
```

FIGURE 15.13 **Output from Program P15-04**

```
                    SAVINGS ACCOUNT MASTER
          DATE   3/04/92                          PAGE   1


                                DATE OF LAST
ACCOUNT          CURRENT        TRANSACTION      DEPOSITOR NAME
NUMBER           BALANCE         YR   MO   DA

 00007           1,007.84        91   09   15    ROSEBUCCI
 00014             990.00-       91   09   16    ROBERT DAVIS M.D.
 00015             700.00        91   09   15    LENORE MILLER
 00020             800.00        91   09   15    LENORE MILLER
 00021           1,027.50        91   09   16    ROSEMARY LANE
 00022           1,000.00        91   09   15    ROSEMARY LANE
 00023           1,100.00        91   09   15    ROSEMARY LANE
 00028           5,654.36        91   09   16    MICHAEL SMITH
 00032              25.00        91   09   16    GENE GALLI
 00035             150.00        91   09   15    JOHN J. LEHMAN
 00056               1.00        91   09   15    EVELYN SLATER
 00070             500.00        91   09   15    PATRICK J. LEE
 00077             160.37        91   09   16    LESLIE MINSKY
 00084           5,074.29        91   09   16    JOHN & SALLY DUPRINO
 00091           2,300.00        91   09   16    JOE'S DELI
 00092             432.00        91   09   16    GENE GALLI
 00096             871.00        91   09   15    GENE GALLI
 00098             500.00        91   09   16    GEORGE & ANN CULHANE
 00105              50.00        91   09   15    ONE DAY CLEANERS
 00112             250.00        91   09   15    ROSEMARY LANE
 00126           1,100.00        91   09   16    JAMES BUDD
 00133           3,563.00        91   09   16    PAUL LERNER, D.D.S.
 00140              25.75        91   09   16    BETH DENNY
 00161           1,280.84        91   09   16    ROBERT RYAN
 00175             202.02        91   09   16    MARY KEATING
 00189              35.00        91   09   15    J. & L. CAIN
 00199              21.00        91   09   15    COMMUNITY DRUGS
 00210           1,000.00        91   09   16    JERRY PARKS
 00220                .00        91   09   16    GENE & THERESA GALLI
 00231             555.00        91   09   15    BILL WILLIAMS



                    SAVINGS ACCOUNT MASTER
          DATE   3/04/92                          PAGE   2


                                DATE OF LAST
ACCOUNT          CURRENT        TRANSACTION      DEPOSITOR NAME
NUMBER           BALANCE         YR   MO   DA

 00245              35.00        91   09   15    FRANK CAPUTO
 00252              15.00        91   09   15    GENE GALLI
 00266              99.57        91   09   15    MARTIN LANG
 00273           2,000.00        91   09   16    VITO CACACI
 00280           2,337.00        91   09   16    COMMUNITY DRUGS
 00306             493.00        91   09   15    COMMUNITY DRUGS
 00308           2,050.00        91   09   16    JOE GARCIA
 00315             250.00        91   09   15    GRACE MICELI
 00329              10.00        91   09   15    GUY VOLPONE
 00343           1,000.00        91   09   15    JOE & MARY SESSA
 00349           1,234.00        91   09   15    COMMUNITY DRUGS
 00350           2,500.00        91   09   15    ROGER SHAW
 00371              10.00        91   09   16    THOMAS HERR
 00391           1,284.00        91   09   16    GENE GALLI
 00392              75.00        91   09   16    INEZ WASHINGTON
 00398              10.00        91   09   16    JUAN ALVAREZ
 00410             318.00        91   09   15    GENE GALLI
 00413             100.00        91   09   16    BILL HAYES
 00420           1,500.00        91   09   16    JOHN RICE
```

EXERCISE *4*

Write a program to list the complete contents of the master files created in Exercises 1 and 2 in this chapter. For each record listed, have your program determine whether the Quantity on Hand is equal to or less than the Reorder Point and print a message REORDER if it is.

Other Operations on Indexed Files

Several kinds of input and output operations on indexed files that are supported by COBOL have not been referred to in this chapter. They are:

a. READing a record randomly on an alternate key

b. Rewriting a record in sequential access mode

c. Deleting a record in sequential access mode

Each of these operations has its own STATUS code values. For details on these operations and their STATUS codes, see your COBOL manual.

Summary

Files with indexed organization have most of their records stored in order on their prime RECORD KEY. An indexed file is equipped with indexes, which permit COBOL to access the file sequentially or randomly. An indexed file may have one or more ALTERNATE RECORD KEYs. The ALTERNATE RECORD KEYs permit COBOL to access the file sequentially or randomly on those KEYs.

An indexed file may be created sequentially or randomly. If the file is created sequentially, the first WRITE statement issued by the program places the first record onto the file. The prime key of each record written after the first must be greater than the prime key of the previous record written. If the file is created randomly, records may be placed onto the file in any order, and COBOL will insert each record into its proper place in sequence. The prime key of each record written must not be a duplicate of a prime key already on the file.

An indexed file may be updated in place. To process a transaction to change an existing master record, COBOL brings the master record in from the file. The record may then be updated in the File Section or in working storage and rewritten onto the file, replacing the old record. To process a transaction to delete an existing master record, COBOL physically removes the record from the file.

To process a transaction to create a new master record, the program builds the new record in the File Section or in working storage. A WRITE statement then directs COBOL to find the place on the file where the new record should be slipped in and to move some existing records around, if necessary, to make room for it.

Some applications require that an indexed file be accessed dynamically. Then a random READ statement or a START statement can find any record on the file on the basis of the prime key or one of the alternate keys. READ . . . NEXT statements can then bring in records sequentially from that record.

All operations, OPEN, CLOSE, READ, READ . . . NEXT, WRITE, REWRITE, and DELETE, set the STATUS code if one is provided for the file. The meanings of the STATUS code depend on the operation being performed. The program may test the STATUS code at any time and take appropriate action.

Fill-In Exercises

1. The three types of file organization supported by COBOL are ______, ______, and ______.
2. The three types of file access supported by COBOL are ______, ______, and ______.
3. The field on which the records in an indexed file are ordered is called the ______.
4. A field that may be used to access records in an indexed file but is not used for ordering them is called a(n) ______.
5. The ______ clause in the FILE-CONTROL entry for a file tells whether the file is indexed.
6. The ______ clause in the FILE-CONTROL entry for a file tells whether records will be read and written randomly, sequentially, or dynamically.
7. The STATUS field is ______ characters long.
8. Every ______ statement to a file attempts to place a new record onto the file.
9. Every ______ statement to a file attempts to replace an existing record on the file.
10. A ______ statement may be used to locate a record randomly on an indexed file but not bring the record in from the file.
11. The ______ ______ phrase is used to indicate that more than one record in an indexed file may contain the same value of an ALTERNATE RECORD KEY.
12. The OPEN mode used for updating records in an indexed file in place is ______.
13. The ______ ______ clause is used to indicate which field is the STATUS field for a file.
14. The OPEN mode used to add records sequentially to the end of a sequential file is ______.
15. The verb that can be used physically to remove a record from an indexed file is ______.

Review Exercises

1. Write a program to create an indexed file of alumni records. Use the same formats for transaction and master records that you used when you created your sequential alumni file in Review Exercise 2, Chapter 13, page 476.

   Have your program check for the presence of all fields in each input record. Have your program print reports showing the records written onto the file and the erroneous transactions.

   In your program specify the Major Department field and the Year of Graduation field as ALTERNATE RECORD KEYs.
2. Write a program to update the indexed file you created in Review Exercise 1. Use the same transaction formats you used when you updated your sequential alumni file in Review Exercise 4, Chapter 14, page 536.

   Have your program make all suitable validity checks on each transaction. For any change to an existing master record, have your program print the Social Security Number and the contents of the changed field from the master record. For a record deleted from the master file, have your program print the Social Security Number, the Student Name, and the Year of Graduation from the master file.

Include among your update transactions at least one that changes a Major Department field in an existing master record and at least one that changes a Year of Graduation field in an existing master record.

3. Write a program to list selected records from the alumni master files produced by the programs in Review Exercises 1 and 2. Have your program accept listing requests in the following formats:

Positions	Field
1	Code A
2–10	Social Security Number
11–80	spaces
1	Code B
2–3	Major Department
4–80	spaces
1	Code C
2–3	Year of Graduation
4–80	spaces

The meanings of the transaction codes are:

A—list the record for this Social Security Number

B—list all records having this Major Department Code

C—list all records having this Year of Graduation

Include among your transactions a request to list, by Year of Graduation, at least one of the records whose Year of Graduation field was changed in Review Exercise 2 and a request to list, by Major Department Code, at least one of the records whose Major Department Code was changed in Review Exercise 2.

4. Modify your solution to Review Exercise 3, so that the selected records are sorted into alphabetic order on Student Name before being listed.

5. Write a program to list, in sequence on Social Security Number, the complete contents of all records on the master files produced in Review Exercises 1 and 2 of this chapter.

6. Write a program to create an indexed inventory master file randomly. Use the same formats for transaction and master records that you used in Exercise 3, Chapter 13, page 457. Have your program accept transactions in random, unSORTed order. Specify the City-State-Zip field as an alternate key WITH DUPLICATES, and specify the Customer Name as an alternate key and do not include the WITH DUPLICATES phrase. Have your program

test for erroneous duplicate values of Customer Name if your COBOL system has facilities for doing so.

Project

Rewrite your solution to the Project in Chapter 13, page 477, creating an indexed file instead of a sequential file. Specify the Customer Number as the prime RECORD KEY, and the third name-and-address line as the ALTERNATE RECORD KEY.

CHAPTER 16

Relative Files

HERE ARE THE KEY POINTS YOU SHOULD LEARN FROM THIS CHAPTER

1. What a relative file is
2. Why relative files are useful
3. How to get COBOL to create a relative file
4. How to access a relative file randomly
5. How to update a relative file
6. How to process a relative file sequentially

KEY WORDS TO RECOGNIZE AND LEARN

relative record number
RELATIVE
RELATIVE KEY
SEQUENTIAL
division/remainder method
prime number
home slot
synonym

A relative file may be thought of as consisting of a number of slots into which records may be placed. The slots are numbered from 1 to the last slot in the file. At any one time, any slot may contain a record or it may be empty. Once COBOL places a record into a slot, COBOL will not move the record to another slot unless directed to do so by a program. Relative files can be accessed sequentially, randomly, and dynamically. COBOL can randomly WRITE a record into any empty slot, REWRITE a record into a slot that already contains a record, DELETE an existing record from a slot and make that slot available for a new record, and READ a record from any slot in the file.

The sequential operations on a relative file are WRITE, REWRITE, START, DELETE, and READ. The dynamic access operations include all the sequential and random operations and also READ . . . NEXT. A relative file must be stored on a direct-access storage device.

A record in a relative file is referred to by its **relative record number,** not by any key field. The relative record number of a record is the number of the slot that the record is in. So if slots 1 and 2 of a relative file are empty, and the first record of the file is in slot number 3, the relative record number of that record is 3. The relative record number need not be stored as a field in the record.

The main advantage of relative files over indexed files is the speed with which records in a relative file may be accessed. In a relative file, there is no need for COBOL to refer to indexes to locate a record. Another difference between relative files and indexed files, which may be an advantage or a disadvantage, is that in a relative file the programmer is responsible for the location of each record. COBOL will not move a record from one slot to another automatically, or keep track of the locations of records.

Using a Relative File

In this first application of a relative file, we will assume that an instructor wants to be able to use a computer to compute students' grades at the end of each term. The instructor plans to accumulate and store each student's examination grades and homework grades in a master file during the term. The master file will have relative organization and one record for each student. The students in the class are numbered 1 through 21.

At the beginning of the term the instructor will establish a relative file containing one record for each student. Each record will have room for 5 exam grades, 12 homework grades, course or section identification, and a count field telling how many records there are in the file. At the start of the term all fields except the identification and count fields will contain zeros. During the term the instructor will update the file, inserting grades into the file when exams are given and when homework assignments are graded. If a student drops the course after a record has been established for that student, the instructor will remove the student's record from the file. Occasionally a grade in the file will have to be changed, as when the instructor makes a mistake entering a grade.

At the end of the term the instructor will run a program that examines the exam and homework grades for each student, gives each grade a weight as indicated by the instructor, and computes a letter grade.

Creating a Relative File Sequentially

Program P16-01 creates a relative file containing master records full of zero grades. Program P16-01 reads only one input record, whose format is as follows:

Positions	Field
1	Code "N"
2–4	Number of Students
5–10	Course or Section
11–80	spaces

The record contains the code "N" in column 1. Columns 2 through 4 say how many records Program P16-01 should create on the master file, and columns 5 through 10 give the course code or section number for identification purposes.

The report output produced by Program P16-01 consists of a report heading and one or two lines telling what happened. The format of the report output is shown in Figure 16.1. Only one of the messages shown is printed by Program P16-01 in any one run.

FIGURE 16.1 Report output format for Program P16-01

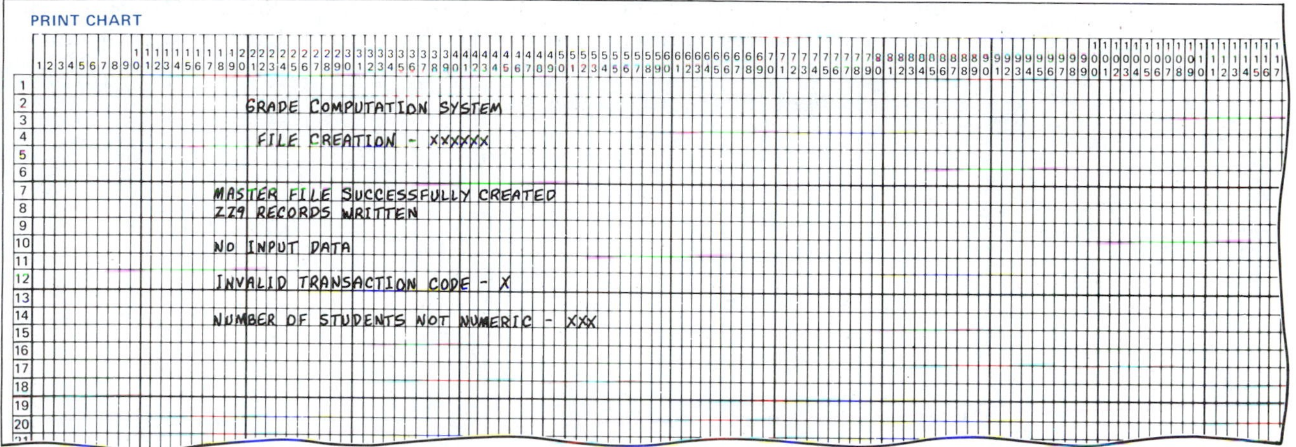

A hierarchy diagram for Program P16-01 is shown in Figure 16.2. It is very straightforward. The "Initialization" procedure reads and checks the one input record. If the record is valid, "Produce grades file" writes master records sequentially onto the master file and prints the appropriate message.

FIGURE 16.2 Hierarchy diagram for Program P16-01

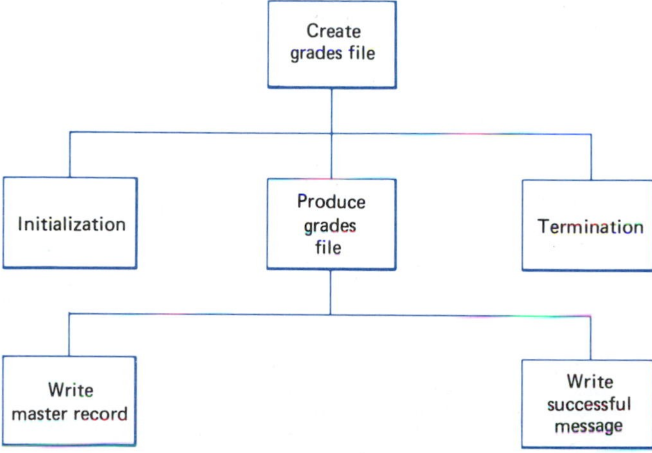

Program P16-01 is shown in Figure 16.3. The FILE-CONTROL entry at line 00130 shows the use of the ORGANIZATION **RELATIVE** clause. There is no RECORD KEY clause in the FILE-CONTROL entry because COBOL does not examine or process record key values in a RELATIVE file.

The master record, GRADES-RECORD-OUT, is defined at line 00480. The fields EXAM-GRADE and HOMEWORK-GRADE are included here only to show the format of the master record. They did not have to be defined in this program, for the field names are not referred to. Notice that the student number does not appear in the record, since the location of the record in the file tells which student the record belongs to.

FIGURE *16.3* **Program P16-01**

```
S COBOL II RELEASE 3.1 09/19/89                  P16001   DATE SEP 28,1991 T
----+-*A-1-B--+----2----+----3----+----4----+----5----+----6----+----7-|--+

00010  IDENTIFICATION DIVISION.
00020  PROGRAM-ID.  P16-01.
00030 *
00040 *     THIS PROGRAM CREATES A RELATIVE FILE SEQUENTIALLY
00050 *
00060 ******************************************************************
00070
00080  ENVIRONMENT DIVISION.
00090  INPUT-OUTPUT SECTION.
00100  FILE-CONTROL.
00110      SELECT TRANSACTION-FILE-IN  ASSIGN TO INFILE.
00120      SELECT REPORT-FILE-OUT      ASSIGN TO PRINTER.
00130      SELECT GRADES-FILE-OUT      ASSIGN TO DISKUNIT
00140          ORGANIZATION RELATIVE
00150          STATUS IS MASTER-FILE-CHECK.
00160
00170 ******************************************************************
00180
00190  DATA DIVISION.
00200  FILE SECTION.
00210  FD  TRANSACTION-FILE-IN.
00220
00230  01  TRANSACTION-RECORD-IN                     PIC X(80).
00240
00250  FD  GRADES-FILE-OUT
00260      LABEL RECORDS ARE STANDARD.
00270
00280  01  MASTER-RECORD-OUT                         PIC X(60).
00290
00300  FD  REPORT-FILE-OUT.
00310
00320  01  REPORT-RECORD-OUT                         PIC X(51).
00330
00340  WORKING-STORAGE SECTION.
00350  01  MASTER-FILE-CHECK                         PIC XX.
00360      88 MASTER-FILE-IS-OPENED                  VALUE "00".
00370      88 WRITE-WAS-SUCCESSFUL                   VALUE "00".
00380
00390  01  CODE-N-RECORD-W.
00400      88  INPUT-RECORD-MISSING VALUE HIGH-VALUES.
00410      05  TRANSACTION-CODE-W                    PIC X.
00420          88  CODE-N          VALUE "N".
00430      05  NUMBER-OF-STUDENTS-W                  PIC 9(3).
00440      05  NUMBER-OF-STUDENTS-X REDEFINES NUMBER-OF-STUDENTS-W
00450                                                PIC X(3).
00460      05  COURSE-OR-SECTION-W                   PIC X(6).
```

FIGURE 16.3 ***continued***

```
 01  GRADES-RECORD-OUT            VALUE ZEROS.
     05  COURSE-OR-SECTION                          PIC X(6).
     05  NUMBER-OF-STUDENTS                         PIC 9(3).
     05  EXAM-GRADE      OCCURS 5 TIMES             PIC 9(3).
     05  HOMEWORK-GRADE OCCURS 12 TIMES             PIC 9(3).
 01  PAGE-HEADING-1.
     05                  VALUE SPACES               PIC X(20).
     05
         VALUE "GRADE COMPUTATION SYSTEM"           PIC X(24).
 01  PAGE-HEADING-2.
     05                  VALUE SPACES               PIC X(21).
     05                  VALUE "FILE CREATION -"
                                                    PIC X(16).
     05  COURSE-OR-SECTION-OUT                      PIC X(6).
 01  SUCCESSFUL-MESSAGE-1.
     05                  VALUE SPACES               PIC X(17).
     05
         VALUE "MASTER FILE SUCCESSFULLY CREATED"
                                                    PIC X(32).
 01  SUCCESSFUL-MESSAGE-2.
     05                  VALUE SPACES               PIC X(17).
     05  NUMBER-OF-STUDENTS-OUT                     PIC ZZ9B.
     05                  VALUE "RECORDS WRITTEN"
                                                    PIC X(15).
 01  NO-INPUT-DATA.
     05              VALUE SPACES                   PIC X(17).
     05              VALUE "NO INPUT DATA"          PIC X(13).
 01  INVALID-CODE-LINE.
     05              VALUE SPACES                   PIC X(17).
     05              VALUE "INVALID TRANSACTION CODE -"
                                                    PIC X(27).
     05  TRANSACTION-CODE-OUT                       PIC X.
 01  NUMBER-OF-STUDENTS-INVALID.
     05              VALUE SPACES                   PIC X(17).
     05              VALUE "NUMBER OF STUDENTS NOT NUMERIC -"
                                                    PIC X(33).
     05  NUMBER-OF-STUDENTS-X-OUT                   PIC X(3).
*****************************************************************
 PROCEDURE DIVISION.
 CREATE-GRADES-FILE.
     PERFORM INITIALIZATION
     IF NOT INPUT-RECORD-MISSING
         PERFORM PRODUCE-GRADES-FILE
     END-IF
     PERFORM TERMINATION
     STOP RUN
     .
```

continued

The paragraph READ-TRANSACTION-FILE, line 01220, READs the one input record into CODE-N-RECORD-W and checks it for validity. If the record is found to be in error, READ-TRANSACTION-FILE prints an error message and sets CODE-N-RECORD-W to HIGH-VALUES to indicate that there is no valid input record.

The WRITE statement at line 01480 sets the STATUS field MASTER-FILE-CHECK. The ANSI standard meanings of the STATUS codes related to writing a relative file sequentially are given in Table 16.1.

FIGURE ***16.3*** ***continued***

```
S COBOL II RELEASE 3.1 09/19/89                    P16001    DATE SEP 28,1991 T
----+-*A-1-B--+----2----+----3----+----4----+----5----+----6----+----7-|--+

01050  INITIALIZATION.
01060      OPEN INPUT  TRANSACTION-FILE-IN
01070           OUTPUT REPORT-FILE-OUT
01080                  GRADES-FILE-OUT
01090      IF NOT MASTER-FILE-IS-OPENED
01100          DISPLAY " MASTER FILE OPEN STATUS = ", MASTER-FILE-CHECK
01110          CLOSE TRANSACTION-FILE-IN
01120                REPORT-FILE-OUT
01130                GRADES-FILE-OUT
01140          STOP RUN
01150      END-IF
01160      WRITE REPORT-RECORD-OUT FROM PAGE-HEADING-1 AFTER PAGE
01170      PERFORM READ-TRANSACTION-FILE
01180      MOVE COURSE-OR-SECTION-W TO COURSE-OR-SECTION-OUT
01190      WRITE REPORT-RECORD-OUT FROM PAGE-HEADING-2 AFTER 2
01200       .
01210
01220  READ-TRANSACTION-FILE.
01230      READ TRANSACTION-FILE-IN INTO CODE-N-RECORD-W
01240          AT END
01250              SET INPUT-RECORD-MISSING TO TRUE
01260              PERFORM WRITE-NO-INPUT-DATA
01270          NOT AT END
01280             IF NOT CODE-N
01290                 PERFORM WRITE-INVALID-CODE-LINE
01300                 SET INPUT-RECORD-MISSING TO TRUE
01310             ELSE
01320             IF NUMBER-OF-STUDENTS-W NOT NUMERIC
01330                 PERFORM WRITE-NO-OF-STUDENTS-INVALID
01340                 SET INPUT-RECORD-MISSING TO TRUE
01350             END-IF
01360             END-IF
01370       END-READ
01380       .
01390
01400  PRODUCE-GRADES-FILE.
01410      MOVE NUMBER-OF-STUDENTS-W TO NUMBER-OF-STUDENTS
01420      MOVE COURSE-OR-SECTION-W TO COURSE-OR-SECTION
01430      PERFORM WRITE-MASTER-RECORD NUMBER-OF-STUDENTS-W TIMES
01440      PERFORM WRITE-SUCCESSFUL-MESSAGE
01450      .
01460
01470  WRITE-MASTER-RECORD.
01480      WRITE MASTER-RECORD-OUT FROM GRADES-RECORD-OUT
01490          INVALID KEY CONTINUE
01500      END-WRITE
01510      IF NOT WRITE-WAS-SUCCESSFUL
01520          DISPLAY  " MASTER FILE WRITE STATUS = ",
01530                     MASTER-FILE-CHECK
01540          PERFORM TERMINATION
01550          STOP RUN
01560      END-IF
01570      .
```

FIGURE 16.3 *continued*

```

 TERMINATION.
     CLOSE TRANSACTION-FILE-IN
           REPORT-FILE-OUT
           GRADES-FILE-OUT
     .

 WRITE-NO-INPUT-DATA.
     WRITE REPORT-RECORD-OUT FROM NO-INPUT-DATA AFTER 2
     .

 WRITE-INVALID-CODE-LINE.
     MOVE TRANSACTION-CODE-W TO TRANSACTION-CODE-OUT
     WRITE REPORT-RECORD-OUT FROM INVALID-CODE-LINE AFTER 2
     .

 WRITE-NO-OF-STUDENTS-INVALID.
     MOVE NUMBER-OF-STUDENTS-X TO NUMBER-OF-STUDENTS-X-OUT
     WRITE REPORT-RECORD-OUT FROM NUMBER-OF-STUDENTS-INVALID
     .

 WRITE-SUCCESSFUL-MESSAGE.
     MOVE NUMBER-OF-STUDENTS-W TO NUMBER-OF-STUDENTS-OUT
     WRITE REPORT-RECORD-OUT FROM SUCCESSFUL-MESSAGE-1 AFTER 3
     WRITE REPORT-RECORD-OUT FROM SUCCESSFUL-MESSAGE-2
     .
```

TABLE 16.1 ANSI standard STATUS codes related to writing a relative file sequentially

Status Code	Meaning
00	Successful completion
24	Invalid key—boundary violation (attempt to WRITE past the physical end of the file)
30	Permanent error (hardware malfunction)
48	File not OPENed as OUTPUT, I-O, or EXTEND

Your COBOL system may have additional codes in the range 90 through 99.

Program P16-01 was run with the input data shown in Figure 16.4 and produced the report output shown in Figure 16.5.

FIGURE 16.4 Input to Program P16-01

```
--------------------------------------------------------------------------------
         1         2         3         4         5         6         7         8
12345678901234567890123456789012345678901234567890123456789012345678901234567890
--------------------------------------------------------------------------------
N021CS302
```

FIGURE 16.5 Report output from Program P16-01

```
   GRADE COMPUTATION SYSTEM

    FILE CREATION - CS302


MASTER FILE SUCCESSFULLY CREATED
 21 RECORDS WRITTEN
```

EXERCISE 1

Write a program to create a relative file of 135 master records, one record for each cash register in a chain of supermarkets. The format of the record is:

Starting cash balance—9(4)V99
Sales
  Grocery—9(4)V99
  Produce—9(4)V99
  Meat—9(4)V99
  Dairy—9(4)V99
Tax—9(3)V99
Bottle and can deposits—9(3)V99
Coupons—9(3)V99
Deposit returns—9(3)V99
Adjustments—S9(3)V99
Ending cash balance—9(4)V99

Create the file with all zero values in all fields. After the file is created, have your program print a message so indicating. Save the file for use later in this chapter.

Updating a Relative File Randomly

In Program P16-02, we will show how the file created by Program P16-01 can have grades inserted and changed, and how a student's record can be deleted. Program P16-02 accepts transactions in random order in the following formats:

Positions	Field
1	Code "E"
2–4	Student Number
5	Exam-Homework Type
6–7	Exam-Homework Number
8–10	Grade
11–80	spaces
1	Code "C"
2–4	Student Number
5	Exam-Homework Type
6–7	Exam-Homework Number
8–10	Grade
11–80	spaces
1	Code "D"
2–4	Student Number
5–80	spaces

The transaction codes are:

E—enter one exam or homework grade into the file

C—change an existing exam or homework grade in the file

D—delete this student's record from the file

All three types of transactions contain a Student Number in positions 2 through 4. Transaction types E and C contain, in positions 5 through 7, an indication of which exam or homework grade is being entered or changed. Position 5 contains the letter E or H to say whether the transaction relates to an exam grade or a homework grade, and positions 6 and 7 say to which exam number (1 through 5) or homework number (1 through 12) the transaction relates.

Program P16-02 produces a transaction register in the format shown in Figure 16.6. The first line in the body of the report shows the successful entering of an exam grade. The second line shows the entering of a homework grade. The next two lines show the changing of an exam grade and a homework grade. The program also produces an error report in the format shown in Figure 16.7. The body lines, containing error messages, show all the errors that can be detected by the program. The last line on the format shows an attempt to change a grade that is not in the file; the second from the last line shows an attempt to insert a grade for an exam or homework that already has a grade entered.

A hierarchy diagram for "Apply transaction" for Program P16-02 is shown in Figure 16.8. It resembles the other "Apply transaction" boxes in the hierarchy diagrams for previous update programs. A difference is in the procedure for checking the validity of the E- and C-type transactions. It turns out that certain validity checks on the two types of transactions are identical, so "Test for valid input" is used for both. If an input transaction is free of errors, the program then enters or changes an exam grade or a homework grade, as appropriate.

FIGURE 16.6 **Output format for transaction register for Program P16-02**

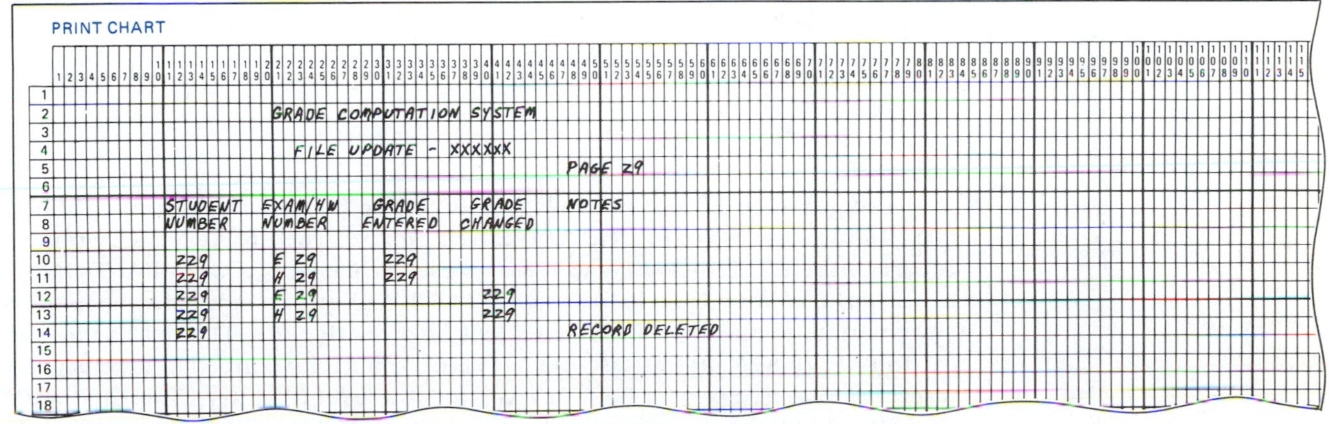

FIGURE 16.7 Output format for error report for Program P16-02

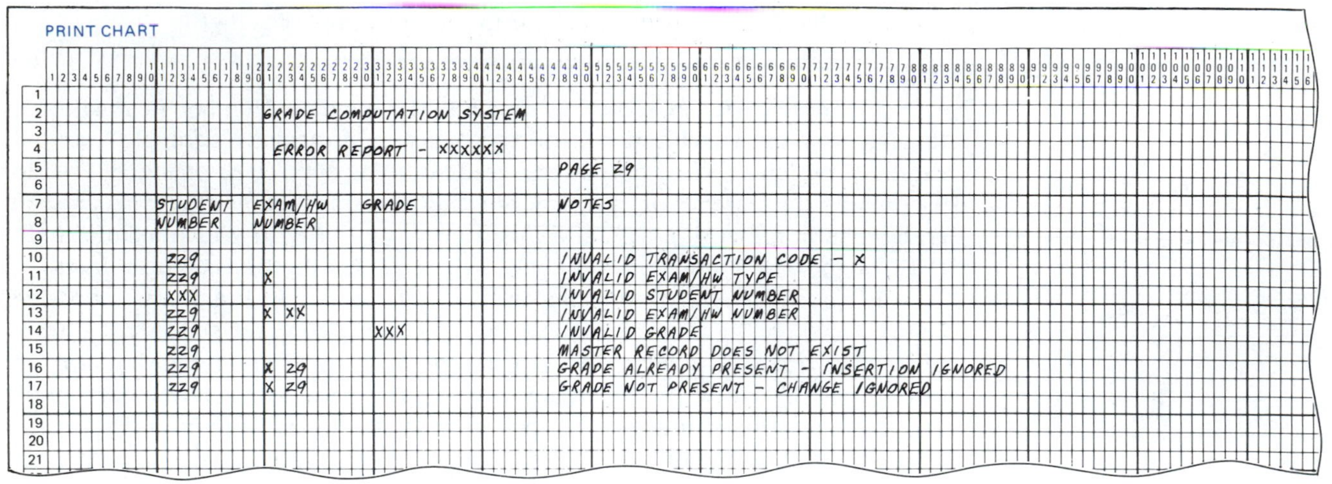

PRINT CHART
GRADE COMPUTATION SYSTEM
ERROR REPORT - XXXXXX
PAGE Z9
STUDENT NUMBER
EXAM/HW NUMBER
GRADE
NOTES
ZZ9
INVALID TRANSACTION CODE - X
ZZ9 X
INVALID EXAM/HW TYPE
XXX
INVALID STUDENT NUMBER
ZZ9 X XX
INVALID EXAM/HW NUMBER
ZZ9 XXX
INVALID GRADE
ZZ9
MASTER RECORD DOES NOT EXIST
ZZ9 X Z9
GRADE ALREADY PRESENT - INSERTION IGNORED
ZZ9 X Z9
GRADE NOT PRESENT - CHANGE IGNORED

FIGURE 16.8 Hierarchy diagram for "Apply transaction" for Program P16-02

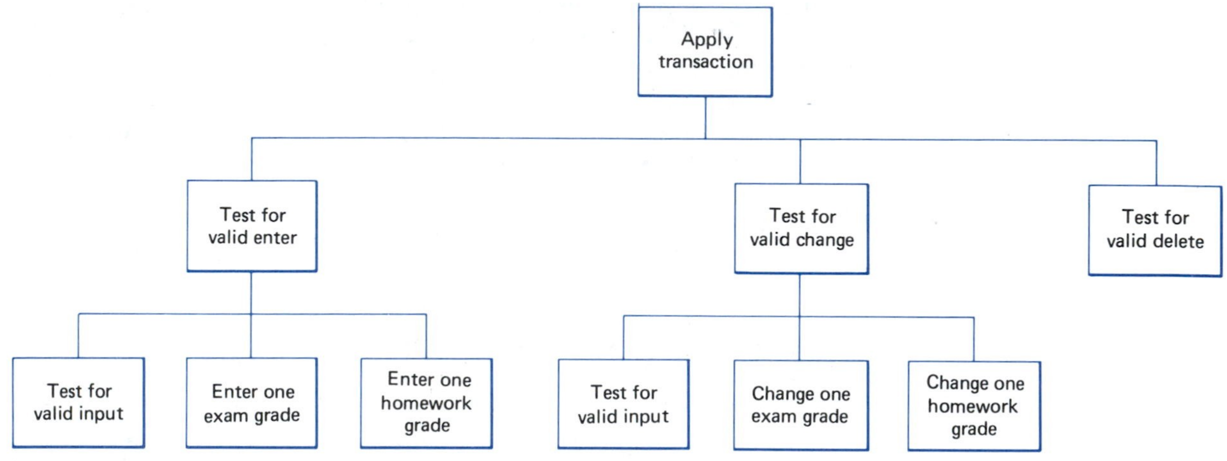

Program P16-02 is shown in Figure 16.9. The FILE-CONTROL entry at line 00140 shows the use of the **RELATIVE KEY** phrase. The RELATIVE KEY phrase is part of the ACCESS clause and must be used whenever ACCESS RANDOM or ACCESS DYNAMIC is specified. The RELATIVE KEY phrase must also be used in any program that uses a START statement on a relative file. The field named as the RELATIVE KEY, in this case RELATIVE-KEY, must be defined as an unsigned integer and must not be a field that is part of a level-01 entry associated with this file. When the file is accessed randomly, the value of the RELATIVE KEY indicates the record to be accessed.

FIGURE 16.9 **Program P16-02**

```
S COBOL II RELEASE 3.1 09/19/89                 P16002   DATE SEP 28,1991 T
----+-*A-1-B--+----2----+----3----+----4----+----5----+----6----+----7-|--+

  IDENTIFICATION DIVISION.
  PROGRAM-ID.  P16-02.
 *
 *     THIS PROGRAM UPDATES A RELATIVE FILE RANDOMLY
 *
 ************************************************************************

  ENVIRONMENT DIVISION.
  INPUT-OUTPUT SECTION.
  FILE-CONTROL.
      SELECT TRANSACTION-FILE-IN  ASSIGN TO INFILE.
      SELECT REPORT-FILE-OUT      ASSIGN TO PRINTER1.
      SELECT ERROR-FILE-OUT       ASSIGN TO PRINTER2.
      SELECT GRADES-FILE-I-O      ASSIGN TO DISKUNIT
          ORGANIZATION RELATIVE
          ACCESS DYNAMIC
          RELATIVE KEY IS RELATIVE-KEY
          STATUS IS MASTER-FILE-CHECK.

 ************************************************************************

  DATA DIVISION.
  FILE SECTION.
  FD  TRANSACTION-FILE-IN.

  01  TRANSACTION-RECORD-IN                          PIC X(80).

  FD  GRADES-FILE-I-O
      RECORD CONTAINS 60 CHARACTERS
      LABEL RECORDS ARE STANDARD.

  01  GRADES-RECORD-I-O                              PIC X(60).

  FD  REPORT-FILE-OUT.

  01  REPORT-RECORD-OUT                              PIC X(61).

  FD  ERROR-FILE-OUT.

  01  ERROR-RECORD-OUT                               PIC X(88).

  WORKING-STORAGE SECTION.
  01  PAGE-LIMIT                  VALUE 50           PIC S99 COMP SYNC.
  01  RELATIVE-KEY                                   PIC 9(3).
  01  PACKED-DECIMAL.
   02 REPORT-PAGE-COUNTER         VALUE 0            PIC S99.
   02 ERROR-PAGE-COUNTER          VALUE 0            PIC S99.
  01  LINE-COUNT-ER                                  PIC S99 COMP SYNC.
  01  ERROR-LINE-COUNTER                             PIC S99 COMP SYNC.
  01  MASTER-FILE-CHECK                              PIC XX.
      88 MASTER-FILE-IS-OPENED                       VALUE "00".
      88 READ-WAS-SUCCESSFUL                         VALUE "00".
      88 FILE-OPERATION-SUCCESSFUL                   VALUE "00".
      88 NO-MASTER-RECORD-FOUND                      VALUE "23".
  01  IS-MASTER-RECORD-IN-THE-FILE                   PIC X.
      88 MASTER-RECORD-IS-IN-THE-FILE                VALUE "Y".
      88 MASTER-RECORD-ISNT-IN-THE-FILE              VALUE "N".
  01  IS-MASTER-RECORD-IN-WORK-AREA                  PIC X.
      88 MASTER-RECORD-IS-IN-WORKAREA                VALUE "Y".
      88 MASTER-RECORD-ISNT-IN-WORKAREA              VALUE "N".
  01  ERROR-FLAG                                     PIC X.
      88 NO-ERRORS-IN-INPUT                          VALUE "Y".
      88 ERROR-IN-INPUT                              VALUE "N".
```

continued

In the TRANSACTION-INPUT-AREA, which starts at line 00650, the Student Number is defined as both numeric and alphanumeric, at lines 00720 through 00740. We use the numeric definition when we do arithmetic or numeric editing, and the alphanumeric definition when STUDENT-NUMBER-X might contain HIGH-VALUES or other nonnumeric data. The field EXAM-HW, line 00750, refers to positions 5 through 7 of the transaction. Position 5, EXAM-HW-TYPE, is to contain either an E or an H and tells whether the transaction refers to an exam grade or a homework grade. Positions 6 and 7, EXAM-HW-NUMBER, tell which exam or homework number the transaction refers to. If to an exam, EXAM-HW-NUMBER must be a number 1 through 5; if to homework, EXAM-HW-NUMBER must be a number 1 through 12.

FIGURE *16.9* ***continued***

```
S COBOL II RELEASE 3.1 09/19/89                   P16002   DATE SEP 28,1991 T
----+-*A-1-B--+----2----+----3----+----4----+----5----+----6----+----7-|--+

00650  01  TRANSACTION-INPUT-AREA.
00660      88  NO-MORE-TRANSACTION-RECORDS              VALUE HIGH-VALUES.
00670      88  NO-TRANSACTION-RECORDS                   VALUE HIGH-VALUES.
00680      05  TRANSACTION-CODE-T                       PIC X.
00690          88  TRANSACTION-IS-ENTER         VALUE "E".
00700          88  TRANSACTION-IS-CHANGE        VALUE "C".
00710          88  TRANSACTION-IS-DELETE        VALUE "D".
00720      05  STUDENT-NUMBER-T                         PIC 9(3).
00730      05  STUDENT-NUMBER-X REDEFINES STUDENT-NUMBER-T
00740                                                   PIC X(3).
00750      05  EXAM-HW.
00760          10  EXAM-HW-TYPE                         PIC X.
00770              88  EXAM                     VALUE "E".
00780              88  HOMEWORK                 VALUE "H".
00790              88  EXAM-HW-TYPE-VALID       VALUES "E", "H".
00800          10  EXAM-HW-NUMBER                       PIC 99.
00810              88  EXAM-NUMBER-VALID                VALUES 1 THRU 5.
00820              88  HOMEWORK-NUMBER-VALID            VALUES 1 THRU 12.
00830          10  EXAM-HW-NUMBER-X REDEFINES EXAM-HW-NUMBER
00840                                                   PIC XX.
00850      05  GRADE-T                                  PIC 9(3).
00860      05  GRADE-X REDEFINES GRADE-T                PIC X(3).
00870
00880  01  GRADES-RECORD-M.
00890      05  COURSE-OR-SECTION-M                      PIC X(6).
00900      05  NUMBER-OF-STUDENTS-M                     PIC 9(3).
00910      05  EXAM-GRADE      OCCURS 5 TIMES           PIC 9(3).
00920      05  HOMEWORK-GRADE  OCCURS 12 TIMES          PIC 9(3).
00930
00940  01  PAGE-HEADING-1.
00950      05                  VALUE SPACES             PIC X(20).
00960      05
00970          VALUE "GRADE COMPUTATION SYSTEM"         PIC X(24).
00980
00990  01  REPORT-PAGE-HEADING-2.
01000      05                  VALUE SPACES             PIC X(22).
01010      05                  VALUE "FILE UPDATE -"    PIC X(14).
01020      05  COURSE-OR-SECTION-M-OUT                  PIC X(6).
01030
01040  01  ERROR-PAGE-HEADING-2.
01050      05                  VALUE SPACES             PIC X(21).
01060      05                  VALUE "ERROR REPORT -  "
01070                                                   PIC X(15).
01080      05  COURSE-OR-SECTION-M-OUT                  PIC X(6).
01090
```

FIGURE *16.9* *continued*

```
       01  PAGE-HEADING-3.
           05                      VALUE SPACES          PIC X(47).
           05                      VALUE "PAGE"          PIC X(5).
           05  PAGE-NUMBER-OUT                           PIC Z9.

       01  REPORT-PAGE-HEADING-4.
           05                      VALUE SPACES          PIC X(10).
           05                      VALUE "STUDENT"       PIC X(9).
           05                      VALUE "EXAM/HW"       PIC X(10).
           05                      VALUE "GRADE"         PIC X(9).
           05                      VALUE "GRADE"         PIC X(9).
           05                      VALUE "NOTES"         PIC X(5).

       01  ERROR-PAGE-HEADING-4.
           05                      VALUE SPACES          PIC X(10).
           05                      VALUE "STUDENT"       PIC X(9).
           05                      VALUE "EXAM/HW"       PIC X(10).
           05                      VALUE "GRADE"         PIC X(18).
           05                      VALUE "NOTES"         PIC X(5).

       01  REPORT-PAGE-HEADING-5.
           05                      VALUE SPACES          PIC X(10).
           05                      VALUE "NUMBER"        PIC X(9).
           05                      VALUE "NUMBER"        PIC X(9).
           05                      VALUE "ENTERED"       PIC X(9).
           05                      VALUE "CHANGED"       PIC X(7).

       01  ERROR-PAGE-HEADING-5.
           05                      VALUE SPACES          PIC X(10).
           05                      VALUE "NUMBER"        PIC X(9).
           05                      VALUE "NUMBER"        PIC X(9).

       01  NO-TRANSACTIONS.
           05                  VALUE SPACES              PIC X(17).
           05                  VALUE "NO TRANSACTIONS"   PIC X(15).

       01  ERROR-LINE.
           05                  VALUE SPACES              PIC X(11).
           05  STUDENT-NUMBER-E                          PIC ZZ9B(6).
           05  STUDENT-NUMBER-E-X REDEFINES STUDENT-NUMBER-E
                                                         PIC X(3)B(6).
           05  EXAM-HW-TYPE-E                            PIC XB.
           05  EXAM-HW-NUMBER-E                          PIC Z9B(6).
           05  GRADE-E                                   PIC ZZ9B(14).
           05  GRADE-X-E REDEFINES GRADE-E               PIC X(3)B(14).
           05  MESSAGE-E                                 PIC X(41).

       01  INVALID-CODE-MESSAGE.
           05                  VALUE "INVALID TRANSACTION CODE -"
                                                         PIC X(27).
           05  TRANSACTION-CODE-E                        PIC X.

       01  GRADE-ENTERED-LINE.
           05                  VALUE SPACES              PIC X(11).
           05  STUDENT-NUMBER-T                          PIC ZZ9B(6).
           05  EXAM-HW-TYPE                              PIC XB.
           05  EXAM-HW-NUMBER                            PIC Z9B(6).
           05  GRADE-T                                   PIC ZZ9.

       01  GRADE-CHANGED-LINE.
           05                  VALUE SPACES              PIC X(11).
           05  STUDENT-NUMBER-T                          PIC ZZ9B(6).
           05  EXAM-HW-TYPE                              PIC XB.
           05  EXAM-HW-NUMBER                            PIC Z9B(15).
           05  GRADE-T                                   PIC ZZ9.

      *****************************************************************
```

continued

The Procedure Division, which starts at line 01780, follows the hierarchy diagram. The paragraph READ-A-TRANSACTION-RECORD, line 02390, uses a validity-checking technique similar to the one used in Program P15-03. READ-A-TRANSACTION-RECORD does not simply READ the next record on the input transaction file and return it to the higher-level paragraph in the program. Instead, READ-A-TRANSACTION-RECORD returns only transaction records having a numeric Student Number. READ-TRANSACTION-FILE, line 02460, checks the Student Number in each transaction after it has been read. If the Student Number is not numeric, READ-TRANSACTION-FILE prints an error message and READs another transaction.

FIGURE 16.9 *continued*

```
S COBOL II RELEASE 3.1 09/19/89                    P16002   DATE SEP 28,1991 T
----+-*A-1-B--+----2----+----3----+----4----+----5----+----6----+----7-|--+


01770
01780  PROCEDURE DIVISION.
01790  UPDATE-GRADES-FILE.
01800      PERFORM INITIALIZATION
01810      PERFORM PROCESS-ONE-KEY UNTIL NO-MORE-TRANSACTION-RECORDS
01820      PERFORM TERMINATION
01830      STOP RUN
01840      .
01850
01860  INITIALIZATION.
01870      OPEN INPUT  TRANSACTION-FILE-IN
01880           OUTPUT REPORT-FILE-OUT
01890                  ERROR-FILE-OUT
01900           I-O    GRADES-FILE-I-O
01910      IF NOT MASTER-FILE-IS-OPENED
01920          DISPLAY " MASTER FILE OPEN STATUS = ", MASTER-FILE-CHECK
01930          PERFORM TERMINATION
01940          STOP RUN
01950      END-IF
01960      READ GRADES-FILE-I-O NEXT INTO GRADES-RECORD-M
01970      IF NOT READ-WAS-SUCCESSFUL
01980          DISPLAY " NO MASTER RECORDS "
01990          PERFORM TERMINATION
02000          STOP RUN
02010      END-IF
02020      MOVE COURSE-OR-SECTION-M
02030           TO COURSE-OR-SECTION-M-OUT OF REPORT-PAGE-HEADING-2
02040              COURSE-OR-SECTION-M-OUT OF ERROR-PAGE-HEADING-2
02050      PERFORM PRODUCE-ERROR-HEADINGS
02060      PERFORM PRODUCE-REPORT-HEADINGS
02070      PERFORM READ-A-TRANSACTION-RECORD
02080      IF NO-TRANSACTION-RECORDS
02090          PERFORM WRITE-NO-TRANSACTIONS
02100      END-IF
02110      .
02120
```

FIGURE 16.9 *continued*

```
PRODUCE-REPORT-HEADINGS.
    WRITE REPORT-RECORD-OUT FROM PAGE-HEADING-1 AFTER PAGE
    ADD 1 TO REPORT-PAGE-COUNTER
    MOVE REPORT-PAGE-COUNTER TO PAGE-NUMBER-OUT
    WRITE REPORT-RECORD-OUT FROM REPORT-PAGE-HEADING-2 AFTER 2
    WRITE REPORT-RECORD-OUT FROM PAGE-HEADING-3
    WRITE REPORT-RECORD-OUT FROM REPORT-PAGE-HEADING-4 AFTER 2
    WRITE REPORT-RECORD-OUT FROM REPORT-PAGE-HEADING-5
    MOVE SPACES TO REPORT-RECORD-OUT
    WRITE REPORT-RECORD-OUT
    MOVE 8 TO LINE-COUNT-ER
    .

PRODUCE-ERROR-HEADINGS.
    WRITE ERROR-RECORD-OUT FROM PAGE-HEADING-1 AFTER PAGE
    ADD 1 TO ERROR-PAGE-COUNTER
    MOVE ERROR-PAGE-COUNTER TO PAGE-NUMBER-OUT
    WRITE ERROR-RECORD-OUT FROM ERROR-PAGE-HEADING-2 AFTER 2
    WRITE ERROR-RECORD-OUT FROM PAGE-HEADING-3
    WRITE ERROR-RECORD-OUT FROM ERROR-PAGE-HEADING-4 AFTER 3
    WRITE ERROR-RECORD-OUT FROM ERROR-PAGE-HEADING-5
    MOVE SPACES TO ERROR-RECORD-OUT
    WRITE ERROR-RECORD-OUT
    MOVE 9 TO ERROR-LINE-COUNTER
    .

READ-A-TRANSACTION-RECORD.
    MOVE SPACES TO STUDENT-NUMBER-X
    PERFORM READ-TRANSACTION-FILE UNTIL
        STUDENT-NUMBER-T IN TRANSACTION-INPUT-AREA IS NUMERIC OR
        NO-MORE-TRANSACTION-RECORDS
    .

READ-TRANSACTION-FILE.
    READ TRANSACTION-FILE-IN INTO TRANSACTION-INPUT-AREA
        AT END
            SET NO-MORE-TRANSACTION-RECORDS TO TRUE
        NOT AT END
            IF STUDENT-NUMBER-T IN TRANSACTION-INPUT-AREA
                 NOT NUMERIC
                PERFORM WRITE-INVALID-STUDENT-NO-LINE
            END-IF
    .

PROCESS-ONE-KEY.
    PERFORM PROCESS-MASTER
    PERFORM PROCESS-TRANSACTION
    PERFORM CHECK-TO-WRITE-MASTER
    .

```

continued

The READ statement at line 02660 is a random READ. When a relative file is read randomly, COBOL uses the value of the RELATIVE KEY field to know which record in the file to READ. Similarly, the REWRITE statement at line 02890 and the DELETE statement at line 02930 are random operations. COBOL uses the value of the RELATIVE KEY field to know which record to REWRITE or DELETE. READ, REWRITE, and DELETE all set the STATUS field if one is specified for the file. The ANSI standard meanings of the STATUS codes for random READ, REWRITE, and DELETE statements on a relative file are given in Tables 16.2 and 16.3. Your COBOL system may have additional codes in the range 90 through 99.

FIGURE *16.9* ***continued***

```
S COBOL II RELEASE 3.1 09/19/89                  P16002   DATE SEP 28,1991 T
----+-*A-1-B--+----2----+----3----+----4----+----5----+----6----+----7-|--+

02630  PROCESS-MASTER.
02640      MOVE STUDENT-NUMBER-T IN TRANSACTION-INPUT-AREA
02650           TO RELATIVE-KEY
02660      READ GRADES-FILE-I-O INTO GRADES-RECORD-M
02670          INVALID KEY CONTINUE
02680      END-READ
02690      IF READ-WAS-SUCCESSFUL
02700          SET MASTER-RECORD-IS-IN-THE-FILE TO TRUE
02710          SET MASTER-RECORD-IS-IN-WORKAREA TO TRUE
02720      ELSE
02730      IF NO-MASTER-RECORD-FOUND
02740          SET MASTER-RECORD-ISNT-IN-THE-FILE TO TRUE
02750          SET MASTER-RECORD-ISNT-IN-WORKAREA TO TRUE
02760      ELSE
02770          DISPLAY " MASTER FILE READ STATUS = ", MASTER-FILE-CHECK
02780          PERFORM TERMINATION
02790          STOP RUN
02800      END-IF
02810      END-IF
02820      .
02830
02840  CHECK-TO-WRITE-MASTER.
02850      MOVE ZEROS TO MASTER-FILE-CHECK
02860      EVALUATE MASTER-RECORD-IS-IN-WORKAREA ALSO
02870               MASTER-RECORD-IS-IN-THE-FILE
02880      WHEN TRUE ALSO ANY
02890          REWRITE GRADES-RECORD-I-O FROM GRADES-RECORD-M
02900              INVALID KEY CONTINUE
02910          END-REWRITE
02920      WHEN FALSE ALSO TRUE
02930          DELETE GRADES-FILE-I-O
02940              INVALID KEY CONTINUE
02950          END-DELETE
02960      WHEN OTHER
02970          CONTINUE
02980      END-EVALUATE
02990      IF NOT FILE-OPERATION-SUCCESSFUL
03000          DISPLAY " MASTER FILE WRITE STATUS = ", MASTER-FILE-CHECK
03010          PERFORM TERMINATION
03020          STOP RUN
03030      END-IF
03040      .
03050
03060  PROCESS-TRANSACTION.
03070      PERFORM APPLY-TRANSACTION
03080      PERFORM READ-A-TRANSACTION-RECORD
03090      .
03100
```

FIGURE 16.9 *continued*

```
APPLY-TRANSACTION.
    EVALUATE TRUE
    WHEN TRANSACTION-IS-ENTER
        PERFORM TEST-FOR-VALID-ENTER
    WHEN TRANSACTION-IS-CHANGE
        PERFORM TEST-FOR-VALID-CHANGE
    WHEN TRANSACTION-IS-DELETE
        PERFORM TEST-FOR-VALID-DELETE
    WHEN OTHER
        PERFORM WRITE-INVALID-CODE-LINE
    END-EVALUATE
    .

TEST-FOR-VALID-ENTER.
    SET NO-ERRORS-IN-INPUT TO TRUE
    PERFORM TEST-FOR-VALID-INPUT
    IF NO-ERRORS-IN-INPUT
        IF EXAM
            PERFORM ENTER-ONE-EXAM-GRADE
        ELSE
            PERFORM ENTER-ONE-HOMEWORK-GRADE
        END-IF
    END-IF
    .

```

continued

TABLE 16.2 **ANSI standard STATUS codes relating to random READ operations on a relative file**

Status Code	Meaning
00	Successful completion
23	Invalid key—no record found
30	Permanent error (hardware malfunction)
47	File not OPENed as INPUT or I-O

TABLE 16.3 **ANSI standard STATUS codes relating to random REWRITE and DELETE operations on a relative file**

Status Code	Meaning
00	Successful completion
23	Invalid key—no record found
30	Permanent error (hardware malfunction)
49	File not OPENed as I-O

The paragraphs ENTER-ONE-EXAM-GRADE, line 03360, and ENTER-ONE-HOMEWORK-GRADE, line 03460, enter a grade into the file only if there is not already a grade there for that exam or homework number. The paragraphs CHANGE-ONE-EXAM-GRADE, line 03690, and CHANGE-ONE-HOMEWORK-GRADE, line 03800, change a grade in the file only if there is already a grade entered. Otherwise, the program prints an error message.

FIGURE *16.9* ***continued***

```
S COBOL II RELEASE 3.1 09/19/89                P16002   DATE SEP 28,1991 T
----+-*A-1-B--+----2----+----3----+----4----+----5----+----6----+----7-|--+

03360  ENTER-ONE-EXAM-GRADE.
03370      IF EXAM-GRADE (EXAM-HW-NUMBER IN TRANSACTION-INPUT-AREA) = 0
03380          MOVE GRADE-T IN TRANSACTION-INPUT-AREA TO
03390            EXAM-GRADE (EXAM-HW-NUMBER IN TRANSACTION-INPUT-AREA)
03400          PERFORM WRITE-GRADE-ENTERED-LINE
03410      ELSE
03420          PERFORM WRITE-GRADE-PRESENT-LINE
03430      END-IF
03440      .
03450
03460  ENTER-ONE-HOMEWORK-GRADE.
03470      IF HOMEWORK-GRADE (EXAM-HW-NUMBER IN TRANSACTION-INPUT-AREA)
03480      = 0
03490          MOVE GRADE-T IN TRANSACTION-INPUT-AREA TO
03500          HOMEWORK-GRADE (EXAM-HW-NUMBER IN TRANSACTION-INPUT-AREA)
03510          PERFORM WRITE-GRADE-ENTERED-LINE
03520      ELSE
03530          PERFORM WRITE-GRADE-PRESENT-LINE
03540      END-IF
03550      .
03560
03570  TEST-FOR-VALID-CHANGE.
03580      SET NO-ERRORS-IN-INPUT TO TRUE
03590      PERFORM TEST-FOR-VALID-INPUT
03600      IF NO-ERRORS-IN-INPUT
03610          IF EXAM
03620              PERFORM CHANGE-ONE-EXAM-GRADE
03630          ELSE
03640              PERFORM CHANGE-ONE-HOMEWORK-GRADE
03650          END-IF
03660      END-IF
03670      .
03680
03690  CHANGE-ONE-EXAM-GRADE.
03700      IF EXAM-GRADE (EXAM-HW-NUMBER IN TRANSACTION-INPUT-AREA) NOT
03710      = 0
03720          MOVE GRADE-T IN TRANSACTION-INPUT-AREA TO
03730            EXAM-GRADE (EXAM-HW-NUMBER IN TRANSACTION-INPUT-AREA)
03740          PERFORM WRITE-GRADE-CHANGED-LINE
03750      ELSE
03760          PERFORM WRITE-GRADE-NOT-PRESENT-LINE
03770      END-IF
03780      .
03790
03800  CHANGE-ONE-HOMEWORK-GRADE.
03810      IF HOMEWORK-GRADE (EXAM-HW-NUMBER IN TRANSACTION-INPUT-AREA)
03820      NOT = 0
03830          MOVE GRADE-T IN TRANSACTION-INPUT-AREA TO
03840          HOMEWORK-GRADE (EXAM-HW-NUMBER IN TRANSACTION-INPUT-AREA)
03850          PERFORM WRITE-GRADE-CHANGED-LINE
03860      ELSE
03870          PERFORM WRITE-GRADE-NOT-PRESENT-LINE
03880      END-IF
03890      .
```

FIGURE 16.9 *continued*

```
TEST-FOR-VALID-DELETE.
     IF MASTER-RECORD-ISNT-IN-WORKAREA
          PERFORM WRITE-MASTER-MISSING-LINE
     ELSE
          SET MASTER-RECORD-ISNT-IN-WORKAREA TO TRUE
          PERFORM WRITE-RECORD-DELETED-LINE
     END-IF
     .

TEST-FOR-VALID-INPUT.
     IF MASTER-RECORD-ISNT-IN-WORKAREA
          SET ERROR-IN-INPUT TO TRUE
          PERFORM WRITE-MASTER-MISSING-LINE
     END-IF
     IF NOT EXAM-HW-TYPE-VALID
          SET ERROR-IN-INPUT TO TRUE
          PERFORM WRITE-INVALID-TYPE-LINE
     END-IF
     IF EXAM-HW-NUMBER IN TRANSACTION-INPUT-AREA NOT NUMERIC
          SET ERROR-IN-INPUT TO TRUE
          PERFORM WRITE-INVALID-EXAM-HW-NUMBER
     END-IF
     IF GRADE-T IN TRANSACTION-INPUT-AREA NOT NUMERIC
          SET ERROR-IN-INPUT TO TRUE
          PERFORM WRITE-INVALID-GRADE-LINE
     END-IF
     IF EXAM AND NOT EXAM-NUMBER-VALID
          SET ERROR-IN-INPUT TO TRUE
          PERFORM WRITE-INVALID-EXAM-HW-NUMBER
     END-IF
     IF HOMEWORK AND NOT HOMEWORK-NUMBER-VALID
          SET ERROR-IN-INPUT TO TRUE
          PERFORM WRITE-INVALID-EXAM-HW-NUMBER
     END-IF
     .

TERMINATION.
     CLOSE TRANSACTION-FILE-IN
            REPORT-FILE-OUT
            ERROR-FILE-OUT
            GRADES-FILE-I-O
     .

WRITE-INVALID-CODE-LINE.
     MOVE SPACES TO ERROR-LINE
     MOVE TRANSACTION-CODE-T TO TRANSACTION-CODE-E
     MOVE INVALID-CODE-MESSAGE TO MESSAGE-E
     MOVE STUDENT-NUMBER-T IN TRANSACTION-INPUT-AREA
       TO STUDENT-NUMBER-E
     PERFORM WRITE-ERROR-LINE
     .

WRITE-NO-TRANSACTIONS.
     WRITE ERROR-RECORD-OUT FROM NO-TRANSACTIONS
     .

WRITE-INVALID-STUDENT-NO-LINE.
     MOVE SPACES TO ERROR-LINE
     MOVE STUDENT-NUMBER-X TO STUDENT-NUMBER-E-X
     MOVE "INVALID STUDENT NUMBER" TO MESSAGE-E
     PERFORM WRITE-ERROR-LINE
     .
```

continued

FIGURE 16.9 *continued*

```
S COBOL II RELEASE 3.1 09/19/89                 P16002   DATE SEP 28,1991 T
----+-*A-1-B--+----2----+----3----+----4----+----5----+----6----+----7-|--+

 WRITE-GRADE-PRESENT-LINE.
     MOVE SPACES TO ERROR-LINE
     MOVE STUDENT-NUMBER-T IN TRANSACTION-INPUT-AREA
       TO STUDENT-NUMBER-E
     MOVE EXAM-HW-TYPE IN TRANSACTION-INPUT-AREA
       TO EXAM-HW-TYPE-E
     MOVE EXAM-HW-NUMBER IN TRANSACTION-INPUT-AREA
       TO EXAM-HW-NUMBER-E
     MOVE "GRADE ALREADY PRESENT - INSERTION IGNORED"
                         TO MESSAGE-E
     PERFORM WRITE-ERROR-LINE
     .

 WRITE-ERROR-LINE.
     IF ERROR-LINE-COUNTER + 1 > PAGE-LIMIT
         PERFORM PRODUCE-ERROR-HEADINGS
     END-IF
     WRITE ERROR-RECORD-OUT FROM ERROR-LINE
     ADD 1 TO ERROR-LINE-COUNTER
     .

 WRITE-GRADE-ENTERED-LINE.
     MOVE CORRESPONDING TRANSACTION-INPUT-AREA
          TO GRADE-ENTERED-LINE
     MOVE CORRESPONDING EXAM-HW TO GRADE-ENTERED-LINE
     IF LINE-COUNT-ER + 1 > PAGE-LIMIT
         PERFORM PRODUCE-REPORT-HEADINGS
     END-IF
     WRITE REPORT-RECORD-OUT FROM GRADE-ENTERED-LINE
     ADD 1 TO LINE-COUNT-ER
     .

 WRITE-GRADE-NOT-PRESENT-LINE.
     MOVE SPACES TO ERROR-LINE
     MOVE STUDENT-NUMBER-T IN TRANSACTION-INPUT-AREA
       TO STUDENT-NUMBER-E
     MOVE EXAM-HW-TYPE IN TRANSACTION-INPUT-AREA
       TO EXAM-HW-TYPE-E
     MOVE EXAM-HW-NUMBER IN TRANSACTION-INPUT-AREA
       TO EXAM-HW-NUMBER-E
     MOVE "GRADE NOT PRESENT - CHANGE IGNORED"
          TO MESSAGE-E
     PERFORM WRITE-ERROR-LINE
     .

 WRITE-GRADE-CHANGED-LINE.
     MOVE CORRESPONDING TRANSACTION-INPUT-AREA
          TO GRADE-CHANGED-LINE
     MOVE CORRESPONDING EXAM-HW TO GRADE-CHANGED-LINE
     IF LINE-COUNT-ER + 1 > PAGE-LIMIT
         PERFORM PRODUCE-REPORT-HEADINGS
     END-IF
     WRITE REPORT-RECORD-OUT FROM GRADE-CHANGED-LINE
     ADD 1 TO LINE-COUNT-ER
     .

 WRITE-MASTER-MISSING-LINE.
     MOVE SPACES TO ERROR-LINE
     MOVE STUDENT-NUMBER-T IN TRANSACTION-INPUT-AREA
       TO STUDENT-NUMBER-E
     MOVE "MASTER RECORD DOES NOT EXIST" TO MESSAGE-E
     PERFORM WRITE-ERROR-LINE
     .
```

FIGURE ***16.9*** ***continued***

```
WRITE-RECORD-DELETED-LINE.
    MOVE SPACES TO ERROR-LINE
    MOVE STUDENT-NUMBER-T IN TRANSACTION-INPUT-AREA
      TO STUDENT-NUMBER-E
    MOVE "RECORD DELETED" TO MESSAGE-E
    IF LINE-COUNT-ER + 1 > PAGE-LIMIT
        PERFORM PRODUCE-REPORT-HEADINGS
    END-IF
    WRITE REPORT-RECORD-OUT FROM ERROR-LINE
    ADD 1 TO LINE-COUNT-ER
    .

WRITE-INVALID-TYPE-LINE.
    MOVE SPACES TO ERROR-LINE
    MOVE STUDENT-NUMBER-T IN TRANSACTION-INPUT-AREA
      TO STUDENT-NUMBER-E
    MOVE EXAM-HW-TYPE IN TRANSACTION-INPUT-AREA
      TO EXAM-HW-TYPE-E
    MOVE "INVALID EXAM/HW TYPE" TO MESSAGE-E
    PERFORM WRITE-ERROR-LINE
    .

WRITE-INVALID-EXAM-HW-NUMBER.
    MOVE SPACES TO ERROR-LINE
    MOVE STUDENT-NUMBER-T IN TRANSACTION-INPUT-AREA
      TO STUDENT-NUMBER-E
    MOVE EXAM-HW-TYPE IN TRANSACTION-INPUT-AREA
      TO EXAM-HW-TYPE-E
    MOVE EXAM-HW-NUMBER IN TRANSACTION-INPUT-AREA
      TO EXAM-HW-NUMBER-E
    MOVE "INVALID EXAM/HW NUMBER" TO MESSAGE-E
    PERFORM WRITE-ERROR-LINE
    .

WRITE-INVALID-GRADE-LINE.
    MOVE SPACES TO ERROR-LINE
    MOVE STUDENT-NUMBER-T IN TRANSACTION-INPUT-AREA
      TO STUDENT-NUMBER-E
    MOVE GRADE-X           TO GRADE-X-E
    MOVE "INVALID GRADE"   TO MESSAGE-E
    PERFORM WRITE-ERROR-LINE
    .
```

Program P16-02 was run with the transaction data shown in Figure 16.10 and the master file created by Program P16-01. Program P16-02 produced the report output shown in Figure 16.11.

FIGURE 16.10 **Transaction input to Program P16-02**

```
--------------------------------------------------------------------------------
         1         2         3         4         5         6         7         8
12345678901234567890123456789012345678901234567890123456789012345678901234567890
--------------------------------------------------------------------------------
D002
E001E01090
E003E02065
E003E04066
E010H04090
E011E01079
E012H10099
E017E02078
E020H02070
E001E04081
E003H07071
E010H01078
E011H07083
E012E02088
E017H04089
E020E01060
D004
E001E05093
E003E03050
E010E01093
E011E03094
D005
E020H09067
D021
E017H07090
E011H09098
D014
E012E04061
E020H05080
E008E02081
E013H04090
D006
T016E02090
C008E02090
E0ABE02086
C016E03100
E008E01095
E008H11079
E003H16095
E019H07070
D018
E001H12088
E020E04089
E017E05080
C017E05090
E001H020A2
E013H09069
E019N05088
D009
E011E05091
E001H09079
D015
C013H09070
C010H01085
E071E05090
E010E03089
E017E03094
E003H06059
E012H11076
E020H09067
E010H05069
E012H12069
E016E01098
D007
E001E02100
E001H03100
```

FIGURE 16.10 *continued*

```
--------------------------------------------------------------------------------
         1         2         3         4         5         6         7         8
12345678901234567890123456789012345678901234567890123456789012345678901234567890
--------------------------------------------------------------------------------
E001H04097
E001H05065
E001H06075
E001H07088
E003E01075
E003E05075
E003H02065
E003H03075
E003H04088
E003H05073
E003H06075
E003H07085
E003H08089
E003H09095
E008E03075
E008E04085
E008H01065
E008H02075
E008H03088
E008H04073
E008H05075
E008H06085
E008H07089
E008H08095
E010E02088
E010E04075
E010E05085
E010H06075
E010H07088
E010H08073
E010H09075
E010H10085
E010H11089
E010H12095
E010H13090
E011H01073
E011H02075
E011H03085
E011H04089
E012E01073
E012E03075
E012E05085
E013E01075
E013E02085
E013E03089
E013E04095
E013E05090
E013H05065
E013H06075
E013H07088
E013H08073
E017E01089
E017E04095
E017H08085
E017H09089
E017H10095
E017H11090
E017H12095
E020E02073
E020E03075
E020E01085
E020H06065
E020H07075
E020H08088
E017H01100
E017H02100
E017H03100
```

FIGURE 16.11 Report output from Program P16-02

```
                GRADE COMPUTATION SYSTEM

                  FILE UPDATE - CS302
                                           PAGE  1

STUDENT   EXAM/HW    GRADE     GRADE      NOTES
NUMBER    NUMBER    ENTERED   CHANGED

    2                                      RECORD DELETED
    1      E  1       90
    3      E  2       65
    3      E  4       66
   10      H  4       90
   11      E  1       79
   12      H 10       99
   17      E  2       78
   20      H  2       70
    1      E  4       81
    3      H  7       71
   10      H  1       78
   11      H  7       83
   12      E  2       88
   17      H  4       89
   20      E  1       60
    4                                      RECORD DELETED
    1      E  5       93
    3      E  3       50
   10      E  1       93
   11      E  3       94
    5                                      RECORD DELETED
   20      H  9       67
   21                                      RECORD DELETED
   17      H  7       90
   11      H  9       98
   14                                      RECORD DELETED
   12      E  4       61
   20      H  5       80
    8      E  2       81
   13      H  4       90
    6                                      RECORD DELETED
    8      E  2                  90
    8      E  1       95
    8      H 11       79
   19      H  7       70
   18                                      RECORD DELETED
    1      H 12       88
   20      E  4       89
   17      E  5       80
   17      E  5                  90
   13      H  9       69
```

FIGURE 16.11 *continued*

GRADE COMPUTATION SYSTEM

FILE UPDATE - CS302

PAGE 2

STUDENT NUMBER	EXAM/HW NUMBER	GRADE ENTERED	GRADE CHANGED	NOTES
9				RECORD DELETED
11	E 5	91		
1	H 9	79		
15				RECORD DELETED
13	H 9		70	
10	H 1		85	
10	E 3	89		
17	E 3	94		
3	H 6	59		
12	H 11	76		
10	H 5	69		
12	H 12	69		
16	E 1	98		
7				RECORD DELETED
1	E 2	100		
1	H 3	100		
1	H 4	97		
1	H 5	65		
1	H 6	75		
1	H 7	88		
3	E 1	75		
3	E 5	75		
3	H 2	65		
3	H 3	75		
3	H 4	88		
3	H 5	73		
3	H 8	89		
3	H 9	95		
8	E 3	75		
8	E 4	85		
8	H 1	65		
8	H 2	75		
8	H 3	88		
8	H 4	73		
8	H 5	75		
8	H 6	85		
8	H 7	89		
8	H 8	95		
10	E 2	88		
10	E 4	75		
10	E 5	85		
10	H 6	75		

continued

FIGURE 16.11 *continued*

```
                    GRADE COMPUTATION SYSTEM

                      FILE UPDATE - CS302
                                                   PAGE   3

STUDENT   EXAM/HW    GRADE      GRADE      NOTES
NUMBER    NUMBER     ENTERED    CHANGED

  10        H  7        88
  10        H  8        73
  10        H  9        75
  10        H 10        85
  10        H 11        89
  10        H 12        95
  11        H  1        73
  11        H  2        75
  11        H  3        85
  11        H  4        89
  12        E  1        73
  12        E  3        75
  12        E  5        85
  13        E  1        75
  13        E  2        85
  13        E  3        89
  13        E  4        95
  13        E  5        90
  13        H  5        65
  13        H  6        75
  13        H  7        88
  13        H  8        73
  17        E  1        89
  17        E  4        95
  17        H  8        85
  17        H  9        89
  17        H 10        95
  17        H 11        90
  17        H 12        95
  20        E  2        73
  20        E  3        75
  20        H  6        65
  20        H  7        75
  20        H  8        88
  17        H  1       100
  17        H  2       100
  17        H  3       100
```

```
              GRADE COMPUTATION SYSTEM

               ERROR REPORT - CS302
                                              PAGE   1

STUDENT   EXAM/HW    GRADE               NOTES
NUMBER    NUMBER

   16                                    INVALID TRANSACTION CODE - T
  0AB                                    INVALID STUDENT NUMBER
   16      E  3                          GRADE NOT PRESENT - CHANGE IGNORED
    3      H 16                          INVALID EXAM/HW NUMBER
    1                 0A2                INVALID GRADE
   19      N                             INVALID EXAM/HW TYPE
   71                                    MASTER RECORD DOES NOT EXIST
   20      H  9                          GRADE ALREADY PRESENT - INSERTION IGNORED
    3      H  6                          GRADE ALREADY PRESENT - INSERTION IGNORED
    3      H  7                          GRADE ALREADY PRESENT - INSERTION IGNORED
   10      H 13                          INVALID EXAM/HW NUMBER
   20      E  1                          GRADE ALREADY PRESENT - INSERTION IGNORED
```

EXERCISE 2

Write a program to update the file you created in Exercise 1. Have your program accept transactions in the following formats:

Positions	Field
1–2	Transaction code
	01—Starting cash balance
	02—Ending cash balance
	03—Grocery sale
	04—Produce sale
	05—Meat sale
	06—Dairy sale
	07—Tax
	08—Bottle and can deposit
	09—Coupon
	10—Deposit return
	11—Adjustment
3–5	Register Number
6–11	Amount (in dollars and cents)
6–9	Amount dollars (sign in position 6)
10–11	Amount cents
12–80	spaces

The format for a deletion transaction is:

Positions	Field
1–2	Code 12
3–5	Register Number

For transaction types 01 and 02, have your program replace the corresponding field in the master record with the Amount field in the transaction. For transaction types 03 through 10, have your program add the Amount field in the transaction to the corresponding field in the master record. In transactions of type 11, adjustments may be positive or negative; have your program add the Amount field in the transaction to the Adjustments field in the master record. For transaction type 12, have your program remove the master record from the file.

Have your program make all suitable validity checks on each transaction. Have your program print reports showing erroneous transactions and all changes made to the master file. Save the updated master file for use later in this chapter.

Processing a Relative File Sequentially

Program P16-03 computes student grades from the updated master file produced by Program P16-02. In many ways, processing a relative file sequentially is the same as processing any file sequentially. But there is one interesting characteristic of a relative file that gives the programmer an option when the file is processed sequentially. Remember that a relative file may have some of its slots empty. Sequential READs to a relative file bring in only records that are actually in the file. Empty slots are skipped over and ignored by the READ statements. At the option of the programmer, COBOL can be asked to provide the program with the relative record number (the slot number) of each record that is read. Program P16-03 will use that option, so that as each student's record is read the program can know the Student Number of the record.

Program P16-03 computes and prints a letter grade for each student. The letter grade depends one-third on the final exam (exam number 5), one-third on the average of the other four exams, and one-third on the homework. If a student missed an exam, the grade on that exam is taken as zero. Letter grades correspond to the following numeric ranges:

90 or higher	A
80 or higher and below 90	B
70 or higher and below 80	C
60 or higher and below 70	D
below 60	F

If a student dropped the course, the program assigns a grade of W. The grade listing has the format shown in Figure 16.12. It shows that every Student Number is assigned some grade, either W or a letter A through F. If a particular Student Number has no record in the file, that number is assigned a grade of W. If a Student Number has a record in the file, a grade A through F is computed and printed along with the numeric values that were used in the computation.

FIGURE *16.12* **Output format for Program P16-03**

PRINT CHART

```
                                GRADE COMPUTATION SYSTEM
                             FINAL LETTER GRADES - XXXXXX
                                                         PAGE Z9

      STUDENT     FINAL       4-EXAM     HOMEWORK      FINAL      FINAL
      NUMBER      EXAM        AVERAGE    AVERAGE       AVERAGE    GRADE

           1      ZZ9         ZZ9.9      ZZ9.9         ZZ9.9        X
           2      ZZ9         ZZ9.9      ZZ9.9         ZZ9.9        X
           3                                                        W
           4      ZZ9         ZZ9.9      ZZ9.9         ZZ9.9        X
           5                                                        W
           6      ZZ9         ZZ9.9      ZZ9.9         ZZ9.9        X
           .
           .
           .
         ZZ9      ZZ9         ZZ9.9      ZZ9.9         ZZ9.9        X
```

A hierarchy diagram for Program P16-03 is shown in Figure 16.13. For each Student Number, the box "Produce a final grade" determines whether a W grade or a letter grade A to F is to be assigned, depending on whether that Student Number has a record in the master file.

FIGURE 16.13 Hierarchy diagram for Program P16-03

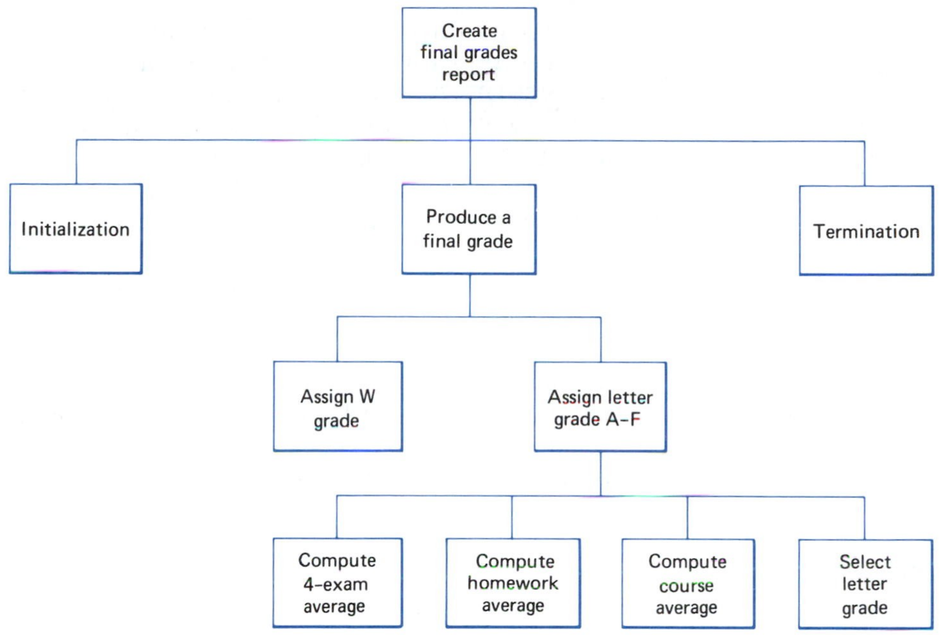

Program P16-03 is shown in Figure 16.14. The FILE-CONTROL entry for the master file contains the clause ACCESS **SEQUENTIAL**, at line 00190. In most programs, no ACCESS SEQUENTIAL clause is needed, for if ACCESS SEQUEN-

FIGURE 16.14 Program P16-03

```
S COBOL II RELEASE 3.1 09/19/89                    P16003   DATE SEP 30,1991 T
----+-*A-1-B--+----2----+----3----+----4----+----5----+----6----+----7-|--+

00010  IDENTIFICATION DIVISION.
00020  PROGRAM-ID.  P16-03.
00030 *
00040 *     THIS PROGRAM PROCESSES A FILE OF EXAM AND HOMEWORK
00050 *     GRADES AND PRODUCES A LETTER GRADE FOR EACH STUDENT.
00060 *
00070 ******************************************************************
00080
00090  ENVIRONMENT DIVISION.
00100  INPUT-OUTPUT SECTION.
00110  FILE-CONTROL.
00120      SELECT LETTER-GRADES-FILE-OUT ASSIGN TO PRINTER.
00130      SELECT GRADES-MASTER-FILE-IN  ASSIGN TO DISKUNIT
00140          ORGANIZATION RELATIVE
00150          ACCESS SEQUENTIAL
00160          RELATIVE KEY IS STUDENT-NUMBER-W
00170          STATUS IS MASTER-FILE-CHECK.
00180
00190 ******************************************************************
```

continued

TIAL is omitted, sequential access is assumed. But in this program we need a RELATIVE KEY, and the RELATIVE KEY phrase is part of the ACCESS clause. So in order to have a RELATIVE KEY you must include an ACCESS clause. The general rule is that whenever you have ACCESS RANDOM or ACCESS DYNAMIC you must have a RELATIVE KEY phrase, and whenever you need a RELATIVE KEY for any reason, you must have some form of ACCESS clause. You are permitted to have ACCESS SEQUENTIAL without a RELATIVE KEY phrase.

When a relative file is read sequentially, each READ statement brings in the next record that is actually in the file. In Program P16-03 we have a RELATIVE KEY, STUDENT-NUMBER-W. Each time a record is read from the master file, COBOL will place the relative record number of that record into STUDENT-NUMBER-W. You will see when we look at the Procedure Division how the program uses STUDENT-NUMBER-W to determine whether there are any Student Numbers to be given grades of W.

In the Working Storage Section the field STUDENT-COUNTER, line 00430, is used to ensure that every Student Number is assigned a grade. During execution of the program, STUDENT-COUNTER is varied from 1 on up in increments of 1, and some grade is printed for each different value of STUDENT-COUNTER, whether or not there is a record in the master file for that Student Number. The field NUMBER-OF-STUDENTS-W, line 00450, is used to show how many records the master file contained when it was created, that is, the number of students represented in the file before any withdrawals.

FIGURE *16.14* ***continued***

```
S COBOL II RELEASE 3.2 09/05/90                P16003    DATE SEP 17,1992 T
----+-*A-1-B--+----2----+----3----+----4----+----5----+----6----+----7-|--+

00200
00210  DATA DIVISION.
00220
00230  FILE SECTION.
00240  FD  GRADES-MASTER-FILE-IN
00250      RECORD CONTAINS 60 CHARACTERS
00260      LABEL RECORDS ARE STANDARD.
00270
00280  01  GRADES-RECORD-IN                              PIC X(60).
00290
00300  FD  LETTER-GRADES-FILE-OUT.
00310
00320  01  GRADES-RECORD-OUT                             PIC X(62).
00330
00340  WORKING-STORAGE SECTION.
00350  01  PAGE-LIMIT                     VALUE 50       PIC S99 COMP SYNC.
00360  01  LINE-COUNT-ER                                 PIC S99 COMP SYNC.
00370  01  MASTER-FILE-CHECK                             PIC XX.
00380      88 MASTER-FILE-IS-OPENED       VALUE "00".
00390      88 READ-WAS-SUCCESSFUL         VALUE "00".
00400      88 END-OF-MASTER-INPUT-FILE    VALUE "10".
00410  01  PACKED-DECIMAL.
00420   02 PAGE-NUMBER-W                  VALUE 0        PIC S99.
00430   02 STUDENT-COUNTER                               PIC S9(3).
00440   02 STUDENT-NUMBER-W                              PIC 9(3).
00450   02 NUMBER-OF-STUDENTS-W       VALUE ZERO         PIC S9(3).
00460   02 NUMBER-OF-HOMEWORKS        VALUE 12           PIC 99.
00470  01  HOMEWORK-SUBSCRIPT                            PIC S99 COMP SYNC.
00480  01  LETTER-GRADE                                  PIC X.
00490
```

FIGURE 16.14 *continued*

```
 01  GRADES-RECORD-M.
     05  COURSE-OR-SECTION-M                          PIC X(6).
     05  NUMBER-OF-STUDENTS-M                         PIC 9(3).
     05  EXAM-GRADE       OCCURS 5 TIMES              PIC 9(3).
     05  HOMEWORK-GRADE OCCURS 12 TIMES               PIC 9(3).

 01  ARITHMETIC-RESULTS.
     05  4-EXAM-AVERAGE                               PIC S9(3)V9.
     05  HOMEWORK-AVERAGE                             PIC S9(3)V9.
     05  HOMEWORK-TOTAL                               PIC S9(4).
     05  COURSE-AVERAGE                               PIC S9(3)V9.
         88  GRADE-IS-EXCELLENT          VALUES 90 THRU 999.9.
         88  GRADE-IS-GOOD               VALUES 80 THRU 89.9.
         88  GRADE-IS-AVERAGE            VALUES 70 THRU 79.9.
         88  GRADE-IS-LOWEST-PASSING     VALUES 60 THRU 69.9.

 01  PAGE-HEADING-1.
     05                    VALUE SPACES               PIC X(20).
     05
         VALUE "GRADE COMPUTATION SYSTEM"             PIC X(24).

 01  PAGE-HEADING-2.
     05                    VALUE SPACES               PIC X(18).
     05                    VALUE "FINAL LETTER GRADES -"
                                                      PIC X(22).
     05  COURSE-OR-SECTION-M-OUT                      PIC X(6).

 01  PAGE-HEADING-3.
     05                    VALUE SPACES               PIC X(49).
     05                    VALUE "PAGE"               PIC X(5).
     05  PAGE-NUMBER-OUT                              PIC Z9.

 01  PAGE-HEADING-4.
     05                    VALUE SPACES               PIC X(4).
     05                    VALUE "STUDENT"            PIC X(10).
     05                    VALUE "FINAL"              PIC X(10).
     05                    VALUE "4-EXAM"             PIC X(10).
     05                    VALUE "HOMEWORK"           PIC X(13).
     05                    VALUE "FINAL"              PIC X(10).
     05                    VALUE "FINAL"              PIC X(5).

 01  PAGE-HEADING-5.
     05                    VALUE SPACES               PIC X(4).
     05                    VALUE "NUMBER"             PIC X(10).
     05                    VALUE "EXAM"               PIC X(10).
     05                    VALUE "AVERAGE"            PIC X(11).
     05                    VALUE "AVERAGE"            PIC X(11).
     05                    VALUE "AVERAGE"            PIC X(11).
     05                    VALUE "GRADE"              PIC X(5).

 01  LETTER-GRADE-LINE.
     05                VALUE SPACES                   PIC X(5).
     05  STUDENT-COUNTER-OUT                          PIC ZZ9B(7).
     05  EXAM-GRADE-5-OUT                             PIC ZZ9B(7).
     05  4-EXAM-AVERAGE-OUT                           PIC ZZ9.9B(5).
     05  HOMEWORK-AVERAGE-OUT                         PIC ZZ9.9B(7).
     05  COURSE-AVERAGE-OUT                           PIC ZZ9.9B(7).
     05  LETTER-GRADE-OUT                             PIC X.

 01  NO-INPUT-DATA.
     05                VALUE SPACES                   PIC X(17).
     05                VALUE "NO INPUT DATA"          PIC X(13).

*****************************************************************
```

continued

The Procedure Division begins at line 01150. The PERFORM statement at line 01180 causes a grade to be produced for every Student Number that was originally in the master file.

The READ statement at line 01580 is a sequential READ. Each time it executes, COBOL brings in from the file the next record actually in the file, skipping over and ignoring any empty slots. Since there is a RELATIVE KEY given for this file, the READ statement updates the RELATIVE KEY field by placing into it the relative record number of the record just read. A sequential READ statement to a relative file sets the STATUS field if one is specified for the file. The ANSI standard meanings of the STATUS codes related to READing a relative file sequentially are given in Table 16.4.

TABLE *16.4*
ANSI standard STATUS codes related to READing a relative file sequentially

Status Code	*Meaning*
00	Successful completion
10	At end—end-of-file encountered
30	Permanent error (hardware malfunction)
47	File not OPENed as INPUT or I-O

Your own COBOL system may have other codes in the range 90–99.

The paragraph PRODUCE-A-FINAL-GRADE begins at line 01700. The IF statement at line 01710 determines whether the Student Number that is next to be assigned a grade has a record in the master file. It does this by comparing STUDENT-COUNTER (whose value is the Student Number next to be assigned a grade) to STUDENT-NUMBER-W (whose value is the Student Number of the master record now in GRADES-RECORD-M). If the Student Numbers are not EQUAL, it means that the student's record has been removed from the master file and the student should be assigned a grade of W.

FIGURE *16.14*

continued

```
S COBOL II RELEASE 3.2 09/05/90                P16003   DATE SEP 17,1992 T
----+-*A-1-B--+----2----+----3----+----4----+----5----+----6----+----7-|--+

01140
01150  PROCEDURE DIVISION.
01160  CREATE-FINAL-GRADES-REPORT.
01170      PERFORM INITIALIZATION
01180      PERFORM PRODUCE-A-FINAL-GRADE
01190          VARYING STUDENT-COUNTER FROM 1 BY 1 UNTIL
01200          STUDENT-COUNTER GREATER THAN NUMBER-OF-STUDENTS-W
01210      PERFORM TERMINATION
01220      STOP RUN
01230      .
01240
```

FIGURE 16.14 *continued*

```
INITIALIZATION.
    OPEN INPUT  GRADES-MASTER-FILE-IN
        OUTPUT LETTER-GRADES-FILE-OUT
    IF NOT MASTER-FILE-IS-OPENED
        DISPLAY " MASTER FILE OPEN STATUS = ", MASTER-FILE-CHECK
        CLOSE LETTER-GRADES-FILE-OUT,
              GRADES-MASTER-FILE-IN
        STOP RUN
    END-IF
    PERFORM READ-MASTER-FILE
    IF END-OF-MASTER-INPUT-FILE
        WRITE GRADES-RECORD-OUT FROM NO-INPUT-DATA AFTER PAGE
    ELSE
        MOVE COURSE-OR-SECTION-M  TO COURSE-OR-SECTION-M-OUT
        MOVE NUMBER-OF-STUDENTS-M TO NUMBER-OF-STUDENTS-W
        PERFORM PRODUCE-PAGE-HEADINGS
    END-IF
    .

PRODUCE-PAGE-HEADINGS.
    ADD 1 TO PAGE-NUMBER-W
    MOVE PAGE-NUMBER-W TO PAGE-NUMBER-OUT
    WRITE GRADES-RECORD-OUT FROM PAGE-HEADING-1 AFTER PAGE
    WRITE GRADES-RECORD-OUT FROM PAGE-HEADING-2
    WRITE GRADES-RECORD-OUT FROM PAGE-HEADING-3
    WRITE GRADES-RECORD-OUT FROM PAGE-HEADING-4 AFTER 4
    WRITE GRADES-RECORD-OUT FROM PAGE-HEADING-5
    MOVE SPACES TO GRADES-RECORD-OUT
    WRITE GRADES-RECORD-OUT
    MOVE 9 TO LINE-COUNT-ER
    .

READ-MASTER-FILE.
    READ GRADES-MASTER-FILE-IN INTO GRADES-RECORD-M
    IF READ-WAS-SUCCESSFUL OR
       END-OF-MASTER-INPUT-FILE
        CONTINUE
    ELSE
        DISPLAY " MASTER FILE READ STATUS = ",
                  MASTER-FILE-CHECK
        PERFORM TERMINATION
        STOP RUN
    END-IF
    .

PRODUCE-A-FINAL-GRADE.
    IF STUDENT-COUNTER NOT EQUAL TO STUDENT-NUMBER-W
        PERFORM ASSIGN-W-GRADE
    ELSE
        PERFORM ASSIGN-LETTER-GRADE-A-F
        PERFORM READ-MASTER-FILE
    END-IF
    .

ASSIGN-LETTER-GRADE-A-F.
    PERFORM COMPUTE-4-EXAM-AVERAGE
    PERFORM COMPUTE-HOMEWORK-AVERAGE
    PERFORM COMPUTE-COURSE-AVERAGE
    PERFORM SELECT-LETTER-GRADE
    .

COMPUTE-4-EXAM-AVERAGE.
    COMPUTE 4-EXAM-AVERAGE ROUNDED =
        (EXAM-GRADE (1) +
         EXAM-GRADE (2) +
         EXAM-GRADE (3) +
         EXAM-GRADE (4)) / 4
    .
```

continued

FIGURE 16.14 *continued*

```
S COBOL II RELEASE 3.2 09/05/90                P16003   DATE SEP 17,1992 T
----+-*A-1-B--+----2----+----3----+----4----+----5----+----6----+----7-|--+


       COMPUTE-COURSE-AVERAGE.
           COMPUTE COURSE-AVERAGE ROUNDED =
               (EXAM-GRADE (5) +
                4-EXAM-AVERAGE +
                HOMEWORK-AVERAGE) / 3
           .

       SELECT-LETTER-GRADE.
           EVALUATE TRUE
           WHEN GRADE-IS-EXCELLENT
               MOVE "A" TO LETTER-GRADE
           WHEN GRADE-IS-GOOD
               MOVE "B" TO LETTER-GRADE
           WHEN GRADE-IS-AVERAGE
               MOVE "C" TO LETTER-GRADE
           WHEN GRADE-IS-LOWEST-PASSING
               MOVE "D" TO LETTER-GRADE
           WHEN OTHER
               MOVE "F" TO LETTER-GRADE
           END-EVALUATE
           PERFORM WRITE-LETTER-GRADE-LINE
           .

       COMPUTE-HOMEWORK-AVERAGE.
           MOVE 0 TO HOMEWORK-TOTAL
           PERFORM ACCUMULATE-HOMEWORK-GRADES
               VARYING HOMEWORK-SUBSCRIPT FROM 1 BY 1 UNTIL
               HOMEWORK-SUBSCRIPT GREATER THAN NUMBER-OF-HOMEWORKS
           COMPUTE HOMEWORK-AVERAGE ROUNDED =
               HOMEWORK-TOTAL / NUMBER-OF-HOMEWORKS
           .

       ACCUMULATE-HOMEWORK-GRADES.
           ADD HOMEWORK-GRADE (HOMEWORK-SUBSCRIPT) TO HOMEWORK-TOTAL
           .

       ASSIGN-W-GRADE.
           MOVE SPACES TO LETTER-GRADE-LINE
           MOVE STUDENT-COUNTER TO STUDENT-COUNTER-OUT
           MOVE "W"             TO LETTER-GRADE-OUT
           PERFORM WRITE-GRADE-LINE
           .

       WRITE-GRADE-LINE.
           IF LINE-COUNT-ER + 1 > PAGE-LIMIT
               PERFORM PRODUCE-PAGE-HEADINGS
           END-IF
           WRITE GRADES-RECORD-OUT FROM LETTER-GRADE-LINE
           ADD 1 TO LINE-COUNT-ER
           .

       WRITE-LETTER-GRADE-LINE.
           MOVE STUDENT-COUNTER TO STUDENT-COUNTER-OUT
           MOVE EXAM-GRADE (5)   TO EXAM-GRADE-5-OUT
           MOVE 4-EXAM-AVERAGE   TO 4-EXAM-AVERAGE-OUT
           MOVE HOMEWORK-AVERAGE TO HOMEWORK-AVERAGE-OUT
           MOVE COURSE-AVERAGE   TO COURSE-AVERAGE-OUT
           MOVE LETTER-GRADE     TO LETTER-GRADE-OUT
           PERFORM WRITE-GRADE-LINE
           .

       TERMINATION.
           CLOSE GRADES-MASTER-FILE-IN
                 LETTER-GRADES-FILE-OUT
           .
```

Program P16-03 was run with the updated master file created by Program P16-02. Program P16-03 produced the output shown in Figure 16.15.

FIGURE *16.15* **Output from Program P16-03**

```
                    GRADE COMPUTATION SYSTEM
                  FINAL LETTER GRADES - CS302
                                                  PAGE  1


STUDENT    FINAL      4-EXAM     HOMEWORK     FINAL      FINAL
NUMBER     EXAM       AVERAGE     AVERAGE     AVERAGE    GRADE

   1        93         67.8        49.3        70.0        C
   2                                                       W
   3        75         64.0        51.3        63.4        D
   4                                                       W
   5                                                       W
   6                                                       W
   7                                                       W
   8         0         86.3        60.3        48.9        F
   9                                                       W
  10        85         86.3        68.7        80.0        B
  11        91         43.3        41.9        58.7        F
  12        85         74.3        20.3        59.9        F
  13        90         86.0        38.4        71.5        C
  14                                                       W
  15                                                       W
  16         0         24.5         0.0         8.2        F
  17        90         89.0        77.8        85.6        B
  18                                                       W
  19         0          0.0         5.8         1.9        F
  20         0         74.3        37.1        37.1        F
  21                                                       W
```

EXERCISE *3*

Write a program to process the master file you updated in Exercise 2 and produce a report in the format shown in Figure 16.E3. Have your program print a line for every cash register number 1 through 135. If any register has no record in the master file, have your program print a message REGISTER OUT OF SERVICE for that register.

For each register having a record in the master file, have your program carry out the following processing:

1. Print the Starting Cash Balance, Adjustments, and Ending Cash Balance from the master record.

2. In the column headed CASH ADDITIONS, print the total of all Sales fields, Tax, and Bottle and Can Deposits from the master record.

3. In the column headed CASH REMOVALS, print the total of the Coupons field and the Deposit Returns field from the master record.

4. Compute a trial sum of the Starting Cash Balance, plus Cash Additions, minus Cash Removals, plus Adjustments.

5. If the trial sum is not equal to the Ending Cash Balance, subtract the trial sum from the Ending Cash Balance and print the difference in the column headed OUT OF BALANCE. If the trial sum is equal to the Ending Cash Balance, print nothing in the OUT OF BALANCE column.

FIGURE ***16.E3*** **Output format for Exercise 3**

PRINT CHART

```
                    DAILY REGISTER BALANCE REPORT
                                                      PAGE Z9

 REGISTER   STARTING     CASH        CASH      ADJUSTMENTS   ENDING     OUT OF
   NUMBER    BALANCE   ADDITIONS   REMOVALS                  BALANCE    BALANCE

        1   Z,ZZZ.99   ZZ,ZZZ.99   Z,ZZZ.99     Z,ZZZ.99-   Z,ZZZ.99
        2   Z,ZZZ.99   ZZ,ZZZ.99   Z,ZZZ.99     Z,ZZZ.99-   Z,ZZZ.99   Z,ZZZ.99-
        3   Z,ZZZ.99   ZZ,ZZZ.99   Z,ZZZ.99     Z,ZZZ.99-   Z,ZZZ.99
        4                                                              REGISTER OUT OF SERVICE
        5   Z,ZZZ.99   ZZ,ZZZ.99   Z,ZZZ.99     Z,ZZZ.99-   Z,ZZZ.99   Z,ZZZ.99-
        .
        .
        .
      ZZ9   Z,ZZZ.99   ZZ,ZZZ.99   Z,ZZZ.99     Z,ZZZ.99-   Z,ZZZ.99
```

An Application Using Randomizing

In the grades file we have used so far, the students were numbered consecutively, from 1 through 21, with every number being used. Similarly, in Exercises 1 through 3, the cash registers were also numbered consecutively, from 1 through 135. In the real world it does not always happen that the objects to be described in a master file are numbered consecutively. More often there are gaps, sometimes quite large gaps, in the numbering.

Consider the savings-account master file we used in Chapters 13 through 15. There we had a five-digit account number, but we did not use all the 100,000 different numbers from 00000 to 99999. We didn't even come close to using all of the numbers. In fact, we had at most not more than 55 accounts in the master file. If we wanted to store the savings-account master as a relative file using only the techniques we have studied so far, we would have to set up a file with 100,000 slots (99,999 slots actually, because there cannot be any slot number 0), and put records into only about 55 of them.

Fortunately, well-known techniques exist that permit this kind of situation to be adapted for use in a relative file. One of the simplest of such techniques is called the **division/remainder method.** It proceeds as follows:

1. Determine the number of slots needed in the file. Often, a relative file using the division/remainder method should contain about 20% more slots than there are records in the file. If 20% turns out not to be a satisfactory figure for a particular file, it can be changed. You will see later why the extra slots are needed and how to tell whether 20% is enough. For our file of 55 savings account records, a file with 66 slots should be suitable to start with.
2. Select the nearest **prime number** that is less than the number of slots selected in step 1. A prime number is a number divisible only by itself and the integer 1. The nearest prime less than 66 is 61, so we select it.

3. Then, to find which slot any particular account record should go into, divide the account number by the prime number chosen in step 2, ignore the quotient, add 1 to the remainder, and use that as the slot number for the record. So if we wanted to determine into which slot to place the record for account number 00298, we divide 298 by 61 (which gives a quotient of 4 and a remainder of 54). Thus the record for account number 00298 should be stored in slot number 55. Table 16.5 shows some possible account numbers and the slots they would go into.

TABLE *16.5*
Some Account Numbers and the relative record numbers of their records, using the division/remainder method with a divisor of 61

Account Number	Remainder After Dividing by 61	Slot Number
00001	1	2
00013	13	14
00060	60	61
00080	19	20
00122	0	1
00123	1	2
00202	19	20
00250	6	7

You can see that when the division/remainder method is used, different record keys can sometimes yield the same **home slot** number. Any two or more record keys that yield the same home slot number are called **synonyms.** There is no way to avoid synonyms when the division/remainder method is used, but you will see how the conflict for slots is resolved when we do a program using the division/remainder technique.

The division/remainder method can be used even if a record key contains one or more nonnumeric characters. The procedures involved are beyond the scope of this book, but can be found in any complete book on systems design.

Creating a Relative File Randomly

Program P16-04 creates a savings-account master file as a relative file, using the file specifications developed in the preceding section. The logic in Program P16-04 is very similar to that in Program P13-02, which created a sequential savings-account master file. The input to Program P16-04 is the same as to Program P13-02, records representing new accounts (the input format is described on page 446). In Program P16-04, as in Program P13-02, the input transactions are SORTed on Account Number and checked for duplicate keys and other errors. If an input record is found to be error-free, the program constructs a master record and writes it to the output master file. In Program P13-02, master records were written sequentially onto an output tape. But in Program P16-04, each master record is instead written into a particular slot in a relative file, and the slot number is computed for each record by the division/remainder method described in the preceding section.

Program P16-04 is shown in Figure 16.16. The FILE-CONTROL entry for the master file, at line 00160, specifies ACCESS RANDOM. For even though the input records will be processed in ASCENDING Account Number sequence, in general the master records will not go into sequential slots in the master file.

ACCOUNT-NUMBER-IN is defined as a numeric field at line 00360 and redefined as alphanumeric at line 00370. We refer to the Account Number as numeric for purposes of arithmetic. We use the alphanumeric form in the SORT to ensure that the SORT statement will operate on the Account Number fields exactly as they appear in the input, with no modifications of form for the purpose of performing numeric comparisons on them.

The COMPUTATIONAL SYNCHRONIZED fields in lines 00710 through 00770 are all used in connection with placing each master record into its correct slot in the file. SLOT-NUMBER is the RELATIVE KEY. INTEGER-QUOTIENT, INTEGER-REMAINDER, and DIVISOR are used for computing the home slot number of each master record before it is written.

FIGURE *16.16* **Program P16-04**

```
S COBOL II RELEASE 3.2 09/05/90                  P16004    DATE MAR 04,1992 T
----+-*A-1-B--+----2----+----3----+----4----+----5----+----6----+----7-|--+


00010  IDENTIFICATION DIVISION.
00020  PROGRAM-ID.  P16-04.
00030 *
00040 *     THIS PROGRAM CREATES A RELATIVE
00050 *     MASTER FILE OF SAVINGS ACCOUNT RECORDS.
00060 *
00070 *****************************************************************
00080
00090  ENVIRONMENT DIVISION.
00100  INPUT-OUTPUT SECTION.
00110  FILE-CONTROL.
00120      SELECT SAVINGS-ACCOUNT-DATA-FILE-IN  ASSIGN TO INFILE.
00130      SELECT SORT-WORK-FILE                ASSIGN TO SORTWK.
00140      SELECT TRANSACTION-REGISTER-FILE-OUT ASSIGN TO PRINTER1.
00150      SELECT ERROR-FILE-OUT                ASSIGN TO PRINTER2.
00160      SELECT ACCOUNT-MASTER-FILE-OUT       ASSIGN TO DISKOUT
00170          ORGANIZATION RELATIVE
00180          ACCESS RANDOM
00190          RELATIVE KEY IS SLOT-NUMBER
00200          STATUS IS FILE-CHECK.
00210
00220 *****************************************************************
00230
00240  DATA DIVISION.
00250  FILE SECTION.
00260  FD  SAVINGS-ACCOUNT-DATA-FILE-IN.
00270
00280  01  SAVINGS-ACCOUNT-DATA-RECORD-IN      PIC X(80).
00290
00300  SD  SORT-WORK-FILE
00310      RECORD CONTAINS 80 CHARACTERS.
00320
00330  01  SORT-WORK-RECORD.
00340      05  CODE-IN                         PIC X.
00350          88  CODE-VALID                  VALUE "1".
00360      05  ACCOUNT-NUMBER-IN               PIC 9(5).
00370      05  ACCOUNT-NUMBER-X   REDEFINES ACCOUNT-NUMBER-IN
00380                                          PIC X(5).
00390      05  AMOUNT-IN                       PIC 9(6)V99.
00400      05  AMOUNT-IN-X REDEFINES AMOUNT-IN PIC X(8).
00410      05  DEPOSITOR-NAME-IN               PIC X(20).
00420          88  DEPOSITOR-NAME-MISSING      VALUE SPACES.
```

FIGURE ***16.16*** ***continued***

```

FD  ACCOUNT-MASTER-FILE-OUT
    LABEL RECORDS ARE STANDARD
    RECORD CONTAINS 39 CHARACTERS.

01  ACCOUNT-MASTER-RECORD-OUT                      PIC X(39).

FD  TRANSACTION-REGISTER-FILE-OUT.

01  REGISTER-RECORD-OUT                            PIC X(72).

FD  ERROR-FILE-OUT.

01  ERROR-RECORD-OUT                               PIC X(84).

WORKING-STORAGE SECTION.
01  PACKED-DECIMAL.
  02 AMOUNT-TOTAL-W              VALUE 0           PIC S9(7)V99.
  02 REGISTER-PAGE-NUMBER-W      VALUE 0           PIC S99.
  02 ERROR-PAGE-NUMBER-W         VALUE 0           PIC S99.
  02 NUMBER-OF-INPUT-RECORDS-W                     PIC S9(3)    VALUE ZERO.
  02 NUMBER-OF-ERRONEOUS-RECORDS-W                 PIC S9(3)    VALUE ZERO.
  02 NUMBER-OF-NEW-ACCOUNTS-W                      PIC S9(3)    VALUE ZERO.
01  REGISTER-PAGE-LIMIT          VALUE 35          PIC S99 COMP SYNC.
01  LINE-COUNT-ER                                  PIC S99 COMP SYNC.
01  ERROR-PAGE-LIMIT             VALUE 50          PIC S99 COMP SYNC.
01  ERROR-LINE-COUNTER                             PIC S99 COMP SYNC.
01  BLANK-LINE                   VALUE " "         PIC X.
01  SLOT-NUMBER                                    PIC 99     COMP SYNC.
01  INTEGER-QUOTIENT                               PIC S9(4)  COMP SYNC.
01  INTEGER-REMAINDER                              PIC S99    COMP SYNC.
01  DIVISOR                      VALUE 61          PIC 99     COMP SYNC.
01  EXTENDED-SEARCH-LIMIT                          PIC S99    COMP SYNC.
01  EXTENDED-SEARCH-STEPS        VALUE 10          PIC S99    COMP SYNC.
01  NUMBER-OF-SLOTS-IN-FILE      VALUE 66          PIC S99    COMP SYNC.
01  FILE-CHECK                                     PIC XX.
    88 MASTER-FILE-IS-OPENED                       VALUE "00".
    88 WRITE-WAS-SUCCESSFUL                        VALUE "00".
    88 SLOT-ALREADY-FILLED                         VALUE "22".
01  MORE-INPUT                                     PIC X        VALUE "Y".
    88 THERE-IS-NO-MORE-INPUT                      VALUE "N".
    88 THERE-IS-NO-INPUT                           VALUE "N".
01  ANY-ERRORS                                     PIC X.
    88 NO-ERROR-IN-INPUT                           VALUE "N".
    88 ERROR-IN-INPUT                              VALUE "Y".
01  ACCOUNT-NUMBER-SAVE              PIC 9(5)      VALUE 99999.
01  TODAYS-DATE.
    05  TODAYS-YEAR                                PIC 99.
    05  TODAYS-MONTH-AND-DAY                       PIC 9(4).
```

continued

EXTENDED-SEARCH-LIMIT and EXTENDED-SEARCH-STEPS are used to resolve space conflicts when more than one Account Number yields the same home slot number. Master records are of course written onto the file one at a time as each input transaction is processed. If some Account Number yields a home slot that is already occupied by a master record, the program will examine slots in the master file immediately following the home slot, looking for an empty one. The number of such slots to be examined is given in the field EXTENDED-SEARCH-STEPS. The field EXTENDED-SEARCH-LIMIT is used to record the number of the last slot that would be examined in such a search. If no empty slot is found within the specified limit, the program terminates with a message that there is no room for this particular master record. There is nothing to do then but increase the size of the file (increase the VALUE of NUMBER-OF-SLOTS-IN-FILE), choose a new higher DIVISOR (a prime number less than the new NUMBER-OF-SLOTS-IN-FILE), and create the file from scratch all over again.

The choice of the number of slots to examine when looking for an empty one is a systems design problem and is beyond the scope of this book. In general, if the number of steps is made too small, the probability is increased that some master record will have no place to go and the program will terminate. If the number of steps is made too large, many master records might end up being stored far from their home slots; thus, finding them later would take a lot of computer time.

FIGURE *16.16* ***continued***

```
S COBOL II RELEASE 3.2 09/05/90                    P16004   DATE MAR 04,1992 T
----+-*A-1-B--+----2----+----3----+----4----+----5----+----6----+----7-|--+


 01  MASTER-RECORD-W.
     05  ACCOUNT-NUMBER                        PIC 9(5).
     05  DEPOSITOR-NAME                        PIC X(20).
     05  DATE-OF-LAST-TRANSACTION              PIC 9(6).
     05  CURRENT-BALANCE                       PIC S9(6)V99.

 01  REPORT-HEADING-1.
     05               PIC X(39) VALUE SPACES.
     05               PIC X(17) VALUE "ROBBEM STATE BANK".

 01  REPORT-HEADING-2.
     05               PIC X(39) VALUE SPACES.
     05               PIC X(17) VALUE "106 WEST 10TH ST.".

 01  REPORT-HEADING-3.
     05               PIC X(38) VALUE SPACES.
     05               PIC X(19) VALUE "BROOKLYN, NY  11212".

 01  REGISTER-PAGE-HEADING-1.
     05               PIC X(29) VALUE SPACES.
     05               PIC X(36)
                      VALUE "SAVINGS ACCOUNT MASTER FILE CREATION".

 01  ERROR-PAGE-HEADING-1.
     05               PIC X(30) VALUE SPACES.
     05               PIC X(34)
                      VALUE "SAVINGS ACCOUNT MASTER FILE ERRORS".

 01  PAGE-HEADING-2.
     05                       PIC X(17) VALUE SPACES.
     05                       PIC X(5)  VALUE "DATE".
     05  TODAYS-MONTH-AND-DAY       PIC Z9/99/.
     05  TODAYS-YEAR      PIC 99B(35).
     05                       PIC X(5)  VALUE "PAGE".
     05  PAGE-NUMBER-OUT            PIC Z9.

 01  REGISTER-PAGE-HEADING-3.
     05                       PIC X(24) VALUE SPACES.
     05                       PIC X(12) VALUE "ACCOUNT".
     05                       PIC X(12) VALUE "INITIAL".
     05                       PIC X(5)  VALUE "NOTES".

 01  ERROR-PAGE-HEADING-3.
     05                       PIC X(24) VALUE SPACES.
     05                       PIC X(24) VALUE "ACCOUNT".
     05                       PIC X(5)  VALUE "NOTES".
```

FIGURE 16.16 *continued*

```
       01  REGISTER-PAGE-HEADING-4.
           05                       PIC X(24) VALUE SPACES.
           05                       PIC X(12) VALUE "NUMBER".
           05                       PIC X(7)  VALUE "DEPOSIT".

       01  ERROR-PAGE-HEADING-4.
           05                       PIC X(24) VALUE SPACES.
           05                       PIC X(6)  VALUE "NUMBER".

       01  NEW-ACCOUNT-LINE.
           05                  PIC X(25)       VALUE SPACES.
           05  ACCOUNT-NUMBER-OUT-G            PIC X(5)B(5).
           05  AMOUNT-OUT-G                    PIC ZZZ.ZZZ.99B(3).
           05                  PIC X(11)       VALUE "NEW ACCOUNT".

       01  ERROR-LINE.
           05                  PIC X(25) VALUE SPACES.
           05  ACCOUNT-NUMBER-OUT-E PIC X(5)B(18).
           05  MESSAGE-E            PIC X(36).

       01  INVALID-CODE-MSG.
           05                  PIC X(13) VALUE "INVALID CODE".
           05  CODE-OUT        PIC X.

       01  AMOUNT-NOT-NUMERIC-MSG.
           05                  PIC X(28) VALUE "INITIAL DEPOSIT NOT NUMERIC".
           05  AMOUNT-OUT-X         PIC X(9).

       01  FINAL-LINE-1.
           05                       PIC X(23) VALUE SPACES.
           05                       PIC X(10) VALUE "TOTAL".
           05  AMOUNT-TOTAL-OUT          PIC Z,ZZZ,ZZZ.99.

       01  FINAL-LINE-2.
           05                       PIC X(40) VALUE SPACES.
           05                       PIC X(14) VALUE "CONTROL COUNTS".

       01  FINAL-LINE-3.
           05                       PIC X(34) VALUE SPACES.
           05                       PIC X(28) VALUE "NUMBER OF NEW ACCOUNTS".
           05  NUMBER-OF-NEW-ACCOUNTS-OUT PIC ZZ9.

       01  FINAL-LINE-4.
           05                       PIC X(34) VALUE SPACES.
           05                       PIC X(28)
                                    VALUE "NUMBER OF ERRONEOUS RECORDS".
           05  NUMBER-OF-ERRONEOUS-RCDS-OUT PIC ZZ9.

       01  FINAL-LINE-5.
           05                       PIC X(34) VALUE SPACES.
           05                       PIC X(28) VALUE "TOTAL".
           05  NUMBER-OF-INPUT-RECORDS-OUT PIC ZZ9.

       01  NO-INPUT-DATA.
           05                       PIC X(21) VALUE SPACES.
           05                       PIC X(13) VALUE "NO INPUT DATA".

       01  INSUFFICIENT-FILE-SPACE.
           05                       PIC X(21) VALUE SPACES.
           05                       PIC X(23) VALUE "INSUFFICIENT FILE SPACE".

      ******************************************************************
```

continued

The Procedure Division starts at line 02030. The WRITE statement at line 03030 is a random WRITE. Each time it executes, COBOL uses the current value of the RELATIVE KEY, SLOT-NUMBER, to know which slot to WRITE the record into. The value of SLOT-NUMBER is computed under control of the PERFORM statement at line 02930. A WRITE statement sets the STATUS field if one is specified for the file. The ANSI standard meanings of the STATUS codes for random WRITEs to a relative file are given in Table 16.6. Your system may have additional codes in the range 90–99.

FIGURE *16.16* ***continued***

```
S COBOL II RELEASE 3.2 09/05/90                 P16004    DATE MAR 04,1992 T
----+-*A-1-B--+----2----+----3----+----4----+----5----+----6----+----7-|--+

02020
02030  PROCEDURE DIVISION.
02040  CREATE-MASTER-FILE.
02050      SORT SORT-WORK-FILE
02060           ASCENDING KEY ACCOUNT-NUMBER-X
02070           USING SAVINGS-ACCOUNT-DATA-FILE-IN
02080           OUTPUT PROCEDURE IS PRODUCE-MASTER-FILE
02090      STOP RUN
02100      .
02110
02120  PRODUCE-MASTER-FILE.
02130      PERFORM INITIALIZATION
02140      PERFORM PROCESS-A-RECORD UNTIL THERE-IS-NO-MORE-INPUT
02150      PERFORM TERMINATION
02160      .
02170
02180  INITIALIZATION.
02190      OPEN OUTPUT ACCOUNT-MASTER-FILE-OUT
02200                  ERROR-FILE-OUT
02210                  TRANSACTION-REGISTER-FILE-OUT
02220      IF NOT MASTER-FILE-IS-OPENED
02230          DISPLAY " MASTER FILE OPEN STATUS = ", FILE-CHECK
02240          CLOSE TRANSACTION-REGISTER-FILE-OUT
02250                ERROR-FILE-OUT
02260                ACCOUNT-MASTER-FILE-OUT
02270          STOP RUN
02280      END-IF
02290      ACCEPT TODAYS-DATE FROM DATE
02300      MOVE CORRESPONDING TODAYS-DATE TO PAGE-HEADING-2
02310      PERFORM PRODUCE-REPORT-HEADINGS
02320      PERFORM READ-A-RECORD
02330      IF THERE-IS-NO-INPUT
02340          WRITE ERROR-RECORD-OUT FROM NO-INPUT-DATA
02350      END-IF
02360      .
02370
02380  PRODUCE-REPORT-HEADINGS.
02390      PERFORM PRODUCE-REGISTER-HEADINGS
02400      PERFORM PRODUCE-ERROR-HEADINGS
02410      .
02420
```

FIGURE 16.16 *continued*

```
PRODUCE-REGISTER-HEADINGS.
    WRITE REGISTER-RECORD-OUT FROM REPORT-HEADING-1 AFTER PAGE
    WRITE REGISTER-RECORD-OUT FROM REPORT-HEADING-2
    WRITE REGISTER-RECORD-OUT FROM REPORT-HEADING-3
    ADD 1 TO REGISTER-PAGE-NUMBER-W
    MOVE REGISTER-PAGE-NUMBER-W TO PAGE-NUMBER-OUT
    WRITE REGISTER-RECORD-OUT FROM REGISTER-PAGE-HEADING-1
                              AFTER 2
    WRITE REGISTER-RECORD-OUT FROM PAGE-HEADING-2
    WRITE REGISTER-RECORD-OUT FROM REGISTER-PAGE-HEADING-3
                              AFTER 3
    WRITE REGISTER-RECORD-OUT FROM REGISTER-PAGE-HEADING-4
    WRITE REGISTER-RECORD-OUT FROM BLANK-LINE
    MOVE 11 TO LINE-COUNT-ER
    .

PRODUCE-ERROR-HEADINGS.
    WRITE ERROR-RECORD-OUT FROM REPORT-HEADING-1 AFTER PAGE
    WRITE ERROR-RECORD-OUT FROM REPORT-HEADING-2
    WRITE ERROR-RECORD-OUT FROM REPORT-HEADING-3
    ADD 1 TO ERROR-PAGE-NUMBER-W
    MOVE ERROR-PAGE-NUMBER-W TO PAGE-NUMBER-OUT
    WRITE ERROR-RECORD-OUT FROM ERROR-PAGE-HEADING-1 AFTER 2
    WRITE ERROR-RECORD-OUT FROM PAGE-HEADING-2
    WRITE ERROR-RECORD-OUT FROM ERROR-PAGE-HEADING-3 AFTER 3
    WRITE ERROR-RECORD-OUT FROM ERROR-PAGE-HEADING-4
    WRITE ERROR-RECORD-OUT FROM BLANK-LINE
    MOVE 11 TO ERROR-LINE-COUNTER
    .

PROCESS-A-RECORD.
    ADD 1 TO NUMBER-OF-INPUT-RECORDS-W
    SET NO-ERROR-IN-INPUT TO TRUE
    PERFORM CHECK-INPUT-FOR-VALIDITY
    IF NO-ERROR-IN-INPUT
        PERFORM BUILD-NEW-ACCOUNT-RECORD
        PERFORM WRITE-NEW-ACCOUNT-RECORD
    END-IF
    MOVE ACCOUNT-NUMBER-IN TO ACCOUNT-NUMBER-SAVE
    PERFORM READ-A-RECORD
    .

BUILD-NEW-ACCOUNT-RECORD.
    MOVE ACCOUNT-NUMBER-IN TO ACCOUNT-NUMBER
    MOVE DEPOSITOR-NAME-IN TO DEPOSITOR-NAME
    MOVE AMOUNT-IN         TO CURRENT-BALANCE
    MOVE TODAYS-DATE       TO DATE-OF-LAST-TRANSACTION
    .

WRITE-NEW-ACCOUNT-RECORD.
    PERFORM COMPUTE-SLOT-NUMBER
    PERFORM WRITE-A-MASTER-RECORD
    IF SLOT-ALREADY-FILLED
        PERFORM EXTENDED-WRITE-SEARCH
    END-IF
    ADD 1 TO NUMBER-OF-NEW-ACCOUNTS-W
    PERFORM WRITE-NEW-ACCOUNT-LINE
    .

WRITE-A-MASTER-RECORD.
    WRITE ACCOUNT-MASTER-RECORD-OUT FROM MASTER-RECORD-W
        INVALID KEY CONTINUE
    END-WRITE
    IF WRITE-WAS-SUCCESSFUL OR SLOT-ALREADY-FILLED
        CONTINUE
    ELSE
        DISPLAY " MASTER FILE WRITE STATUS = ", FILE-CHECK
        PERFORM TERMINATION
        STOP RUN
    END-IF
    .
```

continued

TABLE 16.6
ANSI standard STATUS codes related to writing a relative file randomly

Status Code	Meaning
00	Successful completion
22	Invalid key—an attempt has been made to WRITE a record into an occupied slot
24	Invalid key—boundary violation (attempt to WRITE beyond the physical end of the file)
30	Permanent error (hardware malfunction)
48	File not OPENed as OUTPUT, I-O, or EXTEND

The paragraph EXTENDED-WRITE-SEARCH, line 03150, executes if a WRITE statement returns a STATUS code of 22. EXTENDED-WRITE-SEARCH first computes EXTENDED-SEARCH-LIMIT, the highest slot number that it will examine while looking for an empty slot. It then PERFORMs the paragraph WRITE-A-MASTER-RECORD UNTIL an empty slot is found or all of the examined slots are found to be occupied.

FIGURE 16.16 *continued*

```
S COBOL II RELEASE 3.2 09/05/90                    P16004   DATE MAR 04,1992 T
----+-*A-1-B--+----2----+----3----+----4----+----5----+----6----+----7-|--+

03140
03150  EXTENDED-WRITE-SEARCH.
03160      ADD SLOT-NUMBER TO EXTENDED-SEARCH-STEPS
03170          GIVING EXTENDED-SEARCH-LIMIT
03180      PERFORM WRITE-A-MASTER-RECORD
03190          VARYING SLOT-NUMBER FROM SLOT-NUMBER BY 1
03200              UNTIL
03210                  WRITE-WAS-SUCCESSFUL OR
03220                  SLOT-NUMBER GREATER THAN
03230                      EXTENDED-SEARCH-LIMIT OR
03240                      NUMBER-OF-SLOTS-IN-FILE
03250      IF WRITE-WAS-SUCCESSFUL
03260          CONTINUE
03270      ELSE
03280          PERFORM WRITE-INSUFFICIENT-FILE-SPACE
03290          DISPLAY " MASTER FILE WRITE STATUS = ", FILE-CHECK
03300          PERFORM TERMINATION
03310          STOP RUN
03320      END-IF
03330      .
03340
03350  COMPUTE-SLOT-NUMBER.
03360      DIVIDE ACCOUNT-NUMBER-IN BY DIVISOR
03370          GIVING INTEGER-QUOTIENT
03380          REMAINDER INTEGER-REMAINDER
03390      ADD 1 TO INTEGER-REMAINDER GIVING SLOT-NUMBER
03400      .
03410
```

FIGURE 16.16 *continued*

```
CHECK-INPUT-FOR-VALIDITY.
    IF ACCOUNT-NUMBER-IN NOT NUMERIC
        SET ERROR-IN-INPUT TO TRUE
        PERFORM WRITE-INVALID-KEY-LINE
    END-IF
    IF NOT CODE-VALID
        SET ERROR-IN-INPUT TO TRUE
        PERFORM WRITE-INVALID-CODE-LINE
    END-IF
    IF ACCOUNT-NUMBER-IN = ACCOUNT-NUMBER-SAVE
        SET ERROR-IN-INPUT TO TRUE
        PERFORM WRITE-DUPLICATE-ERROR-MESSAGE
    END-IF
    IF DEPOSITOR-NAME-MISSING
        SET ERROR-IN-INPUT TO TRUE
        PERFORM WRITE-NAME-ERROR-MESSAGE
    END-IF
    IF AMOUNT-IN NOT NUMERIC
        SET ERROR-IN-INPUT TO TRUE
        PERFORM WRITE-AMOUNT-MESSAGE
    END-IF
    IF ERROR-IN-INPUT
        ADD 1 TO NUMBER-OF-ERRONEOUS-RECORDS-W
    END-IF
    .

WRITE-NEW-ACCOUNT-LINE.
    MOVE ACCOUNT-NUMBER-IN TO ACCOUNT-NUMBER-OUT-G
    MOVE AMOUNT-IN         TO AMOUNT-OUT-G
    ADD AMOUNT-IN          TO AMOUNT-TOTAL-W
    IF LINE-COUNT-ER + 1 > REGISTER-PAGE-LIMIT
        PERFORM PRODUCE-REGISTER-HEADINGS
    END-IF
    WRITE REGISTER-RECORD-OUT FROM NEW-ACCOUNT-LINE
    ADD 1 TO LINE-COUNT-ER
    .

WRITE-INVALID-CODE-LINE.
    MOVE ACCOUNT-NUMBER-IN    TO ACCOUNT-NUMBER-OUT-E
    MOVE CODE-IN              TO CODE-OUT
    MOVE INVALID-CODE-MSG TO MESSAGE-E
    PERFORM WRITE-ERROR-LINE
    .

WRITE-ERROR-LINE.
    IF ERROR-LINE-COUNTER + 1 > ERROR-PAGE-LIMIT
        PERFORM PRODUCE-ERROR-HEADINGS
    END-IF
    WRITE ERROR-RECORD-OUT FROM ERROR-LINE
    ADD 1 TO ERROR-LINE-COUNTER
    .

WRITE-DUPLICATE-ERROR-MESSAGE.
    MOVE ACCOUNT-NUMBER-IN TO ACCOUNT-NUMBER-OUT-E
    MOVE "DUPLICATE ACCOUNT NUMBER" TO MESSAGE-E
    PERFORM WRITE-ERROR-LINE
    .

WRITE-NAME-ERROR-MESSAGE.
    MOVE ACCOUNT-NUMBER-IN TO ACCOUNT-NUMBER-OUT-E
    MOVE "DEPOSITOR NAME MISSING" TO MESSAGE-E
    PERFORM WRITE-ERROR-LINE
    .

WRITE-AMOUNT-MESSAGE.
    MOVE ACCOUNT-NUMBER-IN TO ACCOUNT-NUMBER-OUT-E
    MOVE AMOUNT-IN-X        TO AMOUNT-OUT-X
    MOVE AMOUNT-NOT-NUMERIC-MSG TO MESSAGE-E
    PERFORM WRITE-ERROR-LINE
    .
```

continued

FIGURE 16.16 *continued*

```
S COBOL II RELEASE 3.2 09/05/90                  P16004   DATE MAR 04,1992 T
----+-*A-1-B--+----2----+----3----+----4----+----5----+----6----+----7-|--+


WRITE-INVALID-KEY-LINE.
    MOVE ACCOUNT-NUMBER-X TO ACCOUNT-NUMBER-OUT-E
    MOVE "ACCOUNT NUMBER NOT NUMERIC" TO MESSAGE-E
    PERFORM WRITE-ERROR-LINE
    .

WRITE-INSUFFICIENT-FILE-SPACE.
    WRITE ERROR-RECORD-OUT FROM INSUFFICIENT-FILE-SPACE
    .

PRODUCE-FINAL-LINES.
    MOVE AMOUNT-TOTAL-W TO AMOUNT-TOTAL-OUT
    MOVE NUMBER-OF-INPUT-RECORDS-W
         TO NUMBER-OF-INPUT-RECORDS-OUT
    MOVE NUMBER-OF-ERRONEOUS-RECORDS-W
         TO NUMBER-OF-ERRONEOUS-RCDS-OUT
    MOVE NUMBER-OF-NEW-ACCOUNTS-W TO NUMBER-OF-NEW-ACCOUNTS-OUT
    WRITE REGISTER-RECORD-OUT FROM FINAL-LINE-1 AFTER 2
    WRITE REGISTER-RECORD-OUT FROM FINAL-LINE-2 AFTER 2
    WRITE REGISTER-RECORD-OUT FROM FINAL-LINE-3 AFTER 2
    WRITE REGISTER-RECORD-OUT FROM FINAL-LINE-4 AFTER 2
    WRITE REGISTER-RECORD-OUT FROM FINAL-LINE-5 AFTER 2
    .

TERMINATION.
    PERFORM PRODUCE-FINAL-LINES
    CLOSE ACCOUNT-MASTER-FILE-OUT
          ERROR-FILE-OUT
          TRANSACTION-REGISTER-FILE-OUT
    .

READ-A-RECORD.
    RETURN SORT-WORK-FILE
       AT END
           SET THERE-IS-NO-MORE-INPUT TO TRUE
    .
```

Program P16-04 was run with the input data shown in Figure 16.17 and produced the report output shown in Figure 16.18. Notice that several of the Account Numbers are synonyms, requiring extended search (for example 00080, 00202, and 06180).

FIGURE *16.17* **Input to Program P16-04**

```
--------------------------------------------------------------------------------
         1         2         3         4         5         6         7         8
12345678901234567890123456789012345678901234567890123456789012345678901234567890
--------------------------------------------------------------------------------
10008000005000LENORE MILLER
10020200025000ROSEMARY LANE
3122960CA00000MICHELE CAPUANO
10618000075000JAMES BUDD
14674900100000PAUL LERNER, D.D.S.
17549500002575BETH FALLON
12701300002000JANE HALEY
15002700005000ONE DAY CLEANERS
13394600002450ROBERT RYAN
17054900012550KELLY HEDERMAN
19668100001000MARY KEATING
20293300007500BOB LANIGAN
17203200003500J. & L. CAIN
14396700015000IMPERIAL FLORIST
12505500000500JOYCE MITCHELL
13478000025000JERRY PARKS
16574500005000CARL CALDERON
13280900017550JOHN WILLIAMS
17688400015000JOHN J. LEHMAN
16416500002500JOSEPH CAMILLO
18829800015000JAY GREENE
16756600000100EVELYN SLATER
19675200007500
13091700050000PATRICK J. LEE
16695200001037LESLIE MINSKY
11962500150000JOHN DAPRINO
13612600010000JOE'S DELI
11886200050000GEORGE CULHANE
10016900009957MARTIN LANG
16871800027500VITO CACACI
10005400002000COMMUNITY DRUGS
13149000001500SOLOMON CHAPELS
16171400150000JOHN BURKE
100IEROFG15750PAT P. POWERS
15549600200000JOE GARCIA
13823400025000GRACE MICELI
11469700002000
19023000001000GUY VOLPONE
135101))))!%))SALVATORE CALI
19023000055500BILL WILLIAMS
13310000001000KEVIN PARKER
13510100003500FRANK CAPUTO
11510900001500GENE GALLI
13665000002937
11168200100784ROSEBUCCI
16683500001000ROBERT DAVIS M.D.
18191900012500LORICE MONTI
16017500700159MICHAEL SMITH
17666000100000JOE & MARY SESSA
14749100250000ROGER SHAW
```

FIGURE *16.18* **Report output from Program P16-04**

```
                    ROBBEM STATE BANK
                    106 WEST 10TH ST.
                   BROOKLYN, NY  11212

              SAVINGS ACCOUNT MASTER FILE ERRORS
DATE  3/04/92                                      PAGE  1

       ACCOUNT                 NOTES
       NUMBER

        OOIER                  ACCOUNT NUMBER NOT NUMERIC
        OOIER                  INITIAL DEPOSIT NOT NUMERIC OFG15750
        02933                  INVALID CODE 2
        12296                  INVALID CODE 3
        12296                  INITIAL DEPOSIT NOT NUMERIC OCAO0000
        14697                  DEPOSITOR NAME MISSING
        35101                  INITIAL DEPOSIT NOT NUMERIC ))))!%))
        35101                  DUPLICATE ACCOUNT NUMBER
        36650                  DEPOSITOR NAME MISSING
        90230                  DUPLICATE ACCOUNT NUMBER
        96752                  DEPOSITOR NAME MISSING


                    ROBBEM STATE BANK
                    106 WEST 10TH ST.
                   BROOKLYN, NY  11212

             SAVINGS ACCOUNT MASTER FILE CREATION
DATE  3/04/92                                      PAGE  1

       ACCOUNT     INITIAL     NOTES
       NUMBER      DEPOSIT

        00054         20.00    NEW ACCOUNT
        00080         50.00    NEW ACCOUNT
        00169         99.57    NEW ACCOUNT
        00202        250.00    NEW ACCOUNT
        06180        750.00    NEW ACCOUNT
        11682      1,007.84    NEW ACCOUNT
        15109         15.00    NEW ACCOUNT
        18862        500.00    NEW ACCOUNT
        19625      1,500.00    NEW ACCOUNT
        25055          5.00    NEW ACCOUNT
        27013         20.00    NEW ACCOUNT
        30917        500.00    NEW ACCOUNT
        31490         15.00    NEW ACCOUNT
        32809        175.50    NEW ACCOUNT
        33100         10.00    NEW ACCOUNT
        33946         24.50    NEW ACCOUNT
        34780        250.00    NEW ACCOUNT
        36126        100.00    NEW ACCOUNT
        38234        250.00    NEW ACCOUNT
        43967        150.00    NEW ACCOUNT
        46749      1,000.00    NEW ACCOUNT
        47491      2,500.00    NEW ACCOUNT
        50027         50.00    NEW ACCOUNT
        55496      2,000.00    NEW ACCOUNT
```

FIGURE 16.18 *continued*

```
                    ROBBEM STATE BANK
                    106 WEST 10TH ST.
                   BROOKLYN, NY  11212

          SAVINGS ACCOUNT MASTER FILE CREATION
DATE  3/04/92                                        PAGE  2

       ACCOUNT      INITIAL      NOTES
       NUMBER       DEPOSIT

        60175        7,001.59    NEW ACCOUNT
        61714        1,500.00    NEW ACCOUNT
        64165           25.00    NEW ACCOUNT
        65745           50.00    NEW ACCOUNT
        66835           10.00    NEW ACCOUNT
        66952           10.37    NEW ACCOUNT
        67566            1.00    NEW ACCOUNT
        68718          275.00    NEW ACCOUNT
        70549          125.50    NEW ACCOUNT
        72032           35.00    NEW ACCOUNT
        75495           25.75    NEW ACCOUNT
        76660        1,000.00    NEW ACCOUNT
        76884          150.00    NEW ACCOUNT
        81919          125.00    NEW ACCOUNT
        88298          150.00    NEW ACCOUNT
        90230          555.00    NEW ACCOUNT
        96681           10.00    NEW ACCOUNT

      TOTAL         22,291.62

                        CONTROL COUNTS

                NUMBER OF NEW ACCOUNTS          41

                NUMBER OF ERRONEOUS RECORDS      9

                TOTAL                           50
```

EXERCISE 4

Write a program to create a relative inventory file. Use the same formats for input transactions and master records that you used when you created your sequential inventory master file in Exercise 3, Chapter 13, page 457.

Select a file size (number of slots) suitable to the largest number of records you expect your master file to contain. Select a divisor suitable to the number of slots in the file.

Have your program perform the same validity checks as did your program for Exercise 3, Chapter 13. In addition, have your program check that each Account Number is numeric before you divide it by the divisor. Have your program produce reports in the same format that you used in Exercise 3, Chapter 13.

Updating a Randomized Relative File

Program P16-05 updates our relative savings-account master file with additions, changes, and deletions. The input transactions come in from the transaction file in random Account Number sequence, and master records are read from the master file randomly as needed.

To find the master record having a particular Account Number, Program P16-05 must do some of the same steps that Program P16-04 did when it originally put records onto the file. Given an Account Number, Program P16-05 computes the home slot number of the master record and then READs the contents of that slot. If the desired master record is not found in its home slot, the program must then carry out an extended search to determine whether the record is in a nearby slot or not in the file at all.

To add a new savings-account record to the master file, Program P16-05 must find space for it the same way that Program P16-04 found space for master records when it first created the file. Program P16-04 uses the same WRITE logic that Program P16-04 did. Given an Account Number, Program P16-05 computes the home slot number of the master record and then tries to WRITE it in that slot. If the slot is already occupied, Program P16-05 carries out an extended search to determine whether there is a vacant slot nearby. If not, it writes a message INSUFFICIENT FILE SPACE. In that case, the master file must be made larger and recreated.

Program P16-05 is shown in Figure 16.19. Its high-level logic is similar to that used in Program P15-02, a random update to an indexed file. In the Working Storage Section, you can find the usual flags and counters in lines 00580 through 00820. The fields needed for converting Account Numbers to slot numbers and for carrying out extended searches are found in lines 00500 through 00560.

FIGURE *16.19* **Program P16-05**

```
S COBOL II RELEASE 3.2 09/05/90                    P16005    DATE MAR 06,1992 T
----+-*A-1-B--+----2----+----3----+----4----+----5----+----6----+----7-|--+

00010  IDENTIFICATION DIVISION.
00020  PROGRAM-ID.  P16-05.
00030 *
00040 *     THIS PROGRAM UPDATES A RELATIVE MASTER FILE ON DISK
00050 *     WITH ADDITIONS, CHANGES, AND DELETIONS.
00060 *
00070 *****************************************************************
00080
00090  ENVIRONMENT DIVISION.
00100  INPUT-OUTPUT SECTION.
00110  FILE-CONTROL.
00120      SELECT ACCOUNT-MASTER-FILE-I-O           ASSIGN TO MSTRDISK
00130          ORGANIZATION RELATIVE
00140          STATUS IS FILE-CHECK
00150          ACCESS RANDOM
00160          RELATIVE KEY IS SLOT-NUMBER.
00170      SELECT TRANSACTION-FILE-IN               ASSIGN TO TFILEIN.
00180      SELECT TRANSACTION-REGISTER-FILE-OUT     ASSIGN TO PRINTER1.
00190      SELECT ERROR-REPORT-FILE-OUT             ASSIGN TO PRINTER2.
00200
00210 *****************************************************************
```

FIGURE 16.19 *continued*

```
DATA DIVISION.
FILE SECTION.
FD  ACCOUNT-MASTER-FILE-I-O
    LABEL RECORDS ARE STANDARD
    RECORD CONTAINS 39 CHARACTERS.

01  ACCOUNT-MASTER-RECORD-I-O.
    05  ACCOUNT-NUMBER-M                    PIC 9(5).
    05  ACCOUNT-NUMBER-MX REDEFINES ACCOUNT-NUMBER-M
                                            PIC X(5).
    05  DEPOSITOR-NAME-M                    PIC X(20).
    05  DATE-OF-LAST-TRANSACTION-M          PIC 9(6).
    05  CURRENT-BALANCE-M                   PIC S9(6)V99.

FD  TRANSACTION-FILE-IN.

01  TRANSACTION-RECORD-IN                   PIC X(80).

FD  TRANSACTION-REGISTER-FILE-OUT.

01  TRANSACTION-REGISTER-REC-OUT            PIC X(76).

FD  ERROR-REPORT-FILE-OUT.

01  ERROR-REPORT-RECORD-OUT                 PIC X(102).

WORKING-STORAGE SECTION.
01  SLOT-NUMBER                                  PIC 99     COMP SYNC.
01  INTEGER-QUOTIENT                             PIC S9(4)  COMP SYNC.
01  INTEGER-REMAINDER                            PIC S99    COMP SYNC.
01  DIVISOR                          VALUE 61    PIC 99     COMP SYNC.
01  EXTENDED-SEARCH-LIMIT                        PIC S99    COMP SYNC.
01  EXTENDED-SEARCH-STEPS            VALUE 10    PIC S99    COMP SYNC.
01  NUMBER-OF-SLOTS-IN-FILE          VALUE 66    PIC S99    COMP SYNC.
01  BLANKS                                      PIC X      VALUE " ".
01  FILE-CHECK                                  PIC XX.
    88  NO-FILE-OPERATION                       VALUE "00".
    88  MASTER-FILE-IS-OPENED                   VALUE "00".
    88  FILE-OPERATION-WAS-SUCCESSFUL           VALUE "00".
    88  SLOT-ALREADY-FILLED                     VALUE "22".
    88  MASTER-RECORD-NOT-FOUND                 VALUE "23".
    88  FILE-OPERATION-FAILED                   VALUES "10" THRU "99".
01  IS-MASTER-RECORD-IN-WORK-AREA               PIC X.
    88  MASTER-RECORD-IS-IN-WORKAREA             VALUE "Y".
    88  MASTER-RECORD-ISNT-IN-WORKAREA          VALUE "N".
01  IS-MASTER-RECORD-IN-THE-FILE                PIC X.
    88  MASTER-RECORD-IS-IN-THE-FILE             VALUE "Y".
    88  MASTER-RECORD-ISNT-IN-THE-FILE          VALUE "N".
01  PACKED-DECIMAL.
 02 NUMBER-OF-INPUT-RECORDS-W                   PIC S9(3) VALUE ZERO.
 02 NUMBER-OF-ERRONEOUS-RECORDS-W               PIC S9(3) VALUE ZERO.
 02 DEPOSIT-TOTAL-W         VALUE 0             PIC S9(7)V99.
 02 WITHDRAWAL-TOTAL-W      VALUE 0             PIC S9(7)V99.
 02 NUMBER-OF-DEPOSITS-W                        PIC S9(3) VALUE 0.
 02 NUMBER-OF-WITHDRAWALS-W                     PIC S9(3) VALUE 0.
 02 NUMBER-OF-NEW-ACCOUNTS-W                    PIC S9(3) VALUE 0.
 02 NUMBER-OF-NAME-CHANGES-W                    PIC S9(3) VALUE 0.
 02 NUMBER-OF-DELETIONS-W                       PIC S9(3) VALUE 0.
 02 REGISTER-PAGE-COUNTER                       PIC S99 VALUE 0.
 02 ERROR-REPORT-PAGE-COUNTER                   PIC S99 VALUE 0.
01  TODAYS-DATE.
    05  TODAYS-YEAR                             PIC 99.
    05  TODAYS-MONTH-AND-DAY                    PIC 9(4).
```

continued

Notice that ACCOUNT-NUMBER-M, line 00300, and ACCOUNT-NUMBER-T, line 00940, are both defined as numeric and redefined as alphanumeric. That is because they must sometimes be treated as numeric (for division) and sometimes as alphanumeric (such as when assigned HIGH-VALUES). In programs in previous chapters the key field was defined only as alphanumeric because it was never used for arithmetic.

FIGURE *16.19* *continued*

```
S COBOL II RELEASE 3.2 09/05/90                   P16005   DATE MAR 06,1992 T
----+-*A-1-B--+----2----+----3----+----4----+----5----+----6----+----7-|--+

00860
00870  01  TRANSACTION-INPUT-AREA.
00880      05  TRANSACTION-CODE                  PIC X.
00890          88  NEW-ACCOUNT                   VALUE "1".
00900          88  DEPOSIT                       VALUE "2".
00910          88  WITHDRAWAL                    VALUE "3".
00920          88  NAME-CHANGE                   VALUE "4".
00930          88  DELETION                      VALUE "5".
00940      05  ACCOUNT-NUMBER-T                  PIC 9(5).
00950      05  ACCOUNT-NUMBER-X REDEFINES ACCOUNT-NUMBER-T
00960                                            PIC X(5).
00970          88 NO-MORE-TRANSACTION-RECORDS VALUE HIGH-VALUES.
00980          88 NO-TRANSACTION-RECORDS      VALUE HIGH-VALUES.
00990      05  DEPOSIT-AND-WITHDRAWAL-AMTS.
01000          10  DEPOSIT-AMOUNT                PIC 9(6)V99.
01010          10  DEPOSIT-AMOUNT-X     REDEFINES DEPOSIT-AMOUNT
01020                                            PIC X(8).
01030          10  WITHDRAWAL-AMOUNT    REDEFINES DEPOSIT-AMOUNT
01040                                            PIC 9(6)V99.
01050          10  WITHDRAWAL-AMOUNT-X REDEFINES DEPOSIT-AMOUNT
01060                                            PIC X(8).
01070      05  DEPOSITOR-NAME-NEW-ACCOUNT        PIC X(20).
01080          88  DEPOSITOR-NAME-MISSING        VALUE SPACES.
01090  01  TRANSACTION-4-INPUT-AREA REDEFINES TRANSACTION-INPUT-AREA.
01100      05                                    PIC X(6).
01110      05  DEPOSITOR-NAME                    PIC X(20).
01120          88  REPLACEMENT-NAME-MISSING VALUE SPACES.
01130      05                                    PIC X(8).
01140
01150  01  REGISTER-LINE-LIMIT                   PIC S99 VALUE 37 COMP SYNC.
01160  01  LINE-COUNT-ER                         PIC S99          COMP SYNC.
01170  01  ERROR-REPORT-LINE-LIMIT               PIC S99 VALUE 56 COMP SYNC.
01180  01  ERROR-LINE-COUNTER                    PIC S99          COMP SYNC.
01190
01200  01  REPORT-HEADING-1.
01210      05              PIC X(39) VALUE SPACES.
01220      05              PIC X(17) VALUE "ROBBEM STATE BANK".
01230
01240  01  REPORT-HEADING-2.
01250      05              PIC X(39) VALUE SPACES.
01260      05              PIC X(17) VALUE "106 WEST 10TH ST.".
01270
01280  01  REPORT-HEADING-3.
01290      05              PIC X(38) VALUE SPACES.
01300      05              PIC X(19) VALUE "BROOKLYN, NY  11212".
01310
01320  01  REGISTER-PAGE-HEAD-1.
01330      05              PIC X(29) VALUE SPACES.
01340      05              PIC X(36)
01350                      VALUE "SAVINGS ACCOUNT TRANSACTION REGISTER".
01360
```

FIGURE ***16.19*** ***continued***

```
       01  PAGE-HEAD-2.
           05                 PIC X(17)      VALUE SPACES.
           05                 PIC X(5)       VALUE "DATE".
           05  TODAYS-MONTH-AND-DAY          PIC Z9/99/.
           05  TODAYS-YEAR                   PIC 99B(35).
           05                 PIC X(5)       VALUE "PAGE".
           05  PAGE-NUMBER-OUT               PIC Z9.
       01  REGISTER-PAGE-HEAD-3.
           05                     PIC X(20) VALUE SPACES.
           05                     PIC X(12) VALUE "ACCOUNT".
           05                     PIC X(14) VALUE "DEPOSITS".
           05                     PIC X(18) VALUE "WITHDRAWALS".
           05                     PIC X(5)  VALUE "NOTES".
       01  PAGE-HEAD-4.
           05                     PIC X(20) VALUE SPACES.
           05                     PIC X(6)  VALUE "NUMBER".
       01  ERROR-REPORT-PAGE-HEAD-1.
           05                     PIC X(33) VALUE SPACES.
           05                     PIC X(28) VALUE
                                  "SAVINGS ACCOUNT ERROR REPORT".
       01  ERROR-REPORT-PAGE-HEAD-3.
           05                     PIC X(20) VALUE SPACES.
           05                     PIC X(44) VALUE "ACCOUNT".
           05                     PIC X(5)  VALUE "NOTES".
       01  NEW-ACCOUNT-LINE.
           05                     PIC X(21) VALUE SPACES.
           05  ACCOUNT-NUMBER-OUT           PIC 9(5)B(5).
           05  DEPOSIT-AMOUNT-OUT           PIC ZZZ,ZZZ.99B(21).
           05                     PIC X(11) VALUE "NEW ACCOUNT".
       01  DEPOSIT-LINE.
           05                     PIC X(21) VALUE SPACES.
           05  ACCOUNT-NUMBER-M-OUT         PIC 9(5)B(5).
           05  DEPOSIT-AMOUNT-OUT           PIC ZZZ,ZZZ.99.
       01  WITHDRAWAL-LINE.
           05                     PIC X(21) VALUE SPACES.
           05  ACCOUNT-NUMBER-M-OUT         PIC 9(5)B(19).
           05  WITHDRAWAL-AMOUNT-OUT        PIC ZZZ,ZZZ.99.
       01  NAME-CHANGE-LINE.
           05                     PIC X(21) VALUE SPACES.
           05  ACCOUNT-NUMBER-M-OUT         PIC 9(5)B(5).
           05  DEPOSITOR-NAME-OUT           PIC X(20)B(11).
           05                     PIC X(11) VALUE "NAME CHANGE".
       01  DELETION-LINE.
           05                     PIC X(21) VALUE SPACES.
           05  ACCOUNT-NUMBER-M-OUT         PIC 9(5)B(19).
           05  CURRENT-BALANCE-M-OUT        PIC ZZZ,ZZZ.99B(7).
           05                     PIC X(14) VALUE "ACCOUNT CLOSED".
       01  ERROR-MESSAGE-LINE.
           05                 PIC X(21) VALUE SPACES.
           05  ACCOUNT-NUMBER-T-E   PIC X(5)B(36).
           05  ERROR-MESSAGE-OUT    PIC X(52).
       01  DEPOSIT-AMOUNT-INVALID-MSG.
           05                 PIC X(29) VALUE
                              "DEPOSIT AMOUNT NOT NUMERIC -".
           05  DEPOSIT-AMOUNT-X-E   PIC X(8).
```

continued

FIGURE 16.19 *continued*

```
S COBOL II RELEASE 3.2 09/05/90                P16005   DATE MAR 06,1992 T
----+-*A-1-B--+----2----+----3----+----4----+----5----+----6----+----7-|--+
 01  WITHDRAWAL-AMOUNT-INVALID-MSG.
     05                PIC X(32) VALUE
                       "WITHDRAWAL AMOUNT NOT NUMERIC -".
     05  WITHDRAWAL-AMOUNT-X-E PIC X(8).
 01  INVALID-CODE-MSG.
     05                PIC X(27) VALUE "INVALID TRANSACTION CODE -".
     05  TRANSACTION-CODE-E   PIC X.
 01  FINAL-LINE-1.
     05                      PIC X(17) VALUE SPACES.
     05                      PIC X(12) VALUE "TOTALS".
     05  DEPOSIT-TOTAL-OUT         PIC Z,ZZZ,ZZZ.99BB.
     05  WITHDRAWAL-TOTAL-OUT      PIC Z,ZZZ,ZZZ.99.
 01  FINAL-LINE-2.
     05                      PIC X(40) VALUE SPACES.
     05                      PIC X(14) VALUE "CONTROL COUNTS".
 01  FINAL-LINE-3.
     05                      PIC X(34) VALUE SPACES.
     05                      PIC X(26)
                             VALUE "NUMBER OF NEW ACCOUNTS".
     05  NUMBER-OF-NEW-ACCOUNTS-OUT PIC ZZ9.
 01  FINAL-LINE-4.
     05                      PIC X(34) VALUE SPACES.
     05                      PIC X(26)
                             VALUE "NUMBER OF DEPOSITS".
     05  NUMBER-OF-DEPOSITS-OUT   PIC ZZ9.
 01  FINAL-LINE-5.
     05                      PIC X(34) VALUE SPACES.
     05                      PIC X(26)
                             VALUE "NUMBER OF WITHDRAWALS".
     05  NUMBER-OF-WITHDRAWALS-OUT PIC ZZ9.
 01  FINAL-LINE-6.
     05                      PIC X(34) VALUE SPACES.
     05                      PIC X(26)
                             VALUE "NUMBER OF NAME CHANGES".
     05  NUMBER-OF-NAME-CHANGES-OUT PIC ZZ9.
 01  FINAL-LINE-7.
     05                      PIC X(34) VALUE SPACES.
     05                      PIC X(26)
                             VALUE "NUMBER OF CLOSED ACCOUNTS".
     05  NUMBER-OF-DELETIONS-OUT  PIC ZZ9.
 01  FINAL-LINE-8.
     05                      PIC X(34) VALUE SPACES.
     05                      PIC X(26)
                             VALUE "NUMBER OF ERRORS".
     05  NUMBER-OF-ERRONEOUS-RCDS-OUT
                                   PIC ZZ9.
 01  FINAL-LINE-9.
     05                      PIC X(34) VALUE SPACES.
     05                      PIC X(24) VALUE "TOTAL".
     05  NUMBER-OF-INPUT-RECORDS-OUT PIC Z,ZZ9.
 01  NO-TRANSACTIONS.
     05                      PIC X(21) VALUE SPACES.
     05                      PIC X(15) VALUE "NO TRANSACTIONS".
```

FIGURE 16.19 *continued*

```
 01  INSUFFICIENT-FILE-SPACE.
     05                   PIC X(21) VALUE SPACES.
     05                   PIC X(23) VALUE "INSUFFICIENT FILE SPACE".

*****************************************************************

 PROCEDURE DIVISION.
 UPDATE-MASTER-RECORDS.
     PERFORM INITIALIZATION
     PERFORM PROCESS-ONE-KEY UNTIL NO-MORE-TRANSACTION-RECORDS
     PERFORM TERMINATION
     STOP RUN
     .

 INITIALIZATION.
     OPEN INPUT  TRANSACTION-FILE-IN
          OUTPUT TRANSACTION-REGISTER-FILE-OUT
                 ERROR-REPORT-FILE-OUT
          I-O    ACCOUNT-MASTER-FILE-I-O
     IF NOT MASTER-FILE-IS-OPENED
         DISPLAY " MASTER FILE OPEN STATUS = " FILE-CHECK
         CLOSE TRANSACTION-FILE-IN,
               TRANSACTION-REGISTER-FILE-OUT
               ACCOUNT-MASTER-FILE-I-O
         STOP RUN
     END-IF
     ACCEPT TODAYS-DATE FROM DATE
     MOVE CORRESPONDING TODAYS-DATE TO PAGE-HEAD-2
     PERFORM WRITE-REGISTER-PAGE-HEAD
     PERFORM WRITE-ERROR-REPORT-PAGE-HEAD
     PERFORM READ-A-TRANSACTION-RECORD
     IF NO-TRANSACTION-RECORDS
         WRITE ERROR-REPORT-RECORD-OUT FROM NO-TRANSACTIONS
     END-IF
     .

 WRITE-REGISTER-PAGE-HEAD.
     WRITE TRANSACTION-REGISTER-REC-OUT FROM REPORT-HEADING-1
                                        AFTER PAGE
     WRITE TRANSACTION-REGISTER-REC-OUT FROM REPORT-HEADING-2
     WRITE TRANSACTION-REGISTER-REC-OUT FROM REPORT-HEADING-3
     ADD 1 TO REGISTER-PAGE-COUNTER
     MOVE REGISTER-PAGE-COUNTER TO PAGE-NUMBER-OUT
     WRITE TRANSACTION-REGISTER-REC-OUT
           FROM REGISTER-PAGE-HEAD-1 AFTER 2
     WRITE TRANSACTION-REGISTER-REC-OUT FROM PAGE-HEAD-2
     WRITE TRANSACTION-REGISTER-REC-OUT
           FROM REGISTER-PAGE-HEAD-3 AFTER 3
     WRITE TRANSACTION-REGISTER-REC-OUT FROM PAGE-HEAD-4
     WRITE TRANSACTION-REGISTER-REC-OUT FROM BLANKS
     MOVE 11 TO LINE-COUNT-ER
     .

 WRITE-ERROR-REPORT-PAGE-HEAD.
     WRITE ERROR-REPORT-RECORD-OUT FROM REPORT-HEADING-1
                                   AFTER PAGE
     WRITE ERROR-REPORT-RECORD-OUT FROM REPORT-HEADING-2
     WRITE ERROR-REPORT-RECORD-OUT FROM REPORT-HEADING-3
     ADD 1 TO ERROR-REPORT-PAGE-COUNTER
     MOVE ERROR-REPORT-PAGE-COUNTER TO PAGE-NUMBER-OUT
     WRITE ERROR-REPORT-RECORD-OUT FROM ERROR-REPORT-PAGE-HEAD-1
           AFTER 2
     WRITE ERROR-REPORT-RECORD-OUT FROM PAGE-HEAD-2
     WRITE ERROR-REPORT-RECORD-OUT FROM ERROR-REPORT-PAGE-HEAD-3
           AFTER 3
     WRITE ERROR-REPORT-RECORD-OUT FROM PAGE-HEAD-4
     WRITE ERROR-REPORT-RECORD-OUT FROM BLANKS
     MOVE 11 TO ERROR-LINE-COUNTER
     .
```

continued

In PROCESS-MASTER-RECORD, line 03500, the program tries to READ a record from the master file. If it succeeds in finding a record key equal to the Account Number in the transaction on the first try, it sets the appropriate flags, in lines 03540 and 03550. Otherwise, it PERFORMs an extended search to try to find the desired master record. If the record is found, 1 is SUBTRACTed from SLOT-NUMBER because the extended search leaves the value of SLOT-NUMBER greater by 1 than the number of the slot that the record was found in. To see why, look at the PERFORM statement at line 03860.

FIGURE *16.19* ***continued***

```
S COBOL II RELEASE 3.2 09/05/90                    P16005    DATE MAR 06,1992 T
----+-*A-1-B--+----2----+----3----+----4----+----5----+----6----+----7-|--+

03380
03390   PROCESS-ONE-KEY.
03400       PERFORM PROCESS-MASTER-RECORD
03410       PERFORM PROCESS-TRANSACTION-RECORD
03420       PERFORM CHECK-TO-WRITE-MASTER
03430       .
03440
03450   PROCESS-TRANSACTION-RECORD.
03460       PERFORM APPLY-TRANSACTION
03470       PERFORM READ-A-TRANSACTION-RECORD
03480       .
03490
03500   PROCESS-MASTER-RECORD.
03510       PERFORM COMPUTE-SLOT-NO-FOR-READ
03520       PERFORM READ-A-MASTER-RECORD
03530       IF ACCOUNT-NUMBER-MX IS EQUAL TO ACCOUNT-NUMBER-X
03540           SET MASTER-RECORD-IS-IN-THE-FILE
03550               MASTER-RECORD-IS-IN-WORKAREA TO TRUE
03560       ELSE
03570           PERFORM EXTENDED-READ-SEARCH
03580           IF ACCOUNT-NUMBER-MX IS EQUAL TO ACCOUNT-NUMBER-X
03590               SET MASTER-RECORD-IS-IN-THE-FILE
03600                   MASTER-RECORD-IS-IN-WORKAREA TO TRUE
03610               SUBTRACT 1 FROM SLOT-NUMBER
03620           ELSE
03630               SET MASTER-RECORD-ISNT-IN-THE-FILE
03640                   MASTER-RECORD-ISNT-IN-WORKAREA TO TRUE
03650           END-IF
03660       END-IF
03670       .
03680
03690   COMPUTE-SLOT-NO-FOR-READ.
03700       DIVIDE ACCOUNT-NUMBER-T BY DIVISOR
03710           GIVING INTEGER-QUOTIENT
03720           REMAINDER INTEGER-REMAINDER
03730       ADD 1 TO INTEGER-REMAINDER GIVING SLOT-NUMBER
03740       .
03750
03760   COMPUTE-SLOT-NO-FOR-WRITE.
03770       DIVIDE ACCOUNT-NUMBER-M BY DIVISOR
03780           GIVING INTEGER-QUOTIENT
03790           REMAINDER INTEGER-REMAINDER
03800       ADD 1 TO INTEGER-REMAINDER GIVING SLOT-NUMBER
03810       .
03820
```

FIGURE ***16.19*** ***continued***

```
EXTENDED-READ-SEARCH.
    ADD SLOT-NUMBER TO EXTENDED-SEARCH-STEPS
        GIVING EXTENDED-SEARCH-LIMIT
    PERFORM READ-A-MASTER-RECORD
        VARYING SLOT-NUMBER FROM SLOT-NUMBER BY 1
            UNTIL
                ACCOUNT-NUMBER-MX IS EQUAL TO ACCOUNT-NUMBER-X OR
                SLOT-NUMBER GREATER THAN
                    EXTENDED-SEARCH-LIMIT OR
                    NUMBER-OF-SLOTS-IN-FILE
    .

READ-A-MASTER-RECORD.
    READ ACCOUNT-MASTER-FILE-I-O
        INVALID KEY CONTINUE
    END-READ
    IF FILE-OPERATION-WAS-SUCCESSFUL OR
       MASTER-RECORD-NOT-FOUND
        CONTINUE
    ELSE
        DISPLAY " MASTER FILE READ STATUS = ", FILE-CHECK
        PERFORM TERMINATION
        STOP RUN
    END-IF
    .

CHECK-TO-WRITE-MASTER.
    EVALUATE MASTER-RECORD-IS-IN-WORKAREA ALSO
             MASTER-RECORD-IS-IN-THE-FILE
    WHEN TRUE ALSO FALSE
        PERFORM WRITE-NEW-ACCOUNT-RECORD
    WHEN TRUE ALSO TRUE
        REWRITE ACCOUNT-MASTER-RECORD-I-O
    WHEN FALSE ALSO TRUE
        DELETE ACCOUNT-MASTER-FILE-I-O
    WHEN OTHER
        SET NO-FILE-OPERATION TO TRUE
    END-EVALUATE
    IF FILE-OPERATION-FAILED
        DISPLAY " MASTER FILE WRITE STATUS = ", FILE-CHECK
        PERFORM TERMINATION
        STOP RUN
    END-IF
    .

WRITE-NEW-ACCOUNT-RECORD.
    PERFORM COMPUTE-SLOT-NO-FOR-WRITE
    PERFORM WRITE-A-MASTER-RECORD
    IF SLOT-ALREADY-FILLED
        PERFORM EXTENDED-WRITE-SEARCH
    END-IF
    .

WRITE-A-MASTER-RECORD.
    WRITE ACCOUNT-MASTER-RECORD-I-O
        INVALID KEY CONTINUE
    END-WRITE
    IF FILE-OPERATION-WAS-SUCCESSFUL OR
       SLOT-ALREADY-FILLED
        CONTINUE
    ELSE
        DISPLAY " MASTER FILE WRITE STATUS = ", FILE-CHECK
        PERFORM TEFMINATION
        STOP RUN
    .
```

continued

FIGURE 16.19 *continued*

```
S COBOL II RELEASE 3.2 09/05/90                 P16005   DATE MAR 06,1992 T
----+-*A-1-B--+----2----+----3----+----4----+----5----+----6----+----7-|--+

       EXTENDED-WRITE-SEARCH.
           ADD SLOT-NUMBER, EXTENDED-SEARCH-STEPS
               GIVING EXTENDED-SEARCH-LIMIT
           PERFORM WRITE-A-MASTER-RECORD
               VARYING SLOT-NUMBER FROM SLOT-NUMBER BY 1
                   UNTIL
                       FILE-OPERATION-WAS-SUCCESSFUL OR
                       SLOT-NUMBER GREATER THAN
                           EXTENDED-SEARCH-LIMIT OR
                           NUMBER-OF-SLOTS-IN-FILE
           IF FILE-OPERATION-WAS-SUCCESSFUL
               CONTINUE
           ELSE
               PERFORM WRITE-INSUFFICIENT-FILE-SPACE
               DISPLAY " MASTER FILE WRITE STATUS = ", FILE-CHECK
               PERFORM TERMINATION
               STOP RUN
           .

       READ-A-TRANSACTION-RECORD.
           MOVE SPACES TO ACCOUNT-NUMBER-X
           PERFORM READ-TRANSACTION-FILE UNTIL
               ACCOUNT-NUMBER-T IS NUMERIC OR
               NO-MORE-TRANSACTION-RECORDS
           .

       READ-TRANSACTION-FILE.
           READ TRANSACTION-FILE-IN INTO TRANSACTION-INPUT-AREA
               AT END
                   SET NO-MORE-TRANSACTION-RECORDS TO TRUE
               NOT AT END
                   ADD  1 TO NUMBER-OF-INPUT-RECORDS-W
                   IF ACCOUNT-NUMBER-T NOT NUMERIC
                       ADD 1 TO NUMBER-OF-ERRONEOUS-RECORDS-W
                       PERFORM WRITE-INVALID-KEY-LINE
                   END-IF
            .

       APPLY-TRANSACTION.
           EVALUATE TRUE
           WHEN NEW-ACCOUNT
               PERFORM CHECK-FOR-VALID-NEW-ACCOUNT
           WHEN DEPOSIT
               PERFORM CHECK-FOR-VALID-DEPOSIT
           WHEN WITHDRAWAL
               PERFORM CHECK-FOR-VALID-WITHDRAWAL
           WHEN NAME-CHANGE
               PERFORM CHECK-FOR-VALID-NAME-CHANGE
           WHEN DELETION
               PERFORM CHECK-FOR-VALID-DELETION
           WHEN OTHER
               ADD 1 TO NUMBER-OF-ERRONEOUS-RECORDS-W
               PERFORM WRITE-INVALID-CODE-LINE
           END-EVALUATE
           .
```

FIGURE *16.19* ***continued***

```
CHECK-FOR-VALID-NEW-ACCOUNT.
     EVALUATE TRUE
     WHEN MASTER-RECORD-IS-IN-WORKAREA
          ADD 1 TO NUMBER-OF-ERRONEOUS-RECORDS-W
          PERFORM WRITE-NEW-ACCT-INVALID-LINE
     WHEN DEPOSIT-AMOUNT NOT NUMERIC
          ADD 1 TO NUMBER-OF-ERRONEOUS-RECORDS-W
          PERFORM WRITE-DEPOSIT-INVALID-LINE
     WHEN DEPOSITOR-NAME-MISSING
          ADD 1 TO NUMBER-OF-ERRONEOUS-RECORDS-W
          PERFORM WRITE-NAME-MISSING-LINE
     WHEN OTHER
          MOVE ACCOUNT-NUMBER-T TO ACCOUNT-NUMBER-M
          MOVE DEPOSITOR-NAME-NEW-ACCOUNT
               TO DEPOSITOR-NAME-M
          MOVE TODAYS-DATE TO DATE-OF-LAST-TRANSACTION-M
          MOVE DEPOSIT-AMOUNT TO CURRENT-BALANCE-M
          PERFORM WRITE-NEW-ACCOUNT-LINE
          SET MASTER-RECORD-IS-IN-WORKAREA TO TRUE
     END-EVALUATE
     .

CHECK-FOR-VALID-DEPOSIT.
     IF DEPOSIT-AMOUNT NOT NUMERIC
          ADD 1 TO NUMBER-OF-ERRONEOUS-RECORDS-W
          PERFORM WRITE-DEPOSIT-INVALID-LINE
     ELSE
     IF MASTER-RECORD-ISNT-IN-WORKAREA
          ADD 1 TO NUMBER-OF-ERRONEOUS-RECORDS-W
          PERFORM WRITE-MASTER-MISSING-LINE
     ELSE
          ADD DEPOSIT-AMOUNT TO CURRENT-BALANCE-M
          MOVE TODAYS-DATE TO DATE-OF-LAST-TRANSACTION-M
          PERFORM WRITE-DEPOSIT-LINE
     END-IF
     END-IF
     .

 CHECK-FOR-VALID-WITHDRAWAL.
     IF WITHDRAWAL-AMOUNT NOT NUMERIC
          ADD 1 TO NUMBER-OF-ERRONEOUS-RECORDS-W
          PERFORM WRITE-WITHDRAWAL-INVALID-LINE
     ELSE
     IF MASTER-RECORD-ISNT-IN-WORKAREA
          ADD 1 TO NUMBER-OF-ERRONEOUS-RECORDS-W
          PERFORM WRITE-MASTER-MISSING-LINE
     ELSE
          SUBTRACT WITHDRAWAL-AMOUNT FROM CURRENT-BALANCE-M
          MOVE TODAYS-DATE TO DATE-OF-LAST-TRANSACTION-M
          PERFORM WRITE-WITHDRAWAL-LINE
     END-IF
     END-IF
     .

CHECK-FOR-VALID-NAME-CHANGE.
     IF REPLACEMENT-NAME-MISSING
          ADD 1 TO NUMBER-OF-ERRONEOUS-RECORDS-W
          PERFORM WRITE-NAME-MISSING-LINE
     ELSE
     IF MASTER-RECORD-ISNT-IN-WORKAREA
          ADD 1 TO NUMBER-OF-ERRONEOUS-RECORDS-W
          PERFORM WRITE-MASTER-MISSING-LINE
     ELSE
          MOVE DEPOSITOR-NAME TO DEPOSITOR-NAME-M
          MOVE TODAYS-DATE TO DATE-OF-LAST-TRANSACTION-M
          PERFORM WRITE-NAME-CHANGE-LINE
     END-IF
     END-IF
     .
```

continued

A PERFORM . . . VARYING statement changes the value of its VARYING field after it carries out the PERFORMed paragraph and before it tests the UNTIL conditions. So if READ-A-MASTER-RECORD brings in a record whose Account Number IS EQUAL TO ACCOUNT-NUMBER-X, SLOT-NUMBER is nonetheless increased by 1 before the UNTIL tests are made.

The MOVE statement at line 06410 demonstrates that it is legal to MOVE a numeric source, or sending, field (ACCOUNT-NUMBER-T) to an alphanumeric receiving field. If a numeric field is defined as an unsigned integer and is of USAGE DISPLAY, as ACCOUNT-NUMBER-T is, the value of the field will be transferred to the alphanumeric field exactly as it appears in the numeric field, with no change in its form, whether the contents of the sending field are actually numeric or nonnumeric.

FIGURE *16.19* ***continued***

```
S COBOL II RELEASE 3.2 09/05/90                P16005   DATE MAR 06,1992 T
----+-*A-1-B--+----2----+----3----+----4----+----5----+----6----+----7-|--+

05750
05760  CHECK-FOR-VALID-DELETION.
05770      IF MASTER-RECORD-ISNT-IN-WORKAREA
05780          ADD 1 TO NUMBER-OF-ERRONEOUS-RECORDS-W
05790          PERFORM WRITE-MASTER-MISSING-LINE
05800      ELSE
05810          PERFORM WRITE-DELETION-LINE
05820          SET MASTER-RECORD-ISNT-IN-WORKAREA TO TRUE
05830      END-IF
05840      .
05850
05860  WRITE-NEW-ACCOUNT-LINE.
05870      MOVE ACCOUNT-NUMBER-T TO ACCOUNT-NUMBER-OUT
05880      MOVE DEPOSIT-AMOUNT
05890           TO DEPOSIT-AMOUNT-OUT OF NEW-ACCOUNT-LINE
05900      ADD 1 TO NUMBER-OF-NEW-ACCOUNTS-W
05910      ADD DEPOSIT-AMOUNT TO DEPOSIT-TOTAL-W
05920      IF LINE-COUNT-ER + 1 > REGISTER-LINE-LIMIT
05930          PERFORM WRITE-REGISTER-PAGE-HEAD
05940      END-IF
05950      WRITE TRANSACTION-REGISTER-REC-OUT FROM NEW-ACCOUNT-LINE
05960      ADD 1 TO LINE-COUNT-ER
05970      .
05980
05990  WRITE-DEPOSIT-LINE.
06000      MOVE ACCOUNT-NUMBER-M
06010           TO ACCOUNT-NUMBER-M-OUT OF DEPOSIT-LINE
06020      MOVE DEPOSIT-AMOUNT TO DEPOSIT-AMOUNT-OUT OF DEPOSIT-LINE
06030      ADD 1 TO NUMBER-OF-DEPOSITS-W
06040      ADD DEPOSIT-AMOUNT TO DEPOSIT-TOTAL-W
06050      IF LINE-COUNT-ER + 1 > REGISTER-LINE-LIMIT
06060          PERFORM WRITE-REGISTER-PAGE-HEAD
06070      END-IF
06080      WRITE TRANSACTION-REGISTER-REC-OUT FROM DEPOSIT-LINE
06090      ADD 1 TO LINE-COUNT-ER
06100      .
06110
```

FIGURE *16.19* ***continued***

```
WRITE-WITHDRAWAL-LINE.
    MOVE ACCOUNT-NUMBER-M
         TO ACCOUNT-NUMBER-M-OUT OF WITHDRAWAL-LINE
    MOVE WITHDRAWAL-AMOUNT TO WITHDRAWAL-AMOUNT-OUT
    ADD 1 TO NUMBER-OF-WITHDRAWALS-W
    ADD WITHDRAWAL-AMOUNT TO WITHDRAWAL-TOTAL-W
    IF LINE-COUNT-ER + 1 > REGISTER-LINE-LIMIT
        PERFORM WRITE-REGISTER-PAGE-HEAD
    END-IF
    WRITE TRANSACTION-REGISTER-REC-OUT FROM WITHDRAWAL-LINE
    ADD 1 TO LINE-COUNT-ER
    .

WRITE-DEPOSIT-INVALID-LINE.
    MOVE DEPOSIT-AMOUNT-X TO DEPOSIT-AMOUNT-X-E
    MOVE ACCOUNT-NUMBER-T TO ACCOUNT-NUMBER-T-E
    MOVE DEPOSIT-AMOUNT-INVALID-MSG TO ERROR-MESSAGE-OUT
    PERFORM WRITE-ERROR-LINE
    .

WRITE-WITHDRAWAL-INVALID-LINE.
    MOVE WITHDRAWAL-AMOUNT-X TO WITHDRAWAL-AMOUNT-X-E
    MOVE ACCOUNT-NUMBER-T TO ACCOUNT-NUMBER-T-E
    MOVE WITHDRAWAL-AMOUNT-INVALID-MSG TO ERROR-MESSAGE-OUT
    PERFORM WRITE-ERROR-LINE
    .

WRITE-NAME-MISSING-LINE.
    MOVE "DEPOSITOR NAME MISSING" TO ERROR-MESSAGE-OUT
    MOVE ACCOUNT-NUMBER-T TO ACCOUNT-NUMBER-T-E
    PERFORM WRITE-ERROR-LINE
    .

WRITE-NAME-CHANGE-LINE.
    MOVE ACCOUNT-NUMBER-M
         TO ACCOUNT-NUMBER-M-OUT IN NAME-CHANGE-LINE
    MOVE DEPOSITOR-NAME   TO DEPOSITOR-NAME-OUT
    ADD 1 TO NUMBER-OF-NAME-CHANGES-W
    IF LINE-COUNT-ER + 1 > REGISTER-LINE-LIMIT
        PERFORM WRITE-REGISTER-PAGE-HEAD
    END-IF
    WRITE TRANSACTION-REGISTER-REC-OUT FROM NAME-CHANGE-LINE
    ADD 1 TO LINE-COUNT-ER
    .

WRITE-DELETION-LINE.
    MOVE ACCOUNT-NUMBER-M
         TO ACCOUNT-NUMBER-M-OUT IN DELETION-LINE
    MOVE CURRENT-BALANCE-M TO CURRENT-BALANCE-M-OUT
    ADD 1 TO NUMBER-OF-DELETIONS-W
    ADD CURRENT-BALANCE-M TO WITHDRAWAL-TOTAL-W
    IF LINE-COUNT-ER + 1 > REGISTER-LINE-LIMIT
        PERFORM WRITE-REGISTER-PAGE-HEAD
    END-IF
    WRITE TRANSACTION-REGISTER-REC-OUT FROM DELETION-LINE
    ADD 1 TO LINE-COUNT-ER
    .

WRITE-INVALID-CODE-LINE.
    MOVE TRANSACTION-CODE TO TRANSACTION-CODE-E
    MOVE ACCOUNT-NUMBER-T TO ACCOUNT-NUMBER-T-E
    MOVE INVALID-CODE-MSG TO ERROR-MESSAGE-OUT
    PERFORM WRITE-ERROR-LINE
    .

WRITE-MASTER-MISSING-LINE.
    MOVE "MASTER RECORD DOES NOT EXIST" TO ERROR-MESSAGE-OUT
    MOVE ACCOUNT-NUMBER-T TO ACCOUNT-NUMBER-T-E
    PERFORM WRITE-ERROR-LINE
    .
```

continued

FIGURE 16.19 *continued*

```
S COBOL II RELEASE 3.2 09/05/90                  P16005   DATE MAR 06,1992 T
----+-*A-1-B--+----2----+----3----+----4----+----5----+----6----+----7-|--+


 WRITE-NEW-ACCT-INVALID-LINE.
     MOVE
     "ACCOUNT NUMBER ALREADY IN FILE NEW ACCOUNT INVALID" TO
         ERROR-MESSAGE-OUT
     MOVE ACCOUNT-NUMBER-T TO ACCOUNT-NUMBER-T-E
     PERFORM WRITE-ERROR-LINE
     .

 WRITE-ERROR-LINE.
     IF ERROR-LINE-COUNTER + 1 > ERROR-REPORT-LINE-LIMIT
         PERFORM WRITE-ERROR-REPORT-PAGE-HEAD
     END-IF
     WRITE ERROR-REPORT-RECORD-OUT FROM ERROR-MESSAGE-LINE
     ADD 1 TO ERROR-LINE-COUNTER
     .

 WRITE-INSUFFICIENT-FILE-SPACE.
     MOVE "INSUFFICIENT FILE SPACE" TO ERROR-MESSAGE-OUT
     MOVE ACCOUNT-NUMBER-T          TO ACCOUNT-NUMBER-T-E
     PERFORM WRITE-ERROR-LINE
     .

 WRITE-INVALID-KEY-LINE.
     MOVE ACCOUNT-NUMBER-X             TO ACCOUNT-NUMBER-T-E
     MOVE "ACCOUNT NUMBER NOT NUMERIC" TO ERROR-MESSAGE-OUT
     PERFORM WRITE-ERROR-LINE
     .

 TERMINATION.
     PERFORM PRODUCE-FINAL-LINES
     CLOSE TRANSACTION-FILE-IN
           ERROR-REPORT-FILE-OUT
           ACCOUNT-MASTER-FILE-I-O
           TRANSACTION-REGISTER-FILE-OUT
     .

 PRODUCE-FINAL-LINES.
     MOVE  DEPOSIT-TOTAL-W TO DEPOSIT-TOTAL-OUT
     MOVE WITHDRAWAL-TOTAL-W TO WITHDRAWAL-TOTAL-OUT
     WRITE TRANSACTION-REGISTER-REC-OUT FROM FINAL-LINE-1 AFTER 3
     WRITE TRANSACTION-REGISTER-REC-OUT FROM FINAL-LINE-2 AFTER 2
     MOVE NUMBER-OF-NEW-ACCOUNTS-W TO NUMBER-OF-NEW-ACCOUNTS-OUT
     WRITE TRANSACTION-REGISTER-REC-OUT FROM FINAL-LINE-3 AFTER 2
     MOVE NUMBER-OF-DEPOSITS-W TO NUMBER-OF-DEPOSITS-OUT
     WRITE TRANSACTION-REGISTER-REC-OUT FROM FINAL-LINE-4 AFTER 2
     MOVE NUMBER-OF-WITHDRAWALS-W TO NUMBER-OF-WITHDRAWALS-OUT
     WRITE TRANSACTION-REGISTER-REC-OUT FROM FINAL-LINE-5 AFTER 2
     MOVE NUMBER-OF-NAME-CHANGES-W TO NUMBER-OF-NAME-CHANGES-OUT
     WRITE TRANSACTION-REGISTER-REC-OUT FROM FINAL-LINE-6 AFTER 2
     MOVE NUMBER-OF-DELETIONS-W TO NUMBER-OF-DELETIONS-OUT
     WRITE TRANSACTION-REGISTER-REC-OUT FROM FINAL-LINE-7 AFTER 2
     MOVE NUMBER-OF-ERRONEOUS-RECORDS-W
          TO NUMBER-OF-ERRONEOUS-RCDS-OUT
     WRITE TRANSACTION-REGISTER-REC-OUT FROM FINAL-LINE-8 AFTER 2
     MOVE NUMBER-OF-INPUT-RECORDS-W
          TO NUMBER-OF-INPUT-RECORDS-OUT
     WRITE TRANSACTION-REGISTER-REC-OUT FROM FINAL-LINE-9 AFTER 2
     .
```

Program P16-05 was run with the input transactions shown in Figure 16.20 and the master file created by Program P16-04. Program P16-05 produced the report output shown in Figure 16.21.

FIGURE *16.20* **Transaction input to Program P16-05**

```
--------------------------------------------------------------------------------
         1         2         3         4         5         6         7         8
12345678901234567890123456789012345678901234567890123456789012345678901234567890
--------------------------------------------------------------------------------
20042600015000
24749100015000
70038500007500JAMES WASHINGTON
10039200007500INEZ WASHINGTON
476660JOHN & SALLY DUPRINO
26017500125634
34749100150050
10042000150000JOHN RICE
38191900002460
26683500357429
28191900150000
436650BETH DENNY
10039900014Z00GARY NASTI
200007)))$%)))
20039100064200
31510900100000
23310000012750
39023000002735
70042700002500GREG PRUITT
23510100256300
414697GENE & THERESA GALLI
23823400035000
35549600011000
461714
23149000015327
20005400120000
26871800025000
20016900025000
10009200043200GENE GALLI
30009200050000
20009200172500
418862GEORGE & ANN CULHANE
536126
21962500019202
536126
26695200025000
23612600231700
80031500013798
230917
5
20030800005000
400308GENE GALLI
10040600120000
37688400015025
23280900001006
10014100035075IRVING STURDUVAN
```

FIGURE 16.21 Report output from Program P16-05

```
                         ROBBEM STATE BANK
                         106 WEST 10TH ST.
                        BROOKLYN, NY  11212

                  SAVINGS ACCOUNT TRANSACTION REGISTER
DATE  3/06/92                                             PAGE  1

   ACCOUNT      DEPOSITS       WITHDRAWALS       NOTES
   NUMBER

    47491         150.00
    00392          75.00                       NEW ACCOUNT
    76660      JOHN & SALLY DUPRINO            NAME CHANGE
    60175       1,256.34
    47491                        1,500.50
    00420       1,500.00                       NEW ACCOUNT
    81919                           24.60
    66835       3,574.29
    81919       1,500.00
    15109                        1,000.00
    33100         127.50
    90230                           27.35
    38234         350.00
    55496                          110.00
    31490         153.27
    00054       1,200.00
    68718         250.00
    00169         250.00
    00092         432.00                       NEW ACCOUNT
    00092                          500.00
    00092       1,725.00
    18862      GEORGE & ANN CULHANE            NAME CHANGE
    36126                          100.00      ACCOUNT CLOSED
    19625         192.02
    66952         250.00
    32809          10.06

                         ROBBEM STATE BANK
                         106 WEST 10TH ST.
                        BROOKLYN, NY  11212

                  SAVINGS ACCOUNT TRANSACTION REGISTER
DATE  3/06/92                                             PAGE  2

   ACCOUNT      DEPOSITS       WITHDRAWALS       NOTES
   NUMBER

    00141         350.75                       NEW ACCOUNT


TOTALS         13,346.23       3,262.45

                             CONTROL COUNTS

                      NUMBER OF NEW ACCOUNTS       4

                      NUMBER OF DEPOSITS          14

                      NUMBER OF WITHDRAWALS        6

                      NUMBER OF NAME CHANGES       2

                      NUMBER OF CLOSED ACCOUNTS    1

                      NUMBER OF ERRORS            19

                      TOTAL                       46
```

FIGURE *16.21* ***continued***

```
                    ROBBEM STATE BANK
                    106 WEST 10TH ST.
                   BROOKLYN, NY  11212

             SAVINGS ACCOUNT ERROR REPORT
DATE  3/06/92                                  PAGE  1

   ACCOUNT                               NOTES
   NUMBER

    00426                              MASTER RECORD DOES NOT EXIST
    00385                              INVALID TRANSACTION CODE - 7
    36650                              MASTER RECORD DOES NOT EXIST
    00399                              DEPOSIT AMOUNT NOT NUMERIC - 00014Z00
    00007                              DEPOSIT AMOUNT NOT NUMERIC - )))$%)))
    00391                              MASTER RECORD DOES NOT EXIST
    00427                              INVALID TRANSACTION CODE - 7
    35101                              MASTER RECORD DOES NOT EXIST
    14697                              MASTER RECORD DOES NOT EXIST
    61714                              DEPOSITOR NAME MISSING
    36126                              MASTER RECORD DOES NOT EXIST
    36126                              MASTER RECORD DOES NOT EXIST
    00315                              INVALID TRANSACTION CODE - 8
    30917                              DEPOSIT AMOUNT NOT NUMERIC -
                                       ACCOUNT NUMBER NOT NUMERIC
    00308                              MASTER RECORD DOES NOT EXIST
    00308                              MASTER RECORD DOES NOT EXIST
    00406                              DEPOSITOR NAME MISSING
    76884                              WITHDRAWAL AMOUNT NOT NUMERIC - 00015025
```

EXERCISE *5*

Write a program to update the master file you created in Exercise 4, this chapter. Use transactions in the same format you used when you updated your sequential master file in Exercise 3, Chapter 14, page 528.

Have your program make all suitable validity checks on input transactions, and produce suitable reports.

Listing the Contents of a Relative File

A relative file may be accessed sequentially, as we have seen in Program P16-03 when we produced a list of letter grades for students. But if we were to access our savings-account master file sequentially, we would get the records in slot number sequence rather than in sequence on Account Number. ACCESS SEQUENTIAL on a relative file means in sequence on slot number.

Program P16-06 lists our savings-account master records in sequence on Account Number. It does so by SORTing the entire master file on Account Number, using a SORT statement. The SORT then RETURNs the master records one at a time, sequenced on Account Number, to be printed.

Program P16-06 is shown in Figure 16.22. The FILE-CONTROL entry at line 00160 contains no RELATIVE KEY clause, because in this program we have no need to refer to the slot numbers of the records. We therefore need no ACCESS clause. Also, a STATUS field would be of no use, since the SORT is going to be OPENing and READing this file, and we would have no opportunity to test the STATUS field anyway.

FIGURE *16.22* **Program P16-06**

```
S COBOL II RELEASE 3.1 09/19/89                 P16006    DATE OCT 04,1991 T
----+-*A-1-B--+----2----+----3----+----4----+----5----+----6----+----7-|--+

00010  IDENTIFICATION DIVISION.
00020  PROGRAM-ID.  P16-06.
00030
00040 *     THIS PROGRAM LISTS A RELATIVE FILE IN SEQUENCE ON
00050 *     ITS RECORD KEY.  THE PROGRAM FIRST SORTS THE FILE
00060 *     INTO SEQUENCE ON ITS KEY, AND THEN LISTS THE SORTED
00070 *     RECORDS.
00080 *
00090 ******************************************************************
00100
00110  ENVIRONMENT DIVISION.
00120  INPUT-OUTPUT SECTION.
00130  FILE-CONTROL.
00140      SELECT LIST-FILE-OUT    ASSIGN TO PRINTER.
00150      SELECT SORT-WORK-FILE   ASSIGN TO SORTWK.
00160      SELECT MASTER-FILE-IN   ASSIGN TO DISKUNIT
00170          ORGANIZATION RELATIVE.
00180
00190 ******************************************************************
00200
00210  DATA DIVISION.
00220  FILE SECTION.
00230  FD  MASTER-FILE-IN
00240      LABEL RECORDS ARE STANDARD
00250      RECORD CONTAINS 39 CHARACTERS.
00260
00270  01  MASTER-RECORD-IN                                 PIC X(39).
00280
00290  SD  SORT-WORK-FILE
00300      RECORD CONTAINS 39 CHARACTERS.
00310
00320  01  SORT-WORK-RECORD.
00330      05  ACCOUNT-NUMBER-M                             PIC X(5).
00340      05  DEPOSITOR-NAME-M                             PIC X(20).
00350      05  DATE-OF-LAST-TRANSACTION-M.
00360          10  TRANSACTION-YEAR-M                       PIC 99.
00370          10  TRANSACTION-MONTH-M                      PIC 99.
00380          10  TRANSACTION-DAY-M                        PIC 99.
00390      05  CURRENT-BALANCE-M                            PIC S9(6)V99.
00400
00410  FD  LIST-FILE-OUT.
00420
00430  01  LIST-RECORD-OUT                                  PIC X(81).
00440
00450  WORKING-STORAGE SECTION.
00460  01  PAGE-LIMIT       VALUE 38   COMP SYNC            PIC S99.
00470  01  LINE-COUNT-ER               COMP SYNC            PIC S99.
00480  01  PAGE-NUMBER-W    VALUE 0                         PIC S99.
00490  01  MORE-INPUT       VALUE  "Y"                      PIC X(3).
00500      88 THERE-IS-NO-MORE-INPUT   VALUE "N".
00510      88 THERE-IS-NO-INPUT        VALUE "N".
```

FIGURE 16.22 *continued*

```
 01  RUN-DATE.
     05  RUN-YEAR                                       PIC 99.
     05  RUN-MONTH-AND-DAY                              PIC 9(4).

 01  HEADING-1.
     05                 VALUE SPACES                    PIC X(40).
     05                 VALUE  "SAVINGS ACCOUNT MASTER"
                                                        PIC X(22).

 01  HEADING-2.
     05                 VALUE SPACES                    PIC X(28).
     05                 VALUE  "DATE"                   PIC X(5).
     05  RUN-MONTH-AND-DAY                              PIC Z9/99/.
     05  RUN-YEAR                                       PIC 99B(21).
     05                 VALUE  "PAGE"                   PIC X(5).
     05  PAGE-NUMBER-OUT                                PIC Z9.

 01  HEADING-3.
     05                 VALUE SPACES                    PIC X(46).
     05                 VALUE  "DATE OF LAST"           PIC X(12).

 01  HEADING-4.
     05                 VALUE SPACES                    PIC X(20).
     05                 VALUE  "ACCOUNT"                PIC X(13).
     05                 VALUE  "CURRENT"                PIC X(13).
     05                 VALUE  "TRANSACTION"            PIC X(15).
     05                 VALUE  "DEPOSITOR NAME"         PIC X(14).

 01  HEADING-5.
     05                 VALUE SPACES                    PIC X(20).
     05                 VALUE  "NUMBER"                 PIC X(13).
     05                 VALUE  "BALANCE"                PIC X(14).
     05                 VALUE  "YR  MO  DA"             PIC X(10).

 01  DETAIL-LINE.
     05              VALUE SPACES                     PIC X(21).
     05  ACCOUNT-NUMBER-OUT                           PIC X(5)B(4).
     05  CURRENT-BALANCE-OUT                          PIC Z,ZZZ,ZZZ.99-.
     05              VALUE SPACES                     PIC X(4).
     05  TRANSACTION-YEAR-OUT                         PIC 99BB.
     05  TRANSACTION-MONTH-OUT                        PIC 99BB.
     05  TRANSACTION-DAY-OUT                          PIC 99B(4).
     05  DEPOSITOR-NAME-OUT                           PIC X(20).

 01  NO-INPUT-DATA.
     05              VALUE SPACES                     PIC X(21).
     05              VALUE "NO INPUT DATA"            PIC X(13).

*****************************************************************

 PROCEDURE DIVISION.
 SORT-STATEMENT-PARAGRAPH.
     SORT SORT-WORK-FILE
          ASCENDING KEY ACCOUNT-NUMBER-M
          USING MASTER-FILE-IN
          OUTPUT PROCEDURE LIST-MASTER-FILE
     STOP RUN
     .

 LIST-MASTER-FILE.
     PERFORM INITIALIZATION
     PERFORM MAIN-PROCESS UNTIL THERE-IS-NO-MORE-INPUT
     PERFORM TERMINATION
     .
```

continued

FIGURE ***16.22*** ***continued***

```
S COBOL II RELEASE 3.1 09/19/89                  P16006   DATE OCT 04,1991 T
----+-*A-1-B--+----2----+----3----+----4----+----5----+----6----+----7-|--+

       INITIALIZATION.
           OPEN OUTPUT LIST-FILE-OUT
           ACCEPT RUN-DATE FROM DATE
           MOVE CORRESPONDING RUN-DATE TO HEADING-2
           PERFORM PRODUCE-PAGE-HEADINGS
           RETURN SORT-WORK-FILE
               AT END
                   SET THERE-IS-NO-INPUT TO TRUE
           END-RETURN
           IF THERE-IS-NO-INPUT
               WRITE LIST-RECORD-OUT FROM NO-INPUT-DATA
           END-IF
           .

       PRODUCE-PAGE-HEADINGS.
           ADD 1 TO PAGE-NUMBER-W
           MOVE PAGE-NUMBER-W TO PAGE-NUMBER-OUT
           WRITE LIST-RECORD-OUT FROM HEADING-1 AFTER PAGE
           WRITE LIST-RECORD-OUT FROM HEADING-2
           WRITE LIST-RECORD-OUT FROM HEADING-3 AFTER 3
           WRITE LIST-RECORD-OUT FROM HEADING-4
           WRITE LIST-RECORD-OUT FROM HEADING-5
           MOVE SPACES TO LIST-RECORD-OUT
           WRITE LIST-RECORD-OUT
           MOVE 8 TO LINE-COUNT-ER
           .

       TERMINATION.
           CLOSE LIST-FILE-OUT
           .

       MAIN-PROCESS.
           MOVE ACCOUNT-NUMBER-M     TO ACCOUNT-NUMBER-OUT
           MOVE CURRENT-BALANCE-M    TO CURRENT-BALANCE-OUT
           MOVE TRANSACTION-YEAR-M   TO TRANSACTION-YEAR-OUT
           MOVE TRANSACTION-MONTH-M  TO TRANSACTION-MONTH-OUT
           MOVE TRANSACTION-DAY-M    TO TRANSACTION-DAY-OUT
           MOVE DEPOSITOR-NAME-M     TO DEPOSITOR-NAME-OUT
           IF LINE-COUNT-ER + 1 > PAGE-LIMIT
               PERFORM PRODUCE-PAGE-HEADINGS
           END-IF
           WRITE LIST-RECORD-OUT FROM DETAIL-LINE
           ADD 1 TO LINE-COUNT-ER
           RETURN SORT-WORK-FILE
               AT END
                   SET THERE-IS-NO-MORE-INPUT TO TRUE
           .
```

Program P16-06 was run with the updated master file produced by Program P16-05. Program P16-06 produced the output shown in Figure 16.23.

FIGURE *16.23* **Output from Program P16-06**

```
                    SAVINGS ACCOUNT MASTER
        DATE   3/06/92                           PAGE   1


                                 DATE OF LAST
ACCOUNT        CURRENT           TRANSACTION        DEPOSITOR NAME
NUMBER         BALANCE            YR   MO   DA

  00054        1,220.00           92   03   06      COMMUNITY DRUGS
  00080           50.00           92   03   04      LENORE MILLER
  00092        1,657.00           92   03   06      GENE GALLI
  00141          350.75           92   03   06      IRVING STURDUVAN
  00169          349.57           92   03   06      MARTIN LANG
  00202          250.00           92   03   04      ROSEMARY LANE
  00392           75.00           92   03   06      INEZ WASHINGTON
  00420        1,500.00           92   03   06      JOHN RICE
  06180          750.00           92   03   04      JAMES BUDD
  11682        1,007.84           92   03   04      ROSEBUCCI
  15109          985.00-          92   03   06      GENE GALLI
  18862          500.00           92   03   06      GEORGE & ANN CULHANE
  19625        1,692.02           92   03   06      JOHN DAPRINO
  25055            5.00           92   03   04      JOYCE MITCHELL
  27013           20.00           92   03   04      JANE HALEY
  30917          500.00           92   03   04      PATRICK J. LEE
  31490          168.27           92   03   06      SOLOMON CHAPELS
  32809          185.56           92   03   06      JOHN WILLIAMS
  33100          137.50           92   03   06      KEVIN PARKER
  33946           24.50           92   03   04      ROBERT RYAN
  34780          250.00           92   03   04      JERRY PARKS
  38234          600.00           92   03   06      GRACE MICELI
  43967          150.00           92   03   04      IMPERIAL FLORIST
  46749        1,000.00           92   03   04      PAUL LERNER, D.D.S.
  47491        1,149.50           92   03   06      ROGER SHAW
  50027           50.00           92   03   04      ONE DAY CLEANERS
  55496        1,890.00           92   03   06      JOE GARCIA
  60175        8,257.93           92   03   06      MICHAEL SMITH
  61714        1,500.00           92   03   04      JOHN BURKE
  64165           25.00           92   03   04      JOSEPH CAMILLO


                    SAVINGS ACCOUNT MASTER
        DATE   3/06/92                           PAGE   2


                                 DATE OF LAST
ACCOUNT        CURRENT           TRANSACTION        DEPOSITOR NAME
NUMBER         BALANCE            YR   MO   DA

  65745           50.00           92   03   04      CARL CALDERON
  66835        3,584.29           92   03   06      ROBERT DAVIS M.D.
  66952          260.37           92   03   06      LESLIE MINSKY
  67566            1.00           92   03   04      EVELYN SLATER
  68718          525.00           92   03   06      VITO CACACI
  70549          125.50           92   03   04      KELLY HEDERMAN
  72032           35.00           92   03   04      J. & L. CAIN
  75495           25.75           92   03   04      BETH FALLON
  76660        1,000.00           92   03   06      JOHN & SALLY DUPRINO
  76884          150.00           92   03   04      JOHN J. LEHMAN
  81919        1,600.40           92   03   06      LORICE MONTI
  88298          150.00           92   03   04      JAY GREENE
  90230          527.65           92   03   06      BILL WILLIAMS
  96681           10.00           92   03   04      MARY KEATING
```

EXERCISE 6

Write a program to list the contents of your accounts-receivable master file. Have your program SORT the file into Account Number sequence before listing. Run the program using the files produced by your programs in Exercises 4 and 5 in this chapter.

Other Operations on Relative Files

There are other operations that may be carried out on a relative file, which have not been discussed in this chapter. Among them are START, the sequential access uses of REWRITE and DELETE, and the dynamic access operations. Details of these may be found in the COBOL manual for your system.

Summary

A relative file may be thought of as consisting of a string of consecutively numbered slots in which records may be stored. A relative file may be accessed sequentially, randomly, and dynamically. Relative files must be stored on direct-access storage devices.

The sequential operations on a relative file are READ, WRITE, REWRITE, DELETE, and START. The random operations are READ, WRITE, REWRITE, and DELETE. The dynamic-access operations include all the sequential and random operations and also READ . . . NEXT.

A RELATIVE KEY field is used with certain operations. All random operations require a RELATIVE KEY to tell COBOL which record on the file to READ, WRITE, REWRITE, or DELETE. Whenever a START statement is used, a RELATIVE KEY field is required to tell COBOL where to START. When READing a relative file sequentially, if the programmer wants COBOL to provide the relative record number of each record as it is read, a RELATIVE KEY field must be used.

The RELATIVE KEY phrase is part of the ACCESS clause. Whenever a RELATIVE KEY phrase is used, an ACCESS clause must appear. Whenever ACCESS RANDOM or ACCESS DYNAMIC is used, a RELATIVE KEY phrase must appear. ACCESS SEQUENTIAL may appear without a RELATIVE KEY phrase. If the ACCESS clause is omitted, sequential access is assumed.

When items to be represented in a relative file are numbered nonconsecutively, a randomizing technique may be used to compute a home slot number for each record. If more than one record key randomizes to the same home slot number, an extended search is required to locate each record near its home slot.

When a relative file is processed sequentially, the records in the file are processed in slot-number order. If processing in record-key order is desired, the file can be SORTed.

Fill-In Exercises

1. A relative file can be thought of as consisting of a number of ______ into which records can be placed.
2. COBOL can ______ a record into any slot that already contains a record.
3. COBOL can ______ a record into any empty slot.
4. A record in a relative file is referred to by its ______ ______ ______.

5. To process a relative file, the FILE-CONTROL entry for the file must contain a(n) ______ clause.

6. A RELATIVE KEY phrase must be used whenever ACCESS ______ or ACCESS ______ is used.

7. In any random operation on a relative file, the ______ ______ field contains the number of the slot to be operated upon.

8. When a relative file is read sequentially, COBOL can place the relative record number of each record into the ______ ______ field as each record is read.

9. If a random READ attempts to READ an empty slot, the STATUS field is set to ______.

10. In the division/remainder method of randomizing, the divisor is a prime number ______ than the number of ______ in the file.

11. The RELATIVE KEY phrase is part of the ______ clause.

12. In the division/remainder method of randomizing, you ignore the ______ and add 1 to the ______.

13. In the division/remainder method of randomizing, each record key yields a ______ ______ number.

14. Randomizing is needed only when the records in a file are ______ ______.

15. The main advantage of relative files over indexed files is the ______ with which records in a relative file may be accessed.

Review Exercises

1. Write a program to list the relative record number and Account Number of each record in the accounts-receivable file of Exercises 4 and 5, this chapter, in relative record number order. Run your program using as input first the file you created in Exercise 4, and then the updated file you created in Exercise 5.

   Have your program READ the file sequentially, without SORTing it. Check whether your randomizing scheme worked and that each Account Number went into its intended slot. Did your file contain any synonyms? What slots did they go into?

2. Write a program to create an alumni file as a relative file. Use the same formats for input transactions and master records that you used when you created your sequential alumni file in Review Exercise 2, Chapter 13, page 476. Choose a file size suitable to the maximum number of alumni records that you expect to have in your file, and choose a divisor suitable to the file size.

   Have your program check for the presence of all fields in each input record and that the Social Security Number is numeric. Have your program print a report showing the records written onto the master file and the erroneous transactions.

3. Write a program to update randomly the alumni file you created in Review Exercise 2. Use the same transaction formats that you used when you updated your alumni file in Review Exercise 4, Chapter 14, page 536. Have your program check that the Social Security Number in each input record

is numeric and also make all other suitable validity checks. Have your program print a suitable report.

4. Write a program to list the relative record number and the Social Security Number of each record in your alumni file, in relative record number order. Run your program using as input first the file you created in Review Exercise 2 and then the updated file you produced in Review Exercise 3.
5. Write a program to list the contents of your alumni file in Social Security Number order. Run your program using as input first the file you created in Review Exercise 2 and then the updated file you produced in Review Exercise 3.

Project

Rewrite your solution to the Project in Chapter 13, page 477, creating a relative file instead of a sequential file. Use Customer Numbers that are wholly numeric, and use the division/remainder method to compute a home slot number for each record.

CHAPTER 17

Introduction to VSAM File Processing

HERE ARE THE KEY POINTS YOU SHOULD LEARN FROM THIS CHAPTER

1. Why VSAM processing is used
2. How to use the Access Method Services program
3. What outputs to expect from Access Method Services
4. How to establish a key-sequenced data set
5. Two ways to establish an alternate index
6. How to establish a relative-record data set

KEY WORDS TO RECOGNIZE AND LEARN

VSAM
Virtual Storage Access Method
OS
VS
Operating System
Virtual Storage
DOS
Disk Operating System
physical sequential
entry-sequenced data set
key-sequenced data set
relative-record data set
VS1
VS2
Access Method Services
unloaded
command
DEFINE
master catalog
user catalog
JOBCAT
STEPCAT
alternate index
PATH
CYLINDER
data component
index component
BLDINDEX
ALTER
PRINT
LISTCAT
VERIFY
DATASET
CLUSTER
ALTERNATEINDEX
base cluster
NAME
VOLUME
primary amount
secondary amount
RECORDSIZE
FREESPACE

control interval	PATHENTRY
control area	UPDATE
INDEXED	NOUPDATE
data organization parameter	INDATASET
NUMBERED	OUTDATASET
NONINDEXED	allocation status
KEYS	condition code
UNIQUE	AIXBLD
SUBALLOCATION	ENTRY
RELATE	INFILE
NONUNIQUEKEY	OUTFILE
UNIQUEKEY	prefix
UPGRADE	

VSAM stands for **Virtual Storage Access Method.** It is an IBM system that can be used to organize files and carry out input and output functions for programs running under **OS/VS (Operating System/Virtual Storage)** and **DOS/** VS (**Disk Operating System**/Virtual Storage). VSAM provides high-speed retrieval and storage of data, several different ways to protect files by using passwords, and device independence. VSAM is used only with IBM systems. If your school has computing equipment of some other manufacturer, you can skip this chapter.

IBM COBOL II, which was used to run most of the programs in this book, has the ability to process the following four types of files:

1. VSAM indexed files
2. VSAM relative files
3. VSAM sequential files
4. **Physical sequential** files (ordinary OS files)

All the sequential files used in this book are physical sequential. If you wish instead to use VSAM sequential files, you must include the letters AS before the ddname in the ASSIGN clause for the file. For example, you might have:

```
SELECT ACCOUNT-MASTER-FILE-IN ASSIGN TO AS-MSTRIN
```

All VSAM files must be on direct-access storage devices. A VSAM sequential file is called an **entry-sequenced data set.** A VSAM indexed file is called a **key-sequenced data set.** And a VSAM relative file is called a **relative-record data set.**

References

To establish and use VSAM files you must have the proper reference materials. This chapter can serve only as an introduction to VSAM to help you understand the relevant IBM manuals. The following five manuals are absolutely essential if you wish to use VSAM files with COBOL:

1. IBM VS COBOL II Application Programming Language Reference, Order No. GC26-4047

2. IBM VS COBOL II Application Programming Guide, Order No. SC26-4045
3. OS/VS1 Access Method Services, Order No. GC26-3840
   or
   OS/VS2 Access Method Services, Order No. GC26-3841
4. OS/VS Virtual Storage Access Method (VSAM) Programmer's Guide, Order No. GC26-3838
5. OS/VS Message Library: VS1 System Messages, Order No. GC38-1001
   or
   OS/VS Message Library: VS2 System Messages, Order No. GC38-1002

You will have to find out whether your school uses **VS1** or **VS2** in order to know which manuals are appropriate.

This chapter assumes that you have some experience with OS JCL, and that you have created, cataloged, and deleted at least one OS file at your school. If not, you may find that you are unable to understand some parts of this chapter. The programming examples given here are very complete, however, and may provide you with all the JCL you need to use VSAM files with COBOL.

These examples show what works at my school. Your school may have different requirements and conventions, and so the coding that worked for me may have to be modified slightly to work in your installation. Your instructor can provide you with the details you need.

Access Method Services

Access Method Services is the name of a big IBM utility program that creates VSAM files and carries out many useful functions in connection with them. Access Method Services is the only program that can create a VSAM file. This is a radical departure from file-handling techniques in existence before VSAM. In older systems, a new file could be created by a COBOL program and the proper JCL by simply OPENing the file as OUTPUT. With VSAM files, however, Access Method Services must first create a file with no records in it, called an **unloaded** file, and then a COBOL program can place records into the file by OPENing it as OUTPUT.

You get Access Method Services to do what you want by giving it one or more **commands.** You will see descriptions and examples of some important Access Method Services commands later in this chapter. The commands are described in complete detail in reference number 3 above.

The command you use to create a VSAM file is the **DEFINE** command. When a DEFINE command executes, Access Method Services reserves space for the file on a direct-access storage device and enters information about the file into the appropriate VSAM catalog. VSAM catalogs are separate from the OS catalogs. Every VSAM file must be cataloged in one of the VSAM catalogs. NonVSAM files may be cataloged in an OS catalog or a VSAM catalog, or not cataloged.

When a file is first DEFINEd, Access Method Services catalogs the file with no extra effort on the part of the programmer. Later, when the file is used, VSAM automatically keeps the catalog information current. One important piece of information contained in a VSAM catalog entry is the amount of space currently occupied by records in the file. Each time a file is CLOSEd, VSAM determines the amount of space occupied in the file and updates the catalog entry to reflect that information. So beware, if for any reason one of your VSAM files does not get CLOSEd, the catalog entry may not be correct and there will be trouble in store when you later try to use the file. You will soon see a simple way to remedy that difficulty.

VSAM Catalogs

An installation can have any number of VSAM catalogs. Each installation must have exactly one **master catalog,** and it may also have one or more **user catalogs.** In most installations the catalogs are established and named by the systems programmers, so a COBOL programmer (you) need not worry about creating one. A VSAM file may be cataloged in the master catalog or in one of the user catalogs.

All of my VSAM files were cataloged in a user catalog named USERCAT. If you are required to know the name of any user catalog you might be using, write it here:

____

You will have to find out whether there are any rules for naming files in your installation. In the installation where I ran the programs in this book all of my file names had to be of the form:

```
VSAM.NY.GSP.xxxxxxxx
```

where xxxxxxxx stands for any legal name. When you see the programming examples later in this chapter, you will see the file names that I used. The file-naming rules that apply to me almost certainly will not apply to you. You will have to find what file-naming rules apply at your school and use them. You can use the following space to write in the required form of the names of your files, if any:

____

____

JCL with VSAM

The JCL used with VSAM is usually very simple. Since all VSAM files used by any COBOL program have already been created and cataloged, the JCL for most VSAM files has the form:

```
//ddname DD DSN=datasetname,DISP=OLD
```

You may instead specify DISP=SHR if sharing is allowed. No further information is needed in the JCL. A disposition of KEEP is implied for all VSAM files and need not be coded. If you should want to DELETE a file, there is no use putting DELETE in the DISP parameter. Only Access Method Services can delete a VSAM file. You must not specify DISP=NEW under any conditions, even if you are using a VSAM file for the first time. If you do, OS will allocate space for the file and the space will not be available to VSAM.

Sometimes it is necessary to include UNIT and VOL parameters in the JCL for a VSAM file. When we look at the programming examples, you will see when those parameters are needed. Of course, OS ordinarily would not examine any catalog entries when UNIT and VOL are given in the JCL, and would thus not know that the file being described is a VSAM file. So whenever you have to use UNIT and VOL in a DD statement, you must also include the parameter AMP='AMORG' to tell OS that this is a VSAM file. The form of the JCL for a VSAM file with the UNIT and VOL parameters is:

```
//ddname DD DSN=datasetname,DISP=OLD,UNIT=unit,VOL=volume,AMP='AMORG'
```

Whenever you use UNIT and VOL, if your file is cataloged in one of the user catalogs, you must tell the system which catalog. There are two statements you can use to tell the system which user catalog your file is cataloged in—the **JOBCAT** statement and the **STEPCAT** statement. An example of a JOBCAT statement specifying a user catalog named USERCAT is:

```
//JOBCAT DD DSN=USERCAT,DISP=SHR
```

An example of a STEPCAT statement is:

```
//STEPCAT DD DSN=USERCAT,DISP=SHR
```

The DISP parameter can also be specified as OLD if sharing is not wanted. The JOBCAT statement tells the system what user catalog is to be used for the entire job. A STEPCAT statement tells the system what user catalog is to be used for a single job step. When both JOBCAT and STEPCAT are specified, the catalog specified by STEPCAT is used for the job step. If your file is cataloged in the master catalog, you never have to indicate that explicitly to the system, and so you can omit JOBCAT and STEPCAT statements.

A JOBCAT statement, if used, is placed after the JOB statement and before the first EXEC statement. Each STEPCAT statement used is placed immediately after the EXEC statement of the step to which it applies.

The installation at my school does not permit the use of JOBCAT and STEPCAT statements because they interfere with the operation of other systems in use here. I can instead designate a user catalog for only a single procedure step by including the following kind of DD statement, with any legal ddname, among the DD statements for that procedure step:

```
//procstepname.anyname DD DSN=VSAM.CATALOG,DISP=SHR
```

To get Access Method Services to run, you must have an EXEC statement of the form:

```
//stepname EXEC PGM=IDCAMS
```

For its message output file Access Method Services needs the DD statement

```
//SYSPRINT DD SYSOUT=A
```

and a DD statement for its input file, which contains the commands to be executed. If the input file is in the input stream, the DD statement is:

```
//SYSIN DD *
```

Usually no other JCL is needed to run Access Method Services.

Access Method Services Commands

In this section we will briefly describe some of the important Access Method Services commands, most of which are used in the programming examples later in the chapter. When we look at the examples, each of the parameters used in each command will be fully explained.

DEFINE

As mentioned earlier, the DEFINE command is used to create a file. The DEFINE command must also be used to reserve direct-access storage space for **alternate indexes,** in connection with ALTERNATE RECORD KEYs in indexed files. When an ALTERNATE RECORD KEY is used, it is also necessary to DEFINE something called a **PATH.** You will see what the PATH is used for when we look at the programming examples. Each ALTERNATE RECORD KEY in an indexed file requires its own alternate index file and at least one PATH.

In the DEFINE command you assign a name to the file or PATH being DEFINEd. You also say how much direct-access storage space is required for the file being DEFINEd (a PATH occupies no storage space). You may specify the space requirement as a certain number of RECORDS, TRACKS, or **CYLINDERS**. You must also say what VOLUME or VOLUMES the file is to reside on.

In the DEFINE command, you tell Access Method Services whether the file is to be sequential, indexed, or relative. If it is to be indexed, then you must provide Access Method Services with additional information, including the size of the prime RECORD KEY and its location in the record. You must also provide similar information about ALTERNATE RECORD KEYs when you DEFINE the alternate indexes.

The DEFINE command has many optional parameters that can be used to improve the speed efficiency of VSAM's record storage and retrieval. We refrain from using them in the programming examples in the interest of programming simplicity and because our files are so small.

The DEFINE command can be used to assign a password to a file and/or its index, and to assign names to the **data component** and **index component** of an indexed file if desired.

DELETE

The DELETE command is used to free direct-access storage space used for a file or an alternate index and to remove from the catalog the entries relating to those objects or to a PATH. Optionally you can have Access Method Services simply release storage space so that it can be used by another file, or actually erase the contents of the storage, presumably for security purposes.

BLDINDEX

The **BLDINDEX** command is used with indexed files to construct alternate indexes in connection with ALTERNATE RECORD KEYs. There are two ways to create an alternate index—the programmer may give the BLDINDEX command or may let Access Method Services do it. The method in which the programmer gives the BLDINDEX command is more efficient in that it uses less virtual storage in its execution and generally runs faster. The other method complies with the ANSI standard. Both methods are shown in the programming examples dealing with the indexed file.

In the first method the programmer first DEFINEs the indexed file, then runs a COBOL program to load the file with records (such as Program P15-01), then DEFINEs the alternate index and its PATH, and then gives the BLDINDEX command to direct Access Method Services to build the alternate index using the data in the indexed file. It is during the building of the alternate index that Access Method Services can detect the presence of duplicate ALTERNATE RECORD KEY values, after the indexed file has already been completely loaded with records.

The ANSI standard, on the other hand, requires that duplicate values of ALTERNATE RECORD KEYs be detected during, not after, the loading of the indexed file. For this reason a less efficient method, in which the programmer does not give the BLDINDEX command, has been provided for those who need such processing. In Program P15-01 we did not need to detect duplicate values of the ALTERNATE RECORD KEY and so were able to use the first method. Both will be shown shortly, however.

ALTER

It is possible, after a file has been DEFINEd, to change its description in the catalog. The particular descriptors that can be **ALTERed** depend on what kind of file has been DEFINEd and which attributes have been permitted to assume their default values.

PRINT

The **PRINT** command allows Access Method Services to list out the contents of all records in a file or just selected records. The records may be listed in character form, in hexadecimal, or in both character and hexadecimal.

LISTCAT

The **LISTCAT** command allows Access Method Services to print the catalog entries for VSAM files. You may request that the entire catalog entry for a certain file be printed, or you may request that only certain parts of the catalog entry be printed.

The LISTCAT command also allows you to request catalog information for a whole group of files with similar names. For example, you could request that the catalog entries for all files whose names begin with VSAM.NY.GSP be printed.

VERIFY

The **VERIFY** command causes Access Method Services to check that the catalog entries for a file agree with the actual state of the file. Access Method Services does this by examining the file and then making any necessary corrections in the catalog. VERIFY then CLOSEs the file, if it is not already CLOSEd.

You may use the VERIFY command if you suspect or know that a VSAM file was not CLOSEd after its last use. There is no harm in using VERIFY freely before any attempt to OPEN a VSAM file.

An example of a VERIFY command, using the reserved word **DATASET,** is:

```
VERIFY DATASET(VSAM.NY.GSP.IMSTR)
```

Creating an Indexed File

This part of the chapter shows how to create the indexed file and the alternate index file and PATH for the programs in Chapter 15. Some of the conventions that are in force in my installation might be different from the ones in yours. Therefore, the Access Method Services commands that work for me might not be exactly what you need. I will explain each of the commands that I used and each parameter in each command, but if you need or want to use others (like passwords or the optional parameters that improve efficiency), see reference 3 on page 671. First we will look at a typical input stream, which might be usable at most schools, and then at the input stream I used.

A typical input stream for Program P15-01 is shown in Figure 17.1. The JOBCAT statement indicates that all files created in this run are to be cataloged in the user catalog USERCAT. If your installation does not require you to specify the user catalog, or if your files are to be cataloged in the master catalog, you should omit the JOBCAT statement. The first EXEC statement, with stepname IDCAMS1, executes Access Method Services. You can see the use of the //SYSPRINT and //SYSIN statements for Access Method Services.

Defining the Indexed File

The first command to Access Method Services is DEFINE **CLUSTER**. Commands must be written in positions 2 through 72. For an indexed file a CLUSTER consists of the file and its index. Later I will DEFINE **ALTERNATEINDEX** and DEFINE PATH for this indexed file. Once an alternate index and a PATH are established, the original CLUSTER created with this DEFINE CLUSTER command is referred to as the **base cluster.**

FIGURE *17.1* Typical input stream to create an indexed file and alternate index

```
//GSPNY438 JOB 'P15X01',REGION=1120K
//JOBCAT DD DSN=USERCAT,DISP=SHR
//IDCAMS1 EXEC PGM=IDCAMS
//SYSPRINT DD SYSOUT=A
//SYSIN    DD *
    DEFINE CLUSTER -
           (NAME(VSAM.NY.GSP.IMSTR) -
           VOLUME(CNY005) -
           RECORDS(100 10) -
           RECORDSIZE(39 39) -
           FREESPACE(25 10) -
           INDEXED -
           KEYS(5 0))
/*
//COBOL1 EXEC COBUCG
//SYSIN DD *
00010  IDENTIFICATION DIVISION.
00020  PROGRAM-ID.  P15-01.
              .
              .
              .
```

FIGURE 17.1 *continued*

```
    COBOL SOURCE PROGRAM
              .
              .
              .
//GO.PRINTER1 DD SYSOUT=A
//GO.PRINTER2 DD SYSOUT=A
//GO.DISKOUT DD DSN=VSAM.NY.GSP.IMSTR,DISP=OLD,
// UNIT=SYSDA,VOL=SER=CNY005,AMP='AMORG'
//GO.SORTWK01 DD UNIT=SYSDA,VOL=SER=SCR001,
//    SPACE=(TRK,(2),,CONTIG)
//GO.SORTWK02 DD UNIT=SYSDA,VOL=SER=SCR001,
//    SPACE=(TRK,(2),,CONTIG)
//GO.SORTWK03 DD UNIT=SYSDA,VOL=SER=SCR001,
//    SPACE=(TRK,(2),,CONTIG)
//GO.SORTLIB DD DSN=SYS1.SORTLIB,DISP=SHR
//GO.SYSOUT DD SYSOUT=A
//GO.INFILE DD *
              .
              .
              .

    INPUT DATA FOR PROGRAM P15-01
              .
              .
              .
//IDCAMS2 EXEC PGM=IDCAMS
//SYSPRINT DD SYSOUT=A
//SYSIN DD *
    DEFINE ALTERNATEINDEX -
           (NAME(VSAM.NY.GSP.IMSTR.ALTIX) -
           RELATE(VSAM.NY.GSP.IMSTR) -
           VOLUME(CNY008) -
           RECORDSIZE(35 75) -
           FREESPACE(25 10) -
           RECORDS(100 10) -
           KEYS(20 5) -
           NONUNIQUEKEY UPGRADE)
    DEFINE PATH -
           (NAME(VSAM.NY.GSP.IMSTR.ALTPATH) -
           PATHENTRY(VSAM.NY.GSP.IMSTR.ALTIX) -
           UPDATE)
    BLDINDEX INDATASET(VSAM.NY.GSP.IMSTR) -
              OUTDATASET(VSAM.NY.GSP.IMSTR.ALTIX)
/*
//
```

This long DEFINE command shows the use of the continuation indicator, the dash. When used, the dash must be the last character on the line except for trailing blanks. Following the word CLUSTER are a number of parameters enclosed in one set of parentheses. You must give the **NAME** of the file and the **VOLUME** on which it is to reside. Just as you will have to make up a suitable name for your own file (my file name may not work in your installation), you will also have to provide a correct VOLUME (you probably don't have a VOLUME called CNY005 in your installation). You will have to find out what VOLUMEs are used for VSAM files in your installation. You can write them here:

____

____

The file size must be given, in numbers of RECORDS, TRACKS, or CYLINDERS. I used RECORDS. The file size can be specified as a **primary amount** and a **secondary amount.** The primary amount specifies the initial amount of space that is to be allocated to the CLUSTER. The secondary amount specifies the amount of space that is to be allocated each time the CLUSTER extends. Here I allowed for a primary amount of 100 Account Numbers.

The **RECORDSIZE** parameter specifies the average size of the records to be placed in the file and the maximum size, in bytes. In our indexed file, the records are fixed-length, 39-byte records, so the average and maximum size are both given as 39. If this parameter is omitted, Access Method Services assumes a RECORDSIZE of 4089 bytes.

The **FREESPACE** parameter tells Access Method Services how much unoccupied file space to provide and where in the file it should be. The empty file space is useful if records in the indexed file later have to be rearranged, as when new records are randomly inserted into the file. The FREESPACE parameter specifies the percentage of unused space that Access Method Services is to allocate in each **control interval** and each **control area** in the file. A control interval is the number of bytes that is read or written by VSAM at one time, and is always a multiple of 512. A control area is usually one cylinder, although under certain conditions it can be less than one cylinder. A control area can never be larger than one cylinder. Here we are asking that 25% of each control interval and 10% of each control area be left unoccupied when the file is initially loaded with records. If the FREESPACE parameter is omitted, Access Method Services allocates no free space.

The next parameter says that this is an **INDEXED** file. Other **data organization parameters** that may be specified are **NUMBERED** for a relative file and **NONINDEXED** for a sequential file. If no data organization parameter is given, INDEXED is assumed.

The **KEYS** parameter allows the programmer to specify the size of the prime RECORD KEY, in bytes, and its location in the record. In our case the prime RECORD KEY, Account Number, is 5 bytes long and starts in position 1 of the record. Position 1 is indicated with a KEYS parameter of 0. If KEYS is omitted, a 64-byte key starting at the beginning of the record is assumed.

The **UNIQUE** attribute is required in some installations, but not in mine. If UNIQUE is required in your installation, you can include it anywhere, as for example:

```
UNIQUE KEYS(5 0))
```

The opposite of UNIQUE is **SUBALLOCATION**. If this parameter is omitted, SUBALLOCATION is assumed. Notice the closing parenthesis that matches the parenthesis before the NAME parameter.

Thus the file VSAM.NY.GSP.IMSTR is established. Program P15-01 then places records into it.

JCL for Execution of Program P15-01

In the JCL for the GO step, you can find the usual statements for the output printer file and the input data file

```
//GO.PRINTER DD SYSOUT=A
```

and

```
//GO.INFILE DD *
```

Notice the DD statement for the output VSAM master file:

```
//GO.DISKOUT DD DSN=VSAM.NY.GSP.IMSTR,DISP=OLD,
// UNIT=SYSDA,VOL=SER=CNY005,AMP='AMORG'
```

The DISP parameter must be OLD, for OLD is always required with VSAM files. But when this job is first run, there is no file with the name VSAM.NY.GSP.IMSTR. It is not OLD. It does not exist.

To prevent the JCL interpreter from examining any catalogs at the very beginning of the run to see whether the file is OLD, we must include UNIT and VOL parameters. As mentioned earlier, whenever you have to include UNIT and VOL, you must also include AMP='AMORG' to tell the system that this is a VSAM file. By the time we get to execute this step, the file will be OLD. It already will have been created by Access Method Services.

Under no circumstances should you specify DISP=NEW. DISP=NEW will satisfy the JCL interpreter, but does not work with VSAM files.

The remaining JCL statements for the GO step are sometimes needed when a SORT statement is used in a COBOL program, as is done in Program P15-01. These are ordinary OS DD statements.

After the CLUSTER VSAM.NY.GSP.IMSTR is loaded, we can DEFINE the alternate index and its PATH, and build the alternate index. All of that is done with another execution of Access Method Services, in the step IDCAMS2.

Defining the Alternate Index

Here we reserve direct-access storage space for the alternate index by saying DEFINE ALTERNATEINDEX. Following the word ALTERNATEINDEX in the DEFINE command are a number of parameters enclosed in one set of parentheses. First, a NAME must be given for the alternate index. This can be any legal made-up NAME and need have no special relationship to the NAME of the base cluster. The **RELATE** parameter must name the base cluster of which this is an alternate index. The VOLUME parameter names the volume on which the alternate index file is to reside. Here I specified CNY008 as the VOLUME. This shows that the alternate index can be on a different VOLUME from the CLUSTER that it is related to. You would of course specify a VOLUME that is legal in your installation, instead of CNY008.

The UNIQUE attribute may be required for an alternate index in your installation. If so, you can include it anywhere, as for a CLUSTER. For example, you could have

```
UNIQUE VOLUME(CNY008) -
```

An alternate index file is itself organized as an indexed file. The programmer must DEFINE a separate alternate index for each ALTERNATE RECORD KEY in the indexed file. Remember that the DEFINE command only reserves file space. Access Method Services builds the alternate index(es) later, when we give the BLDINDEX command. Here is how Access Method Services would build one alternate index:

1. It goes through the base cluster, extracting from each record the prime RECORD KEY and the ALTERNATE RECORD KEY. In this case it would extract the Account Number and the Depositor Name. It builds a small record containing each Depositor Name and its corresponding Account Number.
2. It sorts the small records on the ALTERNATE RECORD KEY, in this case, Depositor Name. If there is not enough internal virtual storage for the sort, the programmer must provide work files. In our case the amount of data to be sorted was so small that it was sorted internally.
3. It builds an alternate index file in ascending order on the ALTERNATE RECORD KEY from the small sorted records. If duplicate values of the ALTERNATE RECORD KEY are not allowed and more than one record contains the same ALTERNATE RECORD KEY value, processing terminates with an error message.

If the ALTERNATE RECORD KEY is defined WITH DUPLICATES, as ours is, then Access Method Services may have to reformat some of the records. Access Methods Services finds whether there are any small records with duplicate values of the ALTERNATE RECORD KEY and if there are it puts them together into a single record. In our case, if there is more than one record with the same Depositor Name, it means that a depositor has more than one account. Access Method Services will construct an alternate index record consisting of the Depositor Name and all its Account Numbers. It then constructs the alternate index file. So the alternate index contains exactly one record for each Depositor Name, and each record contains all the Account Numbers for that Depositor Name. A record in the alternate index is as large as the size of the Depositor Name, plus the size of all the Account Numbers for that Depositor Name, plus 5. The 5 is a constant that applies to all records in all alternate index files.

In the RECORDSIZE parameter we may tell Access Method Services what we guess the average and maximum sizes of the records in the alternate index file will be. If we guess that no depositor will have more than 10 accounts, the largest record in the alternate index file will be the size of the Depositor Name field (20 characters), plus 10 times the size of the Account Number field (10 times 5, or 50), plus 5, a total of 75. If any depositor has more than 10 accounts, only 10 Account Numbers would be entered in the alternate index for that depositor. BLDINDEX would continue to execute and would print a message giving the number of excess Account Numbers not entered in the alternate index. Subsequent processing of the erroneous index entry by a COBOL program may cause the COBOL program to execute incorrectly.

If we guess that the average number of accounts that a depositor may have is 2, the average record size will be 20 plus 10 plus 5, or 35. This guess need not be precise. VSAM can extend the alternate index file as necessary to absorb some of the inaccuracy in the guess. If the guess is much too small, however, VSAM will not be able to extend the file enough times to accommodate all the records needed. If the guess is much too large, Access Method Services will reserve an unnecessarily large amount of direct-access space when it first establishes the file, and you may run into trouble with the space limitations in your installation. Each program and programmer must operate within the space limitations established by the installation.

One way to avoid having to guess at the average and maximum number of prime record keys associated with a given value of an alternate key is to define the data record so that the alternate key field is immediately to the left of the prime key field. Then designate as the ALTERNATE KEY the combination of the alternate key and the prime key in the record. To implement this method in our savings-account master file, we would define the master record as follows:

```
01   ACCOUNT-MASTER-RECORD.
     05 ALTERNATE-KEY.
        10 DEPOSITOR-NAME-M          PIC X(20).
        10 ACCOUNT-NUMBER-M          PIC X(5).
     05 DATE-OF-LAST-TRANSACTION     PIC 9(6).
     05 CURRENT-BALANCE-M            PIC S9(6)V99.
```

Then in the Environment Division we would have:

```
RECORD KEY IS ACCOUNT-NUMBER-M
ALTERNATE RECORD KEY IS ALTERNATE-KEY
```

There would be no WITH DUPLICATES phrase, even if a depositor has more than one account, for the combination of Depositor Name and Account Number is unique. The size of every record in the alternate index file would be equal to the sum of the size of the ALTERNATE-KEY (now 25), the size of the prime key (5), and 5, or 35. This method can be used only when the record contains exactly one alternate key field.

In the DEFINE command, the FREESPACE parameter tells Access Method Services what percentage of unoccupied space to leave in each control interval and each control area when the alternate index is initially constructed. The free space will be needed if records must be moved around later when new Depositor Names are added to the file. The size of the alternate index file must be given in RECORDS, TRACKS, or CYLINDERS. Here I allowed for a primary amount of 100 Depositor Names.

The KEYS parameter allows the programmer to give the size of the ALTERNATE RECORD KEY and its location in the data record in the base cluster. Our Depositor Name is 20 characters long and starts in position 6, so we have KEYS (20 5). The **NONUNIQUEKEY** attribute tells Access Method Services that the ALTERNATE RECORD KEY was defined WITH DUPLICATES in the COBOL program. If the ALTERNATE RECORD KEY had not been defined WITH DUPLICATES, I would have had to say **UNIQUEKEY** here instead. If this attribute is omitted, NONUNIQUEKEY is assumed.

The **UPGRADE** attribute tells Access Method Services that this alternate index is to be kept up-to-date with the base cluster VSAM.NY.GSP.IMSTR. When you use VSAM with COBOL, an alternate index must always be kept up-to-date with the CLUSTER to which it is RELATEd, although in VSAM with Assembler Language it need not be so. UPGRADE tells VSAM that if the base cluster is modified in any way, with additions, changes, or deletions, VSAM should change the alternate index to reflect the modifications. Notice the closing parenthesis following the word UPGRADE. It matches the opening parenthesis before the word NAME.

Defining the PATH

We now DEFINE a PATH for the alternate index. Following the word PATH we have only three parameters enclosed in a set of parentheses. First we give a name for the PATH. The NAME can be any legal name and need not have any relationship to the NAMEs of either the alternate index or the CLUSTER. In the parameter **PATHENTRY** we give the name of the alternate index of which this is a PATH. We then give the **UPDATE** attribute. The UPDATE attribute tells Access Method Services that this PATH will be used with some program that UPDATEs the base cluster. To DEFINE a PATH for a program that does not update the base cluster, you would specify **NOUPDATE** instead. A PATH that is DEFINEd with UPDATE can also be used with a program that does not update the base cluster. You may DEFINE as many PATHs as you like with an alternate index.

We are now ready to build the alternate index.

Building the Alternate Index

As you can see, the BLDINDEX command is simplicity itself. You tell Access Method Services the name of the **INDATASET,** the name of the base cluster from which the alternate index is to be built. Then you tell it the name of the **OUTDATASET,** the name of the alternate index file already DEFINEd. If the indexed file has been defined in the COBOL program with more than one ALTERNATE RECORD KEY, you may build all the required alternate indexes with a single BLDINDEX command by giving the names of all the alternate indexes in the OUTDATASET parameter. For example:

```
OUTDATASET (VSAM.NY.GSP.IMSTR.NAMEIX -
            VSAM.NY.GSP.IMSTR.BALIX -
            VSAM.NY.GSP.IMSTR.DATEIX)
```

Access Method Services Output

The output produced by Access Method Services for the step IDCAMS1 is shown in Figure 17.2. There you can see the original DEFINE CLUSTER command, and the messages from Access Method Services telling us what it did. First, the **allocation status** is given for the data component and the index component of the file. An allocation status of 0 indicates success.

Access Method Services then shows us the long and funny names it generated for the data component and the index component. The names contain the date and time that the CLUSTER was created. If you want to give your own names to data and index components, you can do so when you DEFINE them.

Following the messages about the names is the message FUNCTION COMPLETED. A **condition code** of 0 signals a perfect, clean execution of the command. The other possible condition codes you can get have the following meanings:

4 —Warning message; successful execution is probable.

8 —Serious error, but processing is completed.

12—Terminating error; processing of the command is terminated.

FIGURE 17.2 Output from step IDCAMS 1

```
IDCAMS   SYSTEM SERVICES                                              TIME: 23:27:28

    DEFINE CLUSTER -
           (NAME(VSAM.NY.GSP.IMSTR) -
           VOLUME(CNY005) -
           RECORDS(100 10) -
           RECORDSIZE(39 39) -
           FREESPACE(25 10) -
           INDEXED -
           KEYS(5 0))

IDC0508I DATA ALLOCATION STATUS FOR VOLUME CNY005 IS 0

IDC0509I INDEX ALLOCATION STATUS FOR VOLUME CNY005 IS 0

IDC0512I NAME GENERATED-(D) VSAM.TDCA8768.VDD91255.TA47CFA0

IDC0512I NAME GENERATED-(I) VSAM.TDCA8EF8.VID91255.TA47CFA0

IDC0001I FUNCTION COMPLETED, HIGHEST CONDITION CODE WAS 0


IDC0002I IDCAMS PROCESSING COMPLETE. MAXIMUM CONDITION CODE WAS 0
```

The Access Method Services output from step IDCAMS2 is shown in Figure 17.3. There you can see the original DEFINE ALTERNATEINDEX command and its results. The data component and index component both were allocated space on VOLUME CNY008 and had names made up for them.

The DEFINE PATH command allocates no storage space, for a PATH occupies none. The BUILDINDEX command is seen to have executed successfully.

FIGURE 17.3 **Output from step IDCAMS2**

```
IDCAMS  SYSTEM SERVICES                                          TIME: 23:27:50

    DEFINE ALTERNATEINDEX -
           (NAME(VSAM.NY.GSP.IMSTR.ALTIX) -
           RELATE(VSAM.NY.GSP.IMSTR) -
           VOLUME(CNY008) -
           FREESPACE(25 10) -
           RECORDS(100 10) -
           KEYS(20 5) -
           RECORDSIZE(35 75) -
           NONUNIQUEKEY UPGRADE)

IDC0508I DATA ALLOCATION STATUS FOR VOLUME CNY008 IS 0

IDC0509I INDEX ALLOCATION STATUS FOR VOLUME CNY008 IS 0

IDC0512I NAME GENERATED-(D) VSAM.T219E0A8.VDD91255.TA47CFA2

IDC0512I NAME GENERATED-(I) VSAM.T219E828.VID91255.TA47CFA2

IDC0001I FUNCTION COMPLETED, HIGHEST CONDITION CODE WAS 0


    DEFINE PATH -
           (NAME(VSAM.NY.GSP.IMSTR.ALTPATH) -
           PATHENTRY(VSAM.NY.GSP.IMSTR.ALTIX) -
           UPDATE)

IDC0001I FUNCTION COMPLETED, HIGHEST CONDITION CODE WAS 0


    BLDINDEX INDATASET(VSAM.NY.GSP.IMSTR) -
             OUTDATASET(VSAM.NY.GSP.IMSTR.ALTIX)

IDC0652I VSAM.NY.GSP.IMSTR.ALTIX SUCCESSFULLY BUILT

IDC0001I FUNCTION COMPLETED, HIGHEST CONDITION CODE WAS 0


IDC0002I IDCAMS PROCESSING COMPLETE. MAXIMUM CONDITION CODE WAS 0
```

Creating an Indexed File at CUNY

Figure 17.4 shows the input stream I used to create a VSAM indexed file at my school. It differs from the input stream shown in Figure 17.1 because the conventions here are different from those at other schools.

I have no job name in my JOB statement, for the remote job entry system I use creates and inserts the job name. I have no JOBCAT statement, for it is forbidden in my installation. Instead, I have the DD statement

```
//GO.ANYNAME DD VSAM.CATALOG,DISP=SHR
```

in the procedure step where it is needed. In my EXEC statement for the step COBOL1, I have procedure name COB2CG, for COB2 is the name for the 1985-standard IBM COBOL compiler in my installation, and I have PARM.COB=(QUOTE,FDUMP), which I need to get my system to accept the quote symbol as the delimiter surrounding nonnumeric literals and produce a conveniently formatted dump in case of abnormal run termination. And finally, I have no need for any of the job control statements relating to the SORT, for the sort system in my installation provides its own work areas.

FIGURE 17.4 **Input stream to create an indexed file and alternate index at CUNY**

```
// JOB 'P15X01',REGION=1120K
//IDCAMS1 EXEC PGM=IDCAMS
//SYSPRINT DD SYSOUT=A
//SYSIN    DD *
    DEFINE CLUSTER -
           (NAME(VSAM.NY.GSP.IMSTR) -
           VOLUME(CNY005) -
           RECORDS(100 10) -
           RECORDSIZE(39 39) -
           FREESPACE(25 10) -
           INDEXED -
           KEYS(5 0))
/*
//COBOL1 EXEC COB2CG,PARM.COB=(QUOTE,FDUMP)
//SYSIN DD *
00010  IDENTIFICATION DIVISION.
00020  PROGRAM-ID.  P15-01.
            .
            .
            .

    COBOL SOURCE PROGRAM
            .
            .
            .
//GO.ANYNAME DD DSN=VSAM.CATALOG,DISP=SHR
//GO.PRINTER1 DD SYSOUT=A
//GO.PRINTER2 DD SYSOUT=A
//GO.DISKOUT DD DSN=VSAM.NY.GSP.IMSTR,DISP=OLD,
// UNIT=SYSDA,VOL=SER=CNY005,AMP='AMORG'
//GO.INFILE DD *
            .
            .
            .

    INPUT DATA FOR PROGRAM P15-01
            .
            .
            .
//IDCAMS2 EXEC PGM=IDCAMS
//SYSPRINT DD SYSOUT=A
//SYSIN DD *
    DEFINE ALTERNATEINDEX -
           (NAME(VSAM.NY.GSP.IMSTR.ALTIX) -
           RELATE(VSAM.NY.GSP.IMSTR) -
           VOLUME(CNY008) -
           RECORDSIZE(35 75) -
           FREESPACE(25 10) -
           RECORDS(100 10) -
           KEYS(20 5) -
           NONUNIQUEKEY UPGRADE)
    DEFINE PATH -
           (NAME(VSAM.NY.GSP.IMSTR.ALTPATH) -
           PATHENTRY(VSAM.NY.GSP.IMSTR.ALTIX) -
           UPDATE)
    BLDINDEX INDATASET(VSAM.NY.GSP.IMSTR) -
             OUTDATASET(VSAM.NY.GSP.IMSTR.ALTIX)
/*
//
```

Using an Indexed File

A typical input stream for Program P15-02 is shown in Figure 17.5. This is the program that updates the indexed file created by Program P15-01. In the GO step you can find the usual DD statements for RECORDIN and the PRINTERs.

FIGURE 17.5 **Typical input stream to update an indexed file having an alternate index**

```
//GSPNY452 JOB 'P15X02'
// EXEC COBUCG
//SYSIN DD *
00010  IDENTIFICATION DIVISION.
00020  PROGRAM-ID.  P15-02.
             .
             .
             .

    COBOL SOURCE PROGRAM
             .
             .
             .
//GO.PRINTER1 DD SYSOUT=A
//GO.PRINTER2 DD SYSOUT=A
//GO.MSTRDISK DD DSN=VSAM.NY.GSP.IMSTR,DISP=OLD
//GO.MSTRDIS1 DD DSN=VSAM.NY.GSP.IMSTR.ALTPATH,DISP=OLD
//GO.INFILE DD *
             .
             .
             .

    INPUT DATA FOR PROGRAM P15-02
             .
             .
             .
/*
//
```

There is also a DD statement for the master file:

```
//GO.MSTRDISK DD DSN=VSAM.NY.GSP.IMSTR,DISP=OLD
```

Now, if an indexed file is defined with one or more ALTERNATE RECORD KEYs, each alternate index PATH must have its own DD statement. If there is only one ALTERNATE RECORD KEY, as in this case, the ddname for the alternate PATH must be formed by attaching the number 1 onto the end of the ddname for the base cluster. So in our case, we would attach the number 1 on to the end of the ddname MSTRDISK. But if the combination of the ddname and the number exceeds eight characters, the ddname must be truncated on the right end so that the combination is just eight characters long. Thus the ddname for the alternate PATH is MSTRDIS1 as shown in the DD statement:

```
//GO.MSTRDIS1 DD DSN=VSAM.NY.GSP.IMSTR.ALTPATH,DISP=OLD
```

Notice that it is the name of the alternate PATH, not the alternate index file, that is given in the DSN parameter.

If there is more than one alternate index, the ddnames for their PATHs are formed by attaching 2, 3, and so on to the end of the base cluster's ddname, in the order in which the ALTERNATE RECORD KEY clauses appear in the COBOL program.

Creating an Alternate Index with AIXBLD

As mentioned earlier, there is a way to arrange the alternate index so that VSAM can detect duplicate values of ALTERNATE RECORD KEYs while the base cluster is being initially loaded with records. To do this, the alternate index must be in existence at the time the base cluster is being loaded. But we have seen that an alternate index can be created only after its base cluster has been loaded. The remedy for this is provided by the COBOL execution-time option **AIXBLD.**

When AIXBLD is specified in the COBOL program that initially loads the base cluster, here is what COBOL does. Before executing your COBOL program, it loads the base cluster with dummy records, issues a BLDINDEX command to Access Method Services to build the alternate index with dummy entries, and then erases the dummy records from the base cluster, restoring it to its previously unloaded state.

Then the COBOL program executes and loads the base cluster. As each record is placed into the base cluster, VSAM makes an entry for it in the alternate index and can see when a duplicate value of an ALTERNATE RECORD KEY is processed.

AIXBLD provides one additional service free of charge. Before it loads the base cluster with dummy records, COBOL enters the RECORDSIZE and KEYS parameters into the catalog for the base cluster, and the KEYS parameter for the alternate index. It does this by issuing ALTER commands to Access Method Services to change the catalog entries for the base cluster and the alternate index to their correct values.

An Input Stream with AIXBLD

A typical input stream showing the use of AIXBLD is given in Figure 17.6. You can see that in one execution of Access Method Services we DEFINE the base cluster, the alternate index, and the PATH. We do not specify RECORDSIZE or KEYS parameters in the DEFINE CLUSTER command, or a KEYS parameter in the DEFINE ALTERNATEINDEX command, because AIXBLD will put them into the catalog with an ALTER command.

FIGURE 17.6 **Typical input stream showing the use of AIXBLD**

```
//GSPNY503 JOB 'AIXJOB',REGION=2376K
//JOBCAT DD DSN=USERCAT,DISP=SHR
//IDCAMS EXEC PGM=IDCAMS
//SYSPRINT DD SYSOUT=A
//SYSIN    DD *
    DELETE VSAM.NY.GSP.IMSTR2 CLUSTER
    DEFINE CLUSTER -
           (NAME(VSAM.NY.GSP.IMSTR2) -
           VOLUME(SCR001) -
           RECORDS(100 10) -
           FREESPACE(25 10) -
           INDEXED)
    DEFINE ALTERNATEINDEX -
           (NAME(VSAM.NY.GSP.IMSTR2.ALTIX2) -
           RELATE(VSAM.NY.GSP.IMSTR2) -
           VOLUME(SCR001) -
           RECORDSIZE(35 75) -
           FREESPACE(25 10) -
           RECORDS(100 10) -
           NONUNIQUEKEY UPGRADE)
    DEFINE PATH -
           (NAME(VSAM.NY.GSP.IMSTR2.ALTPATH2) -
           PATHENTRY(VSAM.NY.GSP.IMSTR2.ALTIX2) -
           UPDATE)
```

continued

FIGURE 17.6 *continued*

```
/*
//COBOL EXEC COBUCLG,PARM.COB=FDUMP,PARM.GO='/AIXBLD'
//SYSIN DD *
00010  IDENTIFICATION DIVISION.
00020  PROGRAM-ID.  P15-01.
              .
              .
              .

    COBOL SOURCE PROGRAM
              .
              .
              .
//GO.PRINTER1 DD SYSOUT=A
//GO.PRINTER2 DD SYSOUT=A
//GO.SYSPRINT DD SYSOUT=A
//GO.DISKOUT DD DSN=VSAM.NY.GSP.IMSTR2,DISP=OLD,
//   VOL=SER=SCR001,UNIT=SYSDA,AMP='AMORG'
//GO.DISKOUT1 DD DSN=VSAM.NY.GSP.IMSTR2.ALTPATH2,DISP=OLD,
// VOL=SER=SCR001,UNIT=SYSDA,AMP='AMORG'
//GO.SORTWK01 DD UNIT=SYSDA,VOL=SER=SCR001,
//    SPACE=(TRK,(2),,CONTIG)
//GO.SORTWK02 DD UNIT=SYSDA,VOL=SER=SCR001,
//    SPACE=(TRK,(2),,CONTIG)
//GO.SORTWK03 DD UNIT=SYSDA,VOL=SER=SCR001,
//    SPACE=(TRK,(2),,CONTIG)
//GO.SORTLIB DD DSN=SYS1.SORTLIB,DISP=SHR
//GO.SYSOUT DD SYSOUT=A
//GO.INFILE DD *
    INPUT DATA FOR AIXJOB
              .
              .
              .
/*
//
```

If the UNIQUE attribute is required at your school, you can include it anywhere, for example

```
UNIQUE VOLUME(SCR002) -
```

in both the DEFINE CLUSTER and DEFINE ALTERNATEINDEX commands.

Preceding the DEFINE CLUSTER command is a DELETE command. This removes any copy of VSAM.NY.GSP.IMSTR2 that might be left over from a prior run of this program. If there is no such copy, the DELETE command does no harm.

The EXEC statement with stepname COBOL shows how to use the AIXBLD option. It is included in the PARM.GO parameter, along with any other execution-time options you may be using. Here it is shown without any other execution-time options. The single quotation marks and the slash are required.

If other execution-time options are also used, such as DEBUG, they can be included along with AIXBLD. For example

```
PARM.GO='/DEBUG,AIXBLD'
```

Remember that if PARM.COB is also present in the EXEC statement, it must appear before PARM.GO.

In the GO step, we have DD statements GO.PRINTER1 and GO.PRINTER2. These are for the output from the COBOL program. We also have GO.SYSPRINT. This is for output from Access Method Services. Whenever you use AIXBLD, you must provide a SYSPRINT for the Access Method Services messages.

The DD statement for the base cluster has the ddname DISKOUT. You can see that UNIT and VOL are used, and so AMP='AMORG' is needed also. This DD statement works whether or not the base cluster VSAM.NY.GSP.IMSTR2 is in existence from a previous run. A DD statement for the alternate PATH must now be given as part of the GO step because AIXBLD needs it. You can see that the ddname for the alternate PATH VSAM.NY.GSP.IMSTR2.ALTPATH2 is made up by attaching a 1 to the end of the ddname of the base cluster. The result is DISKOUT1. Notice that DISKOUT did not have to be truncated.

Output from a Run Using AIXBLD

The output from Access Method Services for the step IDCAMs is shown in Figure 17.7. The output from the DELETE command is shown first. There was a VSAM.NY.GSP.IMSTR2 left over from some previous run, and the **ENTRY** codes tell us what type of object was DELETEd. Following the ENTRY code is the name of the DELETEd object. Some of the Access Method Services ENTRY codes are

C CLUSTER

D data component

G alternate index

I index component

R PATH

V VOLUME

U user catalog

M master catalog

A nonVSAM

The rest of the output in Figure 17.7 is entirely routine and identical in all material respects to output we have already seen.

The output from the step COBOL of course includes all the usual COBOL output, not shown here, and also includes the Access Method Services output resulting from the AIXBLD option. The Access Method Services output is shown in Figure 17.8.

In Figure 17.8 you can see the first ALTER command issued. This is to change the RECORDSIZE and KEYS parameters in the base cluster to their correct values, a RECORDSIZE of (39 39) and a KEYS parameter of (5 0). The second ALTER command corrects only the KEYS parameter of the alternate index, because Access Method Services has no way of knowing how big the records in the alternate index file will be. We guessed at that and used a RECORDSIZE parameter of (35 75) in the DEFINE ALTERNATEINDEX command. Notice that the name of the PATH, not of the alternate index file, is used in the second ALTER command.

FIGURE 17.7 **Output from step IDCAMS with AIXBLD in use**

```
IDCAMS  SYSTEM SERVICES                                                    TIME: 00:05:21

    DELETE VSAM.NY.GSP.IMSTR2 CLUSTER

IDC0550I ENTRY (R) VSAM.NY.GSP.IMSTR2.ALTPATH2 DELETED

IDC0550I ENTRY (D) VSAM.TBC3F2E0.VDD91290.TA4A7C17 DELETED

IDC0550I ENTRY (I) VSAM.TBC3FB40.VID91290.TA4A7C17 DELETED

IDC0550I ENTRY (G) VSAM.NY.GSP.IMSTR2.ALTIX2 DELETED

IDC0550I ENTRY (D) VSAM.T5D19AB0.VDD91290.TA4A7C17 DELETED

IDC0550I ENTRY (I) VSAM.T5D1A250.VID91290.TA4A7C17 DELETED

IDC0550I ENTRY (C) VSAM.NY.GSP.IMSTR2 DELETED

IDC0001I FUNCTION COMPLETED, HIGHEST CONDITION CODE WAS 0


    DEFINE CLUSTER -
           (NAME(VSAM.NY.GSP.IMSTR2) -
           VOLUME(SCR001) -
           RECORDS(100 10) -
           FREESPACE(25 10) -
           INDEXED)

IDC0508I DATA ALLOCATION STATUS FOR VOLUME SCR001 IS 0

IDC0509I INDEX ALLOCATION STATUS FOR VOLUME SCR001 IS 0

IDC0512I NAME GENERATED-(D) VSAM.TFE94960.VDD91290.TA4A7C1F

IDC0512I NAME GENERATED-(I) VSAM.TFE950F0.VID91290.TA4A7C1F

IDC0001I FUNCTION COMPLETED, HIGHEST CONDITION CODE WAS 0


    DEFINE ALTERNATEINDEX -
           (NAME(VSAM.NY.GSP.IMSTR2.ALTIX2) -
           RELATE(VSAM.NY.GSP.IMSTR2) -
           VOLUME(SCR001) -
           RECORDSIZE(35 75) -
           FREESPACE(25 10) -
           RECORDS(100 10) -
           NONUNIQUEKEY UPGRADE)

IDC0508I DATA ALLOCATION STATUS FOR VOLUME SCR001 IS 0

IDC0509I INDEX ALLOCATION STATUS FOR VOLUME SCR001 IS 0
```

FIGURE 17.7 *continued*

```
IDCAMS  SYSTEM SERVICES                                          TIME: 00:05:21

IDC0512I NAME GENERATED-(D) VSAM.T7324BF8.VDD91290.TA4A7C20

IDC0512I NAME GENERATED-(I) VSAM.T7325368.VID91290.TA4A7C20

IDC0001I FUNCTION COMPLETED, HIGHEST CONDITION CODE WAS 0

    DEFINE PATH -
           (NAME(VSAM.NY.GSP.IMSTR2.ALTPATH2) -
           PATHENTRY(VSAM.NY.GSP.IMSTR2.ALTIX2) -
           UPDATE)

IDC0001I FUNCTION COMPLETED, HIGHEST CONDITION CODE WAS 0


IDC0002I IDCAMS PROCESSING COMPLETE. MAXIMUM CONDITION CODE WAS 0
```

FIGURE 17.8 **Access Method Services output from procedure step GO with AIXBLD in use**

```
IDCAMS  SYSTEM SERVICES                                          TIME: 00:06:19

 ALTER VSAM.NY.GSP.IMSTR2                                             -
 RECORDSIZE( 00039 00039 ) KEYS( 005 00000)

IDC0531I ENTRY VSAM.NY.GSP.IMSTR2 ALTERED

IDC0001I FUNCTION COMPLETED, HIGHEST CONDITION CODE WAS 0


IDC0002I IDCAMS PROCESSING COMPLETE. MAXIMUM CONDITION CODE WAS 0


IDCAMS  SYSTEM SERVICES                                          TIME: 00:06:24

 ALTER VSAM.NY.GSP.IMSTR2.ALTPATH2                                    -
                            KEYS( 020 00005)

IDC0531I ENTRY VSAM.NY.GSP.IMSTR2.ALTPATH2 ALTERED

IDC0001I FUNCTION COMPLETED, HIGHEST CONDITION CODE WAS 0


IDC0002I IDCAMS PROCESSING COMPLETE. MAXIMUM CONDITION CODE WAS 0


IDCAMS  SYSTEM SERVICES                                          TIME: 00:06:35

 BLDINDEX INFILE( DISKOUT              ) OUTFILE( DISKOUT1          )

IDC0652I VSAM.NY.GSP.IMSTR2.ALTPATH2 SUCCESSFULLY BUILT

IDC0001I FUNCTION COMPLETED, HIGHEST CONDITION CODE WAS 0


IDC0002I IDCAMS PROCESSING COMPLETE. MAXIMUM CONDITION CODE WAS 0
```

Finally COBOL issues the BLDINDEX command. This command uses different parameters from the ones we used in the BLDINDEX command in Figure 17.1. There, we used the following:

```
INDATASET(VSAM.NY.GSP.IMSTR) -
OUTDATASET(VSAM.NY.GSP.IMSTR.ALTPATH)
```

Here, **INFILE** and **OUTFILE** are used instead of INDATASET and OUTDATASET. When you use INFILE and OUTFILE, you then use ddnames inside the parentheses instead of using the names of clusters or PATHs.

Creating a Relative File

Using Access Method Services to create a relative file involves no new concepts. A typical input stream for Program P16-01, which creates a relative file, is shown in Figure 17.9. You can see the use of the NUMBERED attribute for a relative file. There is no KEYS parameter, for COBOL does not process keys in relative files. There is no FREESPACE parameter, for COBOL does not move records around in a relative file.

Notice that we have no JOBCAT or STEPCAT statements. Here we are taking advantage of a feature that permits Access Message Services to locate by itself the correct catalog in which to enter an object. The **prefix** part of a file name, the part before the first dot (in this case VSAM.), can be used to direct Access Method Services to the correct catalog. This feature is set up by the systems programmers at the time the catalogs are established. You can use this feature only if you are not using UNIT, VOL, and AMP='AMORG' in the DD statement for the file, as is the case here.

FIGURE 17.9 Typical input stream to create a relative file

```
//GSPNY678 JOB 'P16X01',REGION=300K
//FILESTEP EXEC PGM=IDCAMS
//SYSPRINT DD SYSOUT=A
//SYSIN DD *
    DELETE VSAM.NY.GSP.RELMSTR CLUSTER
    DEFINE CLUSTER( -
           NAME(VSAM.NY.GSP.RELMSTR) -
           VOLUMES(CNY005) -
           RECORDS(30) -
           RECORDSIZE(60 60) -
           NUMBERED -
           )
/*
//COBSTEP EXEC COBUCG
//SYSIN DD *
00010  IDENTIFICATION DIVISION.
00020  PROGRAM-ID.  P16-01.
00030
             .
             .
             .

    COBOL SOURCE PROGRAM
             .
             .
             .
//GO.PRINTER DD SYSOUT=A
//GO.DISKUNIT DD DSN=VSAM.NY.GSP.RELMSTR,DISP=OLD
//GO.INFILE DD *
N021CS302
/*
//
```

The JCL shown here works only if there is already a file called RELMSTR in existence from some previous run. If there is not, the techniques shown earlier in this chapter must be used instead.

The output from this execution of Access Method Services is shown in Figure 17.10.

FIGURE *17.10* **Output from step FILESTEP**

```
IDCAMS  SYSTEM SERVICES                                                TIME: 07:11:53

    DELETE VSAM.NY.GSP.RELMSTR CLUSTER

IDC0550I ENTRY (D) VSAM.T592025C.VDD91268.TA48D501 DELETED

IDC0550I ENTRY (C) VSAM.NY.GSP.RELMSTR DELETED

IDC0001I FUNCTION COMPLETED, HIGHEST CONDITION CODE WAS 0

    DEFINE CLUSTER( -
           NAME(VSAM.NY.GSP.RELMSTR) -
           VOLUMES(CNY005) -
           RECORDS(400) -
           RECORDSIZE(60 60) -
           NUMBERED -
           )

IDC0508I DATA ALLOCATION STATUS FOR VOLUME CNY005 IS 0

IDC0512I NAME GENERATED-(D) VSAM.TE189E92.VDD91269.TA48DBA1

IDC0001I FUNCTION COMPLETED, HIGHEST CONDITION CODE WAS 0
```

Summary

IBM's Virtual Storage Access Method (VSAM) is a high-speed access method for use with sequential, relative, or indexed files on direct-access storage devices. Management of VSAM files and the VSAM catalogs is carried out by a utility program called Access Method Services. With Access Method Services, you may DEFINE or DELETE a file, build an alternate index in connection with an ALTERNATE RECORD KEY defined in a COBOL program, ALTER a file's catalog entries, PRINT all or part of a file, list the catalog entry for a file, and VERIFY that a file's catalog entry agrees with the physical state of the file.

To run Access Method Services, you must use an EXEC statement specifying PGM=IDCAMS. You must also provide a SYSPRINT DD statement for Access Method Services output messages and a SYSIN DD statement for the input file of Access Method Services commands.

A VSAM file can be created only by Access Method Services. When the file is used in a program, its DD statement must specify DISP=OLD. If for any reason the DD statement must contain UNIT and VOL parameters, then it must also contain the parameter AMP='AMORG'.

Some installations have one or more user catalogs. If a file is to be cataloged in one of the user catalogs, the programmer can include a JOBCAT or STEPCAT statement. If a file is cataloged in a user catalog and AMP='AMORG' is used, then a JOBCAT or STEPCAT statement must be used also. If a file is cataloged in the master catalog, no catalog indication is ever needed.

There are two ways to create an indexed file having an alternate index. In one method the programmer first DEFINEs the base cluster, then loads it, then DEFINEs the alternate index and its PATH, and then builds the alternate index. The other method uses the COBOL execution-time option AIXBLD. With AIXBLD, the programmer DEFINEs the base cluster, the alternate index, and the PATH, and then gives the AIXBLD option as part of the COBOL program that is to load the file with records. With AIXBLD, COBOL first loads the base cluster with dummy records, builds the alternate index, erases the dummy records from the base cluster, and loads the file with data records. Then COBOL calls upon Access Method Services to ALTER the catalog entries of the base cluster and the alternate index, correcting the RECORDSIZE and KEYS parameters to agree with the record definition in the COBOL program.

A relative file may be created with the DEFINE command through the use of the NUMBERED parameter.

Fill-In Exercises

1. To use a VSAM sequential file you must include the letters AS before the ______ name in the ______ clause for the file.
2. The name of the IBM utility program that can create a VSAM file is ______ ______ ______.
3. A VSAM installation must have exactly one ______ catalog and may have any number of ______ catalogs.
4. The data organization parameter used to DEFINE a VSAM relative file is ______.
5. A ______ statement tells the system what user catalog to use for an entire job; a ______ statement tells the system what user catalog to use for a job step.
6. The command that can be used to build an alternate index is ______.
7. The command that can be used to check that a file's catalog entries agree with the physical state of the file is ______.
8. A VSAM indexed file is called a ______ data set.
9. The data organization parameters used to DEFINE a VSAM sequential file is ______.
10. An alternate index can be built only after its base cluster has been ______.
11. The command that is used to create a VSAM file is ______.
12. The command that is used to change catalog entries for a VSAM file is ______.
13. The DISP parameter for a VSAM file may be ______ or ______; it must never be ______.
14. The space requirement for a VSAM file may be given in terms of the number of ______, ______, or ______.
15. The size and location of the record key in an indexed file is given in the ______ parameter.

Project

Rewrite your solution to the Project in Chapter 15, page 595, using AIXBLD.

CHAPTER 18

String Processing

HERE ARE THE KEY POINTS YOU SHOULD LEARN FROM THIS CHAPTER

1. How to use the STRING verb
2. How to use the UNSTRING verb
3. How to use the INSPECT verb

KEY WORDS TO RECOGNIZE AND LEARN

string processing
STRING
OVERFLOW
delimiter
DELIMITED BY
SIZE
POINTER
UNSTRING
COUNT
TALLYING
span
DELIMITER
reference modification
INSPECT
LEADING
REPLACING
CONVERTING
CHARACTERS
INITIAL

The **string processing** features of COBOL permit programs to operate on the individual characters contained in fields. Each field is treated as if it consisted of one or more characters strung together end-to-end—hence the name string processing.

The STRING Statement

The **STRING** verb enables COBOL to attach two or more fields or parts of fields end-to-end to form one large field. The sending fields, the fields to be strung together, must be defined as alphanumeric or unedited integer. The receiving field must be alphanumeric.

When you write a STRING statement, you write the sending fields in the order in which you want them to be strung together. COBOL sends the sending fields to the receiving field in the order in which they appear in the STRING statement, adding each sending field on to the right end of the ever-growing string in the receiving field.

The STRING statement has an optional **OVERFLOW** phrase to handle situations where the sending fields together are all too big to fit into the receiving field.

If only a part of a sending field is to be sent, COBOL must have some way of knowing which part it is. The STRING verb uses one or more **delimiters** to tell COBOL which parts of sending fields to send. A programmer may select any one or more alphanumeric characters or an unedited integer to use as a delimiter.

The format of the STRING statement is as follows:

```
                                                 {identifier-2}
STRING {{identifier-1} ... DELIMITED BY {literal-2   }} ...
        {literal-1   }                   {SIZE        }
   INTO identifier-3
   [WITH POINTER identifier-4]
   [ON OVERFLOW imperative-statement-1]
   [NOT ON OVERFLOW imperative-statement-2]
   [END-STRING]
```

The sending fields in this format are identifier-1 and literal-1. If a figurative constant is used as a sending-field literal, it stands for one character of data (for example, SPACE or HIGH-VALUE).

Each sending field or group of sending fields has its own **DELIMITED BY** phrase. The DELIMITED BY phrases tell whether all or part of each sending field is to be sent to the receiving field. If **SIZE** is used, the entire sending field is added to the right end of the string in the receiving field; if a delimiter is used (identifier-2 or literal-2), only that portion of the sending field up to but not including the first appearance of the delimiter in the sending field is added to the string in the receiving field. If there are no appearances of the delimiter in a sending field, the entire sending field is added to the string in the receiving field.

Identifier-3 is the receiving field. The STRING statement does not blank out the receiving field before placing characters from sending fields into it. The only character positions in the receiving field that are changed by the STRING statement are the ones that have characters from sending fields placed into them.

The optional **POINTER** phrase will be discussed in the next section. All identifiers shown in the format of the STRING statement must be of USAGE DISPLAY except the POINTER, which must be a numeric integer data item of any USAGE.

Using the STRING Verb

Our first application of the STRING verb uses input data in the following format:

Positions	Field
1–6	Date
1–2	MM
3–4	DD
5–6	YY
7–80	spaces

Each input record contains a date in the usual American form MMDDYY. For each record read, Program P18-01 converts the date to English and prints the input and the English date on one line, as shown in Figure 18.1. Notice that there is only one space between the name of the month and the day, regardless of the length of the name or whether the day is a one-digit number or two. The STRING verb allows us to place the output components exactly where we want them in the output field.

FIGURE *18.1* **Output format for Program P18-01**

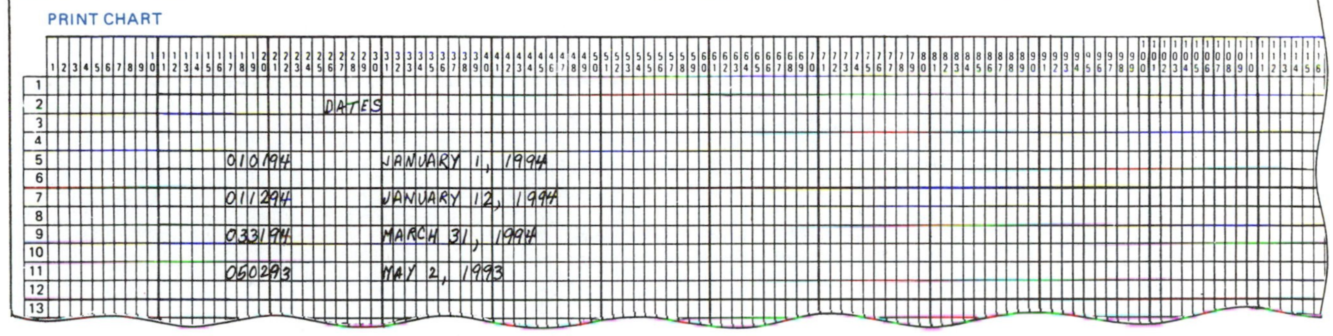

Program P18-01 is shown in Figure 18.2. The names of the 12 months are arranged in a MONTHS-TABLE, lines 00390 through 00540, so that the month number in the input can be used directly as a subscript to obtain the name of the month.

The field ENGLISH-DATE, line 00560, is used for assigning the date in English ready to be printed. ENGLISH-DATE-POINTER, line 00570, is the POINTER, which keeps track of character positions in ENGLISH-DATE as they are used. A POINTER field must be big enough to contain a number one larger than the number of character positions in the receiving field. In this case our receiving field, ENGLISH-DATE, is 18 characters long; so the POINTER field must be big enough to hold the number 19. Unless there is some reason to do otherwise, a POINTER field should always be made COMPUTATIONAL and SYNCHRONIZED, as we have done. You will see the exact function of ENGLISH-DATE-POINTER when we look at the Procedure Division.

The field COMMA-SPACE-CENTURY, line 00580, is a constant that is inserted into every date processed.

FIGURE *18.2* **Program P18-01**

```
S COBOL II RELEASE 3.2 09/05/90                  P18001    DATE SEP 17,1992 T
----+-*A-1-B--+----2----+----3----+----4----+----5----+----6----+----7-|--+

00010  IDENTIFICATION DIVISION.
00020  PROGRAM-ID.  P18-01.
00030 *
00040 *     THIS PROGRAM READS DATES IN MMDDYY FORM
00050 *     AND CONVERTS THEM TO ENGLISH.
00060 *
00070 ******************************************************************
00080
00090  ENVIRONMENT DIVISION.
00100  INPUT-OUTPUT SECTION.
00110  FILE-CONTROL.
00120      SELECT DATE-LIST-FILE   ASSIGN TO PRINTER.
00130      SELECT DATE-FILE-IN     ASSIGN TO INFILE.
00140
00150 ******************************************************************
00160
00170  DATA DIVISION.
00180  FILE SECTION.
00190  FD  DATE-FILE-IN
00200      RECORD CONTAINS 80 CHARACTERS.
00210
00220  01  DATE-RECORD-IN.
00230      05 DATE-IN.
00240         10 MONTH-IN                          PIC 99.
00250         10 DAY-IN.
00260            15 TENS-PLACE                     PIC 9.
00270            15 UNITS-PLACE                    PIC 9.
00280         10 YEAR-IN                           PIC 99.
00290
00300  FD  DATE-LIST-FILE.
00310
00320  01  DATE-RECORD-OUT                        PIC X(48).
00330
00340  WORKING-STORAGE SECTION.
00350  01  MORE-INPUT    VALUE "Y"                PIC X.
00360      88 THERE-IS-NO-MORE-INPUT               VALUE "N".
00370      88 THERE-IS-NO-INPUT                    VALUE "N".
00380
```

FIGURE ***18.2*** ***continued***

```
 01  MONTHS.
         05            VALUE "JANUARY  ."             PIC X(10).
         05            VALUE "FEBRUARY ."             PIC X(10).
         05            VALUE "MARCH  ."               PIC X(10).
         05            VALUE "APRIL  ."               PIC X(10).
         05            VALUE "MAY  ."                 PIC X(10).
         05            VALUE "JUNE  ."                PIC X(10).
         05            VALUE "JULY  ."                PIC X(10).
         05            VALUE "AUGUST  ."              PIC X(10).
         05            VALUE "SEPTEMBER "             PIC X(10).
         05            VALUE "OCTOBER  ."             PIC X(10).
         05            VALUE "NOVEMBER  ."            PIC X(10).
         05            VALUE "DECEMBER  ."            PIC X(10).
 01  MONTHS-TABLE
         REDEFINES MONTHS.
         05 MONTH            OCCURS 12 TIMES          PIC X(10).

 01  ENGLISH-DATE                                     PIC X(18).
 01  ENGLISH-DATE-POINTER    COMP SYNC                PIC S99.
 01  COMMA-SPACE-CENTURY
                             VALUE ", 19"             PIC X(4).

 01  REPORT-HEADING.
         05                  VALUE SPACES             PIC X(25).
         05                  VALUE "DATES"            PIC  X(5).

 01  DETAIL-LINE.
         05                  VALUE SPACES             PIC X(16).
         05  DATE-OUT                                 PIC 9(6)B(8).
         05  ENGLISH-DATE-OUT                         PIC X(18).

  01 NO-INPUT-DATA.
         05                  VALUE SPACES             PIC X(21).
         05                  VALUE "NO INPUT DATA"    PIC X(13).

******************************************************************

 PROCEDURE DIVISION.
 CONTROL-PARAGRAPH.
     PERFORM INITIALIZATION
     PERFORM MAIN-PROCESS UNTIL THERE-IS-NO-MORE-INPUT
     PERFORM TERMINATION
     STOP RUN
     .

 INITIALIZATION.
     OPEN INPUT  DATE-FILE-IN
          OUTPUT DATE-LIST-FILE
     READ DATE-FILE-IN
         AT END
             SET THERE-IS-NO-INPUT TO TRUE
     END-READ
     WRITE DATE-RECORD-OUT FROM REPORT-HEADING AFTER PAGE
     MOVE SPACES TO DATE-RECORD-OUT
     WRITE DATE-RECORD-OUT
     IF THERE-IS-NO-INPUT
         WRITE DATE-RECORD-OUT FROM NO-INPUT-DATA AFTER 2
     END-IF
     .
```

continued

In the MAIN-PROCESS paragraph of the Procedure Division, line 00990, we first blank out ENGLISH-DATE. Then with a series of PERFORM statements, lines 01010 through 01030, we build up the complete date in English in the field ENGLISH-DATE.

In the paragraph STRING-MONTH, line 01120, we first set the POINTER field to 1. When used, the POINTER field always points to the next available character position in the receiving field. As we begin to build up the date in English, we want it to start at the left end (character position 1) of the receiving field, ENGLISH-DATE. The STRING statement at line 01140 first STRINGs all the characters in MONTH (MONTH-IN), up to but not including the first period, INTO the receiving field. If no period is found in the sending field, as in SEPTEMBER, the entire sending field is assigned to the receiving field.

When execution of the STRING statement is complete, COBOL sets the POINTER field to point to the next available unused character position in ENGLISH-DATE.

In the paragraph STRING-DAY, line 01190, one STRING statement or another is executed depending on whether the day of the month has a nonzero tens' place. The phrase DELIMITED BY SIZE causes all characters in the sending field to be added to the string in the receiving field.

The STRING statement at line 01320 shows that more than one sending field in a STRING statement can use the same DELIMITED BY phrase. You may have as many DELIMITED BY phrases as you like in a STRING statement, and each one may have as many fields as you like associated with it.

FIGURE *18.2* ***continued***

```
S COBOL II RELEASE 3.2 09/05/90              P18001   DATE SEP 17,1992 T
----+-*A-1-B--+----2----+----3----+----4----+----5----+----6----+----7-|--+

00980
00990  MAIN-PROCESS.
01000      MOVE SPACES TO ENGLISH-DATE
01010      PERFORM STRING-MONTH
01020      PERFORM STRING-DAY
01030      PERFORM STRING-YEAR
01040      MOVE DATE-IN      TO DATE-OUT
01050      MOVE ENGLISH-DATE TO ENGLISH-DATE-OUT
01060      WRITE DATE-RECORD-OUT FROM DETAIL-LINE AFTER 2
01070      READ DATE-FILE-IN
01080          AT END
01090              SET THERE-IS-NO-MORE-INPUT TO TRUE
01100      .
01110
01120  STRING-MONTH.
01130      MOVE 1 TO ENGLISH-DATE-POINTER
01140      STRING MONTH (MONTH-IN) DELIMITED BY "."
01150          INTO ENGLISH-DATE
01160          POINTER ENGLISH-DATE-POINTER
01170      .
01180
```

FIGURE 18.2 *continued*

```
STRING-DAY.
    IF TENS-PLACE IS EQUAL TO ZERO
        STRING UNITS-PLACE     DELIMITED BY SIZE
            INTO ENGLISH-DATE
            POINTER ENGLISH-DATE-POINTER
    ELSE
        STRING DAY-IN          DELIMITED BY SIZE
            INTO ENGLISH-DATE
            POINTER ENGLISH-DATE-POINTER
    END-IF
    .

STRING-YEAR.
    STRING  COMMA-SPACE-CENTURY
            YEAR-IN            DELIMITED BY SIZE
        INTO ENGLISH-DATE
        POINTER ENGLISH-DATE-POINTER
    .

TERMINATION.
    CLOSE DATE-FILE-IN
          DATE-LIST-FILE
    .
```

Program P18-01 was run with the input data shown in Figure 18.3 and produced the output shown in Figure 18.4.

FIGURE 18.3 **Input to Program P18-01**

```
--------------------------------------------------------------------------------
         1         2         3         4         5         6         7         8
12345678901234567890123456789012345678901234567890123456789012345678901234567890
--------------------------------------------------------------------------------
091593
010295
010194
011294
033194
050294
121495
073195
112494
021495
```

FIGURE 18.4 **Output from Program P18-01**

```
            DATES

091593        SEPTEMBER 15, 1993
010295        JANUARY 2, 1995
010194        JANUARY 1, 1994
011294        JANUARY 12, 1994
033194        MARCH 31, 1994
050294        MAY 2, 1994
121495        DECEMBER 14, 1995
073195        JULY 31, 1995
112494        NOVEMBER 24, 1994
021495        FEBRUARY 14, 1995
```

EXERCISE 1

Write a program to print a list of city names and state abbreviations. Your program should read data in the following format:

Positions	Field
1–20	City Name
21–30	spaces
31–32	State Abbreviation
33–80	spaces

Each input record contains a City Name, some blanks, and a State Abbreviation. For each input record, have your program print the City Name and State Abbreviation separated by a comma and one space, as shown in the format in Figure 18.E1.

FIGURE 18.E1 **Output format for Exercise 1**

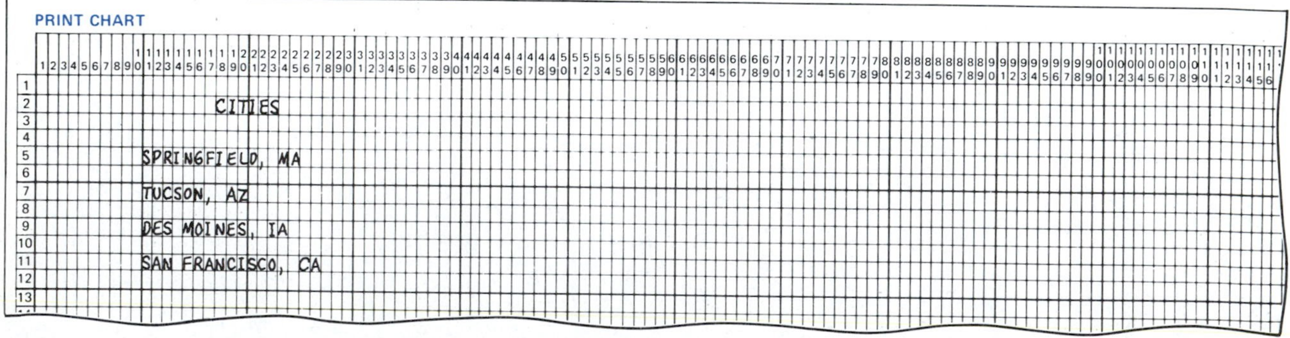

Another Application of the STRING Verb

We now develop a more elaborate application of the STRING verb. Program P18-02 reads input data in the following format:

Positions	Field
1–8	Dollars-and-cents amount
1–6	Dollar amount
7–8	Cents amount
9–80	spaces

Each input record contains an eight-digit dollars-and-cents amount, from $.00 up to $999,999.99. The program is to read each record and print the money amount, edited, and also print the six-digit dollar amount in words, as shown in Figure 18.5.

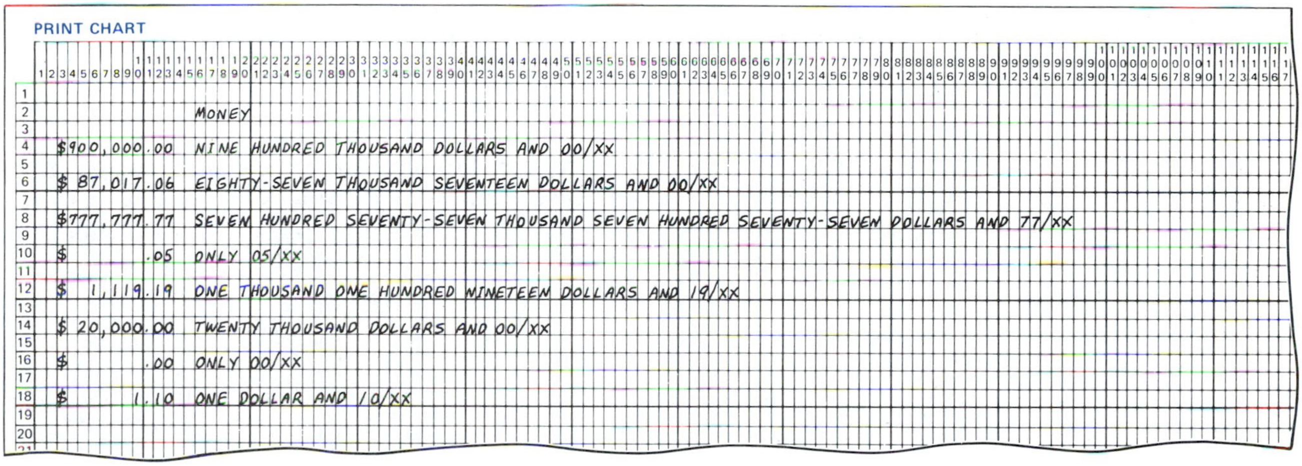

FIGURE *18.5* **Output format for Program P18-02**

PRINT CHART

```
MONEY

$900,000.00  NINE HUNDRED THOUSAND DOLLARS AND 00/XX

$ 87,017.06  EIGHTY-SEVEN THOUSAND SEVENTEEN DOLLARS AND 00/XX

$777,777.77  SEVEN HUNDRED SEVENTY-SEVEN THOUSAND SEVEN HUNDRED SEVENTY-SEVEN DOLLARS AND 77/XX

$        .05  ONLY 05/XX

$   1,119.19  ONE THOUSAND ONE HUNDRED NINETEEN DOLLARS AND 19/XX

$ 20,000.00  TWENTY THOUSAND DOLLARS AND 00/XX

$        .00  ONLY 00/XX

$       1.10  ONE DOLLAR AND 10/XX
```

Peculiarities in the way that numbers are written complicate Program P18-02. For example, the word THOUSAND appears in the number if there are any hundreds of thousands of dollars, tens of thousands of dollars, or thousands of dollars. Every word used in the expression of a number is always followed by a space, except words like TWENTY, THIRTY, FORTY, and so on. They may be followed by a space or a hyphen, depending on the word following. Values between 11 and 19 (and thousands between 11,000 and 19,000) have to be handled in a special way because they are irregular forms.

A hierarchy diagram for the main loop of Program P18-02, "Process a number," is shown in Figure 18.6. The step "String word fields and cent field together" determines which words are needed and STRINGs them INTO an output field for printing.

FIGURE 18.6 **Hierarchy diagram for main loop of Program P18-02**

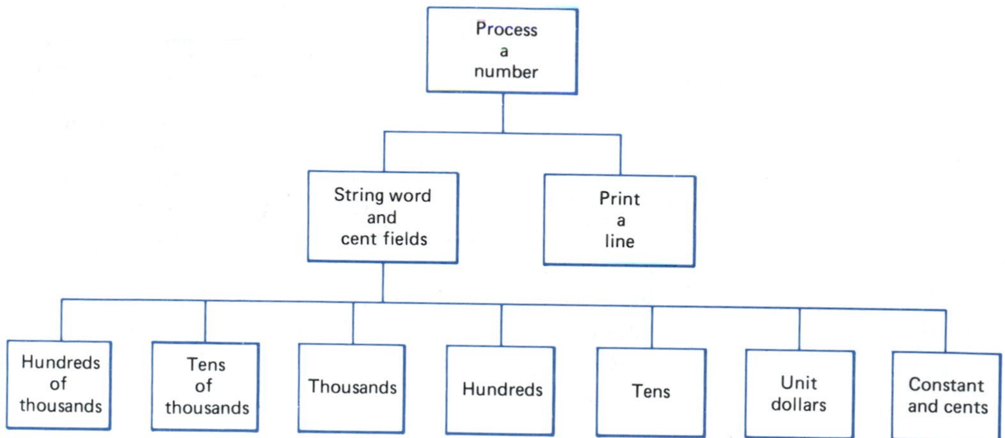

Program P18-02 is shown in Figure 18.7. The field MONEY-IN, line 00230, has been redefined as MONEY-BREAKDOWN, at line 00260. In this way the program can process each of the digits in MONEY-IN individually. Also, the units place and the tens place have been redefined as a single two-digit field so the program can handle the irregular numbers, 11 through 19. Similarly, the thousands place and the tens-of-thousands place have been redefined as a two-digit field so the program can handle thousands from 11 through 19.

A UNITS-PLACE-TABLE and a TENS-PLACE-TABLE have been set up at lines 00530 through 00890 to provide words to be used in the output. We need no table for higher-place values because all the place values higher than tens use the same words as either the units' place or the tens' place. All the numbers up

FIGURE 18.7 **Program P18-02**

```
S COBOL II RELEASE 3.2 09/05/90                  P18002    DATE OCT 22,1991 T
----+-*A-1-B--+----2----+----3----+----4----+----5----+----6----+----7-%--+

00010  IDENTIFICATION DIVISION.
00020  PROGRAM-ID.  P18-02.
00030 *
00040 *     THIS PROGRAM READS IN MONEY AMOUNTS AND PRINTS
00050 *     THEM IN WORDS.
00060 *
00070 ******************************************************************
00080
00090  ENVIRONMENT DIVISION.
00100  INPUT-OUTPUT SECTION.
00110  FILE-CONTROL.
00120      SELECT MONEY-FILE-IN  ASSIGN TO INFILE.
00130      SELECT MONEY-FILE-OUT ASSIGN TO PRINTER.
00140
00150 ******************************************************************
00160
00170  DATA DIVISION.
00180  FILE SECTION.
00190  FD  MONEY-FILE-IN
00200      RECORD CONTAINS 80 CHARACTERS.
00210
```

FIGURE 18.7 *continued*

```
 01  MASTER-RECORD-IN.
     05  MONEY-IN                                     PIC 9(6)V99.
         88  LESS-THAN-A-DOLLAR        VALUES 0 THRU .99.
         88  ONE-DOLLAR                VALUES 1 THRU 1.99.
     05  MONEY-BREAKDOWN REDEFINES MONEY-IN.
         10  HUNDREDS-OF-THOUSANDS-W                  PIC 9.
         10  TEENS-OF-THOUSANDS.
             15  TENS-OF-THOUSANDS-W                  PIC 9.
             15  THOUSANDS-W                          PIC 9.
         10  TEENS-OF-THOUSANDS-W REDEFINES TEENS-OF-THOUSANDS
                                                      PIC 99.
         10  HUNDREDS-W                               PIC 9.
         10  TEENS.
             15  TENS-W                               PIC 9.
             15  UNIT-DOLLARS-W                       PIC 9.
         10  TEENS-W REDEFINES TEENS                  PIC 99.
         10  CENTS-UNEDITED-W                         PIC V99.
         10  WHOLE-CENTS-W
             REDEFINES CENTS-UNEDITED-W               PIC  99.

 FD  MONEY-FILE-OUT.

 01  MONEY-RECORD-OUT                                 PIC X(97).

 WORKING-STORAGE SECTION.
 01  MORE-INPUT          VALUE "Y"                    PIC X.
     88 THERE-IS-NO-MORE-INPUT                       VALUE "N".
     88 THERE-IS-NO-INPUT                            VALUE "N".
 01  MONEY-AMOUNT-IN-ENGLISH                          PIC X(82).
 01  ENGLISH-FIELD-POINTER                            PIC S99.

 01  UNITS-PLACES-TABLE-ENTRIES.
     05              VALUE "ONE ."                    PIC X(10).
     05              VALUE "TWO ."                    PIC X(10).
     05              VALUE "THREE ."                  PIC X(10).
     05              VALUE "FOUR ."                   PIC X(10).
     05              VALUE "FIVE ."                   PIC X(10).
     05              VALUE "SIX ."                    PIC X(10).
     05              VALUE "SEVEN ."                  PIC X(10).
     05              VALUE "EIGHT ."                  PIC X(10).
     05              VALUE "NINE ."                   PIC X(10).
     05              VALUE "TEN ."                    PIC X(10).
     05              VALUE "ELEVEN ."                 PIC X(10).
     05              VALUE "TWELVE ."                 PIC X(10).
     05              VALUE "THIRTEEN ."               PIC X(10).
     05              VALUE "FOURTEEN ."               PIC X(10).
     05              VALUE "FIFTEEN ."                PIC X(10).
     05              VALUE "SIXTEEN ."                PIC X(10).
     05              VALUE "SEVENTEEN "               PIC X(10).
     05              VALUE "EIGHTEEN ."               PIC X(10).
     05              VALUE "NINETEEN ."               PIC X(10).
 01  UNITS-PLACES-TABLE
     REDEFINES UNITS-PLACES-TABLE-ENTRIES.
     05  UNITS-PLACE  OCCURS 19 TIMES                 PIC X(10).

 01  TENS-PLACES-TABLE-ENTRIES.
     05              VALUE "TEN"                      PIC X(7).
     05              VALUE "TWENTY"                   PIC X(7).
     05              VALUE "THIRTY"                   PIC X(7).
     05              VALUE "FORTY"                    PIC X(7).
     05              VALUE "FIFTY"                    PIC X(7).
     05              VALUE "SIXTY"                    PIC X(7).
     05              VALUE "SEVENTY"                  PIC X(7).
     05              VALUE "EIGHTY"                   PIC X(7).
     05              VALUE "NINETY"                   PIC X(7).
 01  TENS-PLACES-TABLE
     REDEFINES TENS-PLACES-TABLE-ENTRIES.
     05  TENS-PLACE OCCURS 9 TIMES                    PIC X(7).
```

continued

through 19 are included in the UNITS-PLACES-TABLE to facilitate programming for the numbers 11 through 19. In this program, all numbers below 20 are treated as units, and programming for the tens' place handles numbers of 20 and larger. A space is included after each word in the UNITS-PLACES-TABLE because the space is part of the field. The units' words are always followed by a space whenever they appear in the output. There is no such space in the entries in the TENS-PLACES-TABLE, because the tens' words are not always followed by a space; they are sometimes followed by a hyphen. An IF test in the Procedure Division determines whether any particular tens' word is to be followed by a space or a hyphen and STRINGs the appropriate character.

In the Procedure Division, the paragraph PROCESS-A-NUMBER, line 01290, follows the hierarchy diagram. In STRING-WORD-AND-CENT-FIELDS, line 01430, the POINTER is set to 1 to point to the first character position of the output field. The PERFORM statements at lines 01460 through 01520 fill the output field with the appropriate words.

In the paragraph HUNDREDS-OF-THOUSANDS, for example, the IF statement at line 01560 determines whether there are any hundreds of thousands of dollars in the number. If there are, it STRINGs the appropriate words into the output field, MONEY-AMOUNT-IN-ENGLISH, and sets the POINTER to point to the first unused character in the output field. The phrase DELIMITED BY "." causes all the characters in the sending field, up to but not including the dot, to be sent to the output field.

FIGURE ***18.7*** ***continued***

```
S COBOL II RELEASE 3.2 09/05/90                  P18002   DATE OCT 22,1991 T
----+-*A-1-B--+----2----+----3----+----4----+----5----+----6----+----7-%--+

00900
00910  01  PAGE-HEADING.
00920      05                  VALUE SPACES              PIC X(15).
00930      05                  VALUE "MONEY"             PIC X(5).
00940
00950  01  DETAIL-LINE.
00960      05                  VALUE SPACES              PIC XX.
00970      05  MONEY-OUT                                 PIC $ZZZ,ZZZ.99BB.
00980      05  MONEY-OUT-IN-ENGLISH                      PIC X(82).
00990
01000  01  NO-INPUT-DATA.
01010      05                  VALUE SPACES              PIC X(15).
01020      05                  VALUE "NO INPUT DATA"     PIC X(13).
01030
01040 ***********************************************************************
01050
01060  PROCEDURE DIVISION.
01070  CONTROL-PARAGRAPH.
01080      PERFORM INITIALIZATION
01090      PERFORM PROCESS-A-NUMBER UNTIL THERE-IS-NO-MORE-INPUT
01100      PERFORM TERMINATION
01110      STOP RUN
01120      .
01130
```

FIGURE 18.7 *continued*

```
INITIALIZATION.
    OPEN INPUT  MONEY-FILE-IN
         OUTPUT MONEY-FILE-OUT
    WRITE MONEY-RECORD-OUT FROM PAGE-HEADING AFTER PAGE
    READ MONEY-FILE-IN
        AT END
            SET THERE-IS-NO-INPUT TO TRUE
            WRITE MONEY-RECORD-OUT FROM NO-INPUT-DATA AFTER 2
    .

TERMINATION.
    CLOSE MONEY-FILE-IN
          MONEY-FILE-OUT
    .

PROCESS-A-NUMBER.
    PERFORM STRING-WORD-AND-CENT-FIELDS
    PERFORM PRINT-A-LINE
    READ MONEY-FILE-IN
        AT END
            SET THERE-IS-NO-MORE-INPUT TO TRUE
    .

PRINT-A-LINE.
    MOVE MONEY-IN                TO MONEY-OUT
    MOVE MONEY-AMOUNT-IN-ENGLISH TO MONEY-OUT-IN-ENGLISH
    WRITE MONEY-RECORD-OUT FROM DETAIL-LINE AFTER 2
    .

STRING-WORD-AND-CENT-FIELDS.
    MOVE SPACES TO MONEY-AMOUNT-IN-ENGLISH
    MOVE 1 TO ENGLISH-FIELD-POINTER
    PERFORM HUNDREDS-OF-THOUSANDS
    PERFORM TENS-OF-THOUSANDS
    PERFORM THOUSANDS
    PERFORM HUNDREDS
    PERFORM TENS
    PERFORM UNIT-DOLLARS
    PERFORM CONSTANT-AND-CENTS
    .

HUNDREDS-OF-THOUSANDS.
    IF HUNDREDS-OF-THOUSANDS-W NOT = 0
        STRING UNITS-PLACE (HUNDREDS-OF-THOUSANDS-W)
                                               DELIMITED BY "."
               "HUNDRED "                      DELIMITED BY SIZE
            INTO MONEY-AMOUNT-IN-ENGLISH
            POINTER ENGLISH-FIELD-POINTER
    END-IF
    .
```

continued

In the paragraph TENS-OF-THOUSANDS, the IF statement at line 01660 determines whether there are any regular tens of thousands of dollars in the number. If there are, it STRINGs the appropriate word into MONEY-AMOUNT-IN-ENGLISH. The IF statement at line 01710 determines whether to STRING a hyphen or a SPACE after it. The IF statement at line 01810 handles the irregular tens of thousands.

FIGURE *18.7* *continued*

```
S COBOL II RELEASE 3.2 09/05/90                 P18002   DATE OCT 22,1991 T
----+-*A-1-B--+----2----+----3----+----4----+----5----+----6----+----7-%--+

01650   TENS-OF-THOUSANDS.
01660       IF TENS-OF-THOUSANDS-W NOT = 0 AND NOT = 1
01670           STRING TENS-PLACE (TENS-OF-THOUSANDS-W)
01680                                                    DELIMITED BY SPACE
01690               INTO MONEY-AMOUNT-IN-ENGLISH
01700               POINTER ENGLISH-FIELD-POINTER
01710           IF THOUSANDS-W NOT = 0
01720               STRING "-"                           DELIMITED BY SIZE
01730                   INTO MONEY-AMOUNT-IN-ENGLISH
01740                   POINTER ENGLISH-FIELD-POINTER
01750           ELSE
01760               STRING SPACE                         DELIMITED BY SIZE
01770                   INTO MONEY-AMOUNT-IN-ENGLISH
01780                   POINTER ENGLISH-FIELD-POINTER
01790           END-IF
01800       END-IF
01810       IF TENS-OF-THOUSANDS-W = 1
01820           STRING UNITS-PLACE (TEENS-OF-THOUSANDS-W)
01830                                                    DELIMITED BY "."
01840               INTO MONEY-AMOUNT-IN-ENGLISH
01850               POINTER ENGLISH-FIELD-POINTER
01860       END-IF
01870       .
01880
01890   THOUSANDS.
01900       IF TENS-OF-THOUSANDS-W NOT = 1
01910           IF THOUSANDS-W NOT = 0
01920               STRING UNITS-PLACE (THOUSANDS-W)     DELIMITED BY "."
01930                   INTO MONEY-AMOUNT-IN-ENGLISH
01940                   POINTER ENGLISH-FIELD-POINTER
01950           END-IF
01960       END-IF
01970       IF HUNDREDS-OF-THOUSANDS-W NOT = 0 OR
01980          TENS-OF-THOUSANDS-W     NOT = 0 OR
01990          THOUSANDS-W             NOT = 0
02000           STRING "THOUSAND "                       DELIMITED BY SIZE
02010               INTO MONEY-AMOUNT-IN-ENGLISH
02020               POINTER ENGLISH-FIELD-POINTER
02030       END-IF
02040       .
02050
02060   HUNDREDS.
02070       IF HUNDREDS-W NOT = 0
02080           STRING UNITS-PLACE (HUNDREDS-W)          DELIMITED BY "."
02090                  "HUNDRED "                        DELIMITED BY SIZE
02100               INTO MONEY-AMOUNT-IN-ENGLISH
02110               POINTER ENGLISH-FIELD-POINTER
02120       END-IF
02130       .
02140
```

FIGURE 18.7 *continued*

```
TENS.
    IF TENS-W NOT = 0 AND NOT = 1
        STRING TENS-PLACE (TENS-W)             DELIMITED BY SPACE
            INTO MONEY-AMOUNT-IN-ENGLISH
            POINTER ENGLISH-FIELD-POINTER
        IF UNIT-DOLLARS-W NOT = 0
            STRING "-"                         DELIMITED BY SIZE
                INTO MONEY-AMOUNT-IN-ENGLISH
                POINTER ENGLISH-FIELD-POINTER
        ELSE
            STRING SPACE                       DELIMITED BY SIZE
                INTO MONEY-AMOUNT-IN-ENGLISH
                POINTER ENGLISH-FIELD-POINTER
        END-IF
    END-IF
    IF TENS-W = 1
        STRING UNITS-PLACE (TEENS-W)           DELIMITED BY "."
            INTO MONEY-AMOUNT-IN-ENGLISH
            POINTER ENGLISH-FIELD-POINTER
    END-IF
    .

UNIT-DOLLARS.
    IF TENS-W NOT = 1
        IF UNIT-DOLLARS-W NOT = 0
            STRING UNITS-PLACE (UNIT-DOLLARS-W) DELIMITED BY "."
                INTO MONEY-AMOUNT-IN-ENGLISH
                POINTER ENGLISH-FIELD-POINTER
        END-IF
    END-IF
    .

CONSTANT-AND-CENTS.
    EVALUATE TRUE
    WHEN LESS-THAN-A-DOLLAR
        STRING "ONLY "                         DELIMITED BY SIZE
            INTO MONEY-AMOUNT-IN-ENGLISH
            POINTER ENGLISH-FIELD-POINTER
    WHEN ONE-DOLLAR
        STRING "DOLLAR AND "                   DELIMITED BY SIZE
            INTO MONEY-AMOUNT-IN-ENGLISH
            POINTER ENGLISH-FIELD-POINTER
    WHEN OTHER
        STRING "DOLLARS AND "                  DELIMITED BY SIZE
            INTO MONEY-AMOUNT-IN-ENGLISH
            POINTER ENGLISH-FIELD-POINTER
    END-EVALUATE
    STRING WHOLE-CENTS-W
           "/XX"                               DELIMITED BY SIZE
        INTO MONEY-AMOUNT-IN-ENGLISH
        POINTER ENGLISH-FIELD-POINTER
    .
```

Program P18-02 was run with the input data shown in Figure 18.8 and produced the output shown in Figure 18.9.

FIGURE 18.8 **Input to Program P18-02**

```
--------------------------------------------------------------------------------
         1         2         3         4         5         6         7         8
12345678901234567890123456789012345678901234567890123456789012345678901234567890
--------------------------------------------------------------------------------
00015890
90000000
08701706
77777777
00000005
00111919
02000000
00000000
00000110
00000099
00000199
00000200
00000100
```

FIGURE 18.9 **Output from Program P18-02**

```
             MONEY

$     158.90 ONE HUNDRED FIFTY-EIGHT DOLLARS AND 90/XX

$900,000.00  NINE HUNDRED THOUSAND DOLLARS AND 00/XX

$ 87,017.06  EIGHTY-SEVEN THOUSAND SEVENTEEN DOLLARS AND 06/XX

$777,777.77  SEVEN HUNDRED SEVENTY-SEVEN THOUSAND SEVEN HUNDRED SEVENTY-SEVEN DOLLARS AND 77/XX

$        .05 ONLY 05/XX

$   1,119.19 ONE THOUSAND ONE HUNDRED NINETEEN DOLLARS AND 19/XX

$ 20,000.00  TWENTY THOUSAND DOLLARS AND 00/XX

$        .00 ONLY 00/XX

$       1.10 ONE DOLLAR AND 10/XX

$        .99 ONLY 99/XX

$       1.99 ONE DOLLAR AND 99/XX

$       2.00 TWO DOLLARS AND 00/XX

$       1.00 ONE DOLLAR AND 00/XX
```

EXERCISE 2 Modify Program P18-02 so that it can handle nine-digit whole dollar amounts, up through $999,999,999.

The UNSTRING Statement

The **UNSTRING** statement can be used to scan a large sending field and break it down into pieces. The UNSTRING statement assigns each piece to a separate receiving field. The scan of the sending field can be based either on one or more delimiters or on size. If based on delimiters, the characters in the sending field are examined from left to right until a delimiter is found. Then, the characters in the sending field up to but not including the delimiter are MOVEd to a receiving field according to the rules of the MOVE statement. A delimiter may be any alphanumeric value or any integer of USAGE DISPLAY. An optional **COUNT** field may be provided, and COBOL will place into the COUNT field the number of characters that were examined before a delimiter was found.

A single UNSTRING statement can have as many receiving fields as desired, and each receiving field may have a COUNT field associated with it. After the first receiving field has had data MOVEd to it, the UNSTRING statement resumes scanning the sending field looking for the next appearance of a delimiter. It then MOVEs to the second receiving field all that portion of the sending field between the first and second appearances of delimiters, and places into the second COUNT field (if one is specified) the number of characters examined between delimiters. If there are no characters between delimiters, then spaces or zeros are moved to the receiving field depending on how the receiving field is defined. The delimiters themselves can optionally be MOVEd to separate receiving fields or not MOVEd. The scan continues until all characters in the sending field have been examined or until all the receiving fields have had data MOVEd to them, whichever comes first.

Receiving fields are listed in an UNSTRING statement in the order in which they are to receive pieces of the sending field. The optional **TALLYING** phrase causes the UNSTRING statement to count how many receiving fields have data MOVEd to them during execution of the statement.

An UNSTRING statement can also break down a large field into pieces of specific sizes, without any consideration of delimiters. There may be as many receiving fields as desired, and they may be of any sizes desired. The UNSTRING statement scans the sending field from left to right and MOVEs to the first receiving field exactly the number of characters that will fit into it. Then the UNSTRING statement continues the scan and MOVEs to the second receiving field exactly the number of characters that will fit into it. The scan continues until all characters in the sending field have been scanned or all of the receiving fields have had data MOVEd to them, whichever comes first. COUNT fields may not be used when an UNSTRING statement is operating on the basis of field sizes. A single UNSTRING statement can operate on the basis of delimiters or sizes, but not both.

An optional OVERFLOW phrase may be used to handle cases where there are more characters in the sending field than can fit into all the receiving fields. An optional POINTER may be used to keep track of which character in the sending field is next to be scanned.

Using the UNSTRING Statement

Program P18-03 shows how a large field may be broken down into smaller fields on the basis of delimiters contained in the large field. Program P18-03 accepts 80-character input records of the kind shown in Figure 18.10. These are selections from poems, written in "prose" format as they might be found in a book review, with slashes between the lines and quotation marks around the whole selection. Notice that some selections extend to more than one input record, but each individual line of poetry is completely contained in one record. A single line of poetry does not **span** records. Program P18-03 reads the selections and prints them in "poetry" format as shown in Figure 18.11. Notice that the program can handle lines up to 37 characters long. If an input record contains a line longer than that, the program prints a message LINE LONGER THAN 37 CHARACTERS.

FIGURE *18.10* **Input to Program P18-03**

```
--------------------------------------------------------------------------------
         1         2         3         4         5         6         7         8
12345678901234567890123456789012345678901234567890123456789012345678901234567890
--------------------------------------------------------------------------------
"SOME PEOPLE/WILL DO ANYTHING/IN ORDER TO SAY/THEY'VE DONE IT."
"LIFE IS FUNNY/THAT WAY.../THERE'S A PIPER/'ROUND EVERY/CORNER/WAITING/
TO BE PAID."
"HOW MANY POETS DOES ONE SMALL PLANET NEED?/WHO KNOWS?/WHO IS ASKING?/
IS ANYONE ANSWERING?"
```

FIGURE *18.11* **Output format for Program P18-03**

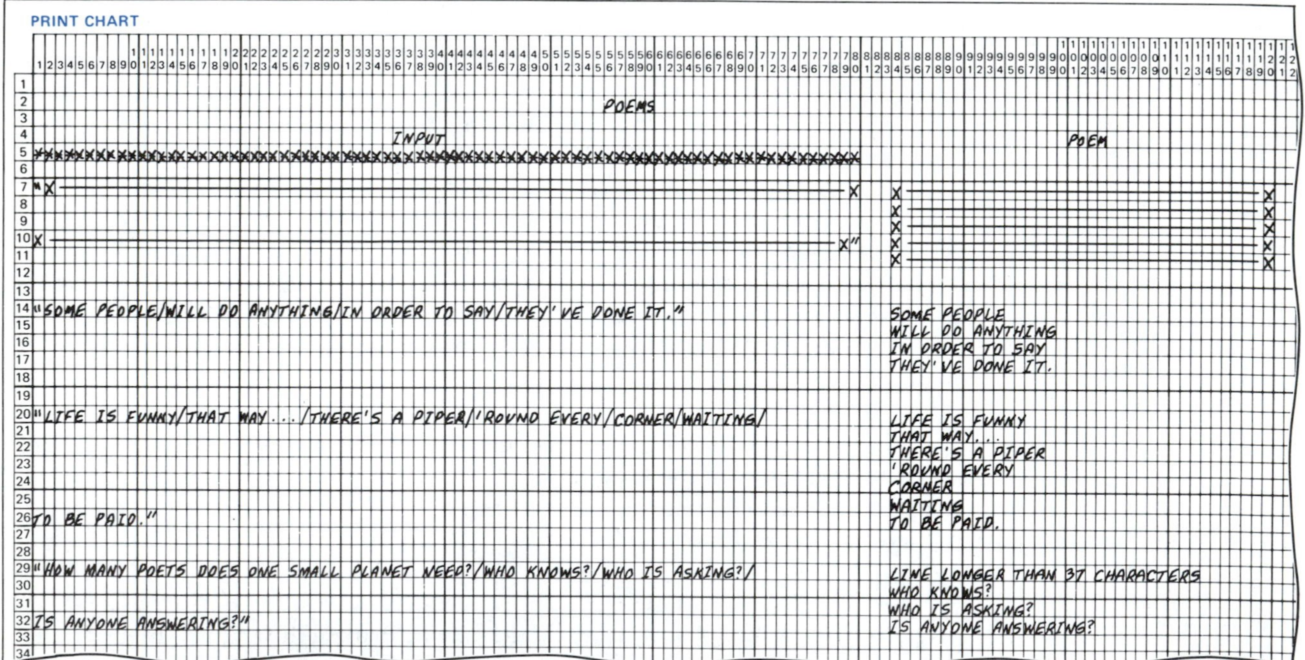

Hierarchy Diagram for Program P18-03

A hierarchy diagram for Program P18-03 is shown in Figure 18.12. The diagram shows how to handle a situation where the input consists of several independent sets of data, as we have here. At the first level of subfunctions, "Initialization" and "Termination" refer to the usual program initialization and termination such as OPENing and closing files, the priming READ, and initializing and terminating the report. "Process all poems" executes until there are no more input data.

At the next level of subfunctions, we must process each poem as a separate set of data. "Initialize for poem" and "Terminate poem" carry out needed functions, which you will see when we look at the program. "Process one poem" executes until the end of a poem is recognized by its closing quotation marks.

At the next level of subfunctions, we must process each of the input records that makes up a poem. Each input record may contain several lines of poetry. "Process one input record" extracts and prints lines of poetry from the input record, and continues to execute until it encounters the end of the record.

FIGURE *18.12* **Hierarchy diagram for Program P18-03**

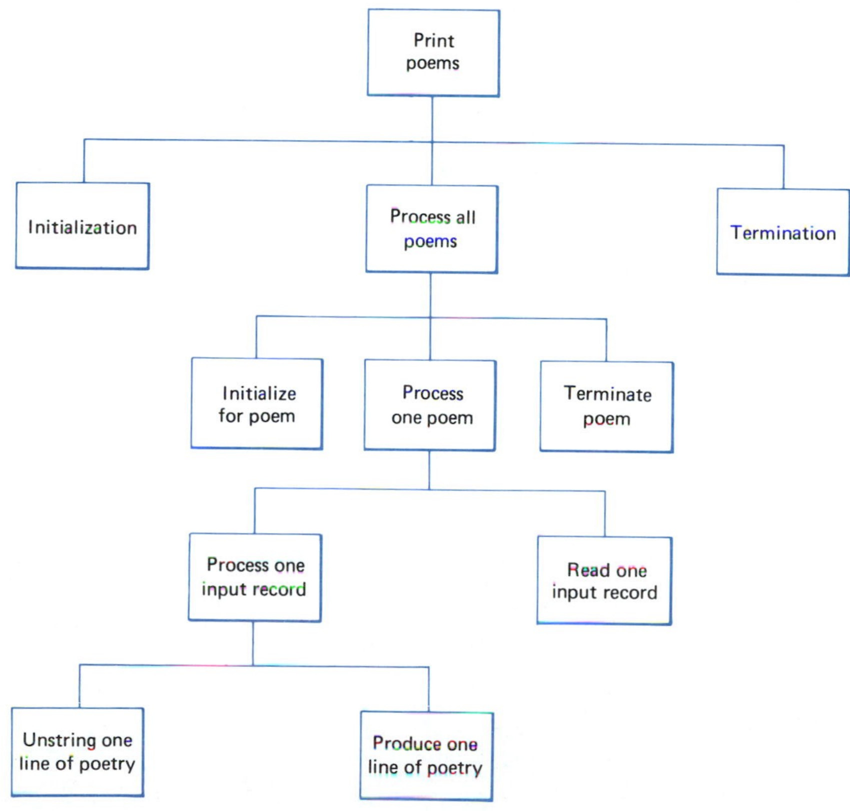

Program P18-03

Program P18-03 is shown in Figure 18.13. In the Working Storage Section are the fields we need to control the repetitive execution of the several loops in this program. MORE-INPUT, line 00300, starts out with VALUE "Y", and the main loop runs UNTIL MORE-INPUT becomes "N".

The field LINE-OF-POETRY, line 00330, is used to assign each line of a poem as it is extracted from an input record. When all the lines of poetry have been extracted from an input record and nothing remains in the input record except perhaps trailing blanks, the program knows that all the lines of poetry have been processed and that a new input record should be read. The program is arranged so that even if there are no trailing blanks in the input record, the end of the record will be detected correctly. You will soon see how.

The field POEMS-LINES, line 00420, is used to store each input record as it comes in from the input file. The field LINE-TERMINATOR, line 00430, is used to indicate whether any particular line of poetry terminates with a slash or with quotation marks. If with quotation marks, the program knows that a complete poem has been processed. Together, POEMS-LINES and LINE-TERMINATOR form an 81-character field that ensures that the end of each input record will be detected even if the poetry goes right up through position 80.

POEMS-LINES-SAVE, line 00450, is part of the coding needed to effect a control break on POEMS-LINES. No totals are taken in this program, and the control break is needed only so that we can get group indication of POEMS-LINES. This means that each different value assigned to POEMS-LINES prints only once, as shown on the print chart in Figure 18.11.

The definition of the print line is shown in lines 00590 through 00610. POEMS-LINE-OUT contains the 80-character input record and three blanks. LINE-OF-POETRY-OUT contains a single line of poetry. Since a single input record will usually contain several lines of poetry, the program is designed to print the input record only with the first line of poetry and to print blanks in the POEMS-LINE-OUT field for all the subsequent lines of poetry in that input record, as shown in Figure 18.11.

FIGURE *18.13* **Program P18-03**

```
S COBOL II RELEASE 3.2 09/05/90                P18003   DATE NOV 01,1991 T
----+-*A-1-B--+----2----+----3----+----4----+----5----+----6----+----7-|--+


00010  IDENTIFICATION DIVISION.
00020  PROGRAM-ID.  P18-03.
00030 *
00040 *     THIS PROGRAM READS POEMS IN "PROSE" FORMAT, WITH
00050 *     EACH PAIR OF LINES OF POETRY SEPARATED BY A SLASH,
00060 *     AND PRINTS EACH POEM IN "POETRY" FORMAT.
00070 *
00080 ******************************************************************
00090
00100  ENVIRONMENT DIVISION.
00110  INPUT-OUTPUT SECTION.
00120  FILE-CONTROL.
00130      SELECT POEMS-FILE-IN  ASSIGN TO INFILE.
00140      SELECT POEMS-FILE-OUT ASSIGN TO PRINTER.
00150
00160 ******************************************************************
```

FIGURE 18.13 *continued*

```
 DATA DIVISION.
 FILE SECTION.
 FD  POEMS-FILE-IN
     RECORD CONTAINS 80 CHARACTERS.
 01  POEMS-RECORD-IN                                 PIC X(80).
 FD  POEMS-FILE-OUT.
 01  POEMS-RECORD-OUT                                PIC X(120).
 WORKING-STORAGE SECTION.
 01  MORE-INPUT          VALUE "Y"                   PIC X.
     88 THERE-IS-NO-MORE-INPUT                       VALUE "N".
     88 THERE-IS-NO-INPUT                            VALUE "N".
 01  LINE-OF-POETRY                                  PIC X(37).
     88 END-OF-INPUT-RECORD                          VALUE SPACE.
 01  LINE-TOO-LONG                                   PIC X(30)
     VALUE "LINE LONGER THAN 37 CHARACTERS".
 01  LINE-LIMIT          VALUE 37                    PIC S99 COMP SYNC.
 01  CHARACTER-COUNTER                               PIC S99 COMP SYNC.
 01  CHARACTER-POINTER                               PIC S99 COMP SYNC.
 01  POEMS-RECORD-W.
     05  POEMS-LINES                                 PIC X(80).
     05  LINE-TERMINATOR                             PIC X.
         88 END-OF-POEM                              VALUE QUOTE.
 01  POEMS-LINES-SAVE                                PIC X(80).
 01  REPORT-HEADING-1.
     05                      VALUE SPACES            PIC X(55).
     05                      VALUE "POEMS"           PIC X(5).
 01  REPORT-HEADING-2.
     05                      VALUE SPACES            PIC X(35).
     05                      VALUE "INPUT"           PIC X(65).
     05                      VALUE "POEM"            PIC X(4).
 01  REPORT-HEADING-3.
     05                      VALUE ALL "*"           PIC X(80).
 01  PRINT-LINE.
     05  POEMS-LINE-OUT                              PIC X(83).
     05  LINE-OF-POETRY-OUT                          PIC X(37).
 01  NO-INPUT-DATA.
     05                      VALUE SPACES            PIC X(9).
     05                    VALUE "NO INPUT DATA"     PIC X(13).
*******************************************************************
```

continued

The Procedure Division is not difficult to follow if the hierarchy diagram of Figure 18.12 is kept near at hand. In the main control paragraph PRINT-POEMS, the PERFORM statement at line 00720 executes UNTIL there are no more data. In PROCESS-ALL-POEMS the PERFORM statement at line 00790 processes each poem UNTIL the end of the poem is recognized by its QUOTE. And in PROCESS-ONE-POEM, the PERFORM statement at line 00840 processes a single input record UNTIL nothing remains of the input record except perhaps trailing SPACES.

Notice the WITH TEST AFTER phrases in the PERFORM statements at lines 00790 and 00840. The phrase is needed in line 00790 because the condition END-OF-POEM may already be true when the program arrives at line 00790, from the end of the previous poem. In order for a PERFORM . . . UNTIL statement to execute the PERFORMed paragraph at least once, the condition either must be false when the program arrives at the PERFORM statement or you must use the WITH TEST AFTER phrase. In line 00840, the condition END-OF-INPUT-RECORD may already be true from the previous input record.

At line 00990 is part of the coding needed to get group indication of the input record, POEMS-LINES. POEMS-LINES is MOVEd both to POEMS-LINES-SAVE and the output print field, POEMS-LINE-OUT. Later, the program will test for a change in value of POEMS-LINE-SAVE and control the printing of POEMS-LINE-OUT appropriately. You will soon see how.

In the paragraph INITIALIZE-FOR-POEM, line 01060, the POINTER is set to 2 so that the first UNSTRING for the poem will begin with character position 2, ignoring the opening quotation marks. Scans of the second and subsequent records for each poem begin in character position 1.

The UNSTRING statement, at line 01230, shows many of the features of UNSTRING. The word following UNSTRING is the sending field. The DELIMITED BY clause, line 01240, lists all of the delimiters to be searched for, separated by OR. The INTO phrase names one receiving field.

Optional phrases follow, at lines 01260 through 01280. The **DELIMITER** phrase tells the system to MOVE, to the field named, each delimiter as it is found. In this case, our delimiters will be MOVEd to LINE-TERMINATOR. Remember that if two delimiters are found right next to each other in the sending field, SPACES will be MOVEd to LINE-OF-POETRY.

The COUNT phrase tells COBOL to MOVE, to the field named, a count of the number of characters scanned in the sending field (excluding the number of characters in the delimiter).

If there were more than one receiving field, each receiving field could have its own DELIMITER field and/or COUNT field.

The POINTER phrase names the field that is used to keep track of the scan in the sending field. After execution of the UNSTRING, the field CHARACTER-POINTER points one character position to the right of the last character scanned.

FIGURE 18.13 *continued*

```
S COBOL II RELEASE 3.2 09/05/90                    P18003   DATE NOV 01,1991 T
----+-*A-1-B--+----2----+----3----+----4----+----5----+----6----+----7-|--+

       PROCEDURE DIVISION.
       PRINT-POEMS.
           PERFORM INITIALIZATION
           PERFORM PROCESS-ALL-POEMS UNTIL THERE-IS-NO-MORE-INPUT
           PERFORM TERMINATION
           STOP RUN
           .

       PROCESS-ALL-POEMS.
           PERFORM INITIALIZE-FOR-POEM
           PERFORM PROCESS-ONE-POEM WITH TEST AFTER UNTIL END-OF-POEM
           PERFORM TERMINATE-POEM
           .

       PROCESS-ONE-POEM.
           PERFORM PROCESS-ONE-INPUT-RECORD WITH TEST AFTER UNTIL
               END-OF-INPUT-RECORD
           MOVE 1 TO CHARACTER-POINTER
           PERFORM READ-ONE-INPUT-RECORD
           .

       INITIALIZATION.
           OPEN INPUT  POEMS-FILE-IN
                OUTPUT POEMS-FILE-OUT
           WRITE POEMS-RECORD-OUT FROM REPORT-HEADING-1 AFTER PAGE
           WRITE POEMS-RECORD-OUT FROM REPORT-HEADING-2 AFTER 2
           WRITE POEMS-RECORD-OUT FROM REPORT-HEADING-3
           MOVE SPACES TO POEMS-RECORD-OUT
           WRITE POEMS-RECORD-OUT
           PERFORM READ-ONE-INPUT-RECORD
           MOVE POEMS-LINES TO POEMS-LINES-SAVE
                               POEMS-LINE-OUT
           IF THERE-IS-NO-INPUT
               WRITE POEMS-RECORD-OUT FROM NO-INPUT-DATA
           END-IF
           .

       INITIALIZE-FOR-POEM.
           MOVE 2 TO CHARACTER-POINTER
           .

       TERMINATION.
           CLOSE POEMS-FILE-IN
                 POEMS-FILE-OUT
           .

       PROCESS-ONE-INPUT-RECORD.
           PERFORM UNSTRING-ONE-LINE-OF-POETRY
           IF NOT END-OF-INPUT-RECORD
               PERFORM PRODUCE-ONE-LINE-OF-POETRY
           END-IF
           .

       UNSTRING-ONE-LINE-OF-POETRY.
           UNSTRING POEMS-RECORD-W
               DELIMITED BY "/" OR QUOTE
               INTO LINE-OF-POETRY
                   DELIMITER LINE-TERMINATOR
                   COUNT     CHARACTER-COUNTER
               POINTER CHARACTER-POINTER
           .

```

continued

The remainder of the coding needed to get group indication of POEMS-LINES is shown in lines 01350–01370 and 01450. POEMS-LINE-OUT gets data MOVEd to it only when its value changes, in the IF statement at line 01350. And at line 01450, POEMS-LINE-OUT is blanked (along with the rest of the output print area), so that it will not print except when it has data MOVEd to it in line 01360.

FIGURE *18.13* ***continued***

```
S COBOL II RELEASE 3.2 09/05/90               P18003   DATE NOV 01,1991 T
----+-*A-1-B--+----2----+----3----+----4----+----5----+----6----+----7-|--+

01310  PRODUCE-ONE-LINE-OF-POETRY.
01320      IF CHARACTER-COUNTER GREATER THAN LINE-LIMIT
01330          MOVE LINE-TOO-LONG TO LINE-OF-POETRY
01340      END-IF
01350      IF POEMS-LINES NOT = POEMS-LINES-SAVE
01360          MOVE POEMS-LINES TO POEMS-LINE-OUT
01370                              POEMS-LINES-SAVE
01380      END-IF
01390      PERFORM PRINT-THE-LINE
01400      .
01410
01420  PRINT-THE-LINE.
01430      MOVE LINE-OF-POETRY TO LINE-OF-POETRY-OUT
01440      WRITE POEMS-RECORD-OUT FROM PRINT-LINE
01450      MOVE SPACES TO PRINT-LINE
01460      .
01470
01480  TERMINATE-POEM.
01490      MOVE SPACES TO POEMS-RECORD-OUT
01500      WRITE POEMS-RECORD-OUT AFTER 2
01510      .
01520
01530  READ-ONE-INPUT-RECORD.
01540      READ POEMS-FILE-IN INTO POEMS-LINES
01550          AT END
01560              SET THERE-IS-NO-MORE-INPUT TO TRUE
01570      .
```

Program P18-03 was run with the input data shown in Figure 18.10 and produced the output shown in Figure 18.14.

FIGURE *18.14* **Output from Program P18-03**

```
                                         POEMS

                              INPUT                                                      POEM
*******************************************************************************

"SOME PEOPLE/WILL DO ANYTHING/IN ORDER TO SAY/THEY'VE DONE IT."          SOME PEOPLE
                                                                         WILL DO ANYTHING
                                                                         IN ORDER TO SAY
                                                                         THEY'VE DONE IT.


"LIFE IS FUNNY/THAT WAY.../THERE'S A PIPER/'ROUND EVERY/CORNER/WAITING/  LIFE IS FUNNY
                                                                         THAT WAY...
                                                                         THERE'S A PIPER
                                                                         'ROUND EVERY
                                                                         CORNER
                                                                         WAITING
TO BE PAID."                                                             TO BE PAID.

"HOW MANY POETS DOES ONE SMALL PLANET NEED?/WHO KNOWS?/WHO IS ASKING?/   LINE LONGER THAN 37 CHARACTERS
                                                                         WHO KNOWS?
                                                                         WHO IS ASKING?
IS ANYONE ANSWERING?"                                                    IS ANYONE ANSWERING?
```

EXERCISE 3

In certain computer systems, the names of data sets consist of one or more components separated by periods. Examples of such names are:

a. DATA

b. DATA.PAYROLL

c. VSAM.DATA.SET

Each component may be from 1 to 8 characters long.

Write a program to read input data records each containing the name of one data set starting in column 1. For each record read, have your program print the data set name and also print each component on a separate line, as shown in the output format in Figure 18.E3. If any component is longer than 8 characters, have your program print a message COMPONENT LONGER THAN 8 CHARACTERS.

FIGURE 18.E3 Output format for Exercise 3

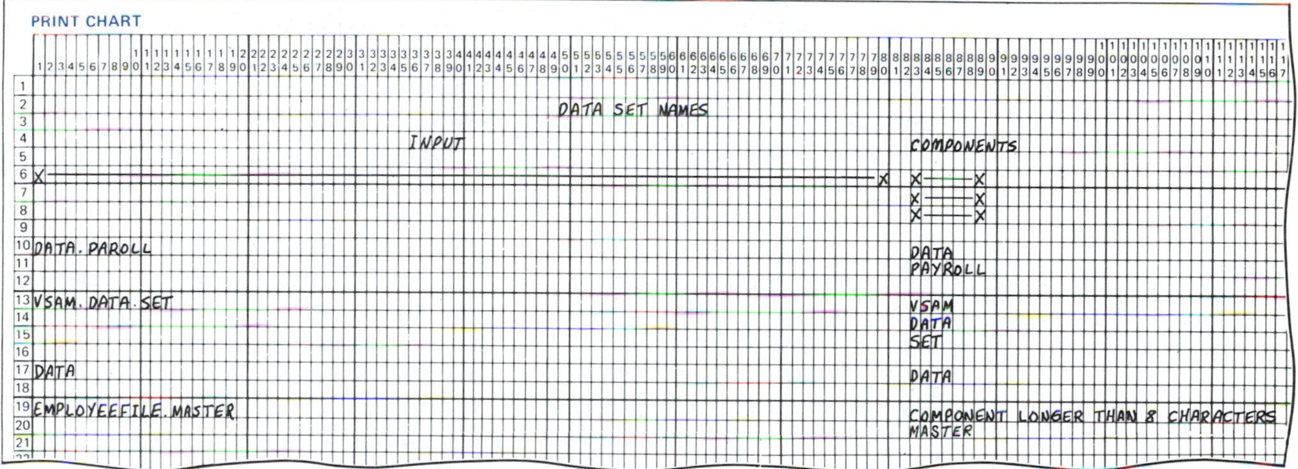

The Format of the UNSTRING Statement

The format of the UNSTRING statement is as follows:

```
UNSTRING identifier-1

   [ DELIMITED BY [ALL] {identifier-2} [OR [ALL] {identifier-3}] ...]
                        {literal-1   }           {literal-2   }

   INTO {identifier-4 [DELIMITER IN identifier-5] [COUNT IN identifier-6]} ...
   [WITH POINTER identifier-7]
   [TALLYING IN identifier-8]
   [ON OVERFLOW imperative-statement-8]
   [NOT ON OVERFLOW imperative-statement-2]
   [END-UNSTRING]
```

This format is difficult to read, because it has many optional words and phrases, and confusing nesting of optional phrases. The format shows that the word UNSTRING is required and that it must be followed by identifier-1, the name of the sending field. The DELIMITED BY clause is shown as optional. If it is omitted, the UNSTRING statement operates on the basis of the sizes of the receiving fields, as described earlier in this chapter. If DELIMITED BY is used, there can be only one such clause in the statement.

A DELIMITED BY clause must contain at least one identifier or literal, and it may contain as many as desired, separated by the word OR. These are shown in the format as identifier-2, literal-1, identifier-3, and literal-2. Any identifier or literal in a DELIMITED BY clause may be preceded by the optional word ALL. If ALL is used, then the UNSTRING statement treats consecutive appearances of the delimiter in the sending field as one appearance of that delimiter.

There must be exactly one INTO clause in an UNSTRING statement. It must contain at least one receiving field, and it may contain as many as desired. The receiving field is shown as identifier-4. Each receiving field may have associated with it an optional DELIMITER phrase and/or an optional COUNT phrase.

Using STRING and UNSTRING Together

We now develop a program to show how STRING and UNSTRING can be used together in one program to edit English prose. Program P18-04 examines English words, phrases, and sentences and replaces all occurrences of the word MAN with the word PERSON and all occurrences of the word MEN with PERSONS. Although the goal of such a program may seem admirable, the results are perhaps not exactly what one would expect or want. Typical input such as

```
MANY DISTINCTLY HUMAN ACTIVITIES EMANATED FROM ERAS
  AS DISTANT AS CAVEMAN DAYS.
MEN AND WOMEN ENGAGED IN MENDING, MANUFACTURING, AND
  MENTAL MANIPULATIONS.
```

and

```
THE MAN-EATING TIGER MANAGED ANYWAY TO MANGLE
   THE WOMAN'S MANDIBLE.
```

would produce output of the kind shown in Figure 18.15.

FIGURE *18.15* **Output format for Program P18-04**

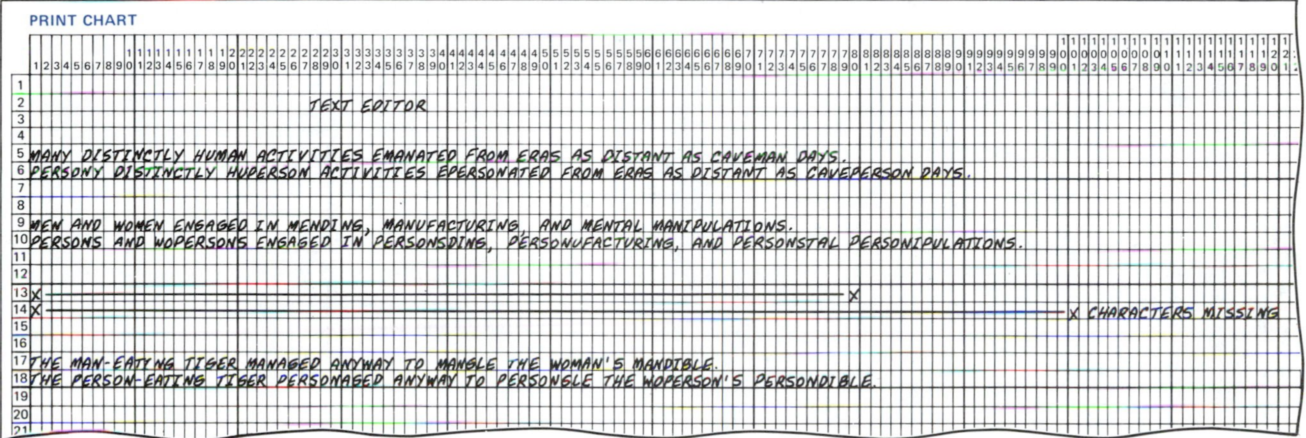

Each selection to be edited is keyed in a single input record starting in position 1. If the edited text occupies more than 120 print positions, Program P18-04 inserts the words CHARACTERS MISSING at the right end of the edited print line.

A hierarchy diagram of the main loop of Program P18-04 is shown in Figure 18.16. For each input record, the program will "Unstring a piece" of the line of text. The first time "Unstring a piece" executes on an input record, it UNSTRINGs all the text up to but not including the first appearance of the word MAN or MEN into a text field, and places the delimiter MAN or MEN into a delimiter field. Each subsequent execution of "Unstring a piece" on the same record UNSTRINGs into the text field all the text between the previous appearance of MAN or MEN up to the next appearance of MAN or MEN, and places the delimiter MAN or MEN into the delimiter field. The text field can sometimes be SPACES, as when MAN and/or MEN begin the input line or when the words MAN and/or MEN are immediately adjacent in the input.

"Replace MAN and MEN" examines the delimiter field for the words MAN and MEN, and replaces MAN with PERSON and MEN with PERSONS. "String a piece" then STRINGs the text field and the word PERSON or PERSONS into an ever-growing output line. "Process line" continues to operate on an input record until the input record is completely processed or the output line grows to more than 120 characters, whichever comes first.

FIGURE 18.16 Hierarchy diagram for main loop of Program P18-04

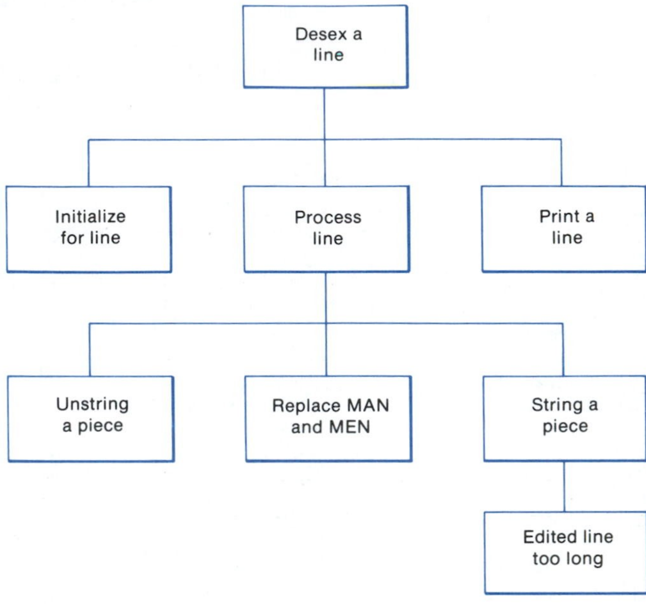

Program P18-04 is shown in Figure 18.17. The field TEXT-RECORD-IN, line 00220, serves as the sending field for the UNSTRING operation. The input record in TEXT-RECORD-IN is broken down and its pieces, namely its delimiters and the text between delimiters, are placed into fields in working storage. The EDITED-LINE, line 00320, is where the edited pieces are strung together for printing.

LINE-BREAKDOWN, line 00330, provides working-storage space for the delimiters (in DELIMITER-W) and the text between them (in LINE-SEGMENT). The field SEGMENT-LENGTH, line 00350, is used by the UNSTRING operation to record the number of characters in each LINE-SEGMENT.

FIGURE 18.17 Program P18-04

```
S COBOL II RELEASE 3.2 09/05/90                    P18004    DATE NOV 07,1991 T
----+-*A-1-B--+----2----+----3----+----4----+----5----+----6----+----7-%--+

00010  IDENTIFICATION DIVISION.
00020  PROGRAM-ID.  P18-04.
00030 *
00040 *     THIS PROGRAM EDITS ENGLISH TEXT, REPLACING ALL
00050 *     APPEARANCES OF MAN WITH PERSON AND ALL APPEARANCES
00060 *     OF MEN WITH PERSONS.
00070 *
00080 ***********************************************************************
```

FIGURE 18.17 ***continued***

```
 ENVIRONMENT DIVISION.
 INPUT-OUTPUT SECTION.
 FILE-CONTROL.
     SELECT TEXT-FILE-OUT  ASSIGN TO PRINTER.
     SELECT TEXT-FILE-IN   ASSIGN TO INFILE.
******************************************************************
 DATA DIVISION.
 FILE SECTION.
 FD  TEXT-FILE-IN.
 01  TEXT-RECORD-IN                         PIC X(80).
 FD  TEXT-FILE-OUT.
 01  TEXT-RECORD-OUT                        PIC X(120).
 WORKING-STORAGE SECTION.
 01  MORE-INPUT               VALUE "Y"     PIC X.
     88 THERE-IS-NO-MORE-INPUT              VALUE "N".
     88 THERE-IS-NO-INPUT                   VALUE "N".
 01  EDITED-LINE                            PIC X(120).
 01  LINE-BREAKDOWN.
     05  LINE-SEGMENT                       PIC X(81).
     05  SEGMENT-LENGTH    COMP SYNC        PIC S99.
     05  DELIMITER-W                        PIC X(7).
 01  SIZES-AND-NUMBERS            COMP.
     05  SIZE-OF-INPUT-RECORD         VALUE 80        PIC S99.
     05  SIZE-OF-EDITED-LINE          VALUE 120       PIC S999.
 01  POINTERS                     COMP.
     05  INPUT-RECORD-POINTER                         PIC S99.
     05  EDITED-LINE-POINTER                          PIC S999.
 01  REPORT-HEADING.
     05              VALUE SPACES           PIC X(27).
     05              VALUE "TEXT EDITOR"    PIC X(11).
 01  TEXT-LINE-OUT                          PIC X(80).
 01  EDITED-LINE-OUT                        PIC X(120).
 01  NO-INPUT-DATA.
     05              VALUE SPACES           PIC X(9).
     05              VALUE "NO INPUT DATA"  PIC X(13).
******************************************************************
```

continued

The Procedure Division, which starts at line 00590, follows the hierarchy diagram. The PERFORM statement at line 00820 operates under control of pointers for the sending and receiving fields of the UNSTRING and STRING operations, respectively. These are initialized in the paragraph INITIALIZE-FOR-LINE, line 00960, to point to the left end of their respective fields.

The UNSTRING statement, line 01090, UNSTRINGs a piece of text and a delimiter. It also places a COUNT of the size of the piece of text into the field SEGMENT-LENGTH. This length can sometimes be zero. In REPLACE-MAN-AND-MEN, line 01170, MAN is replaced by PERSON and MEN by PERSONS. Both IF statements are needed, for DELIMITER-W might contain neither MAN nor MEN. When the UNSTRING statement reaches the end of the sending field without finding a delimiter, it places SPACES into DELIMITER-W.

STRING-A-PIECE, line 01270, determines what to STRING into the output line, if anything. The WHEN phrase at line 01290 determines whether the end of the input record has been reached (and there is nothing more to STRING into the output line), the WHEN phrase at line 01310 determines whether there is some text and a delimiter, and the WHEN phrase at line 01400 takes care of situations where there is a delimiter but no text. If there is some text, the STRING statement at line 01320 places it and PERSON, PERSONS, or SPACES into the output line; if there is no text, the STRING statement at line 01400 places just PERSON, PERSONS, or SPACES into the output line. Notice the use of **reference modification** in line 01320. Reference modification allows a programmer to refer to any part of a field. Here, by using the reference modification 1: SEGMENT-LENGTH on the field LINE-SEGMENT, we refer to that portion of LINE-SEGMENT that begins in position 1 of the field and has a length equal to the

FIGURE *18.17* ***continued***

```
S COBOL II RELEASE 3.2 09/05/90                    P18004   DATE NOV 07,1991 T
----+-*A-1-B--+----2----+----3----+----4----+----5----+----6----+----7-%--+

00580
00590  PROCEDURE DIVISION.
00600  CONTROL-PARAGRAPH.
00610      PERFORM INITIALIZATION
00620      PERFORM DESEX-A-LINE UNTIL THERE-IS-NO-MORE-INPUT
00630      PERFORM TERMINATION
00640      STOP RUN
00650      .
00660
00670  INITIALIZATION.
00680      OPEN INPUT  TEXT-FILE-IN
00690            OUTPUT TEXT-FILE-OUT
00700      READ TEXT-FILE-IN
00710          AT END
00720              SET THERE-IS-NO-INPUT TO TRUE
00730      END-READ
00740      WRITE TEXT-RECORD-OUT FROM REPORT-HEADING AFTER PAGE
00750      IF THERE-IS-NO-INPUT
00760          WRITE TEXT-RECORD-OUT FROM NO-INPUT-DATA
00770      END-IF
00780      .
00790
```

FIGURE 18.17 *continued*

```
DESEX-A-LINE.
    PERFORM INITIALIZE-FOR-LINE
    PERFORM PROCESS-LINE UNTIL
            SPACES = LINE-SEGMENT AND DELIMITER-W
            OR
            INPUT-RECORD-POINTER
                           GREATER THAN SIZE-OF-INPUT-RECORD
            OR
            EDITED-LINE-POINTER
                           GREATER THAN SIZE-OF-EDITED-LINE
    PERFORM PRINT-A-LINE
    READ TEXT-FILE-IN
        AT END
            SET THERE-IS-NO-MORE-INPUT TO TRUE
    .

INITIALIZE-FOR-LINE.
    MOVE SPACES TO EDITED-LINE
    MOVE 1 TO INPUT-RECORD-POINTER
              EDITED-LINE-POINTER
    .

PROCESS-LINE.
    PERFORM UNSTRING-A-PIECE
    PERFORM REPLACE-MAN-AND-MEN
    PERFORM STRING-A-PIECE
    .

UNSTRING-A-PIECE.
    UNSTRING TEXT-RECORD-IN
        DELIMITED BY "MAN" OR "MEN"
            INTO LINE-SEGMENT
                DELIMITER DELIMITER-W
                COUNT     SEGMENT-LENGTH
        POINTER INPUT-RECORD-POINTER
    .

REPLACE-MAN-AND-MEN.
    IF DELIMITER-W = "MAN"
        MOVE "PERSON" TO DELIMITER-W
    ELSE
    IF DELIMITER-W = "MEN"
        MOVE "PERSONS" TO DELIMITER-W
    END-IF
    END-IF
    .

STRING-A-PIECE.
    EVALUATE TRUE
    WHEN SPACES = LINE-SEGMENT AND DELIMITER-W
        CONTINUE
    WHEN SEGMENT-LENGTH NOT = 0
        STRING LINE-SEGMENT (1: SEGMENT-LENGTH)
                            DELIMITED BY SIZE
               DELIMITER-W  DELIMITED BY SPACE
        INTO EDITED-LINE
        POINTER EDITED-LINE-POINTER
        OVERFLOW
           PERFORM EDITED-LINE-TOO-LONG
        END-STRING
    WHEN OTHER
        STRING DELIMITER-W  DELIMITED BY SPACE
        INTO EDITED-LINE
        POINTER EDITED-LINE-POINTER
        OVERFLOW
           PERFORM EDITED-LINE-TOO-LONG
        END-STRING
    END-EVALUATE
    .
```

continued

value in SEGMENT-LENGTH. Reference modifiers always appear in parentheses immediately after the name of the field they are modifying. Remember that SEGMENT-LENGTH contains a COUNT of the size of the piece of text that was unstrung from the input record. The OVERFLOW phrase executes the paragraph EDITED-LINE-TOO-LONG, line 01500, if the EDITED-LINE-POINTER gets to exceed 120. If so, any characters that might have been strung INTO positions 102 through 120 of EDITED-LINE already are replaced by the words CHARACTERS MISSING preceded by a space.

FIGURE *18.17* ***continued***

```
S COBOL II RELEASE 3.2 09/05/90                P18004    DATE NOV 07,1991 T
----+-*A-1-B--+----2----+----3----+----4----+----5----+----6----+----7-%--+

01490
01500     EDITED-LINE-TOO-LONG.
01510         MOVE 102 TO EDITED-LINE-POINTER
01520         STRING " CHARACTERS MISSING" DELIMITED BY SIZE
01530             INTO EDITED-LINE
01540             POINTER EDITED-LINE-POINTER
01550         .
01560
01570    PRINT-A-LINE.
01580         WRITE TEXT-RECORD-OUT FROM TEXT-RECORD-IN AFTER 3
01590         WRITE TEXT-RECORD-OUT FROM EDITED-LINE
01600         .
01610
01620    TERMINATION.
01630         CLOSE TEXT-FILE-IN
01640               TEXT-FILE-OUT
01650         .
```

Program P18-04 was run with the input data shown in Figure 18.18 and produced the output shown in Figure 18.19.

FIGURE *18.18* **Input to Program P18-04**

```
--------------------------------------------------------------------------------
         1         2         3         4         5         6         7         8
12345678901234567890123456789012345678901234567890123456789012345678901234567890
--------------------------------------------------------------------------------
MANY DISTINCTLY HUMAN ACTIVITIES EMANATED FROM ERAS AS DISTANT AS CAVEMAN DAYS.
MEN AND WOMEN ENGAGED IN MENDING, MANUFACTURING, AND MENTAL MANIPULATIONS.
USE MANKIND, HUMANS, OR HUMANKIND INSTEAD OF MAN OR MEN IN WORDS LIKE SALESMEN.
THE MAN-EATING TIGER MANAGED ANYWAY TO MANGLE THE WOMAN'S MANDIBLE.
MAN MEN WOMAN WOMEN MAN WOMAN MAN MEN WOMAN WOMEN MAN MEN WOMAN WOMEN MAN MEN
MENMENMENMENMENMENMENMENMENMENMENMEN
```

FIGURE 18.19 Output from Program P18-04

```
                        TEXT EDITOR

MANY DISTINCTLY HUMAN ACTIVITIES EMANATED FROM ERAS AS DISTANT AS CAVEMAN DAYS.
PERSONY DISTINCTLY HUPERSON ACTIVITIES EPERSONATED FROM ERAS AS DISTANT AS CAVEPERSON DAYS.

MEN AND WOMEN ENGAGED IN MENDING, MANUFACTURING, AND MENTAL MANIPULATIONS.
PERSONS AND WOPERSONS ENGAGED IN PERSONSDING, PERSONUFACTURING, AND PERSONSTAL PERSONIPULATIONS.

USE MANKIND, HUMANS, OR HUMANKIND INSTEAD OF MAN OR MEN IN WORDS LIKE SALESMEN.
USE PERSONKIND, HUPERSONS, OR HUPERSONKIND INSTEAD OF PERSON OR PERSONS IN WORDS LIKE SALESPERSONS.

THE MAN-EATING TIGER MANAGED ANYWAY TO MANGLE THE WOMAN'S MANDIBLE.
THE PERSON-EATING TIGER PERSONAGED ANYWAY TO PERSONGLE THE WOPERSON'S PERSONDIBLE.

MAN MEN WOMAN WOMEN MAN WOMAN MAN MEN WOMAN WOMEN MAN MEN WOMAN WOMEN MAN MEN
PERSON PERSONS WOPERSON WOPERSONS PERSON WOPERSON PERSON PERSONS WOPERSON WOPERSONS PERSON PERSONS WO CHARACTERS MISSING

MENMENMENMENMENMENMENMENMENMENMEN
PERSONSPERSONSPERSONSPERSONSPERSONSPERSONSPERSONSPERSONSPERSONSPERSONSPERSONS
```

EXERCISE *4*

Write a program to read free-form name data, rearrange the fields, and print the name with its first name first. The input name data begins in column 1 of each card and consists of a last name, a first name, an optional middle initial, and an optional tag such as Jr. or CPA. The name is in the following format:

a. Last name followed immediately by a comma and a space.

b. First name followed by a space, if there is a middle initial; first name followed by a space, if there is neither a tag nor a middle initial; first name followed by a comma and a space, if there is a tag but no middle initial.

c. Middle initial, if any, followed by a period. If there is also a tag, the period following the middle initial is followed by a comma and a space.

d. Tag, if any.

Examples of these possibilities are as follows:

Input	*Output*
Popkin, Gary	Gary Popkin
Popkin, Gary S.	Gary S. Popkin
Popkin, Gary, CDP	Gary Popkin, CDP
Popkin, Gary S., CDP	Gary S. Popkin, CDP

In your own input data, make up names of different lengths to be sure your program works. Test your program with very short names and very long ones.

The INSPECT Statement

The **INSPECT** verb has four formats and a lot of capabilities. In general, the INSPECT verb examines a field from left to right looking for characters or groups of characters that are specified by the programmer. The INSPECT verb can be directed to look for ALL appearances of a character or group of characters, or only **LEADING** appearances (as with LEADING SPACES or LEADING ZEROS), or just the FIRST appearance. The INSPECT verb can be directed to confine its search to only a particular portion of the field, BEFORE and/or AFTER the first appearance of some other character or group of characters.

Once the searched-for characters or groups of characters are found, the INSPECT verb can be directed either to count them, replace them with some other specified characters or groups of characters, or first count them and then replace them.

The four formats of the INSPECT statement are shown here.

Format 1:

```
INSPECT identifier-1 TALLYING

 {                    {CHARACTERS [{BEFORE} INITIAL {identifier-4}] ...                  } }
 {identifier-2 FOR    {            {AFTER }         {literal-2   }                       } }...
 {                    {{ALL    } {{identifier-3} [{BEFORE} INITIAL {identifier-4}]...}...} }
 {                    {{LEADING} {{literal-1   } [{AFTER }         {literal-2   }]      } } }...
```

Format 2:

```
INSPECT identifier-1 REPLACING

 {CHARACTERS BY {identifier-5} [{BEFORE} INITIAL {identifier-4}] ...                               }
 {              {literal-3   } [{AFTER }         {literal-2   }]                                   }
 {{ALL    }  {{identifier-3} BY {identifier-5} [{BEFORE} INITIAL {identifier-4}] ...}...           }...
 {{LEADING}  {{literal-1   }    {literal-3   } [{AFTER }         {literal-2   }]    }              }
 {{FIRST  }                                                                                        }
```

Format 3:

```
INSPECT identifier-1 TALLYING

 {                    {CHARACTERS [{BEFORE} INITIAL {identifier-4}] ...                  } }
 {identifier-2 FOR    {            {AFTER }         {literal-2   }                       } }...
 {                    {{ALL    } {{identifier-3} [{BEFORE} INITIAL {identifier-4}]...}...} }
 {                    {{LEADING} {{literal-1   } [{AFTER }         {literal-2   }]      } } }...

  REPLACING

 {CHARACTERS BY {identifier-5} [{BEFORE} INITIAL {identifier-4}] ...                               }
 {              {literal-3   } [{AFTER }         {literal-2   }]                                   }
 {{ALL    }  {{identifier-3} BY {identifier-5} [{BEFORE} INITIAL {identifier-4}]...}...            }...
 {{LEADING}  {{literal-1   }    {literal-3   } [{AFTER }         {literal-2   }]   }               }
 {{FIRST  }                                                                                        }
```

Format 4:

```
INSPECT identifier-1 CONVERTING {identifier-6} TO {identifier-7}
                                {literal-4   }    {literal-5   }
    [{BEFORE} INITIAL {identifier-4}] ...
     {AFTER }         {literal-2   }
```

An INSPECT statement must contain either a TALLYING phrase, a **REPLACING** phrase, a **CONVERTING** phrase, or a TALLYING phrase and a REPLACING phrase. If TALLYING and REPLACING are both specified, all TALLYING is done before any replacement is made.

Identifier-1 is the INSPECTed item. It must be of USAGE DISPLAY. All other identifiers, except identifier-2 (the count field) must be elementary items of USAGE DISPLAY. Each literal must be nonnumeric. Any figurative constant may be used except ALL literal.

The TALLYING option is used to count ALL the appearances or just the LEADING appearances of literal-1 or the contents of identifier-3 in the INSPECTed field, or all **CHARACTERS** in the INSPECTed field. Optionally, the counting can be restricted to that portion of the INSPECTed field BEFORE or AFTER the **INITIAL** appearance of identifier-4 or literal-2.

An INSPECT statement may have no more than one TALLYING phrase. It may have as many count fields as desired, and each count field may serve to count as many different identifiers or literals as desired.

The REPLACING option is used to replace all CHARACTERS in the INSPECTed field BY literal-3 or the contents of identifier-5; or to replace ALL appearances, just the LEADING appearances, or just the FIRST appearance of literal-1 or the contents of identifier-3 in the INSPECTed field BY literal-3 or the contents of identifier-5. Optionally, replacement can be limited to that portion of the INSPECTed field BEFORE or AFTER the INITIAL appearance of literal-2 or the contents of identifier-4 in the INSPECTed field.

The CONVERTING option causes an INSPECT statement to behave as though it was written with the REPLACING phrase and with one or more ALL phrases. For example, the statement

```
INSPECT FIELD-1 CONVERTING
     "ABCD" TO "XYZX" AFTER QUOTE BEFORE "#"
```

is equivalent to

```
INSPECT FIELD-1 REPLACING
     ALL "A" BY "X" AFTER QUOTE BEFORE "#"
     ALL "B" BY "Y" AFTER QUOTE BEFORE "#"
     ALL "C" BY "Z" AFTER QUOTE BEFORE "#"
     ALL "D" BY "X" AFTER QUOTE BEFORE "#"
```

If the initial contents of FIELD-1 is AC''AEBDFBCD#AB''D the contents after execution of the INSPECT statement would be AC''XEYXFYZX#AB''D.

EXERCISE 5

Do the following:

a. Write an INSPECT statement that will count all appearances of the character M in the field WORD-2 and place the count into the field COUNT-2.

b. Write an INSPECT statement that will replace all appearances of leading zeros with the character F after the first appearance of the character M in WORD-3.

c. Write an INSPECT statement that will replace all appearances of the character B with the character H before the first appearance of the character Y in the field WORD-4.

d. Write an INSPECT statement that will count the number of characters in the field WORD-5 after the first appearance of the character K and place the count into the field COUNT-5.

Summary

The STRING verb enables COBOL to attach two or more fields or parts of fields end to end to form one large field. A STRING statement must have at least one sending field and exactly one receiving field; it may have as many sending fields as desired. Any combination of whole fields and parts of fields may be used as sending fields in a single STRING statement. Parts of fields to be sent may be DELIMITED BY one or more characters selected by the programmer. The STRING statement may use an optional POINTER field to keep track of the next available unused character position in the receiving field. An optional OVERFLOW phrase may be used to handle situations where all the sending fields together are too big to fit into the receiving field.

The UNSTRING verb can be used to break down a large field into smaller pieces. An UNSTRING statement must have exactly one sending field and at least one receiving field; it may have as many receiving fields as desired. An UNSTRING statement may have one DELIMITED BY clause, which must contain one or more delimiters. If the DELIMITED BY clause is used, the sending field is broken into pieces based on the appearances of the delimiter(s) in the sending field. For each piece of the sending field that is placed into a receiving field, the UNSTRING statement can also store the associated DELIMITER and a COUNT of the size of the piece.

If the DELIMITED BY phrase is not used, the UNSTRING statement breaks down the sending field on the basis of the sizes of the receiving fields. The DELIMITER and COUNT phrases may not be used when the DELIMITED BY phrase is omitted.

The TALLYING phrase may be used to obtain a count of the number of receiving fields that have data MOVEd to them. The UNSTRING statement does not zero out the TALLYING field but instead adds to its previous contents. An optional POINTER field may be used to keep track of the next character to be scanned in the sending field. An optional OVERFLOW phrase can be used to handle situations where the sending field is too large to fit into all the receiving fields.

The INSPECT verb examines a field from left to right, looking for characters or groups of characters specified by the programmer, and counts and/or replaces them when found. An INSPECT statement can look for ALL appearances of the searched-for character or characters, or it can look only for LEADING appearances. An INSPECT statement can be directed to confine its search to a particular portion of the field, BEFORE or AFTER the first appearance of some character or group of characters.

Fill-In Exercises

1. A STRING statement has exactly one ______ field.
2. The ______ fields in a STRING statement can all use the same ______ clause, or they may use separate ones.
3. The OVERFLOW phrase in a STRING statement handles situations where all the ______ fields cannot fit into the ______ field.
4. The POINTER in a STRING statement keeps track of the next ______ in the ______ field.
5. An UNSTRING statement has exactly one ______ field.
6. The delimiters in the DELIMITED BY clause of an UNSTRING statement are separated by the word ______.
7. The OVERFLOW phrase in an UNSTRING statement handles situations where the ______ field cannot fit into all the ______ fields.
8. The POINTER in an UNSTRING statement keeps track of the next ______ in the ______ field.
9. The TALLYING phrase in an UNSTRING statement counts the number of ______ fields that have data MOVEd to them.
10. The INSPECT statement examines fields from ______ to ______.
11. The ______ and ______ statements can operate on the basis of delimiters or field sizes, but not both.
12. If an INSPECT statement contains both a TALLYING option and a REPLACING option, all ______ is done before any ______ is done.
13. If the DELIMITER IN option is used in an UNSTRING statement and no delimiter is found in the sending field, the field named in the DELIMITER IN phrase is filled with ______ or ______.
14. A STRING statement must have at least one ______ field, and may have as many as desired.
15. An UNSTRING statement must have at least one ______ field, and may have as many as desired.

Review Exercises

1. Write a program to read four-digit numbers with two decimal places and print the amount in words. Typical input and output are shown in Figure 18.RE1.
2. Write a program to read and process input records, each record containing three unsigned integers separated from one another by one blank. The first integer starts in column 1 and the integers may be from 1 to 5 digits in length. For each record read, have your program UNSTRING and ADD the three integers, and print on one line the three integers and their sum.

FIGURE *18.RE1* **Output format for Review Exercise 1**

PRINT CHART

```
                     DECIMALS

          12.20   TWELVE AND TWO TENTHS

           2.50   TWO AND ONE HALF

          24.75   TWENTY-FOUR AND THREE QUARTERS

          19.45   NINETEEN AND FORTY-FIVE ONE-HUNDREDTHS

            .60   SIX TENTHS

          99.25   NINETY-NINE AND ONE QUARTER

           1.10   ONE AND ONE TENTH

           6.00   SIX EXACTLY

           7.01   SEVEN AND ONE HUNDREDTH

           8.02   EIGHT AND TWO HUNDREDTHS
```

3. Modify Program P18-04 so that only if a blank or period follows MAN will it be replaced by PERSON, and only if a blank or period follows MEN will it be replaced by PERSONS. The change improves the program somewhat but still leaves it far from perfect.

4. Do the following:
   a. Write an INSPECT statement that will replace all appearances of the character B with the character C after the first appearance of the character K.
   b. Write an INSPECT statement that will replace all appearances of Y by X, Z by B, and Q by W after the first appearance of the character S.
   c. Write an INSPECT statement that will replace all characters before the first appearance of the character B with the character C.

Project

Write a program to read name and address records in the format shown on page 477. There may be three, four, or five input records for a single name and address. The first input record for each name and address contains a Code 1 in position 1. Have your program strip the trailing blanks from each input record and STRING together and print the records for a single name and address separated by asterisks. For example, the three input records

```
1Gary S. Popkin
21921 President Street
3Brooklyn, NY 11221
```

should produce the following output:

```
Gary S. Popkin*1921 President Street*Brooklyn, NY 11221
```

CHAPTER 19

Subprograms

HERE ARE THE KEY POINTS YOU SHOULD LEARN FROM THIS CHAPTER

1. The several ways that subprograms are useful
2. How to write a subprogram in COBOL
3. How to link a subprogram to a calling program

KEY WORDS TO RECOGNIZE AND LEARN

subprogram
calling program
called program
call
main program
link
run unit
LINKAGE SECTION
EXIT PROGRAM
CALL
BY REFERENCE
BY CONTENT
calling sequence
last-used state
CANCEL

A **subprogram,** in any programming language, is a program that cannot be executed by itself but must execute under control of some other program. A program that controls the execution of a subprogram is referred to as a **calling program.** The subprogram itself is sometimes referred to as the **called program.** We say that the calling program **calls** the subprogram.

A subprogram may itself control the execution of some other subprogram. In that case, the higher-level subprogram becomes a calling program for a lower-level subprogram. The highest-level program, the one that operates on its own and under the control of no other, is called a **main program.** All the programs we have seen so far in this book are main programs. A hierarchy of programs is shown in Figure 19.1.

FIGURE 19.1 **Hierarchy of calling programs and called programs**

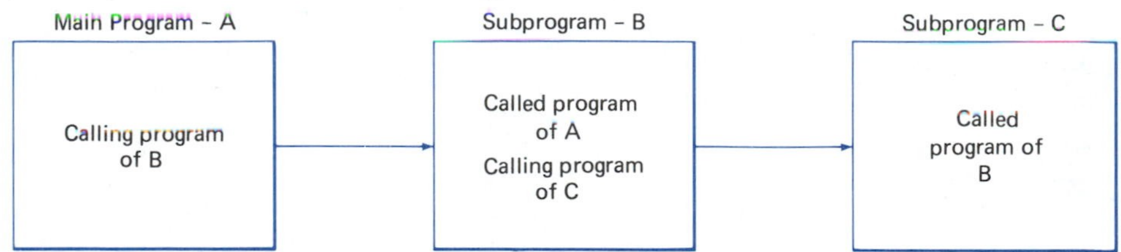

The Uses of Subprograms

There are about four main reasons why a computer installation might use subprograms written in COBOL. Different installations would find these four different reasons to have different degrees of importance.

First, a subprogram is portable. That is, it can be hooked on to, or **linked,** to whatever calling program needs it. To see how this feature can be useful, imagine a computer installation where many programmers are working on a large payroll system that contains many dozens of programs. Some of the programs might process only hourly-paid employees, some of the programs might process only employees paid semimonthly, and some might process all others. Several programs in the system might need to be able to compute employee withholding taxes. It would be very useful if a single routine could be written that would compute withholding taxes and that it be hooked on to each of the programs in the system that needed it. By writing the routine as a subprogram, exactly that result can be accomplished. In general, any procedure that is carried out by several programs should be written as a subprogram and made available to any program that needs it.

Another reason for using subprograms arises when a very large program is to be written. Often, such a program will be tested piece by piece. As each piece is found to work there is no need to test it further. Thus one piece of the program can be written as a main program and all the other pieces as subprograms. Each subprogram can be tested separately, without the need to recompile and retest other portions of the program that are known to work. When all the pieces of the program have been tested, they can be linked together and tested as a single **run unit.**

Later, if a modification needs to be made to this giant program, perhaps all the changes can be confined to just one or two of the subprograms in the run unit. Then it would be necessary to recompile and test only the subprograms that were changed. The remainder of the program, known to be working, would be left untouched.

A third reason for the use of subprograms is related to the second. Some programmers and managers think that breaking a big program into subprograms encourages good programming habits. They are probably right, though a programmer who is determined to make a mess of a program cannot be wholly stopped.

The final reason to use subprograms occurs when more than one language is needed to write a program. This can happen if a program written mainly in COBOL needs some coding in another language to carry out some processing that is either inconvenient or impossible in COBOL. Then a subprogram could be written in the other language and linked to a COBOL calling program. It can also happen that a program written mainly in some language other than COBOL would like to use some COBOL feature. Then a COBOL subprogram could be written and linked to a calling program in the other language.

EXERCISE 1

Try to think of other procedures, such as the preceding withholding tax example, that would be useful in more than one program and that should be written as subprograms. What about some of the procedures in the COBOL programs you have written? Are any of them used in more than one program? If you were to write any of those procedures as a subprogram, do you think there might be students in other COBOL classes in your school who could use your subprogram in their programs? And what about students who are going to take this course next year? Could they use your subprogram? Could students who are studying COBOL at another college use it?

Passing Data Between Programs

A calling program and its subprograms are compiled separately. During their compilations, the programs have nothing to do with one another. They may use the same or different names for files, records, paragraphs, data items, anything, and the names in one program will not interfere with the names in the other. When the programs are finally linked together to form a run unit, usually they must have some way of passing data between them. In the withholding tax example of the preceding section, a calling program would have to pass to its subprogram a worker's gross pay and perhaps some other data. After the subprogram computed the withholding tax, it would pass the results of its computation back to the calling program for further processing. The passing of data is accomplished not on the basis of the names that the data items have in the calling and called programs. You will see later how data are passed.

There can be situations where no data are passed between the calling program and the called program, and some where data are passed only one way—either from the calling program to the called program or from the called program to the calling program. It is this last case that we will see in our first example of a subprogram, Program P19-01.

Writing a Subprogram in COBOL

For this example, we will assume that a certain computer installation has many programs that need the time of day as one piece of data. Let's say that each of these programs prints the time of day as part of its output. Now, the COBOL statement "ACCEPT identifier FROM TIME" inserts the time of day into the field named as the identifier, but in a rather peculiar form, not a form that is suitable for printing directly onto an output report. So we can use a subprogram to ACCEPT the time of day, convert the TIME into printable form, and pass the printable time to any calling program that needs it.

The TIME, as provided by the ACCEPT statement, is an eight-digit field in the following form:

```
01  TIME-OF-DAY.
    05  HOUR                PIC 99.
    05  MINUTE              PIC 99.
    05  SECOND              PIC 99.
    05  100THS-OF-SECOND PIC 99.
```

There is no punctuation in the field, and, to make matters worse, the HOUR field is given in 24-hour military time (0 hours to 23 hours). Thus 2:41 PM would be expressed in eight digits as 14410000. Let us say that we would like our subprogram to ACCEPT the time, convert the time to a printable format such as that shown in Table 19.1, and pass the whole printable field to a calling program. Seconds and hundredths of a second are to be ignored in printing the time.

TABLE *19.1*
TIME as ACCEPTed into a COBOL program and in printable form

Eight-Digit Time	Printable Time
14410000	2:41 PM
02414567	2:41 AM
00101234	12:10 AM
00000000	12:00 AM
12000000	12:00 PM
12302345	12:30 PM
13450000	1:45 PM

You can see that converting the eight-digit time to printable form is not very easy. The program has to determine whether the time is AM or PM. That part is not too difficult, since all HOURs 0 through 11 are AM, and all HOURs 12 through 23 are PM. But then, if the time is PM, the program must adjust the HOUR figure to civilian time. Also, if the HOUR is 00, the program must print it as 12 AM (12 midnight). If the coding for this procedure had to appear in every program that prints the time, there would be a lot of unnecessary duplicate code.

Let us write this procedure as a subprogram so that it can be used by any calling program that needs it. Program P19-01A will be a calling program that we will write later to use the subprogram. Program P19-01B, which is shown in Figure 19.2, is the subprogram.

Notice that there is no Environment Division in this subprogram. That is because this program uses no input or output files, nor do we have need for any of the other entries in the Division. The program only ACCEPTs the TIME, prepares it for printing, and hands it to the calling program. The calling program can then do anything it likes with the field that it has been handed. The calling program will probably print it. The calling program will thus contain the definition of the output file.

In general, a subprogram can do anything that a main program can do. It can OPEN and CLOSE files, perform input and output operations, and have all of the same sections that a main program has. It just happens that this particular subprogram has no input or output operations to perform.

The Working Storage Section, line 00110, contains space for the TIME to be assigned to by the ACCEPT statement. TIME-OF-DAY-W, line 00120, is defined as eight digits long. Since we will not be using seconds or hundredths of a second in this program, the last four digits have been made nameless.

The Linkage Section

The Data Division of this subprogram contains no File Section, for there are no files in this subprogram. There is a new section at line 00190, however, the **LINKAGE SECTION.** A Linkage Section may appear only in a subprogram. The Linkage Section may appear in the Data Division along with any of the other sections in that division. If used, the Linkage Section must appear after the Working Storage Section and before the Report Section.

The Linkage Section must contain the definitions of all data fields that are passed in either direction between the calling program and the called program. If no data are passed, the Linkage Section can be omitted. In this case, we want only to pass a printable time-of-day field to the calling program. This field is defined as TIME-OF-DAY-L, at line 00200. It consists of two characters for the HOUR, one character for a colon, two characters for the MINUTE, and three characters for a space and the letters AM or PM. This is the format of the field as it will be passed to the calling program, ready for printing by the calling program.

FIGURE *19.2*

Program P19-01B

```
S COBOL II RELEASE 3.2 09/05/90                  P1901B   DATE NOV 08,1991 T
----+-*A-1-B--+----2----+----3----+----4----+----5----+----6----+----7-|--+

00010  IDENTIFICATION DIVISION.
00020  PROGRAM-ID.  P1901B.
00030 *
00040 *     THIS SUBPROGRAM ACCEPTS THE TIME OF DAY IN 8-DIGIT
00050 *     FORM AND CONVERTS IT TO HOURS AND MINUTES, AM OR PM,
00060 *     IGNORING SECONDS AND HUNDREDTHS OF A SECOND.
00070 *
00080 ***********************************************************************
00090
00100  DATA DIVISION.
00110  WORKING-STORAGE SECTION.
00120  01  TIME-OF-DAY-W.
00130      05  HOUR                     PIC 99.
00140          88  AM        VALUES 0  THRU 11.
00150          88  PM        VALUES 12 THRU 23.
00160      05  MINUTE                   PIC 99.
00170      05                           PIC 9(4).
00180
00190  LINKAGE SECTION.
00200  01  TIME-OF-DAY-L.
00210      05  HOUR                     PIC Z9.
00220      05  COLON-L                  PIC X.
00230      05  MINUTE                   PIC 99.
00240      05  AM-OR-PM                 PIC X(3).
00250
00260 ***********************************************************************
```

continued

Any entries that are legal in the definitions of input and output records in the File Section may be used in the Linkage Section. This means that any PICTURE, OCCURS, REDEFINES, COMP, SYNC, and level-88 entries, among others, may be used. Especially important is the fact that the VALUE clause must not be used in the Linkage Section except in connection with a level-88 entry, as in the File Section.

Procedure Division USING

The Procedure Division header, line 00280, contains a USING phrase. A USING phrase must appear in the Procedure Division header of a called program whenever data are to be passed in either direction between the calling program and the called program. The USING phrase must name all of the data fields that are to be passed, or else name group-level items that include all the data fields that are to be passed. Here we list only TIME-OF-DAY-L in the USING phrase. TIME-OF-DAY-L is a group-level name that includes all the elementary fields that are to be passed to the calling program.

The remainder of the Procedure Division looks unusual because there is no initialization to be done and no repetitive loop to be PERFORMed. Instead, the TIME is ACCEPTed into TIME-OF-DAY-W and processed into printable form in TIME-OF-DAY-L.

The **EXIT PROGRAM** statement at line 00450 terminates execution of this subprogram. Execution of a subprogram may be terminated with an EXIT PROGRAM statement or a STOP RUN statement. An EXIT PROGRAM statement returns control to the calling program and permits further processing. A STOP RUN statement, as usual, terminates the run unit. An EXIT PROGRAM statement must be the only statement in the paragraph in which it appears. Thus the EXIT PROGRAM statement in this subprogram is in its own paragraph, which here is EXECUTION-COMPLETE. The PERFORM statement in line 00350 is not strictly needed, because the flow of execution in COBOL programs proceeds from one paragraph to the next in the absence of any procedure branching statements such as PERFORM, STOP RUN, or EXIT PROGRAM. The PERFORM statement was included here only for consistency of programming style.

FIGURE ***19.2*** ***continued***

```
S COBOL II RELEASE 3.2 09/05/90                  P1901B   DATE NOV 08,1991 T
----+-*A-1-B--+----2----+----3----+----4----+----5----+----6----+----7-|--+

00270
00280  PROCEDURE DIVISION USING TIME-OF-DAY-L.
00290  CONTROL-PARAGRAPH.
00300      ACCEPT TIME-OF-DAY-W FROM TIME
00310      PERFORM SET-AM-OR-PM
00320      PERFORM FIX-HOUR
00330      MOVE CORR TIME-OF-DAY-W TO TIME-OF-DAY-L
00340      MOVE ":" TO COLON-L
00350      PERFORM EXECUTION-COMPLETE
00360      .
00370
00380  EXECUTION-COMPLETE.
00390      EXIT PROGRAM
00400      .
00410
```

FIGURE 19.2 ***continued***

```
SET-AM-OR-PM.
     IF AM
          MOVE " AM" TO AM-OR-PM
     ELSE
          MOVE " PM" TO AM-OR-PM
     END-IF
     .

FIX-HOUR.
     IF PM
          SUBTRACT 12 FROM HOUR OF TIME-OF-DAY-W
     END-IF
     IF HOUR OF TIME-OF-DAY-W IS EQUAL TO 0
          MOVE 12 TO HOUR OF TIME-OF-DAY-W
     END-IF
     .
```

Writing a Calling Program

Now that we have a subprogram that can provide the time of day to any calling program, let us write a calling program to use the subprogram. The calling program can be as complicated as we like. It can do any kind of processing, and when it needs the time of day, it can call upon the subprogram to provide it. Since right now we are mainly interested in seeing how the subprogram works, we can make our calling program very simple. The simplest possible calling program would be one that just has the subprogram hand the time of day to it, and then prints it. But to check that the subprogram is converting the time correctly, we will have our calling program do two things. It will call upon the subprogram to provide the time of day in printable form, and it will also ACCEPT the time of day itself and print the time in eight-digit form. Then we will be able to see whether the subprogram is doing the time conversion correctly. Program P19-01A, the calling program, will produce its output in the format shown in Figure 19.3.

FIGURE 19.3 **Output format for Program P19-01A**

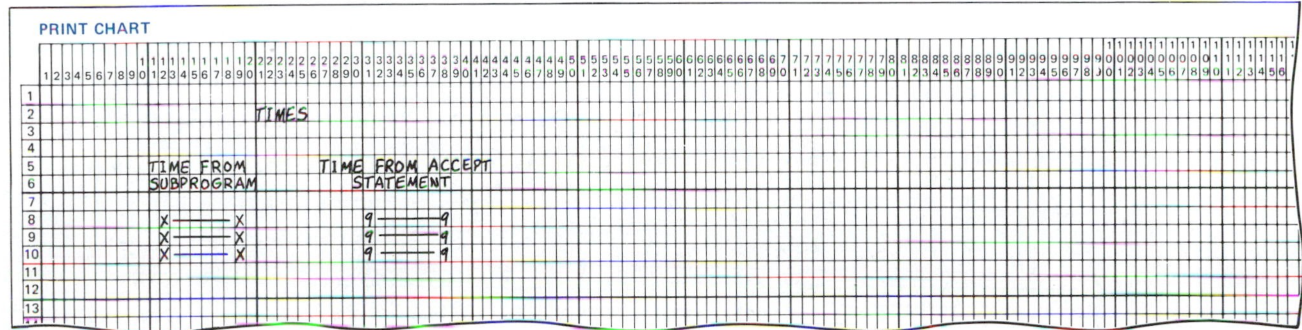

Program P19-01A is shown in Figure 19.4. PRINTABLE-TIME, line 00250, is the field that gets handed to Program P19-01A by the subprogram. In the print line, PRINTABLE-TIME-OUT, line 00430, gets the printable time MOVEd to it from PRINTABLE-TIME, and the field TIME-OF-DAY-OUT, line 00450, is used by Program P19-01A to ACCEPT the TIME into. Notice that we could choose the names of these fields in the main program without regard to what names were used in the subprogram. The field that is passed from the subprogram to the main program is called PRINTABLE-TIME in the main program and TIME-OF-DAY-L in the subprogram. This shows that the names in the main programs and subprograms are unrelated.

In the Procedure Division, line 00490, we execute the main loop, PRINT-TIME, enough TIMES to see what it is doing. PRINT-TIME, line 00650, ACCEPTs the TIME into TIME-OF-DAY-OUT and also calls upon the subprogram to provide the time in printable form. The **CALL** statement at line 00670 transfers control to the subprogram.

Following the word CALL you may have the PROGRAM-ID of the subprogram, in quotation marks. Then a USING phrase must follow, if any data are to be passed in either direction between the calling program and the called program. The USING phrase must contain the names of all the data fields that are to be passed or else name group-level items that include all the data fields that are to be passed. When there is only one item in the USING phrase of the CALL statement, as in this case, it must be defined as being the same length as the field named in the USING phrase of the Procedure Division header in the called program. Here, both are eight-character fields. The items named in the USING phrase of a CALL statement or a Procedure Division header must all be at the 01 level.

Execution of an EXIT PROGRAM statement in a subprogram returns control to the statement in the calling program immediately following the CALL. In our case, the EXIT PROGRAM statement in the subprogram returns control to the MOVE statement at line 00680. Execution proceeds normally in the calling program.

FIGURE 19.4 **Program P19-01A**

```
S COBOL II RELEASE 3.2 09/05/90                  P1901A   DATE NOV 08,1991 T
----+-*A-1-B--+----2----+----3----+----4----+----5----+----6----+----7-|--+

00010  IDENTIFICATION DIVISION.
00020  PROGRAM-ID.  P1901A.
00030 *
00040 *     THIS MAIN PROGRAM OBTAINS THE TIME OF DAY IN PRINTABLE
00050 *     FORM FROM SUBPROGRAM P1901B AND PRINTS IT.  IT ALSO OBTAINS
00060 *     THE 8-DIGIT TIME VIA AN ACCEPT STATEMENT AND PRINTS IT.
00070 *
00080 ******************************************************************
00090
00100  ENVIRONMENT DIVISION.
00110  INPUT-OUTPUT SECTION.
00120  FILE-CONTROL.
00130      SELECT TIME-FILE-OUT ASSIGN TO PRINTER.
00140
00150 ******************************************************************
```

FIGURE 19.4 *continued*

```

DATA DIVISION.
FILE SECTION.
FD  TIME-FILE-OUT.

01  TIME-RECORD-OUT            PIC X(42).

WORKING-STORAGE SECTION.
01  BLANK-LINE                 PIC X      VALUE SPACE.
01  PRINTABLE-TIME             PIC X(8).

01  REPORT-HEADING-1.
    05                         PIC X(20)  VALUE SPACES.
    05                         PIC X(50)  VALUE "TIMES".

01  REPORT-HEADING-2.
    05                         PIC X(10)  VALUE SPACES.
    05                         PIC X(16)  VALUE "TIME FROM".
    05                         PIC X(16)  VALUE "TIME FROM ACCEPT".

01  REPORT-HEADING-3.
    05                         PIC X(10)  VALUE SPACES.
    05                         PIC X(19)  VALUE "SUBPROGRAM".
    05                         PIC X(9)   VALUE "STATEMENT".

01  DETAIL-LINE.
    05                         PIC X(11)  VALUE SPACES.
    05  PRINTABLE-TIME-OUT     PIC X(8).
    05                         PIC X(11)  VALUE SPACES.
    05  TIME-OF-DAY-OUT        PIC 9(8).

*****************************************************************

PROCEDURE DIVISION.
CONTROL-PARAGRAPH.
    PERFORM INITIALIZATION
    PERFORM PRINT-TIME 35 TIMES
    PERFORM TERMINATION
    STOP RUN
    .

INITIALIZATION.
    OPEN OUTPUT TIME-FILE-OUT
    WRITE TIME-RECORD-OUT FROM REPORT-HEADING-1 AFTER PAGE
    WRITE TIME-RECORD-OUT FROM REPORT-HEADING-2 AFTER 3
    WRITE TIME-RECORD-OUT FROM REPORT-HEADING-3
    WRITE TIME-RECORD-OUT FROM BLANK-LINE
    .

PRINT-TIME.
    ACCEPT TIME-OF-DAY-OUT FROM TIME
    CALL "P1901B" USING PRINTABLE-TIME
    MOVE PRINTABLE-TIME TO PRINTABLE-TIME-OUT
    WRITE TIME-RECORD-OUT FROM DETAIL-LINE
    .

TERMINATION.
    CLOSE TIME-FILE-OUT
    .
```

Program P19-01B was linked to Program P19-01A one night and run as a single run unit. The output shown in Figure 19.5 was produced. This is hardly an adequate test of the subprogram. The program would have to be run morning, noon, and night (and at midnight) for a more thorough check. The output does show the speed of execution of the program, though. At least 35 lines of output were produced inside of 0.01 second.

FIGURE *19.5* **Output produced by a run unit consisting of Programs P19-01A and P19-01B**

```
            TIMES


TIME FROM         TIME FROM ACCEPT
SUBPROGRAM           STATEMENT

 11:05 PM             23051501
 11:05 PM             23051501
 11:05 PM             23051501
 11:05 PM             23051501
 11:05 PM             23051501
 11:05 PM             23051501
 11:05 PM             23051501
 11:05 PM             23051501
 11:05 PM             23051501
 11:05 PM             23051501
 11:05 PM             23051501
 11:05 PM             23051501
 11:05 PM             23051501
 11:05 PM             23051501
 11:05 PM             23051501
 11:05 PM             23051501
 11:05 PM             23051501
 11:05 PM             23051501
 11:05 PM             23051501
 11:05 PM             23051501
 11:05 PM             23051501
 11:05 PM             23051501
 11:05 PM             23051501
 11:05 PM             23051501
 11:05 PM             23051501
 11:05 PM             23051501
 11:05 PM             23051501
 11:05 PM             23051501
 11:05 PM             23051501
 11:05 PM             23051501
 11:05 PM             23051501
 11:05 PM             23051501
 11:05 PM             23051501
 11:05 PM             23051501
 11:05 PM             23051501
```

The CALL Statement

The format of the CALL statement used in the programs in this chapter is as follows:

```
CALL {identifier-1} [USING {[BY REFERENCE] {identifier-2} ...} ...]
     {literal-1   }         {BY CONTENT {identifier-2} ...   }

    [ON OVERFLOW imperative-statement-1]
    [END-CALL]
```

The subprogram being CALLed may be referred to by way of a literal, as we do in the examples in this chapter, or by an identifier. If an identifier is used, it must contain the name of the subprogram being CALLed.

The format shows that the USING phrase is optional. We know that it is needed only when data are to be passed between the calling program and the called program. A USING phrase must contain at least one data name and may contain as many as desired. The data names may be qualified if they name items in the File Section. In Program P19-01 the USING phrase contains only one data name. In Program P19-02 you will see how more than one data name is used.

The programs in this chapter both pass data **BY REFERENCE,** which is the default and is assumed if the BY phrase is omitted. If instead data are passed **BY CONTENT,** the field(s) so passed cannot be changed in the calling program by the called program. The corresponding fields in the called program can be changed by the called program, however.

The OVERFLOW phrase is executed if there is no room in primary storage into which to load the subprogram when it is CALLed.

EXERCISE *2*

Write a subprogram to ACCEPT the TIME and convert it into printable form as shown in Table 19.E2. Notice that seconds and hundredths of a second are included in the printable time.

TABLE *19.E2*
TIME as ACCEPTed into a COBOL program and in printable form, with seconds and hundredths of a second

Eight-Digit Time	Printable Time
14410000	2:41:00.00 PM
02414567	2:41:45.67 AM
00101234	12:10:12.34 AM
00000000	12:00:00.00 AM
12000000	12:00:00.00 PM
12302345	12:30:23.45 PM
13450000	1:45:00.00 PM

Then write a calling program to use your subprogram. Having your calling program print the time as given to it by the subprogram, and also print the time in eight-digit form.

Passing Data in Both Directions

We will now write a subprogram that gets data passed to it by its calling program and hands results back to the calling program. Subprogram P19-02B will be similar to subprogram P19-01B, but will have the ability to hand the time of day to the calling program either in military form or standard form. Table 19.2 shows how Program P19-02B can pass the time to its calling program.

Main program P19-02A will CALL subprogram P19-02B in much the same way that Program P19-01A CALLed Program P19-01B. But now when P19-02A CALLs P19-02B, the calling program will have to tell the called program whether it wants the printable time in standard form or military form. For that purpose

TABLE 19.2
TIME as ACCEPTed into a COBOL program and in two printable forms

Eight-Digit Time	Time in Standard Form	Time in Military Form
14410000	2:41 PM	1441
02414567	2:41 AM	0241
00101234	12:10 AM	0010
00000000	12:00 AM	0000
12000000	12:00 PM	1200
12302345	12:30 PM	1230
13450000	1:45 PM	1345

a one-character field is set up in the calling program to signal the called program. If the one-character field contains an S when the subprogram is CALLed, that tells the subprogram that the printable time is wanted in standard form. If the field contains an M, then military form is wanted.

In order to test the subprogram to see whether it can produce printable time in both standard form and military form, we will have the main program call upon the subprogram for times in both forms. Our main program now will ACCEPT the time into itself, CALL the subprogram to hand it the time in standard form, then CALL the subprogram again, this time asking for the time in military form, and then print all three. The output format for Program P19-02 is shown in Figure 19.6.

FIGURE 19.6 **Output format for Program P19-02**

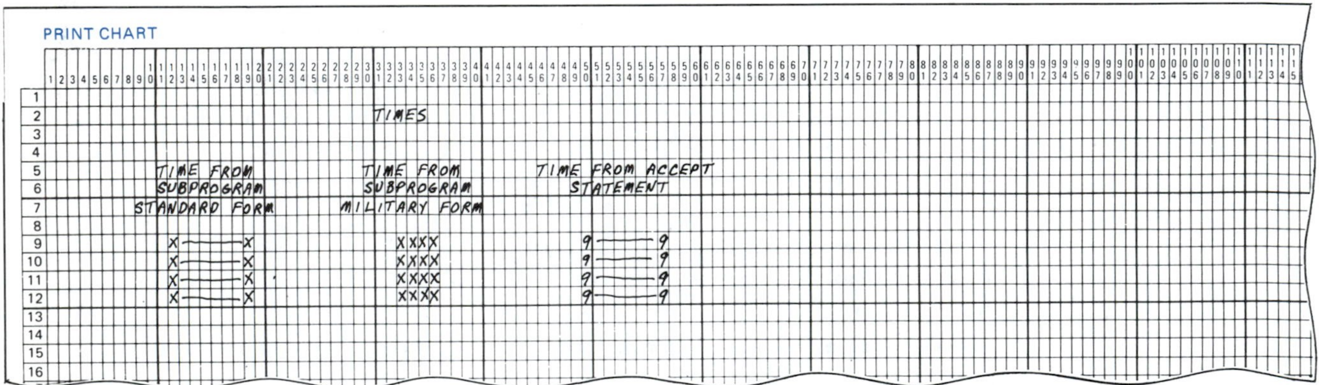

Main program P19-02A is shown in Figure 19.7. There are now two fields into which the program can be handed the time in printable form. STANDARD-FORM-TIME, line 00250, is used to obtain from the subprogram the time in standard form, and MILITARY-FORM-TIME, line 00260, is used to obtain from the subprogram the time in military form. STANDARD-FORM-INDICATOR and MILITARY-FORM-INDICATOR, lines 00270 and 00280, are used to tell the subprogram which form is wanted. When the subprogram is CALLed, one or another of these indicators will be passed to the subprogram. The subprogram will then pass back to the calling program (we hope) printable time in the form requested.

FIGURE *19.7*

Program P19-02A

```
S COBOL II RELEASE 3.2 09/05/90                    P1902A    DATE NOV 11,1991 T
----+-*A-1-B--+----2----+----3----+----4----+----5----+----6----+----7-|--+

 IDENTIFICATION DIVISION.
 PROGRAM-ID.  P1902A.

*    THIS MAIN PROGRAM OBTAINS THE TIME OF DAY IN STANDARD
*    FORM AND IN MILITARY FORM FROM SUBPROGRAM P1902B
*    AND PRINTS BOTH.  IT ALSO OBTAINS
*    THE 8-DIGIT TIME VIA AN ACCEPT STATEMENT AND PRINTS IT.
*
****************************************************************

 ENVIRONMENT DIVISION.
 INPUT-OUTPUT SECTION.
 FILE-CONTROL.
     SELECT TIME-FILE-OUT ASSIGN TO PRINTER.

****************************************************************

 DATA DIVISION.
 FILE SECTION.
 FD  TIME-FILE-OUT.

 01  TIME-RECORD-OUT            PIC X(61).

 WORKING-STORAGE SECTION.
 01  STANDARD-FORM-TIME         PIC X(8).
 01  MILITARY-FORM-TIME         PIC X(8).
 01  STANDARD-FORM-INDICATOR    PIC X           VALUE "S".
 01  MILITARY-FORM-INDICATOR    PIC X           VALUE "M".
 01  BLANK-LINE                 PIC X           VALUE SPACE.

 01  REPORT-HEADING-1.
     05                         PIC X(30)       VALUE SPACES.
     05                         PIC X(5)        VALUE "TIMES".

 01  REPORT-HEADING-2.
     05                         PIC X(10)       VALUE SPACES.
     05                         PIC X(19)       VALUE "TIME FROM".
     05                         PIC X(16)       VALUE "TIME FROM".
     05                         PIC X(16)
                                VALUE "TIME FROM ACCEPT".

 01  REPORT-HEADING-3.
     05                         PIC X(10)       VALUE SPACES.
     05                         PIC X(19)       VALUE "SUBPROGRAM".
     05                         PIC X(19)       VALUE "SUBPROGRAM".
     05                         PIC X(9)        VALUE "STATEMENT".

 01  REPORT-HEADING-4.
     05                         PIC X(8)        VALUE SPACES.
     05                         PIC X(19)
                                VALUE "STANDARD FORM".
     05                         PIC X(13)
                                VALUE "MILITARY FORM".

 01  DETAIL-LINE.
     05                         PIC X(11)       VALUE SPACES.
     05  STANDARD-FORM-TIME-O   PIC X(8)B(12).
     05  MILITARY-FORM-TIME-O   PIC X(5)B(13).
     05  TIME-OF-DAY-O          PIC 9(8).

****************************************************************
```

continued

The CALL statements at lines 00820 through 00850 show USING phrases containing more than one data name. Whenever a USING phrase contains more than one data name, the data names must be listed in a certain order. The order in which the data names must be listed is made up by the programmer and is called the **calling sequence.** Whenever the subprogram is CALLed, the data names must be listed in the same order in the USING phrase. Here we have established that the indicator field must be first in the calling sequence, and the field that is to contain the printable time must be second. That is, the main program will use the first data name in the calling sequence to tell the subprogram what form it wants the time in, and the subprogram will place the printable time into the field named as the second data name in the calling sequence.

Notice that in the two CALL statements to the subprogram, the names of the first and second data names are different. This is one of the important features of subprograms. The calling program can use any names it likes, regardless of what names are used in the subprogram.

FIGURE *19.7* ***continued***

```
S COBOL II RELEASE 3.2 09/05/90                 P1902A    DATE NOV 11,1991 T
----+-*A-1-B--+----2----+----3----+----4----+----5----+----6----+----7-|--+

00620
00630  PROCEDURE DIVISION.
00640  CONTROL-PARAGRAPH.
00650      PERFORM INITIALIZATION
00660      PERFORM PRINT-TIME 35 TIMES
00670      PERFORM TERMINATION
00680      STOP RUN
00690      .
00700
00710  INITIALIZATION.
00720      OPEN OUTPUT TIME-FILE-OUT
00730      WRITE TIME-RECORD-OUT FROM REPORT-HEADING-1 AFTER PAGE
00740      WRITE TIME-RECORD-OUT FROM REPORT-HEADING-2 AFTER 3
00750      WRITE TIME-RECORD-OUT FROM REPORT-HEADING-3
00760      WRITE TIME-RECORD-OUT FROM REPORT-HEADING-4
00770      WRITE TIME-RECORD-OUT FROM BLANK-LINE
00780      .
00790
00800  PRINT-TIME.
00810      ACCEPT TIME-OF-DAY-O FROM TIME
00820      CALL "P1902B" USING STANDARD-FORM-INDICATOR
00830                          STANDARD-FORM-TIME
00840      CALL "P1902B" USING MILITARY-FORM-INDICATOR
00850                          MILITARY-FORM-TIME
00860      MOVE STANDARD-FORM-TIME TO STANDARD-FORM-TIME-O
00870      MOVE MILITARY-FORM-TIME TO MILITARY-FORM-TIME-O
00880      WRITE TIME-RECORD-OUT FROM DETAIL-LINE
00890      .
00900
00910  TERMINATION.
00920      CLOSE TIME-FILE-OUT
00930      .
```

Subprogram P19-02B is shown in Figure 19.8. The LINKAGE SECTION, line 00200, must now contain both TIME-OF-DAY-L as before and the INDICATOR field, since two fields are now passed between the calling program and the called program. The fields may appear in the LINKAGE SECTION in any order.

This LINKAGE SECTION shows that the REDEFINES clause and level-88 entries may be used in the usual way.

The USING phrase in the Procedure Division header now must of course contain the names of both of the fields being passed. And most importantly, the names of the fields must be in the same order in this USING phrase as they are in the USING phrase in the calling program. Once the calling sequence is established, it must be adhered to in every USING phrase in the CALL statements and the Procedure Division header. It is the calling sequence, the order in which the data names are written, that permits the calling program and the called program to use any names they like for the data fields that are passed between them.

When USING phrases contain more than one data name, the lengths of corresponding fields must be the same. That is, the length of the first field in the USING phrase of the CALL statement must be the same as the length of the first field in the USING phrase of the Procedure Division header. Here they are both one character in length. The length of the second field in the USING phrase of the CALL statement must be the same as the length of the second field in the USING phrase of the Procedure Division header. Here they are both eight characters long.

FIGURE 19.8 **Program P19-02B**

```
S COBOL II RELEASE 3.2 09/05/90                  P1902B   DATE NOV 11,1991 T
----+-*A-1-B--+----2----+----3----+----4----+----5----+----6----+----7-|--+

 IDENTIFICATION DIVISION.
 PROGRAM-ID.  P1902B.
*
*     THIS SUBPROGRAM ACCEPTS THE TIME OF DAY IN 8-DIGIT
*     FORM AND CONVERTS IT TO HOURS AND MINUTES
*     IN STANDARD FORM OR MILITARY FORM
*     IGNORING SECONDS AND HUNDREDTHS OF A SECOND.
*
*****************************************************************

 DATA DIVISION.
 WORKING-STORAGE SECTION.
 01  TIME-OF-DAY-W.
     05  HOUR-W                      PIC 99.
         88  AM          VALUES 0  THRU 11.
         88  PM          VALUES 12 THRU 23.
     05  MINUTE-W                    PIC 99.
     05                              PIC 9(4).

 LINKAGE SECTION.
 01  TIME-OF-DAY-L.
     05  HOUR-M                      PIC B99.
     05  STANDARD-HOUR REDEFINES HOUR-M.
         10  HOUR-S                  PIC Z9.
         10  COLON-L                 PIC X.
     05  MINUTE-L                    PIC 99.
     05  AM-OR-PM                    PIC X(3).

 01  INDICATOR                       PIC X.
     88  MILITARY-FORM-REQUESTED             VALUE "M".
     88  STANDARD-FORM-REQUESTED             VALUE "S".

*****************************************************************
```

continued

FIGURE ***19.8*** ***continued***

```
S COBOL II RELEASE 3.2 09/05/90                P1902B   DATE NOV 11,1991 T
----+-*A-1-B--+----2----+----3----+----4----+----5----+----6----+----7-|--+

       PROCEDURE DIVISION USING INDICATOR  TIME-OF-DAY-L.

       CONTROL-PARAGRAPH.
           ACCEPT TIME-OF-DAY-W FROM TIME
           PERFORM SET-AM-OR-PM
           IF STANDARD-FORM-REQUESTED
               MOVE ":" TO COLON-L
               PERFORM FIX-HOUR
           END-IF
           PERFORM MOVE-TIME-OF-DAY
           PERFORM EXECUTION-COMPLETE
           .

       EXECUTION-COMPLETE.
           EXIT PROGRAM
           .

       SET-AM-OR-PM.
           IF STANDARD-FORM-REQUESTED
               IF AM
                   MOVE " AM" TO AM-OR-PM
               ELSE
                   MOVE " PM" TO AM-OR-PM
               END-IF
           ELSE
               MOVE SPACES TO AM-OR-PM
           END-IF
           .

       FIX-HOUR.
           IF PM
               SUBTRACT 12 FROM HOUR-W
           END-IF
           IF HOUR-W IS EQUAL TO 0
               MOVE 12 TO HOUR-W
           END-IF
           .

       MOVE-TIME-OF-DAY.
           IF MILITARY-FORM-REQUESTED
               MOVE HOUR-W TO HOUR-M
           ELSE
               MOVE HOUR-W TO HOUR-S
           END-IF
           MOVE MINUTE-W TO MINUTE-L
           .
```

Program P19-02A was linked to Program P19-02B one night and run as a single run unit. The output shown in Figure 19.9 was produced.

FIGURE 19.9 **Output produced by a run unit consisting of Programs P19-02A and P19-02B**

```
                                TIMES

   TIME FROM                  TIME FROM            TIME FROM ACCEPT
  SUBPROGRAM                 SUBPROGRAM               STATEMENT
 STANDARD FORM              MILITARY FORM

   12:36 AM                      0036                  00361729
   12:36 AM                      0036                  00361729
   12:36 AM                      0036                  00361729
   12:36 AM                      0036                  00361729
   12:36 AM                      0036                  00361729
   12:36 AM                      0036                  00361729
   12:36 AM                      0036                  00361729
   12:36 AM                      0036                  00361729
   12:36 AM                      0036                  00361729
   12:36 AM                      0036                  00361729
   12:36 AM                      0036                  00361729
   12:36 AM                      0036                  00361729
   12:36 AM                      0036                  00361729
   12:36 AM                      0036                  00361729
   12:36 AM                      0036                  00361729
   12:36 AM                      0036                  00361729
   12:36 AM                      0036                  00361729
   12:36 AM                      0036                  00361729
   12:36 AM                      0036                  00361729
   12:36 AM                      0036                  00361729
   12:36 AM                      0036                  00361729
   12:36 AM                      0036                  00361729
   12:36 AM                      0036                  00361729
   12:36 AM                      0036                  00361729
   12:36 AM                      0036                  00361729
   12:36 AM                      0036                  00361729
   12:36 AM                      0036                  00361729
   12:36 AM                      0036                  00361730
   12:36 AM                      0036                  00361730
   12:36 AM                      0036                  00361730
   12:36 AM                      0036                  00361730
   12:36 AM                      0036                  00361730
   12:36 AM                      0036                  00361730
   12:36 AM                      0036                  00361730
   12:36 AM                      0036                  00361730
```

EXERCISE 3

Rewrite your solution for Exercise 3, Chapter 13, page 457, as a main program and a subprogram. Put all the validity checking in the subprogram. Have the main program pass the input record to the subprogram for validity checking. Have the subprogram check the record and return a flag to the main program to say if the record is error-free. If there is an error in the record, have your subprogram stop checking the record when it finds the first error and return to the main program a flag saying that an error has been found, and also return an error message that the main program can print.

Define all possible error messages in working storage in the subprogram. When an error is found, have your program MOVE the appropriate message to the Linkage Section to be passed to the main program.

The Use of the CANCEL Statement

When a subprogram is CALLed more than once from a calling program, or when a single copy of a subprogram in storage is CALLed from more than one calling program, the subprogram is ordinarily in its **last-used state** each time it is CALLed. That is, if the subprogram has any fields in its File Section or Working Storage Section that are changed by the subprogram, those changes stay there and are present the next time the subprogram is CALLed.

For example, if a subprogram has an accumulator field in working storage defined with VALUE 0, and the subprogram ADDs to the accumulator in the course of execution, the sum stays in the accumulator after the subprogram has finished executing. The next time the subprogram is CALLed, the accumulator starts out not with zero, but with the old total.

It is possible to get a fresh copy of a subprogram, if one is needed, by using a **CANCEL** statement. A CANCEL statement is given in the calling program and has the effect of wiping out all traces of previous uses of the subprogram. The next CALL to the subprogram begins execution with a fresh copy. In the programs in this chapter, we had no need of the CANCEL statement because neither of our subprograms changed the contents of their Working Storage Section, nor did they have any File Section to change.

The format of the CANCEL statement is as follows:

```
       {identifier-1}
CANCEL {literal-1   } ...
```

The format shows that when a CANCEL statement is used, at least one subprogram must be CANCELed, and you may cancel as many as desired. The subprogram(s) can be referred to by way of literals, as we have done in the examples in this chapter, or by identifiers. If identifiers are used, they must contain the names of the subprograms to be CANCELed.

Summary

Subprograms can be used when two or more programs need identical computational procedures, when a very large program is to be divided into smaller units for efficiency, when a program is to be written in more than one language, or to encourage good programming practices.

A subprogram operates under control of a calling program, which CALLs the subprogram when needed. A subprogram may in turn be the calling program of another subprogram. A subprogram terminates execution with an EXIT PROGRAM statement or a STOP RUN statement. An EXIT PROGRAM statement must be the only statement in the paragraph in which it appears. A program that executes without being CALLed is a main program.

Data may be passed between the calling program and the called program by way of a USING phrase in the CALL statement of the calling program and a USING phrase in the Procedure Division header of the called program. Both USING phrases must list all the data fields that are to be passed in either direction, or else name group-level items that include all data fields to be passed. The data fields must be listed in the same order in all USING phrases. Items in corresponding positions in all USING phrases must be the same length. The order in which the data fields are listed is called the calling sequence. If no data are passed, the USING phrases may be omitted.

In the called program, all data fields that are passed in either direction must be defined in the Linkage Section. If no data are passed, the Linkage Section may be omitted. If used, the Linkage Section must appear after the Working Storage Section and before the Report Section.

The CANCEL statement may be used to wipe out a previous use of a subprogram so that a later CALL statement can obtain a fresh copy of the subprogram.

Fill-In Exercises

1. A program that requests execution of a subprogram is called a(n) _____ program.
2. A program that is not a subprogram to any other is called a(n) _____ program.
3. The statement that is used to begin execution of a subprogram is the _____ statement.
4. Statements that can be used to terminate execution of a subprogram are _____ and _____.
5. All data fields that are passed between the calling program and the called program must be defined in the _____ Section of the _____ program.
6. A USING phrase appears in the _____ header of the _____ program if there are any data to be passed.
7. A USING phrase appears in the _____ statement in the _____ program if there are any data to be passed.
8. Data are passed between a calling program and a subprogram not on the basis of the _____ of the data fields.
9. The order in which data fields must be named in USING phrases is called the _____ _____.
10. Any clauses that may be used in a _____ Section may be used in a Linkage Section.
11. A subprogram that executes under control of a calling program is called a _____ program.
12. When a subprogram completes executing, it is left in its _____-_____ state.
13. When there is only one item in the USING phrase of a CALL statement, it must be the same _____ as the item in the USING phrase of the _____ _____ header in the called program.
14. A main program linked with all of the subprograms it needs for execution is called a _____ _____.
15. Some programmers and managers think that breaking a large program into subprograms encourages _____ _____ _____.

Review Exercises

1. Write a main program that CALLs two different subprograms (with separate CALL statements). Have the programs pass no data.

   Have your main program call one of the subprograms every 0.01 second, and call the second subprogram every 0.02 second. Have each subprogram print the time that it was called, in any form you desire, on a separate output file. Have your main program OPEN both output files in its initialization routine, and CLOSE both output files in its termination routine. Do not let your program run for more than one-tenth of a second.

2. Modify your solution for Review Exercise 1 so that each output file is OPENed by the program that uses it. Define a flag in each subprogram to say whether its output file has already been OPENed. Start the flag with VALUE 0. When the subprogram is CALLed the first time, have it OPEN its output file and set the flag to indicate that the file is now OPEN. The file then remains OPEN and must not be OPENed again on subsequent CALLs to the subprogram. Remember that a flag in working storage remains unchanged between CALLs.

   Why can the subprograms not CLOSE their output files? Why must the output files be CLOSEd by the main program?

3. Write a subprogram that reverses the order of the characters in an 80-character record and returns the reversed record to the calling program. Use only one data field to pass the data in both directions; that is, have the calling program hand an 80-character record to the subprogram, and have the subprogram hand the reversed 80-character record back to the main program in the same 80-character field. For each record have the main program print on one line the original record and the record with its characters reversed.

Project

Rewrite your solution to the Project in Chapter 11, page 385, as a calling program and a subprogram. Have the calling program read each input record and pass the Gross Pay to the subprogram. Include the tax tables in the subprogram, and have the subprogram compute the tax and pass it to the calling program. Have the calling program print output in the same format as in the Project in Chapter 11.

CHAPTER 20

RM/COBOL-85

HERE ARE THE KEY POINTS YOU SHOULD LEARN FROM THIS CHAPTER

1. How to write a program using RM/COBOL-85
2. How to use RM/CO*

KEY WORDS TO RECOGNIZE AND LEARN

RM/COBOL-85	insert mode
RM/CO*	syntax-check
directory	compile
project	warning
member	interactive debugger
extension	program stepping
full-screen edit	breakpoint

RM/COBOL-85 is one of many COBOL systems available for use on microcomputers. It is the most modern COBOL system manufactured by the Ryan McFarland Corporation. You can buy a copy of the student edition of RM/COBOL-85 at student discount prices for use on your home computer by using the coupon in the back of this book.

If you are using RM/COBOL-85 in your COBOL course at school, this chapter will provide you with the details you need to write and run programs. The student edition of RM/COBOL-85 contains excellent documentation that provides many more details than can be contained just in this one chapter. The additional details will make your use of RM/COBOL-85 much more efficient.

*Creating a Project Using RM/CO**

The best way to develop new programs in RM/COBOL-85 is to use the project-management system called **RM/CO*** (pronounced RM/Co-star). RM/CO* provides a variety of valuable services that we will discuss as we go along. To use RM/CO*, you must first use a DOS command to enter the **directory** where RM/CO* is located on your PC. In this book RM/CO* is located in the directory called C:\EDUC\RMCBL85. Your instructor will give you the information you need to enter the directory where RM/CO* is located at your school. Then, you type the command RMCOSTAR and press the Enter key. Your screen should look something like Figure 20.1.

FIGURE *20.1* **Opening screen of RM/CO***

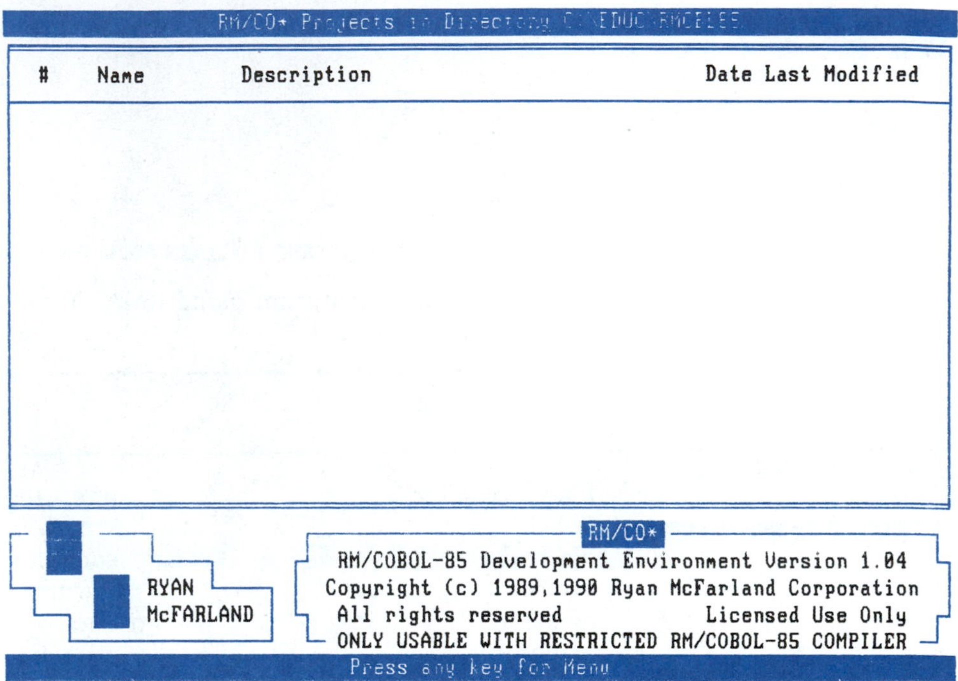

Now, we are going to create what RM/CO* calls a **project.** Your first project will consist of nothing more than your first programming assignment. For the sample first project here I will use just Program P01-01 described in Chapter 1 of this book. To create a project, first follow the instruction on the screen that says *Press any key for Menu.* Your screen should now look something like Figure 20.2.

You are now going to want to create a new project, so you will want to select the menu option *New.* Notice that the entire word "New" is highlighted, but just the Q in "Quit" is highlighted. To select *Quit,* which we don't want to do right now, you would press Q on your keyboard. To select *New,* you could press N, but since the entire word "New" is highlighted you could select *New* also by pressing the Enter key. In any RM/CO* menu, when an entire menu item is highlighted, you can select that item either by pressing its first letter or the Enter key. Now press N or the Enter key. Your screen should look like Figure 20.3.

You can see that RM/CO* is asking you to make up a name for this project. Since your project is going to consist of just your first programming assignment, you can key in a name for the project such as ASSG1 or COB1, or any name up to eight characters long. Use the backspace key to correct errors. I will use the name P0101 for my project here. After you key in your project name and press Enter, your screen should look similar to Figure 20.4.

FIGURE 20.2 Project Directory

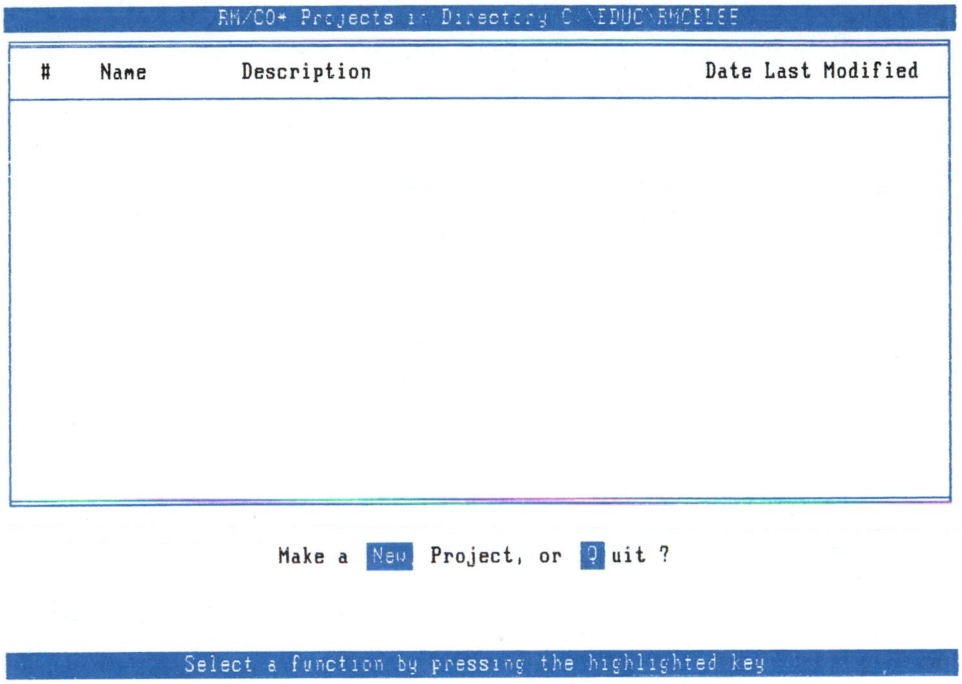

RM/CO* Projects in Directory C:\EDUC\RMCEL66

#	Name	Description	Date Last Modified

Make a New Project, or Quit ?

Select a function by pressing the highlighted key

FIGURE 20.3 Project Directory with prompt for project name

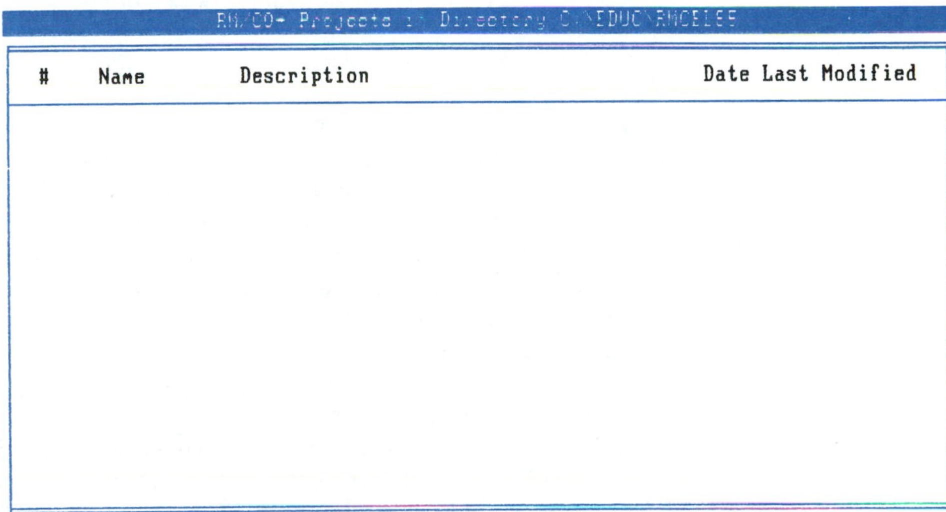

Type a name for the new Project (up to 8 letters/numbers)

(Press Enter when done, Esc to cancel)

Project Name (1-8 Characters):

FIGURE 20.4 Project Directory with prompt for project description

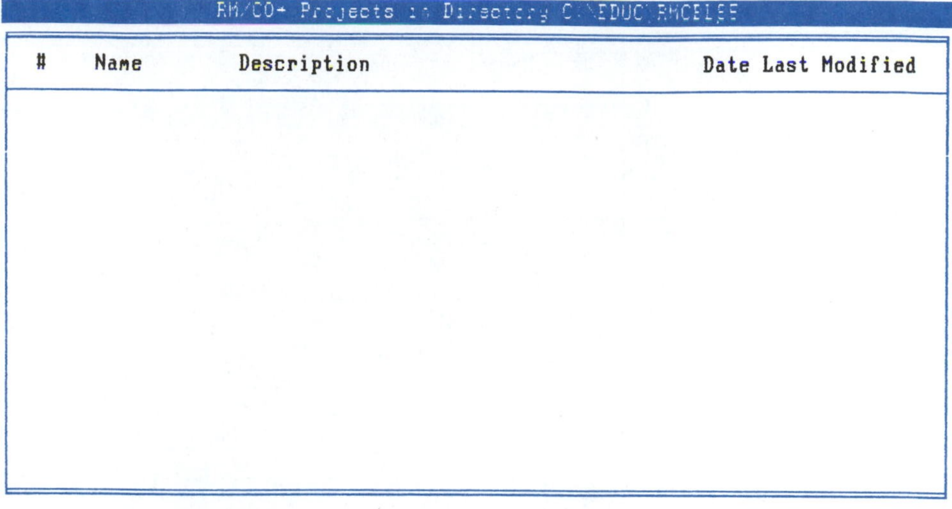


```
            Type a description of the new Project

         (Press Enter when done, Esc to cancel)

Project Description (1-40 Characters):
```

Now type a description of the project. The description need not be fancy. Something like "COBOL Programming Assignment 1" will do. I used "Program P01-01". Press Enter when done, and your screen should look similar to Figure 20.5.

You have now created your first project. The project will remain in RM/CO* until you delete it. Any time you want to work on this project you can access it easily. You will never have to create the project again. As you proceed through your COBOL course you will probably create a new project for each programming assignment you do. This screen will show you the name and description of all the projects you have, and the date and time each was last modified. Right now it shows the date and time the project was created. Now *Enter* the project, by pressing E or the Enter key. Later, if you want to work on this project again, you can *Enter* it in the same way. Your screen should now look similar to Figure 20.6.

Now we are ready to add a **member** to the project. In this project there will be only one member and it will be your first program that you are going to key in. Now press A, and your screen should look similar to Figure 20.7.

Now where it says *Pathname,* enter the name of the program that you are going to key in and press Enter. I used the name P0101. The name of your program can be the same as the name of your project, too. Your screen should look similar to Figure 20.8.

RM/CO* tells you that your program does not exist. You know that. Of course it doesn't exist. You haven't keyed it in yet. RM/CO* asks if it should create the program (notice that RM/CO* adds the CBL **extension**). RM/CO*

FIGURE *20.5* **Project Directory showing project P0101**

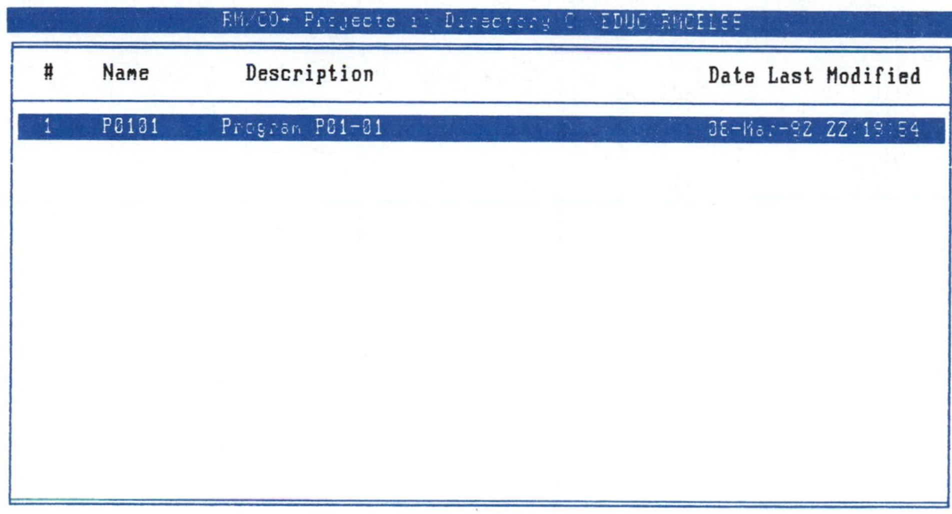

Enter Project, Make a N ew Project, or Q uit ?

Project "P0101" created

FIGURE *20.6* **Project Commands**

P0101: 0 Members 03/08 22:35

#	Member Name	U	Last Edit: Lines	C	Last Comp: Err Wng	Options

Project Commands

A dd Member	O ptions	U pdate	S yntax-Check
D rop Member	Q uit Project	V iew Status/File	C ompile
Enter Member		X ecute OS Command	R un

Project Empty: Press [A] to Add a File

FIGURE 20.7

Prompt for member name

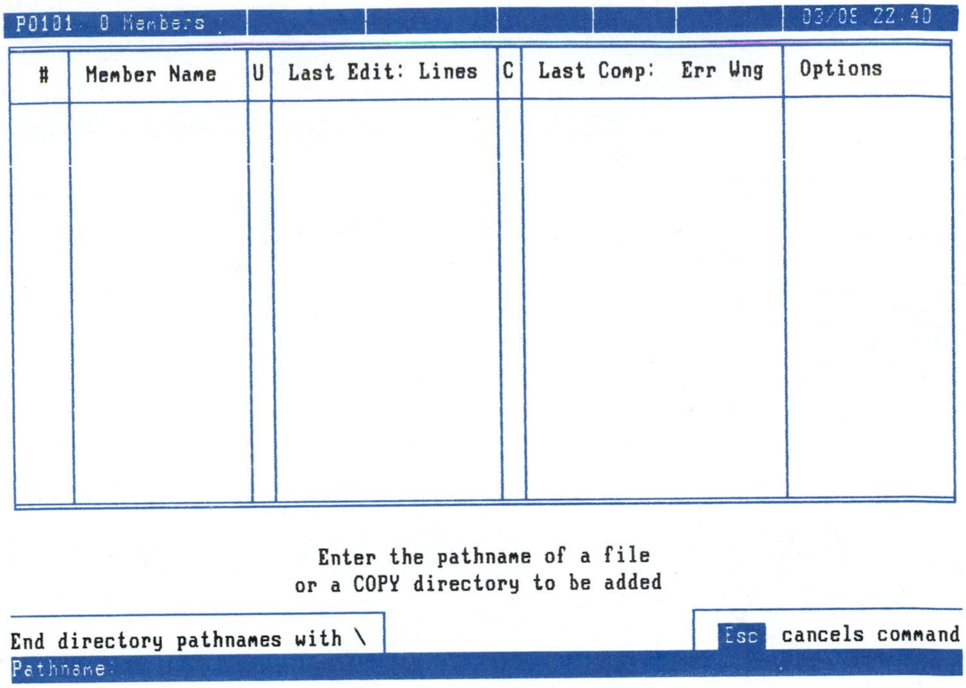

```
P0101  0 Members                                              03/08 22:40

| # | Member Name    | U | Last Edit: Lines | C | Last Comp:  Err Wng | Options |

                    Enter the pathname of a file
                    or a COPY directory to be added

End directory pathnames with \                         Esc cancels command
Pathname:
```

FIGURE 20.8

Prompt for creation of new member

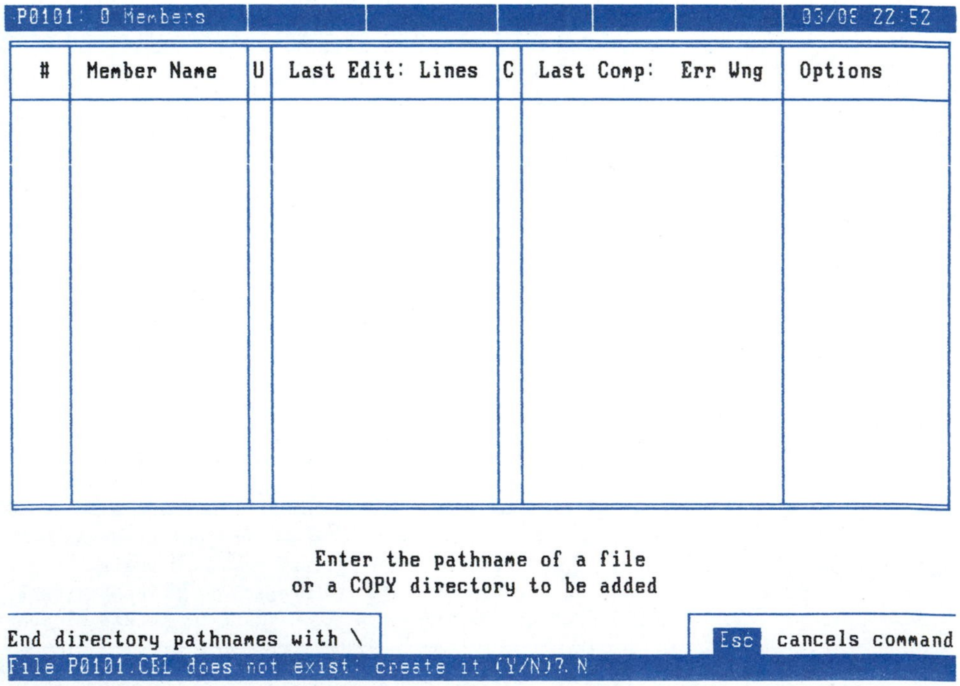

```
P0101: 0 Members                                              03/08 22:52

| # | Member Name    | U | Last Edit: Lines | C | Last Comp:  Err Wng | Options |

                    Enter the pathname of a file
                    or a COPY directory to be added

End directory pathnames with \                         Esc cancels command
File P0101.CBL does not exist: create it (Y/N)?. N
```

offers you the answer N. If you wanted to answer No you could just press Enter. But since you want to answer Yes, type Y and press Enter. Your screen should look similar to Figure 20.9.

FIGURE *20.9* One member entered into project

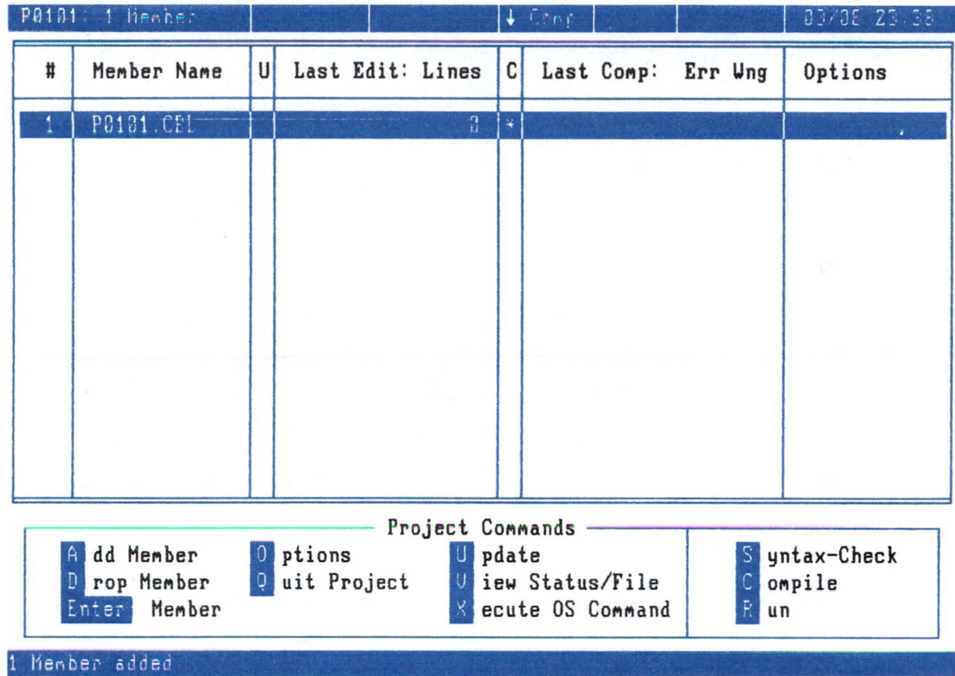

You have now added a member to your project. The member will remain part of the project until you delete it. Any time you want to work on this member you can access it easily. You will never have to add this member again. Now we want to *Enter* the member so press E or the Enter key. Later, if you want to work on this member again, you can just *Enter* it in the same way. Your screen should now look similar to Figure 20.10.

FIGURE 20.10 Edit Commands

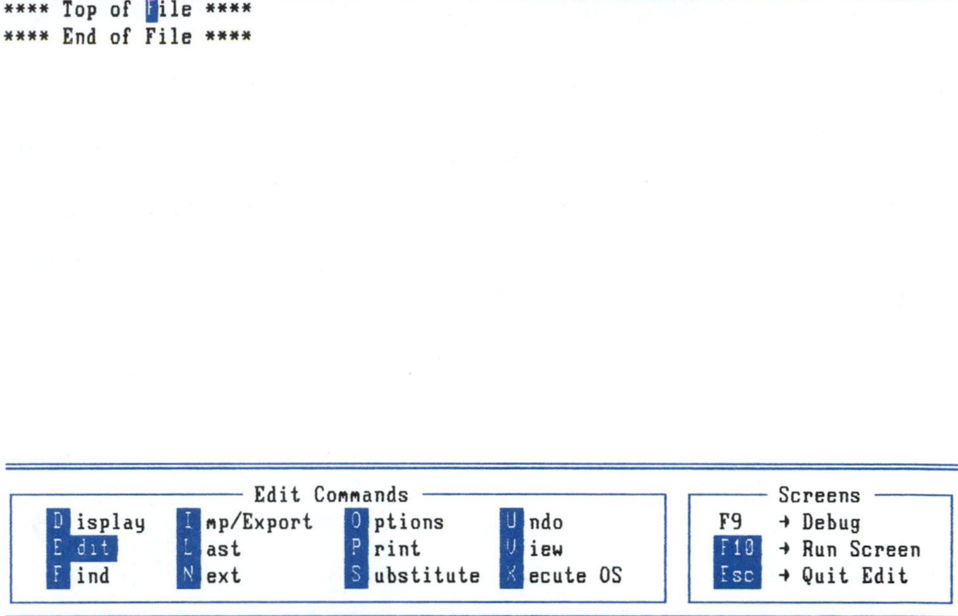

Keying in a Program

Press E or the Enter key to select *Edit* so that you may key in your first programming assignment. Your screen should look like Figure 20.11.

In the upper-right corner of the screen you see 01,08. This tells you that the cursor is in position 8 of line 1. The **full-screen edit** menu is shown at the bottom left of the screen, and the Screens menu is shown at the bottom right of the screen. The word *Alt* at the left side of the screen tells you that you must hold down the Alt key while you press any of the keys in the edit menu. If you now hold down the Alt key and press A, the cursor moves to position 8 of line 2 and you can key the Identification Division header starting in area A where it belongs. When you are working in RM/CO* there is usually no reason to key sequence numbers (positions 1 through 6). The editor always starts you at position 8 of each new line. If you want to key something into position 7 of a line, you must backspace or use the left-arrow key to get there.

After you key the Identification Division header, press Enter. The cursor moves to position 8 of the next line. Thus you can key in your entire program.

FIGURE 20.11 Full-screen edit

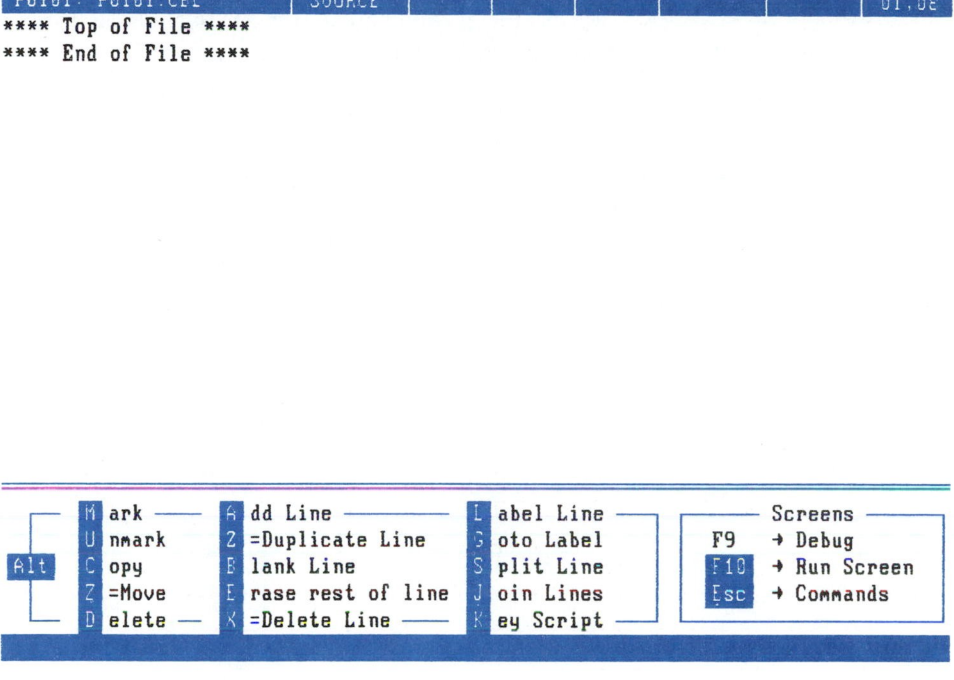

Correcting Errors

If you make an error while you are keying a line, use the backspace key to erase it. If you discover an error in a line after you have keyed it in and pressed Enter, use the arrow keys (left, right, up, and down) to move the cursor to the location of the error. You may then type a correction right over the error, or you may use the Del key to delete the character at the cursor location and close up the line. The backspace key deletes the character to the left of the cursor location and closes up the line. To delete an entire line, hold down Alt and press X.

You can insert characters into lines, too. Press and release the Ins key, and you will see the cursor get taller and the word "INSERT" appear at the top of the screen. This tells you that you are in **insert mode.** Characters that you key now will be inserted into the line at the cursor location. To leave insert mode, press and release the Ins key again.

After moving the cursor around and making corrections, if you want to add more lines to your program, position the cursor on the line after which you want to add lines, hold down Alt, and press A. The editor positions the cursor at position 8 of the new line.

Program P01-01 in RM/COBOL-85

Program P01-01 as written in RM/COBOL-85 is shown in Figure 20.12. The only difference between Program P01-01 here and the version in Chapter 1 is in the Environment Division. The ASSIGN clause now reads ASSIGN TO PRINT, ''PRINTER''. You can use this ASSIGN clause for your printer output file if your computer has a printer directly attached. If your printer is somewhere else, not directly attached to your computer, you may have to use a different ASSIGN clause. Your instructor will give you the details you need.

FIGURE *20.12* **Program P01-01 in RM/COBOL-85**

```
 IDENTIFICATION DIVISION.
 PROGRAM-ID.  P01-01.

*  THIS PROGRAM PRINTS THE AUTHOR'S NAME AND
*    (FICTITIOUS) ADDRESS, ON THREE LINES.  ZIP CODE IS
*    INCLUDED IN THE ADDRESS.
*
*****************************************************************

 ENVIRONMENT DIVISION.
 INPUT-OUTPUT SECTION.
 FILE-CONTROL.
     SELECT COMPLETE-ADDRESS ASSIGN TO PRINT, "PRINTER".

*****************************************************************

 DATA DIVISION.
 FILE SECTION.
 FD  COMPLETE-ADDRESS.

 01  ADDRESS-LINE          PICTURE X(120).

*****************************************************************

 PROCEDURE DIVISION.
 EXECUTABLE-PROGRAM-STEPS.
     OPEN OUTPUT COMPLETE-ADDRESS
     MOVE "G. S. POPKIN"          TO ADDRESS-LINE
     WRITE ADDRESS-LINE
     MOVE "1921 PRESIDENT ST."    TO ADDRESS-LINE
     WRITE ADDRESS-LINE
     MOVE "BROOKLYN, NY  11221"   TO ADDRESS-LINE
     WRITE ADDRESS-LINE
     CLOSE COMPLETE-ADDRESS
     STOP RUN
     .
```

After you have keyed in the entire program and made all desired corrections, press Esc twice to exit from the editor. Your screen should look similar to Figure 20.13.

FIGURE *20.13* **Project Commands showing P0101 edited**

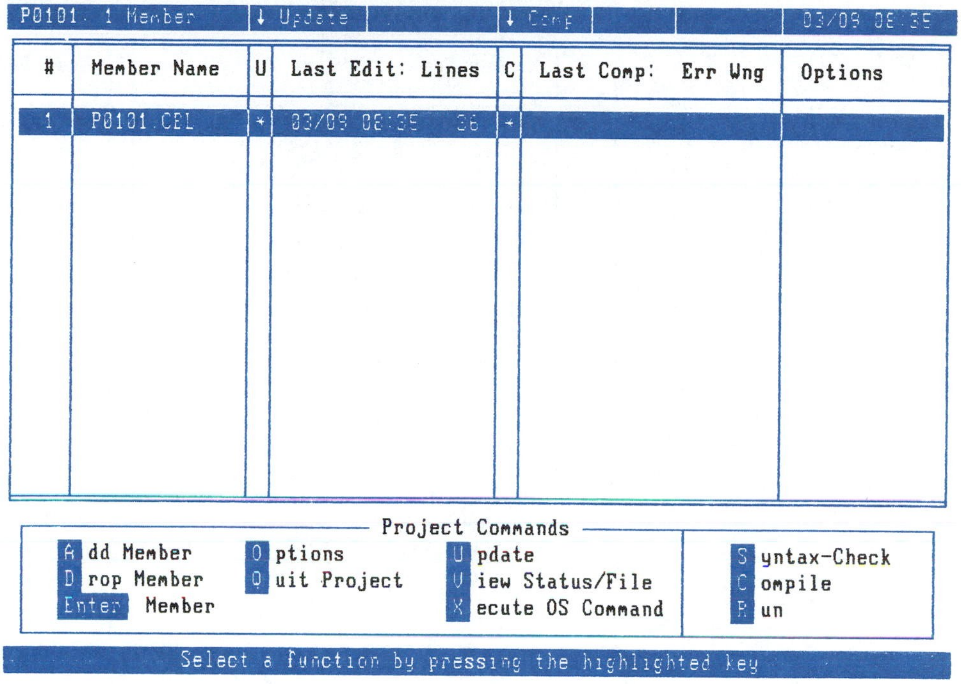

```
 P0101. 1 Member    | ↓ Update |          | ↓ Comp |        |        | 03/08 08:35

 #  | Member Name | U | Last Edit: Lines | C | Last Comp:  Err Wng | Options
 1  | P0101.CBL   | * | 03/08 08:35   36 | * |                     |

                           Project Commands
 A dd Member       O ptions          U pdate               S yntax-Check
 D rop Member      Q uit Project     V iew Status/File     C ompile
 Enter  Member                       X ecute OS Command    R un

              Select a function by pressing the highlighted key
```

Checking a Program for Syntax Errors

Notice that the project screen shows how many lines your program contains and when you last edited it. You are now ready to **syntax-check** your program. RM/CO* will check your program for syntax errors, that is, errors in the use of the COBOL language. Press S, and your screenm should look similar to Figure 20.14.

You now have an opportunity to check the syntax of just one file, all files, or all files that you have changed since they were last **compiled,** or translated. Files that have been changed since they were last compiled are marked with an asterisk in the column headed "C". In this case, all three menu choices give the same result, since all files are the same as one file, and the one file has been changed since it was last compiled (it has not yet ever been compiled). If you press O, the one highlighted file will be checked for syntax. So press Enter, or C, or O, or A.

Figure 20.15 shows the results of the syntax check. The appearance of the word "Check" in the column headed "Options" tells that this was a syntax-checking operation. The check found no errors or **warnings** in my program. Warnings usually will not interfere with proper operation of a program and often can be left uncorrected, but if you have any errors you must eliminate them before you can go on to compile your program. Whether or not you have any errors or warnings, press Esc now to see the Project Commands. If you have no errors or warnings, you can skip the next section.

FIGURE ***20.14*** **Prompt for syntax-check**

```
P0101: 1 Member   | ↓ Update |  | ↓ Comp |  | 03/10 08:49
```

#	Member Name	U	Last Edit: Lines	C	Last Comp: Err Wng	Options
1	P0101.CBL	▸	03/09 08:35 36	▸		

```
Syntax-check Changed Files, One File, or All Files ?

                                        Esc cancels command
```

FIGURE ***20.15*** **Results of syntax-check of Program P01-01**

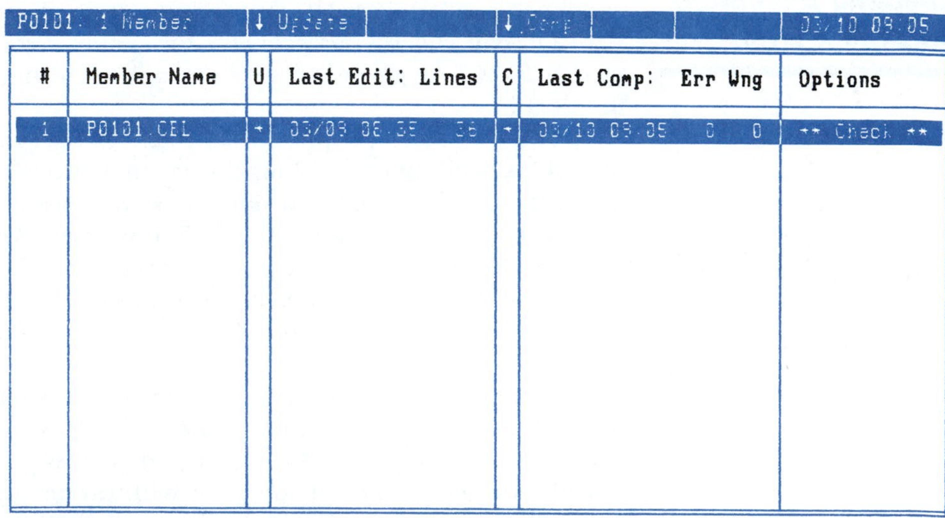


```
Educational Version - Restricted Usage
(c) Copyright 1985, 1989 by Ryan McFarland Corp.  All rights reserved.
Registration Number: CY-0000-01194-01
Syntax-Checking: P01-01
Compilation Complete: 1 Program, 0 Errors, 0 Warnings.
1 File Syntax-Checked: Total of 0 Errors, 0 Warnings issued (Press [ESC])
```

Correcting Syntax Errors and Warnings

Press Enter to see your program on the screen. To locate each error and warning in your program, you will use the edit command *Next.* First *Find* the beginning of the program by pressing F and then keying -* and pressing Enter. (Type first F, then when RM/CO* asks for a Target, type a hyphen and an asterisk with no space between them, and then press Enter.) Then, to find the first error or warning in your program, press N and then D. Do whatever is necessary to correct the error, or to correct the warning if you like—use the arrow keys to move the cursor, the Ins and Del keys, or add a line by holding down Alt and pressing A, or deplete a line by holding down Alt and pressing X, or whatever else is needed.

When you have made the desired correction to the first error or warning, press Esc and then N and then D to locate the next error or warning. Continue to correct all your errors and any of your warnings that you want. You may at any time move the cursor to anywhere in your program by using the up- and down-arrow keys or PgUp and PgDn. When you have made all desired corrections, press Esc once or twice until you see the Project Commands. Then have RM/CO* check your program for syntax errors again. Then you must correct any errors it finds. Continue checking for syntax and correcting errors until no errors are found in the syntax check. When you have no errors in your syntax check, so that your screen looks similar to Figure 20.15, press Esc to see the Project Commands as in Figure 20.13. You are now ready to compile your program.

Compiling a Program

With the Project Commands showing on the screen, press C to compile. As before, you have the choice of compiling just one file, all files, or all files that you have changed since they were last compiled. Also as before, all three menu choices give the same result. If you press O, the one highlighted file will be compiled. So press Enter, or C, or O, or A.

Figure 20.16 shows the results of the compilation. Of course there should be no errors, since the program was previously checked for syntax. If by some chance there are errors, though, you can correct them the same way you would correct errors after a syntax check. Notice that the asterisk in the column headed "C" has disappeared, showing that this file has not been changed since it was last compiled. The "Y" in the "Options" column shows that certain information was included in the compilation that will make the next steps, the ones described in the next sections, easier for you. The word "Run" in the top line tells you that your program is now ready to run. Press Esc to see the Project Commands.

FIGURE 20.16 Results of compilation of Program P01-01

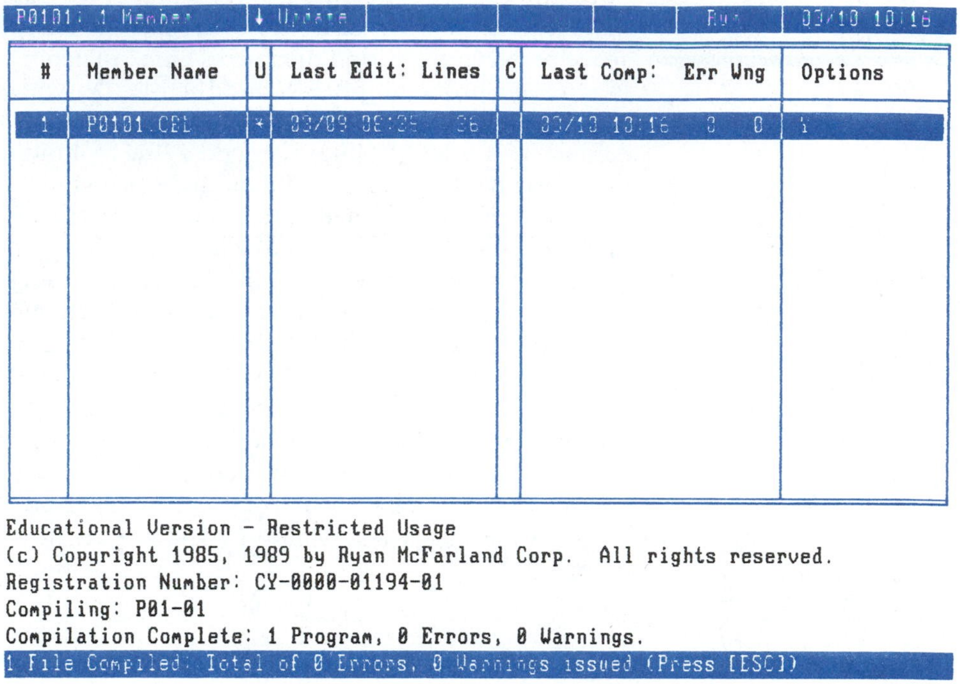

```
P0101: 1 Member    | ↓ Update |          |          |          | Run  | 03/10 10:16

  #  | Member Name | U | Last Edit:  Lines | C | Last Comp:   Err Wng | Options
  1  | P0101.CBL   | * | 03/09 08:35    36 |   | 03/10 10:16    0   0 | Y

Educational Version - Restricted Usage
(c) Copyright 1985, 1989 by Ryan McFarland Corp.  All rights reserved.
Registration Number: CY-0000-01194-01
Compiling: P01-01
Compilation Complete: 1 Program, 0 Errors, 0 Warnings.
1 File Compiled: Total of 0 Errors, 0 Warnings issued (Press [ESC])
```

Running a Program

You are now ready to run your program. RM/CO* always runs programs under control of the **interactive debugger,** which allows you to see what your program is doing at each step. With the Project Commands showing on the screen, press R and then Enter. Your screen should look similar to Figure 20.17.

The debug screen that you see is horizontally divided in two. The upper portion shows your program, with the name of the first paragraph of the Procedure Division highlighted. As the program executes, the highlight moves so that it always marks the line that is about to be executed. The lower portion of the screen is for debugger commands and debugger output. The bottom line on the screen tells you what line number in the program is about to be executed; in this case, line 26. Also, the bottom line on the screen tells you that by pressing the function key labeled F9 you can edit your program, and by pressing the function key F10 you can see what your screen would look like if you were running this program without the debugger.

The second line from the bottom contains the code "ST", to indicate that **program stepping** is active, meaning that you are now executing the program one step at a time; the line number about to be executed, in my program, 26; the program name, in my program, P01-01; and C, a prompt for a command. The debugger is waiting for you to give it a debug command.

The most commonly used debug command is "S", for "Step." This causes the program to execute one statement. Type S now and press Enter. You see that the highlight advances to the next statement, and a new line appears in the debugging window. There exists also a command "SP", for "Step paragraph,"

FIGURE 20.17 **Running Program P01-01 with the interactive debugger**

```
 P0101: P0101.CBL          LISTING                                        01.01
0022
0023      ******************************************************************
0024
0025       PROCEDURE DIVISION.
0026       EXECUTABLE-PROGRAM-STEPS.
0027           OPEN OUTPUT COMPLETE-ADDRESS
0028           MOVE "G. S. POPKIN"        TO ADDRESS-LINE
0029           WRITE ADDRESS-LINE
0030           MOVE "1921 PRESIDENT ST."  TO ADDRESS-LINE
0031           WRITE ADDRESS-LINE
0032           MOVE "BROOKLYN, NY  11221" TO ADDRESS-LINE
0033           WRITE ADDRESS-LINE
0034           CLOSE COMPLETE-ADDRESS
0035           STOP RUN
0036           .
READ ONLY SIZE =                     398 (X"0000018E") BYTES
READ/WRITE SIZE =                    274 (X"00000112") BYTES




ST 26 P01-01 C?
At line 26 in Program P01-01 Keys: [F9]=Edit [F10]=Show Run
```

which causes the program to finish the remainder of the paragraph it is now executing. Now continue pressing S and Enter until the highlight advances to the first WRITE statement in your program. At this point your name should have been MOVEd to your output record area by the MOVE statement immediately preceding the WRITE.

You can view the contents of the output record area, or of any field described in the Data Division, by using the "D" command, for "Display." Now type D, then a space, then the name of the field to be displayed, in this case the name of your output record as you defined it at the 01 level in the File Section, and press Enter. You should see your name, preceded by the code "ANS," meaning the field is defined as alphanumeric, with the PICTURE character X. (Other common field types are GRP for group item, NSU for numeric unsigned, NS for numeric signed, and NSE for numeric edited.) Now give two more Step commands, so that the highlight advances to the next WRITE statement. Now display your output record area and see that it contains your address.

You can direct the debugger to cease stepping and to execute your program without stopping at each line. The "R" command, for "Resume," does this. Type R now and press Enter. The program executes and stops at the STOP RUN statement. The prompt line shows the code "SR" for "STOP RUN." Type R again and press Enter to finish executing the program. The bottom line of the screen should now contain the instruction "Press any key to continue." Do so, and then press Esc to see the Project Commands.

When you are stepping through a program, you might notice an error that you want to correct. To do so, press function key F9 to enter the editor. You may then move the cursor anywhere in your program and make changes in the usual way. To return to the debugger, press key F9 again. Any changes you make to your program in this way will not take effect until you recompile the program later.

Other Debug Commands

When you are in the debugger, there are other commands in addition to S, SP, and R that you will find very helpful. With one of them the debugger allows you to set **breakpoints** at program line numbers you specify. For example, if you set a breakpoint at line 31 and the debugger is executing your program as a result of an R command, the debugger would stop before executing line 31 and await a debug command from you. When a program stops executing at a breakpoint the prompt line shows the code ''BP.'' The debug command to set a breakpoint at line 31 is

```
B 31
```

To see all the breakpoints that you have set, type B and press Enter. To clear a breakpoint at line 31, type

```
C 31
```

To clear all breakpoints, type C and press Enter.

The command ''Q'' causes program execution to quit immediately. It behaves as though a STOP RUN command has been executed. The command ''E'' causes the program to execute to completion without stopping at any breakpoints or the STOP RUN statement.

Updating Your Program File

When your program is working, you can update your program file. Any program that has an asterisk in the column headed ''U'' needs to be updated. With the Project Commands showing on the screen, press U. You will be presented with the usual choices. Press Enter, or C, or O, or A.

It is good practice to update your program files occasionally even if your program is not working. During a long session at the computer you should update your program after every several hundred changes. Also, if you find it necessary to terminate your RM/CO* session before your program is working, you can update your program before terminating but it is not necessary to do so. If you terminate your RM/CO* session without updating your program, the program will still be available to you correctly in your next session.

Updating a program takes about as much time as a syntax-check, and updating too often wastes computer time unnecessarily. Updating a program too seldom increases, only slightly, the amount of time it takes to enter the editor. When in doubt, update less often rather than more.

Terminating Your RM/CO* Session

With the Project Commands showing on the screen, press Q to quit from this project. You will then be presented with the opportunity to enter another project, or return to the one you were working on. Press Q to exit from RM/CO*.

EXERCISE *1*

Write and execute the programming assignment in Exercise 2, Chapter 1, page 8, using RM/COBOL-85 and RM/CO*.

Summary

RM/COBOL-85 is the most modern of the Ryan McFarland COBOL systems for microcomputers. To develop a program in RM/COBOL-85 you would use the RM/CO* project manager. The project manager contains an editor which allows you to key in your program and make corrections and additions. The project manager provides information about each program such as which have been changed since they were last compiled, when each was last compiled, and when each was last changed.

You key programs and correct errors and warnings by using RM/CO*'s full-screen editor. The editor allows you to move to any part of the program using the arrow keys and the PgUp and PgDn keys, to change, insert, or delete characters, and to add or delete lines.

To run most of the programs in this book using RM/COBOL-85, you need change only the ASSIGN clauses in the Environment Division. Output printer files should be ASSIGNed to PRINT, ''PRINTER''.

The syntax-checker indicates errors and warnings in your program. You can use the edit commands Find and Next to locate the errors and warnings for correction.

Programs are run under control of RM/CO*'s interactive debugger. This allows you to see the operation of your program step by step. You can execute one statement at a time, one paragraph at a time, or to the STOP RUN statement. RM/CO* allows you to set one or more breakpoints in your program. You can then execute your program and the debugger will halt execution at every breakpoint. You can also execute your program to completion with no stops at breakpoints or the STOP RUN statement. Whenever the debugger halts execution of your program, you can display the contents of any field defined in your Data Division.

Fill-In Exercises

1. When you use RM/CO*, each of your programs must be a member of a(n) ______.

2. In RM/CO*'s full-screen editor, the key combination for adding one or more lines to your program is Alt-______.

3. In RM/CO*'s full-screen editor, the key combination for duplicating a line in your program is Alt-______.

4. In RM/CO*'s full-screen editor, the key combination for blanking an entire line in your program is Alt-______.

5. In RM/CO*'s full-screen editor, the key combination for blanking from the cursor location to the end of a line is Alt-______.

6. In RM/CO*'s full-screen editor, the key combination for deleting a line from your program is Alt-______.
7. Before compiling a program, you should have RM/COBOL-85 check it for ______ errors.
8. Commonly used commands in the interactive debugger are S for ______, SP for ______ ______, D for ______, R for ______, Q for ______, and E for ______.
9. Codes used by RM/CO* when displaying data fields are ANS for ______, GRP for ______, NSU for ______ ______, NS for ______, and NSE for ______ ______.
10. When only the first letter of a word is highlighted in an RM/CO* menu, you may select that menu item by pressing the ______.
11. When an entire word is highlighted in an RM/CO* menu, you may select that menu item by pressing ______ or the first ______ of the word.
12. Project names in RM/CO* may be up to ______ characters long.
13. In full-screen editing, the Delete key deletes the character ______ the cursor location; the Backspace key deletes the character to the ______ of the cursor location.
14. The command to see all breakpoints is ______; the command to clear all breakpoints is ______.
15. The debugger will stop executing your program before each breakpoint when your program is executing as a result of a(n) ______ command.

CHAPTER 21

Interactive COBOL

HERE ARE THE KEY POINTS YOU SHOULD LEARN FROM THIS CHAPTER

1. How to use the terminal-I/O form of the DISPLAY statement
2. How to use ACCEPT and DISPLAY statements with a Screen Section

KEY WORDS TO RECOGNIZE AND LEARN

terminal-I/O	BACKGROUND
Screen Section	BLANK SCREEN
LINE SEQUENTIAL	REMAINDER
FOREGROUND	AUTO
WHITE	BLINK
BLACK	HIGHLIGHT
BLUE	intensity
GREEN	NO
CYAN	ERASE
RED	LOW
MAGENTA	HIGH
BROWN	

COBOL systems that run on PCs can show output on the computer monitor and can also permit the program user to key input during program execution. Such systems usually have two forms of the ACCEPT statement that can be used for input to a program from the keyboard and two forms of the DISPLAY statement that can be used for output from a program onto the monitor. These are in addition to the ANSI standard ACCEPT statement described in Chapter 4 and the ANSI standard DISPLAY statement described in Chapter 15. There is nothing in the standard regarding keyboard input or screen output, and these extra forms of ACCEPT and DISPLAY are extensions to the standard.

The two extra forms of the ACCEPT statement are called ACCEPT ***terminal-I/O*** and ACCEPT *screen-name*. The two extra forms of the DISPLAY statement are called DISPLAY *terminal-I/O* and DISPLAY *screen-name*. To use the two screen-name forms you must include a **Screen Section** in the Data Division of your program. The Screen Section is used to describe what the screen will look like at different times during execution of the program. The Screen Section is an optional section, itself an extension to the standard, and when used must be the last section in the Data Division.

A Program with Screen Input and Output

Program P21-01 processes employee input records in the following format:

Positions	Field
1–9	Social Security Number
10–34	Employee Name
35–39	Employee Number
40–46	Annual Salary (to two decimal places)

The program will read each record and display the Employee Number on the screen. Then the program will stop and ask the user to type N to see the next Employee Number in the file, Q to cease processing and exit the program, or D to see on the screen all four fields in the record. Figure 21.1 shows what the screen will look like when the program is displaying an Employee Number and waiting for user input.

FIGURE *21.1* Main menu screen for Program P21-01

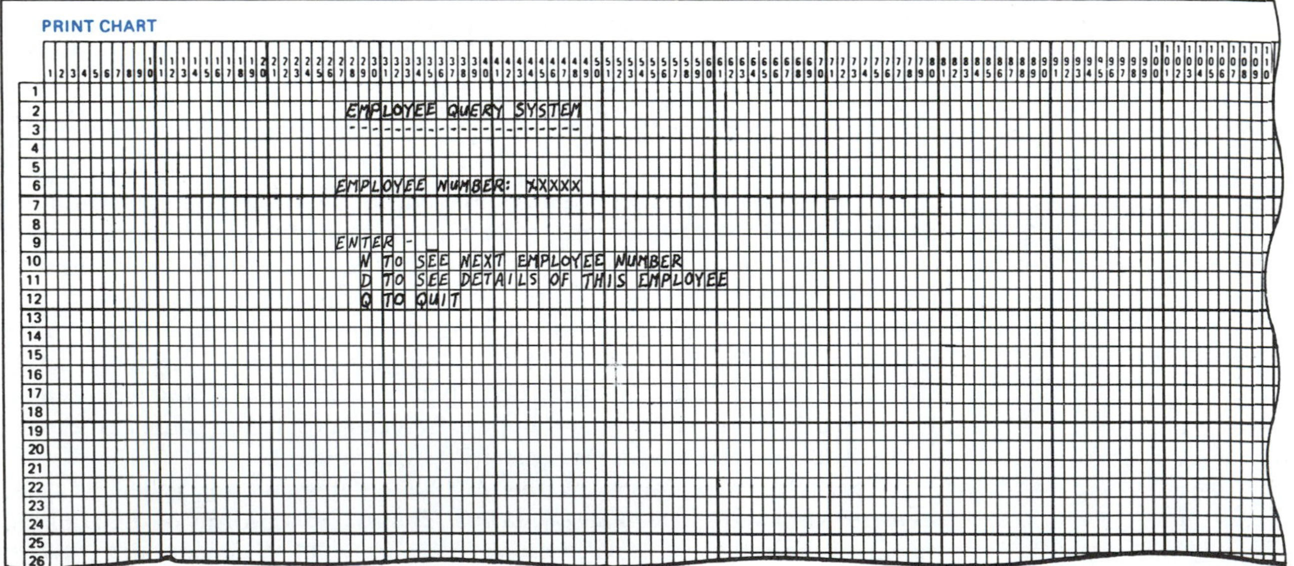

Most screens on most computers in current use are capable of showing 80 columns and 25 lines. Figure 21.1 uses an ordinary print chart to show the location on the screen of each constant and variable. Notice the location of the cursor in line 9, column 35, waiting for user input from the keyboard.

If the user enters an erroneous response, not N or D or Q, the program will blink the message PLEASE ENTER N OR D OR Q in bright white on the screen until a correct response is entered. The appearance of the screen under these conditions is shown in Figure 21.2.

FIGURE *21.2* **Main menu screen with erroneous response**

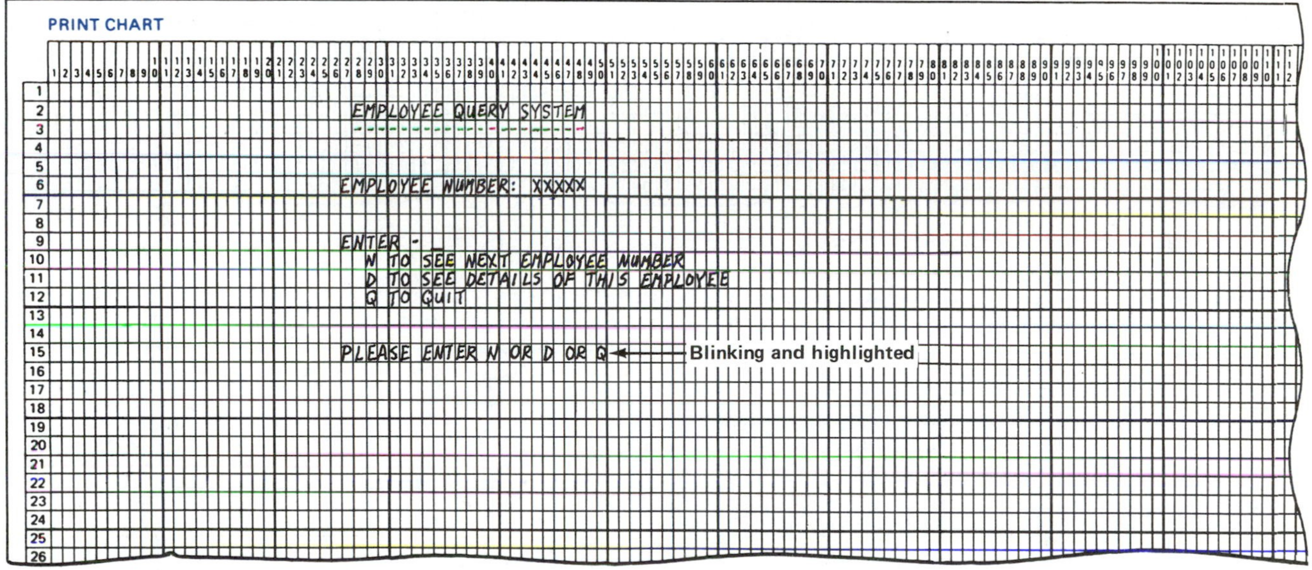

If the user enters D to see all the fields of the record, they will be displayed in the format shown in Figure 21.3. Notice here that the cursor does not appear on the screen, since the user is requested to PRESS ANY KEY TO RETURN TO MENU. When the user presses any key, the appearance of the screen returns to that of Figure 21.1 with the same Employee Number still showing.

The hierarchy diagram for Program P21-01 is shown in Figure 21.4. The subfunction "Main loop" executes once for each input record. For each record, the Employee Number is displayed and a menu selection ACCEPTed. If the user requests a display of the entire record, it is displayed. If not, the next record is read. Remember that when the entire record is displayed, the user may PRESS ANY KEY TO RETURN TO MENU, which is to return to the subfunction "Accept menu selection." So it is possible for the program to go back and forth between "Accept menu selection" and "Display detail" for one input record.

FIGURE *21.3* **Screen showing all fields of input record in Program P21-01**

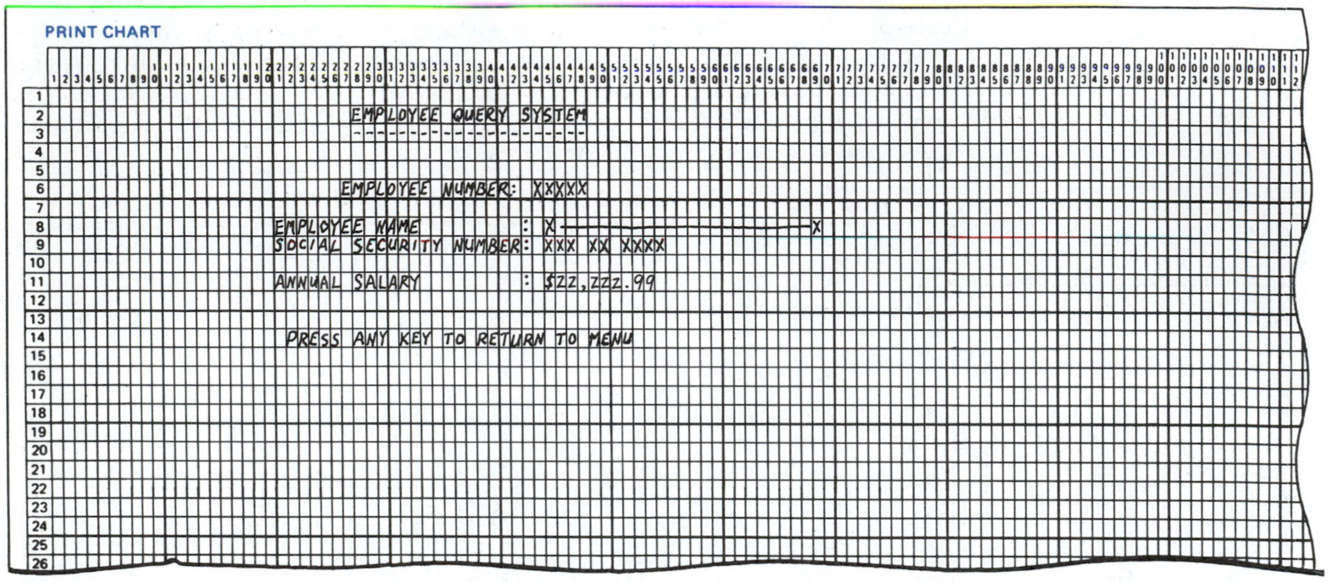

FIGURE *21.4* **Hierarchy diagram for Program P21-01**

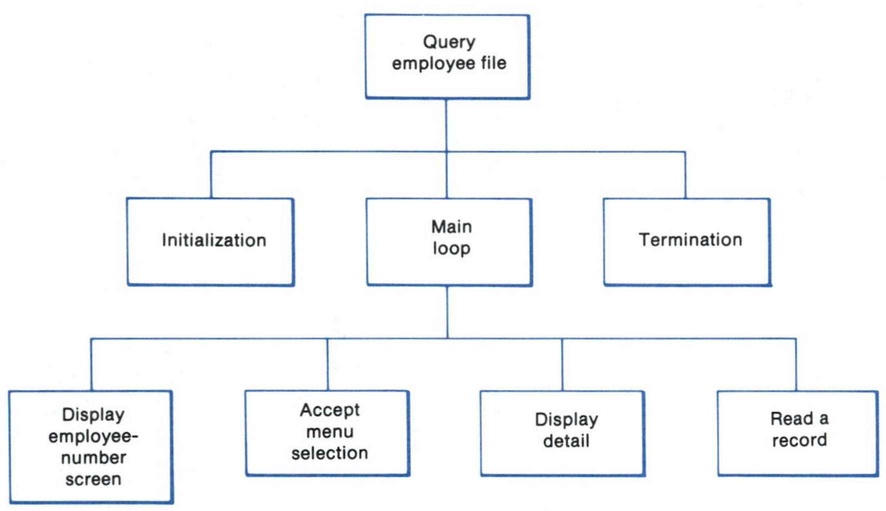

Program P21-01

Program P21-01 is shown in Figure 21.5. In the FILE-CONTROL paragraph, line 21, you can see an ASSIGN clause for a customary type of input file used by COBOL programs on the PC. The complete name of the file is given in the ASSIGN clause, line 22. If the input file is in some different directory from the COBOL program, or on a different drive, you would include drive and directory information with the file name in the usual DOS format, for example "C:\EDUC\

FIGURE 21.5 **Program P21-01**

```
RM/COBOL-85 (Version 4.10.06) For DOS 2.00+    03/10/92  11:35:50 Page 1
Source File: P2101.CBL                       Options: (P Y O=.\ )

LINE    DEBUG     PG/LN  A...B.......2.........3.........4.........5.........6.........7..ID.....8

                         IDENTIFICATION DIVISION.
                         PROGRAM-ID.  P21-01.
                        *
                        *     THIS PROGRAM READS INPUT RECORDS IN THE FOLLOWING FORMAT:
                        *
                        *     POS. 1-9           SOCIAL SECURITY NUMBER
                        *     POS. 10-34         EMPLOYEE NAME
                        *     POS. 35-39         EMPLOYEE NUMBER
                        *     POS. 40-46         ANNUAL SALARY
                        *
                        *     FOR EACH RECORD, THE EMPLOYEE NUMBER IS DISPLAYED AND THE
                        *     USER IS PROMPTED FOR A RESPONSE OF:
                        *         N TO SEE THE NEXT EMPLOYEE NUMBER
                        *         D TO SEE DETAILS OF THE CURRENT EMPLOYEE NUMBER
                        *         Q TO QUIT PROCESSING
                        *
                        ******************************************************************

                         ENVIRONMENT DIVISION.
                         INPUT-OUTPUT SECTION.
                         FILE-CONTROL.
                             SELECT EMPLOYEE-DATA-IN ASSIGN TO INPUT, "DATA2001.DAT"
                                ORGANIZATION IS LINE SEQUENTIAL.

                        ******************************************************************

                         DATA DIVISION.
                         FILE SECTION.
                         FD  EMPLOYEE-DATA-IN
                             RECORD CONTAINS 80 CHARACTERS.

                         01  EMPLOYEE-RECORD-IN.
                             05 SOCIAL-SECURITY-NUMBER-IN.
                                10 SS-NO-1       PIC XXX.
                                10 SS-NO-2       PIC XX.
                                10 SS-NO-3       PIC X(4).
                             05 EMPLOYEE-NAME-IN                 PIC X(25).
                             05 EMPLOYEE-NUMBER-IN               PIC X(5).
                             05 ANNUAL-SALARY-IN                 PIC 9(5)V99.
```

continued

RMCBL85\DATA2001.DAT". The ORGANIZATION clause is required for this file. The clause ORGANIZATION IS **LINE SEQUENTIAL** means that the file is an ordinary ASCII file, keyed in on any ordinary word processor and saved in ASCII format.

Only one file is defined in this program, the input file. There is no output file. Displays to the screen and input from the keyboard are not file operations. A DISPLAY statement can send to the screen any field defined in the File Section, Working Storage Section, or Screen Section. An ACCEPT statement can ACCEPT keyed data into any field in the File Section or Working Storage Section.

FIGURE 21.5 *continued*

```
RM/COBOL-85 (Version 4.10.06) For DOS 2.00+     03/10/92  11:35:50 Page 2
Source File: P2101.CBL                      Options: (P Y O=.\ )

 LINE    DEBUG      PG/LN  A...B.......2.........3.........4.........5.........6.........7..ID.....8

42                           WORKING-STORAGE SECTION.
43                           01  MORE-INPUT                          PIC X     VALUE "Y".
44                               88 THERE-IS-NO-MORE-INPUT           VALUE "N".
45                           01  RESPONSE                            PIC X.
46                               88 SEE-NEXT-RECORD                  VALUE "N" "n".
47                               88 SEE-DETAIL                       VALUE "D" "d".
48                               88 QUIT-PROCESSING                  VALUE "Q" "q".
49                               88 VALID-RESPONSE                   VALUE "N" "D" "Q"
50                                                                         "n" "d" "q".
51                           01  GO-ON                               PIC X.
52
53
54                           SCREEN SECTION.
55                           01  SCREEN-TITLE FOREGROUND WHITE.
56                               05 BLANK SCREEN LINE 2 COLUMN 28 VALUE
57                                  "EMPLOYEE QUERY SYSTEM".
58                               05 LINE PLUS 1 COLUMN 28 VALUE
59                                  "---------------------".
60                               05 LINE 6 COLUMN 27 VALUE
61                                  "EMPLOYEE NUMBER:".
62
63                           01  EMPLOYEE-NUMBER-SCREEN.
64                               05 LINE 6  COLUMN 44 PIC X(5) FROM EMPLOYEE-NUMBER-IN.
65                               05 LINE 15            BLANK LINE.
66
67                           01  PROMPT-SCREEN FOREGROUND WHITE.
68                               05 LINE 8             BLANK REMAINDER.
69                               05 LINE 9  COLUMN 27 VALUE
70                                  "ENTER -".
71                               05 LINE 10 COLUMN 29 VALUE
72                                  "N TO SEE NEXT EMPLOYEE NUMBER".
73                               05 LINE PLUS 1 COLUMN 29 VALUE
74                                  "D TO SEE DETAILS OF THIS EMPLOYEE".
75                               05 LINE PLUS 1 COLUMN 29 VALUE
76                                  "Q TO QUIT".
77                               05 LINE 9  COLUMN 35 AUTO PIC X USING RESPONSE.
78
79                           01  BLINK-LINE.
80                               05 BLINK HIGHLIGHT LINE 15 COLUMN 27 VALUE
81                                  "PLEASE ENTER N OR D OR Q".
82
```

continued

In the Working Storage Section we have the usual flag to detect end-of-file on the input file. We have also a field called RESPONSE, line 45, to ACCEPT from the keyboard the N or D or Q that the user is supposed to key in. Notice in the level-88 entries for RESPONSE that even though the user is supposed to key in uppercase N, D, or Q, it is polite to allow the user to key in lowercase letters as well.

We also have GO-ON, which will ACCEPT the ANY KEY that the user is supposed to press to return to the menu.

We now come to the Screen Section. Here we define what the different screens are to look like when DISPLAYed. The level numbers allowed in the Screen Section are the same as in the Working Storage Section, except that level number 88 is not allowed in the Screen Section. Screens defined in this section can be the object of a DISPLAY or ACCEPT verb in the Procedure Division. A DISPLAY statement naming one of the screens here will send constants and output fields to the screen; an ACCEPT verb naming one of the screens will position the cursor and allow the user to key input into a field in the File or Working Storage Sections. A screen definition may contain both input and output fields. The output fields are activated only when the screen name is the object of a DISPLAY verb; the input fields are activated only when the screen name is the object of an ACCEPT verb.

The first level-01 entry in the Screen Section, at line 55, defines the first screen. This screen consists of fields that are DISPLAYed only once at the beginning of execution of the program and remain on the screen until execution is finished. In line 55 we give a name to the screen, SCREEN-TITLE, and use the reserved words **FOREGROUND WHITE** to specify the color of the fields. Ordinarily, the FOREGROUND color defaults to WHITE, but in this program we will be changing FOREGROUND colors and want to be sure that it will be WHITE here regardless of what has come before. Other reserved color names are **BLACK, BLUE, GREEN, CYAN, RED, MAGENTA,** and **BROWN; BACKGROUND** is a reserved word also.

The SCREEN-TITLE screen consists of three constants, given with VALUE clauses and nonnumeric literals. When this screen is DISPLAYed, the reserved words **BLANK SCREEN** in line 56 clear the screen before any other action takes place. BLANK SCREEN may be used only at the elementary level. Next we use the LINE and COLUMN clauses to say where each constant should appear on the screen. No PICTURE clause is allowed when you use a VALUE clause in a screen definition, for the compiler counts the size of the literal. Notice the form of the LINE clause in line 58. The reserved word PLUS tells the system to position the output on the screen in relation to the line on which the previous output appears.

The EMPLOYEE-NUMBER-SCREEN, line 63, is used to DISPLAY each Employee Number as it is read from the input file. The PICTURE clause in line 64 uses the word FROM to designate the field as an output field and to tell what data is to be sent to the screen when this is DISPLAYed. Line 65 shows the use of the BLANK LINE clause. Line 65 is included in EMPLOYEE-NUMBER-SCREEN because under certain conditions LINE 15 of the screen must be blanked when a new Employee Number is DISPLAYed.

The PROMPT-SCREEN, line 67, defines the menu. In addition, line 68 directs the system to BLANK the **REMAINDER** of the screen from LINE 8 to the end. This erases the previous contents of the screen before DISPLAYing the menu. Lines 69 through 76 define the menu, and line 77 defines how the user response will be handled. The LINE and COLUMN clauses position the cursor for the user's input. The reserved word **AUTO** tells the system that as soon as the input field is filled the input operation is considered complete. The user does not have to press Enter. The PICTURE clause here has the word USING, which designates the field as both an input and output field. It causes the current value of RESPONSE to be shown at the cursor location and also causes the user's keyed input to be placed into RESPONSE.

In line 79 is defined the warning line that appears if the user keys an incorrect response to the menu, using the reserved word **BLINK.** The reserved word **HIGHLIGHT** causes the message to appear in bright white. The default brightness **intensity** for DISPLAY *screen-name* operations is **NO** HIGHLIGHT; the default intensity for ACCEPT *screen-name* operations is HIGHLIGHT.

Finally we come to the screen that defines the detailed DISPLAY of the input record. Line 86 of the definition shows that the LINE clause need not always be included in the definition. LINE 8 is assumed because line 84 of the definition placed the cursor on that line. Line 91 of the definition also omits the LINE clause. LINE 9 is assumed because line 88 of the definition placed the cursor on that line. Lines 92 through 95 omit both the LINE and COLUMN clauses, and the system infers the position of the cursor from its previous locations. The fields defined in lines 91 through 95 appear on the screen on a line one immediately after the other with no space between them.

Line 103 of the definition allows the user to press any key to continue execution of the program. We make the cursor disappear with FOREGROUND BLACK NO HIGHLIGHT. The AUTO clause makes it unnecessary for the user to press Enter after pressing ANY KEY. The word TO in the PICTURE clause designates this field as an input field and causes the user's input to be placed in GO-ON.

It is legal for a PICTURE clause to contain both a FROM phrase and a TO phrase. When a PICTURE clause contains a FROM phrase, the field being defined is an output field and is active during DISPLAY operations. When a PICTURE clause contains a TO phrase, the field being defined is an input field and is active during ACCEPT operations. When a PICTURE clause contains both a FROM and a TO phrase, the field is thus defined for input and output. Its contents are shown on the screen during DISPLAY operations, and the cursor is positioned there for input during ACCEPT operations. A field can be defined for both input and output with a USING phrase, also. A USING phrase in a PICTURE clause has the same effect as a FROM and a TO phrase both naming the same field.

FIGURE *21.5* ***continued***

```
RM/COBOL-85 (Version 4.10.06) For DOS 2.00+     03/10/92  11:35:50 Page 3
Source File: P2101.CBL                        Options: (P Y O=.\ )

 LINE   DEBUG     PG/LN  A...B.......2.........3.........4.........5.........6.........7..ID.....8

   83                     01  DETAIL-SCREEN.
   84                         05 LINE 8 COLUMN 21 BLANK REMAINDER VALUE
   85                            "EMPLOYEE NAME".
   86                         05         COLUMN 43 VALUE ": ".
   87                         05                   PIC X(25) FROM EMPLOYEE-NAME-IN.
   88                         05 LINE 9 COLUMN 21 VALUE
   89                            "SOCIAL SECURITY NUMBER:".
   90                         05 SOCIAL-SECURITY-NUMBER-EDITED.
   91                            10      COLUMN 45 PIC XXX  FROM SS-NO-1.
   92                            10                VALUE "-".
   93                            10                PIC XX   FROM SS-NO-2.
   94                            10                VALUE "-".
   95                            10                PIC X(4) FROM SS-NO-3.
   96                         05 LINE 11 COLUMN 21 VALUE
   97                            "ANNUAL SALARY".
   98                         05          COLUMN 43 VALUE ": ".
   99                         05                    PIC $ZZ,ZZZ.99 FROM
  100                                                      ANNUAL-SALARY-IN.
  101                         05 LINE PLUS 3 COLUMN 22 VALUE
  102                            "PRESS ANY KEY TO RETURN TO MENU".
  103                         05 FOREGROUND BLACK NO HIGHLIGHT AUTO
  104                                           PIC X TO GO-ON.
  105
  106                    *****************************************************************
  107
```

FIGURE *21.5* ***continued***

```
108                      PROCEDURE DIVISION.
109     000002           QUERY-EMPLOYEE-FILE.
110     000005               PERFORM INITIALIZATION
111     000008               PERFORM MAIN-LOOP UNTIL THERE-IS-NO-MORE-INPUT OR
112                                                 QUIT-PROCESSING
113     000034               PERFORM TERMINATION
114     000037               STOP RUN
115                          .
116
117     000040           INITIALIZATION.
118     000043               DISPLAY SCREEN-TITLE
119     000048               DISPLAY PROMPT-SCREEN
120     000059               OPEN INPUT EMPLOYEE-DATA-IN
121     000066               PERFORM READ-A-RECORD
122                          .
123
124     000071           READ-A-RECORD.
125     000074               READ EMPLOYEE-DATA-IN
126                              AT END
127                                  SET THERE-IS-NO-MORE-INPUT TO TRUE
128                          .
129
130     000091           TERMINATION.
131     000094               CLOSE EMPLOYEE-DATA-IN
132     000101               DISPLAY "THANK YOU FOR USING THE EMPLOYEE QUERY SYSTEM"
133                                  ERASE LOW LINE 13 POSITION 16
134                          .
135
136     000116           MAIN-LOOP.
137     000119               DISPLAY EMPLOYEE-NUMBER-SCREEN
138     000130               PERFORM ACCEPT-MENU-SELECTION WITH TEST AFTER
139                                                    UNTIL VALID-RESPONSE
140     000175               EVALUATE TRUE
141                             WHEN SEE-DETAIL
142                                 PERFORM DISPLAY-DETAIL
143                             WHEN SEE-NEXT-RECORD
144                                 PERFORM READ-A-RECORD
145                          END-EVALUATE
146                          .
147
148     000215           ACCEPT-MENU-SELECTION.
149     000218               ACCEPT PROMPT-SCREEN
150     000229               IF NOT VALID-RESPONSE
151                              DISPLAY BLINK-LINE
152                          END-IF
153                          .
154
155     000279           DISPLAY-DETAIL.
156     000282               DISPLAY DETAIL-SCREEN
157     000315               ACCEPT  DETAIL-SCREEN
158     000326               DISPLAY PROMPT-SCREEN
159                          .
```

The Procedure Division, line 108, follows the hierarchy diagram. Notice that DISPLAY statements in lines 118 and 119 appear before the OPEN statement. This shows that DISPLAY statements require no OPEN file. Also, the DISPLAY statement in line 132 is given after the input file is CLOSEd. Line 132 is an example of a terminal-I/O DISPLAY statement. It uses no screen name. The entire output is shown right here. It is the closing thank-you message. The reserved word **ERASE** clears the screen before anything else is done. **LOW** intensity is specified because the default intensity for all terminal-I/O operations is **HIGH**.

The PERFORM statement in line 138 requires a WITH TEST AFTER clause because the condition may already be satisfied by a previous response to the menu prompt.

Program P21-01 was run with the same input data as Program P02-03. The first screen that appears is shown in Figure 21.6. The screen that appears if the user presses an invalid code such as F is shown in Figure 21.7. The screen that appears if the user then presses D is shown in Figure 21.8. The screen that appears if the user presses Q is shown in Figure 21.9.

FIGURE *21.6* **Main menu screen with prompt**

```
 EMPLOYEE QUERY SYSTEM
 ---------------------


EMPLOYEE NUMBER: 10503


ENTER - _
  N TO SEE NEXT EMPLOYEE NUMBER
  D TO SEE DETAILS OF THIS EMPLOYEE
  Q TO QUIT
```

FIGURE *21.7* **Main menu screen with erroneous response**

```
 EMPLOYEE QUERY SYSTEM
 ---------------------


EMPLOYEE NUMBER: 10503


ENTER - F
  N TO SEE NEXT EMPLOYEE NUMBER
  D TO SEE DETAILS OF THIS EMPLOYEE
  Q TO QUIT


PLEASE ENTER N OR D OR Q
```

← Blinking and highlighted

FIGURE *21.8* **All fields of input record**

```
      EMPLOYEE QUERY SYSTEM
      ---------------------


     EMPLOYEE NUMBER: 10503

EMPLOYEE NAME         : MORALES, LUIS
SOCIAL SECURITY NUMBER: 100-04-0002

ANNUAL SALARY         : $50,000.00


 PRESS ANY KEY TO RETURN TO MENU
```

FIGURE 21.9 **Final screen when Program P21-01 is run with the "Kill announcement" execution option of RM/CO***

```
THANK YOU FOR USING THE EMPLOYEE QUERY SYSTEM




Press any key to continue
```

EXERCISE 1

Write a program for an on-screen calculator. Have your program prompt the user to key in a number, then one of the arithmetic operators +, −, *, /, or **, then a second number. Have your program carry out the indicated arithmetic and DISPLAY the result on the screen. Design your screen(s) before you begin coding.

Summary

PC COBOL systems contain extensions to ANSI standard COBOL that allow for convenient screen output from and keyboard input to programs. These include the Screen Section and the terminal-I/O and screen-name forms of the ACCEPT and DISPLAY statements. Input files for PC COBOL systems can be created on a word processor and saved as ASCII files.

In the Screen Section, you give each different screen a name and a level number. Optional clauses tell at which LINE and COLUMN an output field will be DISPLAYed or an input field ACCEPTed, or specify the FOREGROUND and BACKGROUND colors. The three BLANK clauses direct the system to BLANK SCREEN, BLANK LINE, or BLANK REMAINDER of the screen from a specified LINE and/or COLUMN. The AUTO clause specifies that as soon as an input field is filled the input operation is assumed to be complete, so the user need not press Enter.

The PICTURE clause in the Screen Section designates a field as input, output, or both. A PICTURE clause containing the word FROM designates the field as output and tells what field should show on the screen. A PICTURE clause containing the word TO designates the field as input and says where the user's keyed data should be stored. And a PICTURE clause containing the word USING designates the field as input and output; the current contents of the field are DISPLAYed on the screen, and the user's input is ACCEPTed into the same field, replacing what was there.

The reserved words BLINK and HIGHLIGHT can be used to draw attention to particular parts of the output. The default intensity for DISPLAY *screen-name* operations is NO HIGHLIGHT; the default intensity for ACCEPT *screen-name* operations is HIGHLIGHT.

The terminal-I/O form of the DISPLAY statement can show output on the screen without the need for an entry in the Screen Section. The DISPLAY statement contains all the details of the DISPLAY. The reserved word ERASE may be used in such a statement to ERASE the screen, and LOW may be used to DISPLAY the output in ordinary brightness. The default intensity for all terminal-I/O operations is HIGH.

Fill-In Exercises

1. Most microcomputer screens have ______ columns and ______ lines.
2. A clause used to describe an input file in ASCII format is ORGANIZATION IS ______ ______.
3. Level number ______ is permitted in the File Section and Working Storage Section but not in the Screen Section.
4. A screen name defined in the Screen Section can be the object of a(n) ______ verb or a(n) ______ verb.
5. An output field in the Screen Section can have the word ______ or ______ in its PICTURE clause; an input field in the Screen Section can have the word ______ or ______ in its PICTURE clause.
6. The three forms of the BLANK clause that BLANK some portion of the screen are BLANK ______, BLANK ______, and BLANK ______.
7. The reserved word ______, when used with an input field, makes it unnecessary for the user to press Enter.
8. The default intensity for DISPLAY *screen-name* operations is ______; the default intensity for ACCEPT *screen-name* operations is ______.
9. The default intensity for all terminal-I/O operations is ______.
10. In terminal-I/O, the reserved word ______ clears the entire screen.
11. The form of DISPLAY statement that executes without a Screen Section is DISPLAY ______.
12. To have output flash on and off on the screen, include the reserved word ______ in its field definition.
13. The eight screen colors usually supported by PC COBOL systems are ______, ______, ______, ______, ______, ______, ______, and ______.
14. A DISPLAY statement can send to the screen any field defined in the ______ Section, the ______ Section, or the ______ Section.
15. An ACCEPT statement can ACCEPT keyed data into any field in the ______ Section or ______ Section.

CHAPTER 22

The ANSI Debugging Feature

HERE ARE THE KEY POINTS YOU SHOULD LEARN FROM THIS CHAPTER

1. Why the ANSI debugging feature is useful
2. When to use the ANSI debugging feature
3. What ANSI debugging facilities are available
4. How to program using the ANSI debugging feature

KEY WORDS TO RECOGNIZE AND LEARN

debugging line	ALL REFERENCES
debugging section	explicit reference
WITH DEBUGGING MODE	ALL PROCEDURES
computer-name	object-time switch
DEBUG-ITEM	USE FOR DEBUGGING
monitor	USE DEBUGGING

In this chapter we discuss the ANSI standard debugging feature. The ANSI debugging feature is available on many large COBOL systems. The feature is considered an obsolete element of standard COBOL, because individual manufacturers of COBOL compilers are more and more providing their own debugging aids, as for example the Ryan/McFarland aids discussed in Chapter 20. The ANSI debugging feature will be dropped from the next COBOL standard.

The ANSI standard provides two types of debugging aids—**debugging lines** and **debugging sections.** Since debugging lines are the easier to understand and code, we will do those first.

Debugging Lines

When you are developing a new program or modifying an existing one, you will sometimes want to have the program produce some output that is to be used only for debugging. That is, you may want your program to produce, in addition to the output that it was designed to produce, extra output that will help you to find and correct errors in the program. Then, when the program is working correctly, you will want the program to cease producing the extra output. Debugging lines give you a way to control the production of the debug output.

To use this feature, you write into your program all the lines of code that you want for debugging, and put a D in position 7 of each line to indicate to COBOL that the lines are being used for debugging purposes only and are not meant to be part of the normal running of the program. Debugging lines may be written only after the OBJECT-COMPUTER paragraph, or where the paragraph would be if it is omitted, and may be written in the Environment, Data, and Procedure Divisions. If a single debugging statement takes more than one line, each line must have a D in position 7. You cannot use the continuation indicator in debugging lines. But the continuation indicator is rarely used, and anything you can do by using a continuation indicator can be done with other (less convenient) coding techniques anyway. The continuation indicator is discussed fully in Chapter 5.

Then, when you run your program in the ordinary way that we have been doing so far, COBOL will ignore the debugging lines. The lines will appear in your program listing where you wrote them but they will not be executed. To get COBOL to execute the debugging lines you must include, in the Environment Division of your program, a Configuration Section with a SOURCE-COMPUTER paragraph containing a **WITH DEBUGGING MODE** clause.

The format of the SOURCE-COMPUTER paragraph is as follows:

```
SOURCE-COMPUTER. [computer-name [WITH DEBUGGING MODE].]
```

The **computer-name** is provided by the manufacturer. Your instructor will give you the computer name to use for your particular computer. Now, if we have a program that contains debugging lines we can use the WITH DEBUGGING MODE clause to tell COBOL that we want the debugging lines executed. Then, when the program in working correctly we can remove the WITH DEBUGGING MODE clause and COBOL will ignore the debugging lines. Notice that only the words DEBUGGING and MODE are required in the WITH DEBUGGING MODE clause.

The main advantage of using debugging lines is that the lines can stay in the program permanently, and be activated and deactivated by proper use of the WITH DEBUGGING MODE clause. So if some change is to be made to the program in the future, the same debugging that was used originally can easily be reactivated again.

This advantage has a disadvantage. If, when the program is to be changed in the future, some different debugging is wanted instead, all the old debugging lines will have to be laboriously removed by the most junior programmer in the installation, probably you.

The use of debugging lines has another drawback: If the debugging lines are not removed from the program after debugging is completed, the program becomes difficult to read. Position 7 of the line is not where your eye normally falls when you are reading COBOL code, and the Ds there will be easy to overlook. Extra lines in the Environment and Data Divisions don't do much harm, but extra lines in the Procedure Division can make the program very confusing indeed.

These disadvantages can be overcome through the use of debugging sections, which will be discussed later. But first let's look at a program that contains debugging lines.

A Program with Debugging Lines

We will use Program P10-01 to show how debugging lines can be added to a program for use during program development and testing. Review Program P10-01 before going on. The input format for Program P10-01 is given on page 292; the output format in Figure 10.1; Program P10-01 is shown in Figure 10.2; the input data, Figure 10.3; and the output in Figure 10.4. For Program P22-01, we will add debugging lines to Program P10-01 to enable us to check on the calculation of COMMISSION-FOR-SALESPERSON to see that it is working as we expect it to. COMMISSION-FOR-SALESPERSON is calculated at line 01530 in Program P10-01.

Program P22-01 will produce two reports. One will contain the original output of Program P10-01, and the other will contain just debug output.[1] The debug output will have the format shown in Figure 22.1.

FIGURE *22.1* Output format for debug output of Program P22-01

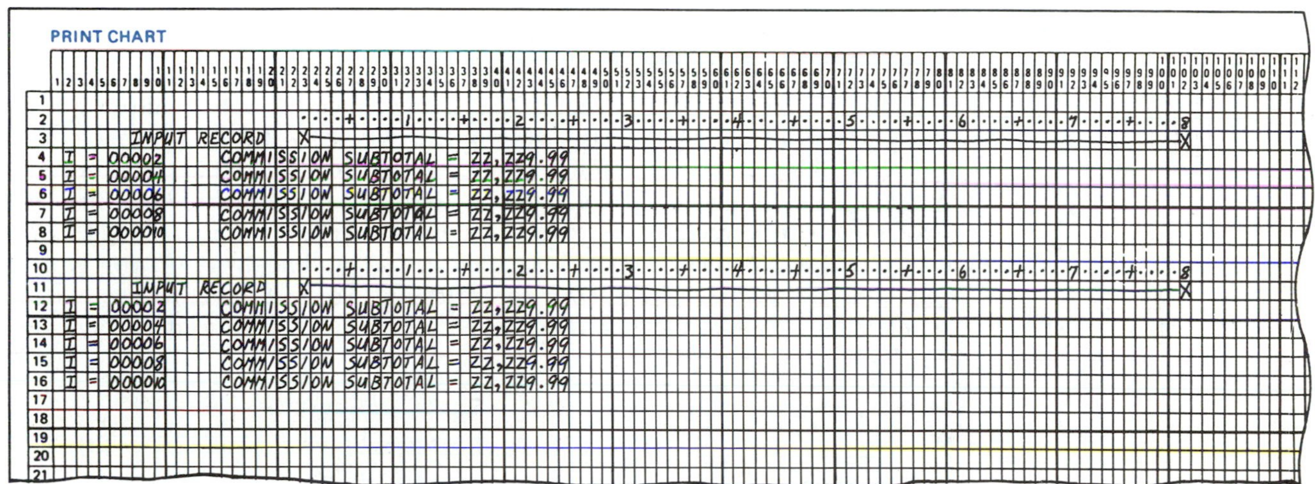

The Debug Output

Program P22-01 will print seven lines of debug output for each salesperson. One of the lines of debug output is labeled INPUT RECORD. Whenever you are doing debugging, you should print out each input record in the exact form in which it was read, with no editing and no reformatting. That way you can see whether

[1]The two reports will print one after the other on the same printer if the printer is not under direct control of your program. If only one printer under direct control of your program is available, the report lines will be interleaved in an unpredictable manner.

you have all your input data in the correct positions. Also, if there are any IF statements in your program that test the input data, you can see which way the IF statements should come out. In general, when you have your input record before your eyes, you can know what the program is supposed to do and can check that it is doing it.

Immediately above the line called INPUT RECORD is a line of 80 dots, + signs, and numbers to make it easy for us to find any particular position of the input record. Immediately following the line called INPUT RECORD are five lines that should show us how COMMISSION-FOR-SALESPERSON is computed from that input record.

COMMISSION-FOR-SALESPERSON is calculated in the paragraph COMMISSION-CALCULATION, which executes under control of the PERFORM . . . VARYING statement at line 01200 in Program P10-01. The paragraph COMMISSION-CALCULATION uses I as a subscript in its COMPUTE statements. In the normal execution of Program P10-01, COMMISSION-CALCULATION executes 10 times for each input record, with I set to 1, 2, 3, and so on to 10. Program P22-01 prints one line of debug output the second, fourth, sixth, eighth, and tenth times that COMMISSION-CALCULATION executes for each input record. Each line shows the value of I and the value of the field COMMISSION-FOR-SALESPERSON. Remember that COMMISSION-FOR-SALESPERSON is zeroed for each input record and is used to accumulate the commission amounts as they are computed for a single salesperson from the 10 Sale Amounts.

Programming for Debug Output

Program P22-01 is shown in Figure 22.2. To produce the debug output we use the WITH DEBUGGING MODE clause in the SOURCE-COMPUTER paragraph, and some debugging lines in the Working Storage Section and in the Procedure Division. In working storage we define the GUIDE-LINE that is to be printed immediately before each input record, at lines 004705 through 004715. We also define COMMISSION-FOR-SALESPERSON-E, at line 004720, for editing COMMISSION-FOR-SALESPERSON for printing. You will see why we need COMMISSION-FOR-SALESPERSON-E when we look at the Procedure Division.

FIGURE *22.2*

Program P22-01

```
S COBOL II RELEASE 3.2 09/05/90                    P22001   DATE MAR 09,1992 T
-----+-*A-1-B--+----2----+----3----+----4----+----5----+----6----+----7-|--+


00010  IDENTIFICATION DIVISION.
00020  PROGRAM-ID.  P22-01.
00030 *AUTHOR. DEBORAH ANN SENIOR.
00040 *
00050 *     THIS PROGRAM PRODUCES A SALESPERSON COMMISSION
00060 *     REPORT SHOWING TEN COMMISSION AMOUNTS
00070 *     AND THE TOTAL FOR EACH SALESPERSON.
00080 *
00090 *
00100 ******************************************************************
```

FIGURE 22.2 ***continued***

```
       ENVIRONMENT DIVISION.
       CONFIGURATION SECTION.
       SOURCE-COMPUTER. IBM-360 WITH DEBUGGING MODE.

       INPUT-OUTPUT SECTION.
       FILE-CONTROL.
           SELECT SALES-FILE-IN                ASSIGN TO INFILE.
           SELECT COMMISSION-REPORT-FILE-OUT   ASSIGN TO PRINTER.

      *****************************************************************

       DATA DIVISION.
       FILE SECTION.
       FD  SALES-FILE-IN
           RECORD CONTAINS 80 CHARACTERS.

       01  SALES-RECORD-IN.
           05  SALESPERSON-NUMBER-IN    PIC X(7).
           05  SALE-AMOUNT-IN           PIC 9(4)V99     OCCURS 10 TIMES.

       FD  COMMISSION-REPORT-FILE-OUT.

       01  REPORT-LINE                  PIC X(119).

       WORKING-STORAGE SECTION.
       01  MORE-INPUT                   PIC X           VALUE "Y".
           88 THERE-IS-NO-MORE-INPUT    VALUE "N".
       01  PACKED-DECIMAL-CONSTANTS     PACKED-DECIMAL.
           05  COMMISSION-RATE-1        PIC V99         VALUE .05.
           05  COMMISSION-RATE-2        PIC V99         VALUE .10.
           05  BRACKET-MAXIMUM          PIC 999V99      VALUE 100.00.
       01  NUMBER-OF-SALES              PIC S99         VALUE 10
                                        COMP            SYNC.
       01  GRAND-TOTAL-COMMISSIONS-W    PIC S9(6)V99    PACKED-DECIMAL
                                                        VALUE 0.
       01  COMMISSION-AMOUNT-W          PIC S9(4)V99    PACKED-DECIMAL.
       01  COMMISSION-FOR-SALESPERSON   PIC S9(5)V99    PACKED-DECIMAL.
       01  I                            PIC S99         COMP SYNC.
       01  LINE-SPACING  VALUE 1        PIC S9          COMP SYNC.
       01  GUIDE-LINE                   PIC X(102)
           VALUE "                        ....+....1....+....2....+....3..
      -        "..+....4....+....5....+....6....+....7....+....8".
       01  COMMISSION-FOR-SALESPERSON-E                 PIC ZZ,ZZ9.99.

       01  PAGE-HEADING-1.
           05          PIC X(51)       VALUE SPACES.
           05          PIC X(17)       VALUE "COMMISSION REPORT".

       01  PAGE-HEADING-2.
           05          PIC X(39)       VALUE "SALES-".
           05          PIC X(73)
               VALUE "C O M M I S S I O N S   O N   S A L E S".
           05          PIC X(5)        VALUE "TOTAL".

       01  PAGE-HEADING-3.
           05          PIC X(10)       VALUE "PERSON".
           05          PIC X(10)       VALUE "SALE 1".
           05          PIC X(10)       VALUE "SALE 2".
           05          PIC X(10)       VALUE "SALE 3".
           05          PIC X(10)       VALUE "SALE 4".
           05          PIC X(10)       VALUE "SALE 5".
           05          PIC X(10)       VALUE "SALE 6".
           05          PIC X(10)       VALUE "SALE 7".
           05          PIC X(10)       VALUE "SALE 8".
           05          PIC X(10)       VALUE "SALE 9".
           05          PIC X(11)       VALUE "SALE 10".
           05          PIC X(7)        VALUE "COMMIS-".
```

continued

In the Procedure Division we need statements that will print each input record and the GUIDE-LINE above it. When you are doing debugging, one way to make sure you print each and every input record is to find the paragraph that contains the nonpriming READ statement or a nonpriming PERFORM of a READ statement. Then print the input record at the very beginning of that paragraph.

We will use DISPLAY statements to print all our debug output. Although DISPLAY has severe limitations which make it unsuitable for printing normal report output, it has two important advantages when used in debugging, as you will see.

The three DISPLAY statements at lines 011805, 011810, and 011815 print first a line of blanks, then the GUIDE-LINE, and finally the line labeled INPUT RECORD. Each DISPLAY statement starts printing on a new line. Remember that, if necessary, you can use a DISPLAY statement before you have OPENed your print file and after you have CLOSEd it.

One of the limitations of the DISPLAY statement is that it automatically single-spaces before printing. No other kind of spacing or skipping is available. That is why we need a DISPLAY statement to print a line of blanks; there is no other way to double-space when using DISPLAY. Another difficulty with DISPLAY is that it does not provide convenient line-formatting capability; you certainly have nothing like the convenience or precision of output-record field definitions when using DISPLAY.

FIGURE 22.2 ***continued***

```
S COBOL II RELEASE 3.2 09/05/90                  P22001    DATE MAR 09,1992 T
----+-*A-1-B--+----2----+----3----+----4----+----5----+----6----+----7-|--+


00720
00730  01   PAGE-HEADING-4.
00740       05            PIC X(112)       VALUE "NUMBER".
00750       05            PIC X(4)         VALUE "SION".
00760
00770  01   DETAIL-LINE.
00780       05  SALESPERSON-NUMBER-OUT  PIC X(9).
00790       05  COMMISSION-AMOUNT-OUT   PIC Z,ZZ9.99BB
00800                                   OCCURS 10 TIMES.
00810       05  COMMISSION-FOR-SALESPERSON-OUT
00820                                   PIC BZZ,ZZ9.99.
00830
00840  01   NO-INPUT-DATA.
00850       05                          PIC X(53) VALUE SPACES.
00860       05                          PIC X(13) VALUE "NO INPUT DATA".
00870
00880  01   TOTAL-LINE.
00890       05                          PIC X(68) VALUE SPACES.
00900       05                          PIC X(41)
00910       VALUE "TOTAL COMMISSION FOR ALL SALESPERSONS".
00920       05  GRAND-TOTAL-COMMISSIONS PIC ZZZ,ZZ9.99.
00930
00940 *****************************************************************
00950
```

FIGURE 22.2 ***continued***

```
PROCEDURE DIVISION.
CONTROL-PARAGRAPH.
    PERFORM INITIALIZATION
    PERFORM MAIN-PROCESS UNTIL THERE-IS-NO-MORE-INPUT
    PERFORM TERMINATION
    STOP RUN
    .

INITIALIZATION.
    OPEN INPUT  SALES-FILE-IN
         OUTPUT COMMISSION-REPORT-FILE-OUT
    WRITE REPORT-LINE FROM PAGE-HEADING-1 AFTER PAGE
    WRITE REPORT-LINE FROM PAGE-HEADING-2 AFTER 4
    WRITE REPORT-LINE FROM PAGE-HEADING-3
    WRITE REPORT-LINE FROM PAGE-HEADING-4
    MOVE 2 TO LINE-SPACING
    PERFORM READ-A-RECORD
    IF THERE-IS-NO-MORE-INPUT
        WRITE REPORT-LINE FROM NO-INPUT-DATA AFTER 2
    END-IF
    .

MAIN-PROCESS.
D   DISPLAY SPACE
D   DISPLAY GUIDE-LINE
D   DISPLAY "       INPUT RECORD    "  SALES-RECORD-IN
    MOVE ZERO TO COMMISSION-FOR-SALESPERSON
    PERFORM COMMISSION-CALCULATION
        VARYING I FROM 1 BY 1 UNTIL
        I IS GREATER THAN NUMBER-OF-SALES
    PERFORM PRODUCE-THE-REPORT
    PERFORM READ-A-RECORD
    .

TERMINATION.
    PERFORM PRODUCE-FINAL-TOTAL-LINE
    CLOSE SALES-FILE-IN
          COMMISSION-REPORT-FILE-OUT
    .

READ-A-RECORD.
    READ SALES-FILE-IN
        AT END
            SET THERE-IS-NO-MORE-INPUT TO TRUE
    .

```

continued

We now need a statement that will print the values of I and the commission subtotals. The statement would have to be in the paragraph COMMISSION-CALCULATION, and the IF statement at line 015305 is it. The IF statement tests to see whether this particular execution of COMMISSION-CALCULATION is one that is supposed to cause a line of debug output to print, and then DISPLAYs a debug line if it is.

The statement at line 015320 shows another limitation of the DISPLAY verb. DISPLAY does not allow you to do output editing directly. The ANSI standard says nothing about editing in connection with the DISPLAY verb. In the COBOL system used to run the programs in this book, DISPLAY edits all numeric output as it thinks best. DISPLAY can be counted on to do a reasonable job of editing a numeric field (but not an excellent one) only if the field is defined as COMPUTATIONAL. If the field is not COMPUTATIONAL, DISPLAY will sometimes make a mess of editing it. That is why we first MOVE COMMISSION-FOR-SALESPERSON to COMMISSION-FOR-SALESPERSON-E before DISPLAYing it. You will see how DISPLAY edits I when we look at the output.

FIGURE 22.2 ***continued***

```
S COBOL II RELEASE 3.2 09/05/90                P22001    DATE MAR 09,1992 T
----+-*A-1-B--+----2----+----3----+----4----+----5----+----6----+----7-|--+

01390   COMMISSION-CALCULATION.
01400       IF SALE-AMOUNT-IN (I) IS NOT GREATER THAN BRACKET-MAXIMUM
01410           COMPUTE
01420             COMMISSION-AMOUNT-W ROUNDED
01430             COMMISSION-AMOUNT-OUT (I) ROUNDED
01440                 = SALE-AMOUNT-IN (I) * COMMISSION-RATE-1
01450       ELSE
01460           COMPUTE
01470             COMMISSION-AMOUNT-W ROUNDED
01480             COMMISSION-AMOUNT-OUT (I) ROUNDED
01490                 = BRACKET-MAXIMUM * COMMISSION-RATE-1 +
01500                   (SALE-AMOUNT-IN (I) - BRACKET-MAXIMUM) *
01510                   COMMISSION-RATE-2
01520       END-IF
01530       ADD COMMISSION-AMOUNT-W TO COMMISSION-FOR-SALESPERSON
015305D     IF I = 2 OR 4 OR 6 OR 8 OR 10
015310D         MOVE COMMISSION-FOR-SALESPERSON TO
015315D              COMMISSION-FOR-SALESPERSON-E
015320D         DISPLAY " I = " I
015325D                 "      COMMISSION SUBTOTAL = "
015330D                 COMMISSION-FOR-SALESPERSON-E
015335D     END-IF
01540       .
01550
01560   PRODUCE-THE-REPORT.
01570       MOVE SALESPERSON-NUMBER-IN TO SALESPERSON-NUMBER-OUT
01580       MOVE COMMISSION-FOR-SALESPERSON TO
01590            COMMISSION-FOR-SALESPERSON-OUT
01600       ADD COMMISSION-FOR-SALESPERSON TO GRAND-TOTAL-COMMISSIONS-W
01610       WRITE REPORT-LINE FROM DETAIL-LINE AFTER LINE-SPACING
01620       MOVE 1 TO LINE-SPACING
01630       .
01640
01650   PRODUCE-FINAL-TOTAL-LINE.
01660       MOVE GRAND-TOTAL-COMMISSIONS-W TO GRAND-TOTAL-COMMISSIONS
01670       WRITE REPORT-LINE FROM TOTAL-LINE AFTER 4
01680       .
```

Program P22-01 was run using the same input as Program P10-01, and produced the normal report output shown in Figure 22.3 and the debug output shown in Figure 22.4. For each line of normal print output, you can find the seven lines of debug output. Notice how the DISPLAY verb edited I.

Now the WITH DEBUGGING MODE clause can be removed from Program P22-01, and the debugging lines will be ignored. The program would then produce just the normal report output.

FIGURE *22.3* **Normal output from Program P22-01**

COMMISSION REPORT

SALES-PERSON NUMBER	SALE 1	SALE 2	SALE 3	SALE 4	SALE 5	SALE 6	SALE 7	SALE 8	SALE 9	SALE 10	TOTAL COMMIS-SION
				C O M M I S S I O N S O N S A L E S							
0001289	495.75	0.63	795.10	43.71	176.49	0.30	6.00	2.40	5.50	82.59	1,608.47
0942386	5.00	195.00	46.93	4.78	1.40	15.00	7.50	36.23	3.00	31.15	345.99
3684420	15.00	7.17	3.75	5.00	0.00	0.00	0.00	0.00	0.00	0.00	30.92
5236714	4.21	2.26	67.37	3.43	24.52	0.00	0.00	0.00	0.00	0.00	101.79
6612364	0.50	17.36	0.94	94.50	3.26	19.51	5.37	4.50	12.36	55.29	213.59
7747119	2.60	11.50	114.50	3.68	39.90	7.50	3.44	0.71	5.00	0.00	188.83

TOTAL COMMISSION FOR ALL SALESPERSONS 2,489.59

FIGURE *22.4* **Debug output from Program P22-01**

```
                                ....+....1....+....2....+....3....+....4....+....5....+....6....+....7....+....8
         INPUT RECORD    0001289500750001256800100048712181492000600011000004800010500087593
I = 00002        COMMISSION SUBTOTAL =      496.38
I = 00004        COMMISSION SUBTOTAL =    1,335.19
I = 00006        COMMISSION SUBTOTAL =    1,511.98
I = 00008        COMMISSION SUBTOTAL =    1,520.38
I = 00010        COMMISSION SUBTOTAL =    1,608.47

                                ....+....1....+....2....+....3....+....4....+....5....+....6....+....7....+....8
         INPUT RECORD    0942386010000200000051927009550002795020000012500041225006000036150
I = 00002        COMMISSION SUBTOTAL =      200.00
I = 00004        COMMISSION SUBTOTAL =      251.71
I = 00006        COMMISSION SUBTOTAL =      268.11
I = 00008        COMMISSION SUBTOTAL =      311.84
I = 00010        COMMISSION SUBTOTAL =      345.99

                                ....+....1....+....2....+....3....+....4....+....5....+....6....+....7....+....8
         INPUT RECORD    3684420020000012165007495010000000000000000000000000000000000000000
I = 00002        COMMISSION SUBTOTAL =       22.17
I = 00004        COMMISSION SUBTOTAL =       30.92
I = 00006        COMMISSION SUBTOTAL =       30.92
I = 00008        COMMISSION SUBTOTAL =       30.92
I = 00010        COMMISSION SUBTOTAL =       30.92

                                ....+....1....+....2....+....3....+....4....+....5....+....6....+....7....+....8
         INPUT RECORD    5236714008412004519072368006850029518000000000000000000000000000000
I = 00002        COMMISSION SUBTOTAL =        6.47
I = 00004        COMMISSION SUBTOTAL =       77.27
I = 00006        COMMISSION SUBTOTAL =      101.79
I = 00008        COMMISSION SUBTOTAL =      101.79
I = 00010        COMMISSION SUBTOTAL =      101.79

                                ....+....1....+....2....+....3....+....4....+....5....+....6....+....7....+....8
         INPUT RECORD    6612364001000022358001873099500006515024512010368008995017360060287
I = 00002        COMMISSION SUBTOTAL =       17.86
I = 00004        COMMISSION SUBTOTAL =      113.30
I = 00006        COMMISSION SUBTOTAL =      136.07
I = 00008        COMMISSION SUBTOTAL =      145.94
I = 00010        COMMISSION SUBTOTAL =      213.59

                                ....+....1....+....2....+....3....+....4....+....5....+....6....+....7....+....8
         INPUT RECORD    7747119005200016500119500007350044895012500006875001425009999000000
I = 00002        COMMISSION SUBTOTAL =       14.10
I = 00004        COMMISSION SUBTOTAL =      132.28
I = 00006        COMMISSION SUBTOTAL =      179.68
I = 00008        COMMISSION SUBTOTAL =      183.83
I = 00010        COMMISSION SUBTOTAL =      188.83
```

EXERCISE *1*

Add debugging lines to your solution to Exercise 3, Chapter 10, page 301, so that the program produces a debug output report as well as the normal output. On the debug output report have your program print each input record and an 80-position guide line. Also for each input record, have your program print the number of hours worked on Tuesday and on Friday. If the number of hours worked is greater than 8 on either of those days, have your program print also the effective hours. Have your program produce its debug output in the format shown in Figure 22.E1.

FIGURE *22.E1* **Debug output format for Exercise 1**

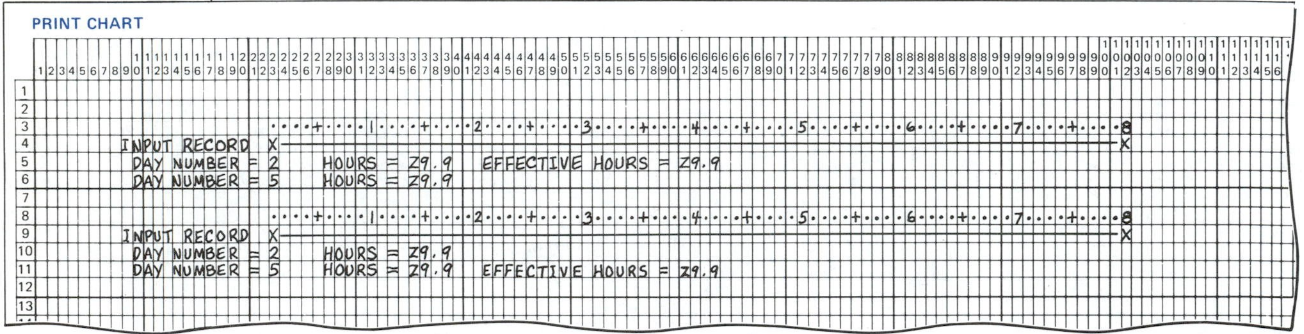

Debugging Sections

It was mentioned earlier that debugging lines in the Procedure Division of a program can make the program difficult to read once the debugging lines have been deactivated. Debugging sections, on the other hand, allow the programmer to group all the debugging code in the Procedure Division into one place, where it can easily be ignored by a reader of the program. Also, debugging sections provide some additional capabilities not conveniently available with debugging lines. In Program P22-02 we will show, by using two debugging sections, how the debugging code in the Procedure Division of a program can be grouped all together and out of the way.

Debugging sections and debugging lines may be used together in the same program. When both are used, it is possible to have

a. The sections and the lines activated

b. The sections and the lines deactivated

c. The sections deactivated and the lines activated

It is not possible to have debugging sections activated while debugging lines are deactivated. It is not necessary to have a D in position 7 in debugging sections, although including the D may save some computer time when both the sections and lines are deactivated.

The Special Register DEBUG-ITEM

Whenever you set up one or more debugging sections in a program, COBOL automatically establishes a special storage area called **DEBUG-ITEM.** No matter how many debugging sections you have in a program, only one DEBUG-ITEM is established. COBOL assigns data to the fields in DEBUG-ITEM when your debugging sections are executed, and you may use the contents of those fields as you wish. We will discuss later what kind of data COBOL assigns to the fields in DEBUG-ITEM.

You must not define the field DEBUG-ITEM in your working storage or anywhere. COBOL defines it automatically. DEBUG-ITEM does not appear in your program listing, but it is there for you to use. The ANSI definition of DEBUG-ITEM is as follows:

```
01  DEBUG-ITEM.
    02  DEBUG-LINE      PICTURE IS X(6).
    02                  PICTURE IS X  VALUE SPACE.
    02  DEBUG-NAME      PICTURE IS X(30).
    02                  PICTURE IS X  VALUE SPACE.
    02  DEBUG-SUB-1     PICTURE IS S9999 SIGN IS LEADING SEPARATE CHARACTER.
    02                  PICTURE IS X  VALUE SPACE.
    02  DEBUG-SUB-2     PICTURE IS S9999 SIGN IS LEADING SEPARATE CHARACTER.
    02                  PICTURE IS X  VALUE SPACE.
    02  DEBUG-SUB-3     PICTURE IS S9999 SIGN IS LEADING SEPARATE CHARACTER.
    02                  PICTURE IS X  VALUE SPACE.
    02  DEBUG-CONTENTS PICTURE IS X(n).
```

The long form of the preceding PICTURE clauses, PICTURE IS, means exactly the same as the shorter forms, PICTURE and PIC.

COBOL adjusts the size of DEBUG-CONTENTS each time it assigns something to it, so that the data fit. The name DEBUG-ITEM and the names of all its elementary fields are reserved words. Notice that DEBUG-ITEM is defined so that you can just print the whole thing out on one line if you like. We will instead print out just the elementary fields as we need them.

DEBUG-ITEM and the fields subordinate to it may be referred to only in debugging sections. This is the other reason for using DISPLAY instead of, let's say, GENERATE, to print debug output. DEBUG-ITEM and its subordinate fields may not be used as SOURCE fields.

Execution of Debugging Sections

Debugging sections may be set up to **monitor** one or more files defined in the File Section, one or more paragraphs or sections in the Procedure Division, and/or one or more fields. The next several pages explain what it means to monitor a field, file, paragraph, or section. A single debugging section may monitor any combination of files, fields, paragraphs, or sections. Whenever you set up a debugging section in a program, you must tell COBOL which file(s), field(s), paragraph(s), and/or section(s) the debugging section is monitoring.

Monitoring a File

When a debugging section is used to monitor a file, COBOL executes the debugging section after it executes any statement that refers to the file name as it appears in the FD entry, except when a READ statement detects an end-of-file or an invalid key. Here's what COBOL does when it comes to a statement that names a file that is being monitored:

1. It executes the statement.
2. If a READ statement detects an end-of-file or invalid key, COBOL skips steps 3 and 4 below.
3. COBOL assigns data to the fields in DEBUG-ITEM as follows:
   a. To the field DEBUG-LINE, it assigns the sequence number (positions 1 through 6) of the statement just executed.
   b. To the field DEBUG-NAME, it assigns the file name.
   c. To DEBUG-SUB-1, DEBUG-SUB-2, DEBUG-SUB-3, it assigns spaces.
   d. To DEBUG-CONTENTS, it assigns the contents of the input record if the statement executed was a READ, and assigns spaces if the statement executed was any other.
4. It executes the debugging section that is monitoring the file.
5. It goes on to the next statement in the program.

A file name defined with an SD entry may not be monitored.

Monitoring a Field

When a debugging section is used to monitor a field, we have a choice. We can tell COBOL to execute the debugging section only when the program comes to statements that explicitly refer to the field and change its contents, or we can use the **ALL REFERENCES** option to tell COBOL to execute the debugging section when the program comes to ALL statements that explicitly refer to the field. An **explicit reference** to a field is one in which the name of the field actually appears in the statement. Statements like MOVE CORRESPONDING, ADD CORRESPONDING, SUBTRACT CORRESPONDING, READ, GENERATE, and group level MOVEs, which may act upon a field but not name it, do not cause execution of the debugging section that is monitoring that field.

Any field defined anywhere in the Data Division may be monitored, except that in the Report Section only fields defined as sum counters may be monitored. Here's what COBOL does when it comes to a statement that names a field that is being monitored:

1. It executes the statement.
2. It assigns data to the fields in DEBUG-ITEM as follows:
   a. To DEBUG-LINE, it assigns the sequence number of the statement.
   b. To DEBUG-NAME, it assigns the name of the field being monitored. If the field being monitored is subscripted or indexed, only the data name of the field is assigned to DEBUG-NAME; no subscripts or indexes are assigned to DEBUG-NAME. If the field is qualified, COBOL assigns to DEBUG-NAME as much of the field name as will fit into DEBUG-NAME's 30 character positions, with the qualifiers separated by IN or OF, depending on the COBOL system being used.
   c. If the field being monitored is subscripted or indexed, numbers representing the values of the subscripts or indexes are assigned to DEBUG-

SUB-1, DEBUG-SUB-2, and/or DEBUG-SUB-3, as needed. Unneeded fields are assigned spaces.

   d. To DEBUG-CONTENTS, COBOL assigns the value of the field being monitored. COBOL MOVEs data to DEBUG-CONTENTS from the field being monitored as though the field being monitored were defined with a PICTURE of Xs. This means that under certain conditions DEBUG-CONTENTS will not be printable. The conditions under which DEBUG-CONTENTS is nonprintable are different for different COBOL systems.

3. It executes the debugging section that is monitoring the field.
4. It goes on to the next statement in the program.

If a field being monitored is named in a clause or phrase that is not executed, or is named as a qualifier, or is named in a statement in a debugging section, steps 2 and 3 above are not executed. If a field being monitored is named in the VARYING clause of a PERFORM statement, or in any of the AFTER or UNTIL clauses of a PERFORM statement, steps 2 through 4 above are executed each time after the field is initialized, changed, or evaluated, whether or not the ALL REFERENCES option is specified.

If a field being monitored is explicitly referred to in a WRITE or REWRITE statement the record being written is assigned to DEBUG-CONTENTS even though the record may no longer be available in the output area in the File Section. This holds true whether the field being monitored is the object of the verb or appears after the word FROM in the WRITE or REWRITE statement, and whether or not the ALL REFERENCES option is specified.

Monitoring a Paragraph or Section

A debugging section may be set up to monitor the execution of one or more paragraphs or sections, or to monitor **ALL PROCEDURES.** Here's what COBOL does when it comes to a paragraph or section being monitored:

1. It assigns data to the fields in DEBUG-ITEM as follows:

   a. To DEBUG-NAME, COBOL assigns the name of the paragraph or section being monitored.

   b. To DEBUG-SUB-1, DEBUG-SUB-2, and DEBUG-SUB-3, it assigns spaces.

   c. To DEBUG-CONTENTS, it assigns the words PERFORM LOOP if the paragraph or section being monitored is being executed under control of a PERFORM statement, or it assigns the words USE PROCEDURE if the paragraph or section being monitored is among the DECLARATIVES, or it assigns the words START PROGRAM if the first nondeclarative paragraph or section in the program is being monitored and this is the first execution of that paragraph or section, or it assigns the words SORT INPUT, SORT OUTPUT, or MERGE OUTPUT if the section being monitored is an INPUT PROCEDURE of a SORT or an OUTPUT PROCEDURE of a SORT or a MERGE.

   d. To DEBUG-LINE, COBOL assigns a sequence number that depends on the words that were assigned to DEBUG-CONTENTS in (c). If the words PERFORM LOOP were assigned to DEBUG-CONTENTS, COBOL assigns to DEBUG-LINE the sequence number of the PERFORM statement. If the words USE PROCEDURE were assigned to DEBUG-CONTENTS, COBOL assigns to DEBUG-LINE the sequence number of the statement that caused the declarative procedure to be executed. If the words START PROGRAM were assigned to DEBUG-CONTENTS, COBOL assigns to DEBUG-LINE the sequence number of the first nondeclarative statement in the program. If the words SORT INPUT, SORT OUTPUT, or MERGE OUTPUT were assigned to DEBUG-CONTENTS, COBOL assigns to DEBUG-LINE the sequence number of the SORT or MERGE statement.

2. COBOL executes the debugging section that is monitoring this paragraph or section.
3. It executes the paragraph or section being monitored.
4. It goes on to the next statement in the program.

You may not monitor a paragraph that is part of a debugging section, nor may you monitor a debugging section. You may monitor a USE BEFORE REPORTING or USE AFTER ERROR PROCEDURE section, or a paragraph that is part of such a section.

Using Debugging Sections

For Program P22-02 we will once again modify Program P10-01. This time, let's use the special register DEBUG-ITEM to DISPLAY the name of each paragraph as the program executes it, so that we can trace the progress of program execution. In addition, let's DISPLAY the contents of the input-record area each time the program enters the main-loop paragraph, called MAIN-PROCESS. There is only one slight difficulty here, and that is that the paragraph COMMISSION-CALCULATION is executed 10 times for each input record, and there really is no need to DISPLAY its name 10 times in a row to trace program execution. So let's say we will DISPLAY the name of the paragraph COMMISSION-CALCULATION only the first time it is executed for each input record, that is, when I is equal to 1.

Program P22-02 was run with the same input data as Program P22-01 and produced the debug output shown in Figure 22.5. Most lines show the name of the paragraph or section being executed. In addition, when a paragraph is being executed under control of a PERFORM statement, the value shown for SEQ NO. is the sequence number of the PERFORM statement that is executing the paragraph. When a paragraph or section is executing not under control of a PERFORM statement, the value shown for SEQ NO. is the sequence number of the first statement in that paragraph or section.

The lines labeled INPUT RECORD show the contents of the input record area as they were each time the program entered the paragraph MAIN-PROCESS.

FIGURE 22.5 Debug output from Program P22-02

```
SEQ NO. = 009800                            NONDECLARATIVE
SEQ NO. = 009800                            CONTROL-PARAGRAPH
SEQ NO. = 009800                            INITIALIZATION
SEQ NO. = 011200                            READ-A-RECORD

                                            ....+....1....+....2....+....3....+....4....+....5....+....6....+....7....+....8
                             INPUT RECORD   000128950075000125680010004871218149200060001100000480001050008759З
SEQ NO. = 009900                            MAIN-PROCESS
SEQ NO. = 012000                            COMMISSION-CALCULATION
SEQ NO. = 012300                            PRODUCE-THE-REPORT
SEQ NO. = 012400                            READ-A-RECORD

                                            ....+....1....+....2....+....3....+....4....+....5....+....6....+....7....+....8
                             INPUT RECORD   094238601000020000005192700955000279502000001250004122500600003б150
SEQ NO. = 009900                            MAIN-PROCESS
SEQ NO. = 012000                            COMMISSION-CALCULATION
SEQ NO. = 012300                            PRODUCE-THE-REPORT
SEQ NO. = 012400                            READ-A-RECORD

                                            ....+....1....+....2....+....3....+....4....+....5....+....6....+....7....+....8
                             INPUT RECORD   3684420020000012165007495010000000000000000000000000000000000000
SEQ NO. = 009900                            MAIN-PROCESS
SEQ NO. = 012000                            COMMISSION-CALCULATION
SEQ NO. = 012300                            PRODUCE-THE-REPORT
SEQ NO. = 012400                            READ-A-RECORD

                                            ....+....1....+....2....+....3....+....4....+....5....+....6....+....7....+....8
                             INPUT RECORD   5236714008412004519072368006850029518000000000000000000000000000
SEQ NO. = 009900                            MAIN-PROCESS
SEQ NO. = 012000                            COMMISSION-CALCULATION
SEQ NO. = 012300                            PRODUCE-THE-REPORT
SEQ NO. = 012400                            READ-A-RECORD

                                            ....+....1....+....2....+....3....+....4....+....5....+....6....+....7....+....8
                             INPUT RECORD   6612364001000022358001873099500006515024512010368008995017360060287
SEQ NO. = 009900                            MAIN-PROCESS
SEQ NO. = 012000                            COMMISSION-CALCULATION
SEQ NO. = 012300                            PRODUCE-THE-REPORT
SEQ NO. = 012400                            READ-A-RECORD

                                            ....+....1....+....2....+....3....+....4....+....5....+....6....+....7....+....8
                             INPUT RECORD   7747119005200016500119500007350044895012500006875001425009999000000
SEQ NO. = 009900                            MAIN-PROCESS
SEQ NO. = 012000                            COMMISSION-CALCULATION
SEQ NO. = 012300                            PRODUCE-THE-REPORT
SEQ NO. = 012400                            READ-A-RECORD
SEQ NO. = 010000                            TERMINATION
SEQ NO. = 012800                            PRODUCE-FINAL-TOTAL-LINE
```

A Program with a Debugging Section

Program P22-02 is shown in Figure 22.6. The WITH DEBUGGING MODE clause must be included to indicate to COBOL that debugging sections (and of course debugging lines) are to be executed. But in addition, COBOL requires that something called an **object-time switch** be on in order for the debugging sections to be executed. Each COBOL system has its own object-time switch outside of the COBOL language.[2] If the object-time switch is off, the debugging sections are deactivated, but the debugging lines, if any, will execute. If the WITH DEBUGGING MODE clause is removed, both the sections and the lines are deactivated and the object-time switch has no effect.

[2]In IBM COBOL II, the object-time switch is the operand PARM.GO='/DEBUG' or PARM.GO='/NODEBUG' in the EXEC statement. In NCR VRX COBOL, the object-time switch is the operand OPTS=00000001 or OPTS=00000000 in the JOB statement.

FIGURE 22.6 **Program P22-02**

```
S COBOL II RELEASE 3.2 09/05/90                  P22002     DATE 03/09/92  TI
----+-*A-1-B--+----2----+----3----+----4----+----5----+----6----+----7-|--+

000100 IDENTIFICATION DIVISION.
000200 PROGRAM-ID.  P22-02.
000300*AUTHOR. DEBORAH ANN SENIOR.
000400*
000500*     THIS PROGRAM PRODUCES A SALESPERSON COMMISSION
000600*     REPORT SHOWING TEN COMMISSION AMOUNTS
000700*     AND THE TOTAL FOR EACH SALESPERSON.
000800*
000900*
001000*****************************************************************
001100
001200 ENVIRONMENT DIVISION.
001205 CONFIGURATION SECTION.
001210 SOURCE-COMPUTER. IBM-360 WITH DEBUGGING MODE.
001215
001300 INPUT-OUTPUT SECTION.
001400 FILE-CONTROL.
001500     SELECT SALES-FILE-IN                 ASSIGN TO INFILE.
001600     SELECT COMMISSION-REPORT-FILE-OUT    ASSIGN TO PRINTER.
001700
001800*****************************************************************
001900
002000 DATA DIVISION.
002100 FILE SECTION.
002200 FD  SALES-FILE-IN
002300     RECORD CONTAINS 80 CHARACTERS.
002400
002500 01  SALES-RECORD-IN.
002600     05  SALESPERSON-NUMBER-IN    PIC X(7).
002700     05  SALE-AMOUNT-IN           PIC 9(4)V99     OCCURS 10 TIMES.
002800
002900 FD  COMMISSION-REPORT-FILE-OUT.
003000
003100 01  REPORT-LINE                  PIC X(119).
003200
003300 WORKING-STORAGE SECTION.
003400 01  MORE-INPUT                   PIC X           VALUE "Y".
003500     88 THERE-IS-NO-MORE-INPUT    VALUE "N".
003600 01  PACKED-DECIMAL-CONSTANTS     PACKED-DECIMAL.
003700     05  COMMISSION-RATE-1        PIC V99         VALUE .05.
003800     05  COMMISSION-RATE-2        PIC V99         VALUE .10.
003900     05  BRACKET-MAXIMUM          PIC 999V99      VALUE 100.00.
004000 01  NUMBER-OF-SALES              PIC S99         VALUE 10
004100                                  COMP            SYNC.
004200 01  GRAND-TOTAL-COMMISSIONS-W    PIC S9(6)V99    PACKED-DECIMAL
004300                                                  VALUE 0.
004400 01  COMMISSION-AMOUNT-W          PIC S9(4)V99    PACKED-DECIMAL.
004500 01  COMMISSION-FOR-SALESPERSON   PIC S9(5)V99    PACKED-DECIMAL.
004600 01  I                            PIC S99         COMP SYNC.
004700 01  LINE-SPACING  VALUE 1        PIC S9          COMP SYNC.
004705 01  GUIDE-LINE                   PIC X(116)
004710     VALUE "                                         ....+....1....+...
004715-          ".2....+....3....+....4....+....5....+....6....+....7..
004720-          "..+....8".
004800
004900 01  PAGE-HEADING-1.
005000     05           PIC X(51)       VALUE SPACES.
005100     05           PIC X(17)       VALUE "COMMISSION REPORT".
005200
005300 01  PAGE-HEADING-2.
005400     05           PIC X(39)       VALUE "SALES-".
005500     05           PIC X(73)
005600         VALUE "C O M M I S S I O N S   O N   S A L E S".
005700     05           PIC X(5)        VALUE "TOTAL".
005800
```

FIGURE *22.6* ***continued***

```
       01  PAGE-HEADING-3.
           05            PIC X(10)        VALUE "PERSON".
           05            PIC X(10)        VALUE "SALE 1".
           05            PIC X(10)        VALUE "SALE 2".
           05            PIC X(10)        VALUE "SALE 3".
           05            PIC X(10)        VALUE "SALE 4".
           05            PIC X(10)        VALUE "SALE 5".
           05            PIC X(10)        VALUE "SALE 6".
           05            PIC X(10)        VALUE "SALE 7".
           05            PIC X(10)        VALUE "SALE 8".
           05            PIC X(10)        VALUE "SALE 9".
           05            PIC X(11)        VALUE "SALE 10".
           05            PIC X(7)         VALUE "COMMIS-".

       01  PAGE-HEADING-4.
           05            PIC X(112)       VALUE "NUMBER".
           05            PIC X(4)         VALUE "SION".

       01  DETAIL-LINE.
           05  SALESPERSON-NUMBER-OUT  PIC X(9).
           05  COMMISSION-AMOUNT-OUT   PIC Z,ZZ9.99BB
                                       OCCURS 10 TIMES.
           05  COMMISSION-FOR-SALESPERSON-OUT
                                       PIC BZZ,ZZ9.99.

       01  NO-INPUT-DATA.
           05                          PIC X(53) VALUE SPACES.
           05                          PIC X(13) VALUE "NO INPUT DATA".

       01  TOTAL-LINE.
           05                          PIC X(68) VALUE SPACES.
           05                          PIC X(41)
           VALUE "TOTAL COMMISSION FOR ALL SALESPERSONS".
           05  GRAND-TOTAL-COMMISSIONS PIC ZZZ,ZZ9.99.

      ************************************************************************

```

continued

The Procedure Division begins at line 009600. Debugging sections are always written into the Procedure Division as DECLARATIVES. A debugging section consists of a section header followed by a USE sentence, followed by one or more paragraphs. The USE sentence in a debugging section must contain the reserved words **USE FOR DEBUGGING** or **USE DEBUGGING,** followed by the name(s) of the file(s), field(s), paragraphs(s), or section(s) being monitored, or the words ALL PROCEDURES. Our MONITOR-ALL-THE-PARAGRAPHS SECTION, line 009606, is being used to monitor all the procedures in the Procedure Division, that is, all the sections and paragraphs. The complete format of the USE FOR DEBUGGING sentence will be given shortly.

Immediately following the USE sentence there must be zero, one, or more paragraphs containing the executable steps of the debugging section. The end of a debugging section is indicated by the beginning of another section or the words END DECLARATIVES.

USE FOR DEBUGGING sections, USE BEFORE REPORTING sections, and USE AFTER ERROR PROCEDURE sections may all appear together in the same program. If they do, all the USE FOR DEBUGGING sections must come before any of the others, immediately following the DECLARATIVES header. The USE BEFORE REPORTING sections and USE AFTER ERROR PROCEDURE sections may appear in any order.

FIGURE 22.6 ***continued***

```
S COBOL II RELEASE 3.2 09/05/90                  P22002     DATE 03/09/92  TI
----+-*A-1-B--+----2----+----3----+----4----+----5----+----6----+----7-|--+

009600 PROCEDURE DIVISION.
009602
009604 DECLARATIVES.
009606 MONITOR-INPUT-FILE SECTION.
009608     USE FOR DEBUGGING ALL PROCEDURES.
009610 MONITOR-PROGRAM-EXECUTION.
009612     EVALUATE DEBUG-NAME ALSO I = 1
009614         WHEN "MAIN-PROCESS" ALSO ANY
009616             DISPLAY SPACES
009618             DISPLAY GUIDE-LINE
009620             DISPLAY "   SEQ NO. = "  DEBUG-LINE
009622                     "   INPUT RECORD  "  SALES-RECORD-IN
009624         WHEN "COMMISSION-CALCULATION" ALSO TRUE
009626             DISPLAY "   SEQ NO. = "  DEBUG-LINE
009628                     "                  "  DEBUG-NAME
009630         WHEN "COMMISSION-CALCULATION" ALSO FALSE
009632             CONTINUE
009634         WHEN OTHER
009636             DISPLAY "   SEQ NO. = "  DEBUG-LINE
009638                     "                  "  DEBUG-NAME
009640     END-EVALUATE
009642     .
009644 END DECLARATIVES.
009646
009648 NONDECLARATIVE SECTION.
009700 CONTROL-PARAGRAPH.
009800     PERFORM INITIALIZATION
009900     PERFORM MAIN-PROCESS UNTIL THERE-IS-NO-MORE-INPUT
010000     PERFORM TERMINATION
010100     STOP RUN
010200     .
010300
```

FIGURE 22.6 *continued*

```
INITIALIZATION.
    OPEN INPUT  SALES-FILE-IN
         OUTPUT COMMISSION-REPORT-FILE-OUT
    WRITE REPORT-LINE FROM PAGE-HEADING-1 AFTER PAGE
    WRITE REPORT-LINE FROM PAGE-HEADING-2 AFTER 4
    WRITE REPORT-LINE FROM PAGE-HEADING-3
    WRITE REPORT-LINE FROM PAGE-HEADING-4
    MOVE 2 TO LINE-SPACING
    PERFORM READ-A-RECORD
    IF THERE-IS-NO-MORE-INPUT
        WRITE REPORT-LINE FROM NO-INPUT-DATA AFTER 2
    END-IF
    .

MAIN-PROCESS.
    MOVE ZERO TO COMMISSION-FOR-SALESPERSON
    PERFORM COMMISSION-CALCULATION
        VARYING I FROM 1 BY 1 UNTIL
        I IS GREATER THAN NUMBER-OF-SALES
    PERFORM PRODUCE-THE-REPORT
    PERFORM READ-A-RECORD
    .

TERMINATION.
    PERFORM PRODUCE-FINAL-TOTAL-LINE
    CLOSE SALES-FILE-IN
          COMMISSION-REPORT-FILE-OUT
    .

READ-A-RECORD.
    READ SALES-FILE-IN
        AT END
            SET THERE-IS-NO-MORE-INPUT TO TRUE
    .

COMMISSION-CALCULATION.
    IF SALE-AMOUNT-IN (I) IS NOT GREATER THAN BRACKET-MAXIMUM
        COMPUTE
         COMMISSION-AMOUNT-W ROUNDED
         COMMISSION-AMOUNT-OUT (I) ROUNDED
            = SALE-AMOUNT-IN (I) * COMMISSION-RATE-1
    ELSE
        COMPUTE
         COMMISSION-AMOUNT-W ROUNDED
         COMMISSION-AMOUNT-OUT (I) ROUNDED
            = BRACKET-MAXIMUM * COMMISSION-RATE-1 +
              (SALE-AMOUNT-IN (I) - BRACKET-MAXIMUM) *
              COMMISSION-RATE-2
    END-IF
    ADD COMMISSION-AMOUNT-W TO COMMISSION-FOR-SALESPERSON
    .

PRODUCE-THE-REPORT.
    MOVE SALESPERSON-NUMBER-IN TO SALESPERSON-NUMBER-OUT
    MOVE COMMISSION-FOR-SALESPERSON TO
         COMMISSION-FOR-SALESPERSON-OUT
    ADD COMMISSION-FOR-SALESPERSON TO GRAND-TOTAL-COMMISSIONS-W
    WRITE REPORT-LINE FROM DETAIL-LINE AFTER LINE-SPACING
    MOVE 1 TO LINE-SPACING
    .

PRODUCE-FINAL-TOTAL-LINE.
    MOVE GRAND-TOTAL-COMMISSIONS-W TO GRAND-TOTAL-COMMISSIONS
    WRITE REPORT-LINE FROM TOTAL-LINE AFTER 4
    .
```

In this program, the debugging procedure is simple enough that it fits into one paragraph. When more than one paragraph is required in a debugging section, remember the rule: PERFORM statements in a debugging section may refer only to paragraphs that are among the DECLARATIVES. The PERFORMed paragraph need not be in the same section as the PERFORM statement.

The USE FOR DEBUGGING Sentence

The format of the USE FOR DEBUGGING sentence is as follows:

```
                         ⎧cd-name-1                           ⎫
                         ⎪[ALL REFERENCES OF] identifier-1    ⎪
USE FOR DEBUGGING ON     ⎨file-name-1                         ⎬ ...
                         ⎪procedure-name-1                    ⎪
                         ⎩ALL PROCEDURES                      ⎭
```

If a field being monitored is named more than once in a single statement, the debugging section for that field is executed only once. Within an imperative statement, each occurrence of an imperative verb is considered to begin a new statement for debugging purposes. Table 22.1 shows all the imperative verbs defined in the 1985 ANSI standard. Some COBOL systems may make additions to or deletions from this list.

TABLE 22.1
The 1985 ANSI standard list of imperative verbs

ACCEPT	GENERATE	REWRITE (2)
ADD (1)	GO TO	SEND
ALTER	INITIALIZE	SET
CALL (7)	INITIATE	SORT
CANCEL	INSPECT	START (2)
CLOSE	MERGE	STOP
COMPUTE (1)	MOVE	STRING
CONTINUE	MULTIPLY (1)	SUBTRACT (1)
DELETE (2)	OPEN	SUPPRESS
DISABLE	PERFORM	TERMINATE
DISPLAY	PURGE	UNSTRING (3)
DIVIDE (1)	READ (5)	WRITE (6)
ENABLE	RECEIVE (4)	
EXIT	RELEASE	

(1) Without the optional ON SIZE ERROR and NOT ON SIZE ERROR phrases.
(2) Without the optional INVALID KEY and NOT INVALID KEY phrases.
(3) Without the optional ON OVERFLOW and NOT ON OVERFLOW phrases.
(4) Without the optional NO DATA and WITH DATA phrases.
(5) Without the optional AT END, NOT AT END, INVALID KEY, and NOT INVALID KEY phrases.
(6) Without the optional INVALID KEY, NOT INVALID KEY, END-OF-PAGE, and NOT END-OF-PAGE phrases.
(7) Without the optional ON OVERFLOW, ON EXCEPTION, and NOT ON EXCEPTION phrases.

Table 22.2 shows all the explicit scope terminators in the 1985 standard.

TABLE 22.2
The 1985 ANSI standard list of explicit scope terminators

END-ADD	END-MULTIPLY	END-SEARCH
END-CALL	END-PERFORM	END-START
END-COMPUTE	END-READ	END-STRING
END-DELETE	END-RECEIVE	END-SUBTRACT
END-DIVIDE	END-RETURN	END-UNSTRING
END-EVALUATE	END-REWRITE	END-WRITE
END-IF		

When a subscripted or indexed field is being monitored, its name must be entered in the USE FOR DEBUGGING sentence without any subscripts or indexes.

Statements appearing outside debugging sections must not refer to paragraphs or sections defined within debugging sections.

Although a single debugging section may refer to any number of files, fields, paragraphs, and/or sections, there may be at most only one debugging section for any one file, field, paragraph, or section. That means that if there is some debugging section monitoring ALL PROCEDURES, no debugging section may monitor a specific paragraph.

EXERCISE 2

Modify your solution to Exercise 3, Chapter 10, page 301, to monitor ALL PROCEDURES. Have your program DISPLAY the input record each time the program enters the main-loop paragraph. Have your program print the name of each paragraph as it executes, except the name of any paragraph that executes more than once for any one input record. For any such paragraph that executes more than once for one input record, print its name only once for that input record.

Use the Debugging Feature

You can now use the debugging feature in any or all of the programming assignments in this book, even when the assignment does not call for it. Use the debugging feature as you see fit to help you test your programs, or as your instructor requires.

Summary

As an aid in testing programs, debugging lines and/or debugging sections may be used to cause a program to produce debug output. Debugging lines may be activated and deactivated by use of the WITH DEBUGGING MODE clause, and debugging sections may be activated and deactivated by use of the object-time switch.

Debugging lines may appear anywhere after the OBJECT-COMPUTER paragraph, and may be written in the Environment, Data, and Procedure Divisions. Debugging lines must have a D in position 7.

The best verb to use for producing debug output is DISPLAY. Although DISPLAY has severe limitations that make it unsuitable for producing normal report output, it has two advantages that make it very useful for producing debug output. The advantages are that you may DISPLAY data on the high-speed printer before the printer file is OPENed and after it is CLOSEd, and that you may refer to the fields in DEBUG-ITEM conveniently within the DECLARATIVES.

A debugging section may be set up to monitor one or more files, fields, paragraphs, or sections. The USE FOR DEBUGGING sentence indicates which files, fields, paragraphs, and/or sections are being monitored by a particular debugging section. Any one file, field, paragraph, or section may be monitored by not more than one debugging section. When COBOL executes a debugging section it assigns data to the fields in DEBUG-ITEM to provide information about the conditions causing execution of the debugging section.

Fill-In-Exercises

1. Debugging lines may appear anywhere after the ______ paragraph.
2. The clause that activates and deactivates debugging lines is the ______ ______ ______ clause.
3. Whenever your program produces debug output, it should always print each ______ record soon after it has been read.
4. Three limitations of the DISPLAY verb are ______, ______, and ______.
5. The field in DEBUG-ITEM to which COBOL assigns the name of the file, field, paragraph, or section being monitored is ______.
6. The field in DEBUG-ITEM to which COBOL assigns a line sequence number is ______.
7. The field in DEBUG-ITEM to which COBOL assigns the value of a field being monitored is ______.
8. The field in DEBUG-ITEM to which COBOL assigns the words PERFORM LOOP is ______.
9. The ______ ______ ______ sentence names the files, fields, paragraphs, and/or sections that are being monitored by a particular debugging section.
10. The ______ ______ option may be used to indicate that a debugging section is monitoring all paragraphs and all sections in a program (except debugging sections, which cannot be monitored).
11. Debugging lines contain the letter ______ in position ______.
12. The phrase that activates and deactivates debugging lines is part of the ______ paragraph.
13. The switch that activates and deactivates debugging sections is called a(n) ______ switch.
14. Fields in DEBUG-ITEM can be referred to only within ______ ______.
15. COBOL assigns the values of subscripts of fields being monitored to ______, ______, and ______.

Review Exercises

1. For this exercise assume that FIELD-1 is the name of a field in working storage in some program and that PARAGRAPH-1 is the name of a paragraph in that program.

Tell whether each of the following is a legal USE FOR DEBUGGING sentence:

a. USE FOR DEBUGGING PARAGRAPH-1, FIELD-1.

b. USE FOR DEBUGGING PARAGRAPH-1, ALL FIELD-1.

c. USE FOR DEBUGGING ALL PARAGRAPH-1, FIELD-1.

d. USE FOR DEBUGGING ALL PROCEDURES, PARAGRAPH-1.

e. USE FOR DEBUGGING ALL PROCEDURES, FIELD-1.

2. Using the names of the field and paragraph in Review Exercise 1, write a USE FOR DEBUGGING sentence that will monitor all statements that refer to FIELD-1 and all the paragraphs and sections in the program.

3. This Review Exercise refers to Program P10-03, Figure 10.10, page 310. Describe the debug output that would be produced if the following statement were added to Program P10-03 at the line sequence numbers indicated:

```
012805D        DISPLAY "STATE-CODE-IN = ",
012810D                STATE-CODE-IN,
012815D                "NAME OF STATE = ",
012820D                STATE-NAME (STATE-NAME-INDEX)
```

4. Write a debugging section that will produce the same debug output as the debugging lines in Review Exercise 3. Be careful in selecting the name to specify in your USE FOR DEBUGGING sentence.

Project

Modify your solution to the Project in Chapter 11 to monitor the SEARCH through the tax table. Write a USE FOR DEBUGGING section so that it prints one line of debug output each time the Gross Pay field is compared to a field in the tax table as the tax table is being SEARCHed. Have each line of debug output contain the following fields:

a. The line sequence number of the SEARCH statement

b. The value of Gross Pay

c. The value of the table index

d. The field in the tax table against which the Gross Pay is being compared

Have your program print identifying information with each field of debug output so it can be identified easily.

APPENDIX A

American National Standard List of COBOL Reserved Words

This list of reserved words is the 1985 ANSI standard. Your own COBOL system may make additions to or deletions from this list.

ACCEPT
ACCESS
ADD
ADVANCING
AFTER
ALL
ALPHABET
ALPHABETIC
ALPHABETIC-LOWER
ALPHABETIC-UPPER
ALPHANUMERIC
ALPHANUMERIC-EDITED
ALSO
ALTER
ALTERNATE
AND
ANY
ARE
AREA
AREAS
ASCENDING
ASSIGN
AT
AUTHOR

BEFORE
BINARY
BLANK
BLOCK
BOTTOM
BY

CALL
CANCEL
CD
CF
CH
CHARACTER
CHARACTERS
CLASS
CLOCK-UNITS
CLOSE
COBOL
CODE
CODE-SET
COLLATING
COLUMN
COMMA
COMMON
COMMUNICATION
COMP
COMPUTATIONAL
COMPUTE
CONFIGURATION
CONTAINS
CONTENT

CONTINUE
CONTROL
CONTROLS
CONVERTING
COPY
CORR
CORRESPONDING
COUNT
CURRENCY

DATA
DATE
DATE-COMPILED
DATE-WRITTEN
DAY
DAY-OF-WEEK
DE
DEBUG-CONTENTS
DEBUG-ITEM
DEBUG-LINE
DEBUG-NAME
DEBUG-SUB-1
DEBUG-SUB-2
DEBUG-SUB-3
DEBUGGING
DECIMAL-POINT
DECLARATIVES
DELETE
DELIMITED
DELIMITER
DEPENDING
DESCENDING
DESTINATION
DETAIL
DISABLE
DISPLAY
DIVIDE
DIVISION
DOWN
DUPLICATES
DYNAMIC

EGI
ELSE
EMI
ENABLE
END
END-ADD
END-CALL
END-COMPUTE
END-DELETE
END-DIVIDE
END-EVALUATE
END-IF
END-MULTIPLY
END-OF-PAGE
END-PERFORM
END-READ
END-RECEIVE
END-RETURN
END-REWRITE
END-SEARCH
END-START
END-STRING
END-SUBTRACT
END-UNSTRING
END-WRITE
ENTER
ENVIRONMENT
EOP
EQUAL
ERROR
ESI
EVALUATE
EVERY
EXCEPTION
EXIT
EXTEND
EXTERNAL

FALSE
FD
FILE
FILE-CONTROL
FILLER
FINAL
FIRST
FOOTING
FOR
FROM

GENERATE
GIVING
GLOBAL
GO
GREATER
GROUP

HEADING
HIGH-VALUE
HIGH-VALUES

I-O
I-O-CONTROL
IDENTIFICATION
IF
IN
INDEX
INDEXED
INDICATE
INITIAL
INITIALIZE
INITIATE
INPUT
INPUT-OUTPUT
INSPECT
INSTALLATION
INTO
INVALID
IS

JUST
JUSTIFIED

KEY

LABEL
LAST
LEADING
LEFT
LENGTH
LESS
LIMIT
LIMITS
LINAGE
LINAGE-COUNTER
LINE
LINE-COUNTER
LINES
LINKAGE
LOCK
LOW-VALUE
LOW-VALUES

MEMORY
MERGE
MESSAGE
MODE
MODULES
MOVE
MULTIPLE
MULTIPLY

NATIVE
NEGATIVE
NEXT
NO
NOT
NUMBER
NUMERIC
NUMERIC-EDITED

OBJECT-COMPUTER
OCCURS
OF
OFF
OMITTED
ON
OPEN
OPTIONAL
OR
ORDER
ORGANIZATION
OTHER
OUTPUT
OVERFLOW

PACKED-DECIMAL
PADDING
PAGE
PAGE-COUNTER
PERFORM
PF
PH
PIC
PICTURE
PLUS
POINTER
POSITION
POSITIVE
PRINTING
PROCEDURE
PROCEDURES
PROCEED
PROGRAM
PROGRAM-ID

PURGE

QUEUE
QUOTE
QUOTES

RANDOM
RD
READ
RECEIVE
RECORD
RECORDS
REDEFINES
REEL
REFERENCE
REFERENCES
RELATIVE
RELEASE
REMAINDER
REMOVAL
RENAMES
REPLACE
REPLACING
REPORT
REPORTING
REPORTS
RERUN
RESERVE
RESET
RETURN
REVERSED
REWIND
REWRITE
RF
RH
RIGHT
ROUNDED
RUN

SAME
SD
SEARCH
SECTION
SECURITY
SEGMENT
SEGMENT-LIMIT
SELECT
SEND
SENTENCE
SEPARATE
SEQUENCE
SEQUENTIAL
SET
SIGN
SIZE
SORT
SORT-MERGE
SOURCE
SOURCE-COMPUTER
SPACE
SPACES
SPECIAL-NAMES
STANDARD
STANDARD-1
STANDARD-2
START
STATUS
STOP
STRING
SUB-QUEUE-1
SUB-QUEUE-2
SUB-QUEUE-3
SUBTRACT
SUM
SUPPRESS
SYMBOLIC
SYNC
SYNCHRONIZED

TABLE
TALLYING
TAPE
TERMINAL
TERMINATE
TEST
TEXT
THAN
THEN
THROUGH
THRU
TIME
TIMES
TO
TOP
TRAILING
TRUE
TYPE

UNIT
UNSTRING
UNTIL
UP
UPON
USAGE
USE
USING

VALUE
VALUES
VARYING

WHEN
WITH
WORDS
WORKING-STORAGE

WRITE

ZERO
ZEROES
ZEROS

+
−
*
/
**
>
<
=
>=
<=

APPENDIX B

Complete ANSI Reference Summary

This appendix contains complete 1985 ANSI standard formats of all elements of the COBOL language. The appearance of the italic letter *S, I, R,* or *W* to the left of the format for the verbs CLOSE, OPEN, READ, REWRITE, USE, and WRITE indicates that the format is used with sequential files, indexed files, relative files, or in Report Writer, respectively.

General Format for Identification Division

```
IDENTIFICATION DIVISION.

PROGRAM-ID. program-name [IS {|COMMON |} PROGRAM] .
                             {|INITIAL|}

[AUTHOR. [comment-entry] ... ]

[INSTALLATION. [comment-entry] ... ]

[DATE-WRITTEN. [comment-entry] ... ]

[DATE-COMPILED. [comment-entry] ... ]

[SECURITY. [comment-entry] ... ]
```

General Format for Environment Division

```
[ENVIRONMENT DIVISION.

[CONFIGURATION SECTION.

[SOURCE-COMPUTER.  [computer-name  [WITH DEBUGGING MODE].]]

[OBJECT-COMPUTER.  [computer-name

     [                       { WORDS      } ]
     [ MEMORY SIZE integer-1 { CHARACTERS } ]
     [                       { MODULES    } ]

     [PROGRAM COLLATING SEQUENCE IS alphabet-name-1]

     [SEGMENT-LIMIT IS segment-number].]]

[SPECIAL-NAMES.  [[ implementor-name-1

     { IS mnemonic-name-1 [ON STATUS IS condition-name-1 [OFF STATUS IS condition-name-2]] } ]
     { IS mnemonic-name-2 [OFF STATUS IS condition-name-2 [ON STATUS IS condition-name-1]] } ] ...
     { ON STATUS IS condition-name-1 [OFF STATUS IS condition-name-2]                      } ]
     { OFF STATUS IS condition-name-2 [ON STATUS IS condition-name-1]                      } ]

     [ALPHABET alphabet-name-1 IS

         { STANDARD-1                                                  } ]
         { STANDARD-2                                                  } ]
         { NATIVE                                                      } ]
         { implementor-name-2                                          } ] ...
         {   {             [ { THROUGH }  literal-2 ] }                } ]
         {   { literal-1   [ { THRU    }            ] } ...            } ]
         {   {             [ {ALSO literal-3} ...   ] }                } ]

     [ SYMBOLIC CHARACTERS {{symbolic-character-1} ... { IS  } {integer-1} ... } ...
     [                                                  { ARE }
           [IN alphabet-name-2] } ] ...

     [ CLASS class-name-1 IS {literal-4 [ { THROUGH } literal-5 ] } ... ] ...
     [                                  [ { THRU    }           ]        ]

     [CURRENCY SIGN IS literal-6]

     [DECIMAL-POINT IS COMMA].]]]
```

```
[INPUT-OUTPUT SECTION.

 FILE-CONTROL.

    {file-control-entry} ...

[I-O-CONTROL.

    [[RERUN [ON {file-name-1           }] EVERY {{[END OF] {REEL} } OF file-name-2}]] ...
                {implementor-name-1    }        {{         {UNIT} }                }
                                                {{integer-1 RECORDS}               }
                                                {integer-2 CLOCK-UNITS             }
                                                {condition-name-1                  }

    [SAME [RECORD    ] AREA FOR file-name-3 {file-name-4} ... ] ...
          [SORT      ]
          [SORT-MERGE]

    [MULTIPLE FILE TAPE CONTAINS {file-name-5 [POSITION integer-3]} ... ] ... .]]]]
```

General Format for File Control Entry

Sequential file:

```
SELECT [OPTIONAL] file-name-1

   ASSIGN TO {implementor-name-1} ...
             {literal-1         }

   [RESERVE integer-1 [AREA ]]
                      [AREAS]

   [[ORGANIZATION IS] SEQUENTIAL]

   [PADDING CHARACTER IS {data-name-1}]
                         {literal-2  }

   [RECORD DELIMITER IS {STANDARD-1        }]
                        {implementor-name-2}

   [ACCESS MODE IS SEQUENTIAL]

   [FILE STATUS IS data-name-2].
```

Relative file:

```
SELECT  [OPTIONAL]  file-name-1

    ASSIGN TO {implementor-name-1} ...
              {literal-1         }

    [RESERVE integer-1 [AREA ]]
                       [AREAS]

    [ORGANIZATION IS]  RELATIVE

    [ACCESS MODE IS {SEQUENTIAL  [RELATIVE KEY IS data-name-1]}]
    [               {{RANDOM }                                }]
    [               {{DYNAMIC}   RELATIVE KEY IS data-name-1  }]

    [FILE STATUS IS data-name-2].
```

Indexed file:

```
SELECT  [OPTIONAL]  file-name-1

    ASSIGN TO {implementor-name-1} ...
              {literal-1         }

    [RESERVE integer-1 [AREA ]]
                       [AREAS]

    [ORGANIZATION IS]  INDEXED

    [ACCESS MODE IS {SEQUENTIAL}]
    [               {RANDOM    }]
    [               {DYNAMIC   }]

    RECORD KEY IS data-name-1

    [ALTERNATE RECORD KEY IS data-name-2  [WITH DUPLICATES]] ...

    [FILE STATUS IS data-name-3].
```

Sort or merge file:

```
SELECT file-name-1  ASSIGN TO {implementor-name-1} ... .
                              {literal-1         }
```

Report file:

```
SELECT [OPTIONAL] file-name-1

    ASSIGN TO {implementor-name-1} ...
              {literal-1         }

    [RESERVE integer-1 [AREA ]]
                       [AREAS]

    [[ORGANIZATION IS] SEQUENTIAL]]

    [PADDING CHARACTER IS {data-name-1}]
                          {literal-2  }

    [RECORD DELIMITER IS {STANDARD-1         }]
                         {implementor-name-2 }

    [ACCESS MODE IS SEQUENTIAL]

    [FILE STATUS IS data-name-2].
```

General Format for Data Division

```
[DATA DIVISION.

[FILE SECTION.

[file-description-entry {record-description-entry} ...                   ]     ]
[sort-merge-file-description-entry {record-description-entry} ...         ] ... ]
[report-file-description-entry                                            ]     ]

[WORKING-STORAGE SECTION.

[77-level-description-entry]     ]
[record-description-entry  ] ... ]

[LINKAGE SECTION.

[77-level-description-entry]     ]
[record-description-entry  ] ... ]

[COMMUNICATION SECTION.

[communication-description-entry [record-description-entry] ... ] ... ]

[REPORT SECTION.

[report-description-entry {report-group-description-entry} ... ] ... ]]
```

General Format for File Description Entry

Sequential file:

```
FD  file-name-1

    [IS EXTERNAL]

    [IS GLOBAL]

    [BLOCK CONTAINS [integer-1 TO] integer-2 {RECORDS   }]
                                             {CHARACTERS}]

    [        {CONTAINS integer-3 CHARACTERS                                         }]
    [RECORD  {IS VARYING IN SIZE [[FROM integer-4] [TO integer-5] CHARACTERS]       }]
    [        {    [DEPENDING ON data-name-1]                                        }]
    [        {CONTAINS integer-6 TO integer-7 CHARACTERS                            }]

    [LABEL {RECORD IS  } {STANDARD}]
    [      {RECORDS ARE} {OMITTED }]

    [VALUE OF {implementor-name-1 IS {data-name-2}} ...]
    [                                {literal-1  }     ]

    [DATA {RECORD IS  } {data-name-3} ...]
    [     {RECORDS ARE}                  ]

    [LINAGE IS {data-name-4} LINES [WITH FOOTING AT {data-name-5}]
    [          {integer-8  }       [                {integer-9  }]

        [LINES AT TOP {data-name-6}] [LINES AT BOTTOM {data-name-7}]]
        [             {integer-10 }] [                {integer-11 }]]

    [CODE-SET IS alphabet-name-1].
```

Relative file:

```
FD  file-name-1

    [IS EXTERNAL]

    [IS GLOBAL]

    [BLOCK CONTAINS [integer-1 TO] integer-2 {RECORDS   }]
                                            {CHARACTERS}

    [        {CONTAINS integer-3 CHARACTERS                                          }]
    [        {IS VARYING IN SIZE [[FROM integer-4] [TO integer-5] CHARACTERS]       }]
    [RECORD  {    [DEPENDING ON data-name-1]                                         }]
    [        {CONTAINS integer-6 TO integer-7 CHARACTERS                             }]

    [LABEL {RECORD IS   } {STANDARD}]
    [      {RECORDS ARE } {OMITTED }]

    [VALUE OF {implementor-name-1 IS {data-name-2}} ...]
    [                                {literal-1  }     ]

    [DATA {RECORD IS  } {data-name-3} ...].
    [     {RECORDS ARE}                  ]
```

Indexed file:

```
FD  file-name-1

    [IS EXTERNAL]

    [IS GLOBAL]

    [BLOCK CONTAINS [integer-1 TO] integer-2 {RECORDS   }]
                                             {CHARACTERS}

    [         {CONTAINS integer-3 CHARACTERS                                       }]
    [         {IS VARYING IN SIZE [[FROM integer-4] [TO integer-5] CHARACTERS]     }]
    [RECORD   {     [DEPENDING ON data-name-1]                                     }]
    [         {CONTAINS integer-6 TO integer-7 CHARACTERS                          }]

    [LABEL {RECORD IS   } {STANDARD}]
    [      {RECORDS ARE } {OMITTED }]

    [VALUE OF {implementor-name-1 IS {data-name-2}} ...]
    [                                {literal-1  }     ]

    [DATA {RECORD IS  } {data-name-3} ...] .
    [     {RECORDS ARE}                  ]
```

Sort-merge file:

```
SD  file-name-1

    [         {CONTAINS integer-1 CHARACTERS                                       }]
    [         {IS VARYING IN SIZE [[FROM integer-2] [TO integer-3] CHARACTERS]     }]
    [RECORD   {     [DEPENDING ON data-name-1]                                     }]
    [         {CONTAINS integer-4 TO integer-5 CHARACTERS                          }]

    [DATA {RECORD IS  } {data-name-2} ...] .
    [     {RECORDS ARE}                  ]
```

Report file:

```
FD  file-name-1

    [IS EXTERNAL]

    [IS GLOBAL]

    [BLOCK CONTAINS  [integer-1 TO]  integer-2 {RECORDS   }]
                                               {CHARACTERS}

    [RECORD  {CONTAINS integer-3 CHARACTERS              }]
             {CONTAINS integer-4 TO integer-5 CHARACTERS }

    [LABEL {RECORD IS   } {STANDARD}]
           {RECORDS ARE } {OMITTED }

    [VALUE OF {implementor-name-1 IS {data-name-1}} ...]
                                     {literal-1  }

    [CODE-SET IS alphabet-name-1]

    {REPORT IS   }  {report-name-1} ...   .
    {REPORTS ARE }
```

General Format for Data Description Entry

Format 1:

```
level-number  [data-name-1]
              [FILLER     ]

     [REDEFINES data-name-2]

     [IS EXTERNAL]

     [IS GLOBAL]

     [{PICTURE} IS character-string]
     [{PIC    }                   ]

     [               {BINARY        }]
     [               {COMPUTATIONAL }]
     [[USAGE IS]     {COMP          }]
     [               {DISPLAY       }]
     [               {INDEX         }]
     [               {PACKED-DECIMAL}]

     [[SIGN IS]  {LEADING }  [SEPARATE CHARACTER]]
     [           {TRAILING}                      ]

     [OCCURS integer-2 TIMES                                            ]
     [                                                                  ]
     [     [{ASCENDING }  KEY IS  {data-name-3} ... ] ...               ]
     [     [{DESCENDING}                            ]                   ]
     [                                                                  ]
     [     [INDEXED BY  {index-name-1} ... ]                            ]
     [                                                                  ]
     [OCCURS integer-1 TO integer-2 TIMES DEPENDING ON data-name-4      ]
     [                                                                  ]
     [     [{ASCENDING }  KEY IS  {data-name-3} ... ] ...               ]
     [     [{DESCENDING}                            ]                   ]
     [                                                                  ]
     [     [INDEXED BY  {index-name-1} ... ]                            ]

     [{SYNCHRONIZED}  [LEFT ]]
     [{SYNC        }  [RIGHT]]

     [{JUSTIFIED}  RIGHT]
     [{JUST     }       ]

     [BLANK WHEN ZERO]

     [VALUE IS literal-1].
```

Format 2:

```
66 data-name-1 RENAMES data-name-2 [{THROUGH} data-name-3] .
                                    {THRU   }
```

Format 3:

```
88 condition-name-1 {VALUE IS  } {literal-1 [{THROUGH} literal-2]} ... .
                    {VALUES ARE}             {THRU   }
```

General Format for Communication Description Entry

Format 1:

```
CD cd-name-1

                          [[SYMBOLIC QUEUE IS data-name-1]
                               [SYMBOLIC SUB-QUEUE-1 IS data-name-2]
                               [SYMBOLIC SUB-QUEUE-2 IS data-name-3]
                               [SYMBOLIC SUB-QUEUE-3 IS data-name-4]
                               [MESSAGE DATE IS data-name-5]
                               [MESSAGE TIME IS data-name-6]
                               [SYMBOLIC SOURCE IS data-name-7]
   FOR [INITIAL] INPUT         [TEXT LENGTH IS data-name-8]
                               [END KEY IS data-name-9]
                               [STATUS KEY IS data-name-10]
                               [MESSAGE COUNT IS data-name-11]]
                          [data-name-1, data-name-2, data-name-3,
                               data-name-4, data-name-5, data-name-6,
                               data-name-7, data-name-8, data-name-9,
                               data-name-10, data-name-11]
```

Format 2:

```
CD  cd-name-1 FOR OUTPUT

    [DESTINATION COUNT IS data-name-1]

    [TEXT LENGTH IS data-name-2]

    [STATUS KEY IS data-name-3]

    [DESTINATION TABLE OCCURS integer-1 TIMES

        [INDEXED BY  {index-name-1} ... ]]

    [ERROR KEY IS data-name-4]

    [SYMBOLIC DESTINATION IS data-name-5].
```

Format 3:

```
CD  cd-name-1

                              ┌[[MESSAGE DATE IS data-name-1]                  ┐
                              │                                                │
                              │     [MESSAGE TIME IS data-name-2]              │
                              │                                                │
                              │     [SYMBOLIC TERMINAL IS data-name-3]         │
                              │                                                │
                              │     [TEXT LENGTH IS data-name-4]               │
    FOR  [INITIAL]  I-O       │                                                │
                              │     [END KEY IS data-name-5]                   │
                              │                                                │
                              │     [STATUS KEY IS data-name-6]]               │
                              │                                                │
                              │[data-name-1, data-name-2, data-name-3,         │
                              │                                                │
                              └     data-name-4, data-name-5, data-name-6]     ┘
```

General Format for Report Description Entry

```
RD  report-name-1

    [IS GLOBAL]

    [CODE literal-1]

    [{CONTROL IS   } {{data-name-1} ...           }]
    [{CONTROLS ARE } {FINAL [data-name-1] ...     }]

    [ PAGE [LIMIT IS  ] integer-1 [LINE ] [HEADING integer-2]
    [      [LIMITS ARE]           [LINES]
    
         [FIRST DETAIL integer-3]  [LAST DETAIL integer-4]

         [FOOTING integer-5]                               ] .
```

General Format for Report Group Description Entry

Format 1:

```
01  [data-name-1]

    [LINE NUMBER IS  { integer-1   [ON NEXT PAGE] } ]
                     { PLUS integer-2             }

    [NEXT GROUP IS  { integer-3       } ]
                    { PLUS integer-4  }
                    { NEXT PAGE       }

                 { { REPORT HEADING }                                   }
                 { { RH             }                                   }
                 {                                                      }
                 { { PAGE HEADING }                                     }
                 { { PH           }                                     }
                 {                                                      }
                 { { CONTROL HEADING }  { data-name-2 }                 }
                 { { CH              }  { FINAL       }                 }
                 {                                                      }
     TYPE IS     { { DETAIL }                                           }
                 { { DE     }                                           }
                 {                                                      }
                 { { CONTROL FOOTING }  { data-name-3 }                 }
                 { { CF              }  { FINAL       }                 }
                 {                                                      }
                 { { PAGE FOOTING }                                     }
                 { { PF           }                                     }
                 {                                                      }
                 { { REPORT FOOTING }                                   }
                 { { RF             }                                   }

    [[USAGE IS]  DISPLAY].
```

Format 2:

```
level-number  [data-name-1]

    [LINE NUMBER IS  { integer-1   [ON NEXT PAGE] } ]
                     { PLUS Integer-2             }

    [[USAGE IS]  DISPLAY].
```

Format 3:

```
level-number  [data-name-1]

    {PICTURE}
    {PIC    }  IS character-string

    [[USAGE IS]  DISPLAY]

    [[SIGN IS]  {LEADING }  SEPARATE CHARACTER]
                {TRAILING}

    [{JUSTIFIED}  RIGHT]
     {JUST     }

    [BLANK WHEN ZERO]

    [LINE NUMBER IS  {integer-1  [ON NEXT PAGE]}]
                     {PLUS integer-2           }

    [COLUMN NUMBER IS integer-3]

    {SOURCE IS identifier-1                                                 }
    {VALUE IS literal-1                                                     }
    {{SUM  {identifier-2} ...  [UPON {data-name-2} ... ]} ...               }
    {        [RESET ON  {data-name-3}]                                      }
    {                   {FINAL      }                                       }

    [GROUP INDICATE].
```

General Format for Procedure Division

Format 1:

```
[PROCEDURE DIVISION  [USING  {data-name-1} ... ].

[DECLARATIVES.

{section-name SECTION [segment-number].

     USE statement.

[paragraph-name.

     [sentence] ... ] ... } ...

 END DECLARATIVES.]

{section-name SECTION [segment-number].

[paragraph-name.

     [sentence] ... ] ... } ... ]
```

Format 2:

```
[PROCEDURE DIVISION  [USING  {data-name-1} ... ].

{paragraph-name.

     [sentence] ... } ... ]
```

General Format for COBOL Verbs

```
ACCEPT identifier-1  [FROM mnemonic-name-1]
```

```
                           ⎧DATE        ⎫
ACCEPT identifier-2 FROM   ⎨DAY         ⎬
                           ⎪DAY-OF-WEEK ⎪
                           ⎩TIME        ⎭
```

```
ACCEPT cd-name-1 MESSAGE COUNT
```

```
ADD  {identifier-1}  ...   TO  {identifier-2 [ROUNDED]} ...
     {literal-1   }

   [ON SIZE ERROR imperative-statement-1]

   [NOT ON SIZE ERROR imperative-statement-2]

   [END-ADD]
```

```
ADD  {identifier-1}  ...   TO {identifier-2}
     {literal-1   }           {literal-2   }

   GIVING  {identifier-3 [ROUNDED]} ...

   [ON SIZE ERROR imperative-statement-1]

   [NOT ON SIZE ERROR imperative-statement-2]

   [END-ADD]
```

```
ADD  {CORRESPONDING}  identifier-1 TO identifier-2 [ROUNDED]
     {CORR         }

   [ON SIZE ERROR imperative-statement-1]

   [NOT ON SIZE ERROR imperative-statement-2]

   [END-ADD]
```

```
ALTER  {procedure-name-1 TO  [PROCEED TO]  procedure-name-2} ...
```

```
CALL {identifier-1} [USING {[BY REFERENCE] {identifier-2} ...} ...]
     {literal-1   }        {BY CONTENT    {identifier-2} ...}

    [ON OVERFLOW imperative-statement-1]

    [END-CALL]
```

```
CALL {identifier-1} [USING {[BY REFERENCE] {identifier-2} ...} ...]
     {literal-1   }        {BY CONTENT    {identifier-2} ...}

    [ON EXCEPTION imperative-statement-1]

    [NOT ON EXCEPTION imperative-statement-2]

    [END-CALL]
```

```
CANCEL {identifier-1} ...
       {literal-1   }
```

```
SW CLOSE {file-name-1 [{REEL} [FOR REMOVAL]      ]} ...
         {            [{UNIT}                    ]}
         {            [                          ]}
         {            [WITH {NO REWIND}          ]}
         {            [     {LOCK     }          ]}
```

```
RI CLOSE {file-name-1 [WITH LOCK]} ...
```

```
COMPUTE {identifier-1 [ROUNDED]} ... = arithmetic-expression-1

    [ON SIZE ERROR imperative-statement-1]

    [NOT ON SIZE ERROR imperative-statement-2]

    [END-COMPUTE]
```

```
CONTINUE
```

```
DELETE file-name-1 RECORD

   [INVALID KEY imperative-statement-1]

   [NOT INVALID KEY imperative-statement-2]

   [END-DELETE]
```

```
         ⎧INPUT [TERMINAL]⎫
DISABLE  ⎨I-O TERMINAL    ⎬  cd-name-1  ⎡WITH KEY ⎧identifier-1⎫⎤
         ⎩OUTPUT          ⎭             ⎣         ⎩literal-1   ⎭⎦
```

```
DISPLAY  ⎧identifier-1⎫ ...   [UPON mnemonic-name-1]  [WITH NO ADVANCING]
         ⎩literal-1   ⎭
```

```
DIVIDE  ⎧identifier-1⎫  INTO  {identifier-2 [ROUNDED]} ...
        ⎩literal-1   ⎭

   [ON SIZE ERROR imperative-statement-1]

   [NOT ON SIZE ERROR imperative-statement-2]

   [END-DIVIDE]
```

```
DIVIDE  ⎧identifier-1⎫  INTO  ⎧identifier-2⎫
        ⎩literal-1   ⎭        ⎩literal-2   ⎭

   GIVING  {identifier-3 [ROUNDED]} ...

   [ON SIZE ERROR imperative-statement-1]

   [NOT ON SIZE ERROR imperative-statement-2]

   [END-DIVIDE]
```

```
DIVIDE  ⎧identifier-1⎫  BY  ⎧identifier-2⎫
        ⎩literal-1   ⎭      ⎩literal-2   ⎭

   GIVING  {identifier-3 [ROUNDED]} ...

   [ON SIZE ERROR imperative-statement-1]

   [NOT ON SIZE ERROR imperative-statement-2]

   [END-DIVIDE]
```

```
DIVIDE {identifier-1} INTO {identifier-2} GIVING identifier-3 [ROUNDED]
       {literal-1   }      {literal-2   }

    REMAINDER identifier-4

    [ON SIZE ERROR imperative-statement-1]

    [NOT ON SIZE ERROR imperative-statement-2]

    [END-DIVIDE]
```

```
DIVIDE {identifier-1} BY {identifier-2} GIVING identifier-3 [ROUNDED]
       {literal-1   }    {literal-2   }

    REMAINDER identifier-4

    [ON SIZE ERROR imperative-statement-1]

    [NOT ON SIZE ERROR imperative-statement-2]

    [END-DIVIDE]
```

```
       {INPUT [TERMINAL]}
ENABLE {I-O TERMINAL    } cd-name-1 [WITH KEY {identifier-1}]
       {OUTPUT          }                     {literal-1   }
```

```
ENTER language-name-1  [routine-name-1].
```

```
         {identifier-1}  [      {identifier-2}]
         {literal-1   }  [      {literal-2   }]
EVALUATE {expression-1}  [ALSO  {expression-2}] ...
         {TRUE        }  [      {TRUE        }]
         {FALSE       }  [      {FALSE       }]

  {{WHEN

    {ANY                                                                                           }
    {condition-1                                                                                   }
    {TRUE                                                                                          }
    {FALSE                                                                                         }
    {      {{identifier-3             } [{THROUGH} {identifier-4             }]}                   }
    {[NOT] {{literal-3                } [{THRU   } {literal-4                }]}                   }
    {      {{arithmetic-expression-1  } [          {arithmetic-expression-2  }]}                   }
```

```
[ALSO

    {ANY                                                                                      }  ]        }
    {condition-2                                                                              }  ]        }
    {TRUE                                                                                     }  ]  ...   } ...
    {FALSE                                                                                    }  ]        }
    {[NOT] {{identifier-5            } [{THROUGH} {identifier-6            }]}}  ]        }
    {      {{literal-5               } [{THRU   } {literal-6               }]}}  ]        }
    {      {{arithmetic-expression-3 } [          {arithmetic-expression-4 }]}}  ]        }

  imperative-statement-1} ...

[WHEN OTHER imperative-statement-2]

[END-EVALUATE]


EXIT


EXIT PROGRAM


GENERATE {data-name-1  }
         {report-name-1}


GO TO [procedure-name-1]


GO TO {procedure-name-1} ... DEPENDING ON identifier-1


IF condition-1 THEN {{statement-1} ...} {ELSE {statement-2} ... [END-IF]}
                    {NEXT SENTENCE    } {ELSE NEXT SENTENCE              }
                                        {END-IF                          }


INITIALIZE {identifier-1} ...

   [             {{ALPHABETIC          }                                  }    ]
   [             {{ALPHANUMERIC        }                                  }    ]
   [ REPLACING   {{NUMERIC             } DATA BY {identifier-2}           } ...]
   [             {{ALPHANUMERIC-EDITED }         {literal-1   }           }    ]
   [             {{NUMERIC-EDITED      }                                  }    ]


INITIATE {report-name-1} ...
```

```
INSPECT identifier-1 TALLYING

  {identifier-2 FOR {CHARACTERS [{BEFORE|AFTER} INITIAL {identifier-4|literal-2}] ...
                    {{ALL|LEADING} {identifier-3|literal-1} [{BEFORE|AFTER} INITIAL {identifier-4|literal-2}] ...} ...} ...} ...
```

```
INSPECT identifier-1 REPLACING

  {CHARACTERS BY {identifier-5|literal-3} [{BEFORE|AFTER} INITIAL {identifier-4|literal-2}] ...
  {{ALL|LEADING|FIRST} {{identifier-3|literal-1} BY {identifier-5|literal-3} [{BEFORE|AFTER} INITIAL {identifier-4|literal-2}] ...} ...} ...
```

```
INSPECT identifier-1 TALLYING

  {identifier-2 FOR {CHARACTERS [{BEFORE|AFTER} INITIAL {identifier-4|literal-2}] ...
                    {{ALL|LEADING} {identifier-3|literal-1} [{BEFORE|AFTER} INITIAL {identifier-4|literal-2}] ...} ...} ...} ...

  REPLACING

  {CHARACTERS BY {identifier-5|literal-3} [{BEFORE|AFTER} INITIAL {identifier-4|literal-2}] ...
  {{ALL|LEADING|FIRST} {{identifier-3|literal-1} BY {identifier-5|literal-3} [{BEFORE|AFTER} INITIAL {identifier-4|literal-2}] ...} ...} ...
```

```
INSPECT identifier-1 CONVERTING {identifier-6|literal-4} TO {identifier-7|literal-5}

    [{BEFORE|AFTER} INITIAL {identifier-4|literal-2}] ...
```

```
MERGE file-name-1 {ON {ASCENDING|DESCENDING} KEY {data-name-1} ...} ...

    [COLLATING SEQUENCE IS alphabet-name-1]

    USING file-name-2 {file-name-3} ...

    {OUTPUT PROCEDURE IS procedure-name-1 [{THROUGH|THRU} procedure-name-2]}
    {GIVING {file-name-4} ...                                              }
```

```
MOVE {identifier-1} TO {identifier-2} ...
     {literal-1   }

MOVE {CORRESPONDING} identifier-1 TO identifier-2
     {CORR         }

MULTIPLY {identifier-1} BY {identifier-2 [ROUNDED]} ...
         {literal-1   }

    [ON SIZE ERROR imperative-statement-1]

    [NOT ON SIZE ERROR imperative-statement-2]

    [END-MULTIPLY]

MULTIPLY {identifier-1} BY {identifier-2}
         {literal-1   }    {literal-2   }

    GIVING {identifier-3 [ROUNDED]} ...

    [ON SIZE ERROR imperative-statement-1]

    [NOT ON SIZE ERROR imperative-statement-2]

    [END-MULTIPLY]

S OPEN  {INPUT  {file-name-1 [REVERSED        ]} ...          } ...
        {                    [WITH NO REWIND  ]               }
        {OUTPUT {file-name-2 [WITH NO REWIND]} ...            }
        {I-O {file-name-3} ...                                }
        {EXTEND {file-name-4} ...                             }

RI OPEN {INPUT {file-name-1} ...  } ...
        {OUTPUT {file-name-2} ... }
        {I-O {file-name-3} ...    }
        {EXTEND {file-name-4} ... }

W OPEN  {OUTPUT {file-name-1 [WITH NO REWIND]} ... } ...
        {EXTEND {file-name-2} ...                  }

PERFORM [procedure-name-1 [{THROUGH} procedure-name-2]]
                          [{THRU   }                 ]

    [imperative-statement-1 END-PERFORM]
```

```
PERFORM [procedure-name-1 [{THROUGH | THRU} procedure-name-2]]
    {identifier-1 | integer-1} TIMES [imperative-statement-1 END-PERFORM]

PERFORM [procedure-name-1 [{THROUGH | THRU} procedure-name-2]]
    [WITH TEST {BEFORE | AFTER}] UNTIL condition-1
    [imperative-statement-1 END-PERFORM]

PERFORM [procedure-name-1 [{THROUGH | THRU} procedure-name-2]]
    [WITH TEST {BEFORE | AFTER}]
    VARYING {identifier-2 | index-name-1} FROM {identifier-3 | index-name-2 | literal-1}
            BY {identifier-4 | literal-2} UNTIL condition-1
        [AFTER {identifier-5 | literal-3} FROM {identifier-6 | index-name-4 | literal-3}
            BY {identifier-7 | literal-4} UNTIL condition-2] ...
    [imperative-statement-1 END-PERFORM]

PURGE cd-name-1

SRI READ file-name-1 [NEXT] RECORD [INTO identifier-1]
    [AT END imperative-statement-1]
    [NOT AT END imperative-statement-2]
    [END-READ]
```

```
R READ file-name-1 RECORD  [INTO identifier-1]

     [INVALID KEY imperative-statement-3]

     [NOT INVALID KEY imperative-statement-4]

     [END-READ]

I READ file-name-1 RECORD  [INTO identifier-1]

     [KEY IS data-name-1]

     [INVALID KEY imperative-statement-3]

     [NOT INVALID KEY imperative-statement-4]

     [END-READ]

  RECEIVE cd-name-1 {MESSAGE} INTO identifier-1
                    {SEGMENT}

     [NO DATA imperative-statement-1]

     [WITH DATA imperative-statement-2]

     [END-RECEIVE]

  RELEASE record-name-1  [FROM identifier-1]

  RETURN file-name-1 RECORD  [INTO identifier-1]

     AT END imperative-statement-1

     [NOT AT END imperative-statement-2]

     [END-RETURN]

S REWRITE record-name-1  [FROM identifier-1]
```

```
RI  REWRITE record-name-1  [FROM identifier-1]

        [INVALID KEY imperative-statement-1]

        [NOT INVALID KEY imperative-statement-2]

        [END-REWRITE]

    SEARCH identifier-1 [ VARYING { identifier-2 } ]
                                  { index-name-1 }

        [AT END imperative-statement-1]

        { WHEN condition-1 { imperative-statement-2 } } ...
                           { NEXT SENTENCE          }

        [END-SEARCH]

    SEARCH ALL identifier-1  [AT END imperative-statement-1]

                 { data-name-1 { IS EQUAL TO } { identifier-3           } }
        WHEN     {             { IS =        } { literal-1              } }
                 {                             { arithmetic-expression-1 } }
                 { condition-name-1                                       }

         [       { data-name-2 { IS EQUAL TO } { identifier-4            } } ]
         [ AND   {             { IS =        } { literal-2               } } ] ...
         [       {                             { arithmetic-expression-2 } } ]
         [       { condition-name-2                                        } ]

         { imperative-statement-2 }
         { NEXT SENTENCE          }

        [END-SEARCH]

    SEND cd-name-1 FROM identifier-1

                                             { WITH identifier-2 }
    SEND cd-name-1  [FROM identifier-1]      { WITH ESI          }
                                             { WITH EMI          }
                                             { WITH EGI          }

        [ { BEFORE }  ADVANCING  { { identifier-3 } [ LINE  ] } ]
        [ { AFTER  }             { { integer-1    } [ LINES ] } ]
        [                        { { mnemonic-name-1 }        } ]
        [                        { { PAGE            }        } ]
```

```
    [REPLACING LINE]

SET  {index-name-1}  ...   TO  {index-name-2}
     {identifier-1}            {identifier-2}
                               {integer-1   }

SET  {index-name-3} ...  {UP BY  }  {identifier-3}
                         {DOWN BY}  {integer-2   }

SET  {{mnemonic-name-1} ...   TO  {ON }} ...
                                  {OFF}

SET  {condition-name-1} ...   TO TRUE

SORT file-name-1  {ON {ASCENDING } KEY  {data-name-1} ... } ...
                      {DESCENDING}

    [WITH DUPLICATES IN ORDER]

    [COLLATING SEQUENCE IS alphabet-name-1]

    { INPUT PROCEDURE IS procedure-name-1  [{THROUGH} procedure-name-2] }
    {                                       {THRU   }                   }
    { USING  {file-name-2} ...                                          }

    { OUTPUT PROCEDURE IS procedure-name-3  [{THROUGH} procedure-name-4] }
    {                                        {THRU   }                   }
    { GIVING  {file-name-3} ...                                          }

                          [      { IS EQUAL TO                  }              ]
                          [      { IS =                         }              ]
                          [      { IS GREATER THAN              }              ]
START file-name-1         [ KEY  { IS >                         }  data-name-1 ]
                          [      { IS NOT LESS THAN             }              ]
                          [      { IS NOT <                     }              ]
                          [      { IS GREATER THAN OR EQUAL TO  }              ]
                          [      { IS >=                        }              ]

    [INVALID KEY imperative-statement-1]

    [NOT INVALID KEY imperative-statement-2]

    [END-START]
```

```
STOP {RUN      }
     {literal-1}

STRING {{identifier-1} ... DELIMITED BY {identifier-2}} ...
       {{literal-1   }                  {literal-2   }}
                                        {SIZE        }}

    INTO identifier-3

    [WITH POINTER identifier-4]

    [ON OVERFLOW imperative-statement-1]

    [NOT ON OVERFLOW imperative-statement-2]

    [END-STRING]

SUBTRACT {identifier-1} ...  FROM {identifier-3 [ROUNDED]} ...
         {literal-1   }

    [ON SIZE ERROR imperative-statement-1]

    [NOT ON SIZE ERROR imperative-statement-2]

    [END-SUBTRACT]

SUBTRACT {identifier-1} ...  FROM {identifier-2}
         {literal-1   }           {literal-2   }

    GIVING {identifier-3 [ROUNDED]} ...

    [ON SIZE ERROR imperative-statement-1]

    [NOT ON SIZE ERROR imperative-statement-2]

    [END-SUBTRACT]

SUBTRACT {CORRESPONDING} identifier-1 FROM identifier-2 [ROUNDED]
         {CORR         }
    [ON SIZE ERROR imperative-statement-1]

    [NOT ON SIZE ERROR imperative-statement-2]

    [END-SUBTRACT]
```

```
SUPPRESS PRINTING

TERMINATE {report-name-1} ...

UNSTRING identifier-1

    [DELIMITED BY [ALL] {identifier-2} [OR [ALL] {identifier-3}] ...]
                        {literal-1   }            {literal-2   }

    INTO {identifier-4 [DELIMITER IN identifier-5] [COUNT IN identifier-6]} ...

    [WITH POINTER identifier-7]

    [TALLYING IN identifier-8]

    [ON OVERFLOW imperative-statement-1]

    [NOT ON OVERFLOW imperative-statement-2]

    [END-UNSTRING]


                                                         {{file-name-1} ...}
                                                         {INPUT            }
SRI USE [GLOBAL] AFTER STANDARD {EXCEPTION} PROCEDURE ON {OUTPUT           }
                                {ERROR    }              {I-O              }
                                                         {EXTEND           }


                                                {{file-name-1} ...}
W USE AFTER STANDARD {EXCEPTION} PROCEDURE ON {OUTPUT           }
                     {ERROR    }              {EXTEND           }


USE [GLOBAL] BEFORE REPORTING identifier-1


                       {cd-name-1                           }
                       {[ALL REFERENCES OF] identifier-1    }
USE FOR DEBUGGING ON   {file-name-1                         } ...
                       {procedure-name-1                    }
                       {ALL PROCEDURES                      }
```

```
S WRITE record-name-1  [FROM identifier-1]

    [ {BEFORE}  ADVANCING  { {identifier-2} [LINE ] } ]
    [ {AFTER }             { {integer-1   } [LINES] } ]
    [                      { {mnemonic-name-1}      } ]
    [                      { {PAGE           }      } ]

    [AT {END-OF-PAGE} imperative-statement-1]
    [   {EOP        }                       ]

    [NOT AT {END-OF-PAGE} imperative-statement-2]
    [       {EOP        }                       ]

    [END-WRITE]
```

```
RI WRITE record-name-1  [FROM identifier-1]

    [INVALID KEY imperative-statement-1]

    [NOT INVALID KEY imperative-statement-2]

    [END-WRITE]
```

General Format for Copy and Replace Statements

```
COPY text-name-1  [ {OF} library-name-1 ]
                  [ {IN}                ]

    [ REPLACING  { {==pseudo-text-1==}  BY  {==pseudo-text-2==} } ... ]
    [            { {identifier-1     }      {identifier-2     } }     ]
    [            { {literal-1        }      {literal-2        } }     ]
    [            { {word-1           }      {word-2           } }     ]

REPLACE  {==pseudo-text-1==  BY  ==pseudo-text-2==} ...

REPLACE OFF
```

General Format for Conditions

Relation condition:

```
                             IS [NOT] GREATER THAN
                             IS [NOT] >
                             IS [NOT] LESS THAN
{identifier-1            }   IS [NOT] <                   {identifier-2            }
{literal-1               }   IS [NOT] EQUAL TO            {literal-2               }
{arithmetic-expression-1 }   IS [NOT] =                   {arithmetic-expression-2 }
{index-name-1            }   IS GREATER THAN OR EQUAL TO  {index-name-2            }
                             IS >=
                             IS LESS THAN OR EQUAL TO
                             IS <=
```

Class condition:

```
                         {NUMERIC          }
                         {ALPHABETIC       }
identifier-1 IS [NOT]    {ALPHABETIC-LOWER }
                         {ALPHABETIC-UPPER }
                         {class-name-1     }
```

Condition-name condition:

```
condition-name-1
```

Switch-status condition:

```
condition-name-1
```

Sign condition:

```
                                   {POSITIVE}
arithmetic-expression-1 IS [NOT]   {NEGATIVE}
                                   {ZERO    }
```

Negated condition:

```
NOT condition-1
```

Combined condition:

```
condition-1  { {AND}  condition-2 } ...
             { {OR }              }
```

Abbreviated combined relation condition:

```
relation-condition  { {AND}  [NOT]  [relational-operator]  object } ...
                    { {OR }                                       }
```

General Format for Qualification

Format 1:

```
                        ⎧ ⎧ ⎧IN⎫                 ⎫       ⎡ ⎧IN⎫ ⎧file-name-1⎫ ⎤ ⎫
                        ⎪ ⎨ ⎨OF⎬  data-name-2    ⎬ ...   ⎢ ⎨OF⎬ ⎨cd-name-1  ⎬ ⎥ ⎪
⎧data-name-1      ⎫     ⎨ ⎩ ⎩  ⎭                 ⎭       ⎣ ⎩  ⎭ ⎩           ⎭ ⎦ ⎬
⎩condition-name-1 ⎭     ⎪   ⎧IN⎫  ⎧file-name-1⎫                                   ⎪
                        ⎩   ⎩OF⎭  ⎩cd-name-1  ⎭                                   ⎭
```

Format 2:

```
paragraph-name-1  ⎧IN⎫  section-name-1
                  ⎩OF⎭
```

Format 3:

```
text-name-1  ⎧IN⎫  library-name-1
             ⎩OF⎭
```

Format 4:

```
LINAGE-COUNTER  ⎧IN⎫  file-name-2
                ⎩OF⎭
```

Format 5:

```
⎧PAGE-COUNTER⎫  ⎧IN⎫  report-name-1
⎩LINE-COUNTER⎭  ⎩OF⎭
```

Format 6:

```
             ⎧ ⎧IN⎫  data-name-4  ⎡⎧IN⎫  report-name-2⎤ ⎫
data-name-3  ⎨ ⎩OF⎭               ⎣⎩OF⎭               ⎦ ⎬
             ⎪ ⎧IN⎫  report-name-2                      ⎪
             ⎩ ⎩OF⎭                                     ⎭
```

Miscellaneous Formats

Subscripting:

```
⎧condition-name-1⎫  (  ⎧integer-1                          ⎫
⎩data-name-1     ⎭     ⎨data-name-2 [{±} integer-2]        ⎬  ... )
                       ⎩index-name-1  [{±} integer-3]      ⎭
```

Reference Modification:

```
data-name-1 (leftmost-character-position: [length])
```

Identifier:

```
              ┌ ┌ IN ┐                 ┐       ┌ ┌ IN ┐ ┌ cd-name-1     ┐ ┐
data-name-1   │ │ OF │  data-name-2   │ ...   │ │ OF │ │ file-name-1   │ │
              └ └    ┘                 ┘       └ └    ┘ └ report-name-1 ┘ ┘

    [({subscript} ... )]  [(leftmost-character-position: [length])]
```

General Format for Nested Source Programs

```
 IDENTIFICATION DIVISION.

 PROGRAM-ID.  program-name-1  [IS INITIAL PROGRAM].

[ENVIRONMENT DIVISION.  environment-division-content]

[DATA DIVISION.  data-division-content]

[PROCEDURE DIVISION.  procedure-division-content]

[[nested-source-program] ...

 END PROGRAM program-name-1.]
```

General Format for Nested Source Programs

```
 IDENTIFICATION DIVISION.

 PROGRAM-ID.  program-name-2  [IS {|COMMON |} PROGRAM] .
                                  {|INITIAL|}

[ENVIRONMENT DIVISION.  environment-division-content]

[DATA DIVISION.  data-division-content]

[PROCEDURE DIVISION.  procedure-division-content]

[nested-source-program] ...

 END PROGRAM program-name-2.
```

General Format for a Sequence of Source Programs

```
{IDENTIFICATION DIVISION.

 PROGRAM-ID. program-name-3 [IS INITIAL PROGRAM].

[ENVIRONMENT DIVISION. environment-division-content]

[DATA DIVISION. data-division-content]

[PROCEDURE DIVISION. procedure-division-content]

[nested-source-program] ...

 END PROGRAM program-name-3.} ...

 IDENTIFICATION DIVISION.

 PROGRAM-ID. program-name-4 [IS INITIAL PROGRAM].

[ENVIRONMENT DIVISION. environment-division-content]

[DATA DIVISION. data-division-content]

[PROCEDURE DIVISION. procedure-division-content]

[[nested-source-program] ...

 END PROGRAM program-name-4.]
```

APPENDIX

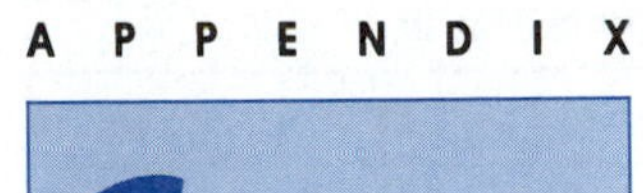

C Permissible Input-Output Operations

The input and output statements permitted on any file depend on the ORGANIZATION, ACCESS MODE, and OPEN mode of the file. Permissible statements are indicated by the presence of an X in the following tables:

TABLE C.1
Permissible statements on files with ORGANIZATION SEQUENTIAL

STATEMENT	OPEN MODE			
	Input	Output	I-O	Extend
READ	X		X	
WRITE		X		X
REWRITE			X	

TABLE C.2
Permissible statements on files with ORGANIZATION INDEXED or ORGANIZATION RELATIVE

FILE ACCESS MODE	STATEMENT	OPEN MODE			
		Input	Output	I-O	Extend
Sequential	READ	X		X	
	WRITE		X		X
	REWRITE			X	
	START	X		X	
	DELETE			X	
Random	READ	X		X	
	WRITE		X	X	
	REWRITE			X	
	START				
	DELETE			X	
Dynamic	READ	X		X	
	WRITE		X	X	
	REWRITE			X	
	START	X		X	
	DELETE			X	

APPENDIX D Input Data for Selected Programming Exercises

FIGURE *D.1* Input data for Exercise 5, Chapter 2

```
--------------------------------------------------------------------------------
         1         2         3         4         5         6         7         8
12345678901234567890123456789012345678901234567890123456789012345678901234567890
--------------------------------------------------------------------------------
00102001BASE MOUNT FOR FAN              203
00102002BLADE                           129
10100012MOTOR                           320
20100013SWITCH PANEL                    529
3021230 SHAFT                           010
```

FIGURE *D.2* Input data for Review Exercise 5, Chapter 3

```
--------------------------------------------------------------------------------
         1         2         3         4         5         6         7         8
12345678901234567890123456789012345678901234567890123456789012345678901234567890
--------------------------------------------------------------------------------
008549912120080080080080080
265362322023084037199023000
103381716240239000000080082
```

FIGURE D.3 Input data for Review Exercise 2, Chapter 4

```
--------------------------------------------------------------------------------
         1         2         3         4         5         6         7         8
12345678901234567890123456789012345678901234567890123456789012345678901234567890
--------------------------------------------------------------------------------
0085499121200800800800080080
2653623222023084037199023000
1033817162402390000000080082
4567821230830920810791011 00
8235792150800800800080080080
9455327560800800800080079078
1235765120790650000000080000
6912766640690000981020000090
1376517920800800800080080080
9681453520800790780000080080
5689365510801001040000000089
8965653171021001001000000000
5136876530870900480920080080
6355847820801230800001230090
4754528530800000800000080000
4517789650000800000080000080
5637895120800800800080080080
1458689770800900900900080000
4158795690800800800080080080
8947561442390000000000000000
4178956890000000000000000240
5847895310800800800080081000
```

FIGURE D.4 Input data for Review Exercise 3, Chapter 5

```
--------------------------------------------------------------------------------
         1         2         3         4         5         6         7         8
12345678901234567890123456789012345678901234567890123456789012345678901234567890
--------------------------------------------------------------------------------
003682528V00950000
117260098Z01500000
265348425W01999999
229650287X02000000
009516254702235000
128659821
032002658401500000
038565462502000000
106562249203000000
756123422Z00500000
```

FIGURE *D.5* **Input data for Review Exercise 2, Chapter 7**

```
--------------------------------------------------------------------------------
         1         2         3         4         5         6         7         8
12345678901234567890123456789012345678901234567890123456789012345678901234567890
--------------------------------------------------------------------------------
-02005   0003034
 02005   0000000
 02005   9876201
-02005   0000006
-02005   8923551
 02005   3485910
 04502   9999999
-04502   0008399
-04502   4567212
-12121   7549900
-12121   0000002
-12121   0000000
 12121   2341111
 12121   0006667
-12121   6666222
 19596   9292929
-19596   1254720
-19596   2348764
-19596   0000020
 19596   0000239
 19596   0021345
-20023   9999999
-20023   8765499
-20023   8686868
 20023   8888880
 20023   8855332
 20023   5678923
-23456   0000211
-23456   0000453
-23456   0001200
 23456   0000012
 23456   0001800
 23456   0000054
-30721   0000101
 30721   0009912
-30721   0009844
-40101   0034287
 40101   0021245
-40101   6000201
 40101   0006700
-40101   3234323
 40101   9002341
-67689   0001114
 67689   0101010
-67689   0003335
 67689   0220330
-67689   0304020
 67689   1000000
-72332   0000004
 72332   0004444
-72332   0044444
 72332   0000444
-72332   0000044
 72332   0404040
```

FIGURE *D.6* Input data for Review Exercise 5, Chapter 8

```
--------------------------------------------------------------------------------
         1         2         3         4         5         6         7         8
12345678901234567890123456789012345678901234567890123456789012345678901234567890
--------------------------------------------------------------------------------
34ABA 06543X843961V
78121H10000003874523
00000ACDEFGHIJKLMNO
14758522342101000000
45541504592186542l6
9#121H19087055O8973
91A00A08749002384OO
99121H19087045O8973
82423617142139999999
73315604396040000000
64876D       0100004
67456509535600000025
55252E054320043#0066
46701F21005054365 28
374   31732990727982
00322A00000149999999
28421B06923Z5000000
14756A08994307059 24
89   6 9"94211764297
78932ZA932416763207
569$2 0094325923965
15008B07076306804 29
05))6L0*92357009215
03442403500040000 01
19123G17036705376 54
```

FIGURE *D.7* Input data for Review Exercise 6, Chapter 9

```
--------------------------------------------------------------------------------
         1         2         3         4         5         6         7         8
12345678901234567890123456789012345678901234567890123456789012345678901234567890
--------------------------------------------------------------------------------
ABC1234  365-09       900000010
CVNMR-D  2.CHJK       000009345
09G8239  6-7YT7       800001050
23879-J  JKSDF7       056000000
WQWEIOU  N-AFDH       990101010
ADJKGLE  512TYN       980200000
AKLJKNU  7-6DFE       XYXYXYXYX
ADGH784  1AN-07       050025000
9675473  S-1287       006700029
```

FIGURE *D.8* Input data for Review Exercise 4, Chapter 10

```
--------------------------------------------------------------------------------
         1         2         3         4         5         6         7         8
12345678901234567890123456789012345678901234567890123456789012345678901234567890
--------------------------------------------------------------------------------
0011
0021
0031
0041
0051
0061
0071
0081
1783
0153
0223
0017
0027
0037
0047
0057
0067
0087
0097
0016
0026
0076
0086
0096
0077
0015
0025
0035
0045
0055
0065
0075
0085
0095
0012
0022
0032
0042
0052
0062
0072
0082
0092
```

FIGURE *D.9* Input data for Review Exercise 2, Chapter 11

```
--------------------------------------------------------------------------------
         1         2         3         4         5         6         7         8
12345678901234567890123456789012345678901234567890123456789012345678901234567890
--------------------------------------------------------------------------------
024563200186400357906486204567000000123758
064352606456300000013684500364209781405689 7
```

FIGURE *D.10* Input data for Review Exercise 3, Chapter 12

```
--------------------------------------------------------------------------------
         1         2         3         4         5         6         7         8
12345678901234567890123456789012345678901234567890123456789012345678901234567890
--------------------------------------------------------------------------------
45124N351
51302E285
65421N421
98741N438
19850E159
48932N375
26418N374
96127N376
10127E400
04575N400
45225N399
42598N401
00456E401
86156N401
```

FIGURE *D.11* **Input data for Review Exercise 2, Chapter 13**

```
--------------------------------------------------------------------------------
         1         2         3         4         5         6         7         8
12345678901234567890123456789012345678901234567890123456789012345678901234567890
--------------------------------------------------------------------------------
1001050000MILLER L  22 WEST 23RD STREET           COLUMBIA SC  29210  AD77
1001120002LANE R    1633 BROADWAY                 E BRUNSWICK NJ 08816DP68
Y         CAPUANO M 1 BISCAYNE TOWER              MIAMI FL  33168     AC65
1001260007BUDD J    875 AVENUE OF THE AMERICAS    NEW YORK NY  10014  DDZZ
1001330010LERNER P  432 PARK AVENUE SOUTH         TUCKAHOE NY  10707  OD
1001050000MILLER L  22 WEST 23RD STREET           COLUMBIA SC  29210  AD77
1001400000FALLON B  60 EAST 42 STREET             CHICAGO IL  60609   ET56
1000980000HALEY J   1300 NEWARK TURNPIKE          AMBLER PA  19002    EM73
1001050000          165 NAGLE AVENUE              FLEMINGTON NJ  08822NU80
7001610000RYAN R    45 FAIRVIEW AVENUE            SOMERVILLE NJ  08876SG78
1001680001HEDERMAN K17 FORT GEORGE HILL           PITTSBURGH PA  15237MK59
1001750000KEATING M 223 ELWOOD STREET             DOWNRS GRVE IL 60515DP81
2001820000LANIGAN B 84 VERMILYEA AVENUE           BROOKLYN NY  11211     81
1002030000MITCHELL J587A WEST 207TH STREET        YONKERS NY  10710   HT79
1002100002PARKS J   3 HAVEN PLAZA                 NEW ROCHLLE NY 10804CT75
1002170000CALDERON C252 BROOME STREET             PRESIDIO CA  91127  DD55
1002240001WILLIAMS J94 MADISON AVENUE             SN FRANCSCO CA 94131AD59
1000350001LEHMAN J J689 COLUMBUS AVENUE           WESTFIELD CN  07090 NU60
1000490001GREENE J  40 CRANE AVENUE               LOUISVILLE KY  40206AC65
1000560000SLATER E                                                    DP
9                   27 HALLADAY STREET            KEY BSCAYNE FL 33149GA
1000700005LEE P J   67-35 YELLOWSTONE BLVD                              67
1000770000MINSKY J  1188 FIRST AVENUE             FREEHOLD NJ  07728  LA53
1000840015DAPRINO J 205 WEST END AVENUE           PITTSBURGH PA  15237LT78
1000980005CULHANE G 509 LAKE STREET               CHICAGO IL  60614   HT70
1002660000LANG M    68 BOWERY                     STATN ISLND NY 10306DL81
1002730002CACACI V  148 DELANCEY STREET           SAN DIEGO CA  92109 DH73
1002940015BURKE J   31 SAINT MARKS PLACE          ARLINGTON VA  02174 DL74
7003010FG1POWERS P P575 LEXINGTON AVENUE          ELMHURST NY  11313
1003080020GARCIA J  262 PARK WEST AVENUE          HARTSDALE NY  10530 EA79
9003150002MICELI G  8532 HAMILTON PARKWAY         NEW HAVEN CN  06575 HT75
3003220000                                        MILFORD NJ  08848   PM72
1003290000VOLPONE G 420 AVENUE L                                      MT80
1003368378CALI S    162 PRESIDENT STREET          CITY ISLAND NY 10464CT49
5002310005WILLIAM B 21 NEW YORK AVENUE            NEW MILFORD NJ 07646DP50
1002380000PARKER K  551 LORIMER STREET                                AC55
0002450000          23 SHERIDAN AVENUE                                MK57
1002520000GALLI G   406 DAHILL ROAD               MANHASSET NY  11030 EM51
1002590000          9219 RIDGE BLVD               WINOOSKI VT  05404  ET69
1000070010BUCCI R   1764 GERRITSEN AVENUE         S NYACK NY  10960   DD67
1000140000DAVIS R   195 ADAMS STREET              S ORANGE NJ  07079  GA66
1000210004MONTI L   381 MARLBOROUGH ROAD          ALEXANDRIA VA  22314SG77
1000280070SMITH M   66 BAY 22ND STREET            OAKLAND CA  94612   HT47
4003430010SESSA J   15 3RD PLACE                  SCARSDALE NY  10583 MK68
1003500025SHAW R    47 LANCASTER AVENUE           NEW PALTZ NY  12561 DH73
```

FIGURE *D.12* **Input data for Review Exercise 4, Chapter 14**

```
--------------------------------------------------------------------------------
         1         2         3         4         5         6         7         8
12345678901234567890123456789012345678901234567890123456789012345678901234567890
--------------------------------------------------------------------------------
2001120002MAME R L
30021000027 HAVEN PLAZA
2001260007
1003920000WASH'TON I3 HAVEN PLAZA                 ARLINGTON VA  02174 DL66
30008432457 HAVEN PLAZA
4000070010MANHASSET NY   11030
4001750000S NYACK NY  10960
1004200015RICE J    49 LANCASTER AVENUE           ALEXANDRIA VA  22314HT58
1004200015PRICE J   49 LANCASTER AVE.             ALEXANDRIA VA  22314AD58
2004200015PRICE J
300420001551 LANCASTER AVENUE
5000490001SG
5002520000
6000700005%)
600014000079
7001050000
7001750000
3000770000111 EIGHTH AVENUE
7000770000
1013457892          53 LANCASTER AVENUE           ALEXANDRIA VA  223140D69
```

FIGURE D.13 Input data for Review Exercise 1, Chapter 15

```
--------------------------------------------------------------------------------
         1         2         3         4         5         6         7         8
12345678901234567890123456789012345678901234567890123456789012345678901234567890
--------------------------------------------------------------------------------
1001050000MILLER L  22 WEST 23RD STREET           COLUMBIA SC  29210  AD78
1001120002LANE R    1633 BROADWAY                 E BRUNSWICK NJ 08816DP48
Y         CAPUANO M 1 BISCAYNE TOWER              MIAMI FL  33168     AC80
1001260007BUDD J    875 AVENUE OF THE AMERICAS    NEW YORK NY  10014  DD76
1001330010LERNER P  432 PARK AVENUE SOUTH         TUCKAHOE NY  10707  OD65
1001400000FALLON B  60 EAST 42 STREET             CHICAGO IL  60609   ET76
1000980000HALEY J   1300 NEWARK TURNPIKE          AMBLER PA  19002    EM79
1001050000          165 NAGLE AVENUE              FLEMINGTON NJ  08822NU66
7001610000RYAN R    45 FAIRVIEW AVENUE            SOMERVILLE NJ  08876SG53
1001680001HEDERMAN K17 FORT GEORGE HILL           PITTSBURGH PA  15237MK((
1001050000MILLER L  22 WEST 23RD STREET           COLUMBIA SC  29210  AD78
1001750000KEATING M 223 ELWOOD STREET             DOWNRS GRVE IL 60515DP71
2001820000LANIGAN B 84 VERMILYEA AVENUE           BROOKLYN NY  11211     72
1002030000MITCHELL J587A WEST 207TH STREET        YONKERS NY  10710   HT64
1002100002PARKS J   3 HAVEN PLAZA                 NEW ROCHLLE NY 10804CT81
1002170000CALDERON C252 BROOME STREET             PRESIDIO CA  91127  DD62
1002240001WILLIAMS J94 MADISON AVENUE             SN FRANCSCO CA 94131AD49
1000350001LEHMAN J J689 COLUMBUS AVENUE           WESTFIELD CN  07090 NU52
1000490001GREENE J  40 CRANE AVENUE               LOUISVILLE KY  40206AC65
1000560000SLATER E                                                    DPoo
9                   27 HALLADAY STREET            KEY BSCAYNE FL 33149GA73
1000700005LEE P J   67-35 YELLOWSTONE BLVD                              70
1000770000MINSKY J  1188 FIRST AVENUE             FREEHOLD NJ  07728  LA55
1000840015DAPRINO J 205 WEST END AVENUE           PITTSBURGH PA  15237LT77
1000980005CULHANE G 509 LAKE STREET               CHICAGO IL  60614   HT74
1002660000LANG M    68 BOWERY                     STATN ISLND NY 10306DL80
1002730002CACACI V  148 DELANCEY STREET           SAN DIEGO CA  92109 DH81
1002940015BURKE J   31 SAINT MARKS PLACE          ARLINGTON VA  02174 DL78
7003010FG1POWERS P P575 LEXINGTON AVENUE          ELMHURST NY  11313     73
1003080020GARCIA J  262 PARK WEST AVENUE          HARTSDALE NY  10530 EA79
9003150002MICELI G  8532 HAMILTON PARKWAY         NEW HAVEN CN  06575 HT74
3003220000                                        MILFORD NJ  08848   PM49
1003290000VOLPONE G 420 AVENUE L                                      MTZZ
1003368378CALI S    162 PRESIDENT STREET          CITY ISLAND NY 10464CT62
5002310005WILLIAM B 21 NEW YORK AVENUE            NEW MILFORD NJ 07646DP65
1002380000PARKER K  551 LORIMER STREET                                AC73
0002450000          23 SHERIDAN AVENUE                                MK79
1002520000GALLI G   406 DAHILL ROAD               MANHASSET NY  11030 EM82
1002590000          9219 RIDGE BLVD               WINOOSKI VT  05404  ET82
1000070010BUCCI R   1764 GERRITSEN AVENUE         S NYACK NY  10960   DD77
1000140000DAVIS R   195 ADAMS STREET              S ORANGE NJ  07079  GA75
1000210004MONTI L   381 MARLBOROUGH ROAD          ALEXANDRIA VA  22314SG76
1000280070SMITH M   66 BAY 22ND STREET            OAKLAND CA  94612   HT67
4003430010SESSA J   15 3RD PLACE                  SCARSDALE NY  10583 MK64
1003500025SHAW R    47 LANCASTER AVENUE           NEW PALTZ NY  12561 DH60
```

FIGURE *D.14* **Input data for Review Exercise 2, Chapter 15**

```
--------------------------------------------------------------------------------
         1         2         3         4         5         6         7         8
12345678901234567890123456789012345678901234567890123456789012345678901234567890
--------------------------------------------------------------------------------
2001120002MAME R L
30021000027 HAVEN PLAZA
2001260007
1003920000WASH'TON I3 HAVEN PLAZA                 ARLINGTON VA  02174 DL66
30008432457 HAVEN PLAZA
4000070010MANHASSET NY  11030
4001750000S NYACK NY  10960
1004200015RICE J    49 LANCASTER AVENUE           ALEXANDRIA VA  22314HT58
2004200015PRICE J
300420001551 LANCASTER AVENUE
5000490001SG
5002520000
6000700005%)
600014000079
7001050000
7001750000
3000770000111 EIGHTH AVENUE
7000770000
1013457892          53 LANCASTER AVENUE           ALEXANDRIA VA  223140D69
1002030000MITCHELL J587A WEST 207TH STREET        YONKERS NY  10710   HT64
```

FIGURE *D.15* **Input data for Review Exercise 2, Chapter 16**

```
--------------------------------------------------------------------------------
         1         2         3         4         5         6         7         8
12345678901234567890123456789012345678901234567890123456789012345678901234567890
--------------------------------------------------------------------------------
1001050000MILLER L  22 WEST 23RD STREET           COLUMBIA SC  29210  AD78
1001120002LANE R    1633 BROADWAY                 E BRUNSWICK NJ 08816DP48
Y         CAPUANO M 1 BISCAYNE TOWER              MIAMI FL  33168     AC80
1001260007BUDD J    875 AVENUE OF THE AMERICAS    NEW YORK NY  10014  DD76
1001330010LERNER P  432 PARK AVENUE SOUTH         TUCKAHOE NY  10707  OD65
1001400000FALLON B  60 EAST 42 STREET             CHICAGO IL  60609   ET76
1000980000HALEY J   1300 NEWARK TURNPIKE          AMBLER PA  19002    EM79
1001050000          165 NAGLE AVENUE              FLEMINGTON NJ  08822NU66
7001610000RYAN R    45 FAIRVIEW AVENUE            SOMERVILLE NJ  08876SG53
1001680001HEDERMAN K17 FORT GEORGE HILL           PITTSBURGH PA  15237MK((
1001750000KEATING M 223 ELWOOD STREET             DOWNRS GRVE IL 60515DP71
2001820000LANIGAN B 84 VERMILYEA AVENUE           BROOKLYN NY  11211    72
1002030000MITCHELL J587A WEST 207TH STREET        YONKERS NY  10710   HT64
1002100002PARKS J   3 HAVEN PLAZA                 NEW ROCHLLE NY 10804CT81
1002170000CALDERON C252 BROOME STREET             PRESIDIO CA  91127  DD62
1002240001WILLIAMS J94 MADISON AVENUE             SN FRANCSCO CA 94131AD49
1000350001LEHMAN J J689 COLUMBUS AVENUE           WESTFIELD CN  07090 NU52
1000490001GREENE J  40 CRANE AVENUE               LOUISVILLE KY  40206AC65
1000560000SLATER E                                                    DP00
9                   27 HALLADAY STREET            KEY BSCAYNE FL 33149GA73
1000700005LEE P J   67-35 YELLOWSTONE BLVD                              70
1000770000MINSKY J  1188 FIRST AVENUE             FREEHOLD NJ  07728  LA55
1000840015DAPRINO J 205 WEST END AVENUE           PITTSBURGH PA  15237LT77
1000980005CULHANE G 509 LAKE STREET               CHICAGO IL  60614   HT74
1002660000LANG M    68 BOWERY                     STATN ISLND NY 10306DL80
1002730002CACACI V  148 DELANCEY STREET           SAN DIEGO CA  92109 DH81
1002940015BURKE J   31 SAINT MARKS PLACE          ARLINGTON VA  02174 DL78
7003010FG1POWERS P P575 LEXINGTON AVENUE          ELMHURST NY  11313    73
1003080020GARCIA J  262 PARK WEST AVENUE          HARTSDALE NY  10530 EA79
9003150002MICELI G  8532 HAMILTON PARKWAY         NEW HAVEN CN  06575 HT74
3003220000                                        MILFORD NJ  08848   PM49
1003290000VOLPONE G 420 AVENUE L                                      MTZZ
1003368378CALI S    162 PRESIDENT STREET          CITY ISLAND NY 10464CT62
5002310005WILLIAM B 21 NEW YORK AVENUE            NEW MILFORD NJ 07646DP65
1002380000PARKER K  551 LORIMER STREET                                AC73
0002450000          23 SHERIDAN AVENUE                                MK79
1002520000GALLI G   406 DAHILL ROAD               MANHASSET NY  11030 EM82
1002590000          9219 RIDGE BLVD               WINOOSKI VT  05404  ET82
1000070010BUCCI R   1764 GERRITSEN AVENUE         S NYACK NY  10960   DD77
1000140000DAVIS R   195 ADAMS STREET              S ORANGE NJ  07079  GA75
1000210004MONTI L   381 MARLBOROUGH ROAD          ALEXANDRIA VA  22314SG76
1000280070SMITH M   66 BAY 22ND STREET            OAKLAND CA  94612   HT67
4003430010SESSA J   15 3RD PLACE                  SCARSDALE NY  10583 MK64
1003500025SHAW R    47 LANCASTER AVENUE           NEW PALTZ NY  12561 DH60
```

FIGURE *D.16* **Input data for Review Exercise 3, Chapter 16**

```
--------------------------------------------------------------------------------
         1         2         3         4         5         6         7         8
12345678901234567890123456789012345678901234567890123456789012345678901234567890
--------------------------------------------------------------------------------
2001120002MAME R L
30021000027 HAVEN PLAZA
2001260007
1003920000WASH'TON I3 HAVEN PLAZA                 ARLINGTON VA  02174 DL66
30008432457 HAVEN PLAZA
4000070010MANHASSET NY  11030
4001750000S NYACK NY  10960
1004200015RICE J    49 LANCASTER AVENUE           ALEXANDRIA VA  22314HT58
2004200015PRICE J
300420001551 LANCASTER AVENUE
5000490001SG
5002520000
6000700005%)
600014000079
7001050000
7001750000
3000770000111 EIGHTH AVENUE
7000770000
1013457892          53 LANCASTER AVENUE           ALEXANDRIA VA  223140D69
1002030000MITCHELL J587A WEST 207TH STREET        YONKERS NY  10710   HT64
```

FIGURE *D.17* **Input data for Review Exercise 2, Chapter 18**

```
--------------------------------------------------------------------------------
         1         2         3         4         5         6         7         8
12345678901234567890123456789012345678901234567890123456789012345678901234567890
--------------------------------------------------------------------------------
2 3 4
12 12 12
99999 99999 99999
0 0 0
```

FIGURE *D.18* **Input data for Review Exercise 3, Chapter 19**

```
--------------------------------------------------------------------------------
         1         2         3         4         5         6         7         8
12345678901234567890123456789012345678901234567890123456789012345678901234567890
--------------------------------------------------------------------------------
             A PALINDROME READS THE SAME WAY BACKWARDS AS FORWARDS.
                           ABLE WAS I ERE I SAW ELBA.
             A MAN, A PLAN, A CANAL - PANAMA.
```

Index

A

B

C

E

F

G

H

I

J

K

L

M

N

O

P

S

T

U